Germany

Andrea Schulte-Peevers

Kerry Christiani, Marc Di Duca, Anthony Haywood,
Catherine Le Nevez, Daniel Robinson, Caroline Sieg

SYLT (p719)
Enjoy a ramble among the sandy dunes, hit the crashing surf or quite literally walk on the ocean floor on this glamorous, windswept North Sea island

HAMBURG (p674)
Let your hair down on a tour of this vibrant city's eclectic bar and pub scene

BREMEN (p660)
Savour the relaxed spirit of this 'metropolis in miniature' with its lovely red-brick and art-nouveau architecture and sizzling alternative nightlife

LÜBECK (p701)
Catch the Hanseatic spirit in this Unesco-recognised town known for its delicious marzipan confections

RÜGEN ISLAND (p747)
Explore the many faces of this fascinating island, including its rugged chalk cliffs, windswept beaches, Romantic-era spa architecture and tree-lined country roads

MÜRITZ NATIONAL PARK (p733)
Hit the slow lane on a leisurely paddling-and-camping trip around this watery paradise teeming with birds

BERLIN (p99)
Visit world-class museums by day and bustling bars, pubs and clubs by night

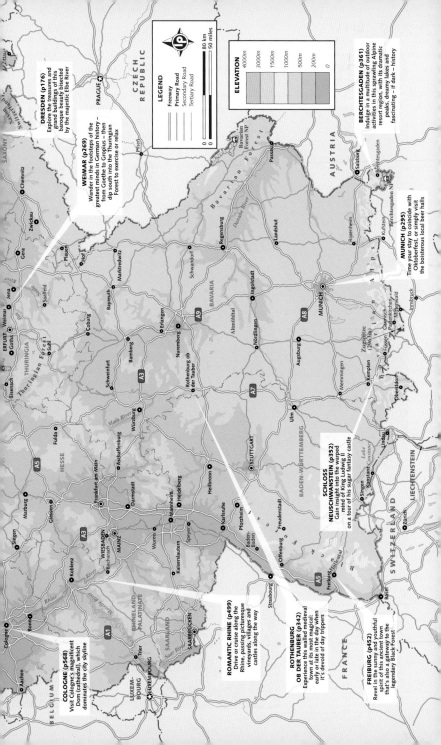

DRESDEN (p176)
Explore the treasures and grand buildings of this baroque beauty bisected by the majestic Elbe River

WEIMAR (p269)
Wander in the footsteps of the greatest minds in German history – from Goethe to Gropius – then dip south into the Thuringian Forest to exercise or relax

BERCHTESGADEN (p361)
Indulge in a multitude of outdoor activities in this sprawling Alpine resort region, with its dramatic peaks, dreamy lakes and fascinating – if dark – history

MUNICH (p295)
Time your stay to coincide with Oktoberfest, or simply visit the boisterous local beer halls

SCHLOSS NEUSCHWANSTEIN (p352)
Gain insight into the warped mind of King Ludwig II on a tour of his sugar fantasy castle

ROTHENBURG OB DER TAUBER (p342)
Experience this walled medieval town at its most magical: early or late in the day when it's devoid of day trippers

ROMANTIC RHINE (p499)
Drive or cruise along the Rhine, passing picturesque vineyards, villages and castles along the way

FREIBURG (p452)
Revel in the sunny and youthful spirit of this ancient town that's also a gateway to the legendary Black Forest

COLOGNE (p568)
Visit Cologne's magnificent Dom (cathedral), which dominates the city skyline

LEGEND
Freeway
Primary Road
Secondary Road
Tertiary Road

ELEVATION
4000m
3000m
1500m
1000m
500m
200m
0

80 km
50 miles

On the Road

ANDREA SCHULTE-PEEVERS
Coordinating Author
Wherever you go in Berlin, you're surrounded by an enormous sense of history, from medieval times to reunification. You may be rushing off to dinner with friends or to a frenetic club when suddenly you find yourself ensnared by something of monumental importance to the world. Here, in the warped labyrinth of the Holocaust Memorial (p115), I feel an extraordinary stillness and the presence of uncounted souls.

KERRY CHRISTIANI On one of the hottest days of summer, we'd headed into the woods close to home in Villingen (p462) to pick bilberries and take a cool stroll among the fir trees. Recent thunderstorms made the Black Forest seem greener and wilder than ever. This is me soaking up the day's last sun.

MARC DI DUCA As a Lonely Planet author I've been to some pretty spectacular places, but nothing I've seen around the world quite compares to the drama of the Alps. While hitting the trails takes you into some magnificent backcountry, you're never really far away from a cosy tavern and a hot meal. Here am I, fresh from a bracing ascent of Germany's highest mountain, the Zugspitze (p356). But I have to fess up – I cheated. I took the train.

ANTHONY HAYWOOD Seagulls cried in the darkness of evening: 'Give me your tired, your poor, your huddled masses yearning to breathe free.' This guy was not the most talkative fellow passenger at Bremerhaven's German Emigration Centre (p670), but perhaps he had good reason to be so contemplative: he was about to board a ship and sail to an unknown future in the New World. The lifelike models on the dock are part of the interesting recreation of events in the centre's exhibition.

CATHERINE LE NEVEZ Germany is synonymous with awe-inspiring castles and frothy beer. But beach-fringed islands? Not so much. Yet Germany's North Sea and Baltic islands, like Rügen (p747), behind me in this photo, are idyllic end-of-the-earth retreats. In true German style, ultra-efficient and ecofriendly public transport makes them a cinch to reach from the mainland.

DANIEL ROBINSON Interviewing locals – especially old-timers – for tips on their favourite eateries is an important part of researching a guidebook. I ran into this particular fellow outside Frankfurt's Senckenberg Museum (p534) and, feeling that day like a Frankfurter, decided to ask him where he goes for the city's tastiest *Worscht* (known elsewhere in Germany as *Wurst*). He said he had something in mind – and then took out a giant bottle of curry sauce.

For full author biographies see p802

Germany Highlights

No matter whether you seek an adrenaline-fuelled foray on the autobahn or a leisurely ride on its latest-generation trains, Germany is a land that demands exploration. Just pack your curiosity and an open mind and we guarantee you'll have a ball. Here's what our authors, staff and travellers loved most about it.

RICHARD N

① BRANDENBURG GATE, BERLIN

The city of Berlin is utterly amazing. There's history everywhere, whether it is something you didn't know or something sad and horrible. I love being able to walk everywhere, enjoying an amazing building or other piece of architecture, like the Brandenburg Gate (p114), at every corner, or being part of history everywhere you stop and just open your eyes and look. The amalgamation of the old and new works so well – your heart wants to cry for the history and smile for the present and future.

Fabre Aurelien,
Traveller, France

RICHARD NEBESKY

② BERLIN WALL

It's been 20 years since the Berlin Wall (p126) collapsed but you can still sense the ghosts of the Cold War when standing in the shadow of a surviving section of this grim and grey divider of humanity.

**Andrea Schulte-Peevers,
Lonely Planet Author, Germany**

A EASTLAND / ALAMY

③ STASI MUSEUM, BERLIN

They hid tiny cameras in watering cans and flower-pots, stole keys from schoolchildren to install listening devices in their homes and collected body-odour samples from suspects' groins. East Germany's Ministry for State Security, better known as the Stasi, was truly an all-pervasive power with an all-out zeal and twisted imagination when it came to controlling, manipulating and repressing its own people. Get the full low-down at the exhibit set up inside the original Stasi headquarters (p129) in Berlin.

**Andrea Schulte-Peevers,
Lonely Planet Author, Germany**

④ ZWINGER, DRESDEN

I was on my first visit to the history-filled city of Dresden with my Lonely Planet *Germany* guide in hand and not too sure what there was to see! Well, if you are like me and enjoy art, architecture and history and want to be blown away, then the Zwinger (p181) is a must-do. It is truly a jaw-dropping sight to see – I was in awe. If it wasn't a beautiful fountain (and there are many), then it was a cute cherub to look at. You can walk around or just sit and stare or do both. The Zwinger has so much going on and it's so easy to get lost in time – make sure you have lots of time in this city because there is a lot to see at the Zwinger alone.

**Clara Monitto,
Traveller, Germany**

5 SCHLOSS NEUSCHWANSTEIN, FÜSSEN

We were stoked to get our rental car upgraded to a Mercedes – what could be more perfect for the autobahn? We quickly discovered that while the car was comfortable at very high speeds, our nerves were not and we had to frequently let old jalopies whiz past us. The other lesson we learned was to not ignore umlauts – those two dots above vowels. Typing Fussen instead of Füssen into our GPS cost us a few hours. But ever since I saw a picture of Schloss Neuschwanstein (p352) 10 years earlier, I was determined to make it there. When we finally arrived, the sheer magnificence (and gaudiness) of the castle was all the more amazing.

Michaela Caughlan,
Lonely Planet Staff, USA

6 SANSSOUCI, POTSDAM

This glorious park and palace ensemble (p157) is what happens if a king has good taste, plenty of cash and access to the finest architects and artists of the day. I never tire of the view of Frederick the Great's petite retreat atop the vine-draped terraces or of discovering yet another romantic corner in the rambling park.

Andrea Schulte-Peevers,
Lonely Planet Author, Germany

EATING WURST FROM A SAUSAGE STAND

Every time my husband and I travel back to Germany, visiting a sausage stand is one of our top priorities. There are lots of varieties (see p79), but my favourite is *Currywurst*, pork sausage cut into slices and topped with ketchup and curry powder, best enjoyed with *Pommes rot-weiss* (French fries with mayonnaise and ketchup).

Birgit Jordan,
Traveller, Australia

JOEFOXBERLIN / ALAMY

8

BAUHAUS BUILDINGS, DESSAU

Chances are you have a little Bauhaus in your house: perhaps the chair you sit on or the table at which you dine. 'Form follows function' was the main credo of the Bauhaus school, perhaps the most influential movement of architecture and design in the 20th century. Come to Dessau (p223) to see where Gropius, Klee, Kandinsky and their colleagues did their best work.

Andrea Schulte-Peevers, Lonely
Planet Author, Germany

EDDIE GERALD / ALAMY

KEITH VAN-LOEN / ALAMY

9

BAUHAUS

7

HOFBRÄUHAUS, MUNICH

A quintessentially Bavarian experience, a night out on the steins at the celebrated Hofbräuhaus (p309) is unmissable. Even the most ubercool, kitsch-hating teetotaller will sooner or later gravitate to the world's most famous beer hall out of sheer curiosity. Order a large wet one, have a sway to the oompah band and watch as the tourists and *Stammgäste* (regular patrons) become ever tipsier and more boisterous as the evening progresses. Raucous laughter, compulsory; red-faced antics, a must.

Marc Di Duca,
Lonely Planet Author, United Kingdom

NIKOLAIKIRCHE, LEIPZIG

The first time I walked into the Nikolaikirche (p197), I was mesmerised. I'm not sure what impressed me more – the arched ceiling painted like a frosted, pastel wedding cake or the palm-like pillars towering above me. Then I found out about the peace prayers it has hosted since 1982 and the infamous demonstrations in 1989, and it all came together: this church is an exquisite element of history, and a constant source of tranquillity.

Caroline Sieg, Lonely Planet Author, Germany

10

IMAGEBROKER / ALAMY

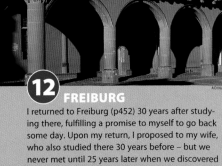

ADINA TOVY

12 FREIBURG

I returned to Freiburg (p452) 30 years after studying there, fulfilling a promise to myself to go back some day. Upon my return, I proposed to my wife, who also studied there 30 years before – but we never met until 25 years later when we discovered we shared an interest in Freiburg and Germany. We now travel there for several weeks each year, visiting friends in Freiburg and all over Germany. A promise fulfilled!

Robert Purrenhage, Traveller, USA

MANFRED GOTT

11 HEIDELBERG

The first glimpse of the bridge over the Neckar River in Heidelberg (p414), the university city that inspired Turner's paintbrush with its whimsical castle and Mark Twain's pen with its raucous nightlife.

Kerry Christiani, Lonely Planet Author, Germany

CRUISIN' AROUND HAMBURG ON A BIKE

Getting around Germany's sprawling 'harbouropolis' (p674) is a breeze, thanks to simple, cheap and often wonderfully scenic transport options, including boat, rail and bus networks. But perhaps the most enjoyable way to explore the country's second-largest city is under your own steam.

Catherine Le Nevez,
Lonely Planet Author, France

13

MARK DAFFEY

AACHEN CATHEDRAL

Charlemagne's palace chapel and burial site (p586) is one of Germany's most famous churches and is a rare example of Carolingian architecture. No matter how many times I set foot inside this majestic space, I'll always be awed by the harmony of its design, the iridescent stained-glass windows, the precious works of art and the momentous sense of history that hangs above it all.

Andrea Schulte-Peevers,
Lonely Planet Author, Germany

14

EYEWAVE / ALAMY

(15) OKTOBERFEST

Are you a beer lover? Well, Munich's Oktoberfest (p314) is the festival for you! Twenty-odd beer halls hold thousands of like-minded beer lovers. Once you settle in for your first stein, you realise this is more about the people than the beer. I spent my first day in the company of some locals who were here for their 27th straight year and after 10 minutes they treated me like a life-long friend. Then with three hours sleep, I woke up and did it again, only to find another amazing bunch of friends.

**Damian Hughes,
Traveller, Australia**

Contents

Regional Map Contents

Schleswig-Holstein p701
Hamburg p675
Bremen p661
Mecklenburg-Western Pomerania p727
Lower Saxony pp614-15
Berlin p103
Saxony-Anhalt p218
Brandenburg p156
North Rhine–Westphalia p558
Harz Mountains p241
Saxony p176
Thuringia p262
Hesse p528
Rhineland-Palatinate & Saarland p481
Bavaria pp296-7
Baden-Württemberg p404

Destination Germany

With nine European borders and a location smack dab in the heart of the continent, Germany could stake a convincing claim to being the most 'European' of all countries. Packing over 80 million people into a pretty tight frame, it's an economic and political powerhouse with bewitching scenery, pulsating cities, progressive culture and an awareness of a historic legacy teetering between horror and greatness.

Few countries have had as much impact on the world as Germany, a land of innovation that has given us the printing press, the automobile, aspirin and MP3 technology. It's the birth place of Martin Luther, Albert Einstein, Karl Marx, Goethe, Beethoven, the Grimm brothers and other players on the world stage. As you travel around, you'll have plenty of brushes with such genius but, perhaps, Germany's scenery lifts the spirit even more. The jagged peaks of the big-shouldered Bavarian Alps unfold above flowering mountain pastures where cows graze lazily. Mighty rivers flow through romantic valleys, past steep vineyards and fairy-tale forests. You'll encounter history in towns where streets were laid out before Columbus set sail and in mighty castles looming above prim, half-timbered villages. Vibrant cities like Berlin, Hamburg, Munich and Cologne are cultural cauldrons offering a kaleidoscope of experiences, from high-brow opera to underground dance parties.

Solidly democratic, Germany has long been a driving force behind European integration and, for much of its recent history, has fashioned itself as a model of national integration into the European Union (EU). Since reunification in 1990, however, it has also been focusing more attention upon itself as a nation, especially by questioning whether or not it should have a stronger voice in Europe and the world. The German National Army *(Bundeswehr)*, for instance, has been involved in military conflicts since 2001, most notably in Afghanistan. With more than 3000 soldiers in charge of operations in the northern region, the German contingent is the third largest within the International Security Assistance Force (ISAF). Images of flag-draped coffins have launched an increasingly spirited debate about whether Germany should be part of armed conflict at all. The soul-searching reached a new peak in late 2009, when an air strike ordered by a German officer resulted in Afghan civilian casualties.

Looking inward, there's considerable discontent among Germans when it comes to assessing the economic and societal progress made since reunification. A major study by the Deutsches Institut für Wirtschaftsforschung (DIW; German Institute for Economic Research) revealed that less than half of the population considers themselves better off now than in 1990. One in four ex-GDR citizens felt that they had a better life in East Germany. The perception is not helped by the fact that there's still a considerable income gap between the two former Germanys (€1444 monthly household net income in the former West versus €1149 in the former East).

For the past two decades, Germany's political landscape has been evolving from a three party system – the Sozialdemokratische Partei Deutschlands (SPD; Social Democratic Party of Germany); the Christlich Demokratische Union Deutschlands (CDU; Christian Democratic Union of Germany) and the CDU's Bavarian sister party, the Christlich-Soziale Union (CSU; Christian Social Union); and the Freie Demokratische Partei (FDP; Free Democratic Party) – into a five party system that includes Bündnis 90/Die Grünen (Alliance 90/The Greens) and the relative newcomer, Die Linke (The Left). The Left grew out of the Sozialistische Einheitspartei Deutschlands

FAST FACTS

Area: 357,045 sq km

Population: 82.7 million

GDP: €2.49 trillion (2008)

Inflation: 0% (April 2009)

Unemployment: 8.35% (August 2009)

Life expectancy: women 82.42 years, men 76.26 years

Most famous civil criminal: Fritz Haarmann (1879–1925), who killed at least 24 people and supposedly drank their blood

Percentage of children born outside marriage: 30%

Number of bicycles: 68 million (2008)

Most popular children's names: Marie and Leon (2008)

(SED; Socialist Unity Party of Germany), the former communist party of East Germany.

When the 2005 election failed to produce a clear winner, a grand coalition of the SPD and CDU/CSU was formed under the leadership of Angela Merkel, Germany's first woman chancellor. Germans, who at the time were overwhelmingly in favour of a grand coalition, hoped that the two largest parties would bury their hatchets and work together to tackle the country's most pressing problems: long-term unemployment, health and pension systems sorely in need of financial reform, migration and citizenship issues, as well as such hot potatoes as a tax system many believe is skewed to benefit the better-off, a hefty national debt, declining real income and a perceived lack of economic incentives for individuals and small business. As it turned out, successes were modest since compromises outnumbered gutsy reforms. As one minister put it, the grand coalition was something between a forced and an arranged marriage.

Then came the financial crisis of 2008–09, which drove up the public debt as massive amounts of money were pumped into ailing German banks. One of the more populist government responses to the crisis was the so-called *Abwrackprämie* (literally 'scrap premium', akin to the US 'cash for clunkers' scheme). Car owners willing to scrap their vehicle if older than nine years received €2500 towards the purchase of a brand-new one. Almost two million Germans took advantage of this scheme, which was intended to boost business for domestic car manufacturers and dealers and push polluters off the road. On the whole, the short-term result was positive, but many economists doubt the program's long-term usefulness.

The 2009 elections showed people's disillusionment with the grand coalition by putting a centre-right alliance of CDU/CSU and FDP into power. While the former dropped a couple of percentage points to 33.8%, support for the pro-business FDP grew by a third to 14.6%, thereby increasing its political strength within the coalition. It was a personal victory for the socially liberal but free-market-fixated FDP, which is led by Guido Westerwelle, one of Germany's few openly gay politicians. The junior party's new self-confidence makes it more difficult for Merkel – who's often criticised for her low-profile political style – to set the political agenda. One of the more controversial goals of the FDP is to weaken the laws that protect workers from dismissal. The party is also in favour of lowering taxes, despite the enormous national debt. CDU/CSU party leaders hope that Merkel will show some teeth and adopt a clearer political stance, even if that means losing her title as 'mother of the nation'.

The SPD, meanwhile, suffered its worst election outcome since the founding of the Federal Republic of Germany in 1949 and will be part of the opposition for the first time since 1998. Unable to define itself to voters on the left, it garnered a paltry 23%, haemorrhaging votes to both Alliance 90/The Greens and the Left.

One of the most divisive topics during the election was nuclear energy and waste. In the 1990s the SPD and Alliance 90/The Greens coalition had passed legislation to take the country's nuclear-power stations off-line by 2020. Under the new CDU/CSU and FDP government, however, this deadline is expected to be extended, at least for some power stations, so as to bridge possible shortfalls until alternative energy sources mature.

Wind and solar energy are growing industries in Germany, and Alliance 90/The Greens in particular see these and other environmentally friendly sources as a driving force in job creation. By late 2009 household solar collectors were contributing about 6000 megawatts each year to Germany's needs – the equivalent of about seven medium-sized nuclear-power stations.

Meanwhile, Gorleben, Germany's controversial intermediate nuclear-waste disposal site in Lower Saxony, is claimed by some in Germany's antinuclear movement to be potentially unsafe. To make matters worse, the nearby Asse storage facility – where radioactive waste was deposited when the nuclear-power industry was in its infancy – was found to be flooded with water and dangerously near collapse. Nuclear energy and Gorleben, which for many years have been the focus of large-scale and often violent demonstrations, are likely to remain hotly debated issues in the future, long after the dust from Germany's 2009 election has settled.

Getting Started

No matter whether you're a backpacker, a three-button suit, a lifestyle jet-setter, a trendy urban nomad or travelling with the tots, you'll find all your travel needs and expectations met in Germany. Reservations for rooms and travel arrangements are recommended between June and early September and around major holidays, but otherwise you can keep your advance planning to a minimum.

WHEN TO GO

See Climate Charts (p763) for more information.

Any time is a good time to visit Germany, even though most people prefer to come between May and September, when sunny skies and warm weather are most likely. Much of life moves outdoors: beer gardens and outdoor cafes are in full swing; festivals and alfresco events enliven cities and villages. This is also the best time for hiking, cycling, water sports and other outdoor pursuits. On the downside, you may have to deal with clogged roads, expensive and elusive lodging and crowds at castles, theme parks and other major attractions.

The shoulder seasons (March to May, and October) bring fewer tourists, often surprisingly pleasant weather and a riot of colour: wildflowers and blooming trees in spring, foliage in autumn.

With the exception of winter sports, activities between November and early March are likely to focus more on culture and city life. Expect reduced opening times or seasonal closures at museums and other sightseeing venues. Some smaller lodging properties, especially in rural areas, close down through November until early December, when they reopen for the holiday season. The ski season usually kicks off in early to mid-December, moves into full swing after New Year's and winds down sometime in March.

For related information, see p763 and p766, and the Events Calendar on p24.

COSTS & MONEY

If you're used to £5 pints, $12 glasses of cabernet or €8 lattes, you're in for a pleasant surprise when visiting Germany. You should be able to live quite comfortably on €120 to €150 per day (per person, travelling as an adult couple). For mere survival, budget on between €40 and €70, which will have you camping or hostelling, preparing your own meals and limiting your entertainment. For ideas on how to stretch your euro further, see p765.

HOW MUCH?

Adult admission to Schloss Neuschwanstein €9

Berlin's best doner kebab €2.80

Bike rental per day €6-12

Mass (1L) of beer at Oktoberfest €8.60

Cinema ticket €6-10

Comfortable midrange accommodation starts at about €80 for a double with breakfast (€60 in some rural areas). Many hostels and hotels have special 'family' rooms with three or four beds, or they can supply sleeping cots for a small extra fee. For more on travelling with kids, see p763.

A two-course meal in an average restaurant costs between €20 and €30 per person, including a beverage. The bill will be lower if you stick to cafes or casual eateries and skip alcoholic drinks. Kids' menus or dishes are quite common.

Museum admission ranges from €0.50 in small local-history museums to €15 for international blockbuster exhibits. Some sights and museums are free, or have admission-free days, and discounts are offered for children, teens, students and seniors.

Car-hire costs vary widely, but you should figure on spending at least €45 per day for a medium-sized vehicle. Flick to p781 in the Transport chapter for more details.

TRAVELLING RESPONSIBLY

Hotels, restaurants and sights that go the extra mile when it comes to being green are listed in our GreenDex (see p826). Another excellent source is the booklet *Tips for Green Travel in Germany*, available as a free download from www.cometogermany.com/pdf/Broschuere_Green_Travel_Tips.pdf.

Accommodation

Many properties follow simple eco-initiatives, such as offering you the option of reusing your towels and sheets, switching to soap dispensers, replacing plastic or styrofoam cups with glass and dropping prepackaged items from the breakfast buffet. Guests can often borrow bicycles for free or a small fee. Newer hotels are sometimes built using local and/or ecofriendly materials. Recycling is *de rigueur*.

You can help raise awareness among hotel staff by thanking them for any ecofriendly programs they offer; if they don't have any, politely encourage them to do so and provide a few constructive hints.

Organisations that certify ecofriendly lodgings include www.biohotels.info, www.viabono.de (in German) and www.ecocamping.de (in German).

Food

Whenever possible eat at locally owned restaurants to support the local economy. Take fast food off the menu. The German word for organic is *'bio'* and you'll see it everywhere these days, even in discount supermarkets like Plus or Aldi. Many chefs have gone 'locavore', meaning they'll source their meat and produce from small regional farms rather than importing it from who knows where. Farmers markets abound and local farmers often set up roadside stands. Germany's water is perfectly safe and clean. If carrying a bottle of water, refill it in bathrooms or at water fountains.

Transport

Even if you're travelling by car, consider ditching it at least part of the time. Getting around between towns or to tourist attractions and trail heads by train or bus is usually uncomplicated and inexpensive since timetables are often designed with visitors' needs in mind. Low-emission or alternative-fuel bus fleets are increasingly common. If you rent a car, spend a little extra on a hybrid or at least get a fuel-efficient model.

The least polluting way to travel is, of course, by bicycle. Bicycle touring has exploded in popularity in Germany in recent years. There are dozens of signposted long-distance routes, plenty of bike rental shops (indicated throughout this book) and hotels that cater specifically for cycle tourists. Get the low-down on p780.

> 'Bicycle touring has exploded in popularity in Germany in recent years'

TRAVEL LITERATURE

To get you in the mood for your trip, consider reading some of these titles written by travellers who have visited Germany before you.

A Tramp Abroad by Mark Twain is a literary classic that includes keen and witty observations about Germany garnered during his travels in Europe, including a walking tour of the Black Forest in the 1880s. Twain's postscript 'The Awful German Language' is a hilarious read.

Mr Norris Changes Trains and *Goodbye to Berlin* are by Christopher Isherwood, who lived in Berlin during the Weimar years and whose stories inspired the movie *Cabaret*. The book brilliantly and often entertainingly chronicles the era's decadence and despair.

For a different take on the same era, try *What I Saw: Reports from Berlin 1920–1933* by Joseph Roth, a dynamic and insightful chronicler.

TOP 10

GERMANY

Berlin •

Belgium

Luxemb

Poland

MUST-SEE GERMAN MOVIES

Planning and dreaming about your trip to Germany is best done in a comfy living room with a bowl of popcorn in one hand and a remote in the other. Go for a classic or pick from among the great crop of recent made-in-Germany flicks. Look for brief reviews on p63.

1 *Metropolis* (1927) Director: Fritz Lang

2 *Die Legende von Paul und Paula* (1973) Director: Heiner Carow

3 *Das Boot* (1981) Director: Wolfgang Petersen

4 *Der Himmel über Berlin* (*Wings of Desire;* 1987) Director: Wim Wenders

5 *Lola Rennt* (*Run Lola Run;* 1998) Director: Tom Tykwer

6 *Good Bye, Lenin!* (2003) Director: Wolfgang Becker

7 *Der Untergang* (*Downfall;* 2004) Director: Oliver Hirschbiegel

8 *Sophie Scholl – Die Letzten Tage* (*Sophie Scholl – The Final Days;* 2005) Director: Marc Rothemund

9 *Das Leben der Anderen* (*The Lives of Others;* 2006) Director: Florian von Donnersmarck

10 *Der Baader-Meinhof Complex* (*The Baader-Meinhof Complex;* 2008) Director: Uli Edel

TOP READS

One of the best ways to learn about a country's culture and grasp a sense of a people is to immerse yourself in a good book. The following Top 10 – from classics to contemporary works – have won kudos and critical acclaim in Germany and abroad. See p61 for more details.

1 *Grimms Märchen* (*Grimm's Fairy Tales;* 1812) Jacob and Wilhelm Grimm

2 *Der Prozess* (*The Trial;* 1925) Franz Kafka

3 *Berlin Alexanderplatz* (1929) Alfred Döblin

4 *Im Westen Nichts Neues* (*All Quiet on the Western Front;* 1929) Erich Maria Remarque

5 *Die Blechtrommel* (*The Tin Drum;* 1959) Günter Grass

6 *Kindheitsmuster* (*Patterns of Childhood;* 1976) Christa Wolf

7 *Der Mauerspringer* (*The Wall Jumper;* 1995) Peter Schneider

8 *Russendisko* (*Russian Disco;* 2000) Wladimir Kaminer

9 *Der Vorleser* (*The Reader;* 2002) Bernhard Schlink

10 *Stasiland* (2004) Anna Funder

OUR FAVOURITE FESTIVALS & EVENTS

Germans really know how to let their hair down, and there's almost always something interesting happening around the country. Here are 10 festivals worth planning a trip around. Also see the various destination chapters and the Events Calendar on p24.

1 Berlinale (International Film Festival; Berlin), February (p134)

2 Cannstatter Volksfest, Stuttgart (Baden-Württemberg) September/October (p408)

3 Karneval/Fasching (various regions), Cologne (p575), Munich (p319)

4 Frankfurt Book Fair, Frankfurt am Main (Hesse), September–October (p536)

5 Hamburger Dom (Hamburg), March (p685)

6 Karneval der Kulturen (Berlin), late May (p134)

7 Kieler Woche, Kiel (Schleswig-Holstein), June (p709)

8 Bach Festival, Leipzig (Saxony), around Ascension Day (p201)

9 Landshuter Hochzeit, Landshut (Bavaria), every four years in July (p394)

10 Munich Oktoberfest (Bavaria), mid-September (p319)

DON'T LEAVE HOME WITHOUT...

- Valid travel and health insurance (p767)
- Memorising at least a few basic words of German (p791)
- Loose pants to accommodate a growing beer belly
- Hotel or camping reservations if travelling outside the cities in summer (p756)
- Nerves of steel for driving on the autobahns (p784)
- Towel and soap if staying in hostels, private rooms or cheap *Pensionen*
- Good maps or a GPS for finding your way on country roads (p768)
- A set of smart clothes and shoes for hitting big-city clubs, the opera or fancy restaurants
- Emergency drug prescriptions and spare glasses or contact lenses

---

There's also *The Temple,* an autobiographical novel by one of Britain's most celebrated 20th-century poets, Stephen Spender. It is based on his travels to Germany in the late 1920s and his encounters with, among others, Isherwood.

It's a tough slog, but Claudio Magris' *Danube* certainly has its moments. Part travelogue, part meditation, it follows the great river through Bavaria and beyond, reflecting on the events that took place along it and the people who've lived there.

The Bells in Their Silence: Travels Through Germany (2004) was written by Michael Gurra, an American literature professor who spent a year living and travelling around Germany in the early 1990s. This travelogue combines a literary tour of the country with impressionistic observations about daily life.

Patrick Leigh Fermor's *A Time of Gifts* (1977) is a keen and readable account of the author's epic journey on foot from Holland to Turkey, passing through the Rhine and Danube valleys, in the years before WWII.

INTERNET RESOURCES

Deutsche Welle (www.dw-world.de) The online version of the German international broadcasting service has news and background information about Germany, on-demand audio and video feeds and newsletter sign-ups.

Deutschland Online (www.magazine-deutschland.de) Online version of *Deutschland Magazine,* with interesting features on culture, business and politics.

Deutschland Portal (www.deutschland.de) The ultimate gateway to online information about Germany.

Facts about Germany (www.tatsachen-ueber-deutschland.de) An excellent and comprehensive reference about all aspects of German society, including education, culture, media, foreign policy and the economy.

German National Tourist Office (www.germany-tourism.de) Official site packed with information on all aspects of travel to and within Germany.

Online German Course (www.deutsch-lernen.com) Free language lessons for absolute beginners and moderately advanced students.

Events Calendar

Germany has a packed schedule of festivals and special events. Mentioned here are those celebrated either throughout the nation or in specific regions. For more merriment, see the Festivals & Events sections in the destination chapters.

JANUARY TO MARCH

KARNEVAL/FASCHING   Feb or Mar
The pre-Lenten season is celebrated with costumed street partying, parades, satirical shows and general revelry, primarily in Düsseldorf, Cologne (p575) and Mainz, but also in the Black Forest and Munich.

APRIL

WALPURGISNACHT   30 Apr
The pagan Witches' Sabbath festival (p259) has Harz villages roaring to life as young and old dress up as witches and warlocks and parade through the streets singing and dancing.

MAIFEST   30 Apr
Villagers celebrate the end of winter by chopping down a tree (Maibaum), painting, carving and decorating it, and staging a merry revelry with traditional costumes, singing and dancing.

MAY

MUTTERTAG   2nd Sun
Mothers are honoured, much to the delight of florists, sweet shops and greeting-card companies.

HAFENGEBURTSTAG   early May
Five-day festival in the Hamburg harbour area (p685).

WAVE-GOTIK-TREFFEN   late May
The world's largest Goth gathering (p201) takes over Leipzig during the long Whitsuntide (Pentecost) weekend.

JUNE

VATERTAG   May/early Jun
Father's Day, now also known as Männertag (Men's Day), is essentially an excuse for men to get liquored up with the blessing of the missis. It's always on Ascension Day.

AFRICA-FESTIVAL   early Jun
Europe's largest festival of African music (p340), held in Würzburg.

KIELER WOCHE   late Jun
Kiel Week (p709) is a huge festival for salty types, with yachting regattas and nonstop partying on the Baltic Sea.

CHRISTOPHER STREET DAY   late Jun
Major gay-pride celebrations erupt in Berlin, Cologne and Hamburg, but also in Dresden, Munich, Stuttgart and Frankfurt.

JULY & AUGUST

SHOOTING FESTIVALS
Over a million Germans (mostly men) belong to shooting clubs and show off their skills at marksmen's festivals. The biggest one is in Hanover; the oldest, in Düsseldorf.

WINE FESTIVALS
As soon as the grapes have been harvested, the wine festival season starts, with wine tastings, folkloric parades, fireworks and the election of local and regional wine queens. The Dürkheimer Wurstmarkt (p495) is one of the biggest and most famous.

**SCHLESWIG-HOLSTEIN
MUSIC FESTIVAL**   mid-Jul–Aug
Leading international musicians and promising young artists perform during this festival (p710) in castles, churches, warehouses and animal barns throughout Germany's northernmost state.

SAMBA FESTIVAL   mid-Jul
This orgy of song and dance (p381) draws around 90 bands and up to 200,000 visitors to Coburg.

KINDERZECHE   3rd week of Jul
Ten-day festival (p346) with children performing in historical re-enactments, a pageant and the usual merriment, held in Dinkelsbühl.

WAGNER FESTIVAL   late Jul-Aug
This prestigious opera and music festival (p379) is held in Bayreuth.

SEPTEMBER, OCTOBER & NOVEMBER

ERNTEDANKFEST   late Sep/early Oct
Rural towns celebrate the harvest festivals with decorated church altars, processions (*Erntedankzug*) and villagers dressed in folkloric garments.

OKTOBERFEST   mid-Sep–early Oct
Munich's legendary beer-swilling party (p314). Enough said.

FRANKFURT BOOK FAIR   mid-Oct
The world's largest book fair (p536), with 7300 exhibitors from over 100 countries, comes to Frankfurt.

ST MARTINSTAG   10-11 Nov
This festival honours the 4th-century St Martin, known for his humility and generosity, with a lantern procession and a re-enactment of the famous scene where he cuts his coat in half to share with a beggar. This is followed by a big feast of stuffed, roasted goose.

DECEMBER

NIKOLAUSTAG   5-6 Dec
On the eve of 5 December, German children put their boots outside the door hoping that St Nick will fill them with sweets and small toys overnight. Ill-behaved children, though, may find only a prickly rod left behind by St Nick's helper, Knecht Ruprecht.

CHRISTMAS MARKETS   late Nov-24 Dec
Mulled wine, spicy gingerbread cookies, shimmering ornaments – these and lots more are typical features of German Christmas markets, held from late November until 24 December. Nuremberg's Christkindlmarkt (p370) is especially famous.

SILVESTER   31 Dec
In Germany, New Year's Eve is called Silvester in honour of the 4th-century pope under whom the Romans adopted Christianity as their official religion. The new year is greeted with fireworks launched by thousands of amateur pyromaniacs.

Itineraries
CLASSIC ROUTES

CITY DELIGHTS
Two Weeks / Berlin to Hamburg

Bookended by great cities, this route offers some of the best culture, character and architecture the country has to offer. Kick off in **Berlin** (p99) with its top-notch museums, old and bold architecture and nice-to-naughty nightlife. From here head south to **Dresden** (p176), sitting proud and pretty in its baroque splendour right on the Elbe River. Next stop is **Munich** (p295), where an evening in a beer garden is the perfect finish to a day of palace and museum hopping. Next up is the Romantic Road, where medieval **Rothenburg ob der Tauber** (p342) is a veritable symphony of half-timbered houses. Cut west to historic **Heidelberg** (p414), idyllically serenaded by an ancient fortress, then north to **Worms** (p487) and **Mainz** (p482), with their fantastic Romanesque cathedrals. Follow the Rhine River through the fairy-tale scenery of the Middle Rhine to cosmopolitan **Cologne** (p568) for a spin around Germany's grandest Gothic cathedral. Wrap up your trip in lovable **Bremen** (p661) and open-minded **Hamburg** (p674), which welcome you with maritime charm.

Prepare for a roller coaster of urban treasures on this 1700km journey that takes in progressive big-city beauties, medieval metropolises mired in history and elegant residential towns shaped by royal visions.

BIGGEST HITS OF THE SOUTH Two Weeks / Frankfurt to Frankfurt

Start your exploration in **Frankfurt** (p528), where you can soak up culture in world-class museums, potent cider in traditional taverns and views of the spectacular city skyline from the river promenade. Next up is **Koblenz** (p501), dramatically located at the confluence of the Rhine and Moselle Rivers. It's the gateway to the **Romantic Rhine** (p499), a scene-stealing combo of steeply terraced vineyards, lordly medieval castles and cute higgledy-piggledy villages. Follow the river south, perhaps stopping in postcard-pretty **St Goar** (p506) and **Bacharach** (p508). Next, follow in the footsteps of Mark Twain in bewitching **Heidelberg** (p414), Germany's oldest university town. Take a break from culture in the celebrity haven of **Baden-Baden** (p443), the legendary spa resort where you can soothe sore muscles in luxurious bathing temples. The town is also the northern gateway to the Black Forest, where you should stop in almost ridiculously picturesque **Gengenbach** (p451) and **Triberg** (p460) on your way to vibrant **Freiburg** (p452), with its imposing minster and fabulous alfresco life in cobbled streets as tangled as computer cables. From here cut east to the vast **Lake Constance** (p467) and follow its scenic northern shore to lovely **Lindau** (p477), a teensy island laced with a maze of cobbled alleys jutting into the water. You're now in Bavaria, en route to the fairy-tale castle of Füssen's **Neuschwanstein** (p352) and **Garmisch-Partenkirchen** (p355), where a train-and-cable-car combo delivers you to the top of the Zugspitze, Germany's highest mountain. Come back down to earth in a beer hall in **Munich** (p295), before wrapping up your journey by oohing and ahing your way up the Romantic Road. Essential stops include **Rothenburg ob der Tauber** (p342) and **Würzburg** (p337), from where it's a quick drive back to Frankfurt.

Germany's southern half presents the mother lode of historic cities, soul-stirring scenery and spirit-lifting culture, as this grand, 1500km loop reveals. It can be 'done' in two weeks, but more time lets you connect more deeply with this land and its feast of treats, treasures and temptations.

ROADS LESS TRAVELLED

MID-GERMAN MEANDERINGS
Two Weeks / Düsseldorf to
Lutherstadt Wittenberg

Kick off your west–east passage in bustling **Düsseldorf** (p558), a magnet for fans of art, shopping and a good time. Those with a penchant for the off-beat will hit the mother lode on the Industrial Heritage Trail through the nearby **Ruhrgebiet** (p590). Quirky delights include former **gas tanks filled with art** (p597) in Oberhausen, blast furnaces turned into **free-climbing zones** (p598) in Duisburg and a colliery turned **museum and adventure playground** (p591) in Essen. East along the A44, stop in **Soest** (p604) and **Paderborn** (p605), both famous for their churches. Plunge into the world of fairy tales in **Hamelin** (p623), the Renaissance town of *The Pied Piper of Hamelin* fame. Close by is restored **Hildesheim** (p633), celebrated for the huge bronze door gracing its cathedral. Continue on to charming **Goslar** (p242), with a 1000-year-old mine and an 11th-century palace. It's also the gateway to the **Harz Mountains** (p240), whose natural splendours are perfect for spending a day or two in the slow lane. Don't leave without sampling the small-town beauty of **Wernigerode** (p249), famous for its colourfully painted medieval houses and as the terminus of the narrow-gauge Harzquerbahn railway to Nordhausen in Thuringia. Continue on to charming **Quedlinburg** (p254), a well-preserved ensemble of half-timbered houses. Then make a beeline straight for **Dessau-Rosslau** (p223), a city that's synonymous with the Bauhaus school of architecture. Ramble around the lush gardens of **Gartenreich Dessau-Wörlitz** (p227) before finishing up in the birthplace of the Reformation, **Lutherstadt Wittenberg** (p229).

This itinerary proves that 'lesser known' doesn't have to mean 'lesser'. Classic and quirky discoveries abound along this 600km-long belt cinched around Germany's surprising middle.

BEST OF THE BALTIC   Two Weeks / Flensburg to Greifswald

Though no stranger to domestic tourism, Germany's towns and resorts fringing the Baltic Sea rarely make it onto international travellers' itineraries – undeservedly so. The first stop, **Flensburg** (p715), easily reached by train or autobahn from Hamburg, is Germany's northernmost town and beckons with a handsome Altstadt. **Schleswig** (p712), a quick hop south, cradles a huge fjord and boasts the intriguing Viking Museum and art-filled Schloss Gottorf. Next up is **Lübeck** (p701), a highlight on this route, with a fairy-tale skyline, enchanting old town and delicious marzipan. East of here, Swedish-flavoured **Wismar** (p741) woos you with a postcard-pretty setting and a lovely step-gabled old town. En route to Rostock, stop in **Bad Doberan** (p740), with its great red-brick minster, quirky Frank Zappa memorial and kid-friendly narrow-gauge train. Though aesthetically challenged, **Rostock** (p733) does have some interesting sights and serves as the region's nightlife hub. **Stralsund** (p744), by contrast, is more sedate but has a very attractive Altstadt and is also the gateway to **Rügen Island** (p747), with its tree-lined country roads, long sandy beaches and mysterious chalk cliffs. To truly traipse off the beaten path, head out to the remote **Darss-Zingst Peninsula** (p743), where nature puts on an especially handsome show. Conclude these meanderings with a stop in **Greifswald** (p754), an old university town close to beach-fringed **Usedom Island** (p755), a popular holiday island that Germany shares with Poland.

A ride along Germany's magical Baltic coast reveals eye candy at every bend of the road. Take your sweet time as you travel along this 500km route from Germany's border with Denmark to where it rubs shoulders with Poland.

TAILORED TRIPS

CASTLES & PALACES

Until unification in 1871, Germany was a mosaic of fiefdoms, whose overseers ruled from the comfort of their Schloss (palace) or *Burg* (castle). A sentimental favourite among Germans is the **Wartburg** (p281) in Eisenach, where Martin Luther translated the Bible into German while in hiding. Less well known but equally impressive is Saxony's **Festung Königstein** (p192), which overlooks the Elbe and is so big, bold and formidable that nobody ever dared attack it. More refined are **Schloss Sanssouci** (p159) in Potsdam and **Schloss Charlottenburg** (p126) in Berlin, both impressive residences of the Prussian Hohenzollern clan. The family's ancestral seat, medieval-looking **Burg Hohenzollern** (p438) near Tübingen

is actually a 19th-century neo-Gothic confection, the original having been destroyed long ago. A similar fate befell **Schloss Heidelberg** (p415), although much of it survives as a romantic ruin. For more romance, visit the robber-baron hang-outs along the Romantic Rhine, especially St Goar's rambling **Burg Rheinfels** (p506) and Braubach's pristine **Marksburg** (p504), which, like the fairy-tale **Burg Eltz** (p520) near the Moselle, has never been destroyed. Germany's most famous palace may be Füssen's **Schloss Neuschwanstein** (p352), but King Ludwig II's more playful **Schloss Linderhof** (p359) or his grand **Schloss Herrenchiemsee** (p334) on Lake Chiemsee are even nicer. Another big Bavarian delight is the baroque **Würzburg Residenz** (p337), designed by star architect Balthasar Neumann.

CATHEDRALS & CHURCHES

Germany has a wealth of houses of worship, the most magnificent of which lift the spirit with their harmonious architecture and priceless treasures. Germany's best-known church, the **Kölner Dom** (p569) in Cologne, is also its biggest: its twin spires dominate the city's distinctive skyline. Another exquisite Gothic cathedral is **Freiburg's Münster** (p453), which has similarly awesome stained-glass windows. The title of 'world's tallest steeple' (reached by 768 steps!) belongs to **Ulm's Münster** (p439), while the **Berliner Dom** (p117) in Berlin claims to be Germany's largest Protestant cathedral. Older than all by several centuries is Charlemagne's octagonal palace chapel, now part of **Aachen's Dom** (p586).

Fans of Romanesque architecture will hit the trifecta along the Rhine with the awe-inspiring cathedrals of **Mainz** (p484), **Worms** (p488) and **Speyer** (p490). Bavaria brims with baroque churches; the **Asamkirche** (p311) in Munich and the **Wieskirche** (p354) in Steingaden are both standouts. The landmark **Frauenkirche** (p180) in Dresden, levelled during WWII, was triumphantly reopened in 2005. Also in former East Germany, the **Schlosskirche** (p230) in Lutherstadt Wittenberg, where Luther published his *Ninety-Five Theses* and found his final resting place, is a major pilgrimage site for Protestants.

Churches with amazing carved altars include the **Jakobskirche** (p343) in Rothenburg ob der Tauber, the **St Nikolaikirche** (p567) in Kalkar and the **Petrikirche** (p595) in Dortmund.

GERMANY IN THE SLOW LANE

Like a fine wine, some of Germany's most memorable destinations are best appreciated in leisurely sips, not quick gulps. So say goodbye to the automobile and hello to the slow lane as you embark on a journey of discovery that will enrich you personally while also lowering your carbon footprint. **Hiddensee** (p753), a tiny island on the Baltic Sea, for instance, is an entirely car-free zone, making bicycle the best way to get around. At the other end of the country, **Oberstdorf** (p360) in the Allgäu has also banned cars, as have most of the **East Frisian Islands** (p656). Germany is crisscrossed with long-distance hiking trails, including the **Rennsteig** (p282) in the Thuringian Forest, one of the oldest and most famous trails in the country. The **Rheinhöhenweg** (p500), along the Romantic Rhine, and the **Rotweinwanderweg** (p496), through the Ahr Valley, also open up lots of fantastic views and have the added benefit of traversing wine regions. If you prefer to two-wheel it, there are plenty of long-distance cycle trails. The nicest of them parallel bodies of water, such as the epic **Elberadweg** (p228), along the Elbe, and the romantic **Neckartal-Radweg** (p403), along the Neckar River. The **Bodensee-Radweg** (p467) around Lake Constance is another popular route. The ultimate in slow travel, though, is canoeing. There's some fantastic terrain to explore along the spidery waterways of the **Spreewald** (p166), while, further south, the whimsically eroded canyon of the **Altmühltal** (p382) provides an even more evocative setting for extended nature explorations afloat.

WORLD HERITAGE SITES

Germany has 33 sites recognised by Unesco for their historical, cultural or natural importance. The latest addition, in 2009, was the **Wattenmeer** (Wadden Sea; p656) in Lower Saxony. Of historical importance is **Trier** (p512), famous for its well-preserved Roman ruins. Several medieval towns have also got the nod, including **Quedlinburg** (p254), **Goslar** (p242), **Bamberg** (p374), **Lübeck** (p701) and **Regensburg** (p388). Take in the lifestyles of the rich and powerful at the baroque palaces of **Schloss Sanssouci** (p159) in Potsdam and **Schloss Augustusburg** (p579) in Brühl, and the medieval castles along the **Romantic Rhine** (p499). The bulging coffers of the Church financed the cathedrals of **Aachen** (p586), **Cologne** (p569), **Hildesheim** (p634) and **Speyer** (p490), the monastery on **Reichenau Island** (p472), the prince-bishops' **Residenz** (p337) in Würzburg and the **Wieskirche** (p354) in Steingaden. Sites honouring Protestant reformer Martin Luther include the **Wartburg** (p281) in Eisenach and memorials in **Lutherstadt Eisleben** (p236) and **Lutherstadt Wittenberg** (p229). **Weimar** (p269) drew a who's who of German thinkers in the 18th century and is the birthplace of the Bauhaus. The **Dessau-Rosslau's Bauhaus buildings** (p224) are also on Unesco's list, as is the grand **Museumsinsel** (p116) in Berlin.

For a change of pace visit Essen's **Zollverein** (p591) colliery and the **Völklinger Hütte** (p525) in Völklingen in the Saarland, both considered outstanding 'cathedrals of industry'.

History

Germany's colourful history begins in a land of forests, windswept coasts and mountains inhabited by Celts and Germanic tribes, who fought the legions of the Roman Empire. By the 9th century, regions east of the Rhine developed their own identity and, for the first time, it became possible to talk about 'German' rulers. But the fortunes of Germany long remained in the hands of feudal rulers, who pursued their own interests at the expense of a unified state. The Middle Ages were a bleak, barbaric time characterised by squabbling princes, religious wars, plague and cultural darkness. Once a federal state did take shape in the 19th century, Germany trod a tumultuous path from unification to war, from democracy to fascism and into WWII, and from there to chilly Cold War division, peaceful reunification and the country that we know today.

The Roman Empire and Its Germanic Peoples by Herwig Wolfram and Thomas Dunlap (translator) is an authoritative history spanning five centuries of Germanic tribe migrations and the foundations of the Roman Empire.

TRIBES & THE ROMANS

The early inhabitants of Germany were Celts and, later, the Germanic tribes. In the Iron Age (from around 800 BC), Germanic tribes on the North German Plain and in the Central Uplands lived on the fringes of Celtic regions and were influenced by the culture without ever melting into it. Evidence of this is still apparent today in Thale, in the Harz Mountains (p258).

The Romans fought pitched battles with the Germanic tribes from about 100 BC. The Germanic tribes east of the Rhine and the Romans fought for control of territory across the river until AD 9, when the Roman general Varus lost three legions – about 20,000 men – in the bloody Battle of the Teutoburg Forest and the Romans abandoned their plans to extend eastwards (see the boxed text, p34). By AD 300, four main groups of tribes had formed: Alemans, Franks, Saxons and Goths.

Two Lives of Charlemagne edited by Betty Radice is a striking biography of Charlemagne, beautifully composed by a monk and a courtier who spent 23 years in Charlemagne's court.

The Roman presence is evoked today in the thermal baths and amphitheatre of Augusta Treverorum (today's Trier), and other Roman relics in Aachen, Xanten, Cologne, Bonn, Mainz (where 4th-century Roman shipwrecks can be viewed), Bingen (prized for its Roman surgical instruments), Koblenz, Augsburg and Regensburg. The Rhine and Moselle vineyards are a lasting tribute to the Romans' penchant for a tipple or two.

THE FRANKISH REICH

Based on the Rhine's western bank, the Frankish Reich became Europe's most important political power in medieval times. This was due, in part, to the Merovingian king Clovis (r 482–511), who united diverse populations. In its heyday the Reich included present-day France, Germany, the Low Countries and half the Italian peninsula. Missionaries such as St Boniface

TIMELINE

800–300 BC	100 BC–AD 9	4th century
Germanic tribes and Celts inhabit large parts of northern and central Germany, but, by around 300 BC, the Celts have been driven back to regions south of the Main River.	Romans and Germanic tribes clash until defeat at the Battle of the Teutoburg Forest halts Roman expansion eastwards. The Romans consolidate territory south of the Limes.	The arrival of Hun horsemen triggers the Great Migration and Germanic tribes are displaced and flee to various parts of the Western Roman Empire. The Lombards settle in northern Italy.

(675–754) – considered the father of German Christianity – crossed the Rhine to convert pagans.

When fighting broke out among aristocratic clans in the 7th century, the Merovingians were replaced by the Carolingians, who introduced hierarchical Church structures. Kloster Lorsch (p546) in present-day Hesse is one fine relic of this era. From his grandiose residence in Aachen, Charlemagne (r 768–814), the Reich's most important king, conquered Lombardy, won territory in Bavaria, waged a 30-year war against the Saxons in the north and was crowned Kaiser by the pope in 800. The cards were reshuffled in the 9th century, when attacks by Danes, Saracens and Magyars threw the eastern portion of Charlemagne's empire into turmoil and four dominant duchies emerged – Bavaria, Franconia, Swabia and Saxony.

Charlemagne's burial in Aachen Dom (Aachen Cathedral; p586) turned a court chapel into a major pilgrimage site (and it remains so today). The Treaty of Verdun (843) saw a gradual carve-up of the Reich and, when Louis the Child (r 900–11) – a grandson of Charlemagne's brother – died heirless, the East Frankish (ie German) dukes elected a king from their own ranks. Thus, the first German monarch was created.

EARLY MIDDLE AGES

Strong regionalism in Germany today has its roots in the early Middle Ages, when dynasties squabbled and intrigued over territorial spoils, watched on helplessly by a toothless, Roman-inspired central state.

The symbolic heart of power was Aachen Dom, which hosted the coronation and burial of dozens of German kings from 936. Otto I was first up in the cathedral. In 962 he renewed Charlemagne's pledge to protect the papacy and the pope reciprocated with a pledge of loyalty to the Kaiser. This made the Kaiser and pope strange and often acrimonious bedfellows for the next 800 years and created the Holy Roman Empire, a nebulous state that survived until 1806 (see the boxed text, p35).

A power struggle between pope and Kaiser, who also had to contend with the local princes or clergy-cum-princes, was behind many of the upheavals in the early Middle Ages. In the Investiture Conflict under the reign of the Salian Heinrich IV (r 1056–1106), the pope cracked down on the practice of simony (selling religious pardons and relics). Heinrich, excommunicated and contrite, stood barefoot in the snow for three days in Canossa in Italy begging forgiveness. He was absolved, but the Reich was convulsed by a 20-year civil war on the issue, which was finally resolved in a treaty signed in the Rhineland-Palatinate town of Worms in 1122. The graves of Heinrich and other Salian monarchs can today be found in the spectacular cathedral in nearby Speyer (p490).

Under Friedrich I Barbarossa (r 1152–90), Aachen assumed the role of Reich capital and was granted its rights of liberty in 1165, the year

The first rulers to promote a strong German identity were Charlemagne's grandson, Louis the German (r 843–76), and Konrad I (r 911–18).

Hildesheim was a centre of power in the Ottonian period (900–1050). Bishop Bernward raised young Otto III (r 983–1002) and graced the town with treasures to befit a new Rome, such as his famous Bernwardstüren in the Hildesheimer Dom.

The use of the title Kaiser was a direct legacy of Roman times (the German word *Kaiser* meaning 'emperor' is derived from 'Caesar').

482	486	716–54
Clovis becomes king of the Franks and unites diverse populations to lay the foundations for a Frankish Reich that begins conquering lands in Western Europe ruled by the crumbling Roman Empire.	Clovis defeats the Romans in the Battle of Soissons in France, the last vestiges of the Western Roman Empire collapse and Romans seek protection among resettled Germanic tribes.	The English Benedictine monk St Boniface undertakes a journey to preach Christianity in Frisia, Hesse, Thuringia and Bavaria. His missionary activities end when he is killed in Frisia.

ROMAN LEGIONS

For many years, Mount Grotenburg near Detmold in North Rhine–Westphalia was thought to be the scene of the Battle of the Teutoburg Forest, but no one can really say for sure where it happened. The most likely candidate is Kalkriese, north of Osnabrück in Lower Saxony, where in the 1990s archaeologists found face helmets, breast shields, bone deposits and other grisly battle remains. Today the site is a **museum and park** (www.kalkriese-varusschlacht.de).

In AD 1 the Romans started building what is today central Europe's largest archaeological site – a wall running 568km from Koblenz on the Rhine to Regensburg on the Danube. Some 900 watchtowers and 60 forts studded this frontier line, dubbed Der Limes (The Limes). The 800km-long Deutsche Limes-Strasse (German Limes Road) cycling route runs between Regensburg in the south and Bad Hönningen in the north (near Koblenz), largely tracing the tower- and fortress-studded fortification. See www.limesstrasse.de for more about the Limes and routes along the wall. Another 280km-long cycling route links Detmold with Xanten (where there's an archaeological park), taking cyclists past various Roman remains and monuments.

Charlemagne was canonised. Meanwhile, Heinrich der Löwe (Henry the Lion), a Welf with an eye for Saxony and Bavaria, extended influence eastwards in campaigns to Germanise and convert the Slavs who populated much of today's eastern Germany. A Slavic minority, the Sorbs, can still be found in the Spreewald region of eastern Germany today. Heinrich, who was very well connected – his second, English wife Mathilde was Richard the Lionheart's sister – founded not only Braunschweig (p635; where his grave is today), but Munich, Lübeck and Lüneburg, too. At the height of his reign, his domain stretched from the north and Baltic coasts to the Alps, and from Westphalia to Pomerania (in Poland).

The Reich gained territory to the east and in Italy, but soon fell apart because of early deaths, squabbling between Welf and Hohenstaufen pretenders to the throne and the election of a king and pope-backed anti-king. At this time kings were being elected by *Kurfürsten* (prince-electors) but crowned Kaiser by the pope – a system that made an unwilling lackey out of a Kaiser. In 1245 the Reich plunged into an era called the Great Interregnum, or the Terrible Time, when Pope Innocent IV annulled his own Kaiser, the Reich was flush with kings, and central authority collapsed into a political heap.

Although the central Reich was only a shadow of its former self, expansion eastwards continued unabated. Land east of the Oder River (now Germany's eastern border) had been settled by German peasants and city dwellers in the mid-12th century. In the 13th century Teutonic knights pushed eastwards, establishing fortress towns such as Königsberg (present-day Kaliningrad). At its peak, the unified state of the knights stretched from the Oder to Estonia. (Later, in the 17th century, a large swathe of this land would become part of Brandenburg-Prussia.)

Heinrich IV's *Gang nach Canossa* is now a German expression to describe doing penance – 'to go to Canossa'.

What's in a name? Past German monarchs include Karl the Fat (r 881–87), Arnulf the Evil and Friedrich the Handsome (both medieval anti-kings), and the righteous Heinrich the Holy (r 1014–24).

732

Charles Martel, king of the Franks, wins the decisive Battle of Tours and stops the progress of Muslims into Western Europe from the Iberian Peninsula, preserving Christianity in the Frankish Reich.

773–800

The Carolingian Charlemagne, grandson of Charles Martel, answers a call for help from the pope. In return he is crowned Kaiser by the pope and under him the Frankish Reich grows in power and extent.

911

Louis the Child dies heirless at the age of 18 and Frankish dukes in the eastern Reich by-pass Charles the Simple in favour of their own monarch, electing the first truly German ruler.

THE HOUSE OF HABSBURG

In 1273 a Habsburg dynasty emerged from the royal heap, mastered the knack of a politically expedient arranged marriage, and dominated European affairs until the 20th century. The arrival of Rudolf (r 1273–91) ended the Terrible Time, but more importantly the Declaration of Rhense (1338) dispensed with the pope's role in crowning a Kaiser. Now the king, elected by the *Kurfürsten*, was automatically Kaiser. In 1356 the Golden Bull set out precise rules for elections and defined the relationship between the Kaiser and the princes. It was an improvement but the Kaiser was still dancing to the tune of the princes.

Dancing, however, was the last thing on the minds of ordinary Germans. They battled with panic lynching, pogroms against Jews and labour shortages – all sparked off by the plague (1348–50) that wiped out 25% of Europe's population. While death gripped the (Ger)man on the street, universities were being established all over the country around this time. The first was in Heidelberg, making it Germany's oldest – and arguably its most spectacular – university city.

A QUESTION OF FAITH

The religious fabric of Germany was cut from a pattern created in the 16th-century Reformation. In the university town of Wittenberg in 1517, German theology professor Martin Luther (1483–1546) made public his *Ninety-Five Theses*, which questioned the papal practice of selling indulgences to exonerate sins. Threatened with excommunication, Luther refused to recant, broke from the Catholic Church and was banned by the Reich, only to be hidden in Wartburg castle (outside Eisenach, in Thuringia; p281), where he

Heinrich the Fowler: Father of the Ottonian Empire by Mirella Patzer brings 10th-century Germany to life in a heady blend of history and fiction.

Once asked who he thought would win an Austria versus Hungary football match, Otto von Habsburg (1912–), the surviving head of the Habsburg family today, is said to have replied: 'Who are we playing?'

WHAT WAS THE HOLY ROMAN EMPIRE?

It was an idea, mostly, and not a very good one. It grew out of the Frankish Reich, which was seen as the successor to the defunct Roman Empire. When Charlemagne's father, Pippin, helped a beleaguered pope (Charlemagne would later do the same), he received the title *Patricius Romanorum* (Protector of Rome), virtually making him Caesar's successor. Having retaken the papal territories from the Lombards, he presented them to the Church (the last of these territories is the modern Vatican state). Charlemagne's reconstituted 'Roman Empire' then passed into German hands.

The empire was known by various names throughout its lifetime. It formally began (for historians, at least) in 962 with the crowning of Otto I as Holy Roman Emperor and finally collapsed in 1806, when Kaiser Franz II abdicated the throne. The empire sometimes included Italy as far south as Rome. Sometimes it didn't – the pope usually had a say in that. It variously encompassed present-day Netherlands, Belgium, Switzerland, Lorraine and Burgundy (in France), Sicily, Austria and an eastern swathe of land that lies in the Czech Republic, Poland and Hungary. It was also known as the 'First Reich' (not to be confused with Otto von Bismarck's Second Reich or Adolf Hitler's Third Reich).

919–1125	1165	1241
Saxon and Salian emperors rule Germany, creating the Holy Roman Empire in 962 when Otto I is crowned Holy Roman Emperor by the pope, reaffirming the precedent established by Charlemagne.	Friedrich I Barbarossa is crowned in Aachen; he canonises Charlemagne and later drowns while bathing in a river in present-day Turkey while co-leading the Third Crusade.	Hamburg and Lübeck sign an agreement to protect their ships and trading routes, creating the basis for the powerful Hanseatic League, which dominates politics and trade across much of Europe.

THE HANSEATIC LEAGUE

The origins of the Hanseatic League go back to various guilds and associations established from about the mid-12th century by out-of-town merchants to protect their interests. After Hamburg and Lübeck signed an agreement in 1241 to protect their ships and trading routes, they were joined in their league by Lüneburg, Kiel and a string of Baltic Sea cities east to Greifswald. By 1356 this had grown into the Hanseatic League, encompassing half a dozen other large alliances of cities, with Lübeck playing the lead role.

At its zenith, the league had about 200 member cities. It earned a say in the choice of Danish kings after fighting two wars against the Danes between 1361 and 1369. The resulting Treaty of Stralsund in 1370 turned it into northern Europe's most powerful economic and political entity. Some 70 inland and coastal cities – mostly German – formed the core of the Hanseatic League, but another 130 beyond the Reich maintained a loose association, making it truly international. During a period of endless feudal squabbles in Germany, it was a bastion of political and social stability. The Lübeck-born author Thomas Mann admired it for having created 'a humane, cosmopolitan society'.

By the 15th century, however, competition from Dutch and English shipping companies, internal disputes and a shift in the centre of world trade from the North and Baltic Seas to the Atlantic had caused decline. The ruin and chaos of the Thirty Years War in the 17th century delivered the final blow, although Hamburg, Bremen and Lübeck retained the 'Hanse City' title. Since reunification, however, well over a dozen cities have decided to adopt the title once again.

The name Habsburg (Hapsburg) originates from *Habichts Burg* (literally 'Hawk Castle'), the spot on the Rhine (in present-day Switzerland, immediately across the border from Germany) from where the great Swabian family first hailed.

The first potato was planted in Germany in 1621, the Gregorian calendar was adopted in 1700 and Germany's first cuckoo clock started ticking in 1730.

translated the New Testament into German. Today, the death mask of Luther can be viewed in the Marktkirche in Halle; another can be seen at Luthers Sterbehaus in Eisleben (p237).

It was not until 1555 that the Catholic and Lutheran churches were ranked as equals, thanks to Karl V (r 1520–58), who signed the Peace of Augsburg (1555), allowing princes to decide the religion of their principality. The more secular northern principalities adopted Lutheran teachings, while the clerical lords in the south, southwest and Austria stuck with Catholicism.

But the religious issue refused to die. Rather, it degenerated into the bloody Thirty Years War, which Sweden and France had joined by 1635. Calm was restored with the Peace of Westphalia (1648), signed in Münster and Osnabrück, but it left the Reich – embracing more than 300 states and about 1000 smaller territories – a nominal, impotent state. Switzerland and the Netherlands gained formal independence, France won chunks of Alsace and Lorraine, and Sweden helped itself to the mouths of the Elbe, Oder and Weser Rivers.

THE ENLIGHTENMENT TO THE INDUSTRIAL AGE

In the 18th century the Enlightenment breathed new life into Germany, inspiring a rabble of autocratic princes to build stunning grand palaces

1245–73	1273	1338
The chaotic period of the Great Interregnum begins when Pope Innocent IV deposes Friedrich II and a string of anti-kings are elected. Local bishops and dukes grab more power, weakening central rule.	The Great Interregnum ends when the House of Habsburg takes over the reins of the Reich and begins its rise to become Europe's most powerful dynasty.	The Declaration of Rhense ends the need for the pope to confirm the Reich's elected Kaiser, abolishing the dependence whereby the pope crowned the Kaiser in exchange for loyalty and protection.

and gardens across the German lands. Berlin's Schloss Charlottenburg, Potsdam's Sanssouci Park and Dresden's Zwinger are fine examples of the spirit of this new age. Meanwhile, Johann Sebastian Bach and Georg Friedrich Händel were ushered on stage and a wave of *Hochkultur* (high culture) swept through society's top sliver. For the time being, however, the masses remained illiterate.

Brandenburg-Prussia became an entity to be reckoned with, kick-started by the acquisition of former Teutonic Knights' territories and assisted by Hohenzollern king Friedrich Wilhelm I (the Soldier King) and his son, Friedrich II (r 1740–86). After the Seven Years' War (1756–63) with Austria, Brandenburg-Prussia annexed Silesia and sliced up Poland.

At the behest of French emperor Napoleon Bonaparte during the Napoleonic Wars, an imperial deputation secularised and reconstituted German territory between 1801 and 1803. In 1806 the Confederation of the Rhine eradicated about 100 principalities. Sniffing the end of the Holy Roman Empire, Kaiser Franz II (r 1792–1806) packed his bags for Austria, renamed himself Franz I of Austria and abdicated the throne. That same year Brandenburg-Prussia fell to the French, but humiliating defeat prompted reforms that brought it closer to civil statehood: Jews were granted equality and bonded labour was abolished.

In 1813, with French troops driven back by the Russians, Leipzig witnessed one of Napoleon's most significant defeats. At the Congress of Vienna (1815), Germany was reorganised into a confederation of 35 states and an ineffective Reichstag (legislative assembly) was established in Frankfurt, an unsatisfactory solution that only minimally improved on the Holy Roman Empire. The Reichstag poorly represented the most populous states and failed to rein in Austro-Prussian rivalry.

By the mid-19th century, the engines of the modern, industrial age were purring across the country. A newly created urban proletarian movement fuelled calls for central government, while the Young Germany movement of satirists lampooned the powerful of the day and called for a central state.

Berlin, along with much of the southwest, erupted in riots in 1848, prompting German leaders to bring together Germany's first ever freely elected parliamentary delegation in Frankfurt's Paulskirche. Austria, meanwhile, broke away from Germany, came up with its own constitution and promptly relapsed into monarchism. As revolution fizzled in 1850, Prussian king Friedrich Wilhelm IV drafted his own constitution, which would remain in force until 1918.

'HONEST OTTO' VON BISMARCK

The creation of a unified Germany with Prussia at the helm was the glorious ambition of Otto von Bismarck (1815–98), a former member of the

For a comprehensive overview of German history, see the German Culture website www .germanculture.com.ua.

Did you know that 9 November is Germany's 'destiny date'? It was the day of the uprising in 1848, the failed revolution in 1918, Hitler's Munich Putsch in 1923, the Night of Broken Glass in 1938, and the day the Wall fell in 1989.

'Laws are like sausages. It's better not to see them being made.'
OTTO VON BISMARCK

1348–50	1356	1414–18
The plague wipes out 25% of Europe's population. Pogroms are launched against Jews, who are accused of poisoning wells. The loss of workers leads to improved circumstances for those able-bodied who survive.	The Golden Bull, formalises the election of the Kaiser. The prince-electors are the archbishops of Cologne, Trier and Mainz, the rulers of Bohemia, Saxony and Brandenburg, and the count of Palatinate.	The so-called 'Great Schism', which has plagued the Catholic Church since 1378, is resolved at the Council of Constance in southern Germany. In 1415 the Bohemian reformer Jan Hus is burned on the stake.

Reichstag and Prussian prime minister. An old-guard militarist, he used intricate diplomacy and a series of wars with neighbours Denmark and France to achieve his aims. In 1871 – later than most other European countries – Germany was unified, with Berlin the proud capital of Western Europe's largest state. At that time, Germany extended from Memel (Klaipėda in present-day Lithuania) to the Dutch border, including Alsace-Lorraine (southwest) in present-day France and Silesia (southeast) in present-day Poland. The Prussian king was crowned Kaiser of the Reich – a bicameral, constitutional monarchy – at Versailles on 18 January 1871 and Bismarck became its 'Iron Chancellor'. Suffrage was limited to men in the new Reich and the national colours were black, white and red.

Bismarck's power was based on the support of merchants and *Junker*, a noble class of nonknighted landowners. An ever-skilful diplomat and power broker, Bismarck achieved much through a dubious 'honest Otto' policy, whereby he brokered deals between European powers and encouraged colonial vanities to distract others from his own deeds. He belatedly graced the Reich of Kaiser Wilhelm I with a few African jewels after 1880, acquiring colonies in central, southwest and east Africa as well as numerous Pacific paradises, such as Tonga, where a weary Prussian prince might one day lay down his steel helmet and relax in the sun.

When pressed, Bismarck made concessions to the growing and increasingly antagonistic socialist movement, enacting Germany's first modern social reforms, but this was not his true nature. By 1888 Germany found itself burdened with a new Kaiser, Wilhelm II, who wanted to extend social reform, and an Iron Chancellor who wanted stricter antisocialist laws. Finally, in 1890, the Kaiser's scalpel excised Bismarck from the political scene. After that, the legacy of Bismarck's brilliant diplomacy unravelled and a wealthy, unified and industrially powerful Germany paddled into the new century with incompetent leaders at the helm.

THE GREAT WAR

Technological advances and the toughening of Europe into colonial power blocs made WWI far from 'great'. The conflict began with the assassination of the heir to the Austro-Hungarian throne, Archduke Franz-Ferdinand, in Sarajevo in 1914 and quickly escalated into a European and Middle Eastern affair: Germany, Austria-Hungary and Turkey against Britain, France, Italy and Russia. In 1915 a German submarine attack on a British passenger liner killed 120 US citizens. By 1917 the USA had also entered the war.

The seeds of acrimony and humiliation that later led to WWII were sown in the peace conditions of the Great War. Russia, in the grip of revolution, accepted humiliating peace terms from Germany. Germany, militarily broken, itself teetering on the verge of revolution and caught in a no man's land between monarchy and modern democracy, signed

---

The record for longevity in Germany is held by Maria Laqua (1889–2002), born just after Germany's last Kaiser, Wilhelm II, was crowned. She died at the age of 112, three days before her 113th birthday.

Bismarck to the Weimar Republic is the focus of Hans-Ulrich Wehler's *The German Empire 1871–1918*, a translation of an authoritative German work. For a revealing study of the Iron Chancellor himself, read *Bismarck, the Man and the Statesman* by Gordon Craig.

Marc Ferro's *The Great War 1914–18* is a compelling account of WWI.

1455	1499	1517
Johannes Gutenberg of Mainz prints 180 copies of the Gutenberg Bible in Latin using a moveable type system that revolutionises book printing and allows books to be published in large quantities.	Switzerland fights a war against the ruling Habsburgs and, after defeating the Swabian League (a confederation that comes to the aid of the Habsburgs), declares its independence from the Holy Roman Empire.	Martin Luther makes public his *Ninety-Five Theses* in the town of Wittenburg. His ideas challenge the selling of indulgences, capturing a mood of disillusionment with the Church and the clergy.

THE NIGHT OF THE LONG KNIVES

Conceived to police public meetings and enforce law, the brown-shirted Nazi state police, the Sturmabteilung (SA), had by 1934 become a troublesome bunch – for Germans and their dictator alike. So much so that, on the night of 30 June 1934, Hitler ordered Schutzstaffel (SS) troops to round up and kill high-ranking SA officers. Their leader, Ernst Röhm, was shot and 76 others were hacked to death, knifed or shot.

Hitler hushed up the gruesome night (dubbed 'The Night of the Long Knives') until 13 July when he announced to the Reichstag that the SA (who numbered two million, easily outnumbering the army) would, from that time forth, serve under the command of the army, which, in turn, would swear an oath of allegiance to Hitler. Justice would be executed by himself and the black-shirted SS under the leadership of former chicken-farmer Heinrich Himmler, effectively giving the SS unchallenged power and making it Nazi Germany's most powerful – and feared – force.

---

the Treaty of Versailles (1919), which made it responsible for all losses incurred by its enemies. Its borders were trimmed back and it was forced to pay high reparations. To allow negotiations, a chancellor was appointed who for the first time was responsible to parliament. A mutiny by sailors in the bustling port of Kiel in 1919 triggered a workers' revolt and a revolution in Berlin, spelling a bitter end for Germany's Kaiser, who abdicated the throne and went to the Netherlands.

After abdicating, Kaiser Wilhelm II could settle in Utrecht (in the Netherlands) on the condition that he didn't engage in political activity. One of his last acts was to send a telegram to Hitler congratulating him on the occupation of Paris.

WEIMAR & THE RISE OF HITLER

The end of the war did not create stability – or peace – in Germany. Socialist and democratic socialist parties fought tooth and nail, while the radical Spartacus League (joined by other groups in 1919 to form the German Communist Party; KPD) sought to create a republic based on Marx' theories of proletarian revolution. Following the bloody quashing of an uprising in Berlin, Spartacus founders 'Red' Rosa Luxemburg (1871–1919) and Leipzig-born Karl Liebknecht (1871–1919) were arrested and murdered en route to prison by *Freikorps* soldiers (right-leaning war volunteers). Their bodies were dumped in Berlin's Landwehr canal, only to be recovered several months later and buried in Berlin.

Meanwhile, in July 1919, in the Thuringian city of Weimar (where the constituent assembly briefly sought refuge during the Berlin chaos), the federalist constitution of a new democratic republic was adopted.

The so-called Weimar Republic (1919–33) was governed by a coalition of left and centre parties headed by President Friedrich Ebert of the Sozialdemokratische Partei Deutschlands (SPD; German Social Democratic Party) until 1925 and then by Field Marshal Paul von Hindenburg, a gritty 78-year-old monarchist. The republic, however, pleased neither communists nor monarchists.

In 1923 a postage stamp cost 50 billion marks, a loaf of bread cost 140 billion marks and US$1 was worth 4.2 trillion marks. In November, the new Rentenmark was traded in for one trillion old marks.

1524–25	1555	1618–48
Inspired by the Reformation, peasants in southern and central Germany rise up against their masters, demanding the end of bonded labour. Luther at first supports the peasants but later switches sides.	The Peace of Augsburg allows princes to decide their principality's religion, putting Catholicism and Protestantism on an equal footing. Around 80% of Germany's population is Protestant.	The Thirty Years War sweeps through Germany and leaves it with a depleted population and vast regions reduced to wasteland. The Reich disintegrates into 300-plus states.

JEWS IN GERMANY

The first Jews arrived in present-day Germany with the conquering Romans, settling in important Roman cities on or near the Rhine, such as Cologne, Trier, Mainz, Speyer and Worms. As non-Christians, Jews had a separate political status. Highly valued for their trade connections, they were formally invited to settle in Speyer in 1084 and granted trading privileges and the right to build a wall around their quarter. A charter of rights granted to the Jews of Worms in 1090 by Henry IV allowed local Jews to be judged according to their own laws.

The First Crusade (1095–99) brought pogroms in 1096, usually against the will of local rulers and townspeople. Many Jews resisted before committing suicide once their situation became hopeless. This, the *Kiddush ha-shem* (martyr's death), established a precedent of martyrdom that became a tenet of European Judaism in the Middle Ages.

In the 13th century Jews were declared crown property by Frederick II, an act that afforded protection but exposed them to royal whim. Rabbi Meir of Rothenburg, whose grave lies in Europe's oldest Jewish cemetery in Worms, fell foul of King Rudolph of Habsburg in 1293 for leading a group of would-be emigrants to Palestine; he died in prison. The Church also prescribed distinctive clothing for Jews at this time, which later meant that in some towns Jews had to wear badges.

Things deteriorated with the arrival of the plague in the mid-14th century, when Jews were persecuted and libellous notions circulated throughout the Christian population. The 'blood libel' accused Jews of using the blood of Christians in rituals. The even more bizarre 'host-desecration libel' accused Jews of desecrating or torturing Christ by, among other dastardly deeds, sticking pins into communion wafers, which then wept tears or bled.

Money lending was the main source of income for Jews in the 15th century. Expulsions remained commonplace, however, with large numbers emigrating to Poland, where the Yiddish

---

William Shirer's definitive 1000-plus-page The Rise and Fall of the Third Reich remains a powerful reportage. His depiction of the Berlin of those times is the literary equivalent of the brutal north face of the Eiger.

The first blow to the new republic came in 1920, when right-wing militants forcibly occupied the government quarter in Berlin in the failed 'Kapp Putsch'. In 1923 hyperinflation rocked the republic. That same year Adolf Hitler (1889–1945), an Austrian-born volunteer in the German army during WWI, launched the Munich Putsch with members of his National Socialist German Workers' Party (NSDAP). Hitler wound up in jail for two years, where he wrote his nationalist, anti-Semitic tome, *Mein Kampf*. Once out, he began rebuilding the party.

Hitler's NSDAP gained 18% of the vote in the 1930 elections, prompting him to run against Hindenburg for the presidency in 1932, when he won 37% of a second-round vote. A year later, Hindenburg appointed Hitler chancellor, with a coalition cabinet of Nationalists (conservatives, old aristocrats and powerful industrialists) and National Socialists (Nazis). When Berlin's Reichstag mysteriously went up in flames in March 1933, Hitler had the excuse he needed to request emergency powers to arrest all communist and liberal opponents and push through his proposed Enabling Law, allowing him to decree laws and change the constitution without consulting parliament. The Nazi dictatorship

---

1648	1740–86	1789–1815
The Treaty of Westphalia formalises the independence of Switzerland, and of the Netherlands, ruled by Spain from the early 16th century when Karl V (Carlos I) was also king of Spain and its colonies.	Brandenburg-Prussia becomes a mighty power under Friedrich the Great. Berlin advances to an 'Athens on the Spree' as Absolutism in Europe gives way to the Enlightenment, heralding an explosion in culture and arts.	The French Revolution and, from 1803, the Napoleonic Wars destroy the last vestiges of the Middle Ages in Europe. Napoleon Bonaparte takes Berlin in 1806 and pays homage at the grave of Friedrich the Great.

language developed. The Reformation (including a hostile Martin Luther) and the Thirty Years War brought difficult times for Jewish populations, but by the 17th century they were valued again for their economic contacts.

Napoleon granted Germany's Jews equal rights, but the reforms were repealed by the 1815 Congress of Vienna. Anti-Jewish feelings in the early 19th century coincided with German nationalism and a more vigorous Christianity, producing a large number of influential assimilated Jews, such as the Düsseldorf-born poet Heinrich Heine (1797–1856).

By the late 19th century, Jews had equal status in most respects and Germany had became a world centre of Jewish cultural and historical studies. There was a shift to large cities, such as Leipzig, Cologne, Breslau (now Wrocław in Poland), Hamburg, Frankfurt am Main and the capital, Berlin, where a third of German Jews lived.

Germany became an important centre for Hebrew literature after Russian writers and academics fled the revolution of 1917. The Weimar Republic brought emancipation for the 500,000-strong Jewish community, but by 1943 Adolf Hitler had declared Germany *Judenrein* (literally 'clean of Jews'). This ignored the hundreds of thousands of Eastern European Jews incarcerated on 'German' soil. Around six million Jews died in Europe as a direct result of Nazism and its barbarity.

The number of Jews affiliated with the Jewish community in Germany is currently around 100,000 – the third largest in Europe – but the real number is probably twice that. Many Jews arrived from the former Soviet Union in the 1990s.

There are particularly informative Jewish museums in Berlin (p124) and Frankfurt (p532).

had begun. When Hindenburg died a year later, Hitler fused the offices of president and chancellor to become Führer of the Third Reich.

Nazis in Power

The thumbscrews slowly tightened around Germany. In the 12 short years of what Hitler envisaged as the 'Thousand Year Reich', massive destruction would be inflicted upon German and other European cities; political opponents, intellectuals and artists would be murdered or forced to go underground or into exile; a culture of terror and denunciation would permeate almost all of German society; and Europe's rich Jewish heritage would be decimated.

In April 1933 Joseph Goebbels, head of the well-oiled Ministry of Propaganda, announced a boycott of Jewish businesses. Soon after, Jews were expelled from public service and 'non-Aryans' were banned from many professions, trades and industries. The Nuremberg Laws (1935) deprived non-Aryans of German citizenship and forbade them to marry or have sexual relations with Aryans – anyone who broke these race laws faced the death penalty (and had to pay their own trial and execution costs to boot).

The Colditz Story (1955), directed by Guy Hamilton, is a gripping if sobering watch. Based on the book *The Colditz Story* (1952) by prison escapee Pat Reid, it portrays the escapes of Allied prisoners of war during WWII from the Nazis' legendary high-security prison in Western Saxony.

1806–13	1813 & 1815	1834
The Holy Roman Empire collapses and Napoleon creates the 16-member Confederation of the Rhine after defeating Austrian and Russian troops in the Battle of Austerlitz.	Napoleon is defeated near Leipzig in 1813 and in 1815 at Waterloo. The post-Napoleon Congress of Vienna redraws the map of Europe, creating in the former Reich the German Alliance with 35 states.	The German Customs Union is formed under the leadership of Prussia, making much of Germany a free-trade area and edging it closer to unification; the Union reinforces the idea of a Germany without Austria.

> **THE NIGHT OF BROKEN GLASS**
>
> Nazi horror escalated on 9 November 1938 with the Reichspogromnacht (often called Kristallnacht or the 'Night of Broken Glass'). In retaliation for the assassination of a German consular official by a Polish Jew in Paris, synagogues and Jewish cemeteries, property and businesses across Germany were desecrated, burnt or demolished. About 90 Jews died that night. The next day another 30,000 were incarcerated, and Jewish businesses were transferred to non-Jews through forced sale at below-market prices.

Hitler won much support among the middle and lower-middle classes by pumping large sums of money into employment programs, many involving rearmament and heavy industry. In Wolfsburg, Lower Saxony, affordable cars started rolling out of the first Volkswagen factory, founded in 1938.

That same year, Hitler's troops were welcomed into Austria. Foreign powers, in an attempt to avoid another bloody war, accepted this *Anschluss* (annexation) of Austria. Following this same policy of appeasement, the Munich Agreement was signed in September 1938 by Hitler, Mussolini (Italy), Neville Chamberlain (UK) and Eduardo Daladier (France), and the largely ethnic-German Sudetenland of Czechoslovakia was relinquished to Hitler. By March 1939, he had also annexed Moravia and Bohemia.

Chester Wilmot presents an interesting account of WWII in *The Struggle for Europe*, told from the perspective of an Australian journalist slap bang in the thick of things.

WWII
Early Years

A nonaggression pact was signed between Hitler and Stalin's USSR in August 1939, whereby the Tokyo-Berlin-Rome axis (Hitler had already signed agreements with Italy and Japan) was expanded to include Moscow. Soviet neutrality was assured by a secret Soviet-German protocol that divided up Eastern Europe into spheres of interest.

In late August an SS-staged attack on a German radio station in Gleiwitz (Gliwice), Poland, gave Hitler the excuse to march into Poland. This proved the catalyst for WWII; three days later, on 3 September 1939, France and Britain declared war on Germany.

German engineers don't always get it right. The *U-1206*, a WWII submarine, was sunk off the coast of Scotland after its complicated toilet system malfunctioned and the submarine had to surface.

Poland, but soon also Belgium, the Netherlands and France, quickly fell to Germany. In June 1941 Germany broke its nonaggression pact with Stalin by attacking the USSR. Though successful at first, Operation Barbarossa soon ran into problems and Hitler's troops retreated. With the defeat of the German 6th Army at Stalingrad (today Volgograd) the following winter, morale flagged at home and on the fronts.

The Final Solution

At Hitler's request, a conference in January 1942 on Berlin's Wannsee came up with a protocol clothed in bureaucratic jargon that laid the basis for the

1848	1848	1866
In London *The Communist Manifesto* on class struggle and capitalism, by Trier-born Karl Marx and fellow countryman Friedrich Engels, is published by a group of Germans living in exile in Britain.	The March Revolution breaks out mainly in the Rhineland and southwest German provinces. Nationalists and reformers call for far-reaching changes; a first parliamentary delegation meets in Frankfurt.	Following a successful war against Denmark, Prussia defeats Austria in the Austro-Prussian War, and chancellor Otto von Bismarck, creates a North German Confederation that excludes Austria.

murder of millions of Jews. The Holocaust was a systematic, bureaucratic and meticulously documented genocidal act carried out by about 100,000 Germans, but with the tacit agreement of a far greater number.

Jewish populations in occupied areas were systematically terrorised and executed by SS troops. Hitler sent Jews to concentration camps in Germany (including Sachsenhausen, Buchenwald and Mittelbau Dora) and Eastern Europe. Sinti and Roma (gypsies), political opponents, priests, homosexuals, resistance fighters and habitual criminals were also incarcerated in a network of 22 camps, mostly in Eastern Europe. Another 165 work camps (such as Auschwitz-Birkenau in Poland) provided labour for big industry, including IG Farbenindustrie AG, producer of the cyanide gas Zyklon B that was used in gas chambers to murder more than three million Jews. The former headquarters of this conglomerate is now part of Frankfurt am Main's university campus (see p535). Of the estimated seven million people sent to camps, 500,000 survived.

Resistance to Hitler was quashed early by the powerful Nazi machinery of terror, but it never vanished entirely. On 20 July 1944, Claus Schenk Graf von Stauffenberg and other high-ranking army officers tried to assassinate Hitler and were executed. The mass extermination of Jews and other Nazi atrocities were outlined in the anti-Nazi leaflets distributed in Munich and other cities by the White Rose, a group of Munich university students, whose resistance attempts cost most of them their lives (see the boxed text, p313).

DEFEAT & OCCUPATION

Systematic air raids on German cities followed the invasion of Normandy in France in June 1944, and the return of the Allies to the European mainland. The brunt of the bombings was suffered by the civilian population; Dresden's Frauenkirche (p180), Germany's greatest Protestant church, was destroyed during a British raid in February 1945 that killed 35,000 people, many of them refugees. Today, this church has been painstakingly reconstructed after its haunting ruins for so long stood as a symbol for the destructiveness of war.

With the Russians advancing on Berlin, a defeated and paranoid Führer and his new bride Eva Braun committed suicide on 30 April 1945 in Hitler's Berlin bunker and, on 7 May 1945, Germany capitulated and peace was signed at the US headquarters in Rheims and again in Berlin in what is now the Museum Berlin-Karlshorst (a German-Soviet history museum).

At the Yalta Conference (February 1945), Winston Churchill, Franklin D Roosevelt and Joseph Stalin agreed to carve up Germany and Berlin into four zones of occupation controlled by Britain, the USA, the USSR and France. By July 1945, Stalin, Clement Attlee (who replaced Churchill after a surprise election win) and Roosevelt's successor Harry S Truman were at the table in Schloss Cecilienhof in Potsdam (Brandenburg) to hammer out the details. At Stalin's insistence, France received its chunk from the Allied regions. Regions

Of the dozens of books covering Nazi concentration camps, I Never Saw Another Butterfly: Children's Drawings and Poems from Terezin Concentration Camp 1942–1944, edited by Yana Volakova, says it all. This Way for the Gas, Ladies and Gentlemen by Tadeusz Borowski is equally chilling.

One of a clutch of fabulous films by Germany's best-known female director, Margarethe von Trotta, Rosenstrasse (2003) is a portrayal of a 1943 protest by a group of non-Jewish women against the deportation of their Jewish husbands.

German Boy: A Child In War by Wolfgang Samuel is the true tale of a German family, told through the eyes of the young Wolfgang, who fled Berlin as the Red Army approached.

1870–71	1890–91	1914–18
Through brilliant diplomacy and the Franco-Prussian War, Bismarck creates a unified Germany, with Prussia at its helm and Berlin as its capital. Wilhelm I, king of Prussia, becomes Kaiser Wilhelm I.	Developing out of workers' parties that sprang up in the mid-19th century, the Sozial-demokratische Partei Deutschlands (SPD) adopts its present name and a program strongly influenced by Marx' writings.	WWI: Germany, Austria-Hungary and Turkey go to war against Britain, France, Italy and Russia. Germany is defeated. Over eight million soldiers and many times that number of civilians die.

Keep on top of
everything German –
culture, politics,
lifestyle and more –
at www.germany.info.

east of the Oder and Neisse Rivers (where the border is today) went to Poland as compensation for earlier territorial losses to the USSR.

THE BIG CHILL

In 1948 the Allies put together an economic aid package, the Marshall Plan, and created the basis for West Germany's *Wirtschaftswunder* (economic miracle). Meanwhile, German cities were rising out of the rubble and first steps were being taken to re-establish elected government. These advances widened the rift between Allied and Soviet zones; in the latter inflation still strained local economies, food shortages affected the population, and the Communist Party of Germany (KPD) and Social Democratic Party of Germany (SPD) were forced to unite as the Sozialistische Einheitspartei Deutschlands (SED; Socialist Unity Party).

A Train of Powder by Rebecca West ranks as one of the most informative books on the Nuremberg trials.

The showdown came in June 1948 when the Allies introduced the Deutschmark (DM) in their zones. The USSR saw this as a breach of the Potsdam Agreement, whereby the powers had agreed to treat Germany as one economic zone. The USSR issued its own currency and promptly announced a full-scale economic blockade of West Berlin. To ensure West Berlin's food supplies, the Allies responded with the remarkable Berlin airlift, whereby American, British, Canadian and some Australian air crews flew into Berlin's Tempelhof Airport (where there's a monument of the event today) the equivalent of 22 freight trains of 50 carriages daily, at intervals of 90 seconds.

A NEW EAST & WEST GERMANY

In this frosty East–West climate, the Rhineland town of Bonn hosted West German state representatives in September 1948 who met to hammer out a draft constitution for a new Federal Republic of Germany (FRG; BRD by its German initials). A year later, 73-year-old Konrad Adenauer (1876–1967), a Cologne mayor during the Weimar years, was elected as West Germany's first chancellor. Bonn – Adenauer's home town – was the natural candidate for the FRG's provisional capital.

Interviews with former Stasi men in the mid-1990s form the basis of Australian journalist Anna Funder's *Stasiland* – crammed with fresh and alternative insights into what the men of the Stasi did after it was disbanded.

East Germany reciprocated by adopting its own constitution for the German Democratic Republic (GDR; DDR by its German initials). On paper, it guaranteed press and religious freedoms and the right to strike. In reality, such freedoms were limited and no one dared strike. In its chosen capital of Berlin, a bicameral system was set up (one chamber was later abolished) and Wilhelm Pieck became the country's first president. From the outset, however, the Socialist Unity Party led by party boss Walter Ulbricht dominated economic, judicial and security policy.

In keeping with centralist policies, the East German states of Saxony, Mecklenburg–Western Pomerania, Saxony-Anhalt and Thuringia were divided into 14 regional administrations and the notorious Ministry for State Security (Ministerium für Staatssicherheit, also known as the Stasi)

1915 & 1917	1918–19	1918–19
A German submarine sinks the RMS *Lusitania*, a British passenger ship carrying 1198 passengers, among them over 120 Americans. The submarine campaign by Germany draws the USA into the war.	Sailors' revolts spread across Germany, Kaiser Wilhelm II flees to the Netherlands, and a democratic Weimar Republic is founded. Women receive suffrage and human rights are embedded in law.	According to the 'war guilt' clause of the Treaty of Versailles, Germany and its allies are made financially responsible for all loss and damage suffered by its enemies, putting the new republic on an unstable footing.

GERMANY'S CHANGING BORDERS

HOLY ROMAN EMPIRE AT THE END OF THE THIRTY YEARS WAR (PEACE OF WESTPHALIA, 1648)

Past Borders
Swedish possession
Present borders

GERMAN EMPIRE 1871–1918

Past Borders
Present borders

GERMANY AFTER THE TREATY OF VERSAILLES (1919–38)

Past Borders
Present borders

WEST GERMANY AND EAST GERMANY 1945–89

East Germany
West Germany
Present borders

was created in 1950 to ensure SED loyalty (see the boxed text, p46). Workers became economically dependent on the state through the collectivisation of farms, and nationalisation of production such as the Horch car factory in Zwickau near Leipzig (which later produced Trabants as the GDR answer to the West Germany's Volkswagen).

Mid-1920s	1933	1933–34
Amid the troubles of the Weimar Republic, Germans discover flamboyant pursuits. Cinemas attract two million visitors daily and cabaret and the arts flourish, but ideological differences increase.	Hitler becomes chancellor of Germany and creates a dictatorship through the Enabling Law. Only the 94 SPD Reichstag representatives present – those not yet in prison or forced into exile – oppose the act.	The Nazi *Gleichschaltung* (enforced conformity) begins, spelling the death of tolerance and pluralism. The federal states become powerless, and opposition parties and free-trade unions are banned.

STASI SECRETS

The Ministry of State Security, commonly called the Stasi, was based on the Soviet KGB and served as the 'shield and sword' of the SED. Almost a state within the state, it boasted an astonishing spy network of about 90,000 full-time employees and 180,000 *inoffizielle Mitarbeiter* (unofficial co-workers) by 1989. Since 1990, only 250 Stasi agents have been prosecuted and since the 10-year limit ended in 2000, future trials are unlikely.

When it came to tracking down dissidents, there were no limits. One unusual collection of files found in its Berlin archive kept a record of dissidents' body odour. Some dissidents who had been hauled in for interrogation were made to deliver an odour sample, usually taken with a cotton-wool pad from the unfortunate victim's crotch. The sample was then stored in a hermetic glass jar for later use if a dissident suddenly disappeared. To track down a missing dissident by odour, Stasi sniffer dogs were employed. These specially trained groin-sniffing curs were euphemistically known as 'smell differentiation dogs'.

What happened to the dogs after the Stasi was disbanded is unclear. What happened to the six million files the Stasi accumulated in its lifetime is a greater cause for concern. In January 1990, protestors stormed the Stasi headquarters in Berlin (today a museum, memorial and research centre – see p197 for details), demanding to see the files. Since then, the controversial records have been assessed and safeguarded by a Berlin-based public body. In mid-2000, 1000-odd information-packed CDs, removed by the US Central Intelligence Agency's (CIA's) Operation Rosewood immediately after the fall of the Wall in 1989, were returned to Germany. A second batch of CIA files (apparently acquired by the CIA from a Russian KGB officer in 1992) were handed over in 2003. The files, for the first time, matched code names with real names. Some of those with an *inoffizieller Mitarbeiter* file are fully fledged informants; others are 'contact' people who either knew they were giving information to someone from the Stasi or were unfortunate enough to be pumped of information without knowing it.

In Soviet zones the task of weeding out Nazis tended to be swift and harsh. In the west the Allies held war-crimes trials in courtroom 600 of Nuremberg's Court House (open to visitors today).

THE 1950S

For an informative overview of the Berlin Wall, see www.berlin .de/mauer on the Berlin city website.

The economic vision of Bavarian-born (from Fürth), cigar-puffing Ludwig Erhard (1897–1977) unleashed West Germany's *Wirtschaftswunder*. Between 1951 and 1961 the economy averaged an annual growth rate of 8%.

Erhard was economic minister and later vice-chancellor in Konrad Adenauer's government. His policies encouraged investment and boosted economic activity to support West Germany's system of welfare-state capitalism. He helped create the European Coal and Steel Community to regulate coal and steel production with France, Italy, West Germany and the Benelux countries, and in 1958 West Germany joined the European Economic

1935	1937–45	1939–45
The Nuremberg Laws are enacted. A law for the 'protection of German blood and honour' forbids marriage between 'Aryans' and 'non-Aryans'. Another law deprives Jews and other 'non-Aryans' of German nationality.	Nazi Germany and Italy sign an agreement that allows several hundred thousand guest workers from Mussolini's Italy to arrive to boost labour for mainly war industries. Later, they become forced labourers.	WWII: Hitler invades Poland. France and Britain declare war on Germany. Millions of Jews are murdered during the Holocaust and 62 million civilians and soldiers die – 27 million in the former Soviet Union alone.

Community (the EU today). Adenauer's deep-rooted fear of the USSR saw him pursue a determined policy of integration with the West.

In East Germany, Stalin's death in 1953 raised unfulfilled hopes of reform. Extreme poverty and economic tensions merely persuaded the government to set production goals higher. Smouldering discontent erupted in violence on 17 June 1953 when 10% of GDR workers took to the streets. Soviet troops quashed the uprising, with scores of deaths and the arrest of about 1200 people. Economic differences widened into military ones when West Germany joined NATO in 1955 and East Germany moved into the fold of the Warsaw Pact, where it remained from 1956 to 1990.

THE WALL

The exodus of young, well-educated and employed East German refugees seeking a better fortune in West Germany strained the troubled GDR economy so much that the GDR government – with Soviet consent – built a wall to keep them in. The Berlin Wall, the Cold War's most potent symbol, went up between East and West Berlin on the night of 12 August 1961. The inner-German border was fenced off and mined.

Berlin and the Wall by Ann Tusa is a saga about the events, trials and triumphs of the Cold War, the building of the Wall and its effects on the people and the city of Berlin.

Having walled in what was left of the struggling population (330,000 East Germans had fled to the west in 1953 alone, and in 1960 almost 200,000 voted with their feet), the East German government launched a new economic policy in a bid to make life better. And it did. The standard of living rose to the highest in the Eastern bloc and East Germany became its second-largest industrial power (behind the USSR).

The appointment of Erich Honecker (1912–94) in 1971 opened the way for rapprochement with the West and enhanced international acceptance of the GDR. Honecker fell in line with Soviet policies (replacing reunification clauses in the East German constitution with a declaration of irrevocable alliance to the USSR in 1974), but his economic policies did promote a powerful economy until stagnation took root in the late 1980s.

'Berlin is the testicle of the West. When I want the West to scream, I squeeze on Berlin'.

NIKITA KHRUSHCHEV, SOVIET COMMUNIST PARTY SECRETARY (1953–64)

ON THE WESTERN SIDE

Meanwhile, West Germany was still in the aged but firm hands of Konrad Adenauer, chancellor from 1949 until 1963, and whose economics minister, Ludwig Erhard, once the Father of the Economic Miracle, was now importing foreign workers. By doing this he was making a post-hoc name for himself as the father of a multi-ethnic German society. About 2.3 million *Gastarbeiter* (guest workers) came to West Germany until the early 1970s, mainly from Italy, Spain, Turkey, Portugal, Morocco and former Yugoslavia, injecting new life into a host German culture that was slowly stirring after the strictures of the Nazi years. While Ludwig Erhard's guest workers arrived from one direction, young Germans who had been children under the Nazis now rode

1945	1948–49	1949
Hitler kills himself in a Berlin bunker while a defeated Germany surrenders; Germany is split into Allied- and Soviet-occupied zones. Berlin has its own British, French, US and Soviet zones with checkpoints.	The Soviet Union blocks land routes to Allied sectors of Berlin after cooperation between Allied and Soviet occupiers breaks down. Over 260,000 US and British flights supply West Berlin during the Berlin airlift.	Allied-occupied West Germany becomes the FRG, with its capital in Bonn and Konrad Adenauer its first chancellor. A separate East Germany is founded in the Soviet-occupied zone, with Berlin as its capital.

their imported Vespa motorcycles to Italy on holiday to bring home a piece of Europe for themselves.

In 1963 Adenauer was eased out by Ludwig Erhard, by then also his vice-chancellor, but in 1966 a fluctuating economy was biting deeply into Erhard's credibility, and Germany's first grand coalition government of Christian Democrats (CDU/CSU) and SPD took office, with Kurt Georg Kiesinger (CDU; 1904–88) as chancellor and Willy Brandt (SPD; 1913–92) as vice-chancellor. The absence of parliamentary opposition fuelled radical demands by the student movement for social reform.

The turning point came in 1969 when the SPD under Willy Brandt formed a new government with the Free Democratic Party (FDP). The Lübeck-born, 1971 Nobel Peace Prize winner spent the Hitler years working in exile as a journalist in Scandinavia, where he was stripped of his citizenship for anti-Nazi writings. Normalising relations with East Germany (his East-friendly policy was known as *Ostpolitik*) was his priority and in December 1972 the Basic Treaty was signed, paving the way for both countries to join the UN in 1973. The treaty guaranteed sovereignty in international and domestic affairs (but fudged formal recognition since it was precluded by the West German constitution).

Brandt was replaced by Helmut Schmidt (b 1918) in 1974 after a scandal (one of Brandt's close advisers turned out to be a Stasi spy). The 1970s saw antinuclear and green issues move onto the agenda, opposed by Schmidt, and ultimately leading to the election of Greens party representatives to the Bonn parliament in 1979. In 1974 West Germany joined the G8 group of industrial nations. But the 1970s were also a time of terrorism in Germany, and several prominent business and political figures were assassinated by the anticapitalist Red Army Faction.

Brandt's vision of East–West cordiality was continued by Chancellor Helmut Kohl (b 1930) who, with his conservative coalition government from 1982, groomed relations between the East and the West, while dismantling parts of the welfare state at home. In the West German capital in 1987, Kohl received East German counterpart Erich Honecker with full state honours.

REUNIFICATION

It was clear that the hearts and minds of Eastern Europeans had long been restless for change, but the events leading up to German reunification caught even the most knowledgeable political observers by surprise.

The so-called *Wende* ('change', ie the fall of communism) in Germany and reunification came about perhaps in the most German of ways: a gradual development that culminated in a big bang. Reminiscent of the situation in Berlin in the 1950s, East Germans began leaving their country in droves. They fled not across a no man's land of concrete, weeds and death strips between East and West this time but through an open border between Hungary and Austria. The SED was helpless to stop the flow of people wanting to leave,

Behind-the-scene footage, interviews, an account of the Wall's fall and shots of the 2500-brick wall rebuilt during the show is included on *The Wall: Live in Berlin,* the DVD of Pink Floyd's electrifying concert in Berlin in 1990.

After the Wall by Marc Fisher is an account of German society, with emphasis on life after the *Wende* (fall of communism). Fisher was bureau chief for the *Washington Post* in Bonn and presents some perceptive social insights.

1950	1951–61	1953
The CDU is founded at federal level in West Germany and Konrad Adenauer, known for his support for strong relationships with France and the US, is elected its first national chairman.	The economic vision of Ludwig Erhard unleashes West Germany's *Wirtschaftswunder*. Between 1951 and 1961 the economy averages an annual growth rate of 8%.	Following the death of Stalin and unfulfilled hopes for better conditions in the GDR, workers and farmers rise up, strike or demonstrate in 560 towns and cities across the country. Soviet troops quash the uprising.

KEEN ON 'GREEN'

Love them or hate them, the Greens party has changed the face of German politics since the mid-1970s, when the party first emerged from the left-wing environmentalist and peace movements. Two figures that capture the spirit of the party best are Franco-German Daniel Cohn-Bendit (b 1945) and former Greens party politician and German foreign minister Joschka Fischer (b 1948).

Cohn-Bendit was a leader in France's student uprising in 1968 (the French government later tossed him out) and is co-president of the Greens party's European faction. He's still very much a grass-roots type of Green, and you often glimpse him on the street in Frankfurt's Bockenheim district. Joschka Fischer, one-time foreign minister, taxi driver and son of a butcher (of German ancestry, but from Hungary) earned notoriety for his time as a member of a *Putzgruppe* (clean-up mob), who battled it out with police in squatter clashes in Frankfurt's Westend. Ironically, this elegant and, in parts, upmarket suburb today owes its existence to the rebel squatters who fought tooth and nail to stop the bulldozers in the 1970s. Fischer is alleged to have punched a policeman in one violent clash (in an odd twist of fate, the policeman's surname was Marx). After a highly popular stint as Germany's foreign minister from 1998 to 2005, Fischer – five times married and, witty tongues might quip, the only Greens politician to practice his party's principle of leadership rotation – has now retired from parliament.

Given the party's provenance, an SPD shade of light red would seem the preferred colour of the Greens. Although it has yet to join forces with conservative parties at state or federal level, the Greens are no strangers to coalitions with 'black' (conservative) parties in city governments. In Hamburg, the Grün-Alternative Liste (Green Alternative List; GAL), a party that is not strictly the Greens but represents Alliance 90/The Greens in that state, is currently in a coalition with the CDU. Now even the conservative parties, once the mortal enemies of the movement, are openly talking about federal coalitions if need be. The atomic energy issue, however, is one where the attraction cools somewhat. Following the election of 2009, which saw the party receive almost 11% of the vote, the Greens declared their intention to fight in opposition any attempt to reverse laws it helped pass to phase out nuclear-power stations by 2020.

some of whom sought refuge in the West German embassy in Prague. Around the same time, East Germans took to the streets in Monday demonstrations following services in Leipzig's Nikolaikirche and other churches in East Germany, safe in the knowledge that the Church supported their demands for improved human rights.

Something had to give, and it did. With the demonstrations spreading and escalating into violence, Erich Honecker accepted the inevitable, relinquishing his position to Egon Krenz (b 1937). And then the floodgates opened: on the fateful night of 9 November, 1989, party functionary Günter Schabowski informed GDR citizens they could travel directly to the West. Tens of thousands of East Germans jubilantly rushed through border points in Berlin and elsewhere in the country, bringing to an end the long, chilly phase of German division.

1954	**1961**	**1963**
West Germany wins the World Cup, a victory which is to become known as the 'miracle of Bern'.	On the night of 12 August, the GDR government begins building the Berlin Wall between East and West Germany. Work soon starts on concrete sections, the beginning of a 155km wall surrounding West Berlin.	US President John F Kennedy declares in Berlin: 'All free men, wherever they may live, are citizens of Berlin. And therefore, as a free man, I take pride in the words, *'Ich bin ein Berliner'*.

ANGELA MERKEL – THE ENIGMATIC CHANCELLOR

Some say that she's enigmatic; others, that she likes to keep a low profile when political dissonance breaks out, especially within her own party. Indisputable, however, is that Angela Merkel's rise to become German chancellor in 2005 brought a number of firsts. She was Germany's first woman and first former East German in the job and, because of the latter, she also became the first Russian-speaking German chancellor.

Merkel was born in Hamburg in 1954 but grew up in the boondocks – in the Uckermark region (in Brandenburg, near the Polish border), where her father had a posting as a pastor in East Germany. She studied physics in Leipzig (quantum chemistry), entering politics as the GDR was falling apart. Soon she was honing her political skills in the ministries of a reunified Germany (Women and Youth was one; Environment, Natural Protection and Reactor Safety was another) under Helmut Kohl, which is why she's sometimes called 'Kohl's foster child'. Her breakthrough came in the late 1990s when the reputations of several CDU high-flyers suffered as a result of a party slush fund.

While political commentators outside Germany have often compared her to the former UK prime minister Margaret Thatcher, Merkel's leadership style rarely has the bite of Britain's 'Iron Lady' (although some state heads, like France's Nicolas Sarkozy and Russia's Vladimir Putin, might disagree on that). What Thatcher and Merkel do have in common, though, is that both have ranked among the *Forbes* 100 most powerful women in the world – Angela Merkel has topped the list no less than three times.

The unified Germany of today with 16 states (five of which are in eastern Germany and called the 'new states') was hammered out after volatile political debate at home and a series of treaties to end post-WWII occupation zones. The days of occupation by the four powers were now consigned to the past. Berlin acquired the status it has today of a separate city-state and, following reunification on 3 October 1990, it was restored as the capital of Germany.

Germany is a constitutional democracy with a president and bicameral system based on the Bundestag (popularly elected lower house of 598 members) and the Bundesrat (upper house of delegates nominated by 16 states).

The single most dominant figure throughout reunification and the 1990s was Helmut Kohl, whose CDU/CSU and FDP coalition was re-elected to office in December 1990 in Germany's first postreunification election.

Under Kohl's leadership, East German assets were privatised; oversubsidised state industries were radically trimmed back, sold or wound up completely; and infrastructure was modernised (and in some cases over-invested in) to create a unification boom that saw the former East Germany grow by up to 10% each year until 1995. Growth slowed dramatically from the mid-1990s, however, creating an eastern Germany that consisted of unification winners and losers. Those who had jobs did well, but unemployment was high and the lack of opportunities in regions such as the eastern Harz Mountains or in cities such as Magdeburg and Halle (both in Saxony-Anhalt) are still causing many young people from the former East Germany to try their luck in western Germany or in boom towns, such as Leipzig in Saxony. Berlin,

1972	**1974**	**1977**
Social Democrat chancellor Willy Brandt's *Ostpolitik* thaws relations between the two Germanys. The Basic Treaty is signed in East Berlin, paving the way for both countries to join the UN.	West Germany joins the G8 group of industrialised nations, and hosts and wins the FIFA World Cup.	The *Deutscher Herbst* (German Autumn) envelops West Germany when a second generation of the left-wing Red Army Faction (RAF) murders key business and state figures.

although economically shaky, is the exception. Many public servants have since relocated there from Bonn to staff the ministries, and young people from all over Germany are attracted by its vibrant cultural scene.

Helmut Kohl also sought to bring former East German functionaries to justice, notably Erich Honecker, who fled after he resigned and lived an ailing and nomadic existence that culminated in his death in Chile in 1994. His court case had by then been abandoned due to his ill health.

The unification legacy of Helmut Kohl is indisputable. His involvement in a party slush-fund scandal in the late 1990s, however, financially burdened his own party and resulted in the CDU stripping him of his position as lifelong honorary chairman. In 1998, a coalition of the SPD and Bündnis 90/Die Grünen (Alliance 90/The Greens) parties defeated the CDU/CSU and FDP coalition.

THE NEW MILLENNIUM

With the formation of a coalition government of SPD and Alliance 90/The Greens in 1998, Germany reached a new milestone. This was the first time an environmentalist party had governed nationally – in Germany or elsewhere in the world. Two figures dominated the seven-year rule of the coalition: Chancellor Gerhard Schröder (b 1944) and the Greens party vice-chancellor and foreign minister Joschka Fischer (b 1948). Schröder's role model was Willy Brandt; Fischer's – because he was the Greens party's first minister in the job – was, by necessity, himself. Despite his provenance from the left-wing house-squatting scene in Frankfurt am Main of the 1970s, he enjoyed widespread popularity among ordinary Germans of all political colours.

Under the leadership of Gerhard Schröder, Germany began to take a more independent approach to foreign policy, steadfastly refusing to become involved in the invasion of Iraq, but supporting the USA, historically its

A man, it would seem, for a financial crisis, Horst Köhler headed the International Monetary Fund (IMF), based in Washington DC, before becoming postwar Germany's ninth president after WWII.

COLOURFUL COALITIONS

Germans describe their coalition governments in colourful but sometimes confusing ways. 'Grand coalition' is self-explanatory, meaning a coalition of the two largest parties (CDU/CSU and SPD). Colour combinations like 'red-red-green' (SPD–The Left–Alliance 90/The Greens), 'black-yellow' (CDU/CSU-FDP) and 'red-yellow' (SPD-FDP) are understood immediately by almost every German. A 'traffic-light coalition' is a coalition of red (SPD), yellow (FDP) and green (Alliance 90/The Greens). There is also something called a 'black traffic light' coalition (as per the German neologism 'Schwampel', from schwarz 'black' and Ampel 'traffic light'), aka 'Jamaica traffic light' (look at the Jamaican flag and you get the idea). In 2001 a Jamaica traffic-light coalition surfaced in Frankfurt am Main for one day before it fell apart. This type of constellation was also known briefly as the 'Africa' or 'Senegal' coalition. Since the national election of 2005, however, 'Jamaica coalition' has become the usual description.

1982

A 'constructive vote of no confidence' brings down the SPD/FDP coalition under Helmut Schmidt. A conservative coalition government is formed in West Germany under Christian Democrat Helmut Kohl.

1985

Boris Becker wins Wimbledon tennis tournament and becomes the youngest player and first German to do so. West Germany receives its biggest confidence boost since its 1954 World Cup victory.

1989

Demonstrations are held in Leipzig and other East German cities. Hungary opens its border with Austria, and East Germans are allowed to travel to the West, prompting the fall of the Berlin Wall.

closest ally, in Afghanistan and the war in Kosovo. Its stance on Iraq – which reflected the feelings of the majority of Germans – caused relations with the US administration of George W Bush to be strained.

In some respects, reunification had kept Germany in its own orbit and had distracted the country from changes occurring in the global economy during the 1990s. At home, Germany sought to adapt the social market economy to what it perceived as new needs in a global economy, notably through a series of labour-market reforms. The fourth of these reforms, popularly known as 'Hartz IV', was intended to streamline unemployment and other social-benefits systems and help the long-term unemployed find work. In practice, however, the Hartz IV reform measures of the Schröder government (which are still in force) proved unwieldy, bureaucratic and, at times, harsh on recipients, and they contributed to a gradual drift of traditional SPD voters to smaller parties left of centre. During the election of 2009 the Hartz IV laws, as well as legislation that made Germans only eligible for state pensions from the age of 67, caused many voters to turn to parties they perceived as having fairer social policies. One of these is Die Linke (The Left), which grew out of the former East German SED and a successor party later uniting with a left grouping in western Germany. Together as The Left party they are challenging the social and labour market policies of the traditional workers' and social democratic party, the SPD.

A key environmental and energy reform of the SPD and Alliance 90/Greens government of 1998–2005 was legislation to close all nuclear-power plants in Germany by 2020. This remains a controversial step and there will be pressure to reverse the decision in an anticipated coalition government of CDU/CSU and FDP. All these parties favour extending the shelf-life of the nuclear-power plants, saying this is necessary to bridge an energy gap until alternative sources become better established.

The rise of the Greens and, more recently, The Left has changed the political landscape of Germany dramatically, making absolute majorities by the 'big two' all the more difficult to achieve. In 2005 the CDU/CSU and SPD formed a grand coalition led by Angela Merkel (b 1954), the first woman, former East German, Russian speaker and quantum physicist in the job (see the boxed text, p50). While many Germans hoped this would resolve a political stalemate that had existed between an opposition-led upper house (Bundesrat) and the government, political horse trading shifted away from the political limelight and was mostly carried out behind closed doors.

When the financial crisis struck in 2008–09, the German government pumped hundreds of billions of euros into the financial system to prop up the banks. Other measures allowed companies to put workers on shorter shifts without loss of pay and pumped money into the economy by encouraging Germans to scrap older cars and buy new ones.

Keep abreast with current affairs at www.dw-world.de.

Discover stat after stat on the Germany of a new Europe at the website of the *Statistisches Bundesamt Deutschland* (Federal Statistical Office), www.destatis.de.

1990	1998	2005
Berlin becomes the capital of reunified Germany. Helmut Kohl's conservative coalition promises East–West economic integration, creating unrealistic expectations of a blossoming economic landscape in the east.	After its popularity wanes during the first decade of reunification, Helmut Kohl's CDU/CSU & FDP coalition is replaced by an SPD and Bündnis 90/Die Grünen government.	Angela Merkel becomes Germany's first woman chancellor, leading a grand coalition of major parties after the election results in neither the SPD nor the CDU/CSU being able to form its own government.

The export industries Germany relies on so heavily for its wealth – Germany, the world's third-largest economy after Japan and the USA, is consistently the world's largest exporter – have suffered badly during the crisis and, if the predictions of the Organisation for Economic Co-Operation and Development (OECD) are a good indication, unemployment in Germany will rise to almost five million or 11.8% of the working population some time in 2010. Other predictions are less dramatic.

The election of 2009 confirmed the trend towards smaller parties and a five-party political system in Germany. The CDU/CSU achieved its second-worst result in the history of the party (around 34% of the vote) and the SPD achieved its worst result in its almost 150-year history, receiving around 23% of the vote. Support for The Left has been consistently strong in eastern Germany over the years, but success in the federal elections of late 2009 allowed it to establish itself at federal level. The Left received around 12% of the vote and is the second-strongest opposition party after the SPD. It nudged close to the FDP (just under 15%), whereas Alliance 90/The Greens, despite picking up a few disillusioned SPD voters, received around 11% and became the smallest of the opposition parties.

Despite having lost support, the CDU/CSU will foreseeably rule in coalition with the FDP, with Angela Merkel retaining the job of chancellor. The influence of a strong FDP on Germany is likely to be a greater focus on neo-liberal economic policies, but also on citizens' rights – traditionally part of the FDP platform. Its leader, Guido Westerwelle (b 1961) is likely to become foreign minister and Germany's vice chancellor. Although sexual orientation scarcely plays a role in German politics, Westerwelle makes no secret of his homosexuality and therefore will probably become Germany's first openly gay vice chancellor.

The five-party system will probably be a long-term feature of the political landscape of Germany, and the SPD will continue to face the prospect of having to enter into coalition agreements with The Left in any future SPD-led government. It has refused so far, but this is likely to change, especially if Berlin's governing mayor, Klaus Wowereit (b 1953) becomes chancellor candidate – he is thought to have good chances – during the next election, scheduled for 2013. At present, Wowereit heads a coalition of the SPD and The Left in Berlin. Sigmar Gabriel (b 1959) and Olaf Scholz (b 1958), both ministers in the earlier grand coalition, are also likely to become key players in any SPD revival.

Two of the best websites for current reports and facts about Germany are *The Economist* magazine's country profile at www.economist.com/countries/germany and the BBC News website (follow the Europe/Country Profile links) at http://news.bbc.co.uk.

'If the Austrians should ever demand reparations from us, I'll send them the bones of Adolf Hitler.'
KONRAD ADENAUER (FORMER GERMAN CHANCELLOR)

2006	2008	2009
Germans proudly fly their flag as the country hosts the FIFA World Cup for the first time as a unified nation.	The economic crisis bites deeply into German export industries. German banks are propped up by state funds as unemployment and state debt begin to rise again.	The CDU/CSU and FDP achieve a majority in the federal election and are poised to form a new coalition government – paving the way for Angela Merkel to be re-elected as chancellor in the Bundestag.

The Culture

THE NATIONAL PSYCHE

The German state of mind is always a favourite for speculation – two 20th-century wars and the memory of the Jewish Holocaust are reasons. Throw in the chilling razor's edge of Cold War division, a modern juggernaut economy that draws half of Europe in its wake and pumps more goods into the world economy than any other, and a crucial geographical location at the crossroads of Europe and this fascination becomes understandable.

Often, though, it pays to ignore the stereotypes, jingoism and those occasional headlines at home describing Germany in military terms – and maybe even forgive Germans for the systematic way they clog up a football field or conduct jagged discussion. Sometimes it helps to see the country through its regional nuances. Germany was very slow to become a nation, so, if you look closely, you will begin to notice many different local cultures within the one set of borders. You will also find that it's one of Europe's most multicultural countries (p59), with Turkish, Greek, Italian, Russian and Balkan influences.

Around 15 million people today live in the former GDR, a part of Germany where, until 1989, travel was restricted, the state was almighty, and life was secure – but also strongly regulated – from the cradle to the grave. Not surprisingly, therefore, many former East Germans – particularly males – are still coming to terms with a more competitive, unified Germany. According to one poll conducted by the Emnid research group, 49% of eastern Germans say the GDR had more good sides than bad, and 8% say they were happier or lived better at that time (see the boxed text, opposite).

The former East Germany continues to lose people hand over fist. In the past, badly affected regions have even tried to lure their youngest and brightest back from cities like Munich and Stuttgart with novel ideas such as a 'returnees package' – containing things like mouse pads, internet links, and local newspaper subscriptions – but the trend is irreversible. According to some estimates, Saxony-Anhalt and the Chemnitz region can expect to lose a quarter of their population by 2030, and Thuringia will shrink by about 20%.

Germans as a whole fall within the mental topography of northern Europe and are sometimes described as culturally 'low context'. That means, as opposed to the French or Italians, Germans like to pack what they mean right into the words they use rather than hint or suggest. Facing each other squarely in conversation, firm handshakes, and a hug or a kiss on the cheek among friends are also par for the course.

Most Germans look fondly upon the flourishing tradition of the apprentice carpenters who travel throughout Germany and Europe on *Wanderschaft* (wanderings) to acquire foreign skills, or the traditionally attired chimney sweeps (some of them women these days) in towns and villages dressed in pitch-black suits and top hats. Even an otherwise ordinary young Bavarian from, say, the finance department of a DAX (Deutscher Aktien Index; German stock index) 30 company might don the Dirndl (traditional Bavarian skirt and blouse) around Oktoberfest time (p314) and swill like a hearty, rollicking peasant. On Monday she'll be soberly back at the desk crunching the numbers like it was all just good fun – which it was, of course.

For all this popular tradition, Germans are not prudish. Nude bathing on beaches and naked mixed saunas are both commonplace, although many women prefer single-sex saunas (usually a particular day at a mixed sauna). Wearing your swimming suit or covering yourself with a towel in the sauna is definitely not the done thing.

GERMAN HUMOUR

'According to a study by the Forsa-Institut, one in 10 Germans has no problem with the idea that the Germans are dying out. Maybe after Germany loses the (football) match against the USA tonight it'll be one in five.'

FROM THE GERMAN CULTURE PROGRAM *KULTURZEIT* (2006)

Better than the reputation? About two million Germans can expect to suffer from an obsessive-compulsive disorder in their lifetime.

Ingo Schulze's *Simple Storys* (Simple Stories; 2001) focuses on life after reunification (unemployment, racial violence etc) in the small Thuringian town of Altenburg.

OSTALGIE

Who would want to go back to East German times? Well, very few people, but there was more to the GDR (German Democratic Republic; the former East Germany) than simply being a 'satellite of the Evil Empire', as Cold War warriors from the 1980s would portray it.

The opening lines of director Leander Haussmann's film *Sonnenallee* (1999) encapsulate this idea: 'Once upon a time, there was a land and I lived there and, if I am asked how it was, I say it was the best time of my life because I was young and in love.' Another film, the smash hit *Good Bye, Lenin!* (2003), looked at the GDR with humour and pathos. It also gave Ostalgie – from *Ost* (East) and *Nostalgie* (nostalgia) – the kick it needed to become a more or less permanent cultural fixture in Germany.

Whether it be in the form of grinning Erich Honecker doubles at parties, Spreewald cucumbers and GDR Club Cola, or the *Ampelmännchen* – the little green man that helped East German pedestrians cross the road – Ostalgie is here to stay. For a taste of what the East offered in daily life – and former East Germans are finding hard to leave behind – check out the DDR Museum Berlin (p118).

LIFESTYLE

The German household fits into the mould of households in other Western European countries. A close look, however, reveals some distinctly German quirks, whether that be a compulsion for sorting and recycling rubbish, a love of fizzy mineral water or filter coffee (a German, Melitta Bentz from Dresden, invented the coffee filter), or perhaps even an abhorrence of anything (but especially eggs) prepared in a frying pan before noon.

Tradition is valued, so in this household Grandma's clock might grind and chime the morning hours somewhere in the room, although these days Grandma herself contemplatively sucks on her false teeth (which she might have had done cheaply in Poland) in an old-age home or discovers the benefits of having a voluble Romanian carer in her own home. A TV will sit squarely in the living room and a computer somewhere else in the house (about 50% of households have one); maybe this is one of the 42 million internet surfers. Eight in 10 Germans own a bike, and a car is also likely to be parked nearby, embodying the German belief that true freedom comes on four wheels and is best expressed tearing along a ribbon of autobahn at 200km/h or more while (illegally) talking on a mobile phone. In every 10th home, a mobile phone has replaced use of the landline network.

When it comes to hammering nails in coffins, about 28% of Germans are smokers.

With such high unemployment and many economically depressed regions in eastern Germany, there are large differences in the standard of living among Germans. The average gross monthly income for a German working in the industrial or service sector is €3127, but over 40% of that would disappear in tax and social security deductions; if the woman of the house also works – which could be difficult if the children are at preschool or half-day school – she might earn €2637. In eastern Germany, the average for both is €2366 per month.

The birth rate is low (1.37 children per woman), on par with Spain. On the face of it, though, the traditional nuclear family is still the most common model in Germany: 63% of children grow up with married parents and at least one sibling. But there's a big difference between eastern and western Germany. While 66% of children in western Germany have this upbringing, only 45% of eastern German kids do. People everywhere are marrying later, with men and women tying the knot at the average ages of 33 and 30 respectively.

After 14 days of bad weather your average German would be prepared to pay €33.45 for a sunny day, according to the weather site www .donnerwetter.de.

Women's issues are lobbied by the 52-member association Deutscher Frauenrat (German Women's Council; www .deutscher-frauenrat.de).

WHEN NAKED VEGETARIANS PUMP IRON

The idea of strapping young Germans frolicking unselfconsciously naked in the healthy outdoors is not new. A German *Körperkultur* (physical culture) first took shape in the late 19th century to remedy industrial society's so-called 'physical degeneration'. Out of this, Germany's modern *Freikörper* (naturist) movement was born.

The early movement was something of a right-wing, anti-Semitic animal, whose puritanical members were scorned by some outsiders as 'the lemonade bourgeoisie'. Achieving total beauty was the name of the game. Anathema to the movement, for example, was someone with a lascivious 'big-city lifestyle' that included smoking, fornicating, eating meat, drinking, and wearing clothes made of synthetic fibres, or anyone with predilections for artificial light. Early naturism also sprouted Germany's first vegetarian *Reform* restaurants and shops.

The most interesting characters to develop out of this odd era were bodybuilders – predominantly vegetarian and naturist, but internationalist in spirit. Some achieved fame abroad under pseudonyms. Others were immortalised in Germany by sculptors, who employed them as models for their works.

Famous pioneers of the movement in Germany include Kaliningrad-born Eugene Sandow (1876–1925), who died trying to pull a car out of a ditch; Berlin-born Hans Ungar (1878–1970), who became famous under the pseudonym Lionel Strongfort; and Theodor Siebert (1866–1961), from Alsleben, near Halle, in eastern Germany.

Abortion is illegal (except when a medical or criminal indication exists), but it is unpunishable if carried out within 12 weeks of conception and after compulsory counselling. Rape within marriage is punishable. Same-sex marriage (in the form of legally recognised same-sex partnerships) has been possible since 2001. Gays and lesbians walk with ease in most cities, especially Berlin, Hamburg, Cologne and Frankfurt am Main, although homosexuals do encounter discrimination in certain eastern German areas.

The country's first gay publication, *Der Eigene*, went to press in 1896 for the first time and – with a few interruptions in between – was published until the early 1930s and the rise of the Nazis.

German school hours, which are usually from 8am to 1pm (until 4pm for the less common 'all day' schools), and the underfunding of child care make combining career and children difficult for German women. The plus side is that parents enjoy equal rights for maternity and paternity leave.

On the whole, the number of women employed is increasing. About 61% of working-age women are employed – high for an EU country, but lower than in the USA and Scandinavia. Almost half of these women work part-time, and in eastern Germany women tend to have more of a presence on the managerial floors.

Currently, most Germans have retired by the age of 63, but changes to retirement ages are gradually increasing this to 67 for those retiring from 2029.

POPULATION

Germany is densely populated – 230 people for every square kilometre (compared with 116 per square kilometre in the expanded EU), although a far greater wedge is crammed into western Germany. The most densely populated areas are Greater Berlin, the Ruhr region, the Frankfurt am Main area, Wiesbaden and Mainz, and another region taking in Mannheim and Ludwigshafen. In eastern Germany, about 20% of the national population lives on 33% of the country's overall land.

Germany has about 20 million old-age pensioners, who account for around a quarter of the population. About 32.5 million Germans (39% of the population) earn their own living.

Most people live in villages and small towns, and German cities are modest by world standards: Berlin aside (3.4 million), the biggest cities are Hamburg (1.75 million), Munich (1.35 million) and Cologne (989,000).

The population in the former East Germany fell below the 1906 level after reunification as easterners moved to the more lucrative west. Oddly, Berlin's

---

DOS & DON'TS

- Germans draw a fat line between *Sie* and *du* (both meaning 'you'). Addressing an acquaintance with the formal *Sie* is a must, unless invited to do otherwise. Muttering a familiar *du* (reserved for close friends and family) to a shop assistant will only incite wrath and bad service, although *du* is often acceptable in young-people-packed bars. If in doubt, use *Sie*.

- Push firmly but politely with German bureaucracy; shouting will only slam down the shutters. Germans lower (rather than raise) their voices when mad.

- Give your name at the start of a phone call, even when calling a hotel or restaurant to book a room or table.

---

postreunification population boom has been offset by the exodus of young families from the capital to the surrounding countryside. Due to declining immigration, the total population figure has been slipping downwards since 2003 and, according to the most recent projections, will hit 74 million by 2050 (compared with today's 82.32 million).

For more on Germany's foreign population, see p59.

SPORT

Germany, always a keen sporting nation, has hosted the summer Olympics and football World Cup two times apiece. Although football (soccer) is easily the most popular sport, tennis, basketball and ice hockey also have strong followings.

Football

Football ignites the passion of Germans everywhere and has contributed much to building Germany's self-confidence as a nation. Its national team has won the World Cup three times, in 1954, 1974 and 1990. West Germany's first victory against Hungary in Bern, Switzerland, was unexpected and miraculous for a country slumbering deeply in post-WWII depression. The 'miracle of Bern' – as the victory is called – sent national morale soaring.

West Germany also won the 1974 World Cup in Munich, the home town of Franz Beckenbauer (b 1945) – dubbed 'Emperor Franz' for his outstanding flair and elegance. A third win in 1990 was remarkable because, for the first time since 1945, Germany fielded a unified team from East and West.

Another highlight of German football was the *Sommermärchen* (Summer Fairy Tale) World Cup of 2006, hosted by Germany. Although it didn't win, Germans rediscovered the art of flag-waving (long a sensitive issue due to its history as a nation) and celebrated one of their best national parties in recent times. National co-trainer at the time, Jürgen Klinsmann (b 1964), who is based in Huntington Beach, California, spent much of the 2008–09 season training Bayern-München – also known as FC Hollywood, and arguably one of the most difficult jobs in German football – before departing.

Another key football figure in Germany is the Dresden-born Matthias Sammer (b 1967), currently responsible for German football's junior talent as sports director for the DFB (German Football Association). Sammer, whose father was a highly successful trainer of the GDR team Dynamo Dresden (for whom Matthias Sammer also played), is often touted as a candidate for national trainer. If he ever gets the post, this would be another unique achievement for the fiery Saxon, who was the last player to kick a goal for East Germany and the first former East German to play in the reunified German national team.

West Germany's 1954 World Cup victory provides the backdrop for Sönke Wortmann's *Das Wunder von Bern* (The Miracle of Bern; 2003), a family drama about a WWII prisoner of war returning to a football-crazy son he no longer recognises.

Bundesliga scoreboards, rankings and fixtures are found online at www .germansoccer.net (in English) and www .bundesliga.de (in German).

CAREFUL WITH THAT DU, DIETER!

It's definitely not a good idea to use the familiar *du* form with the police – this could land you in court. In one bizarre case, the German pop singer and music producer Dieter Bohlen was charged with offensive behaviour when he used the familiar form with a police officer after being approached about a parking offence. The judge let Bohlen off the hook because '*du*' is part of his style. Impolite, yes; offensive, no.

In 2009 the German under 21 national team defeated England 4–0 in the European Championship final, led by trainer Horst Hrubesch (b 1951) and an exciting new generation of German players, of the likes of Gonzalo Castro (b 1987), Sami Khedira (b 1987) and Mesut Özil (b 1988). The names tell part of the story: the vast majority of this German U21 team had a migrant background, and many are set to become part of the next generation of the German national A-team. If all goes to plan, Germany can look optimistically into the future, and Hrubesch's success and popularity with the young players may well make him a future candidate for the trainer position with the national A-team.

When Berlin football club Hertha BSC played a UEFA Europa League home match against Istanbul's Galatasaray in 2008 in Berlin, 60,000 spectators tuned up. Around 40,000 of these were Germans or German residents with an ethnic Turkish background.

Women's football is growing in popularity, partly because of the success of the women's national team. Along with the USA, Germany has won the title twice to date. In 2011 Germany will host the FIFA Women's World Cup (www.fifa.com/womensworldcup), with games to be played in Augsburg, Berlin, Bochum, Dresden, Frankfurt, Leverkusen, Moenchengladbach, Sinsheim and Wolfsburg. All going according to plan, this might be a summer football party just as enjoyable as the men's Summer Fairy Tale of 2006.

Friday-night, Saturday and Sunday games are televised live on pay TV at sports bars all over Germany, whereas round-ups of the weekend matches are broadcast on the *Sportschau* on ARD (German National TV Consortium; see p60) around 6pm on Saturday and Sunday. German national team matches and UEFA Europa League matches are broadcast on free-to-air TV, as well as some UEFA Champions League matches.

Tennis

Tennis was a minor sport in Germany until 1985 when the unseeded 17-year-old Boris Becker (b 1967), from Leimen near Heidelberg, became Wimbledon's youngest-ever men's singles champion. Suddenly every German kid aspired to be the next Boris Becker. The red-headed mentor went on to win five more grand-slam titles in his career.

For a cracking read about football, the great football rivalry between England and Germany, and that famous match in 1966 with the controversial Wembley Goal, delve into Geoff Hurst's *1966 and All That.*

Becker was as colourful off the court as he was on it. His 'affair' in a broom closet with a Russian model in a London hotel in the mid-1990s produced a daughter and newspaper headlines that claimed 'sperm theft', while his tragic – and not surprising, given the broom-closet drama – marital breakdown culminated in a humiliating televised courtroom drama. His fiercest German opponent during the early 1990s (and fellow Wimbledon champion) was Michael Stich (b 1968); since their departure, however, the popularity of tennis has plunged.

Only the lingering, warm afterglow of Mannheim-born Steffi Graf (b 1969) currently lights the tennis darkness. Graf is among the few women to win all four grand-slam events in one year, and in 1988 – after also winning gold in Seoul at the Olympic Games – she became the only player ever to win the 'golden slam'. Germans had always secretly hoped for a Boris-Steffi marriage that might have produced a Teutonic tennis wunderkind. For better or worse, it didn't happen, but Steffi Graf did marry Becker's arch-rival from the USA, Andre Agassi and, unlike Becker, seems to be living happily ever after.

Other Sports

Though a relatively minor sport in Germany, basketball is gaining in popularity, boosted by the star US NBA (National Basketball Association) player for the Dallas Mavericks, Würzburg-born Dirk Nowitzki (b 1978). In 2007 he won the NBA's Most Valuable Player Award, and he was the first European player to be selected for the All-NBA First Team, made up of the best players of a season.

Cycling boomed after Rostock-born Jan Ullrich (b 1973) became the first German to win the Tour de France in 1997. He has also been five times runner up – three times to US cyclist Lance Armstrong. Like Armstrong, Ulrich has often faced allegations of having used illegal performance enhancers, and, in Germany as elsewhere, the public image of cycling has suffered due to allegations and high-profile confessions. Ulrich has consistently rejected such allegations both in and out of court; he retired from professional cycling in 2007 after state prosecutors in Bonn said a DNA test on blood confiscated during a Spanish doping case matched his own. Erik Zabel (b 1970), who comes from Berlin's Prenzlauer Berg district, achieved the remarkable by winning the green jersey six years in a row from 1996 to 2001 in the Tour de France and publicly admitted to experimenting briefly with the doping substance EPO in the 1990s.

With no fewer than seven World Championship titles and more than 50 Grand Prix wins, Michael Schumacher (b 1969) was the most successful Formula One racing driver ever to have taken to the circuit. Schumacher announced his retirement in 2006 and these days is a hobby motorcycle racer. No stranger to charitable causes, in 2009 he donated a few locks of hair so a Swiss company could process the carbon into a diamond for a multiple-sclerosis society.

In Germany Formula One races are held at the Hockenheim circuit, which hosts the German Grand Prix every two years in alternation with Nürburgring, which is where the European Grand Prix is held.

Ice-hockey fans will need no introduction to the IIHF World Championship, being held in May 2010 in Cologne and Mannheim. A crowd of 75,976 is expected for the kick-off Germany versus USA match at the Veltins-Arena (AufSchalke) football arena, topping the current outdoor record of 74,554 from a Michigan State University versus University of Michigan match in 2001 in the USA.

MULTICULTURALISM

Germany would seem more a country of emigrants than immigrants. Not so: it has always attracted immigrants, be it French Huguenots escaping religious persecution (about 30% of Berlin's population in 1700 was Huguenot), 19th-century Polish miners who settled in the Ruhr region, post-WWII asylum seekers, or foreign *Gastarbeiter* (guest workers) imported during the 1950s and 1960s to resolve labour shortages. After reunification, the foreign population soared (from 4.5 million in the 1980s to 7.3 million in 2002), as emigrants from the collapsed USSR and the then war-ravaged Yugoslavia sought shelter. Currently about 3000 *Spätaussiedler* (people of German heritage, mainly from Eastern Europe and Kazakhstan) enter the country each year.

About 6.7 million foreigners (just under 9% of the population) live in Germany, almost a third of these from EU countries and almost half from Europe. Ethnic Turks form the largest single group (1.71 million or 25%), followed by former Yugoslavians (10%), Italians (8%), Poles (6%) and Greeks (5%). Ironically, over 20% of the 'foreign' population is actually German-born, reflecting poor progress on the integration of – mainly – ethnic Turks in the large cities.

Germany's most successful golfer, Bernhard Langer, is the son of a Russian prisoner of war who jumped off a Siberia-bound train and settled in Bavaria.

The Olympic torch was lit for the first time at the 1936 Olympics: 3000 athletes carried the flame from Olympia (Greece) to Berlin, where medallists were later awarded a laurel crown and potted oak tree.

'Jürgen wanted his team to play vertically, but he flew out horizontally.'

TRAINER LEGEND OTTO REHHAGEL, DESCRIBING THE ENFORCED HOLIDAY OF FORMER BAYERN-MÜNCHEN COACH JÜRGEN KLINSMANN

Despite some changes to Germany's antiquated 'blood based' citizenship laws, conservative elements in German society are preventing the introduction of truly modern laws, with state political campaigns having been fought and won at the expense of foreigners, foreigners having to renounce previous citizenship before they can become German, and recurring violence by extreme right-wing groups in eastern Germany directed (mainly) against foreigners – whose numbers rarely rise above a few percent of the population in towns there. Laws that disallow dual nationality for foreigners from Turkey and other non-EU countries are seen as the main reason why so few foreigners take steps to become Germans.

Debate regularly takes place as to whether Germany should promote a German *Leitkultur* (lead culture) as opposed to multiculturalism. Also frequently discussed are the high proportion of ethnically non-German pupils in some schools (in some Berlin schools 80% of pupils are foreigners) and poor German skills among foreigners in the classroom.

On the whole, Germany, whose citizens achieved the remarkable by coping with up to 500,000 former Yugoslavian refugees *each year* in the early 1990s, treats foreigners with respect, even if it still has some political catching up to do.

The Bambi awards – Germany's annual media awards – see national celebrities such as Düsseldorf-born supermodel Claudia Schiffer proffer statuettes of fawns to showbiz stars and other celebrities.

MEDIA

Germany's former chancellor, Gerhard Schröder, the so-called 'media chancellor', is reported to have said that all he needed to govern the country were *Bild*, the Sunday edition of *Bild* (called *Bild am Sonntag; BamS*) and *die Glotze* (the idiot box). If it were that easy, however, we'd all be doing it.

Licence fees subsidise the country's two public TV broadcasters, ARD (known as the first channel) and ZDF (the second channel). Unlike Mainz-based ZDF, ARD groups together several regional public stations, which contribute to the nationwide programs shown on the first channel, as well as the wholly regional shows transmitted on the so-called third channel. Due to the sheer choice of channels, private ownership is relatively diverse and pay TV low on impact; ProSiebenSat.1 Media and the Bertelsmann AG groups have the largest portfolios.

For an overview of media ownership in Germany, go to the English pages of www.kek-online.de.

About six million households are able to receive some form of digital TV (cable, satellite or terrestrial), which is set to replace analogue broadcasting within the next few years. According to plans, this will replace analogue broadcasting in 2010, although it is unlikely to be fully introduced until after that.

For better or worse, it's still possible to fall asleep reading German newspapers, which have mastered the art of dry, factual reporting. Print media has a strong regional bias, but overt backing for particular political parties by newspapers is rarely at the expense of the hard facts. The most influential newspaper is the aforementioned *Bild*, whose circulation exceeds four million. The other main politically conservative newspaper choices are the *Frankfurter Allgemeine Zeitung* and *Die Welt*. In the centre you find the *Süddeutsche Zeitung* and *Frankfürter Rundschau*, and left of these is *die tageszeitung (taz)*, founded in West Berlin in 1978. Both the press and broadcasters are independent and free of censorship.

Old Catholics (www .alt-katholisch.de), of which there are 15,000 in Germany today, rejected papal infallibility to break away from the Catholic Church in 1871. Female priests were ordained from 1996.

RELIGION

The constitution guarantees religious freedom, the main religions being Catholicism and Protestantism, each with about 26 million adherents (around a third of the country's total population each). Religion has a stronger footing in western Germany, especially Catholic Bavaria.

Unlike the Jewish community, which has grown since the early 1990s due to immigration from the former Soviet Union, the Catholic and Protestant

---

A WAY WITH 'UNWORDS'

Each year the Gesellschaft für deutsche Sprache (Society for German Language; www.gfds.de, in German) publishes an *Unwort des Jahres* (Unword of the Year) and several runners up – usually unloved words that dominated the media that year.

In the early 1990s unwords like *ausländerfrei* (free of foreigners), *ethnische Säuberung* (ethnic cleansing) and *Überfremdung* (too many foreigners) reflected a mood of hostility towards foreigners and the break-up of Yugoslavia. By the late 1990s, a *Rentnerschwemme* suggested a flood of pensioners was laying waste to the land, *Wohlstandsmüll* (rubbish of affluence) rather harshly described the large number of incapacitated workers, and *sozialverträgliches Frühableben* (socially compatible early death) offered a glimpse into the German angst that pensioners might be a drain on society by not shuffling off this mortal coil early enough. German *Leitkultur* (lead culture) emerged around 2000, although a proponent of creating a strong German host culture to lead the minority soon became known as a *Leithammel* (bellwether) – a castrated ram that wears a bell and leads the flock. *Ich AG* (Me Inc) was coined to describe a newly introduced legal form of corporation, the single-employee business, and an *Abweichler* became someone who dissents in an act seemingly akin to 'political heresy'. If you received a *Herdprämie* (stove premium), you were probably a woman being given incentives to stay at home like a good housewife and mother. Recently, *notleidende Banken* (banks in a crisis) topped the list of qualifiers, ahead of *Rentnerdemokratie* (pensioner democracy, a new angle on the socially compatible early death, describing how one generation of pensioners dominates and plunders the younger generation). Both came in ahead of *Karlsruhe-Touristen* – defenders of constitutional rights who frequently bring cases to the constitutional court, situated in the northern Baden-Württemberg town of Karlsruhe.

---

churches are losing worshippers. This is attributed partly to the obligatory church tax (8% or 9% of total income tax paid) paid by those belonging to a recognised denomination. Most German Protestants are Lutheran, headed by the Evangelische Kirche (Protestant Church), an official grouping of a couple of dozen Lutheran churches with headquarters in Hanover. In 2005, for the first time in almost five centuries, a German, Joseph Ratzinger (b 1927) became pope, taking the name Pope Benedict XVI.

The head of the Jewish community's Berlin-based umbrella organisation, the Zentralrat der Juden in Deutschland (Central Council of Jews in Germany), is Charlotte Knobloch (b 1932). The largest Jewish communities are in Berlin, Frankfurt am Main and Munich. Countrywide, 80 or more congregations are represented by the council, known for its conservatism (see p40).

Up to 4.3 million Muslims live in Germany. In the past, no single national body had existed to represent the fragmented Muslim community, but in 2007 a Coordinating Council of Muslims in Germany (Koordinationsrat der Muslime in Deutschland) was established by the four largest organisations. This grew out of the so-called Islam Conference, initiated by the Ministry of the Interior to create a dialogue between the state and Germans of the Muslim faith.

> The German Protestant Church is online at www.ekd.de; the Catholics are at www.catholic-hierarchy.org/country/de.html; and the Central Council of Jews at www.zentralratdjuden.de (in German).

ARTS
Literature
EARLY LITERATURE

Oral literature during the reign of Charlemagne (c 800) and secular epics performed by 12th-century knights are the earliest surviving literary forms, but the man who shook up the literary language was Martin Luther, whose 16th-century translation of the Bible set the stage for German writers.

In the 17th century, Christoph Martin Wieland (1733–1813) penned his *Geschichte des Agathon* (Agathon; 1766–67), a landmark in German literature

> Luther said, 'Look at their gobs to find out how they speak, then translate so they understand and see you're speaking to them in German.
>
> OPEN LETTER FROM LUTHER ON TRANSLATION, NUREMBERG, 15 SEPTEMBER 1530.

because it was the first *Bildungsroman* (a novel showing the development of the hero); Wieland was also the first to translate Shakespeare into German.

Shortly after Wieland was summoned to Weimar in 1772, Johann Wolfgang von Goethe (1749–1832) rose to become Germany's most powerful literary figure, later joining forces with Friedrich Schiller (1759–1805) in a celebrated period known as Weimarer Klassik (Weimar classicism; p272).

Writing in Goethe's lifetime, the lyricist and early Romantic poet, Friedrich Hölderlin (1770–1843), created delicate balance and rhythms. Interestingly, he was largely ignored from the mid-19th century, only to be rediscovered in the early 20th century and misused by Hitler for Nazi propaganda.

A 600km-long tourist route called Fairy-Tale Road (p622) leads literary travellers around Germany in the footsteps of the Grimm brothers, Jakob (1785–1863) and Wilhelm (1786–1859). Serious academics who wrote *German Grammar* and *History of the German Language,* they're best known for their collection of fairy tales, myths and legends.

The Düsseldorf-born Heinrich Heine (1797–1856) produced one of Germany's finest collections of poems when he published *Buch der Lieder* (Book of Songs) in 1827, but it was his politically scathing *Deutschland: Ein Wintermärchen* (Germany: A Winter's Tale) that contributed to his work being banned in 1835. By that time, Heine – one of Germany's most famous Jews – was in Paris, in love with an illiterate salesgirl, and was surrounded by pesky German spies.

MODERN & CONTEMPORARY

The Weimar years witnessed the flowering of Lübeck-born Thomas Mann (1875–1955), recipient of the Nobel Prize for Literature in 1929, whose greatest novels focus on social forms of the day. For Mann, 'Germany's first lady' was writer and poet Ricarda Huch (1864–1947), a courageous opponent of Nazism. Mann's older brother, Heinrich (1871–1950), adopted a stronger political stance than Thomas in his work; his *Professor Unrat* (1905) provided the raw material for the Marlene Dietrich film *Der Blaue Engel* (The Blue Angel; p65).

Berlin's underworld during the Weimar Republic served as the focus for the novel *Berlin Alexanderplatz* (1929) by Alfred Döblin (1878–1957). Hermann Hesse (1877–1962), another Nobel prize winner, adopted the theme of the outsider in *Steppenwolf* (1927) and imbued New Romantic spirituality into his work after a journey to India in 1911. Antiwar novel *Im Westen nichts Neues* (All Quiet on the Western Front; 1929) by Osnabrück-born Erich Maria Remarque (1898–1970) was banned in 1933 and remains one of the most widely read German books.

Of the generation that has established itself in the literary scene since 1945, Günter Grass (b 1927) is the most celebrated. Grass burst into the literary limelight with his first novel, *Die Blechtrommel* (Tin Drum; 1959) and grew to become a postwar moral icon – until this was called into question by his youthful membership of the Waffen-SS, which he revealed in his latest book, *Beim Häuten der Zwiebel* (Peeling the Onion; 2006).

Although East Germany no longer exists, the country managed to bring forth some fine writers. Christa Wolf (b 1929) is the best known and most controversial; she admitted to working as an informer for East Germany's secret police briefly in the late 1950s before the state got heavy on artists, and she later spoke out for dissidents. Like Wolf, Sarah Kirsch (b 1935) supported the cause of singer and songwriter Wolf Biermann (b 1936) during the furore that led to his loss of GDR citizenship.

Thomas Brussig (b 1964), a novelist and screenwriter from Berlin, rose to prominence in the mid-1990s with *Helden wie Wir* (Heroes like Us; 1995).

Read Simplicissimus *(Adventures of a Simpleton) by Hans Jacob Christoffel von Grimmelshausen as an appetiser to the early German novel.*

A vivid picture of mid-19th-century German society is painted in Heinrich Heine's Deutschland: Ein Wintermärchen *(Germany: A Winter's Tale), based on a trip the writer took from Aachen to Hamburg.*

Günter Grass' Ein weites Feld *(Too Far Afield; 1992) addresses 'unification without unity' after the fall of the Wall.*

He also wrote the screenplay for the film *Sonnenallee* (p66) and is a member of the Lübeck-based Gruppe 05 – cofounded in 2005 by Günter Grass with other writers to get more young scribes involved in politics. Other members of the group whose works reward exploration include Burkhard Spinnen (b 1956), who has published more than a dozen novels and essays; and novelist, poet and essayist Matthias Politycki (b 1955).

Skipping back to a few relative old-timers for a moment, a trio of contemporary literary figures was born in 1944: the strongly mystic Botho Strauss, crime novelist and Berlin professor Bernhard Schlink (whose books have won prizes and much praise), and novelist WG Sebald (1944–2001), who assured his place as one of Germany's best writers with his powerful portrayal of four exiles in *Die Ausgewanderten* (Emigrants). Munich-based writer and playwright, Patrick Süskind (b 1949) achieved international acclaim with *Das Parfum* (Perfume), his extraordinary tale of a psychotic 18th-century perfumer.

Russian-born Wladimir Kaminer (b 1967) is a popular and interesting author who hit Berlin in the early 1990s. He left the Soviet Union, acquired refugee status in East Germany, then after reunification he began a regular disco with Russian beats in Berlin's Mitte district. Kaminer's first collection of stories was the highly popular *Russendisko* (Russian Disco; 2000), and today he continues to spin vinyl at the disco and elsewhere. His most recent work includes *Es gab keinen Sex im Sozialismus* (There Was No Sex in Socialism; 2009).

Feridun Zaimoglu (b 1964) is Turkish born, wrote an intriguing first novel using the language of German rappers (*Kanak Sprak;* 1995) and is today one of Germany's most important writers of the new generation. He narrowly escaped death in a bus crash in Turkey, which inspired the beginning of his recent work *Liebesbrand* (Blazing Love; 2008).

Zaimoglu is strongly influenced by the work of fellow Turkish-German author and playwright Emine Sevgi Özdamar (b 1946), whose *Das Leben ist eine Karawanserei* (Life is a Kervansaray; 1992) was *Times Literary Supplement* Novel of the Year in 1994. In 2009 she was awarded the Berliner Kunstpreis (Berlin Art Prize).

The Deutscher Buchpreis (German Book Award), the equivalent of Britain's Booker Prize and the US National Book Awards (in fiction), is a good guide to what's new each year. Usually about 130 works of fiction are entered and a short list of five selected. A few recent winners are Uwe Tellkamp (b 1968) for *Der Turm* (The Tower; 2008) and Julia Franck for *Die Mittagsfrau* (Lady Midday; 2007). You can find other short-listed and winning authors on the official website, www.deutscher-buchpreis.de.

Cinema

German film has a long, illustrious and colourful history, perhaps explaining why local productions are popular and account for about 20% of box-office sales, even though budgets are tiny compared to Hollywood productions.

Germany's rich cinematic heritage began in the UFA (Universum Film AG) studio in Babelsberg (Potsdam; p161), founded in 1911 and now a large studio and multimedia complex. One early classic produced by UFA is Fritz Lang's silent classic *Metropolis* (1927), about a subterranean proletarian subclass – it's the first film to use back projection (also see p162).

In the early 1930s film *Der Blaue Engel* (Blue Angel; 1930), directed by Josef von Sternberg, Marlene Dietrich (p65) wooed the audience with hypnotic sensuality and became a star overnight. The 1930s were productive but difficult years. The premier of Fritz Lang's talkie, *Das Testament des Dr Mabuse* (Testament of Dr Mabuse; 1933), about a psychiatric patient with

Meaty Thomas Mann starters include Buddenbrooks, Der Zauberberg (Magic Mountain), and his menacing Doktor Faustus, in which the central character exchanges health and love for creative fulfilment.

Berlin Alexanderplatz: The Story of Franz Biberkopf by Alfred Döblin is a masterful epic set in 1920s Berlin (film-maker Rainer Fassbinder made a 15-hour film version of it).

The Wonderful, Horrible Life of Leni Riefenstahl (1993), directed by Ray Muller, is a stunning three-hour epic about the controversial film-maker who rose to prominence during the Third Reich.

plans to take over the world, had to be shifted to Austria because of some out-of-joint Nazi noses. Hitler would also drive acting greats like Peter Lorre (1904–64; an ethnic German Hungarian) and Billy Wilder (1906–2002; an ethnic Austro-German who wrote scripts in Berlin) to Hollywood exile.

In the 1960s film again entered a new age that brought forth the New German Cinema movement (Junger deutscher Film) and directors Rainer Werner Fassbinder (1945–82), Wim Wenders (b 1945), Volker Schlöndorff (b 1939), Werner Herzog (b 1942) and director-actor Margarethe von Trotta (b 1942). All except Fassbinder, Germany's *enfant terrible* of film who lived hard and left behind a cocaine-spiked wreck, are working today. The resonance of Fassbinder's *Die Sehnsucht der Veronika Voss* (Longing of Veronica Voss; 1981), Wenders' narrative classics *Paris Texas* (1984) and *Der Himmel über Berlin* (Wings of Desire; 1987), Herzog's *Aguirre, der Zorn Gottes* (Aguirre, the Wrath of God; 1972) and Schlöndorff's film rendition of the Günter Grass novel *Die Blechtrommel* (Tin Drum; 1979) can still be felt in local productions today.

The 1990s saw the arrival on the scene of Tom Tykwer (b 1965), whose *Lola Rennt* (Run Lola Run; 1998) established his reputation as one of Germany's best new directors. Since then his work has included a film version of the Patrick Süskind novel *Das Parfum* (Perfume: The Story of a Murderer; 2006) and the US-German production *The International* (2009) on the highly contemporary theme of bad bankers and monetary empires.

A handful of exciting directors emerged in Germany from the late 1990s to join figures like director Doris Dörrie (b 1955) and producer, director and screenwriter Bernd Eichinger (b 1949) in shaping the contemporary scene. These include Christian Petzold (b 1960), Marc Rothemund (b 1968), Fatih Akın (b 1973), Oliver Hirschbiegel (b 1957) and Florian von Donnersmarck (b 1973).

Petzold directed one of Germany's best films of recent years, *Yella* (2007), an evocative, amusing and intelligent work with excellent acting about a woman (played by Nina Hoss) who sort of leaves East Germany, teaming up by chance with a businessman (Devid Striesow). Marc Rothemund's highly acclaimed *Sophie Scholl – Die letzten Tage* (Sophie Scholl: The Final Days; 2005) portrays the interrogation, trial and judgement of Scholl's brave act of resistance against Nazism through her own eyes (see p313).

Fatih Akın's (b 1973) German-Turkish-Italian produced *Auf der anderen Seite* (The Other Side of Heaven; 2007) won the Best Screenplay award at Cannes. Akin is the most prominent of the Turkish-German directors and in 2009 won the Special Jury Prize at the Venice International Film Festival for his romantic comedy *Soul Kitchen* (2009). The film is set in a Hamburg restaurant, with the role of a Greek crook and gambler on parole played by Moritz Bleibtreu (b 1971), one of the most interesting actors in Germany today. Bleibtreu also played the challenging role of Andreas Baader in *Der Baader Meinhof Komplex* (The Baader Meinhof Complex; 2008), directed by Ulrich Edel (b 1947) and based on a book by Stephan Aust (b 1946) about the Red Army Faction (RAF) group of terrorists active in the late 1960s and early 1970s. Bernd Eichinger wrote the screenplay, and the film was nominated for an Oscar in 2009 for the Best Foreign Language Film.

The most visible international face of contemporary German film is Wolfgang Becker's laconic and highly successful *Good Bye, Lenin!* (2003), with its recreation of GDR life for a bed-ridden mother. Oliver Hirschbiegel's *Der Untergang* (Downfall; 2004) is a chilling account of Hitler's last 12 days – from his final birthday to his suicide – mostly in his Berlin bunker. Florian von Donnersmarck's *Das Leben der Anderen* (Lives of Others; 2006) portrays the Stasi and its network of informants five years prior to the fall of the Berlin Wall.

Die Ausgewanderten (Emigrants; 1997) by WG Sebald addresses the lost homeland of an exile in his vivid portrayal of four different journeys by Jewish emigrants – it's a good introduction to this weighty but wonderful novelist.

Frankfurt has hosted the world's largest literary marketplace, the international book fair (www.frankfurt-book-fair.com), since 1949. Leipzig, earlier the traditional book capital, hosts its own fair (www.leipziger-buchmesse.de) in March each year.

Read what the critics say about 500-plus German films at www.german-cinema.de.

MARLENE DIETRICH

Marlene Dietrich (1901–92), born Marie Magdalene Dietrich into a good middle-class family in Berlin, was the daughter of a Prussian officer. After acting school, she worked in the silent-film industry in the 1920s, stereotyped as a hard-living, libertine flapper. But she soon carved a niche in the film fantasies of lower-middle-class men as the dangerously seductive *femme fatale*, best typified by her appearance in the 1930 talkie *Der Blaue Engel* (Blue Angel), which turned her into a Hollywood star.

The film was the start of a five-year collaboration with director Josef von Sternberg, during which time she built on her image of erotic opulence – dominant and severe, but always with a touch of self-irony. Dressed in men's suits for *Marocco* in 1930, she lent her 'sexuality is power' attitude bisexual tones, winning a new audience overnight.

Dietrich stayed in Hollywood after the Nazi rise to power, though Hitler, no less immune to her charms, reportedly promised perks and the red-carpet treatment if she moved back to Germany. She responded with an empty offer to return if she could bring Sternberg – a Jew and no Nazi favourite. She took US citizenship in 1937 and sang on the front to Allied GIs.

After the war, Dietrich retreated slowly from the public eye, making occasional appearances in films, but mostly cutting records and performing live. Her final years were spent in Paris, bedridden and accepting few visitors, immortal in spirit as mortality caught up with her.

Studio Babelsberg in Potsdam (p161) and film museums in Berlin (p122), Potsdam (p161) and Frankfurt am Main (p534) are good starting points for anything to do with the German film tradition.

Television

For a general overview of German media, see p60.

Social etiquette in Germany demands that you never telephone a friend at 8pm – this is when the state-funded ARD broadcasts its *Tagesschau* news program. German TV itself is unlikely to knock you off your lounge room chair, but it will give some interesting insights into the country. As elsewhere, reality TV and casting shows are popular staples. At the high end, one area where Germany excels is in pan-European broadcasting, such as its *Kulturzeit* (Culture Age; 3Sat, various times) collaboration with Austria and Switzerland, and the ARTE channel collaboration with France.

Watch the news with ZDF at www.zdf.de or ARD at www.ard.de (in German).

The long-running *Tatort* (ARD, 8.15pm Sunday) police series is a top-rating show that rotates between a dozen or more German cities, plus Vienna. The opening music and graphic are from the first show in 1970. The Cologne, Münster and Berlin productions are excellent, but each *Tatort* has its own regional character and flavour.

Although production stopped in 1998, the crime classic *Derrick* remains the most successful German TV production ever.

Read what's on the box this week with the online German TV program guide at www.tvtv.de (in German).

Music

LOVE BALLADS TO CONTEMPORARY CLASSICAL

German music in the 12th century is closely associated with Walther von der Vogelweide (c 1170–1230), who achieved renown with love ballads. A more formalised troubadour tradition followed, but it was baroque organist Johann Sebastian Bach (1685–1750), born in Eisenach, who influenced early European music most. His legacy can be explored in Leipzig's Bach-Museum (p198) in the house in which he died. Another museum in Eisenach (p282) is dedicated to his life and work.

Georg Friedrich Händel (1685–1759) was a contemporary of Bach who hailed from Halle in Saxony-Anhalt (his house is also now a museum), but lived and worked almost exclusively in London from 1714.

TOP FIVE GDR RETRO FILMS

For more on Ostalgie, see p55.

- Leander Haussmann's *Sonnenallee* (Sun Alley; 1999) is set in a fantastical Wall-clad East Berlin in the 1970s, and evokes everything nostalgic for the former GDR.

- *Helden wie Wir* (Heroes like Us; 1999), directed by Sebastian Peterson and based on the novel by Thomas Brussig, sees the protagonist (who claims to have been Erich Honecker's personal blood donor) recount the story of his life, including how his penis allegedly leads to the collapse of the Berlin Wall.

- Dull lives are led in dull Frankfurt an der Oder in dull East Germany – until Ellen and Chris are caught doing it. Laughs abound in *Halbe Treppe* (Grill Point; 2001), directed by East German–born Andreas Dresen.

- The Wall falls the day the bartending lead actor hits 30 in West Berlin's bohemian Kreuzberg district. Haussmann's humorous *Herr Lehmann* (Berlin Blues; 2003) is based on a cult book by Element of Crime lead singer Sven Regener.

- *Good Bye, Lenin!* (2003), the cult box-office smash hit by Wolfgang Becker, revolves around a son trying to recreate the GDR for a bedridden ailing mother whose health couldn't stand the shock of a fallen Wall.

Händel's music found favour in the circle of Vienna's classical composers, and it was Joseph Haydn (1732–1809) who taught Bonn-born Ludwig van Beethoven (1770–1827), whose work reflects the Enlightenment. Beethoven is also the most important of the composers who paved the way for Romanticism. His birth house in Bonn is also a museum now (p580).

Among the Romantic composers, Hamburg-born Felix Mendelssohn-Bartholdy (1809–47) is hailed as a sheer genius. He penned his first overture at the age of 17 and later dug up works by JS Bach to give the latter the fame he enjoys today.

Born in Leipzig and dying in Venice, Richard Wagner (1813–83) dominates 19th-century music. Other composers ignored him at their peril. Hitler, who picked up on an anti-Semitic essay and some late-life ramblings on German virtues, famously turned Wagner into a post-mortem Nazi icon. A summer music festival in Bayreuth celebrates Wagner's life and works (p379). For more on the man, see p379.

Hamburg brought forth Johannes Brahms (1833–97) and his influential symphonies, and chamber and piano works. Two figures whose legacies can be explored today in cities such as Bonn, Leipzig and Zwickau are composer Robert Schumann (1810–56) and his gifted pianist-spouse Clara Wieck (1819–96). Schumann (born in Zwickau) and Wieck (born in Leipzig) are buried in Bonn's Alter Friedhof (p583). Pulsating 1920s Berlin ushered in Vienna-born Arnold Schönberg (1874–1951), inventor of a new tonal relationship that turned music on its head. One of his pupils, Hanns Eisler (1898–1962), went into exile in 1933 but returned to East Berlin to teach in 1950. Among his works was the East German national anthem, *Auferstanden aus Ruinen* (Resurrected from Ruins), lyricless from 1961 when its proreunification words fell out of favour with party honchos.

Hanau-born Paul Hindemith (1895–1963) was banned by the Nazis and composed his most important orchestral compositions outside his homeland. The Hindemith Institute (www.hindemith.org) in Frankfurt am Main promotes his music and safeguards his estate. Perhaps better known is Dessau-born Kurt Weill (1900–50), another composer who fled the Nazi terror. He teamed up with Bertolt Brecht (p77) in the 1920s and wrote the music for *Die Morität von Mackie Messer* (Mack the Knife) in Brecht's

Fourteen informative essays bring the vibrant musical age of Luther et al alive in the 300-plus-page *Music in the German Renaissance*, edited by John Kmetz.

Visit the website of violinist Anne-Sophie Mutter (http://anne-sophie-mutter.com) to begin exploring the contemporary classical music scene.

Dreigroschenoper (Threepenny Opera). Weill ended up in New York, where he wrote successful Broadway musicals.

Germany's most prestigious orchestra, the Berliner Philharmoniker (1882; p147), was shaped by conductor Wilhelm Furtwängler (1886–1954) and, from 1954 until his death in 1989, the illustrious Herbert von Karajan (1908–89). Dresden opera orchestra (p188) and the Leipzig Gewandhausorchester (p204) are also important stops on the classical trail. The young Kammersymphonie Berlin (Berlin Chamber Symphony), established in 1991, recaptures the multifaceted music scene of 1920s Berlin through its focus on less common orchestral works. Violinist Anne-Sophie Mutter (b 1963) is the unchallenged star of the modern contemporary scene, performing with the Berlin Symphony Orchestra (founded 1966) at the age of 14 and more recently performing the works of Russian-born Sofia Asgatowna Gubaidulina (b 1931), who has lived and worked in Germany since the early 1990s and is one of its most exciting composers.

> Since 1980 the average male chest has increased in size by 7.3 cm (to 106.1 cm); women's chest size has expanded by 2.3cm (to 98.7 cm).

CONTEMPORARY

Jazz is popular in Germany, and most towns have a jazz club or two. Till Brönner (b 1971) – who studied at the Cologne Music School – has trumpeted, sung and composed his way to renown, recording his *Oceana* album (2006) in Los Angeles with contributions from Madeleine Peyroux (b 1974) and singing Italian model and First Lady of France Carla Bruni (b 1967).

On the downtempo scene, where you find various blends of jazz, dub, hip hop, house and African music, Jazzanova (www.jazzanova.net) is the undisputed master, with remixes and original tunes. It founded the Sonar Kollektiv label (www.sonarkollektiv.com) in the late 1990s, which today includes German acts like Micatone (www.micatone.de, in German) and international figures like Daniel Paul, Georg Levin and Forss. For its 10th anniversary, the label put together the Sonar Kollektiv Orchester with artists such as Clara Hill (www.clarahill.com) and Thief (based around Sascha Gottschalk).

> For more information, practical and historical, on the Berlin Philharmonic Orchestra, tune to www.berlin-philharmonic.com.

These contemporaries complement the soaring sounds of musicians such as Albert Mangelsdorff (1928–2005), saxophonist Heinz Sauer (b 1932), and Klaus Doldinger (b 1936) who formed the legendary fusion band Passport. JazzFest (p135) Berlin brings the best of German and European jazz to the capital each November.

One big question facing most German rock bands is whether to sing in German, English or both. Scorpions, probably the most successful band abroad, sang in English. A contemporary band who chose to sing in German and found success abroad is Rammstein, part of a 'New German Hard' (Neue deutsche Härte) movement that combines industrial rock, metal and dance. The band, which – it says – is mistakenly seen as being right wing and nationalistic and sees itself as outside these labels or even left of the political spectrum, is known for its provocative lyrics and intense sounds. Two other highly successful bands abroad that didn't really have this dilemma were the (mostly) instrumental Tangerine Dream and Kraftwerk. Tangerine Dream has the honour of being the first band to cut a chart success with Virgin Records in the 1970s. About three decades before its time, Düsseldorf-based Kraftwerk created the musical foundations for techno, which in turn spawned Berlin's legendary techno-orientated Love Parade in 1989.

> Thinking of studying in Germany, want to know how many breweries there are in Germany or what life's like in Germany's university towns? See the German Academic Exchange Service website, www.daad.de.

Members of the Neue Deutsche Welle (NDW; German New Wave) always sang in German – although Nena, its tame international mother ship, successfully recorded her hit single '99 Luftballons' in English, too. The movement spawned the Hamburger Schule (Hamburg School) of musicians, with recognised acts such as Blumfeld, Die Sterne and the Tocotronic still going strong since emerging in the 1990s. Die-hard legends gathering no moss are Germany's most enduring punk band, Düsseldorf-based Die Toten Hosen; punk queen Nina Hagen (b 1955), whose transformations still seem ahead of their time; and Die Ärzte. Meanwhile, Herbert Grönemeyer (b 1956), 'Germany's Springsteen' (also a decent actor) and leather legend Udo Lindenberg (b 1946) – who has resided in Hamburg's Hotel Atlantic (p689) longer than some of us have been alive – are still kicking on.

As well as language, another choice facing bands is whether to base themselves in Hamburg or Berlin. Both cities are important capitals for rock bands but exert different influences – the Berlin sound is generally somewhat harder, while Hamburg bands often retain stronger shades of German New Wave, with a punk or lighter pop flavour. Giessen-bred Juli is one soft-rock band that works out of Hamburg, where the sound is often more melodic. Bautzen-born Silbermond is based in Berlin, whereas Wir Sind Helden, considered one of the best pop-rock bands around in Germany at the moment, started in Hamburg and shifted to Berlin.

Element of Crime, led by multitalented Sven Regener (b 1961), has probably had more influence on the arts spectrum than anyone else, having composed and played scores for films including Leander Haussmann's *Sonnenallee* (Sun Alley) and *Herr Lehmann* (Regener also wrote the book and script of the latter).

Huddled between the popular rock, orchestral and electronic dance genres is Barbara Morgenstern (b 1971), who began her career singing a cappella in Hamburg before moving to Berlin, where she branched out into a solo career.

Since Tangerine Dream and Kraftwerk, new generations of electronic musicians have moved into the limelight, making music spawned from techno but inhabiting splinter genres. Berlin-based Apparat (Sascha Ring) is closely associated with the charmingly named Shitkatapult records, one of the top labels for techno and post-techno sounds since the late 1990s. His experiments with sound and vocals result in vivid, melodic techno and rich electropop. The release *Walls* (2007) was one of the top electro albums and has since been followed by *Things to be Frickled* and more recently *Moderat*, which he released on BPitch Control, another top label, as a collaboration with Modeselektor (www.modeselektor.de, in German). The latter churns out IDM (intelligent dance music) influenced by electro and hip hop.

A founder and main act of the BPitch Control label is Ellen Allien (b 1969) (www.ellenallien.de, in German), a DJane who lives in Berlin and has been on the scene since its earliest days. Monika Kruse (b 1971), another of the DJanes, was born in Berlin and grew up in Munich. Her *Changes of Perception* album from 2008 was rated one of the best that year. André Galluzzi, who comes from Frankfurt am Main, has been a resident at the Cocoon Club (p541), the location cofounded by Sven Väth in Frankfurt.

Good places in Berlin to catch some of these are Berghain (p146), where Galluzzi has recently been resident, and Watergate (p146). Also look for gigs by musicians/DJs such as the trance pioneer Paul van Dyk (www.paul vandyk.de, in German) or DJ Tanith (www.tanith.org, in German).

The rap scene in Germany is never short of a protagonist and a tough plot – Germany has lots of rappers, some of dubious quality and politics. Heidelberg's Advanced Chemistry and Stuttgart-bred Die Fantastischen Vier are the mild-mannered godfathers of the form in Germany (some would say still the best), paving the way for a younger, more sinewy breed of gangsta rappers like Bushido (b 1978), Sido (b 1980) and his colleague Fler (b 1982), who are all Berlin-based, or Frankfurt-based Azad (b 1974). Deichkind, a foursome from Hamburg, has some of the best lyrics. Mannheim has produced a raft of rappers, including the soul-influenced Xavier Naidoo (b 1971),

Watch the videos and hear the music of Germany's most influential electro band at www .kraftwerk.com.

'These guys are the greatest German bubblegum-neo-glam-goth-emo boy band. Ever.'

ROLLING STONE MAGAZINE, REVIEWING THE TOKIO HOTEL ALBUM *SCREAM*

'Once every generation, a German band achieves worldwide success... Yes, it's Nietzsche Rock!'

NME MUSIC MAGAZINE ON THE POPULAR METAL BAND RAMMSTEIN

EXPLORING GERMAN MUSIC IN 10 ALBUMS

Stack your CD player with the following, sit back and take a whirlwind tour through German musical history:

■ *Crusaders: In Nomine Domini & German Choral Song around 1600* by various composers (Christophorus label)

■ *Brandenburg Concertos* by JS Bach

■ *Water Music* by Händel

■ *Beethoven: Nine Symphonies* performed by the Berlin Philharmonic Orchestra

■ *Tannhäuser und der Sägerkrieg auf dem Wartburg* (Tannhäuser and the Song Contest of the Wartburg) by Richard Wagner

■ *Brahms: Violin Concerto, Double Concerto* performed by Anne-Sophie Mutter, Antonio Meneses and the Berlin Philharmonic Orchestra

■ *Passport on Stage* by Passport (live sax and jazzy stuff; 2008)

■ *Tour de France Soundtracks* by Kraftwerk (track nine is about a heart monitor)

■ *Nomad Songs* by Micatone (the third album from this Berlin nu-jazz band; 2005)

■ *Soundso* by Wir sind Helden (pop and rock with intelligent lyrics; 2007)

---

who began with Söhne Mannheims (Sons of Mannheim). Interestingly – and partly evident in his style of prose – writer Feridun Zaimoglu (p62) emerged from a small, ethnic-Turk rap scene in Kiel.

Architecture
CAROLINGIAN TO ART NOUVEAU

Among the grand buildings of the Carolingian period, Aachen's Byzantine-inspired cathedral (p586) – built for Charlemagne from 786 to about 800 – and Fulda's Michaelskirche (p553) are surviving masterpieces. A century on, Carolingian, Christian (Roman) and Byzantine influences flowed together in a more proportional interior with integrated columns, reflected in the elegant Stiftskirche St Cyriakus in Gernrode (p258) and the Romanesque cathedrals in Worms (p488), Speyer (p490) and Mainz (p484).

The Unesco-listed Kloster Maulbronn (p424) in Baden-Württemberg, built in 1147, is considered the best preserved monastery of its ilk north of the Alps.

Early Gothic architecture, slow to reach Germany from its northern-French birthplace, kept many Romanesque elements, as the cathedral in Magdeburg (p219) illustrates. Later churches have purely Gothic traits – ribbed vaults, pointed arches and flying buttresses to allow greater height and larger windows, seen in Cologne's cathedral (Kölner Dom; p569), Marburg (Elisabethkirche; p550), Trier (Liebfrauenkirche; p515), Freiburg (Münster; p453) and Lübeck (Marienkirche; p702). From the 15th century, elaborately patterned vaults and hall churches emerged. Munich's Frauenkirche (p311) and Michaelskirche (p310) are typical of this late Gothic period.

The Renaissance reached Germany around the mid-16th century, bestowing Heidelberg and other southern cities with buildings bearing ornate leaf work and columns, while in northern Germany the secular Weser Renaissance style produced the ducal palace (Schloss) in Celle (p627).

From the early 17th century to the mid-18th century, feudal rulers ploughed their wealth into residences. In Baden-Württemberg, the residential retreat of Karlsruhe (p423) was dreamt up, while Italian architect

Pick up *Der geteilte Himmel* (Divided Heaven), by East German writer Christa Wolf, to discover the fate of a woman's love for a man who fled to West Germany.

COLLECTIVE MEMORY

Unesco's 'Memory of the World' program safeguards the world's most precious documentary heritage. German contributions include the following:

■ A unique collection of 145,000 pieces of music from around the world (excluding Western art and pop) in Berlin's Ethnologisches Museum (Museum of Ethnology; p129), recorded between 1893 and 1952 (listed in 1999).

■ Goethe's literary estate (listed in 2001), stashed in the Goethe and Schiller Archives in Weimar's Klassik Stiftung Weimar (p271).

■ Beethoven's Ninth Symphony (listed in 2001), the score of which is kept in the Alte Staatsbibliothek (Old National Library in Berlin; p115).

■ The negative of the reconstructed version of Lang's silent film, *Metropolis* (1927), pieced together from a fragmented original (listed in 2001).

■ The 1282-page *Gutenberg Bible* – Europe's first book to be printed with moveable type – is one of four of the original 30 to survive. Learn about the digital version at www.gutenberg digital.de (listed in 2001); the original cannot be viewed.

Barelli started work on Munich's Schloss Nymphenburg (p315). In northern Germany, buildings were less ornamental, as the work of baroque architect Johann Conrad Schlaun (1695–1773) in Münster or Dresden's treasure trove of baroque architecture demonstrates. One of the finest baroque churches, Dresden's Frauenkirche (p180), built in 1743, was destroyed in the 1945 firebombing of the city, and was reconstructed and finally reopened in 2005. Late baroque ushered in Potsdam's rococo Schloss Sanssouci (p159).

Berlin's Brandenburg Gate, based on a Greek design, is a brilliant showcase of neoclassicism. This late-18th-century period saw baroque folly and exuberance fly out the window – and strictly geometric columns, pediments and domes fly in. The colonnaded Altes Museum (p117), Neue Wache (p116) and the Konzerthaus Berlin (p147) – all designed by leading architect Karl Friedrich Schinkel (1781–1841) – are other pure forms of neoclassicism still gracing the capital. In Bavaria, Leo von Klenze (1784–1864) chiselled his way through virtually every ancient civilisation, with eclectic creations such as the Glyptothek and Propyläen on Munich's Königsplatz (p311).

A wave of derivative architecture based on old styles swept through late-19th-century Germany. A German peculiarity was the so-called rainbow style, which blended Byzantine with Roman features. Renaissance revivalism found expression in Schloss in Schwerin (p726), by Georg Adolph Demmler (1804–86); while sections of Ludwig II's fairy-tale concoction Neuschwanstein (p352) are neo-Romanesque.

Germany's iconic Reichstag building (p120), built in 1894, was designed by Paul Wallot (1841–1912) in the Wilhelmian style with neobaroque and neo-Renaissance elements; it was restored in the 1990s with a stunning glass-and-steel cupola (inspired by the original) by internationally acclaimed British architect Norman Foster. Wallot's use of steel to create a greater span and large glass surface was subsequently adopted by the early-20th-century art-nouveau movement, which created some of the country's most impressive industrial architecture: look no further than Berlin's Wertheim bei Hertie department store on Kurfürstendamm (p128).

Slavonic Sorbs live in pockets of Saxony and Brandenburg, and a small Danish minority can be found around Flensburg (Schleswig-Holstein) on the Danish border.

MODERN & CONTEMPORARY

No architectural movement has had greater influence on modern design than Bauhaus, which was spearheaded by the son of a Berlin architect, Walter

Gropius (1883–1969). Through his founding in 1919 of the Staatliches Bauhaus – a modern architecture, art and design institute in Weimar – Bauhaus pushed the industrial forms of art nouveau to a functional limit and sought to unite architecture, painting, furniture design and sculpture. Critics claimed Bauhaus was too functional and impersonal, relying too heavily on cubist and constructivist forms. But any visit to the Bauhaus Building

---

UNESCO WORLD HERITAGE SITES IN GERMANY

Following is a list of Germany's fabulous treasures and the years in which their Unesco status was declared:

- Aachen Dom (Cathedral; 1978; p586)
- Augustusburg and Falkenlust castles in Brühl (1984; p579)
- Bamberg (1993; p374)
- Bauhaus sites in Weimar and Dessau (1996; p272 and p224)
- Berlin's Museumsinsel (Museum Island; 1999; p116) and Siedlungen der Berliner Moderne (Berlin Modernism Housing Estates; 2008)
- Bremen Rathaus and Rolandstatue (2004; p663)
- Classical Weimar (1998; p271)
- Collegiate Church, Castle and Old Town of Quedlinburg (1994; p254)
- Cologne Dom (1996; p569)
- Garden kingdom of Dessau-Wörlitz (2000; p227)
- Goslar Altstadt and mines of Rammelsberg (1992; p242 and p243)
- Hildesheim's Dom and St Michaeliskirche (1985; p634)
- Kloster Maulbronn (1993; p424)
- Lorsch Abbey and Altenmünster (1991; p546)
- Lübeck (1987; p701)
- Luther memorials in Eisleben and Lutherstadt Wittenberg (1996; p236 and p229)
- Messel Pit fossil site (1995; p546)
- Muskauer Park in Bad Muskau (2004; p214)
- Potsdam's parks and palaces (1990; p157)
- Regensburg (2006; p388)
- Reichenau Island (2000; p472)
- Speyer's Kaiserdom cathedral (1981; p490)
- Trier's Roman monuments, Dom and Liebfrauenkirche (1986; p514)
- Upper Germanic-Rhaetian Limes (2005; p34)
- Upper Middle Rhine Valley (Oberes Mittelrheintal; 2002; p499)
- Völklinger Hütte ironworks (1994; p525)
- Wadden Sea (2009; p656 and p717)
- Wartburg castle (1999; p281)
- Wieskirche, Wies' pilgrimage church (1983; p354)
- Wismar and Stralsund historic centres (2002; p741 and p744)
- Würzburg's Residenz and Court Gardens (1981; p339)
- Zollverein colliery complex in Essen (2001; p591)

Erich Mendelsohn and the Architecture of German Modernism by Kathleen James zooms in on Mendelsohn's expressionist buildings in Berlin and Frankfurt.

in Dessau (p224), where the institute was based after 1925, or the nearby Meisterhäuser (Master Craftsmen's Houses; p225), where teachers from the school lived (such as painters Kandinsky and Klee), instantly reveals just how much the avant-garde movement pioneered modern architecture. In Berlin, the Bauhaus Archive/Museum of Design (p124), which Gropius designed himself in 1964, is a must-see. Also see Design for Life (p224).

The Nazis shut down the Bauhaus school in 1932 and rediscovered the pompous and monumental. One of the most successful attempts was the 1934 Olympiastadion Berlin (Berlin Olympic Stadium; p128), designed by Werner March (1894–1976). In time for the FIFA World Cup 2006, the ageing stadium was rejuvenated with new roofing, restoration of original materials, and the lowering of the playing field to intensify the atmosphere.

The monumental efforts of another political persuasion are captured attractively today in the buildings that line Berlin's (former East German) Karl-Marx-Allee (p125). Yet another highlight that outlived the country that created it is the 368m-high TV Tower on Alexanderplatz (p117), built in 1969. One structure that was much less successful – and has survived history only in fragments – is that most potent symbol of the Cold War, the Berlin Wall (p126).

Experimental design took off in the 1960s in Düsseldorf with slender Thyssenhaus (1960), designed by Hubert Petschnigg (1913–1997), which inspired Tel Aviv's Eliyahu House. In 1972 Munich was graced with its splendid tent-roofed Olympiastadion (p313), which visitors can today scale with a rope and snap hook or abseil down for an architectural kick of the hair-raising sort. In the meantime, Bayern-München football team has sailed over to the Allianz Arena (p316), a remarkable rubber-dinghy-like translucent object that will please football fans with more than just an architectural interest in stadiums. An unusual feature is the hatched entrance to the players' tunnel.

Berlin as it really is leaps off the pages of Wladimir Kaminer's highly readable and humorous short stories in *Russendisko* (Russian Disco; 2002).

Frank Gehry (b 1929) has left exciting imprints on German cities over the past two decades, first through the 1989 Vitra Design Museum in Weil am Rhein (p460), and later with his wacky 1999 Neue Zollhof (New Customs House; p561) in Düsseldorf, the Gehry-Tower (2001) in Hanover, and the 1999 DZ Bank (p114) on Berlin's Pariser Platz.

Berlin, of course, is the locus of many of the most contemporary building projects in Germany today. On Potsdamer Platz, Italian architect Renzo Piano (b 1937) designed DaimlerCity (1998; p122) and Nuremberg-born Helmut Jahn (b 1940) turned a playful hand to the glass-and-steel Sony Center (2000; p122). Another Jahn creation that raises eyebrows and interest in Berlin is the minimalist and edgy Neues Kranzler Eck (2000).

Two spectacular successes in Germany designed by American star architect Daniel Libeskind (b 1946) are Osnabrück's Felix-Nussbaum-Haus (1998; p648) and his more famous zinc-clad zigzag Jüdisches Museum (2001; p124) in Berlin. His transparent wedged extension to the Militärhistorisches Museum in Dresden is expected to be completed in 2010. Back in Berlin, New York contemporary Peter Eisenman achieved the remarkable by assembling 2711 concrete pillars to create the haunting Holocaust Memorial (2005; p115).

For an informative and illustrated dip into Berlin architecture – past, present and future – visit the Senate Department of Urban Development at www.stadtentwicklung .berlin.de.

In 2006 Berlin christened a new star attraction – the vast Hauptbahnhof (p121), a transparent-roofed, multiple-level *Turmbahnhof* (tower station; the lines cross at different levels) that takes glass-and-steel station architecture to new limits.

The contrast (or collision, depending on your view) of old and new in the extension of Cologne's Wallraf-Richartz-Museum (2001; p572), a design by Oswald Mathias Ungers (1926–2007), is a worthy addition to a city with one of the world's most beautiful cathedrals. In 2003 Dresden-born Axel Schultes (b 1943) and Kiel's Charlotte Frank (b 1959) won the German Architecture Prize for their design of the Bundeskanzleramt (New Chancellery; 2001; p120) dubbed 'the washing machine' by Berliners. Munich architect Stephan Braunfels (b 1950) masterminded Munich's modernist Pinakothek der Moderne (2002; p312). More recently, Munich's Museum Brandhorst (2009; p312), with its 36,000 ceramic square tubes, is a colourful addition to the city's museum district. At the other end of the country, the monumental HafenCity Hamburg project (p680) to redevelop the harbour area is set to extend Hamburg's inner city by about 40% by about 2025.

For an interaction of light and architecture, look out for the Luminale festival in the Rhine-Main region (www.luminale.de), an event held in April each year in which light artists use sound and light to transform buildings, museums and parks into illuminated works of art or 'light laboratories'. Another interesting play on light and architecture is Celle's Kunstmuseum (p627)

The Designpreis der Bundesrepublik Deutschland (German Design Prize) is Germany's most prestigious award for design. It is given annually in two categories – products and people (www .designpreis.de).

Visual Arts
FRESCOS TO EXPRESSIONISTS

Whether it be medieval fresco work, oil-on-canvas masterpieces, eclectic Bauhaus or exciting industrial design and fashion, Germany has visual arts for all tastes and interests.

Germany's earliest fresco work dates from Carolingian times (c 800) and is in Trier's St Maximin crypt, now on display at Trier's Bischöfliches Dom- und Diözesanmuseum (p515), and the Stiftskirche St Georg on Reichenau Island (p472), whereas stained-glass enthusiasts will find colourful religious motifs lighting up Augsburg and Cologne cathedrals. By the 15th century, Cologne artists were putting landscapes on religious panels, some of which are on display in Hamburg's Kunsthalle (p677).

The heavyweight of German Renaissance art is the Nuremberg-born Albrecht Dürer (1471–1528), who was the first to grapple seriously with the Italian masters; the Alte Pinakothek (Munich; p311) has several famous works by Dürer, and his house is today a museum in Nuremberg. In Wittenberg, Dürer influenced Franconian-born court painter Lucas Cranach the Elder (1472–1553) whose *Apollo und Diana in Waldiger Landschaft* (Apollo and Diana in a Forest Landscape; 1530) hangs in Berlin's Gemäldegalerie (Picture Gallery; p123).

The Complete Fairy Tales by Jacob and Wilhelm Grimm is a beautiful collection of 210 fairy tales, passed orally between generations and collected by German literature's most magical brothers.

Two centuries later, sculpture became integrated into Germany's buildings and gardens, creating the inspiration for the imposing work by Andreas Schlüter (1660–1714), *Reiterdenkmal des Grossen Kurfürsten* (Equestrian Monument of the Great Elector), in front of Berlin's Schloss Charlottenburg (p126). The four-horse chariot with Victoria on Berlin's Brandenburg Gate (p114) is the work of Germany's leading neoclassical sculptor, Johann Gottfried Schadow (1764–1850).

During the baroque period (from the 17th to mid-18th century), palace walls were frescoed to create the illusion of generous space. The grand staircase by Balthasar Neumann (1687–1753) in Würzburg Residenz (p339) is arguably the finest example.

In the mid-18th century, neoclassicism ushered back in the human figure and an emphasis on Roman and Greek mythology. Hesse-born Johann Heinrich Tischbein (1751–1829) painted Goethe at this time in a classical landscape surrounded by antique objects. View *Goethe in der Campagna* (1787) in Frankfurt am Main's Städel Museum (p534).

Religious themes, occasionally mystic, dominated 19th-century Romanticism. Goethe hated the works of Caspar David Friedrich (1774–1840), indelicately suggesting they ought to be 'smashed against the table'. A room is dedicated to Friedrich's works in Hamburg's Kunsthalle (p677), and his work is also a highlight of Berlin's Alte Nationalgalerie (p116).

Also in the exciting collection of Hamburg's Kunsthalle are works by the founder of the German Romantic movement, Philipp Otto Runge (1777–1810), as well as intensely religious works by the Nazarener (Nazareths). The museum also showcases some later realistic works of Cologne-born Wilhelm Leibl (1844–1900), who specialised in painting Bavarian folk.

German Impressionists are well represented in the Moderne Galerie of Saarbrücken's Saarland Museum (p522). Key exponents of the late-19th-century movement include Max Liebermann (1847–1935), whose work was often slammed as 'ugly' and 'socialist'; Fritz von Uhde (1848–1911); and Lovis Corinth (1858–1925), whose later work, *Die Kindheit des Zeus* (Childhood of Zeus; 1905) – a richly coloured frolic in nature with intoxicated, grotesque elements – is housed in Bremen's Kunsthalle (p664).

Find reviews of the latest contemporary German titles to be translated into English at www.new -books-in-german.com.

The Dresden art scene spawned Die Brücke (The Bridge) in 1905. Its expressionist members Ernst Kirchner (1880–1938), Erich Heckel (1883–1970) and Karl Schmidt-Rottluff (1884–1976) employed primitivist and cubist elements, but Germany's best expressionist painter, the North Frisian Emil Nolde (1867–1956), was an artistic lone wolf who only fleetingly belonged to Die Brücke and was forbidden from working by the Nazis in 1941. His famous *Bauernhof* (1910) is housed in Museumsberg Flensburg (p715).

Munich's Städtische Galerie im Lenbachhaus (p312) showcases a second group of expressionists, Munich-based Der Blaue Reiter (The Blue Rider), centred on Wassily Kandinsky (1866–1944), Gabriele Münter (1877–1962), Paul Klee (1879–1940) and Franz Marc (1880–1916).

BETWEEN THE WARS

After a creative surge in the 1920s, the big chill of Nazi conformity sent Germany into artistic deep freeze in the 1930s and 1940s. In the capital, many artists were classified as 'degenerate' (see the boxed text, opposite) and forced into exile – where a creative explosion abroad took place especially among the Bauhaus movement protagonists who settled in the USA. Other artists were murdered, retreated from public life or tossed in art altogether. In Quedlinburg a fine collection of works by Lyonel Feininger (1871–1956) survives thanks to a local citizen who hid them from the Nazis (see p256).

Jugendstil – an alternative name in German for art nouveau – takes its name from the arts magazine *Jugend* (the word *Jugend* means 'youth'), first published in Munich in 1896.

One of Germany's most influential visual artists was Käthe Kollwitz (1867–1945), who travelled through naturalism and expressionism to arrive at agitprop and socialist realism. Complete series of her *Ein Weberaufstand* (A Weavers' Revolt; 1897) etchings and lithography based on a play by Gerhart Hauptmann (1862–1946), as well as other works, are showcased in Käthe Kollwitz museums in Berlin (p128) and Cologne (p573).

Berlin's Bauhaus Archive/Museum of Design (p124) and Weimar's Bauhaus Museum (p272) have fascinating exhibits on the Bauhaus movement, which continues to shape art and design. Works by Kandinsky, Hungarian László Moholy-Nagy (1895–1946), Klee and the sculptor Gerhard Marcks (1889–1981) are housed in the Berlin venue. See the boxed text, p224, for more on Bauhaus. Marcks' most visible work is *Die Bremer Stadtmusikanten* (Town Musicians of Bremen; see p663).

MODERN & CONTEMPORARY

Post-1945 the creative influence of expressionists such as Nolde, Schmidt-Rottluff and Kandinsky was revived; and a new abstract expressionism took root in the work of Stuttgart's Willi Baumeister (1889–1955) and Ernst Wilhelm Nay (1902–68) in Berlin.

In the 1950s and 1960s, Düsseldorf-based Gruppe Zero (Group Zero) plugged into Bauhaus, using light and space as a creative basis. The 'light

---

DEGENERATE ART

Abstract expressionism, surrealism and Dadaism – 'Jewish subversion' and 'artistic Bolshevism' in the eyes of the Nazis – were definitely not Hitler's favourite movements. In fact by 1937 such forms of expression fell under the axe of *Entartung* (degeneracy), a German biological term borrowed by the Nazis to describe virtually all modern movements. The same year, paintings by Klee, Beckmann, Dix and others – all supposedly spawned by the madness of 'degenerates' – were exhibited in Munich and promptly defaced in protest. Ironically, the exhibition drew a daily scornful yet curious crowd of 20,000 odd.

A year later, a law was passed allowing for the forced removal of degenerate works from private collections. While many art collectors saved their prized works from Nazi hands, the fate of many other artists' works was less fortunate. Many works were sold abroad to rake in foreign currency and in 1939 about 4000 paintings were publicly burned in Berlin.

---

ballets' of Otto Piene (b 1928), relying on projection techniques, were among the best known. Celle's Kunstmuseum (p627) uses some of his light works for effect.

Arguably Germany's most exciting contemporary painter and sculptor is Anselm Kiefer (b 1945), some of whose works are in Berlin's (confusingly named) Hamburger Bahnhof (p121). His monumental *Census* (1967) consists of massive lead folios arranged on shelves as a protest against a 1967 census in Germany; another, the haunting *Mohn und Gedächtnis* (Poppy and Memory; 1989), is a large lead aircraft with three small glass windows in the side filled with poppy seeds. Both are regularly on display.

The same Berlin museum permanently displays works by Düsseldorf's Joseph Beuys (1921–86). Wherever Beuys laid his trademark hat, controversy erupted. *Strassenbahnhaltestelle* (Tram Stop; 1976) consists of rusty iron tram lines and a cannon with a head poking out of it. Beuys says it was inspired by a childhood experience, but bear in mind that he was a radio operator in a fighter plane shot down over Crimea during WWII. He claims to have been nursed back to health by local Tartars, who covered him in tallow and wrapped him in felt. The largest collections of his work are in Darmstadt's Hessisches Landesmuseum (p544; including his revealing *Stuhl mit Fett*; Chair with Fat; 1963) and in Schloss Moyland (p568), near Kalkar in North Rhine–Westphalia.

Anselm Kiefer remains a key figure in the arts scene, recognised in 2008 when he was awarded the German Book Trade Peace Prize (*Friedenspreis des deutschen Buchhandels*). Jörg Immendorff (1945–2007) – like Kiefer, he has also worked in stage design and was one of Beuys' students – has become one of Germany's most collectable artists.

Two contemporary icons of German painting are Gerhard Richter (b 1932) and Sigmar Polke (b 1941). Richter, who was born in Dresden and fled to West Germany in the early 1960s, recently completed a major new work in Cologne's cathedral (p569) – a vast stained-glass window consisting of 11,500 mesmerising square pieces. Polke, along with Richter and others, relied heavily on pop art and what they dubbed 'capitalist realism' – which they used to describe a counterbalance in the West to socialist realism. The influence of the two is as immeasurable as the prices their works command at auctions today. The Museum Ludwig (p572) in Cologne is where you can see a good range of Polke's works.

Bavarian Florian Thomas (b 1966) is one of a new generation of Germany's contemporary artists who owe much to the ground-breaking work of Richter and Polke. His work can be found in the Museum Frieder Burda in Baden-Baden (p444). His *Lieber Onkel Dieter!* (Dear Uncle Dieter!) and *Arusha* are highlights. In the same museum are works by Eberhard Havekost (b 1967),

'Rubble in itself is the future. Because everything that is passes.'

ANSELM KIEFER

For a comprehensive low-down of Germany's contemporary art scene and events, see www .art-in.de (in German).

who uses digitally reworked images as the basis for some of his photorealist pictures – often playing dramatically with light and shadow. Works by Sorb sculptor and painter Georg Baselitz (b 1938) are other highlights of the Museum Frieder Burda. Baselitz was tossed out of art school in the GDR for his artistic provocations, only to have West German authorities confiscate works from his first exhibition there. Take a look at his *Die Grosse Nacht im Eimer* (Big Night Down the Drain), depicting a masturbating figure, and you can see – if not quite understand – why.

Almost as highly prized by collectors and galleries as Richter and Polke, but from a younger generation, Rosemarie Trockel (b 1952) received the highly regarded Düsseldorf Art Prize in 2009 for her works. Her diverse and experimental works span drawings, sculpture, painting and video art. In Leipzig the Neue Leipziger Schule (New Leipzig School) of artists has emerged recently, achieving success at home and abroad, and includes painters such as Neo Rauch (b 1960).

The Neue Sammlung permanent collections of the double banger Neues Museum in Nuremberg (p369) and Pinakothek der Moderne in Munich (p312) are not to be missed as stations on the contemporary art and design circuit; changing exhibitions have ranged from jewellery through to GDR art-poster design, and from Ikea furniture design through to a retrospective of covers from the magazine *Der Spiegel*.

Photography is another area where Germany excels. In the 1920s and 1930s, German photography took two very different directions. Influenced by the Hungarian László Maholy-Nagy, some photographers adopted a playful approach to light, figure, form and how they developed the resulting images in the darkroom. The other direction was *Neue Sachlichkeit* (New Objectivity), based on a documentary-style approach and the creation of archetypes that help us understand the world. The three main protagonists of the New Objectivity movement were Albert Renger-Patzsch (1897–1966), August Sander (1876–1964) and Werner Manz (1901–83). It is said that subsequent generations of photographers have either built on or challenged the work of these early masters of the art.

Around the time Beuys waved adieu in the 1980s, contemporary photographers Andreas Gursky (b 1955) and Candida Höfer (b 1944) were honing their skills under the next generation of photographers, led by Bernd Becher (b 1931) at Düsseldorf's Kunstakademie (Art Academy). Leipzig-born Gursky's work, which can be seen in Cologne's Museum Ludwig (p572), encompasses superb images of architecture, landscapes and interiors, sometimes reworked digitally. Höfer's work, along with the works of other Becher students, can be found in Hamburg's Kunsthalle.

In 2003 another photographer from the Düsseldorf academy who learned the art under Becher, Thomas Ruff (b 1958), provoked controversy with a series of nudes based on pornographic images he downloaded from the internet. More socially acceptable, London-based Bavarian Juergen Teller (b 1964) is a darling of fashion photography and has shot the musician Björk, tennis icon Boris Becker and a pregnant Kate Moss, among others.

Given Germany's rich collections, travelling the contours of visual arts might be an interesting way to organise a trip. In addition to excellent permanent collections in major museums, you'll find lots of smaller art spaces with changing exhibitions. Venues like Berlin's Kunst-Werke Berlin (p119) and Galerie Eigen+Art (www.eigen-art.com) offer a contemporary 'shock of the new'.

The Art Forum Berlin (p135) showcases video, photography, painting, sculpture, installations, graphics, and multimedia each year in September–October. For household design, the Bauhaus Museum in Weimar (p272)

BERTOLT BRECHT

Bertolt Brecht (1898–1956) is Germany's most controversial 20th-century playwright, poet and drama theorist. He wrote his first play, *Baal*, while studying medicine in Munich in 1918. His first opus to reach the stage, *Trommeln in der Nacht* (Drums in the Night; 1922), won the coveted Kleist Prize, and two years later he moved to the Deutsches Theater in Berlin to work with the Austrian actor and director Max Reinhardt.

Over the next decade, in plays such as *Die Dreigroschenoper* (Threepenny Opera; 1928), Brecht developed his theory of 'epic theatre', which, unlike 'dramatic theatre', forces its audience to detach itself emotionally from the play and its characters and to reason intellectually.

A staunch Marxist, Brecht went into exile during the Nazi years, surfaced in Hollywood as a scriptwriter, then left the USA after being called in to explain himself during the communist witch-hunts of the McCarthy era. The exile years produced many of his best plays: *Mutter Courage und ihre Kinder* (Mother Courage and Her Children; 1941), *Leben des Galilei* (Life of Galileo; 1943/47), *Der gute Mensch von Sezuan* (Good Woman of Setzuan; 1943) and *Der Kaukasische Kreidekreis* (Caucasian Chalk Circle; 1948).

Brecht returned to East Berlin in 1949 where he founded the Berliner Ensemble with his wife, the actress Helene Weigel, who directed it until her death in 1971. During his lifetime Brecht was suspected in the East for his unorthodox aesthetic theories and scorned (and often boycotted) in much of the West for his communist principles. Others again saw him as a pragmatist and opportunist. His influence, however, is indisputable. Brecht's poetry, so little known in English, is also a fascinating string in the bow of German literature.

shows how it all began, and the Vitra Design Museum in Weil am Rhein (p460) has other fascinating exhibits.

Berlin is not just the heart of the thriving art scene in Germany, in 2006 it became Europe's first City of Design as part of the Unesco Creative Cities Network – gaining recognition as a crossroads of design, architecture and the visual and performing arts.

Theatre

With more than 6000 stages across the country, Germany is a paradise for the theatregoer. Most plays are staged in multipurpose theatres (opera and music will often be performed there, too) and are subsidised by the state. The average theatre in the network of city, regional and national spaces will put on about 20 or more plays each year.

Masters of the Enlightenment who frequently get a showing include Saxony's Gotthold Ephraim Lessing (1729–81); Württemberg-born Friedrich Schiller, who features especially strongly in Weimar's theatre landscape today; and, of course, Johann Wolfgang von Goethe, who tinkered with his two-part *Faust* for 60 years of his life and created one of Germany's most powerful and enduring dramas about the human condition.

Woyzeck by Georg Büchner (1813–37) is another popular piece and, having anticipated Theatre of the Absurd, lends itself to innovative staging. In 1894 the director of Berlin's Deutsches Theater hired a young actor, Max Reinhardt (1873–1943), who became German theatre's most influential expressionist director, working briefly with dramatist Bertolt Brecht. Both men went into exile under Nazism – Brecht to try his hand at a couple of Hollywood scripts and to answer for his Marxist politics before the House Committee on Un-American Activities during the McCarthy-era witch hunts. Brecht's *Leben des Galilei* (Life of Galileo; 1943/47) was rewritten with a new ending after atomic bombs fell on Hiroshima and Nagasaki. It was first performed in Beverly Hills.

The Augsburg-born dramatist (his birthplace is a pilgrimage site today) returned after WWII to East Berlin and in the 1950s he created the Berliner Ensemble (p149), a venue that produced his plays and became one of the capital's most vibrant theatres. See the boxed text, p77, for more details about Brecht.

Read up-to-date reviews of the latest plays by German playwrights and other cultural offerings at www.goethe.de /enindex.htm.

Heiner Müller (1929–95), a Marxist who was critical of the reality of the GDR, became unpalatable in both Germanys in the 1950s. In the 1980s, existential works such as *Quartet* (1980) earned him an avant-garde label. In the 1960s, Berlin director Rudolf Noelte (1921–2002) took centre stage as the master of postwar German theatre.

Directors like Peter Stein (b 1937) have earned contemporary German theatre its reputation for producing classic plays in an innovative and provocative manner. Part of the so-called *Junge Wilde* (wild youth) movement in the 1970s and 1980s, Stein founded Berlin's Schaubühne (p149) theatre as a collective in 1970 (even the cleaner had a say as to what went on); today it is one of Germany's best.

Also in the capital, Berlin-born Frank Castorf (b 1951) is arguably Germany's most dynamic contemporary director, heading up Berlin's Volksbühne (p149) and piecing together innovative productions in Germany and elsewhere in Europe. Christoph Schlingensief (b 1960) is the best known of Germany's new breed, having staged productions at Berlin's Volksbühne and elsewhere; he's also active in film and action art. In 2008 he was diagnosed with lung cancer, kept a diary about the experience that is now a book, and is currently engaged in establishing a theatre in Africa (www.festspielhaus-afrika.com).

The most-performed contemporary playwright is the Göttingen-born Roland Schimmelpfennig (b 1967), who has worked at Berlin's Schaubühne and Volksbühne, as well as Vienna's Burgtheater. Other contemporary playwrights to watch out for are Moritz Rinke (b 1967); Munich-born, Berlin-based Rainald Goetz (b 1954); Werner Fritsch (b 1960), whose dark plays portray a violent world, occasionally verging on the obscene; and Simone Schneider (b 1962).

Food & Drink

Unlike France or Italy, Germany has never been a culinary destination. In the international imagination, its food is often just something – usually a wurst (sausage) – to accompany its superlative beer. Relying heavily on meat, cabbage and potato, the country's traditional cuisine has a not entirely undeserved reputation as hearty but dull. As one old saying cruelly has it, the problem with German food is that a week later you want some more!

However, Germany has been redeeming itself gastronomically in the past decade in much the same way as has happened in Britain. Top chefs have been experimenting with time-honoured dishes in a wave that's referred to as the *Neue Deutsche Küche* (New German Cuisine), and *multi-kulti* (multicultural) influences – ranging from Turkish to Mediterranean to Asian – have put baba ganoush, burritos and curries on menus and pesto, coconut milk and coriander on supermarket shelves.

As a rule, you still won't find the love of excellent food – and the ability to produce it – permeating every corner of every neighbourhood restaurant as you will in, say, Italy. But you will find exceptions to this in urban centres like Berlin and Hamburg, and the global trend to source local, seasonal ingredients is gaining strength here, too. The *Imbiss* fast-food stall, however, is a ubiquitous phenomenon, allowing you to eat on the run easily and, if you choose your restaurants with just a little care, it is possible to treat your palate at the same time.

Find the top restaurants in Germany – and in major international cities – at www .restaurant-ranglisten.de (also in English).

STAPLES & SPECIALITIES

Wurst, *Brot, Kartoffeln* and sauerkraut (sausage, bread, potatoes and cabbage): yes, sometimes all the national stereotypes ring true. In Germany you'll certainly find things like *Kalbshaxe* (knuckle of veal) and *Sauerbraten* (roast beef marinated in wine and vinegar), but were you aware that *Quark,* a yoghurt-like curd cheese, accounts for 50% of domestic cheese consumption? Or, did you realise that locals are equally devoted to asparagus, mushrooms, pumpkin and venison?

The modern doner kebab (*Dönerkebab*) doesn't emanate from Turkey, but Germany. In 1971, Turkish immigrants running the Berlin restaurant Hasir introduced salad into an ancient Turkish dish; even outlets in Turkey have been making it this way ever since.

Sausage

In the Middle Ages, German peasants found a way to package and disguise animals' less appetising bits, and the wurst (sausage) was born. Today, it's a noble and highly respected element of German cuisine, with strict rules determining the authenticity of wurst varieties. In some cases, as with the finger-sized Nuremberg sausage, regulations even ensure offal no longer enters the equation.

There are more than 1500 sausage species, all commonly served with bread and a sweet *(süss)* or spicy *(scharf)* mustard *(Senf)*.

Bratwurst, served countrywide, is made from minced pork, veal and spices, and is cooked in different ways (boiled in beer, baked with apples and cabbage, stewed in a casserole or simply grilled or barbecued).

The availability of other sausages differs regionally. A *Thüringer* is long, thin and spiced, while a *Wiener* is what hot-dog fiends call a frankfurter. *Blutwurst* is blood sausage (not to be confused with black pudding, which is *Rotwurst*), *Leberwurst* is liver sausage, and *Knackwurst* is lightly tickled with garlic.

Saxony has brain sausage *(Bregenwurst),* Bavaria sells white rubbery *Weisswurst,* made from veal, and Berlin boasts the *Currywurst* (slices of sausage topped with curry powder and ketchup).

Indisputably *the* handbook of German cuisine since it was published in the 1960s, *Dr Oetker's German Cooking: The Original* was handily re-released in 2003, filling you in on all the basic techniques and classic dishes

Bread

In exile in California in 1941, German playwright Bertolt Brecht confessed that what he missed most about his homeland was the bread. That won't surprise anyone who has sampled the stuff. German bread is a world-beater, in a league of its own. It's tasty and textured, often mixing wheat and rye flour, and is available in 300 varieties.

'Black' rye bread *(Schwarzbrot)* is actually brown, but a much darker shade than the slightly sour *Bauernbrot* – divine with a slab of butter. *Pumpernickel* bread is steam-cooked instead of baked, making it extra moist, and actually is black. *Vollkorn* means wholemeal, while bread coated in sunflower seeds is *Sonnenblumenbrot*. If you insist on white bread *(Weissbrot)*, the Germans have that, too.

Fresh bread rolls *(Brötchen* in the north, *Semmel* in Bavaria, *Wecken* in the rest of southern Germany) can be covered in poppy seeds *(Mohnbrötchen)*, cooked with sweet raisins *(Rosinenbrötchen)*, sprinkled with salt *(Salzstangel)* or treated in dozens of other different ways.

Brezeln are traditional pretzels, covered in rock salt.

Living in the USA? Shop for *Brot und Wurst* as if you're in Germany at www.germandeli.com.

Potato

Germans are almost as keen as Russians about the potato. The *Kartoffel* is not only Vegetable Nummer Eins in any meat-and-three-veg dish, it can also be incorporated into any course of a meal, from potato soup *(Kartoffelsuppe)* as a starter, to potato waffles *(Kartoffelwaffeln)* or potato pancakes *(Reibekuchen)* as a sweet treat.

In between, you can try *Himmel und Erde* (Heaven and Earth), a dish of mashed potatoes and stewed apples served with black pudding, or potato-based *Klösse* dumplings. *Pellkartoffeln* or *Ofenkartoffeln* are jacket potatoes, usually capped with a dollop of *Quark*.

Many potato festivals are held throughout the country.

Discover 101 things to do with a pig in Olli Leeb's *Bavarian Cooking,* jam packed with cultural and culinary insights into one of Germany's most distinctive regional cuisines.

Sauerkraut

Finally comes a quintessential German side dish that many outside the country find impossible to fathom: sauerkraut. Before the 2006 FIFA World Cup, one football magazine suggested, with typical abrasiveness: 'It's pickled cabbage; don't try to make it sound interesting.' Okay, we won't. It's shredded cabbage, doused in white-wine vinegar and slowly simmered. But if you haven't at least tried *Rotkohl* (the red-cabbage version of the white-cabbage sauerkraut), you don't know what you're missing. Braising the cabbage with sliced apples and wine turns it into *Bayrischkraut* or *Weinkraut*.

Regional Dishes

Although contemporary German restaurants offer as much of an international mix as anywhere in the world, the country's traditional cuisine has been much more resistant to outside influences than that of, say, Hungary or Italy. Consequently, traditional regional variations remain quite noticeable.

The food in southern states features many pork and veal dishes, accompanied by noodles or dumplings. It's in the northern states that root vegetables such as potatoes predominate, and there's a much greater focus on fish.

Towards the country's borders, its cuisine does take on French, Scandinavian and even Slavic flavours. But it's a subtle difference and the taste usually remains recognisably German.

Germany's most famous TV chef, Tim Mälzer, updates some standards in his best-selling book, *Born To Cook,* such as making *Kalbshaxe* with star anise and *Labskaus* with poached salmon.

BAVARIA

The Chinese say you can eat every part of the pig bar the oink, and Bavarian chefs seem to be in full agreement. No part of the animal is spared their attention: they cook up its knuckles *(Schweinshax'n)*, ribs *(Rippchen)*, tongue *(Züngerl)* and belly *(Wammerl)*. Pork also appears as *Schweinebraten* (a roast) and the misleadingly named *Leberkäse* (liver cheese), where it's combined with beef in a dish that contains no cheese – and in Bavaria at least – no liver. The Bavarians are also quite fond of veal *(Kalb)*.

Dumplings are another menu staple, from potato-based *Klösse* and *Leberknödel* (liver dumplings) to sweet *Senfknödel*, which is made from *Quark*, flour and eggs, then dunked in milk. Dumplings also make a major appearance in the Franconian favourite of *Hochszeitsuppe* (wedding soup) – a clear meat broth garnished with bread dumplings, liver dumplings and pancakes.

BADEN-WÜRTTEMBERG
Neighbouring influences are evident in Baden-Württemberg. Snail soup *(Schneckensuppe)* crosses the border with Alsace, while locals also enjoy *Geschnetzeltes* (veal slices in a white wine and cream sauce) as much as the Swiss.

Pasta is another recurrent theme, with *Spätzle* (literally 'little sparrows'), a type of egg-based noodle, served as a main meal or used to dress meat or fish. The ravioli-like *Maultaschen* are stuffed with ground meat, onion and spinach.

SAARLAND
Just as in Baden-Württemberg, the food here shows many French influences. Fried goose liver and *coq au vin* are common on menus, as is *Budeng mit Gellenewemutsch*, a boudin (hot black pudding) served with a German mash of carrots and potatoes.

When it comes to the crunch, though, Saarlanders revert to true German form, and *Schwenkbraten* (marinated pork grilled on a spit) is probably their most popular dish.

RHINELAND-PALATINATE
Two former chancellors named dishes from this region as their favourite, selecting two meals as different as the men themselves. Helmut Kohl nominated *Saumagen*, a stuffed pork belly with pickled cabbage that's the German equivalent to Scottish haggis, while postwar chancellor Konrad Adenauer preferred *Reibekuchen*, small potato pancakes served with blueberry or apple sauce.

Despite all this, *Rheinischer Sauerbraten* (roast beef marinated in spiced vinegar and braised) is the region's signature dish.

HESSE & WESTPHALIA
Neighbouring Hesse and Westphalia produce outstanding cured and smoked hams (typically smoking them over juniper berries). In Hesse, they like pig in the form of *Sulperknochen*, a dish from trotters, ears and tails, served with mushy peas and pickled cabbage. Westphalians prefer *Pfefferpotthast*, a meat stew spiced with capers, lemon juice and beer.

HAMBURG & AROUND
No two dishes better sum up northern Germany's warming, seafaring fodder than *Labskaus* and *Grünkohl mit Pinkel*. There are variations, but traditional *Labskaus* from Hamburg is a minced dish of salt herring, corned beef, pig lard, potato and beetroot, topped with gherkins and a fried egg. It's a sailor's favourite and, some locals claim, brilliant hangover food – plenty of salt, plenty of fat and not too hard to chew. *Grünkohl mit Pinkel* combines

Cooking the German Way by Helga Parnell is one of the simpler German cookbooks on the market, ideal for those seeking a basic culinary background of the region. It includes a history as well as recipes for basic German dishes.

When Lübeck started producing marzipan in the Middle Ages, the almond paste was considered a medicine not a sweet. We want to know: can we get it on prescription?

steamed kale with pork belly, bacon and *Pinkelwurst* (a spicy pork, beef, oat and onion sausage from Bremen).

Eel soup *(Aalsuppe)* is sweet-and-sour – it's garnished with bacon and vegetables, and spiced with apricots, pears or prunes.

As you move towards Scandinavia, the German diet begins to encompass Nordic staples such as rollmops and herring *(Hering)* in all its other guises (raw, smoked, pickled or rolled in sour cream).

MECKLENBURG–WESTERN POMERANIA

This northeastern state shares Hamburg's obsession with herring, eel and other types of seafood, throwing in a propensity to smoke its fish and a penchant for Baltic cod. Otherwise, it has a quite distinctive cuisine, with locals famed for liking things sweet and sour.

Take *Mecklenburger Rippenbraten* (rolled pork stuffed with lemons, apples, plums, and raisins), for example; or *Mecklenburgische Buttermilchsuppe*, a sweet buttermilk soup flavoured with spices and jam; or the Russian-style *Soljanka*, sour soup with sausage or fish, garnished with lemon and sour cream.

Other typical mixes include raisins with cabbage, honey with pork, and plums with duck. Even the typical *Eintopf* (stew, often a potato version) is served with sugar and vinegar on the side.

Bread pudding is a very popular dessert throughout the state, but visitors might prefer the more unusual and delicious *Sanddorn* (sea buckthorn). Nicknamed the 'Mecklenburg lemon', this is a shrub berry with a subtle citrus flavour, and is used to great effect in teas, ice creams and other dishes (as well as beauty products).

The New German Cookbook: More than 230 Contemporary and Traditional Recipes by Lamar Elmore, Jean Anderson and Hedy Wuerz, and *The German Cookbook: A Complete Guide to Mastering Authentic German Cooking* by Mimi Sheraton are two handy little recipe numbers to have on your kitchen shelf.

BERLIN

Alongside Hamburg, Berlin has one of the country's most cosmopolitan restaurant scenes, but it can still lay claim to a few local delicacies. First on the list comes *Eisbein* (pigs' knuckles), then *Kohlsuppe* (cabbage soup) and *Erbensuppe* (pea soup).

Ironically, the *Berliner* doughnut, which President John F Kennedy once claimed himself to be, does not emanate from the capital. For something sweet, locals are much more likely to tuck into the coffee cake known as *Kugelhupf* (also spelled *Gugelhupf*). Berlin is also where you'll find the country's highest concentration of Turkish doner kebab *(Dönerkebab)* spots, an essential end to any drink-fuelled night out on the town.

SAXONY & THURINGIA

These regions are slightly less meat-obsessed than some of their cousins. *Kartoffelsuppe* (potato soup) is a favourite, and *Leipziger Allerlei* (Leipzig hotpot) often comes in vegetarian versions. There are even lentils to be found in such dishes as *Linsensuppe mit Thüringer Rotwurst* (lentil soup with Thuringian sausages). For dessert, you can try *Quarkkeulchen,* made from curd, boiled potatoes, flour, sugar, and raisins – although these have spread to other parts of Germany, too.

Seasonal Specialities

In an era in which fruit jets around the globe clocking up frequent-flyer miles, and high-tech farming boosts year-round supplies, Germans remain touchingly devoted to their seasonal specialities.

No period ranks higher on the culinary calendar than *Spargelzeit* (asparagus season), when Germans devour great quantities of mostly white asparagus, which they generally consider tastier than the green variety. The

---

FALSE FRIENDS

When ordering food in parts of the country, sometimes a little knowledge of German can be a dangerous thing. So, don't expect half a chicken when you order a *Halve Hahn* in Cologne – it's a rye-bread roll with gouda cheese, gherkin and mustard. *Kölscher Kaviar* is similarly confusing – it's not caviar, but black pudding. And *Nordseekrabben* in Hamburg and Lower Saxony? They're small prawns…of course.

---

season kicks off with the harvesting of the first crop in mid-April and lasts until 24 June – the feast-day of St John the Baptist – which is fitting, given the almost religious intensity with which this 'king of vegetables' is celebrated. You'll find restaurants with separate asparagus menus and whole books devoted to the subject, while many towns and cities even hold asparagus festivals in May and June.

Herring weeks are frequently held on the Baltic coast in spring. Other notable seasonal specialities include *Pfifferlinge* (chanterelles) and *Kürbis* (pumpkin), an autumn treat.

Sweets

Germans more often exercise their sweet tooth over *Kaffee und Kuchen* (coffee and cakes) than they do after a meal. Desserts (*Nachspeisen* or *Nachtische*) are usually light affairs, say custard and fruit, *Rote Grütze* (a tart fruit compote topped with vanilla sauce), ice cream or a fruit salad.

However, let's not forget that this is the country that brought the world the sugary, creamy, calorie-laden, over-the-top *Schwarzwälder Kirschtorte* (Black Forest gateau).

And if that isn't enough of a calling card for sugar fiends, Germany offers an enormous range of other delicious confections, from *Lebkuchen* (gingerbread) and *Nürnberger Lebkuchen* (soft cookies with nuts, fruit peel, honey and spices from Nuremberg) to *Leckerli* (honey-flavoured ginger biscuits) and *Lübecker Marzipan* (marzipan from Lübeck).

Christmas brings its own specialities. *Stollen* is a spiced cake loaded with sultanas, raisins and candied peel, sprinkled with icing sugar and occasionally spruced up inside with a ball of marzipan. It's rarely baked in German homes today (although when it is, it's exquisite), but you'll find it in abundance in Christmas markets – *Stollen* from Dresden is reputedly the best.

DRINKS

While coffee in Germany is not as strong as that served in France or Italy, you can expect a decent cup. All the usual varieties are on offer, including cappuccinos and lattes, although you still frequently see French-style bowls of milky coffee (*Milchkaffee*).

Tea frequently comes in a glass or pot of hot water, with the tea bag served to the side. East Frisians in Bremen and Lower Saxony are the country's biggest consumers of tea, and have dozens of their own varieties, which they traditionally drink with cream and *Kluntje* (rock sugar).

Germans once almost exclusively drank sparkling mineral water (*Mineralwasser*), with loads of bubbles (*mit Gas* or *mit Kohlensäure*). Truly still mineral water (*stilles* or *ohne Kohlensäure*) has become much more widespread, but it remains harder to find than in some other European countries.

Note that the price of many drinks in plastic bottles includes a *Pfand* (deposit), which will be given back to you if you return the bottle to the shop or another similar outlet. Soft drinks frequently come in cans (*Dosen*), too.

When not guzzling beer or wine (see below and p86), Germans like a shot of *Schnaps* (any hard liquor). This comes in a variety of flavours, from apple *(Apfel)*, pear *(Birne)*, or plum *(Pflaume)* to wheat *(Korn)*.

Digestive herbal drinks, such as Jägermeister, are also still popular, although mainly among the older population.

Beer

It's not as cheap as the Czech Republic's world-famous lagers, but German beer is patently up there with the best and is well worth the premium. Brewing here goes back to Germanic tribes, and later monks, so it follows in a hallowed tradition. Unsurprisingly, a trip to an atmospheric Bavarian beer garden or a Cologne beer hall is one of the first things on many foreign visitors' to-do lists.

The 'secret' of the country's golden nectar dates back to the *Reinheitsgebot* (purity law), demanding breweries use just four ingredients – malt, yeast, hops and water. Passed in Bavaria in 1516, the *Reinheitsgebot* stopped being a legal requirement in 1987, when the European Union struck it down as uncompetitive. However, many German brewers still conform to it anyway, seeing it as a good marketing tool against mass-market, chemical-happy competitors.

Thanks to the tradition of the *Reinheitsgebot*, German beer is supposed to be unique in not giving you a *Katzenjammer* or *Kater* (hangover). However, party-goers downing 5 million litres of the stuff at Munich's Oktoberfest (see the boxed text, p314) must surely disagree!

What did Germany's first railway line carry when it opened between Nuremberg and Fürth in 1835? Beer.

VARIETIES

Despite frequently tying their own hands and giving themselves just four ingredients to play with, German brewers turn out 5000 distinctively different beers.

They achieve this via subtle variations in the basic production process. At the simplest level, a brewer can choose a particular yeast for top or bottom fermenting (the terms indicating where the yeast lives while working – at the top or bottom of the brewing vessel).

The most popular form of brewing is bottom fermentation, which accounts for about 85% of German beers, notably the *Pils* (pilsner) popular throughout Germany, most *Bock* beers and the *Helles* (pale lager) type found in Bavaria.

Top fermentation is used for the *Weizenbier/Weissbier* (wheat/white beer) popular in Berlin and Bavaria, Cologne's *Kölsch* and the very few stouts brewed in the country.

Many beers are regional, meaning a Saxon Rechenberger cannot be found in Düsseldorf, where the locally brewed Altbier is the taste of choice. The following list runs through some interesting varieties.

BEER GLOSSARY

For more bare beer facts, statistics, tips on cooking with beer and more, surf with the German Federation of Brewers (in German) at www.brauer-bund.de.

Alkoholfreies Bier Nonalcoholic beer.

Altbier A dark, full beer with malted barley from the Düsseldorf area.

Berliner Weisse With around 2.8% alcohol content, draught *(Schankbier)* is mostly brewed in and around Berlin. It contains lactic acid, giving it a slightly sour taste, and a blend of malted wheat and barley. Top fermented, it's often drunk *mit Grün* (with green or woodruff syrup), or with a dash *(mit Schuss)* of raspberry *(Himbeeren)* syrup.

Bockbier, Doppelbock These two strong beers are around 7% alcohol, but *Doppelbock* is slightly stronger. There's a 'Bock' for almost every occasion, such as *Maibock* (usually drunk in May/spring) and *Weihnachtsbock* (brewed for Christmas). *Eisbock* is dark and more aromatic. *Bock* beers originate from Einbeck, near Hanover.

Dampfbier (steam beer) Originating from Bayreuth in Bavaria, this is top fermented and has a fruity flavour.

Dunkles Lagerbier (dark lager) *Dunkel* (dark) is brewed throughout Germany, but especially in Bavaria. With a light use of hops, it's full-bodied with a strong malt aroma. Malt is dried at a high temperature, lending it a dark colour.

Export Traditionally with a higher alcohol content to help it survive a long journey, this beer is closely associated today with Dortmund, and is often dry to slightly sweet.

Helles Lagerbier (pale lager) *Helles* (pale or light) refers to the colour, not the alcohol content, which is still around 4.6% to 5%. Brewing strongholds are Bavaria, Baden-Württemberg and the Ruhr region. It has strong malt aromas and is slightly sweet.

Hofbräu This is a brewery belonging to a royal court *(Hof)* – for some time in Bavaria only a few nobles enjoyed the right to brew wheat beer.

Klosterbräu This type of brewery belongs to a monastery.

Kölsch By law, this top fermented beer can only be brewed in or around Cologne. It is about 4.8% alcohol, has a solid hop flavour and pale colour, and is served in small glasses (0.2L) called *Stangen* (literally 'sticks').

Leichtbier (light beer) These low-alcohol beers are about 2% to 3.2% alcohol.

Leipziger Gose An unusual beer, flavoured with salt and coriander, this contrives to have a stingingly refreshing taste, with some plummy overtones. Tart like Berliner Weisse, it's also often served with sweeteners, such as cherry *(Kirsch)* liqueur or the almond-flavoured *Allasch*.

Malzbier (malt beer) A sweet, aromatic, full-bodied beer, this is brewed mainly in Bavaria and Baden-Württemberg.

Märzen (March) Full-bodied with strong malt aromas, this is traditionally brewed in March. Today, it's associated with the Oktoberfest.

Obergäriges Bier Top-fermented beer.

Pils (pilsener) This bottom-fermented full beer, with a pronounced hop flavour and a creamy head, has an alcohol content of around 4.8% and is served throughout Germany.

Rauchbier (smoke beer) This dark beer has a fresh, spicy or 'smoky' flavour.

Schwarzbier (black beer) Slightly stronger, this dark, full beer has an alcohol content of about 4.8% to 5%. Full-bodied, it's fermented using roasted malt.

Untergäriges Bier Bottom-fermented beer.

Weizenbier, Weissbier (wheat beer) Predominating in the south, especially in Bavaria, this is around 5.4% alcohol. A *Hefeweizen* has a stronger shot of yeast, whereas *Kristallweizen* is clearer with more fizz. These wheat beers are fruity and spicy, often recalling bananas and cloves. Decline offers of a slice of lemon as it ruins the head and – beer purists say – the flavour.

Horst Dornbusch's *Prost!: The Story of German Beer* is exactly that.

THE INDUSTRY

German beer is brewed by more than 1200 breweries, although many traditionally family-run concerns have been swallowed up by the big-boy brewers. Bremen-based Beck's, producer of one of Germany's best-known beers since 1873, was bought out by Belgian beer giant Interbrew in 2002, while Hamburg's Holsten (founded 1879) now has its roots firmly embedded in the USA.

BREWERY TOURS

Most visitors to Germany are content just to quaff the country's excellent beer – whether from a huge Bavarian stein or one of Cologne's trademark skinny glasses. The more curious might be interested to see how it's mixed.

You can do this at any of the **Holsten breweries** (www.holsten.de), while Beck's (p664) and Friesisches Brauhaus zu Jever (p655) also run tours. Meanwhile, the art of 19th-century beer-making is unravelled at Maisel's Brauerei-und-Büttnerei-Museum in Bayreuth (p379), the world's most comprehensive beer museum (according to *Guinness World Records*). Tour details are included in the regional chapters.

Still, 11 German monasteries continue to produce beer. Kloster Weltenburg, near Kelheim on the Danube north of Munich, is the world's oldest monastery brewery, whose Weltenburg Barock Dunckel won a medal at the 2006 World Beer Cup in Seattle. This light, smooth beer has a malty, toasty finish.

Other connoisseurs believe the earthy Andechs Doppelbock Dunkel, produced by the Benedictines in Andechs near Munich, to be among the world's best.

Wine

Its name sullied for decades by the cloyingly sugary taste of *Liebfraumilch* white wine, German wine has been making a comeback in the 21st century. Following the 2002 marketing campaign – 'If you think you know German wine, drink again' – in the industry's biggest export market, the UK, sellers have been talking of a renaissance. And although the re-evaluation is still in its beginnings, it's not all public-relations hype. Even discerning critics have been pouring praise on German winemakers, with *Decanter* magazine awarding *Weingut* Meyer-Näkel's Dernauer Pfarrwingert Spätburgunder Grosses Gewächs 2005 the top international trophy for Pinot noir in 2008, much to the astonishment of wine experts globally. It's been reported that a symphony of gasps filled the room when the winner was announced at the prestigious awards ceremony.

Germany is most commonly associated with white wines made from riesling grapes. According to Tim Atkin, wine correspondent for the UK's *Observer* newspaper, wine producers in Australia, Austria and Alsace have recently done Germany a favour in using and promoting the grape. This, he says, 'has helped consumers realise that Germany makes the best rieslings of all'. At the same time, the country itself has had 'a tremendous run of vintages since 2000', and its midrange wines have markedly improved, with brands like **Devil's Rock** (www.devils-rock.com), **Dr Loosen** (www.drloosen.com) and the **Vineyard Creatures series** (www.lingenfelder.com).

Having produced wines since Roman times, Germany now has more than 100,000 hectares of vineyards, mostly on the Rhine and Moselle riverbanks. Despite the common association with riesling grapes (particularly in its best wine regions) the less acidic Müller-Thurgau *(Rivaner)* grape is more widespread. Meanwhile, the Gewürztraminer grape produces spicy wines with an intense bouquet. What Germans call *Grauburgunder* is known to the rest of the world as Pinot gris.

German reds are light and lesser known. *Spätburgunder* (Pinot noir), is the best of the bunch and goes into some velvety, full-bodied reds with an occasional almond taste.

WINE REGIONS

There are 13 official wine-growing areas, the best being the Mosel-Saar-Ruwer region. It boasts some of the world's steepest vineyards, where the predominantly riesling grapes are still hand-picked. Slate soil on the hillsides gives the wines a flinty taste. Chalkier riverside soils are planted with the Elbling grape, an ancient Roman variety.

East of the Moselle, the Nahe region produces fragrant, fruity and full-bodied wines using Müller-Thurgau and Silvaner grapes, as well as riesling.

Riesling grapes are also the mainstay in Rheingau and Mittelrhein (Middle Rhine), two other highly respected wine-growing pockets. Rheinhessen, south of Rheingau, is responsible for *Liebfraumilch,* but also some top rieslings.

Other wine regions include Ahr, Pfalz (both Rheinland-Palatinate), Hessische Bergstrasse (Hesse), Baden (Baden-Württemberg), Würzburg (Bavaria) and Elbtal (Saxony).

Germany's wine market, from medieval times to the present, is the fascinating focus of *The Wines of Germany* by Stephen Brook. Among other things, he addresses the question of why German wine has long been mocked.

BETTER THAN GLÜHWEIN

Served in winter and designed to inure you to the sudden drop in temperatures, hot spiced *Glühwein* is a common commodity at Germany's popular Christmas markets. However, it's not the only mulled wine the country produces. Far more spectacular and intoxicating is *Feuerzangenbowle* (literally 'fire-tongs-punch'), which has become a cult tipple, thanks to a movie of the same name.

Contrary to the usual advice, *do* try this at home – providing you can get hold of the necessary equipment (try a German Christmas market). Fill a large saucepan with two or three bottles of red wine, cloves, a stick of cinnamon and slices of citrus fruit, and gently heat. Place a *Zuckerhut* (sugar cone) into a special silver cradle (the *Feuerzange*, meaning 'fire tongs'), and rest them both horizontally over the saucepan. Pour over-proof rum (between 50% and 60%) over the sugar cone with a ladle (for safety's sake, not straight from the bottle). Let it soak for a minute and then carefully put a lit match over the sugar, igniting it. As the flaming sugar falls into the spiced red wine below, it produces a delicious and heady drink.

The 1944 film *Feuerzangenbowle* has four men reminiscing about their school days over a bowl of the self-same punch; when it transpires that one of them was educated by a private tutor and has no idea what they're talking about, they disguise him and send him back to school as an adult. Long banned for its antiauthoritarian attitudes, it's now screened in cinemas before Christmas.

The Württemberg region, around Stuttgart, produces some of the country's best reds, while Saxony-Anhalt's Saale-Unstrut region is home to Rotkäppchen (Little Red Riding Hood) sparkling wine, a former GDR brand that's been a big hit in the new Germany.

WINE GLOSSARY

Auslese A 'selected harvest', this is usually intense and sweet.

Beerenauslese (BA) Grapes are picked overripe, and it's usually a dessert wine.

Deutscher Landwein (country wine) Landwein is usually dry or semi-dry.

Deutscher Tafelwein (table wine) This is the lowest category of wine, and is of mostly poor to average quality.

Eiswein Grapes are picked and pressed while frozen and it's very sweet; a dessert wine.

QbA (Qualitätswein bestimmter Anbaugebiete) The lowest category of quality wine.

QmP (Qualitätswein mit Prädikat) 'Quality wine of distinction.'

Qualitätswein Wine from one of the 13 defined wine-growing regions, which has to pass a tasting test.

Sekt Sparkling wine.

Spätauslese Literally 'selected late-harvest', this type of wine has concentrated flavours, but is not necessarily sweet.

Trockenbeerenauslese (TBA) The grapes are so overripe they are shrivelled (intensely sweet) and resemble raisins.

For a comprehensive rundown of all German wine-growing regions, grape varieties, news of the hottest winemakers, and information on tours or courses, visit www .winesofgermany.co.uk (interested US citizens could also browse www .germanwineusa.org).

WHERE TO EAT & DRINK

Dining out in Germany these days is little different from visiting a restaurant in the rest of the Western world. Sure, you can try for a little authentic local cuisine in an atmospheric town-hall basement restaurant (*Ratskeller*), although you might often find that your fellow diners aren't locals, but other tourists looking for the same thing. It's much better to ask your hotel for a recommendation. German-only menus (*Speisekarte*) displayed outside an establishment are a good sign; the waiter will almost invariably be able to translate for you.

Diners seeking somewhere less formal can opt for a *Gaststätte*, a relaxed and often more 'local' place to eat with a large menu, daily specials and a beer garden out the back. Equally inviting are small bistros calling themselves

---

TOP FIVE GERMAN WINE PRODUCERS

'Too many people still associate Germany with basic, sugary whites', says Tim Atkin, wine correspondent for the UK's *Observer* newspaper. He points out there's much more to German wine, and suggests keeping a particular eye out for the following producers:

Dönnhoff (☎ 06755-263; www.doennhoff.com; Oberhausen, Nahe region)
Egon Müller Scharzhof (www.scharzhof.de; Saar region)
JJ Prüm (www.jjpruem.de; Bernkastel-Wehlen, Mosel region)
Weingut Meyer-Näkel (☎ 02643-1628; www.meyer-naekel.de; Dernau, Ahr region)
Wittmann (☎ 06244-905036; www.weingutwittman.com; Westhofen bei Worms, Rheinhessen region)

Weinkeller or *Bierkeller* (cellars serving wine or beer), which cook up light meals as well as serving glasses of wine or beer. Most cafes and bars serve coffee and light snacks as well as alcohol.

For information on the customary business hours kept by restaurants and other eateries, see p762 and the Quick Reference guide on the inside front cover.

Quick Eats

A *Stehcafé* is a stand-up cafe where sweet cravers can indulge in coffee and cakes at speed and on the cheap. Stand-up food stalls (*Schnellimbiss* or, simply, *Imbiss*) around town make handy speed-feed stops for savoury fodder. In Berlin and other cities, some stalls cook up quick Greek, Italian, Middle Eastern and Chinese bites.

Germany's Turkish population invented the modern doner kebab (*Dönerkebab*), adding salad and sauces to slices of roasted beef, chicken or lamb sandwiched inside pitta bread. Most kebab joints also do vegie versions.

In the north, herring and other fish snacks abound. The Nordsee chain is found countrywide (as well as in Switzerland), while the similar – but slightly more upmarket – Gosch (see the boxed text, p723) is more of a quintessential German experience.

Bavarian beer gardens typically serve light snacks such as fresh warm pretzels (*Brez'n*), Bavarian-style meatloaf (*Leberkäs*) and radishes (*Radi*) to their beer-swilling clientele.

It's a fast-food nation – but the old yellow arches are clearly second tier. Germans eat between 250 and 350 tonnes of doner kebabs a day – double the amount sold by McDonald's and Burger King put together.

VEGETARIANS & VEGANS

While vegetarians will have few tummy grumbles in Berlin and other major cities, the pickings in provincial Germany might be slimmer. Vegetables cooked with meat are often considered meat-free, while many so-called vegetarian places serve fish or chicken.

But all is not lost in this carnivorous land. Most city-based Thai, Vietnamese and other Asian eateries cook up dishes suitable for vegetarians. A couple of regional dishes also do not – miraculously – contain meat, including *Leipziger Allerlei*, a vegetarian option in Saxony. Vegetarians in Frankfurt can feast on *Grüne Sosse* – a tasty green sauce eaten as a main dish on top of boiled potatoes or hard-boiled eggs. Fresh basil, chives, cress, dill, sorrel, parsley and tarragon are among the wealth of herbs to be found in this green, cream-based sauce – a seasonal dish available early spring to early autumn.

Vegetable- or cheese-stuffed strudel (*Gemüsestrudel* or *Topfenstrudel*), potato pancakes (*Kartoffelpuffer*) and potato and semolina dumplings (*Erdäpfelknödel*) are more widespread veg-inspired offerings.

Vegans should plan on sticking to vegetarian Asian cuisine. Most German vegetarian dishes come with cream or cheese; even salads sometimes come with mayonnaise- or yoghurt-based dressings.

GERMANY'S TOP EATS

Germany's 'best', in the conventional sense, they might not be, but we've followed our stomachs to nose out – several hundred meals later – the following tasty cross-section of tastebud ticklers:

Brauerei im Füchsen (p563) Drink in earthy Rhenish hospitality along with home-brewed suds and finger-licking roast pork knuckle.

Café Kante (p539) A classic neighbourhood cafe in Frankfurt's cosmopolitan Bornheim district.

Cookies Cream (p140) This chic dining spot serves meat-free gourmet fare in a signless, hidden industrial space.

Eisgrubbräu (p486) Enjoy hearty German classics and fine dark and light beers just metres from the vats they were brewed in.

Hotel am Schloss (p428) This Tübingen institution is renowned for making some of Baden-Württemberg's finest *Maultaschen* (German ravioli).

Restaurant La Vie (p650) Meals are culinary fireworks that harmoniously blend European and Asian aromas, textures and techniques.

Le Canard Nouveau (p694) Exquisite innovation and one of Hamburg's best riverside seats.

Restaurant Jörg Müller (Romantik Hotel Jörg Müller; p722) Pedigreed Michelin-starred cuisine on the glamorous North Frisian island of Sylt.

Strandhalle (p751) Fine unfussy dining in a memorably decorated room with views of Binz' sandy shores.

Villa Mittermeier (p345) Top-end dining astride the Romantic Road with a wine list to match.

EATING WITH KIDS

Dining with kids is by no means a whining affair in Germany. High chairs are a permanent fixture in restaurants – upmarket and budget alike – and, if you're lucky, the waiter will come clad with a damp cloth at the end of your meal to wipe sticky little fingers clean. Most *Gaststätte* and less formal restaurants offer a small choice of *Kindermenüs* (children's menus) and dishes for children (*Kinderteller* or *Für unsere kleinen Gäste*) – those that don't will almost certainly try to meet any special small-appetite requirements. Eating establishments are rarely equipped with nappy-changing facilities, but some fast-food and quick-eat places have a fold-down changing table in the women's loo.

Supermarkets sell a vast range of ready-made baby food and toddler meals – predominantly organic – as well as formula milk, organic fruit juices and teas.

HABITS & CUSTOMS

Germans eat three meals a day – breakfast (*Frühstück*), lunch (*Mittagessen*) and dinner (*Abendessen*).

Breakfast at home is served on a wooden board (rather than a plate). Great animal-shaped boards, complete with a hollowed-out eye to prop up a hard-boiled egg, can often be found at markets. Yoghurt, *Quark*, muesli, cereal, fruit salad and other typical breakfast staples feature in hotel buffets.

Traditionally, lunch would be the main meal of the day. In the domestic arena, modern working practices have changed this considerably, although many restaurants still tout lunchtime dishes or a fixed lunch menu (*Gedeck* or *Tagesmenü*).

Dinner is dished up at home around 7pm, and in restaurants between about 6pm and 11pm. Both meals are relaxed, and require few airs and graces beyond the obligatory '*Guten Appetit*' (literally 'good appetite'), exchanged between diners before eating. German workers lunching on shared tables sometimes still exchange a courteous '*Mahlzeit*' (literally 'mealtime') before tucking in.

Tipping is quite an individual matter. Many locals, particularly older Germans, will tip absolutely nothing. Some round up the bill, while others

You don't need your Michelin or Gault Millau guides to check out Germany's best restaurants, the country has its own ratings and guides, including *Der Feinschmecker* (www .der-feinschmecker-club .de), Aral's *Schlemmer Atlas* (www.schlemmer -atlas.de) and *Marcellino's Restaurant Report* (www .marcellinos.de)

DOS & DON'TS

One early-20th-century German book of manners that we have seen exhorts dinner guests not to use their knives to carve their initials into the table of their hosts! Things have, fortunately, moved on somewhat since those days. With good manners now an automatic reflex, there's little need to panic at the dinner table, although the following tips might be helpful for first-time visitors to Germany.

■ Do bring a small gift – a bottle of wine or flowers – if you've been invited to a meal.

■ Do inform your hosts beforehand of any dietary needs.

■ Do say *'Guten Appetit'* (good appetite) before starting to eat, and *'Prost!'* when drinking a toast.

■ Do offer to help wash up afterwards, particularly as locals tend to be quite punctilious about housework.

■ Do specify if you don't want your restaurant dishes slathered in mayonnaise, *Quark* or dressing. Germans are unbelievably generous in this department.

■ Do pay your bill at the table and give any tip directly to the server. Say either the amount you want to pay, or *'Stimmt so'* if you don't want change.

■ Don't expect to get a glass of tap water at a restaurant or cafe; although things are changing, especially in cities, it's still an uncommon request that may be not be understood or honoured.

■ Don't get impatient or testy when waiting in a cafe, where many customers come to linger. If you're in a hurry, go to a *Stehcafé*.

■ Don't assume you can pay by credit card when eating out – few restaurants accept cards. Take enough cash instead.

---

tip between 5% and 10%. Do whatever you're comfortable with, given the service and setting.

EAT YOUR WORDS

Common phrases and pronunciation guidelines are included in the Language chapter (p791).

Food Glossary

STARTERS

Bauernsuppe	bow·ern·zu·pe	cabbage and sausage 'Farmer's soup'
Fleischbrühe	flaish·brew·e	bouillon
Frühlingssuppe/	frü·lings·zu·pe/	vegetable soup
Gemüsesuppe	ge·moo·ze·zu·pe	
Graupensuppe	grow·pen·zu·pe	barley soup
Kieler Sprotten	kee·ler shpro·ten	small smoked herrings
Kohlroulade	kawl·ru·laa·de	cabbage leaves stuffed with minced meat
Vorspeisen	fawr·shpai·zen	starters

MAIN COURSES

Brathuhn	braat·hoon	roast chicken
Eintopf	ain·topf	one-pot meat and veg stew
Hackbraten	hak·braa·ten	meat loaf
Hauptgerichte	howpt·ge·rikh·te	main courses
Holsteiner Schnitzel	hol·shtai·ner shnit·tsel	veal with fried egg, served with seafood
Rheinischer Sauerbraten	rai·ni·sher zow·er·braa·ten	marinated meat, slightly sour and roasted
Schweinshaxen	shvains·hak·sen	crispy Bavarian pork leg with potato dumplings

DESSERTS & CAKES

Aachener Printen	aa·khe·ner prin·ten	cakes with chocolate, nuts, fruit peel, honey and spices
Apfelstrudel	ap·fel·shtroo·del	apple strudel
Cremespeise	kraym·shpai·ze	mousse
Eierkuchen	ai·er·koo·khen	pancake
Eis	ais	ice cream
Frankfurter Kranz	frank·fur·ter krants	sponge cake with rum, butter, cream and cherries
Gebäck	ge·bek	pastries
Kompott	kom·pot	stewed fruit
Kuchen	koo·khen	cake
Nachspeisen	naakh·shpai·zen	desserts
Obatzter	aw·bats·ter	Bavarian soft cheese mousse
Obstsalat	awpst·za·laat	fruit salad
Torte	tor·te	layer cake

BASICS

Brot	brawt	bread
Brötchen	breut·khen	bread roll
Butter	bu·ter	butter
Ei(er)	ai(·er)	egg(s)
Käse	kay·ze	cheese
Milch	milkh	milk
Nudeln	noo·deln	noodles
Pfeffer	pfe·fer	pepper
Reis	rais	rice
Salz	zalts	salt
Senf	zenf	mustard
Zucker	tsu·ker	sugar

FISH

Aal	aal	eel
Dorsch	dorsh	cod
Fisch	fish	fish
Forelle	fo·re·le	trout
Garnele	gar·nay·le	prawn
Hering	hay·ring	herring
Karpfen	karp·fen	carp
Lachs	lakhs	salmon

MEAT

Ente	en·te	duck
Fasan	fa·zaan	pheasant
Filet	fi·lay	fillet, tenderloin
Fleisch	flaish	meat
Gans	gans	goose
Geflügel	ge·flew·gel	poultry
Hackfleisch	hak·flaish	chopped or minced meat
Hähnchen/Huhn	hayn·khen/hoon	chicken
Kalbfleisch	kalp·flaish	veal
Lammfleisch	lam·flaish	lamb
Rindfleisch	rint·flaish	beef
Schinken	shing·ken	ham
Schweinefleisch	shvai·ne·flaish	pork
Wild	vilt	game

FRUIT & VEGETABLES

Apfel	ap-fel	apple
Apfelsine	ap-fel-zee-ne	orange
Artischocke	ar-ti-sho-ke	artichoke
Bohnen	baw-nen	beans
Gurke	gur-ke	cucumber, gherkins
Kartoffel	kar-to-fel	potato
Knoblauch	knawp-lowkh	garlic
Kohl	kawl	cabbage
Rotkohl	rawt-kawl	red cabbage

DRINKS

Apfelwein	ap-fel-vain	apple cider
Bier	beer	beer
Glühwein	glew-vain	mulled wine
Kaffee	ka-fay	coffee
Saft	zaft	juice
Wasser	va-ser	water
Weisswein/Rotwein	vais-vain/rawt-vain	white/red wine

Environment

THE LAND

Germany is not just about the Black Forest, the Alps and the Rhine River. Across its 356,866 sq km, Europe's fourth-largest country boasts moor and heath, mudflats and chalk cliffs, glacial lakes and river wetlands. Hugged by Poland, the Czech Republic, Austria, Switzerland, France, Belgium, the Netherlands, Luxembourg and Denmark, the country is mountainous in the south, but flat in the north. Indeed, many visitors are surprised to learn Germany even possesses low-lying islands and sandy beaches.

True, the stereotypes have been forged in the south, where you'll find the 2962m Zugspitze, the highest peak, as well as the famous mountain resort of Berchtesgaden. However, only a small section of the Alps falls within Germany – compared to neighbouring Austria and Switzerland – and it's all in Bavaria. In the wooded mountain range of the Black Forest (Schwarzwald), in Baden-Württemberg to the west, nothing rises above 1500m.

Starting its journey in Switzerland and travelling through Lake Constance, Germany's largest lake, the 1320km Rhine River winds its way around the Black Forest, before crawling up the west side of the map to drain into the North Sea. The Elbe, Oder and other German rivers likewise flow north, except for the Danube, which flows east.

Moving towards the central belt, you'll find the most memorable vineyards and hiking areas in the warmer valleys around the Moselle River. Just north of here, the land was formed by volcanic activity. To the east, south of Berlin, you'll find the holiday area of the Spreewald, a picturesque wetland with narrow, navigable waterways.

Where Germany meets Holland in the northwest and Denmark in the north, the land is flat; the westerly North Sea coast consists partly of drained land and dykes. To the east, the Baltic Sea coast is first riddled with bays and fjords in Schleswig-Holstein, before it gives way to sandy inlets and beaches. On the country's northeastern tip, Rügen, its largest island, is, like England's Dover, renowned for its chalk cliffs.

In 2009 Dresden was deleted from Unesco's list of World Heritage Sites due to the building of a four-lane bridge in the middle of a cultural area. Read more about Unesco's list at www .unesco.org.

WILDLIFE

Like most Western European countries, Germany has few large animals still living in the wild. Of the 102 German mammals studied for the 2009 IUCN (International Union for Conservation of Nature) 'Red List' of endangered or extinct species, seven are in danger of dying out: the fin whale, North Atlantic right whale, wild horse, Bavarian pine vole, European mink, European ground squirrel and brown bear.

Green information galore is posted on the website of the Federal Environment Agency (*Umweltbundesamt;* www .umweltbundesamt.de).

Animals

Snow hares, marmots and wild goats are found throughout the Alps (the marmot below the tree line, the goat and snow hare above it). The chamois is also fairly common in this neck of the woods, as well as in pockets of the Black Forest, the Swabian Alps and Saxon Switzerland (Sächsische Schweiz), south of Dresden.

A rare but wonderful Alpine treat for patient birdwatchers is the sighting of a golden eagle; Berchtesgaden National Park staff might be able to help you find one. The jay, with its darting flight patterns and calls imitating other species, is easy to spot in the Alpine foothills. Look for the flashes of blue on its wings.

For information on Germany's 101 nature parks, see www.naturparke.de.

SETTING FREE THE BEAR?

Although the bear is the symbol of Berlin, the wild animal hasn't lived on German soil since 1835. That changed briefly in 2006, when a brown bear wandered into Bavaria. However, the short life of 'Bruno', as he was christened by tabloid newspapers like *Bild*, was a rather sad footnote in history.

Bruno (officially code named JJ1) was part of a program to reintroduce bears to the Italian Alps when he ambled into Germany and became the first wild bear there for more than 170 years. Spotted by local photographers, he became a media celebrity.

Animal-rights activists began a strenuous campaign to protect the bear, hoping to capture him alive and move him. Farmers, however, started blaming Bruno for killing livestock and, because of a perceived risk to humans, the Bavarian government gave the go-ahead to shoot him...which hunters eventually did.

Even after his death, the WWF (World Wide Fund for Nature) hopes it can leverage the public affection Bruno engendered to establish a sensible bear repopulation program in Germany. But for some Germans the story of Bruno is an unedifying episode they'd rather just forget.

Pesky but sociable racoons, a common non-native species, scoot about eastern Germany, and soon let hikers know if they have been disturbed with a shrill whistle-like sound. Beavers can be found in wetlands near the Elbe River. Seals are common on the North Sea and Baltic Sea coasts.

The north coast also lures migratory birds. From March to May, and August to October, they stop over in Schleswig-Holstein's Wadden Sea (Wattenmeer) National Park and the Vorpommersche Boddenlandschaft National Park while going to and from southerly regions. Forests everywhere provide a habitat for a wide variety of songbirds, as well as woodpeckers.

The highly unlikely title *Animals in the Third Reich: Pets, Scapegoats, and the Holocaust* by Klaus P Fischer and Boria Sax looks at the treatment of animals under Hitler's Third Reich and Nazism's symbolic use of nature for its own means.

Some animals are staging a comeback. Sea eagles, practically extinct in western Germany, are becoming more plentiful in the east, as are falcons, white storks and cranes. The east also sees wolves, which regularly cross the Oder River from Poland, and European moose, which occasionally appear on moors and in mixed forests.

The wild cat has returned to the Harz Mountains and other forested regions, but you shouldn't expect to see the related lynx. Having died out here in the 19th century, lynxes were reintroduced in the 1980s, only to be illegally hunted to the point of extinction again. Today, a few populate the Bavarian Forest National Park, although chances of seeing one in the wild are virtually zero.

The 2005 book *How Green Were the Nazis?: Nature, Environment, and Nation in the Third Reich* by Franz-Josef Bruggemeier, Mark Cioc and Thomas Zeller (eds) takes a look at the Nazis' love of the great outdoors and explores how fascist and conservationist practices overlap.

Deer are still around, although with dwindling natural habitats and their shrinking gene pool, the **Deutsche Wildtier Stiftung** (German Wild Animal Foundation; www.deutschewildtierstiftung.de, in German) has expressed concern for the animal's future.

Plants

Studded with beech, oak, birch, chestnut (mostly of the inedible horse-chestnut variety), lime, maple and ash trees, German forests are beautiful places to escape the madding crowds and relax. Mixed deciduous forest carpets river valleys at lower altitudes, and coniferous species grow thicker as you ascend. According to the 2009 IUCN 'Red List', only 12 plants might be endangered.

Waldfrüchte (berries) are particularly colourful but are for the most part poisonous. The same applies to mushrooms, which are essential for the development of healthy root systems in trees, especially in deciduous forests. Chanterelle *(Pfifferlinge)* mushrooms are an autumn culinary delight.

Alpine regions burst with wildflowers – orchids, cyclamen, gentians, pulsatillas, alpenroses, edelweiss and buttercups. Meadow species colour spring and summer, and great care is taken these days not to cut pastures until plants have seeded. Visitors should stick to paths, especially in alpine areas and coastal dunes where ecosystems are fragile. In late August, heather blossom is the particular lure of Lüneburg Heath, northeast of Hanover.

NATIONAL PARKS

The country's vast and varied landscapes are protected to varying degrees by 101 nature parks, 14 biosphere reserves and 14 national parks (detailed in the table, p96). The Upper Middle Rhine Valley and the Wadden Sea are both safeguarded as Unesco World Heritage Areas to prevent further damage.

ENVIRONMENTAL ISSUES

Germans are the original Greens. They cannot claim to have invented environmentalism, but they were there at the outset and it was they who coined the word to describe the movement. A few 'Values' and 'Ecology' parties were knocking around beforehand, but it was the group of politicians associated with Rudi Dutschke, Petra Kelly and artist Joseph Beuys who first hit on the name The Greens (Die Grünen) when contesting local and national elections in 1979 and 1980. They gained a strong foothold in Bremen, and other political groups across the world decided they quite liked the moniker. The rest, as they say, is history (see the boxed text 'Keen on Green', p49, for more on Die Grünen).

The Greens' concern for the health of the planet and their strong opposition to nuclear power certainly struck a chord with the local populace. Contemporary Germans recycle vigilantly, often prefer to ride bicycles rather than catch buses, and carry their groceries in reusable cloth shopping bags or rolling canvas baskets; all this is simply second nature here.

Green ideology has also wielded an enormous influence on the political agenda. In the 1990s, Greenpeace Germany made international news trying to stop nuclear-waste transport in Lower Saxony and heavily populated North Rhine–Westphalia. German Greenpeace members also helped scuttle Shell's controversial plans to sink the Brent Spar oil platform in the North Sea.

Even more tellingly, the Greens were in government between 1998 and 2005, as the junior partner in Gerhard Schröder's coalition. Under the leadership of Joschka Fischer, the party had a major say in decisions to cut carbon emissions and to wind down the nuclear industry. Although some of these policies are already being reversed under the new, more conservative 'grand coalition' government of CDU/CSU and SPD under Chancellor Angela Merkel, individual Germans' commitment to green issues remains solid.

Energy

Travelling across Germany, one can't help but be struck by the number of giant wind turbines dotting the landscape, especially in the windswept north. You start to wonder just how many there are. Well, there were more than 23,000 in 2008 – the second-largest number of wind farms in one country after the United States.

While other countries debate its pros and cons, Germany has long embraced this technology. It's the world's leading producer of wind energy, accounting for between 38% and 42% of entire global capacity in 2008 (depending on whose figures you believe). According to the GWEC (Global Wind Energy Council), wind turbines currently provide roughly 7.5% of German electricity. Four states proudly boast that more than a third of their energy is fuelled by wind power: Saxony-Anhalt, Mecklenburg–Western

Ting! Ting! Road rage in ecofriendly Germany often happens on the footpath (sidewalk), when inattentive pedestrians step into an oncoming cyclist's way. Watch out for the red cycle lanes – and stay well out of them!

Consisting mainly of firs and pines, the Black Forest derives its name from the dark appearance of these conifers, especially when seen from the hillsides.

Owls of the World: Their Lives, Behaviour and Survival by James R Duncan makes the ideal companion for wildlife enthusiasts out to spot Germany's eagle owls, Eurasian pygmy owls and other owl species.

NATIONAL PARKS

Park & Website	Features	Activities	Best Time to Visit	Page
Bavarian Forest www.nationalpark -bayerischer-wald.de	mountain forest & upland moors (243 sq km); deer, hazel grouse, foxes, otters, eagle owls, botany	walking, mountain biking, cross-country skiing,	spring & winter	p399
Berchtesgaden www.nationalpark -berchtesgaden.de	lakes, subalpine spruce, salt mines & ice caves (210 sq km); eagles, golden eagles, marmots, blue hares	wildlife spotting, walking, skiing	spring & winter	p361
Eifel www.nationalpark -eifel.de	beech forest (110 sq km); wild cats, beavers, kingfishers, wild yellow narcissus	wildlife & flora spotting, hiking, hydrotherapy spa treatments	spring & summer	p589
Hainich www.nationalpark -hainich.de	mixed deciduous forest (76 sq km); beech trees, black storks, wild cats, rare bats	walking	spring	p279
Hamburg Wadden Sea www.wattenmeer -nationalpark.de	mudflats with meadows & sand dunes (120 sq km); sea swallows, terns	birdwatching, mudflat walking	spring & autumn	p699
Harz www.nationalpark -harz.de	amazing rock formations & caves (247 sq km); deer, black woodpeckers, wild cats	climbing, walking	spring, summer & autumn; not weekends (too busy)	p240
Jasmund www.nationalpark -jasmund.de	landscape of chalk cliffs, forest, creeks & moors (30 sq km); white-tailed eagles	walking, cycling	not summer (paths like ant trails)	p752
Kellerwald Edersee www.nationalpark -kellerwald-edersee.de	beech & other deciduous trees, lake (57 sq km); black stork, wild cats, rare bats, stags	walking, wildlife spotting	spring, summer & autumn	p553
Lower Oder Valley www.nationalpark -unteres-odertal.eu	river plain (165 sq km); black storks, sea eagles, beavers, aquatic warblers, cranes	walking, cycling, birdwatching	winter (bird-watching), spring (other activities)	p173
Lower Saxony Wadden Sea www.nationalpark-watten meer-niedersachsen.de	salt-marsh & bog landscape (2780 sq km); seals, shell ducks	swimming, walking, birdwatching	late spring & early autumn	p656
Müritz www.nationalpark -mueritz.de	beech, bogs & lakes galore (318 sq km); sea eagles, fish hawks, cranes, white-tailed eagles, Gothland sheep	cycling, canoeing, birdwatching, hiking	spring, summer & autumn	p733
Saxon Switzerland www.nationalpark -saechsische-schweiz.de	spectacular sandstone & basalt rock formations (93 sq km); eagle owls, otters, fat dormice	walking, climbing, rock climbing	not summer (throngs with Dresden day trippers)	p190
Schleswig-Holstein Wadden Sea www.wattenmeer nationalpark.de	dramatic seascape of dunes, salt marshes & mudflats (4410 sq km); sea life, migratory birds	mudflat walking, tide watching, birdwatching, swimming	spring & autumn	p719
Vorpommersche Boddenlandschaft www.nationalpark -vorpommersche -boddenlandschaft.de	dramatic Baltic seascape (805 sq km); cranes, red deer, wild boar	birdwatching, water sports, walking	autumn (crane watching), summer (water sports)	p744

Pomerania, Schleswig-Holstein and Brandenburg. Additionally, one of the world's largest wind turbines is being built in Northern Germany.

The federal government also backs research into other alternative energy sources, with some €40 million invested in geothermal energy, solar power, hydroelectricity and biomass projects. One of the world's largest solar plants, Waldpolenz Solar Park, is currently being built on a former military base near Leipzig; when completed in 2010, it is expected to produce about 40MHz of electricity per year. All these initiatives mean Germany is well on track to achieving its target of using 30% renewable electricity by 2020.

The current pre-eminence of renewable energies partly derives from the country's decision in 2001 to shut down its nuclear industry. That year, the so-called red-green government (with red representing Schröder's centre-left SPD party) developed a timetable to phase out all 19 of its nuclear energy plants by 2020. But these reactors provide a third of the country's energy needs, and the government was attempting simultaneously to reduce its carbon-emission levels by 40% from 1990 levels, so it massively stepped up investment in alternative energies.

Each of the 19 nuclear reactors was to be shut down on its 32nd birthday, and the first to go was Stade (outside Hamburg) in November 2003. However, by 2007, with only two other reactors decommissioned, there was a change of government in Berlin and, seemingly, a change of heart. Critics were warning of an energy crisis and in 2006 the nuclear industry was lobbying environment minister Sigmar Gabriel (SPD) to postpone the closures by some five to eight years. Although a staunch nuclear opponent himself, Gabriel admitted to news magazine *Der Spiegel* that not everyone in the grand-coalition government shared his views. In 2008, German chancellor Angela Merkel and the CDU/CSU opted to launch opposition to the planned closures, discarding a compromise proposed by the SPD to postpone the shutdown while endorsing a constitutional ban on new plants. The SPD continues to oppose nuclear power, but with Angela Merkel's re-election in 2009 (see p51), it is expected that her government will aim to reverse the proposed plan to shut down the 17 remaining nuclear-power plants.

For comprehensive details of national parks and hot links to their websites, surf www.germany -tourism.de.

One of the easiest ways to stay up to date with current green issues is to follow your favourite green blog – check out the list at www .bestgreenblogs.com. You can search by various categories, including specific countries like Germany.

HOW TO RECYCLE A TEABAG

It might be something of a national joke, but recycling a teabag really does require all but one of the five rubbish bins found in German homes.

Germans are Europe's biggest recyclers. Into the organic waste bin *(Biomüll)*, goes biodegradable waste – garden rubbish, potato peelings, food leftovers, coffee granules and used tea bags (minus metal clip, string and paper tag). The paper *(Papier)* bin takes recyclable paper, waxed and nonwaxed cardboard and teabag paper tags. There's a third *Grüne Punkt* bin for recyclable items – including packaging materials, margarine tubs, empty food tins, cans and teabag clips. Except for glass – which obviously a tea bag doesn't contain – everything left over, including the synthetic string on a teabag, goes in the fourth bin for residuary waste *(Restmüll)*.

Bins found in train stations and airports are slightly different: *Glas* (glass), *Papier* (paper), *Verpackung* (packaging) and *Restmüll* (residuary waste).

Empty mineral-water bottles (both plastic and glass) plus beer and other bottles are another recycling story. When you buy these in the shop, many have a *Pfand* (returnable deposit), usually between €0.08 and €0.25 per bottle. This is to persuade even the laziest of consumers to return their empties to one of 100,000 specified shops and points of sale countrywide. Germans usually save these up until they have a bag full (or three) to return. Be prepared to wait if you find yourself behind such a customer in a supermarket queue!

Per capita, Germany produces roughly 10kg of rubbish daily (by comparison, the United States produces roughly 15kg, Switzerland 12kg, Finland 8kg and Sweden 7kg).

Pollution

When it comes to addressing pollution, Germany might recently have blotted an otherwise fairly enviable copybook. Until 2006, the country was seen as the European leader in reducing carbon-dioxide emissions and offsetting the effects of acid rain and river pollution. However, new carbon-emission quotas for industry announced in the middle of that year were criticised for being unambitious or even lax. Environmental groups accused Angela Merkel's government of not taking its commitments under the Kyoto Protocol seriously enough.

This controversy is a far cry from the period from 1987 to 2000, when Germany proudly achieved the environmental turnaround of the European century with the success of the Rhine Action Programme. Declared dead by 1970, the Upper Rhine was spawning salmon and sea trout again by 1997 – for the first time in 50 years. The transformation was all the more remarkable given that some 15% of the world's chemical industry plants are settled along its banks.

A longer-term Action Plan High Water was put in place until 2020, working on restoring other riverbanks and important adjoining meadows, in a bid to stave off damaging floods.

In 2002 the government was still polishing its green credentials when it stepped up an ecological tax on petrol, diesel, heating oil, natural gas and electricity. The same year it pledged to reduce Germany's 1990 level of greenhouse gas emissions by 21% between 2008 and 2012 – by 2004, its emissions were already 17.5% down on those notched up in 1990.

But in 2006 the German government dialled down on its greenhouse gas plans, asking that industry cut back only 0.6% on carbon emissions between 2008 and 2012. It also gave many business free carbon allowances and exempted a number of major industrial plants from limits until 2022, causing concerns to be voiced by many international critics. However, in 2008 Germany met its Kyoto targets – successfully reducing its gas emissions by 22% since 1990.

Flora and Vegetation of the Wadden Sea Islands and Coastal Areas, by KS Diikema and WJ Wolff (eds), remains indispensable for anyone spending time in any of the three Wadden Sea (Wattenmeer) National Parks.

Schleswig-Holstein generates nearly 38% of its power from its 2500-plus wind turbines.

Berlin

'Berlin is the newest city I have come across', observed Mark Twain in 1891, and a modern-day visitor to the German capital might well echo the sentiment. Twenty years after German reunification, Berlin is a city throbbing with vitality, still struggling for an identify, yet poised for a great future. Head-spinning museums to eclectic galleries, grand opera to guerrilla clubs, gourmet outposts to ethnic snack shacks – no matter whether your tastes run to posh or punk, you can sate them in this city.

Chronic fiscal woes aside, when it comes to fashion, art, design and music, Berlin is the city to watch. A global influx of creative spirits has turned it into a cauldron of cultural cool on par with New York in the '80s. What draws them is an experimental climate infused with an urban grit that gives this eternally unfinished city its street cred.

All this trendiness is a triumph for a town that's long been in the crosshairs of history: Berlin staged a revolution, headquartered fascists, was bombed to bits, ripped in half and finally reunited – and that was just in the 20th century! Perhaps it's because of its historical burden that Berlin is throwing itself into tomorrow. Cafes are jammed at all hours, drinking is a religious rite and clubs host their scenes of hedonism until the wee hours. Sleep? *Way* overrated.

HIGHLIGHTS

- **Royal Encounters** Make a date with Nefertiti and her entourage at the splendid Neues Museum (p117)

- **Chill-out Float** Let the sights drift by while sipping a cool drink on the deck of a river boat (p134)

- **Life's a Beach** Check out sexy bods while chilling and bronzing on the unique Badeschiff, cargo barge turned lifestyle pool (p131)

- **Fashionista Fever** Put together the distinctive Berlin look by scouring the local designer boutiques of the Scheunenviertel (p119)

- **Panoramic Pleasures** Get high on the knock-out views from the Reichstag roof (p120) or the Fernsehturm (p117), Germany's tallest structure

- **Party Animals** Hit the bars of Kreuzberg for a night of tabloid-worthy drinking and debauchery (p144)

- **Wall Stalker** Look for traces of the elusive Berlin Wall by following a GPS-guided Mauerguide (p126)

- **Eccentric Sleeps** – Spend the night in a floating bed, in a prison cell, a kaleidoscope or any of the other wacky rooms at Propeller Island City Lodge (p138)

- ★ Scheunenviertel
- Neues Museum; River Cruise
- Reichstag ★★ ★ ★ Fernsehturm
- Mauerguide
- Propeller Island ★ ★ ★ Badeschiff
- City Lodge ★ Kreuzberg

■ TELEPHONE CODE: 030	■ POPULATION: 3.43 MILLION	■ AREA: 889 SQ KM

HISTORY

By German standards, Berlin entered onto the stage of history rather late and puttered along in relative obscurity for centuries. Founded in the 13th century as a trading post, it merged with its sister settlement Cölln across the Spree River in 1307. The town achieved a modicum of prominence after the powerful Hohenzollern clan from southern Germany took charge in 1411, at least until the 17th century when it was ravaged during the Thirty Years' War (1618–48) with only 6000 people surviving the pillage, plunder and starvation.

The war's aftermath gave Berlin its first taste of cosmopolitanism. In a clever bit of social engineering, Elector Friedrich Wilhelm (called the Great Elector; r 1640–88) managed to quickly increase the number of his subjects by inviting foreigners to settle in Berlin. Some Jewish families arrived from Vienna, but most of the new settlers were Huguenot refugees from France. By 1700, one in five locals was of French descent.

Elector Friedrich III, the Great Elector's son, presided over a lively and intellectual court, but was also a man of great political ambition. In 1701, he simply promoted himself to become King Friedrich I of Prussia, making Berlin a royal residence and capital of the new state of Brandenburg-Prussia.

His son, Friedrich Wilhelm I (r 1713–40), laid the groundwork for Prussian military might. Soldiers were this king's main obsession and he dedicated much of his life to building an army of 80,000, partly by instituting the draft (highly unpopular even then) and partly by persuading his fellow rulers to trade him men for treasure. History quite appropriately knows him as the *Soldatenkönig* (Soldier King).

Ironically, these soldiers didn't see action until his son Friedrich II (aka Frederick the Great; r 1740–86) came to power in 1740. Friedrich fought tooth and nail for two decades to wrest Silesia from Austria and Saxony. When not busy on the battlefield, 'Old Fritz', as he was also called, sought greatness through building (the best bits of Unter den Linden date back to his reign) and embracing the ideals of the Enlightenment. With some of the day's leading thinkers in town (Gotthold Ephraim Lessing and Moses Mendelssohn among them), Berlin blossomed into a cultural centre some even called 'Athens on the Spree'.

Old Fritz' death sent Prussia on a downward spiral, culminating in a serious trouncing of its army by Napoleon in 1806. The French marched triumphantly into Berlin on 27 October and left two years later, their coffers bursting with loot. The post-Napoleonic period saw Berlin caught up in the reform movement sweeping through Europe. Since all this ferment brought little change from the top, Berlin joined other German cities, in 1848, in a bourgeois democratic revolution. Alas, the time for democracy wasn't yet ripe and the status quo was quickly restored.

Meanwhile, the Industrial Revolution had snuck up on Berliners, with companies like Siemens and Borsig vastly spurring the city's growth and spawning a new working class and political parties such as the Social Democratic Party (SPD) to represent them. Berlin boomed politically, economically and culturally, especially after becoming capital of the German Reich in 1871. By 1900 the population had reached two million.

Once again war, WWI in this case, stifled Berlin's momentum. In its aftermath, the city found itself at the heart of a power struggle between monarchists, ultra-left Spartacists and democrats. Though the democrats won out, the 1920s only brought instability, corruption and inflation. Berliners responded like there was no tomorrow and made their city as much a den of decadence as a cauldron of creativity. Artists of all stripes flocked to this city of cabaret, Dada and jazz.

Hitler's rise to power put an instant damper on the fun. Berlin suffered heavy bombing in WWII and a crushing invasion of 1.5 million Soviet soldiers during the final, decisive Battle of Berlin in April 1945. During the Cold War, it became ground zero for hostilities between the US and the USSR. The Berlin Blockade of 1948 and the construction of the Berlin Wall in 1961 were major milestones in the standoff. For 40 years, East and West Berlin developed as two completely separate cities.

With reunification, Berlin once again became the German capital in 1990 and the seat of the federal government in 1999. Mega-sized construction projects such as the Potsdamer Platz and the government quarters eradicated the scars of division but did little to improve the city's balance sheet or unemployment statistics. Not unlike in the 1920s, Berliners compensated by turning their city into a hotbed of creativity, with unbridled nightlife, an explosive art scene and booming fashion and design industries. They showed off their legendary liberalism at the Love Parade and welcomed the global community to such events as the 2006 FIFA World Cup.

Meanwhile, social woes continue to bedraggle Berlin. Poorly performing schools, violent racial attacks by right-wing groups and a spate of 'honour killings' of young Muslim women for wishing to live a Western lifestyle have all captured the headlines in recent years.

Two decades after the rejoining of the city halves, Berlin is reaching a watershed moment. Districts such as Mitte and Prenzlauer Berg, once pioneers of progressiveness, are now firmly in the grip of gentrification and boho-bourgeois pram-pushers. Global developers are building up the banks of the Spree River, investors from Denmark to Ireland to America are snapping up bargain-priced apartments, and international chains are replacing homespun businesses.

All this begs the question: Can Berlin remain the homeland of social freedom and experimentation while increasingly becoming a more corporate-driven, 'normal' metropolis? Governing mayor Klaus Wowereit famously called Berlin 'poor but sexy'. In 10 years' time it may no longer be poor. But will it still be sexy?

ORIENTATION

Berlin is made up of 12 administrative districts of which the central ones hold the most interest to visitors. Mitte, formerly in East Berlin, is the city's historic core and packs such blockbuster sights as the Brandenburger Tor, the Holocaust Memorial, Unter den Linden boulevard, Museumsinsel and the Fernsehturm (TV Tower). The Scheunenviertel area, anchored by the Hackesche Höfe, is jammed with bars, restaurants, galleries and designer boutiques. To the north, gentrified and family-dominated Prenzlauer Berg beckons with a vibrant cafe culture, a bevy of unique owner-run shops and pockets of nightlife action.

South of Mitte, Kreuzberg counts Checkpoint Charlie and the Jüdisches Museum (Jewish Museum) among its highlights. Eastern Kreuzberg, around Kottbusser Tor, is the hub of Berlin's large Turkish population and the place to get down and dirty in

trashy-chic bars and clubs. Across the Spree River, Friedrichshain is an eccentric mix of Stalinist architecture, gritty squat-style pubs, polished cocktail culture and chilly beach bars. The main sight is the East Side Gallery, the longest surviving section of the Wall.

West of Mitte, Tiergarten boasts most of Berlin's large-scale post-reunification projects, including the government district, the Hauptbahnhof glass palace and Potsdamer Platz. The vast Tiergarten park links Mitte with Charlottenburg, the hub of western Berlin with lively shopping along Kurfürstendamm and the royal splendour of Schloss Charlottenburg. Much of the district is upmarket residential, as are the adjoining quarters of Wilmersdorf and Schöneberg, although the latter includes a throbbing gay district around Nollendorfplatz.

For details about Berlin's airports and train stations, see p153 and p154 respectively.

Maps

The maps in this book should suffice in most cases, although the foldout map available for €1 from the Berlin Infostores (p114) might be a useful supplement; it also indicates the former course of the Berlin Wall.

INFORMATION
Bookshops

Another Country (Map pp110–11; ☎ 6940 1160; Riemannstrasse 7, Kreuzberg) Library-store run by an eccentric Brit.

Berlin Story (Map p108; ☎ 2045 3842; Unter den Linden 26, Mitte) Berlin-related books, maps, videos, guides and magazines, many in English.

Dussmann – Das Kulturkaufhaus (Map p108; ☎ 2025 1111; Friedrichstrasse 90, Mitte; ☯ 10am-midnight Mon-Sat) The ultimate in books and music; lots of reading corners and occasional signings, concerts and other events.

East of Eden (Map pp106–7; ☎ 423 9362; Schreinerstrasse 10, Prenzlauer Berg) Living-room-type store perfect for browsing.

Marga Schoeller Bücherstube (Map p112; ☎ 8862 9320; Knesebeckstrasse 33, Charlottenburg) Literary lair with plenty of English titles.

Schropp (Map pp106–7; ☎ 2355 7320; Potsdamer Strasse 129, Schöneberg) Guidebooks and maps galore.

Discount Cards

Berlin WelcomeCard (www.berlin-welcomecard.com; per 2/3/5 days for zones AB €16.50/22/29.50, for zones ABC €18.50/25/34.50) Entitles you to unlimited public transport within the fare zone and up to 50% discount for 140 sights, attractions and tours. Available at the Berlin Infostores (see Tourist Information, p114), U-Bahn and S-Bahn ticket vending machines, BVG offices and many hotels.

CityTourCard (www.citytourcard.de; per 2/3/5 days for zones AB €15.90/20.90/28.90, for zones ABC €17.90/22.90/33.90) Works in same way as Berlin Welcome Card and is a bit cheaper but offers fewer discounts. Available at some hotels and from U-Bahn and S-Bahn vending machines.

SchauLust Museen Berlin (adult/child €19/9.50) Unbeatable deal for culture vultures. Buys admission to permanent exhibits of about 70 museums on three consecutive opening days; available at Berlin Infostores and participating museums.

Emergency

American Hotline (☎ 0177-814 1510) Crisis hotline and referral service for all English speakers, not just Americans.

BVG Public Transport Lost & Found (Map p143; ☎ 194 49; Potsdamer Strasse 180/182, Schöneberg; ☺ 9am-6pm Mon-Thu, to 2pm Fri; ☺ Kleistpark)

Call-a-Doc (☎ 01804-2255 2362) Non-emergency medical assistance and treatment referral.

Fire brigade & ambulance (☎ 112)

International Helpline (☎ in English 4401 0607; ☺ 6pm-midnight) Volunteer-run, anonymous help for people in any crisis situation.

Municipal Lost & Found (Map pp110-11; ☎ 7560 3101; Platz der Luftbrücke 6, Kreuzberg; ☺ 8am-3pm Mon & Tue, 10am-1pm Wed, 1-5pm Thu, 8am-noon Fri)

Police (☎ 110)

Rape Crisis Hotline (☎ 251 2828, 615 4243, 216 8888)

Wheelchair Breakdown Service (☎ 0180-111 4747)

Internet Access

Many hostels, hotels and cafes offer wireless surfing (called W-LAN in German) and the entire Sony Center at Potsdamer Platz (Map pp110–11) is a free public hot spot. The website www.hotspot-locations.com can help you pin down others.

Internet cafes in Berlin have about the lifespan of a fruit fly, so it's best to ask at the tourist office or your hotel for the nearest one. Also look for coin-operated laptops by **Sidewalk Express** (www.sidewalkexpress.com; per hr €2) usually found in malls (eg Potsdamer Platz Arkaden, Alexa) and train stations (eg Friedrichstrasse, Alexanderplatz). **Fat Tire Bike Tours** (Map p108; ☎ 2404 7991; Panoramastrasse 1a; ☺ 9.30am-7.30pm) below the TV Tower has an all-you-can-surf rate for €1.99.

Internet Resources

3D Stadtmodell (www.3d-stadtmodell-berlin.de) Virtual Google Earth–powered journey through Berlin.

Berlin Hidden Places (www.berlin-hidden-places.de) Ideas for getting off the tourist track.

Berlin Tourism (www.visitberlin.de, www.visitBerlin.tv) Official tourist-office website.

Berlin Unlike (http://berlin-unlike.net) Hip guide with up-to-the-minute reviews and happenings; sign up for a free weekly newsletter.

Gridskipper (www.gridskipper.com/travel/berlin) Urban travel guide to the useful, offbeat, naughty and nice.

I Heart Berlin (www.iheartberlin.de) Lifestyle blog with posts about parties, fashion, art and scene insiders.

Left Luggage

Most central railway stations, including Hauptbahnhof, Friedrichstrasse, Zoo and Ostbahnhof, have coin lockers that cost €2 to €4 for 24 hours. The Hauptbahnhof also has a left-luggage office (€4 per piece per 24 hours) behind the ReiseBank currency exchange on the first upper level, opposite the Reisezentrum. There are also left-luggage stations at the central bus station ZOB and at the airports at Tegel and Schönefeld.

Media

For entertainment-listings zines, see p145.

Berliner Zeitung Left-leaning German-language daily most widely read in the eastern districts.

Der Tagesspiegel Local German-language daily with centre-right political orientation, solid news and foreign section, and decent cultural coverage.

Exberliner English-language magazine about the city; for expats and visitors, with features, essays and listings.

taz Appeals to an intellectual crowd with its unapologetically pink-leaning news analysis and reporting.

Medical Services

The US and UK consulates can provide lists of English-speaking doctors. Listed here are hospitals with 24-hour emergency rooms.

Charité Campus Benjamin Franklin (☎ 844 50; Hindenburgdamm 30; ☺ Botanischer Garten) In the Steglitz district in southern Berlin.

Charité Campus Mitte (Map p108; ☎ 450 50; Charité-Platz 1) The most central of the big hospitals.

Charité Campus Virchow-Klinikum (Map pp106-7; ☎ 450 50; Augustenburger Platz 1; ☺ Amrumer Strasse) In the Wedding district in northern Berlin.

Zahnklinik Medeco (Dental Clinic; Map pp110-11; ☎ 2309 5960; Stresemannstrasse 121; ☺ 7am-9pm) Has several other branches around town.

(Continued on page 114)

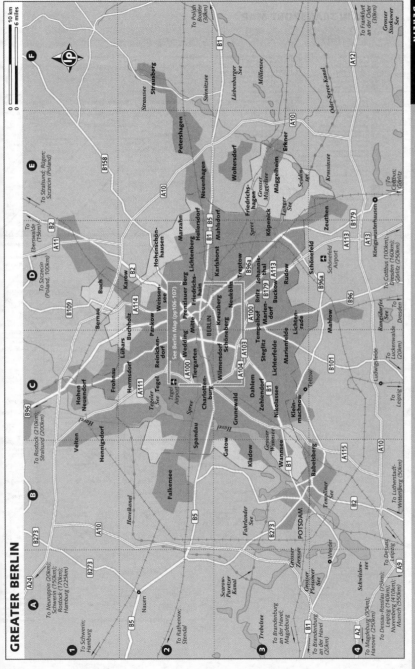

GREATER BERLIN

BERLIN TRANSPORT MAP

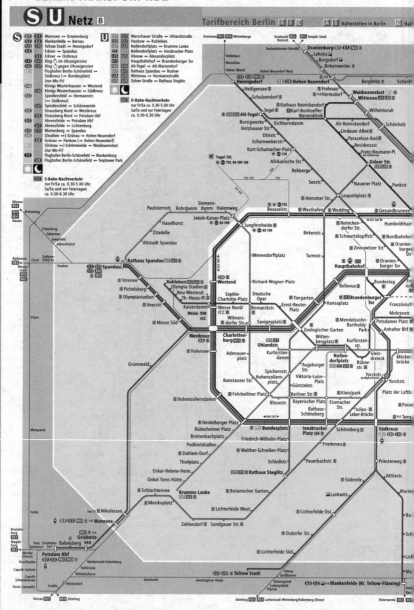

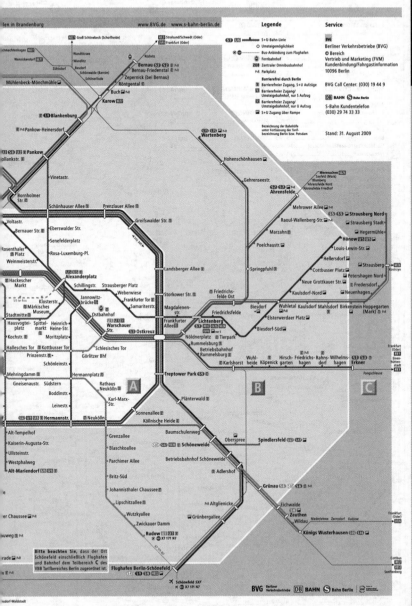

BERLIN

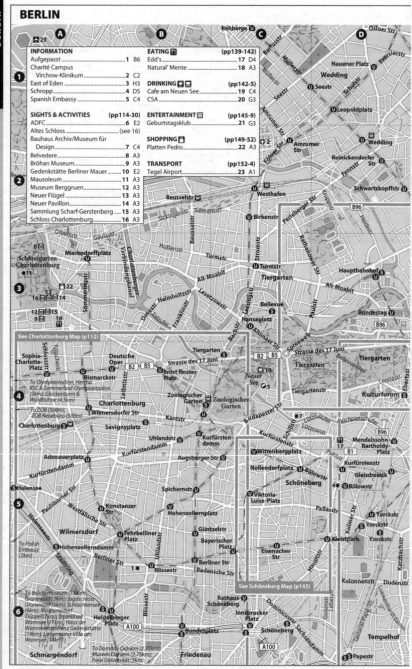

INFORMATION
Aufgepasst	**1** B6
Charité Campus Virchow-Klinikum	**2** C2
East of Eden	**3** H3
Schropp	**4** D5
Spanish Embassy	**5** C4

SIGHTS & ACTIVITIES (pp114–30)
ADFC	**6** E2
Altes Schloss	(see 16)
Bauhaus Archiv/Museum für Design	**7** C4
Belvedere	**8** A3
Bröhan Museum	**9** A3
Gedenkstätte Berliner Mauer	**10** E2
Mausoleum	**11** A3
Museum Berggruen	**12** A3
Neuer Flügel	**13** A3
Neuer Pavillon	**14** A3
Sammlung Scharf-Gerstenberg	**15** A3
Schloss Charlottenburg	**16** A3

EATING (pp139–142)
Edd's	**17** D4
Natural' Mente	**18** A3

DRINKING (pp142–5)
Cafe am Neuen See	**19** C4
CSA	**20** G3

ENTERTAINMENT (pp145–9)
Geburtstagsklub	**21** G3

SHOPPING (pp149–52)
Platten Pedro	**22** A3

TRANSPORT (pp152–4)
Tegel Airport	**23** A1

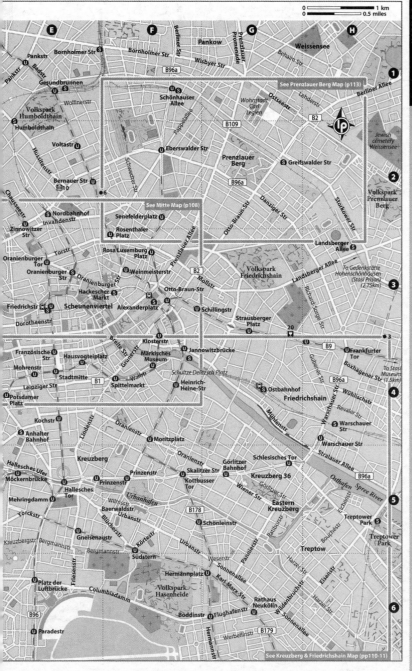

BERLIN

MITTE

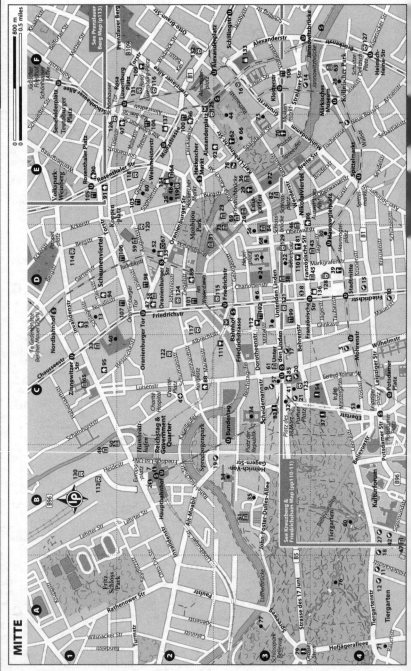

MITTE

KREUZBERG & FRIEDRICHSHAIN

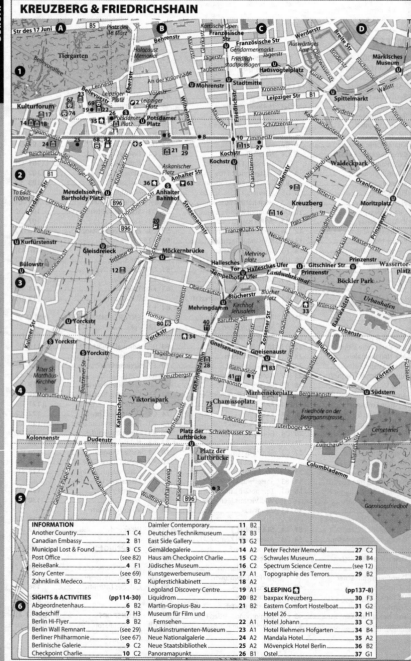

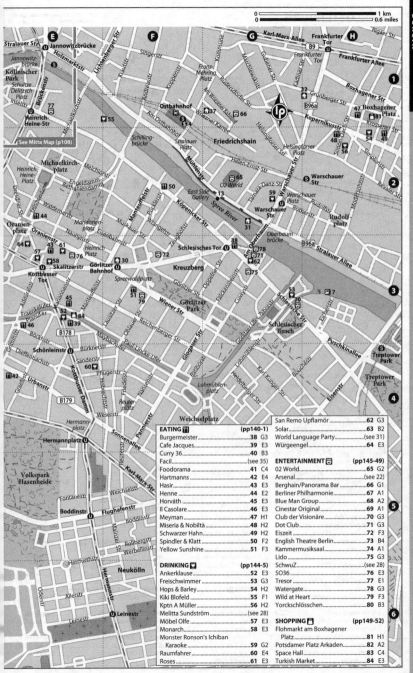

EATING	(pp140-1)
Burgermeister	**38** G3
Cafe Jacques	**39** E3
Curry 36	**40** B3
Facil	(see 35)
Foodorama	**41** C4
Hartmanns	**42** E4
Hasir	**43** E3
Henne	**44** E2
Horváth	**45** E3
Il Casolare	**46** E3
Meyman	**47** H1
Miseria & Nobiltà	**48** H2
Schwarzer Hahn	**49** H2
Spindler & Klatt	**50** F2
Yellow Sunshine	**51** F3

DRINKING	(pp144-5)
Ankerklause	**52** E3
Freischwimmer	**53** G3
Hops & Barley	**54** H2
Kiki Blofeld	**55** F1
Kptn A Müller	**56** H2
Melitta Sundström	(see 28)
Möbel Olfe	**57** E3
Monarch	**58** E3
Monster Ronson's Ichiban Karaoke	**59** G2
Raumfahrer	**60** E4
Roses	**61** E3
San Remo Upflamör	**62** G3
Solar	**63** B2
World Language Party	(see 31)
Würgeengel	**64** E3

ENTERTAINMENT	(pp145-49)
02 World	**65** G2
Arsenal	(see 22)
Berghain/Panorama Bar	**66** G1
Berliner Philharmonie	**67** A1
Blue Man Group	**68** A2
Cinestar Original	**69** A1
Club der Visionäre	**70** G3
Dot Club	**71** G3
Eiszeit	**72** F3
English Theatre Berlin	**73** B4
Kammermusiksaal	**74** A1
Lido	**75** G3
SchwuZ	(see 28)
SO36	**76** E3
Tresor	**77** E1
Watergate	**78** G3
Wild at Heart	**79** F3
Yorckschlösschen	**80** B3

SHOPPING	(pp149-52)
Flohmarkt am Boxhagener Platz	**81** H1
Potsdamer Platz Arkaden	**82** A2
Space Hall	**83** C4
Turkish Market	**84** E3

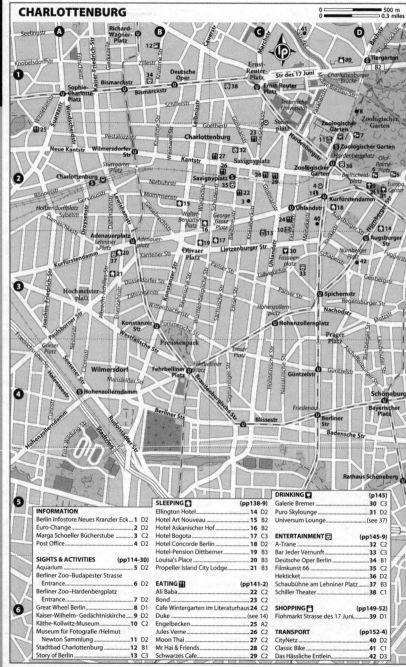

PRENZLAUER BERG

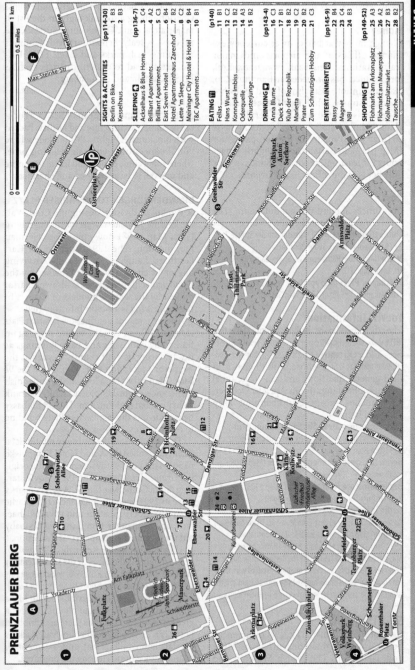

0   0.5 miles

0   1 km

SIGHTS & ACTIVITIES	(pp114–30)
Berlin on Bike	1 B3
Kesselhaus	2 B3

SLEEPING	(pp136–7)
Ackselhaus & Blue Home	3 C4
Brilliant Apartments	4 A2
Brilliant Apartments	5 C3
East Seven Hostel	6 B4
Hotel Apartmenthaus Zarenhof	7 B2
Lette 'm Sleep	8 C2
Meininger City Hostel & Hotel	9 B4
T&C Apartments	10 B1

EATING	(p140)
Fellas	11 B1
Hans Wurst	12 C2
Konnopke Imbiss	13 B2
Oderquelle	14 A3
Schusterjunge	15 B2

DRINKING	(pp143–4)
Anna Blume	16 C3
Deck 5	17 B1
Klub der Republik	18 B2
Marietta	19 C2
Prater	20 B2
Zum Schmutzigen Hobby	21 C3

ENTERTAINMENT	(pp145–9)
Bassy	22 B4
Magnet	23 C4
NBI	24 B3

SHOPPING	(pp149–52)
Flohmarkt am Arkonaplatz	25 A3
Flohmarkt am Mauerpark	26 A2
Kollwitzplatzmarkt	27 B3
Tausche	28 B2

(Continued from page 102)

Money

Change money at banks or at currency exchange offices at the airports and major train stations. **ReiseBank** (www.reisebank.de), for instance, has branches at Bahnhof Zoo, Hauptbahnhof, Ostbahnhof and Bahnhof Friedrichstrasse, while **Euro-Change** (www.euro-change.de) is located in Alexanderplatz and Hauptbahnhof stations, at Friedrichstrasse 80 (Map p108) and inside the Europa-Center (Map p112). ReiseBank keeps slightly longer hours (at least until 8pm); on Sundays your only bet is at the offices in the airports.

Post

Post offices abound throughout Berlin. The most convenient branches for visitors:
Charlottenburg (Map p112; Joachimsthaler Strasse 7; 9am-8pm Mon-Fri, 10am-8pm Sat)
Mitte (Map p108; Rathausstrasse 5; 8am-7pm Mon-Fri, 8am-4pm Sat)
Potsdamer Platz (Map pp110-11; inside Potsdamer Platz Arkaden; 10am-10pm Mon-Sat)

Tourist Information

The city tourist board, **Berlin Tourismus Marketing** (BTM; www.visitberlin.de) operates four walk-in offices and a **call centre** (250 025; 8am-7pm Mon-Fri, 9am-6pm Sat & Sun) whose multilingual staff field general questions and can make hotel and ticket bookings. From April to October, all branches except Hauptbahnhof keep extended hours.
Berlin Infostore Alexa Shopping Center (Map p108; ground fl, Grunerstrasse 20, near Alexanderplatz; 10am-8pm Mon-Sat)
Berlin Infostore Brandenburger Tor (Map p108; south wing; 10am-6pm)
Berlin Infostore Hauptbahnhof (Map p108; ground fl, enter from Europaplatz; 8am-10pm)
Berlin Infostore Neues Kranzler Eck (Map p112; Kurfürstendamm 21; 10am-8pm Mon-Sat, 10am-6pm Sun)
Euraide (Map p108; www.euraide.de; Hauptbahnhof; 10am-7pm daily May-Aug, 11am-6pm Mon-Fri Sep-Apr, closed 23 Dec-15 Feb) Inside the Reisezentrum on the lower level (B1), this independent office is staffed with fluent English speakers eager to assist you with all train-related issues (rail passes, tickets) and other travel-related topics.

SIGHTS

Each of Berlin's districts has its own appeal, but must-see sights concentrate in Mitte and Tiergarten. The Jewish Museum and Checkpoint Charlie in Kreuzberg, and Schloss Charlottenburg also rank high on the list of major attractions. Of the outer districts, the prettiest is leafy Zehlendorf with fabulous museums, lush parks and lakes. For GDR-era relics, head to eastern districts such as Friedrichshain and Lichtenberg.

Mitte

Mitte is the glamorous heart of Berlin, a cocktail of culture, architecture and history. Packed with blockbuster sights, this is likely where you'll concentrate your sightseeing time, where you'll come to play and learn, to admire and marvel, to be astounded and charmed.

BRANDENBURGER TOR & PARISER PLATZ

A symbol of division during the Cold War, the landmark **Brandenburger Tor** (Brandenburg Gate; Map p108) now epitomises German reunification. The 1791 structure by Carl Gotthard Langhans is the only surviving one of 18 city gates and is crowned by the *Quadriga* sculpture, a horse-drawn chariot piloted by the winged goddess of victory. In the south wing is a Berlin Infostore (left).

The gate stands sentinel over **Pariser Platz** (Map p108), an elegant square once again framed by embassies and bank buildings as it was during its 19th-century heyday as the 'emperor's reception hall'. Pop inside the **DZ Bank** (Map p108) for a look at the outlandish conference room US-based architect Frank Gehry created in the atrium. The US Embassy next door was the last Pariser Platz building to open, in July 2008.

The first one was the faithfully rebuilt **Hotel Adlon** (now called the Adlon Hotel Kempinski, p136). This posh caravanserai was the original *Grand Hotel*, where the 1932 movie starring Greta Garbo was filmed. A celeb magnet since its 1907 opening, it has sheltered Charlie Chaplin, Albert Einstein and even Michael Jackson. Remember him dangling his baby out the window? It happened at the Adlon.

US president John F Kennedy of '*Ich bin ein Berliner*' fame is the focus of the small **Kennedy Museum** (Map p108; 2065 3570; www.thekennedys.de; Pariser Platz 4a; adult/concession €7/3.50; 10am-6pm), an intimate, nonpolitical exhibit set up like a walk-through family photo album. Besides a great array of photographs there are scribbled notes, JFK's crocodile-leather briefcase, Jackie's Persian lamb pillbox hat and a *Superman* comic-book edition starring the president.

BERLIN IN...

One Day

Get up early to beat the crowds to the dome of the **Reichstag** (p120), then snap a picture of the **Brandenburger Tor** (opposite) before exploring the maze of the **Holocaust Memorial** (below). From there you're off on a classic saunter along **Unter den Linden** (below) with a detour to **Gendarmenmarkt** (p116) and the glamorous **Friedrichstadtpassagen** (p131). After lunch, take a peek inside the **Berliner Dom** (p117) before being awed by Nefertiti at the **Neues Museum** (p117) and the Pergamon Altar at the **Pergamonmuseum** (p116). Finish up at the **Scheunenviertel** (p119) where you should have no trouble sourcing good spots for dinner, drinks and dancing.

Two Days

Follow the one-day itinerary, then revisit Cold War history at **Checkpoint Charlie** (p124) and the nearby **Haus am Checkpoint Charlie** (p125). Spend the rest of the morning at the amazing **Jüdisches Museum** (p124) before heading off to Berlin's showcase of urban renewal, the **Potsdamer Platz** (p122). Make a stop here at the **Museum für Film und Fernsehen** (p122) or walk a few steps west to the **Kulturforum** (p122) and the superb **Gemäldegalerie** (p123). At night, sample the cuisine and bar scene of **Prenzlauer Berg** (p140 and p143).

Three Days

Follow the two-day itinerary, then devote the morning of day three to **Schloss Charlottenburg** (p126) where you shouldn't miss the Neuer Flügel (New Wing) or a spin around the Schlossgarten (palace park). Spend the afternoon stocking up on souvenirs along the Kurfürstendamm and in the **KaDeWe** (p149), then have an early dinner before catching the latest show at the **Bar Jeder Vernunft** (p148), followed by a nightcap at **Galerie Bremer** (p145).

HOLOCAUST MEMORIAL

The football-field-sized **Memorial to the Murdered European Jews** (Map p108; colloquially known as the Holocaust Memorial) by American architect Peter Eisenman consists of 2711 sarcophagi-like concrete columns rising in sombre silence from undulating ground. You're free to access this maze at any point and make your individual journey through it. For context visit the subterranean **Ort der Information** (information centre; Map p108; ☎ 7407 2929; www.holocaust-mahnmal.de; Cora-Berliner-Strasse 1; admission free, audioguide adult/concession €3/1.50; ☯ 10am-8pm Tue-Sun Apr-Sep, to 7pm Oct-Mar, last admission 45min before closing), whose exhibits will leave no one untouched.

HITLER'S BUNKER

Berlin was burning and Soviet tanks advancing relentlessly when Adolf Hitler, holed up in his bunker (Map p108), put a gun to his head in the final days of WWII. Today, there's just a parking lot on the site along with an information panel (in German and English) with a diagram of the vast bunker network, technical data on how it was constructed and what happened to it after WWII.

UNTER DEN LINDEN

Berlin's most splendid boulevard (Map p108) extends for about 1.5km east of the Brandenburger Tor with grand old buildings lining up like soldiers for inspection. First up, though, is the historical ribbon's newest tourist attraction, **Madame Tussauds** (Map p108; ☎ 4000 4600; www.madametussauds.com/berlin; Unter den Linden 74; adult/child 3-14yr €18.50/13.50; ☯ 10am-7pm, last admission 6pm). Sure, it's an overpriced haven of kitsch and camp, but where else can you cuddle up with Robbie Williams or hug Barack Obama?

High-brow types will likely prefer to steer straight towards the **Deutsche Guggenheim** (Map p108; ☎ 202 0930; www.deutsche-guggenheim.de; Unter den Linden 13-15; adult/concession/family €4/3/8, Mon free; ☯ 10am-8pm Fri-Wed, 10am-10pm Thu), a small, minimalist gallery spotlighting top-notch contemporary artists, such as Eduardo Chillida and Gerhard Richter.

Opposite, the **Alte Staatsbibliothek** (Old State Library; Map p108; Unter den Linden 8) counts the original sheet music of Beethoven's 9th Symphony among its treasures. Next up is the **Humboldt Universität** (Map p108), Berlin's oldest university where Marx and Engels studied and the Brothers Grimm and Albert Einstein taught.

It occupies the palace of Prince Heinrich, brother of King Frederick the Great, whose pompous **equestrian statue** stands on Unter den Linden outside the university.

It was Frederick who created the ensemble of stately structures framing **Bebelplatz** (Map p108), the site of the first big official Nazi book-burning in May 1933. Beneath a glass pane at the square's centre Micha Ullmann's *Empty Library* commemorates the barbaric event. Surrounding the square are the baroque **Alte Königliche Bibliothek** (Old Royal Library; Map p108; 1780), now part of the university; the **Staatsoper Unter den Linden** (State Opera; 1743, p147); and the copper-domed **St Hedwigskirche** (Map p108; 1783).

Just east of here, the perkily turreted **Friedrichswerdersche Kirche** (☎ 2090 5577; Werderscher Markt; admission free; 🕑 10am-6pm) is now a museum of 19th-century German sculptures with works by all of the period's heavyweights. Schinkel groupies should report upstairs to the exhibit on the man's life and accomplishments.

For more Schinkel, return to Unter den Linden and the neoclassical **Neue Wache** (Map p108; admission free; 🕑 10am-6pm). Originally a Prussian guardhouse, it's now an antiwar memorial whose austere interior is dominated by Käthe Kollwitz's emotional sculpture *Mother and her Dead Son*.

If you're wondering what the Germans have been up to for the past 2000 years, pop next door into the excellent **Deutsches Historisches Museum** (German Historical Museum; Map p108; ☎ 203 040; www.dhm.de; Unter den Linden 2; adult/under 18yr €5/free; 🕑 10am-6pm). A startling highlight is the big globe that originally stood in the Nazi Foreign Office with bullet holes where Germany should be. In the courtyard, Andreas Schlüter's baroque mask sculptures of dying soldiers make a strong case against war. High-calibre temporary exhibits take up a strikingly geometrical annexe, called **IM Pei Bau**, named for the architect that designed it.

GENDARMENMARKT

Berlin's most graceful square was once a thriving market place and derives its name from the Gens d'Armes, a Prussian regiment recruited from French Huguenot immigrants. Local Huguenots worshipped at the **Französischer Dom** (French Dome), where the small **Hugenottenmuseum** (Map p108; ☎ 229 1760; adult/concession/family €2/1/3.50; 🕑 noon-5pm Tue-Sat, 11am-5pm Sun) now chronicles their story. The elegant structure is a spitting image of the **Deutscher Dom** (German Dome, Map p108) opposite, home to a hopelessly academic exhibit on German democracy. Completing the trio is Schinkel's beautiful **Konzerthaus Berlin** (p147). Plenty of luxury hotels and fancy restaurants are nearby, as is the sleek new **Emil Nolde Museum** (Map p108; ☎ 4000 4690; www.nolde-stiftung.de; Jägerstrasse 55; adult/concession incl audioguide €10/5; 🕑 10am-7pm), which presents a rotating selection of works by this key German expressionist in a brightly converted 19th-century bank building.

MUSEUMSINSEL

East of the Deutsches Historisches Museum, the sculpture-studded **Schlossbrücke** (Palace Bridge; Map p108) leads to the little Spree island where Berlin's settlement began in the 13th century. Its northern half, Museumsinsel (Museum Island), is a fabulous treasure trove of art, sculptures and objects spread across five museums. A Unesco World Heritage Site since 1999, the complex is undergoing a major update masterminded by British architect David Chipperfield. It will link four of the five museums by a subterranean walkway and add a colonnaded modern central entrance. For a preview, visit www.museumsinsel-berlin.de.

Separate tickets are available for each museum or you can buy a day pass (valid at all except the Neues Museum) for €12 (concession €6). Admission is free if you're under 16 and for everyone during the last four hours on Thursday.

Alte Nationalgalerie

A Greek-temple building by August Stüler is an elegant backdrop for the exquisite collection of 19th-century European art at the **Alte Nationalgalerie** (Old National Gallery; Map p108; ☎ 2090 5577; Bodestrasse 1-3; adult/concession €8/4; 🕑 10am-6pm Tue, Wed & Fri-Sun, 10am-10pm Thu). Drawcards include Caspar David Friedrich's mystical landscapes, sensitive portraits by Max Liebermann and the light-hearted canvasses of Monet and Renoir.

Pergamonmuseum

An Aladdin's cave of treasures from ancient worlds, the **Pergamonmuseum** (Map p108; ☎ 2090 5555; Am Kupfergraben; adult/concession incl audioguide €12/6; 🕑 10am-6pm Fri-Wed, 10am-10pm Thu) is the one museum in Berlin that should not be missed. A feast of classical Greek, Babylonian, Roman, Islamic and Middle Eastern art and architecture, it will amaze and enlighten you. The Pergamon unites three major collections, each with its own signature sights, which are described on the excellent audioguide. Note that some sections may be closed while the museum is undergoing renovation over the next five years.

The undisputed highlight of the Collection of Classical Antiquities is, of course, the museum's namesake, the **Pergamon Altar** (165 BC) from today's Turkey. It's a gargantuan raised marble shrine surrounded by a vivid frieze of the gods doing battle with the giants. The next room is dominated by the immense **Market Gate of Miletus** (2nd century AD), a masterpiece of Roman architecture. Pass through it and enter another culture and century: Babylon during the reign of King Nebuchadnezzar II (604–562 BC). You're now in the Museum of Near Eastern Antiquities where top billing goes to the radiantly blue and ochre **Ishtar Gate**. The strutting lions, horses, and dragons are so striking that you can almost hear the roaring and fanfare.

Upstairs, in the Museum of Islamic Art, standouts include the fortress-like 8th-century **caliph's palace** from Mshatta in today's Jordan, and the **Aleppo Room** from 17th-century Syria with its richly painted, wood-panelled walls.

Altes Museum
Karl Friedrich Schinkel pulled out all the stops for the 1830 **Altes Museum** (Map p108; ☎ 2090 5577; Am Lustgarten; adult/concession €8/4; ☒ 10am-6pm Fri-Wed, 10am-10pm Thu). An architectural highlight is the Pantheon-inspired rotunda, which displays a prized collection of Greek and Roman art and sculpture. As part of the Museumsinsel update, it is scheduled for restoration and may be fully or partly closed in the coming years.

Bodemuseum
On the northern tip of Museumsinsel, this mighty **museum** (Map p108; ☎ 2090 5577; Monbijoubrücke; adult/concession €8/4; ☒ 10am-6pm Fri-Wed, 10am-10pm Thu), in a neobaroque edifice by Ernst von Ihne, houses Byzantine art, a coin collection, old paintings and, most importantly, European sculpture from the Middle Ages to the 18th century. Look out for masterpieces by Tilmann Riemenschneider, Donatello, Giovanni Pisano and Ignaz Günther.

Neues Museum
After 10 years and €200 million, the reconstructed **Neues Museum** (New Museum; Map p108; ☎ 2090 5555; www.smb.spk-berlin.de; adult/concession €10/5; ☒ 10am-6pm Sun-Wed, 10am-8pm Thu-Sat) finally opened in October 2009. David Chipperfield harmoniously incorporated remnants of the war-damaged structure into the new building, which presents the Egyptian Museum (including the famous bust of Queen Nefertiti) and the Papyrus Collection. Eventually, these will be joined by the Museum of Pre- and Early History and works from the Collection of Classical Antiquities.

Berliner Dom
Pompous yet majestic, the 1905 neo-Renaissance **Berliner Dom** (Berlin Cathedral; Map p108; ☎ 2026 9136; Am Lustgarten; adult/concession/under 14yr without audioguide €5/3/free, with audioguide €8/6/free; ☒ 9am-8pm Mon-Sat, noon-8pm Sun Apr-Sep, to 7pm Oct-Mar) was once the royal court church and now does triple duty as house of worship, museum and concert hall. Take a spin around the sombre crypt where dozens of royals are buried in elaborate tombs, then climb up to the outside viewing gallery for glorious city views. The 7269-pipe Sauer organ and the elaborate sarcophagi made for the Great Elector and King Friedrich I and their wives are top draws in the main church hall.

ALEXANDERPLATZ & AROUND
Eastern Berlin's main commercial hub, Alexanderplatz (Map p108) – 'Alex' for short – was named in honour of Tsar Alexander I on his 1805 visit to Berlin. Today it's light years away from the low-life district Alfred Döblin called 'the quivering heart of a cosmopolitan city' in his 1929 novel *Berlin Alexanderplatz*.

Despite post-reunification attempts to temper the socialist look created during the 1960s, Alexanderplatz remains an oddly cluttered, soulless square that's all concrete with no trees. It's littered with stores, a hotel, a fountain, a monument and a huge railway station, and sliced up by roads and tram tracks. Sitting a bit off to the side is the mega-mall Alexa (p149).

The main sight around here is the **Fernsehturm** (TV Tower; Map p108; ☎ 242 3333; adult/child under 16yr €10/5.50, VIP ticket €19.50; ☒ 9am-midnight Mar-Oct, 10am-midnight Nov-Feb), at 368m the tallest

BERLIN

PRUSSIAN POMP, 21 CENTURY STYLE

Nothing of today's Schlossplatz (Map p108) evokes memory of the grand palace where the Prussian rulers made their home for 500 years. Despite international protests, the GDR government razed the barely war-damaged structure in 1951 and replaced it with a modern multi-purpose hall called **Palast der Republik** (Palace of the Republic; Map p108). This was where the GDR parliament hammered out policy and common folk came to hear Harry Belafonte or party on New Year's Eve.

After the fall of the Wall, the Palast closed instantly because of asbestos contamination. Years of debate resulted in the demolition of the behemoth and the plan to build an exact replica of the Prussian palace shell, but with a modern interior. To be called Humboldt Forum, it will shelter art and artefacts from Africa, Asia, Oceania and the Americas that are currently on display at the Museen Dahlem (p129), as well as a library and research facility. For a preview, drop by the **Berliner Schloss Infocenter** (Map p108; ☎ 2067 3093; www.berliner-schloss.de; Hausvogteiplatz 3; admission free; ☺ 9.30am-6pm).

In the meantime, the empty lot is occupied by a big lawn and the **Temporäre Kunsthalle** (Temporary Art Hall; Map p108; ☎ 2045 3650; www.kunsthalle-berlin.com; Schlossplatz; admission varies; ☺ 11am-6pm Sun-Fri, 11am-9pm Sat), which showcases statement-making pieces by international artists living in Berlin.

structure in Germany. Come early (or buy a VIP ticket and skip the line) to beat the queue for the lift to the panorama level at 203m, where views are unbeatable on clear days. Pinpoint city landmarks from here or the upstairs cafe, which makes one revolution in 30 minutes. In sunlight, the steel sphere below the antenna produces the reflection of a giant cross – a source of embarrassment for the secular-minded GDR honchos who built the tower in 1969. West Berliners gleefully dubbed the phenomenon 'the Pope's revenge'.

To find some open space, wander west of the TV Tower and linger among the flower beds and fountains next to the 13th-century **Marienkirche** (Church of St Mary; Map p108; ☎ 242 4467; Karl-Liebknecht-Strasse 8; admission free; ☺ 10am-9pm Apr-Oct, 10am-6pm Nov-Mar), Berlin's second-oldest church. The brick gem is entered via a vestibule spookily decorated with a (badly faded) Dance of Death fresco. Outside, the epic **Neptunbrunnen** (Neptune Fountain; Map p108), created in 1891 by Reinhold Begas is decorated with buxom beauties representing major rivers.

Across Karl-Liebknecht-Strasse, **SeaLife Berlin** (Map p108; ☎ 992 800; Spandauer Strasse 3; adult/concession €17/12; ☺ 10am-7pm, last admission 6pm) is a pricey but entertaining aquarium that follows the Spree River into the North Atlantic. Visits conclude with a glacial lift ride through the AquaDom, a 16m-tall cylindrical tropical fish tank. Catch a free preview from the lobby of the Radisson Blu Hotel.

Below the hotel, the **DDR Museum** (GDR Museum; Map p108; ☎ 847 123 731; Karl-Liebknecht-Strasse 1; adult/concession €5.50/3.50; ☺ 10am-8pm Sun-Fri, 10am-10pm Sat) teaches the rest of us about daily life behind the Iron Curtain. You'll learn that East German kids were put through collective potty training, engineers earned little more than farmers and everyone, it seems, went on nudist holidays. A must for *Good Bye, Lenin!* fans. The entrance is on the Spree bank, opposite the Berliner Dom.

The hulking red building back south across the street is the 1860 **Rotes Rathaus** (Red Town Hall; Map p108; Rathausstrasse 15; closed to the public), the office of Berlin's mayor. The moniker 'red', by the way, was inspired by the colour of its bricks and not (necessarily) the political leanings of its occupants.

The town hall sits on the edge of the twee **Nikolaiviertel** (Nicholas Quarter; Map p108), which is where the GDR regime recreated the city's medieval birthplace in celebration of Berlin's 750th anniversary in 1987. There are only a few original historic buildings, most notably the 1230 **Nikolaikirche** (Map p108; closed for renovation), Berlin's oldest church. All in all, the maze of cobbled lanes is worth a quick stroll, but you won't find too many Berliners patronising the pricey cafes, restaurants and cutesy shops.

It's a bit of a musty, old-fashioned jumble, but the **Märkisches Museum** (March of Brandenburg Museum; Map p108; ☎ 3086 6215; Am Köllnischen Park 5; adult/concession €5/3; ☺ 10am-6pm Tue & Thu-Sun, noon-8pm

Wed) still gives you a grasp on how the tiny trading village of Berlin-Cölln evolved into today's metropolis. A good time to visit is on Sunday afternoons at 3pm when the quirky automatophones (mechanical musical instruments) are launched on their cacophonous journey (separate admission, adult/concession €2/1).

SCHEUNENVIERTEL

It's hard to imagine that, until reunification, the dapper Scheunenviertel (literally 'Barn Quarter') was a neglected, down-at-heel barrio with tumbledown buildings and dirty streets. Fanning out northwest of Alexanderplatz, it's since catapulted from drab to fab and teems with restaurants, bars, clubs, cabarets, concept stores, owner-run boutiques and even a fair amount of resident celebrities. Though fairly quiet in the daytime, it comes to life after dark, especially along the Oranienburger Strasse, the main drag where you may well be sharing the pavement with long-legged sex workers and rowdy 20-somethings on an organised pub crawl.

The Scheunenviertel has also reprised its legacy as a centre of Jewish life with the gleaming gold dome of the **Neue Synagoge** (New Synagogue; Map p108; ☎ 8802 8300; www .cjudaicum.de; Oranienburger Strasse 28-30; adult/concession €3/2; ☑ 10am-8pm Sun & Mon, 10am-6pm Tue-Thu, 10am-5pm Fri Apr-Sep, reduced hr Oct-Mar) being its most striking landmark. Built in Moorish-Byzantine style, the 1866 original seated 3200 and was Germany's largest synagogue. During the 1938 Kristallnacht pogroms, a local police chief prevented Nazi thugs from setting it on fire, an act of courage commemorated by a plaque. It was eventually desecrated anyway but not destroyed until hit by bombs in 1943.

Rebuilt in the 1990s, today's version is not so much a house of worship but a museum and cultural centre called **Centrum Judaicum**. Inside are displays on the building's history and architecture and the lives of the people who worshipped here. The dome can be climbed. From the top you can easily spot a crumbling building that, upon closer inspection, looks like the 'Sistine Chapel of Graffiti'. It's the **Kunsthaus Tacheles** (Map p108; ☎ 282 6185; Oranienburger Strasse 54-56; admission free), a one-time department store turned artists' squat after reunification and now a beloved alternative art and culture space. It may look scary, but don't let that stop you from poking around

the studios, galleries and backyard or to cool your heels in the cafe or beer garden.

The Scheunenviertel's most charismatic side reveals itself in the village-like labyrinth of lanes off Oranienburger Strasse. Embark on an aimless wander and you'll find surprises lurking around every corner: here an intriguing public sculpture, there a cosy watering hole, a 19th-century ballroom or a bleeding-edge gallery such as **Kunst-Werke Berlin** (Map p108; ☎ 243 4590; Auguststrasse 69; adult/concession €6/4; ☑ noon-7pm Tue, Wed & Fri-Sun, to 9pm Thu). A particularly enchanting feature of the Scheunenviertel is the quarter's Höfe, interlinked hidden courtyards filled with cafes, boutiques and party venues. The best known is the **Hackesche Höfe** (Map p108) but also check out the quiet and dignified **Sophie-Gips-Höfe** (Map p108) and the breezy **Heckmannhöfe** (Map p108).

The quarter's Jewish heritage is never far away either. Everywhere you look you'll see small brass **paving stones** commemorating Nazi victims (see boxed text, p120). The great Enlightenment philosopher Moses Mendelssohn was among the 12,000 people buried on **Alter Jüdischer Friedhof** (Map p108); the city's oldest Jewish cemetery on Grosse Hamburger Strasse. Next to the Hackesche Höfe, the small **Museum Blindenwerkstatt Otto Weidt** (Map p108; ☎ 2859 9407; Rosenthaler Strasse 39; admission free; ☑ 10am-8pm) documents how broom and brush maker Otto Weidt saved many of his blind and deaf Jewish workers from the Nazis. And in the same building, the **Anne Frank Zentrum** (Map p108; ☎ 288 865 610; Rosenthaler Strasse 39; adult/concession/family €4/2.50/8; ☑ 10am-6pm Tue-Sun) uses artefacts and photographs to tell the extraordinary story of the famous German-Jewish girl. Museum staff also rents an 'i-guide' tour through the Jewish quarter (€5).

BERLIN

STUMBLING UPON HISTORY

Look down and you'll see them everywhere, but especially in the Scheunenviertel: small brass paving stones engraved with names and placed in front of house entrances. Part of a nationwide project initiated by Berlin-born artist Gunter Demnig, these so-called *Stolpersteine* (stumbling blocks) are essentially mini-memorials to the people (usually Jews) who lived in the building in front of which they're placed before being killed by the Nazis. Berlin's Jewish community suffered tremendously during the Third Reich. In 1933 there were 160,000 Jews living in Berlin; by 1945, 55,000 had been murdered, 100,000 had emigrated and only 5000 remained. Today, about 13,000 Jews live in town, most of them fairly recent arrivals from Russian republics.

ORANIENBURGER TOR AREA

Berlin's traditional theatre district stretches along Friedrichstrasse, south of Oranienburger Tor (Map p108). Major venues include the flashy Friedrichstadtpalast (p148), the eccentric Admiralspalast (p148) and the Berliner Ensemble (p149), founded by Bertolt Brecht in the 1950s.

In fact Brecht, one of Germany's seminal 20th-century playwrights, lived just up the street in what is now the memorial **Brecht-Weigel Gedenkstätte** (Map p108; ☎ 200 571 844; Chausseestrasse 125; tours adult/concession €3/1.50; ☺ tours half-hourly 10-11.30am Tue-Fri, 5-6.30pm Thu, 10am-3.30pm Sat, hourly 11am-6pm Sun). Tours take you into Brecht's office, library and the bedroom where he died in 1956. Downstairs are the cluttered quarters of his actress wife Helene Weigel who lived here until her death in 1971. Call ahead about English-language tours.

The couple is buried in the adjacent **Dorotheenstädtischer Friedhof** (Map p108; Chausseestrasse 126; ☺ 8am-dusk, 8pm latest), the cemetery with the greatest concentration of celebrity corpses in Berlin. Architect Friedrich Schinkel, writer Heinrich Mann and former German president Johannes Rau are among the famous 6ft-under residents.

North of here, you can meet dinosaurs and travel back to the beginning of time at the beautiful **Museum für Naturkunde** (Natural History Museum; Map p108; ☎ 2093 8591; Invalidenstrasse 43; adult/concession/family €3.50/2/7; ☺ 9.30am-5pm Tue-Fri, 10am-6pm Sat & Sun). Star of the show is the world's largest mounted lizard, a 23m-long and 12m-high Brachiosaurus, who's joined by a dozen other Jurassic buddies and an ultra-rare archaeopteryx. Other halls demystify the Big Bang or answer such age-old questions as why zebras are striped.

REICHSTAG & GOVERNMENT QUARTER

Germany's federal government quarter snuggles into the Spreebogen, a horseshoe-shaped bend of the Spree River. A leisurely stroll along the **river promenade** takes you past beer gardens and beach bars and allows for interesting perspectives.

The quarter's historical anchor is the 1894 **Reichstag** (Map p108; Platz der Republik 1), where the German parliament, the Bundestag, has been hammering out its policies since 1999. This followed a total makeover by Lord Norman Foster who preserved only the building's historical shell while adding the striking glass dome. It's well worth queuing for the **lift ride** (admission free; ☺ 8am-midnight, last entry 10pm) to the top to take in the knock-out panorama and close-ups of the dome and the mirror-clad funnel at its centre. Queues are shortest early morning and at night. You can skip 'em altogether if you're disabled, happen to have a kid in a stroller, are on an organised tour or have reservations for the pricey restaurant on top. In these cases, proceed straight to the left entrance.

The Reichstag has been the setting of numerous milestones in German history. After WWI, Philipp Scheidemann proclaimed the German Republic from one of its windows. The Reichstag fire on the night of 27 February 1933 allowed Hitler to blame the communists and seize power. A dozen years later, the victorious Soviets nearly obliterated the building. Restoration – without the dome – wasn't finished until 1972. At midnight on 2 October 1990 the reunification of Germany was enacted here. In summer 1995, the artist Christo and his wife, Jeanne-Claude, wrapped the edifice in fabric for two weeks. Lord Norman set to work shortly thereafter.

In the 1990s, several other government buildings sprouted around the Reichstag, most notably the **Bundeskanzleramt** (Federal Chancellery; Map p108; Willy-Brandt-Strasse 1), an unusual H-shaped compound where Germany's chancellor keeps their office.

HIDDEN BERLIN: MY FAVOURITE SITES

Henrik Tidefjärd, creator of the Gastro-Rallye (p134) and owner of **Berlinagenten** (www.berlinagenten .de), which specialises in customised lifestyle tours, reveals his favourite spots in his adopted home town:

Berlin is a truly electric city full of creative people, crazy parties and historical spots. It's magnetic, alluring and filled with individual discoveries. I'm a true traveller and I think no other city has such a diversity of people, cultural life and environments. It's hard to believe it all exists in one single city. Ah Berlin, you are my inspiration in life!

- I love to eat in either hidden dining locations or in boho-trendy restaurants. **Tartane** (p140) and its show kitchen are a bit of both and fulfil most of my expectations. The quirky dining section upstairs reminds me of the elevator scene in *Being John Malkovich*…

- I like to shake my booty at **Tape Club** (p146), a club in the new emerging industrial area of Berlin. If I'm in the mood for a more thrilling and crazy night out, I head for legendary hot spot **Berghain/Panorama Bar** (p146). The doorman will tell you if you fit in…

- **Schlesische Strasse** (Map pp110–11) is another tip for rather new experiences. Different kinds of alternative bars, beer gardens, clubs, shops à la Berliner Style attract a laid-back scene. I'm especially fond of the **Club der Visionäre** (p146) in the summer, because I can chill out on the river pontoons outdoors and soak up the real living culture.

- The medieval town of **Werder** (Map p103), 45 minutes away from Berlin by train, is my absolute favourite place for relaxing off the beaten track. Situated on an island in the river delta, this place is a true treasure for romantic walks along picturesque streets and for dining on fish in one of the restaurants along the quay.

From Moltkebrücke bridge or the northern river promenade you can best appreciate the circular openings that inspired the building's nickname 'washing machine'. Eduardo Chillida's rusted-steel *Berlin* sculpture graces the forecourt.

The eccentric building with a gravity-defying parabolic roof west of the chancellery is the **Haus der Kulturen der Welt** (House of World Cultures; Map p108; ☎ 397 870; John-Foster-Dulles-Allee 10; admission varies; ⏲ 10am-9pm Tue-Sun). Originally a congress hall, it's now a cultural space with dance performances, readings, films, exhibits and theatre from Latin America, Asia and Africa. Chime concerts ring out at noon and 6pm daily from the nearby 68-bell carillon.

North of the Spree looms the spaceship-like **Hauptbahnhof** (main train station; Map p108), which looks most impressive at night. East of here, a defunct 19th-century train station has been reborn as Berlin's hotbed of contemporary art. Called the **Hamburger Bahnhof** (Map p108; ☎ 3978 3439; Invalidenstrasse 50-51; adult/concession/ under 16yr €8/4/free, last 4hr Thu free; ⏲ 10am-6pm Tue-Fri, 11am-8pm Sat, 11am-6pm Sun), it displays career-spanning bodies of work by Andy Warhol, Roy Lichtenstein, Anselm Kiefer, Joseph Beuys and other 20th-century heavyweights. Also check out the galleries in the Halle am Ufer (Map p108) behind the museum.

Potsdamer Platz & Tiergarten

Potsdamer Platz is Berlin's newest quarter, built on terrain once bifurcated by the Berlin Wall. It became a showcase of urban renewal in the late 1990s, drawing some of the world's finest architects, including Renzo Piano, Richard Rodgers and Helmut Jahn. Today's Potsdamer Platz is a modern reinterpretation of the historic original, which was the equivalent of New York's Times Square until WWII sucked all life out of the area.

A visit to Potsdamer Platz is easily combined with the Kulturforum, a cluster of museums and concert halls, including the famous Philharmonie. Black limousines are a common sight further west in the Diplomatenviertel (Diplomatic Quarter) whose streets are studded with some fine contemporary architecture. And if your head is spinning after all that cultural stimulus, the leafy paths of the glorious Tiergarten, one of the world's largest city parks, will likely prove to be a restorative antidote.

BERLIN

POTSDAMER PLATZ

Although critics complain about Potsdamer Platz' commercialisation and its relatively unspectacular architecture, Berliners and visitors have by and large embraced the new quarter. Up to 100,000 people barrel through its streets and squares daily, shopping at the Potsdamer Platz Arkaden (p149), challenging Lady Luck at the roulette tables or taking in a flick, for instance at the all-English Cinestar Original (p148).

For the best bird's-eye views in the city, take what is billed as Europe's fastest lift to the observation deck of the **Panoramapunkt** (Map pp110–11; ☎ 2529 4372; www.panoramapunkt.de; Potsdamer Platz 1; adult/concession €5/4; ☹ 11am-8pm). From this vantage point it's also easy to see that Potsdamer Platz 2.0 is divided into three slices: **DaimlerCity**, where you are right now, with the mall and lots of public art, the flashy **Sony Center** with its canopied central plaza that's illuminated at night; and the **Beisheim Center**, which was inspired by classic American skyscraper design.

Every February, glamour comes to town, when Brangelina, Madonna and Tomkat sashay down the red carpet to attend premieres at the Potsdamer Platz theatres during the Berlinale international film festival. Germany's film history, meanwhile, gets the star treatment year-round in the engaging **Museum für Film und Fernsehen** (Museum of Film & TV; Map pp110–11; ☎ 300 9030; Potsdamer Strasse 2; adult/concession/family €6/4.50/12; ☹ 10am-6pm Tue, Wed & Fri-Sun, to 8pm Thu) in the Sony Center. Make use of the excellent audioguide as you skip around galleries dedicated to pioneers such as Fritz Lang, ground-breaking movies such as *Olympia* by Leni Riefenstahl and legendary divas such as Marlene Dietrich. The TV exhibit is not nearly as engrossing, although if you ever wondered what *Star Trek* sounds like in German, this is your chance.

The elementary-school set will likely be more enthralled by the nearby **Legoland Discovery Centre** (Map pp110–11; ☎ 301 0400; Sony Center, Potsdamer Strasse; adult/child €14.50/11; ☹ 10am-6pm, last admission 5pm). It's a cute indoor amusement park with a 4-D cinema, a Lego 'factory', a Jungle Trail where Lego crocs lurk in the dark and a mini-Berlin with landmarks made entirely from those little plastic bricks.

Fans of 20th-century abstract, conceptual and minimalist art should pop into the **Daimler Contemporary** (Map pp110–11; ☎ 2594 1420;

Weinhaus Huth, Alte Potsdamer Strasse 5; admission free; ☹ 11am-6pm), a quiet, loft-style gallery space at the top of the only surviving historic structure on Potsdamer Platz. Ring the bell to be buzzed in.

TOPOGRAPHIE DES TERRORS & AROUND

A short walk south from Potsdamer Platz along Stresemannstrasse gets you to Niederkirchner Strasse. Here, next to a short stretch of Berlin Wall, once stood some of the most feared institutions of Nazi Germany, including the Gestapo headquarters and the SS central command. Since 1997, a harrowing open-air exhibit called **Topographie des Terrors** (Topography of Terror; Map pp110–11; ☎ 2548 6703) has documented the impact of these brutal organisations. In 2010, an expanded version is expected to open in a proper documentation centre constructed on the site.

Next to these sinister grounds, the Italian Renaissance-style **Martin-Gropius-Bau** (Map pp110–11; ☎ 254 860; Niederkirchner Strasse 7; admission varies; ☹ hrs vary) presents travelling shows of international stature. Across the street is the **Abgeordnetenhaus** (Map pp110–11), the seat of Berlin's state parliament.

KULTURFORUM

It's easy to spend a day or more mingling with masters old and modern in the five top-notch museums that make up this stellar cultural complex just west of Potsdamer Platz. Also incorporating Berlin's premier classical music venue, the Philharmonie, it was masterfully planned by Hans Scharoun in the 1960s. A ticket to any of the Kulturforum museums entitles you to same-day admission to the permanent collections of the other four. Admission is free the last four opening hours on Thursdays and to anyone under 16 at any time.

The first of the Kulturforum museums to be completed was the **Neue Nationalgalerie** (New National Gallery; Map pp110–11; ☎ 266 2651; Potsdamer Strasse 50; adult/concession €8/4; ☹ 10am-6pm Tue, Wed & Sun, 10am-10pm Thu, 10am-8pm Fri & Sat), an edgy glass temple by Ludwig Mies van der Rohe that shelters early-20th-century European paintings and sculpture. Expect all the usual suspects from Picasso to Dalí, plus an outstanding collection of German expressionists such as Georg Grosz and Ernst Ludwig Kirchner. Note that the permanent collection occasionally yields to visiting blockbuster shows.

Older masters grace the walls of the **Gemäldegalerie** (Picture Gallery; Map pp110-11; ☎ 266 2951; Matthäikirchplatz 8; adult/concession incl audioguide €8/4; ☉ 10am-6pm Tue, Wed & Fri-Sun, 10am-10pm Thu), a gallery of European art from the 13th to the 18th centuries that is famous for its exceptional quality and breadth. Take advantage of the audioguide to get the low-down on selected works by Rembrandt, Dürer, Hals, Vermeer and Gainsborough. And wear comfy shoes: a tour of all 72 rooms covers almost 2km.

Nearby, the cavernous **Kunstgewerbemuseum** (Museum of Decorative Arts; Map pp110-11; ☎ 266 2951; Tiergartenstrasse 6; adult/concession €8/4; ☉ 10am-6pm Tue-Fri, 11am-6pm Sat & Sun) brims with precious objects created through the ages from gold, silver, ivory, wood, porcelain and other fine materials. From medieval gem-encrusted crosses to art-deco ceramics and Philippe Starck furniture, it's all here.

Across the plaza, the **Kupferstichkabinett** (Museum of Prints & Drawings; Map pp110-11; ☎ 266 2951; Matthäikirchplatz; adult/concession €8/4; ☉ 10am-6pm Tue-Fri, 11am-6pm Sat & Sun) has one of the world's largest and finest collections of art on paper, including exceptional works by Dürer, Rembrandt, Picasso and other top practitioners.

The honey-coloured building east of here is Scharoun's famous **Berliner Philharmonie** (Map pp110-11). Its auditorium feels like the inside of a finely crafted instrument and boasts supreme acoustics and excellent sightlines thanks to a clever terraced vineyard design. Scharoun also provided the blueprint for the adjacent 1987 **Kammermusiksaal** (Chamber Music Hall; Map pp110-11), the 1978 **Neue Staatsbibliothek** (New National Library; Map pp110-11; ☎ 2660; Potsdamer Strasse 33; ☉ 9am-9pm Mon-Fri, 9am-7pm Sat) across Potsdamer Strasse, and the **Musikinstrumenten-Museum** (Musical Instruments Museum; Map pp110-11; ☎ 2548 1178; Tiergartenstrasse 1; adult/concession incl audioguide €4/2; ☉ 9am-5pm Tue, Wed & Fri, 9am-10pm Thu, 10am-5pm Sat & Sun). The last can be fun even if the only instrument you play is the triangle. Look for a glass harmonica invented by Ben Franklin, a flute played by Frederick the Great, and Johann Sebastian Bach's cembalo. The Mighty Wurlitzer organ is cranked up at noon on Saturdays.

TIERGARTEN PARK

Berlin's rulers used to hunt boar and pheasants in the rambling Tiergarten until Peter Lenné got to landscape the grounds in the 18th century. Today, Berlin's more charming equivalent of New York's Central Park is a popular place for strolling, jogging, picnicking, Frisbee tossing, grill parties and, yes, gay cruising (especially around the Löwenbrücke). Walking across the entire park takes about an hour, but even a shorter stroll has its rewards. The most idyllic spots include the **Rousseauinsel** (Map p108), a memorial to the 18th-century French philosopher, and the flowery **Luiseninsel** (Map p108). The largest lake is the **Neuer See** (Map pp106–7) where you can rent boats to take your sweetie for a spin or quaff a cold one in the Café am Neuen See (p144).

Tiergarten is bisected east–west by Strasse des 17 Juni, home to a Soviet WWII memorial and the Flohmarkt Strasse des 17 Juni (p151). Big festivals and the annual Christopher Street Day parade (p134) are staged along here, usually culminating at the landmark **Siegessäule** (Victory Column; Map p108; ☎ 391 2961; adult/concession €2.20/1.50; ☉ 9.30am-6.30pm Mon-Fri, 9.30am-7pm Sat & Sun Apr-Oct, 10am-5pm Mon-Fri, 10am-5.30pm Sat & Sun Nov-Mar), a triumphal column envisioned as a monument to Prussian military exploits. The gilded lady on top represents the goddess of victory, but locals irreverently call her 'Gold-Else'. The so-so views from below her skirt take in mostly Tiergarten park.

North of the column, **Schloss Bellevue** (Map p108), a white neoclassical palace from 1785, is the official residence of the German president.

DIPLOMATENVIERTEL

South of Tiergarten park, the Diplomatic Quarter is home to several striking embassy buildings. Standouts include the **Nordic embassies** (Map p108; Rauchstrasse 1), with their cantilevered turquoise facades, the temple-like **Egyptian Embassy** (Map p108; Stauffenbergstrasse 6-7) and the **Austrian Embassy** (Map p108; Stauffenbergstrasse 1), a three-part symphony in copper and terracotta.

A few doors down from the last is the **Gedenkstätte Deutscher Widerstand** (Map p108; ☎ 2699 5000; Stauffenbergstrasse 13-14; admission free; ☉ 9am-6pm Mon-Wed & Fri, 9am-8pm Thu, 10am-6pm Sat & Sun) which deals with German Nazi resistance. Exhibits are in the very rooms where high-ranking officers led by Claus Graf von Stauffenberg plotted the ill-fated assassination attempt on Hitler on 20 July 1944. He and his co-conspirators were shot in the courtyard right after the failed coup. The 2008 movie

Valkyrie, starring Tom Cruise, is based on the story.

Architecture buffs, meanwhile, gravitate west along the canal where the **Bauhaus Archiv/ Museum für Gestaltung** (Bauhaus Archive/Museum of Design; Map pp106-7; ☎ 254 0020; Klingelhöferstrasse 14; adult/concession €6/3; ☥ 10am-5pm Wed-Mon) occupies an avant-garde building by Bauhaus school founder Walter Gropius. The study notes, workshop pieces, models, blueprints and other items by Klee, Kandinsky, Schlemmer and other Bauhaus practitioners underline the movement's enormous influence on all aspects of 20th-century architecture and design.

Kreuzberg

Kreuzberg gets its street cred from being delightfully edgy, wacky and, most of all, unpredictable. The western half around Bergmannstrasse and Mehringdamm is solidly in the hands of upmarket bohemians and also harbours the essential-viewing Jewish Museum. Eastern Kreuzberg (still called SO36, after its pre-reunification postal code), by contrast, is a multicultural, multigenerational mosaic with the most dynamic nightlife in town. Dönerias rub up against Brazilian cafes; headscarf-wearing mamas push prams past punks with metal-penetrated faces and black-haired Goths draped in floor-length leather coats chill next to bright-faced students at an outdoor cinema.

For the Schwules Museum (Gay Museum), see the boxed text on p150.

JÜDISCHES MUSEUM

For an eye-opening, emotional and interactive exploration of 2000 years of Jewish history in Germany visit the impressive **Jüdisches Museum** (Jewish Museum; Map pp110-11; ☎ 2599 3300; www.jmberlin .de; Lindenstrasse 9-14; adult/concession/family €5/2.50/10; ☥ 10am-10pm Mon, 10am-8pm Tue-Sun). You'll learn about Jewish cultural contributions, holiday traditions, the difficult road to Emancipation, and outstanding individuals, such as jeans inventor Levi Strauss and philosopher Moses Mendelssohn. Only one section deals directly with the Holocaust, but its horrors are poignantly reflected by Daniel Libeskind's powerful museum building. Essentially a 3-D metaphor for Jewish suffering, its silvery zinc walls are sharply angled, and instead of windows there are only small gashes piercing the building's gleaming skin. The visual allegory continues on the inside where a steep staircase descends to three intersecting walkways – called 'axes' – representing the fates of Jews during the Nazi years: death, exile and continuity. Only the last leads to the actual exhibit.

BERLINISCHE GALERIE

Discover what the Berlin art scene has been up to for, oh, the past century or so at the **Berlinische Galerie** (Map pp110-11; ☎ 7890 2600; Alte Jakobstrasse 124-128; adult/concession/under 18yr €6/3/free; ☥ 10am-6pm) in a converted glass warehouse near the Jewish Museum. It presents a fine overview of various genres – Secessionism, Dadaism and Fluxus art, expressionism, Nazi art and contemporary art – on two floors linked by a pair of intersecting floating stairways.

CHECKPOINT CHARLIE

Checkpoint Charlie (Map pp110–11) was the principal gateway for Allies, other non-Germans

---

KREUZKÖLLN: THE NEW FRONTIER OF HIPNESS

Once boxed in on three sides by the Berlin Wall, Kreuzberg used to be the western city's countercultural catch basin for students, punks, draft dodgers and squatters. No more. The fall of the Wall catapulted it from the city's edge to its centre, eventually entailing rising rents and tendrils of gentrification.

As a result, students, artists, creative types and others longing for cheap flats and the improvisational spirit of the past decades have of late been pushing the frontier further south, into the northern reaches of the bad-rap 'ghetto' of Neukölln. Christened 'Kreuzkölln', the area along Reuterstrasse, Hobrechtstrasse and Weserstrasse is the ever-burgeoning home of a funky anti-scene. With plenty of shoestring, trashy-cool bars, pubs, galleries, shops and cafes popping up all the time, Kreuzkölln is tailor-made for some intense DIY exploring. And you'll be in good company: Michael Elmgreen and Ingar Dragset, the creators of the Memorial for Homosexual Nazi Victims live here, as does Jutta Teschner, owner of the lingerie label Fishbelly, and Beat Gottwald, who manages the Berlin hip-hop band KIZ.

and diplomats between the two Berlins from 1961 to 1990. Unfortunately, this potent symbol of the Cold War has become a tacky tourist trap where uniformed actors pose with tourists (for tips) next to a replica guardhouse.

The Cold War years, especially the history and horror of the Berlin Wall, are haphazardly, but well-meaningly, chronicled in the private **Haus am Checkpoint Charlie** (Map pp110-11; ☎ 253 7250; www.mauermuseum.de; Friedrichstrasse 43-45; adult/concession €12.50/9.50; ⊙ 9am-10pm). The best bits are about ingenious escapes to the West through tunnels, in hot-air balloons, concealed compartments in cars and even a one-man submarine. You can get similar information for free from the temporary **open-air exhibit** set up along Friedrichstrasse, Zimmerstrasse and Schützenstrasse.

One block west along Zimmerstrasse, you can drift up but not away aboard the **Berlin Hi-Flyer** (Map pp110-11; ☎ 5321 5321; cnr Wilhelmstrasse & Zimmerstrasse; adult/concession €19/13; ⊙ 10am-10pm Sun-Thu, 10am-12.30am Fri & Sat Mar-Nov, 11am-6pm Sun-Thu, 11am-7pm Fri & Sat Dec-Feb), a helium-filled balloon that remains tethered to the ground as it lifts you noiselessly 150m into the air for panoramas of the historic city centre. There are no flights in windy conditions, so confirm ahead by calling the wind hotline at ⊙ 226 678 811.

DEUTSCHES TECHNIKMUSEUM
Fantastic for kids, the **Deutsches Technikmuseum** (German Museum of Technology; Map pp110-11; ☎ 902 540; Trebbiner Strasse 9; adult/concession €4.50/2.50, under 18yr after 3pm free; ⊙ 9am-5.30pm Tue-Fri, 10am-6pm Sat & Sun) is a giant shrine to technology that counts the world's first computer, an entire hall of vintage locomotives and extensive exhibits on aviation and navigation among its top attractions. At the adjacent **Spectrum Science Centre** (Map pp110-11; enter from Möckernstrasse 26; admission incl; ⊙ as above) you can participate in some 250 experiments.

Friedrichshain
Friedrichshain, in the former East Berlin, is a shape-shifter, a slippery creature, still unsettled in its world view and offering a rambunctious stage for good times and DIY surprises. It celebrates its underground-punk-squatter roots in the derelict industrial outposts along **Revaler Strasse** (Map pp110-11) and the graffiti-slathered funky town around Ostkreuz. Mere steps away, **Simon-Dach-Strasse** (Map pp110-11)

is a bar-laden stumbling zone where the young and the restless drink, dance and flirt with all the mad exuberance of a stag party.

Conventional tourist sites are limited to the **East Side Gallery**, the longest remaining stretch of the Berlin Wall (see p126), and the **Karl-Marx-Allee** (Map pp110-11), a grand boulevard built between 1952 and 1960 that is the epitome of Stalinist pomposity. At 90m wide, it runs for 2.3km between Alexanderplatz and Frankfurter Tor and was a source of considerable national pride for the East Germans, providing modern flats for thousands of comrades and also serving as a backdrop for vast military parades. The exhibit at Cafe Sybille at No 72 has more background.

Pockets of open space include the **Volkspark Friedrichshain** (Map pp106-7), a wonderland of tamed wilderness filled with trails, playgrounds, tennis courts, a half-pipe, an outdoor cinema and lots of greenery for sunning, grilling and picnicking.

Prenzlauer Berg
Ageing divas know that a face-lift can quickly pump up a drooping career, and it seems the same can be done with entire neighbourhoods. It helps that Prenzlauer Berg has always had great bone structure, so to speak. Badly pummelled but not destroyed during WWII, the district was among the first to show up in the crosshairs of developers after the Wall collapsed. Now pretty as a polished penny, its townhouses sparkle in prim pastels, their sleekly renovated apartments and lofts the haunts of urbanites, gays, creative types, families and professionals.

It's these bourgeois bohemians who keep alive a burgeoning scene of world-cuisine restaurants, trendy bars, cultural venues, designer boutiques and 'bio' (organic) supermarkets. Berliners may whisper behind raised palms that Prenzlauer Berg is losing its edge but that isn't stopping them from coming here.

Charlottenburg
The glittering heart of West Berlin during the Cold War, glitzy Charlottenburg has fallen a bit off the tourist radar since reunification. Compared to the wild-child character of the eastern districts, it seems like a middle-aged burgher happy with the status quo. Experimentation is elsewhere.

BERLIN

THE BERLIN WALL

It's more than a tad ironic that Berlin's most popular tourist attraction is one that no longer exists. For 28 years, the Berlin Wall, the most potent symbol of the Cold War, divided not only the city but the world. Construction began shortly after midnight of 13 August 1961, when East German soldiers rolled out miles of barbed wire that would soon be replaced with prefab concrete slabs. The Wall was a desperate measure launched by the GDR government to stop the sustained brain and brawn drain it had experienced since its founding in 1949. Some 3.6 million people had already left for the West, putting the country on the verge of economic and political collapse.

Euphemistically called 'Anti-Fascist Protection Barrier', the Wall was a 155km-long symbol of oppression that turned West Berlin into an island of democracy within a sea of socialism. Continually reinforced and refined over time, it eventually grew into a complex border security system that included a 'death strip' made up of trenches, floodlights, patrol roads, attack dogs, electrified fences and watchtowers staffed by trigger-happy guards.

The first would-be escapee was shot only a few days after 13 August, but the full extent of the system's cruelty became blatantly clear on 17 August 1962 when 18-year-old Peter Fechtner was shot and wounded and then left to bleed to death while the East German guards looked on. There's a **memorial** in the spot where he died on Zimmerstrasse, near Markgrafenstrasse (Map pp110–11). Another **Wall Victims Memorial** (Map p108) is just south of the Reichstag, on the eastern end of Scheidemannstrasse.

The demise of the Wall came as unsuspectedly as its creation. Once again the GDR was losing its people in droves, this time via Hungary which had opened its borders with Austria. At the same time, East Germans took to the streets by the tens of thousands demanding improved human rights and an end to the SED monopoly. On 9 November 1989 SED spokesperson Günter

Still, Charlottenburg's long-time draws are in no danger of disappearing. Catch a cabaret at Bar jeder Vernunft, Anna Netrebko at the Deutsche Oper or international jazz greats at A-Trane. Shopaholics can get their kicks on Kurfürstendamm, 'royal' groupies continue to delight in Schloss Charlottenburg and, though now fully grown, polar bear Knut still delights visitors with his antics at the Berlin Zoo. City planners are also keeping their fingers crossed that Great Wheel Berlin, the world's largest Ferris wheel, which is expected to go live in 2010, will retrain some of the spotlight on Charlottenburg.

SCHLOSS CHARLOTTENBURG

The grandest of Berlin's surviving nine former royal pads is **Schloss Charlottenburg** (Charlottenburg Palace; Map pp106–7; ☎ 320 911; www.spsg.de; Spandauer Damm; day pass adult/concession €12/9; ⊕ Richard-Wagner-Platz, then ☐ 145). It consists of the main palace and two outbuildings in the lovely Schlossgarten (palace park). Each building charges separate admission, but it's best to invest in the *Tageskarte* that gives you an entire day to see everything except the Neuer

Flügel (New Wing). Come early on weekends and in summer. A palace visit is easily combined with a spin around the trio of nearby museums, described below.

The Schloss began as the summer residence of Sophie Charlotte, wife of King Friedrich I. Their baroque living quarters in the palace's oldest section, the **Altes Schloss** (Old Palace; ☎ 320 911; adult/concession incl guided tour or audioguide €10/7; ⊗ 10am-6pm Tue-Sun Apr-Oct, to 5pm Nov-Mar), are an extravaganza in stucco, brocade and overall opulence. Highlights include the Oak Gallery, a wood-panelled festival hall draped in family portraits; the lovely Oval Hall with views of the gardens; Friedrich I's bedchamber, with the first-ever bathroom in a baroque palace; and the fabulous Porcelain Chamber, smothered top to bottom in Chinese and Japanese blue ware. Head upstairs to admire the paintings, vases, tapestries, weapons, porcelain and other items essential to a royal lifestyle in the old apartments of Friedrich Wilhelm IV.

The most beautiful rooms, though, are the flamboyant private chambers of Frederick the Great in the **Neuer Flügel** (☎ 320 911; adult/concession incl audioguide €6/5; ⊗ 10am-6pm Wed-Mon Apr-Oct, to

Schabowski made a surprise announcement on GDR TV: all travel restrictions to the West had been lifted – effective immediately. Amid scenes of wild partying and mile-long parades of GDR-made Trabant cars, the two Berlins came together again. The dismantling of the hated barrier began almost immediately.

Only little more than 1.5km of the Berlin Wall still stands as a symbol of the triumph of freedom over oppression. The longest, best-preserved and most interesting stretch is the **East Side Gallery** (Map pp110–11), a 1.3km-long section paralleling the Spree, which was turned into an open-air gallery by international artists in 1990.

Over the past 20 years, the two city halves have visually merged so perfectly that in many places it takes a keen eye to tell East from West. Fortunately, there's help in the form of a **double row of cobblestones** that guides you along 5.7km of the Wall's course.

If you're feeling ambitious, follow all or sections of the 160km-long **Berliner Mauerweg** (Berlin Wall Trail; www.berlin.de/mauer, link to English), a signposted walking and cycling path along the former border fortifications with 40 multilingual information stations posted throughout.

A high-tech way to walk the Wall is with the **Mauerguide** (www.mauerguide.de; adult/concession per 4hr €8/5, per day €10/7), a nifty handheld mini-computer that maps its course via GPS and provides intelligent commentary and historic audio and video. Rental stations include Checkpoint Charlie and the Brandenburger Tor. Call or check the website to confirm locations and opening hours.

For more background, swing by the **Gedenkstätte Berliner Mauer** (Map pp106–7; ☎ 464 1030; www.berliner-mauer-gedenkstaette.de; Bernauer Strasse 111; admission free; ☽ 10am-6pm Apr-Oct, 10am-5pm Nov-Mar), a soon-to-be-expanded memorial that combines a documentation centre, an art installation, a short section of original Wall, a chapel and an outdoor gallery. The Mauermuseum, aka **Haus am Checkpoint Charlie** (p125) also chronicles the Cold War period.

5pm Nov-Mar), designed by star architect du jour Georg Wenzeslaus von Knobelsdorff in 1746. The austere neoclassical ones of his successor, Friedrich Wilhelm II, in the same wing, pale in comparison.

Adjacent to the Neuer Flügel, the Schinkel-designed **Neuer Pavillon** (New Pavilion; ☎ 3209 1443; call for hrs and admission costs) served as a summer retreat of Friedrich Wilhelm III and now houses paintings from the Romantic and Biedermeier periods. Closed for renovation during our visit, it should have reopened by the time you're reading this.

In fine weather, a spin around the sprawling **Schlossgarten** (palace park) with its shady walkways, flower beds and manicured lawns is a must. In the northeast corner, you'll stumble upon the pint-size palace called **Belvedere** (☎ 3909 1445; adult/concession €3/2.50; ☽ 10am-6pm Tue-Sun Apr-Oct, noon-4pm Tue-Sun Nov-Mar), now an elegant setting for porcelain masterpieces by the royal manufacturer KPM.

Across the carp pond awaits the sombre **Mausoleum** (☎ 3209 1446; adult/concession €2/1.50; ☽ 10am-5pm Tue-Sun Apr-Oct), where various royals, including Emperor Wilhelm I and his wife, are entombed in fancy marble sarcophagi.

SCHLOSS AREA MUSEUMS

South of the palace, the **Museum Berggruen** (Map pp106–7; ☎ 3269 5815; www.smb.museum/mb; Schlossstrasse 1; adult/concession/under 16yr €8/4/free, last 4hr Thu free; ☽ 10am-6pm Tue-Sun) exhibits major classical modern art with a special focus on Picasso, Klee, Matisse and Giacometti.

The Berggruen ticket is also good for same-day admission to the **Sammlung Scharf-Gerstenberg** (Map pp106–7; ☎ 3435 7315; www.smb.museum/ssg; Schlossstrasse 70; adult/concession/under 16yr €8/4/free, last 4hr Thu free; ☽ 10am-6pm Tue-Sun), and vice versa. Open since 2008, this stellar museum trains the spotlight on surrealist artists with an impressive body of works by Magritte, Max Ernst, Dalí, Dubuffet and their 18th-century precursors such as Goya and Piranesi. (If you have time, you can also use the ticket to visit the Museum für Fotografie/Helmut Newton Sammlung, p128, on the same day.)

While in the neighbourhood, also pop by the **Bröhan Museum** (☎ 3269 0600; www.broehan-museum.de; Schlossstrasse 1a; adult/concession €6/4; ☽ 10am-6pm Tue-Sun), which displays an outstanding collection of furniture and decorative objects from the art-nouveau, art-deco and Functionalism periods (1889–1939).

BERLIN

KURFÜRSTENDAMM & AROUND

The 3.5km-long Kurfürstendamm (Ku'damm for short) is a ribbon of commerce that began as a bridle path to the royal hunting lodge in the Grunewald forest. In the early 1870s, Bismarck had it widened, paved and lined with fancy residential buildings, apparently in an attempt to one-up the French and their Champs-Elysée.

On Breitscheidplatz, the boulevard's eastern terminus, the bombed-out tower of the landmark **Kaiser-Wilhelm-Gedächtniskirche** (Emperor-William-Memorial-Church; Map p112; admission free; ☺ 9am-7pm) serves as an antiwar memorial, standing quiet and dignified amid the roar. Built in 1895, it was once a real beauty as you'll be able to tell from the before-and-after pictures in the memorial hall on the ground floor. Also duck into the adjacent octagonal **hall of worship**, added in 1961, to admire its midnight-blue glass walls and giant floating Jesus.

Near the church, an exotic Elephant Gate leads inside the **Berlin Zoo** (Map p112; ☎ 254 010; enter on Hardenbergplatz or on Budapester Strasse; adult/student/child zoo or aquarium €12/9/6, zoo & aquarium €18/14/9; ☺ 9am-7pm mid-Mar–mid-Oct, 9am-6pm mid-Sep–mid-Oct, 9am-5pm mid-Oct–mid-Mar), Germany's oldest animal park. Some 14,000 furry, feathered and flippered creatures from all continents, 1500 species in total, make their home here. Knut, the polar bear born at the zoo in 2006, and Bao Bao, a giant panda from China, are among the biggest celebrities, but cheeky orang-utans, endangered rhinos and playful penguins are also perennial crowd pleasers. At the adjacent **Aquarium** (Map p112; Budapester Strasse 32; adult/student/child €12/9/6, zoo & aquarium €18/14/9; ☺ 9am-6pm) dancing jelly fish, iridescent poison frogs and real-life Nemo clownfish should thrill even the most PlayStation-jaded youngsters.

Entertainment for grown-ups awaits at the **Museum für Fotografie/Helmut Newton Sammlung** (Museum of Photography; Map p112; ☎ 3186 4825; Jebensstrasse 2; adult/concession/under 16yr €8/4/free, last 4hr Thu free; ☺ 10am-6pm Tue, Wed & Fri-Sun, to 10pm Thu), behind Zoo station. Built as a Prussian officer's casino and later used as an art library, this imposing neoclassical building now houses changing photography exhibits of international stature upstairs in the Kaisersaal (Emperor's Hall), a barrel-vaulted banqueting hall. The ground floor is dedicated to the works of Helmut Newton, the Berlin-born *enfant terrible* of fashion photography. Tickets

are also good for same-day admission to the Museum Berggruen (p127) and Sammlung Scharf-Gerstenberg (p127).

Art fans also flock to the exquisite **Käthe-Kollwitz-Museum** (Map p112; ☎ 882 5210; Fasanenstrasse 24; adult/concession €5/2.50; ☺ 11am-6pm). It presents the works of one of Germany's greatest women artists, whose social and political awareness lent a tortured power to her work. After losing both her son and grandson on the battlefields of Europe, death and motherhood became recurring themes in her work.

Further west on Ku'damm, the **Story of Berlin** (Map p112; ☎ 8872 0100; Kurfürstendamm 207-208; adult/concession/family €9.80/8/21; ☺ 10am-8pm, last admission & bunker tour 6pm) is a multimedia museum that breaks down some 800 years of Berlin history into bite-sized chunks that are easy to swallow but substantial enough to be satisfying. The Cold War comes creepily to life during a tour of a still fully functional atomic bunker beneath the building. The museum entrance is inside the Ku'damm Karree mall.

OLYMPIASTADION

Built for the 1936 Olympic Games, the **Olympiastadion** (Olympic Stadium; off Map pp106-7; ☎ 2500 2322; www.olympiastadion-berlin.de; adult/concession €4/3, tours in German €8/7; ☺ 9am-8pm Jun–mid-Sep, to 7pm mid-Mar–May & mid-Sep–Oct, to 4pm Nov–mid-Mar on non-event days; ☑ ☺ Olympiastadion) emerged from a major makeover just in time for the 2006 FIFA World Cup. The most notable addition is the spidery oval roof that softens the bombastic bulk of the Colisseum-like Nazi-era structure. On non-event days you can explore the stadium on your own or with an audioguide (€2.50). Guided tours are also available, taking you into locker rooms, warm-up areas and VIP areas that are otherwise off-limits. The gate is on the east side of the stadium. Call ahead to make sure that the stadium is open for touring before making the long journey out here.

The best views of the stadium are from the 77m-high **Glockenturm** (Clock Tower; off Map pp106-7; ☎ 305 8123; adult/concession €3.50/1.50; ☺ 9am-6pm; ☑ Pichelsberg), where interesting exhibits document the 1936 Olympic Games and the history of the grounds. Northwest of here, the **Waldbühne** (☎ tickets 01805-570 070; www.eventim .de) is a lovely outdoor amphitheatre used for summer concerts, film screenings and other cultural events.

Southwestern Berlin

Much of Berlin's southwest is covered by forest, rivers and lakes. Besides the **Freie Universität** and the **Botanischer Garten** (☎ 8385 0100; Königin-Luise-Strasse 6-8; adult/concession/family €5/2.50/10; 🕙 9am-dusk; 🚇 Botanischer Garten), you'll find several excellent museums here.

MUSEEN DAHLEM

Unless some mad scientist invents a magic time-travel-teleporter machine, the **Museen Dahlem** (☎ 830 1438; Lansstrasse 8; adult/concession/under 16yr €6/3/free, last 4hr Thu free; 🕙 10am-6pm Tue-Fri, 11am-6pm Sat & Sun; 🚇 Dahlem Dorf), which displays pre-industrial, non-European art and objects, will be your best bet for exploring the world in a single afternoon.

Exhibits combine the collections of two museums: the Museum of Ethnology and the Museum of Asian Art. There are lots of highlights, but must-sees include the masks, ornaments, vases, musical instruments and other objects of ceremonial and everyday life in the **Africa exhibit** and the cult objects, outriggers and other handcrafted vessels in the **South Seas** hall. Another wing houses **Asian art**, including such prized items as exquisite terracottas, stone sculptures and bronzes as well as wall paintings and sculptures scavenged from Buddhist cave temples along the Silk Route.

Attention-span-challenged kids should make a beeline for the basement to have their horizons broadened by the touchy-feely exhibits in the **Junior Museum** (🕙 1-6pm Tue-Fri, 11am-6pm Sat & Sun).

ALLIIERTEN MUSEUM

The original Checkpoint Charlie guard cabin, a Berlin Airlift plane and a reconstructed spy tunnel are among the dramatic exhibits at the **Alliierten Museum** (Allied Museum; ☎ 818 1990; Clayallee 135; admission free; 🕙 10am-6pm Thu-Tue; 🚇 Oskar-Helene-Heim, then any bus north on Clayallee). Exhibits document the history and challenges faced by the Western Allies during the Cold War.

BRÜCKE MUSEUM

In 1905 Karl Schmidt-Rottluff, Erich Heckel and Ernst Ludwig Kirchner founded Germany's first modern-artist group, called Die Brücke. Rejecting the techniques taught in stuffy academies, they experimented with bright, emotional colours and warped perspectives that paved the way for German expressionism and other art genres. Schmitt-

Rottluff's personal collection forms the basis of the exquisite **Brücke Museum** (☎ 831 2029; Bussardsteig 9; adult/concession €4/2; 🕙 11am-5pm Wed-Mon; 🚇 Oskar-Helene-Heim, then bus 115 to Pücklerstrasse). A visit here is easily combined with a stroll over to the Jagdschloss Grunewald and the Grunewaldsee (swimming allowed), a paradise for joggers and doggies.

HAUS DER WANNSEEKONFERENZ GEDENKSTÄTTE

In January 1942, a group of elite Nazi officials met in a stately villa on Wannsee to hammer out the details of the 'Final Solution' – the systematic deportation and murder of European Jews in eastern Europe. Today the same building houses the memorial **Haus der Wannseekonferenz Gedenkstätte** (☎ 805 0010; www.ghwk.de; Am Grossen Wannsee 56-58; admission free; 🕙 10am-6pm; 🚉 Wannsee, then bus 114 to Haus der Wannsee-Konferenz). You can stand in the room where discussions took place and study the conference minutes. Other rooms chronicle the horrors leading up to – and perpetrated during – the Holocaust.

LIEBERMANN-VILLA AM WANNSEE

If you need a mood-enhancer after visiting the Haus der Wannseekonferenz, head over to the nearby **Liebermann Villa** (☎ 8058 5900; www.max-liebermann.de; Colomierstrasse 3; adult/concession/family €6/4/14, audioguide €3; 🕙 11am-6pm Wed-Mon, to 8pm Thu Apr-Sep, 11am-5pm Wed-Mon Oct-Mar; 🚉 Wannsee, then 🚌 114 to Colomierstrasse), the summer home of Berlin Secession founder Max Liebermann from 1909 until his death in 1935. Influenced by French Impressionism, Liebermann loved the lyricism of nature and gardens in particular and often painted the scenery right outside his window. In summer, there are few more languid spots than the cafe terrace overlooking the formal garden facing the Wannsee.

Eastern Berlin

Anyone interested in GDR history, and the Stasi in particular, should head out to the following two chilling sites.

The former head office of the Ministry of State Security is now the **Stasi Museum** (☎ 553 6854; Ruschestrasse 103, House 1; adult/concession €3.50/3; 🕙 11am-6pm Mon-Fri, 2-6pm Sat & Sun; 🚇 Magdalenenstrasse), where you can marvel at cunningly low-tech surveillance devices (hidden in watering cans, rocks, even neckties), a prisoner transport van with teensy, lightless cells and the obsessively neat offices of Stasi chief Erich Mielke. Panelling is in German only and exhibits are not always self-explanatory, so you may want to invest a few euros in the English-language booklet. From the U-Bahn station, turn north on Ruschestrasse, then turn right after about 100m and walk another 50m across a parking lot towards the buildings straight in front of you.

Victims of Stasi persecution often ended up in the grim **Stasi Prison** (☎ 9860 8230; Genslerstrasse 66; tour adult/concession €4/2, Mon free; ⏰ tours 11am & 1pm Mon-Fri, also 3pm Mar-Dec, hourly 10am-4pm Sat & Sun), now a memorial site officially called Gedenkstätte Hohenschönhausen. Tours (in English at 2pm Saturday and sometimes during the week; call ahead) reveal the full extent of the terror and cruelty perpetrated upon thousands of suspected regime opponents, many utterly innocent. To get here, take tram M5 from Alexanderplatz to Freienwalder Strasse, then walk 10 minutes along Freienwalder Strasse.

ACTIVITIES
Cycling

Berlin is flat and bike-friendly, with special bike lanes and quiet side streets for stress-free riding. There are even eye-level miniature traffic lights at intersections. Still, it pays to keep your wits about you (and preferably with a helmet on) when negotiating city streets. Getting a tyre caught in the tram tracks is particularly nasty.

Of course it's far more relaxing to pedal around leafy suburbs. The Grunewald forest, for instance, with its many lakes, is a great getaway. Or follow the course of the former Berlin Wall along the marked Berliner Mauerweg (p126). For more ideas, consult the guide published by the bicycle club **ADFC** (Map pp106-7; ☎ 448 4724; www.adfc-berlin.de; Brunnenstrasse 28; ⏰ noon-8pm Mon-Fri, 10am-4pm Sat). It's available at their offices, bookshops and bike stores. For guided bike tours, see p134.

Bicycles (Fahrräder) may be taken aboard designated U-Bahn and S-Bahn cars (though not on buses) for the price of a reduced single ticket (see the table, p154). Deutsche Bahn charges €4.50 for a bike ticket (Fahrradkarte) on regional RE and RB trains.

Many hostels and hotels rent bicycles to their guests or can refer you to an agency. Expect to pay from €10 per day and €50 per week. A minimum cash deposit and/or ID is required. One reliable outfit with English-speaking staff and six branches throughout central Berlin is **Fahrradstation** (☎ central reservations 0180-510 8000; www.fahrradstation.de). Alternatively, try **Little John Bikes** (☎ 7889 4123; www.little-john-bikes.de, in German) with branches in Schöneberg, Mitte and Kreuzberg.

To buy a used bike, try the Mauerpark flea market (p150), www.zweitehand.de or www .craigslist.de.

Running

Berlin offers great running terrains in its many parks. Flat and spread out, the Tiergarten (Map p108) is among the most popular and convenient, although the Grunewald in southwest Berlin is even prettier. The trip around the scenic Schlachtensee (in Grunewald) is 5km. The park of Schloss Charlottenburg (Map pp106-7) is also good for a nice, easy trot. More challenging is Volkspark Friedrichshain (Map pp106-7), which has stairs, hills and even a fitness trail.

Swimming

Berlin has lots of indoor and outdoor public pools. Opening hours vary widely by day, time and pool, so call ahead before setting out. Many facilities also have saunas, which generally cost between €10 and €15.

Sommerbad Olympiastadion (off Map pp106-7; ☎ 3006 3440; Osttor, Olympischer Platz; adult/concession €4/2.50; ⏰ 8am-8pm May-Sep; ⊕ ⛁ Olympiastadion) Do laps in the 50m pool built for the 1936 Olympic athletes.

Stadtbad Charlottenburg (Map p112; ☎ Alte Halle 3438 3860, Neue Halle 3438 3865; Krumme Strasse 10; adult/concession €4/2.50; ⏰ 8am-8pm) Alte Halle is a beautiful art-nouveau pool with colourful tiles and popular with gay men on nude bathing nights; Neue Halle is modern with a 50m lap pool and sauna.

Strandbad Wannsee (off Map pp106-7; ☎ 803 5612; Wannseebadweg 25, Zehlendorf; adult/concession €4/2.50; ⏰ 8am-8pm May-Sep; ⛁ Nikolassee, then bus 513) Possibly Europe's largest lakeside lido with 1km of sandy beach and plenty of infrastructure and concessions.

WALKING TOUR

This meander takes in all of central Berlin's blockbuster sights, plus some fabulous hidden corners. From Potsdamer Platz it winds through the Government Quarter to Unter den Linden into historic Berlin, ending in the Scheunenviertel. Along the way, you'll be treated to great views, tremendous archi-

---

PLAY IT COOL BY THE POOL

Viva Berlin! Take an old river barge, fill it with water, moor it in the Spree and – voilà – an urban lifestyle pool is born. In summer, a hedonistic Ibiza-vibe reigns at the artist-designed **Badeschiff** (Map pp110-11; ☎ 533 2030; www.arena-berlin.de; Eichenstrasse 4; admission €3; ☺ from 8am), with bods bronzing in the sand or cooling off in the water and a bar to fuel the fun. On scorching days, come before noon or risk a long wait. After-dark action includes parties, bands, movies and simply chilling. In winter, an ethereally glowing plastic membrane covers up the pool and a deliciously toasty chill zone with saunas and bar.

Any time of year is a fine time to feel your daily cares slip away at **Liquidrom** (Map pp110-11; ☎ 258 007 820; www.liquidrom-berlin.de; Möckernstrasse 10; 2hr/4hr/day pass €17.50/20.50/22.50; ☺ 10am-midnight Sun-Thu, 10am-1am Fri & Sat), a stylishly minimalist day spa that's the perfect mood enhancer on a rainy day. There are a couple of saunas, dipping pools and lounge areas, but the star of the show is the darkened domed hall where you float in a saltwater pool while being showered with soothing sounds and psychedelic light projections. Pure bliss.

---

tecture, interesting nosh spots and plenty of places you might recognise from the history books.

Kick off your tour at **Potsdamer Platz** (1; p122), Berlin's newest quarter and a showcase of contemporary architecture. Check out the section of the **Berlin Wall (2)** outside the S-Bahn station entrance, the public art in **DaimlerCity** (3; p122) and the tented plaza at the **Sony Center** (4; p122). Continue north on Ebertstrasse to the gargantuan **Holocaust Memorial** (5; p115) where you should wander among the concrete blocks for the full visual and emotional impact. Next, get your camera ready for the majestic **Brandenburger Tor** (6; Brandenburg Gate; p114), the ultimate symbol of German reunification. It anchors **Pariser Platz** (7; p114), a harmoniously proportioned square where you should gawk at Frank Gehry's eye-popping atrium inside the **DZ Bank (8)**. Continue north on Ebertstrasse past the moving **Wall Victims Memorial (9)**, which honours those who died trying to escape the GDR. The hulking **Reichstag** (10; p120), where the German parliament meets, looms nearby.

Walk north to the **Paul-Löbe-Haus (11)**, where members of parliament keep their offices, then west on Paul-Löbe-Allee to the **Bundeskanzleramt (12; p120)**, the office of the German chancellor. Head north across Otto-von-Bismarck-Allee to the **Spreebogenpark (13)** with the sweeping glass roof of the **Hauptbahnhof (14)** in full view across the Spree River.

Follow the river promenade east past the **Marie-Elisabeth-Lüders-Haus (15)**, home of the parliamentary library, to Luisenstrasse. Cross the bridge, which offers good views back to the Reichstag. Continuing south on Luisenstrasse soon takes you to **Unter den Linden (16**; p115), Berlin's grand historic boulevard. Turn left, walk past the monumental **Russian Embassy (17)** and hook a right onto Friedrichstrasse.

Soon you'll arrive at the **Friedrichstadtpassagen**, a trio of spectacularly designed – on the inside, anyway – shopping complexes called 'quartiers', which are linked by a subterranean walkway. **Galeries Lafayette** (18; p149) centres on Jean Nouvel's giant plexiglass funnel that reflects light like some mutated hologram. Next door, **Quartier 206** (19) is a dazzling art-deco-inspired symphony in glass and marble beneath a tented glass roof. **Quartier 205 (20)** has a lofty atrium dominated by John Chamberlain's three-storey tall tower created from crushed automobile parts.

For a dose of Cold War history, carry on along Friedrichstrasse for another 500m to the site of **Checkpoint Charlie** (21; p124), the most famous ex–border crossing between East and West Berlin. The nearby **Haus am Checkpoint Charlie** (22; p125) has haphazard but interesting exhibits about the history of the Berlin Wall and spectacular escape attempts.

Otherwise proceed from Quartier 205 by turning left on Mohrenstrasse to get to **Gendarmenmarkt** (p116), Berlin's most beautiful square. It's anchored by Schinkel's **Konzerthaus Berlin** (23; p147) and the sumptuous towers of the **Deutscher Dom** (24; p116) and the **Französischer Dom** (25; p116).

Walk north on Markgrafenstrasse, then east on Behrenstrasse to **Bebelplatz** (p116), site of the infamous Nazi book burnings in 1933. A trio of imposing 18th-century buildings stand on this austere square: the **Alte**

BERLIN WALKING TOUR

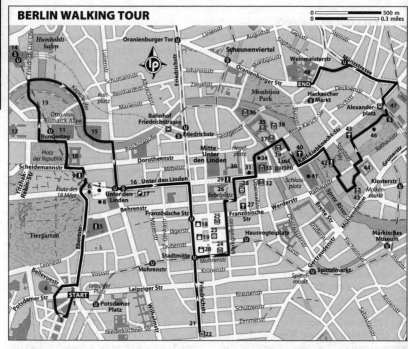

WALK FACTS

Start Potsdamer Platz (🔵 🔴 Unter den Linden)

Finish Hackesche Höfe (🔴 Hackescher Markt)

Distance 9km

Duration Three to four hours without museums, all day with some museums

Königliche Bibliothek (26; Old Royal Library), the **St-Hedwigskirche (27)** and the **Staatsoper Unter den Linden (28**; p147). Nearby is the epic **Reiterdenkmal Friedrich des Grossen (29)**, an equestrian statue of the king who financed this lovely ensemble.

On the north side of Unter den Linden are the **Humboldt Universität (30**; p115) and, a bit further east, Schinkel's **Neue Wache (31**; p116). Across the street is the **Kronprinzenpalais (32)**, a one-time royal palace, while the pink building opposite is the Zeughaus, an armoury converted into the **Deutsches Historisches Museum (33**; p116) with a modern extension by IM Pei, the **IM Pei Bau (34**; p116).

Now walk east towards the river and cross the bridge to the **Museumsinsel** (p116), a cluster of world-class repositories of art and sculpture. On your left are the **Pergamonmuseum (35**; p116), a treasure trove of antiquities, and the **Bodemuseum (36**; p117) with centuries of European art. In front is the resurrected **Neues Museum (37**; p117), which is most famous for its ancient Egyptian collection. Behind it, the **Alte Nationalgalerie (38**; p116) has famous 19th-century paintings, while the **Altes Museum** on your right **(39**; p117) introduces you to art from ancient Greece and Rome.

Turn right behind the Altes Museum to arrive at the magnificent **Berliner Dom (40**; p117), the former royal church and burial place of many Hohenzollern rulers. Across from the cathedral once stood a hideous GDR-era parliamentary and cultural building called Palast der Republik, and before that the royal city palace; a replica of the latter will soon be reconstructed and opened as the **Humboldt Forum (41**; p118).

Behind the ex-palace, turn right for the **Marx-Engels-Forum (42)**, walking past the statue of Karl Marx and Friedrich Engels to the **Nikolaiviertel** (43; Nikolai Quarter; p118), where Berlin was founded in the 13th century. Make your way towards the **Rotes Rathaus** (44; p118), home of the city government, to the **Marienkirche** (45; p118), Berlin's oldest still-operating church. Continue east, perhaps stopping off to catch a ride up the **Fernsehturm** (46; p117), to **Alexanderplatz** (47; p117), once the commercial heart of communist Berlin.

From here follow Münzstrasse to the **Scheunenviertel** (p119), Berlin's historic Jewish quarter and now a vibrant part of town, with plenty of eating, shopping and nightlife. Its hub is the **Hackesche Höfe** (48; p119), a beautifully restored series of courtyards where cafes invite you to cool your heels and wrap up your grand tour.

BERLIN FOR CHILDREN

Travelling to Berlin with tots can be child's play, as there's certainly no shortage of fun things to do around town. Parks and imaginative playgrounds abound in all neighbourhoods and the vast Tiergarten is great for picnics or paddling around the Neuer See lake.

Animal lovers gravitate towards Berlin Zoo (p128), home to the polar-bear celebrity Knut, a petting corral and an adventure playground. The adjacent Aquarium (p128) has lots more crowd-pleasers, but to prevent exhaustion save a visit here for another day.

Finny friends also take centre stage at Sea Life Berlin (p117), whose smaller size makes it suitable for the kindergarten set, as does the company's Legoland Discovery Centre (p122).

Kid-friendly museums include the Museum für Naturkunde (Museum of Natural History; p120) with its giant dinosaurs; the Deutsches Technikmuseum (German Museum of Technology; p124) with its planes, trains and automobiles; and the **Domäne Dahlem** (off Map pp106-7; ☎ 666 3000; Königin-Luise-Strasse 49; adult/concession €2/1, Wed free; ☒ 10am-6pm Wed-Mon; ⊙ Dahlem-Dorf), an outdoor museum where they can watch daily farm-life unfold and meet their favourite barnyard animals. There's also **Museumsdorf Düppel** (off Map pp106-7; ☎ 802 6671; Clauertstrasse 11; adult/concession €2/1; ☒ 3-7pm Thu, 10am-5pm Sun Apr-Oct; ☒ Zehlendorf, then bus 115), a recreated medieval village with Sunday craft demonstrations, games and tours.

Older kids might get a kick out of the Haus am Checkpoint Charlie (p125) with its Cold War spy and escape exhibits. Follow up a visit here with a trip around Berlin's 'Wild East' in a quaint GDR-era car on a Trabi Safari (p134). And your music-loving teens will think you're way cool if you take them on the Fritz Music Tour (p134). For more ideas, see www.visit berlin.de or www.travelforkids.com.

If you need a babysitter, ask at your hotel for a referral or try **Kinder-Hotel** (Map p108; ☎ 4171 6928; www.kinderinsel.de; Eichendorffstrasse 17, Mitte), which has 24-hour day care in 17 languages for kids aged up to 14. Fees are €13 per hour and €69 overnight (14 hours).

TOURS
Bus Tours
CITY CIRCLE TOURS

You'll see them everywhere around town: colourful buses (in summer often open-top double-deckers) that tick off all the key sights on two-hour loops with basic taped commentary in eight languages. You're free to get off and back on at any of the stops. Buses depart roughly every 15 or 30 minutes between 10am and 5pm or 6pm daily. Day tickets cost €15 or €20 (half-price for teens, free for children). Companies include **BBS Berliner Bären Stadtrundfahrt** (☎ 3519 5270; www.sightseeing.de), **Severin + Kühn** (☎ 880 4190; www.severin-kuehn-berlin.de) and **Tempelhofer Reisen** (☎ 752 4057; www.tempelhofer.de). For details, call, check the websites or look for flyers in hotel lobbies and at the Berlin Infostores (p114).

BUS 100 & 200

One of Berlin's best bargains is a self-guided city tour aboard public buses 100 or 200, whose routes check off nearly every major sight in the city centre for the price of a standard bus ticket (€2.10, day pass €6.10).

Bus 100 travels from Bahnhof Zoo to Alexanderplatz, passing by the Gedächtniskirche, Tiergarten (with the Siegessäule), the Reichstag, the Brandenburger Tor and Unter den Linden. A tour on bus 200 also links Bahnhof Zoo and Alexanderplatz but takes a more southerly route via the Kulturforum and Potsdamer Platz. Without traffic, trips take about 30 minutes. These buses get crowded, so watch out for pickpockets.

Bike Tours

Companies listed below operate various English-language tours. Reservations are recommended.

Berlin on Bike (Map p113; ☎ 4373 9999; www.berlin onbike.de; Knaackstrasse 97; tours incl bike €17, with own bike €12, discounts available for children, students and Berlin Welcome Card holders; ☒ Apr–Oct)

Fat Tire Bike Tours (Map p108; ☎ 2404 7991; www .fattirebiketoursberlin.com; Panoramastrasse 1a; tours incl bike & insurance adult/student €20/18)

Boat Tours

A lovely way to experience Berlin on a warm day is from the deck of a boat cruising along the city's rivers, canals and lakes. Tours range from one-hour spins around the historic centre (from €7) to longer trips to Schloss Charlottenburg and beyond (from €16). Most offer live commentary in English and German. **Stern & Kreisschiffahrt** (www.stern undkreis.de) is one of the main operators. The season runs from April to mid-October. Our maps indicate embarkation points.

Walking Tours

Several walking-tour companies run introductory spins that take in both blockbuster and offbeat sights, plus themed tours (eg Third Reich, Cold War, Sachsenhausen, Potsdam). Guides are fluent English speakers, well informed, sharp-witted and keen to answer your questions. Tours don't require reservations – just show up at one of the meeting points. Since these change quite frequently, keep an eye out for flyers in hotel or hostel lobbies or at the tourist offices or contact the companies directly. Some tours are free (well, the guides work for tips, so give what you can) but most cost between €10 and €15.

Berlin Walks (☎ 301 9194; www.berlinwalks.de) The first English-language walking-tour company founded after the fall of the Wall, and still tops.

Brewer's Berlin Tours (☎ 0177-388 1537; www .brewersberlintours.com) Home of the epic all-day Best of Berlin tour (foot massage not included) and shorter free tour.

Insider Tour (☎ 692 3149; www.insidertour.com) Also does bike tours and a pub crawl.

New Berlin Tours (☎ 0179-973 0397; www.newberlin tours.com) Pioneered the concept of the 'free tour' and the notorious pub crawl.

Speciality Tours

Berlinagenten (☎ 4372 0701; www.berlinagenten .com) Get under the skin of Berlin's lifestyle scene with clued-in guides that whisk you off the beaten track and into unique bars, boutiques, restaurants and clubs, even private homes. For an insider's primer on the culinary scene, book their Gastro-Rallye, where you enjoy one course each at three or four restaurant stops. Four-course dinner tours cost €160 per person for groups of two, less for bigger groups; advance booking required. Also see our interview with company founder Henrik Tidefjärd (p121)

Berliner Unterwelten (☎ 4991 0518; www.berliner -unterwelten.de; adult/concession €9/7) Explore Berlin's dark and dank underbelly by picking your way past hospital beds, wartime helmets and filter systems on a tour of WWII-era underground bunkers.

Fritz Music Tours (☎ 3087 5633; www.musictours -berlin.com; bus/walking tour €19/12) Berlin music expert Thilo Schmid gives you the low-down on Berlin's legendary music history – from Iggy and Bowie to U2 and Depeche Mode, from cult clubs to the Love Parade – on a dynamic 2½-hour bus tour. There are also two-hour walking tours leaving from the Kesselhaus club (Map p113; Schönhauser Allee 36-39) in the Kulturbrauerei as well as private minibus tours (per person €45, by arrangement) and monthly tours of the Hansa Studios (€10). The bus tour is held 12.30pm Saturday; reservations required. Walking tours are held in English 2pm Friday and in German 2pm Wednesday and Saturday.

Trabi Safari (☎ 2759 2273; www.trabi-safari.de; cnr Wilhelmstrasse & Zimmerstrasse; 1/2/3/4 passengers per person €60/40/35/30) Spend an hour exploring Berlin's Wild East behind the wheel – or as a passenger – of a GDR-era Trabant (Trabi for short). Live commentary is piped into your vehicle.

FESTIVALS & EVENTS

Berlin is very much a party town with a busy year-round calendar of concerts, street parties, mega sports events, trade shows and festivals celebrating everything from film to fetish, music to movies, travel to fashion. Berlin's **tourist office** (www.visitberlin.de) has a searchable events calendar and can also help you book tickets. To get you planning, we've listed a few highlights.

Berlinale (☎ 259 200; www.berlinale.de) The world's stars and starlets, directors and critics invade in February for Berlin's glamorous international film festival.

Internationale Tourismusbörse (☎ 303 80; www.itb -berlin.com) A virtual trip around the globe at the world's largest travel expo (more than 10,000 exhibitors) held in February or March and open to the public at the weekend.

Karneval der Kulturen (☎ 6097 7022; www .karneval-berlin.de) Exuberant three-day festival in the streets of Kreuzberg culminating in a parade of costumed dancers, singers, DJs and musicians. Pentecost weekend in May or June.

Christopher Street Day (☎ 2362 8632; www .csd-berlin.de) People of every sexual orientation paint the town pink at one of Europe's biggest gay-pride parades and parties held in late June.

Internationale Funkausstellung (☎ 3069 6924; www.ifa-berlin.de) Huge international consumer electronics fair in early September showcases the latest gadgets everyone will want for Christmas.

Berlin Marathon (www.berlin-marathon.com) Some 50,000 runners sweat it out at Germany's biggest street race that has seen nine world records set since 1977; in September.

Art Forum Berlin (☎ 303 80; www.art-forum-berlin .com) This established international contemporary art fair brings together leading galleries, collectors and the merely curious; September or October.

Jazzfest Berlin (☎ 2548 9100; www.jazzfest-berlin.de) This top-rated jazz festival doo-wops through Berlin with performances by fresh and big-time talent in November.

Christmas Markets Plenty of shimmering ornaments and potent mulled wine at dozens of Yuletide markets held throughout December in such locales as Breitscheidplatz (Map p112) and Alexanderplatz (Map p108).

SLEEPING

Berlin boasts more than 100,000 beds and plenty more are scheduled to come online in the next few years. Just about every international chain now has a flagship in the German capital, but more interesting options that better reflect the city's verve and spirit abound. You can sleep in a former bank, boat or factory, in the home of a silent-movie diva, in a 'flying bed' or even a coffin. Standards are high but fierce competition has kept prices low compared to other capital cities.

In fact, Berlin is nirvana for budget travellers. The hostel scene is the most vibrant in Europe and consists of both classic backpacker hostels with alternative flair, and modern 'flashpacker' hostels catering for lifestyle-savvy city-breakers. Of late, new competition has come from budget designer hotels, such as the Motel One chain.

Design-minded travellers with deeper pockets can choose from plenty of lifestyle and boutique hotels as well as *Kunsthotels* (art hotels), which are either designed by artists and/or liberally sprinkled with original art.

Nostalgic types seeking a unique 'Old Berlin' flavour should check into a charismatic B&B, called *Hotel-Pension* or simply *Pension*. They typically occupy one or several floors of historic residential buildings and offer local colour and personal attention galore. Amenities, room size and decor vary, although many have been updated and now feature wi-fi, cable TV and other mod cons.

Also increasingly popular among short-term visitors are furnished flats that give you the benefit of space, privacy and independence, making them especially attractive to families and self-caterers.

Berlin's excellent public transport system puts you within easy reach of everything, so you don't have to be too fussy about which district to base yourself in. Prices noted below are guidelines only and may vary depending on the season, day of the week or trade show or special events activity.

Mitte
BUDGET

baxpax downtown (Map p108; ☎ 2787 4880; www .baxpax.de; Ziegelstrasse 28; dm €16-31, s €42-57, d €69-82, discounts Nov-Feb, breakfast €5.50; ⊠ ▣ 🤶) Baxpax was among the first in town to take budget hospitality to a whole new level. Meet other globetrotters in the fireplace cafe, the courtyard lounge (with stylish pods for chilling) or the rooftop terrace before retiring to modern, spacious rooms and dorms outfitted with flat-screen TV, a table and bedside reading lamps. Some have private bathrooms.

Wombat's City Hostel Berlin (Map p108; ☎ 8471 0820; www.wombats-hostels.com; Alte Schönhauser Strasse 2; dm/d €21/58, apt with kitchen €100, discounts Nov-Feb; ⊠ ▣ 🤶) Wombat's knows how to do hostelling right. From backpack-sized in-room lockers to individual reading lamps and a guest kitchen, the attention to detail is impressive. Spacious rooms have their own bathrooms and freebies include linen, wi-fi (lobby only) and a welcome drink, best enjoyed with fellow party pilgrims in the 7th-floor Wombar.

We also like the following:

Citystay Hostel (Map p108; ☎ 2362 4031; www .citystay.de; Rosenstrasse 16; dm €17-21, s/d with bathroom €55/64, linen €2.50; ⊠ ▣ 🤶) Central hostel and Busabout stop (p776).

Circus Hostel (Map p108; ☎ 2839 1433; www .circus-berlin.de; Weinbergsweg 1a; dm €19-25, s/d with bathroom €50/70, 2-/4-person apt €85/140; ⊠ ▣ 🤶) Brought to you by the Circus Hotel folks, this splendid and central budget abode fires on all cylinders.

MIDRANGE

Motel One Berlin-Alexanderplatz (Map p108; ☎ 2005 4080; www.motel-one.de; Dircksenstrasse 36; d €74-124, breakfast €6.50; P ✕ ✕ 🛈) This stylish crash pad for the cash-strapped has smallish rooms but up-to-the-minute touches (flat-screen TVs, rainforest showers) that are normally the staple of posher players. The lobby takes on a second life as a breakfast area and chill zone.

Circus Hotel (Map p108; ☎ 2839 1433; www.circus -berlin.de; Rosenthaler Strasse 1; s €68, d €78-98; ✕ 🛈) The Circus crew has upped the ante once again with this awesome outpost perfect for grown-up backies. It gets rave reviews for its friendly, professional staff, colour-drenched rooms, excellent breakfast, eco-conscious approach and progressive touches, such as iPod and baby-phone rentals.

Arte Luise Kunsthotel (Map p108; ☎ 284 480; www .luise-berlin.com; Luisenstrasse 19; s €80-115, d €100-210, breakfast €11; P ✕ 🛈) At this 'gallery with rooms' you might sleep in a bed built for giants, in the company of astronauts or inside a boudoir-red 'Cabaret'. Each unit reflects the vision of a different artist, who receives royalties whenever it's rented. Smaller, bathless rooms are also available. Courtyard rooms are quieter.

Honigmond Garden Hotel (Map p108; ☎ 2844 5577; www.honigmond-berlin.de; Invalidenstrasse 122; s €105-175, d €125-235; P ✕ 🛈 🛈) Never mind the busy thoroughfare: this 20-room guesthouse is a sweet retreat where antique-filled rooms overlook a flowery garden with koi pond. The clubby lounge with honour bar and magazines is tailor-made for trading tips with other guests.

Arcotel John F (Map p108; ☎ 405 0460; www .arcotel.at; Werderscher Markt 11; r €108-280, breakfast €18; P ✕ ✕ 🛈 🛈) This urbane lifestyle hotel pays homage to John F Kennedy with plenty of whimsical detail, including hand-carved rocking chairs (because the President used one to combat a bad back) and curvaceous lamps inspired by Jackie's ball gown. Rooms are smartly dressed in black, white, silver and dark zebrano wood and feature plenty of mould-breaking extras.

The following are also recommended:

Hotel Honigmond (Map p108; ☎ 284 4550; www .honigmond-berlin.de, in German; Tieckstrasse 12; s €95-165, d €145-235; P ✕ 🛈 🛈) This sister property of Honigmond Garden scores a perfect 10 on our 'charmometer' for its familial yet elegant ambience.

Arcotel Velvet (Map p108; ☎ 278 7530; www.arcotel .at; Oranienburger Strasse 52; r €108-220, breakfast €15; P ✕ ✕ 🛈 🛈) Supercentral cool-magnet with bold colours and edgy custom design inspired by prominent Berliners.

TOP END

Adlon Hotel Kempinski (Map p108; ☎ 226 10; www .hotel-adlon.de; Unter den Linden 77; s €320-440, d €370-490, breakfast €32; P ✕ ✕ 🛈 🛈 🛈) Close to embassies, the government quarter and, well, just about everything else, the Adlon has been Berlin's most high-profile defender of the grand tradition since 1907. A sleek day spa, the Felix club-restaurant (p146) and a Michelin-starred gourmet outpost have added 21st-century spice to what can otherwise be a rather stodgy ambience.

Hotel de Rome (Map p108; ☎ 460 6090; www.hotel derome.com; Behrensstrasse 37; r €395-495, breakfast €26; P ✕ ✕ 🛈 🛈) If you have coin, set up shop in this 19th-century bank HQ where designer Tommaso Ziffer has created a delightful alchemy of historic and contemporary flair. The former vault is now the pool/spa area and the directors' rooms (still with wartime-era shrapnel wounds in the wainscoting) are now the luxury suites. Great cocktails in the Bebel Bar (p143).

Prenzlauer Berg

East Seven Hostel (Map p113; ☎ 9362 2240; www.east seven.de; Schwedter Strasse 7; dm €17, s/d/tr/q €37/50/51/78, winter discounts, linen €3; ✕ 🛈 🛈) Friendly, convivial and fun, this small hostel is within strolling distance of hip hang-outs and public transport. Cultural and linguistic barriers melt quickly in the idyllic back garden, the guest kitchen (with dishwasher!) or the retro lounge. Come sleepy-time, retreat to comfy pine beds in brightly painted dorms or private rooms.

Lette 'm Sleep (Map p113; ☎ 4473 3623; www.back packers.de; Lettestrasse 7; dm €17-21, tw/apt €49/69, discounts Nov-Mar; ✕ 🛈 🛈) One of our long-time favourites, this is a textbook boho hostel: friendly, earthy, chilled and right on hip Helmholtzplatz. Coffee, tea and internet are free.

Meininger City Hostel & Hotel (Map p113; ☎ 6663 6100; www.meininger-hostels.de; Schönhauser Allee 19; dm €19, s/d/tr €52/70/102, breakfast €3.50; P ✕ 🛈 🛈) Run with panache and professionalism, this top-flight hotel–hostel combo is ideal for savvy nomads seeking plenty of comfort without dropping buckets of cash. A lift whisks you to mod rooms and dorms (all with attached bathrooms) with plenty of space, quality furnishings, flat-screen TVs and even blackout blinds to combat jetlag (or hangovers). Other assets: the all-day cafe-bar, guest kitchen and spot-on location close to sights, eats and party. Check the website for the other four Berlin locations, including a new one at the Hauptbahnhof.

Hotel Apartmenthaus Zarenhof (Map p113; ☎ 802 0880; www.apartmenthaus-zarenhof.de; Schönhauser Allee 140; r €80-160, breakfast €11; ✕ ▯) At this homage to Russian Tsar Nicholas II, rooms pair a regal red-and-blue colour scheme with such 21st-century amenities as plasma TVs. Most units wrap around a central courtyard and come with kitchenettes and small balconies. The gut-buster breakfasts feature such Russian specialities as *blinis* (pancakes) and even caviar.

Ackselhaus & Blue Home (Map p113; ☎ 4433 7633; www.ackselhaus.de; Belforter Strasse 21; 1-/2-room apt from €110-180; ▯) This charismatic contender brings 'sexy' back to the bedroom in 10 apartments spread across two 19th-century buildings. Themed from naughty to nautical, elegant to eastern, each sports a small living room and kitchenette. Breakfast is served until 11am (12.30pm on weekends).

Potsdamer Platz & Tiergarten

Mövenpick Hotel Berlin (Map pp110-11; ☎ 230 060; www.moevenpick-berlin.com; Schöneberger Strasse 3; d €115-200, breakfast €21; ℗ ✕ ✕ ▯) This snazzy hotel cleverly marries bold contemporary design with the industrial aesthetic of the historic Siemenshöfe, making it a chic base of operation for both the suit brigade and city-breakers. Rooms vamp it up with glass cube walls and sensuous olive wood furniture. Tip: the top-floor Atelier Rooms come with Philippe Starck–designed free-standing tubs.

Mandala Hotel (Map pp110-11; ☎ 590 050 000; www.themandala.de; Potsdamer Strasse 3; ste €270-580, breakfast €21; ℗ ✕ ✕ ▯ ▯) How 'suite' it is to be staying at this discrete retreat, a place of casual sophistication and unfussy ambience. Six sizes of suites are available, each outfitted for maximum comfort and ideal working conditions in case you're here to ink that deal. Perks: a Michelin-star restaurant, a snazzy hotel bar and a world-class day spa.

Kreuzberg

baxpax Kreuzberg (Map pp110-11; ☎ 6951 8322; www.baxpax.de; Skalitzer Strasse 104; dm €9-22, s €29-37, d €42-60, discounts Nov-Feb; ✕ ▯ ▯) Small, artsy and chilled-out, this sociable hostel in an old factory puts you smack-dab into Kreuzberg's party zone. It has great security, fanciful murals and one of the most original beds in town: it's inside a genuine Volkswagen bug! Cook up a storm in the kitchen, then meet fellow travellers on the terrace.

Hotel Johann (Map pp110-11; ☎ 225 0740; www.hotel-johann-berlin.de; Johanniterstrasse 8; s €70-90, d €95-105; ✕ ▯) This 33-room hotel consistently tops the popularity charts thanks to its eager-to-please service and gorgeous rooms, some with scalloped ceilings, exposed brick walls and other historic touches. The small garden is perfect for summery breakfasts, while happening Bergmannstrasse and the Jewish Museum are just quick strolls away.

Hotel Riehmers Hofgarten (Map pp110-11; ☎ 7809 8800; www.riehmers-hofgarten.de; Yorckstrasse 83; s €100, d €138-145; ℗ ✕ ▯) Near Viktoriapark, this charismatic boutique hotel is part of a protected 1891 building complex with a lush inner courtyard certain to delight romantics. Large double French doors lead to mostly spacious, high-ceilinged rooms that are modern but not stark. Gourmet restaurant.

Friedrichshain

Ostel (Map pp110-11; ☎ 2576 8660; www.ostel.eu; Wriezener Karree 5; dm €9, s/d without bathroom €33/54, with bathroom €40/61, breakfast €4.50; ℗ ✕ ▯ ▯) Ostel resuscitates GDR charm with original furnishings sourced from flea markets, grannies' attics and eBay. With portraits of party apparatchiks peering down on you, you can stay in a Pioneer Room dorm, a '70s holiday apartment, a prefab flat or the bugged Stasi Suite. Just like staying on the set of *Good Bye, Lenin!*

Eastern Comfort Hostelboat (Map pp110-11; ☎ 6676 3806; www.eastern-comfort.com; Mühlenstrasse 73-77; dm €16-19, 2nd-class s/d/tr/q €50/58/69/76, 1st-class s/d €64/78, linen €5; ✕ ▯ ▯) Moored right by the East Side Gallery, this floating hostel puts you within staggering distance of top party venues. Cabins are carpeted and trimmed in wood, but pretty snug (except for '1st-class'); all but the dorms have their own shower and loo. Private rooms are also available in the Western Comfort boat across the river. Also see p145.

Hotel 26 (Map pp110-11; ☎ 297 7780; www.hotel26-berlin.de; Grünberger Strasse 26; s/d from €70/90; ℗ ✕ ▯) This modern hotel decked out in cheery citrus colours may seem sparse and no-nonsense, but

---

HOLIDAY FLATS

For self-caterers, independent types, wallet-watchers, families and anyone in need of plenty of privacy, a short-term furnished-flat rental may well be the cat's pyjamas. Plenty of options have been popping up lately, but these are our favourites:

■ **Brilliant Apartments** (☎ 8061 4796; www.brilliant-apartments.de; apt €80-120; ☒ ☜) The name is the game in these eight stylish and modern units with full kitchens that sleep up to six and are located on Oderberger Strasse and Rykestrasse, both hip drags in Prenzlauer Berg that put you close to everything.

■ **Miniloft Berlin** (Map p108; ☎ 847 1090; www.miniloft.de; Hessische Strasse 5; apt from €105) Fourteen architect-designed lofts in an energy-efficient building, some with south-facing panorama windows, others with cosy alcoves, all outfitted with modern designer furniture and kitchenettes.

■ **T&C Apartments** (Map p113; ☎ 405 046 612; www.tc-apartments-berlin.de; Kopenhagener Strasse 72; apt from €50) Huge selection of stylish, hand-picked one- to four-room apartments in Mitte, Prenzlauer Berg, Tiergarten and Schöneberg; headquarters located in Prenzlauer Berg.

---

it has a lot going on that doesn't immediately meet the eye, including an eco-conscious approach to hospitality. Rooms are nonsmoking and the breakfast is entirely organic.

Charlottenburg

our pick **Propeller Island City Lodge** (Map p112; ☎ 891 9016 8am-noon, ☎ 0163-256-5909 noon-8pm; www.propeller-island.de; Albrecht-Achilles-Strasse 58; r €65-180, breakfast €7; ☒) The name was inspired by a novel by the master of imagination, Jules Verne, and indeed each of the 32 rooms is a journey to a unique, surreal and slightly wicked world. To be stranded on Propeller Island means waking up on the ceiling, in a prison cell or inside a kaleidoscope. This is no conventional hotel, so don't expect pillow treats or other trappings.

Hotel Bogota (Map p112; ☎ 881 5001; www.hotel-bogota.de; Schlüterstrasse 45; s €66-98, d €90-150; ☒ ☒ ☐ ☜) Helmut Newton studied with fashion photographer Yva here in the 1930s and to this day this rambling landmark hosts glam-mag photo shoots. It oozes vintage charm from every nook and cranny and is one of our favourite budget picks in town. Room sizes and amenities vary greatly (cheaper ones share a bathroom), so inspect a few before settling in.

Hotel-Pension Dittberner (Map p112; ☎ 884 6950; www.hotel-dittberner.de; Wielandstrasse 26; s €67-87, d €95-120; ☜) It's hard not to be completely charmed by this hushed 3rd-floor *Pension* presided over by the super-friendly Frau Lange. The soaring ceilings, plush oriental rugs and armloads of paintings and lithographs ooze genuine Old Berlin flair.

All in all, a great base of operation for city explorations.

Hotel Askanischer Hof (Map p112; ☎ 881 8033; www.askanischer-hof.de; Kurfürstendamm 53; s €105-130, d €117-155; ☒ ☒ ☜) In a city that likes to teeter on the cutting edge, this 17-room jewel warps you back in time to the roaring '20s, albeit with updated amenities. Still, the look is all Old Berlin: eclectic antiques, lacy drapes, gaudy chandeliers and oriental rugs. For extra privacy, order breakfast in bed.

Hotel Art Nouveau (Map p112; ☎ 327 7440; www.hotelartnouveau.de; Leibnizstrasse 59; s €96-146, d €126-176, tr €151-191; ☒ ☒ ☐ ☜) A rickety belle-époque lift drops you off at one of Berlin's finest boutique *Pensionen*. Its rooms neither skimp on space nor on charisma and offer a unique blend of youthful flair and tradition. The honour bar is handy for feeding late-night cravings, and coffee and tea are free.

Ellington Hotel (Map p112; ☎ 683 150; www.ellington-hotel.com; Nürnberger Strasse 50-55; s €120-250, d €130-270, breakfast €19; ☒ ☒ ☒ ☜) Duke and Ella gave concerts in the 'Badewanne' (bath tub) jazz cellar and Bowie and Prince partied in the 'Dschungel' night club, then the lights went out in the '90s. Now the handsome 1920s building has been reborn as a high-concept jewel that wraps all that's great about Berlin – history, innovation, elegance, the art of living – into one attractive package.

Louisa's Place (Map p112; ☎ 631 030; www.louisas-place.de; Kurfürstendamm 160; ste €135-425, breakfast €20; ☒ ☒ ☐ ☜ ☒) Louisa's is a discrete deluxe hideaway that dazzles with class not glitz, perfect for sharp dressers tired of anonymous big-city hotels. Few properties put more emphasis on customising guest services. They'll even send you a pre-arrival questionnaire asking for your likes and dislikes. Suites here are huge, the spa heavenly and the library regal.

Hotel Concorde Berlin (Map p112; ☎ 800 9990; www.berlin.concorde-hotels.com; Augsburger Strasse 41; r from €160; P ✕ ✕ ▢ ☜) If you like designer boutique hotels but value the amenities of a big-city property, the Concorde should fit the bill. Designed by Jan Kleihues, from the curved limestone facade to the door knobs, it channels New York efficiency, French *savoir vivre* and Berlin-style unpretentiousness. The 311 rooms are super-sized, warmly furnished and decorated with contemporary German art prints.

EATING

Once considered a gastronomic wasteland, Berlin now packs in a lot of flavour as bright young chefs have become bolder and more experimental in their kitchens. Even those finicky Michelin testers have confirmed that Berlin is ripe for the culinary big league by awarding coveted stars to 10 chefs. Fortunately, you don't need deep pockets to please your tummy since some of the best eating is actually done in neighbourhood restaurants like Cafe Jacques (p141).

Berlin's multicultural tapestry has brought the world's foods to town, from Austrian schnitzel to Zambian zebra steaks. Vegetarian restaurants are sprouting as fast as alfalfa, as are 'bio' (organic) eateries. In fact, Berlin lays claim to being home to Germany's first organic fast-food restaurant, Yellow Sunshine (p141) and first carbon-neutral restaurant, Foodorama (p141).

Another hot trend: Asian lifestyle eateries. The concept – soups plus a few daily changing specials served in designer ambience – was pioneered a few years back by Monsieur Vuong (right) and has since been copied ad nauseam.

One of life's little luxuries is a leisurely breakfast, and Berliners have just about perfected the art – especially on Sundays when many cafes dish out lavish all-you-can-eat buffets. International fast-food chains are ubiquitous, but the most beloved homegrown fast-food is *Currywurst*, a slivered, subtly spiced pork sausage swimming in tomato sauce and sprinkled with curry powder.

Another local favourite is the *Döner* (doner kebab), a lightly toasted bread pocket stuffed with thinly shaved veal or chicken and salad and doused with garlicky yoghurt sauce.

Mitte

Café Nord-Sud (Map p108; ☎ 9700 5928; Auguststrasse 87; 3-course meal €7.50; ☽ lunch & dinner Mon-Sat) Truth be told, this place we'd rather keep secret. It's just one of those little gems, you know, always packed to the rafters thanks to Jean-Claude's Gallic charm, the kitchen's formidable talents and the rock-bottom prices.

Schwarzwaldstuben (Map p108; ☎ 2809 8084; Tucholskystrasse 48; mains €7-14; ☽ 9am-midnight; ☜) The tongue-in-cheek olde-worlde decor is as delicious as the authentic southern German food served in gut-busting portions at this cosy corner joint. We can't get enough of the *geschmelzte Maultaschen* (sautéed ravioli-like pasta) but all goes down well with a Rothaus Tannenzäpfle beer, straight from the Black Forest.

Ishin (Map p108; ☎ 2067 4829; Mittelstrasse 24; platters €7-18; ☽ 11am-8pm Mon-Sat) This cafeteria-style sushi parlour scores two for looks and 10 for freshness and value. Prices drop even lower during Happy Hour (all day Wednesday and Saturday and 11am to 4pm on other days). Nice touch: the unlimited free green tea.

Monsieur Vuong (Map p108; ☎ 3087 2643; Alte Schönhauser Strasse 46; mains €7.50; ☽ noon-midnight) This upbeat Indochina nosh stop hasn't lost a step despite becoming a fixture on the tourist circuit. From the flavour-packed soups to the fragrant rice and noodle dishes, it's all delicious even if the steady

---

BERLIN'S BEST...

- Asian – Edd's (p140)
- Celebrity Spotting – Grill Royal (above)
- Currywurst – Curry 36 (p141)
- *Döner* – Schlemmerbuffet (p140)
- German – Engelbecken (p142)
- Gourmet – Facil (p140)
- Neighbourhood restaurant – Cafe Jacques (p141)
- Riverside dining – Spindler & Klatt (p141)
- Vegetarian – Cookies Cream (p140)

BERLIN

queue does not make for leisurely meals. Afternoons are slowest.

Tartane (Map p108; ☎ 4472 7036; Torstrasse 225; mains €8-18; ⏱ 6pm-2am) The lamps and Meissen tile mural are scavenged from the demolished GDR-era Palast der Republik, but otherwise this stylish gastro pub is very much in the here and now. Most nights tables buzz with an arty, local crowd wolfing Tartane's luscious signature burgers and downing glasses of refreshing Kölsch beer from Cologne.

Zur Letzten Instanz (Map p108; ☎ 242 5528; Waisenstrasse 14-16; mains €9-18; ⏱ noon-1am Mon-Sat) Oozing folksy Old Berlin charm, this rustic eatery has been an enduring hit since 1621 and has fed everyone from Napoleon to Angela Merkel. It's one of the best places in town for classic Berlin fare.

Kasbah (Map p108; ☎ 2759 4361; Gipsstrasse 2; mains €11-16; ⏱ dinner Tue-Sun) Take your tastebuds on a magic carpet ride at this exotic salon where owner Driss welcomes each guest with a big smile. Eating here is a sensory immersion that starts with rinsing your hands in rosewater before digging into such tasty treats as flaky *b'stilla* (chicken-stuffed filo) or tangy *tagine* (stew). The Moroccan wine is excellent too.

Cookies Cream (Map p108; ☎ 2749 2940; Friedrichstrasse 158; 3-course meal €30; ⏱ dinner Tue-Sat) Combining coolness with substance, this great hidden eatery is reached via the service alley of the Westin Grand Hotel. Upstairs awaits an elegantly industrial space where flesh-free but flavour-packed dishes are brought to linen-draped tables. It's all so good and gorgeous, even diehard meatheads should have no complaints.

Grill Royal (Map p108; ☎ 2887 9288; Friedrichstrasse 105b; mains €16-48; ⏱ dinner) A platinum card is a handy accessory at this 'look-at-me' temple, where politicians, Russian oligarchs, pouting models and 'trustafarians' can be seen slurping oysters and tucking into *wagyū* steak. The entrance is on the canalside below the hotel.

Other faves:

Schlemmerbuffet (Map p108; ☎ 283 2153; Torstrasse 125; *Döner* €2.50; ⏱ 24hr) The best *Döner* in town. Enough said.

Dolores (Map p108; ☎ 2809 9597; Rosa-Luxemburg-Strasse 7; dishes €6; ⏱ 11.30am-10pm Mon-Fri, 1-10pm Sat & Sun) Build-your-own burritos.

Prenzlauer Berg

Konnopke Imbiss (Map p113; ☎ 442 7765; Schönhauser Allee 44a; dishes €1.30-3.90; ⏱ 6am-8pm Mon-Fri, noon-7pm Sat) Legendary *Currywurst* kitchen.

Hans Wurst (Map p113; ☎ 4171 7822; Dunckerstrasse 2a; mains €4-9; ⏱ noon-midnight Tue-Sun) The name is a bit of a tease, for you definitely won't find any wurst (sausage) in this stylish vegan cafe. In fact, Michael Ristock is a veritable genius when it comes to coaxing maximum flavour out of organic, fair-trade and animal-free ingredients. Perks: great music, relaxed crowd and pizza too.

Schusterjunge (Map p113; ☎ 442 7654; Danziger Strasse 9; mains €4-12; ⏱ 11am-midnight) This rustic corner joint doles out authentic Berlin charm with as much abandon as the delish home cooking. Big platters of goulash, pork roast and *Sauerbraten* (vinegar-marinated and braised beef) feed both tummy and soul, and so do the locally brewed Bürgerbräu and Bernauer Schwarzbier.

Fellas (Map p113; ☎ 4679 6314; Stargarder Strasse 3; mains €7-18; ⏱ 10am-1am; ⏱) This unhurried bistro employs cooks surely destined for fancier places. The regular menu has great salads and schnitzel, but the most creativity goes into the big-flavoured weekly specials. Or come just for a snack and wine.

Oderquelle (Map p113; ☎ 4400 8080; Oderberger Strasse 27; mains €8-16; ⏱ dinner) If this restaurant weren't so darn popular, you'd just pop in for a beer and a casual but well-crafted German meal. But, alas, without a reservation, chances of scoring a table after 8pm are practically nil, although the bar stools might do in a pinch.

Potsdamer Platz & Tiergarten

Edd's (Map pp106-7; ☎ 215 5294; Lützowstrasse 81; mains €14-25; ⏱ lunch Tue-Fri, dinner Tue-Sun) Edd's grandma used to cook for Thai royals and the man himself has regaled Berlin foodies for over three decades with such palate-pleasers as twice-roasted duck, chicken steamed in banana leaves and curries that are poetry on a plate. Reservations essential.

Facil (Map pp110-11; ☎ 590 051 234; 5th fl, Mandala Hotel, Potsdamer Strasse 3; 1-/2-course lunch €18/28, 4-/7-course dinner €80/120; ⏱ lunch & dinner Mon-Fri) With its sleek Donghia chairs, alabaster lamps and honey-hued natural stone, this glass garden at the Mandala Hotel (p137) is as breathtaking as Michael Kempf's Michelin-starred fare. Budget gourmets should come for lunch.

Kreuzberg

Burgermeister (Map pp110-11; ☎ 2243 6493; Oberbaumstrasse 8; burger €3; ⏱ 11am-2am or later) A burger joint in a century-old public toilet on a traffic island below the elevated U-Bahn tracks? Don't fret, don't shudder, for the patties here are big and delicious.

Yellow Sunshine (Map pp110-11; ☎ 6959 8720; Wiener Strasse 19; dishes €3.50-7; ☺ noon-midnight) Healthy fast food is not an oxymoron at this certified organic meat-free diner. Their vegie burgers are slobberingly yummy and the *seitan* steak and tofu *Currywurst* might even get hard-core carnivores salivating.

Foodorama (Map pp110-11; ☎ 6900 1100; Bergmannstrasse 94; mains €5-14; ☺ 9am-11pm) What looks like a postmodern school cafeteria is actually Germany's first certified carbon-neutral restaurant. Pop by for organic spins on local faves such as *Currywurst* and potato salad or travel the globe via yakitori and Viennese schnitzel. Quality is uneven but your conscience will be clear.

Henne (Map pp110-11; ☎ 614 7730; Leuschnerdamm 25; half chicken €7.50; ☺ dinner Tue-Sun) At this Berlin institution the name is the menu: roast chicken it is, take it or leave it. It's a concept that's been a cult for over a century, so who are we to argue? Eat in the garden or the original interior from 1907. Reservations highly advised.

Cafe Jacques (Map pp110-11; ☎ 694 1048; Maybachufer 8; mains €7.50-15; ☺ dinner) Fresh flowers, flattering candlelight, delicious wine – this intimate cafe might just be the perfect date spot. But, frankly, you only have to be in love with good food to enjoy supper choices rooted in French or North African cuisine. Make reservations or hope for a no-show.

Spindler & Klatt (Map pp110-11; ☎ 319 881 860; Köpenicker Strasse 16-17; mains €14-22; ☺ dinner, closed Mon & Tue Nov-Apr) Summers on the riverside terrace are magical in this Prussian bread factory turned trendy nosh and party spot. Sit at a long table or loll on a platform bed while tucking into creative fusion fare. Turns into a dance club on Friday and Saturday nights.

Horváth (Map pp110-11; ☎ 6128 9992; Paul-Lincke-Ufer 44a; mains €20-28, 3-/4-course menu €37/45; ☺ dinner Tue-Sun) At this jewel on 'bistro row' along Landwehr canal, Wolfgang Müller translates influences from Asia, Germany and the Mediterranean into something uniquely his own. Foie gras with scallops and orange-vanilla leeks is a typical outcome.

Hartmanns (Map pp110-11; ☎ 6120 1003; Fichtestrasse 31; 3-/4-/5-/6-course menu €42/49/56/64; ☺ dinner Mon-Sat) Culinary wunderkind Stefan Hartmann became Berlin's Chef of the Year in 2008, a mere year after opening this romantic basement restaurant where he regales patrons with innovative French-Mediterranean cuisine.

We also like these:

Curry 36 (Map pp110-11; ☎ 251 7368; Mehringdamm 36; snacks €2-6; ☺ 9am-4am Mon-Sat, 11am-3am Sun) One of the town's top *Currywurst* purveyors.

Il Casolare (Map pp110-11; ☎ 6950 6610; Grimmstrasse 30; pizzas €4.50-7.50; ☺ noon-midnight) Dynamite pizzas – thin, crispy, cheap and wagon-wheel-sized.

Hasir (Map pp110-11; ☎ 614 2373; Adalbertstrasse 10; mains €5-10; ☺ 24hr) Turkish food from the place that invented the Berlin-style doner kebab.

Friedrichshain

Meyman (Map pp110-11; ☎ 0163-806 1363; Krossener Strasse 11a; dishes €3.50-5; ☺ noon-2am) Popular with bar crawlers, this Friedrichshain nosh spot hopscotches around the Mediterranean with pizza, pasta, shwarma, Moroccan casseroles and other balance-restoring munchies.

Schwarzer Hahn (Map pp110-11; ☎ 2197 0371; Seumestrasse 23; mains €6-12; ☺ 10am-10pm Mon-Sat) The small menu at this personable slow-food bistro is stocked with oldies but goodies updated for the 21st century. Service is impeccable and the friendly owner knows a thing or two about wine.

Miseria & Nobiltà (Map pp110-11; ☎ 2904 9249; Kopernikusstrasse 16; mains €12-22; ☺ dinner Tue-Sun) When Eduardo Scarpetti penned the comedy *Poverty and Nobility* in 1888, he didn't know that it would inspire the name of this popular family-run trattoria. You'll definitely feel more king than pauper here when digging into the deftly prepared southern Italian compositions.

Charlottenburg

Ali Baba (Map p112; ☎ 881 1350; Bleibtreustrasse 45; pizza €3-7; ☺ 11.30am-3am) At this been-there-forever hole-in-the-wall pizza parlour the pies are cheap and piping hot and smiles are free. Popular with party people and posh Charlottenburgers in the mood to go slumming.

Schwarzes Cafe (Map p112; ☎ 313 8038; Kantstrasse 148; dishes €4.50-10; ☺ 24hr) Not many cafes have shown as much staying power as this rambling multi-floor icon which has plied an all-ages cast of natives and tourists with bites, beer and breakfast around the clock since 1978. The toilets are a hoot, the little garden idyllic.

Cafe Wintergarten im Literaturhaus (Map p112; ☎ 882 5414; Fasanenstrasse 23; mains €8-16; ☺ 9.30am-midnight) You don't have to be the literary type

BERLIN

in order to enjoy a coffee or light lunch at this genteel art-nouveau villa. Get a dose of Old Berlin flair in the gracefully stucco-ornamented rooms or repair to the idyllic garden. Breakfast is served until 2pm.

Engelbecken (Map p112; ☎ 615 2810; Witzlebenstrasse 31; mains €8-18; ☽ 4pm-1am Mon-Sat, noon-1am Sun) This lakeside charmer gets top marks for its impeccably crafted German soul food. Locally sourced organic meats and produce find their destiny in classic pork roast, porcini strudel or duck with caramelized onions. Reservations essential.

Bond (Map p112; ☎ 5096 8844; Knesebeckstrasse 16; mains €8-30; ☽ lunch Sun-Sat, dinner nightly) If you're in Berlin *On Her Majesty's Secret Service*, you'll impress *The Living Daylights* out of your date at this chill designer den decked out in royal purple, ebony and gold. The standard menu is heavy on, well, standards, like grilled meats, club sandwiches and burgers, but the specials are more inventive. Cheap it ain't, but remember, *You Only Live Twice*.

Moon Thai (Map p112; ☎ 3180 9743; Kantstrasse 32; mains €10-17; ☽ noon-midnight) This is our favourite Thai nosh spot in the western city. Sunset-coloured walls accented with exotic art create an upbeat ambience that's a perfect foil for dishes so perky they might get you out of the doldrums. Anything revolving around duck or squid gets top marks.

Duke (Map p112; ☎ 683 154 000; Nürnberger Strasse 50-55; 2-/3-course lunch €13/18.50, mains €18-28; ☽ 11.30am-midnight) Hotel restaurants tend to be a snore but not this contender at the Ellington Hotel (p138). Chef Carsten Obermayr pairs punctilious craftsmanship with local farm-fresh ingredients resulting in such dishes as lamb medallions with artichokes and potato-olive puree.

Other recommendations:

Jules Verne (Map p112; ☎ 3180 9410; Schlüterstrasse 61; breakfasts €4-10, mains €8-19; ☽ 9am-1am) Global menu bistro where *Flammkuchen* (Alsatian pizza), Austrian schnitzel and North African couscous are all perennial bestsellers.

Mr Hai & Friends (Map p112; ☎ 3759 1200; Savignyplatz 1; mains €8-16; ☽ 11am-1am) Stylish Vietnamese restaurant packed with trendy locals lusting after the fresh and aromatic fare.

Natural' Mente (Map pp106-7; ☎ 341 4166; Schustehrusstrasse 26; mains €8-12; ☽ lunch only) Uses only organic ingredients for daily changing menu of vegetarian, vegan and macrobiotic dishes.

Schöneberg

Habibi (Map p143; ☎ 215 3332; Goltzstrasse 24; snacks €2.50-5; ☽ 11am-3am Sun-Thu, to 5pm Fri & Sat) This perennially popular snack shack makes soul-sustaining felafel that pair perfectly with a freshly pressed carrot juice.

Trattoria á Muntagnola (Map p143; ☎ 211 6642; Fuggerstrasse 27; mains €12-20; ☽ dinner) Everybody feels like family at this convivial joint where dishes burst with the feisty flavours of southern Italy's sun-baked Basilicata region. Many fine ingredients are imported straight from 'the Boot' and turned into pizzas, pastas and rustic mains like garlic-braised rabbit. Nice touch: the olive-oil trolley.

Renger-Patzsch (Map p143; ☎ 784 2059; Wartburgstrasse 54; mains €13-20; ☽ dinner) This off-the-beaten-path neighbourhood restaurant exudes a refreshing earthiness that matches its robust menu. Try big-hunger mains like red-wine-braised ox cheeks or snack on their excellent *Flammkuchen*.

Cafe Einstein Stammhaus (Map p143; ☎ 261 5096; Kurfürstenstrasse 58; breakfast €6-15, mains €15-23; ☽ 9am-1am) Schnitzels, noodles and warm apple strudels – you'll find them all at this classic Viennese coffee house in a historic garden villa once owned by a 1920s German actress. The setting is stylish but the staff could lay off the snootiness.

Other good nosh spots:

Ousies (Map p143; ☎ 216 7957; Grunewaldstrasse 16; small plates €3-9, mains €10-18; ☽ dinner) Bubbly and kitsch-free *ouzeria*, the Greek spin on the tapas bar. Reservations advised.

La Cocotte (Map p143; ☎ 7895 7658; Vorbergstrasse 10; mains €8-17; ☽ dinner) French restaurant with pretty terrace and food that's more country than *haute*.

DRINKING

Berlin is a great place for boozers. From cosy pubs, riverside beach bars, chestnut-shaded beer gardens, underground dives, DJ bars, snazzy hotel lounges and designer cocktail temples, you're rarely far from a good time. Kreuzberg and Friedrichshain are currently the edgiest bar-hopping grounds, with swanky Mitte and Charlottenburg being more suited for date night than dedicated drinking. The line between cafe and bar is often blurred, with many places changing stripes as the hands move around the clock.

Mitte

Barcomi's Deli (Map p108; ☎ 2859 8363; 2nd courtyard, Sophie-Gips-Höfe; Sophienstrasse 21; ⏲ 9am-9pm Mon-Sat, 10am-9pm Sun) Train your java radar onto this buzzing New York–meets-Berlin deli where latte-rati, families and expats meet for coffee, bagels with lox and some of the best brownies and cheesecake this side of the Hudson River.

Bebel Bar (Map p108; ☎ 460 6090; Behrenstrasse 37; ⏲ from 9am) Channel your inner Cary Grant and belly up to the bar at this mood-lit thirst parlour at the Hotel de Rome (p136). Cocktails here have a progressive, sexy edge that goes over well with the global Armani crowd.

Tausend (Map p108; ☎ 460 6090; Schiffbauerdamm 11; ⏲ from 9pm Tue-Sat) The living room of the see-and-be-seen scene. No sign, no light, no bell, just a heavy steel gate beneath a railway bridge with a small window through which you shall be assessed. Once inside the black and metal tunnel, though, there's expert cocktails and eye-candy fellow sippers.

Other cool drinking dens:

Bar 3 (Map p108; ☎ 2804 6973; Weydinger Strasse 20; ⏲ from 9pm Tue-Sat) Laid-back lair for local lovelies, artists and professionals, with delicious Kölsch beer on tap.

Windhorst (Map p108; ☎ 2045 0070; Dorotheenstrasse 65; ⏲ from 6pm Mon-Fri, 9pm Sat) Postage-stamp sized bar with five-star ambience and killer cocktails.

Prenzlauer Berg

Klub der Republik (Map p113; Pappelallee 81, ⏲ from 10pm) No sign for this ballroom-turned-bar, so just look up until you see some steamy windows, then teeter up the wobbly staircase. Join hormone-happy hipsters amid pure GDR-trash-ostalgia and wall projections for electronic sounds and cheap drinks.

Marietta (Map p113; ☎ 4372 0646; Stargarder Strasse 13; ⏲ from 10am) Retro is now at this self-service retreat where you can check out passing eye-candy through the big window or lug your beverage to the dimly lit back room for quiet bantering. On Wednesday nights it's a launch pad for the gay party circuit (p150).

Deck 5 (Map p113; Schönhauser Allee 80; ⏲ 10am-midnight, in good summer weather only) Soak up the city lights at this beach bar in the sky while sinking your toes into tonnes of sand lugged to the top parking deck of the Schönhauser Arkaden mall. Getting there via a seemingly never-ending flight of stairs on Greifenhagener Strasse will get your heart pumping.

Prater (Map p113; ☎ 448 5688; Kastanienallee 7-9; ⏲ from noon Apr-Sep) Berlin's oldest beer garden (since 1837) oozes traditional charm and is a fun spot for guzzling a cold one beneath

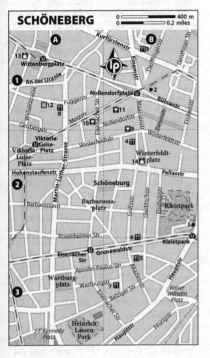

SCHÖNEBERG

0   400 m
0   0.2 miles

the chestnut trees. Bring the kids! There's a small play area just for them.

Anna Blume (Map p113; ☎ 4404 8749; Kollwitzstrasse 83; ☿ 10am-midnight) Named for a Kurt Schwitters poem, this corner cafe lures patrons all day long into its velvety art-nouveau interior perfumed by potent java, homemade cakes and flowers from the attached shop. Its breakfasts are a satisfying affair any time of day; the tiered trays feed two to four. Fantastic people-watching terrace, too.

Potsdamer Platz & Tiergarten

Cafe am Neuen See (Map pp106-7; ☎ 2544930; Lichtensteinallee 2; mains €4-12; ☿ from 10am daily Mar-Oct, Sat & Sun Nov-Feb) This lakeside Bavarian-style beer garden in Tiergarten park feels like a microvacation from the city bustle. Cold beers go well with the bratwurst, pizza and pretzels. Romantic types can even rent a boat and take their sweetie for an aquatic glide.

Solar (Map pp110-11; ☎ 0163-765 2700; www.solar -berlin.de; Stresemannstrasse 76) The door's tight, service slow and the cocktails only so-so but the views – oh, the views – really are worth the vertigo-inducing trip aboard an exterior glass lift to this 17th-floor Manhattan wannabe. The entrance is off-street in an ugly high-rise behind the Pit Stop auto shop.

Kreuzberg & Kreuzkölln

Ankerklause (Map pp110-11; ☎ 693 5649; Kottbusser Damm 104; ☿ from 4pm Mon, from 10am Tue-Sun) This nautical kitsch tavern in an old harbour-master's shack is a great place for quaffing and waving to the boats puttering along the Landwehrkanal. On Thursdays DJs shower attitude-free party people with disco, indie rock and electro.

Freischwimmer (Map pp110-11; ☎ 6107 4309; Vor dem Schlesischen Tor 2; ☿ from 2pm Mon-Fri, from 11am Sat & Sun, winter hr vary) There are few places more idyllic than this rustic ex-boathouse with a sunny terrace floating above a little canal. Come just for drinks, a bite from the global snack menu or Sunday brunch.

Raumfahrer (Map pp110-11; Hobrechtstrasse 54; ☿ from 7pm Mon-Sat) You can't help but see 'red' in this out-there space capsule where drinks may quickly whisk you into Never-Never Land. At this 'low-fi' neighbourhood corner of the world, the beer is cold, the vibe whispers 'good times' and there's an easygoing crowd to match.

Kiki Blofeld (Map pp110-11; Köpenicker Strasse 48/49; ☿ from 2pm Mon-Fri, from noon Sat & Sun) A Spree-side

rendezvous with Kiki will have you swinging in a hammock, lounging on natural grassy benches, chilling on the riverside beach, waving to passing boats from the wooden deck, catching an offbeat flick or shaking it in an East German army boat patrol bunker.

Würgeengel (Map pp110-11; ☎ 615 5560; Dresdner Strasse 122; ☿ from 7pm) For a swanky night out, point the compass to this dimly lit cocktail cave. The interior is pure '50s with a striking glass ceiling, chandeliers and shiny-black tables. The name, by the way, pays homage to the surreal 1962 Luis Buñuel movie, *Exterminating Angel*.

Monarch (Map pp110-11; Skalitzerstrasse 134; ☿ from 9pm Tue-Sat) Bonus points if you can find this upstairs bar right away. Tip: the unmarked entrance is next to the *Döner* shop near the Kaiser's supermarket. Behind the steamed-up windows awaits an ingenious blend of trashy sophistication infused with bouncy electro, strong drinks and a relaxed vibe.

Möbel Olfe (Map pp110-11; ☎ 6165 9612; Reichenberger Strasse 177; ☿ Tue-Sun) An old furniture store has been recast as an always-busy drinking den with cheap libations and a friendly crowd that's mixed in every respect. Beware: those animal skeletons above the bar get downright trippy after a few Polish beers or high-octane vodkas. Enter from Dresdener Strasse.

San Remo Upflamör (Map pp110-11; ☎ 7407 3088; Falckensteinstrasse 46; ☿ 10am-2am) Gather your posse at this laid-back hang-out before heading out into the long Kreuzberg night. If chill clientele, nice waiters, DJ sessions and cold beers won't get you in party mood, what will? Coffee and cake in the daytime.

Friedrichshain

CSA (Map pp106-7; ☎ 2904 4741; Karl-Marx-Allee 96; ☿ from 8pm May-Oct, from 7pm Nov-Apr) Friedrichshain's fanciest bar has been carved out of the former Czechoslovakian national airline office and exudes an ironic Soviet vintage vibe. Dim lights, clear design lines and strong cocktails make this a favourite of the grown-up set. Check out the tables with built-in ash trays.

Kptn A Müller (Map pp110-11; Simon-Dach-Strasse 32) Ahoy matey, the captain's in town, bringing much needed relief from this strip's cookiecutter cocktail-lounge circuit. Pretensions do not fly at this self-service bar where drinks are cheap (0.5L beer or 0.2L glass of wine €2) and there's no charge for table football or wi-fi.

Monster Ronson's Ichiban Karaoke (Map pp110-11; ☎ 8975 1327; Warschauer Strasse 34; ☒ from 7pm) Knock back a couple of 'brewskis' if you need to loosen your nerves before belting out your best J Lo or Justin at this kooky karaoke joint. *Pop Idol* wannabes can pick from thousands of songs and hit the stage; shy types may prefer renting a private party room (per hour €12).

Hops & Barley (Map pp110-11; ☎ 2936 7534; Wühlischstrasse 38) Conversation flows as freely as the beer (and cider) produced right at this congenial microbrewery. Share a table with low-key locals swilling postwork pints and munching rustic *Treberbrot*, a hearty bread made with a natural by-product from the brewing process.

Charlottenburg & Schöneberg

Galerie Bremer (Map p112; ☎ 881 4908; Fasanenstrasse 37; ☒ from 8pm Mon-Sat) Entering this tiny bar tucked behind an art gallery feels like slipping into a swanky '20s speakeasy. The air, though, is rather genteel, grown-up and completely devoid of debauchery. Vintage fans will adore the original interior by Berliner Philharmonie architect Hans Scharoun.

Universum Lounge (Map p112; ☎ 8906 4995; Kurfürstendamm 153) The curvaceous teak bar and white leather banquettes of this spacey retro-glam libation station fill up quickly after the curtain falls at the Schaubühne theatre located in the same building, a 1920s Bauhaus gem by Erich Mendelssohn.

Green Door (Map p143; ☎ 215 2515; Winterfeldtstrasse 50) A long line of renowned 'mixologists' has tended at this oh-so-stylish drinking establishment. They make you ring the doorbell to gain entry, but once inside you'll find it hard to leave the comfy surrounds

Puro Skylounge (Map p112; ☎ 2636 7875; Tauentzienstrasse 11; ☒ from 8pm Tue-Sat) Puro has quite literally raised the bar in Charlottenburg, by moving it to the top of the Europa Center, that is. It's a great place if you want to trade classic Berlin funky-trash for a high-heeled Chanel world. Mind erasers of choice are Moët, martinis and cosmos. Dress up, or forget about it.

ENTERTAINMENT

Sometimes it seems as though Berliners are the lotus-eaters of Germany, people who love nothing better than a good time. Pack some stamina if you want to join them. With no curfew, this is a notoriously late city where bars stay packed from dusk to dawn and beyond and some clubs don't hit their stride until 4am.

Listings

Zitty (www.zitty.de) and **Tip** (www.tip-berlin.de) are the most widely read of the biweekly German-language listings magazines available at newsstands. Party-oriented **030** (www.berlin030.de) is the best of the free zines, while **Berlin Programm** (www.berlin-programm.de) is a good source for mainstream and high-brow events. For up-to-the-minute happenings, subscribe to the free e-newsletter of **Berlin Unlike** (www.berlin.unlike.net). The English-language monthly **ExBerliner** (www.exberliner.de) also has select listings.

Tickets

Credit-card bookings by telephone or online through a venue's box office are becoming more commonplace in Berlin. Most take reservations over the phone but make you show up in person to pay for and pick up your tickets. Agencies, which are commonly found in shopping malls and department stores such as KaDeWe or Galeria Kaufhof, usually add a steep service charge (up to 20%).

Berlin Infostores (p114) All Berlin Infostores sell tickets to events in person, by phone and online. Discounts of up to 50% are available for select same-day performances.

Hekticket (☎ 230 9930; www.hekticket.de) Alexanderplatz (Map p108; ☎ 2431 2431; Karl-Liebknecht-Strasse 12; ☒ noon-8pm Mon-Sat); Bahnhof Zoo (Map p112; ☎ 230 9930; Hardenbergstrasse 29a; ☒ 10am-8pm Mon-Sat, 2-6pm Sun) Also sells discounted 'last min'

BERLIN'S BOAT OF BABBLE

A fun and easy way to meet friendly locals over beer and bratwurst is at the **World Language Party**, which takes over the retro lounge of the floating Eastern Comfort Hostelboat (p137) every Wednesday from 6pm. It brings together an easygoing, all-ages international crowd, including lots of regulars, but don't be shy – people are friendly and eager to welcome newcomers. Admission is €1, which is added to your first drink. Also check MC Charles' website, www.english-events-in-berlin.de, for updates and additional goings-on.

PARTY MILES

Köpenicker Strasse, Kreuzberg (Map pp110–11) Industrial riverside strip where nights might start with supper at chic Spindler & Klatt (p141), continue with a caipirinha at Kiki Blofeld (p144) and finish with steaming up the dance floor at Tresor (opposite) or, if you're in the mood (and dressed right), the libidinous KitKatClub (below)

Kottbusser Tor/Oranienstrasse, Kreuzberg (Map pp110–11) Grunge-tastic area best suited for dedicated drink-a-thons at Möbel Olfe (p144), Würgeengel (p144) and Monarch (p144). The closest music and dance venue is SO36 (opposite).

Oranienburger Strasse, Mitte (Map p108) Major tourist zone where you have to hopscotch around sex workers and pub crawlers to drown your sorrows in overpriced bars.

Schlesische Strasse, Kreuzberg (Map pp110–11) Freestyle street where you could kick off with beer at Freischwimmer (p144), catch a band at Dot Club (opposite) and dance till sunrise at Watergate (below) or Club der Visionäre (below).

Simon-Dach-Strasse, Friedrichshain (Map pp110–11) If you need a cheap buzz, head to this well-trodden booze strip. Kptn A Müller (p144) is great for escaping the cookie-cutter cocktail lounges.

---

tickets for select same-day performances between 2pm and 7pm.

Nightclubs

Berghain/Panorama Bar (Map pp110-11; www.berghain.de; Am Wriezener Bahnhof, Friedrichshain; ☺ Fri & Sat) According to Britain's *DJ Mag* this is the best club in the world and we have no problem seconding the hype. Only the best techno and house vinyl masters heat up this hedonistic bass junkie haven inside a labyrinthine ex-power plant. Strict door and no cameras.

Clärchens Ballhaus (Map p108; ☎ 282 9295; Auguststrasse 24, Mitte; ☺ from 10pm Mon, from 9pm Tue–Thu, from 8pm Fri & Sat, from 3pm Sun) Yesteryear is now at this late, great 19th-century dance hall where groovers and grannies swing their legs to tango, swing, waltz, disco and pop. In the daytime, the garden's a nice spot for pizza and German soul food (served from 12.30pm).

Club der Visionäre (Map pp110–11; ☎ 6951 8942; Am Flutgraben 1, Kreuzberg; ☺ daily) This summertime chill and party playground in an old canalside boat shed is great for a drink or two at any time of day or night. On weekends, they practically never close, making it one of the best Sunday after-party spots in town.

Cookies (Map p108; www.cookies-berlin.de; Friedrichstrasse 158-164, Mitte; ☺ Tue, Thu & Sat) This legendary party palace used to be midweek only but now also runs a Saturday party called 'Crush'. There's no sign, a tough door, great cocktails, and a grown-up ambience. Enter next to the KPM store.

Felix clubrestaurant (Map p108; ☎ 206 2860; Behrenstrasse 72, Mitte; ☺ Thu-Sat) Once past the velvet rope of this exclusive supper club at the Adlon, you too can be shaking that booty to 'international club sounds', sip champagne cocktails and – who knows? – maybe even meet your very own Carrie or 'Mr Big'. Great after-work party on Thursday (from 9pm).

KitKatClub @ Sage (Map p108; ☎ 278 9830; www .kitkatclub.de; Köpenicker Strasse 76, enter from Brückenstrasse, Mitte; ☺ Fri & Sat) This 'kitty' is naughty, sexy, decadent, listens to techno and house and fancies leather and lace, vinyl and whips. Berlin's infamous erotic nightclub currently hides out at Sage Club with its multiple dance floors, shimmering pools and fire-breathing dragon. Check the website for dress code instructions.

Tape Club (Map p108; www.tapeberlin.de; Heidestrasse 14, Mitte; ☺ from midnight Sat, sometimes Fri) There's a tantalising underground vibe to this dancing den where top local and visiting DJs get clubbers going with Chicago- and Detroit-influenced house, deep house, dub house and dub techno. Watch out for the 'Tape Modern' party series, a fusion of club and art expo.

Watergate (Map pp110–11; ☎ 6128 0394; www.water -gate.de; Falckensteinstrasse 49a, Kreuzberg; ☺ Fri & Sat) Watergate has a fantastic location with a lounge overlooking the Spree and a floating terrace actually on it. Top DJs keep the two floors hot and sweaty with a head-spinning mix of techno, breakbeat, house and drum 'n' bass.

Weekend (Map p108; www.week-end-berlin.de; Am Alexanderplatz 5, Mitte; ☺ Thu-Sat) This hot 'n' heavy club in a GDR-era office building delivers awesome views, sleek design and high-profile spinners such as Dixon, Phonique and Tiefschwarz. There are three floors: the 12th with its panoramic windows, the inky black 15th and the rooftop lounge.

Also recommended:

2BE (Map p108; www.2be-club.de; Heidestrasse 73, Mitte; Fri & Sat) The 'place to be' for bootylicious hip hop, R&B and dancehall.

Kaffee Burger (Map p108; ☎ 2804 6495; www.kaffeeburger.de, in German; Torstrasse 60; daily) Fun-for-all party pen and home to the famous Russendisko (Russian Disco).

Tresor (Map pp110-11; ☎ 6953 7713; Köpenicker Strasse 70, Mitte; from midnight Wed, Fri & Sat) The techno pioneer is back in the dark industrial maze of a former power station.

Live Music
ROCK & POP

Lido (Map pp110-11; ☎ 6956 6840; Cuvrystrasse 7, Kreuzberg) A 1950s cinema has been recycled into a rock-indie-electro-pop mecca with mosh-pit electricity and a crowd that cares more about the music than about looking good.

Dot Club (Map pp110-11; ☎ 7676 6267; Falckensteinstrasse 47, Kreuzberg) If you want to catch tomorrow's bands today, head to this newish club, which does triple-duty as concert hall, recording studio and restaurant. It also does party nights and jam sessions, all amid superb acoustics and decor teetering somewhere between kitsch and cult.

Magnet (Map p113; ☎ 4400 8140; Greifswalder Strasse 212-213, Prenzlauer Berg) Small, cheap and dingy, this indie bastion is known for bookers with an astronomer's vision to detect stars in the making. LCD Soundsystem and The Presets had early performances here. After the show, the rambling, multi-floor venue morphs into a dance club with DJs hopscotching from punk to pop to electro.

SO36 (Mapp110-11; ☎ 6140 1306; Oranienstrasse 190, Kreuzberg) Check in your attitude at the door of scruffy 'Esso' where the Dead Kennedys and the Toten Hosen were playing gigs when many of today's patrons were still in diapers. Overall, though, who goes when depends on what's on that night: a solidarity concert, a lesbigay theme party, a night flea market: anything goes at SO36.

Wild at Heart (Map pp110-11; ☎ 611 9231; Wiener Strasse 20, Kreuzberg) Named for a David Lynch road movie, this one-room kitsch-cool dive hammers home punk, rock, ska and rocka-billy. Touring bands, including such top acts as Girlschool and Dick Dale, bring in the tattooed set several times weekly.

JAZZ

A-Trane (Map p112; ☎ 313 2550; www.a-trane.de, in German; Bleibtreustrasse 1, Charlottenburg; 9pm-2am Mon-Thu, open till late Fri & Sat) Herbie Hancock and Diana Krall have anointed the stage of this intimate jazz club but mostly it's emerging talent bringing their A-game to the A-Trane. Entry is free on Monday when local boy Andreas Schmidt is playing, and after 12.30am on Saturday for the late-night jam session.

B-flat (Map p108; ☎ 283 3123; www.b-flat-berlin.de; Rosenthaler Strasse 13, Mitte; from 8pm) Cool cats of all ages come out to this intimate venue where you'll be quite literally sitting within spitting distance of the performers. The emphasis is on acoustic music; mostly jazz, world beats, Afro-Brazilian and other soundscapes. Wednesday's free jam session often brings down the house.

Yorckschlösschen (Map pp110-11; ☎ 215 8070; www.yorckschloesschen.de; Yorckstrasse 15, Kreuzberg; from 5pm Mon-Sat, from 10am Sun) This knick-knack-laden watering hole has plied an all-ages, all comers crowd of jazz and blues lovers with tunes and booze for over a century. There's live music on Wednesday and weekends, pub grub till 1am, a pool table out back and a garden in summer.

CLASSICAL & OPERA

Berliner Philharmonie (Map pp110-11; ☎ 2548 8999; www.berliner-philharmoniker.de; Herbert-von-Karajan-Strasse 1, Tiergarten; tickets €7-150) The Philharmonie is arguably the finest place in town to hear classical music, thanks to its supreme acoustics. It's home base for the legendary Berliner Philharmoniker, currently led by Sir Simon Rattle. Bonus: free lunchtime concerts Tuesdays at 1pm (September to June).

Konzerthaus Berlin (Map p108; ☎ 203 090; www.konzerthaus.de; Gendarmenmarkt 2, Mitte; tickets €10-100) Another supreme music venue, the Schinkel-designed Konzerthaus has the Konzerthausorchester as its 'house band' but others, such as the Rundfunk-Sinfonieorchester Berlin, perform here as well.

Staatsoper Unter den Linden (Map p108; ☎ 2035 4555; www.staatsoper-berlin.org; Unter den Linden 7, performances at Schiller Theater, Bismarckstrasse 110; tickets €5-160) While the grand dame of Berlin's opera houses is getting a facelift (probably until 2013), you'll have to travel to the Schiller Theater in Charlottenburg (Map p112) to attend the high-calibre productions staged under Daniel Barenboim. All operas are sung in their original language.

Deutsche Oper Berlin (Map p112; ☎ 3438 4343; www .deutscheoperberlin.de; Bismarckstrasse 35, Charlottenburg; tickets €12-118) The acoustics of Berlin's largest opera house are the stuff of every tenor's dreams and thanks to its first-ever female boss, Kirsten Harms, its stuffy image has been dropped. All operas are performed in the original language.

Cabaret & Varieté

Admiralspalast (Map p108; ☎ 4799 7499; www.admirals palast.de, in German; Friedrichstrasse 101-102) This beautifully restored 1920s party palace stages crowd-pleasing plays, concerts and musicals in its elegant historic hall, and more intimate shows – including comedy, readings, dance, concerts and theatre – on two smaller stages.

Bar Jeder Vernunft (Map p112; ☎ 883 1582; www.bar-jeder-vernunft.de, in German; Schaperstrasse 24, Charlottenburg) Life's still a cabaret at this intimate 1912 art-nouveau mirrored tent, which puts on song-and-dance shows, comedy and chanson evenings plus the famous *Cabaret* cult musical itself.

Blue Man Group (Map pp110-11; ☎ 01805-4444; www .bluemangroup.de; Marlene-Dietrich-Platz 4, Mitte) This musical and visual extravaganza, starring slightly nutty and energetic guys dipped in Smurf-blue latex suits, performs at its own permanent theatre, a converted IMAX now called Bluemax.

Chamäleon Varieté (Map p108; ☎ 4000 5930; www .chamaeleon-variete.de; Rosenthaler Strasse 40/41, Mitte) An alchemy of art-nouveau charms and high-tech theatre, this intimate former ballroom presents classy variety shows – comedy, juggling acts and singing – often in sassy, sexy and unconventional fashion.

Friedrichstadtpalast (Map p108; ☎ 2326 2326; www .friedrichstadtpalast.de; Friedrichstrasse 107) Marlene Dietrich and Ella Fitzgerald have graced the stage of this 1920s vintage palace. Today, Europe's largest revue theatre does mostly glitzy-glam Vegas-style productions with leggy showgirls in skimpy costumes and feather boas. Since it's hard to fill the 2000 seats, its future is uncertain.

Cinemas

Going to the movies is pretty pricey, with Saturday-night tickets at the multiplexes costing up to €11. Almost all cinemas also add a sneaky *Überlängezuschlag* (overrun supplement) of €0.50 to €1 for films longer than 90 minutes. Go before 5pm or on *Kinotag* (film day, usually Monday to Wednesday) to save up to 50%. Indie theatres are usually cheaper than the megaplexes. In summer, watching movies alfresco in a *Freiluftkino* (outdoor cinema) is a venerable tradition.

Most cinemas show mainstream Hollywood fare dubbed into German. Movies screened in their original language are denoted in listings by the acronym 'OF' (*Originalfassung*) or 'OV' (*Originalversion*); those with German subtitles are marked 'OmU' (*Original mit Untertiteln*).

The venues listed here all screen English-language films.

Arsenal (Map pp110-11; ☎ 2695 5100; Filmhaus, Potsdamer Strasse 2, Sony Center, Tiergarten) Nonmainstream fare from around the world.

Babylon Mitte (Map p108; ☎ 242 5969; Rosa-Luxemburg-Strasse 30, Mitte) Modern art-house fare, silent films, themed screenings and literary readings.

Cinestar Original (Map pp110-11; ☎ 2606 6260; www .cinestar.de; Potsdamer Strasse 4, Tiergarten) Hollywood blockbusters, all in English, all the time.

Eiszeit (Map pp110-11; ☎ 611 6016; Zeughofstrasse 20, Kreuzberg) Obscure, alternative and experimental films.

Filmkunst 66 (Map p112; ☎ 882 1753; Bleibtreustrasse 12, Charlottenburg) Indie house known for offbeat flicks and annual film festival.

Theatre

Berlin has more than 100 theatres, many of which are dark on Mondays and from mid-July to late August. Good seats are often available on performance day from the theatre's box office. Some venues offer discounts of up to 50% for students and seniors. Listed here are the main drama drags; for fringe and experimental stages flick through the listings magazines.

Deutsches Theater (Map p108; ☎ 2844 1225; www .deutschestheater.de, in German; Schumannstrasse 13a, Mitte) Berlin's top theatre has reeled in numerous thespian awards, including Theatre of the Year in 2008. Plays are also performed in the smaller Kammerspiele, next door, and at Box + Bar, an 80-seat space with cocktail bar that presents edgy and experimental fare.

Berliner Ensemble (Map p108; ☎ 2840 8155; www .berliner-ensemble.de, in German; Bertolt-Brecht-Platz 1, Mitte) Brecht's former theatre presents works by him and other European 20th-century playwrights, sprinkled with the occasional play by Shakespeare, Schiller or Lessing. The building itself is gorgeous.

Volksbühne am Rosa-Luxemburg-Platz (Map p108; ☎ 2406 5777; www.volksbuehne-berlin.de, in German; Rosa-Luxemburg-Platz, Mitte) Nonconformist, radical and provocative; Volksbühne's head and Dostoyevsky fan Frank Castorf wouldn't have it any other way. Performances here are not for those squeamish about blood and nudity.

Schaubühne am Lehniner Platz (Map p112; ☎ 890 020; www.schaubuehne.de; Kurfürstendamm 153, Charlottenburg) The western city owes any cutting-edge theatrical credentials to this former 1920s cinema, rescued from bland obscurity under the forceful leadership of director Thomas Ostermeier. Some performances feature English surtitles.

English Theatre Berlin (Map pp110-11; ☎ 691 1211; Fidicinstrasse 40, Kreuzberg) The repertoire of Berlin's oldest English-language stage includes classics, physical theatre, comedy and works by emerging writers and directors, many based in Berlin.

Sport

Hertha BSC (off Map pp106-7; ☎ 01805-189 200; www.hertha bsc.de; Olympiastadion; 🚇 ♿ Olympiastadion) Berlin's long-standing *Bundesliga* (National League) football (soccer) team plays home games at the Olympic Stadium. Tickets are usually available on game day and start at €10.

Alba Berlin (Map pp110-11; ☎ 01805-969 000 111; www.albaberlin.de; Mühlenstrasse 12-30; tickets €10-35) Berlin's top basketball team competes hard on a European level and has a solid winning record. Since 2008, fans have been flocking to the sparkling O2 World arena for home games.

Eisbären Berlin (Map pp110-11; ☎ 9718 4040; www .eisbaeren.de; O2 Platz 1; tickets €15-30) Fervent ice-hockey fans have cheered their team all the way to the national champion title in 2005, 2006, 2008 and 2009. Home games, now in the sleek O2 World arena, practically explode with atmosphere.

SHOPPING

The closest the German capital comes to having a retail spine is Kurfürstendamm and its extension, Tauentzienstrasse. Getting the most out of shopping here means venturing into the various districts, each of which has its own identity and mix of stores calibrated to the needs, tastes and pockets of locals. Go to Charlottenburg for international couture, Kreuzberg for second-hand fashions, and to Mitte and Prenzlauer Berg for indie designers. Schöneberg has the fabulous KaDeWe department store, but its side streets are also lined with niche shops.

Note that some smaller stores do not accept credit cards.

Department Stores & Malls

KaDeWe (Kaufhaus des Westens; Map p143; ☎ 212 10; Tauentzienstrasse 21) This century-old department store has an assortment so vast that a pirate-style campaign is the best way to plunder its bounty, especially in the legendary 6th-floor gourmet food hall

Alexa (Map p108; ☎ 269 3400; Grunerstrasse 20) Power shoppers love this XXL-sized mega-mall that cuts a rose-hued presence near Alexanderplatz. Besides the usual mainstream retailers, there's also a store by German rapper Bushido, the Kindercity interactive indoor playground and Loxx, the world's largest model railway.

Galeries Lafayette (Map p108; ☎ 209 480; Friedrichstrasse 76) The Berlin branch of the exquisite French emporium is centred on a glass cone shimmering with kaleidoscopic intensity. Aside from racks packed with Prada and the like, you can get your mitts on sexy Agent Provocateur lingerie, edgy Berlin fashions and gourmet treats in the food hall.

Potsdamer Platz Arkaden (Map pp110-11; ☎ 255 9270; Alte Potsdamer Strasse) This pleasant indoor mall brims with mainstream chains and also has two supermarkets, a food court and possibly the best ice-cream parlour in town, the upstairs Caffe & Gelato.

Farmers Markets

Winterfeldtmarkt (Map p143; Winterfeldtplatz, Schöneberg; ☯ 8am-2pm Wed, 8am-4pm Sat) Spending Saturdays at this upscale farmers and crafts market is a ritual for many Berliners. Do as they do and cap off a spree with coffee or breakfast in a nearby cafe.

Turkish Market (Map pp110-11; Maybachufer, Kreuzberg; ☯ noon-6.30pm Tue & Fri) Olives, feta spreads, loaves of fresh bread and mountains of fruit and vegetables, all at bargain

GAY & LESBIAN BERLIN

Berlin's legendary liberalism has spawned one of the world's biggest, most fabulous and diverse LGBT playgrounds. Anything goes in 'Homopolis' (and we *do* mean anything), from the highbrow to the hands-on, the bourgeois to the bizarre, the mainstream to the flamboyant.

The rainbow flag has proudly flown in Motzstrasse and Fuggerstrasse in Schöneberg since the 1920s. Prenzlauer Berg has the hippest gay scene in eastern Berlin, with hubs along Greifenhagener Strasse, Gleimstrasse and Schönhauser Allee. Kreuzberg has more of an alt-flavoured feel (Oranienstrasse, Mehringdamm), while Friedrichshain's small but up-and-coming scene is student-driven.

Berlin's gayscape runs the entire spectrum from mellow cafes, campy bars and cinemas, to saunas, cruising areas, clubs with dark rooms and all-out sex venues. In fact, sex and sexuality are entirely everyday matters to the unshockable city folks and there are very few, if any, itches that can't be quite openly and legally scratched. As elsewhere, gay men have more options for having fun, but grrrls – from lipstick lesbians to hippie chicks to bad-ass dykes – won't have to feel left out.

Except for the hard-core places, gay spots get their share of opposite-sex and straight patrons, drawn by gay friends, the fabulousness of the venues, abundant eye candy and, for women in gay bars, a non-threatening atmosphere.

Information

Mann-O-Meter (Map p143; ☎ 216 8008; Bülowstrasse 106) One-stop information centre that also operates a hotline to report attacks on gays (☎ 216 3336)

Out in Berlin (www.out-in-berlin.de) This English/German booklet and website is an indispensable guide to the queer scene in town.

Siegessäule (www.siegessaeule.de) The bible for all things gay and lesbian in Berlin.

Festivals

In mid-June, huge crowds turn out for the **Schwul-Lesbisches Strassenfest** (Gay-Lesbian Street Fair) in Schöneberg, which basically serves as a warm-up for **Christopher Street Day** (p134) later that month.

Sights

A great place to learn about Berlin's queer history is the nonprofit **Schwules Museum** (Gay Museum; Map pp110-11; ☎ 693 1172; Mehringdamm 61; adult/concession €5/3; ☒ 2-6pm Wed-Mon), which is museum, archive and community centre all in one.

In June 2008, the **Denkmal für Homosexuelle NS Opfer** (Memorial for Homosexual Nazi Victims; Map p108) was unveiled on the edge of the Tiergarten park along Ebertstrasse. The off-kilter concrete box echoes the design of the Holocaust Memorial across the street until you look through a window at the looped video showing two men kissing tenderly.

Drinking

Heile Welt (Map p143; ☎ 2191 7507; Motzstrasse 5, Schöneberg) This laid-back lair gets high marks for its flirt factor and sensuous fur-covered walls; it's a great warm-up spot for the long night ahead.

Roses (Map pp110-11; ☎ 615 6570; Oranienstrasse 187, Kreuzberg) The ultimate in kitsch, Roses is a glittery fixture on the local lesbigay booze circuit with bartenders that pour with a generous elbow.

---

prices, are what you'll find at this colourful canalside market.

Kollwitzplatzmarkt (Map p113; Wörther Strasse btwn Knaackstrasse & Kollwitzstrasse, Prenzlauer Berg; ☒ noon-8pm Thu, 9am-4pm Sat) Velvety gorgonzola, juniper-berry-smoked ham, crusty sourdough bread and all manner of organic produce are the kinds of exquisite morsels scooped up by locals at this posh market.

Flea Markets

Flohmarkt am Mauerpark (Map p113; Bernauer Strasse 63; ☒ 10am-5pm Sun) This flea market has all sorts of vendors, with everything from T-shirt designers and families who've cleaned out their closets to down-at-heelers hawking trash. Follow up your shopping with a drink at the outdoor cafe or a nap in the Mauerpark.

Zum Schmutzigen Hobby (Map p113; Rykestrasse 45, Prenzlauer Berg) Local trash drag deity Nina Queer presides over this louche den of kitsch and glam with decor, clientele and goings-on that aren't for the faint-of-heart (check out the porno wallpaper in the men's room). On Wednesdays at 9pm it's standing-room only for Nina's 'glamour trivia quiz'.

Melitta Sundström (Map pp110-11; ☎ 692 4414; Mehringdamm 61, Kreuzberg; ✿ from 2.30pm) This cheerful cafe is busy at all hours but never more so than on Saturday nights when it's a preferred fuelling-up stop for parties at SchwuZ (opposite) out back.

Hafen (Map p143; ☎ 211 4118; Motzstrasse 19, Schöneberg) An essential component of the Schöneberg party scene, the friendly Harbour is a great first stop to dock at before launching into a raucous night on the razzle. On Mondays, quizmaster Hendryk tests your trivia knowledge with his hilarious Quizzorama shows (in English on the first Monday of the month).

Nightclubs

For a review of Berghain/Panorama Bar, see p146.

Ackerkeller (Map p108; ☎ 3646 1356; Bergstrasse 68, Mitte; ✿ from 9pm Tue, from 10pm Fri & Sat) This alt-pub spins into a party venue thrice weekly with rock, pop, electro and even Balkanbeats keeping the dance floor grooving. Best day is Tuesday.

SchwuZ (Map pp110-11; ☎ 629 0880; Mehringdamm 61, Kreuzberg; ✿ Fri & Sat) Fortify yourself at Melitta Sundström (opposite), then head to the basement to work the dance floors. A good place to ease into the scene for all comers.

Connection (Map p143; ☎ 218 1432; Fuggerstrasse 33, Schöneberg; ✿ Fri & Sat) This classic men-only disco was a techno pioneer way back in the '80s and still hasn't lost its grip on the scene. The labyrinth of underground darkrooms is legendary.

Parties

Some of the best queer club nights are independent of the venues they use and may move around. We've given locations current at the time of writing, but it's best to check the websites or the listings mags for the latest scoop. There are also frequent gay parties at SO36 (p147).

Berlin Hilton (Map p113; ☎ 4405 1681; www.berlinhilton.de, in German; Schönhauser Allee 36, Prenzlauer Berg; ✿ Wed) On hump day, 'Hiltonistas' descend upon the small and low-tech NBI club for a heady dance mix of electro-rock and campy singalongs. Would Paris approve?

Chantals House of Shame (Map p113; ☎ 281 8323; www.siteofshame.com; Schönhauser Allee 176a, Prenzlauer Berg; ✿ Thu) Chantal's legendary party (currently at Bassy) is beloved not so much for its glam factor as for the over-the-top trannie shows and the hotties who love 'em.

GMF (Map p108; www.gmf-berlin.de, in German; ✿ Sun) Currently at Weekend (p146), Berlin's premier Sunday club is known for excessive SM (standing and modelling). Predominantly boyz, but girls OK.

Irrenhaus (Map pp106-7; ; www.ninaqueer.com, in German; Am Friedrichshain 33, Friedrichshain; ✿ 3rd Sat of month) The name means 'insane asylum' and they're not kidding. Party hostess with the mostest, trash queen Nina Queer, puts on nutty, naughty shows that are not for the faint of heart. Expect the best; fear the worst.

Flohmarkt am Boxhagener Platz (Map pp110-11; Boxhagener Platz, Friedrichshain; ✿ 9am-4pm Sun) There are few too many pros, but that just means you'll have to dig a little harder for the cool finds. On the plus side: prices are rock bottom.

Flohmarkt am Arkonaplatz (Map pp106-7; Arkonaplatz; ✿ 10am-5pm Sun) Easily combined with the Mauerpark flea market, this one feeds the retro frenzy with plenty of groovy furniture, accessories, clothing, vinyl and books, including plenty of GDR memorabilia.

Flohmarkt Strasse des 17 Juni (Map p112; ✿ 10am-5pm Sat & Sun) West of the Tiergarten S-Bahn station, this big market is a tourist favourite, making bargains as rare as tulips in Tonga. Come here for Berlin memorabilia, stuff from granny's closet and jewellery.

Made in Berlin

Bonbonmacherei (Map p108; ☎ 4405 5243; Oranienburger Strasse 32, Heckmannhöfe, Mitte) The old-fashioned art of handmade sweets has been lovingly revived in this basement-store-cum-show-kitchen. Watch candy masters Katja and Hjalmar using their antique equipment to churn out such tasty treats as the signature leaf-shaped *Maiblätter* (May leaves).

Berlinerklamotten (Map p108; www.berlinerklamotten .de; Court III, Hackesche Höfe, Mitte) Flip through the racks of this arbiter of fashion-cool to dig up urban, cheeky outfits and accessories made right here in the German capital. On weekends, a DJ pumps out high-energy sounds to get you into party mood.

Tausche (Map p113; ☎ 4020 1770; Raumerstrasse 8, Prenzlauer Berg) Heike Braun and Antje Strubels, both landscape architects by training, make by hand cool bags in various sizes that are practical, durable and stylish. Best of all, they're kitted out with exchangeable logo flaps that zip on and off in seconds.

IC! Berlin (Map p108; ☎ 2472 7200; Max-Beer-Strasse 17, Mitte) With no less a luminary than determined fashion chameleon Madonna among its fans, the IC! Berlin brand is *the* place to go for fashion-forward sunglasses, smart screwless specs and a solid dose of Berlin design cool.

Music

Platten Pedro (Map pp106-7; ☎ 344 1875; Tegeler Weg 102, Charlottenburg) Vinyl purists happily make the trip out to this cultish store packed to the rafters with vintage albums, from pop to punk to polka – and not a CD in sight! It's near Schloss Charlottenburg.

Space Hall (Map pp110-11; ☎ 694 7664; Zossener Strasse 33, Kreuzberg) This galaxy for electronic-music gurus has four floors filled with everything from acid to techno by way of drum 'n' bass, neotrance, dubstep and so on. A dozen or so players stand by for easy pre-purchase listening.

GETTING THERE & AWAY
Air

Berlin has two international airports, Tegel (TXL; Map pp106–7), about 8km northwest from the city centre, and Schönefeld (SFX, Map p103), about 22km southeast. For information about either, go to www.berlin-airport .de or call ☎ 0180-500 0186. Schönefeld is

currently being expanded and rebranded as Berlin Brandenburg International (BBI), scheduled to start operation in late 2011. Once BBI is open, Tegel will close.

Most major international airlines serve Berlin, as do discount carriers Ryanair, easyJet, Air Berlin and Germanwings. For airline contact information, see p773.

Bus

Berlin's central bus station, **ZOB** (off Map pp106-7, Masurenallee 4-6; ⊖ Kaiserdamm, ⓡ Messe Nord/ICC) is anything but. In fact, it's in deepest western Berlin, next to the trade-fair grounds, about 4km west of Bahnhof Zoo.

Tickets are available from travel agencies in town and from the on-site **ZOB Reisebüro** (☎ 301 0380; ⓨ 6am-9pm Mon-Fri, 6am-8pm Sat & Sun). The main operators are **BerlinLinienBus** (☎ 861 9331; www.berlinlinienbus.de) and **Gulliver's** (☎ 311 0211; www.eurobusexpress.de).

Backpacker-oriented hop-on, hop-off service **Busabout** (☎ in the UK 08450 267 514; www .busabout.com) stops at the Citystay Hostel (p135) in Mitte.

Car & Motorcycle

The A10 ring road links Berlin with other German and foreign cities, including the A11 to Szczecin (Stettin) in Poland; the A12 to Frankfurt an der Oder; the A13 to Dresden; the A9 to Leipzig, Nuremberg and Munich; the A2 to Hanover and the Ruhrgebiet cities; and the A24 to Hamburg.

Citynetz (Map p112; ☎ 194 44; www.mfz-citynetz.de; Joachimstaler Strasse 4; ⓨ 9am-8pm Mon-Fri, 10am-4pm Sat & Sun) provides ride-share services.

HIRE

All the major international chains maintain branches at the airports, major train stations and throughout town. Check the Yellow Pages (under *Autovermietung*) for local branches or call the central reservation numbers (see p783).

Their vehicles are not the latest models and may have more dents than amenities, but prices are hard to beat at local independent **Das Hässliche Entlein** (Map p112; ☎ 0180-343 3683; www.die-ente.de, in German; Lietzenburger Strasse 29; ⓨ 9am-6pm Mon-Fri). Daily rentals start at €15, including full insurance, VAT and unlimited kilometres; new cars start at €20. Make reservations as early as possible because they only have a smallish fleet.

If you get 'Harley hunger', head to **Classic Bike** (Map p112; ☎ 616 7930; www.classic-bike.de; Salzufer 6; 🚇 Tiergarten). Daily (24-hour) rates range from €70 to €135.

Train

Berlin is well connected by train to other German cities, as well as to popular European destinations, including Prague, Warsaw and Amsterdam.

The futuristic Hauptbahnhof (central train station) has great infrastructure, but with five floors of tracks and services it can be confusing. North- and southbound trains depart from the bottom floor, while east- and westbound trains, as well as the S-Bahn, run from platforms on the top level. Buy tickets in the *Reisezentrum* (Travel Centre) located between tracks 14 and 15 on the first upper floor (1F) and first lower floor (B1). The latter also has a Euraide desk (p114).

The left-luggage office (€4 per piece per 24 hours) is behind the ReiseBank currency exchange on the first upper level, opposite the *Reisezentrum*. Lockers are hidden on the lower level of the parking garage accessible near the Kaiser's supermarket on the first lower floor. Other services include a 24-hour pharmacy, a Berlin Infostore tourist office (p114), a supermarket and other stores open daily from 8am to 10pm. The TXL bus to Tegel airport leaves from Europaplatz (exit north entrance).

While all long-distance trains converge at the Hauptbahnhof, some also stop at other stations such as Spandau, Ostbahnhof, Gesundbrunnen and Südkreuz. Of these, Ostbahnhof has the second-best infrastructure.

GETTING AROUND
To/From the Airports
SCHÖNEFELD

Schönefeld airport is served twice hourly by the AirportExpress train from Bahnhof Zoo (30 minutes), Friedrichstrasse (23 minutes), Alexanderplatz (20 minutes) and Ostbahnhof (15 minutes). Note that these are regular Regionalexpress (RE) or Regionalbahn (RB) designated as Airport Express trains in the timetable. There are more frequent S9 trains, but the service is slower (40 minutes from Alexanderplatz, 50 minutes from Bahnhof Zoo). The S45 line goes straight to the trade-fair grounds.

Trains stop about 400m from the terminals, which are served by a free shuttle bus every 10 minutes. Walking takes about five to 10 minutes.

Buses 171 and X7 link the terminals directly with the U-Bahn station Rudow (U7) with onward connections to central Berlin. The fare for any of these trips is €2.80.

Budget about €35 for a cab ride to central Berlin.

TEGEL

Tegel is connected to Mitte by the JetExpressBus TXL (30 minutes) and to Bahnhof Zoo in Charlottenburg by express bus X9 (20 minutes). Bus 109 also serves the western side of the city but is slower and useful only if you're headed somewhere along the Kurfürstendamm (30 minutes). Tegel is not directly served by U-Bahn, but both bus 109 and X9 stop at Jakob-Kaiser-Platz (U7), the station closest to the airport. Any of these trips cost €2.10.

Taxi rides cost about €20 to Bahnhof Zoo and €23 to Alexanderplatz.

Car & Motorcycle

Driving in Berlin is more hassle than it's worth, especially since parking is hard to find and expensive (about €1 to €2 per hour), so we highly recommend you make use of the excellent public transport system instead.

Central Berlin (defined as the area bounded by the S-Bahn rail ring) is a restricted low-emission zone, which means all cars entering it need an *Umweltplakette* (emission sticker). See p783 for details on how to obtain one.

Public Transport

Berlin's public transport system is run by **BVG** (☎ 194 49; www.bvg.de) and consists of the U-Bahn, S-Bahn, regional trains, buses and trams.

BUYING & USING TICKETS

Bus drivers sell single tickets and day passes, but all other tickets must be purchased before boarding, either from orange vending machines (with instructions in English) located in U- or S-Bahn stations or from any kiosk or shop bearing the BVG logo.

Tickets must be stamped (validated) at station platform entrances. The on-the-spot

BERLIN

fine for getting caught without a valid ticket is €40.

FARES & TICKETS

The network is divided into fare zones A, B and C, with tickets available for zones AB, BC and ABC. Unless you're venturing to Potsdam or Schönefeld airport, you only need the AB ticket, which is valid for two hours. The short-trip ticket (*Kurzstreckenticket*, €1.30) is good for three stops on any U-Bahn or S-Bahn or six on any bus or tram. The group day pass is valid for up to five people travelling together. Children aged six to 14 qualify for reduced (*ermässigt*) rates, while kids under six travel for free.

Ticket type	AB	BC	ABC
single	€2.10	€2.50	€2.80
reduced single	€1.40	€1.7	€2
day pass	€6.10	€6.30	€6.50
group day pass	€15.90	€15.40	€16.10
7-day pass	€26.20	€27	€32.30

BUSES & TRAMS

Buses run frequently between 4.30am and 12.30am. From Sunday to Thursday, night buses take over in the interim, running roughly every 30 minutes. Buses N2, N5, N6, N8 and N9 follow more or less the routes of the U2, U5, U6, U8 and U9. Nightline route maps are available from BVG offices and are also displayed on station platforms.

Trams only operate in the eastern districts. The M10, N54, N55, N92 and N93 offer continuous service nightly.

S-BAHN & REGIONAL TRAINS

S-Bahn trains make fewer stops than U-Bahns and are therefore handy for longer distances, but they don't run as frequently. They operate from around 4am to 12.30am and all night on Friday, Saturday and public holidays.

Destinations further afield are served by Regionalbahn (RB) and Regionalexpress (RE) trains. You'll need an ABC or Deutsche Bahn ticket to use these trains.

U-BAHN

The most efficient way to travel around Berlin is by U-Bahn. Trains operate from 4am until about 12.30am and throughout the night on Friday, Saturday and public holidays (all lines except the U4).

Taxi

You'll find taxi ranks at airports and major train stations and throughout the city. At night, cabs often line up outside theatres, clubs and other venues.

Flag fall is €3.20, then it's €1.58 per kilometre up to 7km and €1.20 for each kilometre after that. Taxis can also be ordered on ☎ 443 322, 210 202 or 263 000. There are no surcharges for night trips but bulky luggage costs an extra €1 per piece.

For short hops you can use the €4 *Kurzstreckentarif* (short-trip rate), which entitles you to ride for up to 2km. You must flag down a moving taxi and request this special rate before the driver has activated the metre. If you want to continue past 2km, regular rates apply to the entire trip.

Brandenburg

Although its land surrounds bustling Berlin, the Brandenburg state of mind is as far from the German capital as Shangri-La. It's a quiet, gentle state with vast expanses of unspoilt scenery, much of it in protected nature reserves. Its landscape is quilted in myriad shades, from emerald beech forest to golden fields of rapeseed and sunflowers, but it's also rather flat, windswept and perhaps even a bit melancholic.

This is a region shaped by water – not only by the rippling Oder, Havel and Spree Rivers that sinuously wend through it, but also by the thousands of ponds and lakes and the labyrinthine waterways connecting them. Water also characterises the Spreewald, where indigenous Sorbs keep alive their customs in island hamlets, and the Lower Oder Valley National Park, whose idyllic wetlands provide shelter for rare and endangered bird species. Like a fine wine, Brandenburg is best appreciated in sips, not gulps. It invites slowing down and exploring by bike, boat or on foot.

As the germ cell of Prussia, and thus modern Germany, Brandenburg is a land of great culture. Nowhere is this more apparent than in off-the-charts Potsdam, the 'German Versailles', with its wealth of parks, museums, stately palaces and resurrected film studio. Fine architecture awaits in the Rheinsberg palace and the Chorin monastery, while the Niederfinow ship-lift ranks as one of the great technological monuments of the early 20th century.

HIGHLIGHTS

■ **Royal Riches** Drain your camera batteries as you try to capture the magnificence of Potsdam's Schloss Sanssouci and the park that surrounds it (p157)

■ **Watery Ramblings** Pull up for a forest beach picnic while kayaking through the idyllic Spreewald Biosphere Reserve (p166)

■ **Techno Marvel** Rub your eyes in disbelief while watching entire barges being hoisted 60m in the air at the massive ship-lift (p174) in Niederfinow

■ **Monastery Magic** Feast your ears on classical music during a summer concert at the romantically ruined medieval monastery at Chorin (p174)

■ **Scorching Skates** Combine exercise with sightseeing while skating or cycling along the car-free trail network of Flaeming Skate (p166)

■ POPULATION: 2.53 MILLION | ■ AREA: 29,478 SQ KM

BRANDENBURG

BRANDENBURG

Information

The excellent website maintained by **Tourismus Marketing Brandenburg** (☎ 0331-200 4747; www.brandenburg-tourism.com) should satisfy all your pretrip planning needs and also has a room-booking function.

Getting Around

The **Brandenburg-Berlin Ticket** (www.bahn.de; online or at station vending machines €27, from a Reisezentrum ticket agent €29) entitles you and up to four accompanying passengers (or one or both parents or grandparents plus all their children or grandchildren under 15 years old) to one day of travel anywhere within Berlin and Brandenburg on local and regional public transport from 9am to 3am the following day

(midnight to 3am the following day on weekends). It is valid in 2nd class on RE, RB and S-Bahn trains as well as buses, U-Bahn and trams. There's now also the **Brandenburg-Berlin Ticket Nacht** (€20), which is valid any day from 6pm to 6am. The 1st-class versions cost €47 in the daytime and €40 at night. For timetable information, see www.vbb-online.de.

POTSDAM & HAVELLAND

The prime attraction of Brandenburg state and the most popular day trip from Berlin, Potsdam is a mere 24km southwest of the capital's city centre and easily accessible by S-Bahn. If time allows, venture another 36km west to the historic city of Brandenburg an der Havel, the centre of the watery Havelland region. Picturesque and less tourist-saturated than Potsdam, it's a perfect introduction to the state for which it's named.

POTSDAM
☎ 0331 / pop 152,000

Potsdam, on the Havel River just southwest of Greater Berlin, is the capital and crown jewel of the state of Brandenburg. Scores of visitors arrive every year to admire the stunning architecture of this former Prussian royal seat and to soak up the elegant air of history that hangs over its parks and gardens. A visit here is essential if you're spending any time in the region at all. All this splendour didn't go unnoticed by Unesco, which gave World Heritage status to large parts of the city in 1990.

No single individual shaped Potsdam more than King Friedrich II (Frederick the Great), the visionary behind many of Sanssouci's fabulous palaces and parks. In April 1945, Royal Air Force bombers devastated the historic centre, including the City Palace on Am Alten Markt, but fortunately most other palaces escaped with nary a shrapnel wound. When the shooting stopped, the Allies chose Schloss Cecilienhof for the Potsdam Conference of August 1945, which set the stage for the division of Berlin and Germany into occupation zones.

Potsdam was also the centre of Germany's influential film industry from the very early days of the medium when the mighty UFA studio was based here. After reunification, the dream factory was resurrected as Studio Babelsberg and is now producing or coproducing such international blockbusters as Quentin Tarantino's *Inglorious Basterds*, Stephen Daldry's *The Reader* and Roman Polanski's Academy Award–winner *The Pianist*.

Orientation
Potsdam Hauptbahnhof (central train station) is just southeast of the Altstadt, across the Havel River. Park Sanssouci is west of the historic centre, while the Neuer Garten with Schloss Cecilienhof is north. Babelsberg is about 4km east of central Potsdam.

Information

BOOKSHOPS
Das Internationale Buch (☎ 291 496; cnr Friedrich-Ebert-Strasse & Brandenburger Strasse) Great selection of maps and travel books.

DISCOUNT CARDS
Potsdam Card (2/3 days €9.60/12.30) This card buys unlimited public transport plus discounts to sights, restaurants, tours and hotels and is sold at the tourist office, hotels and participating venues.

EMERGENCY
Fire & ambulance (☎ 112)
Police (☎ 110)

INTERNET ACCESS
Bagels & Coffee (☎ 887 1612; Friedrich-Ebert-Strasse 92; per hr €1.50; ☺ 7am-10pm Mon-Thu, 7am-11pm Fri, 8.30am-11pm Sat, 8.30am-10pm Sun)

MEDICAL SERVICES
Klinikum Ernst-von-Bergmann (☎ 2410; Charlottenstrasse 72) General hospital and 24-hour emergency room.

MONEY
Commerzbank (☎ 281 90; Lindenstrasse 45)
Eurochange (☎ 280 4033; Brandenburger Strasse 29; ☺ 9.30am-6pm Mon-Fri, 9.30am-4pm Sat)

POST
Main post office (Am Kanal 16-18; ☺ 9am-6.30pm Mon-Fri, 9am-1pm Sat)

TOURIST INFORMATION
For pretrip planning, visit www.potsdam tourismus.de.
Sanssouci Besucherzentrum (☎ 969 4200; www .spsg.de; An der Orangerie 1; ☺ 8.30am-5pm Mar-Oct, 9am-4pm Nov-Feb)
Tourist office Brandenburger Tor (☎ 275 580; Brandenburger Strasse 3; ☺ 9.30am-6pm Mon-Fri, to 4pm Sat & Sun Apr-Oct, 10am-6pm Mon-Fri, 9.30am-2pm Sat & Sun Nov-Mar)
Tourist office Potsdam Hauptbahnhof (☎ 275 580; Bahnhofspassagen, Babelsberger Strasse 16; ☺ 9.30am-8pm Mon-Fri, 9am-8pm Sat) Next to platform 6.

Sights

PARK SANSSOUCI
Park Sanssouci is the oldest and most splendid of Potsdam's many gardens, a vast landscaped expanse of mature trees, rare plants and magnificent palaces. Its trump card is Schloss

POTSDAM

BRANDENBURG

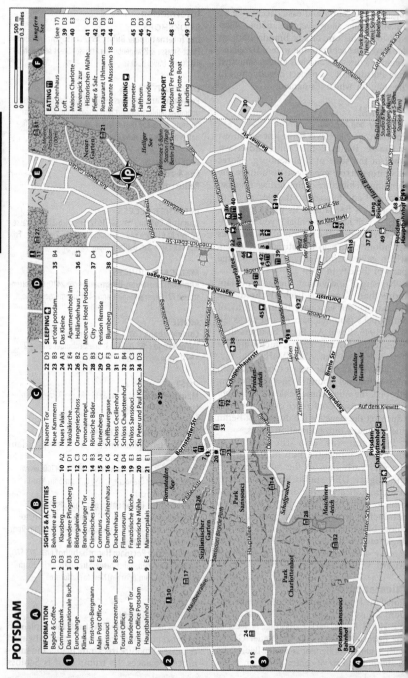

0   500 m
0   0.3 miles

anssouci, Frederick the Great's favourite
ummer retreat, a place where he could be
sans souci' (without cares). In the 19th cen-
ury, Friedrich Wilhelm IV also left his mark
n the park by adding a few buildings

The park is open from dawn till dusk year-
ound. Admission is free, but there are ma-
hines by the entrance where you can make
a voluntary donation of €2. The palaces and
utbuildings all have different hours and ad-
nission prices. Most are closed on Monday
and some of the lesser sights open only at
weekends and on holidays outside the main
season. A one-day pass valid at all Potsdam
palaces is €19 (concession €14) and available
only at Schloss Sanssouci. A day pass to all
palaces except Sanssouci is €14 (concession
€10) and sold at any of them, and also at the
Sanssouci Besucherzentrum (p157).

The palaces are fairly well spaced – it's
almost 2km between the Neues Palais (New
Palace) and Schloss Sanssouci. Take your sweet
time wandering along the park's meander-
ng paths to discover your personal favourite
spot. Free maps are available at the tourist
office. Cycling is officially permitted along
Ökonomieweg and Maulbeerallee, which is
also the route followed by bus 695, the main
ine to the park from the Hauptbahnhof.

Schloss Sanssouci & Around

The biggest stunner, and what everyone
comes to see, is **Schloss Sanssouci** (☎ 969 4190;
adult/concession incl audioguide Apr-Oct €12/8, incl tour
or audioguide Nov-Mar €8/5; ☒ 10am-6pm Tue-Sun
Apr-Oct, to 5pm Nov-Mar), the celebrated rococo
palace designed by Georg Wenzeslaus von
Knobelsdorff in 1747. The timed tickets
sometimes sell out by noon – arrive early,
preferably at opening, and avoid weekends
and holidays. You can only enter the palace
at the time printed on your ticket. Only city
tours booked through the tourist office (p157)
guarantee entry to the Schloss.

Among the rooms you'll see on your self-
guided audio tour, the exquisite circular
Bibliothek (Library), with its cedar panelling
and gilded sunburst ceiling, is undoubtedly a
highlight, even if you can only see it through
a glass door. Other favourites include the
Konzertsaal (Concert Room), playfully decorated with vines, grapes, seashells and even a
cobweb where spiders frolic. The most elegant
room is the domed **Marmorhalle** (Marble Hall),
a symphony in white Carrara marble.

The ladies-in-waiting resided in the
Damenflügel (Ladies' Wing; adult/concession €2/1.50;
☒ 10am-6pm Sat & Sun May-Oct), added under
Friedrich Wilhelm IV in 1840. In the eastern
wing is the **Schlossküche** (palace kitchen; adult/con-
cession €3/2.50; ☒ 10am-6pm Tue-Sun Apr-Oct), whose
pièce de résistance is a giant, wood-fired
'cooking machine'.

As you exit the palace, don't be fooled
by the **Ruinenberg**, a pile of classical 'ruins'
looming in the distance: they're merely a
folly conceived by Frederick the Great. East
of the Schloss, the **Bildergalerie** (Picture Gallery;
☎ 969 4181; adult/concession €3/2.50; ☒ 10am-5pm
Tue-Sun May-Oct), completed in 1763, houses a
feast of 17th-century paintings by Rubens,
Caravaggio, van Dyck and others. To the
west, the **Neue Kammern** (New Chambers; ☎ 969
4206; adult/concession incl tour or audioguide €4/3;
☒ 10am-6pm Tue-Sun May-Oct) is a former orangery and guesthouse, whose fancy interior includes the festive *Ovidsaal*, a grand ballroom
with a patterned marble floor surrounded
by gilded reliefs. A bit further on, subtropi-
cal plants thrive in the **Sizilianischer Garten**
(Sicilian Garden).

Orangerieschloss & Around

Maulbeerallee is the only road cutting
straight through Park Sanssouci. North of
it are a number of buildings, starting in
the east with the **Historische Mühle** (☎ 550
6851; adult/child with tour €3/2, without tour €2.50/1.50;
☒ 10am-6pm daily Apr-Oct, 10am-4pm Sat & Sun Nov
& Jan-Mar), a functioning replica of an 18th-
century windmill. Admission lets you examine historic exhibits and, more interestingly,
the enormous grinding mechanism.

The dominant building in this corner of the park is the elegantly ageing
Orangerieschloss (Orangery Palace; ☎ 969 4280; mandatory tour adult/concession €4/3; ☒ 10am-6pm Tue-Sun May-
Oct). It's a 300m-long Renaissance-style palace
built in 1864 by Italophile Friedrich Wilhelm
IV as a guesthouse for visiting royalty. There
are some nice views from the **tower** (admission
€2) but otherwise the most interesting room
is the **Raphaelsaal**, featuring 19th-century
copies of the painter's masterpieces.

From the Orangery, a tree-lined path
forms a visual axis to the rococo **Belvedere auf
dem Klausberg** (☎ 969 4206; admission €2; ☒ 10am-
6pm Sat & Sun May-Oct), a temple-like pavilion
whose sumptuous interior was beautifully
restored following war damage. En route,

BRANDENBURG

you'll pass the **Drachenhaus** (Dragon House; 1770), a fantastical Chinese palace inspired by the Ta-Ho pagoda in Canton and guarded by an entire army of dragons. It now houses a pleasant cafe-restaurant (p163).

Neues Palais

At the far western end of the park, the **Neues Palais** (New Palace; ☎ 969 4361; adult/concession with tour or audioguide €6/5; ☻ 10am-6pm Wed-Mon Apr-Oct, to 5pm Nov-Mar) has made-to-impress dimensions, a central dome and a lavish exterior decorated with a parade of sandstone figures. It was the last palace built by Frederick the Great, but he never really camped out here, preferring the intimacy of Schloss Sanssouci. Later it served as a guesthouse and only the last German Kaiser, Wilhelm II, used it as a residence until 1918.

Inside await about a dozen splendid rooms, the most memorable of which are the **Grottensaal** (Grotto Hall), a rococo delight with shells, fossils and baubles set into the walls and ceilings; the **Marmorsaal**, a large banquet hall of Carrara marble with a wonderful ceiling fresco; and the **Jagdkammer** (Hunting Chamber), with lots of dead furry things and fine gold tracery on the walls. Frederick the Great's **private apartments** (Königswohnung; adult/concession €5/4; ☻ 10am, noon, 2pm & 4pm Wed-Mon Apr-Oct) can only be seen on guided tours.

On weekends, admission also includes a peak inside the **Pesne-Galerie** (gallery only adult/concession €2/1.50; ☻ 10am-5pm Sat & Sun Apr-Oct) with a fine selection of works by this French painter.

The **Schlosstheater** in the south wing is only open during concerts. The pair of lavish buildings behind the Schloss is called the **Communs**. It originally housed the palace servants and kitchens and is now part of Potsdam University.

Park Charlottenhof

South of the Neues Palais, Park Charlottenhof was laid out under Friedrich Wilhelm IV and now blends smoothly with Park Sanssouci. It gets a lot fewer visitors, partly because it lacks the blockbuster sights. Still, the small neoclassical **Schloss Charlottenhof** (☎ 969 4228; mandatory tour adult/concession €4/3; ☻ 10am-6pm Tue-Sun May-Oct) was modelled after a Roman villa and is actually considered one of Karl Friedrich Schinkel's finest works. Note the Doric portico and bronze fountain to the east.

FREDERICK'S POSTMORTEM ODYSSEY

Frederick the Great so loved Sanssouci, he gave specific instructions to be buried – next to his beloved dogs – on the highest terrace of the vineyards in front of the palace. Alas, his nephew and successor blithely ignored his request, putting him instead next to his father, the 'Soldier King' Friedrich Wilhelm I, in a nearby church. In WWII, the sarcophagi of both father and son were moved by German soldiers for safekeeping and, after the war, ended up in the ancestral Hohenzollern castle in southern Germany (p438). Only after reunification, in 1991, did Frederick the Great get his final wish and was reburied in the exact spot he had personally picked out more than 250 years before. It's marked by a simple gravestone.

Schinkel, aided by his student Ludwig Persius, also dreamed up the nearby **Römische Bäder** (Roman Baths; ☎ 969 4225; adult/concession €3/2.50; ☻ 10am-6pm Tue-Sun May-Oct), a picturesque ensemble of Italian country estates and antique Roman villas. The setting next to a pond is pleasant, but don't go out of your way to come here.

A same-day combination ticket for both sites is €5/4 per adult/concession.

Chinesisches Haus

Northeast of the Roman Baths, the adorable **Chinesisches Haus** (Chinese House; ☎ 969 4225; admission €2; ☻ 10am-6pm Tue-Sun May-Oct) reflects the 18th-century fascination with the Far East. It is one of the prettiest and most photographed buildings in the park, largely because of the gilded sandstone figures with oriental dress and shown sipping tea, dancing and playing musical instruments. One of the monkeys allegedly resembles Voltaire! Inside the domed circular pavilion is a precious collection of Chinese and Meissen porcelain.

ALTSTADT

Moving into old town Potsdam, the baroque **Brandenburger Tor** (Brandenburg Gate) on Luisenplatz is actually older than its more famous cousin in Berlin. From this square, the pedestrianised Brandenburger Strasse runs east to the **Sts Peter und Paul Kirche** (Church of Sts Peter & Paul; ☎ 230 7990; admission free; ☻ 10am-5pm

Mon-Sat, 11.30am-3.30pm Sun), dating from 1868. Just to the southeast on Charlottenstrasse, and once the seat of the town's Huguenots, is the **Französische Kirche** (French Church, 1753).

Northwest of the churches, bounded by Friedrich-Ebert-Strasse, Hebbelstrasse, Kurfürstenstrasse and Gutenbergstrasse, is the picturesque **Holländisches Viertel** (Dutch Quarter). It consists of 134 gabled red-brick houses built for Dutch workers who came to Potsdam in the 1730s at the invitation of Friedrich Wilhelm I. The entire district has been done up beautifully and brims with galleries, cafes and restaurants; Mittelstrasse is especially scenic. Further up Friedrich-Ebert-Strasse is the **Nauener Tor** (Nauen Gate, 1755), a fanciful triumphal arch.

Southeast of the GDR-era Platz der Einheit looms the great neoclassical dome of Schinkel's **Nikolaikirche** (☎ 270 8602; Am Alten Markt; �), 9am-7pm Mon-Sat, 11.30am-7pm Sun), built in 1850, complemented by an obelisk and a small pavilion on the old market square.

West of Am Alter Markt in the former *Marstall* (royal stables) is the smallish **Filmmuseum** (☎ 271 8112; www.filmmuseum-potsdam .de; Breite Strasse 1a; adult/concession/family €3.50/2.50/10, film €5/4; �) 10am-6pm) with a permanent exhibit on the history of the UFA and DEFA (the GDR film company) studios in Babelsberg. The cinema shows all sorts of flicks, from silent movies with live organ accompaniment to recent releases.

Further west is the exotic **Dampfmaschinen-haus** (Pump House; ☎ 969 4248; Breite Strasse 28; mandatory tour adult/concession €2/1.50; �), 10am-6pm Sat & Sun May-Oct), the former palace waterworks built to look like a Turkish mosque complete with minaret.

NEUER GARTEN

The winding lakeside Neuer Garten (New Garden), laid out in natural English style on the western shore of the Heiliger See, is another fine park in which to relax. Right on the lake, the neoclassical **Marmorpalais** (Marble Palace; ☎ 969 4246; tour adult/concession €5/4; ☉ 10am-6pm Tue-Sun May-Oct, 10am-4pm Sat & Sun Nov-Apr) was built in 1792 for Friedrich Wilhelm II by Carl Gotthard Langhans (he of Berlin's Brandenburg Gate fame). Though not quite as fancy as Schloss Sanssouci, the interior is still stunning with its grand central staircase, marble fireplaces, stucco ceilings and collection of Wedgwood porcelain. The most fanciful room is the upstairs **Orientalisches Kabinett**, which looks like a Turkish tent.

Further north, **Schloss Cecilienhof** (☎ 969 4200; adult/concession with tour or audioguide €6/5; ☉ 10am-6pm Tue-Sun Apr-Oct, to 5pm Nov-Mar) is a rustic English-style country manor completed in 1917 for crown prince Wilhelm and his wife Cecilie. The couple's **private apartments** (adult/concession €4/3; ☉ 10am, noon, 2pm & 4pm Tue-Sun) can only be seen on a guided tour, but the palace is really more famous for being the site of the 1945 Potsdam Conference where Stalin, Truman and Churchill hammered out Germany's postwar fate. The conference room with its giant round table looks as though the delegates have just left. Bus 692 makes it up here.

A combination ticket for Cecilienhof and the Marmorpalais costs €8/6 adult/concession (available May to October only).

PFINGSTBERG

For the best view over Potsdam and surrounds, head uphill to the beautifully restored **Belvedere Pfingstberg** (☎ 2005 7930; adult/concession €3.50/2.50; ☉ 10am-8pm Jun-Aug, 10am-6pm Apr, May, Sep & Oct, 10am-4pm Sat & Sun Mar & Nov). Built in Italian Renaissance style, this massive twin-towered palace was commissioned by Friedrich Wilhelm IV but not completed until 1863, two years after his death. A series of spiralling wrought-iron staircases leads up to the towers for spectacular 360-degree views. Just below the palace is 1801 **Pomonatempel** (☎ 270 1972; admission free; ☉ 3-6pm Sat & Sun mid-Apr–Oct), which was Karl Friedrich Schinkel's very first architectural commission.

BABELSBERG

Babelsberg is synonymous with film-making. The mighty UFA began shooting flicks here in 1912, and by the 1920s was producing such blockbusters as Fritz Lang's *Metropolis* (see boxed text, p162) and *The Blue Angel* with Marlene Dietrich. After WWII, it became the base of the East German production company DEFA, and today cameras are rolling in what is called **Studio Babelsberg**.

For visitors, the main reason to come here is the attached **Filmpark Babelsberg** (☎ 721 2750; www.filmpark.de; enter on Grossbeerenstrasse; adult/4-14yr/concession €19/13/16; ☉ 10am-6pm Apr-Oct), a movie-themed amusement park with live shows (great stunt show!), a 4-D cinema and a few poky rides. A highlight is the guided tram ride where you'll be whisked past working sound

BRANDENBURG

BRANDENBURG

METROPOLIS

Potsdam isn't readily associated with class warfare, but it was here, at the UFA studios, that Fritz Lang shot much of his allegorical melodrama *Metropolis* (1927), which deals with exactly that. The film depicts a society literally split in two, with the Thinkers living in idle luxury above ground and the Workers toiling in subterranean caverns to serve the terrible Moloch machine. Threatened by nonviolent protest advocated by the saintly Maria, the Thinkers dispatch a robot clone of her to provoke riots. The sheer scale of the film was unprecedented (Lang hired 10,000 extras), and its relevance has endured, not just in its message of class cooperation but also in its themes of revolution, technology and voyeurism. Some elements were far ahead of their time – the robot Futura is a clear predecessor of the Terminator.

---

stages to the studio backlot and such outdoor sets as 'Berlin Wall' and 'Berlin Street'.

The Filmpark is about 4km east of Potsdam's city centre and served by bus 601. Coming from Berlin, hop on a regional train and get off at Medienstadt Babelsberg.

Northwest of here, **Park Babelsberg**, yet another great Potsdam garden, is where you'll find the Schinkel-designed neo-Gothic **Schloss Babelsberg** (☎ 969 4250; adult/concession with tour €4/3.50, without tour €3/2.50; ☽ 10am-6pm Tue-Sun late Jun-Oct), the summer residence of Emperor Wilhelm I. Wilhelm also commissioned the nearby **Flatowturm** (☎ 600 9494; admission €2; ☽ 10am-6pm Sat & Sun May-Oct), a tower modelled after a medieval town gate in Frankfurt am Main.

SCHIFFBAUERGASSE

Ships were built, coffee was produced and soldiers were drilled on a site that's been reborn as a cultural hub called Schiffbauergasse. On the shores of the Tiefer See, about 2.5km north of central Potsdam, the complex unites numerous venues and institutions, most notably the **Hans-Otto-Theater** (www.hans-otto-theater.de), Potsdam's main stage. The **Museum Fluxus+** (☎ 6010890; www.fluxus-plus.de; Schiffbauergasse 6; adult/concession €7.50/3, half-price Tue; ☽ noon-8pm Tue-Sun) presents works by Nam June Paik, Wolf Vostell and other members of this 1960s avant-garde art movement. Exhibits, movies, club nights and concerts take place in the **Waschhaus** (www.waschhaus.de). Tram 93 makes the trip here from the Hauptbahnhof.

Tours

The local tourist office (p157) runs the 3½-hour **Potsdam Sanssouci Tour** (ticket €27; ☽ 11am Tue-Sun Apr-Oct, Fri-Sun Nov-Mar), which guarantees admission to Schloss Sanssouci, and the two-hour **Altstadt Walking Tour** (adult/concession €9/7;

☽ tour 3pm daily Apr-Oct). Tours are in English and German and tickets are available at the tourist office.

Weisse Flotte Potsdam (☎ 275 9210; www.schiffahrt-in-potsdam.de; Lange Brücke 6; ☽ Apr-Oct) operates dozens of boat tours on the Havel and the lakes around Potsdam, including a sightseeing tour passing the various waterside palaces (€11). Boats depart from the docks near Lange Brücke, by the towering Mercure Hotel.

Festivals & Events

Potsdam's biggest annual events include the **Tulip Festival** in the Dutch Quarter in April, the **Musikfestspiele Potsdam Sanssouci** (www.musikfestspiele-potsdam.de) in June and the **Potsdamer Bachtage** (www.bachtage-potsdam.de, in German) in September (see the boxed text, opposite).

Sleeping

Most people visit Potsdam on a day trip from Berlin, but only by spending the night can you savour the town's quiet majesty without the tour-bus crowds. The tourist office books private rooms and hotels in person, by phone (☎ 275 580) or online (www.potsdam-tourismus.de).

DJH hostel (☎ 581 3100; www.jh-potsdam.de, in German; Schulstrasse 9; dm under/over 26yr €15/18; P ⊠ ▣) Potsdam's hostel is a snazzy 152-bed property where rooms come with showers and toilets and sleep only two or four people. It's around the corner from S-Bahn station Babelsberg.

Mercure Hotel Potsdam City (☎ 2722; www.mercure.com; Lange Brücke; r €61-93; P ⊠ ⊠ ▣) Never mind the bland exterior. Rooms in this highrise are smartly dressed in blues and greys and feature flat screens and beds with chic wooden headboards. It's in a busy but central location near the Hauptbahnhof and right next to the tour-boat landing docks.

art'otel potsdam (☎ 981 50; www.parkplaza.com
artotel_potsdam; Zeppelinstrasse 136; r from €75;
P ⊠ ⊠ ☎) This jazzy lifestyle hotel sits in
an enviable location on the Havel River and
has 123 rooms and a superb top-floor gym
and spa area with five saunas, aromatic baths
and treatments. Canvasses by German artist Katharina Sieverding decorate rooms and
public areas.

Pension Remise Blumberg (☎ 2803231;www.pension
blumberg.de; Weinbergstrasse 26; s €70-75, d €85-92;
P ⊠ ☎) Close to Park Sanssouci, this backyard pension may be petite but the rooms, all
with kitchenette, are not. Bike hire is available,
and the leafy courtyard is perfect for sipping
your morning coffee.

Das Kleine Apartmenthotel im Holländerhaus
(☎ 279 110; www.hollaenderhaus.potsdam.de; Kurfürstenstrasse 15; apt €90-170, breakfast €9.50-15; P ⊠ ☎)
This gem combines the charm of a historic
Dutch Quarter building with an edgy, creative
design scheme. Wood, steel and lots of colour
give the good-sized apartments with kitchens
a contemporary look. A small gym, sauna and
leafy courtyard are good unwinding spots.

Eating

Pfeffer & Salz (☎ 200 2777; Brandenburger Strasse 46;
pizza & pasta €6.50-13; 🕑 11am-11pm; ⊠) In a street
of tourist traps, this Italian eatery stands out
for its authenticity. All noodles are homemade daily, the antipasti selection is mouth-
watering and the pizza comes crispy-hot from
the wood-fired oven.

Loft (☎ 951 0102; Brandenburger Strasse 30/31; mains
€8-15; 🕑 10am-midnight Mon-Sat, 10am-10pm Sun; ⊠)
Fine views, bright surroundings and a lovely
terrace make this a favourite place to enjoy
decent food ranging from pasta to steaks.

Meierei Potsdam (☎ 704 3211; Im Neuen Garten
10; snacks €3-8, mains €10-15; 🕑 11am-9.30pm Mon-

Sat, 11am-8.30pm Sun) Near Schloss Cecilienhof,
this brewpub is especially lovely in summer
when you can count the boats sailing on the
Jungfernsee from your beer-garden table. The
hearty dishes are a perfect match for the delicious suds brewed on the premises.

Maison Charlotte (☎ 280 5450; Mittelstrasse 20;
mains €7.50-20; 🕑 noon-11pm; ⊠) This enchanting bistro may be in the Dutch Quarter but
it's so fantastically French you half expect to
see the Eiffel Tower out the door. Oysters and
foie gras make appearances, but so do more
rustic offerings, such as *croques* (toasts) and
Flammkuchen (Alsatian pizzas).

Restaurant Uhlmann (☎ 7304 0253; Jägerstrasse
38; mains lunch €7-8, dinner €8.50-16.50; 🕑 11am-10pm;
⊠) Located in an 18th-century pottery
workshop, this restaurant is a luscious port
of call for modern German fare. The menu,
sourced from farm-fresh ingredients, changes
frequently but may feature such inspired concoctions as rabbit with a kohlrabi-chanterelle
salad, or quail paired with ratatouille and
basil polenta.

Ristorante Massimo 18 (☎ 8171 8981; Mittelstrasse
18; mains €9-18; 🕑 10am-midnight; ⊠) Travel
from Paris to Rome in about two seconds.
Next to Maison Charlotte, Massimo 18 specialises in robust southern Italian *cucina*.
From wafer-thin carpaccio to mounds of
linguine with lobster, and locally sourced
roast lamb with rosemary potatoes, it's all
lip-smacking good.

Recommended eateries in Park Sanssouci:

Drachenhaus (☎ 505 3808; Maulbeerallee 4a; mains
€10-15; 🕑 11am-7pm Mar-Oct, 11am-6pm Tue-Sun Nov-
Feb; ⊠) Coffee, cake and regional cuisine.

Mövenpick Zur Historischen Mühle (☎ 281 493; Zur
Historischen Mühle 2; mains €10-15; 🕑 8am-midnight;
⊠) International cuisine with huge beer garden and
children's playground.

BRANDENBURG

BACH TO THE FUTURE

The state of Brandenburg has links with many influential German composers, most notably Johann
Sebastian Bach. Even the most blinkered techno-head has probably heard of the *Brandenburg
Concertos*, composed in 1721 for Margrave Christian Ludwig of Brandenburg, who was then based
(a tad ironically) at Köthen in Saxony-Anhalt.

Some years later, in 1747, Frederick the Great managed to lure Bach to Potsdam, where the
great composer wrote *The Musical Offering* on a theme proposed by the king himself. Since
then Bach's place in Brandenburg history has been assured, but it's only in recent times that his
legacy has been fully celebrated. Since 2000 the **Potsdamer Bachtage** (Bach Days), a two-week
festival of concerts, workshops and readings, has dedicated itself to making the master's work
accessible to modern audiences.

Drinking

Hafthorn (☎ 280 0820; Friedrich-Ebert-Strasse 90) This low-key pub is great for quaffing a cold one in the funky beer garden or amid masklike sconces wrought from sheet metal. Pick from the snack menu (€2 to €7.50) to stave off that hangover.

Barometer (☎ 270 2880; Gutenbergstrasse 103; ☺ from 8pm) This vaulted cellar lounge is popular with grown-ups willing to peel off the bills for serious cocktails. Access is via the back courtyard.

La Leander (☎ 270 6576; Benkertstrasse 1; ☺ 5pm-2am Mon-Fri, 11am-2am Sat & Sun) The rainbow flags fly proudly over this low-key Dutch Quarter pub that's a good place for plugging into the local lesbigay scene.

Getting There & Away

Regional trains leaving from Berlin-Hauptbahnhof and Zoologischer Garten take only 25 minutes to reach Potsdam Hauptbahnhof; some continue on to Potsdam-Charlottenhof and Potsdam-Sanssouci, which are closer to Park Sanssouci than Hauptbahnhof. The S-Bahn line S7 from central Berlin makes the trip in about 40 minutes. Berlin transit tickets must cover zones A, B and C (€2.80) to be valid for the trip to Potsdam.

Drivers coming from Berlin should take the A100 to the A115.

Getting Around

Buses and trams operate throughout Potsdam. The most useful line is bus 695, which connects the Hauptbahnhof with the Altstadt and Park Sanssouci. Tickets costs €1.70 and a day pass €3.90.

For bike hire, **Potsdam per Pedales** (☎ 748 0057; per day from €8.50) has branches at the **Potsdam Hauptbahnhof** (☺ 9.30am-7pm May-Sep) and at the **Griebnitzsee S-Bahn station** (☺ 9am-6.30pm daily Easter-Oct, Mon-Fri only Nov-Easter).

For a taxi, ring ☎ 292 929.

BRANDENBURG AN DER HAVEL
☎ 03381 / pop 73,000

Brandenburg may not be Venice, but this pretty town some 50km west of Berlin was definitely shaped by water. Set amid a pastoral landscape of lakes, rivers and canals, it has a historic centre with some fine examples of northern German red-brick architecture. First settled by Slavs in the 6th century,

Brandenburg was a bishopric in the early Middle Ages and a margravial capital until the 15th century. Darker times arrived when the Nazis picked the town to carry out their forced euthanasia program for the mentally disabled, killing tens of thousands. Wartime bombing and GDR neglect left their scars, but these have healed nicely, making Brandenburg once again an attractive day trip from Berlin or Potsdam.

Orientation

Brandenburg is split into three sections by the Havel River, the Beetzsee and their various canals. The Neustadt occupies an island in the centre and is connected to the Altstadt by the Jahrtausendbrücke (Millennium Bridge) while the Dominsel is north of the Neustadt. The train station is about 1km south of the central Neustädtischer Markt.

Information

Dresdner Bank (☎ 2670; Neustädtischer Markt 10)
Post office (St Annenstrasse 30-36)
Tourist information (☎ 208 769; www.stg-brandenburg.de, in German; Steinstrasse 66/67; ☺ 9am-7pm Mon-Fri year-round, 10am-3pm Sat & Sun May-Sep, 10am-2pm Sat Oct-Apr)

Sights & Activities

A fine place to kick off your exploration of Brandenburg is at the mostly Gothic **Dom St Peter und St Paul** (Cathedral of Sts Peter & Paul; ☎ 211 2221; Burghof 9; ☺ 10am-5pm) on Dominsel. Treasures include a carved 14th-century Bohemian altar in the south transept, the vaulted and painted Bunte Kapelle (Colourful Chapel), and a fantastic baroque organ (1723). The **Dommuseum** (adult/concession €3/2; ☺ 10am-5pm) has outstanding medieval vestments and a so-called *Hungertuch* (hunger blanket), with embroidered medallions depicting the life of Jesus.

South of here, across Mühlendamm, the octagonal **Mühlentorturm** (Mill Gate Tower) is one of four surviving medieval fortification towers. Just beyond are the Neustädtischer Markt and the **Katharinenkirche** (☎ 521 162; Katharinenkirchplatz 2; ☺ 10am-4pm Mon-Sat, 1-4pm Sun), a vast Gothic brick church with a lavishly detailed and decorated facade. See if you can spot your favourite biblical characters on the 'Meadow of Heaven' painted ceiling.

South of here, a Gothic red-brick monastery has risen from ruins and been recast as the **Archäologisches Landesmuseum Brandenburg** (Archaeological State Museum; ☎ 410 4112; Neustädtische Heidestrasse 28; adult/concession/family €5/3.50/10; 10am-5pm Tue-Sun). The building itself is a highlight, but there's also plenty of excavated treasure to admire, including superrare stone-age textiles, bronze-age gold rings, Germanic tools and medieval coins.

If you start yearning for higher ground, climb up the nearby **Steintorturm** (cnr Steinstrasse & Neustädtische Heidestrasse; adult/concession €3/1; 9am-5pm Tue-Fri, 10am-5pm Sat & Sun), which also has a small exhibit on Havel shipping. Admission here is also good at the main city museum, the **Stadtmuseum im Frey-Haus** (☎ 584 01; Ritterstrasse 96; adult/concession €3/1; 9am-5pm Tue-Fri, 10am-5pm Sat & Sun), reached by following the pedestrianised Hauptstrasse to the Jahrtausendbrücke. It chronicles local lore from prehistory to the end of the GDR era and presents an entire collection of cute mechanical toys produced by Ernst Paul Lehmann, the man who donated the building to the historical society in 1919. Bearing right takes you to the **Altstädtisches Rathaus**, a red-brick gem fronted by a lanky statue of the mythological figure Roland, a symbol of justice and prosperity.

In warm weather, Brandenburg's charms are best appreciated from the water. A number of outfitters rent canoes and kayaks for about €5 per hour or €30 per day. Try Cafébar (right) or **Wasserwanderrastplatz Am Slawendorf** (☎ 0175-215 7774), both near the Jahrtausendbrücke. There's good **lake swimming** in the Freibad Grillendamm on the Kleiner Beetzsee off the northern shore of Dominsel.

Tours

The tourist office rents out free audioguides (deposit required) for a self-guided English-language tour of the city's medieval centre.

From April to October, **Nordstern** (☎ 226 060; www.nordstern-reederei.de, in German) and **Reederei Röding** (☎ 522 331; www.fgs-havelfee.de) operate boat tours around the Havel lakes. Embarkation is at Am Salzhof, just south of the Jahrtausendbrücke. Fares start at €4.50 for a one-hour spin around the old town.

Sleeping

Pension Zum Birnbaum (☎ 527 500; www.pension-zum-birnbaum.de; Mittelstrasse 1; s/d/tr from €28/42/51; breakfast €3; P) A singing host, breakfast under a pear tree and handsomely furnished, if snug, rooms recommend this little historic inn that places you close to the train station and the Neustadt.

Backpacker Hostel Caasi (☎ 3290; www.caasi.de; Caasmannstrasse 7; dm €12-15, linen €5, s/d €30/50, breakfast €5; P X 🖳) On the edge of town, this is a good option for shoestringers, even though many of the 250 rooms are filled with long-term guests. Assets include kitchen access and a pub.

Sorat Hotel Brandenburg (☎ 5970; www.sorat-hotels.com; Altstädtischer Markt 1; s €98-141, d €114-157; P X X 🛜) The top-notch Sorat has 86 bright, modern rooms in pretty surroundings right by the Rathaus. Rates include a champagne breakfast and gym and sauna use; weekend rates drop significantly.

Eating

Cafébar (☎ 229 048; Ritterstrasse 76; snacks €3-6; 8.30am-6.30pm Mon-Fri, from 9.30am Sat & Sun; X) The best place for coffee and homemade cake, this is a teensy kiosk right by the Jahrtausendbrücke with canalside beach chairs in summer.

Herzschlag (☎ 410 414; Grosse Münzenstrasse 17; tapas €4-7, mains €7-13; from 11.30am) Urban sophistication in sleepy Brandenburg? Look no further than this restaurant-bar combo, complete with artsy decor, lounge music, tasty cocktails and a menu featuring everything from tapas to fajitas to crocodile steaks.

An der Dominsel (☎ 891 807; Neustädtische Fischerstrasse 14; snacks €5-7, mains €8-15; 11am-10pm; X) The regional food – especially the fish dishes – is dependable here, but what you'll probably remember most are the fabulous Dom views across the canal. It's right by the Mühlentorturm.

Bismarck Terrassen (☎ 300 939; Bergstrasse 20; mains €8-15, 2-course meals from €8.50; X) Discover your inner Prussian at this traditional restaurant whose proprietor may greet you in Bismarck costume and seat you in a room brimming with Iron Chancellor memorabilia. The kitsch quotient is undeniably there, but the Brandenburg food is authentic, delicious and plentiful.

For a quick fish snack (from €1.50), pop into one of the little **fishing shacks** (usually to 6pm Mon-Fri, to noon Sat) operated by professional fisherfolk along Mühlendamm. In summer, they set up tables on floating pontoons.

BRANDENBURG

BRANDENBURG

FLAMING FLAEMING: THE GREAT SKATE

In-line skating is popular in Germany and its Eldorado is **Flaeming-Skate** (www.flaeming-skate.de), a 210km smooth asphalt trail that winds through forest, meadows and picturesque villages. It's Germany's longest, with side trails adding to the fun of exploration; it's also extremely gentle on the environment.

The epicentre is Luckenwalde, some 50km south of Berlin on the train line to Lutherstadt-Wittenberg. There are numerous routes, from easy 10km jaunts for beginners to thigh-burning day trips. All are well signposted, making navigation a snap. The website has full details, also in English.

A good place to hire skates and protective gear is **Sportmarkt Luckenwalde** (☎ 03371-611 030; Breite Strasse 5, Luckenwalde; per day/weekend/week €8/15/25; ☻ 9am-6pm Mon-Fri, 9am-12.30pm Sat) Also in Luckenwalde, **Hotel Märkischer Hof** (☎ 03371- 6040; www.skatemekka.com; Poststrasse 8; bike rental per day €7, s/d €55/70, mains €4.50-10) has a good-sized fleet of bicycles for rent. The restaurant serves salads and flavoursome mains, and rooms here will give you a good night's sleep, should you decide to stay.

One interesting place to skate or cycle to is Jüterbog, with the 12th-century **Kloster Zinna** (Zinna Monastery; ☎ 03372-439 505; www.jueterbog.eu; Am Kloster 6; adult/concession €5/3.50; ☻ 10am-5pm Tue-Sun). The classical **Kloster-Zinna-Sommermusiken** (☎ 03372-4650; www.kloster-zinna-sommer musiken.de; tickets €7.50-16) concert series is held here from mid-June to late August. The museum sells tickets.

Regional trains make hourly trips to Luckenwalde or Jüterbog from Berlin-Hauptbahnhof (€5.10, 40 minutes). Drivers should follow the B101.

Getting There & Around

Regional trains link Brandenburg twice hourly with all major stations in central Berlin, including Hauptbahnhof (€6.30, 50 minutes), and with Potsdam (€5.10, 35 minutes).

From the station, it's about a 10-minute walk via Geschwister-Scholl-Strasse and St-Annen-Strasse to the Neustädtischer Markt. Trams 6 and 9 will get you there as well. Free parking is available at the corner of Grillendamm and Krakauer Strasse, just north of the Dom.

SPREEWALD

The Spreewald, a unique lacework of channels and canals hemmed in by forest, is the closest thing Berlin has to a backyard garden. Visitors come here in droves to punt, canoe or kayak on more than 970km of waterways, hike countless nature trails and fish in this Unesco biosphere reserve. The region is famous for its gherkins – over 40,000 tonnes of cucumbers are harvested here every year! Lübben and Lübbenau, the main tourist towns, often drown beneath the tides of visitors vying for rides aboard a *Kahn* (shallow punt boat), once the only way

of getting around in these parts. To truly ap preciate the Spreewald's unique charms, hire your own canoe or kayak or get yoursel onto a walking trail. For pretrip research consult www.spreewald.de.

The Spreewald is also home base to large numbers of Germany's Sorbian minority (see the boxed text, opposite).

Getting There & Around

Frequent regional trains depart central Berlin (eg Hauptbahnhof) for Lübben (€9.10, one hour) and Lübbenau (€10.40, 1¼ hours) en route to Cottbus (€13, 1¾ hours). The towns are also linked by an easy 13km trai along the Spree. Cyclists can explore the region by following a section of the 250km Gurkenradweg (Cucumber Trail). Rent bikes from **Spreewaldradler/Vitalpunkt** (☎ 035603-158 790; bikes per day €8-17) right at the Lübber train station.

LÜBBEN

☎ 03546 / pop 14,350

Compared to Lübbenau, about 13km south-east, tidy Lübben feels more like a 'real town and has a history going back at leas two centuries further than its neighbour Activity centres on the Schloss and the adacent harbour area, both about 1.5km east of the train station. Follow Bahnhofstrasse southeast, turn left on Logenstrasse and continue to Ernst-von-Houwald-Damm, where you'll also find the **tourist office** (☎ 3090; www.luebben.de; Ernst-von-Houwald-Damm 15; ☺ 10am-6pm Apr-Oct, to 4pm Mon-Fri Nov-Mar). The Markt and Hauptstrasse are two blocks north.

Sights & Activities

The prettiest building in town is the compact **Schloss** (☎ 187 478; Ernst-von-Houwald-Damm 14; adult/concession €4/2; ☺ 10am-5pm Tue-Sun Apr-Oct, 10am-4pm Wed-Fri, 1-5pm Sat & Sun Nov-Mar), which contains a progressively presented regional history museum; look for the interactive town model and a 2m-long medieval executioner's sword. The real highlight, though, is a (free) wander around the **Schlossinsel**, an artificial archipelago with gardens, a leafy maze, playgrounds, cafes and the harbour area where you can board punts for leisurely tours (from €8/4 per adult/child). If you'd rather go at your own speed, rent a canoe or kayak from **Bootsverleih Gebauer** (☎ 7194; Lindenstrasse 18; per 2hr from €8).

Sleeping

DJH hostel (☎ 3046; www.jh-luebben.de, in German; Zum Wendenfürsten 8; dm €14.50-17.50; ℗ ⊠) This 127-bed hostel is right on the Spree, about 3km south of the train station, and also has campsites (€10, including breakfast).

Hotel Lindengarten (☎ 4172; www.spreewald-luebben.de; Treppendorfer Damm 15; s/d €50/70; ℗ ⊠) This family-run hotel is a class act all around and has bright and airy rooms, youthful flair and a nice restaurant that serves tapas and regional fare.

Spreewaldhotel Stephanshof (☎ 272 10; www.hotel-stephanshof.de, in German; Lehnigksberger Weg 1; s €65, d €90-95, discount Nov-Mar; ℗ ⊠ 🖙) About a 10-minute walk north of the centre, this modern riverside hotel has its own boat landing, a regional restaurant and bike rentals. Some rooms have balconies.

Eating

Ladencafé im Alten Gärtnerhaus (☎ 186 956; Ernst-von-Houwald-Damm 6; mains €4-10; ⊠) Lovingly decorated, this little cottage with a small beer garden out back serves tasty Mediterranean fare and also sells local crafts and handmade products. It's in the former palace gardener's house.

Goldener Löwe (☎ 7309; Hauptstrasse 15; mains €7-11) This old-fashioned restaurant is an ambience-laden purveyor of regional fare, including a fish platter featuring eel, perch and carp. In summer, enjoy your meal in the beer garden. They also have a few rooms for rent (singles/doubles/triples €45/65/95), in case you feel like dawdling.

Bubak (☎ 186 144; Ernst-von-Houwald-Damm 9; mains €5-16; ☺ 11.30am-10pm) Close to the Schloss, this characterful roadside restaurant was named for a local bogeyman and has weekly concerts

BRANDENBURG

THE SORBS

The Spreewald region is part of the area inhabited by the Sorbs, Germany's only indigenous minority. This intriguing group, numbering just 60,000, descends from the Slavic Wends, who settled between the Elbe and Oder Rivers in the 5th century in an area called Lusatia (Luzia in Sorbian).

Lusatia was conquered by the Germans in the 10th century, subjected to brutal Germanisation throughout the Middle Ages and partitioned in 1815. Lower Sorbia, centred around the Spreewald and Cottbus (Chośebuz), went to Prussia, while Upper Sorbia, around Bautzen (Budyšin), went to Saxony. The Upper Sorbian dialect, closely related to Czech, enjoyed a certain prestige in Saxony, but the Kingdom of Prussia tried to suppress Lower Sorbian, which is similar to Polish. The Nazis, of course, tried to eradicate both.

The Sorbs were protected under the GDR and since reunification interest in the culture has been revived through the media and colourful Sorbian festivals such as the *Vogelhochzeit* (Birds' Wedding) on 25 January and a symbolic 'witch-burning' on 30 April.

For further details, contact the **Sorbian Institute** (☎ 03591-497 20; www.serbski-institut.de, in German) in Bautzen or the **Institute of Sorbian Studies** (☎ 0341-973 7650; www.uni-leipzig.de/~sorb) in Leipzig.

starring its singing proprietor. The menu is a mix of typical Spreewald dishes and classic German food, all prepared creatively and using local products whenever possible.

LÜBBENAU

☎ 03542 / pop 17,300

Lübbenau is prettier than Lübben but has more of a model-village air, despite being considerably bigger overall. The entire Altstadt is a forest of signs pointing to hotels, restaurants and other businesses, making navigating a snap. Near the church you'll find the **tourist office** (☎ 3668; www .spreewald-online.de; Ehm-Welk-Strasse 15; ☼ 9am-7pm Mon-Fri, 9am-4pm Sat, 10am-4pm Sun). The train station is on Poststrasse, about 600m south of the Altstadt.

Sights & Activities

Behind the tourist office, the **Haus für Mensch und Natur** (☎ 892 10; Schulstrasse 9; admission free; ☼ 10am-5pm Tue-Sun Apr-Oct) has exhibits and information about the Spreewald Biosphere Reserve. If you're interested in the region's cultural history, visit the **Spreewald-Museum** (☎ 2472; Am Topfmarkt; adult/concession/family €3/2/5; ☼ 10am-6pm Tue-Sun Apr–mid-Sep, to 5pm mid-Sep–Oct) inside a historic brick building that's gone through stints as a courthouse, jail and town hall.

Several operators offer pretty much the same **punt boating** tours, including the popular two-hour trip to Lehde (€8.50), a completely protected village known as the 'Venice of the Spreewald'. Here you'll find the wonderful **Freilandmuseum** (☎ 2472; adult/concession/family €3/2/5; ☼ 10am-6pm Apr–mid-Sep, to 5pm mid-Sep–Oct), an open-air museum of traditional Sorbian houses and farm buildings. Lehde is also reached via an easy 30-minute trail.

The main embarkation points are the **Kleiner Hafen** (☎ 403 710; www.spreewald-web.de; Spreestrasse 10a), about 100m northeast of the tourist office, and the more workmanlike **Grosser Hafen** (☎ 2225; www.grosser-spreewaldhafen.de; Dammstrasse 77a), 300m southeast. Buy tickets at the embarkation points or from the captain. Active types can hire canoes and kayaks from several outfitters, including **Bootsverleih Francke** (☎ 2722; Dammstrasse 72), for €2 to €5 per hour or €12 to €25 per day, depending on size.

Sleeping & Eating

Check with the tourist office about private rooms (from €14) or simply walk about town and look for signs saying *Gästezimmer*.

Naturcamping am Schlosspark (☎ 3533; www .spreewaldcamping.de, in German; Schlossbezirk 20; adult/ child/tent €6/3/6, 2-person cabins €20) This four-star campsite, just east of the Schloss, has lots of amenities, including bike and canoe rentals

Pension am Alten Bauernhafen (☎ 2930; www .am-alten-bauernhafen.de, in German; Stottoff 5; s from €30, d €42-48; **P**) Charmingly decorated, with large rooms and a fantastic riverside location, this big, family-run house is a fine base of operation. The owner couple grows their own organic vegetables and make many of the breakfast products themselves.

Hotel Schloss Lübbenau (☎ 8730; www.schloss -luebbenau.de; Schlossbezirk 6; s €58-92, d €92-148; **P ⊠**) Check in at this handsome palace for a surprisingly reasonable splurge with all the class you can handle amid lovely park surroundings. The restaurant here is your only fine-dining option in Lübbenau (dinner only; mains €15 to €25).

Stadtbrauerei Babben (☎ 2126; Brauhausgasse 2; ☼ from 5pm mid-Mar–Oct) Brandenburg's smallest brewery makes a mean pilsner and seasonal beers, all of them unfiltered, unpasteurised and therefore always fresh. The menu features casual pub eats; upstairs are four cosy rooms for spending the night (singles/doubles €36/56).

COTTBUS

☎ 0355 / pop 99,800

The southern gateway to the Spreewald, Cottbus has a pretty historic centre anchored by the **Altmarkt**, a handsomely restored square hemmed in by baroque and neoclassical town houses. East of here is the late-Gothic **Oberkirche** (☎ 247 14; Gertraudtenstrasse 1; ☼ 10am-5pm) with its climbable tower (€1). The **tourist office** (☎ 754 20; www.cottbus.de; Berliner Platz 6; ☼ 9am-6pm Mon-Fri, to 1pm Sat) is a short walk west of the Altmarkt, behind the Spree-Galerie shopping centre.

Cottbus (aka Chósébuz) is also the unofficial capital of the Sorbian Blota region. To learn about this Slavic group's history, language and culture, visit the **Wendisches Museum** (☎ 794 930; Mühlenstrasse 12; adult/concession/family €2.50/1.50/6; ☼ 8.30am-6pm Tue-Fri, 2-6pm Sat & Sun) or the cultural centre called **Lodka** (☎ 4857 6468; August-Bebel-Strasse 82; ☼ 10am-4.30pm Mon-Fri). Lodka is near the **Staatstheater Cottbus** (☎ 01803-440 344; Schillerplatz 1), an art-nouveau marvel of a theatre. Southeast of the centre, **Branitzer Park** contains a lovely 18th-century

aroque Schloss, the Fürst-Pückler-Museum
nd the *Wasserpyramide*, a curious grass-
overed pyramid 'floating' in a little lake.

Frequent regional trains link central
erlin stations with Cottbus (€13, 1¾ hours),
lso stopping in Lübben and Lübbenau.

Trams 1 and 3 run to the centre from the
ain station.

ROUND COTTBUS

outh of Cottbus, in an area called Fürst
ückler Land, a vast opencast lignite mining
rea is being turned into Germany's largest
rtificial-lake district. Called the **Lausitzer
eenland**, it will become a recreational haven
vith boating, swimming, golfing and other
utdoor activities. You can observe and learn
nore about this fascinating project at the **vis-
ors centre** (☎ 035753-2610; www.iba-see.de; Seestrasse
00; ☻ 10am-6pm Mar-Oct, 10am-4pm Nov-Feb), then
ollow up with a guided **walking tour** (adult/con-
ession €7/5; ☻ 10.15am-4pm Sat & Sun) around what
till resembles a lunar landscape. The visi-
ors centre is in the hamlet of Grossräschen,
bout 30km south of Cottbus, on the B96
ust east off the A13. There's also a regional
rain service, including from Cottbus (€5.10,
ne hour) and Berlin (€14.20, two hours);
t's a 25-minute signposted walk from the
tation to the visitor centre.

For another perspective on this ambi-
ious project, head 20km west on the B96
o Lichterfeld, where you'll spot a huge steel
ontraption looking a bit like a toppled Eiffel
ower. This is the **F60** (☎ 03531-608 00; www.f60
le/index_e.htm; Bergheider Strasse 4; guided tours adult/
oncession/child €8/7/3; ☻ 10am-9pm Mar, Apr, Sep &
ct, to 10pm May-Aug, 11am-7pm Tue, Wed, Fri-Sun Nov-
eb), a 500m-long conveyor bridge used in
ignite mining (incidentally, the Eiffel Tower
s 'only' 320m high). You can take a tour (in
German) of the behemoth and peruse the
xhibits in the **visitors centre** (admission €1.50)
pen the same hours.

ASTERN
BRANDENBURG

BUCKOW

☎ 033433 / pop 1650

Tiny Buckow is the hub of the Naturpark
Märkische Schweiz, a rural expanse of clear
treams, romantic lakes and gently undulat-

ing hills. Its bucolic charms have provided
creative fodder for numerous artists, most
prominently the poet Theodor Fontane,
who praised its 'friendly landscape' in
Das Oderland (1863). In the 1950s Bertolt
Brecht and Helene Weigel spent their summers here, away from Berlin's stifling heat.
Buckow has long been famous for its clean
and fresh air; in fact, in 1854 Friedrich
Wilhelm IV's physician advised the ailing monarch to visit the village, where 'the
lungs go as on velvet'. No surprise, then,
that Buckow has of late reclaimed its position as one of Brandenburg's most popular
resort towns.

Orientation & Information
Buckow is surrounded by five lakes, the
largest being the Schermützelsee. Stop by
the **tourist office** (☎ 575 00; www.amt-maerkische
-schweiz.de; Sebastian-Kneipp-Weg 1; ☻ 9am-5pm Mon-Fri
year-round, 10am-5pm Sat & Sun Apr-Oct, 10am-2pm Sat &
Sun Nov-Mar) for general maps and information
or the **Besucherzentrum Schweizer Haus** (☎ 158
41; Lindenstrasse 33; ☻ 10am-4pm Mon-Fri year-round,
10am-6pm Sat & Sun Apr-Oct) for details about the
nature park.

Sights & Activities
The **Brecht-Weigel-Haus** (☎ 467; Bertolt-Brecht-
Strasse 30; adult/concession €3/2; ☻ 1-5pm Wed-Fri,
1-6pm Sat & Sun Apr-Oct, 10am-noon & 1-4pm Wed-Fri,
11am-4pm Sat & Sun Nov-Mar) is where the couple
summered from 1952 to 1955. Exhibits include photographs, documents and original
furnishings as well as the covered wagon
first used in the 1949 premiere of *Mother
Courage*. In the fine gardens are copper tablets engraved with Brecht poems. En route
to the house, via Ringstrasse and Bertolt-
Brecht-Strasse, you'll pass plenty more posh
prewar villas.

There's some good walking around here.
Stop by the tourist office for advice and
maps. In summer you can hire rowing boats
or go on a cruise on the Schermützelsee with
Seetours (☎ 232; Bertolt-Brecht-Strasse 11; tours adult/
child €6/3; ☻ 10am-6pm Tue-Sun Apr-Oct).

Sleeping & Eating
A *Kurtaxe* (resort tax) of €1 per person per
night is added to hotel bills.

DJH hostel (☎ 286; www.jh-buckow.de, in German;
Berliner Strasse 36; dm under/over 26yr €14.50/17.50; Ⓟ ⊠)
The local hostel is close to the train station and

BRANDENBURG

the Weisser See and can accommodate up to 106 people in rooms sleeping two to eight.

Hotel Bergschlösschen (☎ 573 12; www.berg schloesschen.com, in German; Königstrasse 38; s €55, d €75-85; **P** ⊠) It may resemble the house from *Psycho*, but you'd be mad (ha ha!) to complain about the upstairs views from this excellent hillside hotel. Rooms are spacious and have balconies and there's even a sauna for civilised pampering.

Stobbermühle (☎ 668 33; www.stobbermuehle .de, in German; Wriezener Strasse 2; s €54, d €78-88, apt €88-198, breakfast €11; **P** ⊠) This romantic hotel has charmingly decorated rooms and apartments, some with whirlpool tubs and kitchenettes. The restaurant (mains €9.50 to €18.50; open 11am to midnight) does creative things with classic German dishes; pork tenderloin paired with avocado-tomato salad, gorgonzola sauce and polenta is a typical offering.

Fischerkehle (☎ 374; Fischerberg 7; mains €9-18; ⊙ 11am-7pm May-Sep, 11am-5pm Oct-Apr; ⊠) This popular historic restaurant with a big terrace overlooking the Schermützelsee specialises in locally caught fish and game.

Getting There & Away

Buckow does not have a train station but there's handy hourly train/bus service leaving from U-Bahn and S-Bahn station Berlin-Lichtenberg. Hop on a train to Müncheberg, then change to bus 928 (€6.30, one hour) or, if it's running, to the **Buckower Kleinbahn** (☎ 575 78; www.buckower-kleinbahn.de; adult/child €2.50/2; ⊙ Sat & Sun May-Sep), a nostalgic electric train. Drivers should follow the B1 to Müncheberg, then steer north towards Buckow via Waldsieversdorf.

FRANKFURT AN DER ODER
☎ 0335 / pop 60,500

Germany's 'other' Frankfurt, 90km east of Berlin, was practically wiped off the map in the final days of WWII and never recovered its one-time grandeur as a medieval trading centre and university town. It didn't help that the city was split in two after the war, with the eastern suburb across the Oder River becoming the Polish town of Słubice. The GDR era imposed a decidedly unflattering Stalinist look, but still, the scenic river setting, a few architectural gems and the proximity to Poland (cheap vodka and cigarettes, for all you hedonists) are all good reasons for a stopover.

Orientation & Information
The Hauptbahnhof is on the southwester edge of the city centre. Walking north o Bahnhofstrasse and east on Heilbronne Strasse delivers you to the landmar Oderturm, a GDR-era high-rise. It border the giant Brunnenplatz, where the **tourist o fice** (☎ 325 216; www.frankfurt-oder-tourist.de; Karl-Mar Strasse 1; ⊙ 9am-7pm Mon-Fri, 10am-2pm Sat May-Se 10am-6pm Mon-Fri, to 2pm Sat Oct-Apr) is ensconced i a glass pavilion. The Marktplatz is just north east of the square, a short walk from the Ode River and the bridge to Słubice.

There's 24-hour internet access inside gambling hall called **California** (☎ 685 131 Slubicer Strasse 10-11; per hr €2; ⊙ 24hr).

Sights
Much of Frankfurt might be called 'aestheti cally challenged', but you wouldn't know standing on the Marktplatz. To the sout looms the crenulated tower of the **Marienkirch** (⊙ 10am-8pm), one of Germany's largest bric Gothic hall churches. Ruined by wartime an GDR disregard, it now boasts a proud ne roof and fantastic medieval stained-glass win dows, which had been kept as war booty i Russia and were only recently returned.

Back on Marktplatz, standing almost as ta as the Marienkirche, is the **Rathaus** with its or nate south gable. Besides the mayor's office, houses the **Museum Junge Kunst** (☎ 401 530; www .museum-junge-kunst.de, in German; Marktplatz 1; adult/cor cession €4/3; ⊙ 11am-5pm Tue-Sun), which has one o the most comprehensive collection of art cre ated in eastern Germany since 1945. Works b such artists as Willy Wolff, Werner Tübke an Cornelia Schleime are displayed here and i the riverside **PackHof** (CPE-Bach-Strasse 11; admissio free; ⊙ 11am-5pm Tue-Sun), a short walk east.

Adjacent to the PackHof, in a restored ba roque mansion, the **Museum Viadrina** (☎ 401 560 www.museum-viadrina.de, in German; CPE-Bach-Strasse 11 adult/concession €3/2; ⊙ 11am-5pm Tue-Sun) present regional history in a comprehensive but rathe turgid fashion.

If you're a fan of German dramatis Heinrich von Kleist (1711-1811), you migh want to follow the Oderpromenade river wall south to the **Kleist-Museum** (☎ 531 155; www.kleis -museum.de; Faberstrasse 7; adult/concession €3/2; ⊙ 10am 6pm Tue-Sun), which chronicles the life, work and importance of Frankfurt's famous son.

Kleist contemporary Carl Philipp Emanue Bach (1714-88), Johann Sebastian's secon on, studied in Frankfurt in the 1730s. The local concert hall, the **Konzerthalle CPE ach** (☎ 401 00; Lebuser Mauerstrasse 4; admission €1; ⏲ 9am-7pm), in a Gothic monastery church t the northern end of the Oderpromenade, ast the bridge to Słubice, was named in his onour. It also harbours a small exhibit on his rather quirky composer known for his motionally charged works.

leeping & Eating

ension Am Kleistpark (☎ 238 90; Humboldtstrasse 14; €35-39, d €56-62; ✗) If you put a premium on alue and can do without most mod cons, ou'll be happy in the large and bright ooms at this property opposite Kleistpark.

Hotel Gallus (☎ 561 50; www.hotel-gallus.com; ürstenwalder Strasse 47; s €50-70, d €63-83; P ✗) lso near the Kleistpark, behind a lovely rt-nouveau facade, Gallus has 25 bright nd uncluttered rooms decked out in varm tones.

Frankfurter Kartoffelhaus (☎ 530 757; Holzmarkt , mains €5-19; ⏲ 11.30am-10pm; ✗) The humble ιotato finds its destiny in soups, salads and asseroles, paired with steak or salmon and umpteen other dishes at this congenial bistro ight on the river promenade.

Turm 24 (☎ 504 517; Logenstrasse 8; mains €9-19; ⏲ 11.30am-11.30pm Mon-Sat, to 10pm Sun; ✗) The hef's ambitions are as lofty as the 24th-floor etting of this smart restaurant. The spectacu- ar views definitely compete with such dishes ιs boar with walnut-herb sauce or homemade agliatelle with salmon and lobster.

Getting There & Around

Frankfurt is served twice hourly by regional rains from central Berlin (€9.10, 70 min- ites) and Cottbus (€10.40, 1¼ hours).

Bike hire is available through **Fahrrad Schondau** (☎ 321 184; Winsestrasse 4; per day €7; ⏲ 9am-6pm Mon-Fri, 9am-12.30pm Sat).

NORTHERN BRANDENBURG

SACHSENHAUSEN CONCENTRATION CAMP

In 1936 the Nazis opened a 'model' con- centration camp in Sachsenhausen, near the town of Oranienburg (population 30,000),

about 35km north of Berlin. By 1945 about 220,000 men from 22 countries had passed through the gates, which had signage read- ing, as at Auschwitz, *Arbeit Macht Frei* (Work Sets You Free). About 100,000 were murdered here, their remains consumed by the relentless fires of the ovens.

After the war, the Soviets set up Speziallager No 7 (Special Camp No 7) for ex-Nazis, regime opponents and anyone else who didn't fit into their mould. An estimated 60,000 people were interned at the camp between 1945 and 1950, and up to 12,000 are believed to have died here. There's a mass grave of victims at the camp and another one 1.5km to the north.

Sights

The **Gedenkstätte und Museum Sachsenhausen** (☎ 03301-2000; www.stiftung-bg.de; Strasse der Nationen 22; admission free; ⏲ 8.30am-6pm mid-Mar–mid-Oct, to 4.30pm mid-Oct–mid-Mar, most exhibits closed Mon) consists of several parts. Even before you enter you'll see a **memorial** to the 6000 pris- oners who died on the *Todesmarsch* (Death March) of April 1945, when the Nazis tried to drive the camp's 33,000 inmates to the Baltic in advance of the Red Army.

About 100m inside the camp is a mass grave of 300 prisoners who died in the infir- mary after liberation in April 1945. Farther on, in the camp commander's house and the so-called 'Green Monster' building, SS troops were trained in camp maintenance and other, more brutal, activities. At the end of the road, the **Neues Museum** (New Museum) has a permanent exhibit about the camp's precursor, the KZ Oranienburg, which was set up in a disused brewery shortly after Hitler's rise to power in 1933.

East of the museum are **Barracks 38** and **39**, reconstructions of typical huts housing most of the 6000 Jewish prisoners brought to Sachsenhausen after Kristallnacht in November 1938. North of here is the **prison**, where particularly brutal punishment was meted out to prisoners. A memorial inside the prison yard commemorates homosexual victims. Nearby, the **Lagermuseum** (Camp Museum), in what was once the camp kitchen, houses poignant exhibits illustrating the every- day horrors of life in the camp during its vari- ous phases. There's even artwork produced by the inmates and some of the equipment employed to make their lives so miserable.

BRANDENBURG

Left of the tall and ugly **monument**, erected in 1961 by the GDR in memory of political prisoners interned here, is the **crematorium** and **Station Z extermination site**, a pit for shooting prisoners in the neck with a wooden 'catch' where bullets could be retrieved and recycled.

Getting There & Away

Oranienburg is served every 20 minutes by the S1 from Berlin-Friedrichstrasse (€2.80, 45 minutes) and by hourly regional trains from Berlin-Hauptbahnhof (€2.80, 25 minutes). From Oranienburg station it's a signposted 20-minute walk to the camp; bus 804 comes by hourly.

RHEINSBERG

☎ 033931 / pop 8800

Rheinsberg, a delightful town on Lake Grienerick about 50km northwest of Berlin, has a strong cultural pedigree. Frederick the Great enjoyed giving flute concerts at the Schloss and his brother Heinrich later turned the palace into a 'court of the muses'. The town also inspired Theodor Fontane's gushy travelogue called *Wanderungen durch die Mark Brandenburg* (Walks through the March of Brandenburg) and Kurt Tucholsky's 1912 breakthrough novel *Rheinsberg – ein Bilderbuch für Verliebte* (Rheinsberg – A Picture Book for Lovers). Cultural events, along with the palace, its park, plenty of boating and some top-notch restaurants, still make Rheinsberg a pleasant getaway.

Information

Post office (Paulshorster Strasse 18b; ⊙ 8am-7pm Mon-Fri, 8am-1pm Sat)

Tourist information (☎ 344 890; www.rheinsberg -tourismus.de; Schillerstrasse 8; ⊙ 10am-1pm & 3-7pm) Private tourist office with internet access (€0.50 per 15 minutes).

Tourist office (☎ 2059; www.tourismus-rheinsberg .de; Kavalierhaus des Schlosses, Am Markt; ⊙ 10am-5pm Mon-Thu, 10am-6pm Fri & Sat, 10am-4pm Sun)

Sights

The town's star attraction is the eponymous **Schloss Rheinsberg** (☎ 7260; www.spsg.de; Mühlenstrasse 1; adult/concession/family incl audioguide €6/5/8; ⊙ 10am-6pm Tue-Sun Apr-Oct, 10am-5pm Nov-Mar), prettily set right on Lake Grienerick and surrounded by a sprawling park. Friedrich Wilhelm I purchased it in 1734 for his 22-year-old son, Crown Prince Friedrich, th future Frederick the Great. The prince, wh spent four years here studying and preparin for the throne, later said this period was th happiest of his life. In 1744 he gave the palac to his brother Heinrich, a closet homosexua whom Frederick forced into marriage wit Wilhelmine of Hesse-Kassel. You'll learn th and other juicy tidbits on a self-guided audi tour (available in English).

During GDR times, the palace was used a a sanatorium and, although nicely restore its interior can't quite match what you migh have seen in Schloss Sanssouci or Schlos Charlottenburg. Still, there are a few highlight especially the **Spiegelsaal** (Hall of Mirrors), dec orated with a ceiling fresco by Antoine Pesn and the **Muschelsaal** (Shell Room).

Schloss tickets are also good for the **Tucholsk Literaturmuseum** (☎ 390 07; www.tucholsky-museum.d in German; without Schloss adult/concession/family €3/2/ on the ground floor of the north wing. The ex hibit traces the life of journalist, satirist, poe and social critic Kurt Tucholsky (1890–1935) who went into exile in Sweden when the Naz came to power.

Activities

Reederei Halbeck (☎ 386 19; www.schiffahrt-rheinsberg.d in German; Markt 11; 2hr trip from €6.50), next to th tourist office, offers a range of lake and rive cruises and hires out canoes, paddle-boats an kayaks. **Rheinsberger Adventure Tours** (☎ 392 47 www.rhintour.de, in German; cnr Rhinstrasse & Mühlenstrass hires out boats and bikes and can arrange a sorts of area excursions.

Sleeping & Eating

Pension Holländermühle (☎ 2332; http://rheinsber .de/hollaender-muehle, in German; Holländer Mühle 1; s €4 d €60-70; **P** **⊠**) Expect charm by the buck at this cute B&B where you can either slee in romantic rooms in a historic windmill o in modern ones in an annex. The restauran serves German and regional fare (mains €8.5 to €16, open noon to 7pm).

Zum Jungen Fritz (☎ 4090; www.junger-fritz.de, i German; Schlossstrasse 8; s/d €47/70; **P**) This swee little inn has big-hearted owners and nin cute rooms. Rates include access to the loca gym (with sauna), which could come in handy after a robust meal at their old-tim German restaurant.

Der Seehof (☎ 4030; www.seehof-rheinsberg.com, i German; Seestrasse 18; s €65-75, d €100-110; **P** **⊠** **P**

This top-flight option in a 1750 townhouse has lovely rooms furnished in a modern, uncluttered country style with wooden floors and plenty of natural light. The restaurant (mains €8.50 to €20) serves exceptional meals, many built around locally caught game and fish.

Eisfabrik (☎ 7240; Kurt-Tucholsky-Strasse 36; ✗) To feed your sweet-tooth cravings, swing by Eisfabrik, which makes its own ice cream, including some from herbs, vegetables and other unusual ingredients.

Café Tucholsky (☎ 343 70; Kurt-Tucholsky-Strasse 30a; mains €6-11; ✇ 11am-10pm; ✗) This smart lakeside cafe is an excellent one-size-fits-all option. Come for coffee and cake, a refreshment, a snack or a full meal.

Zum Alten Fritz (☎ 2086; Schlossstrasse 11; mains around €11; ✇ 11.30am-11pm; ✗) The beautiful old porcelain, books, lamps and other traditional decor almost transport you back to the 18th century. Some of the dishes were also inspired by recipes from that era.

Entertainment

Musikakademie Rheinsberg (☎ 7210; www.musik akademie-rheinsberg.de, in German; Kavalierhaus des Schlosses) The academy presents year-round concerts, ballet, musical theatre and other cultural events at the palace theatre, inside the Hall of Mirrors and at other venues. Tickets are available from the tourist office.

Getting There & Around

Getting to Rheinsberg by public transport is time-consuming and requires multiple changes. Call ☎ 030-2541 4141 or visit www vbb-berlin.de for trip-planning assistance. Drivers should head north via the B96 and consult a map or www.maps.google.com for precise directions.

You can hire bikes from **Fahrradhaus Thäns** (☎ 2622; Schlossstrasse 16; per day €6-8; ✇ 9am-12.30pm Mon-Sat, 2-6pm Mon-Fri).

LOWER ODER VALLEY NATIONAL PARK

In the far northeastern corner of Brandenburg, the **Lower Oder Valley National Park** (Nationalpark Unteres Obertal; www.nationalpark-unteres-odertal.eu) is guaranteed to get you away from the tourist crowds. It protects one of the last relatively unspoiled flood plains in Europe and is home to a stunning diversity of flora and fauna. A patchwork of meadows, marshland and deciduous forest, the park hugs the Polish border for 60km but is just 2km to 4km wide. It's

a paradise for birds and the people who love watching them fly and feed, coo and quack, mate and roost. Around 160 feathered species make their home here, including such endangered specimens as sea eagles and black storks. In autumn the sky darkens with more than 100,000 geese, ducks and cranes stopping on their way to warmer climes further south.

Orientation & Information

The gateway town to the park is Schwedt, about 100km northeast of Berlin. Here you'll find most commercial activity as well as the regional **tourist office** (☎ 03332-255 90; www.unteres -odertal.de; Vierradener Strasse 34; ✇ 10am-6pm Mon-Fri, 10am-4pm May-Sep, 10am-5pm Mon-Fri Oct-Apr).

An even better place to get oriented is the **Nationalparkhaus** (☎ 03332-267 70; Park 2; admission free; ✇ 9am-6pm daily Apr-Oct, 10am-5pm Fri-Sun Nov-Mar), about 8km south in Criewen. This is the park's main visitor centre with exhibits and knowledgeable (though not always English-speaking) folks who are happy to suggest activities and hand out maps. A highlight is the giant aquarium with some 20-odd local fish species flitting around.

Activities

The park is best explored by bicycle. The long-distance Oder-Neisse-Radweg passes through it and smaller paths take you straight to wildflower-studded meadows or the polder banks. From mid-July to mid-November, after the end of the breeding season, the park can be explored by canoe. Enquire about guided tours at the tourist office. Bikes can be hired from **Fahrrad- und Touristikcenter Butzke** (☎ 03332-839 500; Kietz 11) in Schwedt from €5 per day.

Sleeping

The tourist office in Schwedt can help you find private or hotel rooms in the entire region.

Campingplatz am Oderstrom (☎ 033332-870 044, 0170 343 7718; www.campingplatz-mescherin.de, in German; Obere Dorfstrasse 17; per person/car €3/2, per tent €3-5) If you want to truly commune with nature, set up your tent in a lovely riverside setting at the park's northern tip in Mescherin, about 30km north of Schwedt.

Pension Moritz (☎ 03332-516 455; www.landpension -moritz.de, in German; Schwedter Strasse 1; s/d €45/62; P ✗) This adorable B&B has country-style rooms in a new building attached to a working farm with a resident stork family. It's in Meyenburg, about 2km south of Schwedt.

Getting There & Around

Regional trains to Schwedt leave hourly from Berlin-Hauptbahnhof (€10.40, 1¼ hours). From Schwedt, bus 468 goes to Criewen in 15 minutes (€1.40). Alternatively, take the regional train to Angermünde and switch to bus 468 there for Criewen (€9.60, 1¾ hours, every two hours).

Drivers should follow the A11 to the Joachimsthal exit, then continue on the B2 towards Angermünde.

CHORIN

☎ 033366 / pop 520

Plenty of people make the day trip from Berlin to the tiny village of Chorin. Their destination: the renowned **Kloster Chorin** (Chorin Monastery; ☎ 703 77; www.kloster-chorin.com; Amt Chorin 11a; adult/concession/family €4/2.50/10; ⏰ 9am-6pm Apr-Oct, 9am-4pm Nov-Mar), a romantically ruined monastery near a little lake and surrounded by a lush park. Some 500 Cistercian monks laboured over six decades starting in 1273 to erect what is widely considered one of the finest red-brick Gothic structures in northern Germany. The monastery was secularised in 1542 and fell into disrepair after the Thirty Years' War. Renovation has gone on in a somewhat haphazard fashion since the early 19th century.

Enter the complex through the ornate step-gabled western facade which leads to the central cloister flanked by the monastic quarters. To the north looms the church with its sleekly carved portals and elongated lancet windows. Both cloister and church are an enchanting setting for classical summer concerts. On weekends from June to August, top talent performs during the **Choriner Musiksommer** (☎ 03334-657 310; www.musiksommer-chorin.de; tickets €7-23). A shuttle bus connects Chorin train station and the Kloster before and after concerts.

If you need to stay or just fancy a bite, steer towards the lakeside **Hotel Haus Chorin** (☎ 033366-500; www.chorin.de; Neue Klosterallee 10; s €41-69, d €49-89; Ⓟ ☒). The kitchen uses organic ingredients in some dishes, and claims to be the world's first 'honey restaurant' where all dishes contain the sweet stuff (mains €7 to €20).

Chorin is about 60km northeast of Berlin. RE trains make hourly trips from Berlin-Hauptbahnhof (€7.70, 40 minutes). Trains are often met by bus 912, which takes you to within a five-minute walk of the monastery. Alternatively, it's a 2.5km walk along a marked trail through the woods. Or rent a two-wheeler from the **bike rental shop** (☎ 033366-537 00; Bahnhofstrasse 2; per day €8.50) in the train station.

NIEDERFINOW

☎ 033362 / pop 650

Tiny Niederfinow, about 20km southeast of Chorin, would be a mere blip on the map were it not for the spectacular **Schiffshebewerk** (ship-lift; ☎ 033362-215; www.schiffshebewerk-niederfinow.info in German; Hebewerkstrasse 52; ⏰ 9am-6pm Apr-Oct, to 4pm Nov, Dec & mid-Feb–Mar), one of the most remarkable feats of engineering from the early 20th century. Looking a bit like the exoskeleton of an aircraft carrier, it was completed in 1934 and measures 60m high, 27m wide and 94m long. Huge barges sail into a sort of giant bathtub, which is then raised or lowered 36m, water and all, between the Oder River and the Oder-Havel Canal.

The lift can be viewed from the street (free) but for better views climb to the upper canal platform (adult/child €1/0.50) and view the 20-minute operation from above. Even more memorable is a trip on the lift itself aboard a little boat operated by **Fahrgastschifffahrt Neumann** (☎ 03334-244 05; www.finowkanalschifffahrt.de in German; adult/child €6/3; ⏰ 11am, 1pm & 3pm late Mar-Oct). Tickets are sold at the information kiosk in the car park.

If you think this ship-lift is impressive come back in 2014 when a second, much bigger one is scheduled to begin operation adjacent to the existing one. The new behemoth will be 130m long and able to accommodate larger barges capable of transporting the equivalent of 50 trucks.

Niederfinow is served by regional train from Berlin-Hauptbahnhof (€6.30, 1¼ hours) with a change in Bernau or Eberswalde, or directly from U-Bahn and S-Bahn station Lichtenberg (€6.30, one hour). The Schiffshebewerk is a scenic 2km walk north of the station; turn left and follow the road.

Saxony

If you're going to visit just one state in the east, make it Saxony. With rejuvenated Dresden providing the culture, prosperous Leipzig laying on the glitz, and the Sorbs injecting a little Slavic colour, Saxony is firmly back on the traveller's map. Away from the cities, the low hills of the Erzgebirge and rock formations of the Saxon Switzerland are a tranquil bliss. And through this eternal landscape zigzags the Elbe River, just beginning its long journey to the North Sea.

Saxony's landscapes have tugged for centuries at the heartstrings of visionaries. Canaletto and Caspar David Friedrich captured Dresden's baroque brilliance and the mystical beauty of Saxon Switzerland on canvas; JS Bach penned some of his most famous works in Leipzig; and the 'musical poet' Robert Schumann grew up in Zwickau. Dresden's famous Semperoper and the Gewandhaus in Leipzig are two of the world's greatest high-brow venues.

Dresden and Leipzig naturally grab top billing when it comes to the region's history. The former became synonymous in the 20th century with the devastation of WWII, but has since resurrected its baroque heritage, most notably the Frauenkirche. The latter sparked the 'peaceful revolution' of 1989, bringing down the Berlin Wall.

Its sooty socialist-era industries mostly cast aside, Saxony now enjoys the most vibrant economy of the former GDR, and rebuilding work continues apace. But Saxony also gives abundant opportunity to indulge in an odd nostalgia for the erstwhile East Germany, with curious museums packed with planned-economy bric-a-brac, the Zwickau car plant that once rolled out the infamous Trabant, and Soviet-tinged Chemnitz still parading its Karl Marx monument.

HIGHLIGHTS

- **Baroque Bash** Revel in the kicking nightlife scene of Dresden's Neustadt (p187), the best in the east outside of Berlin
- **Honecker's Heritage** Travel back in time to the GDR at museums in Leipzig (p197), Pirna (p190) and Radebeul (p190)
- **Giddy Heights** Clamber up the Bastei (p191) for gobsmacking panoramas of the Saxon Switzerland and the Elbe
- **Go Sorbing** Party with Bautzen's Sorbs (p210), German's little-known Slav minority
- **Blinding Beauty** Don sunglasses to view the dazzling treasures at Dresden's Historiches Grünes Gewölbe (p181)
- **That's Neisse** Marvel at the architecture of Görlitz (p212), one of Germany's most attractive cities

★ Leipzig

Radebeul ★   Dresden   Bautzen ★
Pirna ★   ★ Bastei   Görlitz ★

- POPULATION: 4.35 MILLION
- AREA: 18,413 SQ KM

SAXONY

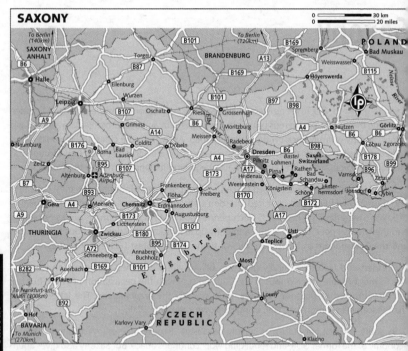

SAXONY

Information

If you need to book a room, or just want more information about Saxony, log on to www .sachsen-tour.de.

Getting Around

An enticement to use public transport is the good-value **Saxony-Ticket** (€28), giving you and up to four accompanying passengers (or one or both parents or grandparents, plus all their children or grandchildren up to 14 years) unlimited train travel during the period of its validity (9am to 3am the next day). Tickets are good for 2nd-class travel throughout Saxony, as well as in Thuringia and Saxony-Anhalt. As well as any regional Deutsche Bahn trains (IRE, RE, RB and S-Bahn), you can also use some private trains, including the LausitzBahn.

CENTRAL SAXONY

DRESDEN

☎ 0351 / pop 512,000

There are few city silhouettes more striking than Dresden's. The classic view from the Elbe's northern bank takes in a playful phalanx of delicate spires, soaring towers and dominant domes belonging to palaces, churches and stately buildings. Numerous artists, most notably the Italian Canaletto, have set up their easels to capture this breathtaking panorama.

'Florence of the north', the Saxon capital was called in the 18th century, when it was a centre of artistic activity presided over by the cosmopolitan Augustus the Strong (August der Starke) and his son Augustus III. Their vision produced many of Dresden's iconic buildings, including the Zwinger, the Frauenkirche and the Hofkirche. But following the seemingly indiscriminate destruction of the city by Allied bombers in 1945 (see boxed text, opposite) during which most of the city centre was turned into landfill, it's a miracle some of these monumental edifices are here today.

But Dresden is a survivor and there is no more potent symbol of its people's determination than the resurrected Frauenkirche. Although the city has been around for eight centuries, it is also forward-looking and sol-

---

MOUNTAIN OF FRAGMENTS

Between 13 and 15 February 1945, British and American planes unleashed 3900 tonnes of explosives on Dresden in four huge air raids. Bombs and incendiary shells whipped up a mammoth firestorm, and ashes rained down on villages 35km away. When the blazes had died down and the dust settled, tens of thousands of Dresdner's had lost their lives, and 20 sq km of this once elegant baroque city lay in smouldering ruins.

Historians still argue over whether this constituted a war crime committed by the Allies on an innocent civilian population. Some claim that with the Red Army at the gates of Berlin, the war was effectively won, and the allies gained little military advantage from the destruction of Dresden. Others have put forward the view that as the last urban centre in the east of the country left intact, Dresden could have provided shelter for German troops returning from the east and was hence a viable target.

As most of the menfolk were at war, it fell to Dresden's women to clear the rubble of their ruined city. Most of the debris was dumped in the west of the city, and came to form the Trümmerberg or 'Mountain of Fragments'. From the top there are views of the Altstadt, including the symbol of Dresden's rebirth, the Frauenkirche.

---

idly rooted in the here and now. There's some great new architecture, a constantly evolving arts and cultural scene, and zinging pub and nightlife quarters.

So take a few days and allow yourself to be caught up in this visual and cultural feast. We promise that Dresden's world-class museums will mesmerise you, its riverside beer gardens relax you, and its light-hearted, almost Mediterranean, disposition, charm you.

Orientation

The meandering Elbe River separates the Altstadt (Old Town) to the south from the Neustadt (New Town) to the north. From the Hauptbahnhof (central train station) it's a 10-minute walk north on pedestrianised Prager Strasse, the main shopping street, to the Frauenkirche and other blockbuster sights.

The main walking bridge to the Neustadt is the Augustusbrücke, just west of the famous riverside promenade called Brühlsche Terrasse, with the Terrassenufer boat landing docks below.

Augustusbrücke segues into pedestrianised Hauptstrasse, the main commercial strip in the so-called Innere Neustadt (Inner New Town), which culminates at Albertplatz. Beyond this lies the Äussere Neustadt (Outer New Town), Dresden's main pub and bar quarter.

About half a kilometre west of Albertplatz is Dresden-Neustadt, the city's second train station (most trains stop at both). Dresden's central bus station is near the Hauptbahnhof.

Dresden airport is 9km north of the city centre.

Information

BOOKSHOPS
Das Internationale Buch (☎ 656 460; Altmarkt 24) Excellent selection of English books.
Der Reisebuchladen (☎ 8996 560; Louisenstrasse 70b) Travel books and maps galore.
Haus Des Buches (☎ 497 360; Dr-Külz-Ring 12; 💻) Lots of Lonely Planet titles, plus internet access.

DISCOUNT CARDS
Dresden City-Card (per 48hr €21) Provides admission to museums, discounted city tours and boats, and free public transport. Buy it at the tourist office.
Dresden Regio-Card (per 72hr €32) Everything offered by the City-Card plus free transport on the entire regional transport network. Valid as far as the Czech border and Meissen.

EMERGENCY
Ambulance (☎ 112/19222)
Police (☎ 110)

INTERNET ACCESS
K&E Callshop (Wiener Passage; per hr €2; 🕐 10am-9pm) In the subterranean passageway outside the Hauptbahnhof.
Telecafé (Böhmische Strasse 3; per hr €2; 🕐 10am-midnight)

LAUNDRY
Crazy Waschsalon (Louisenstrasse 6; 🕐 7am-11pm Mon-Sat)
Eco-Express (Königsbrücker Strasse 2; wash/dry €1.90/0.50; 🕐 6am-11pm) There's also a branch at Rudolf-Leonhard-Strasse 16.

DRESDEN

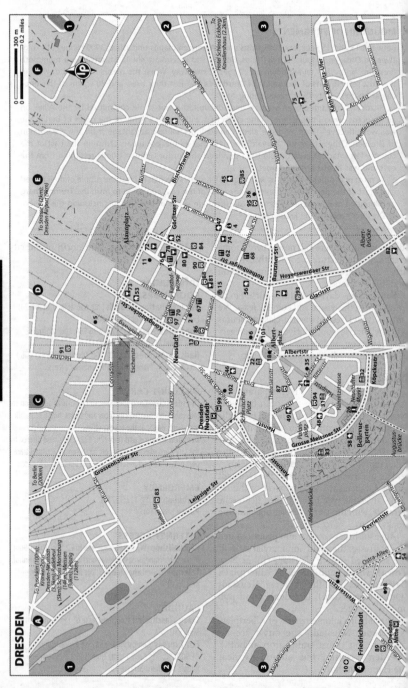

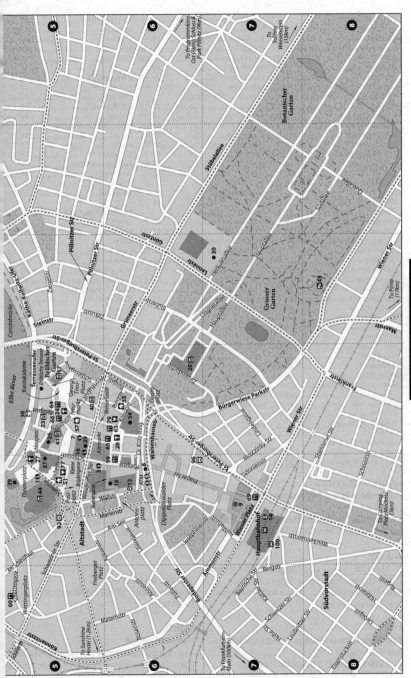

SAXONY

MEDICAL SERVICES

Krankenhaus Dresden-Friedrichstadt (☎ 4800; Friedrichstrasse 41)
Krankenhaus Dresden-Neustadt (☎ 8560; Industrie-strasse 40) Tram 4 to Am Trachauer Bahnhof.

MONEY

Banks and ATMs abound throughout the Altstadt, especially along Prager Strasse.
ReiseBank (Hauptbahnhof; ☺ 8am-8pm Mon-Fri, 8am-6pm Sat, 10am-6pm Sun)

POST

Post Office Altmarkt-Galerie (Altmarkt-Galerie) Enter from Wallstrasse.
Post Office Neustadt (Königsbrücker Strasse 21)

TOURIST INFORMATION

Besucherdienst Semperoper (☎ 4911 705; Schinkel-wache, Theaterplatz 2; ☺ 10am-6pm Mon-Fri, 10am-5pm Sat & Sun) Opera tickets and tours.
Tourist office (☎ 5016 0160; www.dresden-tourist.de; Kulturpalast, Schlossstrasse; ☺ 10am-7pm Mon-Fri, 10am-6pm Sat, 10am-3pm Sun) Also houses the central ticket office.

TRAVEL AGENCY

Neue Reisewelle (☎ 829 720; Alaunstrasse 87) Agents for STA Travel.

Sights

FRAUENKIRCHE

The domed **Frauenkirche** (☎ visitor centre 6560 6100, tickets 6560 6701; www.frauenkirche-dresden.de; admission free; ☺ 10am-noon & 1-6pm Mon-Fri, limited hr on weekends), which is one of Dresden's most beloved symbols, has literally risen from the ashes of the city. The original, designed by Georg Bähr, graced Dresden's skyline for two centuries before collapsing two days after the February 1945 bombing. The GDR left the rubble there as a war memorial, but after reunification a grass-roots movement to rebuild the landmark gained momentum. It was consecrated in November 2005, a year ahead of schedule.

A spitting image of the original, it may not bear the gravitas of age but that only slightly detracts from its festive beauty inside and out. The altar, reassembled from nearly 2000 fragments, is especially striking. The lofty interior, galleried like a theatre, is a wonderful place for concerts, meditations and services, though at other times it's overrun with nattering tourists. Check the website for the current schedule or stop by the **Frauenkirche Visitors Centre** (☺ 9.30am-6pm Mon-Sat) in the Kulturpalast.

Most are satisfied to take a pew to admire and contemplate this remarkable resurrection, but you can also hire an audioguide (€2.50), and climb up to the **copula** (adult/concession/family €8/5/20; ☺ Mar-Oct) for sweeping city views.

RESIDENZSCHLOSS

Home of Saxon kings until 1918, the highlight of the neo-Renaissance **Residenzschloss** is the must-see Grünes Gewölbe (Green Vault), returned to the palace after postwar reconstruction had been completed. Picture it as the real-life equivalent of Aladdin's Cave, a mind-boggling collection of precious objects wrought from gold, ivory, silver, diamonds and other materials. There's so much of it, two separate 'treasure chambers', both in the palace west wing (enter from Sophienstrasse), are needed to display everything.

The **Neues Grünes Gewölbe** (New Green Vault; ☎ 4914 2000; adult/concession incl audioguide €6/3.50; ☺ 10am-6pm Wed-Mon) presents some 1000 objects in 10 modern rooms on the upper floor. Among the most prized items are a frigate fashioned from ivory with wafer-thin sails, a cherry pit with 185 faces carved into it, and an exotic ensemble of 132 gem-studded figurines representing a royal court in India. The artistry of each item is simply dazzling. To avoid the worst crush of people, visit during lunchtime.

A further 3000 items are exhibited below in the show-stopping **Historisches Grünes Gewölbe** (Historical Green Vault; ☎ tickets & information 4914 2000; www.skd-dresden.de; admission incl audioguide €10; ☺ 10am-7pm Wed-Mon), displayed on shelves and tables in a series of increasingly lavish rooms, just as they were during the time of August der Starke. To protect the artworks, which are not behind glass, visitors must pass through a 'dust lock', and numbers are limited to 120 an hour. Admission is by timed ticket only. Advance tickets are available online and by phone, and about a third are sold at the palace box office on the day.

In the same wing, on the top floor, is the **Kupferstichkabinett** (Collection of Prints & Drawings; ☎ 4914 3211; adult/concession €3/2; ☺ 10am-6pm Wed-Mon), which possesses works by some big-hitting names.

For fine views, head up the **Hausmannsturm** (palace tower; adult/concession €2.50/1.50; ☺ 10am-6pm Wed-Mon Mar-Nov). Numismatists might like to peruse the **Münzkabinett** (Coin Collection; ☎ 4914 3231; adult/concession incl tower access €3/2; ☺ 10am-6pm Wed-Mon), also in the tower.

SEMPEROPER

The original **Semperoper** (Opera House; ☎ 491 1496; www.semperoper.de; tours adult/concession €7/3.50) burned down a mere three decades after its 1841 inauguration. When it reopened in 1878, the neo-Renaissance jewel entered its most dazzling period, which saw the premieres of works by Richard Strauss, Carl Maria von Weber and Richard Wagner. Alas, WWII put an end to the fun, and it wasn't until 1985 that music again filled the grand hall.

German-language tours lasting 45 minutes run up to six times a day and explore the most interesting parts of the building. English texts are available.

ZWINGER

Next to the opera house, the sprawling **Zwinger** (☎ 4914 2000; ☺ 10am-6pm Tue-Sun) is among the most ravishing baroque buildings in all of Germany. A collaboration between the architect Matthäus Pöppelmann and the sculptor Balthasar Permoser, it was primarily a party palace for royals, despite the odd name (which means dungeon). Several charming portals lead into the vast fountain-studded courtyard, which is framed by buildings lavishly festooned with baroque sculpture. Atop the western pavilion stands a tense-looking Atlas with the world on his shoulders; opposite him is a cutesy carillon of 40 Meissen porcelain bells, which emit a tinkle every 15 minutes.

Inside, the Zwinger's museum situation has been a bit of a roundabout in recent years, with several comings and goings. The most important permanent collection is the **Gemäldegalerie Alte Meister** (Old Masters Gallery; combined ticket with Rüstkammer adult/concession €7/4.50), which features masterpieces including Raphael's *Sistine Madonna*. Other permanent fixtures include the **Rüstkammer** (Armoury; adult/concession €3/2), a grand collection of ceremonial weapons; the **Porzellansammlung** (Porcelain Collection; adult/concession €6/3.50), a dazzling assortment of Meissen classics and East Asian treasures; and the **Mathematisch-Physikalischer Salon** which normally displays old scientific instruments, globes and timepieces, but was closed at the time of research for renovation.

Until 2009 the Zwinger was also temporary refuge to the **Galerie Neue Meister** and the **Skulpturensammlung**, two exhibitions normally found in the Albertinum. These will remain in limbo until the Albertinum, which suffered damage in the 2002 flood, has been rebuilt, hopefully by summer 2010.

NEUSTADT

Despite its name, Neustadt is actually an older part of Dresden that was considerably less smashed up in WWII than the Altstadt. After reunification it was taken over by the alternative scene, which today still dominates the so-called Äussere (Outer) Neustadt north of Albertplatz. South of here, the Innere (Inner) Neustadt, with Hauptstrasse as its main artery, is now solidly gentrified – especially along Königstrasse, which again sparkles in baroque splendour.

The first thing that catches the eye when crossing Augustusbrücke is the gleaming **Goldener Reiter** (1736) statue of Augustus the Strong. East along the Elbe, the **Museum für Sächsische Volkskunst** (Museum of Saxon Folk Art; ☎ 4914 2000; Köpckestrasse 1; adult/concession €3/2; ☺ 10am-6pm Tue-Sun) displays such quaint things as antique furniture, traditional garments and puppet theatres.

North of the statue, Hauptstrasse is a tree-lined pedestrian shopping street where the **Museum der Dresdner Romantik** (Museum of Dresden Romanticism; ☎ 804 4760; Hauptstrasse 13; adult/concession €3/2; ☺ 10am-6pm Wed-Sun) documents the city's artistic and intellectual movements during the early 19th century.

Further along stands the **Dreikönigskirche** (☎ 812 4102; tower adult/concession €1.50/1; ☺ 11.30am-4pm Tue, 11am-5pm Wed-Sat, 11.30am-5pm Sun May-Oct, shorter hr Nov-Mar) designed by Zwinger-architect Pöppelmann. View the most eye-catching feature, the baroque altar ruined in 1945 and left as a memorial, before scaling the almost 90m-high tower for some panoramic views. Jazz concerts take place here during the Dixieland Festival.

Across Hauptstrasse, the **Neustädter Markthalle**, a gorgeously restored old market hall (enter on Metzer Strasse), provides a laid-back retail experience with stalls selling everything from Russian groceries to kid's wooden toys. There's also a supermarket.

Hauptstrasse culminates at **Albertplatz** with its two striking **fountains** representing turbulent and still waters. Also found here is the interactive **Erich-Kästner-Museum** (☎ 804 5086; Antonstrasse 1; adult/concession €3/2; ☺ 10am-6pm Sun-Tue, 10am-8pm Wed), dedicated to the beloved children's book author, pacifist and outspoken Nazi critic who was born nearby.

Königstrasse runs southwest of Albertplatz, all the way to the not-very-Japanese **Japanisches Palais** (1737). Inside is Dresden's **Museum für Völkerkunde** (Museum of Ethnology; ☎ 814 4814; Palaisplatz 11; adult/concession €4/2; ☺ 10am-6pm Tue-Sun), which boasts well over 70,000 anthropological items from far-flung corners of the world.

North of Albertplatz, the Äussere Neustadt is a spidery web of narrow streets, late-19th-century patrician houses and hidden courtyards, all chock full of pubs, clubs, galleries and one-of-a-kind shops. A highlight here is the **Kunsthofpassage** (enter from Alaunstrasse 70 or Görlitzer Strasse 21), a series of five whimsically designed courtyards each reflecting the vision of a different Dresden artist.

More essential viewing can be found at the **Pfunds Molkerei** (☎ 810 5948; Bautzner Strasse 79; admission free; ☺ 10am-6pm Mon-Sat, 10am-3pm Sun) in the eastern Äussere Neustadt. Hyped up as 'the world's most beautiful dairy shop', it's a riot of hand-painted tiles and enamelled sculpture, all handmade by Villeroy & Boch. The shop sells replica tiles, wines, cheeses and milk. Not surprisingly, the upstairs cafe-restaurant has a strong lactose theme. Slip in between coach tours for a less shuffling look round.

GROSSER GARTEN & AROUND

Southeast of the Altstadt, occupying the former royal hunting grounds, is the aptly named Grosser Garten (Great Garden), a relaxing refuge during the warmer months. A visitor magnet here is the excellent **zoo** (☎ 478 060; Tiergartenstrasse 1; adult/child/concession €8/4/6; ◷ 8.30am-6.30pm Apr-Oct, 8.30am-4.30pm Nov-Mar), where crowds gravitate towards the Africa Hall and the new koala house. At the garden's northwestern corner is the **Botanischer Garten** (botanical garden; admission free; ◷ 10am-dusk). From April to October, a fun way to get around the park is aboard a **miniature train** (☎ 4456 795; adult/concession €3.50/2).

Not, as you might think, an institution dedicated to the history of the GDR's infamously harsh cleaning products, the **Deutsches Hygiene-Museum** (German Hygiene Museum; ☎ 4846 400; www.dhmd.de; Lingnerplatz 1; adult/concession €6/3; ◷ 10am-6pm Tue-Sun), is, in fact, all about you, the human being. The fascinating permanent exhibit is a virtual journey through the body, drawing from anatomy, cultural studies, social science, history and scientific research. You'll learn about various aspects of the human experience, from eating, drinking and thinking to remembering, moving, grooming and dying. Oddly, people seem to linger just a tad longer in the room dealing with sexuality… A highlight is the **Gläserne Mensch** in room 1, the first transparent human model complete with bones, muscles and arteries.

If you've got tots in tow, they're likely to have more fun in the Hygiene Museum's integrated Children's Museum. Located in the basement, it's a highly interactive romp through the mysteries of the five senses.

YENIDZE

Northwest of the Altstadt, you can't miss what looks like a huge kitschy mosque with a great stained-glass onion dome. The **Yenidze** (Weisseritzstrasse 3), the world's first reinforced concrete-framed building, actually started out life in 1907 as a tobacco factory, manufacturing an unsuccessful pseudo-exotic cigarette named Salaam Alakhem. Today it's home to three restaurants and a rooftop beer garden, with cultural events taking place in the dome.

Walking Tour

This Altstadt circuit begins at Altmarkt and makes an arc northwest along the Elbe, taking in the main churches, the Semperoper, the Residenzschloss and the Zwinger. It's a 1½-hour stroll, but with stops you could easily stretch the tour to a day.

The **Altmarkt (1)** was once the historic heart of Dresden. Postwar reconstruction here was heavily influenced by a socialist aesthetic, which meant lots of stark granite, an impractically wide square and the obnoxiously squat **Kulturpalast (2**; ☎ 486 60; www.kulturpalast-dresden.de; Schlossstrasse 2), home to the Dresden Philharmonic Orchestra and the tourist office. The starkness is tempered by streetside cafes, the spanking new **Altmarkt-Galerie (3)** shopping mall and the late-baroque **Kreuzkirche (4**; tower adult/concession €2.50/2; ◷ 10am-5.30pm Mon-Fri, Sat 10am-4.30pm, Sun noon-5.30pm Apr-Oct, shorter hr Nov-Mar). Rebuilt after the war, the church's interior was left deliberately plain and is best enjoyed during a concert, or at 6pm evening prayers (5pm December to March), which are accompanied by the church's world-famous boys' choir, the 700-year-old Kreuzchor.

Following Kreuzstrasse east, you'll soon spot the neo-Renaissance **Neues Rathaus (5**; New Town Hall; ☎ 1905-10; tower adult/concession €3/1.70; ◷ 10am-6pm Apr-Oct) with its 100m-high climbable tower. Cut north through pedestrianised Weisse Gasse, the Altstadt's most delightful dining street, to Wilsdruffer

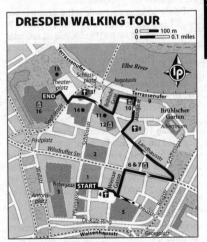

DRESDEN WALKING TOUR

WALK FACTS

Start Altmarkt
Finish Zwinger
Distance 3.5km
Duration 1½ hours

Strasse, where the **Stadtmuseum** (6; ☎ 488 7301; www.museen-dresden.de; Wilsdruffer Strasse 2; adult/concession €4/3; ☷ 10am-6pm Tue-Thu, Sat & Sun, 10am-7pm Fri) presents exhibits on general city history as well as on the reconstruction of the Frauenkirche. Also here is the **Städtische Galerie** (7; ☎ 488 7301; adult/concession €4/3; ☷ 10am-6pm Tue-Thu, Sat & Sun, 10am-7pm Fri), where the baroque city presents its modern side with a respectable collection of 20th-century art. Enter from Landhausstrasse.

Follow Landhausstrasse northwest to Neumarkt, which is again dominated by the landmark **Frauenkirche** (8; p180), whose reconstruction was completed in 2005. On Neumarkt, all around the church, construction is progressing at a steady clip, with sometimes controversial new hotels and shopping complexes springing up. For a preview, check www.neumarkt-dresden.de.

From the north side of Neumarkt, narrow Münzgasse leads straight to the **Brühlsche Terrasse** (9), a spectacular promenade that's been called the 'balcony of Europe', with a pavement nearly 15m above the southern embankment of the Elbe. It's a must for strolling, with expansive views of the river and the Neustadt on the opposite bank.

Beneath the promenade is the Renaissance brick bastion known as the **Festung Dresden** (10; Dresden Fortress; ☎ 438 370 312; adult/child incl audioguide €4/2; ☷ 10am-6pm Apr-Oct, 10am-5pm Nov-Mar), now a museum. The free audioguide helps bring the place to life. Enter from Georg-Treu-Platz.

Otherwise, take the staircase down to Brühlsche Gasse, which leads back to the Neumarkt. From here, turn right onto Augustusstrasse, with its 102m-long **Fürstenzug** (11; Procession of Princes) mural depicted on the facade of the former Stallhof (Royal Stables). The scene, a long row of royalty on horses, was first painted in 1876 by Wullhelm Walther and then transferred to some 24,000 Meissen porcelain tiles in 1904.

Also on Augustusstrasse, you'll find a superb collection of vehicles, including penny-farthings, trams, dirigibles and carriages, at the **Verkehrsmuseum** (12; Transport Museum; ☎ 864 40; www.verkehrsmuseum.dresden.de; Augustusstrasse 1; adult/concession €4.50/2.50; ☷ 10am-5pm Tue-Sun).

Augustusstrasse leads directly to Schlossplatz and the baroque **Hofkirche** (13; ☎ 484 4712; Schlossplatz). Completed in 1755, its crypt contains the heart of Augustus the Strong; his body is in Cracow. You can catch a free organ concert here every Wednesday and Saturday at 11.30am.

Just south of the church is the neo-Renaissance **Residenzschloss** (14), which now houses several museums. These include the must-see Historisches Grünes Gewölbe and Neues Grünes Gewölbe. On the western side of the Hofkirche is Theaterplatz, with Dresden's dramatic and long-suffering **Semperoper** (15). Next to the opera house is the sprawling **Zwinger** (16), a former palace recycled into a major museum complex that includes Dresden's foremost collection of paintings, the Gemäldegalerie Alte Meister.

Tours

The tourist office can help book the following tours:

Barokkokko (☎ 479 8184; www.erlebnisrundgang.de; adult/child €16/9.50) Return to the Dresden of the 18th century on this interactive 1½-hour tongue-in-cheek tour, led by costumed actor-guides who'll even teach you the proper way to curtsey and bow. English-language tours usually run at 6pm Fridays from April to October.

NightWalk Dresden (☎ 8796 867; www.nightwalk -dresden.de; tours €13; ☷ 9pm) Learn all about the intriguing culture and history of the happening Neustadt, one pub at a time, during this fun walk led by clued-in locals. Just show up at Albertplatz near the fountain.

Sächsische Dampfschiffahrt (☎ 866 090; www .saechsische-dampfschiffahrt.de; adult/child €12/6; ☷ Apr-Oct) Ninety-minute river tours on rebuilt paddle-wheel steam boats leave from the Terrassenufer dock at 11am, 1pm, 3pm and 5pm daily. There's also regular service up the Elbe to Schloss and Park Pillnitz (p189) and the Sächsische Schweiz (Saxon Switzerland; p190) and downriver to Meissen (p193).

Stadtrundfahrt Dresden (☎ 899 5650; www.stadt rundfahrt.com; tours €20) This narrated hop-on, hop-off tour has 22 stops in the centre and the elegant outer villa districts along the Elbe. It includes short tours of the Zwinger, Fürstenzug, Frauenkirche and Pfunds Molkerei.

Trabi Safari (☎ 8990 0110; www.trabi-safari.de; per person from €30) Get behind the wheel of the ultimate GDR-mobile for this 1½-hour guided drive.

Festivals & Events

Internationales Dixieland Festival (www.dixieland .de) Early May, with bands from around the world.
Dresdener Musikfestspiele (Music Festival; www .musikfestspiele.com) Held mid-May to June, with mostly classical music.

A BRIDGE TOO FAR

The Saxon heartland, with Dresden at its centre, represents one of the richest cultural tapestries in all of Germany. This fact obviously didn't escape the Unesco officers in charge of designating new World Heritage sites, who in 2004 welcomed a 20km section of the river valley, the Dresdner Elbtal, including Dresden's matchless baroque magnificence, into their exalted club.

But only five years later, in June 2009, the Elbtal joined the most exclusive (and most embarrassing) Unesco club of all. After Oman's Arabian Oryx Sanctuary, Dresden became only the second place on earth (and the first in the developed world) to have its World Cultural Heritage status revoked. The reason? The construction of the controversial four-lane Waldschlösschen Bridge across the river near the scenic spot where Canaletto once immortalised Dresden's fabulous silhouette. Despite Unesco's best efforts at hammering out a compromise solution, even suggesting a tunnel as an acceptable alternative, city leaders remained stubborn. Preparatory construction work on the bridge began in 2007.

Unesco have suggested the city may get the chance to submit a new nomination in future, but with different boundaries. Dresden's red-faced officials will no doubt be eager to regain Unesco-listed status, which not only brings prestige and tourists, but also much-needed federal cash.

Bunte Republik Neustadt (www.brn-dresden.de) The Neustadt's biggest annual bash (mid-June), with lots of free alternative concerts.

Dresdner Stadtfest (City Festival) Mid-August, with something for everyone.

Striezelmarkt (www.striezel-markt.de) In December, one of Germany's oldest Christmas markets and a great place to sample the famous Dresdener Stollen (fruitcake).

Sleeping

Dresden's hotels can be horrendously expensive, with rates among the highest in Germany. Thankfully there are plenty of cheap beds available at the city's superb hostels.

BUDGET

our pick **Hostel & Backpacker Kangaroo-Stop** (☎ 314 3455; www.kangaroo-stop.de; Erna-Berger-Strasse 8-10; dm €12.50-16, s/d/tr €29/38/51, apt €70-84, breakfast €4.90; P ☒ 🖳) With an Australian theme throughout, this superb hostel is spread over two buildings: one for backies, the other for families. Extras include the biggest hostel kitchen-diner you're ever likely to encounter, free internet and several communal areas. The welcoming owner is a mine of information on the city.

Lollis Homestay (☎ 810 8458; www.lollishome.de; Görlitzer Strasse 34; dm €13-19, s €30-38, d €40-42, linen €2, breakfast €3; ☒ 🖳 📶) Dresden's quirkiest hostel has two contenders for Germany's most outlandish dorms – one containing a real Trabant you can bed down in for the night, the other a Giant's Room with oversize furniture that makes guests feel like Tom Thumb. In addition there's free bike rental, a laundry room and the reception desk is made from an old piano.

Hostel Mondpalast (☎ 563 4050; www.mondpalast .de; Louisenstrasse 77; dm €13-19.50, s €29-44, d €37-52, linen €2, breakfast €6; ☒ 🖳) Check in at the out-of-this-world bar-cafe (with cheap drinks) before being 'beamed up' to your room in the Moon Palace – each one dedicated to a sign of the zodiac or some other spacey theme. Bike rentals and large kitchen are also available.

Also recommended:

Campingplatz Mockritz (☎ 4715 250; www.camping -dresden.de; Boderitzerstrasse 30; per adult/tent/car €5.50/2.10/5.50) Friendly little campsite 3km south of the Hauptbahnhof. Take bus 76 from the Hauptbahnhof to 'Campingplatz Mockritz'.

Sunshine Hostel (☎ 880 8981; www.sunshine-hostel .de; Emerich-Ambros-Ufer 2; dm €14-18, s €25-30, d €36-40; P 🖳) Bright new hostel that gets rave reviews but is far from the tourist and nightlife action. Take tram 6 to Wernerstrasse.

Mezcalero (☎ 810 770; www.mezcalero.de; Königs-brücker Strasse 64; dm €18-23, linen €2.50, s/d from €33/58, breakfast €6.50; P ☒) Bizarre Mexican-Aztec B&B, complete with sombreros, festive colours, tiles and tequila bar.

MIDRANGE

Hotel Privat (☎ 811 770; www.das-nichtraucher-hotel.de; Forststrasse 22; s €54-69, d €69-94; P ☒ 🖳) This small, family-run hotel in a quiet residential district has Saxon charm galore and 30 good-sized rooms, some with alcoves and balconies. Tobacco is definitely a no-no here, even in the garden.

Pension am Zwinger (☎ 8990 0100; www.pension -zwinger.de; Ostra-Allee 27; s €70, per extra person €20; P ☒) Self-caterers, families and space-cravers will appreciate these bright, subtly stylish studios with full kitchens. Ring the bell and wait for someone to check you in.

our pick Backstage (☎ 8887 777; www.backstage -dresden.de; Priessnitzstrasse 12; r from €74; **P** **⑤**) A cool converted factory where rooms, each designed by a local artist, will blow your mind but not your budget. One has a four-poster made entirely of bamboo; others have swirling Gaudiesque bathrooms. Breakfast is an extra €6.50.

Hotel Martha Hospiz (☎ 817 60; www.hotel-martha -hospiz.de; Nieritzstrasse 11; s €79-86, d €113-121; **P** **⑤**) Fifty rooms decked out in Biedermeier-style (seven are wheelchair-accessible), an attractive winter garden, a sound on-site restaurant with Saxon cooking and local wine, and a smiley welcome make this a very pleasant place to lay your hat.

RothenburgerHof (☎ 81260; www.rothenburgerhof.de; Rothenburger Strasse 15-17; s €75-115, d €99-140, apt from €140; **P** **✕** **⑧** **☄**) This quiet launch pad for Neustadt explorations counts among its assets apartments with kitchenette and balcony, a Moorish-style steam room and a great pool.

Hotel Schloss Eckberg/Kavaliershaus (☎ 809 90; www.schloss-eckberg.de; Bautzner Strasse 134; s/d from €103/143; **P** **✕** **⬜**) You'll feel like royalty when arriving at this romantic estate set in its own riverside park east of the Neustadt. Rooms in the historic Schloss are pricier and have more flair, but staying in the modern Kavaliershaus lets you enjoy almost as many amenities at the same dreamy setting.

TOP END

Steigenberger Hotel de Saxe (☎ 438 60; www.steigen berger.com; Neumarkt 9; s/d from €150, breakfast €21; **P** **✕** **⑧** **⬜** **⑤**) Wake up to the best views of the Frauenkirche from any hotel window in town, before descending from your sumptuous room to a buffet breakfast costing more than a hostel bed. Unwind after a hard day's sightseeing in the large wellness area.

Radisson Blu Gewandhaushotel (☎ 494 90; www.radissonblu.com; Ringstrasse 1; r €130-300, ste €450-550, breakfast €21; **P** **✕** **⑧** **⬜** **☄**) Another top choice for class and personal service. Housed in a former fabric factory, the public areas are stunning and most Biedermeier-style rooms have whirlpool baths in their marble-fitted bathrooms.

Westin Bellevue (☎ 8050; www.westin.com/dresden; Grosse Meissner Strasse 15; s €150-230, d €180-260, breakfast €19; **P** **✕** **⑧** **⬜** **⑤** **☄**) Baroque and modern elements blend smoothly in this sprawling and elegant property, where the nicest rooms give you unparalleled views of Dresden's famous silhouette.

Hotel Bülow Residenz (☎ 800 30; www.buelow -residenz.de; Rähnitzstrasse 19; s/d €195/250, breakfast €19; **P** **✕** **⑧** **⑤**) This place is a class act all round, from the welcome drink to the cute bears delivered at turndown, the free minibar to free wi-fi. Even the standard rooms are spacious, and the restaurant has a fine reputation as well.

Kempinski Hotel Taschenbergpalais (☎ 491 20; www.kempinski-dresden.de; Taschenberg 3; s €280-370, d €320-400, ste €500-900; **P** **✕** **⑧** **⬜** **⑤** **☄**) This restored 18th-century mansion certainly prickles with wow factor, with views over the Zwinger, incredibly quiet corridors and Bulgari toiletries. In winter, the courtyard turns into an ice rink.

Eating

ALTSTADT

The Altstadt brims with restaurants, most of them targeting the tourist hordes. For a bit more local flavour, try pedestrianised Weisse Gasse, recently declared a *Kneipenviertel* (Pub Quarter), or head to the Neustadt.

SoupCafé (Prager Strasse 2; soups from €3.90; ☽ 11am-9pm daily) Located right by the Hauptbahnhof Nord tram stop, this up-to-the-minute, DayGlo place serves comfort food, such as Saxon potato soup and sponge-cake balls in vanilla sauce, in trendy square bowls.

Ladencafé Aha (☎ 496 0673; Kreuzstrasse 7; mains €5-12; ☽ 10am-midnight) At this warm and cheerful smoke- and stress-free zone above a one-world store, you can sip delicious coffee, pick from the international menu, leaf through the many magazines or watch your kiddies play with the provided toys.

brennNessel (☎ 494 3319; Schützengasse 18; mains €8-12) Housed in Dresden's half-timbered Environmental Centre, this superb vegetarian place with a woodsy interior and leafy cobbled courtyard beer garden is possibly the city's best. It's a favourite hang-out for off-duty Semperoper musicians, whom you can often hear practising nearby.

Sophienkeller (☎ 497 260; Taschenberg 3; mains €8-16) The tourist-oriented 1730s theme with waitresses trussed up in period garb may be a bit overcooked, but the local specialities certainly are not. The highlight of the drinks menu here is the dark Bohemian Krušovice on tap.

Gänsedieb (☎ 485 0905; Weisse Gasse 1; mains €8-17) Worth a gander in the Weisse Gasse, the

'Goose Thief' serves hearty schnitzels, goulash and steaks alongside a full range of Bavarian Paulaner beers. The name was inspired by the fountain outside.

Also recommended:

Barococo (☎ 862 3040; Altmarkt 10; snacks from €5, mains €6-13) Often packed to the gills, this fish restaurant has nice Altstadt views from the upstairs dining room.

Grand Café (☎ 496 2444; An der Frauenkirche 12; mains €10-21; 10am-midnight) Elegant coffee-and-cake stop in the gold-trimmed Coselpalais.

Ogura (☎ 864 2975; An der Frauenkirche 5; meals from €25; noon-2pm & 5.30-10.30pm) Dresden's top sushi restaurant, inside the Hilton.

NEUSTADT

El Perro Borracho (☎ 803 6723; Alaunstrasse 70, Kunsthof; tapas €3.30) Almost blocking an entrance to the Kunsthofpassage, this buzzy eatery is a great place to enjoy a glass of Rioja and a platter of tapas on the cobblestone courtyard when the mercury heads north.

Electric Lotus (Louisenstrasse 58; mains €4-6; 11.30am-11pm) The antidote to conventional fast-food places, this tranquil chapel of ayurvedic, vegan, vegie and organic fare proves that healthy food can also be tasty. It does a brisk trade in takeaways.

ourpick Raskolnikoff (☎ 804 5706; Böhmische Strasse 34; mains €5-14) This bohemian cafe behind an extremely tatty facade was one of the Neustadt's first post-*Wende* (postcommunist) pubs. The menu is sorted by compass direction (borscht to quiche Lorraine to smoked fish), there's a sweet little beer garden out the back, and a gallery and basic guest rooms can be found upstairs (singles and doubles €40 to €55).

PlanWirtschaft (☎ 801 3187; Louisenstrasse 20; mains €7-14; 9am-1am) Only fresh, organic ingredients sourced from local butchers and farmers make it into the international potpourri of dishes at this long-time favourite. There's a romantic courtyard for balmy days.

Villandry (☎ 899 6724; Jordanstrasse 8; mains €8-16; 6.30-11.30pm Mon-Sat) The folks in the kitchen here sure know how to coax maximum flavour out of even the simplest ingredients, and to turn them into super-tasty Mediterranean treats for eyes and palate. Meals are best enjoyed in the lovely courtyard.

Drinking
ALTSTADT

Stadtoase (☎ 0173 404 2380; Terrassenufer; May-Oct) Dump 150 tonnes of sand on the banks of the Elbe, erect a bar and beach volleyball court, and invite the city to party all summer long. Yep, that's Stadtoase.

Fährgarten Johannstadt (☎ 459 6262; Käthe-Kollwitz-Ufer 23b; 10am-1am Apr-Oct) East of the Altstadt, and occasionally too close to the flood-prone Elbe for its own good, this idyllic beer garden pulls great ales and does a mean barbecue.

Rauschenbach Deli (☎ 821 2760; Weisse Gasse 2; mains €7-14; 9am-1am) A cafe by day, this contempo spot morphs into a chic bar with an endless cocktail menu when the moon gets high. Cool terrace, too.

Karl May Bar (☎ 491 2720; Kleine Brüdergasse) If you came to Dresden to relax in sophisticated, dark wood and red leather club surroundings, do it here. The Wild West murals were inspired by the books of Karl May.

NEUSTADT

If you're up for a night on the razzle, head out to the Äussere Neustadt, which is chock-a-block with cafe-bars. Alaunstrasse, Louisenstrasse and Görlitzer Strasse are where it happens.

Bautzner Tor (☎ 8038 202; Hoyerswerdaer Strasse 37) Probably the last GDR-era dive in Dresden to survive ungentrified, this dimly lit but strangely atmospheric museum piece is a nostalgic blast from the past. Food is definitely wallet-friendly and the excellent beer (cheapest in town) is brewed locally by a guy called Lenin.

ourpick Reisekneipe (☎ 267 1930; Görlitzer Strasse 15) Down a few Czech lagers in an African hut or put away a plate of curry in a Siberian log cabin at this travel-bug clinic. Hardened globetrotters give midweek slide-show talks.

Combo (Louisenstrasse 66) Laid-back to the point of toppling, this '70s-retro cafe has enormous windows that fold back when the heat is on, 1960s airport furniture and cool dudes serving the party people. DJs take over after dark.

Scheune (☎ 802 6619; Alaunstrasse 36-40) This former GDR-era youth club is now an artsy pub and alternative rock venue with a beer garden and Indian food on the menu (mains €5 to €10).

Café 100 (☎ 273 5010; Alaunstrasse 100) Wine lovers should make a beeline for this candle-lit pub, with its romantic cavernous cellar and 250 wines on the menu. It's a great place for first dates.

Frank's (☎ 6588 8380; Alaunstrasse 80) Famed for its huge cocktail menu, this is a long-running Neustadt stalwart.

Also recommended:

Café Europa (☎ 804 4810; Königsbrücker Strasse 68; ☻ 24hr; ▢) Smart open-all-hours cafe with newspapers and free internet, but slow service.

Neumanns Tiki (☎ 810 3837; Görlitzer Strasse 21) Polynesian cocktail bar and ice-cream parlour in the Kunsthofpassage.

Entertainment

The finest all-round listings guide to Dresden is *SAX* (www.cybersax.de), sold at newsstands (€1.30). Regular freebies include *Blitz*, *Frizz* and the *Kneipensurfer* and *Use-it* maps. Pick them up at the tourist office, cafes, pubs and hostels.

CLASSICAL MUSIC

Dresdner Philharmonie (☎ 486 6866; www.dresdner philharmonie.de) The city's renowned orchestra performs mostly at the Kulturpalast on Altmarkt. Also check the listings magazines for concerts at the Hofkirche, Dreikönigskirche, Kreuzkirche and Frauenkirche.

Sächsische Staatsoper (☎ 491 1705; www.semper oper.de) Dresden is synonymous with opera, and performances are at the spectacular Semperoper (p181) are brilliant. Tickets are hard to obtain, so plan well ahead or queue for returns.

NIGHTCLUBS

Strasse E (www.strasse-e.de; Werner-Hartmann-Strasse 2) Dresden's most high-octane party zone is in an industrial area between Neustadt and the airport. Half a dozen venues cover the entire sound spectrum, from disco to dark wave, electro to pop. Take tram 7 to Industriegelände. Some of the other clubs reviewed in this section are closer to town.

Puschkin (☎ 205 4587; www.puschkin-club.info; Leipziger Strasse 12) The eclectic mix of gigs on here means it's worth checking the program, whatever you have on your iPod.

Groove Station (☎ 8029 594; Katharinenstrasse 11-13) This popular multipurpose lounge is the oldest live-music club in town. There are foosball and snooker tables and a well-stocked bar.

Down Town (☎ 811 5592; Katharinenstrasse 11-13; ☻ Fri, Sat & Mon) This iconic old factory gives you early *Saturday Night Fever* with its 1970s and '80s nights on Friday. On Monday latex-lovers invade for the legendary Nasty Love Club (closed in summer).

U-Boot (Bautzner Strasse 75; ☻ Fri & Sat) Anything from reggae to nu-punk, catering for the skater crowd.

LIVE MUSIC

Alter Schlachthof (☎ 858 8529; Gothaer Strasse 11) The industrial charm of an old slaughterhouse draws a party-happy crowd for mostly alternative German acts.

Blue Note (☎ 801 4275; www.jazzdepartment.com; Görlitzer Strasse 2b; ☻ to 5am or later) Small, smoky and smooth, this converted smithy has live jazz almost nightly until 11pm, then turns into a night-owl magnet until the wee hours. The talent is mostly regional.

Katy's Garage (☎ 656 7701; Alaunstrasse 48) This rockin' shanty town, a key venue for indie gigs and club nights throughout the week, is centred around a former tyre shop.

Jazzclub Neue Tonne (☎ 802 6017; www.jazzclub tonne.de; Königstrasse 15) Bigger names hit the stage here, and it's a bit more polished than Blue Note.

GAY & LESBIAN VENUES

Dresden's gay scene is concentrated in the Neustadt. For listings, consult **GegenPol** (www .gegenpol.net, in German).

Boy's (☎ 5633 630; www.boys-dresden.de; Alaunstrasse 80; ☻ Tue-Sun) A lively bar-club with parties on Friday and Saturday. A top venue for S&M (standing and modelling; not what you were thinking…).

Queens (☎ 803 1650; Görlitzer Strasse 3) The kitsch decor is the perfect backdrop for this pulsating hot spot, famous for its *Schlager* (schmaltzy German pop songs) parties.

Sappho (☎ 404 5136; Hechtstrasse 23) This women's cafe is an excellent venue on Dresden's thriving lesbigay map.

Valentino (☎ 889 4996; Jordanstrasse 2; ▢) A low-key cafe with great cakes, ice cream and internet access.

CINEMAS

Check www.kinokalender.com for monthly listings. Undubbed English films are shown at the following:

Programmkino Ost (☎ 310 3782; Schandauer Strasse 73) South of the Altstadt.

Quasimodo (☎ 866 0224; Adlergasse 14)
Ufa-Palast (☎ 482 5825; St-Petersburger-Strasse 24a)

THEATRE

Dresden's vibrant theatre scene sees many small companies perform throughout the city; *SAX* has the scoop. Buy theatre tickets at the tourist office or the theatre's box office an hour before performances. Many theatres close from mid-July until early September.

Carte Blanche (☎ 204 720; www.carte-blanche -dresden.de; Priessnitzstrasse 10) Drag-queen shows at their finest.

Schauspielhaus (☎ 491 3555; www.staatsschauspiel dresden.de) Altstadt (Theaterstrasse 2); Neustadt (Glacisstrasse 28) The renowned Staatsschauspiel ensemble plays mostly crowd-pleasers by German playwrights in two venues.

Societätstheater (☎ 803 6810; www.societaets theater.de; An der Dreikönigskirche 1a) A modern and experimental theatre.

Getting There & Away

Dresden airport (☎ 881 3360; www.dresden-airport.de) deals mainly in domestic and charter flights.

Dresden is 2¼ hours south of Berlin-Hauptbahnhof (€36). For Leipzig choose from hourly ICE trains (€29, 1½ hours) or RE trains (€20.80, 1½ hours). The S-Bahn runs half-hourly to Meissen (€5.30, 40 minutes) and Bad Schandau (€5.30, 50 minutes). There are connections to Frankfurt (€85, five hours) and Prague (€30.70, two hours).

Dresden is connected to Leipzig via the A14/A4, to Berlin via the A13/A113, and to the Czech Republic via the B170 south.

For ride-shares contact **Mitfahrzentrale** (☎ 194 30; Dr-Friedrich-Wolf-Strasse 2).

Getting Around

Dresdner Verkehrsbetriebe (DVB; ☎ 857 1011) runs the city's buses and trams as well as a couple of information kiosks, including one on Albertplatz.

The S2 train serves the airport from the Hauptbahnhof and Dresden-Neustadt (€1.80, 22 and 13 minutes respectively). Budget about €18 for a taxi to the Hauptbahnhof.

Single bus and tram tickets cost €1.80, a day pass €4.50. The family day pass, for two adults and up to four kids, is a steal at €6.50. Tickets are available aboard and from vending machines at stops.

The starting rate for taxis is €2.50. There are ranks at the Hauptbahnhof and Neustadt station, or ring ☎ 211 211. For short hops

within the Altstadt, consider a Velotaxi pedicab (rickshaw), which charge €2.50 per person for the first kilometre, then €1 for each additional kilometre.

Antrieb (☎ 8582 059; Könneritzstrasse 7), near the Dresden-Mitte station, hires out bikes for €11 per day.

AROUND DRESDEN
Schloss & Park Pillnitz

Baroque has gone exotic at this **pleasure palace** (☎ 261 3260; park admission free; ⏱ park 5am-dusk, visitors centre 9am-6pm May-Oct, 10am-5pm Nov-Apr), festooned with fanciful Chinese flourishes. This is where the Saxon rulers once lived it up during long hot Dresden summers. A mere 10km southeast of Dresden, Pillnitz is dreamily wedged in between vineyards and the Elbe, and is best reached aboard a steamer (one-way/return €10/16, 1½ hours) operated by **Sächsische Dampfschiffahrt** (☎ 866 090; www.saechsische-dampf schiffahrt.de); boats leave from the Terrassenufer in Dresden (see p184). Otherwise, bus 83 stops at the palace car park.

Guided tours are only for groups of 10 or more, but you can easily explore the wonderful gardens on your own with maps and leaflets from the visitors centre. To learn more about the history of the palace and life at court, visit the **Schlossmuseum** (adult/concession €4/2; ⏱ 10am-5pm Apr-Oct, guided tours 11am & 2pm daily May-Oct, 11am, noon, 2pm & 3pm Sat & Sun Nov-Apr) in the Neues Palais.

Two other buildings, the Wasserpalais and the Bergpalais, house the **Kunstgewerbemuseum** (Arts & Crafts Museum; ☎ 261 30; adult/concession €4/3, more during special exhibits; ⏱ 10am-6pm daily May-Oct), which is filled with fancy furniture and objects from the Saxon court, including Augustus the Strong's throne.

Schloss Moritzburg

Rising assertively from a lake 14km northwest of Dresden, **Schloss Moritzburg** (☎ 035207-873 18; adult/concession/family €6.50/3.50/13; ⏱ 10am-5pm daily Apr-Oct, 10am-4pm Tue-Sun Nov, Dec, Feb & Mar, 10am-4pm Sat & Sun Jan) is yet another baroque playground of August der Starke. The rich interior boasts ornate leather wall coverings, paintings, furniture and the recently restored Federzimmer (Feather Room), featuring August's fanciful bed. An English-language audioguide (€2) is available from the ticket booth. The palace parkland is ideal for drifting around.

SAXONY

Buses 326 and 457 run to Moritzburg from in front of Dresden's Neustadt train station (€3.50, 27 minutes). For a more atmospheric approach, first take the S1 train to Radebeul-Ost (€3.50, 13 minutes), then catch the 1884 narrow-gauge **Lössnitzgrundbahn** (€5.90, 30 minutes) to Moritzburg, from where it's a short walk to the Schloss.

Radebeul

Although a separate town, Radebeul serves as an upmarket bedroom community of Dresden, and has a couple of quirky museums. First up is the **Karl-May-Museum** (☎ 0351-8373 010; Karl-May-Strasse 5; adult/child €7/2.50; ☿ Tue-Sun 9am-6pm Mar-Oct, 10am-4pm Nov-Feb), essentially a tribute to Germany's greatest adventure writer. Though virtually unknown in the English-speaking world, May's rousing tales have sold over 100 million copies worldwide and for generations shaped the image of the American Wild West and the Near East in central European minds. Villa Shatterhand charts his life and work, while Villa Bärenfett has a highly rated exhibition on Native Americans.

Further west along Meissener Strasse, the oddly intriguing, and recently expanded, **Zeitreise Lebensart DDR 1949–1989** (☎ 0351-8351 780; Wasastrasse 50; adult/concession €7.50/5.50; ☿ 10am-6pm Tue-Sun) provides a fascinating glimpse into daily life in the GDR. The four long floors are crammed with four decades' worth of socialist-era flotsam and jetsam, including a fleet of Trabis, ingenious self-contained camping units, plus tonnes of toys, toasters, televisions and other nostalgia-inducing trinkets.

From Dresden, take the S1 train to Radebeul-Ost (€3.50, 13 minutes) or tram 4 from Postplatz to Wasastrasse (€3.50, 28 minutes).

Schloss Weesenstein

A magnificent sight, high above the Müglitz River, **Schloss Weesenstein** (☎ 035027-6260; www .schloss-weesenstein.de; adult/concession €4.50/2.50; ☿ 9am-6pm Apr-Oct, 10am-5pm Nov-Mar) is one of the most undervisited and untouched palaces in Germany. In an amazing alchemy of styles, it blends its medieval roots with later Renaissance and baroque embellishments. This results in an architectural curiosity where the horse stables somehow ended up above a much younger residential tract.

Weesenstein owes much of its distinctive looks to the noble Bünau family, who were granted the palace by the Margrave of Meissen in 1406, and continued to live there for 12 generations until 1772. In the 19th century, it became the home of philosopher-king Johann of Saxony, who also took time off from his royal duties to translate Dante into German. Lavishly furnished and decorated rooms on the ground floor contain an exhibit about the man and life at court. This is accompanied by two or three annually changing exhibits.

There are several restaurants, including a cafe in the former palace prison, a traditional brewpub and the upmarket Königliche Schlossküche. After filling your belly, you can take a digestive saunter in the lovely baroque park.

Schloss Weesenstein is about 16km southeast of Dresden. Coming by train from Dresden requires a change in Heidenau (€5.30, 30 minutes). Weesenstein train station is about 500m south of the castle – follow the road up the hill. By car, take the A17 to Pirna, then head towards Glashütte and follow the signs to the Schloss.

Pirna

En route to or from the Saxon Switzerland you'll probably pass through Pirna, where the **DDR Museum Pirna** (☎ 03501-774 842; www.ddr -museum-pirna.de; Rottwerndorferstrasse 45; adult/concession €4/3; ☿ 10am-6pm Tue-Sun Apr-Oct, 10am-5pm Tue-Thu, Sat & Sun Nov-Mar) is the star attraction.

Though smaller than Radebeul's Zeitreise (left), this is a slightly more structured and digestible look at everyday life in the GDR. If you weren't a resident of East Germany prior to 1989, you might not be overcome with Ostalgie (recent rise of nostalgia for the GDR) at the sight of Eric Honeker's smirking portraits, armchair-size Robotron computers, mock-ups of '80s kitchens and the acres of leatherette and false veneer on show, but you may be accompanied by numerous Saxons who are.

To reach the museum, take the S1 from Dresden's Hauptbahnhof to Pirna (€3.50, 22 minutes), then change onto local bus N to the 'Geibeltbad/Freizeitzentrum' stop.

SAXON SWITZERLAND

Also known as Elbsandsteingebirge (the Elbe Sandstone Mountains), the Saxon Switzerland (Sächsische Schweiz) embraces one of Germany's most unique and evocative landscapes within its 275-sq-km boundaries. This is wonderfully rugged country where Nature has chiselled porous rock into bizarre columns, battered cliffs, tabletop mountains and deep valleys and gorges. The Elbe courses through thick forest, past villages and mighty hilltop castles. No wonder such fabled beauty was a big hit with artists of the Romantic movement, including the painter Caspar David Friedrich and fairy-tale writer Hans Christian Andersen. In 1990, about a third of the area became Saxony's first and only national park. The fun continues on the Czech side of the border in the Czech Switzerland National Park.

You could tick off the area's highlights on a long day trip from Dresden, but to truly 'get' the magic of Saxon Switzerland, consider spending a couple of days here. In addition to hiking, the area is also among the country's premier rock-climbing meccas, offering over 15,000 routes, while cyclists can follow the lovely Elberadweg.

ACTIVITIES

As local hikers and climbers will tell you, the Saxon Switzerland is about much more than the prescribed tourist haunts. For guided nature walks, hikes and climbs, contact **Hobbit Hikes** (☎ 0173 6971 090; www.hobbit-hikes.de) run by two park guides, Daphna and Claudia. Dresden-based **Knotpunkt** (☎ 0177 3478 639; www.knotenpunkt.org) is another small-scale outfit organising climbing courses, nature walks and other outdoor experiences, all with an eco-twist.

GETTING THERE & AROUND

There are only three bridges across the Elbe: two in Pirna and one in Bad Schandau. Passenger ferries (bicycles allowed) cross the Elbe in several other villages.

Boat

From April to October, steamers operated by **Sächsische Dampfschiffahrt** (☎ 0351-866 090) plough up the Elbe several times daily between Dresden and Bad Schandau, stopping in Rathen, Königstein and other towns.

Bus

From mid-April to October, a bus service operated by **Frank Nuhn Freizeit und Tourismus**

> ### WHAT'S IN A NAME?
>
> With its highest peak rising to just 723m, the Saxon Switzerland ain't exactly the Alps. So how did the region get its name? Credit belongs to the Swiss, actually. During the 18th century, the area's romantic scenery, with its needle-nose pinnacles and craggy cliffs, lured countless artists from around the world. Among them was the Swiss landscape artist Adrian Zingg and his friend, the portraitist Anton Graff, who had been hired to teach at Dresden's prestigious art academy. Both felt that the landscape very much resembled their homeland (the Swiss Jura) and voila, the phrase 'Saxon Switzerland' was born. Travel writers picked it up and so it remains to this day.

(☎ 035021-676 14; www.frank-nuhn-freizeit-und-tourismus.de) shuttles between Königstein, Bad Schandau and the Bastei four times daily. The same company also operates the so-called Bastei-Kraxler, which makes hourly runs between 10am and 5pm from the town of Wehlen up to the Bastei. Buy tickets from the driver.

Car & Motorcycle

Towns are linked to Dresden and each other by the B172; coming from Dresden, it's faster to take the A17 and pick up the B172 in Pirna.

Train

The handy S1 connects Bad Schandau, Königstein, Rathen and other Saxon Switzerland towns with Dresden, Radebeul and Meissen every 30 minutes. Bad Schandau is also serviced by long-distance EC trains travelling to Hamburg, Berlin and Vienna.

Bastei

The open fields and rolling hills surrounding the Bastei region, on the Elbe, give little clue as to the drama that lies beyond. Truly one of the most breathtaking spots in Germany, this is a wonderland of fluted pinnacles (up to 305m high) and panoramic views of the surrounding forests, cliffs and mountains – not to mention a magnificent sightline along the river itself. This is the single most popular spot in the national park, so crowds are pretty much guaranteed unless you get here very early or late in the day.

Bastei is an old-fashioned word meaning 'bastion' or 'fortress', in this case the **Felsenburg** (adult/concession €1.50/0.50; ☉ 9am-6pm), a wooden castle occupying this strategic spot from the early 13th century until 1469. These days, a series of footbridges links the crags on which the castle was built, but its remnants are so few that it requires a lot of imagination to picture the place. A highlight is the replica of a catapult once used by castle residents to pelt attackers with ball-shaped rocks. During sieges they would simply destroy the wooden bridges, sending their enemies plummeting to their deaths. Fortunately, these days the much-photographed **Basteibrücke** leading to the castle grounds is made of stone. Assembled in 1850, locals claim the bridge was Europe's first purpose-built tourist attraction.

SLEEPING & EATING

The only sleeping option up here is **Berghotel Bastei** (☎ 035024-7790; www.bastei-berghotel.de; s €49-55, d €82-122; **P**), a nicely spruced-up GDR-era hotel with well-appointed rooms, a tourist-plagued restaurant with fantastic views, plus extras like bowling and a sauna.

Otherwise, you can find rooms from about €12 per person in the convenient but nondescript village of **Lohmen** (☎ tourist office 03501-581 024; Schloss Lohmen 1), a couple of kilometres due northeast, or in nearby **Rathen** (☎ 035024-704 22; Füllhölzelweg 1), a tiny but postcard-pretty resort right on the Elbe. A characterful, good-value option here is **Burg Altrathen** (☎ 035024-7600; www.burg-altrathen.de; Am Grünbach 10-11; s €55-58, d €70-86, tower ste €120; ✕) in a medieval castle above town.

GETTING THERE & AWAY

The nearest train station is in Rathen, where you need to catch the ferry across the Elbe, then follow a sweat-raising 30-minute trail to the top of the Bastei. En route you'll pass the lovely **Felsenbühne** (☎ 035024-7770), an open-air summer theatre that stages light-hearted fare beneath a spectacular rocky backdrop.

To get there by bus, see p191. Public bus 237 also makes the trip to the Bastei from Pirna or Lohmen.

Drivers should arrive before 10am to snag a spot in the inner Bastei car park (€3 for four hours, €5.50 all day), from where it's only a 10-minute walk to the viewpoints. Otherwise, you need to park in the outer lot (€2.50 all day) and catch the frequent shuttle bus (€1 each way) or walk for at least half an hour.

Königstein

South of Rathen, the Elbe has carved an S-curve ending at Königstein 6km away. The town would be unremarkable were it not for the massive citadel built right on a tabletop mountain some 260m above the river. **Festung Königstein** (☎ 035021-646 07; adult/concession/family €5/3/12, audioguide €2.50; ☉ 9am-8pm Apr-Sep, 9am-6pm Oct, 9am-5pm Nov-Mar) is the largest intact fortress in the country, and so imposing and formidable that no-one ever bothered to attack it. Begun in the 13th century, it was repeatedly enlarged and is now a veritable textbook in military architecture, with 30 buildings spread across 9.5 hectares. Highlights include the **Brunnenhaus**, with its seemingly bottomless well, a prickling array of German weaponry from across the centuries, and the **Georgenburg**, once Saxony's most feared prison, whose famous inmates included Meissen porcelain inventor Johann Friedrich Böttger. During WWII, it served as a POW camp and a refuge for art treasures from Dresden. The biggest draw, however, is the widescreen view deep into the national park and across to the Lilienstein tabletop mountain.

There are several eateries up at the fortress and more in the town below. The **tourist office** (☎ 035021-682 61; www.koenigstein-sachsen.de; Schreiberberg 2) can help find lodgings. Pick of the bunch here is **Ferdinands Homestay** (☎ 035022-547 75; www.ferdinandshomestay.de; Halbestadt 51; dm €12.50-17.50, s/d from €25/30, tent/adult €2.50/4.50; **P** ✕), a small and friendly riverside hostel and campsite combo in a secluded, remote spot on the northern bank. Call for directions.

Daily, from April to October, a tourist train makes the steep climb half-hourly, starting at 9am from Reissiger Platz in Königstein (€2). This drops you at the bottom of the fortress, from where you can get a lift or walk.

Alternatively it's a strenuous 30- to 45-minute climb from the bottom. The nearest car park is down below, off the B172.

Bad Schandau

☎ 035022 / pop 3000

Bad Schandau, an unremarkable little spa town on the Elbe just 5km north of the Czech border, is the unofficial capital of the Saxon Switzerland and an ideal base for hikes.

The **tourist office** (☎ 900 30; www.bad-schandau.de; Markt 12; ☉ 9am-9pm daily May-Oct, 9am-6pm daily Apr & Oct, 9am-6pm Mon-Fri, 9am-1pm Sat & Sun Nov-Mar) and the **Nationalparkzentrum** (☎ 502 40; www.lanu.de; Dresdner strasse 2b; adult/concession/family €4/3/7.50; 9am-6pm daily Apr-Oct, 9am-5pm Tue-Sun Nov-Mar, closed Jan) are in the centre of town. The latter has an interactive exhibition on how the sandstone formations were shaped, and introduces visitors to the park's wildlife. An English text is available.

At the southern end of town, the century-old **Personenaufzug** (passenger lift; adult/child return €2.50/2; 9am-6pm Apr & Oct, 9am-7pm May-Sep, 9am-5pm Nov-Mar) whisks you up a 50m-high tower for a commanding view. A footbridge links the structure to a pretty forest path that runs partially along the ridge. A good destination to head for is the **Schrammsteinaussicht**, a viewpoint about an hour's moderately strenuous walk away. It overlooks the rugged Schrammsteine, the densest rock labyrinth in the national park and hugely popular with rock hounds.

The **Kirnitzschtalbahn** is a solar-powered tram (the only one running through any national park in the world) that quaintly trundles 7km northeast along the Kirnitzsch River to the **Lichtenhainer Wasserfall**, a good spot to begin a hike among the sandstone cliffs. Trams run every 30 minutes (one-way/return €3.50/6) from April to early November.

SLEEPING & EATING
Lindenhof (4890; www.lindenhof-bad-schandau.de; Rudolf-Sendig-Strasse 11; s €49-55, d €66-94; P) Smart hotel with a good traditional restaurant.

Elbresidenz (9190; www.elbresidenz-bad-schandau.de; Markt 1-11; s €73-105, d €116-180; P X) This spanking new, top-end hotel on Bad Schandau's main square will satisfy anyone's craving for luxury. Rooms are a lesson in modern elegance and there's a full range of spa cures on tap. Elbe views cost more.

MEISSEN
03521 / pop 29,000
Straddling the Elbe around 25km upstream from Dresden, Meissen is a compact, perfectly preserved Saxon town, popular with day trippers. Crowning a rocky ridge above it is the Albrechtsburg palace, which in 1710 became the cradle of European porcelain manufacture. The world-famous Meissen china, easily recognised by its trademark insignia of blue crossed swords, is still the main draw for coach parties. Fortunately, the Altstadt's cobbled lanes, dreamy nooks and idyllic courtyards make escaping from the shuffling crowds a snap.

Orientation
Meissen's old town occupies the western bank of the Elbe while the train station is on the eastern side. The pedestrian-only Altstadtbrücke (bridge) near the station is the quickest route between the two, and presents you with a picture-postcard view of the town. Follow Elbstrasse west to the central square, Markt, and the tourist office. Drivers need to take the Elbtalbrücke further north.

Information
Dresdner Bank (Heinrichsplatz 7)
Tourist office (419 40; www.touristinfo-meissen.de; Markt 3; 10am-6pm Mon-Fri, 10am-4pm Sat & Sun Apr-Oct, 10am-5pm Mon-Fri, 10am-3pm Sat Nov, Dec, Feb & Mar)

Sights
The Markt is framed by the **Rathaus** (1472) and the Gothic **Frauenkirche** (453 832; tower adult/concession €2/1; 10am-noon & 2-4pm Apr-Oct) whose carillon is the world's oldest made from porcelain; it chimes a different ditty six times daily. Climb the tower for fine red-roof views of the Altstadt.

Even grander vistas will be your reward after schlepping up the Burgberg via a series of steep, stepped lanes. On top, the 15th-century **Albrechtsburg** (470 70; Domplatz 1; adult/concession/family €4/2/9; 10am-6pm Mar-Oct, 10am-5pm Nov-Feb) is considered to be Germany's first residential palace, and it housed the original Meissen porcelain factory from 1710 to 1864. Today it contains displays on the history of porcelain production and temporary shows, with the installation of a major exhibition on Saxon history planned for 2011. Mostly, though, it's the intriguing architecture that's likely to impress, most notably the Grosser Wendelstein staircase and the eye-popping room vaulting.

Next to the palace is Meissen's modest and rather soot-blackened **Dom** (cathedral; 452 490; Domplatz 7; adult/concession/family €2.50/1.50/6; 10am-6pm Mar-Oct, 10am-4pm Nov-Feb), a Gothic masterpiece with medieval stained-glass windows and delicately carved statues in the choir. Combination tickets for both buildings are €6/3/15.

There's no 'quiet time' to arrive at the understandably popular and utterly unmissable **Porzellan-Museum** (468 208; Talstrasse 9; adult/concession/family €8.50/4.50/18; 9am-6pm May-Oct, 9am-5pm Nov-Apr), but it's worth braving the crush (and the waiting) to witness the astonishing artistry and craftsmanship that makes Meissen porcelain truly unique. It's right next to the actual porcelain factory, about 1km south of the Altstadt. You start with a 30-minute tour (with English audioguide) of the Schauwerkstätten, a series of four studios where you can observe live demonstrations of vase throwing, plate painting, figure moulding and the glazing process. This helps you gain a better appreciation for the 3000 pieces, displayed chronologically, at the Schauhalle inside an integrated art-nouveau villa.

Sleeping

Herberge Orange (☎ 454 334; www.herberge-orange.de; Siebeneichener Strasse 34; s/d/tr without bathroom €16/27/40.50; P) This former riverside home of porcelain-factory apprentices, 1.5km south of the Markt, has been converted into a friendly and unassuming hostel-cum-hotel, which is proving a winner with wallet-watching nomads. Towels, sheets and breakfast all cost extra.

Hotel Goldgrund (☎ 479 30; www.hotel-goldgrund -meissen.de; Goldgrund 14; s €41-57, d €59-85; P) On the opposite side of the S-Bahn tracks from the Porcelain Museum, this hotel is surrounded by tranquil woodland. The 21 rooms have high ceilings and new furnishings, and there's a shady summer terrace for evening barbecues.

Hotel Burgkeller (☎ 414 00; www.meissen-hotel.com; Domplatz 11; s/d from €75/125; P) This polished hilltop option has everything you could want – commanding views, elegant rooms, a glorious beer garden and a location adjacent to the cathedral.

Hotel Goldener Löwe (☎ 411 10; www.meissen -hotel.com; Heinrichsplatz 6; s/d from €75/125; P ✂) Everything works like a well-oiled machine at this warm and welcoming hotel in a handsome 17th-century building near the Markt. The 36 rooms have antique-style furnishings and all major amenities.

Eating

our pick **Schloss Taverne** (☎ 402 409; Schlossstufen 1; mains €6-14; ✆ closed Tue) Take a seat on the bench-lined and arcaded inner courtyard, surely Meissen's most atmospheric place to eat, to enjoy goulash, pork chops or Saxon beef joint with dumplings and sauerkraut. Then take it slow with a bottle or two of the region's wine, accompanied by locals on the accordion.

Zollhof (☎ 454 161; Elbstrasse 7; mains €6.50-15.50) The flower-festooned beer garden with its ec-

---

> **DON'T FUMBLE THE FUMMEL!**
>
> The 150-year-old **Café Zieger** (Burgstrasse), by the foot of the Rote Stufen, is sole stockist of a peculiar local patisserie known as the *Meissner Fummel*. Resembling an ostrich egg made of very delicate pastry, legend has it the Fummel was invented in 1710 as a test to stop the royal courier from drinking between deliveries – great care is required if you want to get it home in one piece.

---

centric fountain is the best place to sample the typical German dishes here, or to try lighter ones officially 'stolen' from Jamie Oliver.

Domkeller (☎ 457 676; Domplatz 9; mains €8-16) Meissen's oldest restaurant offers good-value local dishes and views from the leafy terrace to satisfy any vista-junkie; the menu's helpfully 'translated' into Saxon.

Weinschänke Vincenz Richter (☎ 453 285; An der Frauenkirche 12; mains €11-21; ✂) The romance factor is high at this top-flight restaurant, despite the rather martial decor (historic guns and armour) and the decidedly unromantic torture chamber (unless you're into S&M, that is). Expect attentive service, expertly prepared regional cuisine and wines from their own estate.

Getting There & Around

From Dresden, take the half-hourly S1 (€5.30, 37 minutes) to Meissen. For the porcelain factory, get off at Meissen-Triebischtal.

A slower but more fun way to get there is by steam boat operated by **Sächsische Dampfschiffahrt** (☎ 866 090; www.saechsische-dampf schiffahrt.de). These leave the Terrassenufer in Dresden (see p184). Boats return upstream to Dresden at 2.45pm but take three hours to make the trip. Many people opt to go up by boat and back by train.

The hop-on, hop-off **City-Bus Meissen** (adult/concession/family €4.50/3.50/12) links the Albrechtsburg with the porcelain museum every half-hour between 10am and 6pm daily from April to October.

WESTERN SAXONY

LEIPZIG

☎ 0341 / pop 515,000

In Goethe's *Faust*, a character named Frosch calls Leipzig 'a little Paris'. He was wrong – Leipzig is more fun and infinitely less self mportant than the Gallic capital. It's an important business and transport centre, a trade-fair mecca, and arguably the most dynamic city in eastern Germany.

Leipzig became known as the *Stadt der Helden* (City of Heroes) for its leading role n the 1989 'Peaceful Revolution'. Its residents organised protests against the communist regime in May of that year; by October, hundreds of thousands were taking to the streets, placing candles on the steps of Stasi headquarters and attending peace services at the Nikolaikirche.

By the time the secret police got round to pulping their files, Leipzigers were partying n the streets, and they still haven't stopped – from late winter, streetside cafes open their terraces, and countless bars and nightclubs keep the beat going through the night.

Leipzig also stages some of the finest classical music and opera in the country, and its art and literary scenes are flourishing. It was once home to Bach, Schumann, Wagner and Mendelssohn, and to Goethe, who set a key scene of *Faust* in the cellar of his favourite watering hole. The university still attracts students from all over the world and has turned out several Nobel laureates.

Orientation

Leipzig's city centre, and most of the key sights, lies within a ring road tracing the former medieval fortifications. From the Hauptbahnhof on the ring's northeastern edge, simply follow Nikolaistrasse south for a couple of minutes to Grimmaische Strasse, the main east–west artery connecting ex-socialist Augustusplatz with the historic Markt.

The impressive 26-platform Hauptbahnhof (built in 1915, renovated in 1998) isn't just one of the largest passenger terminals in Europe, but also a prime example of how to turn a piece of transport infrastructure into retail space, with more than 150 shops (open until 10pm, with many open on Sunday) spread over two floors.

Leipzig's dazzling Neue Messe (trade-fair grounds) are 7.5km north of the Hauptbahnhof (take tram 16).

Leipzig-Halle airport is 18km to the north of the city (see p204).

Costing over €570 million, the City Tunnel Leipzig will greatly improve public transport links when it opens in 2010. The north–south

tunnel from the Hauptbahnhof to southern suburbs will carry intercity trains and a new S-Bahn service, the latter connecting the airport with the Neue Messe, the Hauptbahnhof and four newly excavated city-centre stations.

Information

BOOKSHOPS

Hugendubel (☎ 01801 484 484; Petersstrasse 12) Three floors of books, including foreign-language novels.
Lehmanns Buchhandlung (☎ 3397 5000; Grimmaische Strasse 10) Great selection of English-language titles.
Ludwig (☎ 2684 6600; Hauptbahnhof) English paperbacks, glossy mags and day-old international press.

DISCOUNT CARDS

Leipzig Card (1/3 days €8.90/18.50) Free or discounted admission to attractions, plus free travel on public transport. Available from the tourist office and most hotels.

EMERGENCY

Police (☎ emergency 110)
Police headquarters (☎ 9660; Dimitroffstrasse 5)

INTERNET ACCESS

Copytel.de (☎ 993 8999; Grimmaische Strasse 23; per hr €1; ☟ 9am-10pm daily)
Intertel Café (☎ 462 5879; Brühl 64; per hr €2; ☟ 10am-10pm)
Webcafé (Reichsstrasse 16-18; per hr €1.50; ☟ 10am-10pm)

LAUNDRY

Maga Pon (☎ 9607 922; Gottschedstrasse 11; wash/dry €3.80/1.80) Laundry or hip cafe? You decide.
Schnell und Sauber (Karl-Liebknecht-Strasse 76; wash €3)

LIBRARIES

Bibliotheka Albertina (☎ 973 0577; Beethovenstrasse 6; ▢) Beautifully restored university library, good for periodicals and foreign-language books.
Deutsche Bücherei (German National Library; ☎ 227 10; Deutscher Platz 1; ▢) The largest library in Germany, with 13.5 million volumes in a fabulously restored building.

MEDICAL SERVICES

Emergency Doctor (☎ 192 92; ☟ 24hr)
Klinikum St Georg (☎ 90900; Delitzscher Strasse 141) Take tram 16 to this hospital.
Universitätsklinikum Leipzig (☎ 971 09; Liebigstrasse 20) Hospital and clinic.

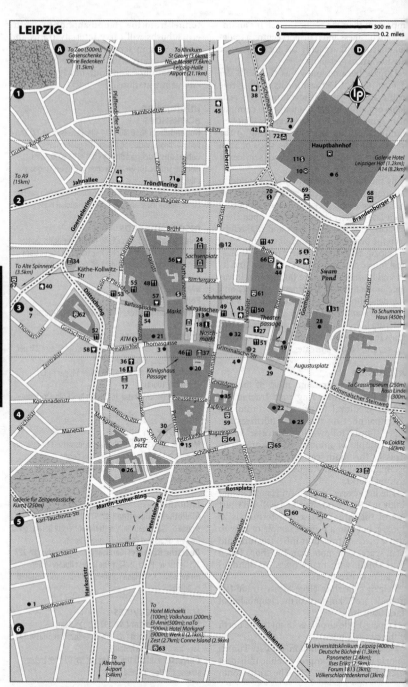

LEIPZIG

SAXONY

MONEY
ReiseBank (Lower Level, west hall, Hauptbahnhof; ⏰ 9am-10pm Mon-Fri, 9.30am-8pm Sat, 1-6pm Sun)

POST
Post Office Augustusplatz (⏰ 9am-8pm Mon-Fri, 9am-3pm Sat)

Post Office Hauptbahnhof (⏰ 9am-10pm Mon-Sat, 1-7pm Sun) Situated at the western end, lower level.

TOURIST INFORMATION
Leipzig Tourist Service (☎ 710 4260; www.lts-leipzig.de; Richard-Wagner-Strasse 1; ⏰ 9.30am-6pm Mon-Fri, 9.30am-4pm Sat, 9.30am-3pm Sun)

Sights
ZEITGESCHICHTLICHES FORUM
Opened in 1999, the excellent **Zeitgeschichtliches Forum** (Forum of Contemporary History; ☎ 222 00; Grimmaische Strasse 6; admission free; ⏰ 9am-6pm Tue-Fri, 10am-6pm Sat & Sun) depicts the history of the GDR from division and dictatorship to fall-of-the-Wall ecstasy and post-*Wende* blues. Highlights include the actual sign from Checkpoint Charlie, film clips showing Berliners looking on in stunned disbelief as the Wall goes up and a mock-up of a GDR-era living room. However, don't get so engrossed by the exhibits that you trip over a piece of the Berlin Wall as you head for the exit.

STASI MUSEUM
In the GDR the walls had ears, as is vividly documented in this **museum** (☎ 961 2443; www.runde-ecke-leipzig.de; Dittrichring 24; admission free; ⏰ 10am-6pm daily) on the all-pervasive power of the Ministry for State Security (Stasi for short), the country's secret police. It's housed in the former Leipzig Stasi headquarters, in a building known as the Runde Ecke (Round Corner). The all-German displays on propaganda, preposterous disguises, cunning surveillance devices, Stasi recruitment among children, scent storage and other chilling machinations reveal the GDR's all-out zeal when it came to controlling, manipulating and repressing its own people.

NIKOLAIKIRCHE
Leipzig's largest church, the **Nikolaikirche** (St Nicholas Church; ☎ 960 5270; ⏰ 10am-6pm), has Romanesque and Gothic roots, but now sports an amazing classical-style interior with palm-like pillars and cream-coloured pews. More recently, the church played a

key role in the nonviolent movement that eventually brought down the GDR regime. In 1982 it began hosting 'peace prayers' every Monday at 5pm (still held today) and in 1989 it became the chief meeting point for peaceful demonstrators. A pamphlet recounts the 'miracle' of 9 October 1989, when 600 SED party faithful, who had been sent to the church to break up the services, ended up listening to the sermon and joining the protesters.

THOMASKIRCHE

The composer Johann Sebastian Bach worked in the **Thomaskirche** (St Thomas Church; ☎ 2222 4200; www.thomaskirche.org; Thomaskirchhof 18; ⌚ 9am-6pm) as a cantor from 1723 until his death in 1750, and his remains lie buried beneath a bronze epitaph near the altar. The Thomanerchor (p204), once led by Bach, is still going strong and now includes 100 boys aged eight to 18. The church tower can be climbed at weekends (€2).

BACH-MUSEUM

Opposite the Thomaskirche, the **Bach-Museum** (☎ 964 110; www.bach-leipzig.de; Thomaskirchhof 16) was receiving a comprehensive refit at the time of writing, but should be back in summer 2010.

MENDELSSOHN-HAUS & SCHUMANN-HAUS

Two other world-famous composers have museums dedicated to them in Leipzig: Felix Mendelssohn-Bartholdy, who lived (and died) in the **Mendelssohn-Haus** (☎ 127 0294; www.mendelssohn-stiftung.de; Goldschmidtstrasse 12; admission €3.50; ⌚ 10am-6pm); and Robert Schumann, who spent the first four years of his marriage to Leipzig pianist Clara Wieck in the **Schumann-Haus** (☎ 393 9620; www.schumann-verein.de; Inselstrasse 18; admission €3; ⌚ 2-5pm Wed-Fri, 10am-5pm Sat & Sun).

GRASSIMUSEUM

The university-run **Grassimuseum** (www.grassimuseum.de; Johannisplatz 5-11; ⌚ 10am-6pm Tue-Sun) unites three very different collections. At the fabulous **Musikinstrumenten-Museum** (☎ 973 0750; adult/concession/family €4/2/8) you can discover music from five centuries in the prestigious and rarity-filled exhibits, in an interactive sound laboratory, and during concerts. At the **Museum für Völkerkunde** (Ethnological Museum; ☎ 973 1900; adult/concession €5/2) you can plunge into an eye-opening journey through the cultures o the world. The **Museum für Angewandte Kuns** (Museum for Applied Arts; ☎ 213 3719; adult/concessio €5/3.50) is the second oldest in Germany an has one of the finest collections of art-nouvea and art-deco furniture, porcelain, glass an ceramics in the country.

MUSEUM DER BILDENDEN KÜNSTE

An edgy glass cube is the home of the **Museum der Bildenden Künste** (Museum of Fine Arts; ☎ 216 990 Katharinenstrasse 10; adult/concession permanent exhib €5/3.50, temporary exhibit from €6/4, combination ticke from €8/5.50; ⌚ 10am-6pm Tue & Thu-Sun, noon-8pr Wed), which has a well-respected collectio of paintings from the 15th century to today including works by Caspar David Friedrich Lucas Cranach the Younger and Claud Monet. Highlights include rooms dedicate to native sons Max Beckmann, Max Klinger whose striking Beethoven monument is veritable symphony of marble and bronze and Neo Rauch, a chief representative of th New Leipzig School.

VÖLKERSCHLACHTDENKMAL

Some 100,000 soldiers lost their lives in th epic 1813 battle that led to the decisive victor of Prussian, Austrian and Russian forces ove Napoleon's army. Built a century later nea the killing fields, the **Völkerschlachtdenkma** (Battle of Nations Monument; ☎ 2416 870; Prager Strasse adult/concession €5/3; ⌚ 10am-6pm Apr-Oct, 10am-4pr Nov-Mar) is a 91m colossus, towering sombrel over southeastern Leipzig like somethin straight out of Gotham City. The nearb **Forum 1813** (adult/concession €3/2, combination ticke €7/4.50) chronicles the events, or else you ca rent an audioguide with English-languag commentary. In June/July, the naTo culture club (p203) hosts its annual 'bath tu race' in the large reflecting pool that sit below the monument. Take tram 15 t Völkerschlachtdenkmal.

ZOO

If you can stomach the hefty admission Leipzig's **zoo** (☎ 593 3385; www.zoo-leipzig.de Pfaffendorfer Strasse 29; adult/child/family €13/9/34 ⌚ 9am-7pm May-Sep, 9am-6pm Apr & Oct, 9am-5pm Nov-Mar), has lots of rare species, plus perennial crowd-pleasers such as tigers, lions and gorillas. The new Gondwanaland tropica species hall has been a highlight since 2009 Take tram 12.

SAXONY

ALTE SPINNEREI

'Cotton to culture' is the motto of the **Alte Spinnerei** (☎ 498 0272; Spinnereistrasse 7; ☱ 11am-5pm Tue-Sat), a 19th-century cotton-spinning factory turned artist colony. Around 80 New Leipzig School artists, including Neo Rauch, have their studios in this huge pile of red-brick buildings, alongside designers, architects, goldsmiths and other creative types whose creations are displayed in 10 galleries. It's in the southwestern district of Plagwitz; take bus 60 from Bayrischer Platz to S-Bahnhof Plagwitz.

PANOMETER

The happy marriage of a *pano*rama (a giant painting) and a gas*ometer* (a giant gas tank) is a **panometer** (☎ 121 3396; www.asisi-factory.de; Richard-Lehmann-Strasse 114; adult/concession €9/7; ☱ 9am-7pm Tue-Fri, 10am-8pm Sat & Sun). The unusual concept is the brainchild of artist Yadegar Asisi, who creates a new image every three or four years. Past examples have included scenes from the Himalayas and ancient Rome. Take tram 16 to Richard-Lehmann-Strasse/Zwickauer Strasse.

OTHER SIGHTS

The **Stadtgeschichtliches Museum** (City History Museum; ☎ 965 130; Markt 1; adult/child €4/3; ☱ 10am-6pm Tue-Sun), found in the Altes Rathaus, chronicles the twists and turns of Leipzig's history. Some temporary themed exhibits are on display nearby in a **new building** (Böttchergässchen 3; adult/concession €3/2; ☱ 10am-6pm Tue-Sun).

Edgy contemporary art in all media is the speciality of the **Galerie für Zeitgenössische Kunst** (☎ 140 810; Karl-Tauchnitz-Strasse 9-11; adult/concession per space €5/3, both spaces €8/4; ☱ noon-7pm Tue-Sun), which has changing exhibits housed in a minimalist container-like space and a late-19th-century villa.

Walking Tour

This circuit starts at the Markt and moves clockwise to Augustusplatz, before exploring the attractive south of the old quarter. It's a 1½-hour walk, but will take the best part of a day if you make all the stops.

On the Markt, the 1556 arcaded Renaissance **Altes Rathaus (1)**, one of Germany's most stunning town halls, houses the Stadtgeschichtliches Museum (above). On the opposite side of the Markt, the **Marktgalerie (2)**

is one of the shiny new shopping complexes that have popped up throughout central Leipzig in recent years.

These modern malls continue the tradition spawned by the historic **Mädlerpassage (3)**, easily among the world's most beautiful shopping arcades. Enter it from Grimmaische Strasse, south of the Markt. A mix of neo-Renaissance and art nouveau, it opened as a trade hall in 1914 and was renovated at great expense in the early 1990s. Today it's home to shops, bars and restaurants, most notably, Auerbachs Keller (p202). There are statues of Faust, Mephistopheles and some students near the Grimmaische Strasse exit; according to tradition you should touch Faust's foot for good luck.

Next door, the **Zeitgeschichtliches Forum (4**; p197) is a must for anyone interested in GDR history. Immediately opposite is the Naschmarkt (snack market) which is dominated by the **Alte Börse (5**; ☎ 9651 322; ☱ by appointment), an ornate former trading house (1687). In front is a 1903 **statue of Goethe (6)**, showing him as a young law student at Leipzig University.

Continue north on Naschmarkt, turn right on Salzgässchen and go to the corner of Reichsstrasse and Schuhmachergässchen, which is dominated by the beautiful art nouveau facade of the **Cafe Riquet (7**; p202). Continue along Reichsstrasse, then turn left into **Specks Hof (8)**, another shopping arcade, where you'll pass a water basin that functions as an upside-down bell; ring it by wetting your hands with the water and running them back and forth over two pommels. If you hit it right, the water starts to fizz. Specks Hof itself contains a beautiful series of tile and stained-glass reliefs by Halle artist Moritz Götze. The eastern portal of Specks Hof takes you straight to the Nikolaikirche (9; p197).

Carry on east through the dank Theaterpassage to reach Augustusplatz, Leipzig's cultural epicentre. The Theaterpassage runs through the 11-storey **Kroch-Haus (10)**, Leipzig's first 'skyscraper', which now houses part of the university's art collection. Topped by a clock and two muscular bronze sentries who bash the bell at regular intervals, the motto (in Latin) reads: 'Work conquers all'.

The behemoth ahead is the functional **Opernhaus (11**; opera house), built from 1956 to 1960, backed by a little park with a pond and a **statue of Richard Wagner (12)**. At the opposite end of Augustusplatz is the boxy 1981 **Neues**

SAXONY

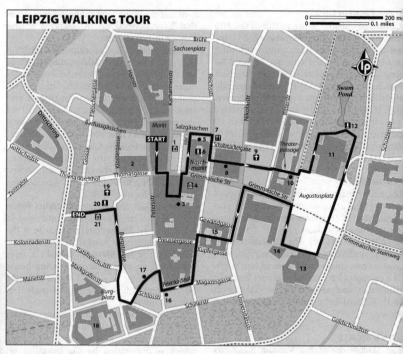

LEIPZIG WALKING TOUR

WALK FACTS

Start Markt
Finish Bach-Museum
Distance 4km
Duration 1½ hours

Gewandhaus (13), home to the world-famous Gewandhaus Orchestra, which was founded in 1743 and is one of Europe's oldest civic orchestras. Next door is the landmark **MDR Hochhaus (14**; 🕑 11am-11pm), a surprisingly attractive skyscraper from 1970, with a viewing platform and restaurant on top.

From Grimmaische Strasse on the western side of Augustusplatz, take a left on Universitätsstrasse and look for the entrance to the **Städtisches Kaufhaus (15**; Universitätsstrasse 16), the site of the city's first cloth exchange (Gewandhaus) and later the inaugural concert hall of the Gewandhaus Orchestra. Composer Felix Mendelssohn-Bartholdy once led a music school here, and there are now free concerts in the summer. The central courtyard is also home to the Strasse der

Stars, Leipzig's version of the Walk of Fame Michael Schumacher, Claudia Schiffer and Mariah Carey are among the celebs whose plaster-cast hands are displayed in a series of cube-shaped cases.

Exit the Städtisches Kaufhaus, head south on Neumarkt, then turn right on Peterskirchhof and you'll come to **arko (16** formerly Café Richter; ☎ 960 5235; Petersstrasse 43 🕑 9.30am-8pm Mon-Fri, 10am-6pm Sat), the oldest coffee retailer in town (since 1879). This fabulous and eclectic building, with its golden iron spiral staircase, is worth a gander; the luscious beans are wonderful too.

From here head north on Petersstrasse, a major shopping boulevard, to the glorious glass-covered **Petersbogen (17)** arcade. This spills out onto Burgplatz, where you confront the impressive 114m-high tower of the neobaroque **Neues Rathaus (18)**, one of the world's largest town halls with some 600 rooms. It was completed in 1905 and stands on the foundations of the Pleissenburg fortress. Recently renovated, it has a rich interior, including a grand staircase straight out of a Donald Trump dream.

From Burgplatz, turn north and walk up Burgstrasse to the **Thomaskirche** (**19**; p198). Outside the church is the 1908 **Bach Memorial** (**20**) showing the composer standing against an organ, with his left-hand jacket pocket turned inside-out (with 20 children from two marriages, the great man always claimed to be broke). The **Bach-Museum** (**21**; p198) is just opposite the church.

Tours

Leipzig Erleben (☎ 7104 280; Richard-Wagner-Strasse 1; www.leipzig-erleben.com; city tour per person €20) Runs four to five bus tours a day, one using an old London Routemaster. Departures are from the tourist office.

Peaceful Revolution Tour (☎ 9612 443; per person €3; ⊗ 2pm Sat) A two-hour German-language walking tour taking in locations that witnessed the key events of 1989. Groups meet at the entrance to the Nikolaikirche.

Trabi Erleben (☎ 1409 0922; www.trabi-stadt rundfahrt.de; 2 people €40) Join a convoy of Trabants belonging to Trabi Erleben for a 90-minute self-drive put-put through Leipzig with live commentary.

Festivals & Events

Highlights of Leipzig's annual events calendar include the **Leipziger Buchmesse** (Book Fair; www.leipziger-buchmesse.de) in late March, the second biggest in the country after Frankfurt. The **Honky Tonk** (www.honky-tonk.de) pub festival in May features dozens of bands and a shuttle bus between drinking holes. On Whitsuntide, a black tide descends on Leipzig for the **Wave-Gotik-Treffen** (www.wave -gotik-treffen.de), the world's largest goth festival, with a pagan village, a medieval market and lots of dark music. The 10-day **Bach Festival** (www.bach-leipzig.de) takes place in late May or early June.

Sleeping

The Leipzig tourist office runs a free **accommodation service** (☎ 710 4255), with singles/doubles from around €25/40.

Mitwohnzentrale (☎ 194 30; Nordstrasse 1; ⊗ 9am-7pm Mon-Fri, 10am-4pm Sat) arranges flat rental (from €20 per person per night).

BUDGET

Central Globetrotter Hostel (☎ 149 9860; www.globe trotter-leipzig.de; Kurt-Schumacher-Strasse 41; dm €12.50-16.50, s/d €27/40, linen €2.50, breakfast €3.50; ✕ 🖳 ☎) This friendly Hauptbahnhof-adjacent hostel has four- to eight-bed dorms, lockers in the corridors and new communal showers. Some

of the singles and doubles have their own facilities. The atmospheric old building also hides a kitchen, laundrette (€3 per load) and common room.

Hostel Sleepy Lion (☎ 993 9480; www.hostel-leipzig .de; Käthe-Kollwitz-Strasse 3; dm €14-18, s/d €30/44, linen €2.50, breakfast €3.50; ✕ 🖳 ☎) Budget-minded nomads will feel welcome at this low-key hostel, with 60 clean and comfy beds in cheerfully painted rooms with private facilities. Major sights and a great party zone are just steps away.

Pension Schlaf Gut (☎ 211 0902; www.schlafgut -leipzig.de; Brühl 64-66; s €31-50, d €46-65; 🅿 ✕) You decide the level of comfort at this modular sleep station. The base rate buys the room; small extra fees are charged for TV, kitchen use, daily cleaning, parking and breakfast.

Motel One (☎ 3374 370; www.motel-one.de; Nikolaistrasse 23; r €59; 🅿 ✕ ⊠ ☎) If you like your design minimalist, your TVs flat screen, your colour schemes edgy but your budget unsqueezed, you'll love this pristine new place right opposite the Nikolaikirche. The 194 rooms have nothing you don't need, the staff are efficiently charming and the location is unsurpassed.

MIDRANGE

Midrange accommodation in the centre is the preserve of the big chains; for something a little more individual you'll have to look a bit further afield.

Hotel Markgraf (☎ 303 030; www.markgraf-leipzig.de; Körnerstrasse 36; s/d €79/90; 🅿 ✕ ☎) This smartly run hotel puts you within staggering distance of the Karl-Liebknecht-Strasse nightlife. Many rooms overlook a pretty little park and there's a sauna for relaxing.

our pick **Galerie Hotel Leipziger Hof** (☎ 697 40; www.leipziger-hof.de; Hedwigstrasse 1-3; s €69-150, d €89-180; 🅿 ✕ 🖳 ☎) Leipzig's most unique place to unpack your bags is this 'gallery with rooms', which brims with originals created by local artists since 1989. It's a first-rate stay, yet relatively affordable, as is the restaurant.

Hotel Michaelis (☎ 267 80; www.hotel-michaelis .de; Paul-Gruner-Strasse 44; s €79-149, d €99-179; 🅿 ✕ ⊠ 🖳) Close to the Karl-Liebknecht-Strasse hipster mile and the city centre, this well-run place gets a big thumbs up for its 62 handsome rooms, well-respected restaurant (with a leafy terrace) and original art collection.

Also recommended:

Dorint Novotel (☎ 995 80; Goethestrasse 11; s/d €64/89, breakfast €14; **P** **X** **X** **Q**) Good value, central and great for families.

Hotel Vier Jahreszeiten (☎ 985 10; Kurt-Schmacher-Strasse 23-29; s €81-118, d €103-156; **P** **X** **☎**) Spotless, well-maintained and near the Hauptbahnhof.

TOP END

Westin Leipzig (☎ 9880; Gerberstrasse 15; r €125-400; **P** **X** **Q** **☎** **Q**) Never mind the bland facade, as this merely conceals Leipzig's most design-conscious hotel, whose mega-cool lobby leads to 436 luxurious rooms. Don't miss having a drink at the Falco bar on the 17th floor with the entire city panorama unfolding below.

Hotel Fürstenhof (☎ 1400; www.luxurycollection .com/fuerstenhof; Tröndlinring 8; r from €200, breakfast €25; **P** **X** **X** **Q** **☎** **Q**) The *dame vieille* of the Leipzig hotel scene, with a 200-year pedigree, finds umpteen ways to spoil its guests. It has updated old-world flair, impeccable service, a gourmet restaurant and an oh-so-soothing grotto-style pool and spa.

Eating

RESTAURANTS

Sol y Mar (☎ 961 5721; Gottschedstrasse 4; mains €5-14; ☺ 9am-late) The soft lighting, ambient sounds and lush interior (including padded pods for noshing in recline) make this a relaxing place to dine. There's lots of choice for non-carnivores and prices are sensible.

India Gate (☎ 9606 065; Nikolaistrasse 10; mains €7-14) Go subcontinental on the 1st floor of the Strohsackpassage, where a smiley welcome awaits curry-aholics at Leipzig's best Indian. Pink tablecloths and a scale model of the Taj Mahal teleport diners to spicier climbs (or perhaps just a British high street).

Gosenschenke 'Ohne Bedenken' (☎ 566 2360; Menckestrasse 5; mains €6-16; ☺ noon-1am) This historic Leipzig institution, backed by the city's prettiest beer garden, is *the* place to sample *Gose*, a local top-fermented beer often served with a shot of liqueur. The menu has a distinctly carnivorous bent. Take tram 12 to Fritz-Seger-Strasse.

Zill's Tunnel (☎ 960 2078; Barfussgässchen 9; mains €9-13; ☺ 11.30am-midnight) Empty tables are a rare sight at this outstanding restaurant offering a classic menu of robust Saxon dishes. Sit on the outside terrace, in the rustic cellar, or in the covered 'tunnel' courtyard.

Zest (☎ 2319 126; Bornaischestrasse 54; mains €10-15) Virtually Leipzig's only vegetarian restaurant is buried deep in the southern suburbs. The perfectly crafted seasonal menu of vegan fare is complimented by carefully selected wines. Alternatively just pop in for a strawberry and basil smoothie. Take tram 10 or 11 south to Pfeffingerstrasse.

Barthel's Hof (☎ 141 310; Hainstrasse 1; mains €7-21; ☺ 7am-11pm) This is a sprawling place with outdoor seating in a courtyard, occasional buffet specials and almost exotic Saxon dishes such as *Heubraten* (marinated lamb roasted on hay). The menu takes some deciphering.

Auerbachs Keller (☎ 216 100; Grimmaische Strasse 2-4, Mädlerpassage; mains €8-25) Founded in 1525, Auerbachs Keller is one of Germany's best-known restaurants. It's cosy and touristy, but the food's actually quite good and the setting memorable. In Goethe's *Faust – Part I*, Mephistopheles and Faust carouse here with some students before they ride off on a barrel. The scene is depicted on a carved tree trunk in what is now the Goethe Room (where the great writer allegedly came for 'inspiration').

Medici (☎ 211 3878; Nikolaikirchhof 5; mains €11-25; ☺ noon-2.30pm & 6-11pm Mon-Sat) The interior may resemble a suspension bridge, but this classy Italian spot gets 10 out of 10 from locals. Mains come in small or large, but serious foodies go for the three- to five-course set menus (€46 to €62).

Also recommended:

Bagel Brothers (☎ 9803 330; Nikolaistrasse 42; bagels €2.50-4; ☺ 6.30am-11pm) Who cares about character when you've a hole to fill. Great people-watching potential outside.

El-Amir (☎ 308 2568; Karl-Liebknecht-Strasse 59; mains €2.50-5) Little hole-in-the-wall place selling Leipzig's biggest and best doner, bar none.

CAFES

Telegraph+++ (☎ 1494 990; Dittrichring 18-20; mains €5-11) This elegantly high-ceilinged cafe serves tasty Austrian favourites and a choice of breakfasts, while you digest international goings-on over an English newspaper.

Café Riquet (☎ 961 0000; Schuhmachergässchen 1; mains €8-12; ☺ 9am-10pm) Two bronze elephants guard the entrance to this Viennese-style coffee house in a superb art-nouveau building.

Zum Arabischen Coffe Baum (☎ 961 0061; Kleine Fleischergasse 4; mains €7.50-17; ☺ 11am-midnight) Hosting six different eateries, Leipzig's oldest inn is as stuffy as your grandma's attic, but he cakes and meals are excellent and there's a free coffee museum to boot. Composer Robert Schumann used to come here for his daily affeine fix.

Drinking

The city centre, especially around Barfuss-gässchen, Kleine Fleischergasse (which make up the famous Drallewatsch) and Gottschedstrasse, has a mix of touristy joints and low-key watering holes. A more alternative vibe rules south, along student-flavoured Karl-Liebknecht-Strasse, sometimes known as Karli or Südmeile. Nearby, Münzgasse is another up-and-coming party strip.

Volkshaus (☎ 2127 222; Karl-Liebknecht-Strasse 32; ☞) Anything goes at this high-ceilinged, big-windowed bar-cafe: drinking, smoking, partying to the wee hours or just hanging out on the Karli. DJs and live footy take over at weekends.

White Chocolate (☎ 2689 085; Gottschedstrasse 1) The white-chocolate interior (complete with Aero bubbles rising to the ceiling interior) at this laid-back bar looks so good, party-goers occasionally try to bite chunks off. Or perhaps it's just the booze…

Spizz (☎ 960 8043; Markt 9) Classic brass instruments dangle above the stage at this city slicker, where you might catch some cool jazz. It has three levels, a good range of wine and beer and slow service (due to sheer numbers).

Cafe Barbakane (☎ 702 5930; Universitätsstrasse 9) Part of the cavernous Moritz-Bastei, this is an always lively cafe-bar with courtyard seating and dirt-cheap yet delicious fare (€3 to €5) to vanquish that hangover.

Sixtina (☎ 0177 476 4855; Katharinenstrasse 11) At some point in the last few years the word 'absinthe' has ceased to mean 'bad idea', and the result is places like Sixtina, wholly dedicated to the deadly green fairy. Smoky, but if you're drinking this stuff, you probably don't care.

Entertainment

The best listings magazine is *Kreuzer*, although the free monthlies *Frizz* and *Blitz* might do just fine.

LIVE MUSIC

Moritz-Bastei (☎ 702 590; www.moritzbastei.de; Universitätsstrasse 9) This classic student club occupies a warren of historic cellars below the old city fortifications. It has live bands or DJs most nights, and the neat Cafe Barbakane (left), and runs films outside in summer.

naTo (☎ 391 5539; www.nato-leipzig.de; Karl-Liebknecht-Strasse 46) The mother of Leipzig's alternative-music pub-clubs, with jazz, experimental and indie sounds alongside films and theatre. Take tram 10 or 11 to Südplatz.

Conne Island (☎ 301 3038; Koburger Strasse 3) This former squatter's haunt has morphed into the city's top venue for punk, indie, ska, rock and hip-hop concerts. It's in the southern suburb of Connewitz; take tram 9 to Koburger Brücke.

Werk II (☎ 3080 140; www.werk-2.de; Kochstrasse 132) This large cultural centre in an old factory is great for catching up-and-coming bands, alternative film and theatre or even circus acts. It's also in Connewitz; take tram 9 to Connewitzer Kreuz.

NIGHTCLUBS

Flower Power (☎ 961 3441; Riemannstrasse 42) It's party time any time at this wackily decorated haunt (check out the old pinball machines). The action doesn't reach a crescendo until 4am and the music tends to be older than the crowd.

Ilses Erika (☎ 306 5111; Bernhard-Göring-Strasse 152) The living-room look makes this small but legendary club feel warm and welcoming. Musicwise, expect indie, retro electronic and whatever the mostly student-age crowd has on their iPod.

Bounce 87 (☎ 149 6687; Nikolaistrasse 12-14) This is a key venue for black music: mellow R&B and soul in the Red Lounge, cool rap classics in the Blue Basement.

GAY & LESBIAN VENUES

GegenPol (www.gegenpol.net, in German) and several free publications keep track of the city's small gay scene. Also check www.gayleipzig.de (in German) for ideas.

Rosa Linde (☎ 879 6982; www.rosalinde.de; Lange Strasse 11) Cafe, culture centre and information point for men and women.

Blaue Trude (☎ 212 6679; Sternwartenstrasse 16) This LGBT club is a scene stalwart, with film and student nights, shows and themed discos.

New Orleans (☎ 960 7989; Brühl 56) A low-key mixed place with a modern interior, some Cajun flavour and flirt-friendly table telephones.

CLASSICAL MUSIC

Gewandhausorchester (☎ 1270 280; www.gewand haus.de; Augustusplatz 8) Led by Ricardo Chailly since 2005, this is one of Europe's finest and oldest orchestras, with a tradition harking back to 1743 – Mendelssohn was one of its conductors. It performs primarily at the Neues Gewandhaus as well as in the Thomaskirche.

Thomanerchor (☎ 9844 211; www.thomaskirche.org; Thomaskirchhof 18) This famous boys' choir performs Bach motets and cantatas at 6pm on Friday and 3pm on Saturday, and also sings during Sunday services at 9.30am and 6pm at the Thomaskirche (p198). Special concerts take place throughout the year.

Oper Leipzig (☎ 126 1261; www.oper-leipzig.de; Augustusplatz 12) Leipzig's Opernhaus (opera house) has a 300-year tradition, though the building only went up in the 1950s. The program is an eclectic mix of classics and contemporary works; the Gewandhausorchester provides the music.

Also check the listings magazines for concerts at the Schumann-Haus (p198), the Mendelssohn-Haus (p198), the Nikolaikirche (p197) and the Bach-Museum (p198) when it reopens.

THEATRE & CABARET

Centraltheater (☎ 1268 168; www.centraltheater-leipzig .de; Bosestrasse 1) The repertory at Leipzig's largest theatre ranges from classics infused with modern elements to new plays by up-and-coming writers.

Skala Theater (☎ 1268 168; Gottschedstrasse 16) The Skala stages sometimes controversial works by contemporary playwrights, often with a critical bent.

Krystallpalast (☎ 140660; www.krystallpalastvariete.de; Magazingasse 4) This company puts on the finest variety shows in town, with snake women, flamenco, trapeze acts and more.

Academixer (☎ 2178 7878; Kupfergasse 3) For a dose of satirical cabaret, head to this place near the university.

Getting There & Away
AIR
Leipzig-Halle airport (☎ 224 1155; www.leipzig-halle -airport.de) is served by domestic and international flights from two dozen airlines, including Lufthansa, Germanwings, Air Berlin, Condor and Austrian Airlines. Ryanair flies into **Altenburg airport** (www.flughafen-altenburg.de) from London-Stansted and Edinburgh.

CAR & MOTORCYCLE
Leipzig lies just south of the A14 Halle Dresden autobahn and 15km east of th A9, which links Berlin to Nuremberg. The garage at the Leipzig Hauptbahnhof charge a maximum of €3 for 24 hours. Between 7am and 11pm, parking at the zoo costs reasonable €3 for four hours.

RIDE SERVICES
The **Mitfahrzentrale** (☎ 194 40; Nordstrasse 1; 9am 8pm) can organise shared rides.

TRAIN
Leipzig is an important link between eastern and western Germany, with connections to all major cities. There are frequent service to Frankfurt (€70, 3½ hours), Munich (€87 five hours), Dresden (€20.80, 1½ hours) and Berlin (€42, 1¼ hours).

Getting Around
TO/FROM THE AIRPORTS
Leipzig-Halle airport is served by RE train twice hourly (€4, 15 minutes), leaving from the Hauptbahnhof. A taxi to or from the city centre costs around €35.

Altenburg airport is located about 50km south of Leipzig and is connected to the city by a special bus (€12, 1¼ hours). It goes to from the central bus station on the eastern side of the Hauptbahnhof, but only at time when flights are arriving or departing. For further information, contact ☎ 03447-85 613 or see www.thuesac.de.

BICYCLE
Zweirad Eckhardt (☎ 961 7274; Kurt-Schumacher-Strasse; 8am-8pm Mon-Fri, 9am-8pm Sat), right by the Hauptbahnhof, hires out bikes for €8 pe 24 hours.

PUBLIC TRANSPORT
Public transport is the responsibility of **LVB** (☎ 194 49; www.lvb.de), which runs an **information kiosk** (8am-8pm Mon-Fri, 8am-4pm Sat) on Willy-Brandt-Platz outside the Hauptbahnhof. The central tram station is here as well. Until the City Tunnel is built, the S-Bahn will only circle the city's outer suburbs.

Single tickets cost €1.40 for up to four stops and an inflated €2 for longer trips day passes are €5.

TAXI

Funktaxi (☎ 4884) and **Löwen Taxi** (☎ 982 22) are the main local firms. There is a €2.10 hire charge and then it's €1.90 per kilometre.

AROUND LEIPZIG

Colditz Escape Museum

High on a crag above the sleepy town of Colditz, some 46km southeast of Leipzig, is the imposing **Schloss Colditz** (☎ 034381-437 77; www.schlosscolditz.com; Schlossgasse 1; adult/concession/family €6/3/12; 🕐 10.30am-5pm daily Apr-Oct, 10am-4pm Nov-Mar), a Renaissance palace that's seen stints as a hunting lodge, a poorhouse and a mental hospital. Mostly, though, it's famous as Oflag IVC, a WWII-era high-security prison for Allied officers, including a nephew of Winston Churchill. Most had already escaped from less secure camps and been recaptured. Some 300 made further attempts, and 31 actually managed to flee. The would-be escapees were often aided by ingenious self-made gadgetry, including a glider fashioned from wood and bed sheets, and a homemade sewing machine for making bogus German uniforms. Most astounding, perhaps, is a 44m-long tunnel below the chapel that French officers dug in 1941–42, before the Germans caught them. You can see some of these contraptions, along with lots of photographs, in the small but fascinating **Fluchtmuseum** (Escape Museum) within the palace. Several inmates wrote down their experiences later, of which Pat Reid's *The Colditz Story* is the best-known account.

A section of the palace now houses a sparkling new 161-bed **DJH hostel** (☎ 034381-450 10; www.colditz.jugendherberge.de; under/over 27yr €21.40/24.90) with incredibly up-to-the-minute facilities.

On weekdays bus 690 runs hourly to Colditz from Leipzig, or alternatively you can take a train to Bad Lausick and catch bus 613 from there. At weekends catch the train to Grossbothen then change to bus 619. The one-way trip takes between 90 minutes and two hours. The town is at the junction of the B107 and B176 roads between Leipzig and Chemnitz.

CHEMNITZ

☎ **0371 / pop 244,000**

Just like the majority of eastern Germany's cities, Chemnitz had to reinvent itself post-*Wende,* and has done so with some measure of success. Known from 1953 to 1990 as Karl-Marx-Stadt, the GDR gave it a Stalinist makeover, and smokestack industries once earned it the nickname of 'Saxon Manchester'. Such scars don't heal easily, and with its thundering boulevards and prefab blocks the town still has a very Soviet feel. In fact every now and then you have to remind yourself you're still in Germany.

But things are gradually improving, and nowhere is this more visible than in the revitalised city centre, now a pedestrianised glass-and-steel shopping and entertainment district. Add to that a lively cultural scene, one of Europe's largest intact art-nouveau quarters and an unpretentious air, and you've got more than a few good reasons for a stopover.

Orientation

The city centre, anchored by the Markt and encircled by a ring road, is about a 10-minute walk south of the train station via Bahnhofstrasse or the Soviet-flavoured Strasse der Nationen. Trams 4, 6 and 522 also link the two; get off at Zentralhaltestelle.

The little Chemnitz River, west of the city centre, flows north–south.

Information

There are several banks with ATMS in the Markt area.

Main post office (Strasse der Nationen 2-4)

ReiseBank (Carolastrasse 2)

Tourist office (☎ 690 680; www.chemnitz-tourismus.de; Markt 1; 🕐 9am-7pm Mon-Fri, 9am-4pm Sat, 10am-4pm Sun)

Sights

KUNSTSAMMLUNGEN CHEMNITZ

A palatial 1909 building, just off the Strasse der Nationen, shelters the **Kunstsammlungen Chemnitz** (Chemnitz Art Museum; ☎ 488 4424; adult/concession €6/3, in combination with Museum Gunzenhauser €12/6; 🕐 11am-6pm Tue-Sun), a high-calibre collection of 19th- and 20th-century German artists. The list of heavy hitters includes Caspar David Friedrich and Lovis Corinth and, most famously, the Chemnitz-born expressionist painter Karl Schmidt-Rottluff, a co-founder of the artist group Die Brücke.

Across town, a second branch, the new **Museum Gunzenhauser** (☎ 488 7024; Stollberger Strasse 2; adult/concession €7/4; 🕐 11am-6pm, closed Tue) displays a private collection of mainly 20th-century art including works by Otto Dix, Alexej von Jawlensky, Max Beckmann, Ernst Ludwig Kirchner and many others.

KARL-MARX-DENKMAL & AROUND

Near the corner of Strasse der Nationen and Brücken-strasse the 7.1m-high **Karl Marx Monument** catches the German philosopher on a very bad hair day in front of a nine-storey frieze, exhorting: 'Workers of all countries, unite!' in several languages. This rare vestige from the GDR era attracts left-wing demonstrators and skateboarders. Plans to remove it have themselves been scrapped.

Across the street, past the Stadthalle/Hotel Mercure complex, is the **Roter Turm**, a medieval defence tower.

DASTIETZ

The **DAStietz** (Moritzstrasse 20) is a former department store reborn as a busy cultural centre. Besides the public library, a university faculty and a few shops, it also harbours the **Neue Sächsische Galerie** (New Saxon Gallery; ☎ 367 6680; adult & concession €2, under 14yr free; ⏰ 10am-8pm Thu-Mon, 10am-8pm Tue), which presents postwar works by Saxon artists. Also here is the **Museum für Naturkunde** (Natural History Museum; ☎ 488 4551; adult/concession/family €4/2.50/8; ⏰ 10am-8pm Mon-Fri, 10am-6pm Sat & Sun, closed Wed), where the most interesting exhibit, the Versteinerter Wald (petrified forest), can be admired for free in the atrium; some of the stony trunks are 290 million years old.

MARKT

Parts of Chemnitz's compact centre have been completely redeveloped since reunification, and have evolved into a modern, though somewhat soulless, commercial hub. Now historic buildings rub shoulders with newcomers such as the glass-and-steel Galeria Kaufhof department store (designed by Helmut Jahn), and the Galerie Roter Turm, a shopping mall sporting a sandstone facade.

Both form part of the ensemble encircling the lively Markt, which is dominated by the **Altes Rathaus** (Old Town Hall), an imposing white 15th-century building with a Renaissance portal, and the **Neues Rathaus** (New Town Hall), which looks older but only dates to 1911. Completing this impressive silhouette is the **Hoher Turm** (High Tower) behind the Altes Rathaus. The adjacent **Jakobikirche** is a Gothic church topped by a neat roof turret and flaunting a rare art-deco facade.

SCHLOSS AREA

Across the river, the **Schlossteich** is a large park-ringed pond, with a music pavilion for summer concerts. Towering over it is the **Schlosskirche** (⏰ 10am-5pm Tue-Sat, 2.30-5.30pm Sun Apr-Oct, 11am-4pm Tue-Sat Nov-Mar), a 12th-century Benedictine monastery later recast into a weighty Gothic hall church. Its treasures include Hans Witten's intriguing sculpture *Christ at the Column* (1515). Just south of the church stands the reconstructed **Schloss** itself, which houses the **Schlossbergmuseum** (☎ 488 4501; Schlossberg 12; adult/concession €3/1.80; ⏰ 11am-6pm Tue-Sun). The vaulted interior rather outshines the historical displays and paintings.

OTHER SIGHTS

Around 2.5km south of the centre the **Henry van de Velde museum** (☎ 488 4424; Parkstrasse 58; admission free; ⏰ 10am-6pm Wed, Fri, Sat & Sun) occupies the 1903 Villa Esche, the Belgian artist's first commission in Germany. The downstairs dining room and music salon have been restored as period rooms, while upstairs you'll find a small collection of crafts and furniture. Take tram 4 to Haydnstrasse.

If you enjoy art-nouveau architecture, you might also find a stroll through the **Kassberg** neighbourhood rewarding; it's about 1km west of the centre (bus 62 or 72 to Barbarossastrasse).

The **Sächsische Eisenbahnmuseum** (Saxony Railway Museum; ☎ 4932 765; www.sem.chemnitz.de; adult/child €5/2; ⏰ 9am-5pm Tue-Sun) is a greasy, hands-off affair housed in two vast semicircular depots. Both contain gargantuan East German steam locos, many of which only clanked and hissed their last for the Deutsche Reichsbahn in the late 1980s.

Take bus 21 from the Zentralhaltestelle to the 'Sächsische Eisenbahnmuseum' stop and follow the signs through the allotments.

Sleeping

Pension Europark (☎ 5228 341; www.europark.de; Schulstrasse 38; s €15-17, d €30-44; **P**) No-frills nomads looking to get their 40 winks for under €40 should head for this unpretentious guesthouse 4km south of the centre, but close to the Altchemnitz Center tram stop (trams 6 and 522). More expensive rooms have private facilities and breakfast is €5 extra.

Hotel Sächsischer Hof (☎ 461 480; www.saechsischer-hof.de; Brühl 26; s €40-57, d €77; **P** ✗) This family-run hotel on a quiet street not far from the Hauptbahnhof and the Schlossberg is one of the best deals in town. Rooms are cheap, clean and airy and there's a decent restaurant.

Hotel Chemnitzer Hof (☎ 6840; www.guennewig.de; Theaterplatz 4; s €89-122, d €99-142; **P** ✗ ▢) Behind the stolid facade awaits this classy establishment, with Bauhaus-style decor, eccentric artworks and 92 comfortable rooms sheathed in warm colours; some overlook Theaterplatz.

Eating & Drinking

Turmbrauhaus (☎ 909 5095; Neumarkt 2; mains €5-13.50) Watch your reflection in the polished copper brewing vats become ever mistier as you down a house ale or two at this upbeat brewpub. The outdoor tables are great for people-watching.

Ratskeller (☎ 694 9875; Markt 1; mains €7.50-18) This slightly touristy pin-up of the Chemnitz dining scene offers huge portions of local cuisine from a suspiciously long menu (over 120 dishes!) You can choose between rustic or sophisticated sections, and the painted and vaulted ceilings are so gorgeous you may want to eat them too.

An der Schlossmühle (☎ 335 2533; Schlossberg 3; mains €8-21) One of several options at the foot of the castle, this 1704 half-timbered gem serves German food and has a woodsy interior and gardenlike terrace.

Getting There & Around

Chemnitz is linked by direct train to Dresden (€13.30, one hour), Leipzig (€15.20, one hour) and Zwickau (€5.40, 30 minutes). The east–west A4 skirts Chemnitz, while the A72 heading south for Munich originates here.

All trams and buses pass through the city-centre Zentralhaltestelle. Single tickets start at €1.30 for short rides; individual day passes are €3.40 per person, or €6.80 for families.

AROUND CHEMNITZ
Augustusburg

About 13km east of Chemnitz, draped across a craggy mountain top above forests and fields, Augustusburg (population 5100) is one of those relatively undiscovered gems people rave about, with friendly locals to boot. The big draw here is the oversized **Schloss** (☎ 037291-380 18; www.die-sehenswerten-drei.de; ⊗ 9.30am-6pm Apr-Oct, 10am-5pm Nov-Mar), built in 1572 as the summer residence of Elector August, the great-great-great grandfather of Saxon ruler Augustus the Strong. Combined admission to the complex's five museums is €6.60 for adults, €5 with a concession and €18 for a family, but individual tickets can be purchased as well.

The Schloss is nicknamed the 'Palace of the Bikers' for good reason. This is where you'll find the **Motorradmuseum** (adult/concession €3.20/2.40), one of the largest and most prestigious collections of motorcycles in Europe. Treasures include classic Horch, DKW (later MZ) and BMW roadsters, and some very rare Harley models. In the former stables, the focus is on a somewhat earlier mode of transportation in the **Kutschenmuseum** (adult/concession €1.60/1.20), which brims with Cinderella-worthy horse-drawn carriages.

Another wing contains the **Jagdtier- und Vogelkundemuseum** (adult/concession €2.80/2.10), which has adorable dioramas featuring local feathered and furry creatures – a likely winner with the kiddies. Admission is also good for several antler-filled rooms dealing with the palace's hunting history. The main reason for coming up here, though, is to see the Venussaal, a vast hall decorated with original 16th-century murals depicting a spooky, mythical mountainscape. Finally, there's the **Kerker** (adult/concession €1.60/1.20), a dank underground prison filled with medieval torture instruments.

Other palace sections can only be seen on **guided tours** (adult/concession €3/2.20) in German. These include the **residential wing**, the **palace church**, which has an altar painting by Lucas Cranach the Younger, and the **Brunnenhaus**,

SAXONY

which still contains the wooden mechanism that once brought water up from a 130m-deep well.

You also have to pay separately (€1) to climb the **Aussichtsturm** (viewing tower) for clear views across the region.

The complex also contains a **DJH hostel** (☎ 202 56; dm under 27yr €15.80-17.80, over 27yr €18.80-20.80; ✖) and several restaurants. For more lodging and eating options, head down into the village, where you'll also find the **tourist office** (☎ 395 50; www.augustusburg.de; Marienberger Strasse 24; ☿ 9am-noon & 1-5pm Mon-Fri).

GETTING THERE & AWAY

Trains run from Chemnitz to Erdmannsdorf (€3.40, 20 minutes), from where you take the *Drahtseilbahn* (funicular) to Augustusburg (one-way/return €4/3).

Coming from Chemnitz, motorists should follow the S236 country road east to the Schloss. From the A4, get off at Frankenberg, take the B169 to Flöha, then switch to the B180 to Augustusburg.

ZWICKAU

☎ 0375 / pop 95,000

A gateway to the Erzgebirge (Iron Ore Mountains), Zwickau has written an especially important chapter in German automobile history. It is the birthplace of both the Audi brand (in 1910) and the GDR-era Trabant, which began rolling, very slowly, off assembly lines in 1957 (see also the boxed text, opposite). The town's sparkling car museum is a must for anyone even remotely interested in the subject. Production continues today courtesy of Volkswagen, which brought much-needed jobs to the area. As a result, Zwickau feels less depressed than other former GDR industrial cities, and also has a fairly lively centre teeming with pubs and restaurants. This, plus an impressive cathedral, the birth house of composer Robert Schumann and some of Germany's oldest homes, make Zwickau worth a stop.

Orientation

The compact and largely pedestrianised Altstadt is encircled by Dr-Friedrichs-Ring. The Hauptbahnhof (central train station) is about 800m west of the ring road; simply follow Bahnhofstrasse then Schumannstrasse.

Vogtlandbahn regional trains to towns in the Czech Republic stop right in the heart of town, just south of the Markt and Rathaus.

Information

Citibank (cnr Innere Plauensche Strasse & Dr-Friedrichs-Ring)

Main post office (Hauptstrasse 18-20)

Telecafé (Leipzigerstrasse 4; per hr €1; ☿ 10am-11pm Mon-Fri, noon-11pm Sat & Sun) Cheap web access.

Tourist office (☎ 271 3240; www.zwickau-tourist.de; Hauptstrasse 6; ☿ 9am-6.30pm Mon-Fri, 10am-4pm Sat)

Sights

AUGUST HORCH MUSEUM

Zwickau's top attraction is this amazing **car museum** (☎ 2717 3812; www.horch-museum.de; Audistrasse 7; adult/concession €5/3.50; ☿ 9.30am-5pm Tue-Sun) that will enlighten and entertain even non-petrolheads. Housed within the original early-20th-century Audi factory, gleaming and imaginatively presented exhibits range from old-timer gems like the 1911 Horch Phaeton to the latest Audi R8. And, of course, there are plenty of Trabants (three million were produced here until 1990) and other cars that gave communism a bad name. You can walk inside an early gas station, inspect Audi founder August Horch's original wood-panelled office, stroll down a 1930s streetscape and even learn how Trabants were made. English-language audioguides are available for €2.50. The museum is about 2.5km north of the Altstadt; take tram 4 to Kurt-Eisner-Strasse.

PRIESTERHÄUSER ZWICKAU

Next to the Dom, the **Priesterhäuser Zwickau** (Priests' Houses; ☎ 834 551; Domhof 5-8; adult/concession/family €4/2/9; ☿ 1-6pm Tue-Sun) gives you a close-up look at medieval living conditions. This ensemble of pint-sized cottages was built between the 13th and 15th centuries, and ranks among the country's oldest surviving residential buildings. Church employees lived here as late as the 19th century. Imagine the people who've come before you as you climb up the creaky stairs, duck into small chambers or inspect the soot-stained kitchen. A modern annex has changing exhibits about the town history.

LORD OF THE RINGS

More than anything else, Zwickau has been shaped by the automobile industry and by one man in particular: August Horch (1868–1951). The first Horch cars rolled into the streets in 1904 and quickly became the queen among luxury vehicles, besting even Mercedes Benz. Horch, alas, was a better engineer than a businessman and in 1909 he was fired by his investors. Not missing a step, he simply opened another factory across town, calling it Audi (Latin for *Horch*, which means 'listen' in German).

Ever wondered why the Audi symbol is four interlinking rings? They stand for Audi, Horch, DKW and Wanderer, the four Saxon car makers who merged into a single company called Auto-Union during the Great Depression. After the war, Audi moved to Ingolstadt in Bavaria. As for Zwickau, it became the birthplace of the Trabant – the GDR's answer to the Volkswagen Beetle. The name means 'satellite' in German, and was inspired by the launch of the world's first satellite (the Soviet Sputnik) in 1957, a year before production started.

By the time it ceased in 1991, more than three million Trabis had rolled off the assembly lines here, most of them for export to other socialist countries – which is why regular GDR folks had to wait up to 13 years (!) to get one.

Because of the country's chronic steel shortage, the Trabi's body was made from reinforced plastic called Duroplast. Powered by a two-stroke engine similar to that of a large lawnmower, this rolling environmental disaster pumped out five times the amount of fumes as the average Western vehicle. Berlin residents still talk of waking up the day the Wall opened to see a vast queue of Trabants stretching down the road, with a dull brown cloud gathering overhead…

ROBERT-SCHUMANN-HAUS

Behind Hauptmarkt is the **Robert-Schumann-Haus** (☎ 215 269; Hauptmarkt 5; adult/concession/family €4/2/9; 10am-5pm Tue-Fri, 1-5pm Sat & Sun), where this renowned composer of the Romantic Age was born and spent the first seven years of his life. Exhibits trace the various life stations of the man who sadly went seriously bipolar in his 30s, and died young in Bonn (p583). A highlight is the piano once played by Schumann's wife, Clara Wieck, herself a noted pianist. There's a monument to the man in the northeast corner of the Hauptmarkt.

DOM ST MARIEN

West of the Schumann-Haus, **Dom St Marien** (Domhof; admission €1; 10am-6pm daily) is a late-Gothic hall church that will quicken the pulse of art fans. Foremost among its treasures is the 1479 altar painting by Michael Wohlgemuth (a teacher of Albrecht Dürer) plus an emotionally charged *pietà* (1502) by famous local sculptor Peter Breuer, and some ultra-rare Protestant confessionals. For details, ask to borrow the English pamphlet.

OTHER SIGHTS

A 10-minute walk north of the Altstadt, the spectacular **Johannisbad** (☎ 272 560; Johannisstrasse 16; adult/concession per hr €3/2.50, per 2hr €4.50/3.50; 10am-10pm Mon & Wed, 8am-10pm Tue & Thu, 10am-11pm Fri, 9am-10pm Sat & Sun) is a beautiful old art-nouveau swimming pool and sauna complex – worth a look even without taking a dip.

On Georgenplatz, 200m northwest of the Dr-Friedrichs-Ring, look out for the dinky **Trabant Monument** in the shape of a bronze family posing gleefully next to their stone Trabi.

Sleeping

Zum Uhu (☎ 295 044; www.zum-uhu.de; Bahnhofstrasse 51; s/d/tr €33/62/75) The rooms at this little family-run inn are looking a bit tired, but it's still the cheapest place to overnight. Book ahead during the week as it's normally full. The traditionally-minded restaurant is as good as it ever was.

Brauereigasthof Zwickau (☎ 303 2032; www.brauhaus-zwickau.de; Peter-Breuer-Strasse 12-16; s/d €45/60;) This is an excellent bargain base. It has five simple but cosy rooms, with ancient exposed beams, above a sprawling restaurant-pub that makes its own beer and schnapps and serves hearty meals in belt-loosening portions (€5 to €14).

Aparthotel 1A (☎ 275 750; www.1a-aparthotel.de; Robert-Müller-Strasse 1A; s/d €57/77;   ) No prizes for originality or flair here, just clean, no-nonsense rooms in a fairly central location, popular with post-credit-crunch business travellers. Rates include breakfast buffet.

SAXONY

Eating & Drinking

Zwickau's almost-hip Kneipenstrasse (pub row), aka Peter-Breuer-Strasse, is good for arm wrestling a few jugs of ale or sipping a cocktail or five. For fast food, try the Zwickau Arcaden shopping mall on Innere-Plauensche-Strasse.

egghead (☎ 303 3386; Peter-Breuer-Strasse 34) One of the best places to party on the Kneipenstrasse, this is a sleek but unpretentious cocktail bar with all kinds of mixed drinks, shakes and tasty crêpes for sustenance.

Wenzel's Prager Bierstuben (☎ 273 7542; Domhof 12; mains €5-12) If you've a big hole to fill, head for this tavern with faux Gothic interiors, old Prague street signs and, most importantly, monster portions of Slavic stodge. Start with some *echt* Carlsbad Becherovka (herbal digestif), followed by a Bohemian belly-stretcher such as beef goulash with dumplings. Swab the decks with a Prague-brewed Staropramen.

Zur Grünhainer Kapelle (☎ 536 1633; Peter-Breuer-Strasse 3; mains €8-14) Feast on Saxon dishes in this former chapel with its cross-vaulted ceilings, fabulous carved furniture and uneven art exhibits. The house speciality is the charmingly named *besoffne Wildsau* (drunken boar)!

Sky Lounge (☎ 390 9969; Peter-Breuer-Strasse 19; dinner mains €10-23; ☽ from 9am) Take the lift to this top-floor hipster haunt where you'll find a lounge, a restaurant and two terraces to catch the morning and afternoon sun. Good for your first and last cup of coffee or breakfast any time of the day.

Drei Schwäne (☎ 204 7650; Tonstrasse 1; mains €18-21) Food fanciers will want to make the trip out to this tip-top place, where the cuisine is inspired by the robust flavours of Provence, Tuscany and the Alsace. Excellent wines and welcoming hosts ensure a memorable evening.

Getting There & Around

Zwickau has direct train links to Leipzig (€15.20, 1½ hours), Chemnitz (€5.40, 30 minutes), Dresden (€21.50, 1½ hours) and towns across the border in the Czech Republic.

Single tickets on trams and buses are €1.70, day passes are €3.40.

EASTERN SAXONY

BAUTZEN

☎ 03591 / pop 42,200

Mustard, prisons and Germany's sole indigenous minority are the unlikely trio that come together in fascinating Bautzen. Rising high above the deep valley of the Spree River, no fewer than 17 towers and much of the town fortification still ring the Altstadt's labyrinth of cobbled lanes that have hardly changed for centuries.

While the town is undeniably German, its heritage is also influenced by the Slavic-speaking Sorbs, (see boxed text, p167) Budyšin, as the Sorb language calls it, is home to several Sorb cultural institutions and public signage is bilingual, though you'd be lucky to hear the language spoken.

Orientation

The Spree River ribbons along the western side of Bautzen's Altstadt, which is centred on the Hauptmarkt. The Hauptbahnhof is a 15-minute walk south of the old quarter and is reached via Bahnhofstrasse, Karl-Marx-Strasse and Lauengraben.

Information

Internetcafé Bautzen (☎ 595 179; Steinstrasse 13; per 30min €1.80; ☽ 10am-10pm Mon-Sat, 5-10pm Sun)
Post office (Postplatz)
Sparkasse (Kornmarkt) A bank.
Tourist office (☎ 420 16; www.bautzen.de; Hauptmarkt 1; ☽ 9am-6pm Mon-Fri, 9am-3pm Sat & Sun Mar-Oct, 1hr shorter hours Nov-Feb) Offers free web access.

Sights

KORNMARKT

The **Stadtmuseum** (city museum; ☎ 498 50; Kornmarkt 1; adult/concession €3.50/2.50; ☽ 10am-6pm Tue-Sun, 6-8pm Thu) reopened in 2009 after a five-year hiatus for restoration. The reinvigorated display looks at the history of the town and region as well as local art in shiny new exhibition spaces.

Nearby, the **Reichenturm** (Reichenstrasse; adult/child €1.40/1; ☽ 10am-5pm Apr-Oct) provides aerial views of the Altstadt. The addition of the baroque cupola in 1718 caused the 53m-high structure to start tilting. Today it deviates 1.4m from the centre, making it one of the steepest leaning towers north of the Alps.

HAUPTMARKT

Reichenstrasse leads west from the tower, past fancy baroque houses to the intimate **Hauptmarkt**, site of the tourist office and thrice-weekly farmers markets. The square is dominated by the impressive **Rathaus**, with an 18th-century baroque exterior that masks a Gothic origin.

The intriguing **sundial** measures time, as well as the lengths of the days and nights for each date.

FLEISCHMARKT & AROUND

North of the Hauptmarkt is the **Fleischmarkt**, the old meat market, dominated by the **Dom St Petri**. This is the only *Simultankirche* in eastern Germany, meaning it serves both Catholics and Protestants. When the Reformation reached Bautzen in 1524, both congregations agreed to share the church, with the Protestants holding services in the nave and the Catholics in the choir. There's a waist-high iron grating separating the two – although it was 4m high until 1952! The spire can be climbed for a small donation.

The Fleischmarkt is also home to the **Bautzner Senfladen** (Bautzen Mustard Shop; ☎ 597 118; Fleischmarkt 5; ☪ 10am-7pm), where you can buy Bautzen's most famous relish and view a free exhibition on mustard production.

North of the square, a lane leads down to the **Nicolaiturm** tower and a cemetery cradled by the romantically ruined **Nicolaikirche**, which was destroyed during the Thirty Years' War. Notice the Sorb inscriptions on many of the headstones.

SCHLOSS ORTENBURG

Further west is Schloss Ortenburg, on a strategic cliff-top spot that's been occupied by a series of castles since the 7th century. You enter the complex through the late-Gothic **Matthiasturm** (Matthias Tower), named for the Hungarian king Matthias Corvinus who ruled over the region in the late 15th century – he's depicted on horseback as a monumental relief on the tower.

The main palace houses a regional courthouse and is closed to the public. A smaller one, off the courtyard, contains the absorbing **Sorbisches Museum** (☎ 424 03; adult/concession €2.50/1.50; ☪ 10am-5pm Mon-Fri, 10am-6pm Sat & Sun Apr-Oct, 10am-4pm Mon-Fri, 10am-5pm Sat & Sun Nov-Mar), with collections and displays on absolutely every aspect of Sorb history and

culture, including a fascinating walk-through section on the history of the Sorbs in the 20th century.

Across the square is Bautzen's shamefully incongruous theatre, whose saving grace is the detailed **neoclassical sandstone frieze** that's been incorporated into the facade. Sculpted by Ernst Rietschel in 1804, it depicts the tragedy of Orest from Ancient Greek mythology and originally adorned the now-destroyed Hoftheater in Dresden.

BAUTZEN PRISONS

It seems incongruous that this pretty, historical town has been known as *Gefängnisstadt* (prison town) for over a century. The first facility, **Bautzen I**, a yellow-brick structure from 1904, gained such notoriety under the Nazis and later the Soviets that it earned the moniker *Gelbes Elend* (Yellow Misery). Completely modernised, it's still used as a correctional facility today.

South of town is **Bautzen II**, which became a Stasi prison in GDR times. Many famous regime opponents – including Rudolf Bahro, who later co-founded the Green Party in West Germany – served their sentences here. Left exactly as it was in the late 1980s, it's now a **Gedenkstätte** (memorial site; ☎ 404 74; www.gedenkstaette-bautzen.de; Weigangstrasse 8a; admission free; ☪ 10am-4pm Tue-Sun) for the victims of political oppression.

OTHER SIGHTS

Slavophiles should head for the **Serbski Dom** (Sorb Cultural Centre; ☎ 421 05; Postplatz 2; ☪ 10am-5pm Mon-Fri) with heaps of information on Sorb-related events, a free exhibition and souvenir shop.

South of the Schloss the **Alte Wasserkunst** (☎ 415 88; adult/concession €2/1.50; ☪ 10am-5pm Apr-Oct, 10am-4pm Nov-Mar) is a tower containing an ingenious and fully functional late-medieval pumping station.

Sleeping

DJH hostel (☎ 403 47; www.bautzen.jugendherberge.de; Am Zwinger 1; dm under/over 27yr €18.80/22.30; ☒) The local hostel has a fairy-tale location in the old ramparts behind the Domstift.

Alte Gerberei (☎ 272 390; www.hotel-alte -gerberei.de; Uferweg 1; s/d €49/67; ℗ ☒) You'll find Old European charm galore in this historic eight-room pension right by the river. The flower-filled courtyard, the river-facing rooms and the wine restaurant are great for unwinding.

Schloss-Schänke (☎ 304 990; www.schloss-schaenke .net; Burgplatz 5; s/d €51/74; (P) (💻) (🛜)) This was once a Franciscan residence, but the 11 renovated rooms are hardly monastic. Some are located in the nearby 17th-century tower, part of the town's erstwhile defences.

Hotel Goldener Adler (☎ 486 60; www.goldener adler.de; Hauptmarkt 4; s/d €75/90; (P) (✗)) History spills from every nook and cranny of this spiffy four-star hotel with its doesn't-get-more-central location. Cap off a day about town with dinner or a drink in the romantic vaulted cellar.

Eating & Drinking

If Bautzen had something like a 'restaurant row', it would be Schlossstrasse, where you'll find about half a dozen internationally themed eateries.

Sam's Bar (☎ 490 964; Fleischmarkt 4; dishes €5-12) For salads, sandwiches and the locally famous 'Samburger', come to this relaxed hang-out that stays open longer than any other place in town.

Bjesada (☎ 470 27; Postplatz 2; mains €7-12) With warm colours, contemporary design and backlit figures from Sorb fairy-tales, the Sorb Cultural Centre restaurant is perhaps not what you'd expect from an eatery celebrating traditional culture. However, the bilingual menu is laden with typical dishes involving herring and beef, with a few token vegie choices thrown in for good measure.

our pick **Wjelbik** (☎ 420 60; Kornstrasse 7; mains €10-16) You can't help but be charmed by your host here, Veronika Mahling, who will greet you, Sorbian style, with a little bread and salt and a hearty *Witajće k nam!* (Welcome!). Enjoy the most Sorbian of dishes, 'Sorbian Wedding' (braised beef with horseradish sauce) in the dining room that manages modern and traditional in one go.

Also recommended:

Bautzner Senfstube (☎ 598 015; Schlossstrasse 3; mains €5-13) Almost all the tasty regional dishes here contain Bautzen's famous mustard.

Zur Apotheke (☎ 480 035; Schlossstrasse 21; mains €10-16) Inside an olde-worlde pharmacy, this progressive eatery takes the medicinal theme to the limit.

Getting There & Away

Regional trains service Bautzen from Görlitz (€7.10, 30 minutes) and Dresden (€10.30, one

hour). The A4 to Dresden or Görlitz runs just south of town. You can park fairly cheaply at Parkplatz Centrum on Äussere Lauenstrasse.

GÖRLITZ

☎ 03581 / pop 56,700

Germany's easternmost city may be somewhat overhyped as the country's most attractive, but few can deny that Görlitz' squares, churches and towers on the Neisse River make for an intriguing halt. It miraculously came through WWII with nary a shrapnel wound and today is a veritable encyclopaedia of European architectural styles. GDR honchos declared the entire city a protected monument, but then invested little in its upkeep. Only after reunification did huge federal cash infusions restore beauty to this ageing *grande dame*. Largely unmarred by the trappings of commercialisation, the nearly 4200 heritage buildings make the place feel almost like a film set. In fact Görlitz stood in for 19th-century Paris and New York in the 2004 remake of *Around the World in 80 Days*, starring Jackie Chan.

The Berlin Wall may have tumbled long ago, but Görlitz is still a divided city. After WWII it was split in two when the Allies made the Neisse River the boundary between Germany and Poland. Görlitz' former eastern suburbs are now the scruffy Polish town of Zgorzelec.

Orientation

The Altstadt spreads to the north of the Hauptbahnhof. From here, Berliner Strasse and Jakobstrasse, the main shopping streets, run south to Postplatz. Beyond, the city is organised around a trio of squares starting with Demianiplatz in the west, followed by Obermarkt and then Untermarkt. From the latter, Neissstrasse leads down to the Neisse River and the Altstadtbrücke, the footbridge to Zgorzelec. If crossing, bring your passport just in case.

Information

There's a Deutsche Bank on Demianiplatz, and a Sparda-Bank on Postplatz.

Görlitz tourist office (☎ 475 70; www.goerlitz.de; Obermarkt 32; ⏰ 9am-7pm Mon-Fri, 9am-6pm Sat & Sun)

I-Vent tourist office (☎ 421 362; www.goerlitz -tourismus.de; Obermarkt 33; ⏰ 9am-7pm Mon-Fri, 9am-5pm Sat, 9.30am-3pm Sun Apr-Oct, 9am-6pm Mon-Fri, 9.30am-3pm Sat Nov-Mar) Private tourist office.

Post office (Postplatz)

Via Regia (☎ 764 762; Brüderstrasse 3; internet per hr
€0.50) Bookshop with internet access.

Sights

OBERMARKT & SOUTHERN ALTSTADT

Obermarkt, Görlitz' largest square, is flanked
by some striking baroque townhouses on its
north side. At the eastern end is the 16th-
century **Dreifaltigkeitskirche** (audioguide €2; ☯ 10am-
5pm Mon-Sat, 11am-5pm Sun), which has a peculiar
layout and an impressive 'Golden Mary' altar.

Punctuating the square's west end like the
dot in an exclamation mark is the 49m-high
Reichenbacher Turm (adult/concession €1.50/1; ☯ 10am-
5pm May-Oct), part of the old fortifications and
still inhabited until 1904. Town-history exhibits on the numerous floors distract few visitors
away from the tower-top views.

Just behind the tower is the 1490
Kaisertrutz, a squat structure also formerly
part of the city's defence system. Behind the
Kaisertrutz stands the **Theater Görlitz** (☎ 474
70; www.theater-goerlitz.de; Demianiplatz 2), which
some consider Dresden's Semperoper in
miniature.

East of here, on Marienplatz, is the **Dicker
Turm** (Fat Tower), with walls almost 6m
thick in some places. Walking south on
Steinstrasse, past the **Frauenkirche**, you'll
soon reach the **Karstadt department store** (An
der Frauenkirche 5-7), which would be unremarkable were it not for its amazing art-nouveau
interior, canopied by a kaleidoscopic glass
ceiling. Another architectural delicacy from
the same period is the sparkling **Strassburg
Passage**, a light-flooded shopping arcade connecting Berliner Strasse and Jacobstrasse.

UNTERMARKT & EASTERN ALTSTADT

The most beautiful patrician houses flank
the Untermarkt, linked to Obermarkt by
Brüderstrasse. The building at the square's
centre is the **Alte Börse** (old stock exchange),
now a hotel.

First up on your right, on the south
side of Untermarkt, is the magnificent
1526 Schönhof, Germany's oldest residential Renaissance structure. It now houses
the **Schlesisches Museum zu Görlitz** (☎ 879 10;
Untermarkt 4; adult/concession €4/2.50; ☯ 10am-5pm
Tue-Sun), which offers a creatively presented
romp through the rich cultural history of
Silesia in 17 themed rooms (start at the top).
English-language audioguides were set to be
introduced in late 2009.

Immediately opposite, taking up the
square's entire western side, is the **Rathaus**
(town hall), begun in 1537 and built in three
sections and styles. If you take a moment
to observe the lower of the two clocks on
the tower, you'll notice that the helmeted
soldier in the middle briefly drops his chin
every minute.

As you continue clockwise, other buildings of note are the peculiar late-Gothic
Flüsterbogen at No 22, where you can whisper sweet nothings to your sweetie via the
reverberating stone arch in the entranceway,
and the Renaissance **Ratsapotheke** (pharmacy)
at No 24, easily recognised by its spidery
sundial.

Circling the square eventually takes you to
Neissstrasse. At No 30 stands the town's only
pure baroque house, the **Barockhaus**. Normally
a museum filled with fancy furniture and art,
it is closed until summer 2011 for renovation.
Also note the Renaissance **Biblisches Haus** next
door, whose facade depicts scenes from the
Bible carved in sandstone. The river and the
Altstadtbrücke are a few more steps downhill.
Cross to get a taste of what Görlitz was like
15 years ago.

Turn left on Kränzelstrasse for the Gothic
Peterskirche (☯ 11am-6pm Mon-Sat, 11.45am-6pm
Sun), where top of the bill is the unusual 'Sun
Organ' fashioned by Silesian-Italian Eugenio
Casparini, with tiny pipes shooting off like
rays. With 6095 tubes, the organ took 11
years to restore (1995–2006) at a cost of 1.5
million euros.

HEILIGES GRAB

A 10-minute walk along Grüner Graben, north
of the Reichenbacher Turm, drops you at the
Heiliges Grab (admission €1.50; ☯ 10am-6pm Mon-Sat,
11am-6pm Sun), an exact replica of the original
Holy Sepulchre in Jerusalem (which has since
been altered repeatedly). It was commissioned
some 500 years ago, by a local mayor in atonement for getting the neighbour's girl knocked
up when he was a youngster.

Tours

Trabant Tour (☎ 642 995; www.trabbitouren.de; Demianiplatz 25) Follow recommended tour routes be-
hind the wheel of your very own Trabi.

Sleeping

Picobello Pension (☎ 420 010; www.picobello-pension.de;
Uferstrasse 32; s/d €25/44, breakfast €5; ℗ ☒ ▣)

lonelyplanet.com

Duvets are thin and water runs lukewarm at this no-frills place down by the river. Some rooms have baths and Poland views. Bike rental and half-board are also available.

Herberge Zum Sechsten Gebot (☎ 764 20; www .boerse-goerlitz.de; s/d €50/65; P ⊠) The name here pays homage to the sixth commandment ('Thou shalt not commit adultery'), but hilariously the spacious, modern rooms are named for famous sinners, such as Henry VIII and the Marquis de Sade.

Gästehaus im Flüsterbogen (☎ 764 20; www.boerse -goerlitz.de; s €60-75, d €85-95; P ⊠) Check in here if you need plenty of elbow room. Antique furnishings combine with modern touches to create character by the armload.

Romantik Hotel Tuchmacher (☎ 473 10; www .tuchmacher.de; Petersstrasse 8; s €88-100, d €118-133; P ⊠ ⊜) The most unusual rooms at this posh oasis of charm in a quiet street near the Peterskirche (bell alert!) sport richly painted baroque ceilings, but others are just as nice with warm hues and classical furnishings. There's a lovely wellness area for relaxing, and a popular restaurant for refuelling.

ourpick Hotel Börse (☎ 764 20; www.boerse-goerlitz .de; Untermarkt 16; s €70-85, d €109-129; P ⊠ ☐) Four-poster beds, huge glass chandeliers, patterned parquet floors and elegant antiques are the hallmarks of this stylish yet spirited hotel. Rooms are named after the cities of Europe.

Also recommended:

Europa (☎ 423 50; www.hotel-europa-goerlitz.de; Berliner Strasse 2; s/d €59/85; ⊠) This sound, if uninspiring, option with modernised rooms is convenient for both the town centre and railway station.

Sorat Hotel Görlitz (☎ 406 577; www.sorat-hotels .com; Struvestrasse 1; s €83-113, d €103-133; P ⊠ ⊜) Days kick off with a champagne breakfast at this central hotel with tasteful, modern rooms (some with wheelchair access).

Eating

Zur Schwarzen Kunst (☎ 418 125; Neissstrasse 22; mains €5-13) Among the many eating options on Neissstrasse is this atmospheric tavern, with rough-hewn stone walls, tiny cellar spaces, candle-in-bottle illumination and an English menu of simple Silesian dishes.

St Jonathan (☎ 421 082; Peterstrasse 16; mains €6-16) Despite its sleek furniture and stunning historic setting, this place only looks expensive. Enjoy delicious German food below the painted vaulted ceiling or, for a romantic tête-à-tête, book the single table inside (!) the

fireplace. Also explore the back of the building with its atrium staircase, where textile merchants used to display their wares.

Vierradenmühle (☎ 406 661; Hotherstrasse 20; mains €9-14) Service is slow but the Saxon and Silesian food is excellent at this place. Sticking out into the Neisse next to the new Altstadtbrücke, it is Germany's easternmost restaurant.

Restaurant Lucie Schulte (☎ 410 260; Untermarkt 22; mains €12-26; ☾ 6pm Mon-Sat) Your tastebuds are likely to do cartwheels when you try the creative flavour pairings at this refreshingly progressive venue. It's set in historic barrel-vaulted rooms off the romantic courtyard of the Flüsterbogen building, and has great wines, too.

Getting There & Away

Trains run regularly between Görlitz and Dresden (€18.30, 1½ hours) via Bautzen (€7.10, 30 minutes). For Berlin (€37.50, three hours), change in Cottbus. Buses and trains also serve Zittau (€5.60, 40 minutes), and there are three cross-border services daily to Wroclaw (Breslau; €18.40, three hours).

Görlitz is just off the A4 autobahn from Dresden; turn off after the Königshainer Berge tunnel, which at 3.3km is currently Germany's second-longest – the longest is the Rennsteig tunnel in Thuringia, an astonishing 7.9km in length! The B6, B99 and B115 converge just north of town.

BAD MUSKAU
☎ 035771 / pop 4000

Squeezed against the border with Poland, drowsy Bad Muskau is a tiny spa-village with one big attraction. Unesco-listed **Muskauer Park** is the verdant masterpiece of 19th-century celebrity landscape gardener, Prince Hermann von Pückler. 'Prince Pickle', as the English dubbed him during a controversial visit to London, toiled on the park for 30 years (from 1815 to 1844), but never completed his 'painting with plants'. He nevertheless set the bar high for European landscapers to follow, even compiling a meticulous instruction manual on landscaping techniques.

In 1945 the park was divided between Germany and Poland when the River Neisse, which bisects Pückler's creation, became the new border.

Start you exploration at the **tourist office** (☎ 504 92; www.badmuskau.info; ☾ 9am-6pm Mon-Fri, 10am-5pm Sat & Sun Apr-Oct, 9am-4pm Mon-Fri

Nov-Mar) in the Altes Schloss where you can pick up a map of the sprawling park. Just across the chateau lake stands the freshly renovated **Neues Schloss**, home to **Pückler!** (☎ 631 00; www.muskauer-park.de; adult/concession €6/3; ☼ 10am-6pm Apr-Oct), an interactive, push-button caper through the action-packed life of the park's much-travelled architect. More of the chateau will be opened up to the public in coming years.

At a whopping 560 hectares, the folly-peppered park is too large to be fully explored on foot. Bike hire (€5 per day) is available at the well-signposted **Schlossvorwerk**, a leafy courtyard where you'll also find a cafe, gift shops and luggage lockers. If crossing to the Polish side of the park, take your passport.

To reach Bad Muskau, first take a train to Weisswasser from Cottbus (€5.15, 30 minutes) or Görlitz (€7.60, 35 minutes), then change onto local bus 250, alighting at Kirchplatz for the tourist office.

ZITTAU
☎ 03583 / pop 30,000
Wedged firmly between Poland and the Czech Republic, sleepy Zittau is an intriguing outpost tucked away in the far-flung Dreiländereck (the bit of Germany TV weather presenters usually cover with their midriff). Undamaged during WWII its largely baroque Altstadt is an original, though GDR-era neglect is still evident in places. Since 1999, the town's star attraction has been the *Grosse Zittauer Fastentuch,* an ultra-rare Lenten veil that was joined by a second, smaller one in 2005. These treasures make Zittau the hub of the Via Sacra, a cross-border holiday route linking sites of religious importance.

Orientation & Information
The Altstadt is a 10-minute walk south of the Hauptbahnhof, via Bahnhofstrasse and Bautzener Strasse.
Post office (Haberkornplatz 1)
Sparkasse (cnr Neustadt & Frauenstrasse) Bank.
Tourist office (☎ 752 137; www.zittau.eu; Markt 1; ☼ 9am-6pm Mon-Fri, 9am-1pm Sat, 1-4pm Sun May-Oct)

Sights & Activities
Zittau's central square, the **Markt**, exudes almost Mediterranean flair thanks to its baroque fountain, patrician townhouses and imposing Italian-palazzo-style **Rathaus** (town

hall), drafted by none other than Prussian master builder Karl Friedrich Schinkel.

Schinkel also designed the **Johanniskirche** (☎ 510 933; tower adult/concession €1.50/1; ☼ noon-6pm Mon-Fri, 10am-4pm Sat & Sun Apr-Oct) north of the Markt. This neoclassical church has two towers that don't match, one of which can be climbed for sweeping views of the mountains. If you're here at noon or 6pm, you might run into the city trumpeter who plays little tunes daily at those times.

East of the Markt, via Frauenstrasse, is the **Neustadt** square, with several fountains and the weighty **Salzhaus** (☼ 8am-6.30pm). Originally a 16th-century salt storage house, it now houses shops, restaurants and the public library.

Continuing on Frauenstrasse soon takes you to the **Museum Kirche zum Heiligen Kreuz** (☎ 500 8920; adult/concession €4/2; ☼ 10am-6pm Tue-Sun Apr-Oct, 10am-5pm Nov-Mar). This former church now shelters Zittau's most famous attraction, the 1472 **Grosses Zittauer Fastentuch** (large Lenten veil). This house-sized painted linen cloth shows a complete illustrated Bible in 90-odd scenes – Genesis to the Last Judgement. Its original purpose was to conceal the altar from the congregation during Lent. Also note the morbidly charming tombstones in the little church cemetery.

Smaller in size, but no less precious or rare, is the 1573 **Kleines Zittauer Fastentuch**, which is the star exhibit at the **Kulturhistorisches Museum Franziskanerkloster** (☎ 554 790; Klosterstrasse 3; adult/concession €2/1.50; ☼ 10am-5pm Apr-Oct, closed Mon Nov-Mar), a short walk west of here. This depicts the crucifixion scene framed by 40 symbols of the Passion of Christ and is one of only six such veils that have survived. Combination tickets for both veils are €5 per adult (€3 concession), which includes an English-language audioguide. The rest of the museum has exhibits chronicling regional history.

Sleeping & Eating
Pension am Markt (☎ 7911 790; www.pension-zittau.de; Markt 11; s/d €33/55; ✗) Post-*Wende* flat-pack furniture may lower the tone here, but you won't find cheaper or more central digs. The vast rooms have preposterously high ceilings, and there's free tea and coffee. Breakfast is down in the 700-year-old cellar.

Hotel Dreiländereck (☎ 5550; www.hotel-dle.de; Bautzener Strasse 9; s €63-65, d €80-90; P ✗) This one-time brewery right in the Altstadt is a top choice, with warmly furnished rooms dressed in green-and-gold hues, and a contemporary brasserie with vaulted ceilings. The only downside is the proximity of the Johanniskirche bells!

Savi (☎ 708 297; Bautzener Strasse 10; meals €2.20-6.50; 🖳) With cheap internet (€2.40 per hour), great coffee, snacks and light meals, an English menu and weekend DJs, you'll wanna go where Zittau's in-crowd go.

Klosterstübl (☎ 517 486; Johannisstrasse 4; mains €5-13) This updated inn has an uncluttered look – all the better to show off the rich oak wainscoting, huge tile oven and hilarious murals featuring frolicking monks. The menu features several regional dishes, including *Wickelklösse* (vegetable-stuffed dumplings).

Dornspachhaus (☎ 795 883; Bautzener Strasse 2; mains €6-17) Situated next to the Johanniskirche, Zittau's oldest eatery oozes history, serves delicious regional cuisine and has a lovely courtyard. The Saxon-dialect menu is hard to decode.

Getting There & Away

A swarm of private train companies operate services out of Zittau, but the entire region is covered by a single tariff system. Direct trains run to Dresden (€18.10, 1½ hours) and Görlitz (€5.60, 40 minutes). Going to Bautzen usually requires a change in Görlitz or Löbau (€7.10, 1½ hours). For Berlin, change in Cottbus (€42.50, four hours).

AROUND ZITTAU
Zittauer Gebirge

South of Zittau, hugging the Czech and Polish borders, the Zittauer Gebirge is the smallest low-mountain range in Europe. With its idyllic gorges, thick forests and whimsical rock formations, it's great for hiking and relaxing.

You can drive or take the bus, but getting there is much more fun aboard the 110-year-old narrow-gauge **Zittauer Schmalspurbahn**. From a diddy timber station in front of Zittau's main terminus, steam locos puff year-round up to the sleepy resort villages of Oybin and Jonsdorf, splitting at Bertsdorf. The service to Oybin (€5.90, 40 minutes) stops at the **Teufelsmühle** (Devil's Mill), built for silver miners in the 17th century; here you can glimpse the **Töpfer peak** (582m) to the east.

Alternatively, you can hike to Oybin on a clearly marked trail, taking you south along the Neisse River before veering off into the hills (11km).

Burg und Kloster Oybin (☎ 7340; www.burgund kloster-oybin.de; adult/concession/family €4/3/10; ⌚ 9am-6pm Apr-Sep, 10am-4pm Oct-Mar), a romantically ruined castle and monastery on a beehive-shaped hill north of the town, was commissioned by Holy Roman Emperor and Czech King Charles IV in the 14th century. The dramatic ensemble is an ideal setting for summer concerts, or just for poking around on your own.

Saxony-Anhalt

Ask a Bavarian or Berliner about Saxony-Anhalt and they'll likely talk about the timeworn (and largely outdated) stereotypes: the industrial legacy, the slag heaps, the high unemployment and the architectural sins committed by GDR town planners. But ask a local about their state, and they'll wax lyrical about its treasures. There'll be talk about taking a gondola ride through the gentle splendours of Wörlitz Park. They'll be proud of the whimsy of the Hundertwasser buildings in Magdeburg and Lutherstadt Wittenberg. They'll encourage you to get on your bike and explore the grandeur of the Elbe River. And they'll toast you with a glass of bubbly made from grapes grown on the sunny slopes around Freyburg.

In the 20 years since reunification, Saxony-Anhalt has gone from humdrum to, well, not quite hip but certainly more happening than its reputation would suggest. Open your eyes and you'll find deep wellsprings of beauty, ingenuity and historical magnitude. After all, Otto I, the first Holy Roman Emperor, is buried in Magdeburg, Martin Luther kick-started the Reformation in Wittenberg and, centuries later, the Bauhaus school revolutionised modern design and architecture from its base in Dessau during its most creative period.

Saxony-Anhalt may not quite have the pulling power of other states but it still packs a punch. Don't just travel through on your way to somewhere else. Lose your preconceptions, unleash your curiosity and you'll discover unique places that'll still resonate with you long after you're back home.

HIGHLIGHTS

- **Grand Visions** Study the origins of modernist architecture by touring Dessau's refurbished Bauhaus gems (p224)

- **Sweet Dreams** Spend the night inside cult architect Hundertwasser's wacky Magdeburg building, Grüne Zitadelle (p219)

- **River Rides** Soak up the mystique of one of Germany's grandest rivers while pedalling along the Elbe River Bike Trail (p228)

- **Pious Peregrinations** Channel Martin Luther while walking in his footsteps in Eisleben (p236) and Wittenberg (p229)

- **Grape Escape** Sample the local product while hopping between small wine estates around Freyburg (p239).

- **Offbeat Journey** Float high above the Elbe River in one of the world's strangest bridges near Magdeburg (p221)

★ Magdeburg

Dessau-Rosslau ★   ★ Lutherstadt Wittenberg

Lutherstadt Eisleben ★

★ Freyburg

- **POPULATION: 2.41 MILLION**
- **AREA: 20,446 SQ KM**

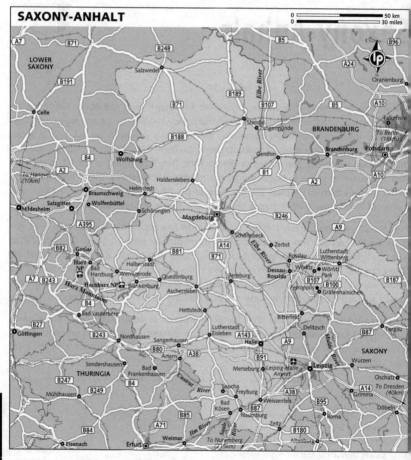

SAXONY-ANHALT

Information

For advance planning, consult the website maintained by the state tourist office at www .sachsen-anhalt-tourismus.de, which comes with a room booking function.

Getting Around

Trains are supplemented by local bus networks and an efficient road system. There are two good-value discount train tickets available in Saxony-Anhalt. The **Sachsen-Anhalt-Ticket** (€28) entitles groups of up to five people to one day of unlimited public transport within the state from 9am to 3am the following day (midnight to 3am the following day on weekends). It is valid in 2nd class on RE, RB and S-Bahn trains as well as buses and trams. The

version for solo travellers costs €19. Another good deal is the **Hopper-Ticket** (€6) which is valid for a day return to any town within 50km of your starting point. All tickets costs €2 more if bought from a train station agent instead of a vending machine.

MAGDEBURG

☎ 0391 / pop 230,000

There's no denying that much of Magdeburg is aesthetically challenged, thanks to WWII bombs and socialist city planners in love with wide boulevards and prefab concrete apartment blocks, the so-called *Plattenbauten*. But don't let this deter you: the capital of Saxony-Anhalt has plenty of surprises in store. This is, after all, one of the country's oldest cities, founded some 1200 years ago and home to the first Gothic cathedral on German soil. Magdeburg's newest architectural attraction, meanwhile, is the whimsical Grüne Zitadelle (Green Citadel), the last building of eccentric artist-architect Friedensreich Hundertwasser.

Thanks to 17,000 students, night owls can look forward to the most happening nightlife between Hanover and Berlin, then nurse their hangover in one of the city's many parks and gardens. There's so much green space here, in fact, that *Men's Health* magazine has named Magdeburg the country's second-greenest city (after Hanover). The Elbe River, too – demoted to industrial waterway in GDR times – is again a vital part of the city, lined by beer gardens, beach bars, a promenade and a paved bikeway.

Back in the 10th century, Otto I, the first Holy Roman Emperor, regarded Magdeburg as his favourite place. Find out why for yourself.

Orientation

Magdeburg's city centre is reasonably compact and easily navigated thanks to the postwar street grid. It's about a 10-minute walk from the train station to the Grüne Zitadelle and Dom and another five to the Elbe River. The main streets are east–west Ernst-Reuter-Allee and north–south Breiter Weg, which links Hasselbachplatz and the university. The city's main parks are all east of the river.

Information

INTERNET ACCESS
Mocc@ (☎ 734 6350; www.mymocca.de; Olvenstedter Strasse 45a; per hr €3; ☒ 10am to last customer Mon-Fri, from 6pm Sat) Terminals and wi-fi.

LAUNDRY
Anne's Waschparadies (☎ 541 2593; Walther- Rathenau-Strasse 60; ☒ 9am-9pm Mon-Fri, 9am-3pm Sat)

MEDICAL SERVICES
Krankenhaus Altstadt (☎ 7910; Max-Otten-Strasse 11-15) Modern, full-service hospital with emergency services.

POST
Post office (Breiter Weg 203-206; ☒ 9am-7pm Mon-Fri, 9am-noon Sat)

TOURIST INFORMATION
Tourist office (☎ 194 33; www.magdeburg-tourist.de; Ernst-Reuter-Allee 12; ☒ 10am-6.30pm Mon-Fri, to 4pm Sat Apr-Oct, 10am-6pm Mon-Fri, to 3pm Sat Nov-Mar)

Sights & Activities

The tourist office publishes free self-guided tour pamphlets that can also be downloaded from their website. Throughout town, bilingual information panels provide background about key sights and instructions for accessing additional details via your mobile phone.

DOM

This grand **cathedral** (☎ 543 0436; admission free; ☒ 10am-6pm May-Oct, 10am-5pm Nov, Dec & Apr; 10am-4pm Jan-Mar) is Magdeburg's main historical landmark and traces its roots to 937 when Otto I (912–73) founded a Benedictine monastery and had it built up into a full-fledged cathedral within two decades. Alas, fire destroyed the original a couple of centuries later. But by then the Gothic style was all the rage, which is why its successor is a three-aisled basilica with transept, choir and pointed windows. The burial place of Otto I and his English wife Editha, it's packed with artistic highlights ranging from the delicate 13th-century **Magdeburg Virgins** sculptures to a haunting **antiwar memorial** by Ernst Barlach. The church also has impressive eco-credentials: in 1990 it became the first one in eastern Germany to get its own solar roof.

Learn more during German-language **tours** (adult/concession €3/1.50; ☒ at 2pm daily, 11.30am Sunday) or ask for an English booklet (€3.50).

GRÜNE ZITADELLE

It's piglet pink and resembles an iced birthday cake accidentally stuck in the oven for a few minutes. It has towers, turrets, golden spheres, trees growing from its facade and meadows sprouting on its rooftops. Right across from the cathedral, the **Grüne Zitadelle** (Green Citadel; ☎ 620 8655; www.gruene-zitadelle.de; Breiter Weg 9; tours adult/concession/child €6/5/2.50; ☒ information office 10am-6pm, tours 11am, 3pm & 5pm Mon-Fri, hourly 10am-5pm Sat & Sun) is Magdeburg's newest, brightest and most inspired landmark. Completed in 2005, it was the final design of Viennese artist Friedensreich Hundertwasser and perfectly reflects his philosophy of creating highly unique spaces in harmony with nature, an 'oasis for humanity', as the master himself put it. Inside are offices, flats and shops, as well as a small hotel (see opposite) and a cafe. If you understand German, join the one-hour guided tours to learn more about the man and his intriguing vision.

HEGELSTRASSE & HASSELBACHPLATZ

Sometimes just turning the corner in Magdeburg can transport you into another century, metaphorically at least. Step onto tree-lined Hegelstrasse, for example, and you'll find yourself back in the early 1900s, with pristine cobbled footpaths and immaculately restored terraced buildings. It's worth continuing on to Hasselbachplatz, the city's pub quarter, where more pretty-as-a-picture historic streets radiate off the square.

ELBAUENPARK & JAHRTAUSENDTURM

One of Magdeburg's finest green patches, the **Elbauenpark** (☎ 593 4263; www.elbauenpark.de, in German; adult/concession incl Jahrtausendturm & butterfly house €3/2; ☼ 9am-8pm May-Sep, reduced hours in winter) has rose, sculpture and other gardens, plus a **butterfly house** (☼ 10am-6pm Tue-Sun Apr-Oct, 10am-4pm Nov-Mar). Its most unusual attraction, though, is the conical **Jahrtausendturm** (Millennial Tower; ☼ 10am-6pm Tue-Sun Apr-Oct), which soars 60m high and bills itself as the world's tallest wooden tower. It's fun to walk up its external spiral walkway and it looks wonderful when lit up at night. German-speakers will also be attracted by the fun, hands-on experiments and physics exhibits within.

Take tram 6 to Messegelände/Elbauenpark.

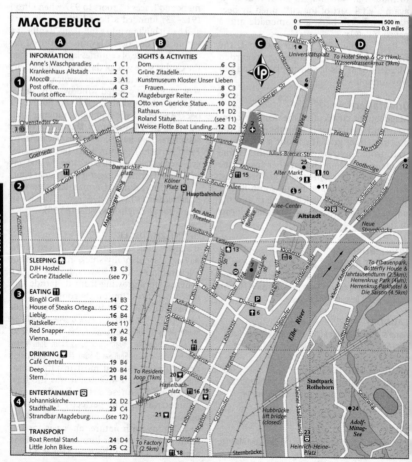

MAGDEBURG

| 0 | 500 m |
| 0 | 0.3 miles |

INFORMATION	
Anne's Waschparadies	1 C1
Krankenhaus Altstadt	2 C1
Mocc@	3 A1
Post office	4 C3
Tourist office	5 C2

SIGHTS & ACTIVITIES	
Dom	6 C3
Grüne Zitadelle	7 C3
Kunstmuseum Kloster Unser Lieben Frauen	8 C3
Magdeburger Reiter	9 C2
Otto von Guericke Statue	10 D2
Rathaus	11 D2
Roland Statue	(see 11)
Weisse Flotte Boat Landing	12 D2

SLEEPING	
DJH Hostel	13 C3
Grüne Zitadelle	(see 7)

EATING	
Bingöl Grill	14 B3
House of Steaks Ortega	15 C2
Liebig	16 B4
Ratskeller	(see 11)
Red Snapper	17 A2
Vienna	18 B4

DRINKING	
Café Central	19 B4
Deep	20 B4
Stern	21 B4

ENTERTAINMENT	
Johanniskirche	22 D2
Stadthalle	23 C4
Strandbar Magdeburg	(see 12)

TRANSPORT	
Boat Rental Stand	24 D4
Little John Bikes	25 C2

To Hotel Sleep & Go (1km); Wasserstrassenkreuz (9km)

To Residenz Joop (1km)

To Factory (2.5km)

To Elbauenpark, Butterfly house & Jahrtausendturm (2.5km); Herrenkrug Park (4km); Herrenkrug-Parkhotel & Die Saison (4.5km)

CANAL IN THE SKY

You'll rub your eyes in disbelief when you first see it: a massive water-filled bridge straddling the Elbe River. About 15km northeast of central Magdeburg, the Wasserstrassenkreuz is Europe's longest canal bridge and a miracle of modern engineering. The 918m-long 'bathtub' links two major shipping canals and has made life a lot easier for barge captains navigating between Berlin and western Germany.

You can drive yourself there (take Magdeburg-Rothensee exit off the A2), take a 4½-hour boat trip with **Weisse Flotte** (☎ 532 8891; www.weisseflotte-magdeburg.de, in German; Petriförder 1; adult/child €20.50/12; ☺ mid-Mar–Oct) or rent a bicycle (see Getting Around, p222) and pedal along the scenic Elberadweg (Elbe River Bicycle Trail).

OTHER PARKS

Closer to town, a long stretch of the eastern river bank is hemmed in by the **Stadtpark Rothehorn**, with playgrounds, picnic areas, the Stadthalle concert hall and a lovely lake where you can take your sweetie for a spin in a rowboat or while away an hour or two in a beer garden. Tram 6 stops about 300m north of the lake. Ride along to the tram terminus to get to **Herrenkrug Park**, another popular spot for strolling and cycling.

OTHER ATTRACTIONS

Magdeburg's oldest building, a decommissioned medieval monastery, is now the **Kunstmuseum Kloster Unser Lieben Frauen** (☎ 565 020; cloister admission free, museum adult/concession €2/1; ☺ 10am-5pm Tue-Sun) and presents regional sculptures and contemporary art from Saxony-Anhalt. The front door, designed by popular local artist Heinrich Apel (b 1935), is fun: you knock with the woman's necklace and push down on the man's hat to enter.

Apel also designed the relief bronze door of the 17th-century **Rathaus** (town hall) on Alter Markt square, which traces the city's history through to 1969, as well as the gilded copy of the **Magdeburger Reiter**, a famous statue of a handsome lad on horseback believed to depict Otto I. The 1240 original is considered the first freestanding equestrian statue north of the Alps. In 2005, the rider was joined on Alter Markt by a butch **Roland** statue, a symbol for municipal independence. Finally, off to the side, is a statue of local boy **Otto von Guericke** (1602–86), the father of vacuum technology.

Sleeping

DJH hostel (☎ 532 1010; www.jugendherberge.de/jh/magdeburg; Leiterstrasse 10; dm/s/tw €20/30/45, over 27yr

extra €3; P X) This large modern hostel is the total package – it's in the middle of town, close to the train station, yet on a quiet street. Rooms have shower and toilet attached, and there's even a family floor with a kiddie romper room.

Hotel Sleep & Go (☎ 537 791; www.hotel-sleep -and-go.de; Rogätzer Strasse 5a; s/d €54/60; P X) If you've outgrown hostels but don't want to drop buckets of money for your overnight digs, this friendly, family-run hotel should fit the bill. Rooms won't win style awards but you'll sleep well beneath fluffy feather duvets and can even dial into CNN on the satellite TV.

Residenz Joop (☎ 626 60; www.residenzjoop.de; Jean-Burger-Strasse 16; s €90-140, d €110-160; P X) Although not related to German clothing designer Wolfgang Joop, this boutique hotel delivers the same kind of discreet elegance and luxury. Stay in this small villa and discover that nothing is too much trouble for your hosts.

Herrenkrug Parkhotel (☎ 850 80; www.herren krug.de, in German; Herrenkrug 3; s €90-132, d €120-180; P X) Rise to chirping birds at this art-deco riverside mansion, then take a wake-up stroll through the lush surrounding park before planning the day at the breakfast buffet. Rooms are spacious and stylish and its restaurant, Die Saison (p222), is among the best in town. Although about 4km from the city centre, it's well connected by public transport.

ourpick Grüne Zitadelle (☎ 620 780; www .hotel-zitadelle.de; Breiter Weg 9; s €105-135, d €125-145, breakfast €11; P X) This hotel right in the Green Citadel channels Hundertwasser with bold colours, organic shapes and all natural materials. The nicest rooms face the inner courtyard and provide access to a grassy terrace. Those facing the street are air-conditioned.

Eating

Bingöl Grill (☎ 555 7913; Breiter Weg 231; dishes €2-5; ☯ 10am-3am Mon, Tue & Sun, to 6am Wed-Sat; ☒) In the wee hours, this unassuming Turkish shop gets howling with night owls hoping to restore balance to the brain with bulging doner kebabs.

Liebig (☎ 555 6754; Liebigstrasse 1-3; snacks €4.50-11, mains €8-12; ☯ from 10am, food until midnight) Tattooed hipsters to helmet-headed grannies, everyone loves Liebig, a trendy cafe-bar-restaurant with large outdoor terrace. Thanks to substantive breakfasts, global fare and cool cocktails it's a good spot no matter where the hands of the clock are.

House of Steaks Ortega (☎ 535 7710; Otto-von-Guericke-Strasse 104; meals €6-15; ☯ 11.30am-midnight; ☒) Surrender helplessly to your inner carnivore at this woodsy pub-style eatery where you'll join a mostly local crowd tucking into yummy cuts of aged Argentine steaks. Cholesterol-watchers can choose from a variety of pizza, pasta and salads.

Vienna (☎ 555 6166; Sternstrasse 24; lunch special €7.50, dinner mains €8-16; ☯ lunch Mon-Fri, dinner daily; ☒) If you thought a schnitzel is a schnitzel is a schnitzel (with apologies to Gertrude Stein), you'll know better after tucking into the huge and juicy contenders at this popular Austrian outpost.

Die Saison (☎ 850 8730; Herrenkrug 3; mains €18-30; ☯ 6.30-10am, noon-2pm & 6.30-10.30pm; ☒) Classic German cuisine gets a modern international twist within the ornately detailed dark-green walls of the Herrenkrug Parkhotel's art-deco dining room. Gourmets on a budget can opt for the three-course menu for €16.50.

Other eating options:

Ratskeller (☎ 568 2323; Alter Markt 6; mains €8-15; ☯ 11am-11pm Mon-Sat, to 9pm Sun) Average German food but all dishes are half price between 3pm and 5pm.

Red Snapper (☎ 737 4884; Maxim-Gorki-Strasse 18; mains €15-25; ☯ lunch Tue-Sat, dinner Mon-Sat; ☒) Romantic gourmet level fish restaurant with summer garden.

Drinking & Entertainment

The nightlife action revolves around the Hasselbachplatz. For listings, pick up a copy of *DATEs*, *Urbanite* or *Kulturfalter* (all free, all in German).

Café Central (☎ 544 2791; Leibnitzstrasse 34; ☯ from 8pm) This hip bar-cum-literary salon recreates the early 1900s with antique velvet sofas, flock wallpaper and Persian carpets. There

are comedy shows, public readings, films or lectures on many evenings, but the decor means it's always worth a visit.

Deep (☎ 0172-393 8695; Breiter Weg 231; ☯ from 7pm) This dimly lit basement bar is trendy but extremely friendly, with DJs at the deck Thursday to Saturday and killer cocktail nightly. Enter via Einsteinstrasse.

Stern (☎ 0173-580 2219; Sternstrasse 9; ☯ from 7pm) For the cheapest beer around Hasselbachplatz, make a beeline for this alt-chic *boît* with two floors of lounges and a dance floor High flirt factor.

Factory (☎ 401 8892; www.factory-magdeburg.de in German; Karl-Schmidt-Strasse 26-29; ☯ from 10pm Fri & Sat) On weekends, shaggy-haired students and skinny-jean hipsters invade this industrial space for concerts and a *Happy Feet*-inducing mix of indie rock, techno and hip hop.

Strandbar (☎ 0175-594 0059; Petriförder 1; ☯ 11am-1pm mid-Apr–Sep, weather permitting) Grab a deck chair and sink your toes into tonnes of sand lugged to this riverside beach bar that's a fine spot for chilling down the day with cocktails and electro beats.

Stadthalle (☎ 593 4520; Heinrich-Heine-Platz 1 Stadtpark Rotehorn) From Mozart to Motörhead – as Magdeburg's premier venue, this 2000-seat venue in the leafy central park has pretty much heard it all.

Johanniskirche (St John's Church; ☎ 593 4650 Jacobstrasse 1) Popular for classical music concerts, this atmospheric church dates back in parts, to 1131.

Getting There & Away

Magdeburg is directly connected to Berlin-Hauptbahnhof (€25, 1¾ hours), Leipzig (€26, 1¼ hours) and Dessau (€10.30, one hour). It's just south of the A2 to Berlin or Hanover and also served by the A14 to Leipzig.

Getting Around

Bus and tram tickets cost €1.70 for a regular single and €3.40 for a day ticket. Buy them from vending machines at each stop.

Little John Bikes (☎ 555 6203; Alter Markt 13-14; ☯ 10am-8pm Mon-Fri, 10am-4pm Sat) is a full-service bike shop that also rents two-wheelers for €10 per day (€25 for three days, €70 for a week).

For a taxi call ☎ 737 373.

DETOUR: THE ALTMARK

An hour's drive north of Magdeburg, the Altmark is an idyllic and sparsely populated region, where flat fields stretch out in all directions and horses outnumber humans. The main hub is **Stendal** (population 36,000), a former Hanseatic trading post with a cluster of splendid medieval structures scattered about its compact Altstadt. Pick up a town map at the train station, then stroll over to the **Tangermünder Tor**, one of two striking town gates; the other is the **Uenglinger Tor** on the north end of the old town.

From Tangermünder Tor, head up Schadewachten and Breite Strasse to the Kornmarkt, where you'll find the **tourist office** (☎ 651 190; www.stendal.de; Kornmarkt 8; ⏱ 9am-6pm Mon-Fri, 10am-1pm Sat, also 10am-1pm Sun Apr-Sep). The square itself is dominated by the late-Renaissance **Rathaus** (town hall), guarded by a monumental Roland statue and the twin-towered late-Gothic brick **Marienkirche**.

A bit further north awaits Stendal's most quirky attraction: a 16m-tall, 45-tonne **Trojan Horse** (the world's largest replica, according to the *Guinness Book of Records*). You can climb into the belly of the horse and enjoy great views from the top. The horse sits on the grounds of the **Winckelmann-Museum** (☎ 215 226; www.winckelmann-gesellschaft.de; Winckelmannstrasse 36-38; adult/concession/family €4/2.50/10; ⏱ 10am-6pm Apr-Sep, to 5pm Oct-Mar), which is otherwise devoted to the father of modern archaeology, local boy Johann Joachim Winckelmann (1717–68).

While you're exploring this remote region, you might as well swing by **Tangermünde** (population 9500), about 11km southeast of Stendal. Its location at the confluence of the Elbe and Tanger Rivers makes it even prettier, although it's quieter still. The second home of Charles IV, the 14th-century king of Bohemia, it's most notable for its surviving town walls, impressive towers and ruined castle. The Altstadt is a five-minute walk south of the Hauptbahnhof, along Albrechtstrasse. Turning right on Mauerstrasse and left on Notpforte takes you to the **tourist office** (☎ 223 93; www.tourismus-tangermuende.de; Markt 2; ⏱ 9am-6pm Mon-Fri, 10am-6pm Sat & Sun Apr-Oct, 10am-5pm Mon-Fri, 10am-4pm Sat, 1-4pm Sun Nov-Mar).

Stendal is directly served by train from Magdeburg (€10.30, 40 minutes). The B188 and B189 (from Magdeburg) intersect in the south of town. Regional trains link Stendal and Tangermünde (€2.10; 12 minutes), as does the B188.

EASTERN SAXONY-ANHALT

DESSAU-ROSSLAU

☎ 0340 / pop 90,000

For Bauhaus junkies, Dessau represents the mother lode. Nowhere else in the world will you find a greater concentration of original 1920s Bauhaus structures than in this city on the Elbe River. Considered the 'built manifesto of Bauhaus ideas', Dessau was the home of the most influential design school of the 20th century during its most creative period from 1925 to 1932.

You could just stop off and see all major Bauhaus sights in the course of a day or stay a bit longer to explore the city's four parks, which form part of the Gartenreich Dessau-Wörlitz (Garden Realm; p227). Alas, the townscape itself is mostly defined by the grey concrete GDR-era aesthetic.

Note that, in 2007, Dessau merged with the smaller town of Rosslau across the Elbe, resulting in an official name change to Dessau-Rosslau.

Orientation

The leading Bauhaus sights are west of the Hauptbahnhof, all within easy walking distance. The town centre lies southeast, about a 15-minute walk away. Pedestrianised Zerbster Strasse is the main drag, leading to the Markt, the town hall and a big shopping mall.

Information

Bauhaus Stiftung (Bauhaus Foundation; ☎ 650 8250; www.bauhaus-dessau.de; Gropiusallee 38; ⏱ 10am-6pm Mon-Fri) For info on, and tours of, Bauhaus buildings (also in English).

Internet cafe (Hauptbahnhof, 1st fl; per hr €2; ⏱ 10am-10pm) Up the spiral stairs of the train station, to the right of the exit doors.

Post office (Kavalierstrasse 30-32; ⏱ 8.30am-6.30pm Mon-Fri, 9am-12.30pm Sat)

SAXONY-ANHALT

Tourist office (☎ 204 1442, accommodation 220 3003; www.dessau-rosslau-tourismus.de; Zerbster Strasse 2c; ☯ 9am-6pm Mon-Fri, 9am-1pm Sat Apr-Oct, 9am-5pm Mon-Fri, 10am-1pm Sat Nov-Mar).

Sights
BAUHAUSGEBÄUDE

Across the world, many modernist masterpieces have fallen into ruin and, for a while, it looked as though a similar fate might befall the seminal **Bauhausgebäude** (Bauhaus Bldg; ☎ 650 8251; www.bauhaus-dessau.de; Gropiusallee 38; admission free; exhibition adult/concession €5/4; ☯ 10am-6pm). Fortunately, major restoration, completed in 2006, successfully staved off the wrecking ball.

If you consider the history of this school building, it's almost impossible to overstate its significance. Two key pioneers of modern architecture, Walter Gropius and Ludwig Mies van der Rohe, served as its directors. Gropius claimed that the ultimate of all artistic endeavours was architecture, and this building was the first real-life example of his vision. It was revolutionary, bringing

industrial construction techniques, such as curtain walling and wide spans, into the public domain and presaging untold buildings worldwide. The school also disseminated the movement's ideals of functionality and minimalism. The tubular steel-frame chair and other enduring industrial designs were born here.

Yet, perhaps more impressive than all these innovations is how contemporary the building looks after more than 80 years. Cubist, concrete and mostly white, it has three interconnecting rectangular wings fronted by plate-glass windows. The grey southern facade boasts the Bauhaus logo; the eastern side has quirky 'swimming pool' balconies.

Today, a smattering of postgrads from an urban studies program use some of the building but much of it is open to the public. The gift shop sells cool trinkets, books, posters and postcards.

You can hire an English-language audioguide (adult/concession €4/3) and tour the building by yourself, but it may be worth-

---

BAUHAUS: DESIGN FOR LIFE

'Less is more' asserted the third and final Bauhaus director, Ludwig Mies van der Rohe. Given that this school survived fewer than 15 years yet exerted more influence on modern design than any other, one has to bow to his logic. As Frank Whitford put it in *Bauhaus: World of Art* (1984): 'Everyone sitting on a chair with a tubular steel frame, using an adjustable reading lamp or living in a house partly or entirely constructed from prefabricated elements is benefiting from a revolution…largely brought about by the Bauhaus.'

Founded in Weimar in 1919 by Berlin architect Walter Gropius, this multidisciplinary school aimed to abolish the distinction between 'fine' and 'applied' arts, and to unite the artistic with the everyday. Gropius reiterated that form follows function and exhorted his students to craft items with an eye toward mass production. Consequently, Bauhaus products stripped away decoration and ornamentation and returned to the fundamentals of design, with strong, clean lines.

From the very beginning, the movement attracted a roll call of the era's greatest talents, including Lyonel Feininger, Wassily Kandinsky, Paul Klee, László Moholy-Nagy, Oskar Schlemmer, plus now legendary product designers Marianne Brandt, Marcel Breuer and Wilhelm Wagenfeld. After conservative politicians closed the Weimar school in 1925, the Bauhaus crew found a more welcoming reception in industrial Dessau.

Even here, though, right-wing political pressure continued against what was seen as the Bauhaus' undermining of traditional values, and Gropius resigned as director in 1928. He was succeeded by Swiss-born Hannes Meyer, whose Marxist sympathies meant that he, in turn, was soon replaced by Ludwig Mies van der Rohe. The latter was at the helm when the school moved to Berlin in 1932 to escape Nazi oppression. To no avail. Just one year later, the Nazis dissolved the school and its leading lights fled the country.

But the movement never quite died. After WWII, Gropius took over as director of Harvard's architecture school, while Mies van der Rohe (the architect of New York's Seagram Building) held the same post at the Illinois Institute of Technology in Chicago. Both men found long-lasting global fame as purveyors of Bauhaus' successor, the so-called International Style.

while joining the one-hour German **tour** (adult/concession €4/3; ☾ tours 11am & 2pm daily year-round, also noon & 4pm Sat & Sun mid-Feb–Oct) to get inside the auditorium, Gropius' office and other rooms that are otherwise off limits.

MEISTERHÄUSER

On leafy Ebertallee, a 15-minute walk west of the Hauptbahnhof, the three remaining **Meisterhäuser** (Masters' Houses; www.meisterhaeuser.de; admission to all 3 houses adult/concession €5/4, combination ticket with Bauhausgebäude €9/6; ☾ 10am-6pm Tue-Sun mid-Feb–Oct, 10am-5pm Nov–mid-Feb) line up for in-spection. The leading lights of the Bauhaus movement lived together as neighbours in these white cubist structures that exemplify the Bauhaus aim of 'design for living' in a modern industrial world.

Originally there was a stand-alone home for Gropius, plus three duplexes, each half of which provided a living/working space for a senior staff member and his family. Gropius' home was destroyed in WWII, along with one-half of the neighbouring duplex. In the febrile environment of the 1920s, you could sit at home here with the Kandinskys, on furniture donated by Marcel Breuer, and with the possibility that Paul Klee or László Moholy-Nagy might drop by for tea.

Unfortunately, the interiors are largely bereft of original furniture, which is too expensive to replace today. All this said, a visit is still an intensely satisfying aesthetic experience, with photos helping to conjure up past interiors.

Haus Feininger, former home of Lyonel Feininger, now pays homage to another German icon with the **Kurt-Weill-Zentrum** (☎ 619 595; Ebertallee 63). There's a room devoted to Dessau-born Weill, who later became playwright Bertolt Brecht's musical collaborator in Berlin, and composed *The Threepenny Opera* and its hit 'Mack the Knife'.

Next up is the **Haus Muche/Schlemmer** (☎ 882 2138; Ebertallee 65/67), which makes it apparent that the room proportions and some of the experiments, such as low balcony rails, don't really cut it in the modern world. At the same time, you also realise how startlingly innovative other features are. The partially black bedroom here is also intriguing; look out for the leaflet explaining the amusing story behind it – Marcel Breuer apparently burst in to paint it when reluctant owner Georg Muche was away on business.

The **Haus Kandinsky/Klee** (☎ 661 0934; Ebertallee 69/71) is most notable for the varying pastel shades in which Wassily Kandinsky and Paul Klee painted their walls (re-created today). There's also biographical information about the two artists and special exhibitions about their work.

One-hour German-language **tours** (adult/concession incl admission €9/6; ☾ 12.30pm Tue-Sun, 12.30pm, 1.30pm & 3.30pm Sat & Sun) meet outside the Bauhausgebäude.

KORNHAUS

Another striking Bauhaus building is the riverside **Kornhaus**, a beer-and-dance hall designed by Carl Flieger, a Gropius assistant. It's about a 20-minute walk north of the Meisterhäuser (via Elballee) and now a restaurant with Elbe views (see p226).

TÖRTEN

If the term 'housing estate' conjures up an image of grim tower blocks, rubbish-blown courtyards and shutters flapping on abandoned shop, leafy Törten, in Dessau's south, might prompt a slight rethink. Built in the 1920s, it is a prototype of the modern working-class estate. Although many of the 300-plus homes have been altered in ways that would have outraged their purist creator Walter Gropius (patios and rustic German doors added to a minimalist facade?), others retain their initial symmetry.

The **Stahlhaus** (Steel House; ☎ 858 1420; Südstrasse 5; admission free; ☾ 10am-6pm Tue-Sun Mar-Oct, to 5pm Nov-Feb) is home to a Bauhaus information centre where you can pick up an English-language pamphlet describing the architecture or join a German-language **tour** (adult/concession €4/3; ☾ tours 3pm Tue-Sun). These take you inside one of Hannes Meyer's red-brick, exterior walkway-access apartment buildings (the so-called *Laubenganghäuser*) as well as to the **Konsumgebäude** (co-op building, still the site of a communal shop) and the **Moses-Mendelssohn-Zentrum** (☎ 850 1199; Mittelring 38; adult/child €2/1; ☾ 10am-7pm Mar-Oct, 1-4pm Nov-Feb). The latter tracks the life and accomplishments of the Dessau-born humanist philosopher Moses Mendelssohn, the godfather of the Jewish Enlightenment.

To reach Törten, take tram 1 towards Dessau Süd (€1.20), get off at Damaschkestrasse and follow the signposts saying 'Bauhaus Architektur'.

OTHER ATTRACTIONS

In 2005 Dessau confirmed its reputation as an architectural trailblazer with the opening of the eye-catching new digs of the **Umweltbundesamt** (Federal Environmental Agency; Wörlitzer Platz 1; ☽ 6am-10pm Mon-Fri, 6am-4pm Sat, 8.30am-4pm Sun). Built using the latest ecological technologies, its coloured and textured facade makes a striking sight as your train pulls into town. Public art graces the parklike outdoor areas, while the lofty, light-flooded forum is open to visitors.

Aviation fans will be wowed by the vintage aircraft at the **Technikmuseum Hugo Junkers** (☎ 661 1982; www.technikmuseum-dessau.de, in German; Kühnauer Strasse 161a; adult/concession/family €3/1.50/8; ☽ 10am-5pm). Tram 1 goes straight to the museum (get off at Junkerspark) from the Hauptbahnhof.

Dessau's centre is rather Eastern Bloc – uninspiring and a mere footnote to its Bauhaus attractions. The **Rathaus**, rebuilt in simplified form after WWII, has a Bauhaus-style clock. The **Anhaltisches Theater Dessau** (☎ 251 110; www .anhaltisches-theater.de, in German; Friedensplatz 1a; tickets €6-27) is a rather pompous neo-Roman structure that was commissioned by the Nazis and is at odds with most of the town's architecture, whether it be Bauhaus or GDR.

Festivals & Events

Although more closely associated with Berlin, and later New York, the composer Kurt Weill was born in Dessau. Every March the city hosts a **Kurt Weill Festival** (www.kurt-weill.de, in German), reprising and updating his collaborations with Bertolt Brecht, such as *The Threepenny Opera*. Performances take place in Dessau and surrounds.

Sleeping

DJH hostel (☎ 619 803; www.jugendherberge.de/jh/dessau; Ebertallee 151; dm under/over 27yr €14/17, breakfast €4.50, linen €3.50; P X ⌨) When it moved to a new address, standards at Dessau's hostel leapfrogged from the 19th to the 21st century. Professionally run by friendly staff, it has 150 beds in cheerful dorms sleeping from two to seven people, each with their own bathroom. The main Bauhaus sights are just a hop, skip and jump away.

Bauhaus dorms (☎ 650 8318; unterkunft@bauhaus -dessau.de; Gropiusallee 38; s/d €25/40; P X) Since the Bauhaus school was renovated, you can channel the modernist dream by staying in the former students' dorms. Don't expect any flights of fancy, though. Rooms are of, shall we say, 'monastic' simplicity.

Hotel-Pension An den 7 Säulen (☎ 619 620; www .pension7saeulen.de, in German; Ebertallee 66; s €47-52, d €65-72; P X) Rooms at this small *Pension* are not of the latest vintage but the garden is pleasant and the breakfast room overlooks the Meisterhäuser across the leafy street. There's an ayurvedic wellness centre on site, should you be in need of a massage.

NH Dessau (☎ 251 40; www.nh-hotels.com; Zerbster Strasse 29; s €72-100, d €86-115; P X ⌨ ⌨ ⌨) The neutral white-and-grey tones somehow feel more stylish than clinical in this modern hotel set in the pedestrianised strip leading to the Rathaus and tourist office. Wrap up a day on the tourist track with a session in the rooftop sauna with attached terrace for cooling down.

Steigenberger Hotel Fürst Leopold (☎ 251 50; www.dessau.steigenberger.de; Friedensplatz; s/d from €90/115, breakfast €16; P X ⌨ ⌨) Dessau's grandest hotel is a modern contender with stylish and spacious rooms dressed in clear lines and subdued blues and reds. It's clearly geared to the suit brigade but with a bar, excellent restaurant, fitness area and beauty spa, there's plenty to appeal to leisure lizards too.

Elbpavilion (☎ 646 150; rohr@ksdw.de; 1-2/3-4 people Apr-Oct & Christmas €150/€200, Nov-Mar €75/120) Feel like a king and queen when staying in this elegant white tower right in Georgium Park, complete with fireplace but no TV or phone.

Eating

Kornhaus (☎ 640 4141; Kornhausstrasse 146; dishes €2.50-11; ☽ 10am-11pm Fri-Wed; X) In an original Bauhaus building right on the Elbe River, this place can't be beat for location, design and ambience even if the food is not terribly inspired. Dine outside on the big terrace or in the dining room with its crazily patterned carpet.

L'Appart (☎ 661 5975; Zerbster Strasse 8; snacks €2.50-6, mains €10-15; ☽ 11.30am-midnight, food to 9pm; X) The jazzy decor is a great foil for the tasty fare at this upbeat French brasserie with a nice terrace overlooking the market square and town hall. Locals in the know invade the place for the €5 weekday lunch specials.

our pick Pächterhaus (☎ 650 1447; Kirchstrasse 1; mains €15-22; ☽ noon-3pm, 5-10pm Tue-Sun; X) Foodies on a mission won't mind making the small detour to this gorgeously restored half-timbered farm house where seasonal and locally sourced ingredients get the gourmet treatment. In fine weather do anything to bag a table on the idyllic terrace beneath a canopy of vines.

The food's only so-so, but Bauhaus fanatics can fuel up right in the storied Bauhausgebäude. Report either to the bright white **Bauhaus Mensa** (☎ 650 8421; Gropiusallee 38; dishes €2.50-5.50; ✆ 8am-2pm Mon-Fri; ✗) or to the slightly more welcoming **Bauhaus Klub** (☎ 650 8444; Gropiusallee 38; dishes €3-9; ✆ 9am-6pm Mon-Fri, 10am-midnight Sat, 10am-6pm Sun; ✗) in the basement.

Getting There & Around
Regional trains serve Dessau from Berlin-Hauptbahnhof (€21, 1¾ hours), Lutherstadt Wittenberg (€6.90, 40 minutes) as well as Leipzig, Halle and Magdeburg (all €10.30, one hour). The Berlin-Munich autobahn (A9) runs east of town.

Single bus and tram tickets cost €1.50, day passes are €4.50. Bikes can be hired from **Mobilitätszentrale** (☎ 213 366; per day €3-7; ✆ 9am-5pm Mon-Fri year-round, 9am-1pm Sat & Sun May-Sep) outside the Hauptbahnhof or from **Beckers Radhaus** (☎ 216 0113; Wilhelm-Feuerherdt-Strasse 13; per day from €6; ✆ 11am-midnight Mon-Fri, 11am-2pm Sat).

GARTENREICH DESSAU-WÖRLITZ
Aside from being a mecca of modern architecture, Dessau and surrounds are home to the Gartenreich Dessau-Wörlitz (Garden Realm), one of the finest garden ensembles in Germany. The parks reflect the vision of Prince Leopold III Friedrich Franz von Anhalt-Dessau (1740–1817). A highly educated man, he travelled to Holland, Italy, France and Switzerland for inspiration on how to apply the philosophical principles of the Enlightenment to the design of a landscape in harmony with nature, architecture and art. In 2000, Unesco recognised his efforts by putting the gardens onto its list of World Heritage Sites. Each of the six English-style gardens comes with its own palace and other buildings, in styles ranging from neoclassical to baroque to neo-Gothic.

The Garden Realm is embraced by the Unesco-protected **Biosphärenreservat Mittlere Elbe** (Biosphere Reserve Middle Elbe; www.biosphaerenreservatmittlereelbe.de, in German). Nature lovers should stop at the **information centre** (☎ 034904-4060; Am Kapenschlösschen 3, Oranienbaum) on the way to Schloss Oranienbaum. There's also a nearby **beaver compound** (adult/child €1/0.50; ✆ 1-4pm Sat & Sun Apr, 11am-5pm Mon-Fri May-Oct, by arrangement at other times), where you can watch the animals through a screen.

Orientation
The six parks are scattered over 142 sq km. The most central is Georgium, being just five minutes' walk from Dessau Hauptbahnhof. The most impressive, Wörlitz, is also the further at about 18km east of town. Mosigkau is about 7km southwest of central Dessau, while Luisium lies 3km east. Oranienbaum is 14km southeast of Dessau or 6km south of Wörlitz. Finally, Grosskühnau is about 5km northwest of central Dessau.

Information
The Dessau tourist office (p224) has all the information you need, or stop by **Wörlitz-Information** (☎ 034905-202 16, room reservations 194 33; www.woerlitz.de; Förstergasse 26; ✆ 9am-6pm Mar-Oct, 9am-4pm Mon-Fri Nov-Jan, 9am-5pm Mon-Fri & 11am-3pm Sat & Sun Feb).

Sights
WÖRLITZ PARK & SCHLOSS
With peacocks feeding on the lawn before a neo-Gothic house, a tree-lined stream flowing towards a Grecian-style temple and a gap in a hedge framing a distant villa, the 112-hectare English-style **Wörlitz Park** (admission free) is the pinnacle of Prince Leopold's garden region. Take your sweet time to saunter among this mosaic of paths, hedges and follies, but don't even think about having a picnic on the sprawling lawns: even walking on them is very much verboten, as is bicycling within park grounds.

Between May and October, hand-cranked **ferries** (tickets €0.60; ✆ 10am-6.30pm daily May-Sep, 11am-5pm daily Apr & Oct, noon-5pm Sat & Sun Mar & Nov) cross the Wörlitzer See, which lies between garden sections. Also during these months, 45-minute **gondola tours** (tickets €6; ✆ 10am-6pm May-Sep, 11am-4pm Apr & Oct) ply the lake, departing when eight people or more gather at the dock – this doesn't take long in summer; indeed the problem is more often too many customers for gondolas. Weekend concerts are another summer highlight.

On the edge of the park nearest the town lies Prince Leopold's former country house, the neoclassical **Schloss Wörlitz** (☎ 034905-4090; tours €4.50; ✆ 10am-6pm Tue-Sun May-Sep, to 5pm Apr & Oct, closed Nov-Mar), which is still filled with original late-18th-century furniture and decorations.

Bus 334 runs from Dessau to Wörlitz roughly every two hours between 6am and 5.30pm (€2, 30 minutes). From late March to early October, there's also train service on Wednesday, Saturday and Sunday (€3, 35 minutes). Check the timetable carefully before heading out or, better yet, check with the information kiosk Mobilitätszentrale (see Getting There & Around, p227) outside the train station. By road from Dessau, take the B185 east to the B107 north, which brings you right into town.

OTHER PARKS & PALACES
Just a five-minute walk from Dessau Hauptbahnhof, the sprawling 18th-century **Georgium** is anchored by the neoclassical **Schloss & Park Georgium** (☎ 0340-613 874; www.georgium.de, in German; Puschkinallee 100; adult/concession/family €3/2/7; ☒ 10am-5pm Tue-Sun), now a picture gallery showcasing German and Dutch old masters, including Rubens and Cranach the Elder. The leafy grounds are also dotted with ponds and fake Roman ruins, including a triumphal arch and a round temple.

Southwest of central Dessau, is **Schloss & Park Mosigkau** (☎ 0340-521 139; Knobelsdorffallee 3, Dessau; admission €4.50; ☒ 10am-5pm Tue-Sun Apr & Oct, 10am-6pm May-Sep, close Nov-Mar), a petite rococo palace that's been called a 'miniature Sanssouci'. Many of the 17 rooms retain their original furnishings, although the highlight is the Galleriesaal with paintings by Rubens and Van Dyck. In summer, play hide-and-seek in the leafy labyrinth. To get there, take bus 16 to Schloss.

East of central Dessau, towards Wörlitz **Schloss & Park Luisium** (☎ 0340-218 3711; Dessau; admission €4.50; ☒ 10am-6pm Tue-Sun May-Sep, to 5pm Apr & Oct, closed Nov-Mar) is an intimate neoclassical refuge framed by an idyllic English garden scattered with neo-Gothic and classical follies it's reached via bus 13 to Vogelherd.

The baroque **Schloss & Park Oranienbaum** (☎ 034904-202 59; admission €4.50; ☒ 10am-5pm Sat & Sun Apr & Oct, 10am-6pm Tue-Sun May-Sep, closed Nov-Mar, is south of Wörlitz and reached by bus 331. **Landschaftspark Grosskühnau** is near the southern end of Kühnau lake; its modest palace is home to administrative offices and not open to the public.

FERROPOLIS
Some 15km south of Wörlitz, Ferropolis answers that nagging question: 'What do you do with an abandoned open-pit GDR coal mine and leftover mining equipment that look like they were dispatched from some postapocalyptic nightmare?'

In 1991, some Bauhaus-inspired designers came up with a solution – a 25,000-seat concert venue and museum…of course! An amphitheatre was built, the mine pit was filled with water diverted from the Mulde River, and the monstrous machines (with charming names like Mad Max, Big Wheel and Medusa) were placed just so.

The **museum** (☎ 034953-351 20; www.ferropolis .com, in German; adult/concession/family €4/3/8; ☒ 10am-6pm Mon-Fri, 10am-7pm Sat & Sun May-Oct, 10am-5pm Nov-Apr) is an interesting monument to mining, and the changes wrought by industrial society. It's also a popular concert and event venue. You can watch a grand ireworks show, catch Linkin Park live or channel a 21st-century Woodstock vibe at uch music festivals as **Splash** (www.splash-festival. e), featuring hip-hop and reggae, and **Melt** www.meltfestival.de).

From Dessau, take bus 331 (in the direction of Gräfenhainichen) to the stop Jüdenberg 107/Ferropolis (€3, 42 minutes); note that his is the third stop with Jüdenberg in its name. From here, it's a dusty 2km walk into he grounds. By car, take the B185 east to the 107 and turn south towards Gräfenhainichen 20 minutes in all); the entrance to Ferropolis s on your left, just past Jüdenberg. Driving rom Lutherstadt Wittenberg, take the B100 o its junction with the B107 and turn north; he entrance is on the right.

UTHERSTADT WITTENBERG
☎ 03491 / pop 47,500

As its full name suggests, Wittenberg is first nd foremost associated with Martin Luther 1483–1546), the monk who triggered the German Reformation by publishing his 95 heses against church corruption (see boxed ext, p232) in 1517. A university town since 502, Wittenberg back then was a hotbed of progressive thinking that also saw priests get married and educators like Luther buddy Philipp Melanchthon argue for schools to accept female pupils. Today, Wittenberg etains its significance for the world's 340 million Protestants, including 66 million Lutherans, as well as for those who simply admire Luther for his principled stand against authority. Sometimes called the 'Rome of the Protestants', its many Reformation-related ites garnered it the World Heritage site nod rom Unesco in 1996.

As a result, Wittenberg's popularity has teadily grown since reunification and – like t or not – even a nascent Luther industry has developed. 'Hier stehe ich. Ich kann nicht anders' (Here I stand. I can do no other), Luther had declared after being asked to renounce his Reformist views at the Diet of Worms. Today, you can buy souvenir socks bearing he same credo.

Orientation

All major sights conveniently line up along Collegienstrasse, which runs east–west and becomes Schlossstrasse west of the Markt. From the Hauptbahnhof it's about a 10-minute signposted walk to Collegienstrasse.

Some trains also stop at Wittenberg-Altstadt, putting you within five minutes of Schlossplatz.

Information

Internetcafé Dot.Komm (☎ 505 052; Fleischerstrasse 6; per hr €3; ☯ 2-11pm Sun-Thu, 2pm-midnight Fri & Sat)
Hospital (Paul-Gerhard-Stiftung; ☎ 500; Paul-Gerhardt-Strasse 42)
Post office (Wilhelm-Weber-Strasse 1)
Tourist office (☎ 498 610; www.wittenberg.de; Schlossplatz 2; ☯ 9am-6.30pm Mon-Fri, 10am-4pm Sat & Sun Apr-Oct, 10am-4pm Mon-Fri, 10am-2pm Sat, 11am-3pm Sun Nov-Mar, closed Sat & Sun Jan & Feb)

Sights
LUTHERHAUS

Even those with no previous interest in the Reformation will likely be fascinated by the state-of-the-art exhibits in the **Lutherhaus** (☎ 420 30; www.martinluther.de; Collegienstrasse 54; adult/concession €5/3; ☯ 9am-6pm daily Apr-Oct, 10am-5pm Tue-Sun Nov-Mar), the former monastery turned Luther family home. Through an engaging mix of accessible narrative (in German and English), spotlit artefacts (eg, his lectern from the Stadtkirche, indulgences chests, Bibles, cloaks), famous oil paintings, and interactive multimedia stations, you'll learn about the man, his times and his impact on world history. Highlights include Cranach's *Ten Commandments* in the refectory and an original room furnished by Luther in 1535. Kids love the new exhibit in the cellar, which uses wooden models and sensor-activated sound effects to depict everyday scenes from the life of the Luther family.

In warm weather, the museum's courtyard cafe is an inviting spot for a pick-me-up and even comes with a view of excavations, including (ahem!) Luther's toilet.

Nearby, on the corner of Lutherstrasse and Am Bahnhof, the **Luthereiche** (Luther Oak) marks the spot where the preacher burned the 1520 papal bull threatening his excommunication; the tree itself, though, was only planted around 1830.

MELANCHTON HAUS

Near the Lutherhaus, the rather text-heavy **Melanchthon Haus** (☎ 403 279; Collegienstrasse 60; adult/concession €2.50/1.50; ☯ 9am-6pm daily Apr-Oct, 10am-5pm Tue-Sun Nov-Mar) discusses the life of university lecturer and humanist Philipp Melanchthon. An expert in ancient languages, Melanchthon helped Luther translate the Bible into German from Greek and Hebrew, becoming the preacher's friend and his most eloquent advocate. Combination tickets with the Lutherhaus are €6 (no concession).

SCHLOSSKIRCHE

Did or didn't he nail those 95 theses to the door of the **Schlosskirche** (Castle Church; ☎ 402 585; Schlossplatz; admission free; ☑ 10am-6pm Mon-Sat, 11.30am-6pm Sun, to 4pm Nov-Easter)? We'll never know for sure, for the original portal was destroyed by fire in 1760 and replaced in 1858 with a massive bronze version inscribed with the theses in Latin. (Also see the boxed text, p232).

Luther himself is buried inside below the pulpit, opposite his friend and fellow reformer Philipp Melanchthon. Pick up an information sheet by the entrance so you don't walk past the other eye-catchers, such as the bronze memorial of Frederick the Wise, by Peter Vischer of Nuremberg, in a niche to the left of the altar.

For a fitness fix, climb up the **Schlossturm** (castle tower; adult/concession €2/1; ☑ noon-4pm Mon-Fri, 10am-5pm Sat & Sun), but be warned that the

floor feels a little shaky in parts, and the view is expansive rather than breathtaking.

STADTKIRCHE ST MARIEN

If the Schlosskirche was the billboard used to advertise the forthcoming Reformation, the twin-towered **Town Church of St Mary** (☎ 40 201; Jüdenstrasse 35; admission free; ☑ 10am-6pm Mon-Sat, 11.30am-6pm Sun, to 4pm Nov-Easter) was where the ecumenical revolution began, with the world's first Protestant worship services in 1521. It was also here that Luther preached his famous Lectern sermons in 1522, and where he married ex-nun Katharina von Bora three years later.

The centrepiece is the large altar, designed jointly by Lucas Cranach the Elder and his son. The side facing the nave shows Luther, Melanchthon and other Reformation figures as well as Cranach himself, in biblical contexts. The altar is also painted on its reverse side. On the lower rung, you'll see a seemingly defaced painting of heaven and hell; medieval students etched their initials into the painting's divine half if they passed their final exams – and into purgatory if they failed.

WITTENBERG WORSHIP

From May to October, a changing roster of Lutheran guest preachers, usually from the US, holds free English-language services in Wittenberg's historic sites. Organised by the **Wittenberg English Ministry** (☎ 498 610; www.wittenberg-english-ministry.com; Schlossplatz 2), these are held at 5pm on Saturday in the Schlosskirche or the Stadtkirche. From Wednesday to Friday, half-hour services are also offered at 4.30pm in the tiny Fronleichnamskapelle (Corpus Christi Chapel) attached to the Stadtkirche.

CRANACH-HÖFE

Lucas Cranach's old residential and work digs have been rebooted as a beautifully restored cultural complex built around two courtyards that often echo with music and readings. There's a permanent **exhibit** (☎ 420 1913; Markt 4; admission €4/3; ☺ 10am-5pm Mon-Sat, 1-5pm Sun Apr-Oct, 10am-1pm Tue-Sat, 1-5pm Sun Nov-Mar) on the man, his life and his contemporaries. Also here is the **Historische Druckerstube** (Historical Print Shop; ☎ 432 917; Schlossstrasse 1; admission free; ☺ 9am-noon, 1-5pm Mon-Fri, 10am-1.30pm Sat), a basement gallery selling ancient-looking black-and-white sketches of Martin Luther, both typeset and printed by hand. A small hotel should have opened on the premises by the time you're reading this.

HAUS DER GESCHICHTE

If you want to catch a glimpse of daily life beyond the Iron Curtain, pop by the **Haus der Geschichte** (House of History; ☎ 409 004; www.pflug ev.de, in German; Schlossstrasse 6; adult/senior & student €5/3.50; ☺ 10am-6pm Mon-Fri, 11am-6pm Sat & Sun). The ground floor is devoted to temporary exhibitions, while the two upper levels take you through recreated GDR-era living rooms, children's rooms and kitchens alongside such environs as a pub, a store, a kindergarten and other public spaces. There's something oddly endearing about the toys, clunky early consumer items, and the tins and jars that would have been sheer gold for the son recreating the good ol' East in the movie *Good Bye, Lenin!*

HUNDERTWASSERSCHULE

How would you like to study grammar and algebra in a building where trees sprout from the windows and gilded onion domes balance above a rooftop garden? This fan-tastical environment is everyday reality for the lucky 1300 pupils of Wittenberg's **Hundertwasserschule** (Hundertwasser School; ☎ 881 131; Strasse der Völkerfreundschaft 130; tours adult/concession €2/1; ☺ 10am-5pm). It was the penultimate work of eccentric Viennese artist, architect and eco-visionary Friedensreich Hundertwasser, who was famous for quite literally thinking 'outside the box'. In Wittenberg, he transformed a boxy GDR-era concrete monstrosity into a colourful and curvy dreamscape. You can view the exterior any time, but tours of the interior wait for at least four participants before they start. Ring ahead for tours in English.

The school is a 20-minute walk northeast of the centre. From the Markt, head east on Jüdenstrasse, turn left into Neustrasse and continue into Geschwister-Scholl-Strasse. Turn left into Sternstrasse, right into Schillerstrasse, and the school is at the next intersection on the left.

Activities

Wittenberg is a key stop on the 860km **Elberadweg** (Elbe River Bike Trail) and a great departure point for shorter excursions along the idyllic river. The tourist office can make suggestions and help with logistics. One particularly fine route is the 43km roundtrip to the Garden Realm Dessau-Wörlitz (p227).

For bike rental, head to **Fahrradhaus Kralisch** (☎ 403 703; www.fahrradhaus-kralisch.de, in German; Jüdenstrasse 11; per 24hr €7; ☺ 9am-noon Mon-Sat, 1-6pm Mon-Fri).

Tours

The tourist office runs various tours, including a standard two-hour **spin around town** (adult/child €8/4.50; ☺ several daily Easter-Oct, in German). DIY types might prefer renting a portable audioguide (€6 and your passport as deposit) with commentary in English and other tongues. If you have your own mobile, you can also get the nitty-gritty on key sights by dialling up ☎ 08122-9999 5682 plus a dedicated extension. The tourist office has a flyer on this particular scheme.

The **MS Lutherstadt Wittenberg** (☎ 769 0433; Schlossstrasse 16; ☺ booking office 10am-5pm Tue-Fri) runs 1½-hour panoramic river cruises (€10) on the Elbe from March to October. Check with the booking office about sailings and how to find the pier in Dessauer Strasse.

Good Bye, Lenin! fans might get a kick out of negotiating Wittenberg's streets squeezed

---

LUTHER LORE

'When the legend becomes fact, print the legend,' a journalist famously tells Jimmy Stewart in the classic Western movie *The Man Who Shot Liberty Valance,* and that is exactly what has happened with Martin Luther and his 95 theses. It's been so often repeated that Luther nailed a copy of his revolutionary theses to the door of Wittenberg's Schlosskirche on 31 October 1517, that only serious scholars continue to argue to the contrary.

Certainly, Luther did write 95 theses challenging some of the Catholic practices of the time, especially the selling of 'indulgences' to forgive sins and reduce the buyer's time in purgatory. However, it's another question entirely as to whether he publicised them in the way popular legend suggests.

Believers point to the fact that the Schlosskirche's door was used as a bulletin board of sorts by the university, that the alleged posting took place the day before the affluent congregation poured into the church on All Saints' Day (1 November), and the fact that at Luther's funeral, his influential friend Philipp Melanchthon said he witnessed Luther's deed.

But Melanchthon didn't arrive in town until 1518 – the year *after* the supposed event. It's also odd that Luther's writings never once mentioned such a highly radical act.

While it's known that he sent his theses to the local archbishop to provoke discussion, some locals think it would have been out of character for a devout monk, interested mainly in an honest debate, to challenge the system so publicly and flagrantly without first exhausting all his options.

In any event, nailed to the church door or not, the net effect of Luther's theses was the same. They triggered the Reformation and Protestantism, altering the way that large sections of the world's Christian population worship to this day.

---

behind the wheel of a tinny East German Trabant car. **Event & Touring** (☎ 03492-266 507; www.event-touring.com; per 3hr from €38) can make it happen. Contact them directly or go through the tourist office.

Festivals & Events

Wittenberg is busiest during **Luthers Hochzeit** (Luther's Wedding festival) in early or mid-June, and for **Reformationsfest** (Reformation Festival) held on 31 October.

Sleeping

The tourist office operates a free room reservation service in person or by phone at ☎ 498 612. Private rooms start at €19 per person.

Brückenkopf Hotel Marina-Camp Elbe (☎ 4540; www.marina-camp-elbe.de; Brückenkopf 1; adult/child €5/4, tent €7-10, car €4, hotel s/d €43/66, breakfast €6; ☻ year-round; ℗ ☒ ⌨) How many camping grounds come with their own wine cellar? This riverside one does, along with a marina, a restaurant, a hotel, holiday apartments, beach volleyball, table tennis, a sauna, laundry facilities and other useful amenities. Bonus: the dreamy views of the town silhouette.

DJH hostel (☎ 403 255; www.jugendherberge .de/jh/wittenberg; Schlossstrasse 14/15; dm under/over 27yr €14/17, s/d €27/54, breakfast €4.50, linen €3.50; ℗ ⌨)

Take crummy old hostel, move into new digs and reboot as bouncy, contemporary shelter. It's a recipe that's worked beautifully for Wittenberg's contender, whose 40 bright rooms sleep up to six people and come with bathrooms, bedside reading lamps and private cabinets.

Pension am Schwanenteich (☎ 402 807; www .wittenberg-schwanenteich.de; Töpferstrasse 1; s €36-47, d €64-74; ℗ ☒ ⌨) At these prices you know you're not getting the Ritz, but if you want friendly and familiar ambience and simple but comfy rooms, this humble *Pension* should fit the bill. The restaurant serves four-course menus of German soul food for €12.50.

Stadthotel Wittenberg Schwarzer Baer (☎ 420 4344; www.stadthotel-wittenberg.de; Schlossstrasse 2; s €56-65, d €69-85; ℗ ☒ ⌨) The modern rooms in this 500-year-old heritage-listed building (no lift) are light, airy and clean-smelling, with wooden floors and cork headboards. Staff are on the ball, too.

our pick **Alte Canzley** (☎ 429 190; www.alte-canzley .de; Schlossplatz 3-5; s €70-125, d €84-139; ℗ ☒ ⌨) The nicest place in town for our money is in a 14th-century building opposite the Schlosskirche. Each of the eight spacious units are furnished in dark woods and natural hues, named for a major historical figure and equipped with a itchenette. The vaulted downstairs harbours axony-Anhalt's first certified organic restau- ant (dishes €4 to €17).

Luther-Hotel (☎ 4580; www.luther-hotel-wittenberg le; Neustrasse 7-10; s €69-104, d €85-122; P X 🛜) 'ou'll sleep like an angel in this sparkling, nodern place affiliated with a Christian harity organisation. Don't expect monas- ic austerity, just good-sized and cheerfully oloured rooms, most of them with unim- •eded Stadtkirche views. A sauna invites •ost-sightseeing unwinding.

ating & Drinking

asinoberg (☎ 400 148; Pfaffengasse 28a; dishes €3-10; ☺ from 6pm) If you like your beer and pub grub with a side of local colour, swing by this water- ng hole presided over by the congenial Willi Vitt. Beer garden in summer.

In Vino Veritas (☎ 769 0565; Mittelstrasse 3; dishes 6-8; ☺ dinner; X) Antipasti, tapas, salads or asta dishes form the perfect accompaniment o the global wine menu at this upmarket nodern bistro. Locals in the know invade for he Friday buffet (€12.90).

Brauhaus Wittenberg (☎ 433 130; Im Beyerhof, Markt ; mains €4-12; ☺ 11am-11pm) This place – with a obbled courtyard, indoor brewery and shiny opper vats – thrums with the noise of people aving a good time. The menu is hearty but lso features smaller dishes for waist-watchers. Jpstairs are a few simple rooms with air-con singles/doubles €50/70).

Café Emmas Bier- & Caféhaus (☎ 419 757; Markt 9; hains €7.50-16; ☺ closed Mon evening; X) Take a step •ack to the 'good old times' in this German ountry kitchen, where servers wear frilly white aprons and the room is chock-full of •ric-a-brac – from dolls and books to irons nd a gramophone.

Café de Marc (☎ 459 114; Pfaffengasse 5; ☺ 10am- pm Tue-Sun; X) This French cafe with its un- •retentious literary vibe is a delightful find or breakfast, java jolts or a refined calvados. When the sun's out, the idyllic courtyard is he place to be.

A series of pubs at the eastern end of Collegienstrasse include **Sweet Apple** (No 38), vhere you can suck on a hookah pipe, and the lt-flavoured **Independent** (☎ 413 257; No 44).

ntertainment

\s you might imagine, Wittenberg is pretty lead after dark, although the cultural centre alled **Barrik** (☎ 403 260; www.barrik.eu; Collegienstrasse

81; ☺ Wed-Sat) does its best to entertain the troops with live comedy, dance, cabaret and transvestite shows.

From May to October, meditate to organ music at 6pm Friday in the Stadtkirche and at 2.30pm Tuesday in the Schlosskirche.

Getting There & Away

Wittenberg is on the main train line to Halle and Leipzig (both €11.30, one hour). ICE (€29, one hour) and RE trains (€20, 1¼ hours) travel to Berlin. Coming from Berlin, be sure to board for 'Lutherstadt- Wittenberg', as there's also a Wittenberge west of the capital.

Getting Around

Lutherstadt Wittenberg is tiny and best ex- plored on foot or by bike. Parking enforce- ment is quite stringent, so use the car parks on the fringes of the Altstadt (such as near Elbtor and along Fleischerstrasse).

SOUTHERN SAXONY-ANHALT

HALLE
☎ 0345 / pop 232,000

It's gradually fading, but even more than two decades after reunification, you can still feel the dread hand of the communist era on Halle more than in other Eastern cit- ies. It was the centre of the GDR's chemical industry and some old-timers still grumble that the town was punished for its 'complic- ity' when losing out to Magdeburg as capital of Saxony-Anhalt in 1990.

Still, anyone who's visited the birth town of composer Georg Friedrich Händel over the past decade would agree that Halle has pulled itself up by its bootstraps, spurred partly by the desire to properly celebrate its 1200th anniversary in 2006. The old town and the market square have been put through a thorough makeover and money was also poured into updating such key cultural institutions as the Händel-Haus and the state art gallery in Moritzburg cas- tle. For culture vultures especially, Halle is increasingly becoming an essential stop on an eastern Germany itinerary.

Orientation

The Altstadt lies northwest of the Haupt-bahnhof. It's about a 15-minute walk to the central Markt and the tourist office; head left from the main entrance and turn left, then follow pedestrianised Leipziger Strasse.

Information

Internetcafe Speed (Am Bauhof 1; per 20min €1; ☑ 10am-midnight Mon-Fri, noon-midnight Sat, 2-10pm Sun)

Post office (Marktplatz 20; ☑ 9.30am-8pm Mon-Sat)

Tourist office (☎ 122 9984; www.stadtmarketing-halle .de; Marktplatz 13; ☑ 9am-8pm Mon-Fri, 10am-4pm Sat year-round, 10am-4pm Sun May-Oct) Sells the Halle Welcome Card (one/three days €7.50/15) good for free public transport and discounted tours and museum admissions.

Sights

MARKTPLATZ

Halle's market square is famous for its 'Five Tower' ensemble formed by the protuber-ances of the **Rote Turm** (Red Tower), a free-standing bell tower, and the **Marktkirche Unser Lieben Frauen** (☎ 517 0894; admission church free, Luther exhibit €2; An der Marienkirche 2; ☑ 10am-5pm Mon-Sat, 3-5pm Sun Mar-Dec, noon-5pm Mon-Sat, 3-5pm Sun Jan & Feb). The latter is a nice enough church that counts Luther's original death mask, made of wax, and the Renaissance pulpit from which he preached, as its most prized possessions. They're displayed in a separate exhibit in the northwest tower. A statue of Händel, who was baptised in the church, graces the square itself, which received a total makeover for the town's 1200th anniversary in 2006. A new fountain recalls Halle's medieval heyday as a major salt-mining and -trading town, while a daily farmers' market adds life, colour and flair.

HÄNDEL-HAUS

The house in which Georg Friedrich Händel (1685–1759) was born in 1685 is now the **Händel-Haus** (☎ 500 900; www.haendelhaus.de, in German; Grosse Nikolaistrasse 5; adult/concession €4/2.50; ☑ 10am-6pm Tue-Sun Apr-Oct, to 5pm Nov-Mar). An exhibit charts the composer's life, achieve-ments and impact on the evolution of clas-sical music with an emphasis on his wider European career. There's the usual assort-ment of artwork, manuscripts, letters, doc-uments and musical instruments, but it's all rather engagingly displayed and made more accessible with the help of a multi-language audioguide. In the second week of

June Halle hosts a prestigious **Händel Festiva** (www.haendelfestspiele.halle.de).

KUNSTMUSEUM MORITZBURG

The late-Gothic Moritzburg castle forms fantastic setting for the superb art collection c the **Kunstmuseum des Landes Sachsen-Anhalt** (Sta Art Museum; ☎ 212 590; www.kunstmuseum-moritzburg.d Friedemann-Bach-Platz 5; adult/concession €5/3; ☑ 10am 8.30pm Tue, 10am-6pm Wed-Sun). The recent addi tion of a glass and aluminium roof over th north and west wings, which had been ruine since the Thirty Years' War (1618–48), nearl doubled the exhibition area. Airy and skyli the new space is entirely dedicated to classica modern art, starting with works by members c the early-20th-century avant-garde group Di Brücke (Kirchner, Heckel, Schmidt-Rottluff and moving on to post-1945 art, primarily b East German artists such as Werner Tübk and Bernhard Heisig. Particularly striking ar Lyonel Feininger's paintings of famous Hall landmarks. Older parts of the castle showcas 19th-century works by Liebermann, Corint and Beckmann as well as medieval paintin and sculpture.

BURG GIEBICHENSTEIN

If it's views of the town and Saale valley yo want, you can't do much better than makin the trip up to this romantically ruined **cast** (☎ 523 3857; Seebener Strasse 1; adult/child €2.10/1.3 ☑ 10am-5pm Tue-Fri, 10am-6pm Sat & Sun Apr-Oct Wander among the remaining fortification and check out the tower and ancient vaulte cellars. Tram 7 will get you here.

Below the castle, at the Giebichenstein brücke (bridge) are the landing docks of th **Reederei Riedel** (☎ 283 2070; www.reederei-riede -halle.de, in German; adult/child €4.50/2.50), which run 45-minute river tours hourly from 10an to 6pm (no tours Monday) between Ma and September. The ticket office is on th Rheinpfalz ship.

BEATLES MUSEUM

Take a 'magical mystery tour' through the lif and music of the Fab Four at the Continent' only full-time **Beatles Museum** (☎ 290 3900; www .beatlesmuseum.net; Alter Markt 12; adult/child €5/3; ☑ 10am 8pm Wed-Sun, last entry 7pm). Uberfan Rainer Moer has amassed enough knick-knacks to cram three floors with baby photos, birth certifi cates, album covers, film posters, wigs, jig saws and even talcum powder – nothing i oo trivial to be displayed. The gift shop sells many Beatles souvenirs.

Sleeping

Citystation Hostel (☎ 315 4413; www.hostel-halle.de; Magdeburger Strasse 28; dm €15-16, s/d/tr €25/38/51, linen 3, breakfast €4; ☒ ☐ ☎) This cute hostel near the train station is a wallet-friendly base of operation with a communal kitchen, bicycle rentals (per day €3) and cheerfully painted rooms sleeping one to six.

Marthahaus (☎ 510 80; www.stiftung-marthahaus.de, German; Adam-Kuckhoff-Strasse 5; s €45-60, d €65-85; ☒) Hospitality is taken very seriously at this quiet hotel run by the Christian mission that manages the adjacent retirement home. It offers fine value for money with soft carpet underfoot, cosy, well-furnished rooms and stained-glass windows in the lounge, stairwell and beautiful dining hall.

Ankerhotel Halle (☎ 232 3200; www.ankerhofhotel.de; Ankerstrasse 2a; s €70-100, d €90-125; ☐ ☒ ☒ ☐) Walls clad in local stone and ceilings supported by heavy wooden beams hark back to the 19th century when this was the Royal Customs Office. Completely modernised, it's now one of Halle's most charming hotels with stylish and good-sized rooms; the nicest have river views. There's even a gym and saunas (yes, plural) for sweating it out.

Apart-Hotel Halle (☎ 525 90; www.apart-halle.de; Kohlschütter Strasse 5-6; s/d/ste from €72/89/115; ☐) If you like a hotel with a flair for the dramatic, this plush villa in a residential quarter some 10 minutes' walk from the centre is your stage. It has classic rooms but also fantastical propelled and mural-swathed themed suites, including 'Serengeti', 'Martin Luther' and 'King Ludwig II'.

Dorint Charlottenhof Halle (☎ 292 30; www.dorint.com/halle; Dorotheenstrasse 12; r €80-130, breakfast €15; ☐ ☒ ☒ ☎ ☒) OK, it's a chain and caters largely to the business brigade, so don't expect too much in terms of character. However, if you're looking for a modern, efficient hotel with lots of amenities – including a pool, gym and sauna for post-sightseeing unwinding – this one should fit the bill nicely.

Kempinski Hotel Rotes Ross (☎ 233 430; www.kempinski-halle.de; Leipziger Strasse 76; r €100-190, breakfast €18; ☐ ☒ ☒ ☎ ☒) With over 300 years' experience in the hospitality business, the Kempinski is Halle's five-star heavyweight with sumptuous public areas and ultra-comfy if rather stuffy rooms with Italian marble baths.

Eating

Café NT (☎ 205 0232; Grosse Ulrichstrasse 51; dishes €3-9; ☒) Exuding the casual charm of a Viennese coffeehouse, this artsy spot affiliated with the edgy Neues Theater is a good place for writing those postcards over coffee, beer or a light meal. After the show, thirsty theatre-lovers invade for heated critiques and cold cocktails.

Sushi Bar am Opernhaus (☎ 681 6627; August-Bebel-Strasse 3; dishes €3-12; ☺ lunch Mon-Fri, dinner daily; ☒ ☑) Piscine morsels as they should be: fresh, without any gimmicks and beautiful to look at. This sushi parlour delivers on all fronts. Greedy guts should come for the all-you-can-eat deal (€15.50) on Tuesday and Sunday nights.

Ökoase (☎ 290 1604; Kleine Ulrichstrasse 2; mains €4.50-12; ☺ 10am-5pm Mon-Sat, 6pm-midnight Wed-Sat; ☒) Hippie types, waist-watchers and enlightened eaters crowd this buzzy vegetarian restaurant to munch on daily organic specials inspired by the world's cuisines. Arabic tomato soup, Greek vegetable stew or Swiss chard coconut soup are typical menu entries.

Hallesches Brauhaus (☎ 212 570; Grosse Nikolaistrasse 2; mains €4-15; ☺ from 11am Mon-Fri, 10am Sat & Sun) Sure, they make their own beer, but that's not the only reason to steer towards this contemporary brewpub. Fortunately, food here is not an afterthought and if you're lusting after hearty German fare, you'll feel quite Piccadilly here.

Palais S (☎ 977 2651; Ackerstrasse 3c; mains €7-14; ☺ from 6pm Mon-Sat, from 10am Sun; ☒) From paella to *pelmeni*, by way of pasta, schnitzels and Argentine steaks – this lively restaurant, in a large half-timbered house on the river, really does offer the 'jungle' of choices it promises. In fine weather, tables on the waterfront terrace are the most coveted. Follow the signs through the business park.

Also recommended:

Wok-Bar (☎ 470 0990; Bernburger Strasse 16; dishes €5-11; ☺ 11.30am-10pm Mon-Fri, from 5.30pm Sat & Sun; ☒) Put together your own stir fry by checking from a list of ingredients.

Chateau & Co (☎ 388 0420; Am Kirchtor 27; mains €9-20; ☺ dinner daily, lunch Sun; ☒) Fresh, seasonal and solid international fare, creative but without culinary pyrotechnics.

Drinking & Entertainment

Finding a party pen to match your mood is easy in Halle's trifecta of fun strips: Kleine Ulrichstrasse, Sternstrasse and the

SAXONY-ANHALT

Bermudadreieck (between Seebener Strasse and Burgstrasse near Burg Giebichstein). Also consult the free zines *Aha!*, *Blitz* or *Frizz*.

Potemkin (☎ 959 8138; Kleine Ulrichstrasse 27; 🕑 9am-1am; ✗) Potemkin has been shaking up Halle's nightlife with libational flights of fancy in an impressive range for many years. In the daytime it's a place for breakfast, panini or a java jolt.

Charivari (☎ 494 8386; Kaulenberg 1; 🕑 from 6pm; ✗) Knock back a couple of 'brewskis' if you need to loosen your nerves before belting out your best J Lo or Justin at this bar-cum-karaoke joint. Featuring over three dozen varieties, the beer menu is not for the indecisive. For sustenance, you can have pasta and pizza delivered from the next-door restaurant.

Objekt 5 (☎ 522 0016; Seebener Strasse 5; ✗) At this alt-flavoured venue you can catch folk, rock and avant-garde concerts and hit the dance floor on Friday and Saturday nights. There's daytime chilling in the beer garden and decent grub (mains €5.50 to €10.50) in the adjacent building. Tram 8 takes you there.

Turm (☎ 202 3737; www.turm-halle.de, in German; Friedemann-Bach-Platz 5; 🕑 from 10pm Wed, Fri & Sat) In the Moritzburg, this old student club flaunts a been-here-forever pedigree but has solidly arrived in the present tense. Three times weekly, DJs spin a heaving mix of techno, house, drum and bass and hip hop for energetic, style-conscious party animals.

Getting There & Away

AIR

Leipzig-Halle Airport (☎ 0341-224 1155; www.leipzig-halle-airport.de) lies about equidistant between both cities, which are about 45km apart. It is served by domestic and international flights from two dozen airlines, including Lufthansa, Germanwings, Air Berlin, Condor and Austrian Airlines.

The airport is linked with Halle Hauptbahnhof at least twice hourly by RE (€3.60, 11 minutes) and IC (€6, 11 minutes) trains.

CAR & MOTORCYCLE

From Leipzig, take the A14 west to the B100. The A14 connects Halle and Magdeburg in about one hour. The B91 runs south from Halle and links up with the A9 autobahn, which connects Munich and Berlin.

TRAIN

Leipzig and Halle are linked by frequen regional (€6, 35 minutes) and IC (€9.50, 2 minutes) trains. Magdeburg is served b IC trains (€19, 50 minutes) and RE train (€15.20, 70 minutes); ICs also go to Berli (€36, 1¼ hours). Local trains serve Eislebe (€6.90, 45 minutes) and Wittenberg (€11.3(one hour).

Getting Around

Trams 2, 5, 7 and 9 run from the train statio to the Marktplatz. Rides cost €1.70 (€1.20 fo rides of up to four stops) or €4 for day cards

For drivers, the one-way street system i Halle is fiendishly complex, and the street busy. Your best bet is to park near th Hauptbahnhof, or at one of the municipa garages, and take trams.

LUTHERSTADT EISLEBEN
☎ 03475 / pop 23,800

It seems odd for a well-travelled man whos ideas revolutionised Europe to have died i the town where he was born. However, a native son Martin Luther (1483–1546) himsel put it before expiring here, *'Mein Vaterlan war Eisleben'* (Eisleben was my fatherland Whereas Lutherstadt Wittenberg has othe distractions, this former mining town focuse on the devout follower these days. Every when you turn, it's Luther, Luther, Luther.

Orientation & Information

Most sights are knotted together aroun the Markt, just north of Hallesche Strasse the main thoroughfare and location of th **tourist office** (☎ 602 124; www.eisleben-tourist.d Hallesche Strasse 4; 🕑 10am-5pm Mon & Wed-Fri, to 6p Tue, 10am-1pm Sat). To get there from the sta tion, it's a 10-minute walk via Bahnhofsrin and Bahnhofstrasse.

Sights

LUTHER SITES

The house where the reformer was born **Luthers Geburtshaus** (☎ 602 124; Lutherstrasse 1! adult/concession €4/2.50; 🕑 10am-6pm daily Apr-Oc 10am-5pm Tue-Sun Nov-Mar) has been a memoria site since 1693. It was recently fully restore and docked to a 19th-century school for th poor via a modern complex. The house itsel is furnished period-style, while exhibits i the annex focus on the family of Luther an aspects of the society in which he grew up.

Luther returned to Eisleben in January 1546 o help settle a legal dispute for the Count of Mansfeld, but he was already ill and died on 8 February, a day after finalising an agreement. Today, **Luthers Sterbehaus** (Luther's Death ouse; ☎ 602 124; Andreaskirchplatz 7; adult/concession 2/1; ☯ 9am-6pm daily Apr-Oct, 10am-5pm Tue-Sun Nov-Mar) contains the reconstructed death chamber with a death mask and the original pall that overed Luther's coffin. Although it was long elieved that this was where Luther departed his world, new research has revealed that he ctually died in a building on the site now occupied by the Hotel Graf von Mansfeld below). With such a long tradition of people aying respects to him here, however, there re no plans to move the exhibition.

MARKT & CHURCHES

Luther delivered his last sermons in the **St ndreaskirche** (Andreaskirchplatz; admission €1; ☯ 10am-oon & 2-4pm Mon-Sat, 10am-1pm & 2-4pm Sun May-Oct), a ate-Gothic hall church on the hill behind the entral Markt. While district vicar, he stayed n the apartments of the **St Annenkirche** (☯ 10am-pm Mon-Fri, 2-4pm Sat May-Oct), 10 minutes west of he Markt. This church also features a stunning Steinbilder-Bibel (stone-picture Bible; 585), the only one of its kind in Europe, nd a wittily decorated pulpit. Finally, see he church where Luther was baptised, the **St etri Pauli Kirche** (Church of Sts Peter & Paul; admission 1; ☯ 10am-noon & 2-4pm Mon-Fri, 11am-4pm Sat & Sun ay-Oct) near the tourist office.

leeping & Eating

Mansfelder Hof (☎ 612 620; www.mansfelderhof.de, in erman; Hallesche Strasse 33; s/d €40/51, breakfast €9; **P**) Behind its vine-covered, faded green stucco acade, the Mansfelder Hof turns out to have modern if rather generic rooms. The restaurant serves Greek food.

Hotel Graf von Mansfeld (☎ 663 00; www.hotel eisleben.de; Markt 56; s/d from €65/95; **P** ✕) Eisleben's remier in-town hotel is a classic outpost of harm and tradition. Although over 500 years ld, it has seriously slicked-up rooms with our-poster beds, and bright and airy flair. The restaurant serves modern international uisine (mains €8.50 to €17).

Hotel an der Klosterpforte (☎ 714 40; www losterpforte.com; Lindenstrasse 44; s €65-85, d €80-120; **P** ✕ ☞) Part of the medieval Helfta monstery, this friendly hotel delivers comforts y the bucket. Plan your next day's adven-ture in the onsite brewery, the restaurant, the beer garden or your spacious and uncluttered room. It's away from the centre, so it helps if you're motorised.

Getting There & Away

There are frequent trains to Halle (€6.90, 45 minutes) where you can change for Lutherstadt Wittenberg (€22, 1¾ hours), Leipzig (€13.30, 70 minutes), Magdeburg (€24, 1¾ hours) and Weimar (€21.20, 2¼ hours).

Eisleben is a half-hour drive west of Halle on the B80.

SAALE-UNSTRUT REGION

It will never rival the likes of Bordeaux as a connoisseur's paradise, but the wine-growing region along the rivers Saale and Unstrut nevertheless provides a wonderfully rural summer retreat. Europe's most northerly wine district produces crisp whites and fairly sharp reds, which you can enjoy at wine tastings, sometimes right at the estates. The 60km bicycle-friendly **Weinstrasse** (Vineyard Rd) meanders through the region, past steeply terraced vineyards, castle-topped hills and small family-owned farms. Local tourist offices sell copies of *Weinstrasse-Land der Burgen*, a regional map showing the main route and associated bicycle paths.

NAUMBURG

☎ 03445 / pop 39,000

At the confluence of the Saale and Unstrut Rivers, today Naumburg sits again as pretty and picturesque as it had for 1000 years. Gone is the pall of heavy industry that hung over the town during the GDR era. Gone too is the stifling presence of the Soviet military that set up a garrison here after WWII. After much restoration and beautification, Naumburg is again ready for its close-up, proud to show off its handsome Altstadt with the striking Renaissance Rathaus and the Marientor double gateway and, most of all, its famous medieval cathedral. In late June, this normally sedate town goes wild during the **Kirschfest** (Cherry Festival; www.kirschfest.de), a celebration of food, drink, music, a parade and fireworks.

Orientation & Information

The Hauptbahnhof is 1.5km northwest of the old town and the Markt, the central square

SAXONY-ANHALT

and site of the **tourist office** (☎ 273 125; www
.naumburg-tourismus.de; Markt 12; ☺ 9am-6pm Mon-Fri,
9am-4pm Sat, 10am-1pm Sun Apr-Oct, 9am-6pm Mon-Fri,
9am-2pm Sat Nov-Mar). To get there, either board
the Naumburger TouristenBahn, a GDR-
era tram (€1.50) or walk along Rossbacher
Strasse (keep bearing left and uphill) past
the cathedral. There's a post office at
Heinrich-von-Stephan-Platz 6.

Sights

DOM

The enormous **Cathedral of Sts Peter & Paul**
(☎ 230 110; Domplatz 16-17; adult/concession/child €4/3/2;
☺ 9am-6pm Mon-Sat, noon-6pm Sun Mar-Oct, 10am-4pm
Mon-Sat, noon-4pm Sun Nov-Feb) is a masterpiece of
medieval architecture and a treasure trove of
superb sculpture. Blueprints were drafted at
a time when the Gothic was supplanting the
Romanesque style. While the crypt and the
east choir, for instance, feature elements of
the latter, the famous west choir is a prime
example from the early Gothic period. This is
where you find the dozen **monumental statues**
of the cathedral founders, including those of a
regal-looking couple called Uta and Ekkehard.
They are the work of the so-called Master
of Naumburg, who also crafted the dizzying
rood screen, which illustrates the Passion with
almost excruciating realism.

The dome's interior exudes a calming seren-
ity achieved by soft light filtering in through
superbly detailed **stained-glass windows**. The
medieval ones were recently joined by ruby-
red modern panes by Neo Rauch, one of the
premier artists of the New Leipzig School.
Look for them in the St Elisabeth Chapel, also
home to one of the oldest statues of the saint,
carved shortly after her canonisation in the
early 13th century.

More riches await in the **Domschatzgewölbe**
(cathedral treasury; adult/concession €2/1; ☺ open same
hours as cathedral), where highlights include an
altar painting by Lucas Cranach the Elder and
a heart-wrenching 14th-century pietà.

NIETZSCHE HAUS

Friedrich Nietzsche (1844-1900) spent most
of his childhood in this modest **home** (☎ 201
638; Weingarten 18; adult/concession €2.50/1; ☺ 2-5pm
Tue-Fri, 10am-4pm Sat & Sun Apr-Oct), acquired by his
mother after the death of her husband. In
1890, she brought her son back here to nurse
him as he was going slowly mad, allegedly as
a result of syphilis. The exhibit consists mostly

of photos, documents and reams of biographi
cal text, and requires a lot of concentration
just like Nietzsche's writings. The emphasis i
more on the man and his life rather than hi
philosophy, controversial works or influenc
on later generations.

Sleeping & Eating

Camping Blütengrund (☎ 261144; www.campingnaumbu
.de, in German; Blütengrund 6; adult/tent/car €5/4.65/2.4C
☺ year-round) This leafy, sport-orientated cam
site, 1.5km northeast of Naumburg at the rive
confluence, has its own canoe and bicycle rent
als. Don't have your own tent? Sleep in a tipi ir
the Indian Village (adult/child €11/8).

DJH hostel (☎ 703 422; www.jugendherberge.de/j
/naumburg; Am Tennisplatz 9; dm under/over 27yr €12/15, s/
€18/30, breakfast €4.50, linen €3.50) Naumburg's larg
and well-equipped hostel is 1.5km south c
the town centre.

Hotel Garni St Marien (☎ 235 40; fax 235 42;
Marienstrasse 12; s/d €45/65; ℗) If you're into Frett
linen and pillow treats, look elsewhere. But i
you consider a friendly welcome, quiet room
and a modest price-tag assets, this little B&
might be where you want to hang your hat.

Hotel Stadt Aachen (☎ 2470; www.hotel-stad
-aachen.de, Markt 11; s/d/tr €62/73/98) Watch the ac
tion on the bustling market square right from
your room window in this traditional inn
with its vine-covered facade. After a heart
dinner in the downstairs restaurant, you ca
retire to good-sized rooms decked out ir
rustic furnishings.

Zur Alten Schmiede (☎ 243 60; www.hotel-zur-alte
-schmiede.de; Lindenring 36-37; s €68, d €90-105; ℗
At the snazziest place to stay in Naumburg
rooms neither skimp on space nor on cha
risma, especially if you can score one of th
newly renovated ones. Robust fare is serve
in the ground-floor restaurant.

Zum Alten Krug (☎ 200 406; Lindenring 44; mains €4-
☒) Although many come here just for a col
beer, this rustic inn also serves a range of cas
ual fare, from succulent ribs to fried sausage
all best paired with their mild sauerkraut.

Getting There & Away

Regional trains chug to Naumburg from Hall
(€7.20, 45 minutes), Jena (€6.90, 45 minutes
and Weimar (€8.40, 30 minutes). A loca
line runs to Freyburg (€2.50, eight minutes
For Leipzig, hop on the fast ICE train (€1
40 minutes).

For boat trips to Freyburg, see opposite.

By road from Halle or Leipzig, take the A9 to either the B87 or the B180 and head west; the B87 is less direct and more scenic, though it's the first exit from the A9.

FREYBURG
☎ 034464 / pop 5200

With its cobblestone streets and medieval castle clinging to vine-covered slopes, Freyburg has a vaguely French atmosphere, the sort of village that puts the 'r' in rustic. Sparkling wine production has been the main source of income here since the middle of the 19th century, and to this day Freyburg is home to Germany's most famous bubbly brand, the Rotkäppchen Sekt (named for the Little Red Riding Hood from the Grimm fairytale). The town seriously comes alive for its wine festival in the second week of September.

Orientation & Information

To reach the town centre from the train station, turn right at RegioBike (see right), left into the park and cross the bridge over the river. For the castle, take the second road to the right (Schlossstrasse). Keep bearing left for the Markt and the **tourist office** (☎ 272 60; www.freyburg-info.de; Markt 2; ☾ 9am-5pm Mon-Thu, to 6pm Fri, 8.30am-2pm Sat).

Sights

Established in 1856, and the biggest sparkling wine producer in Germany, the **Rotkäppchen Sektkellerei** (☎ 340; www.rotkaeppchen.de, in German; Sektkellereistrasse 5; tours €5; ☾ tours 11am & 2pm daily, also 12.30pm & 3.30pm Sat & Sun) is one of the few companies that survived the GDR and, since reunification, has acquired enough muscle to buy other brands, including Mumm.

The two-hour tours take in the historic cellars and the production facilities as well as a two-storey 120,000L oak barrel decorated with ornate carvings (no longer in use) and the Lichthof, a glorious skylit hall used for concerts. In the end, you get a glass of bubbly to quench your thirst. Between 10am and 5pm, you can also taste and buy a whole range of Sekt at the shop out front.

Naumburg's other attraction is the large medieval **Schloss Neuenburg** (☎ 355 30; www .schloss-neuenburg.de; Schloss 25; adult/concession €4/2.50, with tour €6/4.50; ☾ 10am-6pm Apr-Oct, 10am-5pm Tue-Sun Nov-Mar), on the hill above town. It houses an excellent museum that illuminates various aspects of medieval life. There's also a rare Romanesque two-storey (or 'double') chapel and a free-standing tower, the **Dicker Wilhelm** (adult/concession €1.50/1; ☾ 10am-6pm Tue-Sun Apr-Oct), which has further historical exhibitions and splendid views. Castle/tower combination tickets are €5/3.

Getting There & Around

Freyburg is about 9km north of Naumburg and served by trains (€2.50, eight minutes) and buses (€2.50, 23 minutes). The well-marked bicycle route between the two towns makes for a wonderful ride. Bikes can be hired from **RegioBike** (☎ 7080; Bahnhofstrasse 4; per day €8; ☾ 7am-6pm Mon-Fri, 9am-noon Sat).

Perhaps the most scenic way to get to Freyburg is by boat from Blütengrund, at the confluence of the Saale and Unstrut Rivers, just outside Naumburg. The historic, 19th-century **MS Fröhliche Dörte** (☎ 03445-202 830) tootles its way up the Unstrut at 11am, 1.30pm and 4pm daily between April and October. The 70-minute journey costs €6.50 per adult and €3.50 per child one way, and €12 and €7.50 return. It runs back from Freyburg at 12.15pm, 2.45pm and 5.15pm.

Drivers should follow the B180.

SAXONY-ANHALT

Harz Mountains

The Harz Mountains, rising up from the north German Plain as an 'island' of high, forest-clad hills, straddle the states of Saxony-Anhalt, Thuringia and Lower Saxony. They are picturesque rather than spectacular, extending about 100km from west to east and widening to only 30km. Here you find excellent hiking trails in Harz National Park, opportunities for mountain-biking or road cycling, and even the chance to downhill or cross-country ski in a good season.

Many an illustrious visitor has graced the Harz trails. Goethe was frequently seen striding them and set 'Walpurgisnacht', an early chapter of *Faust,* on the highest Harz mountain, the Brocken; later, satirical poet Heinrich Heine spent a well-oiled night on the mountain, as described in *Harzreise* (Harz Journey; 1824).

History, though, is chequered here. From 1952 until reunification, the region was divided between West and East Germany, a single region straddling the Iron Curtain but following two very different paths. Access to border regions of the east were strictly controlled by checkpoints that prevented East German's dashing over to the West.

Today, the mixed deciduous forests and rugged landscape of the eastern regions are strong attractions in the Harz, and revamped infrastructure means interesting hubs in the east like Wernigerode and Quedlinburg are becoming more popular than their counterparts in the west. Nevertheless, the Western Harz has much to offer, and visiting towns such as Goslar, St Andreasberg and Clausthal-Zellerfeld will amply reward the curious traveller.

HIGHLIGHTS

- **Pagan Rituals** Trek to the Brocken or party on Hexentanzplatz, Thale, for Walpurgisnacht (p259)
- **Evening on the Trail** Hike by torchlight through snow outside St Andreasberg for the evening wild deer feeding at the Rehberger Grabenhaus (p248)
- **Views of Past Ages** Stroll among 1400 half-timbered houses from six centuries in Quedlinburg before relaxing with a coffee on a hilltop cafe overlooking town (p255)
- **Free Wheeling** Get on a mountain bike and pedal the forest trails (p251) behind Wernigerode in the Harz National Park
- **Mother Lode** Descend rocky shafts into the mining past in Clausthal-Zellerfeld (p249) and explore 1000 years of mining history in Goslar (p243)
- **Mountain Steaming** Wind through the spectacular wilds of the Selketal from Quedlinburg or Gernrode on a steam train (p250)

HARZ MOUNTAINS

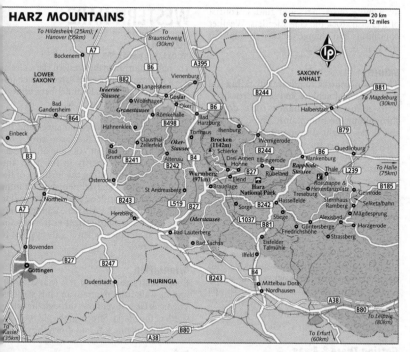

HARZ MOUNTAINS

Information

The main information centre for the Harz Mountains is the **Harzer Verkehrsverband** (☎ 05321-340 40; www.harzinfo.de; Marktstrasse 45; ☼ 8am-5pm Mon-Thu, to 2pm Fri) in Goslar, but information on the Eastern Harz is best picked up in towns there, particularly in Wernigerode.

For information on camping, ask at any tourist office for the free *Der Harz Camping* brochure (in German), which lists major camping grounds and facilities that are open all year.

The kind of map that you choose will depend on the type of activity you have planned. *Der Harz und Kyffhäuser* 1:50,000 map (€5.80) provides a good overview of trails and major sites in the entire Harz.

A local *Kurtaxe* (resort tax; ranging from €0.75 to €3 per night) is charged in most towns. Your resort card will give various discounts on sights and activities. Discount offers include the HarzTourCard (three days, €18), which gives free travel and reduced admission to attractions, and the HarzMobilCard (one month, €13), which is transferable and

entitles the user to concession-priced tickets on buses, trains and any other public transport in the Harz region. A four-day HarzCard (adult/child €27/17) gives free admission to most major museums and includes a return trip on the Brockenbahn to the summit of the Brocken (p253).

Activities
CYCLING

Anyone seeking a challenge will enjoy cycling or mountain biking in the Harz, especially in quieter eastern areas. Buses will transport your bike when space allows.

HIKING

The main attraction in summer is hiking the integrated trail network in the Harz National Park. Trail symbols are colour-coded in red, green, blue and yellow on a square or triangular plate. **Harzklub** (www.harzklub.de, in German) hiking association maps also show trail numbers; the 1:50,000 editions are the best for hikers. Harzklub offices in mountain towns are also good sources of information, including hiking tips, itineraries and the availability of partners and guides. Tourist offices also stock the club's leaflets. Weather conditions can change quickly throughout the year; be prepared.

SKIING
The main centres for downhill skiing are Braunlage, Hahnenklee and St Andreasberg, with many other smaller runs dotted throughout the mountains. The quality of the slopes might disappoint real enthusiasts; conditions for cross-country skiing, however, can be excellent, with lots of well-marked trails and equipment-hire shops. For weather reports and snow conditions, ring the **Harzer Verkehrsverband** (☎ 05321-340 40). There's also a German-language **information service** (☎ 05321-200 24).

SPAS
Often mocked by young Germans as a pensioners' paradise, the Harz is sprinkled with thermal spas and baths where the weary and/or infirm can take a cure. Most spa towns have a *Kurzentrum* (spa centre) or *Kurverwaltung* (spa administration), which often doubles as a tourist office.

Getting There & Away
The area's main towns of Goslar, Wernigerode and Quedlinburg are serviced by frequent trains; contact **Deutsche Bahn** (☎ reservations 118 61, automated timetable information 0800-150 7090; www.bahn.de).

BerlinLinienBus (www.berlinlinienbus.de) connects Berlin with Goslar (one way €29, six hours) and some smaller towns, and there are plenty of regional bus services to take you further into the mountains.

If you're driving, the area's main arteries are the east–west B6 and the north–south B4, which are accessed via the A7 (skirting the western edge of the Harz on its way south from Hanover) and the A2 (running north of the Harz between Hanover and Berlin).

Getting Around
The Harz is one part of Germany where you'll rely on buses as much as trains, and the various local networks are fast and reliable. Narrow-gauge steam trains run to the Brocken and link major towns in the Eastern Harz.

WESTERN HARZ

GOSLAR
☎ 05321 / pop 43,000
The hub of tourism in the Western Harz, Goslar has a charming medieval Altstadt, which, together with its historic Rammelsberg mine, is a Unesco World Heritage Site.

Founded by Heinrich I in 922, the town's early importance centred on silver and the Kaiserpfalz, the seat of the Saxon kings from 1005 to 1219. It fell into decline after a second period of prosperity in the 14th and 15th centuries, reflecting the fortunes of the Harz as a whole, and relinquished its mine to Braunschweig in 1552 and then its soul to Prussia in 1802. The Altstadt, Rammelsberg mine and Kaiserpfalz attract visitors by the busload in summer, when it's always best to reserve ahead.

Orientation
Rosentorstrasse leads to the Markt, a 10 minute walk from the train and bus stations. The small Gose River flows through the centre south of the Markt. Streets in the old town are numbered up one side and down the other.

Information
City-Textilpflege (☎ 242 77; Petersilienstrasse 9; �} 9am-6pm Mon-Fri, 9am-1pm Sat) Laundry.
Deutsche Bank (☎ 757 20; Fischemäkerstrasse 13) Bank services and ATM.
Dr-Herbert-Nieper-Krankenhaus (☎ 440; Kösliner Strasse 12) Medical services, about 6km north of town.
Harzer Verkehrsverband (☎ 340 40; www.harzinfo .de; Bäckergildehaus, Marktstrasse 45; �} 8am-5pm Mon-Thu, to 2pm Fri) Tourist information.
Police (☎ 3390; Heinrich-Pieper-Strasse 1)
Post office (Klubgartenstrasse 10)
Telecenter & Internetcafe (�} 381 80; Breite Strasse 79; per hr €1.80; �} 10am-7.30pm Mon-Sat) Internet access.
Tourist-Information (☎ 780 60; www.goslar.de; Markt 7; �} 9.15am-6pm Mon-Fri, 9.30am-4pm Sat, 9.30am-2pm Sun Apr-Oct, 9.15am-5pm Mon-Fri, 9.30am-2pm Sat Nov-Mar)

Sights
AROUND THE MARKT
One of the nicest things to do in Goslar is to wander through the historic streets around the Markt. **Hotel Kaiserworth** (p244) was erected in 1494 to house the textil

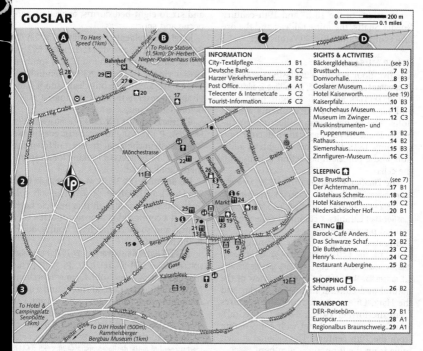

GOSLAR

INFORMATION
City-Textilpflege....................1 B1
Deutsche Bank........................2 C2
Harzer Verkehrsverband.......3 B2
Post Office..............................4 A1
Telecenter & Internetcafe 5 C2
Tourist-Information..............6 C2

SIGHTS & ACTIVITIES
Bäckergildehaus..................(see 3)
Brusttuch..............................7 B2
Domvorhalle...........................8 B3
Goslarer Museum...................9 C3
Hotel Kaiserworth............(see 19)
Kaiserpfalz...........................10 B3
Mönchehaus Museum..........11 B2
Museum im Zwinger...........12 C3
Musikinstrumenten- und
    Puppenmuseum..............13 B2
Rathaus................................14 C2
Siemenshaus........................15 B3
Zinnfiguren-Museum..........16 C3

SLEEPING
Das Brusttuch....................(see 7)
Der Achtermann...................17 B1
Gästehaus Schmitz...............18 C2
Hotel Kaiserworth...............19 C2
Niedersächsischer Hof........20 B1

EATING
Barock-Café Anders...............21 B2
Das Schwarze Schaf.............22 B2
Die Butterhanne...................23 C2
Henry's..................................24 C2
Restaurant Aubergine..........25 B2

SHOPPING
Schnaps und So...................26 B2

TRANSPORT
DER-Reisebüro.....................27 B1
Europcar................................28 A1
Regionalbus Braunschweig..29 A1

guild, and sports almost life-size figures on its orange facade. The impressive late-Gothic **Rathaus** comes into its own at night, when light shining through stained-glass windows illuminates the stone-patterned town square. The highlight inside is a beautiful cycle of 16th-century religious paintings in the **Huldigungssaal** (Hall of Homage; adult/child €3.50/1.50; 11am-3pm Mon-Fri & 10am-4pm Sat & Sun Apr-Oct & Dec).

The **market fountain**, crowned by an ungainly eagle symbolising Goslar's status as a free imperial city, dates from the 13th century – the eagle itself is a copy – the original is on show in the Goslarer Museum (p244). Opposite the Rathaus is the **Glockenspiel**, a chiming clock depicting four scenes of mining in the area. It plays at 9am, noon, 3pm and 6pm.

The baroque **Siemenshaus** (Schreiberstrasse 12) is the 17th-century ancestral home of the Siemens industrial family, but the interior is unfortunately closed to visitors. The **Brusttuch** (p244), at Hoher Weg 1, and the **Bäckergildehaus**, on the corner of Marktstrasse and Bergstrasse, are two fine early 16th-century houses.

KAISERPFALZ

Goslar's pride and joy is the reconstructed 11th-century Romanesque palace, **Kaiserpfalz** (311 9693; Kaiserbleek 6; adult/concession €4.50/2.50; 10am-5pm Apr-Oct, 10am-4pm Nov-Mar). After centuries of decay into a historic pile of rubble, this palace was resurrected in the 19th century and adorned with interior frescoes of idealised historical scenes. On the southern side is **St Ulrich Chapel**, housing a sarcophagus containing the heart of Heinrich III. Below the Kaiserpfalz is the recently restored **Domvorhalle**, displaying the 11th-century Kaiserstuhl, the throne used by Salian and Hohenstaufen emperors. Behind the palace, in pleasant gardens, is an excellent sculpture by Henry Moore called the *Goslarer Krieger* (Goslar Warrior).

RAMMELSBERGER BERGBAU MUSEUM

About 1km south of the town centre, the shafts and buildings of this 1000-year-old **mine** (7500; www.rammelsberg.de; Bergtal 19; adult/concession €11/6.50; 9am-6pm, last admission 4.30pm) are now a museum and Unesco World Heritage Site. Admission to the mine includes a German-language tour and a pamphlet with English

HARZ MOUNTAINS

explanations of the 18th- and 19th-century Roeder Shafts, the mine railway and the ore processing section. Bus 803 stops here.

OTHER MUSEUMS

The five-floor private **Musikinstrumenten- und Puppenmuseum** (☎ 269 45; Hoher Weg 5; adult/child €3/1.50; ⏰ 11am-5pm) will delight both kids and fans of musical instruments and/or dolls. The owner began collecting instruments about 50 years ago; the doll collection spanning 1835-1935 is his daughter's addition, and a porcelain collection is housed in the cellar.

The **Zinnfiguren-Museum** (☎ 258 89; www.zinn figurenmuseum-goslar.de, in German; Klapperhagen 1; adult/concession €4/2; ⏰ 10am-5pm Tue-Sun Apr-Oct, to 4pm Nov-Mar) exhibits a colourful collection of painted pewter figures.

Situated just east of the Zinnfiguren-Museum, the **Goslarer Museum** (☎ 433 94; König-strasse 1; adult/concession €4/2; ⏰ 10am-5pm Tue-Sun Apr-Oct, to 4pm Nov-Mar) offers a good overview of the natural and cultural history of Goslar and the Harz. One room contains the treasures from the former Goslar Dom (cathedral), and there's also a cabinet with coins dating from the 10th century. The original golden eagle from the fountain is also here.

The **Mönchehaus Museum** (☎ 295 70; Mönchestrasse 3; adult/child €5/1.50; ⏰ 10am-5pm Tue-Sat), in a 16th-century half-timbered house, has changing exhibits of modern art, including works by the most recent winner of the prestigious Kaiserring art prize – past winners include Henry Moore, Joseph Beuys and Rebecca Horn. Look for the interesting sculptures in the peaceful garden.

For a real 'scream', take a look inside the **Museum im Zwinger** (☎ 431 40; www.zwinger .de; Thomasstrasse 2; adult/child €2/1.60; ⏰ 10am-5pm Apr-Oct, 10am-4pm Mar, closed mid-Nov–Feb), a 16th-century tower that was once part of the ramparts, which has a collection of such late-medieval delights as torture implements, coats of armour and weapons used during the Peasant Wars.

Sleeping

DJH hostel (☎ 222 40; jh-goslar@djh-hannover.de; Rammelsberger Strasse 25; under/over 27yr dm €20.10/23.10, s €25.10/28.10, d €22.60/25.60; P ✗ 💻) Take bus 803 to Theresienhof to reach this pretty hostel out near the mining museum. Facilities are excellent, with single and twin rooms

and six to eight-bed dorms, as well as barbecue and sports areas.

Hotel & Campingplatz Sennhütte (☎ 225 02; Clausthaler Strasse 28; adult/child €5/2, car/tent €3/2, s/d €25/50) This camping ground is 3km south of Goslar via the B241 (bus 830 to Sennhütte). The rooms are simple but clean, and it's advisable to reserve through the tourist office before setting out.

Gästehaus Schmitz (☎ 234 45; Kornstrasse 1; s/d/tr €40/52/65; P) This slightly eccentric guesthouse is an excellent choice in the heart of town, for those on low budgets or looking for an apartment. Book ahead.

Das Brusttuch (☎ 346 00; www.brusttuch.de; Hoher Weg 1; s €71, d €119-152; P ✗ 🍴) The soft colours and smart rooms in this historic hotel make it a comfortable snooze-zone. It's very central and some rooms have double doors to the hallway.

our pick Hotel Kaiserworth (☎ 7090; www.kaiser worth.de; Markt 3; s €81-101, d €122-182; P ✗ 🛜) This magnificent 500-year-old former merchant guild building has tasteful rooms and a good restaurant open daily from 6am to 11pm. For insomniacs and barflies there's the dungeon-like Dukaten Bar, which is open till 6am.

Niedersächsischer Hof (☎ 3160; www.nieder saechsischer-hof-goslar.de; Rosentorstrasse 20; s €86, d €117; P ✗ 🛜) Opposite the train station, the 'Hof' toys with the idea of being an art hotel (the kids will love the piece near the foyer with the cindered toy cars) and has light rooms well insulated against the bustle outside. Prices fluctuate according to date, so call ahead.

Der Achtermann (☎ 700 00; www.der-achtermann .de, in German; Rosentorstrasse 20; s €79-89, d €104-154; P ✗ 🍴 🛜 🍴) The only drawbacks with this otherwise very good hotel are its sprawling size and the number of business conference guests buzzing in swarms between its ample amenities. Wi-fi is expensive at €8 per hour, but internet is free.

Eating & Drinking

Barock-Café Anders (☎ 238 14; Hoher Weg 4; cake from €2.70; ⏰ 8.30am-6pm; ✗) The first thing that strikes you here is the wonderful smell of cakes and confectionery, the delicious specialities.

Das Schwarze Schaf (☎ 319 5111; Jakobikirchhof 7; dishes €4.30-9; ⏰ 11am-8.30pm; ✗ V) This sleek eatery has a large menu of salads, pasta, *Flammkuchen* (Alsatian pizzas), stir-fries and grills, all served at wooden tables in a bright Asian-European crossover atmosphere. It is popular among a broad crowd of all ages for its appetising nosh. Dishes can be ordered takeaway (€13 minimum order).

Die Butterhanne (☎ 228 86; Marktkirchhof 3; mains €8.90-14; ⏲ from 8.30am; ✕) The fare is traditional and regular here, the outdoor seating is nice and on the first Saturday of the month the tables are cleared and the place morphs into a throbbing nightspot from 10pm. The name refers to a famous local frieze showing a milkmaid churning butter while clutching her buttock to insult her employer – don't try it on disco night.

our pick **Henry's** (☎ 317 400; www.henrys-erleben.de, in German; Markt 6; pasta €9-18, mains €17-22; ⏲ 10am-1am Sun-Thu, 10am-3am Fri & Sat; ✕ ⏲) This stylish addition to Goslar's eating and drinking scene serves a peanut-sauce curry along with three different chutneys. The bar and lounge area has a comfortable minimalist edge with sofas for chilling out day and night. Henry's is also a comfortable hotel with doubles for between €125 and €165.

Restaurant Aubergine (☎ 421 36; www.aubergine -goslar.de, in German; Marktstrasse 4; mains €12-19.50; ⏲ noon-2.30pm & 6-11.30pm; ✕) The Mediterranean Aubergine is a favourite among locals and visitors in the region for the good quality of its nontraditional cuisine, crisp table cloths and service, and classy atmosphere.

Shopping

Hoher Weg has shops selling souvenirs, especially puppets and marionettes, many of them portraying witches.

Schnaps und So (☎ 396 636; Hokenstrasse 3) This is a great local booze store, but approach the Harz fruit wines and herbal schnapps with caution – some of them may leave you the worse for wear.

Getting There & Away
BUS

The office of **Regionalbus Braunschweig** (RBB; ☎ 194 49; www.rbb-bus.de, in German; Bahnhof), from where buses depart, has free timetables for services throughout the Harz region. Bus 831 runs between Goslar and Altenau in the south via Clausthal-Zellerfeld; 830 runs to Clausthal-Zellerfeld via Hahnenklee. Change to the 840 at Clausthal-Zellerfeld for St Andreasberg. Trains are easier to get to Bad Harzburg, where you can take bus 820 to Torfhaus. BerlinLinienBus runs daily to Berlin (one way €29 via Magdeburg). For timetables and bookings, refer to **DER-Reisebüro** (☎ 757 90; Bahnhof).

CAR & MOTORCYCLE

The B6 runs north to Hildesheim and east to Bad Harzburg, Wernigerode and Quedlinburg. The north–south A7 is reached via the B82. For Hahnenklee, take the B241. Car rental is available at **Europcar** (☎ 251 38; Lindenplan 3).

TRAIN

Bad Harzburg-Hanover trains stop here often, as do trains on the Braunschweig–Göttingen line. There are frequent direct trains to Wernigerode (€8.40, 45 minutes); for more frequent services change at Vienenburg.

Getting Around

Local bus tickets cost €2.10. To book a taxi, ring ☎ 1313. **Hans Speed** (☎ 685 734; hans-speed@ freenet.de; Kuhlenkamp 1c) rents mountain and city bikes for €10 per day.

HAHNENKLEE

☎ 05325 / pop 1300

Surrounded by forest some 12km southwest of Goslar, this small, if somewhat staid, spa town makes a good day trip from Goslar for skiing in winter or hiking in summer.

The **tourist office** (☎ 510 40; www.hahnenklee.de; Kurhausweg 7; ⏲ 9am-5pm Mon-Fri, 9am-noon Sat & Sun May-Sep, 9am-4pm Mon-Fri, 9am-noon Sat Nov-Apr) is in the Kurverwaltung building off Rathausstrasse.

Apart from hiking and skiing, the main attraction in Hahnenklee is the unusual **Gustav-Adolf-Kirche** (Gustav-Adolf Church; 1907), a Norwegian-style wooden stave church with an interior of Byzantine and Scandinavian features.

In winter, most visitors come for the downhill and cross-country skiing on the Bocksberg. Day tickets for the *Seilbahn* (cable car) and lifts cost €20/13 for an adult/child. **Snow-Fun** (☎ 0178 180 3045) is the main equipment-hire place in town – head to Hindenburgstrasse 4 for nordic skis, and Rathausstrasse 6 for snowboards and alpine skis. **Hahnenkleer Skischule** (☎ 0170 874 4510; Rathausstrasse 6) runs various ski courses.

Hahnenklee is also popular for its hiking, with trails leading to the Bocksberg from the car park near the stave church, and longer trails to Goslar (trail 2G, blue dot, 11km) via Windsattel and Glockenberg. Remember to take the Harzclub 1:50,000 walking map and be prepared for changing weather conditions.

Getting There & Away

Hahnenklee is just west of the B241, between Goslar and Clausthal-Zellerfeld. Bus 830 serves Hahnenklee from Goslar on the way to Clausthal-Zellerfeld. The BEX BerlinLinienBus stops here daily.

BAD HARZBURG

☎ 05322 / pop 22,500

This pretty spa town just 9km from Goslar is a magnet for visitors seeking health and curative spas. Unless you're one of the many cure-seekers, the main attraction will be the nearby Harz National Park and trails, which offer excellent access to some typically picturesque Harz landscapes.

Information

Haus der Natur (☎ 784 337; Berliner Platz; adult/concession €2/1; ⊗ 10am-5pm Tue-Sun) Harz National Park information centre, with a small interactive exhibition that kids will enjoy most.

Spielpunkt (Herzog-Wilhelm-Strasse 42; per hr €2.50; ⊗ 9am-11pm Mon-Sat, 11am-11pm Sun) Internet access.

Tourist-Information (☎ 753 30; www.bad-harzburg .de, in German; Nordhäuser Strasse 4; ⊗ 9am-6pm Mon-Fri, 10am-4pm Sat & Sun Mar–mid-Jan, 9am-5pm Mon-Fri mid-Jan–Feb)

Activities

A nice thing to do here is hike or ride to **Grosser Burgberg**, a hill above Bad Harzburg with ruins of an 11th-century fortress built by Heinrich IV. There's a 481m-long **cable car** (☎ 753 71; adult/child return €3/1; ⊗ 9am-1pm & 1.30-5pm May-Oct, 10am-1pm & 1.30-4pm Nov-Apr) that goes up to the fortress, and it can be reached by walking up Bummelallee to the Kurpark.

Marked hiking trails lead into the national park from Berliner Platz and Grosser Burgberg, the latter just over 3km from Berliner Platz on foot. Among the many walks are those from Berliner Platz to Sennhütte (1.3km), Molkenhaus (3km) and scenic Rabenklippe (7km), overlooking the Ecker Valley. All destinations have restaurants; a board inside the cable-car station indicates which ones are open.

From Grosser Burgberg you can take the Kaiserweg trail, which leads to Torfhaus and connects to the Brocken. A marked trail also leads to the 23m-high **Radau Waterfall**, some 7km from Grosser Burgberg. If snow conditions are good, it's possible to ski cross-country to/from Torfhaus (p254), which has equipment-hire facilities.

Bad Harzburg's **Sole Therme** (☎ 753 60; Nordhäuser Strasse 3; per 2½hr adult/child €7.50/5; ⊗ 8am-9pm Mon-Sat, 8am-7pm Sun) has heated indoor and outdoor saltwater pools, and six types of saunas. Wednesday and Thursday mornings are respectively men- and women-only sauna days.

Sleeping & Eating

Several good hotels are situated west of the tourist office on Am Stadtpark.

Villa Feise (☎ 967 00; www.villa-feise.de; Rudolf-Huch-Strasse 20; s €45, d €76; P ⊠) Given its proximity to the promenade, this place is great value, offering much more comfort and style than some places that charge double the rate. If you don't have a room with a balcony, there's a nice garden down below.

our pick **Hotel Tannenhof-Solehotel** (☎ 968 80; www.solehotels.de, in German; Nordhäuser Strasse 6; s €60, d €99; P ⊠) This friendly and comfortable hotel alongside the tourist office has two outstanding pluses. It caters for mountain bikers, rents out mountain/touring bikes (€10/14 per day) and GPS for navigation, and can help with routes and maps. On top of this, guests have free access to the nearby Sole Therme spa.

Ringhotel Braunschweiger Hof (☎ 7880; www .hotel-braunschweiger-hof.de; Herzog-Wilhelm-Strasse 54; s €92-126, d €138-168; P ⊠ ⊠) You can relax with a spot of luxury here, where you'll find fine rooms, lots of wellness deals, a lovely garden and a good restaurant downstairs (mains €9.50 to €34). Its cheaper guest house next door has singles/doubles from €68/98.

Hexenklause (☎ 2892; Berliner Platz 3; mains €5.20-14.50; ⊗ 11.30am-6pm) This local favourite serves traditional fare that's a notch above the pack along the promenade.

Getting There & Around

The Hauptbahnhof and bus station are on the northern side of town. Bus 810 leaves here regularly for Goslar and goes via the cable car station; bus 877 heads for Wernigerode (€3, one hour). Bus 820 shuttles almost hourly to Braunlage via Radau Waterfall and Torfhaus. Frequent train services link Bad Harzburg with Goslar, Hanover, Braunschweig and Wernigerode.

Bad Harzburg is on the A395 to Braunschweig; the B4 and B6 lead to Torfhaus and Wernigerode, respectively.

See opposite, for bicycle hire at Hotel Tannenhof-Solehotel.

BRAUNLAGE

☎ 05520 / pop 5000

Braunlage is the area's largest winter-sports centre and very popular with hikers in summer. The skiing here is the best in the region, although it can get crowded on the slopes when the snow is good. Braunlage is currently experiencing something of a decline in popularity, perhaps explaining why in 2009 it staged a naked tobogganing competition – for safety reasons, participants had to wear a helmet, gloves and shoes.

Orientation

Braunlage's heart is the junction of Elbingeröder Strasse and the main thoroughfare, Herzog-Wilhelm-Strasse. The latter changes names several times.

Information

Post office (Herzog-Wilhelm-Strasse 14) Post agency inside the souvenir shop.

Spielhalle (Elbingeröder Strasse 5; per 20min €1; ☻ 9am-11pm Mon-Sat, 11am-11pm Sun) Internet access.

Tourist-Information (☎ 930 70; www.braunlage.de; in German; Kurverwaltung, Elbingeröder Strasse 17; ☻ 9am-12.30pm & 2-5pm Mon-Fri, 9am-12.30pm Sat) Helpful staff and sells tickets for the narrow gauge railway.

Volksbank (☎ 8030; Herzog-Wilhelm-Strasse 19) ATM.

Activities

HIKING

The tourist office has two good free leaflets: *Wandervorschläge Rund Um Braunlage* (Hiking Suggestions Around Braunlage), covering trails in the area and restaurant stops; and *Wanderwege Braunlage* (Braunlage Hiking Trails). If you are heading east, a trail follows the B27 to Elend (red triangle, 7km), where you can pick up the narrow-gauge railway to Wernigerode.

SKIING

A cable car will take you up the 971m-high **Wurmberg**, from where you can ski down or use the three lifts on the mountain itself. Return tickets cost €11. Carving ski equipment can be rented near the cable car at **Wurmburg Seilbahn und Gipfelsturmer** (☎ 923 277), at the former pet-

rol station, from €18 a day. Plenty of other places in town rent out skis, including cross-country skis for the many local trails.

Sleeping & Eating

DJH hostel (☎ 2238; jh-braunlage@djh-hannover.de; Von-Langen-Strasse 28; under/over 27yr €19.50/22.50; ✗) This DJH hostel is central to town and located on the edge of spruce forest about 300m south of Elbingeröder Strasse, near hiking and skiing trails. It has a playground for the kids.

our pick Romantik Hotel Zur Tanne (☎ 931 20; www.tanne-braunlage.de; Herzog-Wilhelm-Strasse 8; s €52-149, d €80-199; Ⓟ ✗ 🛜) The three categories of rooms in this centrally located hotel make it a useful crossover from the midrange to the high end, with rooms in three categories of comfort decorated in woods and gentle colours. It also has a Finnish sauna, steam bath and whirlpool.

relaxa Hotel Harz-Wald Braunlage (☎ 8070; braunlage@relaxa-hotel.de; Karl-Röhrig-Strasse 5a; s €79, d €96-129; Ⓟ ✗ 🖳) Located on the northern edge of town, this modern hotel has an abundance of wellness extras and free use of city bikes. All rooms have their own balcony.

Puppe Brotzeitstube (☎ 487; Am Brunnen 2; gourmet snacks €5-9.90; ☻ 9am-9pm Mon-Sat, 11am-9pm Sun) This unusual gourmet sandwich shop does scrumptious, German-style open sandwiches with local cuts of ham, sausage and other products for eat-in, takeaway or picnic.

Getting There & Away

Bus 850 runs to St Andreasberg from the Von-Langen-Strasse or Eisstadion stops. For Torfhaus and Bad Harzburg, take bus 820 from the main bus station about 1km south of Elbingeröder Strasse, or Eisstadion stop, which is just north of Elbingeröder Strasse. The B4 runs north to Torfhaus and Bad Harzburg. The B27 leads southwest to the St Andreasberg turn-off and northeast to the Eastern Harz.

ST ANDREASBERG

☎ 05582 / pop 1950

Known for its mining museums, clean air and hiking and skiing options, this resort sits on a broad ridge surrounded by wistful mountains, 10km west of Braunlage. St Andreasberg is a pleasant town that offers a quiet base for trips into the national park; it's wonderful to visit during a warm snowless spring or a 'golden October'.

The **tourist office** (☎ 803 36; www.sankt-andreas
berg.de; Am Kurpark 9; ☺ 9am-5pm Mon-Fri, weekends during ski season) is in the split-level, wheelchair-
friendly Kurverwaltung building.

Most shops close for several hours around
noon.

Sights & Activities

German-language tours of the interesting
Grube Samson Mining Museum (☎ 1249; tours adult/
concession €4.50/2.25; ☺ 8.30am-4.30pm, tours at 11am
& 2.30pm) take you 20m down to view early
forms of mine transportation. Follow the
signs from Dr-Willi-Bergmann-Strasse.

The nearby **Catharina Neufang tunnel** (adult/
concession €2.75/2; ☺ 1.45pm Mon-Sat) includes a
mining demonstration, and the **Harzer Roller
Kanarien-Museum** (Canary Museum; adult/child €2.75/2;
☺ 8.30am-4pm Mon-Sat, 10.30am-4.30pm Sun) is worthy of its claim of being the world's only
museum dedicated to canaries (used in the
mines). The display takes you back to the
15th century, but the first miners' 'friends'
arrived in St Andreasberg in 1730 with
workers from Tyrol.

The skiing in St Andreasberg can be excellent. The closest piste is on **Mathias-Schmidt-
Berg** (☎ 265); day passes cost €17. You'll
also find pistes that have lifts out of town
on **Sonnenberg** (☎ 513). One of several places
renting out ski and snowboard equipment
is **Sport Pläschke** (☎ 260; www.skischule-harz.de, in
German; Dr-Willi-Bergmann-Strasse 10).

Cross-country skiers should pick up the
Wintersportkarte map (€1) from the tourist office, because it shows both groomed
and ungroomed trails as well as some good
ski hikes.

The Rehberger Grabenweg is a unique
hiking trail that leads into the Harz National
Park and to the **Rehberger Grabenhaus** (☎ 789;
www.rehberger-grabenhaus.com, in German; ☺ closed
Mon), a forest cafe 3km from St Andreasberg
and only accessible on foot. In the evening
from late December to early March you
can sit in the darkened cafe and watch wild
deer feeding outside. To avoid disturbing
the animals, visitors have to arrive by 5pm
and aren't let out until 7pm. Bring a torch
(flashlight) to find your way back.

There are exhibits on the area's cultural
history, plus park information and a multimedia show in the **Nationalparkhaus** (☎ 923
074; www.nationalpark-harz.de, in German; Erzwäsche 1;
☺ 9am-5pm Apr-Oct, 10am-5pm Nov-Mar).

Sleeping & Eating

Hostel (☎ 809 948; www.harz-herbergen.de, in German;
Am Gesehr 37; dm €19) This independent hostel is
popular with school and other groups but
travellers can also stay here.

Pension Haus am Kurpark (☎ 1010; www.haus
.am.kurpark.harz.de; Am Kurpark 1; s €25-32, d €44-60)
Bears on scooters and skis on walls adorn
this quiet, friendly and very well-run *Pension*
just outside the park. There's a choice of
shared and private bathrooms.

our pick **Pension Holloch** (☎ 1005; www.pension
-holloch.harz.de, in German; Glückauf-Weg 21; s €40-45, d
€60-70) Most rooms have a balcony overlook-
ing the valley and ski piste, so you can see
who's breaking a leg – or someone else's
– from this very comfortable, small and
friendly *Pension*. Best to book ahead.

La Piazza (☎ 999 987; Schützenstrasse 35; pizza &
pasta €5-7, mains €7.50-15; ☺ noon-3pm & 5.30-11pm)
On the main street, this restaurant will
give you the carbohydrate boost you need
to tackle or recover from the pistes. The
outdoor seating is popular in summer. For
delivery the minimum order is €9.

Getting There & Away

Bus 850 runs between St Andreasberg and
Braunlage. The frequent bus 840 runs to
Clausthal-Zellerfeld.

St Andreasberg can be reached via the
B27, which winds along the scenic Oder
Valley from Bad Lauterberg to Braunlage.
The L519 (Sonnenberg) leads north to the
B242 and Clausthal-Zellerfeld, to the B4 and
Bad Harzburg, and to Goslar (B241 or the
B498 along the Oker Valley).

CLAUSTHAL-ZELLERFELD

☎ 05323 / pop 15,000

Formerly two settlements, this small university town was once the region's most important mining centre. Its main attractions
today are mineral and spiritual: an excellent
mining museum and a spectacular wooden
church. There are over 60 lakes in the vicinity, mostly created for the mines, and almost
all are now suitable for swimming.

Orientation & Information

As in many similar linear towns in the Harz,
Clausthal-Zellerfeld's main street changes
names several times, with Kronenplatz as
the hub. Clausthal lies to the south, while

HARZ MOUNTAINS

Zellerfeld begins just beyond Bahnhofstrasse, roughly 1km to the north.

The **tourist office** (☎ 810 24; www.oberharz.de, in German; Bergstrasse 31; ⏰ 9am-5pm Mon-Fri, 10am-4pm Sat & Sun) is near the Oberharzer Bergwerks-museum, and the **Harzklub HQ** (☎ 817 58; www .harzklub.de, in German; ⏰ 9am-noon Mon-Fri) is in the former train station, 10 and 15 minutes on foot respectively north of Kronenplatz. **Harz-Agentur** (☎ 982 460; www.harzagentur.de, in German; Bergstrasse 31) upstairs from the tourist office rents out hard-tail and full-suspension moun-tain bikes (€15 to €22 per day).

Sights

The **Oberharzer Bergwerksmuseum** (☎ 989 50; www .oberharzerbergwerksmuseum.de, in German; Bornhardtstrasse 16; adult/concession €4/2; ⏰ 10am-5pm) has an inter-esting open-air exhibition of mine buildings and mining methods, including a horse-driven carousel that was used to power a lift into the mine. The museum has an English-language brochure with background information and explanations on the different buildings, and there are tours in German (translators are available) that take you into the depths.

South of Kronenplatz in the techni-cal university is the **Geosammlung** (☎ 722 737; Adolph-Roemer-Strasse 2a; adult/concession €1.50/1; ⏰ 9.30am-12.30pm Tue, Wed & Fri, 9.30am-12.30pm & 2-5pm Thu, 10am-1pm Sun), Germany's largest collec-tion of mineral samples. Some of the displays are also on the theme of fossils.

Very close by is the baroque **Marktkirche Zum Heiligen Geist** (☎ 7005; Hindenburgplatz 1; ⏰ 10am-5pm Mon-Sat, 1-5pm Sun Apr-Oct), which was consecrated in 1642 and – another local record – is the country's largest wooden church. While some much needed restoration work continues, it will remain closed throughout the winter.

The **Volksbank Arena Harz** (www.volksbank-arena-harz .de, in German) is an 1800km signposted network of mountain bike trails through the Oberharz with three different levels of difficulty. Harz-Agentur (above) and Harzhotel zum Prinzen (below) can help with suggestions.

Sleeping & Eating

our pick **Harzhotel zum Prinzen** (☎ 966 10; www.zum -prinzen.de, in German; Goslarsche Strasse 20; s €50-55, d €72-84; P ⊠ �) This comfortable hotel 250m north of the tourist office in Zellerfeld has a country cottage feel with blonde solid timber furnishings and wooden floors. It caters well for cyclists and motorcyclists,

renting out GPS and offering route sugges-tions – and after pedalling up and down the Harz Mountains you can relax in its excel-lent sauna facilities (€8.50).

Goldene Krone (☎ 9300; goldene.krone@t-online. de; Am Kronenplatz 3; s €59-65, d €79-88, ste €110-125; P ⊠ �) Heinrich Heine graced the pil-lows here while on his Harz journey in 1824. This is not only the best address in town, it's right in the middle of it. Rooms are bright, a very decent size and decorated in tasteful shades of blue. Wi-fi is free. The Italian restaurant downstairs is one of the better places around too, with pasta, pizza and meat dishes (pasta €7.90, mains €9.80 to €22).

Restaurant Glück Auf (☎ 1616; An der Marktkirche 7; mains €11-18; ⏰ 11.30am-2.30pm & 5.30-10pm Thu-Tue) This outstanding traditional restaurant es-tablished in 1720 is almost an attraction in itself: the historic banquet hall holds about 280 people and has galleries and even a stage at one end. The menu has a good choice of game. Downstairs is a surprise for the kids on the theme of Harz folk tales.

Getting There & Around

Regular bus services leave 'Bahnhof', the former train station, and Kronenplatz for Goslar (bus 830). Disembark at Thomas-Merten-Platz for the Bergwerksmuseum. Take bus 840 for St Andreasberg and bus 831 for Altenau. The B241 leads north to Goslar and south to Osterode, while the B242 goes east to Braunlage and St Andreasberg. To reach the A7, take the B242 west.

EASTERN HARZ

WERNIGERODE

☎ 03943 / pop 33,500

A bustling, attractive town on the northern edge of the Harz, Wernigerode is a good starting point for exploring the eastern re-gions of the Harz National Park. The wind-ing streets of the Altstadt are flanked by pretty half-timbered houses, and high above the Altstadt hovers a romantic ducal castle from the 12th century.

During the early Middle Ages Wernigerode was hampered by centuries of royal squab-bles. Fires followed in the 15th and 16th centuries, changing the face of Wernigerode forever, and later the Thirty Years' War took its population to the brink and back.

HARZ MOUNTAINS

Today it is the northern terminus of the steam-powered narrow-gauge Harzquerbahn (see the boxed text, below), which has chugged along the breadth of the Harz for almost a century; the line to the summit of the Brocken (1142m), northern Germany's highest mountain, also starts here.

Orientation
The bus and train stations are on the northern side of town at the end of Rudolf-Breitscheid-Strasse. The ducal castle is southeast of Markt.

Information
Harz-Klinikum Wernigerode (☎ 610; Ilsenburger Strasse 15) Medical services.
Police (☎ 6530; Nicolaiplatz 4)
Post office (Burgstrasse 19)
Tele.Internet Center Westerntor (☎ 625 046; Westernstrasse 36; per 15min €0.50; ☺ 10am-11pm Mon-Sat, 11am-11pm Sun) Internet access with Skype, telephones.
Volksbank (Breite Strasse 4) Banking services and ATM.
Wernigerode Tourismus (☎ 553 7835; www .wernigerode-tourismus.de, in German; Marktplatz 10; ☺ 8.30am-7pm Mon-Fri, 10am-4pm Sat, 10am-3pm Sun May-Oct, 8.30am-6pm Mon-Fri, 10am-4pm Sat, 10am-3pm Sun Nov-Apr) Tourist information, free map and room-booking service.
Zimmervermittlung und Information am Krummelschen Haus (☎ 606 000; Krummelsches Haus, Breite Strasse 70-72; ☺ 10am-6pm May-Oct, 10am-4pm Nov-Apr) Private tourist information and room-booking service.

Sights
ALTSTADT
The colourful and spectacular towered **Rathaus** on Markt began life as a theatre around 1277, but what you see today is mostly late-Gothic from the 16th century. The artisan who carved the town hall's 33 wooden figures was said to have fallen foul of the authorities, and if you look closely you can see a few of his mocking touches. The neo-Gothic **fountain** (1848) was dedicated to charitable nobles, whose names and coats of arms are immortalised on it.

One of the prettiest half-timbered houses in town is in the cosy Oberpfarrkirchhof, which surrounds the **Sylvestrikirche**; here you'll find **Gadenstedtsches Haus** (1582), with its Renaissance oriel. The **Harz Museum** (☎ 654 454; Klint 10; adult/concession €2/1.30; ☺ 10am-5pm Mon-Sat), a short walk away, has some interesting exhibits on local geology, history and half-timbered houses. Crossing Markt to Breite Strasse, the pretty **Café Wien** building (1583) at No 4 is a worthwhile stopover for both architectural and gastronomical reasons. The carved facade of the **Krummelsches Haus** depicts various countries symbolically; America is portrayed, reasonably enough, as a naked woman riding an armadillo.

NARROW-GAUGE RAILWAYS

Fans of old-time trains or unusual journeys will be in their element on any of the three narrow-gauge railways crossing the Harz. This 140km integrated network – the largest in Europe – is served by 25 steam and 10 diesel locomotives, which tackle gradients of up to 1:25 (40%) and curves as tight as 60m in radius. Most locomotives date from the 1950s, but eight historic models, some from as early as 1897, are proudly rolled out for special occasions.

The network, a legacy of the GDR, consists of three lines. The **Harzquerbahn** runs 60km on a north–south route between Wernigerode and Nordhausen. The serpentine 14km between Wernigerode and Drei Annen Hohne includes 72 bends; you'll get dropped off on the edge of Harz National Park.

From the junction at Drei Annen Hohne, the **Brockenbahn** begins the steep climb to Schierke and the Brocken. Direct services to the Brocken can also be picked up from Wernigerode and Nordhausen, or at stations en route; single/return tickets cost €17/26 from all stations.

The third service is the **Selketalbahn**, which begins in Quedlinburg and runs to Eisfelder Talmühle or Hasselfelde. At Eisfelder Tal, you can change trains for other lines. The picturesque Selketalbahn crosses the plain to Gernrode and follows Wellbach, a creek with a couple of good swimming holes, through deciduous forest to Mägdesprung, before joining the Selke Valley and climbing past Alexisbad to high plains around Friedrichshöhe, Stiege and beyond.

Passes for three/five days cost €42/47 per adult (children half-price). Timetables and information can be picked up from **Harzer Schmalspurbahnen** (☎ 03943-5580; www.hsb-wr.de, in German; Hauptbahnhof, Wernigerode) or in Quedlinburg (p254).

HARZ MOUNTAINS

SCHLOSS

Originally built in the 12th century to protect German Kaisers on hunting expeditions, **Schloss Wernigerode** (☎ 553 030; www .schloss-wernigerode.de; adult/concession/child €5/4.50/2; ☺ 10am-6pm May-Oct, 10am-4pm Tue-Fri, 10am-6pm Sat & Sun Nov-Apr) was enlarged over the years to reflect late-Gothic and Renaissance tastes. Its fairy-tale facade came courtesy of Count Otto of Stolberg-Wernigerode in the 19th century. The museum inside includes portraits of Kaisers, beautiful panelled rooms with original furnishings and the opulent **Festsaal** (Banquet Hall).

The stunning **Schlosskirche** (1880) has an altar and pulpit made of French marble. You can climb the castle **tower** (admission €1), but the views from the castle or restaurant terrace (best appreciated late in the day) are free and just as spectacular.

You can walk (1.5km) or take a Bimmelbahn wagon ride (adult/child return €4.50/2) from Marktstrasse. In summer, horse-drawn carts make the trek from Markt.

Activities

The deciduous **forest** behind the castle is crisscrossed with lovely trails and *Forstwege* (forestry tracks). Wernigerode is also a good starting point for hikes and bike rides into the Harz National Park. **Bad-Bikes** (☎ 626 868; www .badbikes-online.de, in German; Breite Strasse 48a) rents good mountain and city bikes for between €10 and €17.50 per day.

Sleeping

DJH hostel (☎ 606 176; www.jugendherberge.de/jh /wernigerode; Am Eichberg 5; dm under/over 27yr €18/21, s €31; ☒) On the edge of the forest about 2.5km west of town in Hasserode, the renovated DJH hostel has two-, three- and four-bed dorms with bathrooms. There's also a sauna and solarium here, and nearby is the large Brockenbad swimming complex. Take bus 1 or 4 towards Hasserode.

Hotel am Anger (☎ 923 20; www.hotel-am-anger.de, in German; Breite Strasse 92; s €50-60, d €90-100; Ⓟ ☒) Labyrinthine it may be, and there's an awful lot of pine in the 40 rooms, but this courtyard hotel is pleasant and some rooms have views of the castle.

Hotel und Restaurant zur Post (☎ 690 40; www .hotelzurpost-wr.de, in German; Marktstrasse 17; s/d €52/89; Ⓟ ☺) This is a very central and comfortable choice that offers great value, with spacious, bright rooms and elegant furnishings in a half-timbered house.

Parkhotel Fischer (☎ 691 350; www.parkhotel-fischer .de, in German; Mauergasse 1; s €65, d €105; Ⓟ ☒ ☒) Rooms here are comfortable and modern, but it's extras like the tranquil indoor swimming pool with fake-Roman pillars and the sauna that make this particularly attractive.

our pick **Hotel Gothisches Haus** (☎ 6750; gothisches -haus@travelcharme.com; Am Markt 1; s €89-191, d €118-282, ste €201-426; Ⓟ ☒ ☺) The warm Tuscan colours and thoughtful design of this luxury hotel make it very attractive. There's a log fire downstairs in the Kaminbar (Fireplace Bar), and two restaurants – one gourmet and seating only 17 people – plus a wine cellar to explore. Two suites have waterbeds.

Eating & Drinking

Biotopf (☎ 626 015; Marktstrasse 13; mains €3.80; ☺ 10.30am-6.30pm Mon-Fri, 10.30am-1.30pm Sat; ☒ Ⓥ) A relative newcomer on the scene, this organic bistro has inexpensive, changing dishes in bright and simple surroundings.

Markt Wirtschaft (☎ 557 788; Marktstrasse 35; mains €7-14; ☺ 11.30am-4pm & 6pm-midnight Tue-Sat, 11.30am-4pm Sun; ☒ Ⓥ) This bistro and bar has an attractive, spacious interior as well as a courtyard and beer garden – all rounded off by a homely Mediterranean ambience. The range of wines is good and it serves a tasty and filling salad with beef strips for €9.80.

Café am Markt & Lounge (☎ 261 690; Marktplatz 6-9; mains €7.50-13.50, brunch €9.50; ☺ 8am-6.30pm Mon-Sat, Baldini brunch 9am-2pm Sun; ☒) This interesting all-rounder started life as a cafe, but seems to have bred with an Italian restaurant next door (Baldinis, which has a smaller but similar menu) to beget a separate lounge area for smokers (upstairs).

Brauhaus (☎ 695 727; www.brauhaus-wernigerode.de; Breite Strasse 24; mains €8-15; ☺ 11.30am-late; ☒ Ⓥ) Here you can expect to find an enormous, multilevel pub and bistro with fairly standard German meat and vegetarian dishes, and – on Saturday from 9pm – a dance floor upstairs. It's easily the best all-round option for a meal and drink, or to get down into Sunday morning.

Altes Amtshaus (☎ 501 200; Burgberg 15; mains €11-20; ☺ 3-11pm Tue-Thu, 11.30am-11pm Fri-Sun; ☒) Game and traditional dishes like a delicious *Tafelspitz* (prime boiled beef) with radish sauce are served in this former ducal courthouse with a lovely ambience.

Weisser Hirsch (☎ 602 020; www.hotel-weisser-hirsch .de; Marktplatz 5; mains €11-23, hare €22.50; ✗) Crisp white tablecloths, glistening cutlery and wild hare on the menu underscore a traditional but enticing culinary approach at the 'White Stag'. Along with the Stuben in Gothisches Haus (p251), this is one of the best places in town for a meal. Four- and five-course menus are also available (from €24.50 to €50).

Ars Vivendi (☎ 626 606; Bahnhofstrasse 33; entry Sat €5; ✶ from 8pm Fri & Sat) Beyond the muscle-clad bouncers you'll find a cocktail bar where the hopeful young, the restless old and the wistful in-betweens tug on straws while hanging onto the bar in decor that might jar.

Getting There & Away

Direct buses run to most major towns in this region; the timetable (€2) available from the **WVB bus office** (☎ 5640; www.wvb-gmbh.de, in German; Hauptbahnhof) includes a train schedule. Bus 253 runs to Blankenburg and Thale, while bus 257 serves Drei Annen Hohne and Schierke.

There are frequent trains to Goslar (€8.40, 45 minutes) and Halle (€19.60, 1¼ hours). Change at Halberstadt for Quedlinburg (€8.40, 45 minutes) and Thale (€10.30, one hour).

Getting Around

Buses 1 and 2 run from the bus station to the Rendezvous bus stop just north of the Markt, connecting with bus 3. Tickets cost €1. For a taxi, call ☎ 633 053.

RÜBELAND CAVES

Rübeland, a small town just 13km south of Wernigerode, has a couple of interesting **caves** (☎ 039454-491 32; www.harzer-hoehlen.de; adult/child €7/4.50; ✶ 9am-5.30pm Jul & Aug, 9am-4.30pm Feb-Jun, Sep & Oct, 9am-3.30pm Nov-Jan). Admission gets you a guided tour, in German, of either cave (note that only one is open from November to April).

Baumannshöhle was formed about 500,000 years ago, and the first tourists visited in 1646. Human presence in the caves dates back 40,000 years. The Goethesaal, which has a pond, is sometimes used for concerts and plays. **Hermannshöhle** was formed 350,000 years ago and was rediscovered in the 19th century. Its stalactites and stalagmites are spectacular, especially in the transparent Kristallkammer. Salamanders, introduced from southern Europe by researchers, inhabit one pond.

WVB bus 265 leaves Wernigerode for Rübeland hourly. You can join the magnificent Bodetal trail (blue triangle, 16km) to Thale at Rübeland, crossing the Rappbodetalsperre, a 106m-high dam wall across the Harz' largest reservoir, on foot.

If driving from Wernigerode, take the B244 south to Elbingerode, then the B27 east.

SCHIERKE

☎ 039455 / pop 700

Situated at 650m in the hills at the foot of the Brocken and just 16km west of Wernigerode, Schierke is a lovely village and the last stop for the Brockenbahn before it climbs the summit. Schierke has an upper town on the main road to the Brocken and a lower town down in the valley of the Kalte Bode River. It is also a popular starting point for exploring the Harz National Park and the home of the ubiquitous 'Schierker Feuerstein' *digestif.*

The **Kurverwaltung** (☎ 8680; www.schierke-am -brocken.de, in German; Brockenstrasse 10; ✶ 9am-noon & 1-4pm Mon-Fri, 10am-noon & 2-4pm Sat, 10am-noon Sun) has tourist information and can help with accommodation in town. **Nationalparkhaus Schierke** (☎ 477; Brockenstrasse; ✶ 8.30am-4.30pm) has hiking brochures and information on the national park. It is situated 1km north of the tourist office towards Brocken.

Schierke is a popular starting point for hikes to Brocken (1142m), Northern Germany's highest mountain (opposite), as well as cross-country skiing on trails through the forests of the Oberharz. Winter **cross-country ski hire** (☎ 409; Brockenstrasse 14a; per day €10; ✶ 9am-5pm Mon-Fri) is available from an outlet alongside the Stöber Eck store.

You can hike to the Brocken via the bitumen Brockenstrasse (12km), closed to private cars and motorcycles. More interesting is the 7km hike via Eckerloch. Marked trails also lead to the rugged rock formations of Feuersteinklippen (30 minutes from the Kurverwaltung) and Schnarcherklippen (1½ hours).

Horse-drawn wagons travel from Schierke to the Brocken and cost €22 return per person.

On the night of 30 April, Walpurgisnacht (see boxed text, p259), Schierke attracts a veritable throng of visitors, most of whom set off on walking tracks to the Brocken.

Sleeping & Eating

There is plenty of accommodation in town, particularly along Brockenstrasse, but you may need to book ahead. There is also no shortage of restaurants, although the repertoire of most adheres to the usual traditional suspects.

Hotel König (☎ 383; www.harz-hotel-koenig.de, in German; Kirchberg 15; s €33-50, d €50-70) This hotel has a remarkable carved foyer and offers clean and comfortable rooms (some have a verandah), with or without bathrooms, and has a decent restaurant.

our pick **Pension Schmidt** (☎ 333; www.pension-schmidt.de, in German; Brockenstrasse 13; s €48, d €67; P ☒) This unprepossessing *Pension* opposite the Kurverwaltung building is among the best in town. It has a lot of indoor greenery, very comfortable rooms, friendly management and a sauna to ease the aching muscles after a strenuous day's hiking or mountain biking.

Getting There & Around

The frequent bus 257 connects Wernigerode and Braunlage. Narrow-gauge railway services between Wernigerode and Schierke cost €6/10 per single/return. Driving from the west, take the B27 from Braunlage and turn off at Elend. From Wernigerode, take Friedrichstrasse.

MITTELBAU DORA

From late in 1943, thousands of slave labourers (mostly Russian, French and Polish prisoners of war) toiled under horrific conditions digging tunnels in the chalk hills north of Nordhausen. From a 20km labyrinth of tunnels, they produced the V1 and V2 rockets that rained destruction on London, Antwerp and other cities during the final stages of WWII, when Hitler's grand plan became to conduct war from production plants below the ground.

The camp, called Mittelbau Dora, was created as a satellite of the Buchenwald concentration camp after British bombers destroyed the missile plants in Peenemünde in far northeastern Germany. During the last two years of the war, at least 20,000 prisoners died at Dora, many having survived Auschwitz only to be worked to death here.

The US army reached the gates in April 1945, cared for survivors and removed all missile equipment before turning the area over to the Russians two months later. Much of the technology was later employed in the US space program.

After years of mouldering away in the GDR period, the memorial has gradually been improved over the years to give a deeper insight into the horror of Hitler's undertaking. Today the memorial complex includes a permanent exhibition in a modern museum building to explain the background of the camp and the experiences of those who were interned here, a multilanguage library and a cafe.

The horrible truth of the place permeates the memorial, and a visit may be among the most unforgettable experiences you have in Germany.

Orientation & Information

Mittelbau Dora is 5km north of Nordhausen, a dull town of interest only as regards changing trains.

Visitors have independent access to the grounds, crematorium and **museum** (☎ 03631-495 820; www.dora.de; admission free; ☽ 10am-6pm Tue-Sun Apr-Sep, 10am-4pm Oct-Mar). The tunnels, which are the diameter of an aircraft hangar, are accessible by guided tour. Within the dank walls you can see partially assembled rockets that have lain untouched for over 50 years.

Free 90-minute tours operate at 11am and 2pm from Tuesday to Friday, and at 11am, 1pm and 3pm on weekends (also 4pm April to September).

Getting There & Away

The Harzquerbahn links Nordhausen with Wernigerode (single/return €10/17, 2¾ hours). The nearest stop to Dora is Nordhausen-Krimderode, which is served by almost hourly trains from Nordhausen-Nord (11 minutes), next to the main station.

From the Krimderode stop, cross the tracks and walk south along Goetheweg, which curves and becomes Kohnsteinweg. Follow this for 1km towards the unassuming hill and you are at the camp.

Trains run to Halle (€16.70, 1¾ hours) and to Göttingen (€20, 1½ hours) from Nordhausen.

BROCKEN & TORFHAUS

There are prettier landscapes and hikes in the Harz, but the 1142m Brocken is what draws the crowds: about 50,000 on a summer's day. When he wasn't exploring mines, Goethe also tested his mettle by scaling the mountain.

Goetheweg from Torfhaus

The 8km Goetheweg trail to the Brocken from the Western Harz starts at Torfhaus. Easier than other approaches, it initially takes you through bog, follows an historic aqueduct once used to regulate water levels for the mines, then crosses the Kaiserweg, a sweaty 11km trail from Bad Harzburg. Unfortunately, your next stop will be a dead forest, though the trail becomes steep and more interesting as you walk along the former border. From 1945 to 1989 the Harz region was a frontline in the Cold War, and the Brocken was used by the Soviets as a military base. For 28 years the summit was off limits and was virtually the only mountain in the world that couldn't be climbed. Hike along the train line above soggy moorland to reach the open, windy summit, where you can enjoy the view, eat pea soup and *Bockwurst* (boiled sausage), and think of Goethe and Heine.

On top is the **Brockenhaus** (☎ 039455-500 05; www.nationalpark-harz.de, in German; adult/child €4/2, concession €3-3.50; ☽ 9.30am-5pm), with a cafe, interactive displays and a viewing platform. In summer (but only in snow-free conditions) rangers conduct one-hour tours of the plateau, which includes the **alpine garden**, or separate tours of the alpine garden. Plateau tours usually depart at 11.30am and 2pm, and garden tours at 11.15am and 1pm. These can change, though, so best to call ahead for times if you want to join one.

Torfhaus itself is a good starting point for **cross-country skiing** or winter ski treks, with plenty of equipment available for hire. Downhill skiing is limited to 1200m (on two pistes); one recommended route is the Kaiserweg. Make sure you pack a good map and take all precautions. The **Nationalparkhaus** (☎ 05320-263; www.nationalpark-harz.de, in German; Torfhaus 21; ☽ 9am-5pm Apr-Oct, 10am-4pm Nov-Mar) has information on the park.

Getting There & Away
Bus 820 stops at Torfhaus on the well-served Bad Harzburg–Braunlage route.

QUEDLINBURG
☎ 03946 / pop 22,000
With its intact Altstadt and over 1400 half-timbered houses dating from six centuries ago, Quedlinburg is a highlight of any trip to the Harz. In 1994 the city became a Unesco World Heritage Site; since then, work to save the crumbling treasures lining its romantic cobblestone streets has gradually progressed.

In the 10th century the Reich was briefly ruled from here by two women, Theophano

and Adelheid, successive guardians of the 10th-century child-king Otto III, and Quedlinburg itself is closely associated with the *Frauenstift*, a medieval foundation for widows and daughters of the nobility that enjoyed the direct protection of the Kaiser.

Although the Altstadt can get crowded in summer and on weekends, any time of year is nice for a visit.

Orientation
The circular medieval centre of the old town is a 10-minute walk from the Hauptbahnhof (central train station) along Bahnhofstrasse. To reach the Markt, follow the road around and turn left into Heiligegeiststrasse after the post office. Hohe Strasse, off the Markt, leads south to the castle.

Information
Harzerschmalspurbahnen (☎ 527 191; www .hsb-wr.de, in German; Marktstrasse 1; ☽ 10am-5pm Nov–mid-Apr, 9am-1pm & 1.30-6pm Mon-Fri, to 5pm Sat & Sun mid-Apr–Oct) Narrow-gauge railway information.
Klinik Dorothea Christiane Erxleben (☎ 9090; Ditfurter Weg 24) Medical services.
Police (☎ 9770; Schillerstrasse 3)
Post office (Bahnhofstrasse)
Quedlinburg-Tourismus (☎ 905 625; www.quedlin burg.de; Markt 2; ☽ 9.30am-6.30pm Mon-Fri, 9.30am-4pm Sat, 9.30am-2pm Sun May-Oct, 9.30am-5pm Mon-Fri, 9.30am-2pm Sat Nov-Apr) Visit here for tourist information.
Sparkasse (☎ 9050; Markt 15) ATM and banking services.
Spielstube (☎ 4401; Breite Strasse 39; per hr €2; ☽ 9am-10pm Mon-Sat, 2-10pm Sun) Internet access.

Sights
AROUND THE MARKT
Built in 1320, the **Rathaus** has been expanded over the years and was adorned with a Renaissance facade in 1616. Inside, the beautiful Festsaal is decorated with a cycle of frescoes focusing on Quedlinburg's colourful history. The **Roland statue** (1426) in front of the Rathaus dates from the year Quedlinburg joined the Hanseatic League.

Behind the Rathaus is the late-Gothic **Marktkirche St Benedikti**. On the tower you'll see a small house used by town watchmen until 1901. The **mausoleum** nearby survived the relocation of the church graveyard during the 19th century.

There are some fine half-timbered buildings near Marktkirche; arguably the most

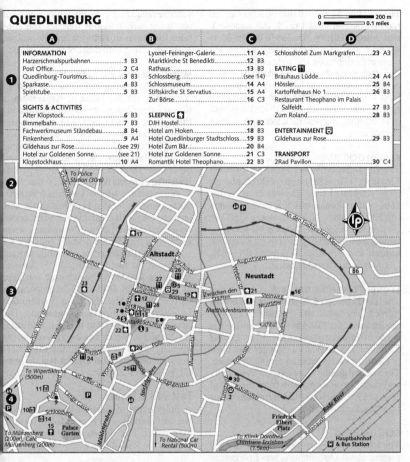

QUEDLINBURG

INFORMATION			SLEEPING			EATING		
Harzerschmalspurbahnen	1	B3	DJH Hostel	17	B2	Brauhaus Lüdde	24	A4
Post Office	2	C4	Hotel am Hoken	18	B3	Hössler	25	B4
Quedlinburg-Tourismus	3	B3	Hotel Quedlinburger Stadtschloss	19	B3	Kartoffelhaus No 1	26	B3
Sparkasse	4	B3	Hotel Zum Bär	20	B4	Restaurant Theophano im Palais		
Spielstube	5	B3	Hotel zur Goldenen Sonne	21	C3	Salfeldt	27	B3
			Romantik Hotel Theophano	22	B3	Zum Roland	28	B3
SIGHTS & ACTIVITIES								
Alter Klopstock	6	B3				ENTERTAINMENT		
Bimmelbahn	7	B3				Gildehaus zur Rose	29	B3
Fachwerkmuseum Ständebau	8	B4						
Finkenherd	9	A4				TRANSPORT		
Gildehaus zur Rose	(see 29)					2Rad Pavillon	30	C4
Hotel zur Goldenen Sonne	(see 21)							
Klopstockhaus	10	A4						

Lyonel-Feininger-Galerie	11	A4
Marktkirche St Benedikti	12	B3
Rathaus	13	B3
Schlossberg	(see 14)	
Schlossmuseum	14	A4
Stiftskirche St Servatius	15	A4
Zur Börse	16	C3

Schlosshotel Zum Markgrafen	23	A3

0 ——— 200 m
0 ——— 0.1 miles

spectacular is the **Gildehaus zur Rose** (1612) at Breite Strasse 39, with a richly carved and panelled interior (see p257).

Return to the Markt and walk through Schuhhof, a shoemakers' courtyard, which is on the east side, and has shutters and stablelike 'gossip doors'. **Alter Klopstock** (1580), which is found at Stieg 28, has scrolled beams typical of Quedlinburg's 16th-century half-timbered houses.

From Stieg 28 (just north of Schuhhof), it's a short walk north along Pölle to Zwischen den Städten, a historic bridge connecting the old town and **Neustadt**, which developed alongside the town wall around 1200 when peasants fled a feudal power struggle on the land. Behind

the Renaissance facade, tower and stone gables of the **Hagensches Freihaus** (1558) is now the Hotel Quedlinburger Stadtschloss (p257). Many houses in this part of town have high archways and courtyards dotted with pigeon towers. Of special note are the **Hotel zur Goldenen Sonne** building (1671; see p256) at Steinweg 11 and **Zur Börse** (1683) at No 23.

There are 45-minute rides through the Altstadt and Neustadt on the **Bimmelbahn** (☎ 918 888; adult/child €5.50/2.50; ☼ 10am-4pm mid-Mar–mid-Nov), leaving hourly from Marktstrasse.

FACHWERKMUSEUM STÄNDEBAU
Germany's earliest half-timbered houses were built using high perpendicular struts.

HARZ MOUNTAINS

The building from 1310 that now houses the **Fachwerkmuseum Ständebau** (☎ 3828; Wordgasse 3; adult/concession €3/2; ☼ 10am-5pm Fri-Wed Apr-Oct, to 4pm Nov-Mar) is one of the oldest, and inside there are exhibits on the style and construction technique. Nearby is **Finkenherd** and a cluster of more recent half-timbered houses, built where Heinrich der Vogler (Henry the Fowler, also Heinrich I; r 919–36) was said to be trapping finches when told he had been elected king.

KLOPSTOCKHAUS
The early classicist poet Friedrich Gottlieb Klopstock (1724–1803) is one of Quedlinburg's most celebrated sons. He was born in this 16th-century house, which is now a **museum** (☎ 2610; Schlossberg 12; adult/concession €3.50/2.50; ☼ 10am-5pm Wed-Sun Apr-Oct, to 4pm Nov-Mar) containing some interesting exhibits on Klopstock himself and Dorothea Erxleben (1715–62), Germany's first female doctor.

LYONEL-FEININGER-GALERIE
The **Lyonel-Feininger-Galerie** (☎ 2384; www.feininger -galerie.de; Finkenherd 5a; adult/concession €6/3; ☼ 10am-6pm Tue-Sun Apr-Oct, 10am-5pm Nov-Mar) houses the work of influential Bauhaus artist Lyonel Feininger (1871–1956). Feininger was born in Germany and became an American citizen. The original graphics, drawings, watercolours and sketches on display are from the period 1906 to 1936, and were hidden from the Nazis by a Quedlinburg citizen.

SCHLOSSBERG
The **Schlossberg** (☼ 6am-10pm), on a 25m-high plateau above Quedlinburg, was first graced with a church and residence under Henry the Fowler. The present-day Renaissance Schloss contains a revamped **Schlossmuseum** (☎ 905 681; adult/concession €4/2.50, combined museum & Stiftskirche €7/4.50; ☼ 10am-6pm Apr-Oct, 10am-4pm Sat-Thu Nov-Mar), with some fascinating Ottonian period exhibits dating from 919 to 1056. A multimedia display explains how the Nazis used the site for propaganda by staging a series of events to celebrate Heinrich – whose life they reinterpreted to justify their own ideology and crimes.

The 12th-century **Stiftskirche St Servatius** (☎ 709 900; adult/concession €4.50/3; ☼ 10am-5.30pm Tue-Sat & noon-5.30pm Sun May-Oct, to 3.30pm Tue-Sun Nov-Mar) is one of Germany's most significant of the Romanesque period. Its treasury contains valuable reliquaries and early Bibles. The crypt has some early religious frescoes and contains the graves of Heinrich and his widow, Mathilde, along with those of the abbesses.

MÜNZENBERG & WIPERTIKIRCHE
Across Wipertistrasse, on the hill west of the castle, are the ruins of **Münzenberg**, a Romanesque convent. It was plundered during the Peasant Wars in 1525, and small houses were later built among the ruins. This fascinating hilltop settlement then became home to wandering minstrels, knife grinders and other itinerant tradespeople. A small private **Münzenberg Museum** (Münzenberg 16; ☼ 10am-noon & 3-5pm Mon, Wed & Fri, 9am-noon & 3-6pm Sat & Sun; admission by donation) is located here behind the cafe (see opposite) – its centrepiece is an excavated skeleton from the 12th or 13th century, when a cemetery was located near the convent.

The **Wipertikirche** crypt was built around 1000, and the **church** (☎ 915 084; ☼ 10am-noon & 2-5pm Mon-Sat, 2-5pm Sun May-Oct) itself was used as a barn from 1812 until its restoration in the 1950s. The church is surrounded by a tranquil cemetery and grounds. The Romanesque crypt from the 11th century is the highlight, which can be viewed during opening hours or by taking the tourist office's **Auf den Spuren der Ottonen tour** (per person €7; ☼ 10am Tue & Sat Apr-Oct).

Festivals & Events
A programme of classical music is held in the Stiftskirche every year from June to September. For tickets and information, contact the tourist office.

Sleeping
DJH hostel (☎ 811 703; jh-quedlinburg@djh-sachsen -anhalt.de; Neuendorf 28; under/over 27yr €16.50/19.50; ☒) This excellent DJH hostel offers four- and 10-bed dorms in a quiet and very central location. It's relatively small and fills quickly in summer.

Hotel zur Goldenen Sonne (☎ 962 50; www.hotel zurgoldenensonne.de, in German; Steinweg 11; s €49-64, d €69-92; ℗ ☒) Both the old and new buildings of this hotel have very decent rooms, but those in the old building are better furnished, have better windows and are mostly away from the restaurant's interior yard.

Hotel am Hoken (☎ 525 40; www.hotel-am-hoken.de; Hoken 3; s €58, d €74-92; ☒) This highly recommended hotel off Markt has elegance, lots of traditional style and some light decorative touches. Floors and furnishings are in attractive timber.

Hotel Zum Bär (☎ 7770; www.hotelzumbaer.de; Markt 8-9; s €58-90, d €85-145; **P**) This traditional hotel situated in the heart of the old town has spacious, well-styled rooms and a good mid-priced restaurant downstairs. Few rooms are specifically nonsmoking though.

Romantik Hotel Theophano (☎ 963 00; www.hotel theophano.de; Markt 13-14; s €69, d €99-140; **P** **X** **▣**) Each room is decorated in an individual style at this rambling, rustic hotel. Most are spacious and very comfortable, but the many staircases (no lift) and low thresholds might be a problem for some. Doubles are reduced Sunday to Thursday.

our pick **Hotel Quedlinburger Stadtschloss** (☎ 526 70; quedlinburgerstadtschloss@precisehotels.com; Bockstrasse 6/Klink 11; s €75-115, d €100-160; **P** **X** **⊙**) Tasteful features and the wellness area (Finnish sauna, steam bath and whirlpool) of this hotel in a restored Renaissance residence make it a great choice in the town centre. Most rooms are designed to accommodate those in wheelchairs. If planning a lot of surfing, note that wi-fi is expensive at €5 per hour.

Schlosshotel Zum Markgrafen (☎ 811 40; www .schlosshotel-zum-markgrafen.de; Wallstrasse 96; s €105, d €150-180; **P** **X**) Some rooms have a whirlpool, most have leadlight windows, and all are comfortable in this neo-Gothic mansion from 1904. You can chill out on the cafe terrace or eat and drink in the hotel restaurant and cocktail bar. Its park is locked after dark and reserved for guests.

Eating & Drinking

our pick **Café Münzenberg** (☎ 907 134; Münzenberg 11/17; snacks €4-8; ☺ 10am-6pm Easter-Oct; **X**) Perched upon the cliff of Münzenberg, this sleek little cafe has outdoor seating, a few snacks and a wonderful view of town. It's well worth the hike up here but hours are subject to change, so ask inside Zum Roland (see right) to find out if it's currently open.

Kartoffelhaus No 1 (☎ 708 334; Breite Strasse 37; mains €2.50-14.50; ☺ 11am-midnight; **X**) Tasty potato and grill dishes – nothing more, nothing less – are served here in large quantities. Enter from Klink.

Hössler (☎ 915 255; Steinbrücke 21; meals €4.60-11; ☺ 9am-7pm Mon-Thu, to 9pm Fri, to 4pm Sat; **X**) This is an excellent fish cafeteria with a restaurant through the passage.

Zum Roland (☎ 4532; Breite Strasse 2-6; mains €6-15, cakes €3; ☺ 10am-10pm; **X**) Sprawling through seven houses and seating over 700 people, this cafe does quite good international nosh and a delicious apple strudel.

Brauhaus Lüdde (☎ 705 206; Blasiistrasse 14; mains €9-16.50; ☺ 11am-midnight Mon-Sat, to 10pm Sun; **X**) After the arrival of a coach group, the average age can soar to 70 years, decreasing slowly as the night grinds on in this lively microbrewery. Decent food and good boutique beer (despite some rather flatulent names for the local drop) are the order of the day in Lüdde.

Restaurant Theophano im Palais Salfeldt (☎ 963 00; Kornmarkt 6; mains €11-35, 6-course menu €46; ☺ 6pm-midnight Tue-Sat; **X**) Belonging to the Romantik Hotel Theophano (see left), this restaurant is housed in a mansion, where it serves fine seasonal dishes.

Entertainment

Unfortunately, Quedlinburg is pretty close to being an entertainment-free zone.

Gildehaus zur Rose (Breite Strasse 39; ☺ from 9pm Fri & Sat) This is your best bet – an occasional venue with DJs and various parties, but the panelled interior alone justifies a visit whenever it's open.

Getting There & Away

For trains to Wernigerode (€8.40, 45 minutes), change at Halberstadt. The narrow-gauge *Selketalbahn* runs to Gernrode (€3, 15 minutes) and beyond; other frequent trains go to Thale (€2.10, 11 minutes). There are no left-luggage lockers, and the station hall isn't always open.

The **QBus** (☎ 2236; www.qbus-ballenstedt.de, in German; Hauptbahnhof) office inside the hall has timetables and information on its frequent regional services. Buses to Thale alternate half-hourly with trains and leave from the bridge in front of the train station (stop 8 and 9).

The **Strasse der Romanik** (Romanesque Road; not to be confused with the Romantic Road in Bavaria) leads south to Gernrode. This theme road follows the L239 south to Gernrode and connects towns that have significant Romanesque architecture. The B6 runs west to Wernigerode, Goslar, the A395 (for Braunschweig) and the A7 between Kassel and Hanover. For Halle take the B6 east, and for Halberstadt the B79 north.

Getting Around

Cars can be hired from **National Car Rental** (☎ 770 70; Gernröder Weg 5b). There are numerous **taxi services** (☎ 707 777, 702 525) in town. **2Rad Pavillon** (☎ 709 507; Bahnhofstrasse 1b) hires out bicycles from €6 per day.

GERNRODE

☎ 039485 / pop 3800

Only 8km south of Quedlinburg, Gernrode makes an ideal day trip. Its Stiftskirche St Cyriakus is one of Germany's finest churches, while hikers, picnickers and steam-train enthusiasts will also enjoy this pretty town, which boasts the largest thermometer and *Skat* (a card game) table in the world.

The **tourist office** (☎ 354; www.gernrode.de; Suderode Strasse 8; ☼ 9am-4pm Mon-Fri) is a 10-minute walk from the Hauptbahnhof and another 10 minutes from the town centre.

Sights & Activities

Stiftskirche St Cyriakus (☎ 275; guided tour €3; ☼ 9am-5pm Mon-Sat, noon-5pm Sun Apr-Oct, tours 3pm daily year-round) is one of the purest examples of Romanesque architecture from the Ottonian period. Construction of the basilica, which is based on the form of a cross, was begun in 959. Especially noteworthy is the early use of alternating columns and pillars, later a common Romanesque feature. The octagonal **Taufstein** (Christening stone), whose religious motifs culminate in the Ascension, dates from 1150. You can also see enclosed in glass **Das Heilige Grab**, an 11th-century replica of Christ's tomb in Jerusalem. The tourist office has information on summer organ concerts and tours.

The **narrow-gauge railway** from Gernrode to Mägdesprung (€3, 30 minutes) is especially picturesque; you can break the trip at Sternhaus Ramberg, where a short trail leads through the forest to **Bremer Teich**, a pretty swimming hole with a camp site and hostel. You can also walk to Mägdesprung and beyond from Gernrode along paths beside the train track.

From the corner of Bahnhofstrasse and Marktstrasse, marked hiking trails lead east to **Burg Falkenstein** (11km), the historic castle in the Selke Valley, and west to Thale (about 13km).

Getting There & Away

Regular QBus services for Thale and Quedlinburg stop at the Hauptbahnhof and in front of the tourist office. The Selketalbahn passes through Gernrode from Quedlinburg (see boxed text, p250); buy tickets at the Hauptbahnhof.

THALE

☎ 03947 / pop 15,200

Situated below the northern slopes of the Harz Mountains, Thale is a small industrial and tourist centre. The main attraction for visitors is the sensational landscape of rugged cliffs and a lush river valley that makes for ideal hiking. On the two cliffs at the head of the valley are Hexentanzplatz and Rosstrappe, both magnets for postmodern pagans, who gather in grand style and numbers each year on 30 April to celebrate Walpurgisnacht (see boxed text, opposite).

Orientation & Information

Thale's two main streets are Poststrasse, which runs diagonally off Bahnhofstrasse (left from the Hauptbahnhof), and Karl-Marx-Strasse, which runs northeast to the Bode River.

The **tourist office** (☎ 2597; www.thale.de; Bahnhofstrasse 3; ☼ 7am-5pm Mon-Fri, 9am-3pm Sat & Sun) is in Friedenspark opposite the Hauptbahnhof. Pick up the English-language brochure

---

HIKING THE HARZER-HEXEN-STIEG

If you feel like hiking but you don't feel up to lugging your pack (or the old knees aren't up to it anymore), then the Harzer-Hexen-Stieg (Harz Witches' Ascent) might be your way to go. The tourist office (above) in Thale regularly organises group hikes that individuals can join. You will arrive in the hut or *Pension* each night to find your luggage awaiting you there. At the end of the 100km hike (usually over seven days) you will also be ferried back to your starting point in Thale. A northern route of the Harzer-Hexen-Stieg goes via Brocken, while the southern route is via St Andreasberg. The size of groups ranges from about five to 20 – the average age is about 50 years, but younger people also join, the folks in Thale say – and the deal is a very reasonable €288 per person in twin-bed rooms.

WITCHES & WARLOCKS

The Bodetal was first inhabited by Celts, whose fortresses were conquered by Germanic tribes and used for pagan rituals before Charlemagne embarked upon campaigns to subjugate and Christianise the local population during the 8th-century Saxon Wars. Harz mythology blends these pagan and Christian elements.

One popular – but misleading – explanation for the Walpurgisnacht festival is that it was an invention of the tribes who, pursued by Christian missionaries, held secret gatherings to carry out their rituals. They are said to have darkened their faces one night and, armed with broomsticks and pitchforks, scared off Charlemagne's guards, who mistook them for witches and devils. In fact the name 'Walpurgisnacht' itself probably derives from St Walpurga, but the festival tradition may also refer to the wedding of the gods Wodan and Freya.

According to local mythology, witches and warlocks gather on Walpurgisnacht at locations throughout the Harz before flying off to the Brocken on broomsticks or goats. There they recount the year's evil deeds and top off the stories with a bacchanalian frenzy, said to represent copulation with the devil. Frightened peasants used to hang crosses and herbs on stable doors to protect their livestock; ringing church bells or cracking whips were other ways to prevent stray witches from dropping by.

One of the best places to celebrate Walpurgisnacht is Thale, where not-so-pagan hordes of 35,000 or more arrive for colourful variety events and the Walpurgishalle tells you all you need to know about sacrifices, rituals and local myths. Schierke, also popular, is a starting point for Walpurgisnacht treks to the Brocken. Wherever you are, expect to see the dawn in with some very strange characters!

Legendary Thale, or book a themed tour with a witch (€4).

There's a Sparkasse bank at the top of Karl-Marx-Strasse; the post office is in the Kaufhaus department store at No 16.

Sights

Hexentanzplatz and **Rosstrappe** are two rugged outcrops flanking the Bode Valley that once had Celtic fortresses and were used by Germanic tribes for occult rituals and sacrifices (see boxed text, above). The landscape also inspired the myth of Brunhilde, who escaped a loveless marriage to Bohemian prince Bodo by leaping the gorge on horseback; her pursuing fiancé couldn't make the jump and plunged into the valley that now bears his name, turning into a hellhound on the way. The impact of Brunhilde's landing supposedly left the famous hoof imprint in the stone on Rosstrappe. It is worth climbing up here for the magnificent views alone.

A **cable car** (return €4.50; ☺ 9.30am-6pm Easter-Sep, 10am-4.30pm Oct-Easter) runs to Hexentanzplatz, or you can take a **chairlift** (return €3.50; ☺ 9.30am-6pm Easter-Sep, 10am-4.30pm Oct-Easter) to Rosstrappe. Go early or late in the day to avoid crowds. Signs direct you from the Hauptbahnhof.

The wooden museum **Walpurgishalle** (Hexentanzplatz; adult/child €1.50/1; ☺ 10am-6pm May-Oct) has exhibitions and paintings on matters heathen (German only), including the *Opferstein*, a stone once used in Germanic sacrificial rituals. Nearby is a 10-hectare **Tierpark** (☎ 2880; www.tierpark-thale.de; adult/concession/child €4/3/2.50; ☺ 10am-7pm Jun-Aug, 9am-6pm May, Sep & Oct, 9am-5pm Feb-Apr, 10am-4pm Nov-Jan) with lynxes, wild cats and other furry friends. The Hexentanzplatz itself is now basically a coach park full of souvenir shops.

Activities

The **hiking** brochures *Wanderführer* (€1) and *Führer durch das Bodetal* (€1.50) are excellent if your German is up to it. Highly recommended is the Bode Valley 'Hexenstieg' walk between Thale and Treseburg (blue triangle, 10km). If you take the bus from Thale to Treseburg, you can walk downstream and enjoy the most spectacular scenery at the end. WVB bus 264 does the trip from April to early November, and QBus 18 runs via Hexentanzplatz from April to October. Another 10km trail (red dot) goes from Hexentanzplatz to Treseburg; combine with the valley walk to make a round trip.

Festivals & Events

The open-air **Harzer Bergtheater** (☎ 2324; www.harzer-bergtheater.de, in German; Hexentanzplatz) has a summer program of music and plays, plus a performance on Walpurgisnacht. Tickets are sold at the venue and the tourist office.

Sleeping & Eating

Book extremely early for Walpurgisnacht. The number of cheap private rooms is limited, but the tourist office can help, especially in finding holiday flats.

DJH hostel (☎ 2881; jh-thale@djh-sachsen-anhalt.de; Bodetal-Waldkater; under/over 27yr €16.50/19.50; P ✗) This DJH hostel is central to the train and bus stations and nestled in lush surroundings where the trail begins for the Bode Valley.

Hotel Haus Sonneneck (☎ 496 10; www.haus-sonnen eck-thale.de, in German; Heimburgstrasse 1a; s €35-49, d €55-80; P ✗) Situated between Friedenspark and the forest, this hotel also has light, wood-panelled interiors, complemented by some antique furnishings and a spacious feel. It is central, quiet and close to the walks and lifts.

Ferienpark Bodetal Thale (☎ 776 60; www.ferien park-bodetal.de, in German; Hubertusstrasse 9-11; s €60-90, d €75-90; P ✗ ♨) Directly across Friedenspark, this modern hotel and holiday apartment complex has very smart rooms with balconies, a children's playground, a restaurant and various health and fitness extras.

Piccola Romantica (☎ 630 99; Musestieg 28; pizza €4.40-9.50, pasta €4.20-6.50, schnitzel €7.60-8.50) Though it's a 20-minute walk northeast from the station along Bahnhofstrasse and Sputnikweg, this Italian restaurant is a good deal for sit down or – if the walk's too much after the hiking – delivery meals.

Both Hexentanzplatz and Rosstrappe have restaurants. The **Berghotel Hexentanzplat** (☎ 4730; Hexentanzplatz; mains €9-13) has outdoor terrace seating in summer and is the best option for a sit-down meal. It also has rooms for €50/80.

Getting There & Around

Frequent trains travel to Halberstadt (€5.10 45 minutes), Quedlinburg (€2.10, 12 minutes), Wernigerode (€10.30, one hour) and Magdeburg (€15.20, 1½ hours). Karl-Marx Strasse leads to the main junction for roads to Quedlinburg and Wernigerode.

The bus station is located alongside the train station. For Wernigerode, take bus WVB 253; to get to Treseburg, take QBus 18. WVB bus 264 goes to Treseburg and Blankenburg via Rosstrappe. For a taxi, call ☎ 2505 or ☎ 2435.

Thuringia

Thuringia's mystique has long been on the radar of German travellers, but, for most foreign visitors, this former East German state is usually *terra incognita*. Those who do visit, however, most surely enjoy what they encounter. Places like Weimar, for instance, which became a keystone of German culture and thought during the Age of Enlightenment and later gave birth to the hugely influential Bauhaus movement. Or Eisenach, remarkable for being both a centre of historic German Lutheranism and of car manufacturing. Jena, of course, has kept alive its legacy as a city of science and optics to this day. And don't forget the state capital, Erfurt, which wears its medieval splendour with pride.

Once you've done cultural and historical Thuringia, however, it's time to shake off all those civilising influences and explore the rich natural offerings of the Thuringian Forest. Its sleepy villages are the portals through which hikers, cyclists and anyone in need of stress relief can indulge their love for the outdoors. You can walk in the footsteps of Johann Wolfgang von Goethe, feeling embraced by thick forest and liberated by vistas that send the spirit soaring.

Although its roads and trails are well trodden and its cities were long ago etched onto the world cultural map, Thuringia brings many unexpected rewards for visitors who put aside frantic activity and immerse themselves in the gentle momentum of slow travel.

HIGHLIGHTS

- **Culture Vulture** Find out why Germany is known as the 'land of poets and thinkers' on a saunter around Weimar (p269)
- **Going for Goethe** Follow in the footsteps of Germany's favourite genius by hiking the Goethewanderweg (p286) from Ilmenau (p285) to Stützerbach
- **Castle Cravings** Go behind the scenes of the Middle Ages at the Wartburg (p281), Martin Luther's one-time hiding place
- **Glamour Grotto** Go hunting for fairies in the underground world of the Feengrotten in Saalfeld (p293)
- **Science, Seriously** Peer through a microscope and into the starry skies in Jena's Optical Museum and planetarium (p290)
- **Rennsteig Ramble** Tackle a leg or two of the Rennsteig (p282), Germany's oldest trail, by foot or on your bike from Eisenach (p280)
- **Wild Ride** Rattle across meadows and through the trees aboard a nostalgic tram (p277) running from Gotha (p276) to beautiful Friedrichroda (p284) and beyond

- POPULATION: 2.28 MILLION
- AREA: 16,172 SQ KM

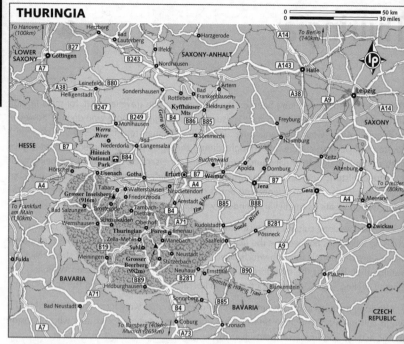

THURINGIA

Information

For pretrip planning needs, the **Thuringia Tourist Board** (www.thuringia-tourism.com) has put together a nifty website. Once you're here, you could also swing by their brick-and-mortar office in Erfurt (opposite). The board issues the **Thüringen Card** (1/3/6 days adult €14/33/53, child €9/20/31), which gives you free admission to more than 200 attractions and also includes some public transportation. It's sold on-line, at local tourist offices, hotels and other participating venues.

Getting There & Away

The only airport is in Erfurt, but it's tiny and, unless you're driving, you're far more likely to arrive by train. All the major towns are served several times daily from Frankfurt, Berlin, Dresden and other cities.

Drivers will find the A4 a handy link between the major towns, from Eisenach in the west to Jena in the east. The new A71 autobahn cuts north–south through the forest from Erfurt to Schweinfurt in northern Bavaria. The Berlin–Munich A9 cuts through the eastern part of Thuringia. The

rural north and mountainous south of the state are criss-crossed by well-maintained 'B' roads.

Getting Around

Trains are supplemented by local bus networks and an efficient road system. There are two good-value discount train tickets available in Thuringia. The **Thüringen-Ticket** (€28) gives up to five people unlimited travel within the state from 9am to 3am the following day or, on Saturday and Sunday, from midnight to 3am the following day. It is valid in 2nd class on RE, RB and S-Bahn trains, as well as on buses and trams. The version for single travellers costs €19. Another good deal is the **Hopper-Ticket** (€6), which is valid for a day return to any town within 50km of your starting point, including places in Saxony-Anhalt. All tickets costs €2 more if bought from a train station agent instead of a vending machine.

Thuringia also has an extensive bike trail system. The website www.rad-thueringen.de has lots of information, but unfortunately only in German.

CENTRAL THURINGIA

ERFURT

☎ 0361 / pop 199,000

Thuringia's capital is a scene-stealing combo of sweeping squares, time-worn alleyways, perky church towers, idyllic river scenery and vintage inns and taverns. On the little Gera River, Erfurt was founded by the indefatigable missionary St Boniface as a bishopric in 742 and was catapulted to prominence and prosperity in the Middle Ages when it began producing a precious blue pigment from the woad plant. In 1392 rich merchants founded the university, allowing students to study common law, rather than religious law. Its most famous graduate was Martin Luther, who studied philosophy here before becoming a monk at the local Augustinian monastery in 1505.

Today Erfurt's looks still very much reflect its medieval roots, but, fortunately, it's anything but ossified. Refounded in 1994, the university is again going strong, with students injecting verve and vigour into the city's cultural life. Erfurt is also a media hub as the seat of KI.KA, a popular children's TV channel, and several radio stations and newspapers. Its numerous sightseeing gems include a lofty cathedral, the winding streets of the restored Altstadt (old town), a spectacular garden and one of Europe's most interesting bridges.

Orientation

The Hauptbahnhof (central train station) is just outside the ring road on the southeastern edge of the town centre. It's a five-minute walk northwest from the Hauptbahnhof along Bahnhofstrasse to Anger, the main shopping artery, and another five minutes to Fischmarkt and the tourist office.

Information

Emergency Clinic (☎ 224 9910; Puschkinstrasse 23; ☻ 24hr)

Erfurt Tourist Office (www.erfurt-tourismus.de) Benediktsplatz (☎ 664 00; Benediktsplatz 1; ☻ 10am-7pm Mon-Fri, 10am-6pm Sat, 10am-4pm Sun Apr-Dec, 10am-6pm Mon-Sat, 10am-4pm Sun Jan-Mar) Petersberg (☎ 6015 384; ☻ 11am-6.30pm Apr-Oct, 11am-4pm Nov & Dec) Sells the ErfurtCard (€12.90 per 48 hours), which includes a city tour, public transport and free or discounted admissions.

Fire & Ambulance (☎ 112)

Habel & Hugendubel (☎ 484 484; Anger 62) Huge bookshop with English-language books.

Internet Café (☎ 262 3834; Ratskellerpassage, Fischmarkt 5; per min €0.05; ☻ 10am-8pm Mon-Fri, 11am-7pm Sat, 3-8pm Sun)

Police (☎ emergencies 110, nonemergencies 6620; Andreasstrasse 38)

Post office (Anger 66; ☻ 9am-7pm Mon-Fri, 9am-1pm Sat)

ReiseBank (☎ 643 8361; Hauptbahnhof; ☻ 8am-8pm Mon-Fri, 9am-4pm Sat) Currency exchange.

Thuringia Tourist Office (☎ 374 2388; Willy-Brandt-Platz 1; ☻ 9am-7pm Mon-Fri, 10am-4pm Sat & Sun) Opposite the Hauptbahnhof.

Sights

MARIENDOM & SEVERIKIRCHE

Erfurt is at its most striking in the vast Domplatz, where the Mariendom and the Severikirche form a photogenic ensemble.

The **Dom** (St Mary's Cathedral; ☎ 646 1265; Domplatz; ☻ 9am-6pm Mon-Sat, 1-6pm Sun May-Oct, 10-11.30am & 12.30pm-4pm Mon-Sat, 2-4pm Sun Nov-Apr) has origins as a simple chapel founded in 742 by St Boniface, but the Gothic pile you see today has the hallmarks of the 14th century. Check out the superb **stained-glass windows** (1370–1420) featuring biblical scenes; the **Wolfram** (1160), a bronze candelabrum in the shape of a man; the **Gloriosa bell** (1497); a Romanesque stucco **Madonna**; and the 14th-century **choir stalls**. The steps buttressing the cathedral make for a dramatic backdrop for the popular **Domstufen-Festspiele** (www.domstufen.de, in German), a classical music festival held every August.

The **Severikirche** (☎ 576 960; Domplatz; ☻ 9am-6pm Mon-Sat, 1-6pm Sun May-Oct, 10-11.30am & 12.30-4pm Mon-Sat, 2-4pm Sun Nov-Apr) is a five-aisled hall church (1280) that counts a stone **Madonna** (1345), a 15m-high baptismal **font** (1467), and the sarcophagus of **St Severus** among its most prized treasures.

ZITADELLE PETERSBERG

On the Petersberg hill northwest of Domplatz, this citadel ranks among Europe's largest and best-preserved baroque fortresses. It sits above a honeycomb of tunnels, which can be explored on **guided tours** (adult/concession €8/4; ☻ 7pm Fri & Sat May-Oct) run by the tourist office. Also up here is the Romanesque **Peterskirche**, which is used as the **Forum for Concrete Art** (☎ 785 2298; admission free; ☻ 10am-6pm Wed-Sun).

THURINGIA

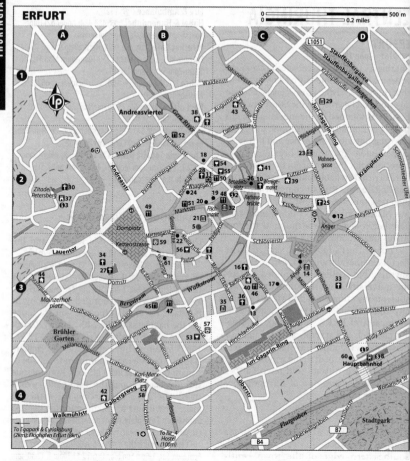

ERFURT

AUGUSTINERKLOSTER

It's Luther lore galore at the **Augustinerkloster**
(Augustinian monastery; ☎ 576 600; Augustinerstrasse
10, enter on Comthurgasse; tours adult/concession €5/3;
☻ tours hourly 10am-noon & 2-5pm Mon-Sat, 11am, 2pm
& 3pm Sun Apr-Oct, to 4pm Mon-Sat Nov-Mar). This is
where the reformer lived from 1505 to 1511,
and where he was ordained as a monk and
read his first mass. You're free to roam the
grounds, visit the church, with its ethereal
Gothic stained-glass windows, and attend
the prayer services held by the resident
Protestant sisters at 7am, noon and 6pm
daily except Tuesday. Guided tours get
you inside the monastery itself, including
the cloister, a recreated Luther cell and
an exhibit on the history of the Bible and
Luther's life in Erfurt. For information on
spending the night, see Sleeping, p267.

KRÄMERBRÜCKE

Even if it could not claim to be the only
bridge north of the Alps lined with houses
on both sides, the medieval **Krämerbrücke**
(merchant bridge) would still be a most
charming spot. You can watch chocolate
makers, potters, jewellers and other artisans
at work in their teensy studios or enjoy a
coffee or glass of wine in a cafe. The 1325
stone bridge used to be bookended by two
churches, of which only the **Ägidienkirche** remains. Climbing up its **tower** (admission €1.50;
☻ 11am-5pm Tue-Sun) is worth the cardio effort,
and not only for shutterbugs.

ALTE SYNAGOGE

The **Alte Synagoge** (Old Synagogue; ☎ 655 1608; http://
alte-synagoge.erfurt.de; Waagegasse 8; admission adult/stu-
dent under 27/child €5/1.50/1.50; ☺ 10am-6pm Tue-Sun)
in Erfurt is one of the oldest Jewish houses
of worship in Europe, with roots in the 12th
century. After the pogrom of 1349, it was converted into a storehouse and, after later standing empty for decades, has now been restored
as an exhibit space and museum. Since late
2009, a new exhibit documents the history of
the building, although an even bigger draw is
the treasure unearthed during recent excavations in Erfurt's Jewish quarter. It includes 600
pieces in all: rings, brooches, cutlery and, most
famously, a super-rare golden Jewish marriage
ring from the early 14th century.

CHURCHES

Erfurt's churches give an interesting insight into the city's history. The old university church **Michaeliskirche** (☎ 346 7212; cnr
Michaelisstrasse & Allerheiligenstrasse; ☺ 11am-4pm Mon-
Sat) boasts a magnificent **organ** (1652), made
by local master Ludwig Compenius, and was a
key gathering place of leading local dissidents
during the final days of the GDR.

The bomb-damaged **Barfüsserkirche** (☎ 554
560; Barfüsserstrasse 20; adult/concession €1/0.50; ☺ 10am-
1pm & 2-6pm Apr-Oct) has a small collection of

medieval art and hosts a summer theatre in
its courtyard.

MUSEUMS

A trio of museums peer into the past of Erfurt
and the region. Inside the magnificent portal
of the Haus am Stockfisch, the **Stadtmuseum** (City
Museum; ☎ 655 5650; Johannesstrasse 169; adult/conces-
sion/family €4/3/12; ☺ 10am-6pm Tue-Sun) has exhibits
ranging from a medieval bone-carver's workshop to displays on Erfurt in GDR times.

The **Angermuseum** (☎ 562 3311; www.anger
museum.de; Anger 18) has been undergoing restoration forever and we don't dare venture
a guess at when it will again present its fine
collections of medieval art, landscape paintings and Thuringian faience (glazed earth-
enware). 'Soon', say the tourist office folk.
Keep us posted.

Meanwhile, you can swing by the **Museum
für Thüringer Volkskunde** (Thuringian Folklore Museum;
☎ 655 5607; Juri-Gagarin-Ring 140a; adult/concession
€1.50/0.75; ☺ 10am-6pm Tue-Sun) for folkloric
costumes, painted furniture and other items
illustrating village life throughout the ages.

EGAPARK ERFURT

It's easy to spend hours amid the kaleidoscopic
flower beds, romantic rose garden, Japanese
rock garden and greenhouses of the rambling

egapark (Erfurter Gartenausstellung; ☎ 564 3737; www
.ega-erfurt.com; Gothaer Strasse 38; adult/concession/family
€6/4.80/14; ☽ 9am-8pm May–mid-Sep, 9am-sunset mid-Sep–
Apr), about 4km west of the city centre (take tram
2 from Anger). It's so huge that there's even a
little trolley to whisk around the foot weary.
Part of the park is the medieval **Cyriaksburg**
citadel, now home to a horticultural museum.
Climb to the top for fantastic views.

Walking Tour

This walking tour checks off all the major
attractions in the heart of the city. Starting at
the Hauptbahnhof, head a short way north on
Bahnhofstrasse to the 14th-century **Reglerkirche
(1)**. The portal and the southern tower of this
former monastery church are Romanesque, and
the large carved altar dates back to 1460.

Bahnhofstrasse intersects with Anger,
Erfurt's busy commercial strip. On your right
looms the big **Anger 1 shopping mall (2)**, right
next to the twin-towered **Kaufmannskirche (3)**.
Cut a left on Anger, shuffle past the yellow
Angermuseum (4; see p265) and note the pretty
facades at No 23 and Nos 37–38. You'll also
pass the **Bartholomäusturm (5)**, a tower with

a 60-bell *Glockenspiel* that chimes its merry
tune daily at 10am, noon and 6pm.

At the **Angerbrunnen (6)** fountain, veer
right and follow Regierungsstrasse past
Wigbertikirche (7) to the Renaissance and baroque **Stadthalterpalais (8)**, now the office of
Thuringia's chancellor. Turn north (right)
into Meister-Eckehart-Strasse, then right into
Barfüsserstrasse, where the hauntingly ruined
Barfüsserkirche (9; p265) awaits. Double back to
Meister-Eckehart-Strasse and turn right, heading past the 13th-century **Predigerkirche (10)**.
Then turn west (left) into Paulstrasse and continue along Kettenstrasse to Domplatz, presided over by the grand combo of **Mariendom
(11**; p263) and **Severikirche (12**; p263).

Northwest of the Dom complex, on another
hill, are the **Zitadelle Petersberg (13**; p263) and
the Romanesque **Peterskirche (14**; p263).

WALK FACTS

Start Hauptbahnhof
Finish Fischmarkt
Distance 3.2km
Duration Two hours

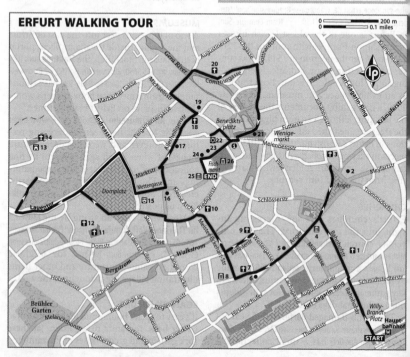

ERFURT WALKING TOUR

Back on the Domplatz, duck into the tiny Mettengasse alley for the **Theater Waidspeicher 15**; p269), now a puppet theatre but formerly a storehouse for woad, the blue dye that made Erfurters rich in the Middle Ages. Nearby, a spectacular portal fronts the 1536 **Haus zum Sonneborn (16)**, where blushing couples now exchange their wedding vows.

At the end of Mettengasse, turn left into Grosse Arche and continue via Allerheiligenstrasse to the Andreasviertel, the former university quarter. At Allerheiligenstrasse 20 is the **Haus zur Engelsburg (17)**, where a group of humanist philosophers met in Luther's day to compose at least two contentious *Dunkelmännerbriefe* (Obscurantists' Letters), satirical letters mocking contemporary theology, science and teaching practices.

A few steps further and you're at the Gothic **Michaeliskirche (18**; p265), the former university church. The original university itself, the **Collegium Majus (19)**, was destroyed by bombs in 1945, leaving only the handsome Gothic portal to admire. The university (founded in 1392, closed in 1816 and reopened in 1994) was so influential that Luther referred to it as 'my mother to whom I owe everything'.

Continue on Michaelisstrasse, cross the idyllic Gera River and hook a right on Comthurgasse to arrive at the **Augustiner-kloster (20**; p264), where Luther was a monk. From Comthurgasse, turn right onto Gotthardtstrasse, which takes you to Wenigemarkt square and the famous **Krämerbrücke (21**; p264). Poke your head inside the little stores, then, at the end of the bridge, turn right onto Michaelisstrasse and immediately left on Waagegasse to the **Alte Synagoge (22**; **p265)** and its famous gold treasure.

Double back, then turn right at the tourist office and head straight to **Fischmarkt**, a medieval market square, home to such pretty buildings as the 1584 **Haus zum Breiten Herd (23)**, with a rich Renaissance facade and a frieze depicting the five human senses. The frieze theme got picked up again in 1892 at the next-door **Gildehaus (24)**, decorated with depictions of the four virtues. On the square's northern side, contemporary art mixes well with the Renaissance setting of the **Haus zum Roten Ochsen (25)**, now home of the **Kunsthalle Erfurt** (☎ 655 5660; www.kunsthalle-erfurt.de; Fischmarkt 7; adult/con-

cession €3/1.50; ☻ 11am-6pm Tue, Wed & Fri-Sun, to 8pm Thu). Opposite, the neo-Gothic **Rathaus (26**; ☻ 8am-6pm Mon, Tue & Thu, to 4pm Wed, to 2pm Fri, 10am-5pm Sat & Sun), built 1870–75, has a series of murals depicting scenes from Luther's life, as well as the Tannhäuser and Faust legends. On the 3rd floor is an extravagant festival hall.

Sleeping
BUDGET
The Erfurt tourist office has access to a large contingent of **private rooms** (☎ 664 0110), starting at €20 per person.

Re_4 Hostel (☎ 600 0110; www.re4hostel.de; Puschkinstrasse 21; dm €13-16, s/d without bathroom €20/40, s/d with bathroom €26/52, linen €2; P ☒ ▯) If you've ever spent a night in a police lock-up, staying in this former police station might give you flashbacks – or not. It's run by an energetic, clued-in crew, happy to help you make the most out of your stay in Erfurt. Room 13 has a chilling surprise. The hostel's about 1.5km from the Hauptbahnhof.

Opera Hostel (☎ 6013 1366; www.opera-hostel.de; Walkmühlstrasse 13; dm €13-18, s/d/tr without bathroom €37/48/66, s/d/tr with bathroom €45/54/75, linen €2.50; ☒ ▯ ☞) Run with smiles and aplomb, this upmarket hostel in a historic building scores big with wallet-watching global nomads. You'll sleep like a log in bright, spacious rooms, many with an extra sofa for chilling, and make friends in the communal kitchen and on-site lounge-bar.

Pension Rad-Hof (☎ 602 7761; www.rad-hof.de, in German; Kirchgasse 1b; s €30-55, d €50-60; ☒ ▯ ☞) The owners of this cyclist-friendly guest house, next to the Augustinian monastery and near the pub quarter, have gone the extra mile in renovating the building with natural materials, such as wood and mud. No two rooms are alike.

Evangelisches Augustinerkloster zu Erfurt (☎ 664 0110; www.augustinerkloster.de; Augustinerstrasse 10; s/tw €48.50/78; P ☒ ☞) This venerable monastery has very much the character of a retreat, with only a Bible and no TV for entertainment in rooms barely larger than a monk's cell. Still, there's something undeniably special about this tranquil place, not in the least because of the bend-over-backwards friendly staff.

MIDRANGE
Hotel Ibis (☎ 664 10; www.accorhotels.com; Barfüsserstrasse 9; s/d from €71/81; P ☒ ▯ ☞) If you've stayed at

other Ibis hotels, you'll be pleasantly surprised by the larger-than-usual rooms and decent bathrooms at this entry in a quiet yet central setting opposite the Barfüsserkirche.

Hotel & Gasthof Nikolai (☎ 5981 7119; www.hotel-nikolai-erfurt.com, in German; Augustinerstrasse 30; s €78-81, d €94-110; P ✗) The location alongside the river, the overall high standard of rooms, and the friendly owners make this a prime choice, even though some rooms are small.

Hotel am Kaisersaal (☎ 658 560; www.hotel-am-kaisersaal.de, in German; Futterstrasse 8; s €84-94, d €100-110; P ✗) Rooms are tip-top and appointed with all expected mod cons in this highly rated hotel. Request a room facing the yard, though, if street noise disturbs.

IBB Hotel (☎ 674 00; www.ibbhotels.com; Gotthardtstrasse 27; s/d €85/106; P ✗ ✗) This saucy lifestyle hotel, near a willow-fringed arm of the Gera River, gets thumbs up from design-minded travellers. Rooms are spread over two buildings, one an annex on the historic Krämerbrücke with cheaper rooms.

TOP END

Pullman Erfurt am Dom (☎ 644 50; www.pullmanhotels .com; Theaterplatz 2; s €100-123, d €100-163; P ✗ ✗) Erfurt's only full-on luxury address has 160 rooms that exude effortless sophistication thanks to classy decor and a soothing natural-hued colour scheme. Sightseeing fatigue quickly fades in the impeccable Zen-inspired wellness area.

Eating

There's a **Rewe supermarket** in the Anger 1 shopping mall and a **Tegut supermarket** at the corner of Marktstrasse and Domplatz.

Henner (☎ 654 6691; Weitergasse 8; dishes €3-6; ☺ 9am-7pm Mon-Fri, 9am-5pm Sat; ✗) This upbeat bistro makes a great daytime pit stop for freshly made sandwiches, homemade soups and crisp salads.

Altstadt Café (☎ 562 6473; Fischersand 1; dishes €3-7.50; ☺ 11am-10pm Mon-Fri, noon-10pm Sat, 2-7pm Sun; ✗) Chatty mothers, foot-weary sightseers and people catching up on their reading gather at this historic cafe in a 14th-century building. The terrace overlooking the Gera is an enchanting spot in fine weather.

Zum Goldenen Schwan (☎ 2623 742; Michaelisstrasse 9; snacks €3-7, mains €6-14; ☺ 11am-1am) This authentic inn serves all the usual Thuringian classics, but, if you're up to mounting your own *Survivor* challenge, try something called

Puffbohnenpfanne (fried broad beans with roast bacon), an Erfurt speciality. Excellen house brews washes everything down well.

Steinhaus (☎ 2447 7112; Allerheiligenstrasse 20-21 mains €4-8; ☺ from 11am-late, food till midnight) The ceiling beams may be ancient, but the crowd i intergenerational at this rambling gastro pub-cum–beer garden in the historic Engelsburg Dips, baguettes, pasta and gratins should keep your tummy filled and your brain balanced.

Zwiesel (☎ 789 7207; Michaelisstrasse 31; mains €6-9 ☺ 11am-1am Sun-Thu, 11am-2am Fri & Sat) Been cut ou of the family will? No problem at this reliable cheapie choice, which has 25 mains costing just €5.95 and drinks prices to match. Ever the rump steak is only €8.95.

Mediterrana (☎ 602 7600; Lange Brücke 37a; main €6-18; ☺ 11am-midnight) Candles, Chianti and a table for two are the hallmarks of a romantic night out. If that and the riverside setting in ar ancient mill don't make your date swoon, a least the delicious Italian food should ensure a fine evening.

Si Ju (☎ 655 2295; Fischmarkt 1; mains €7.50-20 ☺ 9am-late Mon-Sat, 10am-late Sun) This restaurant-lounge combo is a fashionable stop any time for diners and drinkers of all ages. Steals include the breakfast buffet for €6, the business lunch for €7.50 and the all-you-can-eat afternoon coffee and cake for €5.50.

our pick Zum Güldenen Rade (☎ 561 3506; Marktstrasse 50; mains €8.50-15; ☺ 11am-midnight) For the best potato dumplings in town, report to this gorgeous patrician town house that, centuries ago, housed a tobacco factory. Aside from the classic version with gravy, you can also order them with stuffings, such as spinach and salmon, or with black pudding and liver pâté.

Drinking

Just north of Fischmarkt, Erfurt's former university quarter is a hub of nightspots, pubs and bars, especially along Michaelisstrasse and Futterstrasse.

Hemingway (☎ 551 9944; Michaelisstrasse 26) Everything the macho scribe loved is here in abundance: cigar humidors with personal drawers, 148 types of rum, and 30 different daiquiri cocktails. The Africa Lounge has a local Bambi, though, not an elephant bagged beneath Kilimanjaro.

Modern Masters (☎ 550 7251; Michaelisstrasse 48; ☺ from 5pm) Urbane and sophisticated, this cocktail bar has been shaking up Erfurt with flights of fancy in libation through an impressive range of more than 220 concoctions.

Weinstein LeBar (☎ 0152 2332 6707; Kleine Arche 1; ☺ from 7pm Sun-Fri, 8pm Sat; ✂) This is as unassuming a wine bar as wine bars should be: soft music, candlelight and as many as 50 wines by the glass, including some hard-to-get bottles from the nearby Saale-Unstrut Valley. A basic snack menu is available.

Dubliner (☎ 789 2595; Neuwerkstrasse 47a; ☺ from 4pm) On weekends it seems everybody's popping by to knock back pints of Kilkenny or Guinness at this boisterous Irish thirst parlour (is there any other kind?). Whiskey's all the rage downstairs.

Entertainment

Consult the free zines *Dates*, *Takt* and *Blitz* for nightlife and event listings. Throughout summer, from the end of May, classical concerts take place beneath the linden trees in the romantic courtyard of Michaeliskirche (on Fridays). Organ concerts are held year-round in the Predigerkirche and Michaeliskirche (at noon Wednesdays), and in the Dom (Saturdays).

Engelsburg (☎ 244 770; www.eburg.de, in German; Allerheiligenstrasse 20-21) Good times are pretty much guaranteed at this venerable venue, no matter whether you hunker down for beer and talk in the Steinhaus pub (see Eating, opposite), report to the dance floor of the medieval cellar labyrinth or go highbrow at the upstairs Café DuckDich cultural forum.

Presseklub (☎ 789 4565; Dalbergsweg 1) A former gathering spot for media types, this club is now a delightfully dancey party location with a chic interior and salsa and '80s nights.

Theater Waidspeicher (☎ 598 2924; Domplatz 18; tickets adult/concession €9/6.50, children's shows €5/3.50) Not only children will be enchanted by the adorable marionettes and puppets that perform at this cute theatre in a historic woad storehouse (reached via Mettengasse).

DasDie Brettl (☎ 551 166; www.dasdielive.de; Lange Brücke 29) Cabaret, musicals, concerts, transvestite shows and poetry slams heat up the stage of this cultural centre.

Getting There & Away

The tiny **Flughafen Erfurt** (☎ 656 2200; www.flughafen-erfurt.de; Binderlebener Landstrasse 100) is about 6km west of the city centre and is served by Air Berlin and a few charter airlines.

Erfurt has direct IC train links to Berlin-Hauptbahnhof (€54, 2½ hours) and ICE connections with Dresden (€48, 2½ hours) and Frankfurt am Main (€51, 2¼ hours). Direct trains also go to Meiningen (€16.70, 1½ hours) and Mühlhausen (€11.30, 45 minutes). Regional trains to Weimar (€4.40, 15 minutes) and Eisenach (€10.30, 50 minutes) run at least once hourly.

Erfurt is just north of the A4 and is crossed by the B4 (Hamburg to Bamberg) and the B7 (Kassel to Gera). The A71 autobahn runs south to Schweinfurt via Ilmenau, Oberhof and Meiningen.

Getting Around

Tram 4 directly links the airport and Anger in the city centre (€1.70, 20 minutes). Tickets in the central (yellow) zone for trams and buses cost €1.70, or €4.20 for a day pass. To order a taxi, ring ☎ 511 11 or ☎ 555 55.

Bikes can be hired at **Fahrradstation** (Bahnhofstrasse; ☺ 10am-7pm Mon-Fri, 10am-2pm Sat) for €12 per 24 hours and at **Radhaus am Dom** (☎ 602 0640; Kettenstrasse 13; ☺ 10am-6pm Mon-Fri, 10am-2pm Sat) from €9 per 24 hours.

WEIMAR

☎ 03643 / pop 64,000

Neither a monumental town nor a medieval one, Weimar appeals to those whose tastes run to cultural and intellectual pleasures. After all, this is the epicentre of the German Enlightenment, a symbol for all that is good and great in German culture. An entire pantheon of intellectual and creative giants lived and worked here: Goethe, Schiller, Bach, Cranach, Liszt, Nietzsche, Gropius, Herder, Feininger, Kandinsky, Klee…the list goes on (and on, and on). You'll see reminders of them wherever you go – here, a statue; there, a commemorative plaque decorating a house facade – plus scores of museums and historic sites. In summer, Weimar's many parks and gardens lend themselves to taking a break from the intellectual onslaught.

Internationally, of course, Weimar is better known as the place where the constitution of the Weimar Republic was drafted after WWI (see the boxed text, p274), though there are few reminders of this historical moment. The ghostly ruins of the Buchenwald concentration camp, on the other hand, provide haunting evidence of the terrors of the Nazi

THURINGIA

regime. The Bauhaus and classical Weimar locations are protected as Unesco World Heritage Sites.

Orientation

It's about a 20-minute walk south from the Hauptbahnhof to the start of the historic centre at Goetheplatz.

Information

Police (☎ 8820; Markt 13)

Post office (Goetheplatz 7-8; ☽ 9am-6.30pm Mon-Fri, 9am-noon Sat)

Roxanne Internet Café (☎ 800 194; Markt 21; per 30min €1; ☽ 10am-late Mon-Sat year-round, 1pm-late Sun May-Sep, 3pm-late Sun Oct-Apr) Internet terminals and wi-fi. Smoking is permitted.

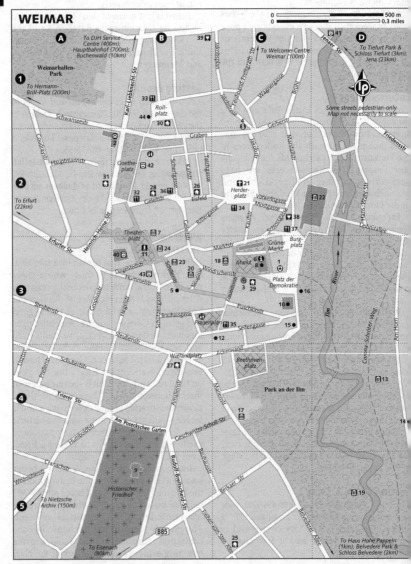

WEIMAR

Sparkasse (Graben 4) Bank with ATM.

Thalia (☎ 828 10; Schillerstrasse 5a) Bookshop.

Tourist office (☎ 7450; www.weimar.de; Markt 10; ✆ 9.30am-6pm Mon-Fri, to 3pm Sat & Sun Apr-Oct, 9.30am-6pm Mon-Fri, to 2pm Sat & Sun Nov-Mar) Sells the WeimarCard (€10 for 72 hours) for free or discounted museum admissions and travel on city buses and other benefits. There are also desks of the Buchenwald Information (☎ 430 200) and the Klassik Stiftung Weimar (☎ 545 407; www.klassik-stiftung.de).

Welcome-Centre Weimar (☎ 7450; Friedensstrasse 1; ✆ 10am-6pm Mon-Sat) This tourist office branch is about 10 minutes south of the train station.

Sights

GOETHE HAUS & NATIONALMUSEUM

No other individual is as closely associated with Weimar as Johann Wolfgang von Goethe, who lived in this town from 1775 until his death in 1832, the last 50 years in what is now the **Goethe Haus** (☎ 545 401; Frauenplan ; adult/concession/under 16 €8.50/7/free; ✆ 9am-6pm Tue-Fri & Sun, 9am-7pm Sat Apr-Sep, 9am-6pm Tue-Sun Oct, 9am-4pm Tue-Sun Nov-Mar). This is where he worked, studied, researched and penned *Faust* and other immortal works. If you're a Goethe fan, you'll get the chills when seeing his study and the bedroom where he died, both preserved in their original state. To get the most from your visit, get the audioguide (€2).

The ticket foyer also gives access to the **Goethe Nationalmuseum**, whose exhibits are expected to get an update in 2010. The focus will be less on the man himself than on his epoch, which is referred to as Weimar Classicism. Goethe, his contemporary Schiller, his ducal patrons (Anna Amalia and Carl August), his muse (Charlotte von Stein) and other cultural spear carriers feature in this loose collection of paintings, books, busts, letters and *objets d'art*. Details about admission and hours were not available at press time.

SCHILLER HAUS

Dramatist and Goethe buddy Friedrich von Schiller lived in Weimar from 1799 until his early death in 1805. Unlike Goethe, however, he had to buy his own house, now the **Schiller Haus** (☎ 545 401; Schillerstrasse 12; adult/concession/under 16 €5/4/free; ✆ 9am-6pm Tue-Fri & Sun, 9am-7pm Sat Apr-Sep, 9am-6pm Tue-Sun Oct, 9am-4pm Tue-Sun Nov-Mar). Study up on the man, his family and life in Thuringia in a new permanent exhibit before plunging on to the private quarters, including the study with his deathbed and the desk where he wrote *Wilhelm Tell* and other famous works.

Both Goethe and Schiller are interred at the **Historischer Friedhof** (Historical Cemetery) in the neoclassical **Fürstengruft** (Am Poseckschen Garten; adult/concession/under 16 €3.50/3/free; ✆ 10am-6pm Apr-Oct, 10am-4pm Nov-Mar), along with Duke Carl August.

PARK AN DER ILM

The sprawling Park an der Ilm (Ilm Park), just east of the Altstadt, is as inspiring and romantic now as it was when Goethe lived here from 1776 until 1782 in what is now **Goethes Gartenhaus** (☎ 545 401; adult/concession/under 16 €4.50/3.50/free; ✆ 10am-6pm Apr-Oct, to 4pm Nov-Mar). By giving him this simple cottage, Carl August successfully induced Goethe to stay in Weimar. It's within view of the **Römisches**

THURINGIA

Haus (☎ 545 401; adult/concession/under 16 €3.50/3/free; ☺ 10am-6pm Tue-Sun Apr-Oct), the duke's summer retreat, built under Goethe's supervision. Perched on top of an artificial bluff, Weimar's first neoclassical house now contains restored period rooms and an exhibit on Ilm Park.

On the western edge of the park, the **Liszt-Museum** (☎ 545 401; Marienstrasse 17; adult/concession/under 16 €4/3/free; ☺ 10am-6pm Wed-Mon Apr-Oct) is where the composer and pianist resided in Weimar in 1848 and again from 1869 to 1886, writing such key works as the *Hungarian Rhapsodies* and the *Faust Symphony*.

ART NOUVEAU IN WEIMAR

Belgian art-nouveau architect, designer and painter, Henry van de Velde is considered a pioneer of modernity. In 1902, he founded the arts and crafts seminar in Weimar that Walter Gropius later developed into the Bauhaus. For nine years, starting in 1908, van de Velde and his family lived in the **Haus Hohe Pappeln** (☎ 545 965; Belvederer Allee 58; adult/concession €2.50/2; ☺ 1-5pm Tue-Sun Apr-Oct), which looks a bit like a ship on its side and features natural stone, stylised chimneys, loggias and oversized windows. One floor is open for touring and features furniture that van de Velde designed for a local family. To get here, take bus 1 or 12 to Papiergraben.

Van de Velde also added an art-nouveau touch to the **Nietzsche Archiv** (☎ 545 401; Humboldtstrasse 36; adult/concession/under 16 €2.50/2/free; ☺ 1-6pm Tue-Sun Apr-Oct), where the philosopher spent his final years in illness.

There's also a cluster of splendidly restored art-nouveau buildings (though not by van de Velde) on Cranachstrasse, Gutenbergstrasse and Humboldtstrasse, just west of the Historischer Friedhof.

BAUHAUS IN WEIMAR

Considering that Weimar is the birthplace of the influential Bauhaus school, the **Bauhaus Museum** (☎ 545 401; Theaterplatz; adult/concession €4.50/3.50; ☺ 10am-6pm) is a rather modest affair. But if all goes according to plan, that'll change when it moves into splashy new digs in 2013. Meanwhile, the old building will present temporary exhibits on the group's profound impact on modern design and construction. How profound? Read up on it in the boxed text, p224.

The only Bauhaus building ever constructed in Weimar is Georg Muche's **Haus am Horn** (☎ 904 056; Am Horn 61; ☺ 11am-5pm Wed Sat & Sun Apr-Sep). Today, it's used for exhibitions and events.

HERZOGIN ANNA AMALIA BIBLIOTHEK

The phoenixlike rebirth of Anna Amalia's precious **library** (☎ 545 401; www.klassik-stiftung.de Platz der Demokratie 1; adult/concession incl audioguide €6.50/5.50; ☺ 10am-3pm Tue-Sun) following a 2004 fire is nothing short of a miracle. These days the magnificent **Rokokosaal** (Rococo Hall) is again crammed with 40,000 tomes once used for research purposes by Goethe, Schiller and other Weimar hotshots. Scholars may still borrow the books; for the rest of us, the fine

---

GOETHE – THE LITERARY LION

Johann Wolfgang von Goethe bestrides German culture like a colossus. He's often called the 'German Shakespeare', but not even Shakespeare lived to be 82, having written novels, essays, literary criticism, philosophical treatises, scientific articles and travelogues, as well as plays and poetry. Goethe was also a consummate politician, town planner, architect, social reformer and scientist. In short, he was the last 'Renaissance' man, able to do everything.

Born in Frankfurt am Main and trained as a lawyer, Goethe quickly overcame the disadvantages of a wealthy background and a happy childhood to become the driving force of the 1770's *Sturm und Drang* (Storm and Stress) literary movement. Though he worked and experimented in various styles throughout his life, his work with Friedrich Schiller fostered the theatrical style known as Weimar classicism. Goethe himself once described his work as 'fragments of a great confession'. He was revered across Europe, even during his own lifetime. Napoléon invited him to France to be the Imperial Laureate. Though fascinated by Napoléon, Goethe was no blind admirer; he didn't go to Paris.

Goethe's defining work was *Faust*, a lyrical but highly charged retelling of the classic legend of a man selling his soul for knowledge. It took Goethe almost his entire life to complete it to his own satisfaction, and it's still a much-performed piece of theatre in Germany today; a fitting legacy for a genuine giant.

busts and paintings of these men are just
as interesting. Entry is by timed ticket and
capped at 250 people per day, so book in
advance or start queuing before the ticket
office opens at 9.30am.

BELVEDERE & TIEFURT PARKS

A short bus ride away (take bus 1 from
Goetheplatz), the lovely Belvedere Park harbours Carl August's former hunting palace,
the **Schloss Belvedere** (☎ 545 401; adult/concession/
under 16 €5/4/free; ⏰ 10am-6pm Tue-Sun Apr-Sep). It displays glass, porcelain, faience and weapons
from the late 17th and 18th centuries.

A few kilometres east of the Hauptbahnhof,
Tiefurt Park is an English-style garden that
embraces **Schloss Tiefurt** (☎ 545 401; Hauptstrasse
14, Weimar-Tiefurt; adult/concession/under 16 €5/4/free;
⏰ 10am-6pm Tue-Sun Apr-Sep), Anna Amalia's
temple of the muses'. The period rooms give
you an impression of the age and her intellectual round-table gatherings where Goethe,
Schiller and Herder were regulars. Bus 3 from
Goetheplatz goes out here.

WEIMAR HAUS

The **Weimar Haus** (☎ 901 890; www.weimarhaus.de;
Schillerstrasse 16; adult/concession €6.50/5.50; ⏰ 10am-
7pm Apr-Sep, 10am-6pm Oct-Mar) is a history museum for people who hate history museums.
Sets, sound and light effects, wax figures
and even an animatronic Goethe accompany you on your 30-minute journey into
Thuringia's past, from prehistory to the
Enlightenment. The production values can
be comical, but the entertainment factor is
unarguably high.

Walking Tour

Our tour begins on Theaterplatz. Here, the
famous **Goethe and Schiller statue** (**1**; 1857)
fronts the **Deutsches Nationaltheater** (**2**; German
National Theatre), best known as the place
where the National Assembly drafted the constitution of the Weimar Republic in 1919.
Goethe was director here from 1791 to 1817,
and Liszt and Strauss were its music directors
in the late 19th century.

Across from here is the **Bauhaus Museum**
(**3**; opposite), adjacent to the baroque
Wittumspalais (**4**; ☎ 545 401; adult/concession/under 16
€5/4/free; ⏰ 10am-6pm Tue-Sun Apr-Sep, 10am-4pm Tue-Sun
Nov-Mar), once a residence of Anna Amalia.

From Theaterplatz, follow Schillerstrasse
past the **Weimar Haus** (**5**; above) to the **Schiller**

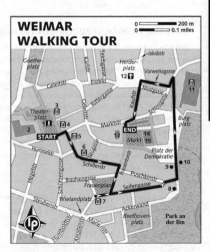

WEIMAR WALKING TOUR

0 —— 200 m
0 —— 0.1 miles

WALK FACTS

Start Theaterplatz
Finish Markt
Distance 1.8km
Duration 1½ hours

Haus (**6**; p271), the one-time home of the famous dramatist. His buddy Johann Wolfgang
von Goethe lived just down the street. Get
there by turning right into Frauentorstrasse
and following it to Frauenplan and the must-
see **Goethe Haus & Nationalmuseum** (**7**; p271).

Goethe's long-time muse (and perhaps
more), Charlotte von Stein, lived close by
in what is now **Haus der Frau von Stein** (**8**) at
the end of Seifengasse For now, it's used by
the Goethe-Institut language school and culture centre, but, since being sold to a private
owner, its fate is uncertain.

Turning left puts you onto the Platz der
Demokratie and thus next to the **Fürstenhaus**
(**9**), a former palace and now home to the prestigious music academy founded by Franz Liszt
in 1872, and the **Herzogin Anna Amalia Bibliothek**
(**10**, opposite).

Continue north to Burgplatz, anchored by
the **Stadtschloss (11)**, the former residence of
the ducal family of Saxe-Weimar. Inside is the
Schlossmuseum (☎ 545 960; Burgplatz 4; adult/conces-
sion/under 16 €6/5/free; ⏰ 10am-6pm Tue-Sun Apr-Oct, to
4pm Nov-Mar) with art by Albrecht Dürer, Dutch
masters and German romanticists. Several
restored rooms are also open for touring.

THURINGIA

HOW THE WEIMAR REPUBLIC GOT ITS NAME

Despite its name, the Weimar Republic (1919–33), Germany's first dalliance with democracy, was never actually governed from Weimar. The town on the Ilm River was merely the place where, in 1919, the National Assembly drafted and passed the country's first constitution.

Assembly delegates felt that the volatile and explosive political climate rocking post-WWI Berlin would threaten the democratic process if it took place there, and looked for an alternative location. Weimar had several factors in its favour: a central location, a suitable venue (the Deutsches Nationaltheater), and a humanist tradition entirely antithetical to the militaristic Prussian spirit that had led to war.

Weimar's spot in the democratic limelight, however, lasted only briefly. With the situation in Berlin calming down, the delegates returned to the capital just one week after passing the constitution on 31 July.

West of here, via Vorwerksgasse, is Herderplatz, dominated by the **Stadtkirche St Peter und Paul** (12; ☎ 851 518; Herderplatz; ⊙ 10am-6pm Mon-Fri, 10am-noon & 2-4pm Sat, to 3pm Sun Apr-Oct, 11am-noon & 3-4pm daily Nov-Mar), popularly known as the Herderkirche after Johann Gottfried Herder, who's buried inside. The church has a famous altarpiece (1555), painted by the Cranach father-and-son team, and a triptych showing Martin Luther as a knight, professor and monk.

Heading south on Kaufstrasse takes you to the Markt, where our tour ends. Treat yourself to a sausage or a cuppa and look around at the gorgeous buildings framing this central square: the neo-Gothic **Rathaus** (13; 1841), the **Stadthaus (14)**, which now houses the tourist office, and the Renaissance **Cranachhaus (15)**, where Cranach the Elder lived for two years before his death in 1553.

Sleeping

Visitors to Weimar pay a supplement of €2 per room per overnight stay for the upkeep of cultural sites.

BUDGET

Weimar has four DJH hostels, which are usually crawling with pimple-faced teens on school excursions. If that doesn't deter you, contact the **DJH Service Centre** (☎ 850 000; www .djh-thuringen.de; Carl-August-Allee 13) for information and reservations. Otherwise try Labyrinth Hostel (below).

Labyrinth Hostel (☎ 811 822; www.weimar-hostel .com; Goetheplatz 6; dm €13-20, s €29-40, s €40-46, linen €2, breakfast €3; ✕ ▢ ☜) Loads of imagination has gone into this professionally run hostel with artist-designed rooms. In one double, for example, the bed perches on stacks of books,

while another comes with a wooden high platform bed. Bathrooms are shared and so are the kitchen and the lovely rooftop terrace Dorm 8 has a balcony.

MIDRANGE

Hotel zur Sonne (☎ 862 90; Rollplatz 2; s €47-52, d €67 86; P ✕ ☜) Although rooms are small and nondescript in this friendly, traditional hotel it's clean, reliable and right in town and has downstairs restaurant.

Hotel Amalienhof (☎ 5490; www.amalienhof-weima .de; Amalienstrasse 2; s €60-75, d €80-105; P ✕) Th charms of this church-affiliated hotel are manifold: classy antique furnishings, richl styled rooms that point to history withou burying you in it, and a late breakfast buffe for those who take their holidays seriously It's a splendid choice.

Hotel Anna Amalia (☎ 495 60; www.hotel-ann -amalia.de; Geleitstrasse 8-12; s €60-75, d €85-120, ap €120-180; P ✕ ☜) The Mediterranean look with its nice, fresh colour scheme, exude feel-good cheer in this family-run hotel nea Goetheplatz. For more panache and elbov room, book one of the apartments, whic sleep up to four.

our pick Casa dei Colori (☎ 0171 930 8036; www.cas -colori.de; Eisfeld 1a; r €65-85, breakfast €9.50; P ✕ ☜ Possibly Weimar's most charming boutiqu *Pension*, the Casa convincingly imports cheer fully exuberant Mediterranean flair to cen tral Europe. The mostly good-sized room are dressed in bold colours and come with small desk, a couple of comfy armchairs an stylish bathrooms.

Art Hotel (☎ 540 60; www.art-hotel-weimar.de Freiherr-vom-Stein-Allee 3a-3b; s €74-99, d €94-119; P ✕ This classy and contemporary art hotel cater for the needs of both tourists and busines travellers. After a day of turf pounding, the fine restaurant and the stress-melting spa and fitness area will compete for your attention. It's about a 10-minute walk south of the centre.

TOP END

Hotel Elephant Weimar (☎ 8020; www.luxurycollection .com/elephant; Markt 19; r €106-259, ste €266-600; **P** ✗ 🖳 🛜) The moment you make your entrance in the elegant art-deco lobby of this charmer, you sense that it's luxury all the way from here to the top. For over 300 years, this classic has wooed statesmen, artists, scholars and the merely rich with first-class service and amenities.

Eating & Drinking

Estragon (☎ 253 212; Herderplatz 3; soups €2.80-5.30; 🕑 10am-7pm Mon-Sat, noon-4pm Sun; ✗) There are days when a bowl of steamy soup feels as warm and embracing as a hug from a good friend. This little soup kitchen turns mostly organic ingredients into delicious flavour combos served in three sizes. It shares digs with a small organic supermarket.

Brasserie Central (☎ 852 774; Rollplatz 8a; breakfast €3-8, mains €6-13; 🕑 10am-1am; ✗) This popular bistro-bar starts the day with breakfast and, as the clock loops the hours, becomes a relaxed eatery, and a place to indulge in coffee, wine or beer.

ACC (☎ 851 161; www.acc-cafe.de; Burgplatz 1; dishes €5-10; 🕑 11am-midnight Mon-Fri, 10am-midnight Sat & Sun; 🖳 🛜) Goethe had his first pad after arriving in Weimar in this building, now home to an alt-vibe, artsy hang-out, where the food and wine are organic whenever possible and the upstairs gallery delivers a primer on the local art scene. The owners also rent out a room and a holiday flat (www.goethezimmer.de), both handsomely furnished.

Residenz-Café (☎ 594 08; Grüner Markt 4; mains €5-16; ✗) The 'Resi', one of Weimar's enduring favourites, is a jack of all trades: everyone should find something to their taste here. The Lovers' Breakfast is €19.50 for two, but the inspired meat and vegetarian dishes may well have you swooning, too.

Jo Hanns (☎ 493 617; Scherfgasse 1; mains €10-20; 🕑 11am-midnight; ✗) The food is satisfying but it's the 130 wines from the Saale-Unstrut Region – many served by the glass – that give Jo Hanns a leg up on the competition. No matter whether you order the classic steak or scallops and shrimp with mint-lime spaghetti, there's a bottle with your name on it.

Gasthaus zum Weissen Schwan (☎ 908 751; Frauentorstrasse 23; mains €11-20; 🕑 noon-midnight Wed-Sun; ✗) At this venerable inn, you can fill your tummy with Goethe's favourite dish, which actually hails from his home town of Frankfurt (boiled beef with herb sauce, red beet salad and potatoes). The rest of the menu, though, is upmarket Thuringian.

Anno 1900 (☎ 903 571; Geleitstrasse 12a; mains €12-19; 🕑 11am-1am Mon-Fri, 10am-1am Sat & Sun; ✗) Send your taste buds on a wild ride in this elegant art-nouveau pavilion. How about emu filet with carrot-rocket fettucine followed by tonka-bean crème brûlée? It's adventurous, but most of the time it works. Breakfast is served until the hangover-friendly time of 2pm.

Planbar (☎ 502 785; Jakobsplan 6; ✗) Past the heavy door awaits this good-looking bar with an unpretentious, all-ages crowd that likes to knock back the mojitos, flirt with the bartenders and wave to the DJs.

Entertainment

Studentenclub Schützengasse (☎ 904 323; www .schuetzengasse.de; Schützengasse 2) The grunge factor is high at this student club, which may be just what the doctor ordered as an antidote to highbrow burnout. Monday movie nights and salsa nights also provide diversions.

Kasseturm (☎ 851 670; www.kasseturm.de; Goetheplatz 10) A little hipper than 'Schütze', Kasse is another venerable student club, with an assorted bag of parties, concerts, drum workshops and whatever else gets people off the couch. Three floors of action, for young and old.

Deutsches Nationaltheater (German National Theatre; ☎ 755 334; www.nationaltheater-weimar.de; Theaterplatz 2; tickets €8-55; 🕑 closed Jul-Aug) Expect a grab bag of classic and contemporary theatre, opera and concerts at this venerable space.

E-Werk (☎ 748 868; www.ewerkweimar.de, in German; Am Kirschberg 4; Rebecca Horn exhibit adult/concession/under 16 €1.50/1/free; 🕑 Rebecca Horn exhibit noon-6pm Sat & Sun May-Oct) The National Theatre also performs in this former tram depot, which also has a cinema, live music, cultural events and an excellent exhibit of works by contemporary avant-garde artist Rebecca Horn.

Getting There & Away

Regular ICE services go to Frankfurt (€55, 2½ hours), Leipzig (€25, 50 minutes) and Dresden (€44, 2¼ hours); the IC train serves Berlin-Hauptbahnhof (€51, 2¼ hours). Erfurt (€5, 15 minutes) and Eisenach (€13.30, 1¼ hours) are served several times hourly, plus there's frequent service to Jena-West (€5, 15 minutes).

Getting Around

For trips outside the centre, there's a good bus system (a single costs €1.70; a day pass, €4.20). For a taxi, call ☎ 903 600.

Grüne Liga (☎ 492 796; Goetheplatz 9b; ☺ 9am-3pm Mon-Fri, 9am-noon Sat) rents out city bikes from €6 per 24 hours (enter from Rollplatz).

Note that driving in the Altstadt is severely restricted, so it's best to park outside the centre. There's a free lot at Hermann-Brill-Platz, about a 10-minute walk northwest from the Altstadt.

BUCHENWALD

The Buchenwald concentration camp **museum and memorial** (☎ 03643-4300; www.buchenwald.de; Ettersberg; admission free; ☺ buildings & exhibits 10am-6pm Tue-Sun Apr-Oct, 10am-4pm Tue-Sun Nov-Mar, grounds open until sunset) are 10km northwest of Weimar. You first pass the memorial erected above the mass graves of some of the 56,500 victims from 18 nations that died here – including Jews, German antifascists and Soviet and Polish prisoners of war. The concentration camp and museum are 1km beyond the memorial. Many prominent German communists and social democrats, Ernst Thälmann and Rudolf Breitscheid among them, were murdered here. After 1943, prisoners were exploited in the production of weapons. Many died during medical experimentation. Shortly before the end of the war, some 28,000 prisoners were sent on death marches. Between 1937 and 1945, more than one-fifth of the 250,000 people incarcerated here died. On 11 April 1945, as US troops approached and the SS guards fled, the prisoners rebelled (at 3.15pm – the clock tower above the entrance still shows that time), overwhelmed the remaining guards and liberated themselves.

After the war, the Soviet victors established Special Camp No 2, in which 7000 so-called anticommunists and ex-Nazis were literally worked to death. Their bodies were found after the *Wende* in mass graves north of the camp and near the Hauptbahnhof.

Pamphlets and books in English are sold at the bookshop, where you can also rent an excellent multilanguage audioguide for €3 (€5 with images). Last admission is 30 minutes before closing.

To get here, take bus 6 (direction Buchenwald) from Goetheplatz in Weimar. By car, head north on Ettersburger Strasse from Weimar train station and turn left onto Blutstrasse.

GOTHA
☎ 03621 / pop 46,250

Gotha was once described in historic documents as Thuringia's wealthiest and most beautiful city. Although it can no longer lay claim to either, it remains a pleasant town, dominated by the grand and gracious Schloss Friedenstein, built by Duke Ernst I (1601–1675), the founder of the House of Saxe-Coburg-Gotha. His descendants reinvented themselves as the House of Windsor after WWI and now occupy the British royal throne. Perhaps because of this circumstance, Gotha was never bombed in WWII. Although the Schloss is clearly Gotha's blockbuster attraction, the town's also a gateway to the Thuringian Forest and the northern terminus of the quirky Thüringerwaldbahn (opposite).

Orientation & Information

The hilltop Schloss Friedenstein and its gardens take up about half of Gotha's city centre, with the Altstadt to the north and the Hauptbahnhof to the south. It's a brisk 15-minute walk from the Hauptbahnhof to the Neumarkt and Hauptmarkt central squares. In the latter, you'll find the **tourist office** (☎ 5078 5712; www.gotha.de; Hauptmarkt 33; ☺ 9am-6pm Mon-Fri, 10am-3pm Sat year-round, plus 10am-2pm Sun May-Sep).

Sights

SCHLOSS FRIEDENSTEIN

This horseshoe-shaped **palace** (☎ 823 414; www.stiftungfriedenstein.de; adult/concession €7/3; ☺ 10am-5pm Tue-Sun May-Oct, to 4pm Nov-Apr) is the largest surviving early baroque palace in Germany. Much of the compound is now the **Schlossmuseum** (Palace Museum), a glorious assembly of art collections displayed in lavish baroque and neoclassical apartments. The picture gallery features priceless works by Rubens, Tischbein, Cranach and other old masters as well as the radiant *Gothaer Liebespaar* (Pair of Lovers) painted around

---

TRAM THROUGH THE TREES

Thuringia's most unusual ride has to be the **Thüringerwaldbahn** (☎ 4310; www .waldbahn-gotha.de). Starting out as ordinary city tram 4 at Gotha's Hauptbahnhof, it curves around the city ring road, crawls through some unlovely suburbs and then just keeps on going – like a local version of the Hogwarts Express – straight into the fairy-tale world of the Thuringian forest, as far as Tabarz.

1480 by an anonymous artist known only as Master of the Housebook.

Climb the stairs to compare the exuberantly stucco-ornamented **Festsaal** (Festival Hall) to the less flashy neoclassical wing whose sculpture collection includes a famous Renaissance work by Conrad Meit called *Adam und Eva*. The **Kunstkammer** is a curio cabinet jammed with exotica like engraved ostrich eggs and a cherry pit engraved with the face of Ernst I.

The **Schlosskirche** (Palace Church) occupies the northeastern corner, while the southwest tower contains the stunning **Ekhof-Theater**, one of the oldest baroque theatres in Europe, dating from the late 1700s. Unfortunately, it only hosts performances during the popular **Ekhof Festival** (www.ekhof-festival.de, in German) in July and August. Upstairs is a regional history and folklore museum with the usual hodgepodge of exhibits. Schloss tickets are also good for the **Museum der Natur** (Natural History Museum; Parkallee 15; ☼ same hours as palace) in an imposing building on the edge of the Gothaer Park.

Individual tickets to the regional history museum, natural history museum or the Ekhof-Theater are available for €3 (concession €2) each.

With prior reservation, you can also take a tour of the eerie **Kasematten** (€3.50; ☼ 1pm Sat & Sun), a warren of defensive underground passages deep below the palace.

HAUPTMARKT

Hauptmarkt is dominated by the picturesque **Rathaus** (town hall) with its colourful Renaissance facade and 35m-tall **tower** (€1; ☼ 11am-6pm Apr-Oct, 11am-4pm Nov-Mar). It started out as a storage house in 1567, later served as ducal pad of Ernst I while Schloss Friedenstein was under construction, and only became a town hall in 1665. The 14th-century

Wasserkunst (cascading fountain) originally supplied the city with water but is now purely decorative; the pump is deep inside the baroque Lucas-Cranach-Haus at No 17. Other houses on Hauptmarkt also reward exploration. If the legs are tired, a picnic lunch in the **Orangerie** of the Schloss is a nice way to enjoy these luscious surroundings.

Sleeping

Café Suzette (☎ 856 755; www.cafe-suzette.com; Bebelstrasse 8; s/d €30/60; **P**) Small but friendly, this cute little *Pension* has minimum-frills rooms above a cafe and cake shop, five minutes from the Hauptbahnhof. They even rent out bikes in case you want to work off the pudge factor of that chocolate cake.

Hotel Am Schlosspark (☎ 4420; www.hotel-am -schlosspark.de; Lindenauallee 20; s €75-90, d €105-115; **P** **⊠**) Rooms in the only central topend choice in Gotha are modern and fully equipped. Head to the spa for an extended relaxation session. Kids, meanwhile, can horse around on the adjacent playground.

Der Lindenhof (☎ 7720; www.lindenhof.bestwestern .de; Schöne Aussicht 5; s €83-93, d €99-129; **P** **⊠** **🖳**) Never mind that this property is in a former military barracks: its bright, well-kept rooms deliver on both space and country-style charisma. We also like the sunny terrace, the small library and the soul-restoring fitness area, with gym, sauna and steam room.

Eating & Drinking

Berggarten Gotha (☎ 744 475; Berggartenweg 50; mains €5-9; ☼ 11am-11pm Mon-Sat, 11am-8pm Sun Apr-Sep & Dec, 11am-7pm Sun-Thu, 11am-11pm Fri & Sat Jan-Mar, Oct & Nov; **⊠**) If you're outdoor bound, point your compass to this congenial inn and beer garden, with a playground and easy access to bike and hiking trails. The menu is all about German comfort food, with cabbage rolls, roast venison and fried plaice all making appearances.

Alte Sternwarte (☎ 723 90; Florschützstrasse 10; mains €7-13; ☼ 5-10pm Mon, 11.30am-10pm Tue-Sat, 11.30am-8pm Sun; **⊠**) You may have to put up with the occasional coach-tourist invasion, but otherwise the 'Old Observatory' is a fine place for a belly-filling meal. Much of the menu is modular: you pick a cut of meat or fish and pair it with your favourite sides and sauce. They also have a few rooms (single/double €64/82).

Carnaby (☎ 706 834; 18-März-Strasse 24) If the locals want to let their hair down, they head to this happening Irish pub to knock back a few pints of Murphy's Irish stout and listen to a wild mix of live bands, from Krautrock to folk.

Getting There & Away

Gotha is linked by regional train to Eisenach (€5.10, 25 minutes), Erfurt (€5.10, 25 minutes), Weimar (€8.40, 45 minutes) and Mühlhausen (€6.90, 20 minutes). IC trains stop en route to Berlin-Hauptbahnhof (€57, three hours), while the ICE serves Frankfurt am Main (€48, two hours). Gotha is just north of the A4 and is crossed by the B247 and B7.

For the Thüringerwaldbahn, see the boxed text, p277.

NORTHERN THURINGIA

MÜHLHAUSEN

☎ 03601 / pop 36,500

Mühlhausen flaunts medieval charisma galore. Its historic centre is a warren of cobbled alleyways linking a proud churches and encircled by nearly intact fortifications. In the early 16th century, the town became a focal point of the Reformation and a launch pad for the Peasants' War of 1525, led by local preacher Thomas Müntzer. The decisive battle took place on the Schlachtberg in nearby Bad Frankenhausen (see Kyffhaüser, opposite), where the rebellion was quickly crushed. Müntzer was decapitated outside the Mühlhausen town gates.

The GDR regime hailed the reformer as a great hero and an early social revolutionary who fought for the rights of the common man. There are still numerous sites in and around the town that uphold his memory. In 1975, Mühlhausen even got the prefix Thomas-Müntzer-Stadt (like Lutherstadt Wittenberg), but this was dropped after reunification. With reunification, though, Mühlhausen became united Germany's most central town, located a mere 5km north of the country's precise geographical centre in Niederdorla.

Information

The **tourist office** (☎ 404 770; www.muehlhausen.de; Ratsstrasse 20; 9am-5pm Mon-Fri, 10am-4pm Sat & Sun Apr-Oct, 9am-5pm Mon-Fri, 10am-2pm Sat Nov-Mar) is about 1km west of the Hauptbahnhof, between Obermarkt and Untermarkt. Steinweg (near Obermarkt) is the main shopping street.

Sights

Key sights cluster in the town centre and can easily be explored on foot. Heading west on Karl-Marx-Strasse from the Hauptbahnhof for about 1km gets you to the Untermarkt and the grand Gothic **Divi-Blasii-Kirche** (☎ 446 516; 10am-noon & 2-5pm Mon-Thu, to 4pm Sat, 1-5pm Sun Jun-Aug, 10am-noon & 2-4pm Mon-Thu, 2-4pm Sun Apr, May, Sep & Oct), built by the Teutonic Knights. A few centuries later, Johann Sebastian Bach did his magic thing on the church organ.

North of Divi-Blasii-Kirche, via the pedestrianised Linsenstrasse, is **Kornmarkt** and the **Kornmarktkirche** (☎ 404 684; Ratsstrasse; adult/concession €3/2; 10am-5pm Tue-Sun), which is no longer a church but a museum about the German Peasants' War and the Reformation.

The tourist office is just north of Kornmarkt in the handsome **Rathaus** (☎ 4520; Ratsstrasse 19; adult/concession €1/0.50; 10am-4pm Tue-Sun), an architecturally intriguing hotchpotch of Gothic, Renaissance and baroque styles. Inside, pay special attention to the Great Hall and the Councillors' Chamber.

Continuing north, you reach **Obermarkt**, lorded over by the five-nave **Marienkirche** (St Mary's Church; ☎ 870 023; adult/concession €3/2; 10am-5pm Tue-Sun), incidentally Thuringia's second-largest church after the Dom in Erfurt. It's now used as a memorial museum to Thomas Müntzer who preached here to his rebel followers in 1525 before the disastrous Schlachtberg battle.

Go west along Herrenstrasse to the **Inneres Frauentor**, where you can access a 330m walkable stretch of the 12th-century **town wall** (☎ 816 020; adult/concession €3/2; 10am-5pm Apr-Oct). Stroll as far as the **Rabenturm**, where you can chart the rest of your explorations of Mühlhausen's fascinating web of medieval lanes from the viewing platform.

Sleeping & Eating

DJH hostel (☎ 813 318; www.muehlhausen.jugendherberge .de, in German; Auf dem Tonberg 1; under/over 26yr incl breakfast & dinner €20/23; P X) This small hostel is about 2.5km west of the Hauptbahnhof. Take bus 5 or 6 to Blobach, then walk 500m.

An der Stadtmauer (☎ 465 00; www.hotel-an -der-stadtmauer.de; Breitenstrasse 15; s/d Mar-Oct €56/77, cheaper Nov-Feb; P X) The tasteful fittings, comfort and old-town location make this a very good choice. Some rooms open onto a courtyard, and there's a small bar and beer garden as well.

Brauhaus zum Löwen (☎ 4710; www.brauhaus -zum-loewen.de, in German; Felchtaer Strasse 2-4; s/d €60/90; P) Conversation flows as freely as the beer at this classic brewery-pub, where you can get fed and fuelled among the copper vats before retiring to boldly pigmented, country-style rooms. Still in a party mood? Join the local cool kids in the adjacent Leo disco (Wednesday to Saturday), the kind of place where, on some nights, 'ladies' get more free drinks the shorter their skirts.

Postkeller (☎ 889 812; Steinweg 6; mains €4.50-12.50; ☺ lunch & dinner) Another food-and-party combo: fuel up on regional food served in the lovely wood-panelled restaurant, decorated with a tiled stove and an entire flea market's worth of knick-knacks; then go dancing and flirting in the PK cocktail bar-cum-club (open Wednesday, Friday and Saturday).

Landhaus Frank 'Zum Nachbarn' (☎ 812 513; Eisenacher Landstrasse 34; mains €12-20; ☺ 11.30am-10pm; ☒) One of the top local restaurants, Zum Nachbarn has moved to new digs on the outskirts of town. It's still worth the trip, however, to indulge in upmarket regional and international cuisine, including specialities such as stuffed rack of lamb paired with herbed tiger shrimp and honey-sage jus.

Getting There & Away
Trains links Mühlhausen with Erfurt (€11.30, 45 minutes) and Gotha, where you have to change if headed for Eisenach (€11.30, 50 minutes). Mühlhausen sits at the crossroads of the B249 from Sondershausen and the B247 from Gotha.

AROUND MÜHLHAUSEN
Hainich National Park
About 15km southwest of Mühlhausen, the **Hainich National Park** (Nationalpark Hainich; ☎ 03603-390 70; www.nationalpark-hainich.de) protects the largest continuous deciduous forest in Germany. There's hiking and cycling, of course, but the main reason for swinging by is to take a walk through the tree tops on the **Baumkronenpfad** (Tree Top Trail; adult/student/family €7.50/5/20; ☺ 10am-7pm Apr-Oct, 10am-4pm Nov-Mar). Two wooden paths meander some 44m above ground, giving you a unique perspective on the forest's flora and fauna, not to mention great views over the park itself. The trail is near Thiemsburg castle, also the site of the park information centre, which has a **nature exhibit** (adult/student/family €2/1.50/5.50; ☺ 10am-7pm Apr-Oct, 10am-4pm Nov-Mar).

On weekends, the Wanderbus (Hiking Bus) makes four trips out here from Mühlhausen. Check the schedule with the Mühlhausen tourist office or call ☎ 03601-801 710.

KYFFHÄUSER MOUNTAINS
It's not particularly mighty or large, but there's an undeniable mystique to the densely forested Kyffhäuser low-mountain range. In history, this rural area is famous as the site of a bloody key battle in the Peasants' War of 1525 that left at least 6000 peasants dead and resulted in the capture and execution of their leader, the radical reformer Thomas Müntzer.

The main town is **Bad Frankenhausen**, where the **regional tourist office** (☎ 034671-717 16; www.kyffhaeuser-tourismus.de; Anger 14; ☺ 10am-6pm Mon-Fri, 10am-3pm Sat, 10am-noon Sun Apr-Oct, 10am-5pm Mon-Fri, 9am-noon Sat Nov-Mar) can help with maps, directions and general information.

Because the area is so sparsely populated, it's poorly served by public transportation, but bike trails and roads lead to all the main sights.

Sights
KYFFHÄUSER DENKMAL
The Kyffhäuser was once home to one of Germany's largest medieval castles, the massive Reichsburg, built in the 12th century during the reign of Emperor Friedrich Barbarossa. It's now merely a romantic ruin but, according to legend, Barbarossa lies in eternal sleep in the belly of the mountain, awaiting the time when he'll be needed to bring honour and prosperity back to his people. In the 19th century, Emperor Wilhelm I was seen as Barbarossa's spiritual successor and a bombastic statue was erected in 1896 on top of the foundations of the medieval castle. Showing the emperor on horseback, the **Kyffhäuser Denkmal** (Kyffhäuser Monument; ☎ 034651-2780; www.kyffhaeuser-denkmal.de; adult/concession/family €5/2.50/13; ☺ 9.30am-6pm Apr-Oct, 10am-5pm Nov-Mar) stands below a 60m-high tower and above a sculpture of Barbarossa sitting on a stone throne. To get to the monument, follow the B85 north from Bad Frankenhausen for about 10km, then turn right at the sign and continue for another 2km.

BARBAROSSAHÖHLE
One of the largest gypsum caves in Europe, the **Barbarossahöhle** (☎ 034671-545 13; www.hoehle.de; Mühlen 6, Rottleben; adult/child/family €7.50/4/21; ☺ 10am-5pm daily Apr-Oct, 10am-4pm Tue-Sun Nov-Mar, tours hourly) was discovered in 1865 and, because of its proximity to the Kyffhäuser mountain, immediately became associated with the Barbarossa legend. Tours last about 50 minutes and take you past shimmering underground lakes and

THURINGIA

bizarre gypsum sheets that hang from the ceiling like drying hides, as well as slabs described by legend as Barbarossa's table and chair. The caves are 7km west of Bad Frankenhausen, north of Rottleben.

PANORAMA MUSEUM

On the very site where thousands of peasants were slaughtered in 1525 now looms the **Panorama Museum** (☎ 034671-6190; www.panorama -museum.de, in German; Am Schlachtberg 9; adult/con-cession/child €5/4/2; ☺ 10am-6pm Tue-Sun Apr-Oct, to 5pm Nov-Mar, also 1-6pm Mon Jul & Aug), one of the Kyffhäuser's unique sights. There's just one painting inside the giant cylindrical structure, but what a painting it is! Called *Frühbürgerliche Revolution in Deutschland* (Early Civil Revolution in Germany), it measures an astonishing 14m by 123m and is painted in a vivid, colourful style reminiscent of Bruegel and Hieronymus Bosch. More than 3000 figures, assembled in numerous scenes, depict not the actual battle but an allegorical interpretation of the tumultuous transition from the Middle Ages to the modern era.

It took artist Werner Tübke and his assistants five years to complete this complex work, which was inaugurated in 1989, just a couple of months before the fall of the Berlin Wall. Its artistic merit and political context have been hotly debated, but its size and ambitious themes do not fail to impress.

The museum is on the Schlachtberg, about 3km north of Bad Frankenhausen.

Sleeping & Eating

A Kurtaxe (spa tax) of €1.50 per person is added to every overnight stay.

Alte Hämmelei (☎ 034671-5120; www.alte-haemmelei .de; Bornstrasse 33, Bad Frankenhausen; dm/s/d/tr €25/42/74/96; Ⓟ) Tradition is worn on the sleeve of this historic half-timbered house with wooden interiors. Private rooms combine rustic and modern elements, while the 12-bed dorm is right below the A-frame rafters. Indulge in deftly prepared regional fare (mains €7.50 to €14), such as the signature dish called Ohle Hämmelei (lamb filet with lima beans and potato pancakes).

Hotel Residenz (☎ 034671-750; www.residenz -frankenhausen.de; Am Schlachtberg 3, Bad Frankenhausen; s/d from €75/105; Ⓟ ✕ ☲) This large hotel is a good midrange choice and often has some tempting last-minute deals and spa packages.

The restaurant does upmarket international food, using fresh and seasonal farm and field products (mains €6 to €17); there's even a decent kids' menu.

Weinlokal Zum Schwan (☎ 034671-624 32; Erfurter Strasse 9, Bad Frankenhausen; mains €8-14; ✕) This restaurant, in one of the oldest half-timbered buildings in town, serves local *Sauerbraten* (sour marinated beef) and juicy steaks, and has about three dozen wines.

Getting There & Around

Bad Frankenhausen is no longer served by train. To get there from, say, Erfurt, first catch a regional train to Sondershausen, Heldrungen, Artern or some other village and then switch to a bus or rent a bicycle. In Sondershausen, **Radwanderzentrum Kyffhäuserkreis** (☎ 034671-509 38; August-Bebel-Strasse 27; ☺ 8am-2pm Mon-Fri & by arrangement) has a sizeable fleet of bicycles and charges between €3 and €5 per day. It also has a **branch** (☎ 034671-777 71; Am Bahnhof 42) in Bad Frankenhausen.

THURINGIAN FOREST

The Thuringian Forest (Thüringer Wald) is about tradition, not trendiness; family, not flings – it's an ingenious blend of nature and culture. Stretching from Eisenach in the northwest to Saalfeld in the southeast, it's a mountainous region, with crags and peaks rising to about 1000m. Germany's most popular trail, the Rennsteig, runs for 169km along spectacular ridges. This and scores of other trails, ski slopes and cycle paths are here for the taking, demanding only that you bring a sense of wonderment and respect for nature.

EISENACH
☎ 03691 / pop 43,500

Eisenach is a small town on the edge of the Thuringian forest whose modest appearance belies its association with two German heavyweights: Johann Sebastian Bach and Martin Luther. Luther went to school here and later returned to protective custody in the Wartburg, now one of Germany's most famous castles and a Unesco World Heritage Site. A century later, Bach, the grandest of all baroque musicians, was born in a wattle-and-daub home and attended the same school as Luther had. Eisenach also has a century-old automotive tradition – the world's first BMW rolled off the local assem-

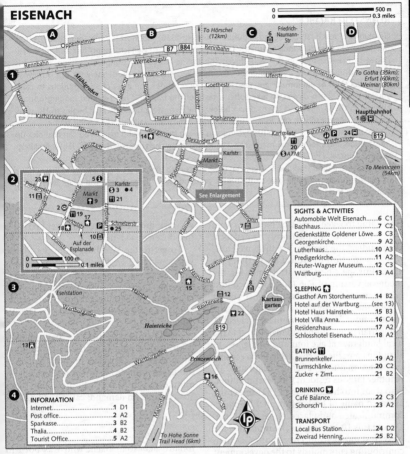

EISENACH

SIGHTS & ACTIVITIES
Automobile Welt Eisenach	**6** C1
Bachhaus	**7** C2
Gedenkstätte Goldener Löwe	**8** C3
Georgenkirche	**9** A2
Lutherhaus	**10** A3
Predigerkirche	**11** A2
Reuter-Wagner Museum	**12** C3
Wartburg	**13** A4

SLEEPING
Gasthof Am Storchenturm	**14** B2
Hotel auf der Wartburg	(see **13**)
Hotel Haus Hainstein	**15** B3
Hotel Villa Anna	**16** C4
Residenzhaus	**17** A2
Schlosshotel Eisenach	**18** A2

EATING
Brunnenkeller	**19** A2
Turmschänke	**20** C2
Zucker + Zimt	**21** B2

DRINKING
Café Balance	**22** C3
Schorsch'l	**23** A2

TRANSPORT
Local Bus Station	**24** D2
Zweirad Henning	**25** B2

INFORMATION
Internet	**1** D1
Post office	**2** A2
Sparkasse	**3** B2
Thalia	**4** B2
Tourist Office	**5** A2

bly line in 1929. And when it's time to shake off culture and civilisation, remember that the famous Rennsteig hiking trail is only a hop, skip and jump away.

Orientation

Except for the Wartburg, which is 2km southwest of town, most sights are concentrated around the Markt, a 15-minute walk west from the Hauptbahnhof. Buses to the Wartburg and the Hohe Sonne trail head stop right outside the Hauptbahnhof.

Information

Internet (Point Shop; Hauptbahnhof; per 30min €1; 5am-8pm Mon-Fri, 8am-8pm Sat, 8am-9pm Sun) Two terminals inside a train station shop.

Post office (Markt 6; 8.30am-6pm Mon-Fri, 8.30am-noon Sat)

Sparkasse (Karlstrasse 2-4) Bank with ATM.

Thalia (711 50; Karlstrasse 6) Bookshop.

Tourist office (792 30; www.eisenach.info; Markt 24; 10am-6pm Mon-Fri, 10am-5pm Sat & Sun) Staff also sell the Classic Card (€19 for 72 hours), which is good for public transport and admission to all the important sights, including the Wartburg.

Sights

WARTBURG

When it comes to medieval castles and their importance in German history, the **Wartburg** (2500; www.wartburg-eisenach.de; tour adult/concession €8/5, museum & Luther study only €4/2.50; tours 8.30am-5pm Mar-Oct, 9am-3.30pm Nov-Feb) is the mother lode.

THURINGIA

RENNSTEIG RAMBLE

Germany's oldest (first mentioned in public records in 1330) and most popular long-distance trail, the 169km Rennsteig winds southeast from Hörschel (near Eisenach) along forested mountain ridges to Blankenstein on the Saale River. The trail is marked by signposts reading 'R', and is best hiked in May/June and September/October. You should be moderately fit, but otherwise no special skills or equipment are needed – just good shoes and a set of strong thighs to carry you for six or seven days. Day hikes offer a taste of the trail, and hiker-geared lodging options abound in the villages and towns down below. The Rennsteig bike trail also begins in Hörschel and travels over asphalt, soft forest soil and gravel, mostly paralleling the hiking trail.

The tourist office in Eisenach has cycling and hiking brochures and maps. You can also pick up information and professional maps from the **Rennsteigwanderhaus** (☎ 036928-911 94; Rennsteig-strasse 9, Hörschel; ⊙ 8.30-5pm).

A time-honoured tradition for Rennsteig ramblers is to pick up a pebble from the Werra River at the beginning of your hike, carry it with you and throw it back into the Saale River upon completing the trail.

According to legend, the first buildings were put up in 1067 by the hilariously named local ruler Ludwig the Jumper (see the boxed text, p284) in an effort to protect his territory. In 1206, Europe's best minstrels met for the medieval version of *Pop Idol*, a song contest later immortalised in Richard Wagner's opera *Tannhäuser*. Shortly thereafter, Elisabeth, the most famous Wartburg woman, arrived. A Hungarian princess, she was married off to the local landgrave at age four and later chose to abandon court life for charitable work, earning canonisation quickly after her death in 1235. Another famous resident was Martin Luther, who went into hiding here in 1521 under the assumed name of Junker Jörg after being ex-communicated and placed under papal ban. During this 10-month stay, he translated the New Testament from Greek into German, contributing enormously to the development of the written German language.

You'll get to see Luther's modest wood-panelled **study** at the end of the guided tour, which is the only way to see the interior of the castle. Many of the rooms contain extravagant 19th-century impressions of medieval life rather than the original fittings. The enormous **banquet hall**, whose great acoustics make it a popular concert space, is just one highlight. There's also a **museum**, where you can admire paintings by Lucas Cranach the Elder and important Christian artefacts from all over Germany.

Budget at least two hours total: one for the guided tour, the rest for the museum and the grounds (views!). From April to October, the 1.30pm tour is in English, other-wise ask the guide for a pamphlet (available in a dozen or so languages).

To get to the Wartburg from the Markt, walk one block west to Wydenbrugkstrasse, then head southwest along Schlossberg through the forest via Eselstation (this takes about 40 minutes, and parts are rather steep). A more scenic route is via the Haintal (50 minutes).

From April to October, bus 10 runs hourly from 9am to 5pm from the Hauptbahnhof (with stops at Karlsplatz and Mariental) to the Eselstation, from where it's a steep 10-minute walk up to the castle. In winter, buses are available on demand; call ☎ 228 822 for a pick-up.

BACHHAUS

Johann Sebastian Bach, who was born in Eisenach in 1685, takes the spotlight in the revamped and enlarged **Bachhaus** (☎ 793 40; www.bachhaus.de; Frauenplan 21; adult/concession/family €6.50/3.50/12; ⊙ 10am-6pm), one of the best biographical museums we've ever seen. Exhibits are set up in the type of wattle-and-daub town house where the Bach family lived (the original was destroyed) and trace both his professional and private life through concise, intelligent and engaging bilingual panelling. Your journey culminates in a modern annexe, where you can sit in suspended bubble chairs and listen to the wide range of musical contributions made by this versatile genius. Admission also includes a 20-minute concert played on antique instruments.

OTHER SIGHTS

The Markt is dominated by the galleried **Georgenkirche** (☎ 732 662; Pfarrberg 2; ☽ 10am-noon & 2-4pm). St Elizabeth and Johann Sebastian Bach were both baptised in this church, where Luther preached while under papal ban. From June to September, free half-hour organ concerts take place at 11am Monday to Saturday.

As a school boy, Luther lived in the half-timbered **Lutherhaus** (☎ 298 30; www.luther haus-eisenach.de; Lutherplatz 8; adult/concession €3.50/2; ☽ 10am-5pm), where a partly interactive exhibit reveals how the eager pupil became one of the world's most influential religious reformers.

Fans of Richard Wagner should flock to the exhibits on the composer's life, times and oeuvre at the **Reuter-Wagner Museum** (☎ 743 293; Reuterweg 2; adult/concession €3/2; ☽ 11am-5pm Tue-Sun). It's in a villa once owned by writer Fritz Reuter located at the foot of the Wartburg, which inspired Wagner's *Tannhäuser*.

Those with a political mind might find it interesting to know that the first nationwide proletarian movement, the Social Democratic Workers' Party of Germany, was founded in Eisenach by August Bebel and Wilhelm Liebknecht in 1869. The **Gedenkstätte Goldener Löwe** (Golden Lion Memorial; ☎ 882 723; Marienstrasse 57; admission free; ☽ 9am-4pm Mon-Fri) has an interesting exhibit covering the 19th-century workers' movement in Germany.

Arty types, meanwhile, should head to the crypt of the **Predigerkirche** (☎ 784 678; Predigerplatz 2; adult/concession/family €2.60/1.50/5.10; ☽ 11am-5pm Tue-Sun), a fine setting for an exquisite collection of medieval sculpture, paintings and liturgical objects.

And then there's cars, cars, cars! Production revved up in Eisenach in 1896 with the Wartburg, a model based on the French Decauville. The **Automobile Welt Eisenach** (☎ 772 12; Friedrich-Naumann-Strasse 10; adult/concession/family €3/2/7; ☽ 11am-5pm Tue-Sun) celebrates this history by displaying pretty much the entire product range, including an 1899 Wartburg Dixi, a 1936 BMW 328 sports car and other rare vintage vehicles and assorted memorabilia, many from the GDR era.

Activities

Eisenach is a handy gateway to the Thuringian Forest. Bus 11 drops you at the Hohe Sonne trail head, right on the Rennsteig hiking trail, although you could also hike there (or back) via the craggily romantic Drachenschlucht gorge. From April to October, buses leave twice in the morning on weekdays and hourly from 8.30am to 4.30pm on Saturday and Sunday.

Sleeping

Gasthof Am Storchenturm (☎ 733 263; www.gasthof -am-storchenturm.de, in German; Georgenstrasse 43a; dm €15.50-18, s/d €23/36, breakfast €5; P ✗) Lots of long-socked hikers pad down the trails for simple but comfortable rooms here in a hostel-type guest house in a spiffed-up barn. Refuel on rustic regional fare in the on-site restaurant (mains €6.50 to €13).

Residenzhaus (☎ 214 133; www.residenzhaus-eisenach .de, in German; Auf der Esplanade; s/d without bathroom €25/50, d with bathroom €60; ✗) If you're into hip decor, fancy linen and chocolate on your pillow, go elsewhere. But if you want modern comforts in a historic, central setting without shelling out big money, lug your luggage up the spiral stone staircase. Some rooms share bathrooms.

Hotel Haus Hainstein (☎ 2420; www.hainstein.de; Am Hainstein 16; s €45-54, d €72-82; P) A stately art-nouveau villa in the leafy, hilly area south of town provides the charismatic setting of this small hotel, which has bright, stylish rooms, its own chapel, a restaurant and views of the Wartburg.

our pick **Hotel Villa Anna** (☎ 239 50; www.hotel-villa -anna.de, in German; Fritz-Koch-Strasse 12; s €75, d €95-115; P ✗ ☎) This boutique hotel at the foot of the Wartburg focuses on delivering amenities and services people actually want and need. Appealing rooms are modern, good sized and outfitted with ultracomfy beds, a big desk and free wi-fi.

Schlosshotel Eisenach (☎ 214 260; www.schlosshotel -eisenach.de; Marktplatz 10; s €75-88, d €114-124, ste €130-190; P ✗) Most rooms, the nicest with balconies, face the quiet inner courtyard in this sprawling central complex. Its upmarket amenities lure business types during the week, but the sauna is perfect any time for unwinding or soothing post-hike muscles.

Hotel auf der Wartburg (☎ 797 223; www.wartburg hotel.de; Auf der Wartburg; s/d from €145/220; P ✗) Built in 1914, this hotel has subdued colours and furnishings to match the historic site. The singles at this luxury address are called 'Luther' rooms, but, for serious opulence, book one in the 'Prince' category.

THURINGIA

LUDWIG DER SPRINGER – TAKING THE JUMP

German gentry is rife with quirky monikers. Henry the Fowler was supposedly out catching birds one day when someone told him he'd just become king. The unfortunate 13th-century Thuringian landgrave, Henry the Illustrious, squabbled for years over Thuringia and other territories, and had a son called Albert the Degenerate. Karl the Bald got his byname for obvious reasons. Ludwig the Rich probably didn't even earn his. But what about Ludwig der Springer (meaning Ludwig the Jumper)? Ludwig supposedly got his jumping-jack moniker when he sprang out of a window into the Saale River in Halle. The great leap occurred after he was jailed for fatally stabbing the margrave Friedrich III in a squabble over Saxony. To make amends for his foul deed against Friedrich, he founded the Benedictine monastery that now lies under the foundations of Schloss Reinhardsbrunn (opposite) in what is now – you guessed it – Friedrichroda.

Eating & Drinking

Zucker + Zimt (☎ 217 588; Markt 2; dishes €2.50-11.50; ☻ 10am-8pm, to 10pm May-Oct; ✗) A whiff of urbanity in stuffy Eisenach, this upbeat cafe, dressed in mod apple green, fully embraces the 'bio' trend. Organic and fair-trade ingredients find their destination in light creative mains, bagel sandwiches, stuffed crêpes and homemade cakes.

Brunnenkeller (☎ 212 358; Markt 10; mains €7.50-16; ☻ 11am-11pm Apr-Oct, lunch Thu-Mon, dinner daily Nov-Mar; ✗) Linen-draped tables beneath an ancient vaulted brick ceiling set the tone of this traditional chow house in a former monastery cellar. Quite predictably, the food is honest-to-goodness German and regional classics.

our pick **Turmschänke** (☎ 213 533; Wartburgallee 2; mains €10-22, 3-/4-course menu €29/35; ☻ dinner Mon-Sat; ✗) This hushed hideaway in Eisenach's only surviving medieval city gate scores a perfect 10 on the 'romance-meter.' Walls panelled in polished oak, beautiful table settings and immaculate service are a perfect foil for Ulrich Rösch's flavour-packed concoctions that teeter between trendy and traditional.

Café Balance (☎ 715 29; Mariental 3; ✗) This congenial cafe in a grand art-nouveau villa makes a great pit stop on your way to or from the Wartburg. The tea selection is stratospheric (more than 150 varieties), but fans of java and homemade cakes will also get their fill.

Schorsch'l (☎ 0173 372 5174; www.schorschl.de; Georgenstrasse 19; ☻ 7pm-2am) Smoke gets in your eyes, but otherwise this is a relaxed pub drawing all comers for drinks, chatter and the occasional live band.

Getting There & Around

Direct regional trains run frequently to Erfurt (€10.30, 45 minutes), Gotha (€5.10, 25 minutes) and Weimar (€13.30, 1¼ hours). ICE trains are faster and also serve Frankfurt am Main (€34, 1¾ hours) while IC trains go to Berlin-Hauptbahnhof (€61, 3¼ hours).

If you're driving, Eisenach is right on the A4 and is crossed by the B7, B19 and B84.

Zweirad Henning (☎ 784 738; Schmelzerstrasse 4-6; ☻ 9am-6pm Mon-Fri, 9am-1pm Sat) rents out bikes for €8 per day and also does repairs. Pick up a cycling map from the tourist office.

FRIEDRICHRODA

☎ 03623 / pop 7500

Dangling down into a valley from wooded slopes about 20km south of Gotha, picturesque Friedrichroda was a busy resort town in GDR days. It fell somewhat out of favour in the 1990s, when East Germans set their sights on Majorca and other beach destinations, but its popularity has since returned, especially with improved infrastructure and the development of health and spa tourism. Friedrichroda is also working towards establishing itself as a winter sports centre.

Orientation & Information

Friedrichroda has two train stations: Bahnhof Friedrichroda in the east and Bahnhof Reinhardsbrunn north of the centre. Both are stops of the Thüringerwaldbahn (which is actually a tram; see the boxed text, p277).

The **tourist office** (☎ 332 00; www.friedrichroda .info, in German; Marktstrasse 13-15; ☻ 9am-5pm Mon-Thu, 9am-6pm Fri, 9am-noon Sat) is in the centre of town. A bank with an ATM is nearby at Hauptstrasse 35-37.

Sights & Activities

Friedrichroda's prime attraction is the **Marienglashöhle** (☎ 311 667; tour adult/concession €6/2.50; ☻ tours 9am-5pm Apr-Oct, to 4pm Nov-Mar), a large gypsum cave featuring an underwater lake and a crystal grotto. You enter the latter in the dark, then – just to give you that otherworldly feel – the theme from *Close Encounters of the Third Kind* plays in the background as the light gradually brightens, unveiling a sparkling universe. Most of the crystallised gypsum here has been harvested and used to decorate statues of the Virgin Mary and altars in the region and beyond. The cave is about a 40-minute walk through the woods from the city centre, and is also a stop on the Thüringerwaldbahn.

In the northern part of town, hemmed in by a lavish English park with ancient trees, the neo-Gothic **Schloss Reinhardsbrunn** (1828) cuts a commanding presence. It was here that Queen Victoria of England first laid eyes on her cousin and future husband, Duke Albert of Saxe-Coburg-Gotha. An English buyer has since bought it and plans to reopen it as a hotel.

The Schloss abuts the lovely landscaped **Kurpark**, home to the Ludowinger spring, where excellent mineral water bubbles up from a depth of 58m. Much of it is bottled, but you're free to fill up from the taps in one of the park's glass pavilions.

For an easy day trip into the forest, take the Thüringer Wald-Express bus (€4.50) to the **Heuberghaus** on the mountain ridge, hike along the ridge to the **Inselsberg** peak (90 minutes), then take the Inselsberg Express bus (€4.50) down to Tabarz and catch the Thüringerwaldbahn back to Friedrichroda (€1.35). (It sounds more complicated than it is.)

Sleeping & Eating

Friedrichroda has good tourism infrastructure but can get deluged with visitors in summer. If you need to satisfy a country hunger, walk along Hauptstrasse, sniff and take your pick. Virtually all restaurants have a traditional atmosphere. The daily spa tax (Kurtaxe) of €1.20 is added to overnight stays.

Pension Feierabend (☎ 304 386; www.pension-feierabend.de, in German; Büchig 1; s €25-30, d €36-40; P) Small but beautiful, this half-timbered family-run house is a class act and is hard to beat for value, comfort and character. It's in a quiet spot, yet is only a saunter from the Kurpark. All rooms have a balcony but rooms 8 and 9 are especially spacious.

Pension Villa Phönix (☎ 200 880; www.villa-phoenix.de; Tabarzer Strasse 3; s/d €35/60) Although this 'phoe-

nix' rises up right alongside the road, double glazing keeps out the street noise. Coloured walls and knick-knacks in the six rooms create the illusion of staying at your friend's pad. Some have enclosed balconies.

Berghotel (☎ 3540; www.a-z-wohlfuehlhotels.de, in German; Zum Panoramablick 1; r €50-80; P ☒ ☲) Rooms come in four categories at this GDR-era behemoth with an enviable hilltop location. None are particularly large, but, with easy access to the outdoors and an activity program that ranges from table-tennis tournaments to dance parties, you probably won't be spending much time in them. The 12th-floor panorama restaurant is a fine spot for sunset dinners (mains €7.50 to €22).

Getting There & Around

The Thüringerwaldbahn (tram 4) serves Gotha (€2.90) and Tabarz (€1.80) several times hourly. The most scenic stretch begins right after Friedrichroda, running through the forest to Tabarz.

If you're driving, take the Waltershausen/Friedrichroda exit off the A4. The town is also on the B88 to Ilmenau.

Fahrzeugwelt am Rennsteig (☎ 309 899; Bahnhofstrasse 30a; ☉ 8am-6pm Mon-Fri, 9am-1pm Sat) rents out mountain and trekking bikes for €8 per day.

ILMENAU

☎ 03677 / pop 26,500

Although home to a small technical university, Ilmenau is most famously associated with Johann Wolfgang von Goethe. The great man visited this sleepy town on the northern slopes of the Thuringian Forest no fewer than 28 times, charged by the court of Saxe-Weimar to revive the local mining industry that had brought great riches to the town in the Middle Ages. The **Goethe Stadtmuseum im Amtshaus** (☎ 600 107; Am Markt 1; adult/concession €3/1.50; ☉ 10am-5pm) chronicles his efforts in the very 1st-floor rooms where he once had his offices. There's also a much-photographed statue of the man in front of the building, which also happens to be the starting point of the famous Goethewanderweg (see the boxed text, p286).

The **tourist office** (☎ 600 300; www.ilmenau.de; Am Markt 1; ☉ 9am-6pm Mon-Fri, 10am-5pm Sat) reserves hotels and private rooms from €28.

The **DJH hostel** (☎ 884 681; www.ilmenau.jugendherberge.de, in German; Am Stollen 49; under/over 26yr incl

GOETHE TRAIL – IN THE FOOTSTEPS OF GENIUS

This lovely and, at times, challenging 18.5km day hike, which takes between five and eight hours depending on fitness levels, follows in the footsteps of Johann Wolfgang von Goethe, who spent much time around Ilmenau in the employ of Carl August, Duke of Saxe-Weimar. The hike encompasses level forest terrain, steep climbs and everything in between; it's marked with the letter 'G' in Goethe's own handwriting. An excellent 1:30,000 hiking map by Grünes Herz is available at the tourist office.

From the **Goethe Stadtmuseum im Amtshaus** (p285) in Ilmenau, the trail heads west via the Schwalbenstein and Emmasteinfelsen peaks to the village of Manebach, where the steep climb up the **Kickelhahn** (861m) begins. Approaching the top, you'll pass the replica of the little forest cabin (Goethehäuschen) where Goethe wrote the famous poem *Wayfarer's Night Song*. At the top, **Berggasthaus Kickelhahn** (☎ 03677-202 034; Kickelhahn 1; ☺ 10am-6pm) and a lookout tower are fine spots for a break.

The trail descends to **Jagdhaus Gabelbach** (☎ 202 626; Waldstrasse 26, Ilmenau; adult/concession €2/1.50; ☺ 10am-5pm Tue-Sun Apr-Oct, to 4pm Nov-Mar), a hunting lodge and former guest house with exhibits on Goethe's scientific research. From here, it meanders south to the village of Stützerbach, where the **Goethe-Museum Stützerbach** (☎ 036784-502 77; Sebastian-Kneipp-Strasse 18, Stützerbach; adult/concession €2/1.50; ☺ 10am-5pm Sat & Sun Apr-Oct, to 3pm Nov-Mar) features rooms (still with the original furnishings) where Goethe used to stay and work.

Check with the tourist office (or online at www.rennsteig-bus.de) about the timetable of bus No 300 back to Ilmenau. You can also walk directly to the Kickelhahn from Ilmenau, bypassing Manebach, in about 1½ hours. Or you can drive up Waldstrasse to the parking lot at Herzogröder Wiesen, from where it's a 25-minute uphill walk to the Kickelhahn peak.

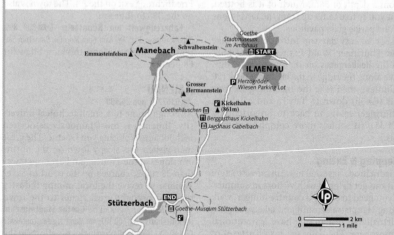

breakfast & dinner €22/25; ☒ ▣) is near the technical university, about 2km east of the train station, to which it's linked by buses A, B and C.

After a tough day on the Goethewanderweg, **Hotel Tanne** (☎ 6590; www.hotel-tanne-thueringen.de; Lindenstrasse 38; s €62, d €84-89; ℗ ☒) has comforts such as sauna, solarium and massage facilities to rejuvenate the body.

Erfurter Bahn trains directly link Ilmenau with Erfurt (€10.30, one hour); change in

Neudietendorf for Eisenach (€15.20, 1½ hours). By car, Ilmenau is served by the A71, which links Erfurt with Schweinfurt via Oberhof and Meiningen.

SCHMALKALDEN
☎ 03683 / pop 10,500

Schmalkalden's old town virtually sighs under the sheer weight of its half-timbered houses and is crowned by a handsome hilltop castle, Schloss Wilhelmsburg. About 40km south of Eisenach, the little town played a big role during the Reformation. It was here in 1531 that the Protestant princes established the Schmalkaldic League to counter the central powers of Catholic emperor Charles V. Although they suffered a daunting military defeat in 1546, they managed to regroup and eventually got the emperor to sign the Peace of Augsburg in 1555 that allowed each of the German states to choose between Lutheranism and Catholicism.

Orientation & Information

It's about a 10-minute walk from the train and bus stations to the Altmarkt central square and another seven minutes to Schloss Wilhelmsburg. There's an ATM on Weidebrunner Gasse, near Lutherplatz, and a post office on Altmarkt.

The **tourist office** (☎ 403 182; www.schmalkalden.de; Mohrengasse 1a; ☯ 9am-6pm Mon-Fri, 10am-3pm Sat & Sun Apr-Oct, 9am-5pm Mon-Fri, 10am-1pm Sat Nov-Mar) is just off Altmarkt.

Sights & Activities

Overlooking the town, the late-Renaissance-style **Schloss Wilhelmsburg** (☎ 403 186; Schlossberg 9; adult/concession €3.50/2; ☯ 10am-6pm daily Apr-Oct, 10am-4pm Tue-Sun Nov-Mar) is Schmalkalden's most imposing building. Landgrave Wilhelm IV of Hessen conceived it as a hunting lodge and summer residence in the 1580s. Since then, the Schloss has largely kept its original design, with lavish murals and stucco decorating most rooms, of which the **Riesensaal**, with its coffered and painted ceiling, is the most impressive. The playfully decorated **Schlosskirche** (palace church) has a rare wood organ that is thought to be the oldest working organ of its type in Europe. There's also an exhibit on life during the Renaissance and Schmalkalden's role in the Reformation, as well as an animated 3-D journey into the world of the Middle Ages.

The **Rathaus** (1419) on Altmarkt functioned as the meeting place of the Schmalkaldic League; nearby the incongruous towers of the late-Gothic **St Georgenkirche**, another place where Luther once preached, also overlook the square.

Schmalkalden is the western terminus of the **Martin-Luther-Weg**, a 17km easy-to-moderate hiking trail that ends at Tambach-Dietharz, from where there are bus services

back to town (weekdays only; the tourist office can help with times).

About 6km north of town, **Neue Hütte** (☎ 403 018; Gothaer Strasse; adult/concession/family €2/1/4; ☯ 10am-5pm Tue-Sun Apr-Oct) will thrill both kids and the technically minded. One of the few surviving 19th-century smelting plants in Europe, it has a waterwheel, turbines and other industrial knick-knacks.

Sleeping & Eating

Teichhotel (☎ 402 661; www.teichhotel.de, in German; Teichstrasse 21; s/d €50/75; P ☒) Just outside the Altstadt, this hotel has plain but comfortable rooms. The restaurant serves well-priced hearty fare to keep hikers and bikers happy.

Stadthotel Patrizier (☎ 604 514; www.stadthotel-patrizier.de, in German; Weidebrunner Gasse 9; s/d €55/82) After a day on the road, linger over wine and light regional classics in the restaurant or the idyllic courtyard, then rest your weary head in your delightfully dapper room. The two suites provide enough elbow room for families.

Maykel's (☎ 608 970; Lutherplatz 1; mains €2.50-9; ☯ 10am-midnight) From clerks to cops to cool kids, everybody's got a soft spot for this relaxed cafe-bar, where breakfast is served until 2pm and there's good pub grub to counteract your alcohol intake.

The Castle (☎ 466 703; Schlossberg 1b; ☯ nightly May-Oct, Mon-Sat Nov-Apr) A youngish crowd gathers for booze, bratwurst and beats at the Castle, which is about as hip as things get in good old Schmalkalden. In summer, the action spills into the yard.

Getting There & Around

Schmalkalden is served by the private Süd-Thüringen-Bahn (www.sued-thueringen-bahn.de). Going to Erfurt (€15.20, 1¾ hours) requires a change in Zella-Mehlis; for Eisenach (€8.40, one hour), you need to change in Wernshausen. Schmalkalden is about 6km east of the B19, which connects Eisenach and Meiningen.

Fahrrad Anschütz (☎ 403 909; Stiller Gasse 17; per day €5-10; ☯ 9am-6pm Mon-Fri, 9am-noon Sat) rents out city, touring and mountain bikes. A recommended route is the 28km Mommelstein-Radweg that follows a former railway line and some forest trails through a tunnel and viaduct (the tourist office has maps and directions).

MEININGEN

☎ 03693 / pop 21,000

Tranquil, idyllic and blessed with vast expanses of parkland, Meiningen is one of the nicest towns in a region rife with rural gems. Some 30km south of Schmalkalden, it's a former ducal residence with a long tradition in the performing arts. The resident theatre, founded in 1866 by Duke Georg II, went on tour, playing before sold-out audiences in London, Vienna, Moscow and other European cities. Georg II also catapulted the court orchestra (the Meininger Hofkapelle) to international fame by appointing pianist-conductor Hans von Bülow as musical director; the baton later passed to Richard Strauss and Max Reger. The theatre festival in early summer draws thousands of fans to the little town on the Werra River.

Orientation & Information

The Schlosspark to the west and the English Garden to the north fringe Meiningen's town centre. The train and bus stations are east of the English Garden, the site of the Meiningen Theater. Signs near the train station point across the English Garden towards the tourist office on Markt, which also has a post office and banks.

The **tourist office** (☎ 446 50; www.meiningen.de; Markt 14; ☽ 11am-6pm Mon-Fri, 10am-5pm Sat year-round, plus 10am-3pm Sun May-Oct) is behind the *Stadtkirche* (parish church). **Das Waschcafé** (☎ 885 571; Anton-Ulrich-Strasse 49; ☽ 9am-10pm Mon-Fri, 10am-10pm Sat) does triple duty as an internet cafe, laundry and travel agency.

Sights

The lavish late-17th-century **Schloss Elisabethenburg** (☎ 503 641; www.meiningermuseen.de; adult/concession/family €4/2.50/7.50; ☽ 10am-6pm Tue-Sun) served as the ducal residence until 1918 and sports neo-Renaissance and other revivalist features in addition to the pure-baroque central floors of the main wing. Some rooms showcase paintings, sculpture, furniture and knick-knacks from throughout the ages, while others deal with Meiningen's music and theatre traditions. Tickets are also good at the **Baumbachhaus** (☎ 502 848; Burggasse 2), a small literature museum.

The nearby **Theatermuseum** (☎ 471 290; tour adult/concession/family €3.50/2/6; ☽ 10am, noon, 2pm & 4pm Tue-Sun) displays some of the 275 original stage backdrops from the early days of the Meiningen Theater, sketches of set designs and costumes drawn by Georg II, and historic photographs of well-known actors.

A combined ticket for the Schloss and museums costs €5.50 (concession €3.50, families €12.50).

Sleeping & Eating

Hotel Schlundhaus & Rautenkranz (☎ 813 838; www.meininger-hotels-mit-flair.de, in German; Schlundgasse 4; s €50-55, d €78-108; P ✗ ☎) Rustic-style rooms with new furnishings in a historic hotel and guest house make this a comfortable place to repose. The restaurant is well priced and claims to be the place where the Thuringian potato dumplings were invented.

Sächsischer Hof (☎ 4570; www.saechsischerhof.com; Georgstrasse 1; s €78-102, d €110-140; P ✗) Life goes from frantic to romantic as soon as you check yourself into this 200-year-old inn, which used to be a postal coach stop. The standard rooms are spacious, others are palatial (most have ante-rooms), even if the bathrooms are a trifle small.

Schloss Landsberg (☎ 440 90; www.meininger-hotels-mit-flair.de, in German; Landsberger Strasse 150; s €100, d €134-168; P ☎) Fancy yourself knight and damsel in this turreted medieval castle on the northern edge of town. The nicer rooms with sumptuous canopy beds, painted walls and dreamy valley views are truly worthy of a princess.

Turmcafé (☎ 881 036; Schloss Elisabethenburg; food €2.50-6; ☽ 11am-6pm Tue-Sat, 11am-5pm Sun; ✗) Over the top in all ways, this baroque cafe high in the Schloss is a lovely stop for coffee and cake or a light meal.

Kutscherstube (☎ 4570; Georgstrasse 1; mains €8-16 ☽ lunch & dinner; ✗) Inside the Sächsischer Hof, this place is an atmosphere-laden port of call for hearty Thuringian cuisine. The dumplings are the star of the menu, of course, and pair beautifully with the uniformly excellent meat dishes.

Posthalterei (☎ 4570; Georgstrasse 1; 3-/4-/5-/6-/7-course menu €35/44/54/64/69; ☽ dinner Tue-Sat, lunch Sun; ✗) Also in the Sächsischer Hof, this gourmet restaurant occupies the building where postal coaches once parked. The cooking is truly wizardly, blending Asian and Mediterranean flavours into what is essentially regional fare.

Getting There & Away

Meiningen is directly linked to Erfurt (€16.70, 1½ hours) and to Eisenach (€11.30, one hour) by the **Süd Thüringen Bahn** (www.sued-thueringen-bahn.de). Coming from Eisenach, drivers should take the B19; from Erfurt, the A71.

THE SAALE VALLEY

JENA

☎ 03641 / pop 102,000

Jena enjoys a lovely setting on the Saale River, flanked by muscular limestone hills and blessed with a climate mild enough for orchids and vines to thrive. A university town since 1558, it may not be as pretty as Weimar, some 20-odd kilometres to the west, but it did attract its own share of 18th-century cultural giants, Schiller and Goethe among them. However, it's really Jena's pedigree as a city of science that sets it apart from other Thuringian towns. This is, after all, the 19th-century birthplace of optical precision technology, pioneered by Carl Zeiss, Ernst Abbe and Otto Schott. Today, several museums and the world's oldest public planetarium attest to this legacy. Although it bears the scars of WWII and GDR aesthetics, Jena's still a beguiling town, with some 20,000 students injecting a large dose of liveliness. Outside the city centre, you'll find lovely art-nouveau neighbourhoods, challenging trails leading to glorious viewpoints and the best nightlife in eastern Thuringia.

Orientation

Jena's main point of orientation is the soaring JenTower, which sits right next to the Markt, the tourist office and the Wagnergasse pub mile. Pretty much all major attractions are within a five- or 10-minute walk from here. Jena has two train stations. Long-distance trains arrive at Jena-Paradies, a 10-minute walk south of the Markt. Regional trains from Erfurt or Weimar stop at the tiny Jena-West station. To get to the centre from Jena-West, turn left onto Westbahnhofstrasse and follow it to Kollegienstrasse, turn right and you'll be at the Markt in a minute.

Information

Bagels & Beans (☎ 219 291; Leutragraben 2-4; per min €0.04, wi-fi per 30min €1.50; ☽ 8am-8.30pm Mon-Fri, 9am-7pm Sat, 8am-6pm Sun) Internet and wi-fi just east of the JenTower.

Police (☎ 810; Am Anger 30)

Post office (Engelplatz 8; ☽ 9am-6.30pm Mon-Fri, 9am-1pm Sat)

Sparkasse (☎ 6790; Ludwig-Weimar-Gasse 5) Bank with ATM.

Tourist office (☎ 498 050; www.jena.de; Markt 16; ☽ 9am-7pm Mon-Fri, 9am-6pm Sat, 10am-3pm Sun) In Jena's oldest building, dating from 1384. Sells the JenaCard (€8.90) for 48 hours of public transport and free and discounted tours and admissions.

Sights

JENTOWER

The 128m-tall cylindrical **JenTower** (lift €3; ☽ 11am-midnight) sticks out from Jena's silhouette like the tall kid in your third-grade picture. In the early 1970s, the medieval Eichplatz was razed to make room for this concrete behemoth, built as a Zeiss research facility. It proved unsuitable, and the building languished for some time before getting a facelift and reopening with an observation platform and the upmarket Scala restaurant (p291). Down at street level is the Neue Mitte shopping mall.

AROUND THE MARKT

Despite the forces of time and developers' bulldozers, the **Markt** still reflects a measure of Jena's medieval heritage. At its southern end stands the **Rathaus** (1380), with an astronomical clock in its baroque tower. Every hour, on the hour, a little door opens and a devil/fool called Schnapphans appears, trying to catch a golden ball (representing the human soul) that dangles in front of him.

The square is anchored by a **statue** of Prince-Elector Johann Friedrich I, founder of Jena's university and popularly known as 'Hanfried'. The handsome building with the half-timbered upper section at the northern end of the square contains the **Stadtmuseum & Kunstsammlung Jena** (City Museum & Art Collection; ☎ 498 050; www.stadtmuseum.jena.de, in German; Markt 7; adult/concession €4/2.50; ☽ 10am-5pm Tue, Wed & Fri, 2-10pm Thu, 11am-6pm Sat & Sun). Learn how the city evolved into a centre of philosophy and science, what the Seven Miracles are all about and check out the latest art exhibit.

North of the museum, the **Stadtkirche St Michael** (Parish Church; Kirchplatz; ☽ 12.30-5pm Mon, 10am-5pm Tue-Sun May-Sep) would be just another Gothic church if it didn't possess Martin Luther's original engraved tombstone (yep, the one in Wittenberg's Schlosskirche is actually a 19th-century replica).

UNIVERSITÄT JENA

Jena's university was founded as Collegium Jenense in 1558, in a former monastery on

Kollegiengasse. Parts of it are still there; enter the courtyard to admire the coat of arms of Johann Friedrich I and to check out the free exhibit (in German) on the university's illustrious history.

West of here across Leutragraben, in an excellent example of urban recycling, the former Zeiss optics factory is now the university's main campus. Buildings wrap around Ernst-Abbe-Platz, dotted with abstract sculptures by Frank Stella; on the south side is the **Goethe Galerie** shopping mall.

The university **headquarters** (Fürstengraben 1) are in a century-old complex on the northeastern edge of the Altstadt. Step inside to admire a Minerva bust by Rodin and a wall-sized painting showing Jena students going off to fight against Napoléon.

GOETHE & SCHILLER

As minister for the elector of Saxe-Weimar, Goethe visited Jena many times, regulating the flow of the Saale, building streets, designing the botanic garden, cataloguing the university library or discovering the obscure human central jawbone. Most of the time, he stayed in the tiny house that's now the **Goethe Gedenkstätte** (Goethe Memorial; ☎ 949 009; Fürstengraben 26; adult/concession €1/0.50; ☽ 11am-3pm Wed-Sun Apr-Oct). Exhibits illustrate his accomplishments as a natural scientist, poet and politician. Goethe himself planted the ginkgo tree just east of here, now part of the **Botanischer Garten** (botanic garden; ☎ 949 274; adult/concession €3/1.50; ☽ 9am-6pm mid-May–mid-Sep, to 5pm mid-Sep–mid-May), the second-oldest in Germany, with more than 12,000 plants from every climatic zone on earth.

Goethe is also credited with recruiting Schiller to Jena University in 1789. The playwright enjoyed Jena so much that he stayed for 10 years, longer than anywhere else, in what is now known as **Schillers Gartenhaus** (Schiller's Garden House; ☎ 931 188; Schillergässchen 2; adult/concession €2.50/1.30; ☽ 11am-5pm Tue-Sun Apr-Oct, 11am-5pm Tue-Sat Nov-Mar). He wrote *Wallenstein* in the little wooden shack in the garden, where he and Goethe liked to wax philosophical.

CITY OF SCIENCE

Carl Zeiss, Ernst Abbe and Otto Schott were three pioneers who put Jena on the scientific map. Zeiss began building rudimentary microscopes in 1846 and, with Abbe's help, developed the first scientific microscope in 1857. Together with Otto Schott, the founder

of Jenaer Glaswerke (glass works), they pioneered the production of optical precision instruments, which eventually propelled Jena to global prominence in the early 20th century.

Their life stories and the evolution of optical technology are the themes of the **Optisches Museum** (Optical Museum; ☎ 443 165; Carl-Zeiss-Platz 12, adult/concession €5/4; ☽ 10am-4.30pm Tue-Fri, 11am-5pm Sat). Tour Zeiss' recreated 1866 workshop, then browse through an engaging collection of microscopes, cameras, spectacles and other optical instruments. Elsewhere you can test your own vision and go on what amounts to a simulated acid trip by exploring mind-bending 3-D holograms. An English-language pamphlet is available. Outside is a commemorative pavilion built by Henry van de Velde, with a bust of Abbe by Max Klinger.

Travel to distant stars and planets in the **Zeiss Planetarium** (☎ 885 488; www.planetarium-jena.de; Am Planetarium 5; adult/concession admission €8/6.50 combination ticket with Optical Museum €11/9, laser show €9/7.50; ☽ hours vary), the world's oldest public planetarium (1926). Its state-of-the-art dome projection system makes it a heavenly setting for cosmic laser shows paying tribute to music legends Pink Floyd and Queen.

Finally, for more on the history, the production and technology of glass, swing by the **Schott Glasmuseum** (☎ 681 1765; Otto-Schott-Strasse 13; admission free; ☽ 1-5pm Tue-Fri), a free interactive multimedia exhibition with audioguides in English.

Festivals & Events

A great time to be in town is for **Kulturarena Jena** (☎ 498 060; www.kulturarena.com), an international music festival – with blues, rock, classical and jazz – that gets the town rocking in July and August.

Sleeping

Alpha One Hostel Jena (☎ 597 897; www.hostel-jena.de, in German; Lassallestrasse 8; dm €15-17, s/d €25/40, linen €2.50, breakfast €3.50; ✗ ⌨) Jena's sparkling new indie hostel is in a quiet street, yet within staggering distance of the Wagnergasse pubs. The decent-sized rooms are splashed in bright colour; those on the third floor have great views and room 16 even has a balcony.

Ibis Hotel City am Holzmarkt (☎ 8130; www.ibishotel.com; Teichgraben 1; r from €59, breakfast €10; ℗ ✗) This chain contender has all the prerequisites

JENA FROM ABOVE

There's plenty of hiking and biking around Jena, but, for a rewarding thigh burner, scoot up the 500 steps to the **Landgrafenturm**, an ancient tower on a hill north of town (approach via Philosophenweg). Called 'Balcony of Jena', this lofty perch treats you to a glorious panorama of the town and surroundings, high above the din of the city and practically at eye level with the top of the JenTower. There are benches for resting and a restaurant, the **Landgrafen Jena** (☎ 507 071; mains €10-18; ☽ 11am-11pm Wed-Sun), for refreshments or light seasonal dishes. Several trails radiate in all directions from up here as well. Less than 3.5km away, for instance, there's the **Papiermühle** (☎ 459 80; Erfurter Strasse 102; mains €7-20, s/d €55/85; ☽ 11.30am-midnight), a charming brewery-pub and beer garden that's a welcome refuelling stop; it even has a few rooms in case you feel like spending the night. Otherwise, it's an easy ride on bus 16 back into town.

to give you a good night's sleep and puts you smack dab in the thick of things.

Gasthaus zur Noll (☎ 597 710; www.zur-noll.de; Oberlauengasse 19; s €60-70, d €70-90; P ⊠ ☎) You'll find classic Thuringian hospitality galore in this historic charmer that gets rave reviews for its breakfast buffet bonanza. Rooms teeter between elegant and rustic and are endowed with all the expected modern trappings. For extra character and space, ask to stay in the wood-clad *Bohlenstube*. The restaurant-pub is perfect for sampling rustic fare, including a vampire-repelling garlic soup (mains €9 to €17).

Steigenberger Esplanade Jena (☎ 8000; www.jena steigenberger.de; Carl-Zeiss-Platz 4; r €90-160; breakfast €16; P ⊠ ⊠ 🖥 ☎) With lots of light, glass and edgy design, Jena's premier abode radiates urban poshness in its public areas and 179 rooms wrapped around a vertigo-inducing atrium. It's inside the Goethe Galerie mall, so shopaholics won't have to lug their bags very far.

Eating & Drinking

There's a supermarket in the basement of the Goethe Galerie.

ourpick **Café Immergrün** (☎ 447 313; Jener Gasse 6; mains €2-5; ☽ 11am-late) Sink deep into a plump sofa for intense tête-à-têtes or gather your posse in the leafy garden at this self-service bistro-pub, tucked off a quiet side street just north of the JenTower. The cheap meals (mostly pasta, rice and baguettes) make it popular with students, but all free spirits are welcome.

Café Stilbruch (☎ 827 171; Wagnergasse 2; dishes €3-23; ☽ 8.30am-1am Mon-Fri, 9am-late Sat & Sun) The competition is great on Wagnergasse, Jena's pub mile, but this multilevel contender is still our favourite stop for drinks and a bite from

the something-for-everybody menu. For privacy, snag the table atop the spiral staircase; for people watching, sit outside.

Roter Hirsch (☎ 443 221; Holzmarkt 10; mains €3.50-13; ☽ 9am-midnight Mon-Sat, 10am-11pm Sun; ⊠) Open the door and feel catapulted back by about 500 years in this charismatic warren of wood-panelled rooms with secluded corners. It's the perfect backdrop for the hearty home cooking; girth-friendly smaller dishes are also available.

Scala (☎ 356 666; JenTower, Leutragraben 1; mains €17-30; ☽ 11am-midnight; ⊠) Other tower restaurants may be higher, but few match the calibre of Scala. The cuisine is globally inspired but doesn't play it safe. Oriental-spice-encrusted duck with linguine in orange-ginger sauce is a typically ambitious flavour pairing.

Entertainment

Rosenkeller (☎ 931 190; Johannisstrasse 13) This historic club in a network of cellars has plied booze and music to generations of students and is still among the best places in town to get into trouble and meet some friendly locals.

Kassablanca Gleis 1 (☎ 282 620; Felsenkellerstrasse 13a) Near Jena-West train station, this joint feeds the cultural cravings of the indie crowd with a potpourri of live concerts, dance parties, readings, experimental theatre, movies and other distractions. Cheap drinks fuel the fun.

Volksbad Jena (☎ 498 060; www.jena.de/volksbad; in German; Knebelstrasse 10) You can't swim in water in this century-old public pool any longer; instead you'll be showered by cultural events ranging from the mainstream to the offbeat.

Getting There & Away

Direct trains to Weimar (€5, 15 minutes), Erfurt (€8.50, 30 minutes) and Eisenach

THURINGIA

depart from Jena-West. ICE trains to Berlin-Hauptbahnhof (€56, 2½ hours) depart from Jena-Paradies, as do twice hourly services to Rudolstadt (€6.90, 35 minutes) and Saalfeld (€8.40, 45 minutes).

Jena is just north of the A4 from Dresden to Frankfurt, and west of the A9 from Berlin to Munich. The B7 links it with Weimar, while the B88 goes south to Rudolstadt and Saalfeld.

Getting Around

Single bus or tram tickets cost €1.70, while a day pass is €4.20. For a taxi, call ☎ 458 888. **Fahrrad Kirscht** (☎ 441 539; Löbdergraben 8; ☽ 9am-7pm Mon-Fri, 9am-4pm Sat) rents out bikes for €15 for the first 24 hours and €10 per day thereafter.

AROUND JENA
Dornburger Schlösser

On a plateau above the Saale River about 15km north of Jena, this trio of **palaces** (☎ 036497-222 91; Dornburg; Renaissance or Rococo Palace adult/concession €2/1.50, combination ticket €3.50/2.50; ☽ 10am-6pm Tue-Sun Apr-Oct) makes for a pleasant excursion in summer. The most interesting is the 1539 **Renaissance Palace**, where Goethe sought solitude after the death of his patron, Duke Carl August. The rooms he stayed in have been restored more or less to their 1828 state. The youngest is the small and attractive **Rococo Palace**, which is used for temporary exhibits, concerts and weddings. The oldest is the aptly named **Altes Schloss**, which blends Romanesque, late-Gothic, Renaissance and baroque elements but can only be viewed from the outside. The **gardens** (admission free; ☽ 8am-dusk) are open year-round.

Trains travel frequently to Dornburg from Jena-Paradies (€3.10, 15 minutes), from where it's a steep 20- to 30-minute climb. Alternatively, combine culture with cardio and hire a bicycle to follow the 32km **Schlösser Tour** (Palace Tour), which starts in central Jena.

RUDOLSTADT

☎ 03672 / pop 26,000

Rural Rudolstadt was, until 1918, the main residence of the princes of Schwarzburg-Rudolstadt, whose baroque hilltop castle is the town's single biggest attraction. In 1788 Goethe and Schiller met in Rudolstadt for the first time. The Rudolstadt theatre also has a pedigree going back to the late 18th

century and once got the creative juices of Liszt, Wagner and Paganini flowing; it's still putting on performances today.

Rudolstadt's **tourist office** (☎ 414 743; www .rudolstadt.de, in German; Marktstrasse 57; ☽ 9am-6pm Mon-Fri, to 1pm Sat) is just west of the Markt.

Sights

Overlooking the town from its lofty perch the baroque **Schloss Heidecksburg** (☎ 429 00 www.heidecksburg.de; Schlossbezirk 1; adult/concession €6/5 ☽ 10am-6pm Tue-Sun Apr-Oct, 10am-5pm Tue-Sun Nov-Mar) is honeycombed with lavishly decorated and furnished rooms and harbours regional history exhibits and collections of paintings porcelain, weapons and minerals. Perhaps the palace's best feature, though, is free: a terrific view over the valley.

Down in the old town, another important port of call is the **Stadtkirche St Andreas** (☎ 412 108; Kirchhof 1; ☽ 2-5pm May-Sep), a late-Gothic hall church that was heavily embellished during the baroque era. Note especially the wall-sized family tree of the local rulers and the ornate epitaphs.

The latest addition to Rudolstadt's cultural landscape is the **Schillerhaus Rudolstadt** (☎ 486 470; Schillerstrasse 25; adult/concession €5/3; ☽ 10am-6pm Tue-Sun Apr-Oct, 10am-5pm Wed-Sun Nov-Mar). It's a small museum in the very house where Schiller first bumped into Goethe, while a guest of the literary-minded sisters Charlotte and Caroline von Lengefeld. Schiller developed a close relationship with both women and, although he ended up marrying Charlotte, rumours of a love triangle have never gone away. Exhibits try to shed some light on this titillating matter.

Sleeping & Eating

DJH hostel (☎ 313 610; www.rudolstadt.jugendherberge .de; Schillerstrasse 50; dm under/over 26yr incl breakfast & dinner €22.50/25.50; ☒ ▣) This small hostel is handily located in the Altstadt, a five-minute walk from the train station.

Hotel Adler (☎ 4403; www.hotel-adler-rudolstadt.de; Markt 17; s €55, d €85-95; Ⓟ) In a 16th-century stone building right on the Markt, this hotel has breezy rooms sheathed in soothing colours and outfitted with heavenly beds, some with a canopy. The on-site restaurant dishes up dependable German classics (mains €7 to €15).

Getting There & Away

Trains depart frequently for Saalfeld (€2.10, nine minutes) and Jena-Paradies (€6.90, 35 minutes).

Rudolstadt is linked to Jena and Ilmenau via the B88 and to Weimar by the B85.

SAALFELD

☎ 03671 / pop 27,500

Gables, turrets and gates provide a cheerful welcome to Saalfeld, which has been sitting prim and pretty along the Saale River for 1100 years. Aside from the handsome medieval town centre, it lures visitors with one of Thuringia's most engrossing natural attractions, the Feengrotten (Fairy Grottoes).

The Hauptbahnhof is east of the Saale River, about a 10-minute walk from the Markt and the **tourist office** (☎ 339 50; www.saalfeld.de; Markt 6; 9am-6pm Mon-Fri, 9am-2pm Sat, 10am-2pm Sun Apr-Oct, am-6pm Mon-Fri, 10am-2pm Sat Nov-Mar).

Sights

The Altstadt can easily be covered on a brief stroll. From the Hauptbahnhof, pass through (maybe even climb up) the 15th-century **Saaltor** (town gate). Just west of here on the Markt is the striking Renaissance **Rathaus**, with its spiked turrets and ornate gables. Opposite is the partly Romanesque **Marktapotheke**, which has been a pharmacy since 1681.

Behind the Markt, the twin towers topping the Gothic **Johanniskirche** (St John's Church; ☎ 455 440; Kirchplatz 3; 11am-5pm Mon-Fri, 11am-4pm Sat, 1-4pm Sun) rise into view. From May to October, every Wednesday at 8pm, concerts ring through this enormous hall church, whose choir ceiling is painted with 200 different plant species in what's called a *Himmelswiese* (heavenly meadow). Also note the life-size carved figure of St John the Baptist.

Brudergasse, west of the Markt, leads uphill to a 13th-century Franciscan monastery, now recycled as the **Stadtmuseum** (City Museum; ☎ 598 471; Münzplatz 5; adult/concession/family €4/2.50/5; 10am-5pm Tue-Sun). Its major allure is the celestial building itself, and the collection of local Late-Gothic carved altarpieces.

FEENGROTTEN

About 3km southwest of the train station, the **Feengrotten** (Fairy Grottoes; ☎ 550 40; www.feengrotten.de; Feengrottenweg 2; tour adult/concession/family €8/6.50/19; 9.30am-5pm daily Apr-Oct, 10.30am-3.30pm daily Nov, Dec, Feb & Mar, 10am-3.30pm Sat & Sun Jan) are Saalfeld's prime attraction. Formerly alum slate mines (from 1530 to 1850), they were opened for tours in 1914 and rank as the world's most colourful grottoes according to no less an authority than *Guinness World Records*. Don't expect Technicolor dreams, though: 'colour' here refers mostly to different shades of brown, ochre and sienna, with an occasional sprinkling of green and blue. Small stalactite and stalagmite formations add to a bizarre and subtly impressive series of grottoes, with names like Butter Cellar and Blue-Green Grotto. The highlight is the Fairytale Cathedral and its Holy Grail Castle.

Above ground, aspiring Harry Potters may well be enchanted by the **Feenweltchen** (Fairy World; adult/concession/family €6/5/14.50, combination ticket with grottoes €12/10.50/29; 9am-6pm May-Oct), a kingdom of elves, fairies and nature spirits waiting to be discovered.

Bus A makes the trip from Saalfeld Bahnhof and Markt to the grottoes every half-hour.

Sleeping & Eating

Zum Pappenheimer (☎ 330 89; www.zum-pappenheimer.de; Fleischgasse 5; s/d €40/55, mains €6-12; 8am-midnight Mon-Sat, 8am-3pm Sun;) This cosy, ceramic-tiled bistro-pub is a good place to start or end an evening. Upstairs are a couple of simple rooms in case you feel like staying.

Hotel am Hohen Schwarm (☎ 2884; www.schwarm hotel.de, in German; Schwarmgasse 18; s €43-53, d €63-73;) Rooms in this family-run hotel are in no danger of appearing in *House Beautiful* any time soon, but they're comfortable, quiet and big enough to give you a good night's sleep.

Hotel Anker (☎ 5990; www.hotel-anker-saalfeld.de; Am Markt 25-26; s/d €54/80;) Emperor Charles V once rested his head in this 15th-century building that's now a gracious hotel-restaurant, with 70 rooms dressed in elegant country style. The nicest are in the older wing of the building. Wrap up a day on the road in the cellar restaurant, whose extensive menu runs from locally caught trout to elk steak (€7 to €20).

Sächsische Kaffeestube (☎ 2944; Saalstrasse 62; 10am-7pm;) This is the place for delicious ice cream and coffee, on a back terrace overlooking the leafy Saale River.

Getting There & Away

Regional trains run frequently to Rudolstadt (€2.10, nine minutes) and Jena (€8.40, 45 minutes). There's also an ICE connection to Berlin-Hauptbahnhof (€62, 2¾ hours). Saalfeld is linked to Rudolstadt and Weimar via the B85 and to Jena by the B88.

Bavaria

From the sky-scraping Alps in the south to the Danube plain and beyond to the dark wooded hills of Franconia, diverse Bavaria (Bayern) is Germany's largest *Land* (state). Gobsmacking Alpine vistas, towns saturated in historical character, and a wealth of castles bequeathed by an odd-ball 19th-century king also make the southern 'free state' one of its most fascinating.

Bavaria enjoys a split personality which sees city dwellers swap weekend lederhosen and frothy steins of beer for nine-to-five laptops and cappuccinos. Munich's provincial power dressers steer an economy bigger than Sweden's, while out in the sticks time stands still.

Bavarians are subdivided into three peoples. Historic Bavaria is centred around Munich, the Alps and the medieval strongholds of Regensburg and Passau. Swabia begins at the old banking powerhouse, Augsburg. To the north, Nuremberg, Bamberg and Würzburg are part of Franconia. But one thing unites all Bavaria's citizens: a love of their traditional way of life.

Slicing through western Bavaria is Germany's most popular holiday route – the Romantic Road. This trail of walled towns and ancient watchtowers culminates in the world's most famous castle, King Ludwig II's dreamy Neuschwanstein. From there the northern reaches of the Alps extend for 250km of show-stopping scenery that has hikers and skiers on cloud nine.

But Munich is Bavaria's real heart and soul. It's a chic metropolis, yet a laid-back place that manages to combine Alpine air with Mediterranean joie de vivre. But wherever your Bavarian travels take you, expect oceans of beer served with legendary, thigh-slapping hospitality.

HIGHLIGHTS

- **Mine's a Stein** Go frothy at the mouth in one of Munich's famous beer halls (p325)

- **Bavaria from Above** Rack and pinion your way to the top of the Zugspitze, Germany's highest peak (p356)

- **Get Loopy** Go full circle around the town walls of dinky Dinkelsbühl (p346)

- **Leafy Escape** Hit the trail through the wilds of the Bavarian Forest (p399)

- **Bird's-Eye View** Soar to the Eagle's Nest (p361) in Berchtesgaden

- **Palatial Perfection** Indulge your romantic fantasies at sugary Schloss Neuschwanstein (p352)

★ Bavarian Forest

★ Dinkelsbühl

★ Munich

★ Schloss Neuschwanstein

★ Zugspitze

★ Berchtesgaden

- POPULATION: 12.5 MILLION
- AREA: 70,549 SQ KM

History

For centuries Bavaria was ruled as a duchy in the Holy Roman Empire, a patchwork of nations that extended from Italy to the North Sea. In the early 19th century, a conquering Napoleon annexed Bavaria, elevated it to the rank of kingdom and doubled its size. The fledgling nation became the object of power struggles between Prussia and Austria and, in 1871, was brought into the German Reich by Bismarck.

Bavaria was the only German state that refused to ratify the Basic Law (Germany's near-constitution) following WWII. Instead, Bavaria's leaders opted to return to its pre-war status as a 'free state', and drafted their own constitution. Almost ever since, the *Land* has been ruled by the Christlich-Soziale Union (CSU), the arch-conservative party that is peculiar to Bavaria. Its dominance of a single *Land*'s (state's) politics is unique in postwar Germany, though Bavarian state elections in 2008 saw the party lose 17% of its vote. Its sister party, the CDU, operates in the rest of the country by mutual agreement.

Getting There & Around

Munich is Bavaria's main transport hub, second only to Frankfurt in flight and rail connections. Rail is the best way to reach Munich from other parts of Germany, and the best means of getting from the Bavarian capital to other parts of Bavaria. Air links within Bavaria are much less extensive.

Without your own set of wheels in eastern Bavaria and the Alps, you'll have to rely on bus services, which peter out in the evenings and at weekends. Trips along the Romantic Road are done by tour bus, although again a car is a better idea. Several long-distance cycling routes cross Bavaria and the region's cities are some of the most cycle-friendly in the world, so getting around on two wheels could not be easier.

If you're travelling in a group, or can assemble one (as many people do pre-departure), you can make enormous savings with the **Bayern-Ticket** (€28). This allows up to five adults unlimited travel on one weekday from 9am to 3am, or from midnight to 3am next day on weekends. It's good for 2nd-class rail travel across Bavaria (regional trains only, no ICs or ICEs) as well as most public transport.

Accommodation

DJH youth hostels in Bavaria accept guests aged over 27 (who pay a €4 surcharge), although priority is still given to younger travellers. Independent, all-age hostels in Munich, Nuremberg, Bamberg and Würzburg are a less institutional alternative.

Bavaria's parks are generally open to free camping. Parks such as the Altmühltal Nature Park restrict camping to designated areas, for a small fee. Be sure to follow the local code of ethics and common decency, and pack up everything you brought along – litter, bottles, cans – and bury human waste before you leave.

Bavaria for Children

Kinderland Bavaria is a classification system for family-friendly sights, hotels, leisure facilities, museums and camp sites. For more information, go to www.kinderland.by.

MUNICH

☎ 089 / pop 1.35 million

Pulsing with prosperity and *Gemütlichkeit* (cosiness), Munich (München) revels in its own contradictions. Folklore and age-old traditions exist side by side with sleek BMWs, designer boutiques and high-powered industry. Its museums include world-class collections of artistic masterpieces, and its music and cultural scenes give Berlin a run for its money.

Despite all its sophistication, Munich retains a touch of provincialism that visitors find charming. The people's attitude is one of live-and-let-live – and Müncheners will be the first to admit that their 'metropolis' is little more than a *Weltdorf*, a world village. During Oktoberfest visitors descend on the Bavarian capital in their thousands to raise a glass to this fascinating city.

HISTORY

It was Benedictine monks, drawn by fertile farmland and the closeness to Catholic Italy, who settled in what is now Munich. The city derives its name from the medieval *Munichen*, or monks. In 1158, the Imperial Diet in Augsburg sanctioned the rule of Heinrich der Löwe, and Munich the city was born.

In 1240, the city passed to the House of Wittelsbach, that would govern Munich

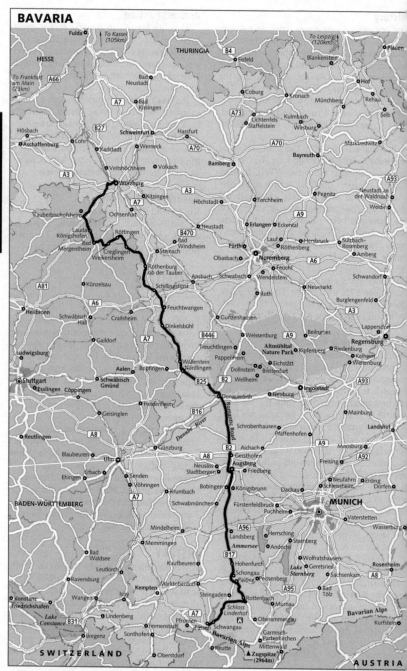

(as well as Bavaria) until the 20th century. Munich prospered as a salt-trading centre but was hit hard by the plague in 1349. The epidemic subsided only after 150 years, whereupon the relieved *Schäffler* (coopers) initiated a ritualistic dance to remind burghers of their good fortune. The *Schäfflertanz* is performed every seven years but it is re-enacted daily by the little figures on the city's *Glockenspiel* (carillon) on Marienplatz.

By the 19th century an explosion of monument-building gave Munich its spectacular architecture and wide Italianate avenues. Things got out of hand after King Ludwig II ascended the throne in 1864, as spending for his grandiose projects (such as Schloss Neuschwanstein) bankrupted the royal house and threatened the government's coffers. Ironically, today they are the biggest money-spinners of Bavaria's tourism industry.

Munich has seen many turbulent times but last century was particularly bumpy. WWI practically starved the city to death, the Nazis first rose to prominence here, and the next world war nearly wiped the city off the map. The 1972 Olympic Games began as a celebration of a new democratic Germany, but ended in tragedy when 17 people were killed in a terrorist hostage-taking incident. In 2006 the city won a brighter place in sporting history, when it hosted the opening game of the FIFA World Cup.

Today, Munich's claim to being the 'secret capital' of Germany is alive and well. The city is recognised for its high living standards, with the most millionaires per capita after Hamburg, and for a haute couture that rivals Paris and Milan. In 2008 the whole city took the summer off to celebrate the 850th birthday of this great metropolis.

ORIENTATION

The Hauptbahnhof (central train station) is less than 1km west of Marienplatz, the heart of the historic Altstadt (old town). North of Marienplatz is the Residenz (the former royal palace), crammed with museums and theatres, and Odeonsplatz with the landmark Theatinerkirche St Kajetan. To the east of Marienplatz is the Platzl quarter, with its traditional taverns and beer halls such as the Hofbräuhaus. Hipper bars and venues are south of the square in the Gärtnerplatzviertel quarter, which, along with the Glockenbachviertel west of here,

form Munich's gay and lesbian area. The
Isar River flows through the eastern part of
the city from south to north.

Munich is divided into various districts,
each with their own distinct character.
Schwabing, north of the Altstadt, is home
to Munich's university and a host of cafes
and restaurants. East of Schwabing is the
Englischer Garten (English Garden), one
of Europe's largest city parks. North of
Schwabing you'll find the Olympiapark,
site of the 1972 Olympic Games, and the
BMW Museum.

East of the Altstadt lies Haidhausen, a
trendy neighbourhood packed with pubs.
South and west of the Altstadt, and near the
Hauptbahnhof, is Ludwigsvorstadt, a half-
seedy, half-lively area packed with shops,
restaurants and hotels. The Westend, further
west, bristles with renovated villas, cool cafes
and wine bars, all near the Theresienwiese,
home of the Oktoberfest.

North of here is cosmopolitan Neuhausen,
a more residential area that's home to
Schloss Nymphenburg (Nymphenburg
Palace) with its lovely gardens a little further
northwest. Munich's airport is almost 36km
northeast of the city.

INFORMATION
Bookshops
Geobuch (Map p302; ☎ 265 030; Rosental 6) Best travel
bookshop in town.
Hugendubel (☎ 01803-484 484) Marienplatz (Map
p302); Karlsplatz (Map p302) National chain with tonnes of
English-language books.
Max & Milian (Map p302; ☎ 260 3320; Ickstattstrasse
2) The city's best gay bookshop.
Munich Readery (Map p306; ☎ 1219 2403; Augusten-
strasse 104) Germany's biggest collection of secondhand
English-language titles.
Words' Worth Books (Map p305; ☎ 283 642; Schell-
ingstrasse 3) An excellent English-language bookshop.

Cultural Centres
Amerika Haus (Map p306; ☎ 552 5370; Karolinenplatz 3)
Goethe-Institut (Map p302; ☎ 551 9030; Sonnen-
strasse 25)
Institut Français (Map p305; ☎ 286 6280; Kaulbach-
strasse 13)

Discount Cards
City Tour Card (1/3 days €9.80/18.80, 3-day card for up
to 5 adults €29) Unlimited public transport and up to 50%
discount on 50 museums and attractions.

Emergency
Ambulance (☎ 192 22)
Fire (☎ 112)
Police (Map p302; ☎ 110; Arnulfstrasse 1) Police station
right beside the Hauptbahnhof.

Internet Access
The city libraries (*Stadtbibliotheken;* below)
have cheap access, but you may have to wait.
Coffee Fellows (Map p302; Schützenstrasse 14; per hr
€2.50; ☑ 7am-11.30pm) Order coffee downstairs, check
emails upstairs.
Cyber!ce-C@fe (Map p305; ☎ 3407 6955; Feil-
itzschstrasse 15; per 30min €2.50; ☑ 9am-midnight) Ice
cream and Apple Macs near the Englischer Garten.

Internet Resources
Munichfound (www.munichfound.com) Expat magazine.
Munich Tourist Office (www.munich-tourist.de)
Munich's official website.

Laundry
Laundries are thin on the ground. Typical
costs are €3 to €4 per load, plus about €0.50
for 10 to 15 minutes' dryer time.
City-SB Waschcenter (Map p302; Paul-Heyse-Strasse
21; ☑ 7am-11pm) Charges €4 per load.
Schnell und Sauber (off Map p302; Parkstrasse 8;
☑ 6am-midnight) A short walk from the Hauptbahnhof.

Left Luggage
Gepäckaufbewahrung (Map p302; ☎ 1308 3468;
Hauptbahnhof; per piece €5; ☑ 8am-8pm Mon-Sat,
8am-6pm Sun) A staffed storage room, in the north part of
the station's main hall.
Lockers (Map p302; Hauptbahnhof; per 24hr €3-10;
☑ 24hr) In the main hall of the station and opposite
tracks 16, 24 and 28-36.

Libraries
Bayerische Staatsbibliothek (Bavarian State Library;
Map p305; ☎ 286 380; Ludwigstrasse 16; ☑ reading
hall 8am-midnight)
Stadtbücherei (City Library; ☑ 10am-7pm Mon-Fri)
Haidhausen (Map p304; ☎ 480 983 313; Rosenheimer
Strasse 5); Schwabing (Map p305; ☎ 4521 3630; Hohen-
zollernstrasse 16); Westend (off Map p302; ☎ 189 378
380; Schrenkstrasse 8)
Universitätsbibliothek (Map p305; ☎ 2180 2429;
Geschwister-Scholl-Platz 1; ☑ 9am-10pm Mon-Fri)

Media
Abendzeitung Light broadsheet that, despite the name,
has a morning delivery.

(Continued on page 307)

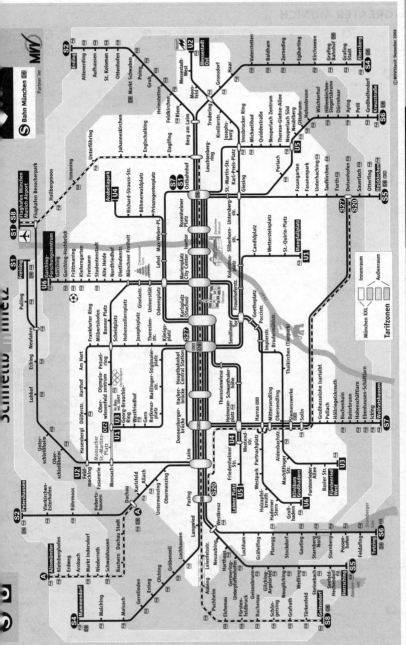

© MVV/Stand: Dezember 2006

GREATER MUNICH

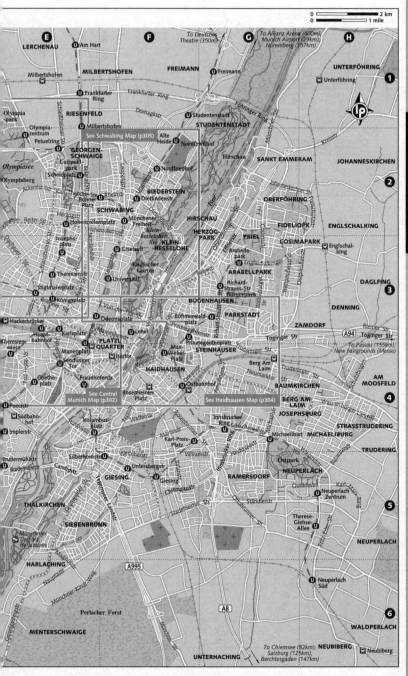

CENTRAL MUNICH

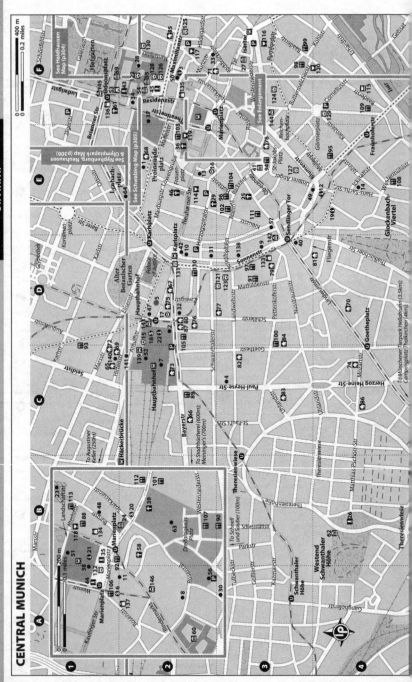

CENTRAL MUNICH

BAVARIA

HAIDHAUSEN

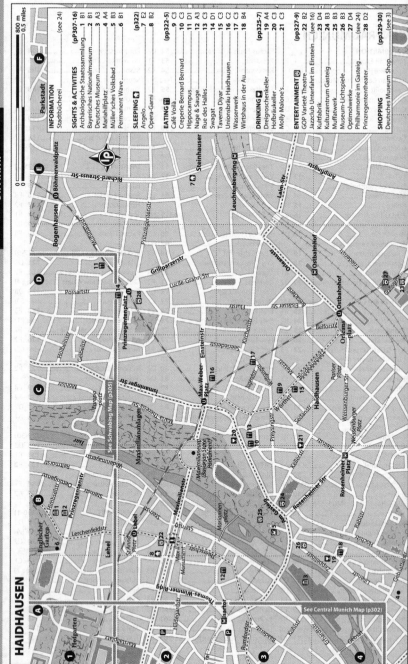

INFORMATION	
Stadtbücherei	(see 24)

SIGHTS & ACTIVITIES	(pp307-16)
Archäologische Staatssammlung	1 B1
Bayerisches Nationalmuseum	2 B1
Deutsches Museum	3 A3
Mariahilfplatz	4 A4
Müller'sches Volksbad	5 B3
Permanent Wave	6 B1

SLEEPING	(p322)
Angelo	7 E2
Opera-Garni	8 B2

EATING	(pp322-5)
Café Voilà	9 C3
Creperie Bernard Bernard	10 D1
Hippocampus	11 D1
Nage & Sauge	12 A3
Rue des Halles	13 C3
Swagat	14 D1
Taverna Diyar	15 D1
Unionsbräu Haidhausen	16 C2
Wasserwerk	17 C3
Wirtshaus in der Au	18 B4

DRINKING	(pp325-7)
Dreigroschenkeller	19 A4
Hofbräukeller	20 C3
Molly Malone's	21 C3

ENTERTAINMENT	(pp327-9)
GOP Varieté Theatre	22 B2
Jazzclub Unterfahrt im Einstein	(see 16)
Kultfabrik	23 D4
Kulturzentrum Gasteig	24 B3
Muffatwerk	25 B3
Museum-Lichtspiele	26 B3
Optimolwerke	27 D4
Philharmonie im Gasteig	(see 24)
Prinzregententheater	28 D2

SHOPPING	(pp329-30)
Deutsches Museum Shop	(see 3)

0 — 800 m
0 — 0.5 miles

Parkstadt

See Schwabing Map (p305)

See Central Munich Map (p302)

SCHWABING

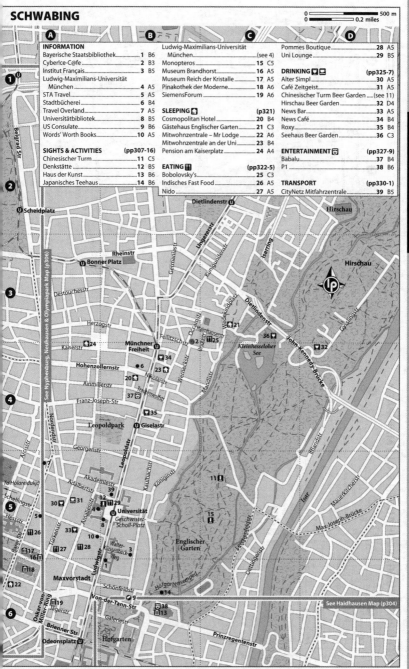

0 — 500 m
0 — 0.2 miles

INFORMATION
Bayerische Staatsbibliothek 1 B6
Cyberlce-C@fe 2 B3
Institut Français 3 B5
Ludwig-Maximilians-Universität
München 4 A5
STA Travel 5 A5
Stadtbücherei 6 B4
Travel Overland 7 A5
Universitätbibliotek 8 B5
US Consulate 9 B6
Words' Worth Books 10 A5

SIGHTS & ACTIVITIES (pp307-16)
Chinesischer Turm 11 C5
Denkstätte 12 B5
Haus der Kunst 13 B6
Japanisches Teehaus 14 B6

Ludwig-Maximilians-Universität
München .... (see 4)
Monopteros 15 C5
Museum Brandhorst 16 A5
Museum Reich der Kristalle 17 A5
Pinakothek der Moderne 18 A6
SiemensForum 19 A6

SLEEPING (p321)
Cosmopolitan Hotel 20 B4
Gästehaus Englischer Garten 21 C3
Mitwohnzentrale – Mr Lodge 22 A6
Mitwohnzentrale an der Uni 23 B4
Pension am Kaiserplatz 24 A4

EATING (pp322-5)
Bobolovsky's 25 C3
Indisches Fast Food 26 A5
Nido 27 A5

Pommes Boutique 28 A5
Uni Lounge 29 B5

DRINKING (pp325-7)
Alter Simpl 30 A5
Café Zeitgeist 31 A5
Chinesischer Turm Beer Garden ..... (see 11)
Hirschau Beer Garden 32 D4
News Bar 33 A5
News Café 34 B4
Roxy 35 B4
Seehaus Beer Garden 36 C3

ENTERTAINMENT (pp327-9)
Babalu 37 B4
P1 .... 38 B6

TRANSPORT (pp330-1)
CityNetz Mitfahrzentrale 39 B5

BAVARIA

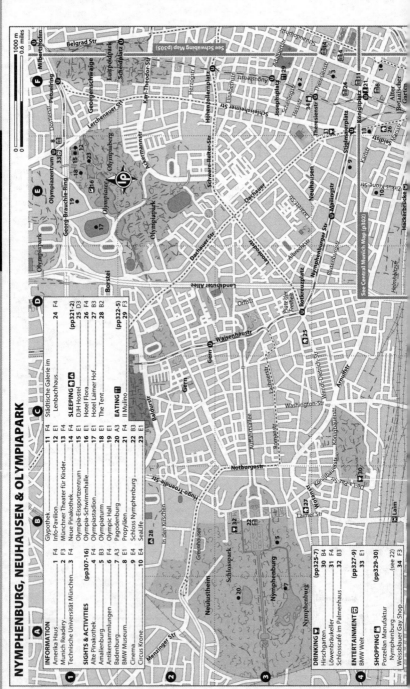

NYMPHENBURG, NEUHAUSEN & OLYMPIAPARK

INFORMATION	
Amerika Haus	1 F4
Munich Readery	2 F3
Technische Universität München	3 F4

SIGHTS & ACTIVITIES	(pp307-16)
Alte Pinakothek	4 F4
Amalienburg	5 B3
Antikensammlungen	6 F4
Badenburg	7 A3
BMW Museum	8 E1
Cinema	9 E4
Circus Krone	10 E4
Glyptothek	11 F4
Info-Pavilion	12 E1
Münchner Theater für Kinder	13 F4
Neue Pinakothek	14 F4
Olympia-Eissportzentrum	15 E1
Olympia-Schwimmhalle	16 E1
Olympiastadion	17 E1
Olympiaturm	18 E1
Olympic Hall	19 E1
Pagodenburg	20 A3
Propyläen	21 F4
Schloss Nymphenburg	22 B3
SeaLife	23 E1
Städtische Galerie Im	
Lenbachhaus	24 F4

SLEEPING	(pp321-2)
DJH Hostel	25 D3
Hotel Flora	26 F4
Hotel Laimer Hof	27 B3
The Tent	28 B2

EATING	(pp322-5)
Il Mulino	29 F3

DRINKING	(pp325-7)
Hirschgarten	30 B4
Löwenbräukeller	31 F4
Schlosscafé im Palmenhaus	32 B3

ENTERTAINMENT	(pp327-9)
BMW Welt	33 E1

SHOPPING	(pp329-30)
Porzellan Manufaktur	
Nymphenburg	(see 22)
Weissblauer Gay Shop	34 F3

(Continued from page 298)

Münchner Merkur The city's arch-conservative daily.
Süddeutsche Zeitung Widely read regional paper with a liberal streak. Monday's edition has a *New York Times* supplement in English.
tz Local tabloid similar to the saucy *Bild,* Germany's biggest-selling paper.

Medical Services

The US and UK consulates have lists of English-speaking doctors. Most pharmacies have employees who speak passable English, but there are several designated as 'international', with staff fluent in English.
Apotheke Hauptbahnhof (Map p302; ☎ 5998 9040; Bahnhofsplatz 7)
Ärztlicher Bereitschaftsdienst (☎ 01805-191 212; ☻ 24hr) Emergency medical service.
Ludwigs-Apotheke (Map p302; ☎ 550 5070; Neuhauser Strasse 11) English-speaking pharmacy.

Money

ATMs are widespread throughout the city; a few key ones are listed below.
American Express (Map p302; ☎ 2280 1465 ; Promenadeplatz 6)
Deutsche Bank (Map p302; Marienplatz)
ReiseBank (Map p302; Hauptbahnhof; ☻ 7am-8pm Mon-Fri, 8am-6pm Sat & Sun)
Sparkasse (Map p302; Sparkassenstrasse 2)

Post

Post office Altstadt (Map p302; Sattlerstrasse 1; ☻ 9am-6pm Mon-Fri, 9am-12.30pm Sat, closed Sun)
Post office Hauptbahnhof (Map p302; Bahnhofplatz 1; ☻ 8am-8pm Mon-Fri, 9am-4pm Sat, closed Sun)

Tourist Information

Bavarian Castles & Museums Infopoint (Map p302; ☎ 2101 4056; Alter Hof 1; ☻ 10am-6pm Mon-Sat) Heaps of info on attractions across Munich and Bavaria.
EurAide (Map p302; ☎ 593 889; www.euraide.de; Arnulfstrasse entrance, Hauptbahnhof; ☻ 9.30am-12.30pm & 3.30-6pm Mon-Fri, 8.30am-12.30pm & 3.30-6pm Sat May-Jul) The office makes reservations and sells tickets for DB trains and tours. EurAide's free newsletter, the *Inside Track,* is packed with practical info about the city and surroundings.
Tourist office Hauptbahnhof (Map p302; ☎ 2339 6500; Bahnhofsplatz 2; ☻ 9am-8pm Mon-Sat, 10am-6pm Sun); Marienplatz (Map p302; ☎ 2339 6500; Neues Rathaus; ☻ 10am-8pm Mon-Fri, 10am-4pm Sat, 10am-2pm Sun)

Travel Agencies

EurAide is the best place to go with complicated rail pass enquiries, or to book train travel in Germany and elsewhere in Europe.

STA Travel (Map p305; ☎ 2880 5870; www.statravel.de; Schellingstrasse 45)
Travel Overland (Map p305; ☎ 2727 6100; www.travel-overland.de; Barer Strasse 73)

Universities

Munich is home to about 90,000 students. The biggest universities are listed below.
Ludwig-Maximilians-Universität München (Map p305; ☎ 218 00; www.uni-muenchen.de; Geschwister-Scholl-Platz 1) Runs German-language courses for foreigners throughout the year.
Technische Universität München (Map p306; ☎ 289 01; Arcisstrasse 21) Renowned faculties of science, engineering and medicine.

DANGERS & ANNOYANCES

During Oktoberfest crime and staggering drunks are major problems, especially at the southern end of the Hauptbahnhof. It's no joke: drunk people in a crowd trying to get home can become violent, and there are dozens of assaults every year. Leave early or stay very cautious, if not sober, yourself.

The *Föhn* is a weather-related annoyance peculiar to southern Germany. Static-charged wind from the south brings exquisite views clear to the Alps and an area of dense pressure that sits on the city. Visiting film-maker Ingmar Bergman wrote that the *Föhn* makes 'nice dogs bite, and cats spew lightning'. Müncheners claim that it simply makes them cranky.

Munich is riddled with bike paths, and Bavaria's speeding cyclists don't expect you to be walking on them. Tangling with a two-wheeler is both embarrassing and potentially dangerous, so watch where you tread.

SIGHTS

Munich's major sights are clustered around the Altstadt, with the main museum district near the Residenz. However, it will take another day or two to explore Bohemian Schwabing, the sprawling Englischer Garten, and trendy Haidhausen to the east. Northwest of the Altstadt you'll find cosmopolitan Neuhausen, the Olympiapark, and one of Munich's jewels – Schloss Nymphenburg.

Marienplatz & Around

The heart and soul of the Altstadt is **Marienplatz** (Map p302), the old town square. At the northwest corner stands the **Mariensäule** (Marian Column), erected in 1638 to celebrate the removal of Swedish forces at the end of the Thirty Years' War. Topped with a golden figure of the Virgin Mary dating from 1590, it was one of the first Marian columns erected north of the Alps.

NEUES RATHAUS

The soot-blackened facade of the neo-Gothic **Neues Rathaus** (New Town Hall; Map p302) is festooned with gargoyles and statues, including a dragon scaling the turrets. Inside, six grand courtyards host festivals and concerts throughout the year. For a good view of the city, ascend the 85m **tower** (adult/concession €2/1; 10am-5pm Mon-Fri Nov-Apr, 10am-7pm May-Oct).

Huge crowds gather on Marienplatz to watch the **Glockenspiel** (carillon). Note the three levels: two portraying the *Schäfflertanz* (see p295) and another the Ritterturnier, a knights' tournament held in 1568 to celebrate a royal marriage. The characters spring into action for a neck-stiffening 12 minutes at 11am and noon (also 5pm November to April). The night scene featuring the Münchener Kindl (a girl in a monk's robe) and a *Nachtwächter* (nightwatchman) runs at 9pm.

ST PETERSKIRCHE

Opposite the Neues Rathaus stands the **St Peterskirche** (Church of St Peter; Map p302). Severely Gothic in inspiration, the baroque interior is a subdued affair compared to some, but does have a magnificent high altar and eye-catching statues of the four church fathers (1732) by Egid Quirin Asam. A clamber up the 297 steps of the rectangular 92m **tower** (adult/concession €1.50/1; 9am-5.30pm), also known as 'Alter Peter', is one for the vistaholics.

FISCHBRUNNEN

Local legend suggests that dipping an empty purse into the **Fischbrunnen** (Fish Fountain; Map p302) on Ash Wednesday guarantees it will always be full. Topped with a preposterously spherical carp, the fountain was used to keep river fish alive during medieval markets, and later as the ceremonial dunking spot for butchers' apprentices.

ALTES RATHAUS

The Gothic **Altes Rathaus** (1474) was destroyed by lightning and bombs, and then rebuilt in a plainer style after WWII. In its south tower is the city's **Spielzeugmuseum** (Toy Museum; Map p302; 294 001; Alter Rathausturm; adult/child/family €3/1.50/7;

10am-5.30pm) with a huge collection of toys, Barbie dolls and teddy bears.

Behind the Altes Rathaus, the **Heiliggeistkirche** (Church of the Holy Spirit; Map p302; Tal 77) was built in 1392. This oasis of city-centre peace and quiet is a riot of pink and beige rococo decoration, with amazing 18th-century frescoes by Cosmas Damian Asam.

Viktualienmarkt & Around

The bustling **Viktualienmarkt** (Map p302) is one of Europe's great food markets. In summer the entire place is transformed into one of the finest and most expensive beer gardens around, while in winter people huddle for warmth and schnapps in the small pubs around the square. The merchandise and food are of the finest quality, and prices tend to be high. The enormous **maypole** bears artisans' symbols and the traditional blue-and-white Bavarian stripes. On the south side of the square you'll see a statue of Karl Valentin, Germany's most celebrated comedian.

The **Schrannenhalle** (Map p302), a reconstructed 19th-century grain hall, stands just off the southwest corner of the market. As well as housing several pricey Thai, Indian and Italian eateries, there's also a stage for live bands and a beer bottle sculpture made entirely from bottle openers.

STADTMUSEUM

To mark the city's 850th birthday in 2008, the **Stadtmuseum** (City Museum; Map p302; 2332 2370; St-Jakobs-Platz; adult/concession €4/2; 10am-6pm, closed Mon) restructured its collections to create the 'Typisch München' (Typically Munich) exhibition. This condenses Munich's tangled past into five easily digestible periods, with a chronological walking route leading through the rambling building. Exhibits in each section represent what is most typical for the time, and explain why.

A separate exhibit, Nazionalsozialismus in München (National Socialism in Munich), explores the darker corners of the city's role in Nazism after 1918. Set in a windowless hall among riveted steel plates, this powerful display taps a vast pool of photographs, uniforms, letters from concentration camp prisoners and many other documents.

JÜDISCHES MUSEUM MÜNCHEN

Many decades in the planning, the **Jüdisches Museum München** (Munich Jewish Museum; Map p302;

MY PERFECT DAY

We asked Gaby Holder, founder and owner of Radius Tours/Original Munich Walks for the past 21 years, how she would spend a day unwinding in the Bavarian capital:

'My perfect day would begin with breakfast at **Café Rischart** (p324), overlooking **Marienplatz** (p307) and the **Glockenspiel** (opposite) tower of the town hall.

Then it's off to spend the morning relaxing at the **Englischer Garten** (p312), maybe pausing to watch the surfers riding the **permanent wave** (p316).

My favourite lunch spot is the **Viktualienmarkt** (opposite), Munich's 200-year-old food market. I'd buy some cheese, olives and bread from the various stands, order an ale at the market beer garden and just sit and watch the world go by. Afterwards, I might find the energy to climb the tower of the nearby **St Peterskirche** (opposite) for the most stunning view of the city.

Suitably fortified, I'd head off on my bike in the afternoon to the vast grounds of **Schloss Nymphenburg** (p315), and maybe relax with a book for an hour or two in the sprawling gardens.

The cosy little tavern beneath the **Bier & Oktoberfestmuseum** (below) is my choice for an evening meal of traditional Bavarian fare. Afterwards I'd hop aboard the S-Bahn to the cool **Optimolwerke** (p328) club near Ostbahnhof, where it's party time until at least 3am.

☎ 2339 6096; www.juedisches-museum-muenchen.de; St Jakobs-Platz 16; adult/concession €6/3; ☾ 10am-6pm, closed Mon) is a major undertaking that attempts to come to terms with one of the most sinister chapters in the city's history. Contained within a modernist glass cube, the exhibits aim to show in a balanced, sensitive fashion the Jewish place in Munich's cultural landscape over the ages, from medieval times through to the horrors of the Third Reich and today's slow regeneration. Next door stands the quite forbidding, stone-clad new synagogue, built to finally replace the Romanesque synagogue that was razed by the Nazis in 1938.

HOFBRÄUHAUS

No visit to Munich would be complete without a visit to the Hofbräuhaus (see p325), Bavaria's (and possibly the world's) most celebrated beer hall. The swigging hordes of tourists tend to eclipse the fabulous interior, where dainty twirled flowers adorn the medieval vaults. The ballroom upstairs was the site of the first large meeting of the National Socialist Party on 20 February 1920. The gift shop sells exorbitantly priced steins and pretzel-shaped postcards.

BIER & OKTOBERFESTMUSEUM

In a 14th-century timber-framed house is the cute little **Bier & Oktoberfestmuseum** (Map p302; ☎ 2423 1607; www.bier-und-oktoberfestmuseum.de; Sterneckerstrasse 2; adult/concession €4/2.50; ☾ 1-5pm Tue-Sat), providing a potted history of Germany's

national tipple. Pore over old brewing vats, historic photos and some of the earliest Oktoberfest regalia. The earthy tavern is open 6pm to midnight (closed Monday).

Max-Joseph-Platz

Munich's glitziest high-end shopping boulevard, Maximilianstrasse, begins at **Max-Joseph-Platz** (Map p302), home to some of the city's most beloved edifices. Among them are the grandiose Nationaltheater (see p328), home to the Bavarian State Opera, and the granddaddy of them all – the Residenz. The square centres on a statue of **Max I Joseph**, the Bavarian king who proclaimed Germany's first constitution in 1818.

RESIDENZ

On the north side of Max-Joseph-Platz looms the oldest section of the **Residenz** (Map p302), the huge palace that housed Bavarian rulers from 1385 to 1918. Statues of **two lions** guard the gates to the palace on Residenzstrasse; rubbing one of their shields is said to bring you wealth. The northern wings open into several interior courtyards – the Emperor, the Apothecary and the Fountain – as well as two smaller ones, Chapel and King's Tract.

Residenzmuseum

The Wittelsbachs' amazing treasures, as well as the trappings of their lifestyles, are on display at the **Residenzmuseum** (Map p302; ☎ 290 671; enter from Max-Josephs-Platz 3; adult/under 18yr with parents/concession €6/free/5, combiticket with

BAVARIA

Schatzkammer €9/free/8; ⏰ 9am-6pm Apr–mid-Oct, 10am-5pm mid-Oct–Mar). The museum has roughly 130 rooms, and is so large that it's divided into two sections. You can see it all with a free audioguide.

The enclosed Grotto Court, one of the first places you'll see when you enter, features the wonderful Perseusbrunnen (Perseus Fountain). Next door is the famous Antiquarium, a lavishly ornamented barrel vault, smothered in frescoes and built to house the Wittelsbachs' huge antique collection. Other highlights include the Ancestral Gallery, with portraits of the rulers of Bavaria including the great conqueror Charlemagne; the Schlachtensäle (Battle Halls); the Porcelain Chambers, containing 19th-century porcelain from Berlin, Meissen and Nymphenburg; and the Asian Collections, with precious Chinese and Japanese porcelain, tapestries and jewellery.

Designed by Belgian architect François Cuvilliés and recently renovated, the **Cuvilliés-Theater** (Map p302; ⏰ 2-6pm Mon-Sat, 9am-6pm Apr–mid-Oct, 2-5pm Mon-Sat, 10am-5pm Sun mid-Oct–Mar) is one of Europe's finest rococo stages. The original theatre building was destroyed in a bombing raid in 1944, but the original finely carved fittings and furnishings, which had been dismantled and kept in a safe place during WWII, witnessed the premiere of Mozart's opera *Idomeneo*.

Schatzkammer der Residenz

The Residenzmuseum entrance also leads to the **Schatzkammer der Residenz** (Residence Treasury; Map p302; ☎ 290 671; enter from Max-Joseph-Platz 3; adult/concession/under 18yr with parents €6/5/free; ⏰ 9am-6pm Apr–mid-Oct, 10am-5pm mid-Oct–Mar). It exhibits an Aladdin's cave of baubles and precious objects. Included among the mind-boggling treasures are portable altars, the pearl-studded golden cross of Queen Gisela of Hungary, the Bavarian crown jewels, and 'exotic handicrafts' from Turkey, Iran, Mexico and India.

Staatliches Museum Ägyptischer Kunst

German explorers of the Near East brought back treasures that made their way into the **Staatliches Museum Ägyptischer Kunst** (Egyptian Art Museum; Map p302; ☎ 298 546; enter from Hofgartenstrasse 1; adult/concession €6/4; ⏰ 9am-5pm Tue-Fri, also 5-9pm Tue, 10am-5pm Sat & Sun). The excellent collection dates from the Old, Middle and New Kingdoms (2670–1075 BC).

Odeonsplatz to Karlsplatz

The elongated square called Odeonsplatz (Map p302) was the site of the so-called Beer Hall Putsch (revolt) by the Nazis in 1923, which landed Hitler in jail. At its southern end looms the **Feldherrnhalle** (Field Marshals' Hall). The statues under its Italian-style arches are of pre-20th-century military heroes Johann von Tilly and Carl Philipp von Wrede, both cast from the copper of melted-down cannon.

The imposing baroque church swelling up on the west side is the **Theatinerkirche St Kajetan** (Map p302; Theatinerstrasse 22), built in the 17th century to commemorate the birth of Prince Max Emanuel. Its massive twin towers flanking a giant cupola are a landmark of Munich's skyline. Inside, the intensely ornate high dome stands above the **Fürstengruft** (royal crypt), containing the remains of Wittelsbach dynasty members. Opposite and a bit to the north, a neoclassical gate leads the way to the former **Hofgarten** (Royal Gardens).

On Theatinerstrasse you'll find the entrance to the **Fünf Höfe** (Map p302), a fashionable shopping mall embracing five courtyards. The sleek glass-and-steel passages are lined with upscale designers, cafes and gift shops. The building also houses the **Kunsthalle der Hypo-Kulturstiftung** (☎ 224 412; www.hypo-kunsthalle .de; Theatinerstrasse 8; ⏰ 10am-8pm), a modern gallery space renowned for quality cross-genre exhibits.

Munich's main shopping drag is Kaufinger Strasse, which becomes Neuhauser Strasse in the west. Along it, the **Michaelskirche** (St Michael's Church; Map p302) is one of the city centre's most spectacular churches. The ceiling is a 20m-wide barrel-vaulted expanse with no supporting columns, thus creating a large, pew-filled space. Drop down into the crypt to find tombs of some members of the Wittelsbach family, including the humble final resting place of castle-crazed King Ludwig II. The facade showing the triumph of Catholicism over Protestantism was receiving a much-needed facelift at the time of writing.

Neuhauser Strasse culminates in Karlsplatz, punctuated by the broken Gothic arch of the **Karlstor** (Map p302), the western gate and perimeter of the Altstadt, and an enormous modern fountain, a favourite meeting point. About 250m north of Karlsplatz stands another fountain, the bombastic **Wittelsbacher Brunnen** (Map p302) that gushes water from beneath some stern-looking mythical figures.

FRAUENKIRCHE

Visible from just about anywhere in the Altstadt, the twin copper onion domes of the **Frauenkirche** (Church of Our Lady; Map p302) are often used as an emblem for the city. In contrast to its redbrick Gothic exterior, the interior is a soaring passage of light. The tomb of Ludwig the Bavarian, guarded by knights and noblemen, can be found in the choir. Near the door, look for the footprint cast in the pavement; according to legend, the devil lost a bet with the architect and stamped out in a huff. The 98m-tall south **tower** (adult/concession €3/1.50; 10am-5pm Mon-Sat Apr-Oct) affords excellent views – on clear days as far as the Alps.

ASAMKIRCHE

Near the **Sendlinger Tor**, a 14th-century gate, you'll come upon the pint-sized St Johann Nepomuk church, better known as the **Asamkirche** (Map p302; Sendlinger Strasse 62). Designed and built in the 18th century as a private chapel by the prolific Asam brothers, who lived next door, the over-the-top baroque interior with not an inch of unembellished wall or column, must have been an awe-inspiring sight for 18th-century Müncheners, as it is today. The narrowness of the nave packed with barley-sugar columns, hovering cherubs and faux marble heightens the riotous effect.

More of the younger Asam's masterful frescoes can be viewed in the riotously baroque **Damenstiftskirche** (Map p302; Damenstiftstrasse 1) just north of Sendlinger Strasse.

Königsplatz & Around

Northwest of the Altstadt is **Königsplatz** (Map p306), a Greek Revivalist square created under King Ludwig I. It is anchored by the Doric-columned **Propyläen** gateway and orbited by three museums. A short walk to the north you'll find the Kunstareal (literally 'Art Area'), home to Munich's three major art museums, the **Pinakotheks** (www.pinakothek.de). To get there, take the U2 or tram 27.

ALTE PINAKOTHEK

The **Alte Pinakothek** (Map p306; 2380 5216; Barer Strasse 27, enter from Theresienstrasse; adult/child €5.50/4, Sun €1; 10am-6pm, to 8pm Tue, closed Mon) is a veritable treasure trove of works by Old European Masters and an unmissable part of any visit to the city. Housed in a neoclassical temple built by King Ludwig I, it is one of the most important collections in the world.

Nearly all the paintings were collected or commissioned by Wittelsbach rulers over the centuries. The strongest section is **Old German Masters**: the four church fathers by Michael Pacher stands out, as does Lucas Cranach the Elder's *Crucifixion* (1503), an emotional rendition of the suffering Jesus.

Albrecht Dürer receives special attention in the **Dürersaal** upstairs. His famous Christ-like *Self-Portrait* (about 1500), showing the gaze of an artist brimming with self-confidence hangs alongside his final major work, *The Four Apostles*.

There is a choice bunch of **Old Dutch Masters**, including an altarpiece by Rogier van der Weyden called *The Adoration of the Magi*, plus *The Seven Joys of Mary* by Hans Memling, *Danae* by Jan Gossaert and *The Land of Cockayne* by Pieter Bruegel the Elder.

Rubens fans have reason to rejoice. At 6m in height, his *Large Last Judgement* (1617) was so big that court architect Leo van Klenze had to design the hall around the canvas. Other Flemish 17th-century artists represented include Anthonis van Dyck and Rembrandt, with his intensely emotional *Passion Cycle*.

Free English-language audioguides with taped commentary about 90 works are available in the lobby.

NEUE PINAKOTHEK

Picking up where the Alte Pinakothek leaves off, the **Neue Pinakothek** (Map p306; 2380 5195; Barer Strasse 29; adult/child €7/5, Sun €1; 10am-6pm, to 8pm Wed, closed Tue) contains an extensive collection of 18th- to early-20th-century paintings and sculpture, from rococo to Jugendstil (art nouveau).

The core of the exhibit is 19th-century German art from the private stock of King Ludwig I, who had nearly 400 paintings when he died in 1868. An entire room is dedicated to Hans Marées (1837–87), whose country scenes are infused with a touch of sentimentality.

Munich society painters Wilhelm von Kaulbach and Karl von Piloty are given space, reflecting a renewed interest in German history in the late 19th century. The king had a special affinity for the 'Roman Germans', a group of neoclassicists centred around Johann Koch, who favoured Italian landscapes.

The most memorable canvases include those by Romantic painter Caspar David Friedrich, such as his *Riesengebirge Landscape with Rising Mist*. Like these landscapes, the works of English portraitist Thomas Gainsborough display strong emotionalism and an ominous mood.

Other masters on display with a high recognition value include Edgar Degas, Gauguin, Manet and Van Gogh; one of the latter's *Sunflowers* (1888) is on display.

A free English-language audioguide can be picked up at the entrance.

PINAKOTHEK DER MODERNE

Opened in 2002 after six years of construction, **Pinakothek der Moderne** (Map p305; ☎ 2380 5360; Barer Strasse 40; adult/child €10/7, Sun €1; ☼ 10am-6pm, to 8pm Thu, closed Mon) is Germany's biggest collection of modern art. The spectacular interior is dominated by a huge eyelike dome, spreading natural light throughout the soft white galleries over four floors.

The museum pools several collections under a single roof: a survey of 20th-century art, plus design, sculpture, photography and video. A variety of sources were tapped, including the Bavarian royal family and the State Graphics Collection of 400,000 drawings, prints and engravings.

There are oils and prints by household names such as Picasso, Dali, Klee, Kandinsky and Warhol, mostly lesser-known works that will be fresh to many visitors. The basement covers the evolution of design from the industrial revolution to today. VW Beetles, Eames chairs and early Apple Macs stand alongside more obscure items such as AEG's latest electric kettles in 1909.

MUSEUM BRANDHORST

Opened next door to the Pinakothek der Moderne in mid-2009, the new multicoloured **Museum Brandhorst** (Map p305; ☎ 2380 5118; www.museum-brandhorst.de; Theresienstrasse 35a; adult/child €7/5, Sun €1; ☼ 10am-6pm, to 8pm Thu, closed Mon) was purpose-built to house a 700-piece private collection of modern and contemporary works belonging to Udo and Annette Brandhorst. Wow-factor is provided by Picasso, Warhol, Cy Twombly and even Damien Hirst, plus a number of lesser-known artists.

SIEMENSFORUM

Southeast of the Pinakotheks is the **SiemensForum** (Map p305; ☎ 6363 2660; Oskar-von-Miller-Ring 20; admission free; ☼ 9am-5pm Mon-Fri). It's a fun, hands-on kind of place, with five floors of promotional exhibits on electronics and microelectronics, ranging from the telegraph to the PC.

LENBACHHAUS

Leading late-19th-century painter Franz von Lenbach used his considerable fortune to construct a residence in Munich in the 1880s. His widow sold it to the city and threw in a bunch of his works as part of the deal. The villa houses the **Städtische Galerie im Lenbachhaus** (Map p306; www.lenbachhaus.de; Luisenstrasse 33), but is closed for vital renovation until at least 2012. When it reopens, the staggering range of 19th-century masterpieces by great artists such as Franz Marc and Wassily Kandinsky will be back on show.

OTHER MUSEUMS

Munich's oldest museum is the **Glyptothek** (Map p306; ☎ 286 100; Königsplatz 3; adult/concession €3.50/2.50, Sun €1, combined with Antikensammlungen €5.50/3.50; ☼ 10am-5pm, 10am-8pm Thu, closed Mon). Like all the buildings on Königsplatz, Glyptothek is a piece of Greek fantasy. Classical busts, portraits of Roman kings and sculptures from a Greek temple in Aegina are among its prize exhibits.

One of Germany's best antiquities collections is housed in the **Antikensammlungen** (Map p306; ☎ 598 359; Königsplatz 1; adult/concession €3.50/2.50, Sun €1; ☼ 10am-5pm, 10am-8pm Wed, closed Mon). It features vases, gold and silver jewellery and ornaments, bronze work, and Greek and Roman sculptures and statues.

The **Museum Reich der Kristalle** (Map p305; ☎ 2394 4312; Theresienstrasse 41; adult/concession €3/1.50; ☼ 1-5pm, closed Mon) has a literally dazzling collection of crystals. A large Russian emerald, meteorite fragments from Kansas and diamonds are also among the museum's most cherished exhibits.

Englischer Garten & Around

The **Englischer Garten** (English Garden; Map p305) is one of Europe's most monumental city parks – bigger even than London's Hyde Park or Central Park in New York. It was laid out in the late 18th century by an American-born physicist, Benjamin Thompson, an adviser to the Bavarian government and at one time its war minister. There are no English flower beds, but it's a great place for strolling, jogging, drinking and even surfing, conveniently located between the Isar River and the Schwabing district. In balmy weather

THE WHITE ROSE

Open resistance to the Nazis was rare during the Third Reich; after 1933, intimidation and the instant 'justice' of the Gestapo and SS served as powerful disincentives. One of the few groups to rebel was the ill-fated Weisse Rose (White Rose), led by Munich University students Hans and Sophie Scholl.

The nonviolent White Rose began operating in 1942, its members stealing out at night to smear 'Freedom!' and 'Down with Hitler!' on the city's walls. Soon they were printing anti-Nazi leaflets on the mass extermination of the Jews and other Nazi atrocities. One read: 'We shall not be silent – we are your guilty conscience. The White Rose will not leave you in peace.'

In February 1943, Hans and Sophie were caught distributing leaflets at the university. Together with their best friend, Christian Probst, the Scholls were arrested and charged with treason. After a summary trial, all three were found guilty and beheaded the same afternoon. Their extraordinary courage inspired the award-winning film *Sophie Scholl – Die Letzten Tage* (Sophie Scholl – The Final Days; 2005).

A memorial exhibit to the White Rose, **DenkStätte** (Map p305; ☎ 2180 3053; Geschwister-Scholl-Platz 1; admission free; ⏲ 10am-4pm Mon-Thu, 10am-3pm Fri) is within the Ludwig-Maximilian-Universität.

you'll see hundreds of naked sunbathers in the park, with their jackets, ties and dresses stacked neatly beside them.

Several follies add some architectural interest. The **Chinesischer Turm** (Chinese Tower) dating back to 1789 rises from a thicket of green benches belonging to the city's best-known beer garden. Just south of here is the heavily photographed **Monopteros**, a faux Greek temple with pearly white columns. The **Japanisches Teehaus** (Japanese Teahouse) was built during the 1972 Olympics, and holds authentic tea ceremonies every second and fourth weekend in summer at 3pm, 4pm and 5pm. You can also rent a paddle boat and navigate the **Kleinhesseloher See**, an idyllic little lake.

On the southern edge of the garden, the monolithic **Haus der Kunst** (House of Art; Map p305; ☎ 2112 7113; Prinzregentenstrasse 1; ⏲ 10am-8pm Mon-Sun, to 10pm Thu) was once a Nazi gallery that ridiculed so-called 'degenerate' art. Today it holds high-calibre shows of paintings, photography and modern art exhibitions.

BAYERISCHES NATIONALMUSEUM

Off the southeastern corner of the Englischer Garten stands the stern building of the **Bayerisches Nationalmuseum** (Bavarian National Museum; Map p304; ☎ 211 2401; Prinzregentenstrasse 3; adult/concession €5/4, Sun €1; ⏲ 10am-5pm Tue-Sun, 10am-8pm Thu). It's chock-full of exhibits showcasing the art, folklore and cultural history of southern Germany, and Bavaria in particular.

The ground floor has treasures from the early Middle Ages to the rococo period, including evocative sculptures by Erasmus

Grasser and Tilman Riemenschneider, two of the greatest artists of the era. Upstairs are 19th-century highlights including Nymphenburg porcelain, precious glass and an exquisite collection of Jugendstil items. A special section is also devoted to possibly the world's greatest collection of church nativity scenes dating from the 17th to the 19th centuries.

ARCHÄOLOGISCHE STAATSSAMMLUNG

Occupying a contender for the world's ugliest museum building, the **Archäologische Staatssammlung** (Map p304; ☎ 211 2402; Lerchenfeldstrasse 2; adult/concession €3/2, Sun €1; ⏲ 9.30am-5pm, closed Mon) traces the settlement of Bavaria from the Stone Age to the early Middle Ages. The exhibition features objects from Celtic, Roman and Germanic civilisations, including the well-preserved body of a ritually sacrificed young girl.

Olympiapark & Around

Almost four decades after the Olympic Games for which it was built, the **Olympiapark** (Map p306) is still an integral part of life in the city. The centrepieces are the 290m Olympiaturm, the massive undulating 'tented' roof covering the west side of the Olympic Stadium, the Olympic hall and swimming centre.

The best place to start is the **Info Pavilion** (☎ 3067 2414; www.olympiapark-muenchen.de; ⏲ 10am-6pm Mon-Fri, 10am-3pm Sat) at the **Olympia-Eissportzentrum** (Ice-Skating Rink; ⏲ open skating sessions 10am-noon & 1.30-4pm Mon-Fri, 8-10.30pm Wed-Sun). Here you can pick up maps, book tours and find out about events happening in the grounds.

OKTOBERFEST

It all started as an elaborate wedding toast – and turned into the world's biggest collective booze-up. In October 1810 the future king, Bavarian Crown Prince Ludwig I, married Princess Therese, and the newlyweds threw an enormous party at the city gates, complete with a horse race. The next year Ludwig's fun-loving subjects came back for more. The festival was extended and, to fend off autumn, was moved forward to September. As the years drew on the racehorses were dropped and sometimes the party had to be cancelled, but the institution called Oktoberfest was here to stay.

Nearly two centuries later, this 16-day extravaganza draws over six million visitors a year to celebrate a marriage of good cheer and outright debauchery. A special beer is brewed for the occasion (Wies'nbier), which is dark and strong. Müncheners spend the day at the office in lederhosen and dirndl in order to hit the festival right after work. It is Bavaria's largest tourist draw, generating about €1 billion in business. No admission is charged, but most of the fun costs something.

On the meadow called Theresienwiese (Wies'n for short), a temporary city is erected, consisting of beer tents, amusements and rides – just what drinkers need after several frothy ones! The action kicks off with the Brewer's Parade at 11am on the first day of the festival. The parade begins at Sonnenstrasse and winds its way to the fairgrounds via Schwanthalerstrasse. At noon, the lord mayor stands before the thirsty crowds at Theresienwiese and, with due pomp, slams a wooden tap into a cask of beer. As the beer gushes out, the mayor exclaims, *O'zapft ist's!* (It's tapped!). The next day resembles the opening of the Olympics, as a young woman on horseback leads a parade of costumed participants from all over the world.

Hotels become booked out very quickly and prices skyrocket, so reserve accommodation as early as you can (like a year in advance). The festival is a 15-minute walk southwest of the Hauptbahnhof, and is served by its own U-Bahn station, Theresienwiese. Trams and buses have signs reading 'Zur Festwiese' (literally 'to the Festival Meadow').

Wandering the grounds is free but you'll have to pay to see inside the **Olympiastadion** (Olympic Stadium; adult/child €2/1; ☺ 9am-4.30pm Oct–mid-Apr, 8.30am-6pm mid-Apr–Sep, closed event days). There are several tours available, but most settle for the one-hour **Stadium Tour** (adult/concession €6/4; ☺ Apr-Nov), which visits the Olympic Stadium, VIP area and locker rooms, or the year-round, self-guided **Audiowalk** (per headphone set €7), which takes in all the Olympiapark's sights on a prescribed route. When the weather plays ball you can enjoy spectacular city vistas from the top of the **Olympiaturm** (Olympic Tower; adult/concession €4.50/2.80; ☺ 9am-midnight, last trip 11.30pm), which houses a restaurant and an incongruous display of rock-music memorabilia (free with tower ticket).

If you're looking to keep the kids amused (and can stomach the budget-busting admission), **SeaLife** (Map p306; ☎ 450 000; adult/child 3-14yr €14.90/9.95; ☺ 10am-7pm) is the place to head. Reef sharks, moray eels and magical sea horses are among the 10,000 creatures on display, all presented in realistic aquariums with recessed glass viewing ports. Tunnel walkways lead you right through some tanks – the next best thing to scuba diving.

BMW MUSEUM
Redesigned from scratch and reopened in 2008, the **BMW Museum** (Map p306; ☎ 0180-211 8822; www.bmw-museum.com; Am Olympiapark 2; adult/child €12/6; ☺ 9am-6pm Tue-Fri, 10am-8pm Sat & Sun) is like no other car museum on the planet. The seven themed 'houses' examine the development of BMW's product line and include sections on motorcycles and motor racing. However, the interior design of this truly unique building, with its curvy retro feel, futuristic bridges, squares and huge backlit wall screens, almost upstages the exhibits.

An undulating bridge leads from the museum to BMW's architectural showpiece, the cloud-shaped **BMW Welt** (Am Olympiapark 1; admission free; ☺ 9am-8pm). Here you'll find interactive exhibits, the latest high-powered cars and motorbikes, a restaurant and a BMW 'lifestyle accessories' shop. This is also the place to arrange a **factory tour** (adult/child €6/3; ☻ 8.30am-8pm Mon-Fri), which demonstrates just how a 'Beamer' is born.

South of the Altstadt

You could spend days exploring the **Deutsches Museum** (Map p304; ☎ 217 91; www.deutsches-museum.de; Museuminsel 1; adult/concession/family €8.50/7/17, child under 6yr free; ☻ 9am-5pm), said to be the world's largest science and technology collection. This vast museum occupies its own island southeast of Isartor (Isar Gate) and features just about anything ever invented. Interactive displays (including glass blowing and paper making), model coal and salt mines, and wonderful sections on musical instruments, caves, geodesy, micro-electronics and astronomy are just some of the delights on offer. Demonstrations take place throughout the day; a popular one is in the power hall where a staff member is raised in the insulated Faraday Cage and zapped with a 220,000V bolt of lightning.

West of the Altstadt
THERESIENWIESE

About 1.5km west of the old town, the gigantic, ear-shaped **Theresienwiese** (Theresa Meadow; Map p302) is the venue for the annual Oktoberfest (see boxed text, opposite) and other events. On the western flank looms the classical **Ruhmeshalle** (Hall of Fame; Map p302; admission free), an open gallery of famous Bavarians whose busts adorn the wall like hunting trophies. The hall curls horseshoelike around the green-tinged **Bavaria statue** (Map p302; adult/under 18yr with parents/concession €2.50/free/1.50; ☻ 9am-6pm Apr-Oct). Climb up to the head cavity to get a great view from her hollow eyes of the 'Wies'n', as the locals call the festival grounds.

VERKEHRSZENTRUM

Sheltered in an historic trade fair complex, the **Verkehrszentrum** (Transport & Mobility Centre; Map p302; ☎ 500 806 762; Theresienhöhe 14a; adult/child €6/3; ☻ 9am-5pm) features some fascinating exhibits, with hands-on displays about pioneering research and famous inventions, plus cars, boats and trains, and the history of car racing. Another section shows off the Deutsche Museum's entire vehicle collection, ranging from the first motorcars to high-speed ICE trains.

Schloss Nymphenburg

Commanding **Schloss Nymphenburg** (Map p306; ☎ 179 080; combined ticket to everything adult/concession €10/8) and its lavish gardens sprawl about 5km northwest of the Altstadt. Begun in 1664 as a villa for Electress Adelaide of Savoy, the palace and gardens were expanded over the next century to create the royal family's summer residence. Franz Duke of Bavaria, the head of the once royal Wittelsbach family, still occupies an apartment within the palace complex. To get there take tram 17 from Karlsplatz.

SCHLOSS

The **main palace building** (adult/concession €5/4; ☻ 9am-6pm Apr–mid-Oct, 9am-4pm mid-Oct–Mar) consists of a large villa and two wings of creaking parquet floors and sumptuous period rooms. Right at the beginning comes the highpoint of the entire Schloss, the **Schönheitengalerie** (Gallery of Beauties), housed in the former apartments of Queen Caroline. Some 38 portraits of beautiful women chosen by an admiring King Ludwig I peer prettily from the walls. The most famous is of Helene Sedlmayr, the daughter of a shoemaker, wearing a lavish frock the king gave her for the sitting. You'll also find Ludwig's beautiful but notorious lover, Lola Montez, as well as 19th-century gossip-column celebrity, Jane Lady Ellenborough, and English beauty Lady Jane Erskine.

Further along the tour route is the **Queen's Bedroom**, which still contains the sleigh bed on which Ludwig II was born, and the **King's Chamber** resplendent with 3-D ceiling frescoes.

Also in the main building, the **Marstallmuseum** (adult/concession €4/3; ☻ 9am-6pm Apr–mid-Oct, 10am-4pm mid-Oct–Mar) displays royal coaches and riding gear (including Ludwig II's over-the-top sleigh) on ground level, and a collection of porcelain from the legendary Nymphenburger Manufaktur on the 1st floor, while the **Museum Mensch und Natur** (Museum of Humankind & Nature; adult/under 18yr with parents/concession €3/free/2; ☻ 9am-5pm Tue-Fri, to 8pm Thu, 10am-6pm Sat & Sun, closed Mon) has child-oriented interactive displays on the animal kingdom, planet earth and the mysteries of the human body (German only).

GARDENS & OUTBUILDINGS

The royal gardens take the form of a magnificently landscaped English-style park. They contain a number of follies, including the **Amalienburg** (Map p306; adult/concession €2/1;

9am-6pm Apr–mid-Oct, 10am-4pm mid-Oct–Mar), a dainty hunting lodge with a domed central room; the **Pagodenburg** Chinese teahouse; and the **Badenburg** (Map p306; adult/concession €2/1; 9am-6pm Apr–mid-Oct) sauna and bathing house.

Other Sights
MÜNCHENER TIERPARK HELLABRUNN
Around 5000 animals inhabit Munich's 'geo-zoo' (one with distinct sections dividing animals by continents). The **Münchener Tierpark Hellabrunn** (Map p300-1; 625 080; Tierparkstrasse 30; adult/concession €9/6; 8am-6pm Apr-Sep, 9am-5pm Oct-Mar), to the south of the city, was one of the first of its kind. The sprawling, well-maintained grounds are home to rhinos, elephants, deer and gazelles, as well as a special petting zoo, full of cuddly sheep, deer and lambs. To get there take the U3 to Thalkirchen or bus 52 from Marienplatz.

ALLIANZ ARENA
Soccer and architecture fans alike should take a side trip to the northern Munich suburb of Fröttmaning to see Munich's showpiece football stadium – already an historic site after hosting the opening game of the World Cup 2006. Nicknamed the 'life belt' and 'rubber boat' (*Schlauchboot*), the state-of-the-art, €340 million **Allianz Arena** (off Map pp300–1) has walls made of inflatable cushions that can be individually lit to match the jerseys of the host team – be it local sides FC Bayern München and TSV 1860 München (who share the stadium) or the national team. Take a **tour** (01805-555 101; adult/child 4-12yr €10/6.50; 1pm in English) of the stadium but expect to queue in summer. To get there take the U6 to Fröttmaning.

ACTIVITIES
Munich makes a perfect base for outdoor exploits. For information about hiking and climbing, contact the Munich branch of the **Deutscher Alpenverein** (German Alpine Club; Map p302; 551 7000; www.alpenverein-muenchen-oberland.de; Bayerstrasse 21V) near the Hauptbahnhof.

Cycling
Munich is an excellent place for cycling. Pumped full of bracing Alpine air and with a network of leafy paths, the Englischer Garten is a good place to start a day's tour.

Mike's Bike Tours (Map p302; 2554 3988; www.mikesbiketours.com; tour €24; Mar–mid-Nov) offers guided bike tours of the city. Its point of contact is **Discover Bavaria** (Map p302; cnr Brauhausstrasse &

Hochbrückenstrasse), but tours leave from the archway of the Altes Rathaus on Marienplatz. The standard four-hour tour is an easy pedal with a 45-minute break at a beer garden. Discover Bavaria also rents out bikes for €9 per day.

Radius Tours & Bike Rental (Map p302; 596 113; www.radiustours.com; 8.30am-6pm Apr–mid-Oct, 8.45am-noon mid-Oct–Mar) hires out bikes for €3 per hour or €14.50 per day, with a €50 deposit. You'll find it at the end of tracks 27 to 36 in the Hauptbahnhof. Staff speak English and are happy to provide tips and advice on pedalling around Munich.

Surfing
At the southern tip of the Englischer Garten (Map p304) is an artificial 'permanent wave' in a frigid arm of the Isar, where crowds gather at weekends to watch neoprene-clad surfers practise their moves.

Swimming
The authorities don't sanction bathing in the crystalline Isar River, but plenty of Müncheners can't resist. On warm days the pebbly islets in the riverbed are lined with natives seeking a healthy glow.

Munich also has many swimming pools to cool your desires. The **Olympia-Schwimmhalle** (Map p306; 3067 2290; Olympiapark; adult/child €3.80/2.90; 7am-11pm) has long laps, or admire the spectacular art nouveau architecture while taking a dip at the **Müller'sches Volksbad** (Map p304; 2361 3434; Rosenheimer Strasse 1; adult/child €3.50/2.80; 7.30am-11pm). Take tram 18 from Karlsplatz to the 'Am Gasteig' stop.

WALKING TOUR
This Altstadt circuit (Map p317) takes in the key sights in Munich's historic centre and the Englischer Garten. If you include visits to all the museums and churches mentioned here, you've got a two-day itinerary on your hands.

Commence at the **Michaelskirche** (**1**; p310), a richly ornamented church with barrel vaults, and the final resting place of King Ludwig II. Proceed east along Sendlinger Strasse, the main shopping drag, passing by the Frauenkirche, Munich's landmark church. The way opens into Marienplatz, the old town square, punctuated by the **Mariensäule** (**2**; p307) in front of the neo-Gothic **Neues Rathaus** (**3**; p308). The blue-bottomed **Fischbrunnen** (**4**; p308) gushes peacefully near the entrance. The steeple of **St Peterskirche** (**5**; p308) affords a

MUNICH ALTSTADT WALKING TOUR

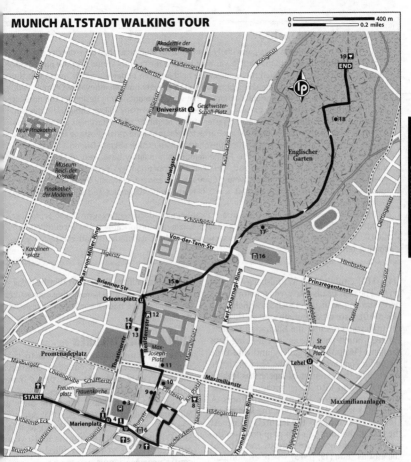

great vista of the old town, including the **Altes Rathaus** (**6**; p308), now home to a toy museum. To see amazing Asam frescoes, peek inside the **Heiliggeistkirche** (**7**; p308).

Head east on Im Tal, taking a left into Maderbräustrasse to Orlandostrasse, site of the **Hofbräuhaus** (**8**; p309), Munich's most (in)famous beer hall. Then zigzag through the backstreets – west on Münzstrasse, left into Sparkassenstrasse and then into the alley Ledererstrasse. At Burgstrasse, turn right into the courtyard of the **Alter Hof** (**9**), the Wittelsbachs' early residence in Munich. Exit north and proceed along Hofgraben, past the former **Münzhof** (**10**; mint). The street opens into the grand Maximilianstrasse and Max-Joseph-Platz, address of the grand

WALK FACTS

Start Michaelskirche
Finish Chinesischer Turm
Distance 5km
Duration 2½ hours

Nationaltheater (**11**; p328) and fine opera. A treasure-filled palace and museum, the **Residenz** (**12**; p309) was the seat of the Wittelsbach rulers for over four centuries.

Stroll north on Residenzstrasse to reach Odeonsplatz, site of the Nazis' first lunge at power. Here looms the **Feldherrnhalle** (**13**; p310), a hulking shrine to war heroes. The bombastic, mustard-yellow **Theatinerkirche St Kajetan**

MUNICH'S OLYMPIC TRAGEDY

The 1972 Summer Olympics were particularly significant for Munich as they gave the city a chance to make a historic break with the past. It was the first time the country would host the prestigious sporting event since 1936, when the Games were held in Berlin under Hitler. The motto was the 'Happy Games', and the emblem was a blue sun spiral. The city built an innovative Olympic Park, which included the tentlike plexiglass canopies that were revolutionary in design for the times. It was the perfect opportunity to present a new, democratic Germany full of pride and optimism.

But in the final week of the Games disaster struck. Members of a Palestinian terrorist group known as 'Black September' killed two Israeli athletes and took nine others hostage at the Olympic Village, demanding the release of political prisoners and an escape aircraft. During a failed rescue attempt by German security forces at Fürstenfeldbrück, a military base west of Munich, all of the hostages and most of the terrorists were killed. Competition was suspended briefly before Avery Brundage, the International Olympic Committee president, famously declared 'the Games must go on'. The bloody incident cast a pall over the entire Olympics and sporting events in Germany for years to follow.

These tragic events are chronicled in an Oscar-winning documentary, *One Day in September* (2000) by Kevin McDonald, as well as in Steven Spielberg's historical fictional account, *Munich* (2005). The killings prompted German security to rethink its methods and create the elite counter-terrorist unit, GSG 9.

(14; p310) contains the Wittelsbachs' family crypt. The tour heads into green territory from here, starting with the neoclassical **Hofgarten** (15; p310). Cross it diagonally and go through the underpass to enter the Englischer Garten. Proceed north past the sinister-looking **Haus der Kunst** (16; p313), a gallery and one-time forum for Nazi art propaganda. The leafy route winds past the ceremonial **Japanisches Teehaus** (17; p313) and into a vast meadow popular with frisbee experts and nude sunbathers. A little hill with a classical folly, the **Monopteros** (18; p313), completes the leisurely scene. At the end of the tour you can plop down in the beer garden alongside the curious, multi-tiered **Chinesischer Turm** (19; p313) where an oompah band pumps out traditional tunes.

COURSES

Large numbers of expats and immigrants who make Munich their home mean there are tens of language schools in the city offering German language courses for all levels. Prices start at around €250 for a four-week course:

DESK (Map p302; ☎ 263 3334; www.desk-sprachkurse.de; Blumenstrasse 1) Tried and tested school with 25 years of experience behind it and a central location.

DeutschAkademie (Map p302; ☎ 2601 8989; www.deutschakademie.de; Sonnenstrasse 8) Small groups, qualified teachers and courses running throughout the day.

Inlingua (Map p302; ☎ 231 1530; www.inlingua.de; Sendlinger-Tor-Platz 6) A national chain with branches in every large city across Germany; serving a more corporate clientele.

Ludwig-Maximilians-Universität München (Map p305; ☎ 2180 2143; www.fremdsprachen.uni-muenchen.de; Schellingstrasse 3) Summer and term-time courses at the university.

MUNICH FOR CHILDREN

Museums with hands-on exhibits to play with, a well-stocked zoo, countless children's theatre events and plenty of parks make Munich a superb city for kiddies.

You can safely leave the little ones at **Münchner Kindl** (Map p302; ☎ 2423 1600; Burgstrasse 6; per hr €7, 1st hr free; ☑ 9am-6pm Mon-Fri, 10am-4pm Sat). Offspring aged 18 months to 10 years old are welcome at this toy-filled childcare centre near Marienplatz.

Sure-fire hits include the **Hellabrunn zoo** (p316), which has a huge Kinderzoo (children's zoo), and **SeaLife** (p314), an entertaining aquarium in the Olympiapark. The **Deutsches Museum** (p315) has lots of interactive science exhibits and a reconstructed coal mine, while the **Spielzeugmuseum** (Toy Museum; p308) should keep the little 'uns mesmerised.

Other entertainment for children includes the following:

Circus Krone (Map p306; ☎ 545 8000; Zirkus-Krone-Strasse 1-6; ☑ Dec-Apr) An enduring favourite and venerable Munich tradition.

Münchner Marionettentheater (Map p302; ☎ 265 712; Blumenstrasse 32) Munich's main puppet theatre often shows Mozart's musical plays.

Münchner Theater für Kinder (Map p306; ☎ 593 8858; www.muenchner-theater-fuer-kinder.de, in German; Dachauer Strasse 46) Children's performances year-round.

TOURS

For a budget tour of Munich's high-brow collections, hop aboard **city bus 100** which runs from the Hauptbahnhof to the Ostbahnhof via 21 of the city's museums and galleries. This includes all three Pinakothek, the Residenz and the Bayerisches Nationalmuseum. As this is an ordinary bus route, the tour costs no more than a public transport ticket.

Radius Tours (Map p302; ☎ 5502 9374; www.radius tours.com) offers a variety of excellent guided city strolls starting from the Hauptbahnhof, track 32–34. The two-hour **Munich Highlights Walk** (adult/concession €10/9; ☼ 10am) takes you through the heart of the city and provides heaps of historical background. The **Third Reich Tour** (adult/concession €12/10; ☼ 3pm Apr-Oct) takes you to Munich's Nazi-related sites including Gestapo HQ and the Hofbräuhaus.

Munich Walk Tours (☎ 2423 1767; www.munich walktours.de) offers a popular **Beer & Brewery Tour** (adult/under 26yr €18/16; ☼ 6.15pm May–mid-Sep). Walks depart from under the Glockenspiel on Marienplatz (Map p302).

Münchener Stadtrundfahrten (Map p302; ☎ 0700-2878 6877; www.sightseeing-munich.com; Schützenstrasse 9; adult/child €13/7) runs Munich hop-on-hop-off bus tours (one hour, every 20 minutes from 9am to 5.30pm) leaving from the Karstadt department store opposite the Hauptbahnhof.

For a more tailor-made approach, try **John's Bavarian Tours** (☎ 0162-320 7323; www.johns -bavarian-tours.com). American landscape artist John Wetstone has lived in the city for over 30 years and puts together expert door-to-door Munich tours for small groups and individuals.

FESTIVALS & EVENTS

Munich always has something to celebrate. The list below gives just a few of the highlights; for more details check www.muenchen -tourist.de.

January/February

Fasching A six-week carnival beginning on 7 January with all kinds of merriment, including costume parades and fancy-dress balls.

February/March

Starkbierzeit Potent spring beers, traditional dancing and stone-lifting contests. The Löwenbräukeller (p326) is the place to experience it all.

April

Frühlingsfest The Theresienwiese (Map p302) fills with beer tents and amusements for the Spring Festival, a two-week mini-Oktoberfest.

May

Maidult A traditional fair on Mariahilfplatz (Map p304), with crafts, antiques and amusement rides.

June/July

Filmfest München (www.filmfest-muenchen.de) World premieres of international and independent films.
Jakobidult Summer fair on Mariahilfplatz much like the Maidult.
Opera Festival (☎ 218 501; www.bayerische .staatsoper.de) A month-long festival of opera concluding on 31 July with Wagner's *Die Meistersinger von Nürnberg*.
Tollwood Summer Festival (☎ 383 8500; www .tollwood.de) A world culture gala with nightly music concerts at the Olympiapark (Map p306).

September

Oktoberfest (www.oktoberfest.de) The legendary beer bash which, despite the name, is actually held from mid-September to the first Sunday in October. Held on the Theresienwiese (Map p302).

November/December

Christkindlmarkt (www.christkindlmarkt.de) A traditional Christmas market on Marienplatz (Map p302).
Tollwood Winter Festival Music festival and Christmas market in tents on the Theresienwiese.

SLEEPING

Room rates in Munich tend to be high, and skyrocket during the Oktoberfest. Book well ahead.

Budget travellers are spoilt for choice around the Hauptbahnhof where the majority of hostels congregate. The Altstadt has the most top-end hotels.

Around the Hauptbahnhof
BUDGET

our pick **Wombat's** (Map p302; ☎ 5998 9180; www .wombats-hostels.com; Senefelderstrasse 1; dm €12-24, d €70; P ⌨ ☎) Munich's most kicking hostel has a convenient location right by the train station.

BAVARIA

All rooms (dorms and doubles only) have Ikea-style furniture and en suite showers and toilets. The newly renovated 24-hour reception, winter chill-out garden, large bar and laundry room (per load €4.50) make for happy stays.

Euro Youth Hotel (Map p302; ☎ 5990 8811; www.euro-youth-hotel.de; Senefelderstrasse 5; dm €12.50-20, s €32-42, d €40-55; ✗ ⊚) Housed in one of the few buildings around the Hauptbahnhof to survive WWII, this atmospheric hostel-hotel oozes history with every dangling chandelier and creaky staircase. The bar is a delightful haunt, and the €2-a-drink happy hour (6pm to 9pm) is understandably popular. Despite having 200 beds spread over 58 well-kept rooms, this place is often full, so book ahead.

Meininger's (off Map p302; ☎ 420 956 053; www.meininger-hostels.de; Landsbergerstrasse 20; dm €16-29, s €43-60, d €31-48; P ✗ ▯ ⊚) About 800m west of the Hauptbahnhof, this energetic hostel-hotel on the doorstep of the Augustiner brewery has interiors and facilities similar to Wombat's, but also a rooftop terrace and underground parking. Take tram 18 or 19 to Holzapfelstrasse.

Easy Palace Station Hotel (Map p302; ☎ 552 5210; www.easypalace.de; Schützenstrasse 7; dm from €19.90, s €35-55, d €49-99; ▯) For low-budget quarters with a touch of vintage character try this hostel based in an aging hotel. Styles run the gamut, from a 1950s brass bed to a rustic oak from the disco era. Only seven of the 55 rooms are dorms (sleeping four to six); the rest are spacious singles and doubles available in three categories of comfort.

Also recommended:

4You Hostel (Map p302; ☎ 552 1660; www.the4you.de; Hirtenstrasse 18; dm €13-24, s €39-45, d €52-64) Once a bit of a grotty crash pad, this rapidly improving place has modernised rooms, a large downstairs bar, 24-hour reception and free Wii.

A&O City Hotel (Map p302; ☎ 4523 5700; www.ao hostels.com; Bayerstrasse 75; dm €12-14, d €44; ▯) Munich's A&O teeters between simple hotel and fancy hostel. The en suite rooms are smallish but well maintained.

MIDRANGE

our pick Cocoon (Map p302; ☎ 5999 3907; www.hotel-cocoon.de; Lindwurmstrasse 35; s/d €69/89; ✗ ▩ ▯ ⊚) If retro-design is your thing, you just struck gold. Things kick off in the reception with the faux '70s veneer and suspended '60s ball chairs, and continue in the rooms, all identical and decorated in cool retro oranges and greens. Every room has LCD TV, iPod dock, 'laptop cabin' and the hotel name above every bed in

1980s robotic lettering. Glass showers are actually in the sleeping area, with only a kitschy Alpine meadow scene veiling life's vitals.

Creatif Hotel Elephant (Map p302; ☎ 555 785; www.creatifelephanthotel.com; Lämmerstrasse 6; s/d €75/85; P ✗) This bright and welcoming hotel is the best of a bunch of midrange options north of the Hauptbahnhof. Simple rooms with bright decor have sound facilities, though nothing to raise the pulse.

Hotel Belle Blue (Map p302; ☎ 550 6260; www.hotel-belleblue.com; Schillerstrasse 21; s from €75, d from €92; P ✗ ▩ ▯) This chic little hotel employs subtle, attractive colour schemes and tasteful furnishings to great effect. The bathrooms are a hit, with their glass cubicle showers, underfloor heating and designer fixtures. All this distracts you from the fact that the rooms are a little snug.

Hotel Hotelissimo (Map p302; ☎ 557 855; www.hotelissimo.com; Schillerstrasse 4; s €68-189, d €98-199; ✗ ▯) A stone's thrown from the Hauptbahnhof, this chic family-run hotel has immaculate rooms and a general feel-good factor. Decor reflects a real appreciation for design, colour and fabrics.

Also recommended:

Hotel Bristol (Map p302; ☎ 5434 8880; www.bristol-muc.com; Pettenkofer Strasse 2; s/d from €69/85; P ▯ ⊚) Comfy, well-furnished rooms with friendly service and generous breakfast.

Hotel Müller (Map p302; ☎ 232 3860; www.hotel-mueller-muenchen.de; Fliegenstrasse 4; s €79, d €99-139; ✗ ⊚) Big, bright business-standard rooms and good price-to-quality ratio.

Hotel Schweiz (Map p302; ☎ 543 6960; www.hotel-schweiz.de; Goethestrasse 26; s €55-68, d €75-98; P ✗ ▯) Bright but cosy hotel with maple-wood furniture, a small wellness area and an open-air terrace.

TOP END

Anna Hotel (Map p302; ☎ 599 940; www.annahotel.de; Schützenstrasse 1; r from €160; P ✗ ▩ ▯ ⊚) Take a top location, add a generous dose of style and trendiness and you've got one killer design hotel. The classy Donghia furniture is dressed in gold, black and burgundy fabrics so rich you want to run your hands over them, while the sensuous bathrooms feature a gushing 'rainforest' shower.

our pick Cortiina (Map p302; ☎ 242 2490; www.cortiina.com; Ledererstrasse 8; s €165-270, d €225-390; P ✗ ▩ ▯) This stunning hotel offers modern stylish elegance minus the usual antique knick-knacks. The design is chic and minimalist without losing any comfort. Dark wood and low lighting run throughout the hotel, while the bedrooms are lined with oak panelling, have parquet floors and individual furnishings, as well as glass-encased bathrooms lined with Jura stone.

Dorint Sofitel (Sofitel Munich Bayerpost; Map p302; ☎ 599 480; www.sofitel.com; Bayerstrasse 12; r €170-450; P ⊠ ⬚ 🖥 🍽) The brilliantly restored neoclassical facade of the former Royal Bavarian Post Office contains a jewel that satisfies all cravings for luxury. The 396 rooms and suites are a cocktail of style, surprise lighting effects and supreme comfort.

Altstadt & Around

Hotel Blauer Bock (Map p302; ☎ 231 780; www.hotelblauerbock.de; Sebastiansplatz 9; s €45-72, d €78-118; P ⊠) This hotel once provided beds for Benedictine monks and coachmen for the grain market nearby. Smart rooms with individual touches overlook the Schrannenhalle, a blink away from the Viktualienmarkt.

Bayerischer Hof (Map p302; ☎ 212 00; www.bayerischerhof.de; Promenadeplatz 2-6; s €221-480, d €338-480; P ⊠ ⬚ 🖥 📶 🍽) Room doors fold away into the stucco mouldings at the Hof, one of the grande dames of the Munich hotel trade. It boasts a super-central location, a pool and a jazz club. Marble, antiques and old paintings abound, and you can dine till you drop at any one of the three fabulous restaurants. Rates include a champagne breakfast. There's wheelchair access.

Kempinski Vier Jahreszeiten München (Map p302; ☎ 212 50; www.kempinski-vierjahreszeiten.de; Maximilianstrasse 17; s/d from €249/252; P ⊠ ⬚ 🖥 🍽) This illustrious hotel has a grand facade featuring statues of the managers, the four seasons and four continents. The rooms don't have as many amenities as you'd think, but the suites are palatial and the rooftop pool is an incredible blue-sky swim.

Schwabing
BUDGET
Pension am Kaiserplatz (Map p305; ☎ 349 190; fax 339 816; Kaiserplatz 12; s €31-47, d €49-59) The facade of this Jugendstil villa is a throwback to more romantic times, when Schwabing was awash with art and culture. The superb-value rooms (just 10, all with hall bathrooms) are lovingly decorated with a family touch, and breakfast is delivered to your door by the congenial host herself.

MIDRANGE
Gästehaus Englischer Garten (Map p305; ☎ 383 9410; www.hotelenglischergarten.de; Liebergesellstrasse 8; s €65-169, d €75-169; P) Wake up to the quack of ducks in the adjacent Englischer Garten at this cosy pension occupying a graceful old ivy-covered mill with a private garden for breakfast (€9.50 extra). Most of the antique-filled rooms have private bathrooms.

Cosmopolitan Hotel (Map p305; ☎ 383 810; www.cosmopolitan-hotel.de; Hohenzollernstrasse 5; s/d from €90/100; P ⊠) Plenty of dark wood and subtle lighting meets the eye at this upmarket art-filled hotel. Rooms are tastefully done out, but can feel a touch cluttered. It's ideally located for Schwabing's nightlife.

Nymphenburg, Neuhausen & Around
BUDGET
DJH hostel (Map p306; ☎ 2024 4490; www.muenchen-city.jugendherberge.de; Wendl-Dietrich-Strasse 20; dm under/over 27yr €25.10/29.10; ☒ closed Dec; ⊠) This is the most central DJH hostel, located in Neuhausen northwest of the Altstadt. Relatively loud and busy, it's also popular and friendly. There's a restaurant, a garden, bikes for hire, and no curfew. Take the U1 to Rotkreuzplatz.

Hotel Flora (Map p306; ☎ 597 067; www.hotel-flora.de; Karlstrasse 49; s €45-60, d €56-80; 🖥) This is a quiet, simple hotel in a venerable complex with good-value rooms, including quads (€88), that are an ideal set-up for families. Rates include breakfast. It's just a five-minute walk north of the Hauptbahnhof.

Other recommendations:

Campingplatz Nord-West (Map pp300-1; ☎ 150 6936; www.campingplatz-nord-west.de; Auf den Schrederwiesen 3; tent €4.50-12, car/person €4/5.20) Pleasant camp site about 2km from Olympiapark and within walking distance of three swimming lakes.

The Tent (Map p306; ☎ 141 4300; www.the-tent.com; In den Kirschen 30; tent bunk/floor space €10.50/7.50, tent €5.50; ☒ Jun-Nov) A kilometre north of Schloss Nymphenburg, this youth-oriented camping ground has classic tent pitches, as well as a 160-bunk main tent with floor space and foam mats for shoestring nomads. Cheapest sleep in town during the Oktoberfest.

MIDRANGE
Hotel Laimer Hof (Map p306; ☎ 178 0380; www.laimerhof.de; Laimer Strasse 40; s/d from €69/89; P) Run by Bavaria's friendliest couple, this cute listed villa has a relaxed country feel, despite being just five minutes' walk from Schloss Nymphenburg. Of

the 23 rooms, those on the upper floors have the most character and best views.

Haidhausen
MIDRANGE

Angelo (Map p304; ☎ 189 0860; www.angelo-munich.com; Leuchtenbergring 20; s/d from €110/130; ✗ ☎) From the open-plan jazz-themed reception-bar to the superbly composed rooms, the restaurant's clean lines to the crisp bathrooms, Munich's newest design hotel is a slick and minimalist affair, but warm and welcoming at the same time. It's already a firm favourite among Bavaria's power dressers. The downside is the location in the unfashionable, traffic-plagued end of Haidhausen, but it's a mere four stops on the S-Bahn from Marienplatz.

TOP END

Opera-Garni (Hotel Opéra; Map p304; ☎ 5210 4940; www.hotel-opera.de; St Annastrasse 10; r €190-275, ste €285-365; ✗ ☎) Step inside the Opera and you'll step back in time. This hotel is pure old-world elegance and refinement. Breakfast is served in the garden between graceful statues, and the rooms are stunningly decorated with individual combinations of rich colours and fabrics, antiques, chandeliers and Persian carpets.

Westend & Ludwigsvorstadt
BUDGET

Pension Westfalia (Map p302; ☎ 530 377; www.pension-westfalia.de; Mozartstrasse 23; s/d from €35/50; ☒) You don't have far to stagger from the Oktoberfest meadow to this stately four-storey villa. Outside the beer festival this cosy, family-run pension is a peaceful base for sightseeing. Rooms are all reached by lift, and most have private bathrooms.

Easy Palace (Map p302; ☎ 558 7970; www.easypalace.de; Mozartstrasse 4; dm €19-27, s/d €59/69; ⓟ ☐) Converted from a hotel, this hostel smells a bit like teen spirit, but has a good range of facilities such as pool tables, bike hire and luggage storage. Dorms are basic but comfy.

MIDRANGE

Hotel-Pension Mariandl (Map p302; ☎ 5529 1053; www.mariandl.com; Goethestrasse 51; s €65-115, d €70-165) Old-world charm, huge rooms with high ceilings and oriel windows make this neo-Gothic mansion a real treat. The downstairs restaurant (Café am Beethovenplatz; p324 and p329) has live jazz or classical music nightly at 8pm. Children are welcome.

Hotel Uhland (Map p302; ☎ 543 350; www.hotel-uhland.de; Uhlandstrasse 1; s €67-145, d €81-190; ⓟ ✗ ☐) A stein's throw from the Theresienwiese, this attractively renovated art nouveau villa has a relaxed atmosphere and English-speaking staff. Some large rooms come with a tiny balcony, and there's a quaint garden.

Southwest of the City
BUDGET

Campingplatz Thalkirchen (Map pp300-1; ☎ 723 1707 www.camping.muenchen.de; Zentralländstrasse 49; tent €3-4, car €4.50, person €4.70-8.30; ☺ mid-Mar–Oct) Scenically located on the Isar River, 5km southwest of the city centre, this popular camp site has all the facilities needed for pleasant nights under rustling nylon. Take the U3 to Thalkirchen and then bus 135, or it's a 15-minute walk.

DJH hostel (Map pp300-1; ☎ 7857 6770; www.muenchen-park.jugendherberge.de; Miesingstrasse 4; dm under/over 27yr €29/33; ⓟ ✗) Still fairly accessible to the centre, the thoroughly modernised München Park Hostel is 5km southwest of the Altstadt in the suburb of Thalkirchen. There's no curfew. Take the U3 to Thalkirchen then follow the signs.

Long-Term Rentals

If you're planning to stay in Munich for a month or longer, you might consider renting through a *Mitwohnzentrale* (flat-sharing agency; p759). Accommodation can be anything from rooms in shared student flats to furnished apartments.

Generally speaking, a room in a flat costs about €350 to €600 per month, while a one-bedroom apartment ranges from €500 to €800. Commission (up to one month's rent) VAT (19%) and, in some cases, a deposit must be added to the rent.

Agencies to try include the following:
City Mitwohnzentrale (Map p302; ☎ 194 30; www.mitwohnzentrale.de; Lämmerstrasse 4)
Mitwohnzentrale an der Uni (Map p305; ☎ 330 3740; www.mwz-munich.de; Fendstrasse 6)
Mitwohnzentrale – Mr Lodge (Map p305; ☎ 340 8230; www.mrlodge.de; Barer Strasse 32)

EATING
Restaurants
AFGHAN

Lemar (Map p302; ☎ 2694 9454; Brunnstrasse 4; mains €5-12; ☺ dinner) Lemar provides an excellent introduction to this little-known but tasty cuisine, serving scrumptious Central Asian

lishes such as spicy lentil soup, chicken kebabs, fried basmati rice with raisins and pista-
hios, and *mantu* (pasta balls filled with meat
nd yoghurt). Rave reviews from all who eat
n the authentic cushion-strewn dining space
mean bookings may be necessary.

ASIAN

wagat (Map p304; ☎ 4708 4844; Prinzregentenplatz
3; mains €10-15) Generally regarded as one of
Munich's best Indians restaurants, Swagat is
ituated in an intimate cellar space bedecked in
ndian fabrics, smiling gods and brass lanterns.
The curry is as hot as Bavarians can take it, and
here's plenty to please noncarnivores.

Sushi & Soul (Map p302; ☎ 201 0992; Klenzestrasse
1; mains €10-20) This stylishly pricey joint wows
vith soft lighting, a long, central table that
points dramatically towards the backlit open
itchen and fabulous sushi. During the long-
tanding and popular happy hour (6pm to
pm) a multicourse Bento palette of sushi, not
o mention all the cocktails, is half-price.

BAVARIAN & GERMAN

Weisses Bräuhaus (Map p302; ☎ 229 9875; Im Tal 10;
mains €6-15) The *Weisswurst* (veal sausage)
erved here sets the city's standard; wash
a pair down with the excellent Schneider
Weissbier. Of an evening the dining halls
re charged with red-faced, beer-fuelled hi-
arity and Alpine whoops to the strains of a
abble-rousing oompah-band.

Fraunhofer (Map p302; ☎ 266 460; Fraunhoferstrasse
?; mains €7.50-16) This bustling restaurant is a
homely place where the old-world atmosphere
and decor (featuring mounted animal heads
and a portrait of Ludwig II) contrasts with the
menu. Its fresh takes on classical fare draw a
hip, intergenerational crowd.

Unionsbräu Haidhausen (Map p304; ☎ 477 677;
insteinstrasse 42; mains €7.50-16.50) This sophis-
icated brewpub has eight separate spaces
where a mixed clientele of business types,
ocals and tourists slurp the house brew and
east on meat platters. There's a jazz club
n the basement (Jazzclub Unterfahrt im
Einstein; p329).

Other recommendations:
Mundskugel (Map p302; ☎ 264 272; Hotterstrasse
8; mains €10-18) Munich's oldest restaurant, founded in
440, feels a bit like an old-fashioned doll's house.
Wirtshaus in der Au (Map p304; ☎ 448 1400;
ilienstrasse 51; mains €8-20) Fewer tourists and creative
avarian cuisine in a faux rural setting.

FRENCH & INTERNATIONAL

Königsquelle (Map p302; ☎ 220 071; Baaderplatz 2;
mains €5-16; ☽ dinner) Something of a Munich
institution for its attentive service and dark,
well-stocked hardwood bar, the food here is
consistently excellent, straightforward but
expertly prepared.

Rue des Halles (Map p304; ☎ 485 675; Steinstrasse
18; mains €17-26) The gourmet French cuisine
draws a high-octane crowd to this designer
restaurant near the Kulturzentrum Gasteig.
Count on about €80 for a three-course meal,
including a glass of wine.

ITALIAN

Café Osteria La Vecchia Masseria (Map p302; ☎ 550
9090; Mathildenstrasse 3; mains €7-15) This is one
of the best Italian places in Munich, loud
but unquestionably romantic. Earthy wood
tables, antique tin buckets, baskets and
clothing irons conjure up the ambience
of an Italian farmhouse. The chef comes
out to greet customers in his trademark
straw hat.

Hippocampus (Map p304; ☎ 475 855; Mühlbaurstrasse
5; mains €14-25) One of Munich's top restaurants is this snazzy, upmarket Italian temple
right near the Prinzregententheater, serving
a pretentious range of Italian specials. It
has a stylish, dark-wood interior, romantic
ambience and wannabe clientele.

Also recommended:
Il Mulino (Map p306; ☎ 523 3335; Görrestrasse 1;
mains €6-20) Classy neighbourhood eatery in Neuhausen,
with an attractive 'look-at-me' decking area out front.
La Fiorentina (Map p302; ☎ 534 185; Goethestrasse
41; mains €6-17) Cosy hang-out with Tuscan country cooking and big-as-your-plate pizzas.

JEWISH

Einstein (Map p302; ☎ 202 400 332; St-Jakobs-Platz 18;
mains €14-23; ☽ closed Sat) Reflected in the plate-
glass windows of the Jewish Museum, this is
the only kosher eatery in the city centre. The
ID and bag search entry process is worth it for
the restaurant's uncluttered lines, smartly laid
tables and soothing ambience.

KURDISH/TURKISH

Taverna Diyar (Map p304; ☎ 4895 0497; Wörthstrasse 10;
mains €10-18) At its best when heaving with punters after 9pm on a Friday and Saturday, and
just as the belly dancer gets into full wobble,
this places cooks up authentic platters of fish,
kebabs and grilled lamb with lots of Kurdish

BAVARIA

and Turkish zing. Try the Turkish wine if you dare.

LATIN AMERICAN

Joe Peña's (Map p302; ☎ 226 463; Buttermelcherstrasse 17; mains €10-17) This festive cantina-style restaurant is considered Munich's best Tex-Mex joint and can get very crowded, especially during happy hour (5pm to 8pm). The food's tasty but calibrated to Central European tastes.

VEGETARIAN

Buxs (Map p302; ☎ 291 9550; Frauenstrasse 9; dishes per 100g €2.30; ⏰ closed Sat evening & Sun; Ⓥ) One of Munich's few outposts of vegie culture, this light-filled self-service place serves 40-plus varieties of soups, salads and antipasti – there are also recipe books on sale so you can enjoy them at home.

Zerwirk (Map p302; ☎ 2323 9195; Ledererstrasse 3; mains €6-12.50; ⏰ closed Sun; Ⓥ) Through a twist of fate the Zerwirk, once a purveyor of wild game, now houses one of Munich's few vegan restaurants. Dishes like pasta carbonara, tofu fennel or rucola chilli are served in elegant minimalist surrounds in the 2nd-floor dining rooms. Downstairs, the vaulted chambers are thrown open every weekend for club nights.

Prinz Myschkin (Map p302; ☎ 265 596; www.prinz myshkin.com; Hackenstrasse 2; mains €10-16; ⏰ closed Sun; Ⓥ) Considered by many to be Munich's best vegetarian restaurant, this spacious, trendy haunt has an impressive Italian- and Asian-influenced menu, including some macrobiotic choices. The menu is available in English.

Cafes & Bistros

Trachtenvogl (Map p302; ☎ 201 5160; Reichenbachstrasse 47; snacks €3-8) A send-up of the Black Forest, complete with cuckoo clock and braying elk, this warped little cafe-lounge has good sandwiches, cakes, milkshakes and 30 different kinds of hot chocolate (cold if you like).

Café Rischart (Map p302; ☎ 231 7000; Marienplatz 18; dishes €4-8) Some of the best views of the Marienplatz combine with Munich's finest cakes and pastries at this city institution. Plan your sightseeing assault on the city over a delicious breakfast.

Isarpost (Map p302; ☎ 4111 8046; Sonnenstrasse 24-26; mains €5-8) Housed in the grand, mid-18th-century building of the former postal office, this foyer cafe is Munich's newest see-and-be-seen venue. Choose from the Italian menu, or just unwind with a macchiato under the stylishly high, light-flooded vaulting.

Creperie Bernard Bernard (Map p304; ☎ 480 1173; Innere-Wiener-Strasse 32; crepes €5-9; ⏰ dinner Mon-Sat) The best crepes in town can be found at this small Parisian place that serves up delicious savouries oozing goat's cheese or shrimp, various fruit-filled galettes and even snails if that's your sort of thing.

Café Voilà (Map p304; ☎ 489 1654; Wörthstrasse 5; mains €5-10) High stucco ceilings, giant mirrors and large windows make this cafe a great place for watching the world go by. It's buzzing for breakfast (€4.50 to €10) and later in the day for fairly priced baguettes, burgers and interesting vegetarian dishes.

Café am Beethovenplatz (Map p302; ☎ 5529 1053; Goethestrasse 51; mains €5-11) This relaxed cafe with a musical theme has high ceilings, chandeliers and a cultivated Central European atmosphere. The breakfast selections are named after famous composers; tasty evening meals are accompanied by live jazz or classical music.

Wasserwerk (Map p304; ☎ 4890 0020; Wolfgangstrasse 19; mains €6-15; ⏰ dinner only) This quirky bistro – strewn with ducts, pipes and wheels – plays up the waterworks theme to marvellous effect. Expect a consistently delicious range of quality international cuisine.

Schlosscafé im Palmenhaus (Map p306; ☎ 175 309; Schloss Nymphenburg; mains €7-12) The glass-fronted 1820 palm house, where Ludwig II used to keep his exotic house plants warm in winter, is now a high-ceilinged and pleasantly scented cafe. It's just behind the palace.

Bobolovsky's (Map p305; ☎ 297 363; Ursulastrasse 11; mains €7.50-12) The varied menu at this bustling bistro includes all the old favourites, such as fajitas, quesadillas and chilli. Portions are very generous and on weekdays this place takes the happy-hour concept to new lengths, with incredibly cheap deals on breakfast, lunch and cocktails.

Nido (Map p305; ☎ 2880 6103; Theresienstrasse 40; mains €7.50-13) This popular place is a trendy spot with lots of brushed aluminium and big picture windows. It serves a small menu of simple Italian-influenced dishes and a large dose of unpretentious cool.

Uni Lounge (Map p305; ☎ 2737 3264; Geschwister Scholl-Platz 1) Enjoy a cheap breakfast, lazy lunch or cocktails to a soundtrack of high-minded conversation beneath the whitewashed vaulting of this student hang-out. The outdoor seating is ringed by grand university buildings.

Nage & Sauge (Map p304; ☎ 298 803; Mariannenstrasse
1 This hip little Italo-cafe is packed every night
with young, creative souls who snuggle up to
the candlelit tables for the 'Ente Elvis' pasta,
altimbocca or a sublime cocktail. It's tucked
way in a side street in Lehel, so quiet you'll
wonder if it's still within the city limits.

Café Zeitgeist (Map p305; ☎ 2865 9873; Türkenstrasse
4) Simply a perfect spot to pore over coffee
nd cake to watch, from a shady courtyard, the
teady flow of students and trendoids pulsing
long Türkenstrasse.

Quick Eats
Throughout the city, branches of **Vinzenzmurr**
Map p302; Sendlinger Strasse 38 & Sonnenstrasse 8;
⊙ 8.15am-6pm) offer the quintessential fast-food
xperience, with favourites like *Weisswurst*,
Leberkäse im Semmel* (spicy meatloaf in a
bun) or *Schweinebraten mit Knödel* (roast
pork with dumplings) among the best lunch
deals in town.

South of the Hauptbahnhof hone in on the
treet window of **Ristorante Ca'doro** (Map p302;
ayerstrasse; pizza slices €2.40-3.80). To the north of
the train station, **Deli Star** (Map p302; Dachauer Strasse
5; snacks €2.50-4; ⊙ Mon-Fri) has soups, bagels and
alads. One of the cheapest bakeries in this
rea is **Best Back** (Map p302; Bayerstrasse; ⊙ 6.30am-
midnight Mon-Fri, 7am-midnight Sat) where you can
narf a few sticky cakes and pastries, washed
own with a coffee for less than €1.

Around Marienplatz the pizza window at **La
izzetta** (Map p302; Tal 1; pizza slices €3) is mobbed at
unchtimes. **Sasou** (Map p302; Marienplatz 28; sushi €3.30-
.40) serves up imaginative sushi palettes and
ther Japanese food and drink just a few steps
rom the main tourist action. **Soupmama** (Map
302; Blumenstrasse 1; soups €2.80-6.90), looking onto
he Viktualienmarkt, uses only organic ingredi-
nts in its broths. **Münchner Suppenküche** (Map p302;
chäfflerstrasse 7; dishes €3-6; ⊙ closed Sun) is another
ood spot, just north of the Frauenkirche. This
elf-service soupery serves chicken casseroles,
hilli con carne and other filling snacks.

Schwabing has lots of cheap places to eat,
ncluding **Pommes Boutique** (Map p305; Amalienstrasse
8; mains €2.20-5), where you can grab some
heap-as-chips fries and a hot dog before
etiring to the adjacent minigolf room.

For affordable Indian takeaway near the
Neue Pinakothek, try **Indisches Fast Food** (Map
305; Barer Strasse 46; mains €5-7.50), where fragrant
basmati rice accompanies full-flavoured
ndian standards.

Self-Catering
At the Viktualienmarkt (Map p302), south
of Marienplatz, deep-pocketed travellers
can put together a gourmet picnic of breads,
cheeses and salad to take off to a beer garden or the Englischer Garten. For cheaper
and fresher fare, head to the Turkish grocery
stores around Schillerstrasse, Goethestrasse
and Landwehrstrasse in Ludwigsvorstadt.

Alois Dallmayr (Map p302; ☎ 213 50; Dienerstrasse
14) For a world-class selection of deli goods
try the legendary Alois Dallmayr with a
spread of exotic foods from every corner
of the earth.

DRINKING
To state the blindingly obvious, beer drinking forms a major part of Munich's nightlife.
Though consumption is falling, Germans still
guzzle an average of 112L of the amber liquid
per person per year, but Bavarians average a
belly-bursting 170L!

Beer Halls & Gardens
One of the most enjoyable ways to sample
Bavaria's best brews is in the local beer halls
and gardens. People come here primarily to
drink and, although food may be served, it is
generally an afterthought – for food options
at beer halls, see the boxed text, p327. A few
places still allow you to bring along a picnic
lunch and just buy the beer, but in most cases
outside food is forbidden.

Most places listed here are either gardens or gardens-cum-restaurants; almost all
open from 10am to at least 10pm. Even in
the touristy places, be careful not to sit at
the *Stammtisch*, a table reserved for regulars
(there will be a brass plaque).

You sometimes have to pay a *Pfand* (deposit) for the glasses (usually €2.50). Beer
costs around €5 to €6.50 per litre.

ALTSTADT
Hofbräuhaus (Map p302; ☎ 221 676; Am Platzl 9) This is
certainly the best-known and most celebrated
beer hall in Bavaria, but apart from a few local
yokels you'll be in the company of tourists. A
live band is condemned to play Bavarian folk
music most of the day.

Augustiner-Grossgaststätte (Map p302; ☎ 2318
3257; Neuhauser Strasse 27) This sprawling place
has a less raucous atmosphere and superior
food to the usual offerings. Altogether it's a
much more authentic example of an old-style

BAVARIA

Munich beer hall, complete with secluded courtyards and hunting trophies.

Braunauer Hof (Map p302; ☎ 223 613; Frauenstrasse 42) This pleasantly warped beer garden has a hedge maze, a bizarre wall mural and a golden bull that's illuminated at night.

ENGLISCHER GARTEN

There are three beer gardens in the park (Map p305).

Chinesischer Turm (☎ 383 8730; Englischer Garten 3) This is an institution known to every Münchener from an early age. The popular watering hole derives extra atmosphere from a classic Chinese pagoda and entertainment by a good-time oompah band (in an upper floor of the tower, fenced in like the Blues Brothers).

There are two other beer gardens better suited for families and sweethearts: **Hirschau** (☎ 369 942; Gysslingstrasse 15) and **Seehaus** (☎ 381 6130; Kleinhesselohe 3) are both on the shores of the park's glistening ponds.

NEUHAUSEN

Augustiner Keller (off Map p302; ☎ 594 393; Arnulfstrasse 52) Every year this leafy 5000-seat beer garden, about 500m west of the Hauptbahnhof, buzzes with activity from the first hint of spring-time. It's a beautiful spot with a laid-back atmosphere ideal for leisurely drinking.

Löwenbräukeller (Map p306; ☎ 526 021; Nymphenburger Strasse 2) This enormous beer hall is a local fixture for its regular Bavarian music and heel-slapping dances. During the Starkbierzeit (the springtime 'strong beer season'), the famous stone-lifting contests are held here. A beer garden rambles round the entire complex.

Hirschgarten (Map p306; ☎ 172 591; Hirschgartenallee 1) Locals and savvy visitors flock to the Hirschgarten, just south of Schloss Nymphenburg. This quaint country beer garden has deer wandering just the other side of the fence. To get there take the S-Bahn to Laim.

HAIDHAUSEN

Hofbräukeller (Map p304; ☎ 448 7376; Innere Wiener Strasse 19) Not to be confused with its better-known cousin in the city centre, this sprawl-ing, very atmospheric restaurant-cum-beer garden retains an early-20th-century air. Locals in *Tracht* (traditional costume) come here to guzzle big mugs of foaming beer alongside the regular specials of roast pork.

Bars & Pubs
ALTSTADT & AROUND

Alter Simpl (Map p305; ☎ 272 3083; Türkenstrasse 57 mains €6-13) This watering hole has good jazz a reasonable menu and an art-house vibe Thomas Mann and Hermann Hesse wer among the writers and artists that used to meet here in the early 20th century.

Dreigroschenkeller (Map p304; ☎ 489 029C Lilienstrasse 2) A cosy and labyrinthine cella pub with rooms based upon Bertolt Brecht' *Die Dreigroschenoper* (The Threepenn Opera), ranging from a prison cell to a re satiny salon. There are nine types of beer t choose from and an extensive menu of heart German soak-up material.

Jodlerwirt (Map p302; ☎ 221 249; Altenhofstrasse ⟨ from 6pm Tue-Sat) One of Munich's earthi est pubs has an accordion-playing host an stand-up comic who spread good cheer i yodelling sessions at the upstairs bar. By th end of the evening you'll find yourself swayin arm-in-arm with complete strangers.

Other recommendations:

Baader Café (Map p302; ☎ 201 0638; Baaderstrasse 47) A literary think-and-drink place with a high celebrity quotient and possibly the best Sunday brunch in town.

Pacific Times (Map p302; ☎ 2023 9470; Baaderstrasse 28) Trendy joint decked out in dark wood and wicker chair to attract the beautiful people.

SCHWABING

If you want a variety of hip bars within spittin distance of each other, then Leopoldstrasse i for you.

Roxy (Map p305; ☎ 349 292; Leopoldstrasse 48) Th place to talent spot and people-watch. Thi slick bar attracts a designer crowd keen to han out, look good and sip cocktails. By day it fers surprisingly good food at decent prices.

News Bar (Map p305; ☎ 281 787; Amalienstrasse 55; main €6-11) This trendy cafe has a great selection c magazines and newspapers (including Englis ones) for sale. It's an ideal spot for brunch or lazy morning poring over a paper.

News Café (Map p305; ☎ 3838 0600; Leopoldstrass 74) Not just another news-bar clone, the plusl leather seating, rows of glowing red lamp and African-inspired art make this hip join a great place to hang out. The €6.90 'busines lunch' is one of the best deals in town.

EXPAT PUBS

Munich has a large English-speaking expa population, and enterprising Irish, Brits and

AND THERE'S FOOD, TOO

In beer gardens, tables laid with a cloth and utensils are reserved for people ordering food. If you're only planning a serious drinking session, or if you have brought along a picnic, don't sit there.

If you do decide to order food, you'll find very similar menus at all beer gardens. Typical dishes include roast chicken (about €9 for a half), spare ribs (about €11.50, and probably not worth it), huge pretzels (about €4) and Bavarian specialities such as *Schweinebraten* (roast pork) and *Schnitzel* (veal; €9 to €12).

Radi is a huge, mild radish that's eaten with beer; you can buy prepared radish for about €4.50. Or, buy a radish at the market and a *Radimesser* at any department store, stick it down in the centre and twist the handle round and round, creating a radish spiral. If you do it yourself, smother the cut end of the radish with salt until it weeps to reduce the bitterness – and increase your thirst!

Obatzda is Bavarian for 'mixed up'. This cream cheeselike speciality is made of butter, ripe Camembert, onion and caraway (about €4 to €6). Spread it on *Brez'n* (a pretzel) or bread.

Another speciality is *Leberkäs* (liver cheese), which is nothing to do with liver or cheese but is instead a type of meatloaf that gets its name from its shape. It's usually eaten with sweet mustard and soft pretzels.

BAVARIA

Aussies have opened numerous just-like-home pubs with a friendly welcome. Most have live music and other events at least once a week.

Molly Malone's (Map p304; ☎ 688 7510; Kellerstrasse 1) If you're pining for shepherd's pie, fish and chips or a curry just two days into a RTW trip, this atmospheric award-winning Irish pub will put you right. The bar stocks over 100 types of whisky.

Ned Kelly's (Map p302; ☎ 2421 9899; Frauenplatz 1) Probably the best expat and traveller scene in town, this Australian bar near the Frauenkirche has live music seven nights a week, live big-screen footy and a menu featuring much of Australasia's iconic fauna. The venue is shared with Kilian's Irish pub.

ENTERTAINMENT

Munich is naturally the cultural epicentre of Bavaria and the Alps. Apart from discos, pubs and beer halls, excellent classical, jazz and opera venues abound.

Listings

Go Muenchen (www.gomuenchen.com; €3) What's-on guide to the city including exhibitions, concerts etc.

In München (www.in-muenchen.de; free) The best source of information; available free at bars, restaurants and ticket outlets.

Konzertnews (www.muenchenmusik.de) Free classical music and opera listings magazine.

München im... (free) Excellent A-to-Z pocket-sized booklet of almost everything the city has to offer.

Munich Found (www.munichfound.de) English-language city magazine with useful listings.

Tickets

Tickets to entertainment venues and sports events are available at official ticket outlets (*Kartenvorverkauf*).

München Ticket (Map p302; ☎ 0180-5481 8181; www.muenchenticket.de; Neues Rathaus) Counter within the Marienplatz tourist office.

Zentraler Kartenvorverkauf (www.zkv-muenchen.de) Karlsplatz (Map p302; ☎ 5450 6060); Marienplatz (Map p302; ☎ 292 540) Branches all over the city and kiosks in these U-Bahn stations.

Cinemas

For information about screenings check any of the Munich listings publications. Admission usually ranges from €6.50 to €8.50, though one day, usually Monday or Tuesday, is 'Kinotag' with reduced prices. Non-German films in mainstream cinemas are almost always dubbed. Films showing in the original language with subtitles are labelled 'OmU' (Original mit Untertiteln); those without subtitles are 'OV' or 'OF' (Originalversion or Originalfassung). Amerika Haus (p298) shows nondubbed films, as do the following movie theatres:

Atlantis (Map p302; ☎ 555 152; Schwanthalerstrasse 2)

Cinema (Map p306; ☎ 555 255; Nymphenburger Strasse 31) The pick of the bunch: comfy and modern, with great balcony seats, ice cream and salty popcorn (not a given).

City Atelier (Map p302; ☎ 591 918; Sonnenstrasse 12)

Filmmuseum (Map p302; ☎ 2332 4150; St-Jakobs-Platz 1) In the Stadtmuseum.

Museum-Lichtspiele (Map p304; ☎ 482 403; Lilienstrasse 2) Small and quirky.

Nightclubs

Munich has a thriving club scene with something to suit most tastes. Bouncers are notoriously rude and 'discerning', so dress to kill (or look, as locals say, *schiki-micki*) and keep your cool. The cover prices for discos vary but average between €5 and €10.

Kultfabrik (Map p304; www.kultfabrik.de; Grafinger Strasse, Haidhausen) and **Optimolwerke** (Map p304; www.optimol werke.de; Grafinger Strasse, Haidhausen) are back-to-back villages of pubs, bars and clubs – nearly 40 in total – near the Ostbahnhof. They're a party animal's mecca, where you can roam from an '80s disco to hip-hop, trance and heavy metal venues. An 'in' spot here is **Drei Türme** (☎ 4502 8817; www.dreituerme.de; ✆ 9pm-4am Tue, 10pm-6am Wed, Fri & Sat), a chic living-room club disguised as a Hollywood castle and lit by a forest of glass-fibre tubes. Alternatively join Munich's huge Russian expat mob for some vodka-fuelled excitement at **Kalinka** (☎ 4090 7260; ✆ 10pm-5am Fri, 10pm-9am Sat), a flashy place decked out with lots of red velvet, dancing girls and a giant bust of Lenin. Other options include **Milch & Bar** (☎ 450 2880; www.milchundbar.de; ✆ 10pm-6am Sun-Thu, 10pm-9am Fri & Sat), a more mainstream choice catering to disco divas; and the padded crimson **Living4** (☎ 4900 1260; www.living4.de; ✆ 10pm-4am Tue-Thu, 10pm-6am Fri & Sat), playing a good mix of hip hop, Latin and house.

Muffatwerk (Map p304; ☎ 4587 5010; www.muffat werk.de; Zellstrasse 4) This is another big complex that holds large concerts and, in summer, an open-air disco on Friday with drum 'n' bass, acid jazz and hip hop (it's always crowded, so expect queues).

P1 (Map p305; ☎ 211 1140; Prinzregentenstrasse 1) A bit of a Munich institution and still the see-and-be-seen place for the city's wannabes with extremely choosy and effective bouncers, snooty staff and the occasional celebrity.

Registratur (Map p302; ☎ 2388 7758; Blumenstrass 4) No mistake, the dusty halls and '60s panelling of this old city building have the charm of an off-location. The humour isn' lost on the (mostly 20s) crowd, who come for a diet of African beats, shock rock and indie pop.

Live Music
CLASSICAL

Philharmonie im Gasteig (Map p304; ☎ 480 98C www.gasteig.de; Rosenheimer Strasse 5) As home to the city's Philharmonic Orchestra, Munich' premier high-brow cultural venue has a packed schedule. The Symphonieorcheste des Bayerischen Rundfunks (Bavariar Radio Symphony Orchestra) is also base here, and performs on Sundays throughou the year.

Nationaltheater (Map p302; ☎ box office 218 501 www.staatsoper.bayern.de; Max-Joseph-Platz 2) The Bayerische Staatsoper (Bavarian State Opera performs here. Its prestigious opera festiva takes place in July. You can buy tickets a regular outlets or at the box office.

Staatstheater am Gärtnerplatz (Map p302; ☎ 218. 1960; www.staatstheater-am-gaetnerplatz.de; Gärtnerplatz 3 This venue focuses on opera, operetta and musicals, with the occasional classical music concert on special occasions.

JAZZ

Munich has a sizzling jazz scene.

Babalu (Map p305; ☎ 172-273 4909; Leopoldstrasse 27) The program is always turbo-charged a

---

his indie club with orange '70s decor.
Vednesdays are a climax of funky, unfet-
:red jazz for the dance-mad. Concerts begin
t 9pm and then, around midnight, DJs take
ver with soulful grooves.

Jazzclub Unterfahrt im Einstein (Map p304; ☎ 448
794; Einsteinstrasse 42) This is perhaps the best-
nown place in town, with live music from
pm and regular international acts. Sunday
ights feature an open jam session.

Jazzbar Vogler (Map p302; ☎ 294 662; Rumfordstrasse
7; ☽ Mon-Sat) Conceived as a 'cultural living
oom' by ex-journalist Vogler, this intimate lit-
le club has grown into one of the city's top jazz
enues. The musicians are some of Munich's
addest cats.

Also recommended:

afé am Beethovenplatz (Map p302; ☎ 552 9100;
oethestrasse 51) Atmospheric cafe with live music most
veekdays and a piano brunch every Sunday.

light Club Bar (Map p302; ☎ 212 0994; Promenade-
latz 2-6) Intimate club in the Hotel Bayerischer Hof where
ou can catch top talent almost nightly.

ROCK

arge rock concerts are staged at the Olympia-
ark (p313), or at venues listed under
Vightclubs (see opposite). The **Brunnenhof**
er Residenz (Map p302; ☎ 936 093; Residenzstrasse
) occasionally hosts open-air performances
anging from rock, jazz and swing to classical
nd opera in stunning surroundings.

heatre

Munich has a dynamic theatre scene, though
`nglish-language performances are very thin
`n the ground. The two biggest companies
`re the Bayerisches Staatsschauspiel and the
Münchener Kammerspiele. The **Bayerisches
`taatschauspiel** (☎ tickets 218 501) performs at the
`esidenztheater** (Map p302; Max-Joseph-Platz 1) and
`t the **Theater im Marstall** (Map p302; Marstallplatz)
`ehind the Nationaltheater.

Münchener Kammerspiele (Map p302; ☎ 2339 6600;
Aaximilianstrasse 28) This theatre stages large-scale
`roductions of heavyweight drama by German
vriters or foreign playwrights translated
nto German.

Deutsches Theater (off Map pp300-1; ☎ 5523 4444;
Verner-Heisenberg-Allee 11) Recently decamped to
` huge tent in Fröttmaning (near the Allianz
`rena), Munich's answer to London's West
`nd has touring road shows (usually popular
`nusicals like *Grease*).

Kulturzentrum Gasteig (Map p304; ☎ 480 980;
Rosenheimer Strasse 5) This is a major cultural
centre with theatre, classical music and
other special events held in several halls with
excellent acoustics.

Other venues include the **Prinzregententheater**
(Map p304; ☎ 2185 2959; Prinzregentenplatz 12) and
the **GOP Varieté Theater** (Map p304; ☎ 210 288 444;
Maximilianstrasse 47), which shows a real jumble
of acts.

SHOPPING

Fashionistas can crunch their credit in
Maximilianstrasse, Theatinerstrasse, Residenzstrasse and Brienner Strasse. For high street
shops and department stores try the pedestrian
area around Marienplatz, Neuhauser Strasse
and Kaufingerstrasse. For streetwear, head
for the indie boutiques around Gärtnerplatz,
Glockenplatz, Schwabing and Haidhausen.
Beer steins and *Mass* (1L tankard) glasses are
available at all the department stores and the
beer halls themselves.

Deutsches Museum Shop (Map p304; ☎ 2138 3892;
Museuminsel 1) Perhaps the most fascinating museum gift shop you'll ever visit with heaps of
man-gadgets, working models, kids' science
sets, unusual toys, unique 3-D postcards and
museum-related knick-knacks and souvenirs.
There's another branch at Rindermarkt 17.

Foto-Video-Media Sauter (Map p302; ☎ 551
5040; Sonnenstrasse 26) This computer and
photographic equipment superstore sells
everything from the smallest memory card
to industrial-size printers.

Holareidulijö (Map p305; ☎ 271 7745; Schellingstrasse
81; ☽ noon-6.30pm Tue-Fri, 10am-1pm Sat) Munich's
only secondhand traditional clothing emporium, and worth a look even if you don't intend
to buy. Apparently, wearing hand-me-down
lederhosen reduces the risk of chafing.

Ludwig Beck (Map p302; ☎ 236 910; Marienplatz 11)
Munich's most venerable department store has
some chic but reasonably priced clothes, a large
CD shop, a trendy coffee bar and restaurant.

Manufactum (Map p302; ☎ 2354 5900; Dienerstrasse
12) Anyone with an admiration for top-
quality German design classics should
make a beeline for this place. Last-a-life-
time household items compete for shelf
space with retro toys, Bauhaus lamps and
times-gone-by stationary.

Porzellan Manufaktur Nymphenburg (Map p306;
☎ 1791 9710; Schloss Nymphenburg; ☽ 10am-5pm Mon-
Fri) It has made fine porcelain for Bavarian

royals and quite a few commoners since being founded in 1747. There's a more central store at Odeonsplatz 1 (Map p302).

Schuster (Map p302; ☎ 237 070; Rosenstrasse 1-5) Get tooled up for the Alps at this sports megastore boasting seven shiny floors of equipment, including cycling, skiing, travel and camping paraphernalia.

GETTING THERE & AWAY
Air
Munich's **international airport** (MUC; ☎ 089-975 00; www.munich-airport.de) is second in importance only to Frankfurt for international and domestic flights. There are direct services to/from many key destinations including most European capitals, New York, Los Angeles, Cape Town and all major German cities.

Almost 90 airlines fly to and from Munich including big-hitters such as Air France, British Airways, Delta Airlines, easyJet, Germanwings, Lufthansa and KLM. For contact details, see p773.

Bus
Sinbad (Map p302; ☎ 5454 8989; Arnulfstrasse 20) specialises in long-distance coach tickets for almost any destination in Europe.

Munich is also a stop for **Busabout** (www.busabout.com), a system of circular routes that takes in Amsterdam, Berlin, Paris, Prague, Rome and Vienna, among other cities (also see p776).

Europabus (see p337) links Munich to the Romantic Road. For details of fares and timetables enquire at **DTG** (Map p302; ☎ 8898 9513; www.touring.de; Hirtenstrasse 14) near the Hauptbahnhof, the agent for Deutsche Touring and Eurolines buses.

BerlinLinienBus (☎ 09281-2252; www.berlinlinienbus.de) runs daily buses between Berlin and Munich (one-way/return €47/88, 9½ hours), via Ingolstadt, Nuremberg, Bayreuth and Leipzig. It picks up from the north side of the Hauptbahnhof.

Car & Motorcycle
Munich radiates autobahns like numbered octopus legs. Take the A9 to Nuremberg, the A92/A3 to Passau, the A8 to Salzburg, the A95 to Garmisch-Partenkirchen and the A8 to Ulm or Stuttgart.

Motorists in need of traffic information should turn to the incredibly dependable **ADAC** (German Auto Association; Map p302; ☎ 767 60; www.adac.de; Sonnenstrasse 23).

All major car-hire companies have office at the airport and/or the 2nd level of Munich Hauptbahnhof, including **Hertz** (☎ 550 2256; ww .hertz.com; 🕑 7am-9pm Mon-Fri, 9am-5pm Sat & Sun), **Avi** (☎ 550 2251; www.avis-europe.com; 🕑 7am-9pm Mon-Fr 8am-5pm Sat & Sun) and **Europcar** (☎ 549 0240; ww .europcar.com; 🕑 7am-9pm Mon-Fri, 8am-7pm Sat & Sun).

For shared rides, consider using on of Munich's *Mitfahrzentralen* (ride-shar agency). The **ADM-Mitfahrzentrale** (Map p30. ☎ 194 40; www.mitfahrzentrale.de; Lämmerstrasse 6) i conveniently near the Hauptbahnhof. **CityNet Mitfahrzentrale** (Map p305; ☎ 194 44; www.cityne -mitfahrzentrale.de; Adalbertstrasse 6) in Schwabin has a good online booking function. Fares ar considerably lower than the train.

Train
Train is by far the best way to get in and ou of Munich. Swift and frequent connection link the Bavarian capital to all major Germa cities as well as European destinations suc as Vienna (€75, five hours), Prague (€60, si to eight hours) and Zürich (€64, four hours) Prices vary according to demand and the clas of train.

There are direct IC and ICE trains to Berli (€113, six hours), Hamburg (€127, six hours) Frankfurt (€89, 3¼ hours) and Stuttgart (€52 2½ hours).

Prague extension passes (add-on tickets t Eurail and German rail passes) are sold at th rail-pass counters in the Reisezentrum at th Hauptbahnhof, or through EurAide (p307).

GETTING AROUND
While central Munich is compact enough fo exploring on foot, the well-regimented publi transport system will zoom you out to th suburbs with swift Teutonic efficiency.

To/From the Airport
Munich's **Flughafen Franz-Josef Strauss** (www .munich-airport.de) is connected by the S8 to th Ostbahnhof, Hauptbahnhof and Marienplat (€9.20). The trip to the Hauptbahnhof take about 40 minutes and trains run every 2 minutes from around 4am until 1am. For northern and eastern suburbs take the S8.

The Lufthansa Airport Bus (Map p302) trav els at 20-minute intervals from Arnulfstrass near the Hauptbahnhof (one-way/retur €10.50/17, 40 minutes) between 5.10am an 8.28pm. A taxi from the airport to the Altstad costs around €60.

ar & Motorcycle

orget about driving in the city centre; many reets are pedestrian-only, ticket enforcement Orwellian and parking is a nightmare. The urist office map shows city car parks, which enerally cost about €1.50 to €2.50 per hour.

ublic Transport

Munich's excellent public transport network un by **MVV** (www.mvv-muenchen.de) makes getting round the city a cinch. The system is zone-ased, but most places of interest to visitors except Dachau and the airport) are within the white' inner-zone (Innenraum).

Tickets are valid for the S-Bahn, U-Bahn, ams and buses, but must be time-stamped in he machines at station entrances and aboard uses and trams before use. Failure to buy nd/or validate a ticket puts you at the mercy f now uniformed ticket inspectors, who will olitely fine you €40 as a *Schwarzfahrer* (liter-lly 'black passenger').

Short rides (four bus or tram stops; two U-Bahn or S-Bahn stops) cost €1.20, while onger trips cost €2.30. It's marginally heaper to buy a strip-card of 10 tickets alled a *Streifenkarte* for €11, and stamp one trip per adult on rides of two or less tram r U-Bahn stops, two strips for longer jour-eys. The MVV was planning price hikes at he time of writing, so check the website for xact prices.

Some of the other deals on offer:

arCard Wochenkarte (€36.60) Weekly pass covering ll four zones, valid Monday until midnight the following unday; if you buy later, it's still only good until Sunday.

ageskarten (day passes) One day (individual/up o 5 people €5/9); Three day (individual/up to 5 people 12.30/21) Valid for the inner zone only.

Rail passes are also valid on S-Bahn trains. A bicycle pass costs €2.50 and is valid all ay except during rush hour (6am to 9am nd 4pm to 6pm Monday to Friday), when ikes are banned.

The U-Bahn ceases operation around 2.30am on weekdays and 1.30am at veekends, but a network of night buses *Nachtbusse)* still operates. Pick up the lat-st route and time schedule from any tourist r MVV office.

axi

axis cost €2.70 at flagfall, plus a per-ilometre price of €1.25 to €1.60. For a radio-dispatched taxi, ring ☎ 216 10 or 194 10. Taxi ranks are indicated on the city's tourist map.

AROUND MUNICH

DACHAU CONCENTRATION CAMP MEMORIAL

The way to freedom is to follow one's orders; exhibit honesty, orderliness, cleanliness, sobriety, truthfulness, the ability to sacrifice and love of the Fatherland.

Inscription from the roof of the concentration camp at Dachau

Dachau was the Nazis' first concentration camp, built by Heinrich Himmler in March 1933 to house political prisoners. All in all it 'processed' more than 200,000 inmates, killing at least 43,000, and is now a haunt-ing memorial. Expect to spend two to three hours here to fully absorb the exhibits. Note that children under 12 may find the experi-ence too disturbing.

A new **visitors centre** (☎ 669 970; www.kz -gedenkstaette-dachau.de; Alte Römerstrasse 75) opened in May 2009 housing a bookshop, cafe and tour booking desk. It's on your left as you enter the main gate.

You pass into the compound itself through the **Jourhaus**, originally the only entrance. Set in wrought iron, the chilling slogan 'Arbeit Macht Frei' (Work Sets You Free) hits you at the gate.

The **museum** (admission free; ☼ 9am-5pm Tue-Sun) is at the southern end of the camp. Here a 22-minute English-language documentary runs at 11.30am, 2pm and 3.30pm. Either side of the small cinema extends an exhibi-tion relating the camp's harrowing story. This includes photographs of the camp, its officers and prisoners, and of horrifying 'scientific experiments' carried out by Nazi doctors. Other exhibits include a whipping block, a chart showing the system of prisoner catego-ries (Jews, homosexuals, Jehovah's Witnesses, Poles, Roma and other 'asocial' types) and documents on the persecution of 'degenerate' authors banned by the party.

Outside, in the former roll call square, is the **International Memorial** (1968), inscribed in English, French, Yiddish, German and Russian, which reads 'Never Again'. Behind the exhibit building, the **bunker** was the notorious camp prison where inmates were tortured. Executions took place in the prison yard.

Inmates were housed in large barracks, now demolished, which used to line the main road north of the roll call square. In the camp's northwestern corner is the **crematorium** and gas chamber, disguised as a shower room but never used. Several religious shrines, including a timber Russian Orthodox church, stand nearby.

Tours

Dachauer Forum (☎ 669 970; €3; ✦ 1.30pm Tue-Fri, noon & 1.30pm Sat & Sun May-Sep, 1.30pm Thu, Sat & Sun Oct-Apr) Tours (2½-hour), by dedicated English-speaking volunteers, depart from the visitors centre. There are also half-hour introductions (€1.50) at 12.30pm Tuesday to Sunday (additionally at 11am Saturday and Sunday) May to October, and Thursday, Saturday and Sunday November to April.

Radius Tours (Map p302; ☎ 089-5502 9374; www .radiustours.com; adult/concession €21/18; ✦ 9.15am & 12.30pm Tue-Sun Apr-Oct, 11am Nov-Mar) Five-hour English-language tours leave from the end of tracks 32-34 at Munich's Hauptbahnhof. They include public transport from Munich.

Self-guided Audio Tour (adult/child €3/2) Covers the history, key buildings and the exhibits (up to two hours). Available from the visitors centre.

Getting There & Away

The westbound S2 makes the journey from Munich Hauptbahnhof to Dachau Hauptbahnhof in 21 minutes. From here change to local bus 726, which runs every 20 minutes. You'll need a two-zone ticket (€4.60, or four strips of a *Streifenkarte*), including the bus connection.

SCHLEISSHEIM
☎ 089 / pop 5700

The northern Munich suburb of Schleissheim is worth a visit for its three palaces and the aviation museum.

The crown jewel of the palatial trio is the **Neues Schloss Schleissheim** (☎ 315 8720; Max-Emanuel-Platz 1; adult/under 18yr/concession €4/free/3, combination ticket for all 3 palaces €6/free/5; ✦ 9am-6pm Apr-Sep, 10am-4pm Oct-Mar, closed Mon). Modelled after Versailles, this pompous pile was dreamed up by prince-elector Max Emanuel in 1701. Inside, you'll be treated to stylish period furniture, a gallery of oil paintings belonging to the Bavarian state

art collection and a vaulted ceiling smothere in 3-D frescoes by the prolific Cosmas Damia Asam. The palace is surrounded by an impres sive manicured park that's ideal for picnics.

Nearby, the **Altes Schloss Schleissheim** (☎ 31 5272; Maximilianshof 1; adult/concession €2.50/1.5 ✦ 9am-6pm Apr-Sep, 10am-4pm Oct-Mar, closed Mo is only a shadow of its former Renaissanc self. It houses exhibits on religious festiva and Prussian culture. On a little island at th eastern end of the Schlosspark stands **Schlos Lustheim** (☎ 315 8720; adult/concession €3/2; ✦ 9am 6pm Apr-Sep, 10am-4pm Oct-Mar, closed Mon), featurin the finest collection of Meissen porcelain afte Dresden's Zwinger museum.

Near the palaces you'll find **Flugwer Schleissheim** (☎ 315 7140; Effnerstrasse 18; adult/co cession €6/3; ✦ 9am-5pm), the aviation branc of the Deutsches Museum (p315). Display are housed in three historical buildings – th command, the tower and the constructio hall – as well as a new hall, and include abou 60 planes and helicopters, plus hang-glider engines, rockets and flight simulators.

To reach Schleissheim take the S1 (toward Freising) to Oberschleissheim. It's about 15-minute walk from the station alon Mittenheimer Strasse towards the palaces.

STARNBERG
☎ 08151 / pop 23,000

Around 25km southwest of central Munich glittering Lake Starnberg (Starnberger See was once the haunt of Bavaria's royal family but now provides a bit of easily accessibl R&R for anyone looking to escape the hurl burly of the Bavarian capital.

At the northern end of the lake the affluen town of Starnberg is the heart of the Fünf Seen-Land (Five-Lakes-District). Beside Lake Starnberg the district comprises th Ammersee and the much smaller Pilsensee Wörthsee and Wesslinger See. Swimming yachting and windsurfing are popular activi ties on all lakes.

The district **tourist office** (☎ 906 00; www.sta .de; Wittelsbacherstrasse 2c, Starnberg; ✦ 8am-6pm Mor Fri, 9am-1pm Sat May–mid-Oct) has a room-findin service.

King Ludwig II famously (and mysteri ously) drowned in Lake Starnberg (see boxe text, p354). The spot where his body wa found, in the town of Berg on the easter shore, is now marked with a memorial cros in the shallows, near the Votivkapelle. To ge there, take bus 961 from Starnberg.

From early May to mid-October, **Bayerische-Seen-Schifffahrt** (☎ 8061) runs boat services from Starnberg to the other lake towns, as well as one- and three-hour tours (€8.50/15.90 respectively). The longer tour, starting from the docks behind the S-Bahn station, takes in five palaces as well as the Ludwig II cross.

If you'd rather get around the lake yourself, you can hire bikes at **Bike It** (☎ 746 430; Bahnhofstrasse 1, Starnberg; per day €15-20). **Paul Dechant** (☎ 121 06; Hauptstrasse 20), near the S-Bahn station, hires rowing, pedal and electric-powered boats from €11 per hour.

Starnberg is 31 minutes on the S6 from Munich Hauptbahnhof (€4.60 or four strips of a *Streifenkarte*). To get to Starnberg by car from Munich, take the A95 and drive about 20km southwest.

ANDECHS

Founded in the 10th century, the gorgeous hilltop monastery of **Andechs** (☎ 08152-3760; www.andechs.de; admission free; ⏰ 8am-6pm Mon-Fri, 9am-5pm Sat, 9.45am-6pm Sun) has long been a place of pilgrimage, though today more visitors come to slurp the Benedictines' fabled ales.

The church owns two relics of enormous importance: branches that are thought to come from Christ's crown of thorns, and a victory cross of Charlemagne, whose army overran much of Western Europe in the 9th century. In the Holy Chapel the votive candles, some of them over 1m tall, are among Germany's oldest. The remains of Carl Orff, the composer of *Carmina Burana*, are interred here as well.

Outside, soak up the magnificent views of the purple-grey Alps and forested hills before plunging into the nearby **Bräustüberl** (☎ 08152-376 261; ⏰ 10am-8.45pm), the monks' beer hall and garden. There are seven varieties of beer on offer, from the rich and velvety Doppelbock dark to the fruity unfiltered Weissbier. The place is incredibly popular, and on summer weekends you may have to join a queue of day-trippers at the door to get in.

The easiest way to reach Andechs is to take the S5 to Herrsching (€6.90, 48 minutes), then change onto bus 951 or the private Ammersee-Reisen bus (€2.20, 11 times daily). Alternatively, it's a pleasant 4km hike south from Herrsching through the protected woodland of the Kiental.

BAD TÖLZ

☎ 08041 / pop 17,600

Situated some 40km south of central Munich, Bad Tölz is a pretty spa town straddling the Isar. The town's gentle inclines provide a delightful spot for its attractive, frescoed houses and the quaint shops of the old town. At weekends thousands flock here from Munich to enjoy the ultramodern swimming complex, Alpine slide and hiking trips down the river. Bad Tölz is also the gateway to the Tölzer Land region and its emerald-green lakes, the Walchensee and the Kochelsee.

Every year on 6 November, its residents pay homage to the patron saint of horses, Leonhard. The famous Leonhardifahrt is a pilgrimage up to the Leonhardi chapel on Kalvarienberg, where townsfolk dress up in traditional costume and ride dozens of garlanded horse carts to the strains of brass bands.

Bad Tölz **tourist office** (☎ 786 70; www.bad-toelz.de; Marktstrasse 48; ⏰ 9am-12.30pm & 1.30-6pm Mon-Fri, 9am-noon Sat) doubles as the museum ticket office.

Sights & Activities
ALTSTADT

Cobble-stoned and car-free, **Marktstrasse** is flanked by statuesque town houses with ornate overhanging eaves that look twice as high on the sloping street. The **Stadtmuseum** (☎ 504 688; Marktstrasse 48; adult/concession €2/1.50; ⏰ 10am-4pm, Tue-Sun) touches on practically all aspects of local culture and history, with a fine collection of painted armoires (the so-called Tölzer Kasten), a 2m-tall, single-stringed *Nonnengeige*, examples of traditional glass painting and a cart used in the Leonhardifahrt.

In a side alley a few steps south of Marktstrasse, through Kirchgasse, is the **Pfarrkirche Maria Himmelfahrt** (Church of the Assumption; Frauenfreithof), a late-Gothic three-nave hall church enduring some serious renovation at the time of research. Wandering down Marktstrasse, you'll soon spot the baroque **Franziskanerkirche** (Franciscan Church; Franziskanergasse 1) across the Isar. Surrounded by lovely gardens, its blanched interior is enlivened by several beautiful altars.

Above the town, on Kalvarienberg, looms Bad Tölz' landmark, the twin-towered

BAVARIA

Kalvarienbergkirche (Cavalry Church). This enormous baroque structure stands side by side with the petite **Leonhardikapelle** (Leonhardi Chapel; 1718), the destination of the Leonhardi pilgrimage.

ALPAMARE

In the spa section of town, west of the Isar River, you'll find the fantastic water complex **Alpamare** (☎ 509 999; www.alpamare.de; Ludwigstrasse 14; 4hr pass adult/child €27/24, day pass €33/24; ⏰ 9.30am-10pm). This huge centre has heated indoor and outdoor mineral pools, a wave and surfing pool, a series of wicked water slides (including Germany's longest, the 330m-long Alpabob-Wildwasser), saunas, solariums and its own hotel. Bus 1 from the train station stops 100m away.

BLOMBERG

Southwest of Bad Tölz, the **Blomberg** (1248m) is a family-friendly mountain that has a natural toboggan track in winter, plus easy hiking and a fun Alpine slide in summer.

Unless you're walking, getting up the hill involves a chairlift ride aboard the **Blombergbahn** (☎ 3726; top station return adult/child €8/3.50, midway one-way €2.50; ⏰ 9am-5pm May-Oct, 9am-4pm Nov-Apr weather permitting). Over 1km long, the fibreglass **Alpine slide** snakes down the mountain from the middle station. You zip down through the 17 hairpin bends on little wheeled bobsleds with a joystick to control braking. You can achieve speeds of up to 50km/h but if you do, chances are you'll ram the rider ahead of you or fly clean off the track. A long-sleeved shirt and jeans provide a little protection. Riding up to the midway station and sliding down costs €4 per adult (€3.50 concession), with discounts for multiple trips.

To reach Blomberg, take RVO bus 9612, 9591 or 9610 from the train station to the Blombergbahn stop.

Getting There & Away

The private **Bayerische Oberlandbahn** (BOB; ⏰ 08024-997 171; www.bayerischeoberlandbahn.de) runs hourly trains between Bad Tölz and Munich Hauptbahnhof (€10.30, 50 minutes). Alternatively, take the S2 from central Munich to Holzkirchen, then change to the BOB. In Holzkirchen make sure you board the Bad Tölz-bound portion of the train.

CHIEMSEE

☎ 08051

Most foreign visitors arrive at the shores of the Bavarian Sea – as Chiemsee is affectionately known – in search of King Ludwig II's Schloss Herrenchiemsee. The lake's natural beauty and water sports make the area popular with stressed-out city dwellers, and many affluent Müncheners own weekend retreats by its shimmering waters.

The towns of Prien am Chiemsee and about 5km south, Bernau am Chiemsee (both on the Munich–Salzburg rail line) are perfect bases for exploring the lake. Of the two towns, Prien is by far the larger and livelier.

Information

All the tourist offices have free internet for brief walk-in use.

Bernau tourist office (☎ 986 80; www.bernau-am-chiemsee.de; Aschauer Strasse 10)

Chiemsee Info-Center (☎ 965 550; www.chiemsee.de; ⏰ 9am-6pm Mon-Fri, 10am-3pm Sat & Sun) On the southern lakeshore, near the Bernau-Felden autobahn exit. Information for the whole area.

Prien tourist office (☎ 690 50; www.tourismus.prien.de; Alte Rathausstrasse 11)

Sights

SCHLOSS HERRENCHIEMSEE

An island just 1.5km across the Chiemsee from Prien, Herreninsel is home to Ludwig II's Versailles-inspired **Schloss Herrenchiemsee** (☎ 688 70; www.herren-chiemsee.de; adult/under 18yr/concession €7/free/6; ⏰ tours continuously 9am-6pm Apr–mid-Oct, 9.40am-4.15pm mid-Oct–Mar). Begun in 1878, it was never intended as a residence but as a homage to absolutist monarchy, as epitomised by Ludwig's hero, the French Sun King, Louis XIV. Ludwig spent only 10 days here and even then was rarely seen, preferring to read at night and sleep all day.

The palace is typical of Ludwig's creations, its design and appearance the product of the Bavarian monarch's romantic obsessions and unfettered imagination. Ludwig splurged more money on this palace than on Neuschwanstein (p352) and Linderhof (p359) combined, but when cash ran out in 1885, one year before his death, 50 rooms remained unfinished.

The rooms that were completed outdo each other in opulence. The vast **Gesandtentreppe** (Ambassador Staircase), a double staircase eading to a frescoed gallery and topped by a glass roof, is the first visual knockout on the guided tour, but that fades in comparison to the stunning **Grosse Spiegelgalerie** (Great Hall of Mirrors). This tunnel of light runs the length of the garden (98m, or 10m longer than that in Versailles). It sports 52 candelabra and 33 great glass chandeliers with 7000 candles, which took 70 servants half an hour to light. In late July it becomes a superb venue for classical concerts.

The **Paradeschlafzimmer** (State Bedroom) features a canopied bed perching altarlike on a pedestal behind a golden balustrade. This was the heart of the palace, where morning and evening audiences were held. But it's the king's bedroom, the **Kleines Blaues Schlafzimmer** (Little Blue Bedroom), that really takes the cake. The decoration is sickly sweet, encrusted with gilded stucco and wildly extravagant carvings. The room is bathed in a soft blue light emanating from a glass globe at the foot of the bed. It supposedly took 18 months for a technician to perfect the lamp to the king's satisfaction.

Admission to the palace also entitles you to a spin around the **König-Ludwig II-Museum**, where you can see the king's christening and coronation robes, more blueprints of megalomaniac buildings and his death mask.

To reach the palace, take the ferry from Prien-Stock (€6.50 return, 15 to 20 minutes) or from Bernau-Felden (€8, 25 minutes, May to October). From the boat landing on Herreninsel, it's about a 20-minute walk through pretty gardens to the palace. Palace tours, offered in German or English, last 30 minutes.

FRAUENINSEL

A third of this tiny island is occupied by **Frauenwörth Abbey**, founded in the late 8th century and one of the oldest in Bavaria. The 10th-century church, whose freestanding campanile sports a distinctive onion-dome top (11th century), is worth a visit. Opposite the church is the AD 860 Carolingian **Torhalle** (☎ 08054-7256; admission €1.50; ⊙ 10am-6pm May-Oct). It houses medieval objets d'art, sculpture and changing exhibitions of regional paintings from the 18th to the 20th centuries.

Return ferry fare, including a stop at Herreninsel, is €7.60 from Prien-Stock and €8 from Bernau-Felden.

Activities

The swimming beaches at Chieming and Gstadt (both free) are the easiest to reach, on the lake's eastern and northern shores respectively. A variety of boats are available for hire at many beaches, for €6 to €20 per hour. In Prien, **Bootsverleih Stöffl** (☎ 2000; www.stoeffl.de; Strandpromenade) is possibly the best company to turn to.

The futuristic-looking glass roof by the harbour in Prien-Stock shelters **Prienavera** (☎ 609 570; Seestrasse 120; 4hr pass adult/concession €9.90/5.50, day pass €11.90/6.50; ⊙ seasonal, usually 10am-9pm), a popular pool complex with a wellness area, water slides and a restaurant.

Sleeping

The tourist offices can set up **private rooms** (per person from €18) in town and in farmhouses.

Panorama Camping Harras (☎ 904 613; www.camping-harras.de; per person/tent/car €5.50/3.60/1.80) This camp site is scenically located on a peninsula with its own private beach, catamaran and surfboard hire. The restaurant has a delightful lakeside terrace.

DJH hostel (☎ 687 70; www.prien.jugendherberge.de; Carl-Braun-Strasse 66; dm under/over 27yr €19/23; ⊙ closed Dec-early Feb) Prien's hostel organises lots of activities and has an environmental study centre for young people. It's in a bucolic spot, a 15-minute walk from the Hauptbahnhof.

Hotel Bonnschlössl (☎ 965 6990; www.alter-wirt-bernau.de; Ferdinand-Bonn-Strasse 2, Bernau; s €47-55, d €81-103; P) Built in 1477, this pocket-sized palace hotel with the faux-turrets once belonged to the Bavarian royal court. Rooms are stylish if slightly overfurnished, and there's a wonderful terrace with a rambling garden.

Hotel Garni Möwe (☎ 5004; www.hotel-garni-moewe.de; Seestrasse 111, Prien; s €50-67, d €73-101; P) This traditional Bavarian hotel right on the lakefront is excellent value, especially the loft rooms. It has its own bike and boat hire, plus a fitness centre, and the large garden is perfect for travellers with children.

Eating

Alter Wirt (☎ 965 6990; Kirchplatz 9, Bernau; mains €7-15, children's menu €3-7; ⊙ closed Mon) This massive half-timbered inn with five centuries of history, situated on the main drag through Bernau, serves up Bavarian meat slabs and international favourites to a mix of locals and tourists.

BAVARIA

Badehaus (☎ 970 300; Rathausstrasse 11, Bernau; mains €7-16) Near the Chiemsee Info-Center and the lakeshore, this contemporary beer hall and garden has quirky decor and gourmet fare enjoyed by a mix of locals and visitors. A special attraction is the 'beer bath', a glass tub filled (sometimes) with a mix of beer and water.

Westernacher am See (☎ 4722; Seestrasse 115, Prien; mains €8-16) This lakeside dining haven has a multiple personality, with a cosy restaurant, cocktail bar, cafe, beer garden and glassed-in winter terrace. Its speciality is modern twists on old Bavarian favourites. They also have spacious double rooms (€90) with splendid views of the Chiemsee.

Getting There & Around

Prien and Bernau are served by hourly trains from Munich (€15.20, one hour). Hourly RVO bus 9505 connects the two lake towns.

Local buses run from Prien Bahnhof to the harbour in Stock. You can also take the historic Chiemseebahn (1887), the world's oldest narrow-gauge **steam train** (one-way €3.30; ⊙ May-Sep).

Chiemsee Schifffahrt (☎ 6090; www.chiemsee-schifffahrt.de; Seestrasse 108) operates hourly ferries from Prien with stops at Herreninsel, Fraueninsel, Seebruck and Chieming on a schedule that changes seasonally. You can circumnavigate the entire lake and make all these stops (getting off and catching the next ferry that comes your way) for €12.40. Children aged six to 15 get a 50% discount.

Chiemgauer Radhaus (☎ 4631; Bahnhofsplatz 6, Prien) and **Chiemgau Biking** (☎ 691 7613; Chiemseestrasse 84, Bernau) hire out mountain bikes for €16 and €22 respectively per day.

THE ROMANTIC ROAD

Two million people ply the Romantic Road (Romantische Strasse) every year, making it by far the most popular of Germany's holiday routes. That means lots of signs in English and Japanese, tourist coaches and kitsch galore. For the most part the trail rolls through pleasant, if not spectacular, landscape that links some of the most picturesque towns in Bavaria and the eastern fringes of Baden-Württemberg.

Despite the hordes of visitors, it's worth falling for the sales pitch – you won't be alone, but you certainly won't be disappointed. For the best trip, pick and choose your destinations carefully, or risk an overdose of the incredible medieval architecture.

Orientation & Information

The Romantic Road runs north–south through western Bavaria, covering 420km between Würzburg and Füssen near the Austrian border. It passes through more than two dozen cities and towns, including Rothenburg ob der Tauber, Dinkelsbühl and Augsburg.

Each town en route has its own local tourist office, in addition to the central **Romantic Road tourist office** (☎ 09851-551 387; www.romantischestrasse.de; Segringerstrasse 19) in Dinkelsbühl.

Getting There & Away

Though Frankfurt is the most popular gateway for the Romantic Road, Munich is a good choice as well, especially if you decide to take the bus (see also opposite).

BICYCLE

With its gentle gradients and bucolic flavour between towns, the Romantic Road is ideal for the holidaying cyclist. Bikes can be hired at many train stations; tourist offices keep lists of bicycle-friendly hotels that permit storage, or check out **Bett und Bike** (089-5586 9010; www.bettundbike.de) predeparture.

BUS

Half a dozen daily buses connect Füssen and Garmisch-Partenkirchen (€9.40, all via Neuschwanstein and most also via Schloss Linderhof). There are also several connections between Füssen and Oberstdorf (via Pfronten or the Tirolean town of Reutte).

BerlinLinienBus (☎ 030-860 6211; www.berlinlinienbus.de) runs buses between Berlin and Rothenburg twice weekly (one-way/return €52/86, seven hours).

TRAIN

Direct trains run from Munich to Füssen (€22.20, two hours) at the southern end of the Romantic Road every two hours, more often if you change in Buchloe. Rothenburg is linked by train to Würzburg (€11.30, one hour), Munich (from €34.40, three hours), Augsburg (€27.50, 2½ hours) and Nuremberg (€17.30, 1¼ to two hours), with at least one change needed in Steinach to reach any destination.

Getting Around
BUS
It *is* possible to do this route using train connections and local buses, but the going is complicated, tedious and slow, especially at weekends. The ideal way to travel is by car, though many foreign travellers prefer to take Deutsche Touring's Europabus, which can get incredibly crowded in summer. From April to October the special coach runs daily in each direction between Frankfurt and Füssen (for Neuschwanstein); the entire journey takes around 11 hours. There's no charge for breaking the journey and continuing the next day.

Reservations & Fares
Tickets are available for short segments of the trip, and reservations are only necessary during peak-season weekends. Reservations can be made through travel agents, **Deutsche Touring** (☎ 069-790 3501; www.touring.de), **EurAide** (☎ 089-593 889; www.euraide.de) in Munich, and Deutsche Bahn's Reisezentrum offices in the train stations.

The most popular halts – along with the one-way and return fares from Frankfurt – are listed below.

Destination	Cost (one-way/return)
Dinkelsbühl	€47/71
Füssen	€98/147
Munich	€81/122
Nördlingen	€54/81
Rothenburg ob der Tauber	€38/56
Würzburg	€24/36

The following are fares from Munich.

Destination	Cost (one-way/return)
Dinkelsbühl	€34/51
Nördlingen	€27/41
Rothenburg ob der Tauber	€43/65
Würzburg	€57/86

Coaches can accommodate bicycles (per 100km €3), but you must give three working days' notice. Students, children, pensioners and rail-pass holders qualify for discounts of between 10% and 50%.

WÜRZBURG
☎ 0931 / pop 134,500
'If I could choose my place of birth I would consider Würzburg', wrote author Hermann Hesse, and it's not difficult to see why. This scenic town straddles the Main River and is renowned for its art, architecture and delicate wines. A large student population guarantees a laid-back vibe, and plenty of hip nightlife pulsates though its cobbled streets.

Würzburg was a Franconia duchy when, in 686, three Irish missionaries tried to persuade Duke Gosbert to convert, and ditch his wife. Gosbert was mulling it over when his wife had the three bumped off. When the murders were discovered decades later, the martyrs became saints and Würzburg was made a pilgrimage city, and, in 742, a bishopric.

For centuries the resident prince-bishops wielded enormous power and wealth, and the city grew in opulence under their rule. Their crowning glory is the Residenz, one of the finest baroque structures in Germany and a Unesco World Heritage Site.

Orientation
Würzburg's centre is compact and, perhaps by more than accident, shaped like a bishop's mitre. The Hauptbahnhof and bus station are at the northern end of the Altstadt. The main shopping street, Kaiserstrasse, runs south from here into the town centre. The Main River forms the western boundary of the Altstadt; the fortress is located on the west bank, with other key sights to the east.

Information
BOOKSHOP
Hugendubel (☎ 354 040; Kürschnerhof 4-6) Megastore with a decent range of English-language paperbacks.

DISCOUNT CARDS
Welcome Card (per 7 days €3) Available from tourist offices; gives reduced admission prices to main sights and tours.

EMERGENCY
Ambulance (☎ 192 22)
Ärztliche Bereitschaftpraxis (Medical Emergency Practice; ☎ 322 833; Domerschulstrasse 1)

INTERNET ACCESS
Log Inn (☎ 205 6923; Häfnergasse 5; per hr €2.90; ☯ 9am-11pm Mon-Sat, 10am-11pm Sun)

LAUNDRY
SB Waschsalon (☎ 416 773; Frankfurter Strasse 13a; per load from €3.80) Browse the internet while you wait.

MONEY
Deutsche Bank (Juliuspromenade 66)

BAVARIA

BAVARIA

WÜRZBURG

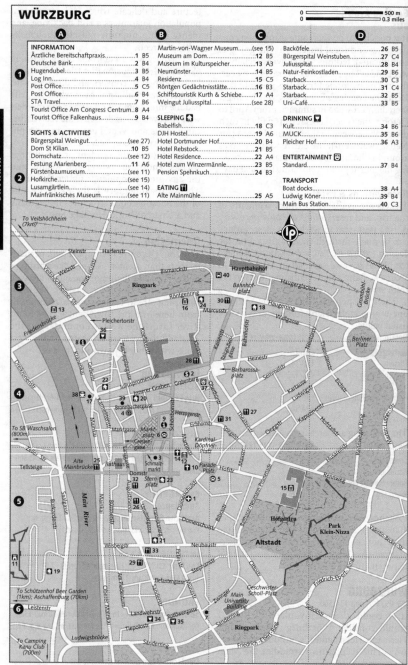

INFORMATION		
Ärztliche Bereitschaftpraxis................**1** B5	Martin-von-Wagner Museum........(see 15)	Backöfele..........................**26** B5
Deutsche Bank....................................**2** B4	Museum am Dom....................**12** B5	Bürgerspital Weinstuben..........**27** C4
Hugendubel..**3** B5	Museum im Kulturspeicher........**13** A3	Juliusspital..........................**28** B4
Log Inn...**4** B4	Neumünster..........................**14** B5	Natur-Feinkostladen..............**29** B6
Post Office..**5** C5	Residenz..............................**15** C5	Starback............................**30** C5
Post Office..**6** B4	Röntgen Gedächtnisstätte........**16** B3	Starback............................**31** C4
STA Travel..**7** B6	Schiffstouristik Kurth & Schiebe..**17** A4	Starback............................**32** B5
Tourist Office Am Congress Centrum..**8** A4	Weingut Juliusspital................(see 28)	Uni-Café............................**33** B5
Tourist Office Falkenhaus..................**9** B4		
	SLEEPING	**DRINKING**
SIGHTS & ACTIVITIES	Babelfish..............................**18** C3	Kult..................................**34** B6
Bürgerspital Weingut..................(see 27)	DJH Hostel............................**19** A6	MUCK................................**35** B6
Dom St Kilian.....................................**10** B5	Hotel Dortmunder Hof............**20** B4	Pleicher Hof........................**36** A3
Domschatz...(see 12)	Hotel Rebstock......................**21** B5	
Festung Marienberg............................**11** A6	Hotel Residence......................**22** A4	**ENTERTAINMENT**
Fürstenbaumuseum.............................(see 11)	Pension Spehnkuch................**24** B3	Standard............................**37** B4
Hofkirche..(see 15)		
Lusamgärtlein....................................(see 14)	**EATING**	**TRANSPORT**
Mainfränkisches Museum.....................(see 11)	Alte Mainmühle......................**25** A5	Boat docks..........................**38** A4
		Ludwig Köner......................**39** B4
		Main Bus Station..................**40** C3

POST
Post office (Marktplatz 20-24 & Paradeplatz 4)

TOURIST INFORMATION
Tourist office Marktplatz (☎ 372 398; www.wuerzburg
.de; Falkenhaus; ☯ 10am-6pm Mon-Fri, 10am-2pm Sat
Apr-Dec & Sun May-Oct, 10am-4pm Mon-Fri, 10am-2pm
Sat Jan-Mar); Am Congress Centrum (☎ 372 335; Am
Congress Centrum; ☯ 8am-5pm Mon-Thu, 8am-1pm Fri)

TRAVEL AGENCY
STA Travel (☎ 521 76; Zwinger 6)

Sights
RESIDENZ
A symbol of wealth and prestige for the
Würzburg bishops, the Unesco-listed **Residenz**
(☎ 355 170; www.residenz-wuerzburg.de; Balthasar-
Neumann-Promenade; adult/concession €5/4; ☯ 9am-6pm
Apr-Oct, 10am-4.30pm Nov-Mar, English-language tours
11am & 3pm) is one of southern Germany's most
important and eye-catching palaces.

Almost immediately upon entering you'll
see the brilliant **grand staircase** come into view
on the left. Miraculously, the vaulted ceiling
survived the war intact and Tiepolo's magnificent fresco *The Four Continents* (1750–53)
– said to be the world's largest above a staircase – dazzles in all its glory. Look closely
to see Balthasar Neumann, architect of the
Residenz, perched smugly on a cannon.

For opulence, the bishops' imperial apartments rivalled those of kings. The **Kaisersaal**
(Imperial Hall) is a combination of marble,
gold stucco and more incredible frescoes. The
Spiegelsaal (Hall of Mirrors) is the most memorable, with gilded stucco dripping from the
ceiling and walls lined with glasslike panels.
In the building's southern wing is the magnificent **Hofkirche** (Court Church; admission free), an
early example of Neumann's penchant for
spatial illusions. The side wings of the altar are
decorated with paintings by Tiepolo.

Next to the church, the **Martin-von-Wagner
Museum** (☎ 312 288; admission free; ☯ closed Mon)
exhibits a minor collection of Greek vases
and graphic art. The museum backs onto the
spectacular French- and English-style gardens
of the **Hofgarten** (☯ dawn-dusk).

FESTUNG MARIENBERG
Perched high on the Main's left bank, the
Festung Marienberg (Marienberg Fortress)
has presided over Würzburg since the city's
prince-bishops commissioned a 'new' castle in

1201. It was only ever taken once, by Swedish
troops in the Thirty Years War. The lovely
walk up from the river via the vine-covered
hill takes 20 minutes, or bus 9 will get you
there from Juliuspromenade.

The fortress is home to two museums. The
Fürstenbaumuseum (☎ 355 1750; adult/concession €4/3;
☯ 9am-6pm Tue-Sun mid-Mar–Oct) serves as the city's
history museum, while the **Mainfränkisches
Museum** (☎ 205 940; adult/concession €4/3, combined
ticket for both museums €5/4; ☯ 10am-7pm Tue-Sun
Apr-Oct, 10am-4pm Tue-Sun Nov-Mar) in the baroque
Zeughaus (armoury) contains a famous collection of works by local 15th-century master sculptor Tilman Riemenschneider. An
exhibit on winemaking can be found in the
Kelterhalle, where grapes once fermented.

CHURCHES
In the Altstadt, the satisfyingly symmetrical
Neumünster (☯ 7am-6pm) stands on the site
where the ill-fated missionaries met their
maker. The baroque interior has busts of
the three martyrs (the three Irish missionaries – Kilian, Colonan and Totnan) on
the high altar and the tomb of St Kilian in
the crypt. The north exit leads to the lovely
Lusamgärtlein with the grave of Walther von
der Vogelweide, one of Germany's most famous minstrels. Even today wreaths of flowers are regularly laid on his tomb.

On the same square is the **Dom St Kilian** (St
Kilian Cathedral), rebuilt in a hotchpotch
of modern, baroque and Romanesque styles
after significant damage during WWII. Of
note are the prince-bishops' tombstones on
the pillars; the two in red marble in the left
aisle are by Riemenschneider.

MUSEUM AM DOM & DOMSCHATZ
Housed in a beautiful building by the cathedral, the **Museum am Dom** (☎ 386 261;
Domerschulstrasse 2; adult/concession €3.50/2.50, combined
ticket with Domschatz €4.50; ☯ 10am-6pm Apr-Oct, 10am-
5pm Nov-Mar, closed Mon) displays collections of
modern art on Christian themes. Works of
international renown by Joseph Beuys, Otto
Dix and Käthe Kollwitz are on display, as
well as masterpieces of the Romantic, Gothic
and baroque periods.

At the Würzburger **Domschatz** (Cathedral
Treasury; ☎ 3856 5600; Plattnerstrasse; adult/student
€2/1.50; ☯ 2-5pm Tue-Sun) you can wander
through a rich display of church artefacts
from the 11th century to the present.

MUSEUM IM KULTURSPEICHER

In a born-again historic granary right on the Main River you'll find the **Museum im Kulturspeicher** (☎ 322 250; Veitshöchheimer Strasse 5; adult/concession €3.50/2; ⏲ 1-6pm Tue, 11am-6pm Wed, 11am-7pm Thu, 11am-6pm Fri-Sun). This fascinating museum has choice artworks from the 19th to the 21st centuries, with an emphasis on German Impressionism, neo-realism and contemporary art. It also houses the post-1945 constructivist works of the Peter C Ruppert Collection, a challenging assembly of computer art, sculpture, paintings and photographs.

RÖNTGEN GEDÄCHTNISSTÄTTE

Würzburg's most famous modern scion is Wilhelm Conrad Röntgen, discoverer of the X-ray. The **Röntgen Gedächtnisstätte** (Röntgen Museum; ☎ 351 1103; Röntgenring 8; admission free; ⏲ 8am-4pm Mon-Thu, 8am-3pm Fri) is a tribute to his life and work.

Tours

Schiffstouristik Kurth & Schiebe (☎ 585 73; www.schiffstouristik.de; €9) offers quick river cruises (40 minutes) to the wine-growing town of Veitshöchheim.

The tourist office runs 1½-hour English-language **guided tours** (adult/child €6/4; ⏲ 1pm Fri & Sat May-Oct) departing from the Falkenhaus. You can also borrow an audioguide with a recorded tour (€5) of all the major sights.

Würzburg is the centre of the Franconian wine industry, and you can sample some of the region's finest vintages on tours of these historic wine cellars (reservations are advised):

Bürgerspital Weingut (☎ 350 3403; Theaterstrasse 19; tours €6; ⏲ tours 2pm Sat Mar-Oct) At the Bürgerspital Weinstuben; includes a small bottle of wine.

Weingut Juliusspital (☎ 393 1400; Juliuspromenade 19; tours €6-10; ⏲ tours in German 5pm Fri & Sat Apr-Dec) In the splendid complex with the Juliusspital wine bar.

Festivals & Events

Africa-Festival Europe's biggest festival of black music (tickets from the tourist office), held in late May and/or early June.

Hoffest am Stein Wine and music festival held in mid-July at the Weingut am Stein (☎ 258 08), 10 minutes' walk north of the Hauptbahnhof.

Mozart Festival (☎ tickets 372 336) Germany's oldest Mozart festival takes place at the Residenz in late May/early June.

Sleeping

Achieving REM sleep in Würzburg comes slightly cheaper than in other Bavarian cities.

BUDGET

Camping Kanu Club (☎ 725 36; Mergentheimer Strasse 13b; per person/tent €3/2.50) The closest camp site to the town centre. Take tram 3 or 5 to the Judenbühlweg stop, which is on its doorstep.

our pick **Babelfish** (☎ 304 0430; www.babelfish-hostel.de; Haugerring 2; dm €16-20, s/d €40/58; ⊠ 💻 📶) Recently moved to flashy premises opposite the train station, the spanking new Babelfish has 74 beds spread over two floors, a sunny rooftop terrace, 24-hour reception, wheelchair-friendly facilities and little extras like card keys and a laundry room. The name comes from a creature in Douglas Adams' novel *The Hitchhiker's Guide to the Galaxy*.

DJH hostel (☎ 425 90; www.wuerzburg.jugendherberge.de; Burkarderstrasse 46; dm under/over 27yr €21.60/25.60) At the foot of the fortress, this well-equipped, wheelchair-friendly hostel has room for 238 snoozers in three- to eight-bed dorms. Take tram 3 or 5 to Sanderring, then it's a five-minute walk north along the river.

Pension Spehnkuch (☎ 547 52; www.pension-spehnkuch.de; Röntgenring 7; s €31-33, d €56-62, tr €78-81; ⊠) More like a home stay with a German family than a *Pension*, this delightful apartment guesthouse has cosy rooms, a sunny breakfast parlour and a genuinely friendly welcome. Bathrooms are shared.

MIDRANGE & TOP END

Hotel Dortmunder Hof (☎ 561 63; www.dortmunder-hof.de; Innerer Graben 22; s €42-65, d €76-100; 📶) In a handy position two blocks from the Markt, this bike-friendly hotel occupies a brightly renovated building with spotless, en suite rooms including cable TV. Parking can be arranged close by, and there's live music in the cellar bar.

Hotel zum Winzermännle (☎ 541 56; www.winzermaennle.de; Domstrasse 32; s €62-75, d €92-105) This former winery was rebuilt in its original style after the war by the same charming family. Rooms range from broom cupboards to palatial but all are tastefully furnished. It's right in the pedestrian zone with parking nearby.

Hotel Residence (☎ 535 46; www.wuerzburg-hotel.de; Juliuspromenade 1; s €67-78, d €88-110; P) With comely dormer windows and royal-hued interiors, this charming hotel, replete with all the trimmings, is a short walk from the river, congress centre and the city's main sights.

Hotel Rebstock (☎ 309 30; www.rebstock.com; Neubaustrasse 7; s €83-119, d €133-169; P) Class, hospitality and a touch of nostalgia are the characteristics of this elegant hotel, one of Würzburg's best snooze temples. Meticulously restored, this rococo mansion has superbly furnished rooms and amenities galore.

Eating

For a town of its size, Würzburg has a bewildering array of enticing pubs, beer gardens, cafes and restaurants, with plenty of student hang-outs among them.

Starback (Kaiserstrasse 33; snacks from €0.69) No German-language skills are required to put together a budget breakfast or lunch at this brilliant self-service bakery. Other branches are found at Spiegelstrasse 1 and Augustinerstrasse 1.

Natur-Feinkostladen (Sanderstrasse 2a; dishes from €3) Come here for wholesome snacks and healthy fare, such as grain burgers; this place also runs the adjacent specialist grocery.

Uni-Café (☎ 156 72; Neubaustrasse 2; snacks €3-8) This is a hugely popular student hang-out on the lively Neubaustrasse strip. It has two floors of chilled-out clientele who come for the cheap snacks, cool music and – most of all – some fun.

our pick **Bürgerspital Weinstuben** (☎ 352 880; Theaterstrasse 19; mains €5-10) The cosy nooks of this labyrinthine medieval place are among Würzburg's most popular eating and drinking spots. Choose from a broad selection of Franconian wines and wonderful regional dishes, including *Mostsuppe*, a tasty wine soup.

Alte Mainmühle (☎ 167 77; Mainkai 1; mains €6-25) Accessed straight from the old bridge, tourists and locals alike cram onto the double-decker terrace suspended above the Main River to savour modern twists on old Franconian favourites. Summer alfresco dining is accompanied by pretty views of the Festung Marienberg; in winter retreat to the snug timber dining room.

Backöfele (☎ 590 59; Ursulinergasse 2; mains €7-20) For romantic atmosphere, it's hard to beat this rustic restaurant set around a pretty courtyard. The menu features innovative twists on traditional game, steak and fish dishes. Marbled slabs of meat are grilled over the wood oven.

Juliusspital (☎ 540 80; Juliuspromenade 19; mains €10-23) This attractive *Weinstube* (traditional wine bar) features fabulous Franconian delicacies. The Juliusspital was first founded as a hospital in 1576 by Julius Echter von Mespelbrunn, whose name pops up everywhere in Würzburg. The basement has a cave-like bakery with a clutch of tables.

Drinking & Entertainment

For more options, grab a copy of the monthly listing magazine *Frizz* (in German).

our pick **Kult** (☎ 531 43; Landwehrstrasse 10; ☼ 9am-late Mon-Fri, 10am-late Sat & Sun) Enjoy a tailor-made breakfast, munch on cheap lunch or party to the wee hours at Würzburg's hippest cafe. The unpretentious interior with its salvaged tables and old beige benches hosts regular fancy-dress parties, table-football tournaments and other off-beat events. DJs take over at weekends.

Schützenhof beer garden (☎ 724 22; Mainleitenweg 48) For a drink with sun and a bucolic view, head for this delightful beer garden about 500m south of the Käppele chapel on the east bank of the Main. The main ingredients are ultra-fresh – listen for the farmyard animals protesting to the rear – and the beer (try the Balthasar Neumann) is served with a donkey-shaped *Brezel* (pretzel).

Pleicher Hof (☎ 465 2510; Pleichertorstrasse 30; ☼ cafe 5pm-1am Tue-Sat, 6pm-1am Sun, bar 9.30pm-4am Wed, Fri & Sat) This cool cafe spreads Med-style vibes during the evening, with light meals and coffees being the favoured fare. In the cellar music bar the agenda goes for the jugular, with heavy garage, funk and amped-up student parties.

MUCK (☎ 465 1144; Sanderstrasse 29) This fun place has loads of board games to while away the hours. One of the earliest openers in town, and serving a mean breakfast from 7am, the cafe morphs into something of an informal party after nightfall.

Standard (☎ 465 1144; Oberthürstrasse 11a) Beneath a corrugated-iron ceiling and stainless-steel fans are newspaper racks, art and soulful jazz, with focaccias and pasta on the menu. Downstairs there's a second, dimly lit bar where bands and DJs perform a couple of times a week.

Getting There & Away

There are frequent train connections to Frankfurt (€27, one hour), Bamberg (€17.60, one hour) and Nuremberg (from €17.80, one hour). Travelling to Rothenburg ob der Tauber (€11.30, 1¼ hours) requires a change in Steinach.

The Romantic Road Europabus stops at the main bus station next to the Hauptbahnhof.

Getting Around

Würzburg is manageable on foot, but you can also take buses and trams for €1.10 (for short journeys) or €2.10 (for regular journeys); the cheaper ticket will do for trips in town. Day passes are €4.30; passes bought on a Saturday can also be used on Sunday. The most useful service is bus 9 which shuttles between the Residenz and the Festung Marienberg. For a taxi call ☎ 194 10.

For bicycle hire head to **Ludwig Köner** (☎ 523 40; Bronnbachergasse 3; bikes per day €10).

ASCHAFFENBURG
☎ 06021 / pop 69,000

With its cobbled lanes and half-timbered houses, this semi-charming town has just enough for a worthwhile trip from Würzburg or Frankfurt. In style terms it's more Hessian than Bavarian, but King Ludwig II was so chuffed with the mild climate he dubbed Aschaffenburg the 'Bavarian Nice'.

The **tourist office** (☎ 395 800; www.info-aschaffenburg.de; Schlossplatz 1; ☼ 9am-5pm Mon-Fri, 10am-1pm Sat) will put you on the right path for Aschaffenburg's most spectacular draw, the magnificent Renaissance **Schloss Johannisburg**. Once the summer residence of the Mainz archbishops, today it's home to the **Schlossmuseum** (☎ 386 570; Schlossplatz 4; adult/concession €4/3, combined ticket with Pompejanum €6/5; ☼ 9am-6pm Tue-Sun Apr-Sep, 10am-4pm Tue-Sun Nov-Mar). The modest interior has the usual oil paintings and period furniture, but the unlikely highlight is a collection of architectural cork models depicting landmarks from ancient Rome.

Behind the beautiful palace garden stands the **Pompejanum** (☎ 386 570; adult/child €4/free; ☼ 9am-6pm Tue-Sun Apr-Sep). Built for folly fan King Ludwig I, this replica of a Pompeii villa comes complete with frescoes, mosaics and Roman antiquities.

From there, follow Schlossgasse into the Altstadt. On Stiftsplatz you'll come upon the **Stiftskirche**. This church has its origins in the 10th century, but is now an oddly skewed but impressive mix of Romanesque, Gothic and baroque styles. The attached **Stiftsmuseum** (☎ 330 463; adult/concession €2.50/1.50; ☼ 11am-5pm Tue-Sun) is home to some intriguing relics and paintings.

Three kilometres west of town lies the **Park Schönbusch**, a shady 18th-century expanse scattered with ornamental ponds and follies, and the **Schlösschen** (☎ 386 570; Kleine Schönbuschallee 1; tours adult/concession €3/2; ☼ 9am-6pm Tue-Sun Apr-Sep), a country retreat of the archbishops. Take bus 3 from the train station.

Filling Franconian fare can be sourced at the tiny **Schlossgass' 16** (☎ 123 13; Schlossgasse 28; mains €5-16) wine tavern, and **Schlappeseppel** (☎ 156 46; Schlossgasse 14; mains €5-13), a long-serving pub pulling pints of local ale.

Trains to and from Würzburg (€21.50, 40 minutes) and Frankfurt (€14, 30 minutes) operate at least hourly. The A3 runs right past town.

ROTHENBURG OB DER TAUBER
☎ 09861 / pop 11,200

A well-polished gem from the Middle Ages, Rothenburg ob der Tauber (meaning 'above the Tauber River') is the main tourist stop along the Romantic Road. With its web of cobbled lanes, higgledy-piggledy houses and towered walls, the town is impossibly charming. Preservation orders here are the strictest in Germany – and at times it feels like a medieval theme park – but all's forgiven in the evenings, when the yellow lamplight casts its spell long after the last tour buses have left.

Orientation

The Hauptbahnhof is a 10-minute walk east of the Altstadt along Ansbacher Strasse. The main shopping drag is Schmiedgasse, which runs south to Plönlein, a scenic fork in the road anchored by a half-timbered ochre cottage and gurgling fountain that's become Rothenburg's unofficial emblem.

Information

Dresdner Bank (Galgengasse 23)

Interplay (☎ 935 599; Milchmarkt 3; per hr €3; ☼ 8am-1am) Internet access.

Post office Altstadt (Rödergasse 11); Bahnhof (Zentro mall, Bahnhofstrasse 15)

Tourist office (☎ 404 800; www.rothenburg.de; Marktplatz 2; ☼ 9am-7pm Mon-Fri, 10am-5pm Sat & Sun May-Oct, 9am-5pm Mon-Fri, 10am-1pm Sat Nov-Apr) Out-of-hours electronic room-booking board in the foyer, plus free internet.

Volksbank (Marktplatz) To the right of the tourist office.

Wäscherei Then (☎ 2775; Johannitergasse 9; per load €3.50) Laundry.

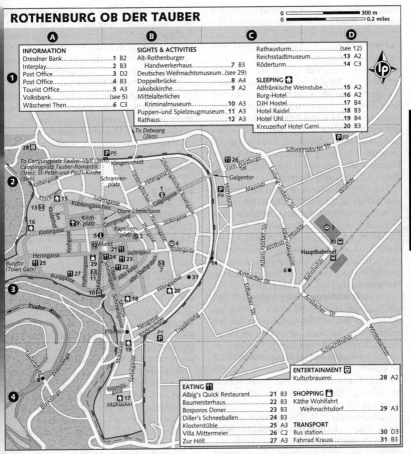

ROTHENBURG OB DER TAUBER

INFORMATION		
Dresdner Bank	1	B2
Interplay	2	B3
Post Office	3	D2
Post Office	4	B3
Tourist Office	5	A3
Volksbank	(see 5)	
Wäscherei Then	6	C3

SIGHTS & ACTIVITIES		
Alt-Rothenburger		
Handwerkerhaus	7	B3
Deutsches Weihnachtsmuseum	(see 29)	
Doppelbrücke	8	A4
Jakobskirche	9	A2
Mittelalterliches		
Kriminalmuseum	10	A3
Puppen- und Spielzeugmuseum	11	A3
Rathaus	12	A3

Rathausturm	(see 12)	
Reichsstadtmuseum	13	A2
Röderturm	14	C3
SLEEPING		
Altfränkische Weinstube	15	A2
Burg-Hotel	16	A2
DJH Hostel	17	B4
Hotel Raidel	18	B3
Hotel Uhl	19	B4
Kreuzerhof Hotel Garni	20	B3

EATING		
Albig's Quick Restaurant	21	B3
Baumeisterhaus	22	B3
Bosporos Doner	23	B3
Diller's Schneeballen	24	B3
Klosterstüble	25	A3
Villa Mittermeier	26	C2
Zur Höll	27	A3

SHOPPING		
Käthe Wohlfahrt		
Weihnachtsdorf	29	A3
TRANSPORT		
Bus station	30	D3
Fahrrad Krauss	31	B3

ENTERTAINMENT		
Kulturbrauerei	28	A2

BAVARIA

Sights

The **Rathaus** on the Markt was begun in Gothic style in the 14th century, and completed during the Renaissance. Climb the 220 steps to the viewing platform of the **Rathausturm** (adult/concession €2/0.50; 9.30am-12.30pm & 1-5pm Apr-Oct & Dec, noon-3pm Nov & Jan-Mar) to be rewarded with widescreen views of the Tauber.

North of the Marktplatz, the recently sandblasted **Jakobskirche** (Klingengasse 1; adult/concession €2/0.50, during services free; 9am-5.15pm Apr-Oct, 10am-noon & 2-4pm Nov & Jan-Mar, 10am-4.45pm Dec) is Rothenburg's major place of pilgrimage. The main draw is the carved **Heilig Blut Altar** (Holy Blood Altar), set on a raised platform at the western end of the nave. It depicts the Last Supper with Judas, unusually, at the cen-

tre, receiving bread from Christ. The rock crystal inside is said to contain a drop of Christ's blood.

Brutal implements of torture and punishment from medieval times are on display at the curiously fascinating **Mittelalterliches Kriminalmuseum** (Medieval Crime Museum; 5359; Burggasse 3; adult/concession €3.80/2.20; 11am-5pm Apr, 10am-6pm May-Oct, 2-4pm Nov, Jan & Feb, 1-4pm Dec). Displays include chastity belts, masks of disgrace for gossips, a cage for errant bakers, a neck brace for quarrelsome women and a beer-barrel pen for drunks. Visitors gain gruesome amusement from having their photo taken in the stocks outside.

Another popular activity is the 2.5km circular walk around the unbroken ring of the town walls. There are good views from the eastern tower, the **Röderturm** (Rödergasse; adult/child €1.50/1; ⊙ 9am-5pm), though it's staffed by volunteers and often closed. For the most impressive views, though, go to the west side of town, where a sweeping view of the Tauber Valley includes the **Doppelbrücke**, a double-decker bridge. Also visible is the head of a trail that leads down the valley and over to the lovely Romanesque **St-Peter-und-Pauls-Kirche** (☎ 5524; Detwang; adult/child €1/0.50; ⊙ 8.30am-noon & 1.30-5pm Apr-Oct, 10am-noon & 2-4pm Nov-Mar, closed Mon) which contains a stunning Riemenschneider altar. There's a beer garden (Unter den Linden) about halfway along the trail.

The city's showcase of local art, culture and history is the **Reichsstadtmuseum** (Imperial City Museum; ☎ 939 043; Klosterhof 5; adult/child €3.50/2; ⊙ 9.30am-5.30pm Apr-Oct, 1-4pm Nov-Mar), which is housed in a former convent. Highlights include the superb *Rothenburger Passion* (1494) by Martinus Schwarz, and the convent rooms themselves, including a 14th-century kitchen. The **gardens** are ideal for a quiet stroll.

The **Alt-Rothenburger Handwerkerhaus** (☎ 5810; Alter Stadtgraben 26; adult/child €2.50/1; ⊙ 11am-5pm Mon-Fri, 10am-5pm Sat & Sun Apr-Oct, 2-4pm daily Dec) reconstructs the working and social life of Rothenburg's medieval citizens. For the nostalgic, the **Puppen-und Spielzeugmuseum** (Doll & Toy Museum; ☎ 7330; Hofbronnengasse 13; adult/child €4/2.50; ⊙ 9.30am-6pm Mar-Dec, 11am-5pm Jan-Feb) has an amazing collection of doll's houses, teddy bears and toy carousels.

Käthe Wohlfahrt Weihnachtsdorf (see opposite) houses the **Deutsches Weihnachtsmuseum** (German Christmas Museum; ☎ 409 365; adult/child €4/2; ⊙ 10am-5.30pm), which traces the development of various Yuletide customs.

Tours

The tourist office runs 90-minute walking tours (€6; in English) at 2pm from April to October. Every evening a lantern-toting *Nachtwächter* dressed in traditional costume leads an entertaining tour of the Altstadt. English tours (€6) meet at the Rathaus at 8pm.

Festivals & Events

The **Historisches Festspiel 'Der Meistertrunk'** (see boxed text, opposite) takes place each year on Whitsuntide, with parades, dances and a medieval market. The highlight, though, is the re-enactment of the mythical Meistertrunk story.

The Meistertrunk play itself is performed three more times: once during the **Reichsstadt-Festtage** in early September, when the entire city's history is re-enacted in the streets, and twice during the Rothenburger Herbst, an autumn celebration in October.

The **Historischer Schäfertanz** (Historical Shepherds' Dance), featuring colourfully dressed couples, takes places on Marktplatz several times between April and October.

Rothenburg's **Christmas market** is one of the most romantic in Germany. It takes place each year around the central Marktplatz from late November until 23 December.

Sleeping

DJH hostel (☎ 941 60; www.rothenburg.jugend herberge.de; Mühlacker 1; dm under/over 27yr €20/24; ▯) Rothenburg's hostel is housed in two enormous old buildings in the south of town. It's agreeably renovated, extremely well equipped and very popular, so book in advance.

our pick **Hotel Raidel** (☎ 3115; www.romanticroad .com/raidel; Wenggasse 3; s with/without bathroom €39/24, d €49/59; Ⓟ) With 500-year-old exposed beams studded with wooden nails, antiques throughout and a welcoming owner, as well as musical instruments for the guests to play, this is the place to check in if you're craving some genuine romance on the Romantic Road.

Hotel Uhl (☎ 4895; www.hotel-uhl.de; Plönlein 8; s €36-59, d €59-79; Ⓟ ⓢ) A quiet family-run hotel with well-appointed, if slightly overfurnished, rooms. The downstairs cafe does a mean *Schneeball* (sweetish dough strip ravelled into a ball and dipped in cinnamon and sugar).

Kreuzerhof Hotel Garni (☎ 3424; www.kreuzerhof -rothenburg.de; Millergasse 4-6; s €40, d €55-68; Ⓟ) Away from the tourist swarms, this quiet family-run place has neat rooms with antique touches in a medieval town house and annexe. There's free tea and coffee and the generous breakfast is a great set-up for the day.

Altfränkische Weinstube (☎ 6404; www.romantic road.com/altfraenkische-weinstube; Am Klosterhof 7; s €58, d €64-75) Hiding in a quiet side street near the Reichsstadtmuseum, this enchantingly characterful inn has atmosphere-laden rooms, all with bathtubs and most with four-poster or canopied beds. The restaurant (open for dinner only) serves up sound regional fare with a dollop of medieval cheer.

Burg-Hotel (☎ 948 90; www.burghotel.rothenburg.de; Klostergasse 1-3; r €100-170; Ⓟ ▯) The best views in

---

DRINK & YE SHALL BE FREE

In 1631 the Thirty Years War – pitching Catholics against Protestants – reached the gates of Rothenburg ob der Tauber. Catholic General Tilly and 60,000 of his troops besieged the Protestant market town and demanded its surrender. The town resisted but couldn't stave off the onslaught of marauding soldiers, and the mayor and other town dignitaries were captured and sentenced to death.

And that's pretty much where the story ends and the legend begins. As the tale goes, Rothenburg's town council tried to sate Tilly's bloodthirstiness by presenting him with a mug of wine fit for a giant. Tilly, after taking a sip or two, presented the men with an unusual challenge, saying: 'If one of you has the courage to step forward and down this mug of wine in one gulp, then I shall spare the town and the lives of the councilmen!' Mayor Georg Nusch accepted – and succeeded! And that's why you can still wander though Rothenburg's wonderful medieval lanes today.

It's pretty much accepted that Tilly was really placated with hard cash. Nevertheless, local poet Adam Hörber couldn't resist turning the tale of the *Meistertrunk* into a play, which since 1881 has been performed every Whitsuntide (Pentecost), the seventh Sunday after Easter. It's also re-enacted several times daily by the clock figures on the tourist office building.

---

town are from this charming 15-room hotel, built right into the town fortifications. All rooms have private sitting areas, and there's an elegant guest lounge with an antique baby grand piano.

In the suburb of Detwang, about 2km north of the Altstadt by car (or a pleasant 3km walk along the Tauber River), you'll find two camping grounds situated in an idyllic natural setting. **Campingplatz Tauber-Idyll** (☎ 3177; www .rothenburg.de/tauberidyll; Detwang 28) and **Campingplatz Tauber-Romantik** (☎ 6191; www.camping-tauber romantik.de; Detwang 39) both charge around €5.50 per person and €5 for a tent, and open Easter to late October.

Eating

Rothenburg's most obvious speciality is *Schneeballen*. Some 23 different types are produced at **Diller's Schneeballen** (☎ 938 010; Hofbronnengasse 16), though a more limited range is available all over town.

Zur Höll (☎ 4229; Burggasse 8; dishes €6-18) This medieval wine tavern, with an appreciation for slow food, is in the town's oldest original building, dating back to the year 900. The menu of regional specialities is limited but refined, though it's the wine that people really come for.

Baumeisterhaus (☎ 947 00; Obere Schmiedgasse 3; mains €9-16) This traditional German inn is one of the town's most atmospheric, and that's saying something. The woody dining area is set around a beautiful vine-clad courtyard and bristles with old hunting relics. The daily menu has a wealth of fine traditional fare.

Klosterstüble (☎ 8890; Heringsbronnengasse 5; mains €11-18) One dining room is a cosy hunting lodge, the other a classy stone affair at this first-rate hotel-restaurant. The Italian mains, veal goulash, and Franconian *Spätzle* (noodles) are owner cooked and complemented by a good selection of Frankish wines. The rooms upstairs are of a similarly high standard.

Villa Mittermeier (☎ 945 40; Vorm Würzburger Tor; mains €18-28) The kitchen dynamos at this classy establishment serve top-notch Michelin-starred cuisine in five settings, including a black-and-white tiled 'Temple', an alfresco terrace and a barrel-shaped wine cellar. The artistic chefs rely on locally harvested produce, and the wine list (400-plus varieties) is probably Franconia's best.

Also recommended:
Albig's Quick Restaurant (Hafengasse 3; dishes €2-7) Central European fast food, Rothenburg style.
Bosporus Doner (☎ 934 716; Hafengasse 2; dishes €3-8) For delicious kebabs and Middle Eastern goodies.

Entertainment
Kulturbrauerei (☎ 919 26; Nuschweg 2; ☯ 2-8pm Fri-Sun) Based in a historic old brewery with faux turrets, and staging anything and everything from cutting-edge art exhibits to jazz and indie pop concerts.

Shopping
Käthe Wohlfahrt Weihnachtsdorf (☎ 4090; Herrngasse 1) With its mind-boggling assortment of Yuletide decorations and ornaments, this shop lets you celebrate Christmas every day of the year (to go with the snowballs). Many

of the items are handcrafted with amazing skill and imagination, and prices are accordingly high.

Getting There & Away

You can go anywhere by train from Rothenburg, as long as it's Steinach. Change here for services to Würzburg (€11.30, one hour). Travel to and from Munich (from €35, three hours) can involve up to three different trains. The Europabus stops in the main bus park at the Hauptbahnhof and on the more central Schrannenplatz. The A7 runs right past town.

Getting Around

The city has five car parks right outside the walls. The town centre is closed to nonresident vehicles from 11am to 4pm and 7pm to 5am weekdays, and all day at weekends; hotel guests are exempt.

Some hotels have bicycle hire, or try **Fahrrad Krauss** (☎ 3495; Wenggasse 42; per half-day/day €5/10). Clamber aboard a horse-drawn carriage at the Markt or hail one down in the street; rides of 25 to 30 minutes cost about €6 per person, but it's worth haggling. Call ☎ 2066 for taxis.

DINKELSBÜHL

☎ 09851 / pop 12,000

Some 40km south of Rothenburg, immaculately preserved Dinkelsbühl proudly traces its roots to a royal residence founded by Carolingian kings in the 8th century. Saved from destruction in the Thirty Years War and ignored by WWII bombers, this is arguably the Romantic Road's quaintest and most authentically medieval halt. For a good overall impression of the town, walk along the fortified walls with their 18 towers and four gates.

Orientation & Information

The Altstadt is five minutes' walk west of the Busbahnhof (bus station), via the town gate called the Wörnitzer Tor. The **tourist office** (☎ 902 440; www.dinkelsbuehl.de; Altrathausplatz 14; ☺ 9am-6pm Mon-Fri, 10am-5pm Sat & Sun Apr-Oct, 10am-5pm daily Nov-Mar) recently moved to the new Haus der Geschichte. Dinkelsbühl is also home to the central **Romantic Road tourist office** (☎ 551 387; Segringer Strasse 19; ☺ 9am-5pm Mon-Thu 9am-1pm Fri). The post office and police station are next to the bus station.

Sights

Near the Wörnitzer Tor, Dinkelsbühl's history comes under the microscope at the new **Haus der Geschichte** (History House; ☎ 902 440; Altrathausplatz 14; adult/child €4/2; ☺ 9am-6pm Mon-Fri, 10am-5pm Sat & Sun May-Oct, 10am-5pm daily Nov-Apr) which occupies the old town hall. There's an interesting section on the Thirty Years War and a gallery with paintings depicting Dinkelsbühl at the turn of the century.

Continue into the historical centre to find the **Weinmarkt**, the main square lined with a row of splendid Renaissance mansions. The corner building is the step-gabled **Ratsherrntrinkstube**, the erstwhile weigh house which later hosted important guests such as Emperor Karl V and King Gustav Adolf of Sweden.

Standing sentry over Weinmarkt is **Münster St Georg**, one of southern Germany's purest late-Gothic hall churches. Rather austere from the outside, the interior stuns with an incredible fan-vaulted ceiling. A curiosity is the **Pretzl Window** donated by the bakers' guild, in the upper section of the last window in the right aisle.

Following Dr-Martin-Luther-Strasse north past the Schranne, you'll reach the **Spitalanlage**. Founded in 1280 as a hospital, this is now a seniors' residence and home to a gallery with changing temporary shows.

Just outside the western town gate, the **Museum of the 3rd Dimension** (☎ 6336; Nördlinger Tor; adult/concession €9/7; ☺ 10am-6pm Apr-Oct, 11am-4pm Sat & Sun Nov-Mar) has three floors of holographic images, stereoscopes and 3-D imagery. The you-must-be-kidding admission includes a pair of red-green-tinted 3-D specs.

Festivals & Events

In the third week of July, the 10-day **Kinderzeche** (Children's Festival; www.kinderzeche.de) celebrates how, during the Thirty Years War, the town's children persuaded the invading Swedish troops to spare Dinkelsbühl from a ransacking. The festivities include a pageant, re-enactments in the festival hall, lots of music and other merriment.

Sleeping & Eating

The tourist office can help find private rooms from €30.

Campingpark 'Romantische Strasse' (☎ 7817; www.campingpark-dinkelsbuehl.de; Kobeltsmühle 6; per tent/person €6.15/4.10) This camping ground is set on the shores of a swimmable lake 1.5km northeast of Wörnitzer Tor.

DJH hostel (☎ 9509; www.dinkelsbuehl.jugend herberge.de; Koppengasse 10; dm €17.70; Ⓨ closed Nov-Feb) Dinkelsbühl's hostel in the western Altstadt occupies a beautifully restored 15th-century granary with doll's house qualities.

Gasthof Goldenes Lamm (☎ 2267; www.goldenes.de; Lange Gasse 26-28; s €38-54, d €64-86) This stress-free family-run oasis has pleasant rooms at the top of a creaky staircase, and a funky rooftop garden deck with plump sofas. The attached restaurant plates up Franconian-Swabian specialities, including a vegie selection.

our pick Dinkelsbühler Kunststuben (☎ 6750; www.kunst-stuben.de; Segringer Strasse 52; s €50, d €55-80; ☒) Personal attention and charm by the bucketload make this one of the best guesthouses on the entire Romantic Road. Furniture (including the four-posters) is all handmade by Voglauer, there's a pretty breakfast room and the cosy library is perfect for curling up in with a good read. The artisan owner will show his Asia travel films if enough guests are interested.

Deutsches Haus (☎ 6058; www.deutsches-haus-dkb.de; Weinmarkt 3; s €79-90, d €129; ☎) This historic building plays games with visitors, thanks to an illusion created by its 13th-century architects: it looks straight but is actually off-kilter. Inside, rooms are superbly equipped with a baroque flourish, and the formal restaurant serves game and fish prepared according to age-old recipes.

Haus Appelberg (☎ 582 838; Nördlinger Strasse 40; dishes €5-10; Ⓨ 6pm-midnight Tue-Sat) At Dinkelsbühl's best-kept dining secret, owners double up as cooks to keep tables supplied with traditional dishes such as local carp, Franconian sausages and *Maultaschen* (pork and spinach ravioli). On warm days swap the rustic interior for the secluded terrace, a fine spot for some evening idling over a local Hauf beer or a Franconian white.

Weib's Brauhaus (☎ 579 490; Untere Schmiedgasse 13; dishes €5-12; Ⓨ closed Tue) A female brew master presides over the copper vats at this lively restaurant-pub. The traditional menu includes the popular *Weib's Töpfle* (woman's pot) of pork and deep-fried mashed potatoes and, of course, the house brew.

Getting There & Away
Despite a railway line cutting through the town, Dinkelsbühl is not served by passenger trains. Regional buses to and from Nördlingen (€6.30, 45 minutes) stop at the Busbahnhof. Reaching Rothenburg (€8.90, two hours) is a real test of patience without your own car. Change from bus 805 to a train in Ansbach, then change trains in Steinach. The Europabus stops right in the Altstadt at Schweinemarkt.

NÖRDLINGEN
☎ 09081 / pop 20,100
Charmingly medieval, Nördlingen sees fewer tourists than its better known neighbours and manages to retain an air of authenticity, which is a relief after some of the Romantic Road's worst excesses. The town lies within the Ries Basin, a massive impact crater gouged out by a meteorite more than 15 million years ago. The crater – some 25km in diameter – is one of the best preserved on earth, and has been declared a special 'geopark'. Nördlingen's 14th-century walls, all original, mimic the crater's rim and are almost perfectly circular.

Incidentally, if you've seen the 1970s film *Willy Wonka and the Chocolate Factory*, you've already looked down upon Nördlingen from a glass lift.

Orientation & Information
Imagine Nördlingen as a cartwheel, with the St Georgskirche as the hub, five main roads radiating out as the spokes, and the ring of covered walls, including 12 completely intact gates, as the wheel's rim. You can circumnavigate the entire town in around an hour by taking the sentry walk (free) on top of the walls all the way. The Hauptbahnhof and main post office are outside the walls to the southeast.

Geopark Ries Information Centre (☎ 273 8200; www.geopark-ries.de; Vordere Gerbergasse 3; Ⓨ 10am-4.30pm Tue-Sun) Has a free exhibition on the crater.

Tourist office (☎ 841 16; www.noerdlingen.de; Marktplatz 2; Ⓨ 10am-6pm Mon-Thu, 10am-4.30pm Fri, 10am-2pm Sat Easter-early Nov, 10am-2pm Sun May-Sep, Mon-Fri only mid-Nov–Easter) Has an out-of-hours foyer with web access and brochures.

Sights
ST GEORGSKIRCHE
The massive late-Gothic **St Georgskirche** is one of the largest churches in southern Germany. Its elaborate baroque organ and the intricate pulpit (1499) are worth a look, but the real draw is the 90m **Daniel Tower** (adult/concession €2/1.40; Ⓨ 9am-6pm Apr-Jun, Sep & Oct, 9am-7pm Jul & Aug, 9am-5pm Nov-Mar). Only from the top can you

appreciate Nördlingen's shape and the gentle landscape of the Ries crater.

RIESKRATER MUSEUM

Situated in an ancient barn, the **Rieskrater Museum** (☎ 273 8220; Eugene-Shoemaker-Platz 1; adult/child €4/1.50; ☯ 10am-4.30pm Tue-Sun) explores the formation of meteorite craters and the consequences of such violent collisions with Earth. Rocks, including a genuine moon rock (on permanent loan from NASA), fossils and other geological displays shed light on the mystery of meteors.

BAYERISCHES EISENBAHNMUSEUM

One of Germany's largest collections of classic steam trains can be found at the **Bayerisches Eisenbahnmuseum** (Bavarian Railway Museum; ☎ 09083-340; www.bayerisches-eisenbahnmuseum.de; Am Hohen Weg 6a; adult/child €5/2.50; ☯ noon-4pm Tue-Sat, 10am-5pm Sun May-Sep, Sat & Sun only Mar, Apr & Oct). Its 100 nostalgic vehicles range from sleek high-speed engines for transporting passengers to cute little railyard shunters. An old-time loco puffs its way to Dinkelsbühl (adult/child €18/12, two hours return) a few weekends in summer. To reach the museum, cross the footbridge at the southern end of the train station.

OTHER MUSEUMS

The **Stadtmuseum** (☎ 273 8230; Vordere Gerbergasse 1; adult/concession €4/1.50; ☯ 1.30am-4.30pm Tue-Sun Mar-early Nov) features costumes and displays on local history. More enlightening is the exhibit on the history of the old town walls and fortifications at the **Stadtmauermuseum** (☎ 9180; Löpsinger Torturm; adult/child €1.50/1; ☯ 10am-4.30pm Apr-Oct).

Festivals & Events

The largest annual celebration is the 14-day **Nördlinger Pfingstmesse** at Whitsuntide/Pentecost. It's an exhibition of regional traders, with a huge market featuring beer tents, food stalls and entertainment.

Sleeping & Eating

Hotel Altreuter (☎ 4319; www.hotel-altreuter.de; Marktplatz 11; s €35-45, d €48-64; ☒) Perched above a busy cafe and bakery, rooms here are of the could-be-anywhere type, but the location next to the Daniel Tower cannot be beaten. Bathrooms are private and the tasty breakfast is served down in the cafe.

Jugend & Familengästehaus (☎ 275 0575; www.jufa.at/noerdlingen; Bleichgraben 3a; s/d €48/67; ☒ ☐)

Located just outside the town walls, this shiny 185-bed hostel-hotel is spacious and clean-cut. There are two- to four-bed rooms, ideal for couples or families, and facilities include bicycle hire, a cafe with internet terminals and even a small cinema. Unless you are travelling with an entire handball team in tow, dorms are off limits to travellers, however hard you plead.

Kaiserhof Hotel Sonne (☎ 5067; Marktplatz 3; s €55-65, d €75-120; Ⓟ ☒) Nördlingen's top sleep has hosted a procession of emperors and their entourages since 1405. Rooms tastefully blend traditional charm with 21st-century comforts, and there's an atmospheric regional restaurant and cellar wine bar.

Café Radlos (☎ 5040; Löpsinger Strasse 8; mains €6-13; ☯ closed Tue) Nördlingen's hippest and most entertaining cafe serves international cuisine and some creative vegie options. Slinky jazz sets a mellow tone for surfing the net (€2 per 30 minutes) or just enjoying a drink in the beer garden.

Sixenbräu Stüble (☎ 3101; Bergerstrasse 17; mains €10-17; ☯ closed Mon) An attractive gabled town house near the Berger Tor houses this local institution, which has been plonking wet ones on the bar since 1545. The pan-Bavarian menu has heavy carnivorous leanings, and there's a beer garden for alfresco elbow bending.

Getting There & Away

Train journeys to and from Munich (€25, two hours) and Augsburg (€13.30, one hour) require a change in Donauwörth. The Europabus stops at the Rathaus. Regional VGN bus 501 goes to Dinkelsbühl (€6.30, 45 minutes).

AUGSBURG

☎ 0821 / pop 269,000

Bavaria's third-largest city is also one of Germany's oldest, founded by the stepchildren of Roman emperor Augustus over 2000 years ago. As an independent city state from the 13th century, Augsburg was free to raise its own taxes. Public coffers bulged on the proceeds of the textile trade, and banking families such as the Fuggers and the Welsers even lent money to kings and countries. However, from the 16th century religious strife and economic decline plagued the city. Augsburg finally joined the Kingdom of Bavaria in 1806.

Today this attractive city of spires and cobbles is an easy day trip from Munich or an engaging stop on the Romantic Road. It's also an alternative accommodation option during the Oktoberfest, though this secret got out long ago.

Orientation

The Hauptbahnhof is at the western end of Bahnhofstrasse, which runs into Fuggerstrasse at Königsplatz, the city's main bus transfer point. The heart of the Altstadt is Rathausplatz, reached on foot from Königsplatz up Annastrasse.

Information

Buchhandlung Rieger & Kranzfelder (☎ 517 880; Maximilianstrasse 36, Fugger Stadtpalast) Guides, maps and two shelves of English-language titles.

Fernweh (☎ 155 035; Dominikanergasse 10) STA Travel representative.

Internetcafé (☎ 319 5665; Bahnhofstrasse 29; per hr €2; ☼ 9am-10pm Mon-Sat, 11am-10pm Sun) Virtually Augsburg's only surviving internet cafe.

Post office (Hauptbahnhof)

Tourist office (☎ 502 070; www.augsburg-tourismus .de; Rathausplatz; ☼ 9am-6pm Mon-Fri, 10am-5pm Sat, 10am-2pm Sun Apr-Oct, 9am-5pm Mon-Fri, 10am-2pm Nov-Mar)

Sights

RATHAUSPLATZ

This square at the city's heart is dominated by the twin onion-dome spires of the Renaissance **Rathaus** (1615–20). Its roof is crowned by a 4m pine cone, Augsburg's emblem and an ancient fertility symbol. Inside, the star attraction is the meticulously restored **Goldener Saal** (Golden Hall; ☎ 349 6398; Rathausplatz; admission €2; ☼ 10am-6pm), the main meeting hall. It's a dazzling space canopied by a gilded and coffered ceiling, interspersed with frescoes.

For widescreen city views, climb the **Perlachturm** (Perlach Tower; Rathausplatz; adult/concession €1/0.50; ☼ 10am-6pm Apr-Nov, 2-6pm Fri-Sun Dec) next door to the Rathaus.

DOM MARIÄ HEIMSUCHUNG

North of Rathausplatz you'll find the cathedral, **Dom Mariä Heimsuchung** (Hoher Weg), which dates back to the 10th century. Architecturally it's a hotchpotch of addition on addition, including the instalment of bronze doors in the 14th century depicting Old Testament scenes. The oldest section is the crypt underneath the west choir, which features a Romanesque Madonna. Other treasures include medieval frescoes, the *Weingartner Altar* by Hans

Holbein the Elder, and – dating from the 12th century – the *Prophets' Windows* (depicting Daniel, Jonah, Hosea and Moses), some of the oldest stained-glass windows in Germany.

ST ANNA KIRCHE

Often regarded as the first Renaissance church in Germany, the rather plain-looking **St Anna Kirche** (Church of St Anna; Im Annahof 2) contains a bevy of treasures as well as the sumptuous **Fuggerkapelle**, where Jacob Fugger and his brothers lie buried, and the lavishly frescoed **Goldschmiedekapelle** (Goldsmiths' Chapel; 1420). The church played an important role during the Reformation. In 1518 Martin Luther, in town to defend his beliefs before the papal legate, stayed at what was then a Carmelite monastery. His rooms have been turned into the **Lutherstiege**, a small museum about the Reformation. The entire complex was under renovation at the time of writing.

FUGGEREI

Built to provide homes for poor Catholics, the **Fuggerei** (☎ 319 8810; adult/child €4/2; ☼ 8am-8pm Apr-Oct, 9am-6pm Nov-Mar) is one of the oldest welfare settlements in the world. Jacob Fugger financed the project in the 16th century and this town within a town is still home to 150 Catholic Augsburgers. Many of the 140 apartments have been modernised but the exterior is pretty much unchanged, with the original bell pulls beside each door. For centuries the rent has remained at one Rhenish Gilder (€1 today) per year, plus utilities and three daily prayers. Sound management means the Fugger Foundation is still going strong, despite the global economic downturn.

To see how Fuggerei residents lived in the past, visit the **Fuggereimuseum** (Mittlere Gasse 14; with Fuggerei admission free; ☼ 9am-8pm Mar-Oct, 9am-6pm Nov-Apr).

MAXIMILIANSTRASSE

Only the richest merchant families could afford to live on this grand boulevard, which is so wide you might mistake it in parts for a square. The former residence of Jakob Fugger, the **Fugger Stadtpalast**, is at No 36-38. It embraces the Damenhof (Ladies' Court), a gorgeous Italian Renaissance-style inner courtyard. A nearby rococo palace, the **Schaetzlerpalais** (☎ 324 4102; Maximilianstrasse 56; adult/ concession €7/5.50; ☼ 10am-8pm Tue, 10am-5pm Wed-Sun)

BAVARIA

was built for a wealthy banker between 1765 and 1770, and today houses the **Deutsche Barockgalerie** (German Baroque Gallery) and the **Staatsgalerie** (Bavarian State Gallery). The pièce de résistance is the 23m-long ballroom – a riot of carved decorations, stucco and mirrors, all topped off with a kinetic ceiling fresco.

OTHER SIGHTS

In a restored patrician's house (1546), **Maximilianmuseum** (☎ 324 4102; Philippine-Welser-Strasse 24; adult/child €7/5.50; ⌚ 10am-8pm Tue, 10am-5pm Wed-Sun) traces the history of Augsburg. It also has a large exhibition of gold and silver work from baroque and rococo masters. A second floor displays sculptures and architectural models.

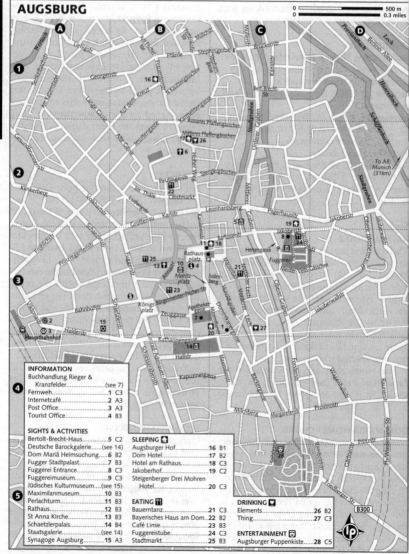

AUGSBURG

Fans of the *Threepenny Opera* will enjoy the **Bertolt-Brecht-Haus** (☎ 324 2779; Auf Dem Rain 7; adult/concession €2/1; ⏰ 10am-5pm Tue-Sun), the birthplace of the famous playwright and poet. Brecht's work was banned by the Nazis for his communist leanings and he was later shunned by West Germans for the same reason (see boxed text, p77).

About 300m east of the main train station, as you head towards the Altstadt you'll come to the **Synagoge Augsburg**, an art nouveau temple built between 1914 and 1917. Inside is the **Jüdisches Kulturmuseum** (Jewish Cultural Museum; ☎ 513 658; Halderstrasse 8; adult/concession €4/2; ⏰ 9am-4pm Tue-Fri, 10am-5pm Sun), with exhibitions on Jewish life in the region, Germany and Central Europe.

Sleeping

Augsburg's hotel owners pump up their prices for Oktoberfest just as much as their Munich counterparts.

Jakoberhof (☎ 510 030; www.jakoberhof.de; Jakoberstrasse 41; s €27-74, d €39-89; P ☐ ☎) The best-value hotel in town is this simple place near the Fuggerei. Bright and airy rooms have few frills and higher rates are for private facilities.

Hotel am Rathaus (☎ 346 490; www.hotel-am-rathaus-augsburg.de; Am Hinteren Perlachberg 1; s €65-98, d €98-125; P ☒ ☐) As central as it gets, and moments away from Rathausplatz, this boutique hotel has fresh neutral decor and a sunny little breakfast room. The trendy Italian restaurant is surprisingly good.

Dom Hotel (☎ 343 930; www.domhotel-augsburg.de; Frauentorstrasse 8; s €72-105, d €92-135; P ☒ ☎ ☒) The bigger the room, the higher the price at these good-value lodgings. The smaller attic rooms have beamed ceilings and great views. Guests have free use of the garden, pool and sauna, and children are welcome.

Steigenberger Drei Mohren Hotel (☎ 503 60; www.augsburg.steigenberger.de; Maximilianstrasse 40; s/d from €90/135; P ☒ ☐ ☎ ☒) This landmark hotel, with luxurious decor, is a stunning place where both Mozart and Goethe once stayed. Marble bathrooms, original art and a beautiful garden terrace are among the elegant touches.

Augsburger Hof (☎ 343 050; www.augsburger-hof.de; Auf dem Kreuz 2; s €90-105, d €99-140; P ☒ ☐) All rooms are business standard, staff are friendly and there are two on-site places to eat at this pretty window-boxed hotel near the Dom. The higher-priced rooms open into the courtyard.

Eating

In the evening, Maximilianstrasse is the place to hang out, with cafes overflowing onto the pavements and Augsburg's young and beautiful watching the world go by.

RESTAURANTS & CAFES

Café Linse (☎ 510 588; Färbergässchen 5; dishes €6-10; ⏰ 9am-7pm Mon-Fri, 9am-6pm Sat) A favourite lunch spot among local office workers, the Linse serves cheap and cheerful mains, coffees, sandwiches and beer at tightly packed cafe tables under whitewashed vaulting.

Bayerisches Haus am Dom (☎ 349 7990; Johannisgasse 4; mains €6-10) Enjoy an elbow massage from the locals at chunky timber benches, while refuelling on Bavarian and Swabian dishes, cheap lunch options (€6) or a sandwich. Erdinger and Andechser are the frothy double-act that stimulates nightly frivolity in the beer garden.

Also recommended:

Bauerntanz (☎ 153 644; Bauerntanzgässchen 1; mains €7-14) A local institution serving big portions of creative Swabian and Bavarian food.

Fuggereistube (☎ 308 70; Jakoberstrasse 26; mains €11-20) Vintage 1970s hunting-lodge decor, with Bavarian food and good service.

QUICK EATS

Cheap eats abound on Bahnhofstrasse, and the local **Stadtmarkt** (btwn Fuggerstrasse & Annastrasse; ⏰ 7am-6pm Mon-Fri, 7am-2pm Sat) is a picnicker's feast. The usual sausage-pizza-*Brezel* culprits cluster around the Hauptbahnhof.

Drinking

Elements (☎ 508 0759; Frauentorstrasse 2) Knock back a cocktail or five at this trendy bar which attracts the beautiful people of an eve. Weekend breakfast is ideal for those who rise at the crack of lunchtime.

Thing (☎ 395 05; Vorderer Lech 45) Augsburg's coolest beer garden sports totem poles and often gets crowded in the evenings.

Entertainment

Augsburger Puppenkiste (☎ 450 3450; www.augsburger-puppenkiste.de; Spitalgasse 15; tickets €9-22) The celebrated puppet theatre holds puppet performances of modern and classic fairy-tales that even non-German speakers will enjoy. Advance bookings are essential.

BAVARIA

BAVARIA

Getting There & Away

Regional trains run hourly between Augsburg and Munich (€11.30, 45 minutes), every other hour to Nuremberg (€23.30, two hours) and several times an hour to Ulm (€15 to €22, 45 minutes to one hour). ICE trains travel to Würzburg (€46, two hours).

The Romantic Road Europabus stops at the Hauptbahnhof and the Rathaus. Augsburg is just off the A8 northwest of Munich.

FÜSSEN

☎ 08362 / pop 17,700

The final halt on the Romantic Road, Füssen is a bustling little tourist town nestled between towering Alpine peaks. It's in the so-called Königswinkel (Royal Corner), home to Germany's biggest tourist attractions: the fantasy castles of Ludwig II (see the boxed text, p354), Neuschwanstein and Hohenschwangau.

Most whiz in and out of the area, checking off fairy-tale castles on a whirlwind coach tour. Those who stay longer escape the crowds into a landscape of gentle hiking trails, Alpine vistas and pretty lakes.

Orientation & Information

The castles are around 4km east of Füssen via the B17 (Münchener Strasse).

Füssen tourist office (☎ 938 50; www.fuessen.de; Kaiser-Maximilian-Platz 1; 🕙 9am-6.30pm Mon-Fri, 10am-2pm Sat, 10am-noon Sun May-Oct, 9am-5pm Mon-Fri, 10am-2pm Sat Nov-Apr)

Hohenschwangau tourist office (☎ 819 765; www .schwangau.de; Alpestrasse; 🕙 11am-7pm May-Oct, 11am-5pm Nov-Apr) At the bus stop below the castles. Provides an informal left-luggage service.

Sights

CASTLES

Schloss Hohenschwangau

Ludwig spent his formative years at the sun-yellow **Schloss Hohenschwangau** (☎ 930 830; adult/concession €9/8, with Neuschwanstein €17/15; 🕙 8am-5.30pm Apr-Sep, 9am-3.30pm Oct-Mar). His father, Maximilian II, rebuilt this palace in a neo-Gothic style from 12th-century ruins left by Schwangau knights. With all this faux medieval imagery filling his childhood, no wonder Ludwig turned out the way he did.

Far less showy than Neuschwanstein, Hohenschwangau has a distinctly lived-in feel and every piece of furniture is a used original. After his father died, Ludwig's main alteration was having stars, illuminated with hidden oil lamps, painted on the ceiling of his bedroom.

Here Ludwig first met Wagner, and the **Hohenstaufensaal** room features a square piano where the hard-up composer would entertain Ludwig with excerpts from his latest oeuvre. Some rooms have frescoes from German history and legend (including the story of the Swan Knight, Lohengrin). The swan theme runs throughout.

Schloss Neuschwanstein

Appearing through the mountaintops like a misty mirage is the world's most famous castle, and the model for Disney's citadel, **Schloss Neuschwanstein** (☎ 930 830; adult/concession €9/8, with Hohenschwangau €17/15; 🕙 8am-5pm Apr-Sep, 9am-3pm Oct-Mar).

Ludwig planned this castle himself, with the help of a stage designer rather than an architect, and it provides a fascinating glimpse into the king's state of mind. Built as a romantic medieval castle, it was started in 1869 and, like so many of Ludwig's grand schemes, was never finished. For all the money spent on it, the king spent just over 170 days in residence.

Ludwig imagined his palace as a giant stage to recreate the world of Germanic mythology in the operatic works of Richard Wagner. Its centrepiece is the lavish **Sängersaal** (Minstrels' Hall), created to feed the king's obsession with Wagner and medieval knights. Wall frescoes in the hall depict scenes from the opera *Tannhäuser*. Concerts are held here every September.

Other completed sections include Ludwig's *Tristan and Isolde*–themed **bedroom**, dominated by a huge Gothic-style bed crowned with intricately carved spires; a gaudy artificial grotto (another nod to *Tannhäuser*); and the Byzantine **Thronsaal** (Throne Room) with an incredible mosaic floor containing over two million stones. Almost every window provides tour-halting views across the plain below.

New features at the end of the tour include a 20-minute **film** on the castle and its creator, a reasonably priced cafe and the inevitable gift shops.

For the postcard view of Neuschwanstein and the plains beyond, walk 10 minutes up to **Marienbrücke** (Mary's Bridge), which spans the spectacular Pöllat Gorge over a waterfall just above the castle. It's said Ludwig liked to

ome here after dark to watch the candlelight
adiating from the Sängersaal.

Tickets & Tours

Both castles must be seen on guided tours
in German or English), which last about 35
minutes (Hohenschwangau is usually first).
Timed tickets are only available from the **Ticket
Centre** (☎ 930 830; www.ticket-center-hohenschwangau.de;
Alpenseestrasse 12) at the foot of the castles. In
summer come as early as 8am to ensure you
get in that day.

When visiting both castles, enough time
s left between tours for the steep 30- to 40-
minute walk between the castles. Alternatively,
you can shell out €4 for a horse-drawn car-
iage ride, which is only marginally quicker.

All Munich's tour companies (p319) run
day excursions out to the castles.

ALTSTADT FÜSSEN

Füssen's compact historical centre is a tangle
of lanes lorded over by the **Hohe Schloss**, a late-
Gothic confection and one-time retreat of the
bishops of Augsburg. The inner courtyard is a
masterpiece of illusionary architecture dating
back to 1499; you'll do a double take before
realising that the gables, oriels and windows
are not quite as they seem. The north wing of
the palace contains the **Staatsgalerie im Hohen
Schloss** (☎ 940 162; Magnusplatz 10; adult/concession
€2.50/2, with Städtische Gemäldegalerie €3) with regional
paintings and sculpture from the 15th and
16th centuries. The **Städtische Gemäldegalerie**
(City Paintings Gallery) below is a showcase of
19th-century artists.

Below the Hohen Schloss, and integrated
into the former Abbey of St Mang, is the
Museum Füssen (☎ 903 146; Lechhalde 3; adult/child
under 14yr €2.50/free; ❧ 11am-5pm Apr-Oct, 1-4pm
Nov-Mar, closed Mon). Füssen's heyday as a 16th-
century violin-making centre is recalled here,
and you can view the abbey's festive baroque
rooms, Romanesque cloister and the St Anna
Kapelle (AD 830).

TEGELBERGBAHN

For fabulous views of the Alps and the
Forggensee, take this **cable car** (☎ 983 60; www
tegelbergbahn.de; one-way/return €10/17; ❧ 8.30am-5pm
Jul-Oct, 9am-5pm Nov-Jun) to the top of the Tegelberg
(1707m), a prime launch point for hang-
gliders and parasailers. From here it's a wonderful hike down to the castles (two to three
hours; follow the signs to Königsschlösser).

To get to the valley station, take RVO bus 73
or 78 from Füssen Bahnhof.

Sleeping

Accommodation in the area is surprisingly
good value and the tourist office can help
track down private rooms from as low as
€15 per person.

House LA (☎ 624 8610; www.housela.de; Welfenstrasse
39; dm €18) A 15-minute walk west of the train
station, this small hostel offers spacious,
rooms (some with balconies) and breakfast
on a rear patio with mountain views. The
owner will pick you up from the station if
you call ahead.

Pension Kössler (☎ 4069; www.pension-koessler.de;
Zalinger Strasse 1; s €35-38, d €70-76; ℗) This small
Pension with a friendly atmosphere offers
outstanding value. Rooms are simple but
comfortable and have private bathroom,
TV, phone and balcony – some overlook
the attractive garden.

Hotel zum Hechten (☎ 916 00; www.hotel-hechten
.com; Ritterstrasse 6; s €46-59, d €86-98; ℗ ✕) This is
one of Füssen's oldest hotels and a barrel of
fun. Public areas are traditional in style but
the bedrooms are mostly airy and brightly
renovated. The owner has decorated part of
the restaurant in campy Ludwig II colours.
Children are welcome.

Hotel Sonne (☎ 9080; www.hotel-sonne.de;
Prinzregentenplatz 1; r €99-189; ℗ ✕ 🖳) Although
traditional-looking from outside, this
Altstadt hotel has undergone a designer
facelift within. Rooms have quality leather
chairs, red-gold royal carpets and fancy flat-
screen TVs, not to mention some kickin'
bathroom fittings.

Campers should head for the following
modern lakeside camp sites, both 4.5km
north of the castles:

Campingplatz Brunnen am Forggensee (☎ 8273;
www.camping-brunnen.de; Seestrasse 81, Schwangau; per
site/person €6/7.50)

Campingplatz Bannwaldsee (☎ 930 00; www
.camping-bannwaldsee.de; Münchner Strasse 151; per
site/person €8.50/7.30)

Eating

Frühlingsgarten (☎ 917 30; Alatseestrasse 8; mains €5-13)
This decent hotel restaurant, 500m south-
west of the Altstadt, serves Allgäu specials
such as *Maultaschen* and *Krautspätzle* (noodles with herbs) indoors or out in the sunny
beer garden.

BAVARIA

LUDWIG II, THE FAIRY-TALE KING

Every year on 13 June, a stirring ceremony takes place in Berg, on the eastern shore of Lake Starnberg. A small boat quietly glides towards a cross just offshore and a plain wreath is fastened to its front. The sound of a single trumpet cuts the silence as the boat returns from this solemn ritual in honour of the most beloved king ever to rule Bavaria – Ludwig II.

The cross marks the spot where Ludwig died under mysterious circumstances in 1886. His early death capped the life of a man at odds with the harsh realities of a modern world no longer in need of a romantic and idealistic monarch.

Prinz Otto Ludwig Friedrich Wilhelm was a sensitive soul, fascinated by romantic epics, architecture and music, but his parents, Maximilian II and Marie, took little interest in his musings and he suffered a lonely and joyless childhood. In 1864, at 18 years old, the prince became king. He was briefly engaged to the sister of Elisabeth (Sisi), the Austrian empress, but as a rule he preferred the company of men. He also worshipped composer Richard Wagner, whose Bayreuth opera house was built with Ludwig's funds.

Ludwig was an enthusiastic leader initially, but Bavaria's days as a sovereign state were numbered, and he became a puppet king after the creation of the German Reich in 1871 (which had its advantages, as Bismarck gave Ludwig a hefty allowance). Ludwig withdrew completely to drink, draw castle plans and view concerts and operas in private. His obsession with French culture and the Sun King, Louis XIV, inspired the fantastical palaces of Neuschwanstein, Linderhof and Herrenchiemsee – lavish projects that spelt his undoing.

Contrary to popular belief, it was only Ludwig's purse – and not the state treasury – that was being bankrupted. However, by 1886 his ever-growing mountain of debt and erratic behaviour had put him at odds with his cabinet. The king, it seemed, needed to be 'managed'.

In January 1886, several ministers and relatives arranged a hasty psychiatric test that diagnosed Ludwig as mentally unfit to rule (this was made easier by the fact that his brother had been declared insane years earlier). That June he was removed to Schloss Berg on Lake Starnberg. A few days later the dejected bachelor and his doctor took a Sunday evening lakeside walk and were found several hours later, drowned in just a few feet of water.

No-one knows with certainty what happened that night. There was no eyewitness nor any proper criminal investigation. The circumstantial evidence was conflicting and incomplete. Reports and documents were tampered with, destroyed or lost. Conspiracy theories abound. That summer the authorities opened Neuschwanstein to the public to help pay off Ludwig's huge debts. King Ludwig II was dead, but the myth was just being born.

Michelangelo (☎ 924 924; Lechhalde 1; mains €7-15) This sophisticated Italian job at the rear of the Rathaus is run by a real Italian chef who plates up some deliciously simple fare, including 38 different pizzas. The tables in the old monastery gardens afford beautiful views high above the river.

Franziskaner Stüberl (☎ 371 24; Kemptener Strasse 1; mains €10-15) This quaint restaurant specialises in *Schweinshaxe* (pork knuckle) and *Schnitzel*, prepared in more varieties than you can shake a haunch at. Non-carnivores go for the excellent *Kässpätzle* (rolled cheese noodles) and the huge salads.

Getting There & Away

If you want to 'do' the castles on a day trip from Munich you'll need to start early. The first train leaves Munich at 4.57am (€22.20, 2½ hours; change in Kaufbeuren), reaching Füssen at 7.24am.

Getting Around

RVO buses 78 and 73 serve the castles from Füssen Bahnhof (€3.50 return), stopping also at the Tegelbergbahn valley station. Taxis to the castles are about €10.

With the Alps on one side and the lake-filled plains on the other, the area around Füssen is a cyclist's paradise. You can hire two-wheelers at the **Radsport Zacherl** (3292 Kemptenerstrasse 19; per day €8).

AROUND FÜSSEN

Known as 'Wies' for short, the **Wieskirche** (☎ 8862-932 930; www.wieskirche.de; Steingaden) is one of Bavaria's best-known baroque churches and a Unesco-listed heritage site. About a million visitors a year flock to see its pride and joy, the monumental work of the legendary artist-brothers, Dominikus and Johann Baptist Zimmermann.

In 1730, a farmer in Steingaden, about 30km northeast of Füssen, witnessed the miracle of his Christ statue shedding tears. So many pilgrims poured into the town that the local abbot commissioned a new church to house the weepy work. Inside, gleaming white pillars are topped by gold capital stones and swirling decorations; the pastel ceiling fresco celebrates Christ's resurrection. Not even the constant deluge of visitors can detract from these charms.

From Füssen regional RVO bus 73 makes the journey up to six times daily. The Europabus also makes a brief stop at the Wieskirche. By car, take the B17 northeast and turn right (east) at Steingaden.

BAVARIAN ALPS

Stretching west from Germany's remote southeastern corner to the Allgäu region near Lake Constance, the Bavarian Alps (Bayerische Alpen) form a stunningly beautiful natural divide along the Austrian border. Ranges further south may be higher, but these mountains shoot up from the foothills so abruptly that the impact is all the more dramatic.

The region is dotted with quaint frescoed villages, spas and health retreats, and possibilities for skiing, snowboarding, hiking, canoeing and paragliding – much of it year-round. The ski season lasts from about late December until April, while summer activities stretch from late May to November.

One of the largest resorts in the area is Garmisch-Partenkirchen, one of Munich's favourite getaway spots. Other superb bases are Berchtesgaden, Füssen (p352) and Oberstdorf.

Most of the resorts have plenty of reasonably priced accommodation, though some places levy a surcharge (usually about €3) for stays of less than two or three days in peak seasons. Most resorts also charge a Kurtaxe (resort tax; less than €2) for overnight stays, but this entitles you to certain perks, like free tours, a city bus service and entry to special events.

Getting Around

There are few direct train routes between main centres, meaning buses are the most efficient method of public transport in the Alpine area. If you're driving, sometimes a short cut via Austria works out to be quicker (such as between Garmisch-Partenkirchen and Füssen or Oberstdorf).

GARMISCH-PARTENKIRCHEN

☎ 08821 / pop 26,000

A much-loved hang-out for outdoor types and moneyed socialites, the double-barrelled resort of Garmisch-Partenkirchen is blessed with a fabled setting a snowball's throw from the Alps. To say you 'wintered in Garmisch' still has an aristocratic ring, and the area offers some of the best skiing in the land, including runs on Germany's highest peak, the Zugspitze (2964m).

The towns of Garmisch and Partenkirchen were merged for the 1936 Winter Olympics, and to this day host international skiing events. Today a clock on Richard-Strauss-Platz is leisurely counting down the hours to the 2011 Alpine World Skiing Championships, the first time the event will have been held here since 1978.

Garmisch-Partenkirchen also makes a handy base for excursions to Ludwig II's palaces, including nearby Schloss Linderhof and the lesser-known Jagdschloss Schachen.

Orientation

The train tracks that divide the two towns culminate at the Hauptbahnhof. From here, turn west on St-Martin-Strasse to get to Garmisch, or east on Bahnhofstrasse to reach Partenkirchen. From the Hauptbahnhof the centre of Garmisch is about 500m away, the centre of Partenkirchen about 1km.

Information

Gräfe & Unzer (☎ 2120; Rathausplatz 15) English books and hiking maps.

Hobis Cyber Café (☎ 2727; Zugspitzstrasse 2; per 1hr €3; ⏱ 5.30am-5.30pm Mon-Fri, 5.30am-noon Sat, 7-11am Sun) Internet access in the town's best bakery.

Klinikum (☎ 770; Auenstrasse 6) Full-service hospital.

Mountain Rescue (☎ 3611; Auenstrasse 7)

Post office (Bahnhofplatz)

Sparda Bank (Hauptbahnhof)

Tourist office (☎ 180 700; www.gapa.de; Richard-Strauss-Platz 2, Garmisch; ⏱ 8am-6pm Mon-Sat, 10am-noon Sun)

BAVARIA

Sights & Activities

ZUGSPITZE

Views from the top of Germany are literally breathtaking, especially during föhn weather when they extend into four countries. Skiing and hiking are the main activities here. To get to the top, you can walk (right), or take the cogwheel train (*Zugspitzbahn*) or a cable car.

The **Zugspitzbahn** (☎ 797 01; www.zugspitze.de; return adult/child €36/20) has its own station right behind the Hauptbahnhof. From here it chugs seven times a day along the mountain base to the Eibsee, a forest lake, then winds its way through a mountain tunnel up to the Schneeferner Glacier (2600m). From there a cable car makes the final ascent to the summit.

Alternatively, the **Eibsee-Seilbahn** (return adult/child €36/20), a steep cable car, sways and swings its way straight up to the summit from the Eibsee lake in about 10 minutes – it's not for the faint-hearted! Most people go up on the train and take the cable car back down, but it works just as well the other way around.

Expect serious crowds at peak times in winter and through much of the summer. Skiers may find it easier, but slower, to schlep their gear up on the train, which offers exterior ski-holders.

SKIING

Garmisch has two big ski fields: the Zugspitze plateau (2964m) and the Classic Ski Area (Alpspitze, 2628m; Hausberg, 1340m; Kreuzeck, 1651m; day pass adult/child €31/17.50). A Happy Ski Card (two days, adult/child €65/39) covers all the slopes, plus other ski areas around the Zugspitze, including Mittenwald and Ehrwald (an incredible 231km of pistes and 106 ski lifts). Local buses serve all the valley stations.

Cross-country ski trails run along the main valleys, including a long section from Garmisch to Mittenwald; call ☎ 797 979 for a weather or snow report.

For ski hire and courses try the following:
Skischule (☎ 4931; www.skischule-gap.de; Am Hausberg 4)
Sport Total (☎ 1425; www.agentursporttotal.de; Marienplatz 18) Also organises paragliding, mountain biking, rafting and ballooning.

HIKING

The area around Garmisch-Partenkirchen is prime hiking and mountaineering territory. Mountain guides are at the tourist office on Monday and Thursday between 4pm and 6pr to give help and information to anyone head ing into the Alps. Brochures and maps are als available with route suggestions for all levels

Hiking to the **Zugspitze summit** is only pos sible in summer and is only recommende for those with experience of mountaineering Another popular route is to King Ludwig II hunting lodge, **Jagdschloss Schachen** (☎ 92 30; adult/concession €4/3; ⏰ Jun-Oct), which can b reached via the Partnachklamm (below) i about a four-hour hike. A plain wooden hu from the outside, the interior is surprisingl magnificent; the **Moorish Room** is somethin straight out of the *Arabian Nights*.

For guided hikes and courses contact th following:
Bergsteigerschule Zugspitze (☎ 589 99; www .bergsteigerschule-zugspitze.de; Dreitorspitzstrasse 74)
Deutscher Alpenverein (☎ 2701; www.alpenverein -ga-pa.de; Hindenburgstrasse 38)

PARTNACHKLAMM

One of the area's main attractions is the dra matically beautiful **Partnachklamm** (☎ 3167 adult/child €2/1), a narrow 700m-long gorg with walls rising up to 80m. A circular wal hewn from the rock takes you through th gorge, which is spectacular in winter whe you can walk beneath curtains of icicles and frozen waterfalls.

Sleeping

The tourist office has a 24-hour outdoo room-reservation board.

Hostel 2962 (☎ 957 50; www.hostel2962.com Partnachauenstrasse 3; dm from €15, d from €58; P) Relaunched in 2008 as a hostel, this is still es sentially a typical Garmisch hotel (former Hote Schell), but a good choice nonetheless. If you can get into the four-bed dorm, it's the cheapes sleep in town. Breakfast is an extra €5.

DJH hostel (☎ 967 050; www.garmisch.jugendherberg .de; Jochstrasse 10; dm under/over 27yr €22.80/26.80 P ☒ ▣) The standards at this smartly re vamped hostel are as good at some chain ho tels. Rooms have Ikea-style furnishings an fruity colour schemes, and there are indoo and outdoor climbing walls if the Alps ar not enough.

Gasthof zum Rassen (☎ 2089; www.gasthof-rasse .de; Ludwigstrasse 45; s €32-53, d €52-90; P ☒) In thi beautifully frescoed 14th-century building the bright, contemporary rooms provide a contrast with the trad style of the public areas

GARMISCH-PARTENKIRCHEN

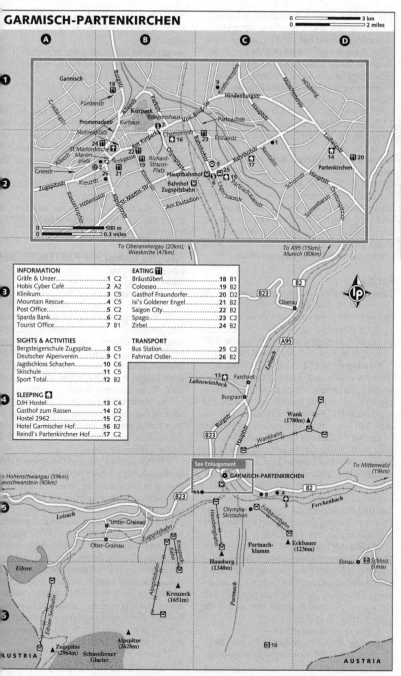

BAVARIA

INFORMATION
Gräfe & Unzer	**1**	C2
Hobis Cyber Café	**2**	A2
Klinikum	**3**	C5
Mountain Rescue	**4**	C5
Post Office	**5**	C2
Sparda Bank	**6**	C2
Tourist Office	**7**	B1

SIGHTS & ACTIVITIES
Bergsteigerschule Zugspitze	**8**	C5
Deutscher Alpenverein	**9**	C1
Jagdschloss Schachen	**10**	C6
Skischule	**11**	C5
Sport Total	**12**	B2

SLEEPING
DJH Hostel	**13**	C4
Gasthof zum Rassen	**14**	D2
Hostel 2962	**15**	C2
Hotel Garmischer Hof	**16**	B2
Reindl's Partenkirchner Hof	**17**	C2

EATING
Bräustüberl	**18**	B1
Colosseo	**19**	B2
Gasthof Fraundorfer	**20**	D2
Isi's Goldener Engel	**21**	B2
Saigon City	**22**	B2
Spago	**23**	C2
Zirbel	**24**	B2

TRANSPORT
Bus Station	**25**	C2
Fahrrad Ostler	**26**	B2

The massive event hall, formerly a brewery, houses the oldest folk theatre in Bavaria.

Hotel Garmischer Hof (☎ 9110; www.garmischer -hof.de; Chamonixstrasse 10; s €59-94, d €94-136; P ☒) Generations of athletes, artists and outdoor enthusiasts have stayed at this refined chateau, property of the Seiwald family since 1928. Tasteful and cosy are the rooms, many with incredible Alpine views. All of them have cable TV, direct-dial phones and safes. Breakfast is served in the vaulted cafe-restaurant with a garden terrace.

Reindl's Partenkirchner Hof (☎ 943 870; www .reindls.de; Bahnhofstrasse 15; s €75-150, d €140-200, ste €210-600; P ☒ ☐ ☎ ☒) It doesn't get much better than this: an elegant, three-winged luxury hotel stacked with perks, a wine bar and a top-notch gourmet restaurant. Rooms are studies in folk-themed elegance and some enjoy gobsmacking mountain views. Most celebrities visiting Ga-Pa pitch up here.

Eating

Colosseo (☎ 528 09; Klammstrasse 7; mains €5-20; ⓨ closed Mon) The faux Roman sculptures, chirpy waiters and mountain views make this upstairs pizzeria a sure winner. The menu is principally pasta-pizza, but there are also delicious fish and meat dishes to choose from.

Bräustüberl (☎ 2312; Fürstenstrasse 23; mains €6-16) This place, a bit outside the centre, is quintessentially Bavarian, complete with enormous enamel coal-burning stove and dirndl-clad waitresses. The dining room is to the right, the beer hall (with more ambience) is to the left.

Gasthof Fraundorfer (☎ 9270; Ludwigstrasse 24; mains €8-16; ⓨ closed Tue) Squeeze yourself in between tourists and the odd yokel for this unmissably kitsch part of the Ga-Pa experience. The multilingual menu has a carnivore bias, the decor ranges from baroque cherubs and hunting trophies to the 'Sports Corner', and there's yodelling, shoe-slapping and Bavarian oompah music, every evening.

Isi's Goldener Engel (☎ 948 757; Bankgasse 5; mains €9-15) This local favourite has hunting-lodge decor that blends frescoes, stag heads and a gilded stucco ceiling. The huge menu ranges from _Leberkäse_ (meatloaf) to pepper steak in cognac cream, though the best deal is the generous lunch special.

Other recommendations:

Saigon City (☎ 969 315; Am Kurpark 17a; mains €5-9; ⓨ closed Mon) No-frills Vietnamese diner serving crispy duck, egg noodles and seafood.

Zirbel (☎ 716 71; Promenadestrasse 2; meals €6.50-15) Popular, tunnel-shaped pub serving snacks and small meals.

Spago (☎ 966 555; Partnachstrasse 50; mains €7-30) Alpine kitsch-free cafe-bistro off the main drag with an international menu and a slick clientele.

Getting There & Around

Garmisch-Partenkirchen enjoys hourly con nections from Munich (€17.60, 1½ hours), an special packages combine the return trip wit a Zugspitze day ski pass. RVO bus 9606 trave to Füssen, with stops at Oberammergau, th Wieskirche and the castles at Neuschwanstei and Hohenschwangau. The A95 from Munic is the direct road route.

Bus tickets cost €1.40 for journeys i town. For bike hire try **Fahrrad Ostler** (☎ 336 Kreuzstrasse 1; per day/week from €10/50).

AROUND GARMISCH-PARTENKIRCHE

Oberammergau

☎ 08822 / pop 5400

Quaint Oberammergau occupies a wid valley surrounded by the dark forests an snow-dusted peaks of the Ammergauer Alp The centre is packed with traditional painte houses, woodcarving shops and awestruc tourists who come here to learn about th town's world-famous Passion Play. It's also great budget base for hikes into easily acce sible Alpine backcountry.

The **tourist office** (☎ 922 740; www.ammergau -alpen.de; Eugen-Papst-Strasse 9a; ⓨ 9am-6pm Mon-F 10am-2pm Sat, 10am-1pm Sun mid-Jun–mid-Oct, 9am-6p Mon-Fri, 10am-1pm Sat mid-Oct–mid-Jun) can hel find accommodation.

A blend of opera, ritual and Hollywood ep the **Passion Play** has been performed every ye ending in a zero since the late 17th century a a collective thank you from the villagers fo being spared the plague. Half the village tak part, sewing amazing costumes and growin hair and beards for their roles (no wigs false hair allowed). The next performanc will take place between May and Octob 2010, but tours of the **Passionstheater** (☎ 923 Passionswiese 1; tours adult/concession €4/1; ⓨ erratic hou call ahead) enable you to take a peek at the co tumes and sets anytime. In the years betwee Passion Plays, spectacular opera events a held monthly from July to September; ask the tourist office for details.

The town's other claim to fame is **Lüftmaler** the eye-popping house facades painted in a lusionist style. Images usually have a religious lavour, but some also show hilarious beer-all scenes or fairy-tale motifs, like *Little Red ₹iding Hood* at Ettaler Strasse 48 or *Hansel & ₹retel* at No 41 down the road. The pick of the ₹op is the amazing **Pilatushaus** (☎ 923 10; Ludwig-₹oma-Strasse 10; admission with museum ticket; ☽ 1-6pm Je-Sat May-Oct), whose painted columns snap ₹to 3-D as you approach. It contains a gallery ₹d several workshops.

Oberammergau is also known for its in-₹icate **woodcarvings**. Workshops abound ₹round town, churning out everything from ₹rkscrews to life-sized saints and nativity ₹enes. Some amazing examples can be seen ₹ the little parish cemetery on Pfarrplatz ₹nd in the **Oberammergau Museum** (☎ 941 36; ₹rfstrasse 8; adult/child €4/1; ☽ 10am-5pm Tue-Sun, ₹osed Feb & Nov).

You can bed down at the **DJH hostel** (☎ 4114; ₹ww.oberammergau.jugendherberge.de; Malensteinweg 10; ₹m under/over 27yr €17.70/21.70) or the exception-₹lly good-value **Gästehaus Richter** (☎ 942 94; ₹aestehaus-richter.de; Welfengasse 2; s €22-35, d €50-70; ☒ ▣ ☞) with immaculate en suite rooms, a ₹est kitchen and filling Alpine breakfast.

Hourly trains connect Munich with ₹berammergau (change at Murnau; €16.70, ¾ hours). RVO bus 9606 goes to Garmisch-₹artenkirchen and Füssen almost hourly.

₹hloss Linderhof

₹ pocket-sized trove of weird treasures, **Schloss ₹inderhof** (☎ 920 30; adult/concession Apr-Sep €7/6, ₹t-Mar €6/5; ☽ 9am-6pm Apr-Sep, 10am-4pm Oct-Mar) ₹as Ludwig II's smallest but most sumptu-₹us palace, and the only one he lived to see ₹lly completed. Finished in 1878, the palace ₹ugs a steep hillside in a fantasy landscape ₹f French gardens, fountains and follies. The ₹eclusive king used the palace as a retreat ₹nd hardly ever received visitors here. Like ₹errenchiemsee (p334), Linderhof was in-₹ired by Versailles and dedicated to Louis ₹IV, the French 'sun king'.

Linderhof's myth-laden, jewel-encrusted ₹ooms are a monument to the king's excesses ₹at so unsettled the governors in Munich. ₹he **private bedroom** is the largest, heavily or-₹amented and anchored by an enormous 108-₹andle crystal chandelier weighing 500kg. An ₹rtificial waterfall, built to cool the room in ₹ummer, cascades just outside the window. ₹he **dining room** reflects the king's fetish for ₹rivacy and inventions. The king ate from

a mechanised dining board, whimsically la-belled 'Table, Lay Yourself', that sank through the floor so that his servants could replenish it without being seen.

Created by the famous court gardener Carl von Effner, the gardens and out-buildings, open April to October, are as fascinating as the castle itself. The highlight is the oriental-style **Moorish Kiosk**, where Ludwig, dressed in oriental garb, would preside over nightly entertainment from a peacock throne. Underwater light dances on the stalactites at the **Venus Grotto**, an artifi-cial cave inspired by a stage set for Wagner's *Tannhäuser*. Now sadly empty, Ludwig's fantastic conch-shaped boat is moored by the shore.

Linderhof is about 13km west of Oberammergau and 26km northwest of Garmisch-Partenkirchen. Bus 9622 travels to Linderhof from Oberammergau nine times a day. If coming from Garmisch-Partenkirchen change in Ettal or Oberammergau.

Mittenwald

☎ 08823 / pop 7900

Nestled in a cul-de-sac under snowcapped peaks, sleepily alluring Mittenwald, 20km southeast of Garmisch-Partenkirchen, is the most natural spot imaginable for a resort. Known far and wide for its master violin makers, the citizens of this drowsy village seem almost bemused by its popu-larity. The air is ridiculously clean, and on the main street the loudest noise is a babbling brook.

The **tourist office** (☎ 339 81; www.mittenwald.de; Dammkarstrasse 3; ☽ 8.30am-6pm Mon-Fri, 9am-noon Sat, 10am-noon Sun Jul-Sep, shorter hours Oct-Jun) has de-tails of excellent hiking and cycling routes. Popular hikes with cable-car access will take you up the granddaddy Alpspitze (2628m), as well as the Wank, Mt Karwendel and the Wettersteinspitze. Return tickets to Karwendel, which boasts Germany's second-highest cable-car route, cost €22/12 per adult/child.

The Karwendel ski field has one of the longest runs (7km) in Germany, but it is primarily for hot doggers and freestyle pros. Day ski passes to the nearby Kranzberg ski fields, the best all-round option, cost €22 per adult and €14 per child. For equipment hire and ski/snowboard instruction contact the **Vereinigte Skischule** (☎ 5772; www.skischulevereinigte .de; Bahnhofsplatz 3).

BAVARIA

The only classic off-piste sight in town is the **Geigenbaumuseum** (Violin-Making Museum; ☎ 2511; Ballenhausgasse 3; adult/concession €4/3; ☻ 10am-5pm Tue-Sun Feb, Mar & May-Oct), a collection of over 200 locally crafted violins and the tools used to fashion them. It's also the venue for occasional concerts.

Behind a very pretty facade, **Hotel-Gasthof Alpenrose** (☎ 927 00; www.alpenrose-mittenwald .de; Obermarkt 1; s €26-48, d €71-89; **P**) has cosy, old-style rooms, a cute restaurant and live Bavarian music almost nightly. Around 1km south of the Obermarkt, **Restaurant Arnspitze** (☎ 2425; Innsbrucker Strasse 68; mains €17-23; ☻ closed Tue) serves award-winning gourmet fare.

Mittenwald is served by hourly trains from Garmisch-Partenkirchen (€3.70, 20 minutes), Munich (€20.50, 1¾ hours) and Innsbruck, across the border in Austria, (€10.20, one hour). Otherwise RVO bus 9605 connects Mittenwald with Garmisch-Partenkirchen (30 minutes) several times a day.

OBERSTDORF

☎ 08322 / pop 11,000

Spectacularly situated in the western Alps, the Allgäu region feels a long, long way from the rest of Bavaria, both in its cuisine (more *Spätzle* than dumplings) and the dialect, which is closer to the Swabian of Baden-Württemberg. The Allgäu's chief draw is the car-free resort of Oberstdorf, a major skiing centre a short hop from Austria.

The **tourist office** (☎ 7000; www.oberstdorf.de; Prinzregenten-Platz 1; ☻ 8.30am-noon & 2-6pm Mon-Fri, 9.30am-noon Sat) and its **branch office** (☎ 700 217; Bahnhof; ☻ 9am-8pm Mon-Sat, 9am-6pm Sun May-Oct, 9am-noon & 2-6pm Nov-Apr) runs a room-finding service.

Oberstdorf is almost ringed by towering peaks and offers superb hiking. For an exhilarating day walk, ride the Nebelhorn **cable car** (adult/child €20/9.50) to the upper station, then hike down via the **Gaisalpseen**, two lovely alpine lakes (six hours).

In-the-know skiers value the resort for its friendliness, lower prices and less-crowded pistes. The village is surrounded by 70km of well-maintained cross-country trails and three ski fields: the **Nebelhorn** (day/half-day passes €33/28), **Fellhorn/Kanzelwand** (day/half-day passes €36/31) and **Söllereck** (day/half-day passes €25/20).

For ski hire and tuition, try **Alpin Skischule** (☎ 952 90; www.alpinskischule.de; Am Bahnhofplatz 1a) opposite the train station.

The **Eislaufzentrum Oberstdorf** (☎ 700 530 behind the Nebelhorn cable-car station, i the biggest ice-skating complex in German with three separate rinks.

Sleeping & Eating

Oberstdorf is chock-full with private guest houses, but owners are usually reluctant t rent rooms for just one night, even in th shoulder seasons.

DJH hostel (☎ 2225; www.oberstdorf.jugendherberge.d Kornau 8; dm under/over 27yr €18.20/22.20; ☻ Jan–mid-No A relaxed, 200-bed chalet-hostel with com manding views of the Allgäu Alps. Take bu 1 to the Reute stop; it's in the Kornau subur near the Söllereck chairlift.

Weinklause (☎ 969 30; www.weinklause.de; Prinze strasse 10; s €55-68, d €42-64; **P** **☒**) Willing to tak one-nighters at the drop of a felt hat, thi superb lodge offers all kinds of rooms an apartments, some with kitchenette, som with jaw-dropping, spectacular alpine view A generous breakfast is served in the restau rant, which comes to life most nights wit local live music.

Filser Kur-und Ferienhotel (☎ 7080; www.fils hotel.de; Freibergstrasse 15; s €84-110, d €83-119; **P** **☒** This is one of many luxurious but good value health resorts in the area, with spar kling facilities, including fitness rooms, poc and sauna. Rooms are high-standard studie in modern simplicity and some sport ele gant traditional touches. There's wheelcha access.

our pick **Weinstube am Frohmarkt** (☎ 3988; A Frohmarkt 2; mains €7-18; ☻ 5pm-1am Thu-Tue) Th musty-sweet aroma of wine, cheese an Tyrolean cured ham scents the air at thi intimate wine bar. Rub shoulders with lo cals over the Törggelen buffet downstairs, o retreat upstairs for a quiet glass of wine.

Imbisstro (☎ 800 718; Oststrasse 19; snacks €3.50-7.5 mains €10-20) With a menu featuring everythin from champagne to *Currywurst* this trend place certainly lives up to the play on word (*Imbiss*, ie stand-up food stall plus bistro) i its name. Grab a cheap bar-stool lunch, o take your time over a steak blow-out unde camp chandeliers or out on the street.

Getting There & Away

There are at least five direct trains dail from Munich (€27.80, 2½ hours), otherwi change in Buchloe. RVO buses 81 and 971

un three times daily between Oberstdorf
and Füssen (one-way/return €10.20/18,
wo hours).

BERCHTESGADEN & BERCHTESGADENER LAND

☎ 08652 / pop 7700

Wedged into Austria and framed by six formidable mountain ranges, the Berchtesgadener
Land is a drop-dead-gorgeous corner of
Bavaria. Local legend has it that angels given
the task of distributing the earth's wonders
were startled by God's order to get a move
on and dropped them all here. These most
definitely included the Watzmann (2713m),
Germany's second-highest mountain, and the
pristine Königssee, perhaps Germany's most
photogenic lake.

Much of the area is protected by law within
the Berchtesgaden National Park, which was
declared a 'biosphere reserve' by Unesco in
1990. The village of Berchtesgaden is the obvious base for hiking circuits into the park; away
from the trails, the main draws are the mountaintop Eagle's Nest, a lodge built for Hitler,
and Dokumentation Obersalzberg, a museum
that chronicles the region's dark Nazi past.

Information

Hypovereinsbank (Weihnachtsschützenplatz 21/2)

Internet Stadl (Königseer Strasse 17; per 15min €1.50;
🕙 9am-8pm) Coin-operated, high-speed internet access.

Nationalpark office (☎ 643 43; www.nationalpark
berchtesgaden.de; Franziskanerplatz 7; 🕙 9am-5pm)
Has a free exhibition and sells hiking maps.

Post office (Franziskanerplatz 21)

Tourist office (☎ 9670; www.berchtesgadener-land.info;
Königsseer Strasse 2; 🕙 8.30am-6pm Mon-Fri, 9am-5pm
Sat, 9am-3pm Sun May–mid-Oct, 8.30am-5pm Mon-Fri,
9am-noon Sat mid-Oct–Apr) Has a free room-booking service
and an electronic room-reservation board outside.

Sights

KÖNIGSSEE

Without doubt the highlight of any visit
to the Berchtesgadener Land is a crossing
of the emerald-green **Königssee**. Contained
by steep mountain walls just 5km south of
Berchtesgaden, it's the country's highest lake
(603m) with pure water shimmering into
fjordlike depths. Departing from the lakeside
village of Schönau (take bus 839 or 841 from
Berchtesgaden), **Bayerische Seen-Schifffahrt**
(☎ 963 60; www.seenschifffahrt.de; return adult/child
€12.50/6.30) runs electric boats year-round to

St Bartholomä, a quaint onion-domed chapel
on the western shore. At one point, the boat
stops while the captain plays a *Flügelhorn*
towards the amazing **Echo Wall** – the melody
bounces back after several seconds. About an
hour's hike from the dock at St Bartholomä is
the **Eiskapelle** (Ice Chapel), where an ice dome
grows every winter to heights of over 200m.
In late summer the ice melts and the water
tunnels a huge opening in the solid ice.

DOKUMENTATION OBERSALZBERG

This should be the first stop on any tour
of Berchtesgadener Land. A quiet mountain retreat 3km east of Berchtesgaden,
Obersalzberg became the southern headquarters of Hitler's government. The fascinating **Dokumentation Obersalzberg** (☎ 947 960;
Salzbergstrasse 41; adult/child under 16yr €3/free; 🕙 9am-
5pm Apr-Oct, 10am-3pm Tue-Sun Nov-Apr) leaves few
stones unturned. The forced takeover of
the area, the construction of the compound
and the daily life of the Nazi elite are documented, and all facets of the Nazi terror
regime – Hitler's near-mythical appeal, his
racial politics, the resistance movement
and the death camps – are covered in extraordinary depth. A section of the underground bunker network is open for touring.
Audioguides are available for €2. To get
there take bus 838 from the Hauptbahnhof.

EAGLE'S NEST

Berchtesgaden's most sinister draw is Mt
Kehlstein, a sheer-sided peak at Obersalzberg
where Martin Bormann, a key henchman of
Hitler's, engaged 3000 workers to build a diplomatic meeting-house for the Führer's 50th
birthday. Perched at 1834m, the innocent-
looking lodge (called Kehlsteinhaus in
German) occupies one of the world's most
breathtaking spots. Ironically, Hitler is said
to have suffered from vertigo and rarely
enjoyed the spectacular views himself.

From mid-May to October, the **Eagle's
Nest** is open to visitors. To get there, drive
or take bus 849 from the Hauptbahnhof to
the Kehlstein bus departure area. From here
the road is closed to private traffic and you
must take a special **bus** (www.kehlsteinhaus.de;
per person €15; 🕙 8.55am-4pm) up the mountain
(35 minutes). The final 124m stretch to the
summit is in a luxurious, brass-clad elevator.
The Eagle's Nest now houses a restaurant
that donates profits to charity.

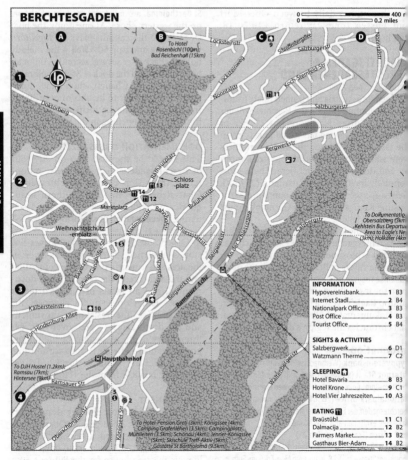

BERCHTESGADEN

INFORMATION
Hypovereinsbank	1 B3
Internet Stadl	2 B4
Nationalpark Office	3 B3
Post Office	4 B3
Tourist Office	5 B4

SIGHTS & ACTIVITIES
Salzbergwerk	6 D1
Watzmann Therme	7 C2

SLEEPING
Hotel Bavaria	8 B3
Hotel Krone	9 C1
Hotel Vier Jahreszeiten	10 A3

EATING
Bräustübl	11 C1
Dalmacija	12 B2
Farmers Market	13 B2
Gasthaus Bier-Adam	14 B2

SALZBERGWERK

Once a major producer of so-called 'white gold', Berchtesgaden has thrown open its **salt mines** (☎ 600 20; adult/child €14/9; ☼ 9am-5pm May-Oct, 11.30-3pm Nov-Apr) for fun-filled tours (90 minutes). The brand-new **SalzZeitReise** exhibition opened here in 2007, and sees visitors donning protective overalls and taking a special train into the depths of the mine. Down below, the highlights include the crossing of a 100m-long illuminated lake containing the same concentration of salt as the Dead Sea, and the brightly lit, interactive treasure chamber where visitors learn about the history of salt mining in the Alps. It's usually only around 12°C down there, so bring a sweater.

Activities

HIKING

The wilds of the 210-sq-km Berchtesgade National Park offer some of the best hiking i Germany. A good introduction is a 2km tra up from St Bartholomä beside the Königsse to the notorious Watzmann-Ostwand, wher scores of mountaineers have met their death Another popular hike goes from the south ern end of the Königssee to the Obersee. Fo details of routes visit the Nationalpark offic (p361), or buy a copy of the *Berchtesgadene Land* (sheet 794) map in the Kompass serie

SKIING

The **Jenner-Königsee area** (☎ 958 10; daily pass adul child €26.50/14.10) at Königssee is the biggest, mos

---

HITLER'S MOUNTAIN RETREAT

Of all the German towns tainted by the Third Reich, Berchtesgaden has a burden heavier than most. Hitler fell in love with nearby Obersalzberg in the 1920s, and bought a small country home, later enlarged into the imposing Berghof.

After seizing power in 1933, Hitler established a part-time headquarters here and brought much of the party brass with him. They bought, or often confiscated, large tracts of land and tore down farmhouses to erect a 7ft-high barbed-wire fence. Obersalzberg was sealed off as the fortified southern headquarters of the NSDAP (National Socialist German Workers' Party). In 1938, British prime minister Neville Chamberlain visited for negotiations (later continued in Munich) which led to the infamous promise of 'peace in our time' at the expense of Czechoslovakia's Sudetenland.

Little is left of Hitler's Alpine fortress today. In the final days of WWII, the Royal Air Force levelled much of Obersalzberg, though the Eagle's Nest, Hitler's mountaintop eyrie, was left strangely unscathed. The historical twist and turns are dissected at the impressive Dokumentation Obersalzberg (p361).

---

aried of five local ski fields. For equipment ire and courses, try **Skischule Treff-Aktiv** (☎ 667 0; www.treffaktiv.de; Jennerbahnstrasse 19, Schönau).

WATZMANN THERME
Berchtesgaden's thermal wellness and fun **pool complex** (☎ 946 40; Bergwerkstrasse 54; tickets per 4/12hr €8.80/11.40/16.30; ☒ 10am-10pm) has several indoor and outdoor pools with various hydrotherapeutic treatment stations, a sauna and inspiring Alpine views.

Tours
Experience the sinister legacy of the Obersalzberg area, including the Eagle's Nest and the underground bunker system, on a four-hour guided tour with **Eagle's Nest Tours** (☎ 649 71; www.eagles-nest-tours.com; adult/concession €48/45; ☒ 1.15pm mid-May–Oct). Buses depart from the tourist office and reservations re advised.

Sleeping
Berchtesgaden has plenty of private rooms from €25 per person; ask at the tourist office. **Campingplatz Mühlleiten** (☎ 4584; www.muehlleiten.eu; Königsseer Strasse 70; campsite/person €7/5.90) and **Camping Grafenlehen** (☎ 4140; www.camping-grafenlehen.de; Königsseer Fussweg 71; campsite/person €7/5.90) are both in Schönau near the Königssee.

DJH hostel (☎ 943 70; www.berchtesgaden.jugend erberge.de; Struberberg 6; dm under/over 27yr €17.90/21.90) This 274-bed hostel is situated in the suburb of Strub, and has great views of Mt Watzmann. It's a 25-minute walk from the Hauptbahnhof or a short journey on bus 839.

Hotel-Pension Greti (☎ 975 297; www.pension greti.de; Waldhauserstrasse 20, Schönau; s €25-39, d €44-

72; **P**) Warm and welcoming, and just a 15-minute walk from the Königssee, Greti's rooms are surprisingly voguish and all have balconies. The cellar bar is perfect for some post-piste unwinding.

Hotel Krone (☎ 946 00; www.hotel-krone-berchtes gaden.de; Am Rad 5; s €38-53, d €70-106; **P**) This family-run gem, a short stroll from the town centre, has wonderful views of the valley and the Alps beyond. Country-cabin-style rooms are generously sized, with carved pine ceilings, niches and bedsteads. The sunny terrace is breakfast paradise.

Hotel Bavaria (☎ 660 11; www.hotelbavaria.net; Sunklergässchen 11; s €46-61, d €64-130; **P**) A short hop from the station, this guesthouse, run by the same family for a century, has romantically beamed rooms with four-poster beds and modern bathrooms. Looking at the views from some of the pricier quarters with balconies, you'd think the hotel had been lined up specially to catch the vistas.

Hotel Vier Jahreszeiten (☎ 9520; www.hotel -vierjahreszeiten-berchtesgaden.de; Maximilianstrasse 20; s €52-73, d €83-104; **P**) For a glimpse of Berchtesgaden's storied past, stay at this traditional Alpine lodge where Bavarian royalty once entertained. Rooms have panoramic views of the mountains and the in-house restaurant couldn't be more atmospheric.

Hotel Rosenbichl (☎ 944 00; www.hotel-rosenbichl .de; Rosenhofweg 24; d €56-68; **P**) This wellness hotel in the middle of the protected nature zone offers exceptional value. Room decor is a bit naff '90s, but you get a lot of floor space for your euro. Guests also have the option of being steamed, boiled and fried in the sauna, whirlpool and solarium.

Eating

Weekly farmers markets selling meats, cheese and other produce are held on the Marktplatz every Friday morning between April and October.

Holzkäfer (☎ 621 07; Buchenhöhe 40; dishes €4-9; ☺ 2pm-late, closed Tue) This funky log-cabin restaurant in the hills around Obersalzberg is a great spot for a night out with fun-loving locals. Crammed with antlers, carvings and backwoods oddities, it's known for its tender pork roasts, dark beers and list of Franconian wines. There's wheelchair access.

Bräustübl (☎ 976 724; Bräuhausstrasse 13; mains €8-14) Enter through the arch painted in Bavaria's white and blue diamonds and pass the old beer barrels to reach a secluded beer garden. The vaulted hall is the scene of heel-whacking Bavarian stage shows every Saturday night.

Gaststätte St Bartholomä (☎ 964 937; St Bartholomä; mains €8-15) On the shore of the Königsee, and reached by boat, this is a tourist haunt that actually serves delicious food made with ingredients picked, plucked and hunted from the surrounding forests and the lake. Savour generous platters of venison in mushroom sauce with dumplings and red sauerkraut, or grilled trout in the large beer garden or indoors.

Other options:

Dalmacija (☎ 976 027; Marktplatz 5; dishes €5-8) Pizzas, pastas and a whiff of the Balkans in a bistro-cafe teeming with young patrons.

Gasthaus Bier-Adam (☎ 2390; Markt 22; mains €9-22) Cheerful place with a good range of traditional fare.

Getting There & Away

Travelling from Munich by train involves a change at Freilassing (€28.50, three hours). There are direct trains from Salzburg (€8.40, one hour), although RVO bus 840 (one-way/return €4.90/8.50) makes the trip in about 45 minutes and has more departures. Berchtesgaden is south of the Munich–Salzburg A8 autobahn.

FRANCONIA

Somewhere between Ingolstadt and Nuremberg, Bavaria's accent mellows, the oompah bands play that little bit quieter and wine competes with beer as the local tipple. This is Franconia (Franken), and as every local will tell you, Franconians, who in habit the wooded hills and the banks of th sluggish Main River in Bavaria's norther reaches, are a breed apart from their bras and extrovert siblings to the south.

In the northwest, the region's wine growers produce some exceptional white sold in a distinctive teardrop-shaped bottle the *Bocksbeutel*. For outdoor enthusiasts the Altmühltal Nature Park offers wonder ful hiking, biking and canoeing. But it i Franconia's old royalty and incredible cities Nuremberg, Bamberg and Würzburg (fo the latter, see p337) – that draw the bigges crowds.

NUREMBERG

☎ 0911 / pop 500,000

Nuremberg (Nürnberg), Bavaria's second largest city and the unofficial capital o Franconia, is an energetic place where th nightlife is intense and the beer is as dar as coffee. As one of Bavaria's biggest draw it is alive with visitors year-round, but es pecially during the spectacular Christma market.

For centuries Nuremberg was the unde clared capital of the Holy Roman Empir and the preferred residence of most Germa kings, who kept their crown jewels here Rich and stuffed with architectural won ders, it was also a magnet for famous art ists, though the most famous of all, Albrech Dürer, was actually born here. 'Nuremberg shines throughout Germany like a su among the moon and stars,' gushed Marti Luther. By the 19th century the city had be come a powerhouse in Germany's industria revolution.

The Nazis saw in Nuremberg a perfec stage for their activities. It was here that th fanatical party rallies were held, the boycot of Jewish businesses began and the infamou Nuremberg Laws outlawing Jewish citizen ship were enacted. On 2 January 1945, Allie bombers reduced the city to landfill, killin 6000 people in the process.

After WWII the city was chosen as the sit of the War Crimes Tribunal, now known a the Nuremberg Trials. Later, the painstakin reconstruction – using the original stone o of almost all the city's main buildings, in cluding the castle and old churches in th Altstadt, returned the city to some of it former glory.

Orientation

Most major sights are within the Altstadt. The Hauptbahnhof is just outside the old city walls to the southeast. From here, pedestrian Königstrasse runs to the city centre, where the shallow Pegnitz River flows from east to west.

About 4km southeast of the centre is the Reichsparteitagsgelände, the Nazi rally grounds also known as Luitpoldhain. The courthouse where the Nuremberg Trials were held is around 2km from the centre of the Altstadt.

Information

BOOKSHOPS

Freytag & Berndt (☎ 202 9709; Königstrasse 85) Huge range of maps and guides including souvenir 3-D plans of Nuremberg (€3.50).

Schmitt & Hahn (☎ 214 6711; Hauptbahnhof; 5.30am-11pm Mon-Fri, 6.30am-11pm Sat, 7am-11pm Sun) Full selection of international press and a decent selection of English-language paperbacks.

INTERNET ACCESS

Tat-s (☎ 815 7521; Hauptbahnhof, upper level; per 5min €1; 24hr) Web access upstairs at the train station.

LAUNDRY

SB Waschsalon (☎ 598 5925; Tafelfeldstrasse 42; per load €4.50; 7am-11pm) Situated 700m southwest of the Hauptbahnhof.

Schnell und Sauber (☎ 180 9400; Sulzbacher Strasse 86; per load €4.50; 6am-midnight) Take tram 8 to Deichslerstrasse.

MEDICAL SERVICES & EMERGENCY

Ambulance (☎ 192 22)

Ärztliches Bereitschaftsdienstzentrum (☎ 01805-191 212; Bahnhofstrasse 11a) Medical centre.

Unfallklinik Dr Erler (☎ 272 80; Kontumazgarten 4-18) Medical centre.

MONEY

Commerzbank (Königstrasse 21)

Hypovereinsbank (Lorenzerplatz 21)

ReiseBank (Hauptbahnhof)

POST

Main post office (Bahnhofplatz 1)

TOURIST INFORMATION

Tourist offices (☎ 233 60; www.tourismus.nuernberg.de) Königstrasse (Königstrasse 93; 9am-7pm Mon-Sat, 10am-4pm Sun); Hauptmarkt (Hauptmarkt 18; 9am-6pm Mon-Sat, 10am-4pm Sun May-Sep) Staff sell the Nürnberg + Fürth Card (€19), good for two days of public transport and admission to museums and attractions in both cities.

Sights

HAUPTMARKT

This bustling square in the heart of the Altstadt is the site of markets including the famous Chriskindlesmarkt (Christmas market). The ornate Gothic **Pfarrkirche Unsere Liebe Frau** (1350–58), better known as the Frauenkirche, was built on the site of a razed synagogue as a repository for the crown jewels of Holy Roman Emperor Charles IV who, fearing theft, sent them instead to his native Prague for safekeeping. Beneath the clock the seven electoral princes march around Charles IV every day at noon.

Protruding from the northwest corner of the square like a half-buried church spire is the 19m **Schöner Brunnen** (Beautiful Fountain). A replica of the late-14th-century original, it is a stunning golden vision of 40 electors, prophets, Jewish and Christian heroes and other allegorical figures. The original, made of badly eroded sandstone, stands in the Germanisches Nationalmuseum (p369). A local superstition has it that if you turn the small **golden rings** on its sides three times your wish will come true.

ALTES RATHAUS & ST SEBALDUSKIRCHE

Beneath the **Altes Rathaus** (1616–22), a hulk of a building with lovely Renaissance-style interiors, you'll find the macabre **Lochgefängnisse** (Medieval Dungeons; ☎ 231 2690; Rathausplatz 2; tours adult/concession €3/1.50; 10am-4.30pm Tue-Sun Apr-Oct, daily during Christkindlesmarkt). This 12-cell death row and torture chamber must be seen on a 30-minute guided tour (held every half-hour) and might easily put you off lunch.

Across the cobbles from the Altes Rathaus rises the 13th-century **St Sebalduskirche**, Nuremberg's oldest church. Check out the ornate carvings over the **Bridal Doorway** to the north, depicting the Wise and Foolish Virgins. The highlight inside is the bronze shrine of **St Sebald**, a Gothic and Renaissance masterpiece that took its maker, Peter Vischer the Elder, as well as his two sons, more than 11 years to complete. The entire piece is carried by a posse of giant snails.

STADTMUSEUM FEMBOHAUS

Set in an ornate 16th-century merchant house, the **Stadtmuseum Fembohaus** (Fembo House Municipal Museum; ☎ 231 2595; Burgstrasse 15; adult/concession €5/2.50; 10am-5pm Tue-Fri, 10am-6pm Sat & Sun) provides an entertaining overview of Nuremberg's

BAVARIA

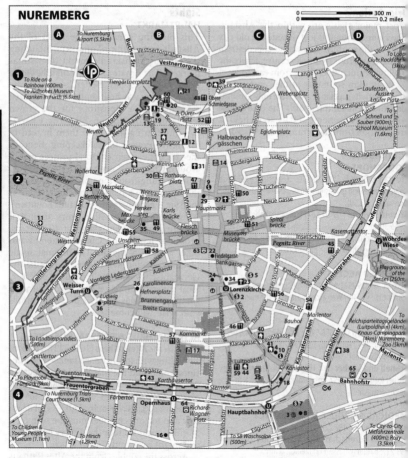

NUREMBERG

950-year history against the backdrop of the restored historic rooms of this 16th-century merchant house. The most innovative part of the museum, a flashy multimedia show called 'Noricama', is a both dramatic and witty 52-minute dash through the main events that have shaped the city.

FELSENGÄNGE

Under the **Albrecht Dürer Monument** on Albrecht-Dürer-Platz are four storeys of dank passageways called the **Felsengänge** (☎ 227 066; adult/concession €4.50/3.50; ☺ tours at 11am, 1pm, 3pm & 5pm, 3-person minimum). Burrowed into the sandstone in the 14th century to house a brewery and beer cellar, they also served as an air-raid shelter during WWII. Down in the

tunnels, which can only be seen on a tour things can get pretty chilly even in summer so take a jacket. Buy tickets from the brewpub **Hausbrauerei Altstadthof** (Bergstrasse 19).

TIERGÄRTNERPLATZ

Framed by charming half-timbered houses the **Tiergärtnertor** is a square tower from the 16th century. The long, dark passage underneath gives a suitable impression of the city's walls, in places up to 6m thick. On the square stands the beautiful late-Gothic half-timbered **Pilatushaus**, owned by a wealthy maker of armour for kings and nobles. In front is Jürgen Goetz' bronze **sculpture** *Der Hase – Hommage à Dürer* (The Hare – A Tribute to Dürer; 1984). This nod to Dürer's watercolour original, called *Junger Feldhase* 1502), shows the dire results of tampering with nature.

A few steps further east is the **Historischer Kunstbunker** (☎ 227 066; Obere Schmiedgasse 52; ours adult/concession €4.50/3.50; ☽ tours 2pm), a climate-controlled bomb shelter used to protect art treasures during WWII. Works by Albrecht Dürer, sculptor Veit Stoss and Martin Behaim, the maker of a bafflingly accurate 15th-century globe, were kept safe here from the allied bombs raining down on the city. Tickets are only available from the Hausbrauerei Altstadthof.

KAISERBURG

Another must-see is the humongous **Kaiserburg** (Imperial Castle; ☎ 244 6590; Burg; adult/concession incl museum €6/5, well & tower only €3/2; ☽ 9am-6pm Apr-Sep, 10am-4pm Oct-Mar). Construction began here during the Hohenstaufen reign in the 12th century, and dragged on for almost four centuries. The complex embraces the Kaiser's living quarters, a Romanesque chapel, the Imperial and Knights' Halls and the **Sinwellturm** (Sinwell Tower; 113 steps). There's also the amazing 48m-deep **Tiefer Brunnen** (Deep Well), which still yields drinking water.

The **Kaiserburg Museum** (☎ 200 9540; Burg; adult/concession €5/4) chronicles the history of the castle and sheds light on medieval defence techniques. The grassy knoll in the southeast corner of the castle gardens is **Am Ölberg**, a great spot to sit and gaze out over the city's rooftops.

ALBRECHT-DÜRER-HAUS

Germany's most famous Renaissance draughtsman, Dürer lived and worked at what is now known as the **Albrecht-Dürer-Haus** (☎ 231 2568; Albrecht-Dürer-Strasse 39; adult/concession €5/2.50; ☽ 10am-5pm Tue-Sun, 10am-8pm Thu) from 1509 till his death in 1528. Several originals and copies of his graphic works are on display, and a multimedia version of Agnes, his wife, takes visitors through the master's recreated workshop.

SPIELZEUGMUSEUM

The **Spielzeugmuseum** (Toy Museum; ☎ 231 3164; Karlstrasse 13-15; adult/concession €5/2.50; ☽ 10am-5pm Tue-Fri, 10am-6pm Sat & Sun) has a vast collection of playthings from many periods – from innocent hoops and sticks to blood 'n' guts computer games. Kids and parents will love the play area.

WEINSTADL & HENKERSTEG

On the north side of the Pegnitz, near the Karlsbrücke, is the impressive half-timbered **Weinstadl**, an old wine depot with two half-timbered storeys jutting out over the river. It has had a storied life, ranging from lepers' refuge to student dorm. Crossing the river is the covered timber **Henkersteg** (Hangman's Bridge), built to keep the hangman's exposure to disease to a minimum.

EHEKARUSSELL BRUNNEN

At the foot of the fortified **Weisser Turm** (White Tower) stands the startlingly grotesque **Ehekarussell Brunnen** (Marriage Carousel Fountain), a large bronze work depicting six interpretations of marriage (from first love to quarrel to death-do-us-part) all based on a verse by Hans Sachs, the medieval cobbler-poet. You soon realise why the artist, Jürgen Weber, faced a blizzard of criticism when the fountain was unveiled in 1984; it's enough to put anyone off tying the knot. On Hefnersplatz, the townsfolk had fewer quibbles with another modern fountain, the **Peter-Henlein-Brunnen** dedicated to the 16th-century tinkerer who is credited with making the first pocket watch.

LORENZKIRCHE

Lorenzer Platz is dedicated to one of the church's first archivists, St Lawrence, a revered Catholic saint. Nuremberg's Catholics were once split into competing factions, one north and the other south of the river; the latter made a statement with the **Lorenzkirche** (Church of St Lawrence), a massive 15th-century church crammed with artistic treasures. Highlights include the stained-glass windows (including a Rosetta window 9m in diameter) and Veit Stoss' *Engelsgruss* (Annunciation), a wooden carving with life-size figures suspended above the high altar.

The **Tugendbrunnen** (Fountain of Virtues), on the north side of the church, shows six ladies (Faith, Hope, Charity, Courage, Temperance and Patience) brazenly spouting water from their breasts in the shadow of a figure representing Justice.

REICHSPARTEITAGSGELÄNDE

If you've ever wondered where the infamous black-and-white images of ecstatic Nazi supporters hailing their Führer were filmed, was here in Nuremberg. This orchestrate propaganda began as early as 1927, but afte 1933 Hitler opted for a purpose-built venu the **Reichsparteitagsgelände** (Nazi Party Rall Grounds). Much of the outsized ground was destroyed during Allied bombing raid but enough is left to get a sense of the mega lomania behind it.

At the northwestern edge was th **Luitpoldarena**, designed for mass SS and S. parades. The area is now a park. South c here, the half-built **Kongresshalle** (Congres Hall) was meant to outdo Rome's Colosseur in both scale and style.

A visit to the **Dokumentationszentru** (Documentation Centre; ☎ 231 5666; Bayernstrasse 11 adult/student €5/2.50; ✆ 9am-6pm Mon-Fri, 10am-6pm S & Sun) in the north wing of the Kongresshall helps to put the grounds into some histori cal context. A stunning walkway of glass cu diagonally through the complex, ending wit an interior view of the congress hall. Insid the exhibit *Fascination and Terror* exam ines the rise of the NSDAP, the Hitler cul the party rallies and the Nuremberg Trial Don't miss it.

East of the Kongresshalle, across th artificial Dutzendteich (Dozen Ponds), i the **Zeppelinfeld**, fronted by a 350m-lon grandstand, the **Zeppelintribüne**, where mos of the big Nazi parades, rallies and event took place. It now hosts sporting events an rock concerts, though this rehabilitation sti causes controversy.

The grounds are bisected by the 60m wide **Grosse Strasse** (Great Road), which cul minates, 2km south, at the **Märzfeld** (Marc Field), which was planned as military ex ercise grounds. West of the Grosse Strass was to have stood the **Deutsches Stadion** with seating capacity of 400,000. Things never go beyond the first excavation, and the hole wa filled with groundwater – today's Silbersee

To get to the grounds, take tram 9 from th Hauptbahnhof to Dokuzentrum.

NUREMBERG TRIALS COURTHOUSE

Nazi war criminals were tried for crime against peace and humanity in th **Schwurgerichtssaal 600** (Courtroom 600; ☎ 231 566 Fürther Strasse 110). The courtroom was closed a time of writing due to building work and th installation of a permanent exhibition, but i scheduled to reopen in early 2010.

Held in 1945–46, the trials resulted in the conviction and sentencing of 22 Nazi leaders and 150 underlings, and the execution of dozens. Among those condemned to death were Joachim von Ribbentrop, Alfred Rosenberg, Wilhelm Frick and Julius Streicher. Hermann Göring, the Reich's field marshal, cheated the hangman by taking cyanide in his cell hours before his scheduled execution.

Many suppose the Allies opted for Nuremberg for symbolic reasons, but their choice may have simply been down to the layout of the building, one of few such complexes to survive the war intact.

To get there, take the U1 to Bärenschanze.

GERMANISCHES NATIONALMUSEUM

One of the most important museums of German culture with over 1.3 million items (not all of which are displayed), the **Germanisches Nationalmuseum** (☎ 133 10; Kartäusergasse 1; adult/concession €6/4; ☽ 10am-6pm Tue-Sun, 10am-9pm Wed) is strangely underrated and undervisited. It features an archaeological collection, arms and armour, musical and scientific instruments and toys – but the jewel in its crown is the **art section**. This varied exhibit not only boasts exquisite paintings, but also sculpture, historical garments, porcelain and glass objects. Long-running renovation work at the museum means some sections may be closed.

As you might expect, local lad Dürer gets top billing. The works on display give an insight into the artist's enormous prestige at the Holy Roman court; his commissions included portraits for emperors Charlemagne and Sigrimund, whose faces appeared on the doors of the imperial chambers. The artist's celebrated *Hercules Slaying the Stymphalian Birds* confirms his superb grasp of anatomical detail and a flash of mischief (Dürer put his own facial features on the Greek hero). The many other gems include Albrecht Altdorfer's *Victory of Charlemagne over the Avars near Regensburg*, whose impossible detail tests the human eye.

The museum's main entrance is on Kartäusergasse, which is dominated by the **Way of Human Rights**, a row of symbolic, white-concrete pillars (and one oak tree) bearing the 30 articles of the Universal Declaration of Human Rights. Each 8m-high pillar is inscribed in German and, in succession, the language of a people whose rights have been violated. The oak represents the languages not explicitly mentioned.

DEUTSCHE BAHN MUSEUM

Nuremberg's impressive **Deutsche Bahn Museum** (German Railways Museum; ☎ 0180-444 2233; www.db -museum.de; Lessingstrasse 6; adult/concession €4/3; ☽ 9am-5pm Tue-Fri, 10am-6pm Sat & Sun) explores the history of Germany's legendary rail system. You'll see the country's first engine, the *Adler*, which ran from Nuremberg to nearby Fürth in 1852. Other fine specimens include Ludwig II's gilded carriage (dubbed the 'rolling Neuschwanstein' for its starry ceiling fresco and lavish decoration) and Bismarck's sober quarters for official visits. A highlight is the hourly demonstration of one of Germany's largest model railways, run by a controller at a huge console of blinking lights and switches.

NEUES MUSEUM

Housed in a spectacularly incongruous building with an all-glass facade, the **Neues Museum** (☎ 240 200; www.nmn.de; Klarissenplatz; adult/concession €4/3, Sun €1; ☽ 10am-8pm Tue-Fri, 10am-6pm Sat & Sun) has the panache of a museum devoted to art and design. The upper floor displays contemporary art (mostly abstracts) while the lower showcases major developments in design since 1945. For a free peek at the exhibits, just stand in the courtyard outside.

HANDWERKERHOF

A recreation of an old-world Nuremberg crafts quarter, the **Handwerkerhof** (☽ 10am-6.30pm Mon-Fri, 10am-4pm Sat) is a self-contained tourist trap by the Königstor. It's about as quaint as a hammer on your thumbnail, but if you're cashed up you may find some decent merchandise.

JÜDISCHES MUSEUM FRANKEN IN FÜRTH

A quick U-Bahn ride away in the neighbouring town of Fürth is the **Jüdisches Museum Franken in Fürth** (Frankish Jewish Museum; ☎ 770 577; Königstrasse 89; adult/concession €3/2; ☽ 10am-5pm Wed-Sun, 10am-8pm Tue). Fürth once had the largest Jewish congregation of any city in southern Germany, and this museum, housed in a handsomely restored building, chronicles the history of Jewish life in the region from the Middle Ages to today. To reach the museum, take the U1 to the Rathaus stop in Fürth.

Walking Tour

This circuit covers the historic centre's key sights over a leisurely 2.5km walk. With visits to all the museums and attractions listed, it could take the best part of two days.

BAVARIA

NUREMBERG ALTSTADT WALKING TOUR

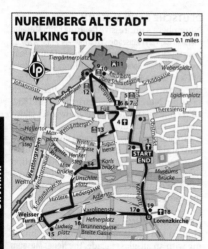

WALK FACTS

Start Hauptmarkt
Finish Hauptmarkt
Distance 2.5km
Duration 2 hours

The tour starts at the Hauptmarkt, the main square. At the eastern end is the ornate Gothic **Pfarrkirche Unsere Liebe Frau** (**1**; p365), or Frauenkirche. The clock's figures spring into action every day at noon. The **Schöner Brunnen** (**2**; p365) rises up from the cobblestones like a buried cathedral. Walk north to the Altes Rathaus, the old town hall with its **Lochgefängnisse** (**3**; p365), the medieval dungeons. Opposite stands the 13th-century **St Sebalduskirche** (**4**; p365), with an exterior smothered in religious sculptures and the bronze shrine of St Sebald inside. Just up Burgstrasse, the **Stadtmuseum Fembohaus** (**5**; p365) covers the highs and lows of Nuremberg's past with a multimedia show. Backtrack south to Halbwachsengässchen and turn right into Albrecht-Dürer-Platz and a dignified statue of the great painter, the **Albrecht Dürer Monument** (**6**; p366). Directly beneath are the **Felsengänge** (**7**; p366), tunnels once used as an old beer cellar and an air-raid shelter.

Moving up Bergstrasse, you'll reach the massive **Tiergärtnertor** (**8**; p366), a 16th-century tower. Nearby is the comely, half-timbered **Pilatushaus** (**9**; p366) and a strange, glassy-eyed hare dedicated to Dürer. A few steps east is the **Historischer Kunstbunker** (**10**; p367) where

precious art was stored in WWII. Looming over the scene is the **Kaiserburg** (**11**; p367) the castle of medieval knights with imperial chambers. Go south to the **Albrecht-Dürer-Haus** (**12**; p367) where the Renaissance genius lived and worked. Continue south along Albrecht Dürer-Strasse, turn left on Füll and skirt the back of Sebalduskirche to Karlsstrasse, where you'll reach the **Spielzeugmuseum** (**13**; p367) with masses of amusing toys.

Cross the Karlsbrücke to enjoy a view of the **Weinstadel** (**14**), an old wine depot overlooking the river. Continue across the Henkersteg (Hangman's Bridge) and wend your way south to Vordere Ledergasse which leads west to the amazing **Ehekarussell Brunnen** (**15**; p368), with its outrageous image of married life. Head east on Ludwigsplatz past the **Peter-Henlein-Brunnen** (**16**; p368), with a statue of the first watchmaker, and proceed along Karolinenstrasse to reach the city's oldest house, **Nassauer Haus** (**17**) at No 2, and the massive **Lorenzkirche** (**18**; p368), a 15th-century tabernacle with a suspended carving of the Annunciation. The **Tugendbrunnen** (**19**; p368), Fountain of the Seven Virtues, is on the north side of the church.

Continuing north up Königstrasse will return you to the Hauptmarkt, your starting point.

Tours

English-language **Old Town walking tours** (adult/child under 14yr €9/free; ☻ 1pm May-Oct) are run by the tourist office, and include admission to the Kaiserburg. Tours leave from the Hauptmarkt branch (see p365) and take 2½ hours.

Other organised tours:

History for Everyone (☎ 307 360; www.geschichte-fuer-alle.de) Intriguing range of themed English-language tours by a nonprofit association. The 'Albrecht Dürer' and 'Life in Medieval Nuremberg' tours come highly recommended.

Nuremberg Tours (☎ 0176-8009 2402; www.nurembergtours.com; tours adult/concession €18/15; ☻ 11am Mon, Thu & Sat mid-Apr–mid-Oct, Thu & Sun mid-Oct–Dec) Four-hour walking and public transport tours taking in the city centre and the Reichsparteitagsgelände. Groups meet at the entrance to the Hauptbahnhof.

Festivals & Events

From late November to Christmas Eve, the Hauptmarkt is taken over by the most famous **Christkindlesmarkt** (Christmas Market; www.christkindlesmarkt.de) in Germany. Yuletide shoppers descend on the 'Christmas City' from all over

NUREMBERG FOR KIDS

No city in Bavaria has more for kids to see and do than Nuremberg. In fact keeping the little 'uns entertained in the Franconian capital is child's play.

Museums

Children & Young People's Museum (☎ 600 0410; www.kindermuseum-nuernberg.de; Michael-Ende-Strasse 17; adult/family €5.80/17; ✆ 2-5.30pm Sat, 10am-5.30pm Sun, closed Jul & Aug) Educational exhibitions and lots of hands-on fun – just a pity it's not open more often.

School Museum (☎ 530 2574; Äussere Sulzbacher Strasse; adult/child €5/2.50; ✆ 9am-5pm Tue-Fri, 10am-6pm Sat & Sun) Recreated classroom plus school-related exhibits from the 17th century to the Third Reich.

Deutsche Bahn Museum (p369) Feeds the kids' obsession for choo-choos.

Play

Playground of the Senses (☎ 231 5445; www.erfahrungsfeld.nuernberg.de; Untere Talgasse 8; adult/child €5.60/3.20; ✆ 9am-6pm Mon-Fri, 1-6pm Sat, 10am-6pm Sun) Some 80 hands-on 'stations' designed to educate children in the laws of nature, physics and the human body. Take the U2 or U3 to Wöhrder Wiese.

Toys

Playmobil (☎ 9666 1700; www.playmobil-funpark.de; Brandstätterstrasse 2-10, Zirndorf; admission per person from €2.50; ✆ 9am-7pm May-Sep, 9am-6pm Oct, 10am-6pm Nov-Apr) Playmobil theme park with life-size versions of the popular toys. Located 9km west of the city centre in Zirndorf – take the U3 to Gustav-Adolf-Strasse, then change to bus 113.

Käthe Wohlfahrt Christmas shop (☎ 4090; www.bestofchristmas.com; Königstrasse 8) The Nuremberg branch of this year-round Christmas shop.

Spielzeugmuseum (p367) Some 1400 sq metres of Matchbox, Barbie, Playmobil and Lego, plus a great play area.

Germanisches Nationalmuseum (p369) Has a new toy section and holds special tours for children.

Zoo

Nuremberg Zoo (☎ 545 46; www.tiergarten.nuernberg.de; Am Tiergarten 30; adult/child €7.50/3.70; ✆ 8am-7.30pm Apr-Sep, 9am-5pm Oct-Mar) An open-air zoo and Dolphinarium with enclosures as close as possible to the animals' natural habitats. Take bus 5 from the Hauptbahnhof.

Europe to seek out unique gifts at the scores of colourful timber trinket stalls that fill the square. The aroma of *Lebkuchen* (large, soft, spicy biscuits), mulled wine and roast sausages permeates the chilly air, while special festive events take place on the square and at other venues around town.

Sleeping

Accommodation gets tight and rates rocket during the Christmas market and toy fair (trade only) in late January to early February. At other times, cheap rooms can be found, especially if you book ahead.

BUDGET

Knaus-Campingpark (☎ 981 2717; www.knauscamp.de; Hans-Kalb-Strasse 56; per tent/person €3.50/6.50) A camping ground near the lakes in the Volkspark,

southeast of the city centre. Take the U1 to Messezentrum, then walk about 1km.

Lette 'm sleep (☎ 992 8128; www.backpackers.de; Frauentormauer 42; dm €16-20, d €49, linen €3; 🖥 🛜) Conveniently located within the old town wall and just five minutes from the Hauptbahnhof, this is a great place to grab some shut-eye and meet fellow travellers. The excellent facilities include a cosy common room, kitchen, bar, free web access and a basement laundry (€5 per load). The rooftop apartments boast their own kitchens and are ideal for groups of friends. Staff are a mine of information on the city and the wider Franconia region.

DJH hostel (☎ 230 9360; www.nuernberg.jugend herberge.de; Burg 2; dm under/over 27yr €21.90/25.90) A 20-minute walk north of the Hauptbahnhof, this spotless youth hostel in the former castle stables has 382 beds in bright airy dorms. It's open year-round.

Probst-Garni Hotel (☎ 203 433; fax 205 9336; Luitpoldstrasse 9; s €46-56, d €59-75) A pleasant, family-run outfit in the old centre, with spacious modern quarters, as clean as a new pin. The 39 rooms, each with a slightly different colour scheme, are spread over three floors and are adequately distant from somewhat sleazy Luitpoldstrasse.

MIDRANGE

Art & Business Hotel (☎ 232 10; www.art-business-hotel.com; Gleissbühlstrasse 15; s €60-89, d €84-145; ✉ ⎙) You don't have to be an artist or a business person to stay at this new, up-to-the-minute place, a retro sport shoe's throw from the Hauptbahnhof. Rooms are a study in diligently composed minimalism, while technicolour art and design brings cheer to the communal spaces. Rates tumble at weekends.

ourpick Hotel Elch (☎ 249 2980; www.hotel-elch.de; Irrerstrasse 9; s/d €69/85; ⎙ ⎙) This dramatically historic hotel, occupying a 14th-century half-timbered house near the Kaiserburg, has petite rooms up a narrow medieval staircase. Breakfast is served in the quaint woody restaurant, the Schnitzelria, which does a good line in Franconian beers and, yes, *Schnitzel*.

Hotel Deutscher Kaiser (☎ 242 660; www.deutscher-kaiser-hotel.de; Königstrasse 55; s €87-162, d €106-188; ⓟ ✉ ⎙) A grand sandstone staircase leads to ornately decorated rooms in this 1880s-built hotel in the Altstadt. The 'Kaiser' rooms are slightly dearer but superior to the standard doubles, with bidets in the bathrooms, brocaded curtains and carved bedsteads. The elegant reading room is a gem.

Hotel Drei Raben (☎ 274 380; www.hotel-drei-raben.de; Königstrasse 63; s & d €100-185; ✉ ⎙) This designer theme hotel builds upon the legend of three ravens perched on the building's chimney stack, who tell each other stories from Nuremberg lore. Each of the 21 rooms uses its style and humour to tell a particular tale – from the life of Dürer to the history of the locomotive.

TOP END

Agneshof (☎ 214 440; www.agneshof-nuernberg.de; Agnesgasse 10; s €90-175, d €112-225; ⓟ ✉ ⎙) The Agneshof is a real pleasure – an oasis of calm with an upbeat artsy air, first-rate facilities and elegant contemporary rooms. If you feel like some pampering, try the whirlpool and in-house health treatments. The comfy Kaiser suites offer unparalleled views of the castle.

Eating
RESTAURANTS

Sushi Glas (☎ 205 9901; Kornmarkt 7; sushi from €4.50 ☺ noon-11pm Mon-Wed, noon-midnight Thu-Sat, 6-10pm Sun) Take a pew in this 21st-century sugar cube to watch the sushi chef deftly craft your order. When the mercury climbs high, enjoy you *nigiri*, sashimi and American sushi beneath the huge sunshades on the Kornmarkt.

Café am Trödelmarkt (☎ 208 877; Trödelmarkt dishes €5-9) A gorgeous spot on a sunny day the 'Fleamarket Cafe' overlooking the covered Henkersteg bridge is an excellent choice for breakfast or lunch. A menu of salads, filled baguettes and a bevy of seasonal dishes such as asparagus or freshwater fish may soon see you back for second helpings.

Barfüsser Kleines Brauhaus (☎ 204 242; Königstrasse 60; mains €6-15) This Nuremberg institution is housed in an atmospheric old grain warehouse packed with copper vats, enamel advertising plaques and oodles of other knick-knacks. The cavernous vaulted cellar is the place to install yourself in the company of an *Eichenholzfässchen*, a 5L oak-wood keg of beer.

Enchilada (☎ 244 8498; Obstmarkt 5; mains €6-18) This Mexican haunt with faux adobe walls does generous taco platters, burritos and nachos in a candlelit setting. Later on, the cocktail lists come out for the patrons flowing in from the Hauptmarkt nearby.

Burgwächter (☎ 222 126; Am Ölberg 10; mains €7-15) Refuel after a tour of the Kaiserburg with prime steaks, *Bratwurst* with potato salad, homemade filled pastas and salads, as you feast your eyes on the best terrace views from any city eatery. With kids in tow, ask for *Kloss*, a simple dumpling with sauce dish (€3.20).

Heilig-Geist-Spital (☎ 221 761; Spitalgasse 12 mains €7-17) Lots of dark carved wood, a herd of hunting trophies and a romantic candlelit half-light make this former hospital one of the most atmospheric dining rooms in town. Sample the delicious, seasonally changing menu inside or out in the pretty courtyard where the tinkle of cutlery on plate competes with a dribbling fountain.

Hütt'n (☎ 201 9881; Burgstrasse 19; mains €7-17) This local haunt is perpetually overflowing with admirers of *Krustenschäufele* (roast pork with crackling, dumplings and sauerkraut salad) so be prepared to queue. It's also a good place to down a few tankards of Franconian *Landbier*.

our pick Marientorzwinger (☎ 274 2784; Lorenzerstrasse 33; mains €8-17) This is the last remaining *Zwinger* eatery (taverns built between the inner and outer walls when they relinquished their military use) in Nuremberg. Chomp on sturdy Franconian staples or a vegie dish in the simple wood-panelled dining room or the leafy beer garden, and swab the decks with a yard of Fürth-brewed Tucher.

Also recommended:

Kettensteg (☎ 221 081; Maxplatz 35; mains €6-14) Nuremberg's best open-air option far from the tourist march serving light seasonal twists on Franconian fare.

Zunftstübchen (☎ 180 9207; Am Ölberg 35; mains €7-10; ✆ closed Mon & Tue) Historic place serving a reassuringly short and simple menu of Central European favourites.

QUICK EATS

Naturkostladen Lotos (☎ 243 598; Unschlittplatz 1; dishes €2.50-7) Unclog arteries and blast free radicals with a blitz of grain burgers, spinach soup or vegie pizza at this health-food shop. The fresh bread and cheese counter is a treasure chest of nutritious picnic supplies.

Souptopia (☎ 240 6697; Lorenzer Strasse 27; soups €2.80-6.50; ✆ closed Sun) Like-granny-used-to-make soups, backed up by a good choice of sandwiches, salads and other vegie options, make this a fantastic hole-filler.

Vegan Imbiss (Luitpoldstrasse 13; dishes €3-6) Wedged between the facades of Luitpoldstrasse, this tiny snack bar offers meat- and dairy-free noodle-rice-veg combinations with a touch of Asian zing.

Sushi Nagoya (☎ 242 5143; Hintere Ledergasse 2; mains €6-20; ✆ 11.30am-3pm & 5.30-11.30pm Mon-Sat) This gaudy sushi bar in a former Bavarian pub has mean deals, such as a 'Bento' – miso soup, three pieces of sushi, a spring roll and chicken teriyaki – for €9.95.

American Diner (Cinecitta Cinema, Gewerbemuseumsplatz 3; burgers €8-12; ✆ 11am-1am Sun-Thu, 11am-2am Fri & Sat) For the juiciest burgers in town head for this retro diner in the Cinecitta Cinema.

NUREMBERG SAUSAGES

There's hot(dog) competition between Regensburg and Nuremberg over whose sausages are best; the latter's are certainly more famous. Sample them for yourself at the following places.

Bratwurstglöcklein im Handwerkerhof (☎ 227 625; Handwerkerhof; dishes €5-11) Despite its location in the folksy Handwerkerhof, the sausages here are first-rate. *Drei im Weckla* (three links in a roll) will cost you loose change.

Bratwursthäusle (☎ 227 695; Rathausplatz 1; dishes €5-11; ✆ closed Sun) Seared over a flaming beechwood grill, the little links sold at this rustic inn arguably set the standards for *Rostbratwürste* across the land. You can dine in the timbered restaurant or on the terrace with views of the Hauptmarkt.

Drinking

Landbierparadies (☎ 287 8673; Rothenburger Strasse 26; mains €6-9; ✆ evenings) A less than inspiring exterior and a spit 'n' sawdust, all-timber saloon detract little from the incredible wellspring of obscure country ales pulled at this pub. Some 'brands' are only available here and in the village where they are brewed.

Treibhaus (☎ 223 041; Karl-Grillenberger-Strasse 28) Well off the path of most visitors, this bustling cafe is a Nuremberg institution. It serves breakfast till evening and caffeinated comfort to students and weary-legged shoppers.

Meisengeige (☎ 208 283; Am Laufer Schlagturm 3) This long-established hole-in-the-wall bar draws an intense crowd of film intellectuals thanks to the tiny indie cinema next door.

Entertainment

The excellent *Plärrer* (www.plaerrer.de; €2), available at newsstands throughout the city, is the best source of information on events around town. Otherwise the free monthly listings magazine *Doppelpunkt* (www.doppelpunkt.de), found in bars, restaurants and the tourist office, does an adequate job.

NIGHTCLUBS

Hirsch (☎ 429 414; Vogelweiherstrasse 66) This converted factory, 2.5km south of the Hauptbahnhof, hosts live alternative music almost daily, including big-name acts such as Suzanne Vega and The Wailers. Take the U1 to Frankenstrasse.

Loop Club (☎ 686 767; Klingenhofstrasse 52; ✆ Thu-Sat) With three dance areas and a languid chill-out zone with lounge music, this place attracts a slightly more mature crowd. Thursdays are 150-Cent night, a collective send-up with cheap mixed drinks flowing to the sound of '80s hits and karaoke. Take the U2 to Herrnhütte, turn right and it's a five-minute walk.

Mach1 (☎ 246 602; Kaiserstrasse 1-9; ◷ Thu-Sat) This legendary dance temple has been around for decades but still holds a spell over fashion victims. Line up and be mustered.

Rockfabrik (☎ 565 056; Klingenhofstrasse 56; ◷ Thu-Sat) Safely out of earshot of the centre, 3.5km to the northeast, this citadel of rock heaves with longhairs who flock here for the weekend 'AC/DC', 'Oldies' and 'Heroes of Rock' nights. Take the U2 to Herrnhütte.

CINEMA

Roxy (☎ 488 40; Julius-Lossmann-Strasse 116) This cinema shows first-run films in the original English version, a rarity in Nuremberg. Take tram 8 to the Südfriedhof stop.

Filmhaus (☎ 231 5823; Königstrasse 93) This small indie picture house shows foreign-language movies plus reruns of cult German flicks and films for kids.

THEATRE & CLASSICAL MUSIC

Staatstheater (State Theatre; www.staatstheater-nuernberg .de; Richard-Wagner-Platz 2) Nuremberg's magnificent Staatstheater serves up an impressive mix of dramatic arts. The renovated art nouveau opera house presents opera and ballet, while the Kammerspiele offers a varied program of classical and contemporary plays. Tickets are available at the box office or by calling ☎ 231 3808. The Nürnberger Philharmoniker also performs here.

Getting There & Away

Nuremberg airport (☎ 937 00), 5km north of the centre, is served by regional and international carriers, including Lufthansa, Air Berlin and Air France.

Trains run at least hourly to/from Frankfurt (€48, two hours) and Munich (€49, one hour). There are direct connections several times daily to Berlin (€89, 4¾ hours) and Vienna (€86, five hours), while a couple of slow trains also go to Prague (€51.40, five hours).

Buses leave for Berlin at 12.10pm (oneway €42, four hours) with BerlinLinienBus, and to destinations across Europe from the spanking-new bus station near the Hauptbahnhof. The **Eurolines/Touring ticket office** (☎ 221 940; Käte-Ströbel-Strasse 4) is nearby.

The **CityToCity Mitfahrzentrale** (☎ 194 40; www .citytocity.de; Hummelsteiner Weg 12; ◷ 9am-6pm Mon-Fri, 9am-1.30pm Sat) ride-share service is right behind the south exit of the Hauptbahnhof.

Getting Around
TO/FROM THE AIRPORT

U-Bahn 2 runs every few minutes from the Hauptbahnhof to the airport (€1.80, 12 minutes). A taxi to/from the airport will cost you about €16.

BICYCLE

The tourist office sells the ADFC's *Fahrrad Stadtplan* (€4.50), a detailed map of the city and surrounding area. It also hands out a list of bicycle-friendly hotels in town that will store bicycles for travellers. For bike hire try the excellent **Ride on a Rainbow** (☎ 397 337; Adam-Kraft-Strasse 55; per day €10-22).

PUBLIC TRANSPORT

The best transport around the Altstadt is at the end of your legs. Tickets on the VGN bus, tram and U-Bahn/S-Bahn networks cost €1.60/1.90 per short/long ride. A day pass costs €3.80. Passes bought on Saturday are valid all weekend.

TAXI

The starting rate for a **taxi ride** (☎ 194 10) is €2.60.

BAMBERG

☎ 0951 / pop 70,000

With a history-steeped centre, a magnificent cathedral and heaps of romantic charm, it's difficult not to be impressed by Bamberg. Clearly one of Germany's most beautiful cities, this Unesco-listed history lesson was built by archbishops on seven hills, earning it the sobriquet of 'Franconian Rome'.

Miraculously, Bamberg emerged from WWII with hardly a scratch, and most of the city's finest buildings are originals. Many unadulterated examples of architecture from the Romanesque era onwards have survived, lending the city a more genuine feel than most. Bamberg is also justly famous for its beer, with 10 breweries in town and another 80 or so in the vicinity.

Orientation

Two waterways bisect the city: the Main-Danube Canal, just south of the Hauptbahnhof, and the Regnitz River, which flows through

BAMBERG

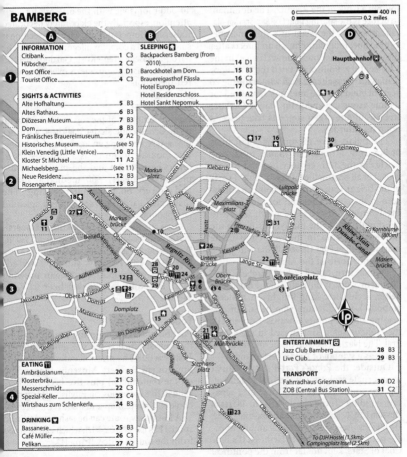

INFORMATION	
Citibank	**1** C3
Hübscher	**2** C2
Post Office	**3** D1
Tourist Office	**4** C3

SIGHTS & ACTIVITIES	
Alte Hofhaltung	**5** B3
Altes Rathaus	**6** B3
Diözesan Museum	**7** B3
Dom	**8** B3
Fränkisches Brauereimuseum	**9** A2
Historisches Museum	(see 5)
Klein Venedig (Little Venice)	**10** B2
Kloster St Michael	**11** A2
Michaelsberg	(see 11)
Neue Residenz	**12** B3
Rosengarten	**13** B3

SLEEPING	
Backpackers Bamberg (from 2010)	**14** D1
Barockhotel am Dom	**15** B3
Brauereigasthof Fässla	**16** C2
Hotel Europa	**17** C2
Hotel Residenzschloss	**18** A2
Hotel Sankt Nepomuk	**19** C3

EATING	
Ambräusianum	**20** B3
Klosterbräu	**21** C3
Messerschmidt	**22** C3
Spezial-Keller	**23** C4
Wirtshaus zum Schlenkerla	**24** B3

DRINKING	
Bassanese	**25** B3
Café Müller	**26** C3
Pelikan	**27** A2

ENTERTAINMENT	
Jazz Club Bamberg	**28** B3
Live Club	**29** B3

TRANSPORT	
Fahrradhaus Griesmann	**30** D2
ZOB (Central Bus Station)	**31** C2

To Kornblume (800m)

To DJH Hostel (1.5km); Campingplatz Insel (2.5km)

BAVARIA

the town centre. The city's bus hub, the Zentraler Omnibusbahnhof (ZOB), is on Promenadestrasse, just off Schönleinsplatz.

Information

Bamberg Card (per 48hr €9) Provides admission to city attractions, use of city buses and a walking tour. It's available from the tourist office.

Citibank (Schönleinsplatz)

Hübscher (☎ 982 250; Grüner Markt 16; internet per 30min €1.50; ☻ 9am-7pm Mon-Fri, 9am-6pm Sat) Large bookshop with English-language titles and internet access upstairs.

Post office (Ludwigstrasse 25)

Tourist office (☎ 297 6200; www.bamberg.info; Geyersworthstrasse 3; ☻ 9.30am-6pm Mon-Fri, 9.30am-2.30pm Sat & Sun)

Sights

ALTSTADT

Bamberg's main appeal lies in its sheer number of fine historic buildings, their jumble of styles and the paucity of modern eyesores. Most attractions are sprinkled along the Regnitz River, but the town's incredibly statuesque **Altes Rathaus** is actually on it, perched on twin bridges like a ship in dry dock (note the cherub's leg sticking out from the fresco on the east side). To the northwest are the charming half-timbered homes of **Klein Venedig** (Little Venice), complete with punts, canals and river docks.

DOM

Bamberg's princely and ecclesiastical roots are felt strongest around Domplatz on the southern bank of the Regnitz. The dominant structure is the soaring **Dom** (� 8am-5pm Nov-Mar, 8am-6pm Apr-Oct), the result of a Romanesque-Gothic duel fought by church architects after the original edifice burnt down (twice) in the 12th century. Politics dictated the final floor plan, which was altered each winter during 20 years of building. The interior is renowned for its fine acoustics, and from May to October free 30-minute organ concerts take place at noon on Saturday.

The pillars have the original light hues of Franconian sandstone thanks to Ludwig I, who in the 19th century ordered the removal of all postmedieval decoration. Traces of the bright 13th-century reliefs can still be seen in the choir. Look out for the **Lächelnde Engel** (Smiling Angel) in the north aisle, who smirkingly hands the martyr's crown to the headless St Denis. In the west choir is the marble tomb of **Pope Clemens II**, the only papal burial spot north of the Alps.

The star turn, however, and Bamberg's enduring mystery, is the statue of the **Bamberger Reiter**, a chivalric king-knight on a steed. Nobody knows for sure who he is, but one leading theory points towards Konrad III, the Hohenstaufen king buried in the cathedral. The Nazis seized on the heroic medieval image as a symbol of Aryan perfection.

Outside, the **Prince's Portal** shows Christ in an ornate sculpture of the Last Judgment. On the south side of the Dom, in a separate building off the cloisters, is the **Diözesan Museum** (☎ 502 316; Domplatz 5; adult/concession €3/2.50; ☺ 10am-5pm Tue-Sun). Top ranking among its ecclesiastical treasures goes to Heinrich II's Blue Coat of Stars, kept not far from the pontifical knee-socks of Clemens II.

AROUND DOMPLATZ

Northwest of the Dom is the **Alte Hofhaltung** (old court hall), a former prince-bishops' palace that contains the **Historisches Museum** (☎ 519 0746; Domplatz 7; adult/concession €3/2; ☺ 9am-5pm Tue-Sun May-Oct). The mixed bag of exhibits includes a model of the pilgrimage church Vierzehnheiligen (p382) and the Bamberger Götzen, ancient stone sculptures found in the region.

Across the square, you'll spot the stately **Neue Residenz** (☎ 519 390; Domplatz 8; adult/concession €4/3; ☺ 9am-6pm Apr-Sep, 10am-4pm Oct-Mar), a huge episcopal palace now housing a significant collection of baroque paintings. The

40-odd rooms vie with the artwork for your attention, especially the elaborately decorated Kaisersaal (Imperial Hall), where the ceiling is smothered in a complex allegorical fresco. The baroque **Rosengarten** (Rose Garden) behind the palace has fabulous views over Bamberg's red-tiled roofs.

MICHAELSBERG

Above Domplatz, at the top of Michaelsberg, is the Benedictine **Kloster St Michael**, a former monastery and now an aged people's home. The monastery church is a must-see, both for its baroque art and the meticulous depictions of nearly 600 medicinal plants and flowers on the vaulted ceiling. The manicured garden terrace boasts a splendid city panorama.

Also up here is the **Fränkisches Brauereimuseum** (Franconian Brewery Museum; ☎ 530 16; Michaelsberg 10f; adult/concession €3/2.50; ☺ 1-5pm Wed-Sun Apr-Oct). Exhibits show plaster(ed) dummies of monks, who began brewing their Benediktiner Dunkel beer as early as 1122.

Tours

Possibly the most tempting tour offered by the tourist office is the self-guided **Brewery Trail** (adult €22). The price includes entry to the Franconian Brewery Museum (depending on the route taken) plus five beer vouchers valid in five brewpubs, an English information booklet, a route map and a souvenir stein.

A less boozy route can be fashioned using a special **PDA** (per 4/8hr €8.50/12), which can be hired from the tourist office. Bring ID.

Sleeping

To book a room (from about €40/60 for singles/doubles) through the room reservations hotline, call ☎ 297 6310.

Campingplatz Insel (☎ 563 20; www.campinginsel.de; Am Campingplatz 1; tents €4-8, adult/car €5/4) This well-equipped place, in a tranquil spot right on the river, is the sole camping option. Take bus 18 to Campingplatz.

Backpackers Bamberg (☎ 222 1718; www.backpackers bamberg.de; Memmelsdorferstrasse 21; dm €16-19; ☺) By the time you read this, Bamberg's only independent hostel will have moved from its delightfully cosy loft to larger premises in Heiliggrabstrasse. New facilities will include bike storage, a fully equipped kitchen and free wi-fi. Check the website for details.

Brauereigasthof Fässla (☎ 265 16; www.faessla.de; Obere Königstrasse 19-21; s/d €40/60; **P**) Those with more than a passing interest in the local brews should try this atmospheric guesthouse, where snug but modern rooms are just up the stairs from the pub and covered courtyard.

Hotel Europa (☎ 309 3020; www.hotel-europa-bamberg.de; Untere Königstrasse 6-8; s €67-71, d €92/97) Bamberg's newest lodgings are a spick-and-span but unfussy affair above the town's most respected Italian restaurant. Ask for a room at the front with views of the Dom and the red-tiled roofs of the Altstadt. Breakfast is in the restaurant or out in the sunny courtyard.

Barockhotel am Dom (☎ 540 31; www.barockhotel.de; Vorderer Bach 4; s/d €72/98; **P** ⊠ 🖵) The sugary facade, a sceptre's swipe from the Dom, gives a hint of the baroque heritage and original details within. Rooms have sweeping views of the Dom or over the roofs of the Altstadt, and breakfast is served in a 14th-century vault.

our pick **Hotel Sankt Nepomuk** (☎ 984 20; www hotel-nepomuk.de; Obere Mühlbrücke 9; s/d €95/145; **P**) Named aptly after the patron saint of bridges, this classy place is located in an A-framed former mill in the middle of the Regnitz. It has rustic rooms, a superb gourmet restaurant on the premises and bicycles for hire.

Hotel Residenzschloss (☎ 609 10; www.residenz schloss.com; Untere Sandstrasse 32; s/d €139/174; **P** ⊠) Opposite the concert hall, one of Bamberg's best hotels occupies a historic former hospital. Its swanky furnishings, from the Roman-style steam bath to the flashy piano bar, have little in common with institutional care.

Eating

Grüner Markt, the main shopping drag, has a daily produce market and a number of fast-food options.

Wirtshaus zum Schlenkerla (☎ 560 60; Dominikanerstrasse 6; dishes €5-10) A local legend that's known nationwide, this dark, rustic 16th-century restaurant with long wooden tables serves tasty Franconian specialities and its own superb *Rauchbier*, poured straight from the oak barrel.

Spezial-Keller (☎ 548 87; Sternwartstrasse 8; dishes €5-11) Quite a hike out of town, but the superb *Rauchbier* served here is your reward, along with great views of the Dom and the Altstadt from the beer garden. Join Bamberg's beer connoisseurs in November to ring in the *Bockbier* (malty beer) season.

Klosterbräu (☎ 522 65; Obere Mühlbrücke 1-3; mains €6-11) This beautiful half-timbered brewery is Bamberg's oldest. It draws *Stammgäste* (regulars local drinkers) and tourists alike who wash down filling slabs of meat and dumplings with its excellent range of ales.

Ambräusianum (☎ 509 0262; Dominikanerstrasse 10; dishes €7-15) This outstanding brewpub does a killer *Weisswurst* breakfast – parsley-speckled veal sausage served with a big freshly baked pretzel and a *Weissbier* (€5.50). Sit next to the copper vat and listen to the beer ferment.

Kornblume (☎ 917 1760; Kapellenstrasse 22; mains €8-10; 🕑 5.30pm-midnight Mon, 11.30am-2pm & 5.30pm-midnight Wed-Sun; **V**) Don't be deterred by the crass decor at this family-run place 1.5km east of the centre, as the tasty food is lovingly prepared and strict organic and eco-friendly principles impeccably upheld. The menu reads like a vegetarian's antioxidant bible, though the occasional meat dish also makes an appearance. Take bus 5 to Wunderberg.

Messerschmidt (☎ 297 800; Lange Strasse 41; mains €15-24) In the house where plane engineer Willy Messerschmidt was born, this stylish gourmet eatery oozes old-world tradition, with dark woods, white linens and formal service. Dine out on the charming alfresco terrace overlooking a pretty park, or in the attached wine tavern with a more relaxed atmosphere.

Drinking & Entertainment

For chilled-out entertainment the best places to head for are Austrasse and Sandstrasse, where the hip hang out by day and night. See Eating, left, for brewpubs.

Café Müller (☎ 202 943; Austrasse 23) Attractive coffee house and cocktail bar that spills out onto the cobbles from late winter.

Bassanese (☎ 509 568; Karolinenstrasse 2) Serves authentic Italian gelato, strudels and handmade chocolates to fans in wicker chairs on the cobblestones near the old town hall.

Other possible options include **Pelikan** (☎ 603 410; Untere Sandstrasse 45), a candlelit pub with occasional local bands, and **Live Club** (☎ 603 410; Oberer Sandstrasse 7), a premier venue for live music. Down the road, **Jazz Club Bamberg** (☎ 537 40; Oberer Sandstrasse 18) is a fixture on the scene for intimate, high-quality acts.

Getting There & Around

There are at least hourly RE and RB trains from Nuremberg (€11.30, 45 to 60 minutes) or from Würzburg (€17.60, one hour), as well

BAVARIA

as ICE trains every hour to/from Munich (€56, two hours) and Berlin (€80, four to five hours).

Several buses, including 1, 2 and 14, connect the train station with the central bus station, ZOB. Bus 10 goes from the ZOB to Domplatz.

Most explore Bamberg on foot, but you can also hire bicycles at **Fahrradhaus Griesmann** (☎ 229 67; Obere Königstrasse 42; per day €9.50). Cars are a colossal pain in town, so park on the outskirts or take a bus (€1.30, or €6.60 for a Tourist Ticket good for 48 hours of unlimited travel). For a taxi, call ☎ 150 15.

BAYREUTH
☎ 0921 / pop 75,000

Even without its Wagner connections, Bayreuth would still be an interesting detour from Nuremberg or Bamberg for its baroque architecture and curious palaces. But it's for the annual Wagner Festival that 60,000 opera devotees make a pilgrimage to this neck of the *Wald*, many having waited years in the ticket lottery to do so.

Bayreuth's glory days began in 1735 when Wilhelmine, sister of King Frederick the Great of Prussia, was forced to marry stuffy Margrave Friedrich. Bored with the local scene, the cultured Anglo-oriented Wilhelmine invited the finest artists, poets, composers and architects in Europe to court. The period bequeathed some eye-catching buildings, still on display for all to see.

Orientation

The Hauptbahnhof is five to 10 minutes' walk north of the historic cobblestone centre. Head south on Bahnhofstrasse to Luitpoldplatz and on to the pedestrianised Maximilianstrasse, the main drag also known as Markt. The Eremitage, a baroque palace with manicured gardens, is about 6km to the east, while the Festspielhaus, the theatre for the Wagner Festival performances, is 1.5km north of the town centre.

Information

Bayreuth Card (72hr €11.50) Good for unlimited trips on city buses, museum entry and a two-hour guided city walk (in German).
Commerzbank (Maximilianstrasse 38)
Internet Telecafé (Maximilianstrasse 85; per hr €1.40; ⏰ 10am-10pm Mon-Sat, noon-10pm Sun)
Post office (Hauptbahnhof & Kanzleistrasse 3)

Tourist office (☎ 885 88; www.bayreuth-tourismus.de; Luitpoldplatz 9; ⏰ 9am-6pm Mon-Fri, 9am-2pm Sat)

Sights
TOWN CENTRE

Outside of the Wagner Festival from late July to the end of August the streets of Bayreuth slip into a kind of provincial slumber, although the town's strong musical traditions ensure there are good dramatic and orchestral performances all year.

Designed by Giuseppe Galli Bibiena, a famous 18th-century architect from Bologna, the **Markgräfliches Opernhaus** (Margravial Opera House; ☎ 759 6922; Opernstrasse; tours adult/under 18yr/concession €5/free/4; ⏰ tours 9am-6pm Apr-Sep, 10am-4pm Oct-Mar) is a stunning baroque masterpiece. Germany's largest opera house until 1871, it has a lavish interior smothered in carved, gilded and marbled wood. Yet Richard Wagner deemed the place too modest for his serious work and conducted here just once. German speakers especially will enjoy the 45-minute sound-and-light multimedia show, which is a glorification vehicle for the Duchess Wilhelmine more than the great composer.

Just south of here is Wilhelmine's **Neues Schloss** (New Palace; ☎ 759 6921; Ludwigstrasse 21; adult/concession €5/4; ⏰ 9am-6pm Apr-Sep, 10am-4pm Tue-Sun Oct-Mar), which opens into the vast **Hofgarten** (admission free; ⏰ 24hr). A riot of rococo style, the margravial residence after 1753 features a collection of 18th-century porcelain made in Bayreuth. The annual VIP opening gala of the Wagner Festival is held in the Cedar Room. Also worth a look is the **Spiegelscherbenkabinett** (Broken Mirror Cabinet), which is lined with irregular shards of broken mirror – supposedly Wilhelmine's response to the vanity of her era.

To learn more about the man behind the myth, visit Haus Wahnfried, Wagner's former home on the northern edge of the Hofgarten. It now houses the **Richard Wagner Museum** (☎ 757 2816; www.wagnermuseum.de; Richard-Wagner-Strasse 48; adult/concession €4/2; ⏰ 9am-5pm, 9am-8pm Tue & Thu Apr-Oct). Wagner had this lovely home built with cash sent by King Ludwig II. Inside is a thorough, if unexciting, exhibit on Wagner's life, with glass cases crammed with documents, photographs, clothing and private effects. The composer and his wife Cosima are buried in an unmarked, ivy-covered tomb in the garden, with the sand-

BAVARIA

RICHARD WAGNER

With the backing of King Ludwig II, Richard Wagner (1813–83), the gifted, Leipzig-born composer and notoriously poor manager of money, turned Bayreuth into a mecca of opera and high-minded excess. Bayreuth profited from its luck and, it seems, is ever grateful.

For Wagner, opera-listening was meant to be work, and he tested his listeners wherever possible. *Götterdämmerung, Parsifal, Tannhäuser* and *Tristan and Isolde* are grandiose pieces that will jolt any audience geared for light entertainment. Four days of *The Ring of the Nibelungen* are good for limbering up.

After poring over Passau and a few other German cities, Wagner designed his own festival hall in Bayreuth. The unique acoustics are bounced up from a below-stage orchestra via reflecting boards onto the stage and into the house. The design took the body density of a packed house into account, still a remarkable achievement today.

Wagner was also a notorious womaniser, an infamous anti-Semite and a hardliner towards 'non-Europeans'. So extreme were these views that even Friedrich Nietzsche called Wagner's works 'inherently reactionary, and inhumane'. Wagner's works, and by extension Wagner himself, were embraced as a symbol of Aryan might by the Nazis, and even today there is great debate among music lovers about the 'correctness' of supporting Wagnerian music and the Wagner Festival in Bayreuth.

stone grave of his loving canine companion Russ standing nearby.

OUTSIDE THE TOWN CENTRE

North of the Hauptbahnhof, the main venue for Bayreuth's annual Wagner Festival is the **Festspielhaus** (☎ 787 80; Festspielhügel 1-2; adult/concession €5/4; ☼ tours 10am & 2pm Dec-Mar, Apr-Aug when rehearsals permit, 10am, 11am, 2pm & 3pm Sep & Oct, closed Mon & Nov), constructed in 1872 with Ludwig II's backing. The structure was specially designed to accommodate Wagner's massive theatrical sets, with three storeys of mechanical works hidden below stage (see boxed text, above). Take bus 5 to Am Festspielhaus.

About 6km east of the centre lies the **Eremitage**, a lush park girding the **Altes Schloss** (☎ 759 6937), Friedrich and Wilhelmine's summer residence. At the time of research its rococo interiors were being returned to their original state with renovation work set to finish by mid-2010. Also in the park is horseshoe-shaped **Neues Schloss** (not to be confused with the one in town), which centres on the amazing mosaic Sun Temple with gilded Apollo sculpture. Around both palaces you'll find numerous grottoes, follies and gushing fountains. To get there take bus 2 from Markt.

For a fascinating look at the brewing process, head to the enormous **Maisel's Brauerei-und-Büttnerei-Museum** (Maisel's Brewery & Coopers Museum; ☎ 401 234; Kulmbacher Strasse 40;

tours adult/concession €4/2) next door to the brewery of one of Germany's finest wheat-beer makers. The 90-minute guided tour (2pm daily, in German) takes you into the bowels of the 19th-century plant, with atmospheric rooms filled with 4500 beer mugs and amusing artefacts.

Festivals & Events

The **Wagner Festival** (www.bayreuther-festspiele.de) has been a summer fixture for over 130 years. The event lasts 30 days, with each performance attended by an audience of 1900. Demand is insane, with an estimated 500,000 fans vying for less than 60,000 tickets. Tickets are allocated by lottery but preference is given to patrons and Wagner enthusiasts. To apply, send a letter (no phone, fax or email) by mid-September for the next year's festival to the Bayreuther Festspiele, Kartenbüro, Postfach 10 02 62, 95402 Bayreuth. You must write in every year until you 'win' and the average waiting period is five to 10 years. Alternatively, you could lay siege to the box office on performance days between 1pm and 4.30pm to snap up cheap returned tickets, but there's no guarantee you'll get in. Lucky ticket holders face another endurance test once in the Festspielhaus – the seats are hard wood, ventilation is poor and there's no air-conditioning.

Sleeping

During the Wagner Festival, beds are as hard to come by as the tickets themselves. Most places are booked out months in advance and all charge 'special' rates for the month-long opera bash.

DJH hostel (☎ 764 380; www.bayreuth.jugendherberge .de; Universitätsstrasse 28; dm €18.40) This excellent 140-bed hostel near the university has comfortable, fresh rooms and a relaxed atmosphere.

Hotel Goldener Hirsch (☎ 1504 4000; www.bayreuth -goldener-hirsch.de; Bahnhofstrasse 13; s €65-85, d €85-110; P ✗) Not far from the train station, this landmark site has had the same name since 1753, and has been a hotel since 1900. Behind its forest-green exterior the '70s and '80s vibe is gradually giving way to clean-cut contemporary decor, but all rooms are spacious and welcoming.

Hotel Goldener Anker (☎ 650 51; www.anker-bayreuth .de; Opernstrasse 6; s €78-128, d €128-198; P ✗) The refined elegance of this hotel, owned by the same family since the 16th century, is hard to beat. It's just a few metres from the opera house, in the pedestrian zone. Many of the rooms are decorated in heavy traditional style with swag curtains, dark woods and antique touches.

Jagdschloss Thiergarten (☎ 09209-9840; www .schlosshotel-thiergarten.de; Oberthiergärtner Strasse 36; r €95-180; P ✗) This former hunting castle is a gorgeous place that has its own white deer wandering in the gardens and luxurious rooms with canopied beds. The gourmet, traditional restaurant has a domed 13m-high ceiling, and there's a library and bar with open fireplace. The hotel is about 5km south of Bayreuth.

Eating

Rosa Rosa (☎ 685 02; Von-Römer-Strasse 2; mains €2.60-6) Join Bamberg's chilled crowd at this bistro-cum-pub for belly-filling portions of salad, pasta and vegie fare, as well as seasonal dishes from the big specials board, or just a Friedenfelser beer in the evening. The poster-lined walls keep you up to date on the latest acts to hit town.

Hansl's Wood Oven Pizzeria (☎ 543 44; Friedrichstrasse 15; pizzas from €4.30) The best pizza in town is found at this hole-in-the-wall. A check-list menu lets you choose your own toppings, and *voilà*, you can name your creation. Look out for the Lonely Planet ads in the tiny dining space.

Kraftraum (☎ 800 2515; Sophienstrasse 16; mains €5.50-8; V) This vegetarian eatery has plenty to tempt even the most committed meat-eater. Pastas and jacket potatoes hold the fort, alongside some amazing salads and antipasti platters. Sunday brunch has a devoted following.

Oskar (☎ 516 0553; Maximilianstrasse 33; dishes €6-15) From the wood-panelled interior to out on the cobbles this updated version of a Bavarian beer hall bustles from morning to night. The menu includes salads and baked potato dishes, but the speciality is anything involving dumplings.

Also recommended:

Miamiam Glouglou (☎ 656 66; Von-Römer-Strasse 28; mains €7-20) Delightful Parisian-style restaurant with an authentically French menu.

Hua Hin (☎ 644 97; Ludwigstrasse 30; mains €8-14; ⏱ 11.30am-2.30pm & 5.30-11.30pm) A temple of tasty Thai food.

Getting There & Away

Bayreuth is well served by rail from Nuremberg (€16.70, one hour). Trains from both Munich (€62, 2½ hours) and Regensburg (€30, 2¼ hours) require a change in Nuremberg.

COBURG

☎ 09561 / pop 42,000

If marriage is diplomacy by another means, Coburg's rulers were surely masters of the art. Over four centuries, the princes and princesses of the house of Saxe-Coburg intrigued, romanced and ultimately wed themselves into the dynasties of Belgium, Bulgaria, Denmark, Portugal, Russia, Sweden and, most prominently, Great Britain. The crowning achievement came in 1857, when Albert of Saxe-Coburg-Gotha took the vows with his first cousin, Queen Victoria, founding the present British royal family. They quietly adopted the less-Germanic name of Windsor during WWI.

Coburg languished in the shadow of the Iron Curtain during the Cold War, all but closed in by East Germany on three sides, but since reunification the town has undergone a revival. Its proud Veste is one of Germany's finest medieval fortresses. What's more, some sources contend that the original hot dog was invented here.

Orientation

Markt is the old town's central square. The Hauptbahnhof lies to the northwest, Veste Coburg to the northeast.

Information

Postbank (Hindenburgstrasse 6)

Stadtbücherei Coburg (☎ 891 421; Herrengasse 17; ⏰ noon-6pm Mon, Tue & Thu, 9am-1pm Wed, 11am-5pm Fri, 9am-noon Sat) Free internet access.

Tourist office (☎ 898 000; www.coburg-tourist.de; Herrengasse 4; ⏰ 9am-6.30pm Mon-Fri, 10am-3pm Sat, 10am-2pm Sun Apr-Oct, 9am-5pm Mon-Fri, 10am-3pm Sat Nov-Mar) Just off Markt.

Sights & Activities

Coburg's epicentre is the magnificent Markt, a cafe-filled square oozing a colourful, aristocratic charm. The fabulous Renaissance facades and ornate oriels of the **Stadthaus** (town house) and the **Rathaus** vie for attention, while a statue of Prince Albert calmly surveys the scene.

The lavish **Schloss Ehrenburg** (☎ 808 832; Schlossplatz; tours in German adult/under 18yr/concession €4/free/3; ⏰ tours hourly 9am-5pm Tue-Sun Apr-Sep, 10am-3pm Tue-Sun Oct-Mar) was once the town residence of the Coburg dukes. Albert spent his childhood in this sumptuous, tapestry-lined palace, and Queen Victoria stayed in a room with Germany's first flushing toilet (1860). The splendid **Riesensaal** (Hall of Giants) has a baroque ceiling supported by 28 statues of Atlas.

Towering above everything is a story-book medieval fortress, the **Veste Coburg** (⏰ courtyard dawn-dusk). With its triple ring of fortified walls, it's one of the most impressive fortresses in Germany, but curiously has a dearth of foreign visitors. It houses the vast collection of the **Kunstsammlungen** (☎ 8790; adult/concession €5/2.50; ⏰ 9.30am-5pm daily Apr-Oct, 1-4pm Tue-Sun Nov-Mar), with works by star painters such as Rembrandt, Dürer and Cranach the Elder. The elaborate Jagdintarsien-Zimmer (Hunting Marquetry Room) is a superlative example of carved woodwork.

Protestant reformer Martin Luther, hoping to escape an imperial ban, sought refuge at the fortress in 1530. His former quarters has a writing desk and, in keeping with the Reformation, a rather plain bed.

The **Veste-Express** (one-way/return €2.50/3.50; ⏰ Apr-Oct), a tourist train, makes the trip to the fortress every 30 minutes. Infrequent bus 8 goes uphill year-round from Herrengasse near the Markt (€1.40 each way). Otherwise it's a steep 3km climb on foot.

Festivals & Events

It may seem an unlikely pairing, but every year in mid-July Coburg explodes into Europe's largest **Samba Festival** (www.samba-festival.de), an orgy of song and dance that attracts almost 100 bands and up to 200,000 bum-wiggling visitors.

Sleeping & Eating

DJH hostel (☎ 153 30; www.coburg.jugendherberge.de; dm under/over 27yr €18.10/22.10) Coburg's spick-and-span hostel is housed in a mock red-brick castle, Schloss Ketschendorf, located some 2km from town. Take bus 1 from the Hauptbahnhof.

Gasthof Fink (☎ 249 40; www.gasthof-fink.de; Lützelbucher Strasse 22; s €32-48.50, d €52-73) This smart English-speaking inn, 4km south of town, consists of a traditional *Gasthof* (inn), with timber-lined rooms, and a light-strewn contemporary hotel with balconies. Take bus 7 from the Hauptbahnhof to Lützelbuch.

our pick **Hotelpension Bärenturm** (☎ 318 401; www.baerenturm-hotelpension.de; Untere Anlage 2; s €75, d €100-120; Ⓟ Ⓧ) For those who prefer their complimentary pillow pack of Gummi Bears served with a touch of history, Coburg's most characterful digs started life as a defensive tower that was expanded in the early 19th century to house Prince Albert's private tutor. Each of the 15 rooms is a gem boasting squeaky parquet floors, antique-style furniture and regally high ceilings.

Café Prinz Albert (☎ 945 20; Ketschengasse 27; dishes €3-5; ⏰ 8am-6.30pm) Coburg's links with the British royals are reflected here in both the decor and menu. The Prince Albert breakfast – a cross-cultural marriage of sausage, egg and Bamberger croissants – is fit for a queen's consort.

Tie (☎ 334 48; Leopoldstrasse 14; mains €14.50-18; ⏰ from 5pm Tue-Sun; Ⓥ) Heavenly (if pricey) food is made with fresh organic ingredients at this bright vegetarian restaurant. Dishes range from vegetarian classics to Asian inspirations, with the odd fish or meat dish for the unconverted.

Getting There & Away

Direct trains to Bamberg (€10.30, 50 minutes) and Nuremberg (€19.90, 1¾ hours) leave Coburg every other hour. The trip to Bayreuth (€15.20, 1½ hours) requires a change in Lichtenfels. BerlinLinienBus links Coburg to Berlin (€41, 5½ hours) twice a week.

AROUND COBURG

About 25km south of Coburg is the ornate, gilded 18th-century pilgrimage church, **Basilika Vierzehnheiligen** (☎ 09571-950 80; admission free; ☾ 6.30am-7pm Apr-Oct, 7.30am-dusk Nov-Mar). It stands on the spot where a local shepherd reported having recurring visions of the infant Jesus flanked by the 14 *Nothelfer* (Holy Helpers), a group of saints invoked in times of adversity since the 14th-century bubonic plague.

The church is one of the masterpieces of Balthasar Neumann, the renowned architect. The intersecting oval rotundas, play of light and trompe l'oeil ceiling create an optical illusion, making the interior appear much larger than it is and creating a sense of constant motion. Statues of the saints line the free-standing central altar, the focal point of the sumptuous interior.

Alte Klosterbrauerei (☎ 09571-3488; snacks €3.50-5; ☾ 10am-8pm) is a wonderful brewery attached to the adjacent convent at the back of Vierzehnheiligen (up past the wooden stands peddling kitsch). Grab a table in the leafy beer garden, order a half-litre of bracing *Nothelfertrunk* beer and drink in the stunning view. Stay long enough and you may glimpse the nun in her habit who lugs in cases for refill.

Getting There & Away

Regional trains connect Coburg with Lichtenfels (€5.10, 20 minutes), from where there are two buses a day to Vierzehnheiligen. A taxi from Lichtenfels is about €8. The basilica is near the town of Staffelstein, just off the B173, about a 30-minute drive from Coburg.

ALTMÜHLTAL NATURE PARK

The Altmühltal Nature Park is one of Germany's largest nature parks and covers some of Bavaria's most gorgeous terrain. The Altmühl River gently meanders through a region of little valleys and hills before joining the Rhine-Main Canal and eventually emptying into the Danube. Outdoor fun on well-marked hiking and biking trails is the main reason to head here, but the river is also ideal for canoeing. There's basic camping in designated spots along the river, and plenty of accommodation in the local area.

The park's main information centre is in Eichstätt (opposite), a charmingly historic town at the southern end of the park that makes an excellent base for exploring.

For information on the park and for help with planning an itinerary, contact the **Informationszentrum Naturpark Altmühltal** (☎ 08421-987 60; www.naturpark-altmuehltal.de; Notre Dame 1, Eichstätt; ☾ 9am-5pm Mon-Sat, 10am-5pm Sun Apr-Oct, 8am-noon & 2-4pm Mon-Thu, 8am-noon Fri Nov-Mar). Upstairs in the centre is a museum of the park's wildlife and habitats, complete with a recreation of landscapes in the garden.

Orientation

The park takes in 2900 sq km of land southwest of Regensburg, south of Nuremberg, east of Treuchtlingen and north of Eichstätt. The eastern boundaries of the park include the town of Kelheim.

There are bus and train connections between Eichstätt and all the major milestones along the river including, from west to east, Gunzenhausen, Treuchtlingen and Pappenheim. North of the river, activities focus around the towns of Kipfenberg, Beilngries and Riedenburg.

Activities

CANOEING & KAYAKING

The most beautiful section of the river is from Treuchtlingen or Pappenheim to Eichstätt or Kipfenberg, about a 60km stretch that you can do lazily in a kayak or canoe in two to three days. There are lots of little dams along the way, as well as some small rapids about 10km northwest of Dollnstein. Signs warn of impending doom, but locals say that if you heed the warning to stay to the right, you'll be safe.

San-Aktiv Tours (☎ 09831-4936; www.san-aktiv-tours .de; Bühringer Strasse 11, 91710 Gunzenhausen) and **Natour** (☎ 09141-922 929; www.natour.de; Gänswirtshaus 12, 91781 Weissenburg) are the largest and best-organised canoe-hire companies in the park, with a network of vehicles to shuttle canoes, bicycles and people around the area. Trips through the park run from April to October, and you can canoe alone or join a group. Packages generally include the canoe, swim vests, maps, instructions, transfer back to the embarkation point and, for overnight tours, luggage transfer and lodgings.

You can hire canoes and kayaks in just about every town along the river. Expect to pay about €15/25 per day for a one/two-person boat, more for bigger ones. Staff will haul you and the boats to or from your embarkation point for a small fee.

You can get a full list of boat-hire outlets from the Informationszentrum Naturpark Altmühltal. Some recommendations include the following:

Bootsverleih Beilngries (☎ 08461-8903; Beilngries)

Bootsverleih Otto Rehm (☎ 08422-987 654; www.rehm-r.de; Dollnstein)

Fahrradgarage (☎ 08421-2110; www.fahrradgarage.de; Eichstätt)

Franken-Boot (☎ 09142-4645; www.frankenboot.de; Treuchtlingen)

CYCLING & HIKING

With around 3000km of hiking trails and 800km of cycle trails criss-crossing the landscape, foot and pedal are the best ways to strike out into the park. Cycling trails are clearly labelled and have long rectangular brown signs bearing a bike symbol. Hiking-trail markers are yellow. The most popular cycling route is the Altmühltal Radweg, which runs parallel to the river for 160km. The Altmühltal-Panoramaweg stretching 200km between Gunzenhausen and Kelheim is a picturesque hiking route, which crosses the entire park from west to east.

You can hire bikes in almost every town within the park, and prices are more or less uniform. Most bike-hire agencies will also store bicycles. Ask for a list of bike-hire outlets at the Informationszentrum Naturpark Altmühltal.

In Eichstätt, Fahrradgarage (above) hires out bicycles for €8 per day. Staff will bring the bikes to you or take you and the bikes to anywhere in the park for an extra fee.

ROCK CLIMBING

The worn cliffs along the Altmühl River offer some appealing terrain for climbers of all skill levels. The medium-grade 45m-high rock face of Burgsteinfelsen, located between the towns of Dollnstein and Breitenfurt, has routes from the fourth to eighth climbing level with stunning views of the valley. The Dohlenfelsen face near the town of Wellheim has a simpler expanse that's more suitable for children. The Informationszentrum Naturpark Altmühltal can provide more details on the region's climbing options.

Getting There & Around

BUS

From mid-April to October the FreizeitBus Altmühltal-Donautal takes passengers and their bikes around the park. Buses normally run three times a day from mid-April to early October (see www.naturpark-altmuehltal.de for a timetable, listed in German under 'Freizeit/Tipp'). Route 1 runs from Regensburg and Kelheim to Riedenburg on weekends and holidays only. Route 2 travels between Eichstätt, Beilngries, Dietfurt and Riedenburg with all-day service on weekends and holidays and restricted service on weekdays. All-day tickets costing €10/7 for passengers with/without bicycles, or €22.50/17 per family with/without bikes, are bought from the driver.

TRAIN

Hourly trains run between Eichstätt Bahnhof and Treuchtlingen (€5.10, 25 minutes), and between Treuchtlingen and Gunzenhausen (€4, 15 minutes). RE trains from Munich that run through Eichstätt Bahnhof also stop in Dollnstein, Solnhofen and Pappenheim.

EICHSTÄTT

☎ 08421 / pop 13,700

Hugging a tight bend in the Altmühl River, Eichstätt radiates a distinct Mediterranean flair. The cobbled streets meander past elegant buildings and leafy squares, giving this sleepy town a general sense of refinement. Italian architects, notably Gabriel de Gabrieli and Maurizio Pedetti, rebuilt the town after Swedes razed the place during the Thirty Years War (1618–48) and it has since remained undamaged. Since 1980 many of its baroque facades have concealed faculties and libraries belonging to Germany's sole Catholic university.

Orientation

Eichstätt has two train stations. Mainline trains stop at the Bahnhof, 5km from the centre, from where coinciding diesel trains shuttle to the Stadtbahnhof. From here walk north across the Spitalbrücke and you'll end up in Domplatz, the heart of town. Willibaldsburg castle is about 1km southwest of the Stadtbahnhof.

Information

Post office (Domplatz 7)

Raiffeisenbank (Domplatz 5)

Tourist office (☎ 600 1400; www.eichstaett.info; Domplatz 8; ⏰ 9am-6pm Mon-Sat, 10am-1pm Sun Apr-Oct, 10am-noon & 2-4pm Mon-Thu, 10am-noon Fri Nov-Mar)

Sights

TOWN CENTRE

Eichstätt's centre is dominated by the richly adorned **Dom**. Standout features include an enormous stained-glass window by Hans Holbein the Elder, and the carved sandstone **Pappenheimer Altar** (1489–97), depicting a pilgrimage from Pappenheim to Jerusalem. The seated statue is of St Willibald, the town's first bishop.

The **Domschatzmuseum** (Cathedral Treasury; ☎ 507 42; Residenzplatz 7; adult/child €2/free; ☒ 10.30am-5.30pm Wed-Fri, 10am-5pm Sat & Sun Apr-Nov) includes the robes of 8th-century English-born bishop St Willibald and baroque Gobelin tapestries.

The **Residenz** (Residenzplatz; admission €1; ☒ tours 10.15am, 11am, 11.45am, 2pm, 2.45pm & 3.30pm Sat & Sun Apr-Oct) is the former prince-bishops' palace, completed in 1736. It has a stunning main staircase and rococo Spiegelsaal (Hall of Mirrors) with a fresco from Greek mythology. In the square is a golden statue of Mary on a 19m-high column.

North of the Dom is another baroque square, the **Markt**, where markets are held on Wednesday and Saturday mornings. About 250m northwest of here, on Westenstrasse, is the **Kloster St Walburga**, burial site of St Willibald's sister and a pilgrimage destination. Every year between mid-October and late February, water oozes from Walburga's relics in the underground chapel and drips down into a catchment. The nuns bottle diluted versions of the so-called *Walburgaöl* (Walburga oil) and give it away to the faithful. A staircase from the lower chapel leads to an off-limits upper chapel where you can catch a glimpse through the grill of beautiful ex-voto tablets and other trinkets left as a thank you to the saint. The main **St Walburga Church** above has a glorious rococo interior.

WILLIBALDSBURG

The hilltop castle of Willibaldsburg (1355) houses two museums. The **Jura-Museum** (☎ 4730; Burgstrasse 19; adult/under 18yr €4/free; ☒ 9am-6pm Apr-Sep, 10am-4pm Nov-Mar, closed Mon) is great, even if fossils usually don't quicken your pulse. Highlights are a locally found archaeopteryx (the oldest-known fossil bird) and aquariums with living specimens of the fossilised animals. Also up here is the **Museum of Pre-History & Early History** with a 6000-year-old mammoth skeleton. Descend to the cellar to find the 76.5m-deep well – toss in a coin and listen for about 10 seconds for the plop. The

Bastiongarten, built on the ramparts, affords fantastic views of Eichstätt.

Looking across the valley, you can make out the **limestone quarry** (adult/child €2/1; ☒ 9am-5pm) where you can dig for fossils. At the base of the quarry is the **Museum Berger** (☎ 4663; Harthof; adult/child €2/0.50; ☒ 10am-5pm daily Jun–mid-Sep, 1.30-5pm Mon-Sat, 10am-5pm Sun Apr, May & mid-Sep–Oct), which displays geological samples.

Sleeping & Eating

Municipal camp site (☎ 908 147; fax 908 146; Pirkheimerstrasse; campsite €7; ☒ Apr-Nov) This basic camping ground is on the northern bank of the Altmühl River, about 1km southeast of the town centre. It closes for 10 days during the Volksfest (a mini-Oktoberfest) in late August or early September.

DJH hostel (☎ 980 410; www.eichstaett.jugendherberge .de; Reichenaustrasse 15; dm under/over 27yr €19.50/23.50; ☒ closed Dec-Jan) This comfy, well-maintained place has 122 beds and commanding views of the Altstadt. The double rooms, if available, have their own shower and toilet.

Fuchs (☎ 6789; www.hotel-fuchs.de; Ostenstrasse 8; s €40-48, d €60-80; ℗ ☒ ☎) A super-central, family-run hotel with underfloor heating in the bathrooms, which adjoins a cake shop with a sunny dining area. It's convenient to a launch ramp on the river, and you can lock your boat in the garage.

Hotel Adler (☎ 6767; www.adler-eichstaett.de, in German; Marktplatz 22; s €67-75, d €91-115; ℗ ☒) A superb ambience reigns at this ornate 300-year-old building right on Markt. The rooms are bright, airy and modern, and it offers all the trappings, including bike and boat hire and a generous breakfast buffet. There's wheelchair access.

Café im Paradies (☎ 3313; Markt 9; mains €5-17) This sophisticated spot on Markt is prime for people-watching. Recharge with a snack or full meal, either in the antique-lined interior or out on the terrace.

Gasthof Krone (☎ 4406; Domplatz 3; mains €6-18) Traditionally garbed waitresses bang down monster platters of local nosh in the beer garden and two-tiered dining room of this lively tavern. Altmühltaler lamb is the speciality here, its meat infused with special flavour by the park's herb-rich meadows.

Getting There & Away

Trains run hourly or more between Ingolstadt and Eichstätt (€5.10, 25 minutes). Alternatively take the hourly, weekday-only Schnellbus

(€4.90, 45 minutes) from Ingolstadt bus station (ZOB) or Eichstätt's Residenzplatz.

INGOLSTADT
☎ 0841 / pop 122,000

Even by Bavaria's elevated standards, Danube-straddling Ingolstadt is astonishingly affluent. Auto manufacturer Audi has its headquarters here, flanked by a clutch of oil refineries in the outskirts. But industry has left few marks on the charming medieval centre, with its cobblestone streets and historic buildings. Ingolstadt's museum church has the largest flat fresco ever made. And few people may know that its old medical school figured in the literary birth of Frankenstein, the monster by which all others are judged.

Orientation

The Hauptbahnhof is 2.5km southeast of the Altstadt; buses 10, 11, 15 and 16 run between them every few minutes (€1.80). The Danube is south of the Altstadt; the Audi factory is about 2km north of the centre.

Information

Dresdner Bank (Rathausplatz 3)
Post office (Am Stein)
Stadtbücherei (☎ 305 3839; Hallstrasse 2-4; internet access per 30min €0.50)
Surfen bei Yorma's (Hauptbahnhof; internet access per hr €3)
Tourist office (www.ingolstadt-tourismus.de) City centre (☎ 305 3030; Rathausplatz 2; ⊙ 9am-6pm Mon-Fri, 10am-2pm Sat & Sun, shorter hours & closed Sun Nov-Mar); Hauptbahnhof (☎ 305 3005; Elisabethstrasse 3; ⊙ 8.30am-6.30pm Mon-Fri, 9.30am-2pm Sat)

Sights

ASAMKIRCHE MARIA DE VICTORIA

The crown jewel among Ingolstadt's sights, the **Asamkirche Maria de Victoria** (☎ 175 18; Neubaustrasse 11/2; adult/concession €2/1.50; ⊙ 9am-noon & 1-5pm Tue-Sun Mar-Oct, 1-4pm Nov-Feb) is a baroque masterpiece designed by brothers Cosmas Damian and Egid Quirin Asam between 1732 and 1736. Its shining glory is the trompe l'oeil ceiling (painted in just six weeks in 1735), the world's largest fresco on a flat surface. The piece is full of stunning optical illusions – stand on the little circle in the diamond tile near the door and everything snaps into 3-D. Focus on anything – the Horn of Plenty, Moses' staff, the treasure chest – and it will alter dramatically when you move around the room. The Asams took the secrets they used to the grave.

Across the street is the **Tilly House** (Neubaustrasse 2), where General Tilly, a famous Field Marshal in the Thirty Years War, died in 1652 from tetanus (the result of a war wound). There's a commemorative plaque around the corner on Johannesstrasse.

DEUTSCHES MEDIZINHISTORISCHES MUSEUM

Located in the stately Alte Anatomie (Old Anatomy) at the university, the **Deutsches Medizinhistorisches Museum** (German Museum of Medical History; ☎ 305 2860; Anatomiestrasse 18/20; adult/concession €4.50/2.25; ⊙ 10am-5pm Tue-Sun) chronicles the evolution of medical science as well as the many (scary) instruments and techniques used. Pack a strong stomach for the visit.

The ground floor eases you into the exhibition with medical delights such as birthing chairs, enema syringes and lancets for blood-letting. Upstairs things get closer to the bone in displays of human skeletons with preserved musculature and organs, foetuses of conjoined twins, a pregnant uterus and a cyclops. Recover in the bucolic medicinal plant garden, which includes a garden of smells and touch designed for the blind.

NEUES SCHLOSS, BAYERISCHES ARMEE MUSEUM & REDUIT TILLY

The ostentatious **Neues Schloss** (New Palace) was built for Duke Ludwig the Bearded in 1418. Fresh from a trip to wealth-laden France, Ludwig borrowed heavily from Gallic design and created a residence with 3m-thick walls, Gothic net vaulting and individually carved doorways. One guest who probably didn't appreciate its architectural merits was future French president Charles de Gaulle, held prisoner of war here during WWI.

Today the building houses the **Bayerisches Armee Museum** (Bavarian Military Museum; ☎ 937 70; Paradeplatz 4; adult/concession €3.50/3, on Sun €2, combined ticket with Reduit Tilly €4.50/3.50; ⊙ 8.45am-5pm Tue-Sun). Exhibits on long-forgotten battles, armaments dating back to the 14th century and legions of tin soldiers pack the rooms.

The second part of the museum is in the **Reduit Tilly** (adult/concession €3.50/3, on Sun €2, combined ticket with Neues Schloss €4.50/3.50; ⊙ 8.45am-5pm Tue-Sun) across the river. This 19th-century fortress has an undeniable aesthetic, having been designed by Ludwig I's chief architect. It was named after

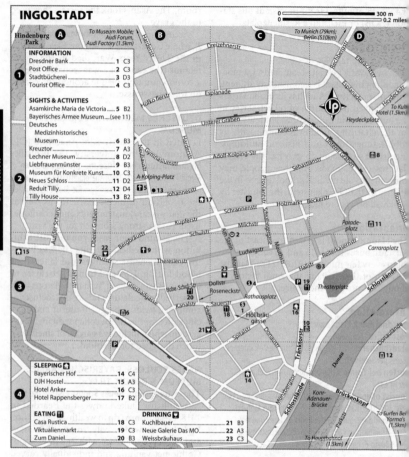

INGOLSTADT

INFORMATION
Dresdner Bank	**1** C3
Post Office	**2** C3
Stadtbücherei	**3** D3
Tourist Office	**4** C3

SIGHTS & ACTIVITIES
Asamkirche Maria de Victoria	**5** B2
Bayerisches Armee Museum	(see 11)
Deutsches Medizinhistorisches Museum	**6** B3
Kreuztor	**7** A3
Lechner Museum	**8** D2
Liebfrauenmünster	**9** B3
Museum für Konkrete Kunst	**10** C3
Neues Schloss	**11** D2
Reduit Tilly	**12** D4
Tilly House	**13** B2

SLEEPING 🛏
Bayerischer Hof	**14** C4
DJH Hostel	**15** A3
Hotel Anker	**16** C3
Hotel Rappensberger	**17** B2

EATING 🍴
Casa Rustica	**18** C3
Viktualienmarkt	**19** C3
Zum Daniel	**20** B3

DRINKING 🍷
Kuchlbauer	**21** B3
Neue Galerie Das MO	**22** A3
Weissbräuhaus	**23** C3

Johann Tilly – a field marshal of the Thirty Years War who was known as the 'butcher of Magdeburg' – and features exhibits covering the history of WWI and post-WWI Germany.

MUSEUM MOBILE

This high-tech car museum is part of the **Audi Forum** (☎ 283 4444; Ettinger Strasse 40; adult/concession €2/1.50, tours €4/3; �%9am-6pm). Exhibits on three floors chart Audi's humble beginnings in 1899 to its latest dream machines such as the R8. Some 50 cars and 20 motorbikes are on display, including prototypes that glide past visitors on an open lift. Take bus 11 or 44 to the terminus from the Hauptbahnhof or Paradeplatz.

The two-hour tours of the **Audi factory** (☎ 0800-282 4444; adult/concession €7/3.50; �%tours in English 11.30am Mon-Fri) take you through the entire production process, from the metal press to the testing station.

LIEBFRAUENMÜNSTER

Ingolstadt's biggest church was established by Duke Ludwig the Bearded in 1425 and enlarged over the next century. A classic Gothic hall church, the **Liebfrauenmünster** (Minster of Our Dear Lady; �%8am-6pm) has a pair of strangely oblique square towers that flank the main entrance. Inside, subtle colours and a nave flooded with light intensify the magnificence of the soaring ceiling vaults and the 'blossoming' stonework of several side chapels. The high altar by Hans Mielich (1560) has a rear panel depicting St Katharina

---

THE BIRTH OF FRANKENSTEIN

Mary Shelley's *Frankenstein*, published in 1818, set a creepy precedent in the world of monster fantasies. The story is well known: young scientist Viktor Frankenstein travels to Ingolstadt to study medicine. He becomes obsessed with the idea of creating a human being and goes shopping for parts at the local cemetery. Unfortunately, his creature is a problem child and sets out to destroy its maker.

Shelley picked Ingolstadt because it was home to a prominent university and medical faculty. In the 19th century, a laboratory for scientists and medical doctors was housed in the Alte Anatomie (now the Deutsches Medizinhistorisches Museum; p385). In the operating theatre, professors and their students carried out experiments on corpses and dead tissue, though perhaps one may have been inspired to work on something a bit scarier...

---

debating with the professors at Ingolstadt's new university, ostensibly in a bid to convert the Protestant faculty to Catholicism – a poke at Luther's Reformation.

KREUZTOR

The redbrick **Kreuztor** (1385), with its Gothic outline of pixie-capped turrets, was just one of four main city gates until the 19th century. The former **fortifications**, which are now flats, still encircle the city.

OTHER ATTRACTIONS

Ingolstadt has two of Germany's leading art galleries for experimental materials. The **Museum für Konkrete Kunst** (Museum of Concrete Art; ☎ 305 1871; www.mkk-ingolstadt.de; Tränktorstrasse 6-8; adult/concession €3/1.50; ☒ 10am-5pm Tue-Sun) features creative abstracts and fascinating 3-D works in concrete, with artists of international renown.

The **Lechner Museum** (☎ 305 2250; www.lechner-museum.de; Esplanade 9; adult/concession €3/1.50; ☒ 11am-5pm Thu-Sun) highlights works cast in steel, a medium that's more expressive than you might think. Exhibits are displayed in a striking glass-covered factory hall from 1953.

Sleeping

DJH hostel (☎ 305 1280; www.ingolstadt.jugendherberge.de; Friedhofstrasse 41/2; dm under/over 27yr €16.90/20.90; ☒ closed mid-Dec–Jan) This beautiful well-equipped and wheelchair-friendly hostel is in a renovated city fortress (1828), about 150m west of the Kreuztor.

Hotel Anker (☎ 300 50; www.hotel-restaurant-anker.de; Tränktorstrasse 1; s €56, d €88-92) Bright rooms, a touch of surrealist art and a great location make this family-run hotel a good central choice. The traditional restaurant attracts a loyal local following, but the lack of English is a downside.

Bayerischer Hof (☎ 934 060; www.bayerischer-hof-ingolstadt.de; Münzbergstrasse 12; s €62-68, d €82-87; P) The corridors here won't win any ambience prizes, but the rooms themselves, located around a Bavarian eatery, are furnished with hard-wood furniture, TVs and modern (albeit brown) bathrooms. Rates come down slightly at weekends.

Hotel Rappensberger (☎ 3140; www.rappensberger.de; Harderstrasse 3; s €85-150, d €110-185; P) This small, stylish hotel specialises in minimalist rooms with designer lighting and traditional German touches. The standard rooms are snug, but things get quite spacious a step up. The attached cafe-restaurant is a byword for chic.

Kult Hotel (☎ 951 00; www.kult-hotel.de; Theodor-Heuss-Strasse 25; s & d from €139-169; P ☒ ☎) Aping the Asamkirche, the most eye-catching feature of rooms at this exciting design hotel, 2km northeast of the city centre, are the painted ceilings, each one a work of art. Otherwise fittings and furniture come sleek, room gadgets are the latest toys, and the restaurant constitutes a study in cool elegance.

Eating & Drinking

Local drinkers are proud that Germany's Beer Purity Law of 1516 was issued in Ingolstadt. To find out why, try a mug of smooth Herrnbräu, Nordbräu or Ingobräu.

For a quick bite head for the Viktualienmarkt, where fast-food stalls provide international flavour.

Zum Daniel (☎ 352 72; Roseneckstrasse 1; mains €8-16; ☒ closed Mon) This is the oldest pub in town and just drips with character and tradition. Locals say Daniel has the town's best pork roast and the seasonal specials are not bad either.

Weissbräuhaus (☎ 328 90; Dollstrasse 3; mains €8.50-16) This modern beer hall serves standard Bavarian dishes, including the delicious *Weissbräupfändl* (pork fillet with homemade *Spätzle*). There's a beer garden with a charming fountain out back.

Neue Galerie Das MO (☎ 339 60; Bergbräustrasse 7) Right opposite the Liebfrauenmünster, this trendy cafe-bar holds art exhibits and has probably the best beer garden in town, amid a copse of chestnut trees.

Also recommended:

Casa Rustica (☎ 333 11; Höllbräugasse 1; mains €5-16) Most agree this is Ingolstadt's best Italian restaurant, with a melting cheese and herb aroma in the air and cosy half-circle box seating.

Kuchlbauer (☎ 335 512; Schäffbräustrasse 11a) A superb brewpub with oodles of neat brewing and rustic knick-knacks hanging from the walls and ceiling.

Getting There & Away

Trains to Regensburg (€13.30, one hour) and Munich (€15.20, one hour) leave at least hourly. A BEX BerlinLinienBus coach leaves for Berlin daily at 10.55am (€47, five hours).

EASTERN BAVARIA

The sparsely populated eastern reaches of Bavaria may live in the shadow of Bavaria's big-hitting attractions, but they hold many historical treasures to rival their neighbours. Top billing goes to Regensburg, a former capital, and one of Germany's prettiest and liveliest cities. From here the Danube gently winds its way to the Italianate city of Passau. Landshut was once the hereditary seat of the Wittelsbach family, and the region has also given the world a pope, none other than incumbent Benedict XVI who was born in Marktl am Inn. Away from the towns, the Bavarian Forest broods in semi-undiscovered remoteness.

Eastern Bavaria was a seat of power in the Dark Ages, ruled by rich bishops at a time when Munich was but a modest trading post. A conquering Napoleon lumped Eastern Bavaria into river districts, and King Ludwig I sought to roll back these changes by recreating the boundaries of a glorified duchy from 1255. Though it brought a sense of renewed Bavarian-ness, the area remained very much on the margins of things, the odd and appealing mixture of ancient Roman cities, undulating farmland and rugged wilderness that it is today.

REGENSBURG

☎ 0941 / pop 130,000

A Roman settlement completed under Emperor Marcus Aurelius, Regensburg was the first capital of Bavaria, the residence of dukes, kings and bishops, and for 600 years an imperial free city. Two millennia of history bequeathed the city some of the region's finest architectural heritage, a fact recognised by Unesco in 2006. Though big on the historical wow-factor, today's Regensburg is a laid-back and unpretentious sort of place, and a good springboard into the wider region.

Oskar Schindler lived in Regensburg for years, and today one of his houses bears a **plaque** (Am Watmarkt 5) to his achievements, commemorated in the Steven Spielberg epic *Schindler's List*.

Orientation

The city is divided by the east-flowing Danube, which separates the Altstadt from the northern banks. Islands in the middle of the river, mainly Oberer and Unterer Wöhrd are populated as well. The Hauptbahnhof is at the southern end of the Altstadt. From there Maximilianstrasse leads north to Kornmarkt, the centre of the historic district.

Information

BOOKSHOPS

Bücher Pustet (☎ 569 70; Gesandtenstrasse 6-8) Good collection of English-language novels and travel books.

Presse + Buch (Hauptbahnhof) Stocks English books, newspapers and magazines.

EMERGENCY

Ambulance (☎ 192 22)

Police (☎ 110; Minoritenweg 1)

INTERNET ACCESS

Lok.in (☎ 5957 9404; 1st fl, Hauptbahnhof; per 30min €2; ☺ 6pm-1am)

LAUNDRY

Münz Wasch Center (Winklergasse 14; per 6kg load €3; ☺ 6am-10pm Mon-Sat)

LIBRARIES

Stadtbücherei (☎ 507 2470; Haidplatz 8, Thon Dittmer Palais)

MEDICAL SERVICES

Evangelisches Krankenhaus (☎ 504 00; Emmeramsplatz) Hospital.

MONEY

More banks are located along Maximilian-strasse.

Sparkasse City Center (Neupfarrplatz)

POST

Post office (Domplatz) Also next to the Hauptbahnhof.

TOURIST INFORMATION

Tourist office (☎ 507 4410; www.tourismus.regensburg de; Altes Rathaus; ⏲ 9am-6pm Mon-Fri, 9am-4pm Sat, 9.30am-4pm Sun)

Sights

DOM ST PETER

Regensburg's soaring landmark, the **Dom St Peter** (☎ 597 1660; Domplatz; admission free) ranks among Bavaria's grandest Gothic cathedrals. Construction dates from the late 13th century, but the distinctive filigree spires weren't added until the 19th century; the extravagant western facade from this period is festooned with sculptures. Inside are kaleidoscopic stained-glass windows above the choir and in the south transept. Another highlight is a pair of charming sculptures (1280), attached to pillars just west of the altar, which features the Angel Gabriel beaming at the Virgin on the opposite pillar as he delivers the news that she's with child.

The **Domschatzmuseum** (Cathedral Treasury; ☎ 576 45; adult/concession €2/1; ⏲ 10am-5pm Tue-Sat, noon-5pm Sun Apr-Nov) brims with monstrances, tapestries and other church treasures.

SCHLOSS THURN UND TAXIS & MUSEUM

In the 15th century, Franz von Taxis (1459–1517) assured his place in history by setting up the first European postal system, which remained a monopoly until the 19th century. In recognition of his services, the family was given a new palace, the former Benedictine monastery St Emmeram, henceforth known as **Schloss Thurn und Taxis** (☎ 504 824; www.thurnund taxis.de; Emmeramsplatz 5; combined ticket adult/concession €11.50/9; ⏲ tours at 11am, 2pm, 3pm & 4pm Mon-Fri, also 10am & 1pm Sat & Sun Apr-Oct, weekends only Nov-Mar). It was soon one of the most modern palaces in Europe, and featured such luxuries as flushing toilets, central heating and electricity. Tours include a look into the Basilika St Emmeram (p390).

The palace complex also contains the **Thurn und Taxis-Museum** (☎ 504 8133; adult/concession €4.50/3.50; ⏲ 11am-5pm Mon-Fri, 10am-5pm Sat & Sun).

The jewellery, porcelain and precious furnishings on display here belonged, for many years, to the wealthiest dynasty in Germany. The fortune, administered by Prince Albert II, is still estimated at well over €1 billion.

DOCUMENT NEUPFARRPLATZ

Regensburg once had a thriving medieval Jewish community centred around Neupfarrplatz. When the city fell on hard economic times in the early 16th century, the townspeople expelled all Jews and burned their quarter to the ground. A multimedia exhibit, the **Document Neupfarrplatz** (☎ 507 3442; tours adult/concession €5/2.50; ⏲ 2.30pm Thu-Sat, additionally Sun & Mon Jul & Aug) explains events on the square from ancient times right up until the formation of the resistance movement in 1942–43. You can visit a Roman legionary fortress, Jewish houses and both Gothic and Romanesque synagogues. Tickets are only available from Tabak Götz at Neupfarrplatz 3.

ALTES RATHAUS & REICHSTAGSMUSEUM

The seat of the Reichstag for almost 150 years, the **Altes Rathaus** is now home to Regensburg's three mayors and the **Reichstagsmuseum** (Imperial Diet Museum; ☎ 507 3442; Altes Rathaus; adult/concession €7.50/4; ⏲ tours in English 3pm Apr-Oct, 2pm Nov-Mar). Tours take in not only the lavishly decorated **Reichssaal** (Imperial Hall) but also the original **torture chambers** in the basement. The interrogation room bristles with tools such as the rack, the Spanish Donkey (a tall wooden wedge on which naked men were made to sit) and spiked chairs.

STEINERNE BRÜCKE

An incredible feat of engineering for its day, Regensburg's **Steinerne Brücke** (Stone Bridge) was at one time the only fortified crossing of the Danube. Ensconced in its southern tower is the **Brückturm-Museum** (☎ 507 5889; Weisse-Lamm-Gasse 1; adult/concession €2/1.50; ⏲ 10am-5pm Apr-Oct), a small historical exhibit about the bridge.

CHURCHES

South of the Dom, the humble exterior of the graceful **Alte Kapelle** (Alter Kornmarkt 8) belies the stunning interior with its rich rococo decorations. The core of the church, however, is about 1000 years old, although the Gothic vaulted ceilings were added in

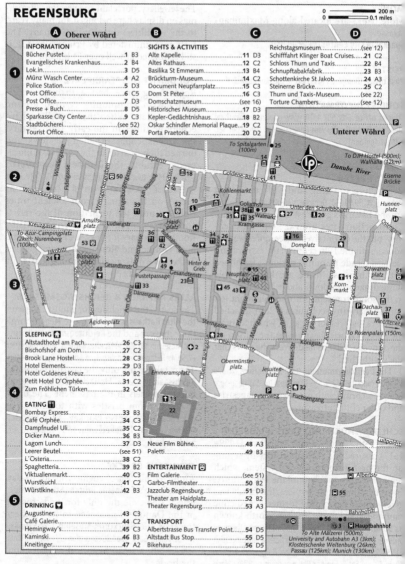

REGENSBURG

0 ____ 200 m
0 ____ 0.1 miles

INFORMATION
Bücher Pustet	1	B3
Evangelisches Krankenhaus	2	B4
Lok.in	3	D5
Münz Wasch Center	4	A2
Police Station	5	D3
Post Office	6	C5
Post Office	7	D3
Presse + Buch	8	D5
Sparkasse City Center	9	C3
Stadtbücherei	(see 52)	
Tourist Office	10	B2

SIGHTS & ACTIVITIES
Alte Kapelle	11	D3
Altes Rathaus	12	C2
Basilika St Emmeram	13	B4
Brückturm-Museum	14	C2
Document Neupfarrplatz	15	C3
Dom St Peter	16	C3
Domschatzmuseum	(see 16)	
Historisches Museum	17	D3
Kepler-Gedächtnishaus	18	B2
Oskar Schindler Memorial Plaque	19	C2
Porta Praetoria	20	D2

Reichstagsmuseum	(see 12)	
Schifffahrt Klinger Boat Cruises	21	C2
Schloss Thurn und Taxis	22	B4
Schnupftabakfabrik	23	B3
Schottenkirche St Jakob	24	A3
Steinerne Brücke	25	C2
Thurn und Taxis-Museum	(see 22)	
Torture Chambers	(see 12)	

SLEEPING
Altstadthotel am Pach	26	C3
Bischofshof am Dom	27	C2
Brook Lane Hostel	28	C3
Hotel Elements	29	D3
Hotel Goldenes Kreuz	30	B2
Petit Hotel D'Orphée	31	C2
Zum Fröhlichen Türken	32	C4

EATING
Bombay Express	33	B3
Café Orphée	34	C3
Dampfnudel Uli	35	C2
Dicker Mann	36	B3
Lagom Lunch	37	D3
Leerer Beutel	(see 51)	
L'Osteria	38	C2
Spaghetteria	39	B2
Viktualienmarkt	40	C3
Wurstkuchl	41	C2
Würstlkine	42	B3

DRINKING
Augustiner	43	C3
Café Galerie	44	C3
Hemingway's	45	C3
Kaminski	46	B3
Kneitinger	47	A2

Neue Film Bühne	48	A3
Paletti	49	B3

ENTERTAINMENT
Film Galerie	(see 51)	
Garbo-Filmtheater	50	B2
Jazzclub Regensburg	51	D3
Theater am Haidplatz	52	B2
Theater Regensburg	53	A3

TRANSPORT
Albertstrasse Bus Transfer Point	54	D5
Altstadt Bus Stop	55	D5
Bikehaus	56	D5

the Middle Ages. The church is open only during services but you can always peek through the wrought-iron grill.

Near the Schloss is a masterpiece by the Asam brothers, the **Basilika St Emmeram** (Emmeramsplatz 3; ☉ closed Fri & Sun morning). There are two giant ceiling frescoes and, sheltered in its crypt, the remains of Sts Emmeram,

Wolfgang and Ramwold, all Regensburg bishops in the early days of Christianity.

The 12th-century main portal of the **Schottenkirche St Jakob** (Jakobstrasse 3) is considered one of the supreme examples of Romanesque architecture in Germany. Its reliefs and sculptures form an iconography that continues to baffle the experts.

OTHER SIGHTS

The most tangible reminder of the ancient Castra Regina (Regen Fortress), where the name 'Regensburg' comes from, is the remaining **Roman wall**, which follows Unter den Schwibbögen and veers south onto Dr-Martin-Luther-Strasse. Dating from AD 179 the rough-hewn **Porta Praetoria** arch is a key reminder of the city's heritage.

The **Historisches Museum** (☎ 507 2448; Dachauplatz 2-4; adult/concession €2.20/1.10; ☻ 10am-4pm Tue-Sun, additionally 4-8pm Thu) has exhibits ranging from the Stone Age to the 19th century, with an emphasis on the Roman period and the city's medieval glory days.

Other worthwhile attractions include the house of astronomer and mathematician Johannes Kepler, now the **Kepler-Gedächtnishaus** (Kepler Memorial House; ☎ 507 3442; Keplerstrasse 5; adult/concession €2.20/1.10; ☻ 10.30am-4pm Sat & Sun), and the unexpected **Schnupftabak-Fabrik** (Snuff Factory; ☎ 507 3442; Gesandtenstrasse 3; adult/concession €5/2.50; ☻ tours 2.30pm Fri, 11am & 2.30pm Sat & Sun), a museum in the old Bernard snuff works packed full of old machines and tobacco-related knick-knacks.

Tours

City walking tours (adult/child €8/5; ☻ in English 11.30pm Wed & Sat May-Oct) Groups meet in front of the Altes Rathaus.

Schifffahrt Klinger (☎ 521 04; www.schifffahrt klinger.de) Offers short cruises (50 minutes) on the Danube (adult/child €7.50/3.20, hourly from 9am to 4pm, April to late October) and to the Walhalla monument (adult/child single €7.50/3.20, return €10.50/4.80; at 10.30am and 2pm, 45 minutes each way plus a one-hour stop at the monument).

Festivals & Events

Dult Oktoberfest-style party with beer tents, carousel rides, entertainment and vendors on the Dultplatz, in May and late August/early September.

Weihnachtsmarkt Christmas Market, with stalls selling roasted almonds, gingerbread and traditional wooden toys. At Neupfarrplatz and Schloss Thurn und Taxis, during December.

Sleeping

BUDGET

Brook Lane Hostel (☎ 690 0966; www.hostel-regensburg.de; Obere Bachgasse 21; dm €15-19, s/d/apt €35/45/140; ☒ ☎) Expanded and thoroughly modernised in 2009, Regensburg's only backpacker hostel has spanking-new dorms and bathrooms, and its very own food store.

Zum Fröhlichen Türken (☎ 536 51; www.hotel-zum -froehlichen-tuerken.de; Fröhliche-Türken-Strasse 11; s €39-58, d €59-82; [P]) With its comfortable, clean quarters, unstinting breakfast and mild-mannered staff, the Jolly Turk will bring a smile to any budget-minded traveller's face. The pricier rooms have private bathrooms.

Also recommended:

Azur-Campingplatz (☎ 270 025; www.azur-camping .de/regensburg; Weinweg 40; per person €5.50-7.50, per tent €6-9) A pretty site about 3km from the Altstadt on the southern bank of the Danube. Take bus 6.

DJH hostel (☎ 574 02; www.regensburg.jugend herberge.de; Wöhrdstrasse 60; dm under/over 27yr €20.40/24.40) Regensburg's 186-bed hostel occupies a beautiful old building on a large island about a 10-minute walk north of the Altstadt. Take bus 3 or 8 from Albertstrasse.

MIDRANGE

Petit Hotel D'Orphée (☎ 596 020; www.hotel-orphee .de; Wahlenstrasse 1; s €35-110, d €70-135) Behind a humble door in the heart of the city lies a world of genuine charm, unexpected extras and real attention to detail. The striped floors, wrought-iron beds, original sinks and common rooms with soft cushions and well-read books give the feel of a lovingly attended home. Another somewhat grander branch of the hotel is located above the Café Orphée (p392).

Hotel Goldenes Kreuz (☎ 558 12; www.hotel-goldenes kreuz.de; Haidplatz 7; s €75-105, d €95-125; ☒ ☎) Surely the best deal in town, the nine fairy-tale rooms here each bear the name of a crowned head and are fit for a Kaiser. Huge mirrors, dark antique and Bauhaus furnishings, four-poster beds, chubby exposed beams and parquet flooring produce a stylish opus in leather, wood, crystal and fabric.

Altstadthotel am Pach (☎ 298 610; www.ampach .de; Untere Bachgasse 9; s €96-158, d €116-178; ☒ ☎) Those who have shaped Regensburg history, from Marcus Aurelius to Emperor Karl V, are commemorated in the 21 rooms of this sleek new hotel. Rooms vary in size but all are warmly furnished with thick carpets, comfy mattresses and a minifridge with complimentary beer and water.

our pick **Hotel Elements** (☎ 941-3819 8600; www .hotel-elements.de; Alter Kornmarkt 3; apt €129-149) Four elements, four rooms, and what rooms they are! This tiny, brand-new theme-hotel breaks new ground with its imaginative design, and is the best-kept secret in Bavaria. 'Fire' blazes in plush crimson and is just the thing for honeymooning couples, while nautically themed 'Water' is splashed with portholes and a Jacuzzi. 'Air' is spacious and light, as opposed to 'Earth' where colonial chocolate browns and bamboo reign.

TOP END

Bischofshof am Dom (☎ 584 60; www.hotel-bischofshof.de; Krauterermarkt 3; s €79-115, d €138-148; ⓟ) The sprawling residence of the former bishops is now a romantic upmarket hotel, with Laura Ashley-style rooms set around a beautiful leafy courtyard. The beer garden is a popular spot on summer evenings, and there's wheelchair access.

Eating

'In Regensburg we ate a magnificent lunch, had a divine musical entertainment, an English hostess and a wonderful Moselle wine,' Mozart wrote to his wife Constance in 1790. Available in Mozart's day, but better washed down with a local Kneitinger Pils, is a delectable *Bratwurstl* (grilled sausage) and *Händlmaier's Süsser Hausmachersenf*, a distinctive sweet mustard.

RESTAURANTS

Spaghetteria (Am Römling 12; dishes €4.90-8.70) Get carbed up at this former 17th-century chapel where you can splatter six types of pasta with 23 types of sauce, and get out the door for the cost of a cocktail in Munich. The entrance fresco has a pasta-sucking character from *Commedia dell' Arte*.

Dicker Mann (☎ 573 70; Krebsgasse 6; mains €6-15) One of the oldest restaurants in town, this stylish, very traditional restaurant has dependable Bavarian food, swift service and a lively flair thanks to its young and upbeat staff. On a balmy evening, grab a table in the lovely beer garden out back.

Café Orphée (☎ 529 77; Untere Bachgasse 8; mains €7-18; ☉ 9am-1am) This delightful brasserie, decked out in red velvet, dark wood and plenty of mirrors, is straight off a Parisian street. Pâtés, snacks, coffee or a light lunch all stem from a menu of appetising Gallic cuisine.

Rosenpalais (☎ 599 7579; Minoritenweg 20; bistro mains €11-20, restaurant mains €20-32; ☉ closed Sun) If it's posh-nosh you're after, try this refined place just off Dachauplatz. Well-heeled clientele head upstairs to the graceful silver-service restaurant, wallet-watching gourmets stay downstairs. Either way the food is superb.

Other recommendations:

L'Osteria (☎ 599 9181; Watmarkt 1; mains €5.50-9.50) It keeps the pizza-pasta combo coming fast at this low-lit, kitsch-free chain *ristorante*.

Leerer Beutel (☎ 589 97; Bertoldstrasse 9; mains €9-17) An imaginative menu and friendly service awaits you in the cavernous interior or out on the car-free cobbles.

QUICK EATS

Wurstkuchl (Thundorfer Strasse 3; 6 sausages €6.90) Justifiably famous for its little sausage grilled over beech wood and served with *Kraut* (cabbage).

Lagom Lunch (Dr-Martin-Luther-Strasse 9; ☉ close Sat & Sun) Smiley, no-frills lunch spot where the sandwiches, vegie dishes and panini come cheap as chips.

Wurstlkine (Rotehahnengasse 2) If Historisch-Wurstküche is closed, head for this sausage stand with cult status among night owls.

Dampfnudel Uli (☎ 532 97; Watmarkt 4; dishes under €5; ☉ closed Sun & Mon) This quirky little noshery serves a mean *Dampfnudel* (steamed doughnut) with custard in a photo- and stein-filled Gothic chamber at the base of the Baumburger Tower.

Bombay Express (☎ 584 0954; Am Ölberg 3; mains €5-8; ☉ 11am-7pm Mon-Sun) Has fragrant Indian curries made with choice ingredients for takeaway or eating at stand-up tables.

Viktualienmarkt (☉ daily) There is a fresh produce market at Neupfarrplatz.

Drinking
BEER GARDENS

Augustiner (☎ 584 0455; Neupfarrplatz 15) This popular fairy-lit beer garden and restaurant (meal €8 to €16) is ideally located in the heart of the city. The sprawling garden and cavernous interior is a fine place to leave your beer glass ring and pack away some gorgeous grub.

Kneitinger (☎ 524 55; Arnulfsplatz 3; ☉ 9am-11pm) This quintessential Bavarian brewpub is the place to go for some hearty home cooking (mains €5.80 to €15), delicious house suds and outrageous oompah frolics. It's been in business since 1530. Tours of its brewery are given Wednesday afternoons at 3pm.

Spitalgarten (☎ 847 74; St Katharinenplatz 1) A veritable thicket of folding chairs and slatted tables by the Danube, this is one of the best places in town for some alfresco quaffing. It claims to have brewed beer (today's Spital) here since 1350, so it probably knows what it's doing by now.

AFES & BARS

afé Galerie (☎ 561 408; Kohlenmarkt 6) With an ce-cream bar, sports TV, dance floor and idewalk tables scattered around a splashing ountain, this multitasking cafe is busy round he clock.

Kaminski (☎ 599 9033; Hinter der Grieb 6) Whether or afternoon coffee, a champagne breakfast or red wine with mussels, this self-assured cafe with pin-striped decor has something for everyone. Breakfast always has a classical soundtrack.

Paletti (☎ 515 93; Pustetpassage; ◉ 8am-1am Mon-at, 3pm-1am Sun) Tucked into a covered passageway off Gesandtenstrasse, this buzzy Italian cafe-bar is a hip hang-out with seen-and-been windows and art-clad walls.

Hemingway's (☎ 561 506; Obere Bachgasse 5) Black wood, big mirrors and lots of photos of Papa himself add to the cool atmosphere of this art-deco-style bar.

Neue Film Bühne (☎ 570 37; Bismarckplatz 9) Theatrical decor and the odd disco ball characterise this funky cafe-bar frequented by an eclectic crowd of students, yuppies and young families. In summer, the terrace overlooking Bismarckplatz is great for lounging.

Entertainment

Ask for a free copy of *Logo*, the local listings mag, in cafes and bars around town.

CINEMAS

Film Galerie (☎ 560 901; www.filmgalerie.de; Bertoldstrasse 9) Part of the Leerer Beutel cultural centre, this cinema concentrates on art-house films, often shown in the original language (including English).

Garbo-Filmtheater (☎ 575 86; Weissgerbergraben 1) This theatre shows classic Hollywood and modern films in English.

LIVE MUSIC & THEATRE

Alte Mälzerei (☎ 788 810; www.alte-maelzerei.de; Galgenbergstrasse 20) Regensburg's top venue for soul, funk, rock, metal and just about any other genre you can imagine, as well as poetry readings and dance events.

Jazzclub Regensburg (☎ 563 375; www.jazzclub -regensburg.de; Bertoldstrasse 9) This jazz club in the Leerer Beutel cultural centre is a vortex of talent, putting on two to three concerts a week.

Theater Regensburg (☎ 507 2424; www.theater -regensburg.de; Bismarckplatz) Runs a varied program of opera, ballet, classical concerts and drama.

Theater am Haidplatz (Haidplatz 8) Also has open-air performances in summer.

The cathedral's famous boys' choir, the Regensburger Domspatzen, sings at 10am Sunday service in the Dom St Peter.

Getting There & Away

Regensburg has direct train links to Frankfurt am Main (€63, three hours), Munich (€23.30, 1½ hours) via Landshut (€11.30, 50 minutes), Nuremberg (€17.60, one to two hours) and Passau (from €20.50, one to two hours).

Regensburg is about an hour's drive southeast of Nuremberg and northwest of Passau via the A3 autobahn. The A93 runs south to Munich.

Getting Around
BICYCLE

At **Bikehaus** (☎ 599 8808; Bahnhofstrasse 18; bikes per day €6-9.50; ◉ 10am-7pm Mon-Sat) you can hire anything from kiddies bikes to fully saddled tourers and even a rickshaw (per day €60) for a novel city tour.

BUS

On weekdays the Altstadtbus somehow manages to squeeze its way through the narrow streets between the Hauptbahnhof and the Altstadt every 10 minutes for €1 a ride. The bus transfer point is one block north of the Hauptbahnhof, on Albertstrasse. Tickets cost €1.90 for journeys in the centre; strip tickets cost €7 for five rides (two strips per ride in town). An all-day ticket (€4 at ticket machines, €5.50 on the bus) is a better deal.

CAR & MOTORCYCLE

The Steinerne Brücke and much of the Altstadt is closed to private vehicles. Car parks in the centre charge from €1.50 per hour and are well signposted.

TAXI

For a taxi, call ☎ 194 10 or 520 52.

AROUND REGENSBURG
Klosterschenke Weltenburg

When you're this close to the world's oldest monastic brewery, there's just no excuse to miss out. **Klosterschenke Weltenburg** (☎ 09441-675 70; www.klosterschenke-weltenburg.de; Asamstrasse 32; ◉ 8am-7pm Apr-Nov, closed Mon-Wed Mar) has been brewing its delicious dark beer since 1050. Now a state-of-the-art brewery, it is a favourite spot for an excursion, and the comely beer garden can get quite crowded on warm weekends and holidays.

Not everyone comes for the brew alone, as the complex is also home to a most magnificent church, **Klosterkirche Sts Georg und Martin**, designed by Cosmas Damian and Egid Quirin Asam. Its eye-popping high altar shows St George triumphant on horseback, with the skewered dragon and rescued princess at his feet. Also worth noting is the oval ceiling fresco, with a sculpture of CD Asam leaning over the railing.

The most dramatic approach to Weltenburg is by boat from the Danube river town of Kelheim (about 30km southwest of Regensburg on the B16) via the **Danube Gorge**, a spectacular stretch of the river as it carves through craggy cliffs and past bizarre rock formations. From mid-March to October, you can take a trip up the gorge for €4.60/8.20 one-way/return; bicycles are an extra €2.10/4.

Walhalla

Modelled on the Parthenon in Athens, the **Walhalla** (adult/child €4/3; ☻ 9am-5.45pm Apr-Sep, 10-11.45am & 1-3.45pm Oct-Mar) is a breathtaking Ludwig I monument dedicated to the giants of Germanic thought and deed. Marble steps seem to lead up forever from the banks of the Danube to this dazzling marble hall, with a gallery of 127 heroes in marble. It includes a few dubious cases, such as astronomer Copernicus, born in a territory belonging to present-day Poland. The latest addition (2009) was romantic poet, Heinrich Heine, whose works were set to music by Strauss, Wagner and Brahms.

To get there take the Danube Valley country road (unnumbered) 10km east from Regensburg to the village of Donaustauf, then follow the signs. Alternatively, you can take a two-hour boat cruise with **Schifffahrt Klinger** (☎ 0941-521 04; €7.50/10.50 one-way/return; ☻ 10am & 2pm Apr–mid-Oct), which includes a one-hour stop at Walhalla.

Befreiungshalle

Perched on a hill above the Danube, this mustard-coloured tankard of a building is the **Befreiungshalle** (Hall of Liberation; ☎ 09441-682 0710; Befreiungshallestrasse 3; adult/concession €3/2.50; ☻ 9am-6pm Apr-Sep, 9am-4pm Oct-Mar). Erected in 1863, it's an outrageous piece of Bavarian nationalism ordered by King Ludwig I to commemorate

the victories over Napoleon (1813–15). Insid you'll find a veritable shrine lorded over b white marble angels modelled on the Roma goddess Victoria.

LANDSHUT
☎ 0871 / pop 62,000

A worthwhile halfway halt between Munic and Regensburg, Landshut (pronounce *lands*-hoot) was the hereditary seat of th Wittelsbach family in the early 13th century and capital of the Dukedom of Bavaria Landshut for over a century. Apart from brief episode as custodian of the Bavarian University two centuries ago, Landshuter have since been busy retreating into provincia obscurity, but the town's blue-blooded past i still echoed in its grand buildings, a histori cal pageant with a cast of thousands and on seriously tall church.

Every four years in July the town host the **Landshuter Hochzeit** (next in 2013), on of Europe's biggest medieval bashes, whic commemorates the marriage of Duke Georg der Reiche of Bavaria-Landshut to Princes Jadwiga of Poland in 1475.

Orientation

The train station is 1.5km northwest of th historical centre. Follow Luitpoldstrasse t the River Isar – you'll find all the town's sight on the other side.

Information

Sparkasse (Bischof-Sailer-Platz 431) A bank.
Tourist office (☎ 922 050; www.landshut.de; Altstadt 315; ☻ 9am-6pm Mon-Fri, 10am-4pm Sat Mar-Oct, 9am-5pm Mon-Fri, 10am-2pm Sat Nov-Feb)

Sights

Coming from the train station, you enter Landshut's historical core through the broken Gothic arch of the stocky **Ländtor**, virtually the only surviving piece of the town's medieval defences. From here, Theaterstrasse brings you to the 600m-long **Altstadt**, one o Bavaria's most impressive medieval marketplaces. Pastel town houses lining its curving cobbled length hoist elaborate gables, every one a different bell-shaped or saw-toothed creation in brick and plaster.

Rising in Gothic splendour at the southern end of the Altstadt is Landshut's recordbreaking **St Martin Church** (☻ 7.30am-6.30pm Apr-Sep, 7.30am-5.30pm Oct-Mar); its spire is the tallest brick tructure in the world at 130.6m and took 55 ears to build. Also gracing the Altstadt is the **tadtresidenz** (☎ 924 110; Altstadt 79; adult/concession 3/2, combination ticket with Burg Trausnitz €7/5; ☺ 9am–pm Apr–Sep, 10am–4pm Oct–Mar), a Renaissance palce built by Ludwig X which hosts temporary xhibitions on historical themes.

Roosting high above the Altstadt is **Burg rausnitz** (Trausnitz Castle; ☎ 924 110; adult/conceson €5/4; ☺ 9am–6pm Apr–Sep, 10am–4pm Oct–Mar), andshut's top attraction. The 50-minute uided tour (in German with English text) akes you through the Gothic and Renaissance alls and chambers, ending at an alfresco arty terrace with bird's-eye views of the town elow. The ticket is also good for the **Kunst-nd Wunderkammer**, a typical Renaissance-era lisplay of exotic curios assembled by the ocal dukes.

leeping & Eating

JH hostel (☎ 234 49; www.landshut.jugendherberge.de; ichard-Schirrmann-Weg 6; under/over 27yr €13.50/17.50) This clean, well-run 100-bed hostel occupies n attractive old villa up by the castle, with iews across town.

Zur Insel (☎ 923 160; www.insel-landshut.de; Badstrasse 6; s €45-90, d €70-95; **P** ✗) On an island in the sar, this is a good-value place to kip with imple folksy rooms and a wood-panelled estaurant.

Goldene Sonne (☎ 925 30; www.goldenesonne.de; eustadt 520; s/d from €89/125; **P** 🖳 🛜) True to ts name, the 'golden sun' fills a magnificent abled town house with light. Rooms sport tylishly lofty ceilings, ornate mirrors and lat-screen TVs. For the price, some of the athrooms could do with an update.

Alt Landshut (☎ 330 6070; Isarpromenade 3; mains 6-14) Sunny days see locals linger over an ugustiner and some neighbourhood nosh utside by the Isar. In winter you can retreat o the simple whitewashed dining room.

Augustiner an der St Martins Kirche (☎ 430 5624; irchgasse 250; mains €7.50-17) This dark wood tavrn at the foot of the St Martin's spire is the est place in town to down a meat-dumpling ombo, washed along with a frothy Munich vet one.

etting There & Away

andshut is a fairly major stop on the mainine between Munich (€13.30, 50 minutes) nd Regensburg (€11.30, 50 minutes). There re direct trains every two hours to Passau

(€19.90, one hour 20 minutes), otherwise change in Plattling.

STRAUBING
☎ 09421 / pop 44,600

Some 30km southeast of Regensburg, Straubing enjoyed a brief heyday as part of a wonky alliance that formed the short-lived Duchy of Straubing-Holland. As a result, the centre is chock-a-block with historical buildings that opened new horizons in a small town. In August, the demand for folding benches soars during the **Gäubodenfest**, a 10-day blow-out that once brought together grain farmers in 1812, but now draws over 20,000 drinkers.

Orientation & Information

Compact and quite walkable, the historical centre is squeezed between the Danube and the Hauptbahnhof. The central square is shaped more like a street and consists of Theresienplatz and Ludwigsplatz.

Tourist office (☎ 944 307; www.straubing.de; Theresienplatz 20; ☺ 9am–5pm Mon–Wed & Fri, 9am–6pm Thu, 10am–2pm Sat) Makes free room referrals.

Sights & Activities

Lined with pastel-coloured houses from a variety of periods, the pedestrian square is lorded over by the Gothic **Stadtturm** (1316). It stands next to the richly gabled **Rathaus**, originally two merchants' homes but repackaged in neo-Gothic style in the 19th century. Just east of the tower is the gleaming golden **Dreifaltigkeitssäule** (Trinity Column), erected in 1709 as a nod to Catholic upheavals during the War of the Spanish Succession.

Straubing has about half a dozen historic churches. The most impressive is **St Jakobskirche** (Pfarrplatz), a late-Gothic hall church with original stained-glass windows but also a recipient of a baroque makeover, courtesy of the frantically productive Asam brothers. The pair also designed the interior of the **Ursulinenkirche** (Burggasse), their final collaboration. Its ceiling fresco depicts the martyrdom of St Ursula surrounded by allegorical representations of the four continents known at the time. Also worth a look is the nearby **Karmelitenkirche** (Hofstatt).

North of here is the former ducal residence **Herzogsschloss** (Schlossplatz), which overlooks the river. This rather austere 14th-century building was once the town's tax office.

One of Germany's most important repositories of Roman treasure is the intimate **Gäubodenmuseum** (☎ 974 10; www.gaeubodenmuseum.de; Frauenhoferstrasse 9; adult/concession €2.50/1.50; ✆ 10am-4pm Tue-Sun). Displays include imposing armour and masks for both soldiers and horses, probably plundered from a Roman store.

Getting There & Away
Straubing is on a regional train line from Regensburg (€8.40, 30 minutes) and Passau (€13.30, one hour). Trains to and from Munich (€23.10, two hours) require a change in Neufahrn or Plattling. Drivers should take the Kirchhof exit off the A3 (the Nuremberg-Passau autobahn). There's free parking at Unter den Hagen, a five-minute walk south of Stadtplatz.

PASSAU
☎ 0851 / pop 51,000

Gathered around the confluence of three rivers, the Danube, Inn and Ilz, Passau was predestined to become a powerful trading post. The waterways and major trade routes that converged here brought wealth, especially from 'white gold' (salt), and Christianity brought prestige as the city evolved into the largest bishopric in the Holy Roman Empire. The handsome old centre has a distinctly Italian look, with a maze of winding medieval cobbled lanes, underpasses and archways away from the main thoroughfares. The *Niebelungenlied*, the epic poem about a dragon-slayer, is believed to originate from here, at the bishop's 13th-century court.

A major river-cruise stop, Passau is often deluged with day visitors. It is also the hub of many long-distance cycling routes, eight of which converge here, and a good springboard for explorations into upper Austria.

Orientation
Passau's Altstadt is a narrow peninsula with the confluence of the three rivers at its eastern tip. The Hauptbahnhof is about a 10-minute walk west of the Altstadt. The Veste Oberhaus is on the Danube's north bank.

Information
Bücher Pustet (☎ 560 890; Nibelungenplatz 1) Large selection of English paperbacks and magazines.
Citibank (Theresienstrasse 1)
Commerzbank (Ludwigstrasse 13)

Post office (Nikolastrasse 2)
Tourist office Altstadt (☎ 955 980; www.passau.de; Rathausplatz 3; ✆ 8.30am-6pm Mon-Fri, 9am-4pm Sat & Sun, reduced hours mid-Oct–Easter); Hauptbahnhof (☎ 95 980; Bahnhofstrasse 28; ✆ 9am-5pm Mon-Fri, 10.30am-3.30 Sat & Sun Easter-Sep, reduced hours Oct-Easter) Staff sell the Passaucard (adult/child 1 day €14.50/10.50, 3 days €26.50/18) valid for several attractions, unlimited use of public transport and a city river cruise.

Sights
VESTE OBERHAUS
This 13th-century fortress, built by the prince bishops, towers over the city with patriarchal pomp. Views are superb, either from the castle tower (€1) or from the **Battalion Linde**, a lookout that gives the only bird's-eye view of the three-way confluence down below.

Inside the bastion is the **Oberhausmuseum** (☎ 4933 5012; Oberhaus 125; adult/concession €5/4; ✆ 9am-5pm Mon-Fri, 10am-6pm Sat & Sun Mar-Nov) Some of the best exhibits here uncover the mysteries of medieval castle-building and knight's rites of passage.

DOM ST STEPHAN
The characteristic green onion domes of Passau's otherwise whitewashed cathedral, the **Dom** (✆ 6.30am-7pm), float serenely above the town silhouette. There has been a church on this spot since the 5th century, but the current baroque look emerged after the Great Fire of 1662. The interior was designed by a crew of Italian artists, notably the architect Carlo Lurago and the stucco master Giovanni Carlone. The frescoes show fascinating scenes of heaven, but the true masterpiece is the industrial-size church organ, one of the world's largest with a staggering 17,97. pipes. Organ recitals are held on weekdays at noon, and on Thursday at 7.30pm from May to October (adult/child €3/1 lunchtime, €5/3 evening).

From the south aisle, a set of corkscrew stairs leads to the **New Bishop's Residence**, which contains the **Domschatz-und Diözesan-museum** (Cathedral Treasury & Museum; adult/concession €2/1; ✆ 10am-4pm Mon-Sat May-Oct). This showcases a range of ecclesiastical finery that illustrates the power and wealth of the Church rulers.

ALTES RATHAUS
The tower carillon in the colourful **Rathaus** chimes several times daily (hours are listed on the wall alongside the historical flood levels -

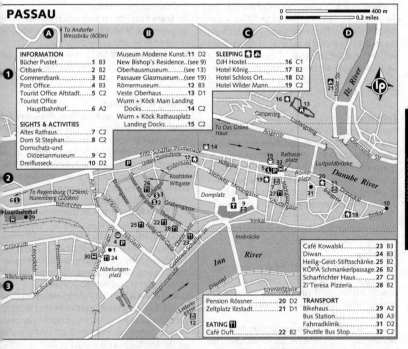

PASSAU

heck out 2002!). Inside, the **Grosser Rathaus
Saal** (Great Assembly Room; adult/concession €2/1.50;
🕙 10am-4pm Apr-Oct) has wonderful murals by
local artist Ferdinand Wagner, showing scenes
from Passau's history with a melodramatic
flourish. If it's not being used for a wedding,
also sneak into the adjacent **Small Assembly
Room** for a peek at the ceiling fresco showing buxom beauties and a fierce-looking man
– meant as allegories of the three rivers.

Wagner, who used to live in the huge building on the north bank of the Danube, just to
the right of where the Luitpoldbrücke suspension bridge is today, threatened to move out
of town if the bridge was built. It was, he did,
and after viewing the paintings, you wonder
whether the city made the right choice.

PASSAUER GLASMUSEUM

If you were wondering why Passau has bilingual signage in Czech and German, visit the
Passauer Glasmuseum (Passau Museum of Glass; 🕾 350
1; Hotel Wilder Mann, Am Rathausplatz; adult/concession
5/4; 🕙 1-5pm), the largest museum of Czech
glass and crystal in the world and a magnet
for Slavic cross-border raiders. Even if you

charge through this amazing collection of
over 30,000 pieces displayed in 380 cases,
you'll need an hour to view the 36 rooms
filled with baroque, classical, art nouveau
and art-deco pieces. There's a luxury bedroom chamber right in the museum that's
let to visiting VIPs as part of the adjacent
Hotel Wilder Mann (p398). Be sure to pick
up a floor plan as it's easy to get lost.

OTHER MUSEUMS

The **Museum Moderne Kunst** (Modern Art Museum;
🕾 383 8790; Bräugasse 17; adult/concession €5/3; 🕙 10am-
6pm Tue-Sun) holds temporary exhibitions with
both a local and international bent in a wonderful hodgepodge of buildings.

Across the Fünferlsteg Inn footbridge,
in the Kastell Boiotro, is the **Römermuseum**
(🕾 347 69; Kastell Boiotro, Lederergasse 43; adult/conces-
sion €2/1; 🕙 10am-4pm Tue-Sun Mar–mid-Nov), which
depicts Passau's original settlement and hosts
temporary shows with a Roman theme.

DREIFLUSSECK

The very nib end of the Altstadt peninsula,
the point where the rivers meet, is known as

the **Dreiflusseck** (Three River Corner). From the north the little Ilz sluices brackish water down from the Bavarian forest, which meets the murky brown Danube as it flows from the west and the pale jade of the Inn from the south, forming an odd murky tricolour. The effect is best observed from the ramparts of the Veste Oberhaus (p396).

Activities

From March to early November, **Wurm + Köck** (☎ 929 292; www.donauschiffahrt.de; Höllgasse 26; adult/child 45min €7.80/3.90, 2hr €11.50/free) operate cruises to the Dreiflusseck from the docks near Rathausplatz, as well as a whole host of other sailings to places along the Danube. The four-hour **evening cruise** (per person €30.50; 🕑 7pm Apr–Oct) with live music and three-course dinner is a romantic experience.

Sleeping

Zeltplatz Ilzstadt (☎ 414 57; Halser Strasse 34; adult/child €8/6.50) This tent-only camping ground has an idyllic spot on the Ilz, about a 15-minute walk from the Altstadt. Catch bus 1, 2 or 4 to Ilzbrücke.

DJH hostel (☎ 493 780; www.passau.jugendherberge.de; Veste Oberhaus 125; dm under/over 27yr €17.90/21.90) This beautifully renovated 132-bed hostel is right in the fortress.

Pension Rössner (☎ 931350; www.pension-roessner.de; Bräugasse 19; s/d €35/60; ⓟ) The price-to-quality ratio is high at this immaculate *Pension* in a restored mansion on the eastern tip of the Altstadt. Each room is uniquely decorated and many also have fortress views. Breakfast is a silly €7 extra.

ourpick **Hotel Wilder Mann** (☎ 350 71; www.wilder-mann.com; Am Rathausplatz; s €50-60, d €80-140; ⓟ) Royalty and celebrities, from Empress Elizabeth of Austria to Mikhail Gorbachev and Henry Kissinger, have stayed at this historic inn. Rooms seek to recapture a lost grandeur, and some of the carved bedsteads are very grand indeed. The glorious Ludwig II and Empress Elizabeth suites cost from €200 a night if you're feeling flush.

Hotel König (☎ 3850; www.hotel-koenig.de; Untere Donaulände 1; s €65-100, d €89-140; ⓟ ✗) Spacious modern rooms, great views over the river and a good central location make this riverside property an excellent choice. The hotel also has a good restaurant with a beautiful dining terrace. There is wheelchair access.

Other recommendations:

Das Grüne Haus (☎ 211 8565; www.bettundbike-passau .de; Angerstrasse 39; dm/d €24/48; ⓟ) Bike-friendly hotel cum-hostel on the north bank of the Danube.

Hotel Schloss Ort (☎ 340 72; www.schlosshotel-passau .de; Im Ort 11; s €68-88, d €97-136; ⓟ) Snug medieval palace housing a stylish hotel a hop from the Dreiflusseck.

Eating & Drinking

Diwan (☎ 490 3280; top fl, Stadtturm, Niebelungenplatz 1; mains €3-7) Climb aboard the high-speed lift from street level to this trendy, high-perched cafe-lounge with by far the best views in town. From the tangled rattan and plush cappuccino culture sofas you can see it all – the Dom, the rivers, the fortress – while you tuck into the offerings of the changing seasonal menu.

Zi'Teresa Pizzeria (☎ 2138; Theresienstrasse 26; meal €5.60-20) Theresienstrasse and its side streets are lined with cafes and restaurants and popular places to just hang out, such as Zi'Teresa. This lively, always-bustling Italian eatery attracts young and old to munch on generously topped pizzas and superb pastas.

Café Kowalski (☎ 2487; Oberer Sand 1; dishes €6-11) Chat flows as freely as wine or beer at this gregarious cafe, a kicker of a nightspot. The giant burgers, *Schnitzels* and salads are best sampled on the terrace overlooking the Ilz.

Andorfer Weissbräu (☎ 754 444; Rennweg 2; mains €6-13) High on a hill 1.5km north of the Altstadt, this rural beer garden attached to the Andorfer brewery serves filling Bavarian favourites, but the star of this show is the outstanding *Weizen* and *Weizenbock* ale brewed metres away. Take bus 7 from the ZOB to Ries-Rennweg.

ourpick **Scharfrichter Haus** (☎ 359 00; Milchgasse 2; mains €7.40-16.50; 🕑 noon-2pm & 6pm-1am) Cafe, cellar restaurant and jazz club rolled into one, this Passau institution draws a sophisticated crowd who enjoy seasonal specials on crisp white linen, before retiring to the intimate cabaret theatre with a glass of Austrian wine.

Heilig-Geist-Stiftsschänke (☎ 2607; Heilig-Geist-Gasse 4; mains €10-19; 🕑 closed Wed) Traditional food is prepared with panache, and served either in the classy walnut-panelled tangle of dining rooms or the leafy beer garden, where hedges create separate dining areas. The candlelit stone cellar is open from 6pm.

Other recommendations:

Café Duft (☎ 346 66; Theresienstrasse 22; mains €3.30-10) A vaulted chamber with low lights, dark wood and a good range of dishes.

KÖPA Schmankerlpassage (Ludwigstrasse 6) Fruit stalls, meat and fish counters to put together a full meal for under €6.

Getting There & Away

TRAIN

Passau is on the main train line to Nuremberg (€32.90 to €43, two hours), Regensburg (€20.50 to €26, one hour) and Vienna (€43.20, three hours). There are also direct trains to Munich (€30.20, 2½ hours). The trip to Zwiesel (€19, 1½ hours) and other Bavarian Forest towns requires a change in Plattling.

Getting Around

Central Passau is sufficiently compact to explore on foot. The CityBus links the Bahnhof with the Altstadt (€0.80) up to four times an hour. Longer trips within Passau cost €1.50; a day pass costs €3.50 (€5 for a family).

The walk up the hill to the Veste or the hostel, via Luitpoldbrücke and Ludwigsteig path, takes about 30 minutes. From April to October, a shuttle bus operates from Rathausplatz (€2/2.50 one-way/return).

There are several public car parks near the train station but only one in the Altstadt at Römerplatz (€1.10/€10 per hour/day).

Bikehaus (☎ 0800-460 8460; Hauptbahnhof platform 1; Apr-Oct) and **Fahrradklinik** (☎ 334 11; Bräugasse 10) both hire out bikes from €12 per day.

MARKTL AM INN
☎ 08678 / pop 2700

On a gentle bend in the Inn, some 60km southwest of Passau, sits the drowsy village of Marktl am Inn. Few people outside of Germany (or indeed Bavaria) had heard of it before 19 April 2005, the day when its favourite son, Cardinal Joseph Ratzinger, was elected as **Pope Benedict XVI**. Literally overnight the community was inundated with reporters, devotees and the plain curious, all seeking clues about the pontiff's life and times. Souvenirs like mitre-shaped cakes, 'Papst-Bier' (Pope's Beer) and religious board games flooded the local shops.

The pope's **Geburtshaus** (Birth House; ☎ 747 680; www.papsthaus.eu; Marktplatz 11; adult/child €3.50/free; ☉ 10am-noon & 2-6pm Tue-Fri, 10am-6pm Sat & Sun Apr-Oct) is the simple but pretty Bavarian home where Ratzinger was born in 1927 and lived for the first two years of his life before his family moved to Tittmoning, another tiny *Burg* (castle). The exhibition kicks off with

a film (in English) tracing the pontiff's early life, career and the symbols he selected for his papacy. You then head into the house proper where exhibits expand on these themes. The modest room where Ratzinger came into the world is on the upper floor.

The **Heimatmuseum** (Local History Museum; Marktplatz 2; adult/child €2/1; ☉ by prior arrangement) is in possession of a golden chalice and a skullcap that was used by Ratzinger in his private chapel in Rome, but is only open to groups of five or more. Visitors should call the **tourist office** (☎ 748 820; www.markt-marktl.de; Marktplatz 1) at least a day ahead to arrange entry. His baptismal font can be viewed at the **Pfarrkirche St Oswald** (Parish Church of St Oswald; Marktplatz 6), which is open for viewing except during church services.

With immaculate rooms and a superb restaurant, family-run **Pension Hummel** (☎ 282; www.gasthof-hummel.de; Hauptstrasse 34; s/d €41/59), a few steps from the train station, is the best spot to get some shut-eye. Wash down simple Bavarian fare with Papst-Bier at **Gasthaus Oberbräu** (☎ 1040; Bahnhofstrasse 2; mains €6-10; ☉ 10am-midnight).

Marktl is a very brief stop on an Inn-hugging branch line between Simbach and Mühldorf (€5.10, 20 minutes), from where there are regular direct connections to Munich, Passau and Landshut.

BAVARIAN FOREST

Together with the Bohemian Forest on the Czech side of the border, the Bavarian Forest (Bayerischer Wald) forms the largest continuous woodland area in Europe. This inspiring landscape of peaceful rolling hills and rounded tree-covered peaks is interspersed with little-disturbed valleys and stretches of virgin woodland, providing a habitat for many species long since vanished from the rest of the region. A large area is protected as the surprisingly wild and remote Bavarian Forest National Park (Nationalpark Bayerischer Wald).

Although incredibly good value, the region sees few international tourists and remains quite traditional. A centuries-old glass-blowing industry is still active in many of the towns along the **Glasstrasse** (Glass Road), a 250km holiday route connecting Waldsassen with Passau. You can visit the studios, workshops, museums and shops and stock up on traditional and contemporary designs.

BAVARIA

Orientation

The low hills of the Bavarian Forest stretch northwest to southeast along the German-Czech border. One of the bigger towns, and an ideal base for its transport links, is Zwiesel.

Information

Grafenau tourist office (☎ 08552-962 343; www .grafenau.de; Rathausgasse 1; ☼ 8am-5pm Mon-Thu, 8am-1pm Fri, 10-11.30am Sat)

Zwiesel tourist office Town centre (☎ 09922-840 523; www.zwiesel-tourismus.de; Stadtplatz 27; ☼ 8.30am-5pm Mon-Fri, 10am-1pm Sat); Zwiesel-Süd (☼ 10am-noon Mon-Fri) The latter has English-speaking staff and is just outside town on the main road towards Regen.

Sights

The forest, local customs and glass making are the main themes of exhibits at Zwiesel's **Waldmuseum** (Forest Museum; ☎ 09922-840 583; Stadtplatz 29; adult/concession €2/1; ☼ 9am-5pm Mon-Fri, 10am-noon & 2-4pm Sat & Sun mid-May–mid-Oct, reduced hours winter). Also in Zwiesel is the **Dampfbier-Brauerei** (☎ 09922-846 60; Regener Strasse 9; tours €3.50; ☼ tours noon Tue & Fri) where you can join a brewery tour and sample its peppery ales.

Frauenau's dazzlingly modern **Glasmuseum** (☎ 09926-941 020; Am Museumspark 1; adult/child €5/2.50; ☼ 9am-5pm Mon-Fri, 10am-4pm Sat & Sun) covers four millennia of glass-making history, starting with the ancient Egyptians and ending with modern glass art from around the world. Demonstrations and workshops for kids are regular features.

On the southern edge of the Bavarian Forest, in Tittling, there's the **Museumsdorf Bayerischer Wald** (☎ 08504-8482; Herrenstrasse 11; adult/child €4/free; ☼ 9am-5pm Apr-Oct). This 20-hectare open-air museum features 150 typical Bavarian Forest timber cottages and farmsteads from the 17th to the 19th centuries, with displays ranging from clothing and furniture to pottery and farming implements. Take frequent RBO bus 6124 to Tittling from Passau Hauptbahnhof.

BAVARIAN FOREST NATIONAL PARK

A paradise for outdoor enthusiasts, the Bavarian Forest National Park stretches for about 24,250 hectares along the Czech border, from Bayerisch Eisenstein in the north to Finsterau in the south. Its thick forest, most of it mountain spruce, is criss-crossed by hundreds of kilometres of marked hiking, cycling and cross-country skiing trails. The three main mountains, Rachel, Lusen and Grosser Falkenstein, rise up to between 1300m and 1450m and are home to deer, wild boar, fox, otter and countless bird species.

Around 1km northeast of the village of Neuschönau stands the **Hans-Eisenmann-Haus** (☎ 08558-961 50; www.nationalpark-bayerischer-wald.de Böhmstrasse 35, Neuschönau; ☼ 9am-5pm), the national park's main visitor centre. The free, but slightly dated, exhibition has a hands-on displays designed to shed light on topics such as pollution and tree growth. There's also a children's discovery room, a shop and a library. See opposite for details about transport in the park.

Activities

Two long-distance hiking routes cut through the Bavarian Forest: the European Distance Trails E6 (Baltic Sea to the Adriatic) and E8 (North Sea to Carpathia). There are mountain huts all along the way. Another popular hiking trail is the Gläserne Steig (Glass Trail) from Lam to Grafenau. Whatever route you're planning, maps produced by Kompass – sheet 185, 195 and 197 (€6 to €7.50) – are invaluable companions. They are available from tourist offices and the park visitor centre.

The Bavarian Forest has seven ski areas, but downhill skiing is low-key, even though the area's highest mountain, the Grosser Arber (1456m), occasionally hosts European and World Cup ski races. The best resorts are in the north, such as Bischofsmais near the Geisskopf (1097m), Bodenmais near the Grosser Arber, and Neukirchen near the Hoher Bogen (1079m). The major draw here is cross-country skiing, with 2000km of prepared routes through the ranges.

Sleeping

Accommodation in this region is a real bargain; Zwiesel and Grafenau have the best choices.

Azur-Ferienpark Bayerischer Wald (☎ 09922-80 595; www.azur-camping.de; Waldesruhweg 34, Zwiesel; per person €6-7.50, tent €4-5.50) About 500m north of the Hauptbahnhof, near public pools and sports facilities.

Rachelblick (☎ 08553-1289; Klingenbrunn Bahnhof 9, Klingenbrunn; s/d €17.50/35; (P)) Situated in the tiny forest hamlet of Klingenbrunn Bahnhof, but just 100m from a halt on the Waldbahn, this cosy family-run guesthouse is an ideal rural escape. Rooms are standard guesthouse issue but have en-suite bathrooms and pretty forest iews. It's a great base for hiking or skiing the ountless trails that criss-cross the forest.

DJH hostel (☎ 08553-6000; www.waldhaeuser.jugend erberge.de; Herbergsweg 2, Neuschönau; dm under/over 27yr ₂0.20/24.20) The only hostel right in the national ›ark and an ideal base for hikers.

Hotel-Gasthaus Zum Kellermann (☎ 08552-967 10; ›ww.hotel-zum-kellermann.de; Stadtplatz 8, Grafenau; s/d 37/60; ☿ closed Wed; Ⓟ) Fresh and airy rooms t very reasonable rates make this simple ³rafenau guesthouse a good bet. There's a ›retty terrace area outside and the restaurant mains €6 to €12) supplies yummy local fare.

Hotel Hubertus (☎ 08552-964 90; www.hubertus ›rafenau.de; Grüb 20, Grafenau; s €47-58, d €78-104; Ⓟ ☖) ⁀his elegant hotel in Grafenau offers incred- ›le value for the weary traveller. The stylish ›ooms are spacious and most have balconies. ³uests are treated to a pool and sauna, and ˙elicious buffet meals.

Hotel Zur Waldbahn (☎ 09922-8570; www.zurwald ⁀hn.de; Bahnhofplatz 2, Zwiesel; s €55-62, d €88-96; Ⓟ ☖) ⁀radition and modern comforts blend seam- ˙essly at this friendly inn, conveniently lo- ˙ated opposite the Hauptbahnhof. The warm, ⁀ood-panelled rooms are tastefully furnished, ⁁he restaurant is top-notch, and just check ›ut that pool.

›ating

⁀einanger (☎ 09922-869 690; Angerstrasse 37, Zwiesel; ⁀ains €6-11; ☿ 7pm-1am Wed-Sat) If your stomach ›raves a lighter dinner, try this cheerful wine ›istro with brick walls and polished wooden

tables. French onion soup, cheeses and ba- guette sandwiches all feature on the menu, and some Fridays there's live jazz.

Dampfbräu (☎ 09922-605 30; Stadtplatz 6, Zwiesel; mains €8-15) Rustic hearts cut out of the chunky timber backrests, murals illustrating local in- dustries, simple belly-fillers caught and picked in the surrounding forests and tankards of locally brewed ale make this the most char- acterful tavern eatery in town. The wild boar goulash in a dark beer sauce, is the best of the Bavarian Forest on a plate.

Getting There & Around

From Munich, Regensburg or Passau, Zwiesel is reached by rail via Plattling; most trains continue to Bayerisch Eisenstein on the Czech border, with connections to Prague. The scenic Waldbahn shuttles directly be- tween Zwiesel and Bodenmais and Zwiesel and Grafenau.

There's also a tight network of regional buses, though service can be infrequent. The Igel-Bus navigates around the national park on four routes. A useful one is the Lusen-Bus (€4/10 per one-/three-day ticket), which leaves from Grafenau Hauptbahnhof and travels to the Hans-Eisenmann-Haus, the Neuschönau hostel and the Lusen hiking area.

The best value is usually the **Bayerwald-Ticket** (€7), a day pass good for unlimited travel on bus and train throughout the forest area. It's available from the park visitor centre, stations and tourist offices throughout the area.

BAVARIA

Baden-Württemberg

If one word could sum up Baden-Württemberg, it would surely be inventive. Some 35,00 years ago, cavemen in the Swabian Alps gave the world figurative art and so sparked string of firsts. Germany's southwesternmost state is the birthplace of Albert Einstein, DN/ (Miescher) and the astronomical telescope (Kepler). It was here that Bosch invented the spar plug; Gottlieb Daimler, the gas engine; and Count Ferdinand, the zeppelin. And where woul(we be without Black Forest cake, cuckoo clocks and the ultimate beer food, the pretzel?

It's as much as travellers can do to tear their gaze away from the bewitching scenery shifting from terraced vineyards between Heidelberg and Stuttgart to the Swabian Alps' mist castle-topped crags and the Upper Danube Valley's precipitous ravines. Swing south to Lak Constance and the pastoral picture becomes one of ripening cornfields and wetlands outline by the jagged Swiss Alps. To the west, the fabled Black Forest serves a soothing tonic c luxuriantly green valleys, where woodsy farmhouses crouch below softly rounded hills.

Let your journey unfold in half-timbered villages stuck in the Middle Ages; in the baroqu palaces in Karlsruhe and Ludwigsburg; in Roman-style decadence in Baden-Baden's spas; c in the here and now exploring Stuttgart's futuristic car museums and the energetic nightlif of university towns Heidelberg, Freiburg and Tübingen. Goethe, Turner, Twain and the Broth ers Grimm drew inspiration from Baden-Württemberg, which time and again amazes wit its roll-call of genius, incredible natural beauty and sweet eccentricities.

HIGHLIGHTS

- Gorge on the one-and-only Black Forest cake and hear the world's biggest cuckoo call in **Triberg** (p460)

- Soak up Altstadt views with a jolly punt along the Neckar in **Tübingen** (p426)

- Abandon modesty for a naked splash in the thermal waters of Baden-Baden's **Roman-Irish Bath** (p446)

- Border hop, bathe and bed down in the straw on **Lake Constance** (p467)

- Strain your neck for a good look at the world's tallest steeple topping Ulm's **Münster** (p439)

★ Baden-Baden

★ Tübingen

★ Ulm

★ Triberg

★ Lake Constance

■ POPULATION: 10.75 MILLION   ■ AREA: 35, 752 SQ KM

Activities

HIKING

Baden-Württemberg practically coined the word wanderlust as the base of the **schwarzwaldverein** (www.schwarzwaldverein.de, in German), Germany's first hiking club founded in Freiburg in 1864. Whether it's to be leisurely strolls through Stuttgart's vineyards and Lake Constance's orchards, or multiday hikes into the darkest depths of the Black Forest, nearly everywhere in this hike-friendly state has well-maintained, signposted trails and lodgings where muddy boots are not an issue.

Local tourist offices stock maps and can suggest day hikes, but for longer treks check the website www.wanderbares-deutschland.de (in German). **Wandern Ohne Gepäck** (www.wandern-ohne-gepaeck.com, in German) is a savvy initiative where walkers can hit the trail without luggage on two Black Forest routes, including a three-day hike from Freudenstadt (p448). The 1:50,000 scale maps produced by the Landesvermessungsgsamt and Kompass are recommended.

CYCLING

Thousands of kilometres of signed cycling routes criss-cross Baden-Württemberg, a great place to exchange autobahn speeding for two-wheel cruising. The state's cycling appeal reaches from gentle spins around Lake Constance to the uphill slog and invigorating scenery of mountain biking in the Black Forest. For free-wheeling with watery views, try these:

Bodensee-Radweg Loops around Lake Constance and through three countries: Germany, Switzerland and Austria (see p467).

Donautal-Radweg (www.donau-radweg.info) Traces the mighty Danube from Donaueschingen (65km east of Freiburg) to Ulm (190km northeast of Donaueschingen), continuing to Vienna, Budapest and beyond.

Neckartal-Radweg (www.neckartal-radweg.de, in German) Shadows the Neckar River for 357km from Villingen-Schwenningen northward to Tübingen, Stuttgart and Heidelberg.

Rheintal-Weg Follows the Rhine from Konstanz westward to Basel and then northward via Freiburg (or Breisach) to Baden-Baden, Heidelberg, Mannheim and beyond.

Veloroute Rhein Traces the Rhine River along its left bank (in France and then Germany) and the right bank from Basel northward to Mannheim (415km).

Getting There & Around

Stuttgart airport (www.stuttgart-airport.com), Baden-Württemberg's largest, is a hub for the low-cost airline **Germanwings** (www.germanwings.com). Frankfurt airport is about 75km north of Mannheim. Other useful airports include the Basel-Mulhouse **EuroAirport** (www.euroairport.com), where budget airlines easyJet and Ryanair operate. **Karlsruhe-Baden-Baden airport** (Baden Airpark; www.badenairpark.de) and **Friedrichshafen airport** (www.fly-away.de) are both served by Ryanair among other airlines.

Trains, trams and/or buses serve almost every city, town and village in this chapter, though public transport across the Black Forest can be slow, and long-distance trips (for instance Freiburg to Konstanz) may involve several changes. Available at train stations, the great-value Deutsche Bahn **Baden-Württemberg Ticket** allows 2nd-class travel on trains and some buses, costing €19 for an individual and €28 for up to five people. Most Black Forest hotels issue guests with the **Schwarzwald-Gästekarte** (p444), providing free use of the local public transport network.

STUTTGART

☎ 0711 / pop 591,100

Ask many Germans their opinion about the Stuttgarters and they will go off on a tangent: they are smooth operators behind a Mercedes wheel, speeding along the autobahn while flashing and gesticulating; they are city slickers in designer suits with a Swabian drawl; they are tight-fisted homebodies who slave away to *schaffe, schaffe, Häusle baue* (work, work, build a house). So much for the stereotypes.

Blessed with a prosperous air, a finger on the pulse of technology and an endearing love of the great outdoors, the real Stuttgart immediately challenges such preconceptions. One minute you're touring space-age car museums, the next you're strapping on boots to hike through vineyards, dining on Michelin-starred cuisine or shimmying beside ubercool 20-somethings in the bars on Theodor-Heuss-Strasse.

Progressive, open-minded and strikingly self-assured, Stuttgart cherishes its traditions, stays true to its rural heritage and embraces innovation with a passion.

BADEN-WÜRTTEMBERG

HISTORY

Whether with trusty steeds or turbocharged engines, Stuttgart was literally born to ride, founded as the stud farm Stuotgarten around 950 AD. Progress was swift: by the 12th century Stuttgart was a trade centre, by the 13th century a blossoming city and by the early 14th century the seat of the Württemberg royal family. Count Eberhard im Bart added sheen to Swabian suburbia by introducing the *Kehrwoche* in 1492, the communal cleaning rota still revered today.

The early 16th century brought hardship, peasant wars, plague and Austrian rulers (1520–1534). A century later, the Thirty Years' War devastated Stuttgart and killed half its population.

In 1818, King Wilhelm I launched the firs the Cannstatter Volksfest to celebrate the en of a dreadful famine. An age of industrialisa tion dawned in the late 19th and early 20th centuries, with Bosch inventing the spark plug and Daimler pioneering the gas engine Heavily bombed in WWII, Stuttgart wa painstakingly reconstructed and became the capital of the new state of Baden-Württember in 1953. Today it is one of Germany's greenes and most affluent cities.

ORIENTATION

The main pedestrian shopping street Königstrasse, extends southwest from the Hauptbahnhof. Public squares on o near Königstrasse include Schlossplat

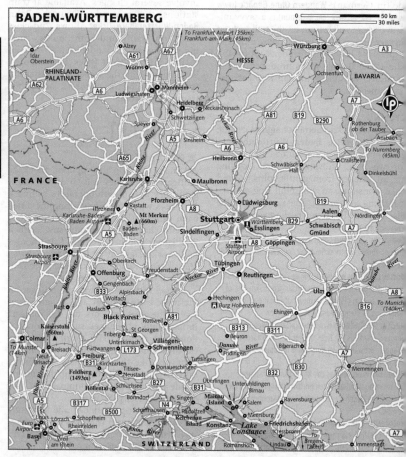

BADEN-WÜRTTEMBERG

and Schillerplatz. The leafy Schlossgarten stretches northeastward from Schlossplatz almost 4km to the Neckar River. The district of Bad Cannstatt straddles the Neckar River about 3km northeast of the Hauptbahnhof.

Steep grades are common on Stuttgart's hillsides: more than 500 city streets end in *Stäffele* (staircases).

INFORMATION
Bookshops
Wittwer (☎ 250 70; Königstrasse 30) A bookshop with foreign-language and travel sections.

Cultural Centres
Deutsch-Amerikanisches Zentrum (German-American Center; ☎ 228 180; www.daz.org; Charlottenplatz 17; ☯ 2-6pm Tue-Thu) Promotes German-American relations.

Discount Cards
Stuttcard (72hr €9.70) Free entry to most museums, plus discounts on events, activities and guided tours. Sold at the tourist office and some hotels.
Stuttcard Plus (72hr €20) Combines the Stuttcard with a three-day pass for bus, tram and U-Bahn travel within the city, including transport to and from the airport.
VVS 3-Day Ticket (72hr inner city/metropolitan area €10.30/13.90) Three-day pass for unlimited use of public transport, available to guests with a hotel reservation.

Internet Access
City Call Internet Center (Eberhardstrasse 14; per hr €2; ☯ 10am-midnight Mon-Sat, 11am-midnight Sun)
Coffee Fellows (☎ 292 743; Hauptbahnhof; per hr €5; ☯ 6am-10pm) Up the stairs behind track 4. Free wi-fi.
Cyber Café (☎ 284 9980; Klett-Passage 29; per hr €2; ☯ 9am-11pm Mon-Sat, 10am-11pm Sun)
Treppe (☎ 222 1646; Kleiner Schlossplatz 13-15; per hr €3; ☯ 9am-midnight Mon-Sat, noon-midnight Sun) Sleek cafe-lounge with high-speed internet.

Laundry
SB-Waschsalon Trieb (☯ 7am-7pm Mon-Fri, 7am-3pm Sat) Self-service laundry in the arcade behind the tourist office. There's also a 24-hour *'Waschbox'*.

Medical Services
Klinikum Stuttgart (☎ 2780; Kriegsbergstrasse 60) The city's largest hospital.

Money
ATMs Königstrasse has many, including one in the tourist office.

ReiseBank & Western Union (Hauptbahnhof, opposite track 11; ☯ 8am-8.30pm, Western Union to 8pm) Currency exchange.

Post
Post office (inside Königsbau Passagen; ☯ 10am-8pm Mon-Fri, 9am-4pm Sat) Slightly northwest of the Schlossplatz. There's also a branch in the Hauptbahnhof, up the stairs behind track 4.

Tourist Information
Baden-Württemberg Tourist Board (www.tourismus-bw.de)
Tourist office (☎ 222 80; www.stuttgart-tourist.de; Königstrasse 1a; ☯ 9am-8pm Mon-Fri, 9am-6pm Sat, 11am-6pm Sun) The staff can help with room bookings and public transport enquiries. Has a list of vineyards open for tastings.
Welcome Information Center (☎ 222 8240; ☯ 8am-7pm Mon-Fri, 9am-noon & 1-6pm Sat & Sun) The tourist office branch at Stuttgart International Airport. Situated in Terminal 3, Level 2 (Arrivals).

SIGHTS
City Centre
A lift races up to the Hauptbahnhof's 10th floor, where an **Aussichtsplatform** (Viewing Platform; admission free; ☯ 10am-9pm Apr-Sep, 10am-6pm Oct-Mar) affords close-ups of the revolving Mercedes logo and far-reaching views over Stuttgart.

East of the station, the fountain-dotted **Mittlerer Schlossgarten** (Middle Palace Garden) draws thirsty crowds to its terrific **beer garden** (p411) in summer. The **Unterer Schlossgarten** (Lower Palace Garden) is a ribbon of greenery rambling northeast to the Neckar River and the **Rosensteinpark**, home to the zoo (p407). Sitting south, the **Oberer Schlossgarten** (Upper Palace Garden) is framed by eye-catching landmarks like the columned **Staatstheater** (State Theatre) and the ultramodern glass-clad **Landtag** (State Parliament).

Stepping east, the neoclassical meets contemporary **Staatsgalerie** (State Gallery; ☎ 470 400; www.staatsgalerie-stuttgart.de; Konrad-Adenauer-Strasse 30-32; adult/concession €5.50/4, special exhibitions €10/7; ☯ 10am-6pm Tue-Sun, to 8pm Tue & Thu) bears British architect James Stirling's curvy, colourful imprint. Alongside big-name exhibitions, the gallery harbours a top-drawer collection of 20th-century art, showcasing works by Rembrandt, Monet, Dalí and pop idols Warhol and Lichtenstein.

Stuttgart's main artery is the shopping boulevard **Königstrasse**, reaching south from

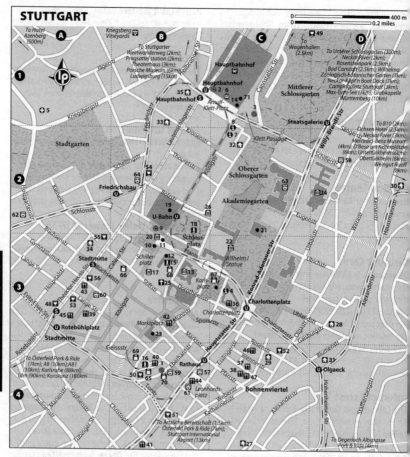

STUTTGART

the Hauptbahnhof. Halfway down is the **Schlossplatz**, a regal plaza crowned by the **König Wilhelm Jubilee Column**, with fountains representing the eight rivers of Baden-Württemberg.

A shimmering glass cube sheltering the **Kunstmuseum Stuttgart** (☎ 2162188; www.kunstmuseum -stuttgart.de; Kleiner Schlossplatz 1; adult/concession €5/3.50, special exhibitions €10/8; ✆ 10am-6pm Tue-Sun, to 9pm Wed & Fri) dominates the square's western flank. The gallery is a romp through modern and contemporary art, with works by Otto Dix and Dieter Roth. For a 360-degree view over Stuttgart, head up to the Cube cafe. Out front, the primary colours and geometric forms of **Alexander Calder's mobile** catch the eye.

Just north of Schlossplatz is the classical, colonnaded **Königsbau**, reborn as an upmarket shopping mall, the **Königsbau Passagen**. Identified by its copper cupola, the **Württembergischer Kunstverein** (☎ 223 370; www.wkv-stuttgart.de; Schlossplatz 2; adult/concession €5/3; ✆ 11am-6pm Tue-Sun, to 8pm Wed) nearby stages thought-provoking contemporary art exhibitions.

Duke Karl Eugen von Württemberg's answer to Versailles was the exuberant three-winged **Neues Schloss** (New Palace), a baroque-neoclassical royal residence that now houses state government ministries. A bronze statue of Emperor Wilhelm I looking dashing on his steed graces nearby **Karlsplatz**.

On the other side of the Renaissance **Alte Kanzlei** (Old Chancellory), south of Schlossplatz, lies cobbled Schillerplatz, where the poet-dramatist Friedrich Schiller is immortalised in bronze. Here an archway leads to the turreted 10th-century **Altes Schloss**, where the **Landesmuseum Württemberg** (☎ 279 3498; www .landesmuseum-stuttgart.de; Schillerplatz 6; adult/under 12yr/ concession €4.50/free/3; ☺ 10am-5pm Tue-Sun) homes in on regional archaeology and architecture. The historic booty comprises Celtic jewellery, Neolithic pottery, diamond-encrusted crown jewels and rare artefacts like 35,000-year-old figurines carved from mammoth ivory. Time your visit to see, from the arcaded courtyard, the rams above the clock tower lock horns on the hour.

Music buffs should catch one of the Friday lunchtime concerts (€3) at the **Instrumenten Museum** (Schillerplatz 1; admission free with Landesmuseum ticket; ☺ 10am-5pm Tue-Sun), occupying a former wine depot topped by a Bacchus statue. Right next door, the sand-hued **Stiftskirche** stands out with its mismatched late-Gothic towers.

Car Museums

A futuristic swirl on the cityscape, the brand-new **Mercedes-Benz Museum** (☎ 173 0000; www .museum-mercedes-benz.com; Mercedesstrasse 100; adult/ concession €8/4; ☺ 9am-6pm Tue-Sun; ☒ Gottlieb-Daimler-

Stadion) takes a chronological spin through the Mercedes empire. Look out for legends like the 1885 Daimler Riding Car, the world's first gasoline-powered vehicle, and the record-breaking Lightning Benz that hit 228km/h on Daytona Beach in 1909. There's a free guided tour in English at 1.45pm.

Like a pearly white spaceship preparing for lift-off, the barrier-free **Porsche Museum** (☎ 9112 0911; www.porsche.com; Porscheplatz 1; adult/concession €8/4; ☺ 9am-6pm Tue-Sun; ☒ Neuwirtshaus) is every little boy's dream. Groovy audioguides race you through the history of Porsche from its 1948 beginnings. Break to glimpse the 911 GT1 that won Le Mans in 1998.

Parks & Gardens

Wilhelma Zoologisch-Botanischer Garten (☎ 540 20; www.wilhelma.de; Rosensteinpark; adult/concession €11.40/5.70, after 4pm & in winter €8/4; ☺ 8.15am-nightfall; ☒ Wilhelma) is a quirky mix of zoo and botanical gardens. Kid magnets include semi-striped okapis, elephants, penguins and a petting farm with Poitou donkeys. Greenhouses sheltering tree ferns, camellias and Amazonian species are among the botanical highlights. Sniff out the gigantic

BADEN-WÜRTTEMBERG

BOHEMIAN BEANS

To really slip under Stuttgart's skin, take a wander through one of the city's lesser-known neigh-bourhoods. Walk south to **Hans-im-Glück Platz**, centred on a fountain depicting the caged Grimm's fairy-tale character Lucky Hans, and you'll soon reach the boho-flavoured **Bohnenviertel** (bean district; www.bohnenviertel.net, in German). This neighbourhood takes its name from the beans that Americans introduced in the 16th century. Back then they were grown everywhere as the staple food of the poor tanners, dyers and craftsmen who lived here. A recent facelift has restored the district's cobbled lanes and gabled houses, which harbour idiosyncratic galleries, workshops, bookstores, wine taverns and cafes. The Bohnenviertel's villagey feel is a refreshing tonic to the big-city feel of central Stuttgart.

---

bloom of the malodorous titan arum in the Moorish Villa.

When temperatures soar, Stuttgarters head to **Max-Eyth-See**, about 7km northeast of the Hauptbahnhof on the U14 line, for pedalo fun on the lake and picnicking in the park beside the Neckar River. Murky water means swimming is out, but there's a worth-while **bike path**, part of the Neckartal-Radweg (p403). The terraced-style vineyards rising above the river are scattered with **Wengerter-Häuschen** (tool sheds); some are more than 200 years old and protected landmarks.

TOURS
Boat
From early May to late October, **Neckar-Käpt'n** (☎ 5499 7060; www.neckar-kaeptn.de) runs boat ex-cursions on the Neckar River (from €8), de-parting from its dock at Wilhelma in Bad Cannstatt on the U14.

Walking & Bus
Sightseeing and walking tours feature the 1½-hour **Stadt-Spaziergang** (City Walk; €8; ☾ 11am Apr-Oct), beginning at the tourist office, and the 2½-hour **Stadt-Rundfahrt** (City Coach Tour; adult/con-cession €18/14.50; ☾ 1.30pm daily Apr-Oct) starting at Hotel am Schlossgarten (opposite). Both are in English and German

FESTIVALS & EVENTS
The following list is a taster of Stuttgart's live-liest events.
Sommerfest Riverside parties, open-air gigs and alfresco feasting are what this four-day August shindig is all about.
Weindorf A 10-day event where wine-makers sell the year's vintages from hundreds of booths on Schlossplatz and the Oberer Schlossgarten. Begins on the last weekend in August.
Cannstatter Volksfest Stuttgart's answer to Oktober-fest, this beer-guzzling bash, held over three consecutive

weekends from late September to mid-October, lifts spirits with oompah music, fairground rides and fireworks.
Weihnachtsmarkt One of Germany's biggest Christmas markets brings festive twinkle to Marktplatz, Schillerplatz and Schlossplatz from late November to 23 December.

SLEEPING
Stuttgart is gradually upping the ante in slumber land but, like it or not, nondescript chains still reign supreme. Expect weekend discounts of 10% to 20% at hotels targeting business travellers. If you're seeking indi-vidual flair and a family welcome, stop by the tourist office for a list of private guesthouses and apartments.

Budget
Campingplatz Stuttgart (☎ 556 696; www.camping platz-stuttgart.de; Mercedesstrasse 40, Bad Cannstatt; per person/tent/car €6.30/4.50/2.50; ☾ year-round) This leafy site, 1km southeast of the Bad Cannstatt S-Bahn station, has a bistro, laun-dry and playground.

DJH hostel (☎ 664 7470; www.jugendherberge-stuttgart .de; Haussmannstrasse 27; dm 1st/subsequent night €22.90/19.60; ☾ 24hr; 🖥) A recent makeover has glammed up this hostel, offering squeaky-clean dorms with private bathrooms. A lounge and a terrace with fab city views add to the sociable vibe. It's 800m southeast of the Hauptbahnhof

Museumstube (☎ 296 810; www.museumstube.de; Hospitalstrasse 9; d €67, s/d without bathroom €32/47) Within staggering distance of pumping Theodor-Heuss-Strasse, this humble abode is kept shipshape by kindly Maria and Drago. Rooms are old fashioned but super-clean. Head downstairs to sample their famous gou-lash. Prices don't include breakfast.

Hostel Alex 30 (☎ 838 8950; www.alex30-hostel.de; Alexanderstrasse 30; dm/s/d €23/35/56, breakfast €7; 🅿 🖥; ⓔ Olgaeck) Backpackers find a relaxed base in these mellow digs with a bar, sundeck and communal kitchen. The 32 citrus-bright rooms are light and contemporary.

Midrange

Abalon Hotel (☎ 217 10; www.abalon.de; Zimmermannstrasse 7-9; s €79-89, d €99-112; P ⬚) Affable staff, a top location and wallet-friendly rates make Abalon a great pick. The bright parquet-floored rooms are large and spotless.

City Hotel (☎ 210 810; www.cityhotel-stuttgart.de; Uhlandstrasse 18; s €79-89, d €99-115) Eschew the anonymity of Stuttgart's cookie-cutter chains for this intimate hotel just off Charlottenplatz. Rooms are light, clean and modern, if slightly lacklustre. Breakfast on the terrace in summer is a bonus.

ourpick Hotel Azenberg (☎ 225 5040; www.hotel azenberg.de, in German; Seestrasse 114-116; s €85-145, d €105-165; P ⬚ ⬚) This family-run retreat has plush, individually designed quarters with themes swinging from English country manor to Picasso. Work off breakfast doing laps in the pool. The hotel is a brisk uphill stroll or a short ride on bus 43 from Stadtmitte to Hölderlinstrasse.

Hotel Unger (☎ 209 90; www.hotel-unger.de, in German; Kronenstrasse 17; s €80-125, d €112-175; P ⬚) Right near the Hauptbahnhof, this hotel's corporate feel is offset by its friendliness and comfort. Guests rave about the generous breakfast with smoked fish, fresh fruit and pastries. Rates drop around 40% at weekends.

Ochsen Hotel (☎ 407 0500; www.ochsen-online.de; Ulmer Strasse 323; s €86-99, d €114-128; P ; ⬚ Inselstrasse) It's well worth going the extra mile to this charismatic 18th-century hotel. Some of the spacious, warm-hued rooms have whirl-pool tubs for a post-sightseeing bubble. The wood-panelled restaurant serves appetising local fare.

Top End

Hotel am Schlossgarten (☎ 202 60; www.hotelschloss garten.com; Schillerstrasse 23; s €120-141, d €164-184; P ⬚) Sidling up to the Schloss, this hotel has swish rooms with above-par perks like free newspapers and chocolate; those facing the park are the quietest. Foodies jostle for a table in the Michelin-starred Zirbelstube restaurant (mains €28 to €52).

Der Zauberlehrling (☎ 237 7770; www.zauberlehrling .de; Rosenstrasse 38; s €115-155, d €145-245, ste €270-420; ⬚) The self-consciously cool sorcerer's apprentice reveals design-driven rooms, from Titanic with its waterbed to the high-tech wizardry of the Media Suite. Yet it's hard to conjure up a smile at reception and the place lacks a little soul. Nice, but not quite magic.

Steigenberger Graf Zeppelin (☎ 204 80; www .stuttgart.steigenberger.de; Arnulf-Klett-Platz 7; s/d from €195/220; P ⬚ ⬚) While its concrete facade won't bowl you over, inside is a different story. This five-star pad facing the Hauptbahnhof is luxury all the way with its snazzy rooms, Zen-style spa and Michelin-starred restaurant, Olivo (p410).

EATING

Stuttgart has become quite experimental in the kitchen, sprouting a crop of avant-garde restaurants where inspired chefs put a creative, seasonal spin on German cuisine. The centre serves up a mix of flavours, from Swabian soul food like *Spätzle* (egg-based noodles) to tangy *Currywurst* (curried sausage). Explore

BADEN-WÜRTTEMBERG

A VINE ROMANCE

To taste the fruity Trollingers and citrusy rieslings produced in the region, factor in a stroll through the vineyards surrounding Stuttgart. The **Stuttgarter Weinwanderweg** (www.stuttgarter -weinwanderweg.de, in German) comprises several walking trails that thread through winegrowing villages. One begins at Pragsattel station (on the U5 or U6 line) and meanders northeast to Max-Eyth-See (opposite), affording fine views from Burgholzhofturm. Visit the website for alternative routes, maps and distances.

From October to March, look out for a broom above the door of **Besenwirtschaften** (*Besa* for short). Run by winegrowers, these rustic bolt-holes are atmospheric places to chat with locals while sampling the new vintage and Swabian home cooking. Some operate every year, but most don't. Check the Besen Kalender website (www.besenkalender.de, in German) during vintage times. Stuttgart-area *Besenwirtschaften* that open annually include the central **City-Besen** (☎ 470 4248; Wilhelmsplatz 1; ⏰ 5pm-midnight Mon-Fri, noon-midnight Sat), an atmospheric vaulted cellar serving home-grown wines.

the Bohnenviertel's narrow lanes for intimate bistros and arty cafes with a youthful buzz.

Budget

Imbiss zum Brunnenwirt (☎ 245 021; Leonhardsplatz 25; sausages €2.40-3.20; ☽ 11am-2am Mon-Thu, 11am-3am Fri & Sat, 4pm-2am Sun) Shabby chic describes this hole-in-the-wall joint in Bohnenviertel, where an eclectic crowd – from passing vagrants to Mercedes coupé drivers – flock for Stuttgart's most famous *Currywurst*.

our pick Bitter Sweet (☎ 222 0888; Wagnerstrasse 38a; snacks €3-4; ☽ 10am-7pm Mon-Sat) Prettier than a little girl's bedroom, this pastel-washed, flower-strewn cafe is shoehorned into a courtyard in Bohnenviertel. Marcel keeps the scones, tarts, aromatic speciality teas and good vibes coming. It doubles as a shop selling homemade jams, chocolate and old-fashioned hard-boiled sweets.

Forum Theater Café (☎ 440 074 992; Gymnasiumstrasse 21; snacks €4-7; ☽ 3pm-11.30pm Mon-Fri, noon-2.30pm Sat; **Ⓥ**) This nature-inspired, kid-friendly cafe in the Forum Theater has a relaxed ambience and rotating art exhibitions. Revive over a yogi tea or organic snacks from wholesome soups to moist blueberry cake.

Deli (☎ 236 0200; Geissstrasse 7; mains €6-13; ☽ 10am-1am Sun-Thu, to 3am Fri & Sat) Overlooking the Hans-im-Glück fountain, this groovy cafe-bar plays mellow lounge music and rustles up dishes from pasta to spicy shrimp curry.

Self-caterers make for the **food market** (Marktplatz; ☽ 7.30am-1pm Tue, Thu & Sat) and the **Markthalle** (market hall; Dorotheenstrasse 4; ☽ 7am-6.30pm Mon-Fri, 7am-4pm Sat), which sells picnic fixings and has Italian and Swabian restaurants.

Midrange

Weinhaus Stetter (☎ 240 163; Rosenstrasse 32; mains €7-13.50; ☽ 3-11pm Mon-Fri, 11am-2pm & 5.30-11pm Sat) No-nonsense Swabian cooking, such as flavoursome *Linsen und Saiten* (lentils with sausage), and wines are the mainstay of this Bohnenviertel tavern. The attached wine shop sells 650 different vintages.

Calwer-Eck-Bräu (☎ 2224 9440; Calwer Strasse 31; mains €9-18.50; ☽ 11am-midnight Mon-Thu, to 1am Fri & Sat, 10am-midnight Sun) Dark polished wood and leather banquettes create a cosy feel in this 1st-floor brewpub. Loosen a belt notch for Swabian-Bavarian dishes like *Maultaschensuppe* (ravioli soup) and *Weisswurst* (white veal-pork sausage), which pair nicely with cloudy pilsners.

Alte Kanzlei (☎ 294 457; Schillerplatz 5a; mains €9.50-17.50; ☽ 10am-midnight Mon-Thu, to 1am Fri & Sat) Empty tables are gold-dust rare at this convivial, high-ceilinged restaurant on Schillerplatz. Feast on Swabian favourites like *Spannpferkel* (roast suckling pig) and *Flädlesuppe* (pancake soup), washed down with regional tipples.

Amadeus (☎ 292 678; Charlottenplatz 17; mains €10-17.50; salads €4.50-8.80; ☽ noon-midnight Mon-Fri, 10am-midnight Sat & Sun) Once an 18th-century orphanage dishing up gruel, this chic, bustling restaurant now serves glorious Swabian food such as *Maultaschen* and riesling-laced *Kutteln* (tripe). The terrace is a big draw in summer.

Basta (☎ 240 228; Wagnerstrasse 39; mains €10-18; ☽ 4pm-1am Mon-Fri, 1pm-2am Sat) The hum of chatter and herby smells fill this snug Bohnenviertel bistro. Each flavour shines through in dishes like wild-garlic *Maultaschen* and glass noodles with sea bream. Wine lovers have plenty of choice.

Weinstube Schellenturm (☎ 236 4888; Weberstrasse 72; mains €10-19; ☽ 5pm-midnight Mon-Sat) Since casting off its *Schellen* (shackles) as a jail, this turreted 16th-century tower has been reincarnated as a wine tavern. Ascend the spiral staircase to feast on regional treats such as hazelnut *Spätzle* and herb-crusted lamb under wood beams.

Weber (☎ 253 6338; Calwer Strasse 52; mains €12-23; ☽ 11am-midnight Mon-Thu, 11am-2am Fri & Sat, 10am-midnight Sun) Jazzy beats play in this hip bistro, sporting a sleek interior with teak tables, olive-black colours and woven screens. Presented in a vinyl cover, the menu gives local flavours a Mediterranean twist – think ostrich filet with lemon *Schupfnudeln* (potato noodles). Brunch favourites include *luxus Eier* (luxury eggs) with truffle oil and parmesan.

Top End

Olivo (☎ 204 8277; Arnulf-Klett-Platz 7; mains €35-44, 3-course lunch/dinner €48/109; ☽ Tue-Sat) Chef Marc Rennhack's Franco-German cuisine is fresh and innovative. The culinary heavyweight packs a Michelin-starred punch with seasonal signature dishes like meltingly tender Charolais beef with scallops, and pollack with *boudin noir*. Crisp white linen and warm orange tones create a slick, modern setting.

our pick Délice (☎ 640 3222 www.restaurant-delice.de; Hauptstätter Strasse 61; ☽ 6.30pm-midnight Mon-Fri) Save your appetite for dinner (presuming you've booked well ahead) at this vaulted Michelin-starred restaurant. Viennese master chef Friedrich Gutscher uses organic ingredients in

THEODOR-HEUSS-STRASSE BAR CRAWL

Crammed with hipper-than-thou lounge bars, Theodor-Heuss-Strasse, just west of Königstrasse, is the centre of Stuttgart's pulsating after-dark scene. Dress the part (jeans and trainers are a no-no in most places) to slip past picky doormen. DJ Amar works the crowd into a sweat spinning house and electro at charcoal-black **7 Grad** (Theodor-Heuss-Strasse 32), while neighbouring **Barcode** (Theodor-Heuss-Strasse 30) fuels the party with decadent cocktails in streamlined surrounds. Good-looking Stuttgarters dance to soul and funk at nouveau Alpine chic **Muttermilch** (Theodor-Heuss-Strasse 23), where the vibe is clubby, and ice-cool **Suite 212** (Theodor-Heuss-Strasse 23). It's less of a beauty contest at relaxed student hang-out **Schaufenster Mitte** (Theodor-Heuss-Strasse 4), hosting upbeat exhibitions and gigs.

taste sensations such as tender pigeon breast on boletus potatoes and curd ice cream with rose water. The sommelier will talk you through the award-winning riesling selection.

DRINKING

Biergarten im Schlossgarten (☎ 226 1274; Mittlerer Schlossgarten; ☼ 10am-1.30am May-Oct) Celebrate summer with beer and pretzels at Stuttgart's best-loved, 2000-seat beer garden in the green heart of the Schlossgarten. Regular live music gets steins a-swinging.

Café Weiss (☎ 244 121; Geissstrasse 16; ☼ 6pm-3am Mon-Thu, to 4am Fri & Sat) Drunken students and punks, hip-hop dudes and glammed-up divas – all love this grungy, borderline sleazy dive. The bartenders can be gruffer than billy goats, but they pour a stiff vodka and lend change for the jukebox.

Hüftengold (☎ 248 6988; Olgastrasse 44; ☼ 7am-midnight Mon-Sat, 10am-10pm Sun) Rumour has it that when the boss fell pregnant, she named her other baby, this lounge cafe, *Hüftengold* (love handles). Bag a log stool in this retro sylvan wonderland for cocktails, chill-out grooves and cosy evening chats by candlelight.

Palast der Republik (☎ 226 4887; Friedrichstrasse 27; ☼ 11am-2am, to 3am Fri & Sat) Named after the former seat of East German parliament, this round kiosk has a less-than-imposing history as a public toilet. It's popular among students and alternative types, who sit at tables or on the ground sipping their brew.

ENTERTAINMENT

For the low-down on events, grab a copy of German-language monthly **Lift Stuttgart** (www.lift-online.de) from the tourist office or news kiosks, or listings magazine **Prinz** (www.prinz.de/stuttgart.html). Events tickets can be purchased at the **Kartenvorverkauf desk** (☎ 222 8243; inside the tourist office; ☼ 9am-8pm Mon-Fri, 9am-4pm Sat).

Nightclubs

Click onto www.subculture.de (in German) for more on Stuttgart's club scene.

Dilayla (☎ 236 9527; Eberhardstrasse 49; admission free; ☼ 9pm-4am, to 6am Fri & Sat nights, from 11pm late May-Sep) Crash on the sofas or get your groove on to '70s and '80s soundtracks at this laid-back, dimly lit basement club. Gets going around midnight.

Die Röhre (☎ 299 1499; www.die-roehre.com, in German; Willy-Brandt-Strasse 2/1; admission varies) A hugely popular, industrial-style concert and party venue under the curved ceiling of an aborted vehicle tunnel or *Röhre* (tube).

King's Club (☎ 226 4558; www.kingsclub-stuttgart.de, in German; Calwer Strasse 21; admission Fri & Sat €10; ☼ 10pm-6am) Scarlet walls create a sultry backdrop at King's, where gays, lesbians and straights dance to house and electro. Picks up after midnight. Enter from Gymnasiumstrasse.

Wagenhallen (☎ 253 7012; www.wagenhallen.de, in German; Innerer Nordbahnhof 1; admission varies) Swim away from the mainstream at this post-industrial space near Eckhardtshaldenweg U-Bahn, where club nights, gigs and workshops skip from Balkan beat parties to poetry slams. There's a relaxed beer garden for summertime quaffing.

Live Jazz

Bix Jazzclub (☎ 2384 0997; www.bix-stuttgart.de, in German; Leonhardsplatz 28; admission €8-25; ☼ 6.30pm-1am Tue-Wed, 6.30pm-3am Thu-Sat) Suave chocolate-gold tones and soft lighting set the scene for first-rate jazz acts at Bix, swinging from big bands to soul and blues.

Kiste (☎ 553 2805; www.kiste-stuttgart.de; Hauptstätter Strasse 35; admission €5; ☼ 6pm-1am Mon-Thu, to 2am Fri & Sat) Jam-packed at weekends, this hole-in-the-wall bar is Stuttgart's leading jazz venue, with nightly concerts (except Sunday), starting at 9.30pm or 10pm.

Performing Arts

Liederhalle (☎ 202 7710; www.liederhalle-stuttgart.de; Berliner Platz 1; ticket prices vary) Jimi Hendrix and Sting are among the stars who have performed at this culture and congress centre. The 1950s venue stages big-name classical and pop concerts, cabaret and comedy.

Staatstheater (☎ 203 20; www.staatstheater-stuttgart .de, in German; Oberer Schlossgarten 6; ticket prices vary) Stuttgart's grandest theatre presents a top-drawer program of ballet, opera, theatre and classical music. The Stuttgart Ballet (www .stuttgart-ballet.de, in German) is hailed one of Europe's best companies.

Theaterhaus (☎ 402 0720; www.theaterhaus.com, in German; Siemensstrasse 11; Ⓜ Maybachstrasse) This dynamic theatre stages live rock, jazz and other music genres, plus theatre and comedy performances.

Variété im Friedrichsbau (☎ 225 7070; www .friedrichsbau.de, in German; Friedrichsstrasse 24; tickets €20–40) Famous for its excellent variety shows and cabaret productions.

SHOPPING

Mosey down plane tree–lined Königstrasse, Germany's longest shopping mile, for high-street brands and department stores, Calwer Strasse for chichi boutiques, and Stifftstrasse for designer labels. The casual Bohnenviertel is the go-to quarter for antiques, galleries, vintage garb and Stuttgart-made crafts.

Brunnenhannes (☎ 273 8435; Geissstrasse 15) Nothing to wear to Oktoberfest? Biker-meets-Bavaria Brunnenhannes has the solution with lederhosen for strapping lads, dirndls for buxom dames and gingham lingerie that is half kitsch, half cool.

Feinkost Böhm (☎ 227 560; Kronprinzstrasse 6) Böhm is a foodie one-stop shop with regional wine, beer, chocolate and preserves, and an appetising deli.

Marcoccino (☎ 5189 0596; Geissstrasse 10; Ⓨ 11am-7pm Mon-Sat) Handmade chilli truffles, goat's cheese pralines, chocolate caviar…however will you choose? The attractively packaged treats in Marco's chandelier-lit store make yummy gifts.

Stilwerk (☎ 253 6713; www.stilwerk.de; Königsbau-passagen; Ⓨ 10am-8pm Mon-Sat) Some of Germany's top design stores cluster under an elliptical glass roof at Stilwerk, specialising in everything from space-age bathrooms to stylish rattan creations.

Tausche (☎ 414 8490; Eberhardstrasse 51; Ⓨ 11am-7pm Mon-Fri, to 6pm Sat) Berlin's snazziest messenger bags have winged their way south. Tausche's walls are a technicolour mosaic of exchangeable flaps: from *die blöde Kuh* (the silly cow) to Stuttgart's iconic Fernsehturm (TV Tower). Pick one to match your outfit and mood.

For outdoor action, there's a bustling **flower market** (Schillerplatz; Ⓨ 7.30am-1pm Tue, Thu & Sat) and a **flea market** (Karlsplatz; Ⓨ to 4pm Sat).

GETTING THERE & AWAY
Air

Stuttgart International Airport (STR; ☎ 01805-948 444; www.stuttgart-airport.com), a major hub for **Germanwings** (www.germanwings.com), is 13km south of the city. There are four terminals, all within easy walking distance of each other.

Car & Motorcycle

The A8 from Munich to Karlsruhe passes Stuttgart, often abbreviated to 'S' on highway signs, as does the A81 from Singen (near Lake Constance) to Heilbronn and Mannheim.

Stuttgart recently boosted its ecofriendly credentials by becoming an **Umwelt Zone** (www .umwelt-plakette.de), where vehicles are graded according to their emissions levels. Expect to pay €6 to €10 for an *Umweltplakette* (environment sticker), which is obligatory in green zones and can be ordered online. See p783 for more details.

Train

IC and ICE destinations include Berlin (€126, 5½ hours), Frankfurt (€56, 1¼ hours) and Munich (€46 to €52, 2¼ hours). There are frequent regional services to Tübingen (€11.30, one hour), Schwäbisch Hall's Hessental station (€13.30, 70 minutes) and Ulm (€16.70, one hour).

GETTING AROUND
To/From the Airport

S2 and S3 trains take about 30 minutes to get from the airport to the Hauptbahnhof (€3.10).

Bicycle

Rent a Bike (☎ 4207 0833; www.rentabike-stuttgart .de, in German; adult 6½hr/full day €12/16, student €9/12) delivers and picks up bikes. Stuttgart has 50 **Call-a-Bike** (☎ 0700 0522 2222; www.callabike .de) stands. The first 30 minutes are free and rental costs around €5 per hour thereafter. Visit the website for maps and details.

It's free to take your bike on *Stadtbahn* lines, except from 6am to 8.30am and 4pm to 6.30pm Monday to Friday. Bikes are allowed on S-Bahn trains (S1 to S6) but you have to buy a *Kinderticket* (child's ticket) from 6am to 8.30am Monday to Friday. You can't take bikes on buses or the *Strassenbahn* (tramway).

Car & Motorcycle

Underground parking costs about €2.50 for the first hour and €2 for each subsequent hour. See www.parkinfo.com (in German) for a list of car parks. The Park & Ride ('P+R') options in Stuttgart's suburbs afford cheap parking; convenient lots include Degerloch Albstrasse (on the B27; take the U5 or U6 into town), which is 4km south of the centre; and Österfeld (on the A81; take the S1, S2 or S3 into the centre).

Avis, Budget, Europcar, Hertz, National and Sixt have offices at the airport (Terminal 2, Level 2). Europcar, Hertz and Avis have offices at the Hauptbahnhof (next to track 16).

Public Transport

From slowest to fastest, Stuttgart's **public transport network** (www.vvs.de, www.ssb-ag.de, in German) consists of a *Zahnradbahn* (rack railway), buses, the *Strassenbahn* (tramway), *Stadtbahn* lines (light-rail lines beginning with U; underground in the city centre), S-Bahn lines (suburban rail lines S1 through to S6) and *Regionalbahn* lines (regional trains beginning with R). On Friday and Saturday there are night buses (beginning with N) with departures from Schlossplatz at 1.11am, 2.22am and 3.33am.

For travel within the city, single tickets are €1.95, and four-ride tickets *(Mehrfahrtenkarte)* cost €6.92. A day pass, good for two zones (including, for instance, the Mercedes-Benz and Porsche Museums), is better value at €5.80 for one person or €9.70 for a group of between two and five.

Taxi

To order a taxi call ☎ 194 10 or ☎ 566 061.

AROUND STUTTGART

Grabkapelle Württemberg

When King Wilhelm I of Württemberg's beloved wife Katharina Pavlovna, daughter of a Russian tsar, died at the tender age of 30 in 1819, the king tore down the family castle and built this domed **burial chapel** (☎ 337 149; adult/concession €2.20/1.10; ☽ 10am-noon Wed, 10am-noon & 1-5pm Fri & Sat, 10am-noon & 1-6pm Sun Mar-Oct). The king was also interred in the classical-style Russian Orthodox chapel decades later. Scenically perched on a vine-strewn hill, the grounds afford long views down to the valley.

Grapkapelle Württemberg is 10km southeast of Stuttgart's centre. Take bus 61 from the Obertürkheim station, served by the S1.

Ludwigsburg
☎ 07141 / pop 87,350

This neat, cultured town is the childhood home of the dramatist Friedrich Schiller. Duke Eberhard Ludwig put it on the global map in the 18th century by erecting a chateau to out-pomp them all: the sublime, Versailles-inspired Residenzschloss. With its whimsical palaces and gardens, Ludwigsburg is baroque in overdrive and a flashback to an age when princes wore powdered wigs and lords went a-hunting.

ORIENTATION & INFORMATION

S-Bahn trains from Stuttgart serve the Hauptbahnhof, 750m southwest of the centre. The Residenzschloss, on Schlossstrasse (the B27) lies 400m northeast of the central Marktplatz.

Ludwigsburg's **tourist office** (☎ 910 2252; www.ludwigsburg.de; Marktplatz 6; ☽ 9am-6pm Mon-Fri, 9am-2pm Sat) has excellent material in English on lodgings, festivals and events such as the baroque Christmas market.

SIGHTS & ACTIVITIES

Nicknamed the Swabian Versailles and *almost* as imposing, the **Residenzschloss** (☎ 182 004; www.schloss-ludwigsburg.de; Schlossstrasse; tours adult/concession/family €6.50/3.30/16.30; ☽ 10am-6pm, last tour at 5pm) is an extravagant 452-room baroque, rococo and Empire affair. The 90-minute chateau tours (in German with an English text) begin half-hourly.

The 18th-century feast continues with a spin of the staggeringly ornate, scarlet and gold **Karl Eugen Apartment**, and three **museums** (adult/concession incl audioguide €3.50/1.80; ☽ 10am-5pm) showcasing everything from exquisite baroque paintings to fashion accessories and majolica.

BADEN-WÜRTTEMBERG

More appealing in summer is a fragrant stroll amid the herbs, rhododendrons and gushing fountains of the **Blühendes Barock** (Blooming Baroque; ☎ 975 650; Mömpelgardstrasse 28; adult/concession €7.50/3.60; ⏲ 7.30am-8.30pm late Mar–Oct) gardens. Kids drag their parents to the fairy-tale theme-park **Märchengarten** (⏲ 9am-6pm) to visit the witch with a Swabian cackle at the gingerbread house and admire their fairness in Snow White's magic mirror. Should you want Rapunzel to let down her hair at the tower, get practising: *Rapunzel, lass deinen Zopf herunter* (The gold-tressed diva only understands – accurately pronounced! – German).

Sitting in parkland, a five-minute walk north of the Residenzschloss, is the petit baroque palace **Schloss Favorite** (☎ 182 004; 30min tour adult/concession €3.50/1.80; ⏲ 10am-12.30pm & 1.30-5pm mid-Mar–Oct, 10am-12.30pm & 1.30-4pm Tue-Sun Nov–mid-Mar), graced with Empire-style furniture. Duke Eugen held glittering parties here.

GETTING THERE & AROUND

Stuttgart's S4 and S5 S-Bahn lines go directly to Ludwigsburg's Hauptbahnhof (€3.20), frequently linked to the chateau by buses 421, 425 and 427. On foot, the chateau is 1km from the train station.

There are two large parking lots 500m south of the Residenzschloss, just off the B27.

NORTHERN BADEN-WÜRTTEMBERG

Straddling the French border, northern Baden-Württemberg is an intriguing mix of rural landscapes and dynamic cities. Heidelberg beckons Mark Twain lovers to its party-mad Altstadt and hypnotic castle, while Mannheim and Karlsruhe appeal to culture buffs with their world-class galleries, progressive culture and splendid baroque palaces. Detour from the well-trodden track to lesser-known towns like Schwäbisch Hall, with half-timbered town houses that mirror its lucrative medieval salt trade.

HEIDELBERG

☎ 06221 / pop 145,300

Whether you go to Heidelberg to tiptoe in the footsteps of Mark Twain, who quipped about its drunken, duelling fraternities and eulogised its ruptured castle in his 1880 novel *A Tramp Abroad*; to see the light of William Turner in the Altstadt and the Neckar River or to crawl the pubs Goethe-style in a quest for enlightenment, this postcard-perfect city obliges. Precisely as it does for the 3.5 million other visitors every year.

Cultured and conservative, rebellious and erudite, philosophical and frivolous sober and smashed: Heidelberg is one city many personalities. With an academic elite to rival the Oxbridges and Harvards of this world, this is Germany's oldest and most famous university city, home to 32,000 students who fizz up the nightlife and uphold the longstanding reputation for academic excellence.

Orientation

Heidelberg's Altstadt spreads along the Neckar River from Bismarckplatz east to the Schloss. Europe's longest pedestrian zone, the 1600m-long Haupstrasse, runs east-to-west through the Altstadt, about 200m south of the Neckar.

Two bridges link the Altstadt with the Neckar's northern bank: at the western end, north of Bismarckplatz, is Theodor-Heuss-Brücke, while north of the Marktplatz is the Alte Brücke (also known as Karl-Theodor-Brücke).

Information

Internet cafes are scattered on and around Hauptstrasse.

Ärztlicher Bereitschaftdienst (☎ 192 92; Alte Eppenheimer Strasse 35; ⏲ 7pm or 8pm-7am, 24hr Sat & Sun) For medical care when most doctors' offices are closed. Situated one block north of the Hauptbahnhof.

Deutsch-Amerikanisches Institut (☎ 607 30; www.dai-heidelberg.de; Sofienstrasse 12; ⏲ library 1-6pm Mon-Fri, to 8pm Wed, 10am-2pm Sat) Has concerts, films, lectures and occasional exhibits.

HeidelbergCard (1/2/4 days €12.50/17/22, 2-day family card €30) Entitles you to unlimited public transport use, free admission to the Schloss and most museums, plus discounts on bike rental and tours.

Internet Lounge (per 5min/hr €0.50/6; ⏲ 7am-midnight) Internet in the Hauptbahnhof.

Main post office (Hugo-Stotz-Strasse 14) To the right as you exit the Hauptbahnhof.

Post office (Sofienstrasse 8-10)

ReiseBank (⏲ 7.30am-8pm Mon-Fri, 9am-5pm Sat, 9am-1pm Sun) In the Hauptbahnhof building; exchanges currency.

Tourist office (☎ 194 33; www.heidelberg-marketing
.de; ⊗ 9am-7pm Mon-Sat, 10am-6pm Sun & holidays
Apr-Oct, 9am-6pm Mon-Sat Nov-Mar) Right outside the
Hauptbahnhof. Out front is a hotel reservation board with
a free telephone. Sells the HeidelbergCard.
Waschsalon (Kettengasse 17; per 7kg €8.50; ⊗ 9am-
.30pm Mon, Tue, Thu & Fri, 9am-1pm Wed & Sat) A
laundry where you can DIY or pick up two hours later.
Wetzlar (☎ 241 65; Plöck 79-81) Specialises in foreign-
language books.

Sights

SCHLOSS

Sticking up above the Altstadt like a picture-
book pop-up against a theatrical backdrop
of wooded hills, the partly ruined, red sandstone **Schloss** (☎ 538 431; www.schloss-heidelberg.de;
adult/concession €3/1.50, gardens free; ⊗ 8am-5.30pm) is
Heidelberg's heart-stealer. Palatinate princes,
stampeding Swedes, Protestant reformers, raging fires and lightning bolts – this
Gothic-Renaissance fortress has seen the
lot. Its tumultuous history, story-book looks
and changing moods have inspired the pens
of Mark Twain and Victor Hugo as well as
Turner's prolific paintbrush.

The Renaissance **Schlosshof** (courtyard) is so
elaborate it often elicits gasps from visitors, as
do the knockout views over Heidelberg and
the Neckar Valley from the **terrace**. The only
way to see the less-than-scintillating interior
is by guided **tour** (adult/concession €4/2; ⊗ 11.15am,
12.15pm, 2.15pm & 4.15pm daily, also 10.15am Sat & Sun,
additional tours at 1.15pm & 3.15pm mid-Apr–mid-Oct). An
audioguide costs €4.

Infinitely more fun than science lessons, the **Deutsches Apothekenmuseum** (German
Pharmacy Museum; ☎ 258 80; admission incl in Schloss
ticket; ⊗ 10.15am-6pm Apr-Oct, 10am-5.30pm Nov-Mar),
off the courtyard, explores chemistry and
pharmacology in centuries past. Look out
for the hands-on kids' pharmacy (healthy
tea anyone?) and miracle cures from opiates
to, hmmm, unicorn. With a capacity of more
than 220,000L, the 18th-century **Grosses Fass**
(Great Vat) is the world's largest wine cask,
shaped from 130 oak trees. Describing it as
being 'as big as a cottage', Mark Twain be-
moaned its emptiness and mused on its possible functions as a dance floor and gigantic
cream churn.

Behind the Schloss, the verdant **Schlossgarten**
(castle garden) is great for a stroll. The **Pulver
Turm** (Gunpowder Tower) was damaged by
French forces in 1693.

To reach the castle you can either hoof it
up the steep, cobbled **Burgweg** in about 10
minutes, or take the **Bergbahn** (funicular railway;
www.bergbahn-heidelberg.de; adult/6-14yr one way €3/2,
return €5/4; ⊗ every 10min) from the Kornmarkt
station.

KÖNIGSTUHL

For views over hill and dale, hop in one of
the century-old rail cars trundling between
the castle and the 550m-high **Königstuhl**. The
return fare, with a stop at the Schloss, is adult
€8 and child six to 14 years €6.

Children adore the kitschy cuteness of
Märchenparadies (Fairy-Tale Park; ☎ 234 16; www
.maerchenparadies.de, in German; adult/2-12yr €3/2;
⊗ 10am-6pm Apr-Nov, 10am-7pm Jul & Aug), a mini-
theme park with gentle rides, play areas and
fairy-tale characters from Snow White to
Rumpelstiltskin.

UNIVERSITY

Despite witty observations about boisterous
student duels and drunkenness, Mark Twain
points out that 'idle students are not the rule'
in Heidelberg in his 1880 novel *A Tramp
Abroad*. Indeed Germany's oldest university,
Ruprecht-Karls-Universität (www.uni-heidelberg.de), established in 1386 by Count Palatinate Ruprecht
I, has plenty of gravitas with a student hall of
fame starring composer Robert Schumann
and chancellor Helmut Kohl. Today it comprises 18 faculties with 32,000 students from
80 nations.

The most historic facilities are on
Universitätsplatz, dominated by the **Neue
Universität** and the 18th-century **Alte Universität**,
the old and new university buildings.

From 1778 to 1914, students convicted
of misdeeds, such as womanising, inebria-
tion or freeing the local pigs, were tossed
into the **Studentenkarzer** (Student Jail; ☎ 543 554;
Augustinergasse 2; adult/concession €3/2.50; ⊗ 10am-6pm
Tue-Sun Apr-Sep, 10am-4pm Tue-Sat Oct-Mar), behind the
Alte Universität, where they were detained
for at least three days and fed only bread and
water. Delinquents doing more time could
interrupt their sentence for critical reasons
(say, to take exams). In certain circles, a stint
in the Karzer was *de rigueur* to prove one's
manhood. Judging by the inventive graffiti and inscriptions, some found their stay
highly entertaining.

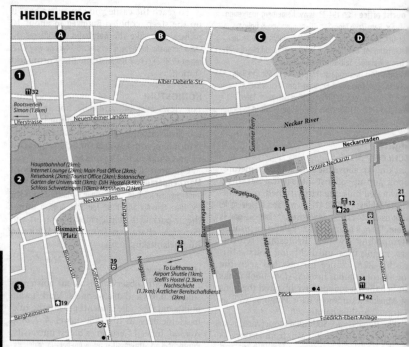

HEIDELBERG

A ticket to the Studentenkarzer also gets you into the richly wood-panelled **Alte Aula** (Old Assembly Hall; Grabengasse 1; ✆ 10am-6pm Tue-Sun Apr-Sep, 10am-4pm Tue-Sat Oct-Mar) and a ho-hum exhibition in German on the history of the university.

A block south, the **Universitätsbibliothek** (University Library; Plöck 107-109; admission free), built from 1901 to 1905, displays rare books and prints from its superb collections in the upstairs corner **Ausstellungsraum** (exhibition room; ✆ 10am-6pm).

Orchids, ferns and Madagascan succulents thrive in the verdant **Botanischer Garten der Universität** (University Botanical Garden; ✆ 545 783; Im Neuenheimer Feld 340; admission free; ✆ outdoor areas open all day, hothouses 9am-4pm Mon-Thu, 9am-2.30pm Fri, 9am-noon & 1-4pm Sun), part of the university's largest campus area. Take tram 4 or 5 to reach the garden, around 1km north of the Hauptbahnhof.

JESUITENKIRCHE

Rising above an attractive square just east of Universitätsplatz, the baroque, red sandstone **Jesuit church** was once the focal point of Heidelberg's Jewish quarter. The **Schatzkammer** (treasury; admission €3; ✆ 10am-5pm Tue-Sat, 1-5pm Sun Jun-Oct, Sat & Sun Nov-May) displays precious religious artefacts.

MARKTPLATZ

Second only to the Schloss on the must-see list is the ochre-red **Heiliggeistkirche** (built 1398–1441) on the Marktplatz, an imposing Gothic church and a Protestant place of worship. See if you can spot the late-medieval markings on the facade, used to ensure that pretzels were of the requisite shape and size. For bird's-eye snapshots of Heidelberg, climb to the top of the **church spire** (adult/student €1/0.50; ✆ 11am-5pm Mon-Sat, 1-5pm Sun mid-Mar–Oct, 11am-3pm Fri & Sat, 12.30-3pm Sun Nov–mid-Mar).

The trickling **Hercules fountain** in the centre of the Marktplatz is where petty criminals were chained and left to face the mob in the Middle Ages. Just south, the former royal **pharmacy** has been reincarnated as a, perhaps not quite as healthy, McDonald's.

ALTE BRÜCKE

On the Altstadt side of the bridge, listen for the giggles and clacking cameras to pinpoint a statue of a **brass monkey** holding a mirror

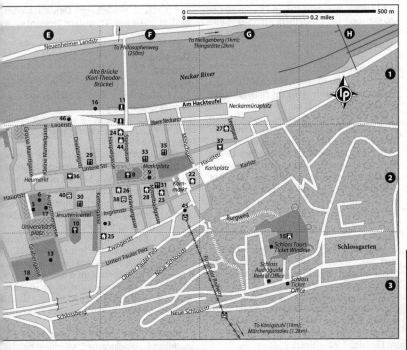

and surrounded by mice: touch the mirror for wealth, the outstretched fingers to ensure you return to Heidelberg and the mice for many children. Speaking of fertility, the **Karl-Theodor-Statue** on the bridge refers to the legend that the prince fathered almost 200 illegitimate children.

KURPFÄLZISCHES MUSEUM

Tucked behind a courtyard, the intriguing **Kurpfälzisches Museum** (Palatinate Museum; ☎ 583 4020; Hauptstrasse 97; adult/concession €3/1.80, on Sun €1.80/1.20; ☉ 10am-6pm Tue-Sun) condenses regional history. Among the highlights are 15th- to 20th-century paintings, Roman and Merovingian artefacts and a copy of the 600,000-year-old Heidelberg Man's jawbone (the original is stored across the river at the palaeontology centre).

PHILOSOPHENWEG

If you need solitude from the crowds, take a contemplative amble along the **Philosophenweg** (Philosophers' Way), on the hillside north of the Neckar River. Snaking through steep vineyards and orchards, the trail commands Kodak views of the Altstadt and the Schloss, which inspired German philosopher Georg Wilhelm Friedrich Hegel. The view is captivating at sundown when Heidelberg is bathed in a reddish glow. The walkway is a well-known lovers' haunt, where many a young local is said to have lost their heart (and virginity!).

Tours

The tourist office's English-language **walking tours** (adult/concession €7/5; ☒ 10.30am Fri & Sat Apr-Oct) of the Altstadt depart in front of the Rathaus on Marktplatz.

A leisurely way to see the sights is to hire a pedalo at **Bootsverleih Simon** (☎ 411 925; 3-/4-person pedalos per 30min €8/10; ☒ 11am-sundown Apr-Sep), on the north shore of the Neckar by Theodor-Heuss-Brücke.

The following companies cruise the Neckar.

Rhein-Neckar Fahrgastschifffahrt (☎ 201 81; www.rnf-schifffahrt.de, in German; adult/4-12yr to Neckarsteinach return €12/6.50; ☒ mid-Apr–late Nov) Boats dock on the south bank of the Neckar midway between the two bridges. It's a worthwhile day trip upriver to Neckarsteinach and its four castles, built by four brothers between 1100 and 1250 as a result of a family feud. Also offers other excursions to towns on the Neckar and Rhine.

Solarschiff (☎ 409 284; www.hdsolarschiff.com; adult/3-14yr/concession €6.50/3/4; ☒ Tue-Sun Mar-Oct) A solar-powered, glass-topped boat whose 50-minute excursions begin next to the Alte Brücke.

Festivals & Events

Heidelberg resounds to bangers, rockets and oohs and ahs at the thrice-yearly **fireworks festivals** (on a Saturday in June, July and September). On the last Saturday in September, **Heidelberger Herbst** is a huge party with music, street entertainment and general drunken merrymaking.

Handmade crafts, donkeys begging a stroke at the live nativity scene on Kornmarkt, and an open-air ice rink on Karlsplatz are part and parcel of Heidelberg's **Christmas market**, held across town from late November to late December.

Sleeping
BUDGET

Bargains are thin on the ground in Heidelberg and finding a bed during high season can be tricky, so it's worth booking ahead. Most hotels charge an extra €8 to €12 for breakfast, but cafes are plentiful if you want to cut costs.

DJH hostel (☎ 651 19; www.jugendherberge-heidelberg.de; Tiergartenstrasse 5; dm 1st/subsequent night €22.90/19.60) Though the schoolkids here are often as night active as the critters in the neighbouring zoo, this is a decent cheapie with impeccable dorms and the occasional passing elephant. Take bus 33 from the Hauptbahnhof.

Steffi's Hostel (☎ 0176-2016 2200; www.hostel heidelberg.de; Alte Eppelheimer Strasse 50; dm €20-24, s/d €29/52; 💻) Backpackers sing the praises of this budget newbie, housed in a one-time brick factory near the Hauptbahnhof. Steffi greets guests warmly with great perks from a shared kitchen and lounge to free internet, bike rental and tea.

Pension Jeske (☎ 237 33; www.pension-jeske -heidelberg.de; Mittelbadgasse 2; s/d without bathroom €25/55, d with bathroom €65) Large, colourful and decorated with flair, the rooms in this 250-year-old house are the antithesis of cookie-cutter blandness.

Hotel Am Kornmarkt (☎ 905 830; www.hotelam kornmarkt.de; Kornmarkt 7; s €65, d €85-110, s/d without bathroom €40/70) The wine-red baroque facade of this hotel is a beacon to euro-conscious travellers. The wood-floored rooms are strictly no frills but they're neat and clean. The priciest have Kornmarkt views, while cheaper ones share bathrooms.

MIDRANGE

Dubliner (☎ 873 0751; www.dublinerheidelberg.com; Hauptstrasse 93; s/d/ste €69/85/100; 💻) Guinness and Irish ditties induce sound slumber at this central fave. Soft lighting, earthy colours and wood floors give the spick-and-span rooms a contemporary touch. Breakfast costs an extra €6.50. There's free wi-fi at the bar.

Hotel Goldener Hecht (☎ 166 025; www.hotel -goldener-hecht.de; Steingasse 2; s €62-77, d €80-100) The area is firmly touristy territory, but it's hard to beat this centuries-old hotel for Neckar views. Goethe was once turned away for lack of space and the well-kept rooms are still sought-after today, so book ahead.

Hotel zum Pfalzgrafen (☎ 204 89; www.hotel-zum-pfalzgrafen.de; Kettengasse 21; s €69-77, d €87-103; **P**) Chalk-white walls and polished pine floors keep the rooms bright and breezy at this family-run place.

Denner Hotel (☎ 604 510; www.denner-hotel.de; Bergheimer Strasse 8; s €90-110, d €110-130, €20 less Fri & Sat; **□**) The chipper team make guests right at home at this boutique hotel. The 19 rooms have creatively painted walls and hardwood floors; some feature neoclassical balconies overlooking Bismarckplatz.

Hotel Goldener Falke (☎ 143 30; www.goldener-falke-heidelberg.de; Am Marktplatz; s €70-85, d €135-155; **□**) Expect a heartfelt welcome at this spruced-up hotel on Marktplatz. Sleek rooms come with flat-screen TVs, gleaming bathrooms and features like slanted wood beams. Light sleepers should forego views for a quieter back room.

Hotel zum Ritter St Georg (☎ 1350; www.ritter-heidelberg.de; Hauptstrasse 178; s €72-93, d €118-144; **□**) Set in a late-Renaissance pile near the Marktplatz, the rooms here are comfy if somewhat an anticlimax given the opulent facade and lobby.

Kulturbrauerei Hotel (☎ 502 980; www.heidelberger-kulturbrauerei.de, in German; Leyergasse 6; s €111-140, d €121-160; **P**) Great beer and grub are a boon at this microbrewery hotel. The stylish rooms are decked out in soft creams with shiny parquet floors and large windows.

TOP END

Hotel zum Sepp'l (☎ 230 85; www.zum-seppl.de, in German; Hauptstrasse 213; s/d €127/165) Steps lead up from this age-old student pub to rooms that ooze historic charm with antique dark-wood furnishings and creaky floors. Plump beds, sunny paint-jobs and marble bathrooms add modern comfort. Rates dip in low season.

ourpick **Hip Hotel** (☎ 208 79; www.hip-hotel.de; Hauptstrasse 115; s €135-180, d €150-210; **□**) Snooze in a Fijian beach shack complete with sandy bay, a woodsy Canadian hunter's cottage, or a topsy-turvy Down Under room where everything (paintings, doors, bed) is upside down. In an age where cities spawn a theme hotel a minute, this place is truly hip. The globetrotting Kischka family's eye for detail shines through, whether you plump for a Swiss ski hut or four-poster romance in Prague.

Eating & Drinking

The Altstadt, especially Steingasse, is chock-full of restaurants, fast-food joints and beer gardens, serving everything from pan-fresh falafel to well-spiced curries. For a more local vibe, head to the leafy district of Neuenheim or the Hauptbahnhof area. Untere Strasse is great for bar hopping.

Schiller's Café (☎ 0175-402 8456; Heiliggeiststrasse 5; snacks €2-4; ⏰ 10am-8pm; **V**) Whisper quietly about this half-timbered cafe, housed in one of Heidelberg's oldest buildings, where the film *Schiller*, produced by ARD, was filmed in 2005. Hot chocolates like cannabis-cinnamon, homemade cakes, quiches, and wines are mostly organic and/or gluten-free.

Raja Rani (☎ 653 0893; Friedrichstrasse 15; mains €2.50-5) Not bad for a cheap, fast korma or masala. The mango lassis are superb.

Café Burkardt (☎ 166 620; Untere Strasse 27; cake & snacks €2.50-8) Full of doily-draped nooks and dark-wood crannies, this nostalgic cafe tempts with Heidelberg's scrummiest tarts and cheesecakes. Opt for a table in the courtyard, where Weimar Republic president Friedrich Ebert was born.

Falafel (☎ 0151-2414 8544; Merianstrasse 3; snacks €3-6; **V**) The chef is quick with his frying pan and witticisms at this laid-back joint opposite the Jesuitenkirche. Go for the wonderfully fresh falafel and free tea.

Green (☎ 433 2545; Marktplatz; light meals €6-8; ⏰ 10am-1am Mon-Thu, 10am-3am Fri & Sat; **V**) Heidelberg locals hang out over brunch and organic smoothies at this cafe, an attention grabber with its lime-green bar, brushed gold walls and aquarium.

Marktstübchen (☎ 653 0893; Marktplatz, Neuenheim; light meals €6-9) Tots whiz past on tricycles as their parents toast summer with cold beers and perfectly crisp *Flammkuchen* (Alsatian pizzas) on the square at this Alsatian-style bistro in Neuenheim.

Café Gekco (☎ 604 510; Bergheimer Strasse 8; mains €7.40-11.50; ⏰ 7am or 8am-1am, to 3am Fri & Sat) Far from the madding crowd, this groovy cafe has a palmlike canopy of halogen lights. It's great for brunch, lunch (€6 to €7), tapas and cocktails.

KulturBrauerei (☎ 502 980; Leyergasse 6; mains €9.90-19.80) With its chandeliers and time-faded frescoes, this high-ceilinged microbrewery is an atmospheric spot for tucking heartily into *Schäufele* (pork shoulder) with sauerkraut, or quaffing home-brews in the beer garden.

Sultana (☎ 208 79; Hauptstrasse 115; mains €14-28; dinner Wed-Mon) Keyhole arches, *tadelakt*-like walls and bursts of hot colour whisk you to Marrakech at this restaurant in the Hip Hotel (p419). The menu is a Moroccan *diffa* (feast) of *tagine*, couscous and meltingly tender *mechoui* lamb.

Destille (☎ 228 08; Untere Strasse 16; ☺ noon-2am, to 3am Fri & Sat) Just like the tree behind the bar, this mellow pub grows on you, especially after a Tabasco schnapps *Warmer Erpel* (warm duck) or three.

MaxBar (☎ 244 19; Marktplatz 5; ☺ 8am-1am, to 2am Fri & Sat) Ah *oui*, this Marktplatz cafe wouldn't be out of place in Paris with its banquettes, Napoleon bust above the bar, cold pastis and authentically arrogant staff.

Zum Sepp'l (☎ 230 85; Hauptstrasse 213; ☺ noon-midnight) Heidelberg's most historic student pub, Sepp'l is worth a beer alone to gawp at the frat photos smothering the dark wooden walls and the names carved into the tables. It exudes the ambience of yesteryear, though these days students are outnumbered by tourists.

Entertainment

Heidelberg's student population fuels the party at the weekend. The city's effervescent cultural scene includes regular concerts, dance and theatre performances. Tickets and event listings are available at **Heidelberg Ticket** (☎ 582 0000; Theaterstrasse 4; ☺ 11am-7pm Mon-Fri, noon-6.30pm Sat).

Cave54 (☎ 27 840; www.cave54.de, in German; Krämergasse 2; admission from €5) Louis Armstrong and Ella Fitzgerald have played the Cave, Germany's oldest student jazz club which opened in 1954. It hosts jam sessions at 8.30pm every Sunday. The DJ pumps out an eclectic mix of rock, blues and oldies until 3am on other nights of the week.

Deep (☎ 651 7760; Hauptstrasse 1; ☺ 11pm-5pm Fri & Sat) Self-consciously trendy, this lounge-club is on a mission to sex up this city with its virginal white decor, eye-candy crowd and uber-picky doormen. House and techno dominate the decks.

Gloria und Gloriette (☎ 253 19; www.cinevent.de, in German; Hauptstrasse 146) A cinema that screens undubbed films three times a week.

Nachtschicht (☎ 438 550; www.nachtschicht.com, in German; Alte Eppelheimer Strasse 5; admission usually €4.50; ☺ 10pm-5am Thu-Sat) Set in a cavernous old tobacco factory, this is one of Heidelberg's most popular clubs, attracting lots of students.

The soundtrack skips from hip hop to house depending on the night.

Shopping

If the Bavarian wench aprons and I-love-Heidelberg T-shirts sold around Marktplatz aren't to your taste, amble down the mile-long, traffic-free Hauptstrasse for high-street brands, or find one-off galleries and speciality shops in the Altstadt's backstreets.

our pick Heidelberger Zuckerladen (☎ 243 65 Plöck 52; ☺ noon-7pm Mon-Fri, 11am-3pm Sat) Kiddie be warned: the dentures and dentist's chair in the window of this cult sweet shop reveal what will happen to your gnashers if you overindulge on the Zuckerladen's bonbons, liquorice laces and fizzy sherbet. Marion Brecht is the eccentric candy man who adds magic to the pick 'n' mix with dice games.

L'Épicerie (☎ 438 357; Hauptstrasse 35; ☺ 10pm 5am Wed-Sat) In a courtyard off Hauptstrasse L'Épicerie attracts foodies with its luscious pralines, spices, oils and preserves.

Sobral (☎ 654 7750; Steingasse 12) Brazilian designer Carlos Alberto Sobral has brought primary colours and pop-art creativity to catwalks across the globe. Find his jelly-bean bright jewellery and home accessories here.

Getting There & Away

Heidelberg is 21km southeast of Mannheim and 120km northwest of Stuttgart.

Lufthansa's Airport Shuttle (☎ 0621-651 620; www .lufthansa-airportbus.de) links the Crowne Plaza Hotel (Kurfürstenanlage 1-3), three blocks southwest of Bismarckplatz, with Frankfurt airport (€20, 1¼ hours, almost hourly).

The north–south A5 links Heidelberg with both Frankfurt and Karlsruhe.

There are at least hourly train services to/ from Baden-Baden (€15.20 to €26, one hour to 1½ hours), Frankfurt (€15.20 to €25.50 one hour to 1½ hours) and Stuttgart (€19.60 to €35, 40 minutes to 1½ hours).

Getting Around

Bikes can be hired from **Eldorado** (☎ 654 4460 www.eldorado-hd.de, in German; Neckarstaden 52; per day €15 ☺ 10am-noon & 2-6pm Tue-Fri, 10am-6pm Sat, 2-6pm Sun) three short blocks west of the Alte Brücke.

The city's underground car parks charge around €1.50 per hour and €16 per day.

Tram 5 and buses 33, 34, 21 and 5 link the Hauptbahnhof with Bismarckplatz, the main hub for **public transport** (www.vrn.de). Single tickets cost €2.10; a 24-hour pass (also valid on Sunday if stamped Saturday) for one/five people costs €5.20/9. Tickets are sold by drivers (except on tram line 5) and at ticket machines.

Taxis (☎ 302 030) line up outside the Hauptbahnhof. It costs about €12 from the Hauptbahnhof to the Alte Brücke.

AROUND HEIDELBERG

The grand summer residence of Prince-Elector Karl Theodor (1724–99), **Schloss Schwetzingen** (☎ 06221-538 431; www.schloesser-und-gaerten.de; adult/concession Apr-Oct €8/4, Nov-Mar €6/3, garden only Apr-Oct €4/2, Nov-Mar €2.50/1.30; ☯ tours 10am-4pm Tue-Fri, 11am-5pm Sat & Sun Apr-Oct, 2pm Fri, 11am, 2pm & 3pm Sat & Sun Nov-Mar, gardens 9am-7.30pm Apr-Oct, to 4.30pm Nov-Mar) is a throwback to the glamorous era of German baroque.

Inspired by Versailles, the whimsical gardens hide follies such as the columned **Temple Apollos** and the **Chinesische Brücke**, an arched Chinese bridge. Inside the **Jagdschloss** (Hunting Palace) is the **Rokokotheater** (1752), with a tunnel illusion that enhances its dimensions.

Schloss Schwetzingen is just off the A6, 10km west of Heidelberg and 8km south of Mannheim. It's linked to Heidelberg's Hauptbahnhof by bus 717 (€3.50, 30 minutes, twice an hour) and to Mannheim's Hauptbahnhof by bus 710 (€3.50, 35 minutes, twice an hour).

MANNHEIM

☎ 0621 / pop 309,800

OK, so the smokestacks and nondescript concrete high-rises aren't scenic Germany at its best, but let's just say you can't take Mannheim at face value. Underpinning the working-class gloom and industrial doom is a dynamic city with big-name shopping, an alphanumeric grid layout that will tickle chess fans for hours, and an energetic cultural scene.

Synagogues, mosques and churches hint at Mannheim's ethnic diversity. Factor in a walk through Jungbusch Turkish quarter, filled with animated street life, cafes and shwarma joints, and you will realise – despite what streets called 'Q3, 16' suggest – that Mannheim is very much a name, not a number.

Orientation & Information

Surrounded by a ring road, Mannheim's centre is sandwiched between the Rhine (southwest) and the Neckar (northeast). It is divided into four quadrants by two largely pedestrianised shopping streets, north–south Breite Strasse and east–west Planken, with Paradeplatz at their intersection. The Hauptbahnhof is at the southern edge of the centre.

Main post office (Q2) Next to Paradeplatz.

Tourist office (☎ 293 8700; www.tourist-mannheim.de; Willy-Brandt-Platz 3; ☯ 9am-7pm Mon-Fri, 10am-1pm Sat) Just outside the Hauptbahnhof. Sells tickets for cultural events.

Sights & Activities

Mannheim's trophy sight is the lemon-and-red sandstone **Schloss** (☎ 655 718; www.schloss-mannheim .de; Bismarckstrasse; adult/concession/family incl audioguide €5/2.50/12.50; ☯ 10am-5pm Tue-Sun), Germany's largest baroque palace. Soon after completion in 1760, Elector Karl Theodor moved his court to Munich. The recently restored state rooms are a baroque-gone-mad feast of stucco, marble, porcelain and chandeliers. Mythological gods dance across the walls of the frilly rococo **Kabinettsbibliothek** (library), while gilt-framed ancestors keep a beady eye on the **Rittersaal** (Hall of Knights).

While you're in a baroque mood, make for the lavishly frescoed **Jesuitenkirche** (www.jesuiten kirchemannheim.de, in German; A4, 2; ☯ 9am-7pm).

Rising gracefully above **Friedrichsplatz**, five blocks northeast of the Hauptbahnhof, is the 60m-high, late-19th-century **Wasserturm** (Water Tower), framed by manicured lawns with two art-nouveau fountains. A handsome ensemble of red sandstone edifices, many with arcades, lines the perimeter.

On Friedrichsplatz' southern side is the acclaimed **Kunsthalle** (☎ 293 6430; www.kunsthalle -mannheim.de, in German; Friedrichsplatz 4; adult/concession/family €7/5/10; ☯ 11am-6pm Tue-Sun), a vast repository of modern and contemporary art by masters such as Cézanne, Degas Manet, Kandinsky and Rodin. The permanent collection is sometimes stored away to make space for blockbuster exhibitions.

Stepping northeast of Friedrichsplatz, the neobaroque **Christuskirche** (Werderplatz), topped by a green dome, has a distinctive outline and is exactly 5m higher than the Wasserturm.

When the sun shines, locals flop on the banks of the Neckar in the **Luisenpark** (adult/concession €5/3.50; ☯ 9am-dusk), a green spine taking in hothouses, gardens, a butterfly hall, an aquarium and a Chinese teahouse. A revolving restaurant is skewered to the 212m-high spike of the **Fernmeldeturm** (telecommunications tower; ☎ 419 290; Hans Reschke Ufer; adult/concession €4/3; ☯ 10am-11pm). Take tram 5 to get there.

BADEN-WÜRTTEMBERG

Sleeping

Mannheim has stacks of corporate hotels but characterful pickings remain slim.

DJH hostel (☎ 822 718; www.jugendherberge -mannheim.de; Rheinpromenade 21; dm 1st/subsequent night €17.90/14.80; ☒ reception 2.30-10pm; **P**) In Schlosspark's green heart, this attractive hostel is a 10-minute walk south of the Hauptbahnhof.

Arabella Pension Garni (☎ 230 50; www.pension -arabella-mannheim.de, in German; M2, 12; s €28-37.50, d €46-59) Super-centrally located two blocks north of the Schloss, Arabella has 18 bright, spacious rooms with shared bathrooms. Prices don't include breakfast.

Maritim Parkhotel (☎ 158 80; www.maritim.de; Friedrichsplatz 2; s €100-€251, d €115-283; **P** ☐ ☒) Venetian crystal, Carrara marble and liveried bellboys – no expense has been spared in the palatial trappings of this art-nouveau pile. Elegant rooms, a swimming pool and live lobby music in the evenings are luxuries that come with the price tag. Prices don't include breakfast.

Eating & Drinking

The Marktplatz is flanked by shwarma joints and cafes with alfresco seating.

Taksim (☎ 279 39; H3, 21; sweets & snacks €1-2; ☒ 8am-9am) There's often a snaking queue for the goodies at this Turkish patisserie. Wait your turn for spinach-cheese *gözleme* cooked fresh in front of you, savoury pides and sticky baklava.

ourpick Café Prag (☎ 178 7724; E4, 17; cake €3.50; ☒ 10am-6pm Mon, 10am-8pm Tue-Sat, 1-6pm Sun) In former Mannheim's a tailor's shop and cigar store, Jugendstil Café Prag is now an arty cafe with cranberry-red walls and a boho feel. The jazz is as smooth as the espresso and as sweet as the legendary rhubarb cake and raspberry tart. A Mannheim must.

Gasthaus Zentrale (☎ 202 43; N4, 15; daily specials €4.50-7, mains €6.30-16.40; ☒ 9.30am-1am) Once a student dive, this rustic gastro pub rustles up decent pizza and steaks, and has a warm-weather beer garden. It's three blocks east of Paradeplatz.

Entertainment

Nationaltheater Mannheim (National Theatre; ☎ 168 00; www.nationaltheater-mannheim.de, in German; Mozartstrasse 9) The granddaddy of Mannheim's performing arts scene, this theatre has been going strong for 300 years and staged Schiller's first major play, *Die Räuber* (The Robbers).

Getting There & Around

Mannheim is a major rail hub on the Hamburg–Basel line. Destinations include Frankfurt (€15.20 to €25.50, 37 to 70 minutes several times hourly) and Freiburg (€38 to €44 1½ hours to 3½ hours, twice hourly). Frequent S-Bahn and RE trains link the Hauptbahnhof with Heidelberg (€6.50, 10 to 17 minutes).

Mannheim is near the junction of the east-west A6, the A67 north to Frankfurt, and the A656 east to Heidelberg. There's free parking about 1km east of the Wasserturm around the Fernmeldeturm (such as along Hans-Reschke-Ufer and Ludwig-Ratzel-Strasse).

KARLSRUHE

☎ 0721 / pop 288,900

When planning this radial city in 1715, the Margraves of Baden placed a mighty baroque palace smack in the middle – an urban layout so impressive it became the blueprint for Washington DC.

Laid-back and cultured, Karlsruhe grows on you the longer you linger, with its rambling parks, museums crammed with futuristic gizmos and French impressionist paintings. The suburbs dotted with art-nouveau town houses are a reminder that France is just 15km away. Some 20,000 students keep the beer cheap and vibe upbeat in the pubs, the dance floors crowded in bass-loaded clubs, and the wheels of innovation in culture and technology turning.

Orientation

From the Schloss, 32 streets radiate like the spokes of a wheel. Karlsruhe's focal point is the Marktplatz, at the intersection of the main east–west shopping street, tram-clogged Kaiserstrasse, and the north–south Karl-Friedrich-Strasse, which links the Schloss with the Hauptbahnhof, 2.5km south. The university campus begins 500m east of the Marktplatz.

Information

ATMs There are several along Kaiserstrasse near the Marktplatz.

Hauptbahnhof tourist office (☎ 3720 5383; www.karlsruhe-tourism.de; Bahnhofplatz 6; ☒ 8.30am-6pm Mon-Fri, 9am-1pm Sat). Across the street from the Hauptbahnhof. The iGuide (€8) is a self-guided audiovisual walking tour of the centre lasting four hours. Also sells the Karlsruher WelcomeCard.

Karlsruher WelcomeCard (€9.50) Good for two days (three days including a weekend), entitling you to public transport use and free or reduced-price entry to museums.

Marktplatz tourist office (☎ 3720 5376; Karl-Friedrich-Strasse 9; ☯ 9.30am-7pm Mon-Fri, 10am-3pm Sat) Offers the same services as the Hauptbahnhof tourist office. Sells events tickets and has a public transport information desk.

Post office (Poststrasse) Just east of the Hauptbahnhof.

Webdome (☎ 161 590; Akademiestrasse 43; per hr €2; ☯ 10am-midnight) Good for two days (three days including a weekend), high-speed internet access.

Sights & Activities

SCHLOSS & MARKTPLATZ

All roads lead to the baroque-meets-neoclassical **Schloss**, which creeps into almost every snapshot. Karl Wilhelm Margrave of Baden-Durlach named his epicentral palace Karlsruhe (Karl's retreat) when founding the city in 1715. Destroyed in the war, the grand palace was sensitively rebuilt. In warm weather, locals play *pétanque* on the fountain-strewn **Schlossplatz** parterre.

Edging north, the **Schlossgarten** is a popular student hang-out and a relaxed spot for walks and picnics. Lush with exotic foliage, the **Botanischer Garten** (☎ 926 3008; gardens free, greenhouses adult/concession €2.20/1.10; ☯ 10am-4.45pm Mon-Fri, 10am-5.45pm Sat & Sun) is speckled with greenhouses – one with a giant Victoria waterlily.

The treasure-trove **Badisches Landesmuseum** (Baden State Museum; ☎ 926 6520; www.landesmuseum.de, in German; adult/concession €4/3, after 2pm Fri free; ☯ 10am-5pm Tue-Thu, 10am-6pm Fri-Sun), inside the Schloss, shelters the jewel-encrusted crown of Baden's grand-ducal ruling family, and spoils of war from victorious battles against the Turks in the 17th century. Scale the **tower** for a better look at Karlsruhe's circular layout and for views reaching to the Black Forest.

A line of 1645 blue majolica tiles, called the **Blaue Linie**, connects the Schloss to the **Museum in der Majolika** (☎ 926 6583; Ahaweg 6; adult/concession €2/1; ☯ 10am-1pm & 2-5pm Tue-Sun), exhibiting glazed ceramics made in Karlsruhe since 1901.

At the northern tip of Marktplatz, **Museum beim Markt** (☎ 926 6578; Karl-Friedrich-Strasse 6; adult/concession €2/1; ☯ 11am-5pm Tue-Thu, 10am-6pm Fri-Sun, after 2pm Fri free) presents an intriguing stash of post-1900 applied arts, from art nouveau to Bauhaus.

The grand neoclassical Marktplatz is dominated by the Ionic portico of the 19th-century **Evangelische Stadtkirche** and the dusky-pink **Rathaus**. The iconic red-stone **pyramid** is an in-congruous tribute to Karl Wilhelm Margrave of Baden-Durlach and marks his tomb.

STAATLICHE KUNSTHALLE

The outstanding **State Art Gallery** (☎ 926 3359; www.kunsthalle-karlsruhe.de, in German; Hans-Thoma-Strasse 2-6; adult/student €6/4; ☯ 10am-5pm Tue-Fri, 10am-6pm Sat & Sun), southwest of the Schloss, harbours a first-class collection; from the canvases of late-Gothic German masters like Matthias Grünewald and Lucas Cranach the Elder to the impressionistic flights of fancy of Degas, Monet and Renoir. Step across to the Orangerie to view Kandinsky's colour-charged works and Max Ernst's surrealist fantasies.

ZENTRUM FÜR KUNST UND MEDIENTECHNOLOGIE

Set in a historic munitions factory, the **ZKM** (Media & Art Centre; ☎ 810 00; www.zkm.de; Lorenzstrasse 19; ☯ 10am-6pm Wed-Fri, 11am-6pm Sat & Sun) is a mammoth exhibition and research complex fusing art and emerging electronic media technologies.

The interactive **Medienmuseum** (Media Museum; adult/7-17yr/concession €5/2/3, after 2pm Fri free) has media art displays including a computer-generated 'legible city' and real-time bubble simulations. The **Museum für Neue Kunst** (Museum for Contemporary Art; adult/7-17yr/concession €5/2/3, incl the Medienmuseum €8/3/5, after 2pm Fri free) hosts first-rate temporary exhibitions of post-1960 art.

Next to the ZKM, the **Städtische Galerie** (☎ 133 4401; www.staedtische-galerie.de, in German; Lorenzstrasse 27; adult/concession €2.60/1.80; ☯ 10am-6pm Wed-Fri, 11am-6pm Sat & Sun) zooms in on local and postwar German art.

Served by tram 2, the ZKM is 2km southwest of the Schloss and a similar distance northwest of the Hauptbahnhof.

Sleeping

Mainly geared towards corporate functions, Karlsruhe's hotels don't rank too highly on the charm-ometer. Ask the tourist office for a list of private guesthouses.

DJH hostel (☎ 282 48; www.jugendherberge-karlsruhe .de; Moltkestrasse 24; dm 1st/subsequent night €20.50/17.60) If you don't mind shortish beds and the odd giggling teenager in your dorm, try this 167-bed hostel, a few blocks west of the Schloss.

Hotel Avisa (☎ 349 77; www.hotel-avisa.de; Am Stadtgarten 5; s/d from €83/112; **P**) Spruce rooms with free wi-fi are the deal at this family-run hotel, two blocks northeast of the Hauptbahnhof.

BADEN-WÜRTTEMBERG

Acora Hotel (☎ 850 90; www.acora.de; Sophienstrasse 69-71; s/d from €96/119; P) Chirpy staff make you feel right at home at this apartment-hotel, featuring bright, modern rooms equipped with kitchenettes.

Eating & Drinking

Café Salomon (☎ 921 2080; Hans-Thoma-Strasse 3; bagels €1–€4.50 Ⓨ 8.30am-6pm Mon-Fri, 9.30am-6pm Sat & Sun) The go-to place for Israeli breakfasts and authentic bagels such as Greek-style with feta and olives.

MoccaSin (☎ 921 2127; Ritterstrasse 6; drinks & snacks €1.70-4; Ⓨ 7.30am-8pm Mon-Fri, 9.30am-8pm Sat, 11am-7pm Sun) Unlike in the 16th century when coffee drinkers were sinners (hence the name), you can sip mochas, smoothies or organic espressos in heathenry peace at this sleek cafe.

our pick **Die Kippe** (☎ 697 829; Gottesauer Strasse 23; daily special €3.90; Ⓨ 8am-1am, to 3am Fri & Sat) Every student has a tale about Kippe, Karlsruhe's best-loved 'dog end', named after the free tobacco behind the bar. Wallet-friendly daily specials might include juicy schnitzels or egg-fried rice. A young crowd gathers in the beer garden in summer. There's live rock at 9pm on Saturdays. Take tram 1 or 2 to Durlacher Tor.

Bray Head (☎ 350 5115; Kapellenstrasse 40; mains €5.90-6.90; Ⓨ 4pm-1am, to 2am Tue-Thu, to 3am Fri & Sat; 🛜) Ferghal's home-brewed stout goes down a treat with grub such as Irish stew and fish 'n' chips at this convivial pub near Kippe. On Saturday there's live rock at 8.30pm.

Oberländer Weinstuben (☎ 250 66; Akademiestrasse 7; mains €26-36; Ⓨ Tue-Sat) Foodies praise this wood-panelled tavern's bulging wine cellar and French-infused menu. Signature dishes like veal carpaccio with snap peas and smoked pigeon breast with Périgord truffles are beautifully cooked and artistically presented.

Entertainment

From rock gigs to Gothic clubs, Karlsruhe has a vibrant music scene. German speakers should check out the website www.ka -nightlife.de.

Badisches Staatstheater (☎ 933 333; www.staats theater.karlsruhe.de, in German; Baumeisterstrasse 11) Karlsruhe's theatre hosts top-drawer opera, dance, music, theatre and ballet performances.

Club Carambolage (☎ 373 227; Kaiserstrasse 21; Ⓨ 9pm-3am or later) Filled with cult kitsch, this popular club opposite the university has billiards, kicker and a diverse playlist skipping from indie to '80s cheese.

Unverschämt (☎ 848 922; Kaiserallee 3; Ⓨ 10pm-5am Wed-Sat) In the dark, dark bowels of Karlsruhe, UV thuds to rock and metal. With leather-clad Goths, whisky-wasted bikers, and diehard head-bangers, the crowd is every bit as shameless as the name suggests.

Getting There & Away

Destinations well-served by rail include Baden-Baden (€9.50 to €14.50, 15 to 30 minutes) and Freiburg (€23 to €33, one to two hours).

Karlsruhe is on the A5 (Frankfurt–Basel) and is the starting point of the A8 to Munich. There are Park & Ride options outside of the city centre; look for 'P+R' signs.

Getting Around

The Hauptbahnhof is linked to the Marktplatz by tram and light-rail lines 2, 3, S1, S11, S4 and S41. Single tickets cost €2.10 for an adult and €1.10 per child between six and 14 years of age; a 24-Stunden-Karte costs €4.70 (€7.10 for up to five people).

There are Park & Ride options outside of the city centre; look for 'P+R' signs.

A relaxed and ecofriendly way to explore Karlsruhe is by bike. Deutsche Bahn has Call-a-Bike stands across the city; for details and rates see p412.

KLOSTER MAULBRONN

Billed as the best-preserved medieval monastery north of the Alps, this one-time **Cistercian monastery** (☎ 07043-926 610; www .schloesser-und-gaerten.de; adult/concession/family €6/3/15; Ⓨ 9am-5.30pm Mar-Oct, 9.30am-5pm Tue-Sun Nov-Feb) was founded by Alsatian monks in 1147, born again as a Protestant school in 1556 and designated a Unesco World Heritage Site in 1993. Its famous graduates include the astronomer Johannes Kepler. Aside from the Romanesque-Gothic portico in the **monastery church** and the weblike vaulting of the **cloister**, it's the insights into monastic life that make this place so culturally stimulating.

Maulbronn is 30km east of Karlsruhe and 33km northwest of Stuttgart, near the Pforzheim Ost exit on the A8. From Karlsruhe, take the S4 to Bretten Bahnhof and from there bus 700 (€4, one hour); from Stuttgart, take the train to Mühlacker and then bus 700.

SCHWÄBISCH HALL

☎ 0791 / pop 36,450

If you could visit just one place in Baden-Württemberg, where might it be? Heidelberg? Stuttgart? The Black Forest? Few would pick Schwäbisch Hall, out on its rural lonesome near the Bavarian border. Yet this medieval time-capsule of higgledy-piggledy lanes, soaring half-timbered houses built high on the riches of salt, and covered bridges that criss-cross the Kocher River is pure Brothers Grimm stuff.

Buzzy cafes and first-rate museums add to the appeal of this town, known for its rare black-spotted pigs and the jangling piggy banks of its nationwide building society.

Orientation & Information

The Kocher River separates the Altstadt, on the right bank, from the Neustadt, on the left bank. The Altstadt's main street, Neue Strasse, links Am Markt square with the river.

Tourist office (☎ 751 246; www.schwaebischhall.de; Am Markt 9; ⏰ 9am-6pm Mon-Fri, 10am-3pm Sat & Sun May-Sep, 9am-5pm Mon-Fri Oct-Apr) On the Altstadt's main square.

Sights & Activities

ALTSTADT

A leisurely saunter will take you along narrow stone alleys, among half-timbered hillside houses and up slopes overlooking the **Kocher River** and its weir. The islands and riverbank parks are perfect for picnics.

Am Markt springs to life with a farmers' market every Wednesday and Saturday morning. On the square, the eye is drawn to the baroque-style **Rathaus**, festooned with coats of arms and cherubs, and the terracotta-hued **Widmanhaus** at No 4, a remnant of the 13th-century Franciscan monastery. The centrepiece is the late-Gothic, rib-vaulted **Kirche St Michael**. The majestic staircase out the front has been used to stage **Freilichtspiele** (open-air theatre performances; www.freilichtspiele-hall.de, in German) every summer since 1925.

Note the **Gotischer Fischbrunnen** (1509), next to the tourist office, a large iron tub once used for storing fish before sale.

Towering above Pfarrgasse, south of Am Markt, is the steep-roofed, 16th-century **Neubau**, built as an arsenal and granary and now used as a theatre. Ascend the stone staircase for dreamy views over red-roofed houses to the former **city fortifications**, the covered **Roter Steg** bridge and the **Henkerbrücke** (Hangman's Bridge).

Down by the river, the well-curated **Hällisch-Fränkisches Museum** (☎ 751 289; Im Keckenhof; adult/student €2.50/1.50; ⏰ 10am-5pm Tue-Sun) traces Schwäbisch Hall's history with its collection of shooting targets, Roman figurines, and rarities including an exquisite hand-painted wooden **synagogue interior** from 1738 and a 19th-century mouse guillotine.

KUNSTHALLE WÜRTH

The brainchild of industrialist Reinhold Würth, this contemporary **gallery** (☎ 946 720; www.kunst.wuerth.com; Lange Strasse 35; admission free; ⏰ 10am-6pm) is housed in a striking limestone building that preserves part of a century-old brewery. Stellar temporary exhibitions have previously spotlighted the work of artists such as David Hockney, Edvard Munch and Georg Baselitz.

HOHENLOHER FREILANDMUSEUM

For a taste of the rural Swabia of yore, visit the **open-air farming museum** (☎ 971 010; adult/concession €6/4; ⏰ 9am-6pm Tue-Sun May-Sep, 10am-5pm Tue-Sun Mar, Apr, Oct & Nov) in Wackershofen. Alongside traditional farmhouses (some hosting demonstrations) are orchards and farmyard animals including local black-spotted pigs. It's 6km northwest of Schwäbisch Hall and served by bus 7.

Sleeping

Campingplatz Am Steinbacher See (☎ 2984; Mühlsteige 26; per person/tent €4.80/6; ⏰ year-round) Overlooking a lake, this back-to-nature site is full of happy campers enjoying facilities including a playground, communal kitchen and bike tours. Take bus 4 to Steinbach Mitte.

DJH hostel (☎ 410 50; www.jugendherberge-schwaebisch-hall.de; Langenfelder Weg 5; dm 1st/subsequent night €20.60/17.50) A cobbled patio, barbecue area and tidy dorms make this hostel a solid choice. It's a 10-minute stroll east of Am Markt.

Hotel Sölch (☎ 946 6466; www.hotel-soelch.de, in German; Hauffstrasse 14; s/d €49/72; P ⏸) A 20-minute stroll from the centre lies this simple, good-value hotel. Bread fresh from the downstairs bakery is served at breakfast.

Hotel Scholl (☎ 975 50; www.hotel-scholl.de; Klosterstrasse 2-4; s €69-79, d €95-115) A snazzy pick behind Am Markt, this family-run hotel has rustic-meets-modern rooms with parquet floors, flat-screen TVs, granite bathrooms and free wi-fi.

Der Adelshof (☎ 758 90; www.hotel-adelshof.de, in German; Am Markt 12; s €80-100, d €125-150; P 🖳) This centuries-old pad is as posh as it gets in Schwäbisch Hall, with a wellness area, gourmet restaurant and plush quarters from the blue-and-white Wedgwood room to the four-poster Turmzimmer.

Eating & Drinking

Gelatarias, bistros and bars vie for attention on Neue Strasse and riverfront Haalstrasse.

Café Am Markt (☎ 66 12; Am Markt 9; cakes €2-3; ☯ 8am-6pm) When the weather warms, nab a patio table facing the church to indulge your sweet tooth with delectable pralines, ice cream and cakes like vanilla-rich *Schmandkuchen* (rich sour-cream cake).

s'Hällische (☎ 946 6521; Neue Strasse 2; lunch plates €4.80; ☯ 8am-6.30pm Mon-Fri, 8am-1.30pm Sat) Great-value lunches like roast chicken and barbecued sausages lure midday crowds to this butcher-deli, famed for its succulent, organic meat.

Olli's (☎ 946 3238; Sparkassenplatz 9 & Untere Herrngasse 2; light meals €3.50-7.30; ☯ cafe 9am-6pm, bar 5pm-1am) Make for this hip cafe and bar duo for appetising salads and snacks by day, or mojitos on the pavement terrace by night.

Sudhaus (☎ 946 7270; Lange Strasse 35; mains €11-24; ☯ 9am-midnight) Part of Kunsthalle Würth, this redbrick microbrewery churns out home brews and Swabian classics like lip-smacking roast suckling pig in beer sauce. Retreat to the beer garden on balmy days or the roof terrace to see the Altstadt twinkle.

Ratskeller (☎ 946 7270; Lange Strasse 35; mains €18-32) Dine under wood beams on seasonal French-style dishes at Der Adelshof's elegant restaurant.

Getting There & Around

The town has two train stations: trains from Stuttgart (€13.30, 1¼ hours, hourly) arrive at Hessental, on the right bank about 7km south of the centre and linked to the Altstadt by bus 1; trains from Heilbronn go to the left-bank Bahnhof Schwäbisch Hall, a short walk along Bahnhofstrasse from the centre. Trains and buses shuttle regularly between the two.

Outfits hiring bikes include **2-Rad Zügel** (☎ 971 400; Johanniterstrasse 55; per day €10; ☯ 9am-12.30pm & 2-7pm Mon-Fri, 9am-2pm Sat), north of the centre on the B19.

SWABIAN ALPS & AROUND

Castle-topped mountains cloaked in fog, prehistoric dripstone caves, Jurassic fossils and two legendary rivers – the Neckar and Danube – give the Swabian Alps an air of mystery. Stretching south of Stuttgart and east of the Black Forest, this region of limestone plateaus, luxuriantly green forests and gently rounded hills is the soul of *Schwabeländle* (dear old Swabia).

Famed as being as tight as their valleys, the locals treasure their rural roots and age-old traditions. Pepping up this vision of pastoral bliss are feisty university cities like party-loving Tübingen and Ulm, birthplace of Einstein. For information and maps, visit the website http://en.s-alb.de.

TÜBINGEN

☎ 07071 / pop 83,800

Liberal students and deeply traditional *Burschenschaften* (fraternities) singing ditties for beloved Germania, eco-warriors and punks – all have a soft spot for this bewitchingly pretty Swabian city, where cobbled alleys lined with gabled town houses twist up to a perkily turreted castle. As did some of the country's biggest brains. It was here that Joseph Ratzinger, now Pope Benedict XVI, lectured theology in the late 1960s before fleeing to Bavaria, scandalised by Marxist-inspired student radicalism; and here that Friedrich Hölderlin studied stanzas, Johannes Kepler planetary motions and Goethe the bottom of a beer glass. Today the hybrid-driving mayor, Boris Palmer, is on his own green mission to cut emissions with clean transport and renewable energy policies.

The finest days unfold slowly in Tübingen with leisurely brunches in Altstadt cafes punting on the willow-lined Neckar River and pretending, as the students so diligently do, to work your brain cells in a chestnut-shaded beer garden.

Orientation

The Neckar River divides Tübingen from east to west. Karlstrasse leads south to the Hauptbahnhof (500m) from Eberhardsbrücke. North up the hill is Mühlstrasse and, to the west, the compact, largely pedestrian-sed Altstadt. The main university area lies urther north (about 1km from the river) long Wilhelmstrasse.

Most of Tübingen's sights concentrate in he Altstadt. The Neckar's northern bank eads steeply up to a ridge, where you'll find (from east to west) the Stiftskirche, Am Markt quare and the Schloss.

nformation

ATMs Around the Hauptbahnhof, Eberhardsbrücke and m Markt.

Osiander (☎ 920 10; Wilhelmstrasse 12-14) Purveyor of ooks since 1596.

Post office (cnr Hafengasse & Neue Strasse) In the Altstadt.

Tourist office (☎ 913 60; www.tuebingen-info.de; An der Neckarbrücke 1; ☺ 9am-7pm Mon-Fri, 10am-4pm Sat, plus 11am-4pm Sun May-Sep) South of Eberhardsbrücke. Has a otel board outside and can provide details on hiking options for example to Bebenhausen or Wurmlinger Kapelle).

Jutel (Mühlstrasse 14; per hr €2; ☺ 10am-10pm Mon-at, noon-10pm Sun) Two other internet cafes are located n the same block.

Waschsalon (Mühlstrasse 18; ☺ 8am-10pm Mon-Sat) elf-service laundry.

Sights & Activities

On its fairy-tale perch above Tübingen, the urreted 16th-century **Schloss Hohentübingen** (Burgsteige 11) overlooks the Altstadt's red rooftops. An ornate Renaissance gate leads to the courtyard and the laboratory where Friedrich Miescher discovered DNA in 1869. Inside, the archaeology **museum** (☎ 297 7384; adult/concession €4/3; ☺ 10am-6pm Wed-Sun May-Sep, 10am-5pm Oct-Apr) hides the 35,000-year-old Vogelherd figurines, the world's oldest figurative artworks. These thumb-sized ivory carvings of mammoths and lions were unearthed in the Vogelherdhöhle caves in the Swabian Alps.

Half-timbered town houses frame the Altstadt's main plaza **Am Markt**, a much-loved student hang-out. Rising above the hubbub is the 15th-century **Rathaus**, with a riotous baroque facade and an astronomical clock. Statues of four women representing the seasons grace the **Neptune Fountain** opposite. Keep an eye out for **No 15**, where a single white window frame identifies a secret room where Jews hid in WWII.

Head east along Kirchgasse to the late-Gothic **Stiftskirche** (Am Holzmarkt; admission free; ☺ 9am-5pm), which shelters the tombs of

the Württemberg dukes and some dazzling medieval stained-glass windows.

Facing the church's west facade, the **Cottahaus** is the one-time home of Johann Friedrich Cotta, who first published the works of Schiller and Goethe. A bit of a lad, Goethe conducted detailed research on Tübingen's pubs during his weeklong stay in 1797. The party-loving genius is commemorated by the plaque *'Hier wohnte Goethe'* (Goethe lived here). On the wall of the grungy student digs next door is the perhaps more insightful sign *'Hier kotzte Goethe'* (Goethe puked here).

Neckargasse links Holzmarkt to the Neckar, the **Eberhardsbrücke** and **Neckarmüller** (p428), one of Tübingen's liveliest beer gardens.

Steps lead down from the bridge to **Platanenallee**, a leafy island on the Neckar shaded by plane trees, where there are views up to the pastel-painted mansions spilling down the hillsides to the river.

On the Neckar's banks sits the silver-turreted **Hölderlinturm**, the former abode of 19th-century German lyric poet Friedrich Hölderlin. Across the river just east of the bridge is **Bootsvermietung Märkle** (☎ 315 29; www .bootsvermietung-tuebingen.de, in German; Eberhardsbrücke 1; ☺ 11am-6pm Apr-Oct, to 9pm in summer). An hour of splashy fun in a rowboat, canoe, pedalo or 12-person *Stocherkähne* (punts) costs €7.50, €7.50, €10 and €48 respectively. Or sign up at the tourist office for an hour's **punting** (adult/under 12yr €6/3; ☺ at 1pm Sat & Sun May-Sep) around the Neckarinsel, beginning at the Hölderlinturm.

Green-fingered students tend to the Himalayan cedars, swamp cypresses and rhododendrons in the gardens and hothouses of the serene **Botanischer Garten** (Botanical Garden; ☎ 297 8822; Hartmeyerstrasse 123; admission free; ☺ 8am-4.45pm daily, to 7pm Sat & Sun in summer), 2km northwest of the centre. Take bus 5, 13, 15 or 17.

In the same neighbourhood, the streamlined **Kunsthalle** (☎ 969 10; Philosophenweg 76; www .kunsthalle-tuebingen.de; admission €6; ☺ 10am-5pm Wed-Sun) stages worthwhile exhibitions of mostly contemporary art.

A great hike is the *Kreuzweg* (way of the cross) to the 17th-century **Wurmlinger Kapelle** (☺ 10am-4pm May-Oct), 6km southwest of Tübingen. A footpath loops up through well-tended vineyards to the whitewashed pilgrimage chapel, where there are long views across the Ammertal and Neckartal valleys.

BADEN-WÜRTTEMBERG

BADEN-WÜRTTEMBERG

MESSING ABOUT ON THE RIVER

Hundreds of competitors descend on the Neckar in fancy dress for June's hilarious **Stocherkahnrennen** (Punt Race). Kicking off upstream, the race begins politely, but too much heave-ho soon brings out the one-upmanship, particularly around the narrow Nadelöhr (needle's eye), where jostling, shoving, dunking, and even breaking your rival's oar are permitted. The first team to reach the Neckarbrücke wins the race, the title and as much beer as they can sink. The losers, much to the crowd's amusement, have to guzzle half a litre of cod-liver oil. Get there early (around 1pm) for a prime spot on Platanenallee and prepare to be splashed.

Festivals & Events

Time your visit to catch the wild **Stocherkahnrennen** (above) in early June, or liberate your duckie from the bathtub at the **Entenrennen** (www.tuebinger-entenrennen.de) on the first Saturday in October, when some 6000 rubber ducks bob from Alleenbrücke to Neckarbrücke. Summer's biggest shindig is the **Stadtfest** in July, with bands, a funfair, fireworks and plentiful bratwurst.

Sleeping

Neckar Camping Tübingen (☎ 43145; www.neckarcamping .de; Rappenberghalde 61; per person/tent/car €6/4.80/3; ⏰ Apr-Oct) You can paddle right up to this tree-fringed site by the river, where first-rate facilities include a communal kitchen, restaurant, bike rental and wi-fi. Bus 9 stops nearby.

DJH hostel (☎ 23002; www.jugendherberge-tuebingen.de; Gartenstrasse 22/2; dm 1st/subsequent night €21.90/18.60; 🖳) Plain the dorms may be, but there are no quibbles about this hostel's brilliant location on the north bank of the Neckar. There's a chilled terrace and cafeteria. Hoof it or take bus 22 from the Hauptbahnhof.

Pension Binder (☎ 526 40; Nonnengasse 4; s €53, d €82-98) Service is borderline matronly (mind your Ps and Qs) but quarters are immaculate, quiet and endearingly old fashioned, especially the beamed attic room. Book well ahead.

our pick Hotel am Schloss (☎ 929 40; www.hotelam schloss.de; Burgsteige 18; s €65-75, d €118-135; P 🖳) Some come for the restaurant's legendary *Maultaschen* (mains €9 to €15), some for peerless castle views, and others for the dapper rooms ensconced in a 16th-century building. Rumour has it Kepler

was partial to the wine here; try a drop yoursel before attempting the tongue twister above th bench outside: *dohoggeddiadiaemmerdohogge* (the same people sit in the same spot). And very nice spot it is, too.

Landhotel Hirsch (☎ 609 30; www.landhotel-hirsc -bebenhausen.de; Schönbuchstrasse 28, Bebenhausen; €92-105, d €142-195; P) Worth the 6km ride t cute-as-a-button Bebenhausen, the Hirsc has bright cottage-style rooms with plum beds and marble bathrooms. Take bus 82 from Tübingen Hauptbahnhof.

Hotel Krone Tübingen (☎ 133 10; www.krone-tuebinge .de; Uhlandstrasse 1; s €107-119, d €139-159; P) If it' good enough for the Dalai Lama and the Duk of Württemberg… In family hands since 1885 this old-world charmer at the southern end o Eberhardsbrücke shelters 43 plush rooms.

Eating

Eiscafé San Marco (☎ 239 47; Nonnengasse 14; ice crear €0.80-9.80; ⏰ 10am-10pm) When the sun's out, si on the terrace at Italian-run San Marco fo creamy gelati made with fresh fruit.

X (☎ 249 02; Kornhausstrasse 6; snacks €1.50-3; ⏰ 11am 1am) Sizzling and frying since 1971, this hole in-the-wall bolt-hole churns out good-valu student fodder including Tübingen's crispes fries, bratwurst and burgers.

Kornblume (☎ 527 08; Haaggasse 15; snacks €2.50-8 ⏰ 11am-8pm Mon-Fri; Ⓥ) Vegies and health conscious locals squeeze into this hobbit like cafe for wholesome soups, vitamin-rich juices and organic salads by the scoopful.

Die Kichererbse (☎ 521 71; Metzgergasse 2; snacks €3-5 ⏰ 8.30am-5.30pm Mon-Fri, to 7pm Sat; Ⓥ) All hail th 'chickpea' for its scrummy falafel. Grab one o the few tables to chomp on a classic (€3).

Asien Haus (☎ 552 086; Schmiedtorstrasse 7; main €4-7.50; ⏰ 11.30am-5pm Mon-Fri, 11.30am-3pm Sa Flaming woks, spicy aromas and inviting clatter lure the midday crowds to this no-frills joint. The Thai curries and stir-fries are cheap and authentic.

Neckarmüller (☎ 278 48; Gartenstrasse 4; mains €7.50 15; ⏰ 10am-1am) Overlooking the Neckar, thi cavernous microbrewery is a summertime magnet for its chestnut-shaded beer garden Come for home brews by the metre and beer laced dishes from (tasty) Swabian roast to (interesting) tripe stew.

Alte Weinstube Göhner (☎ 567 078 Schmiedtorstrasse 5; mains €7.80-10.80; ⏰ 10am-10pm,

(Continued on page 437)

WELCOME TO GERMANY

Whether you're meandering along the Romantic Road, cycling through the magnificent rolling dunes of the North Frisian Islands or sipping a cocktail at one of Berlin's sizzling beach bars, Germany is one fascinating playground of traditional half-timbered villages and sultry, stimulating cities, where bratwurst stands flank busy street corners and time is earmarked for afternoon *Kaffee und Kuchen* (coffee and cake). Weave your way through the old and the new, and be prepared for the unexpected at any given turn.

Food & Drink

Waistlines be damned, this is one exceptional place to indulge in gut-filling meat and potatoes. Recent influxes of immigrants mean tastes are eternally evolving, and Germany's own version of the doner kebab is a fixture all across the country. Get a dose of your favourite staples, but be sure to branch out and try the abundant foreign flavours.

❶ Sausages
Go ahead and indulge in a monstrous plate of German wurst (p79). This simple comfort food is always served in a convivial atmosphere with a satisfying dollop of fresh mustard.

❷ Beer
It really is all about the beer (p84) here. Pilsner, dark or wheat, it's all a gulp of sheer bliss topped off with masses of fluffy white froth. Don't worry if you end up with a white moustache – it's all part of the delicious experience.

❸ Schwarzwälder Kirschtorte
Black Forest gateau is simple – moisten chocolate cake with cherry schnapps, layer it with cherries and hefty slabs of whipped cream, and then top it all off with more whipped cream and maraschino cherries. Finally, unbutton those trousers and ponder why diets were invented.

❹ Doner Kebab
Freshly sliced lamb straight off the spit with chopped cabbage, lettuce, onions, tomatoes and cucumber, topped off with a dollop of hot sauce and cooling yoghurt sauce, all rolled into a toasted flat bread – it's the supreme street food.

Cities

With clubbing for every age group, avant-garde art, traditional beer gardens and a zest for life, German cities pulsate and move to their own special beat – see what the fuss is all about.

❶ Cologne

Be it at Carnival time or just on a lazy mid-summer's day, the Dom in Cologne (p568) wows all senses. Take a rest beneath the remarkable Gothic towers and marvel at the amazing detail.

❷ Hamburg

Take culture and flair, add a hedonistic red-light district and waterways everywhere you turn, stir it all up in a stylish bar shaker and ta-da! – out pours the exhilarating media capital of Germany, Hamburg (p674).

❸ Berlin

Edgy art, throbbing clubs and vibrant cafes – it's all happening in Berlin (p99). The city that dismantled the wall 20 years ago keeps reinventing itself with an intoxicating energy that'll keep you up until dawn.

❹ Munich

Sophisticated yet villagelike (OK, a very large village), Munich (p295) takes you from the gargoyle-covered neo-Gothic Neues Rathaus (New Town Hall) to the exquisite Englischer Garten (English Garden) to the most famous beer hall in the world, the Hofbräuhaus.

The Great Outdoors

Germans love being outside, and they've blazed meticulous walking and cycling trails throughout the vast countryside and mountains. Cliffs aching to be scrambled, rivers begging to be kayaked – there's a pursuit for nature seekers of all kinds.

❷ Bavarian Alps

Whiz down the slopes of this prime skiing and snowboarding territory or scale jagged cliffs – either way, finish off the hard day's work with a mug at one of the oompah-music-playing watering holes in Garmisch-Partenkirchen (p355).

❸ Berchtesgaden National Park

Don those hiking boots and ascend the stunning terrain flanked by sparkling lakes and jagged mountain peaks – Berchtesgaden National Park (p361) is where you'll snap countless photos of divine, natural splendour, with a hefty dose of pure, fresh air.

❹ Spreewald

Punting in the canals near Lübbenau (p168) is like floating through a sea of bucolic green – you glide past ancient houses under a canopy of trees and wonder if life can get much more sublime than this.

❶ Sylt

Salt-clogged wind whips you along your beach stroll right around the corner from a Louis Vuitton shop – Sylt (p719) is the island of extremes. Cycle your way through the undulating dunes and warm up afterwards with a piping-hot mug of Frisian tea.

❺ Black Forest

Thick and dense, with green, velvety landscapes flanked by inky swathes of trees, the Black Forest (p443) is a cycling and hiking utopia – and the region's sublime thermal baths are the perfect antidote to those aching muscles.

Festivals & Events

Germany's vibrant festivities range from rambunctious beer-tent action, rollicking street parties and jazz and pop-music celebrations to a film festival rivalling Cannes and gingerbread-bedecked markets sure to put the holiday spirit into any Scrooge's soul.

❶ Oktoberfest

Wooden tables stretched out beyond your line of vision, hundreds of festive beer drinkers clinking glasses – this festival (p314) is the quintessential image of Germany. And yes, that matron of the golden potion really is carrying six 1L mugs of happiness on tap.

❷ Cologne's Carnival

Young, old and everything in between, everyone comes together for Germany's most entertaining party (p575). Don a fuchsia wig, wriggle into a pair of feather-studded trousers and join the merry revellers in the streets. You only live once.

❸ Christmas Markets

Tree ornaments, arts and crafts, a hand-made wallet – you name it. There's a gift for everyone among the cosy wooden stalls of Germany's Christmas markets (p25). And you can peruse them all with a mug of steaming *Glühwein* (mulled wine).

❹ Christopher Street Day

A fixture of every Berlin summer since 1979, this LGBT (lesbian, gay, bisexual and transgender) celebration (p135) welcomes anyone ready to rejoice and boogie their way across town.

(Continued from page 428)

As down-to-earth and comfy as a Swabian farmer's boots, this 175-year-old haunt is Tübingen's oldest wine tavern. Join the high-spirited regulars to discuss the merits of *Maultaschen*, sip a glass of Trollinger and, if you're lucky, hear someone bashing out golden oldies on the piano.

Wurstküche (☎ 927 50; Am Lustnauer Tor 8; mains €9.50-14.50; ☺ 11am-midnight) The rustic, wood-panelled Wurstküche brims with locals quaffing wine and contentedly munching *Schupfnudeln* (potato noodles) and *Spanpferkel* (roast suckling pig).

Sternwarte (☎ 968 995; Waldhäuserstrasse 70; mains €13-21; ☺ 11.30am-midnight Mon-Sat, 10am-10pm Sun) Stargazers trek north of the centre to this observatory restaurant, serving Med-style specialities like fragrant vegetable couscous and scallop risotto. Round off with drinks at the glass-and-chrome bar. The flowery garden has splendid country views.

Drinking

Tübingen's spirited nightlife centres on bar-lined Haaggasse.

JazzKeller (☎ 550 906; www.jazzclub-tuebingen.de, in German; Haaggasse 15/2; ☺ 7pm-2am Sun-Thu, to 3am Fri & Sat) This mellow Tübingen institution hosts DJs and gigs in the cellar. On Wednesday there's live jazz at 9pm.

Schwärzlocher Hof (☎ 433 62; Schwarzloch 1; ☺ 11am-10pm Wed-Sun) Scenically perched above the Ammertal valley, a 20-minute trudge west of town, this creaking farmhouse is famous for its beer garden. Kids love the resident horses, rabbits and peacocks. The home-pressed *Most* (cider) is lethal.

Storchen (☎ 522 10; Ammergasse 3) Mind your head climbing the stairs to this easygoing student hang-out. This lively spit-and-sawdust bar serves enormous mugs of milky coffee and cheap local brews under wood beams.

Tangente-Night (☎ 230 07; Pfleghofstrasse 10; ☺ 4pm-3am, to 4am Fri & Sat) Totally chilled Tangente-Night enjoys a fierce student following. Belt out a classic at Monday's karaoke party under the motto 'drink faster and sing for your life'. The vibe is clubbier at weekends with music skipping from rock to electro.

Weinhaus Beck (☎ 227 72; Am Markt 1; ☺ 9am-11pm) There's rarely an empty table at this convivial wine tavern beside the Rathaus.

THE WAY TO A SWABIAN'S HEART...

The delights of dialect and cuisine are united in Swabia, where even the simplest restaurant order makes linguistic spaghetti of your schoolbook German. Scrimping grannies have thriftily been raiding cupboards for centuries to concoct dishes that please local palates and puzzle the *Raigschmeckdr* (stranger). Even the great pretzel was born in these parts in the 15th century, when Tübingen university founder, Count Eberhard im Bart, asked a baker from nearby Bad Urach to create a pastry through which the sun could shine three times.

As the Swabian saying goes: *Was der Bauer net kennt frisst er net* (What the farmer doesn't know, he doesn't eat), so find out before you dig in:

■ **Bubespitzle** Officially called *Schupfnudeln*, these short, thick potato noodles – similar to gnocchi, but stodgier – are browned in butter and tossed with sauerkraut. Sounds appetising until you discover that *Bubespitzle* means little boys' penises. No prizes for guessing why…

■ **Gaisburger Marsch** A strong beef stew served with potatoes and *Spätzle*.

■ **Maultaschen** Giant ravioli pockets, stuffed with left-over ground pork, spinach, onions and bread mush. The dish is nicknamed *Herrgottsbeschieserle* (God trickster) because it was a cover-up for eating meat during Lent.

■ **Saure Kuddle** So who is for sour tripe? If you haven't got the stomach, try potato-based, meat-free *saure Rädle* (sour wheels) instead.

■ **Spätzle** Long egg-based noodles thicker than spaghetti. These are fried with onions and topped with cheese in the waistline-expanding favourite *Käsespätzle*.

■ **Zwiebelkuche** Autumnal onion tart with bacon, cream and caraway seeds, which pairs well with *neuer Süsser* (new wine) or *Moschd* (cider).

Entertainment

Tübingen's thriving cultural scene covers the entire spectrum, from rock gigs to bass-loaded club nights and boundary-crossing plays.

Kino Atelier (☎ 212 25; Am Haagtor 1) Under the same roof as boho Café Haag, this independent cinema screens art-house and foreign films, some in their original language.

Südhaus (☎ 746 96; www.sudhaus-tuebingen.de, in German; Hechinger Strasse 203) This arts centre has an eclectic program embracing contemporary dance, concerts, stand-up comedy and club nights. Take bus 3 or 5.

Zoo (☎ 977300; www.zoo-tuebingen.de; Schleifmühleweg 86) Tübingen's funkiest alternative arts venue, Zoo hosts gigs and club nights with DJs pumping out tunes from indie to hip hop. Head for the beer garden if you prefer conversing to cavorting,

Shopping

Tübingen's labyrinthine Altstadt makes for relaxed shopping, dotted with kooky galleries, speciality stores and musty second-hand bookshops.

Ammerkeramik (☎ 255 397; Ammergasse 21; ◷ 10am-1pm & 2.30-6.30pm Mon-Fri, 10am-2pm Sat) Ellen Reinhardt is a whiz on the wheel in her ceramics workshop, stocking quality stoneware, crockery and knick-knacks to brighten up any mantelpiece.

Vinum (☎ 520 52; Lange Gasse 6; ◷ 9.30am-6.30pm Mon-Fri, 9.30am-4pm Sat) Wines and liqueurs share shelf space with mustards, vinegars and oils in this cellar of local goodies.

Wochenmarkt (Marktplatz; ◷ 7am-1pm Mon, Wed & Fri) Bag glossy fruit and veg, oven-fresh bread and local honey and herbs at Tübingen's farmers' market.

Getting There & Around

Tübingen is an easy train ride from Stuttgart (€11.30, 45 to 60 minutes, at least two an hour) and Villingen (€17.80 to €22.50, 1½ to two hours, hourly) in the Black Forest.

The centre is a maze of one-way streets with residents-only parking, so head for a multistorey car park. To drive into Tübingen, you need to purchase an environmentally friendly *Umweltplaketten* (emissions sticker); see p783 for details.

Radlager (☎ 551 651; Lazarettgasse 19-21; ◷ 9.30am-6.30pm Mon, Wed & Fri, 2-6.30pm Tue & Thu, 9.30am-2.30pm Sat) rents bikes for €10 per day.

If you'd rather let someone else do the pedalling, **Riksch-Radsch** (☎ 300 449; Aixer Strasse 198, organise 1½-hour rickshaw tours of the centre (€19.80 per person) and three-hour trips to Bebenhausen (€29.80 per person).

AROUND TÜBINGEN
Naturpark Schönbuch

For back-to-nature hiking and cycling, make for this 156-sq-km **nature reserve** (☎ 07071-602 262; www.naturpark-schoenbuch.de), 6km north of Tübingen. With a bit of luck and a pair of binoculars, you might catch a glimpse of black woodpeckers and yellow-bellied toads.

The nature reserve's beech and oak woods fringe the village of **Bebenhausen** and its well-preserved **Cistercian Abbey** (☎ 07071-602 802 www.kloster-bebenhausen.de; adult/concession €3.50/1.80 ◷ 9am-noon & 1-6pm Mon, 9am-6pm Tue-Sun Apr-Oct, 9am-noon & 1-5pm Nov-Mar). Founded in 1183 by Count Rudolph von Tübingen, the complex became a royal hunting retreat post-Reformation. A visit takes in the frescoed **summer refectory**, the Gothic **abbey church** and intricate star vaulting and half-timbered facades in the **cloister**.

Bebenhausen, 3km north of Tübingen, is the gateway to Naturpark Schönbuch. Buses run at least twice hourly (€2, 13 minutes).

Burg Hohenzollern

Rising dramatically from an exposed crag, its medieval battlements and silver turrets often veiled in mist, **Burg Hohenzollern** (Hohenzollern Castle; ☎ 07471-2428; www.preussen.de) sure is impressive from a distance, but up close it looks more contrived. Dating to 1867, this neo-Gothic castle is the ancestral seat of the Hohenzollern family, the first and last monarchical rulers of the short-lived second German empire (1871–1918).

History fans should take a 35-minute German-language **tour** (adult/6-15yr/concession €8/4/6; ◷ 9am-5.30pm mid-Mar–Oct, 10am-4.30pm Nov-mid-Mar), which takes in towers, overblown salons replete with stained glass and frescoes and the dazzling *Schatzkammer* (treasury) The **grounds** (admission without tour €4) command tremendous views over the Swabian Alps.

Frequent trains link Tübingen, 28km distant with Hechingen (€4, 25 minutes, one or two an hour), about 4km northwest of the castle.

Naturpark Obere Donautal

One word: wow. Theatrically set against limestone, cave-riddled cliffs, dappled with pine and beech woods that are burnished gold in autumn, and hugging the Danube's banks, the **Upper Danube Valley Nature Reserve** (www .oberedonau.de, www.naturpark-obere-donau.de, in German) bombards you with rugged splendour. Stick to the autobahn, however, and you'll be none the wiser. To explore the nature reserve, slip into a bicycle saddle or walking boots, and hit the trail.

One of the finest stretches is between **Fridingen** and **Beuron**, a 12.5km ridge-top walk of three to four hours. The signposted, easy-to-navigate trail runs above ragged cliffs, affording eagle's-eye views of the meandering Danube, which has almost 2850km to go before emptying into the Black Sea. The vertigo-inducing outcrop of **Laibfelsen** is a great picnic spot. From here, the path dips in and out of woodlands and meadows flecked with purple thistles. **Berghaus Knopfmacher** (☎ 1057; Fridingen; mains €8-14) has a terrace for reviving over drinks and Swabian fare, including game in season.

In Beuron the big draw is the working **Benedictine abbey**, one of Germany's oldest dating to 1077. The lavish stucco and fresco **church** (admission free; ☺ 5am-8pm daily) is open to visitors. See the website www.beuron.de (in German) for sleeping options.

Fridingen and Beuron lie on the L277, 75km south of Tübingen and 45km east of Villingen. Frequent trains link Beuron to Tübingen (€25, two hours), Villingen (€29.50, 58 minutes) and Ulm (€20.40, 1¾ hours).

ULM
☎ 0731 / pop 121,500

Starting with the statistics, Ulm has the crookedest house (as listed in *Guinness*) and one of the narrowest (4.5m wide), the world's oldest zoomorphic sculpture (aged 30,000 years) and tallest cathedral steeple (161.5m high), and is the birthplace of the all-time brainiest physicist, Albert Einstein. Relatively speaking, of course.

Superlatives aside, this idiosyncratic city will win your affection with everyday encounters; particularly in summer when your chain sings as you pedal along the Danube and the Fischerviertel's beer gardens hum with animated chatter. One *Helles* too many and you may decide to impress the locals by attempting the tongue twister: '*In Ulm, um Ulm, und um Ulm herum.*' Don't say we didn't warn you.

Orientation

Ulm's Altstadt, on the north bank of the Danube, is delineated by the river (south), the Hauptbahnhof (west) and Olgastrasse (north). The Münster looms above the pedestrianised centre. The Blau River's two channels, lined with quaint houses, meet the Danube about 300m south of the Münster.

Skipping south of the Danube is the comparatively bland, modern city of Neu-Ulm in Bavaria. The two cities share transport systems and municipal facilities.

Information

Eco-Express SB-Waschsalon (Wielandstrasse 29; ☺ 6am-11pm Mon-Sat) A self-service laundry four blocks northeast of Willy-Brandt-Platz.

Herwig (☎ 962 170; Münsterplatz 18) A bookshop with a good selection of travel guides and maps.

Internet Café (Herdbruckerstrasse 26; per hr €1; ☺ 10am-10pm)

Post office (Bahnhofplatz 2) To the left as you exit the Hauptbahnhof.

Tourist office (☎ 161 2830; www.tourismus.ulm.de; Stadthaus, Münsterplatz 50; ☺ 9am-6pm Mon-Sat, 11am-3pm Sun Apr-Oct, 9am-6pm Mon-Fri, 9am-4pm Sat Nov-Mar) Sells the Ulm Card.

Ulm Card (1/2 days €8/12) Offers discounted museum admission and public transport.

Sights
MÜNSTER

Ooh, it's so big…first-time visitors gush as they strain their neck muscles gazing up to the **Münster** (Cathedral; Münsterplatz; admission free; ☺ 9am-4.45pm Jan & Feb, to 5.45pm Mar & Oct, to 6.45pm Apr-Jun & Sep, to 7.45pm Jul & Aug). It is. And rather beautiful. Celebrated for its 161.5m-high steeple, the world's tallest, this Goliath of cathedrals took a staggering 500 years to build from the first stone laid in 1377. Note the **hallmarks** on each stone, inscribed by cutters who were paid by the block. Those intent on cramming the Münster into one photo, filigree spire and all, should lie down on the cobbles.

Only by puffing up 768 spiral steps to the 143m-high viewing platform of the **tower** (adult/student €4/2.50; ☺ last admission 1hr before closing) can you appreciate the Münster's dizzying height. Up top there are terrific views of the Black Forest and, on cloud-free days, the Alps.

The **Israelfenster**, a stained-glass window above the west door, commemorates Jews killed during the Holocaust. The Gothic-style wooden **pulpit canopy**, as detailed as fine lace,

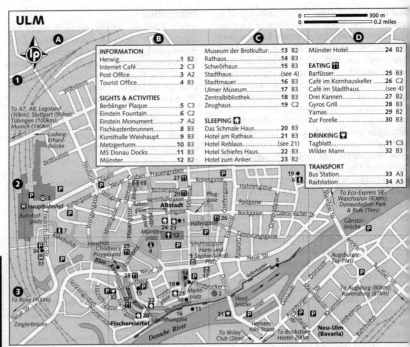

ULM

INFORMATION			Museum der Brotkultur	.13	B2	Münster Hotel	.24	B2
Herwig	.1	B2	Rathaus	.14	B3			
Internet Café	.2	C3	Schwörhaus	.15	B3	**EATING** 🍴		
Post Office	.3	A2	Stadthaus	(see 4)		Barfüsser	.25	B3
Tourist Office	.4	B3	Stadtmauer	.16	B3	Café im Kornhauskeller	.26	C2
			Ulmer Museum	.17	B3	Café im Stadthaus	(see 4)	
SIGHTS & ACTIVITIES			Zentralbibliothek	.18	B3	Drei Kannen	.27	B3
Berblinger Plaque	.5	C3	Zeughaus	.19	C2	Gyros Grill	.28	B3
Einstein Fountain	.6	C2				Yamas	.29	B2
Einstein Monument	.7	A2	**SLEEPING** 🛏			Zur Forelle	.30	B3
Fischkastenbrunnen	.8	B3	Das Schmale Haus	.20	B3			
Kunsthalle Weishaupt	.9	B3	Hotel am Rathaus	.21	B3	**DRINKING** 🍷		
Metzgerturm	.10	B3	Hotel Reblaus	(see 21)		Tagblatt	.31	C3
MS Donau Docks	.11	B3	Hotel Schiefes Haus	.22	B3	Wilder Mann	.32	B3
Münster	.12	B2	Hotel zum Anker	.23	B2			
						TRANSPORT		
						Bus Station	.33	A3
						Radstation	.34	A3

eliminates echoes during sermons. Biblical figures and historical characters such as Pythagoras, who strums a lute, embellish the 15th-century oak **choir stalls**. The impressive **stained-glass windows** in the choir, dating from the 14th and 15th centuries, were removed during WWII.

The Münster's regular **organ concerts** (tickets €5; ⏱ 11.30am most Sun year-round) are a musical treat.

STADTHAUS
Designed by Richard Meier, the contemporary aesthetic of the concrete-and-glass **Stadthaus** is a dramatic contrast to the Münster. The American architect caused uproar by erecting a postmodern building alongside the city's Gothic giant, but the result is both striking and functional. The edifice stages exhibitions and events, and houses the tourist office and a cafe.

MARKTPLATZ
Lording it over the Marktplatz, the 14th-century, step-gabled **Rathaus** (Town Hall) sports an ornately painted Renaissance fa-

cade and a gilded **astrological clock**. Inside there is a replica of **Berblinger's flying machine**. In front is the **Fischkastenbrunnen**, a fountain where fishmongers kept their catch alive on market days. The 36m-high glass pyramid behind the Rathaus is the city's main library, the **Zentralbibliothek**, designed by Gottfried Böhm.

FISCHERVIERTEL & CITY WALL
On the third Monday of July, the mayor swears allegiance to the town's 1397 constitution from the 1st-floor loggia of the early 17th-century baroque **Schwörhaus** (Oath House; Weinhof), three blocks west of the Rathaus.

The charming **Fischerviertel**, Ulm's old fishers' and tanners' quarter, is slightly southwest. Here beautifully restored half-timbered houses huddle along the two channels of the Blau River, traversed by footbridges. Harbouring art galleries, rustic restaurants, courtyards and the crookedest hotel in the world (see p442), the cobbled lanes are ideal for a leisurely saunter.

South of the Fischerviertel, along the Danube's north bank, runs the redbrick

Stadtmauer (city wall), the height of which was reduced in the 19th century after Napoleon decided that a heavily fortified Ulm was against his best interests. Walk it for fine views over the river, the Altstadt and the colourful tile-roofed **Metzgerturm** (Butcher's Tower), doing a Pisa by leaning 2m off-centre.

East of the Herdbrücke, the bridge to Neu-Ulm, a **bronze plaque** marks where Albrecht Berblinger, a tailor who invented a flying machine resembling a hang-glider, attempted to fly over the Danube in 1811. The so-called 'Tailor of Ulm' made an embarrassing splash landing, but his design was later shown to be workable (his failure apparently caused by a lack of thermals on that day).

EINSTEIN FOUNTAIN & MONUMENT

A nod to Ulm's most famous son, Jürgen Goertz's fiendishly funny bronze **fountain** shows a wild-haired, tongue-poking-out Albert Einstein, who was born in Ulm but left when he was one year old. Standing in front of the 16th-century *Zeughaus* (arsenal), the rocket-snail creation is a satirical play on humanity's attempts to manipulate evolution for its own self-interest. Nearby, at Zeughaus 4, is a single stone bearing the inscription *Ein Stein* (One Stone).

On Bahnhofstrasse sits Max Bill's **monument** (1979) to the great physicist, a stack of red-granite pillars marking the spot where Einstein was born.

MUSEUMS

The **Museum Pass** (€12), sold at the tourist office and participating museums, gets you into seven local museums.

It's easy to spend half a day discovering the outstanding **Ulmer Museum** (☎ 161 4330; Marktplatz 9; adult/concession €3.50/2.50, Fri free; ☼ 11am-5pm Tue-Sun, to 8pm Thu), which romps through ancient and modern art, history and archaeology. Standouts feature the 20th-century **Kurt Fried Collection**, starring Klee, Picasso and Lichtenstein works. Archaeological highlights include tiny Upper Palaeolithic figurines, unearthed in caves in the Swabian Alps, including the 30,000-year-old ivory *Löwenmensch* (lion man), the world's oldest zoomorphic sculpture.

The glass-fronted **Kunsthalle Weishaupt** (☎ 161 43 60; www.kunsthalle-weishaupt.de, in German; Hans-und-Sophie-Scholl-Platz 1; adult/concession €6/4; ☼ 11am-5pm Tue-Sun, to 8pm Thu) right opposite unveils the private collection of Siegfried Weishaupt. The accent is on modern and pop art, with bold paintings by Klein, Warhol and Haring.

How grain grows, what makes a good dough and other bread-related mysteries are unravelled at the **Museum der Brotkultur** (Museum of Bread Culture; ☎ 699 55; www.museum-brotkultur.de; Salzstadelgasse 10; adult/concession €3.50/2.50; ☼ 10am-5pm Thu-Tue, to 8.30pm Wed). The collection celebrates bread as the stuff of life over millennia and across cultures, displaying curios from mills to Egyptian corn mummies.

LEGOLAND

A sure-fire kid-pleaser, **Legoland Deutschland** (☎ 08221-700 700; www.legoland.de; adult/3-11yr & senior €34/28; ☼ from 10am-btwn 6pm & 10pm mid-Apr–early Nov) is a pricey Lego-themed amusement park, with shows, splashy rides and a miniature world built from 25 million Lego bricks. It's in Günzburg, 30km northeast of Ulm, just off the A8 and served by bus 850.

SPOT THE SPARROW

You can't move for *Spatzen* (sparrows) in the German language. You can eat like one *(essen wie ein Spatz)* and swear like one *(schimpfen wie ein Rohrspatz)*; there are *Spatzenschleuder* (catapults), *Spätzles* (little darlings) and *Spatzenhirne* (bird brains). Nicknamed *Spatzen,* Ulm residents are, according to legend, indebted to the titchy bird for the construction of their fabulous Münster.

The story goes that the half-baked builders tried in vain to shove the wooden beams for the minster sideways through the city gate. They fretted and struggled, until suddenly a sparrow fluttered past with straw for its nest. Enlightened, the builders carried the beams lengthways, completed the job and placed a bronze statue of a sparrow at the top to honour the bird.

Today there are sparrows everywhere in Ulm: on postcards, in patisseries, at football matches (team SSV Ulm are dubbed *die Spatzen*) and, above all, in the colourful sculptures dotting the Altstadt. Watch out for the birdie as you wander.

Tours

The **MS Donau** (☎ 627 51; adult/child €7.50/4.50; ☻ May–mid-Oct) cruises the Danube at 2pm, 3pm and 4pm daily, and also at 5pm on weekends. The docks are on the Ulm side, just south of the Metzgerturm. **Sportiv Touren** (☎ 970 9298; www.sportivtouren.de, in German; adult/child under 14yr €24.50/17) runs 2½-hour canoe tours from various points on the Danube and Iller Rivers.

Sleeping

With a little pretrip planning, you can eschew chain drabness in favour of quirky digs in Ulm. The tourist office lists holiday apartments and guesthouses that charge around €20 to €25 per person.

Brickstone Hostel (☎ 708 2559; www.brickstone -hostel.de; Schützenstrasse 42; dm €18-22, s/d €30/44; ☎) This converted redbrick house in Neu-Ulm is single-handedly upping the backpacker ante with snazzy rooms, relaxed common areas and perks like bike rental and free tea. Take bus 7 to Schützenstrasse from the Hauptbahnhof.

Hotel zum Anker (☎ 632 97; Rabengasse 2; s with/ without bathroom €48/35, d from €65/55; P) These well-kept digs are popular among cyclists doing the Danube. The recently revamped, parquet-floored rooms represent excellent value. Astronomer Johannes Kepler's first works were printed here in 1627.

Münster Hotel (☎ 641 62; Münsterplatz 14; s with/without bathroom €45/33, d €68-78) Rooms are nothing flash, but there are no arguments about the modest rates, impeccable cleanliness and awesome Münster views at this hotel on the square.

Hotel am Rathaus & Hotel Reblaus (☎ 968 490; www.rathausulm.de, in German; Kronengasse 10; s/d/q €68/88/135, s/d without bathroom €50/70; P) Just paces from the Rathaus, these family-run twins ooze individual charm in rooms with flourishes like stucco and Biedermeier furnishings.

Das Schmale Haus (☎ 175 4940; Fischergasse 27; s €76-81, d €99-104) Measuring just 4.5m across, the half-timbered 'narrow house' is a one-off. The affable Heides have transformed this slender 16th-century pad into a gorgeous B&B, with exposed beams, downy bedding and wood floors in all three rooms. Call ahead and you might just get lucky.

our pick Hotel Schiefes Haus (☎ 967 930; www .hotelschiefeshausulm.de; Schwörhausgasse 6; s/d €125/148) There was a crooked man and he walked a crooked mile…presumably to the world's most crooked hotel. But fear not, ye of littl[e] wonkiness, this 15th-century, half-timbere[d] rarity is not about to topple into the Bla[u] River. And up those creaking wood stairs in your snug, beamed room, you won't hav[e] to buckle yourself to the bed thanks to spiri[t] levels and specially made height adjusters. I[f] you're feeling *really* crooked, plump straigh[t] for room No 6.

Eating & Drinking

Pubs and restaurants are virtually wall to wa[ll] along Neue Strasse and the Blau River.

Gyros Grill (☎ 602 3146; Weinhofberg 5; snacks €2.70[-] 7.80) This hole-in-the-wall joint rustles up tast[y] pitta gyros, haloumi and calamari, and has a[ ] terrace beside the Blau.

Café im Kornhauskeller (☎ 746 78; Hafengass[e] 19; breakfast & snacks €4-8; ☻ 8am-midnight Mon-Sa[t,] 9am-10pm Sun) Art-slung walls and an attrac[-] tive inner courtyard create a laid-back vib[e] at this cafe, great for breakfast (we like the D[a] Vinci with *prosecco*, melon and Parma ham)[,] salads and drinks.

Tagblatt (☎ 746 78; Insel 1, Neu-Ulm; snacks €5-9[;] ☻ 8am-2am Mon-Fri, 5am-2am Sat & Sun) Welcome t[o] Bavaria and one of Ulm's finest riverside bee[r] gardens, with prime views to the Altstadt. Gra[b] a chair outside to quaff a cold one, or chom[p] imaginative salads, schnitzels and burgers.

Drei Kannen (☎ 677 17; Hafenbad 31/1; lunch specia[l] Mon-Fri €5.90, mains €8-17) A rustic Swabian res[-] taurant whose courtyard is overlooked by a[n] Italian-style loggia. Loosen a belt notch fo[r] dishes like pork knuckles and *Schupfnudel[n]* (potato noodles), washed down with malt[y] beers.

Café im Stadthaus (☎ 600 93; Münsterplatz 50; lunc[h] special €7.90; ☻ 8am-midnight Mon-Sat, 10am-9pm Su[n]) This modern glass cube has appetising lunc[h] specials and a terrace offering peerless view[s] of the Münster.

Barfüsser (☎ 602 1110; Lautenberg 1; mains €6[-] 16.50; ☻ 10am-1am, to 2am Thu-Sat) Light bite[s] like *Flammkuchen* and *Käsespätzle* (chees[e] noodles) soak up the prize-winning bee[r] microbrewed in Neu-Ulm, at this brewpu[b.] Tuesday is karaoke night.

Wilder Mann (☎ 205 8743; Fischergasse 2; main[s] €7.50-14.90) Young and lively, this pub host[s] fun events from barbecues to DJ nights. The well-mixed cocktails and people-watching ter[-] race compensate for the so-so food.

Zur Forelle (☎ 639 24; Fischergasse 25; mains €9.5[0-] 21.50; ☻ 11am-3pm & 5pm-midnight) Since 1626, thi[s] low-ceilinged tavern has been convincing wayfarers (Einstein included) about the joys of seasonal Swabian cuisine. Ablaze with flowers in summer, this wood-panelled haunt by the Blau prides itself on its namesake *Forelle* (trout), kept fresh under the bridge.

Yamas (☎ 407 8614; www.yamas-ulm.com, in German; Herrenkellergasse 29; mains €12.50-23.50; ⏰ 10am-1am Sun-Thu, to 2am Fri & Sat) Yamas means 'cheers' in Greek and this slinky glass-walled restaurant is certainly an arrival to toast. Wonderfully fresh seafood, such as baby calamari with home-made pesto, pairs well with zesty wines from the huge cellar. Round out with an unusual brew from the tea menu.

Entertainment

The tourist office sells event tickets and hands out the free German-language monthly *Spazz*, listing cultural happenings.

Roxy (☎ 968 620; www.roxy.ulm.de, in German; Schillerstrasse 1) A huge cultural venue, housed in a former industrial plant 1km south of the Hauptbahnhof, with a concert hall, cinema, disco, bar and special-event forum. Take tram line 1 to Ehinger Tor.

Wiley Club (☎ 867 04; www.wiley-club.de, in German; Wileystrasse 4, Neu-Ulm; ⏰ 11am-1am, to 2am Fri & Sat) On a former US military base, this one-time canteen has a restaurant, cafe-bar and stage, and hosts live music and club nights. Situated 2.5km south of the Altstadt; take bus 6 to the Wiley Club.

Getting There & Away

Ulm, about 90km southeast of Stuttgart and 150km west of Munich, is near the intersection of the north–south A7 and the east–west A8.

Ulm is well-served by ICE trains; major destinations include Stuttgart (€16.70 to €24, one hour, several hourly) and Munich (€24.80 to €34, 1½ hours to two hours, several hourly).

Getting Around

Ulm's ecofriendly trams run on renewable energy. There's a local **transport information counter** (☎ 166 2120; www.swu-verkehr.de, in German) in the tourist office.

Except in parking garages (€0.60 per 30 minutes), the whole city centre is metered; many areas are limited to one hour. There's a Park & Ride lot at Donaustadion, a stadium 1.5km northeast of the Münster and on tram line 1.

You can hire bikes, including tandems, from **Radstation** (☎ 150 0231; Friedrich-Ebert-Strasse; per day €5; ⏰ 6am-8pm Mon-Fri, 9am-7pm Sat, Sun & holidays), between the Hauptbahnhof and the bus station. Bike paths go along the Danube.

To order a taxi, call ☎ 660 66.

NORTHERN BLACK FOREST

Green, rolling and almost soothingly beautiful, the Northern Black Forest scythes through western Baden-Württemberg, from the bubbling thermal baths of Roman-rooted Baden-Baden in the north to the Swiss border in the south. Laced with zigzagging roads that make for memorable driving and cycling, this is a back-to-nature region of mossy fir and beech woodlands, cherry orchards and story-book villages, and tight valleys where only tinkling cowbells interrupt the overwhelming sense of calm.

BADEN-BADEN
☎ 07221 / pop 54,800

'So nice that you have to name it twice', gushed Bill Clinton. Indeed there's no denying Baden-Baden's allure to royals, the rich and celebrities – Obama and Bismarck, Queen Victoria and Victoria Beckham included. Yet nice hardly does bon vivant Baden-Baden justice; it's without doubt one of Baden-Württemberg's most refined cities, lined with chichi boutiques, smart pavement cafes, and manicured gardens where fountains dance and locals walk coiffed poodles.

Locked in an embrace between the Black Forest and France, this grand dame of German spas stills turn heads with her graceful belle époque villas, fortunes in her sumptuous casino, and the moods in her temple-like thermal baths that put the *Baden* (bathe) in Baden.

Orientation

Baden-Baden's heart is Leopoldsplatz, which fans out into pedestrianised shopping streets. Most sights, including Lichtentaler Allee, on the west bank of the Oosbach, are within easy walking distance.

The Bahnhof is in the suburb of Oos, 4km northwest of the centre, with the central bus station out the front.

BADEN-WÜRTTEMBERG

BADEN-WÜRTTEMBERG

BLACK FOREST CENT SAVER

In most parts of the Black Forest your hotel or guesthouse will issue you with the handy **Schwarzwald-Gästekarte** (Guest Card) for discounts or freebies on museums, ski lifts, events and attractions. Versions of the card with the Konus symbol entitle you to free use of public transport.

Almost all tourist offices in the Black Forest sell the three-day **SchwarzwaldCard** (adult/4-11yr/family €32/21/99, incl 1 day at Europa-Park €55.50/45.50/189) for admission to around 150 attractions in the Black Forest, including museums, ski lifts, boat trips, spas and swimming pools. Details on both cards are available at www.blackforest-tourism.com.

Information

Branch tourist office (Kaiserallee 3; 10am-5pm Mon-Sat, 2-5pm Sun) In the Trinkhalle. Sells events tickets.

Internet Café (Lange Strasse 54; per hr €2; 10am-10pm) Internet access at the northern edge of the pedestrianised town centre.

Main tourist office (☎ 275 200; www.baden-baden .com; Schwarzwaldstrasse 52; 9am-6pm Mon-Sat, 9am-1pm Sun) Situated 2km northwest of the centre. If you're driving from the northwest (from the A5) this place is on the way into town. Sells events tickets.

Post office (Lange Strasse 44) Inside Kaufhaus Wagener.

Sights

KURHAUS & CASINO

Corinthian columns and a frieze of mythical griffins grace the belle époque facade of the monumental **Kurhaus** (☎ 353 202; www.kurhaus-baden-baden.de, in German; Kaiserallee 1), which towers above well-groomed gardens. An alley of chestnut trees, flanked by two rows of boutiques, links the Kurhaus with Kaiserallee.

Inside is the sublime **casino** (☎ 302 40; www .casino-baden-baden.de; admission €3; 2pm-2am Sun-Thu, 2pm-3am Fri & Sat, poker tables open 8pm-5am Fri & Sat), which seeks to emulate – indeed, outdo – the gilded splendour of Versailles. Marlene Dietrich called it 'the most beautiful casino in the world'. Gents must wear a jacket and tie, rentable for €8 and €3 respectively. If you're not much of a gambler and want to simply marvel at the opulence, join a **guided tour** (€4; in German), every half-hour from 9.30am (10am from October to March) to 11.30am daily.

In the leafy park just north sits the **Trinkhalle** (Pump Room; Kaiserallee 3), where you can wander a 90m-long portico embellished with 19th-century frescoes of local legends. Baden-Baden's elixir of youth, some say, is the free curative mineral water that gushes from a faucet (10am to 2am, until 3am Friday and Saturday) linked to the springs below. A cafe sells plastic cups for €0.20, or bring your own bottle to fill with super water.

LICHTENTALER ALLEE

Punctuated by grand 19th-century villas, wrought-iron lanterns and cascading fountains, this flowery park promenade shadows the sprightly Oosbach from the Kurhaus to Kloster Lichtenthal, about 3km south. It's ideal for a languid saunter or a picnic, especially in spring when the gardens are awash with daffodils and bluebells.

The gateway to Lichtentaler Allee is **Baden-Baden Theater**, a neobaroque confection whose frilly interior recalls the Opéra-Garnier in Paris.

Voluptuous Joan Miró sculptures guide the eye to the sky-lit **Kunsthalle** (State Art Gallery; ☎ 300 763; www.kunsthalle-baden-baden.de, in German; Lichtentaler Allee 8a; adult/concession €5/4; 11am-6pm Tue-Sun, to 8pm Wed), which hosts rotating exhibitions of contemporary art.

Sidling up to the Kunsthalle is **Museum Frieder Burda** (☎ 398 980; www.museum-frieder-burda.de; Lichtentaler Allee 8b; adult/concession €9/7; 10am-6pm Tue-Sun) lodged in an avant-garde edifice designed by Richard Meier. The star-studded modern and contemporary art collection includes works by Warhol and Picasso, as well as by German artists such as Georg Baselitz, Florian Thomas and Eberhard Havecost.

The **Stadtmuseum** (☎ 932 272; Lichtentaler Allee 10; adult/child €4/2; 10am-6pm Tue-Sun, to 8pm Wed), just south, timelines Baden-Baden's past with exhibits from Roman figurines to belle époque paintings and roulette wheels.

Around 1km south is the **Gönneranlage**, a rose garden perfumed by 400 varieties that thrive in the local microclimate. The Byzantine-style 1882 **Russische Kirche** (Russian Church; Maria-Victoria-Strasse; admission €0.50; 10am-

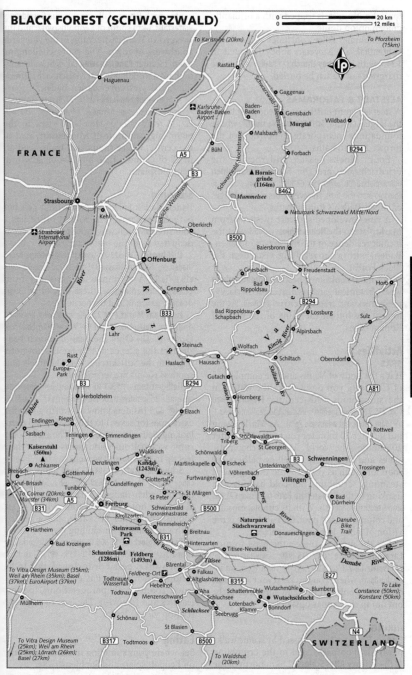

BLACK FOREST (SCHWARZWALD)

0   20 km
0   12 miles

BADEN-WÜRTTEMBERG

6pm), slightly east, is topped with a brilliantly golden onion dome.

Lichtentaler Allee concludes at the **Kloster Lichtenthal**, a Cistercian abbey founded in 1245, with an **abbey church** (☯ daily) where the margraves of Baden lie buried.

ALTSTADT & PANORAMAS

A steepish jaunt northeast of Leopoldsplatz is the largely Gothic **Stiftskirche** (Marktplatz), whose foundations incorporate some ruins of the former Roman baths.

Four blocks east, underneath the Friedrichsbad, are the **Römische Badruinen** (Römerplatz; adult/under 15yr €2.50/1; ☯ 11am-noon & 3-6pm mid-Mar–mid-Nov), the well-preserved vestiges of Baden-Baden's Roman baths.

A vine-enveloped staircase twists up from Marktplatz to the **Neues Schloss** (Schlosstrasse), the former residence of the margraves of Baden-Baden, with a far-reaching vista over the Black Forest.

For more cool views, head to **Florentinerberg** where botanical gardens nurture wisteria, cypress trees and fragrant citrus groves. At the foot of the hill sit the ruins of the original Roman baths.

Activities

SPAS

If it's the body of Venus and the complexion of Cleopatra you desire, take the waters in the sumptuous 19th-century **Friedrichsbad** (☎ 275 920; www.roemisch-irisches-bad.de; Römerplatz 1; ☯ 9am-10pm, last admission 7pm). As Mark Twain put it: 'after 10 minutes you forget time; after 20 minutes, the world'. Modesty, rheumatic aches and the nudity of fellow bathers are soon forgotten as you slip into the regime of steaming, scrubbing, hot-cold bathing and dunking in the **Roman-Irish Bath** (admission €21, incl soap & brush massage €31). With its cupola, mosaics and column-ringed pool, the bathhouse is the vision of a neo-Renaissance palace.

For the modest, there's the glass-fronted **Caracalla-Therme** (☎ 275 940; www.caracalla.de; Römerplatz 11; 2/3/4hr €13/15/17; ☯ 8am-10pm, last admission 8pm), where you can keep your swimsuit on in the pools, grottos and surge channels, but not in the saunas upstairs.

HIKING

Baden-Baden is criss-crossed by scenic walking trails. Footpaths lead to the crumbling 11th-century **Altes Schloss**, 2.5km north of the centre, with Rhine Valley views; the **Geroldsauer waterfalls**, 6km south of Leopoldsplatz; and the overgrown **Yburg** castle ruins, in the vineyards southwest of town. The more challenging 40km circular **Panoramaweg** takes in waterfalls, orchards, woodlands and Malschbach, affording Kodak views over Baden-Baden.

A **Standseilbahn** (cable car; ☎ 2770; www.stadtwerke -baden-baden.de, in German; adult/6-15yr one-way €2/1.30, return €4/2; ☯ 10am-10pm) rises to the 668m-high summit of Mt Merkur, east of the centre, where signposted trails head off in all directions. Take bus 204 or 205 from Leopoldsplatz.

Sleeping

Baden-Baden is jam-packed with hotels but bargains are rare. The tourist office has a room-reservation service, where a 10% fee is deducted from the cost of the room.

DJH hostel (☎ 522 23; www.jugendherberge-baden -baden.de; Hardbergstrasse 34; dm 1st/subsequent night €19.10/15.90) A 10-minute uphill trudge from Grosse Dollenstrasse, these digs offer clean dorms, gardens and barbecue areas.

Hotel am Markt (☎ 270 40; www.hotel-am-markt -baden.de; Marktplatz 18; s/d €44/80, without bathroom €32/64; P ▣) Only the peal of church bells shatters the silence at this family-run hotel opposite the Stiftskirche. The 23 homely and spotless rooms are terrific value.

Heiligenstein (☎ 961 40; www.hotel-heiligenstein.de, in German; Heiligensteinstrasse 19a, Neuweier; s €75-79, d €110-115; P ▣) Insiders know it's worth going the extra mile (or seven) to this sweet hotel overlooking Neuweier's vineyards. The slick rooms come with balconies and guests can put their feet up in the spa and gardens.

Schweizer Hof (☎ 304 60; www.schweizerhof.de; Lange Strasse 73; s €72, d €99-119; ▣) Sitting on one of Baden-Baden's smartest streets, this above-par hotel is a real find, with dapper rooms, chandelier-lit spaces, and a garden with sun lounges for chilling.

Rathausglöckel (☎ 906 10; www.rathausgloeckel.de; Steinstrasse 7; s €85-100, d €110-135; ☏) Tucked down a street near Friedrichsbad, this 16th-century town house has charmingly renovated rooms with parquet floors, period features and free wi-fi. The best rooms have rooftop views.

Eating

See where your rumbling stomach leads you on Leopoldsplatz and Sophienstrasse.

BADEN-WÜRTTEMBERG

Monte Christo (☎ 393 434; Eichstrasse 5; tapas €4.80-9.90; ⏲ 6pm-1am) This cheerful bar whips up tasty tapas from shallot-topped sardines to mussels in red-pepper sauce.

Jensens (☎ 397 900; Sophienstrasse 45; light meals €5-8; ⏲ 10.30am-late; 🛜) Chilli-red walls, wood floors and jazzy music give this cafe a hip feel. Enjoy a beer or *Flammkuchen* (around €6) on the patio.

Café Kunsthalle (☎ 392 000; Lichtentaler Allee 8a; snacks €5.50-9.80; ⏲ 10am-6pm Tue-Sun; Ⓥ) Next to the Kunsthalle, this avant-garde cafe serves yummy salads, baguettes and antipasti. The little heated terrace overlooks the sculpture-dotted park.

Leo's (☎ 380 81; Luisenstrasse 10; mains €11-25; ⏲ 10am-1am Sun-Thu, to 2am Sat) Bill Clinton and a host of other luminaries have dined at this snazzy bistro-cum–wine bar. It rolls out creative salads, pasta and cocktails.

La Provence (☎ 216 515; Schlossstrasse 20; mains €13.50-21.50; ⏲ noon-1am) Candlelight illuminates the vaults and art-nouveau mirrors of this one-time wine cellar, which marries full-bodied wines with French delicacies like garlicky snails and duck breast in honey-coriander sauce.

Rizzi (☎ 258 38; Augustaplatz 1; mains €15-24; ⏲ noon-1am) A summertime favourite, this stout pink villa's tree-shaded patio faces Lichtentaler Allee. Italian numbers such as whole sea bass and saffron-infused risotto pair nicely with local rieslings.

Entertainment

Ensconced in an historic train station and fabled for its acoustics, the **Festspielhaus** (☎ 301 3101; www.festspielhaus.de; Beim Alten Bahnhof 2, Robert-Schumann-Platz) is Europe's second biggest concert hall, seating 2500 theatre-goers, and a lavish tribute to Baden-Baden's musical heritage. Under the direction of Andreas Mölich-Zebhauser, the grand venue hosts a world-class program of concerts, opera and ballet.

The revered **Baden-Badener Philharmonie** (☎ 932 791; www.philharmonie.baden-baden.de) frequently performs in the Kurhaus.

Getting There & Away

Karlsruhe-Baden-Baden airport (Baden Airpark; www.badenairpark.de), 15km west of town, is linked to London and Dublin by Ryanair.

Buses to Black Forest destinations depart from the bus station, next to the Bahnhof.

Baden-Baden is close to the A5 (Frankfurt-Basel autobahn) and is the northern starting point of the zigzagging Schwarzwald-Hochstrasse (see boxed text, below), which follows the B500.

BADEN-WÜRTTEMBERG

TOP FIVE GREAT DRIVES

More than just pretty drives, many of these routes highlight a theme, such as Franco-German friendship, clock-making and winegrowing. Local tourist offices provide details and brochures.

- **Schwarzwald-Hochstrasse** (Black Forest Hwy) Following the B500, this connects Baden-Baden with Freudenstadt, 60km to the south. It affords expansive views of the Upper Rhine Valley and the Vosges Mountains in Alsace (France). The route skirts a number of lakes, including the pine-fringed Mummelsee.

- **Badische Weinstrasse** (Baden Wine Rd) An oenologist's delight. From Baden-Baden south to Lörrach, this 160km route corkscrews through the red-wine vineyards of Ortenau, the Pinot noir of Kaiserstuhl and Tuniberg, and the white-wine vines of Markgräflerland.

- **Schwarzwald-Tälerstrasse** (Black Forest Valley Rd) Twists 100km from Rastatt to Freudenstadt, affording views across steep valleys (the Murgtal and Kinzig), lush woodlands, granite cliffs and gin-clear streams. High points include Gernsbach's half-timbered houses, Forbach's bridge and freshly tapped beer in Alpirsbach.

- **Deutsche Uhrenstrasse** (German Clock Rd) A 320km loop starting in Villingen-Schwenningen that revolves around the story of clock-making in the Black Forest. Stops include Furtwangen and cuckoo-clock capital Triberg.

- **Grüne Strasse** (Green Rd) Links the Black Forest with the Rhine Valley and the Vosges Mountains in France. Popular with hikers and cyclists, this 160km route takes you through Kirchzarten, Freiburg, Breisach, Colmar and Munster.

Baden-Baden is on a major north–south rail corridor. Twice-hourly destinations include Freiburg (€17.80 to €27, 45 to 90 minutes) and Karlsruhe (€9.50 to €14.50, 15 to 30 minutes).

Getting Around

BUS

Stadtwerke Baden-Baden (☎ 2771; www.stadtwerke -baden-baden.de) run local buses that cost €1.60/2.10/4.70 for a one-zone/two-zone/24-hour ticket. A three-zone day pass for up to five people is €7.10.

Bus 201 (every 10 minutes) and other lines link the Bahnhof with Leopoldsplatz. Bus 205 links the Bahnhof with the airport from Monday to Friday.

CAR & MOTORCYCLE

The centre is mostly pedestrianised, so it's best to park and walk. There is a free parking lot north of the centre on Schlossstrasse, close to the Neues Schloss.

Michaelstunnel on the D500 routes traffic away from the centre, ducking underground west of the Festspielhaus and resurfacing just south of the Russische Kirche.

FREUDENSTADT

☎ 07441 / pop 23,700

Duke Friedrich I of Württemberg built a new capital here in 1599, which was bombed to bits in WWII. The upshot is that Freudenstadt's underwhelming centre is offset by its striking Black Forest location and myriad outdoor pursuits. Statistic lovers will delight in ticking off Germany's biggest square (216m by 219m, for the record), dislocated by a T-junction of heavily trafficked roads. Freudenstadt's saucier claim to fame is as the home of the country's first naturist hotel: tan obligatory, clothing *verboten*.

Orientation & Information

Freudenstadt's focal point is the Marktplatz on the B28. The town has two train stations: the Stadtbahnhof, five minutes' walk north of Marktplatz, and the Hauptbahnhof, 2km southeast of Marktplatz at the end of Bahnhofstrasse. The bus station is outside the Stadtbahnhof.

ATMs There are several on the Marktplatz.

Post office (Marktplatz 64)

Tourist office (☎ 8640; www.freudenstadt.de; Marktplatz 64; ☷ 9am-6pm Mon-Fri, 10am-2pm Sat, Sun May-Sep, 10am-5pm Mon-Fri, 10am-1pm Sat, 11am-1pm Sun Oct-Apr) Has an internet terminal (€6 per hour). Hotel reservations are free.

Sights & Activities

At the heart of Freudenstadt, the sprawling, arcaded **Marktplatz** harbours rows of shops, cafes with alfresco seating and a **playground**.

In the southwest corner looms the 17th-century red-sandstone **Stadtkirche** (☷ 10am-5pm), a potpourri of styles, with an ornate 12th-century Cluniac-style **baptismal** font, Gothic windows, Renaissance portals and baroque towers. The two naves are at right angles to each other, an unusual design by the geometrically minded duke.

The glass-fronted **Panorama-Bad** (☎ 921 300; www.panorama-bad.de, in German; Ludwig-Jahn-Strasse 60; adult/6-17yr all day €9.30/8, incl sauna €14.20/10.90; ☷ 9am-10pm Mon-Sat, 9am-8pm Sun) is a relaxation magnet with pools, steam baths and saunas.

While you won't linger for Freudenstadt's sights, the deep forested valleys on its fringes are well worth exploring. Scenic **hiking trails** include a 12km uphill walk to Kniebis on the Schwarzwald-Hochstrasse, where there are superb Kinzig Valley views. Ask the tourist office for details and maps.

Slip into the saddle of a **mountain bike** to tackle routes like the 85km Kinzigtal-Radweg, taking in dreamy landscapes and half-timbered villages, or the 60km Murgtal-Radweg over hill and dale to Rastatt. Both valleys have bike trails and it's possible to return to Freudenstadt by train. **Intersport Glaser** (☎ 918 590; Katherinenstrasse 8), 300m north of Marktplatz, hires mountain bikes for €14 per day.

Sleeping & Eating

There's a hotel board with a free phone outside the tourist office.

Camping Langenwald (☎ 2862; www.camping -langenwald.de; Strasburger Strasse 167; per person/tent/car €6.50/5/3; ☷ Easter-1 Nov) A Rolls-Royce of a campsite, this foresty hideaway has leafy pitches, a nature trail, solar-heated pool and barbecue area. It's 2km from Freudenstadt and served by bus 12 to Kniebis.

Hotel Adler (☎ 915 20; www.adler-fds.de; Forststrasse 15-17; s €42-49, d €68-86; **P**) The Gaiser family extend a warm welcome at this guesthouse with large, comfy rooms, a lounge with free

---

FREUDENSTADT'S FULL MONTY

You can leave your hat on and guard your towel like a hygiene hawk, but otherwise it's birthday suits only at Freudenstadt's soon-to-be naturist hotel, a first in Germany. To the delight of some and disgust of others, **Hotel Rosengarten** (www.naturisten-hotel.de, in German), a former walking hotel, is set to be born again as the stark-naked Black Forest capital of *Freikörperkultur* (FKK; free body culture), with a balmy year-round temperature of 26°C. After stripping gleefully at the reception, guests must obey strict house rules, namely no dangly bits on lounges, sneaky snapshots or public displays of sleaziness. For the last, the punishment is being made to don clothes – oh the shame! – and leave the hotel.

---

tea and a terrace. The bistro (mains €8 to €17) downstairs serves Swabian faves like *Spätzle* (egg noodles).

Hotel Schwanen (☎ 915 50; www.schwanen-freuden stadt.de, in German; Forststrasse 6; s €35-49, d €84-106; ☞) Don't judge this place by its 1970s-style reception, as the rooms are modern with wi-fi. The restaurant (mains €8.50 to €15.50) is famous for its *Riesenpfannkuchen* (giant pancakes).

Turmbräu (☎ 905 121; Marktplatz 64; mains €7-16; ☷ 10am-1am, to 3am Fri & Sat) Stop by this barn-style microbrewery and beer garden for a party vibe, Turmbräu brews (a 5L barrel costs €12.50) and filling grub like pork knuckles and *Maultaschen*.

Getting There & Away

Trains on the Ortenau rail line, serving Offenburg and Strasbourg, depart hourly from the Hauptbahnhof and are covered by the 24-hour Europass. The pass represents excellent value, costing €9.70 for individuals and €15.40 for families. The hourly Murgtalbahn goes to Karlsruhe (€15.20, 1½ hours) from the Stadtbahnhof and Hauptbahnhof.

Freudenstadt marks the southern end of the **Schwarzwald-Hochstrasse** and is a terminus of the gorgeous **Schwarzwald-Tälerstrasse** (see boxed text, p447), which runs from Rastatt via Alpirsbach.

KINZIGTAL

The horseshoe-shaped Kinzigtal (Kinzig Valley) begins south of Freudenstadt and shadows the burbling Kinzig River south to Schiltach, west to Haslach and north to Offenburg. Near Strasbourg, 95km downriver, the Kinzig is eventually swallowed up by the mighty Rhine. The valley's inhabitants survived for centuries on mining and shipping goods by raft.

Lush hills and woodlands that tumble artistically down to half-timbered villages stir the soul in this beautiful valley. The orchards are awash with almond and cherry blossom in spring, while the terraced vineyards flush crimson and gold in autumn.

GETTING THERE & AWAY

The B294 follows the Kinzig from Freudenstadt to Haslach, from where the B33 leads north to Offenburg. If you're going south, pick up the B33 to Triberg and beyond in Hausach.

The hourly Kinzigtal rail line links Freudenstadt's Hauptbahnhof with Offenburg (€13.30, 1¼ hours), stopping in Alpirsbach (€2.85, 16 minutes), Schiltach (€5.10, 27 minutes), Hausach (€6.90, 46 minutes), Haslach (€8.40, 52 minutes), and Gengenbach (€11.30, 65 minutes). From Hausach, trains run roughly hourly southeast to Triberg (€5.10, 22 minutes), Villingen (€10.30, 47 minutes) and Konstanz (€25, two hours).

Alpirsbach

☎ 07444 / pop 7000

Lore has it that Alpirsbach is named after a quaffing cleric who, when a glass of beer slipped clumsily from his hand and rolled into the river, exclaimed: *All Bier ist in den Bach!* (All the beer is in the stream!). A prophecy, it seems, as today Alpirsbacher Klosterbräu is brewed from pure spring water. **Brewery tours** (☎ 671 49; Marktplatz 1; tours €6.50; ☷ 2.30pm daily) are in German, though guides may speak English. Two beers are thrown in for the price of a ticket.

A few paces north, you can watch chocolate being made and scoff delectable beer-filled pralines at **Schau-Confiserie Heinzelmann** (☎ 1599; Ambrosius-Blarer-Platz; ☷ 9am-noon & 2-6pm Mon-Fri, to 5pm Sat).

All the more evocative for its lack of adornment, the 11th-century former Benedictine

Kloster Alpirsbach (☎ 951 6281; www.schloesser
-und-gaerten.de; Klosterplatz 1; adult/concession €4/3.30;
☒ 10am-5.30pm Mon-Sat mid-Mar–Oct, 1-3.30pm Thu, Sat
& Sun Nov–mid-Mar) sits opposite. The monastery
effectively conveys the simple, spiritual life in
its flat-roofed church, spartan cells and Gothic
cloister, which hosts candlelit **concerts** (www
.kreuzgangkonzerte.de, in German) from June to August.
It's amazing what you can find under the floorboards, as the museum reveals with its stash of
16th-century clothing, caricatures (of artistic
scholars) and lines (of misbehaving ones).

The **tourist office** (☎ 951 6281; www.stadt-alpirsbach
.de, in German; Hauptstrasse 20; ☒ 10am-noon & 2-5pm
Mon-Fri, closed Wed afternoon) next to the train station can supply hiking maps and, for cyclists,
information on the 84km Kinzigtalradweg
from Offenburg to Lossburg.

Schiltach

☎ 07836 / pop 4000

Schiltach looks and feels like something out
of a children's fairy story, nestling below thick
forest and hugging the banks of the Kinzig
and Schiltach Rivers. The lovingly restored
half-timbered houses, which once belonged to
tanners, merchants and raft builders, are a riot
of crimson geraniums in summer. Drop off
the map for a spell to unwind in what is, perhaps, the fairest village in the Kinzig Valley.

INFORMATION

The **tourist office** (☎ 5850; www.schiltach.de;
Marktplatz 6; ☒ 9am-noon & 2-5pm Mon-Thu, 9am-noon
Fri) in the Rathaus can help find accom-
modation and offers free internet access.
Hiking options are marked on an enamel
sign just opposite.

SIGHTS & ACTIVITIES

Centred on a trickling fountain, the sloping, triangular **Marktplatz** is Schiltach at its
picture-book best. The frescoes of the step-
gabled, 16th-century **Rathaus** opposite depict
scenes from local history. Clamber south
up **Schlossbergstrasse**, pausing to notice the
plaques that denote the trades of one-time
residents, such as the *Strumpfstricker* (stocking weaver) at No 6, and the sloping roofs
where tanners once dried their skins. Up top
there are views over Schiltach's red rooftops
to the surrounding hills.

Museum am Markt (☎ 5875; Marktplatz 13; admission
free; ☒ 11am-5pm Apr-Oct) romps through local
history with exhibits from antique spinning

wheels to Biedermeier costumes. The highlight is an interactive display on the devilish
Teufel von Schiltach, a woman accused of
witchcraft and of starting a devastating fire
in 1533.

Schiltach is at the confluence of the **Kinzig**
and **Schiltach Rivers**. Until the 19th century,
logging was big business here and enormous
rafts were constructed to ship timber as far
as the Netherlands. The **Schüttesäge Museum**
(☎ 5850; Hauptstrasse 1; admission free; ☒ 11am-5pm Tue-
Sun Apr-Oct) spotlights Schiltach's raft-building
heritage with reconstructed workshops and a
watermill that generates hydroelectricity. The
willow-fringed riverbanks outside attract grey
herons and kids who come to splash in the
shallow water in summer.

SLEEPING & EATING

The Altstadt has some first-rate places to stay
and eat.

Campingplatz Schiltach (☎ 7289; Bahnhofstrasse
6; per person/tent/car €4/3.50/2.50) The affable Brede
family runs this riverside campsite. Tots can
let off steam in the playground and sandpit.

Gasthof Sonne (☎ 957 570; Marktplatz 3; s €42.50-
50, d €72-80) So is it to be the rose-tinged love
nest or the knight's chamber with shining
armour? Pick a room to suit your mood at
this half-timbered guesthouse. The restaurant
(mains €8 to €14.50) serves Swabian fare like
Katzagschroi (beef, onions, egg and fried potatoes); the name refers to the cat's whine when
it finds no leftovers in the kitchen.

ourpick **Weysses Rössle** (☎ 387; www.weysses
-roessle.de; Schenkenzeller Strasse 42; s/d €49.50/74;
P ☐ ☎) Rosemarie and Ulrich are the 19th
generation to run this 16th-century inn.
Rosewood and floral fabrics dress the country-
style rooms, featuring snazzy bathrooms and
free wi-fi. Portraits of great-grandparents
beam down from the walls in the woodsy tavern (mains €10 to €21), where you can tuck
into Baden snail soup or dark-beer roast.

Gutach

☎ 07831 / pop 2300

Well worth the 4km detour south of the Kinzig
Valley, the **Schwarzwälder Freilichtmuseum** (Black
Forest Open-Air Museum; ☎ 935 60; www.vogtsbauernhof.org;
adult/6-17yr/concession/family €6/3/5/13; ☒ 9am-6pm
late Mar-early Nov, to 7pm Aug) spirals around the
Vogtsbauernhof, a self-contained, early-17th-
century farmstead. Farmhouses shifted from
their original locations have been painstak-

BEHOLD THE SUPER BOG

If giant cuckoo clocks and Black Forest cherry cake no longer thrill, how about a trip to the world's largest loo? Drive a couple of minutes south of Gutach on the B33 to Hornberg and there, in all its lavatorial glory, stands the titanic toilet dreamed up by Philippe Starck. Even if you have no interest in designer urinals or home jacuzzis, it's worth visiting the **Duravit Design Centre** (☎ 07833-700; www.duravit.de, in German; Werderstrasse 36, Hornberg; ⏱ 8am-7pm Mon-Fri, noon-4pm Sat) alone for the tremendous view across the Black Forest from the 12m-high ceramic loo.

---

ingly reconstructed, using techniques such as thatching and panelling, to create this authentic farming hamlet and preserve age-old Black Forest traditions.

Explore barns filled with wagons and horn sleds, *Rauchküchen* (kitchens for smoking fish and meat) and the **Hippenseppenhof** (1599) with its eye-catching crucifix, chapel and massive hipped roof constructed from 400 trees. It's a great place for families, with inquisitive farmyard animals to pet, artisans on hand to explain their crafts, and frequent demonstrations from sheep shearing to butter making.

The self-controlled bobs of the **Schwarzwald Rodelbahn** (☎ 965 580; www.schwarzwaldrodelbahn.de; Singersbach 4; adult/child €2.50/2; ⏱ 9am-8pm Apr-Oct, 9am-5pm Nov-Mar), 1.5km north of Gutach, are faster than they look. Lay off the breaks for extra speed.

Haslach

☎ 07832 / pop 7000

Back in the Kinzig Valley, Haslach's 17th-century former Capuchin monastery lodges the **Schwarzwälder Trachtenmuseum** (Black Forest Costume Museum; ☎ 706 172; Im Alten Kapuzinerkloster; admission €2; ⏱ 9am-5pm Tue-Sat, 10am-5pm Sun Apr–mid-Oct, 9am-noon & 1-5pm Tue-Fri mid-Oct–Mar), showcasing flamboyant costumes and outrageous hats, the must-have accessories for the well-dressed *Fräulein* of the 1850s. Look out for the Black Forest *Bollenhut*, a straw bonnet topped with pompons (red for unmarried women, black for married) and the Schäppel, a fragile-looking crown made from hundreds of beads and weighing up to 5kg.

Gengenbach

☎ 07803 / pop 11,100

If ever a Black Forest town could be described as chocolate box, it would surely be Gengenbach, with its scrumptious Altstadt of half-timbered town houses framed by vineyards and orchards. It's fitting, then, that director Tim Burton made this the home of gluttonous Augustus Gloop in the 2005 blockbuster *Charlie and the Chocolate Factory*, though less so that he called it Düsseldorf.

INFORMATION

The **tourist office** (☎ 930 143; www.stadt-gengenbach.de; Im Winzerhof; ⏱ 9am-12.30pm & 1.30-5pm Mon-Fri Sep-Jun, no midday closure Jul & Aug, also 10am-noon Sat May-Oct), is in a courtyard just off Hauptstrasse.

SIGHTS & ACTIVITIES

The best way to discover Gengenbach's historic centre is with a saunter through its narrow backstreets, such as the gently curving **Engelgasse**, off Hauptstrasse, lined with listed half-timbered houses draped in vines and bedecked with scarlet geraniums.

Between the town's two tower-topped gates sits the triangular **Marktplatz**, dominated by the **Rathaus**, an 18th-century, pink and cream confection. The **fountain** bears a statue of a knight, a symbol of Gengenbach's medieval status as a Free Imperial City.

Amble east along Klosterstrasse to spy the former **Benedictine monastery**. Right opposite, the stuck-in-time **Holzofen-Bäckerei Klostermühle** (☎ 3618 Klosterstrasse 7) fills the lanes with wafts of freshly baked bread from its wood-fired oven. Buy a loaf to munch in the calm **Kräutergarten** (Herb Garden; Benedikt-von-Nursia-Strasse), behind the monastery walls, or stroll east to the flowery **park**.

The tourist office has info on the hour-long **Weinpfad**, a wine trail beginning in the Altstadt that threads through terraced vineyards to the Jakobskapelle, a 13th-century chapel commanding views that reach as far as Strasbourg on clear days. The free, lantern-lit **Nachtwächterrundgang** (night watchman's tour) starts at the Rathaus on Wednesday and Saturday at 10pm from May to July and at 9pm from August to October.

SLEEPING & EATING

The Marktplatz and Hauptstrasse are peppered with cafes, pizzerias and *Weinstuben* (wine taverns).

CHRISTMAS COUNTDOWN

Every December, Gengenbach rekindles (and supersizes) childhood memories of opening tiny windows when the Rathaus morphs into the world's biggest **advent calendar**. You can sense the anticipation on the Marktplatz at 6pm daily, when one of the 24 windows is opened to reveal a festive scene. The tableaux are painted by artists or children's-book illustrators such as Tomi Ungerer. From 13 to 23 December, a Christmas market brings extra yuletide sparkle, mulled wine and carols to the Marktplatz. You can admire the calendar until Epiphany (6th January).

DJH hostel (☎ 0781-317 49; www.jugendherberge -schloss-ortenberg.de; Burgweg 21; dm €20; **P** **☐**) The Hogwarts gang would feel at home in 12th-century Schloss Ortenberg, rebuilt in whimsical neo-Gothic style complete with lookout tower and wood-panelled dining hall. A staircase sweeps up to dorms with Kinzig Valley views. Take bus 7134 to Ortenberger Hof, 500m from the hostel.

Pfeffer & Salz (☎ 934 80; www.pfefferundsalz -gengenbach.de, in German; Mattenhofweg 3; s €46-50, d €70-74; **P**) This forest farmhouse is a peaceful hideaway 10 minutes' stroll north of the Altstadt. The modern rooms are quite a bargain, jazzed up with warm colours and flat-screen TVs.

Winzerstüble (☎ 3636; Hauptstrasse 18; Flammkuchen €6.50-9) Jostle for a courtyard table at this convivial wine tavern next to the tourist office. The crisp *Flammkuchen* goes well with local Müller-Thurgau and riesling wines.

SOUTHERN BLACK FOREST

The Southern Black Forest is like a landscape painting come to life. Tucked into the folds of vividly green valleys are wood-shingled farmhouses silhouetted by hazy hills that ripple off into a watercolour distance. Add cow-grazed meadows, forests bristling with fir and pine trees and gemstone lakes to the canvas and you're looking at quite the sylvan masterpiece.

The conservation-oriented, 370,000-hectare **Naturpark Südschwarzwald** (Southern Black Forest Nature Park; www.naturpark-suedschwarzwald .de) spans most of the region, home to vivacious university city Freiburg and medieval Villingen, Breisach's undulating vineyards and the Black Forest's highest peak Feldberg (1493m).

Getting Around
Various public-transport groupings offer extensive, reasonably priced bus and rail links throughout the Southern Black Forest. See p457 for details. Plan your journey with the help of www.efa-bw.de.

FREIBURG
☎ 0761 / pop 213,000
Freiburg is a story-book tableau of gabled town houses, narrow lanes and cobbled squares, given its happy-ever-after by some 22,000 students who add an injection of cool, a love of alfresco dining and attitude-free nightlife to the medieval mix. Crouching at the foot of wooded hills, Freiburg's scenery is pure Black Forest, but its spirit is deliciously southern.

Blessed with 2000 hours of annual sunshine, this is Germany's warmest city. Indeed while neighbouring hilltop villages are still shovelling snow, the trees in Freiburg are clouds of white blossom, and locals are already quaffing in canalside beer gardens or firing up the barbecue. This eco-trailblazer has shrewdly tapped into that natural energy to generate nearly as much solar power as the whole of Britain, making it one of the country's greenest cities.

Orientation
The Altstadt's focal point, two blocks southwest of the Münster, is the intersection of Kaiser-Joseph-Strasse, the centre's main north–south artery. About 600m west is the Hauptbahnhof and bus station, which define the western edge of the Altstadt. The Dreisam River runs along the Altstadt's southern edge.

Information
Herder (☎ 282 820; Kaiser-Joseph-Strasse 180; ⏲ 9.30am-7pm Mon-Sat) Stocks foreign-language books and maps.
Planet Internet Café (Kartäuserstrasse 6; per hr €1.80; ⏲ 9am-midnight Mon-Sat, 11am-midnight Sun) Internet, discount calls, cakes and Turkish tea.

Police station (Rotteckring)
Post office (Eisenbahnstrasse 58-62)
Tee-Online (Grünwälderstrasse 19; per hr €3.50;
🕑 10am-10pm Mon-Sat, noon-8pm Sun) Hip cafe with
speedy internet, wi-fi and free tea.
Tourist office (☎ 388 1880; www.freiburg.de;
Rathausplatz 2-4; 🕑 8am-8pm Mon-Fri, 9.30am-5pm
Sat, 10am-noon Sun Jun-Sep, 8am-6pm Mon-Fri, 9.30am-
2.30pm Sat, 10am-noon Sun Oct-May) Well stocked with
1:50,000-scale cycling maps (€6.95) and the useful booklet
Freiburg – Official Guide (€4).
Wash & Tours (Salzstrasse 22; per hr €3, laundry per
machine €4.50; 🕑 9am-7pm Mon-Sat) A self-service
laundry and internet cafe.

Sights
MÜNSTER
Freiburg's Gothic **Münster** is the monster of all
minsters, a red-sandstone giant that dwarfs
the bustling Münsterplatz, with a riot of
punctured spires that flush scarlet at dusk.
Crane your neck to notice the leering **gargoyles**, including a mischievous one on the
southern flank that once spouted water from
its backside.

The **main portal** is adorned with sculptures depicting Old and New Testament
scenes – note allegorical figures such as
Voluptuousness (the one with snakes on her
back) and Satan himself. Nearby are medieval wall markings once used to ensure that
merchandise (eg loaves of bread) were of the
requisite size.

Square at the base, the sturdy tower becomes an octagon higher up and is crowned by
a filigreed 116m-high spire. Ascend 209 steps
to the **tower** (adult/student €1.50/1; 🕑 9.30am-5pm Mon-
Sat, 1-5pm Sun) for views that reach as far as the
Vosges Mountains in France on a clear day.

Inside the Münster, the kaleidoscopic
stained-glass windows are dazzling. Many were
financed by guilds – in the bottom panels
look for a pretzel, scissors and other symbols
of medieval trades. The high altar features a
masterful triptych of the coronation of the
Virgin Mary by Hans Baldung.

SOUTH OF THE MÜNSTER
Facing the Münster's south side and embellished with polychrome tiled turrets is the
arcaded brick-red **Historisches Kaufhaus**, a 16th-
century merchants' hall. The coats of arms
on the oriels and the four figures above the
balcony symbolise Freiburg's allegiance to
the House of Habsburg.

The sculptor Christian Wentzinger's baroque town house, east of the Kaufhaus, now
shelters the **Museum für Stadtgeschichte** (City
History Museum; ☎ 201 2515; Münsterplatz 30; adult/con-
cession €2/1; 🕑 10am-5pm Tue-Sun), spelling out in
artefacts Freiburg's eventful past. Inside a
wrought-iron staircase guides the eye to an
elaborate ceiling fresco.

Tiptoe south to Augustinerplatz where
the **Augustinermuseum**, housed in a former
monastery, is set to reopen in 2010. The
collection comprises paintings by Matthias
Grünewald and Cranach and a prized
collection of medieval stained glass.

Across the Gewerbekanal, the **Museum
für Neue Kunst** (Museum of Modern Art; ☎ 201 2583;
Marienstrasse 10; adult/concession €2/1; 🕑 10am-5pm
Tue-Sun) highlights 20th-century expressionist
and abstract art, including emotive works by
Oskar Kokoschka and Otto Dix.

A canal babbles west through the charming former fishing quarter of **Fischerau** to
Martinstor (Kaiser-Joseph-Strasse), one of Freiburg's
two surviving town gates, and, slightly north,
Bertoldsbrunnen fountain, which marks where
the city's thoroughfares have crossed since its
foundation in 1091.

Veering east of the Museum für Neue
Kunst brings you to the 13th-century city
gate **Schwabentor**, emblazoned with a mural
of St George slaying the dragon. Trails nearby
twist up to the forested **Schlossberg**, topped
by the **Aussichtsturm**, a lookout tower that's

BADEN-WÜRTTEMBERG

STREETS WORTH SHOPPING

Shoppers find a lot to like about Freiburg's
meandering streets, packed with boutiques and big-name stores. Trams rattle along **Kaiser-Joseph-Strasse** and
Bertoldstrasse, where high-street and
department stores gather. Explore
Schusterstrasse and **Rathausgasse** for
art, jewellery and classic fashion, or amble
east to **Oberlinden** and **Konviktstrasse**
for crafts, delis and antique shops. Edging
south, the quaint lanes of **Gerberau**,
Fischerau and **Marienstrasse** are great
for a lazy mooch, sprinkled with cute boutiques and speciality stores selling everything from hand-crafted ceramics and toys
to chocolate, honey and footwear.

shaped like an ice-cream cone, and commands panoramic views.

WESTERN ALTSTADT

The chestnut-shaded **Rathausplatz** is a popular hang-out. On its western side, the **Neues Rathaus** (New City Hall) comprises two Renaissance town houses with arcades that lead through to a cobblestone courtyard. The tower's tinkling **carillon** plays at noon daily.

Linked to the Neues Rathaus by an over-the-street bridge is the step-gabled, oxblood-red **Altes Rathaus** (Old City Hall; 1559), which shelters the tourist office. Freiburg's oldest edifice, the early 14th-century **Gerichtslaube**, is a short hop west along Turmstrasse.

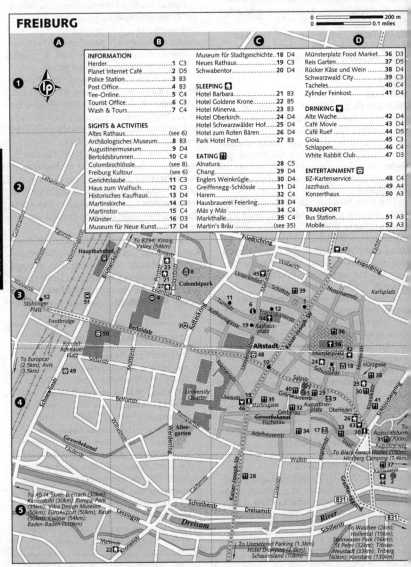

FREIBURG

0 — 200 m
0 — 0.1 miles

INFORMATION	
Herder	1 C3
Planet Internet Café	2 D5
Police Station	3 B3
Post Office	4 C4
Tee-Online	5 D5
Tourist Office	6 C3
Wash & Tours	7 C4

SIGHTS & ACTIVITIES	
Altes Rathaus	(see 6)
Archäologisches Museum	8 B3
Augustinermuseum	9 D4
Bertoldsbrunnen	10 C4
Colombischlössle	(see 8)
Freiburg Kultour	(see 6)
Gerichtslaube	11 C3
Haus zum Walfisch	12 C3
Historisches Kaufhaus	13 D4
Martinskirche	14 C4
Martinstor	15 C4
Münster	16 D3
Museum für Neue Kunst	17 D4

Museum für Stadtgeschichte	18 D4
Neues Rathaus	19 C3
Schwabentor	20 D4

SLEEPING	
Hotel Barbara	21 B3
Hotel Goldene Krone	22 B5
Hotel Minerva	23 B3
Hotel Oberkirch	24 D4
Hotel Schwarzwälder Hof	25 D4
Hotel zum Roten Bären	26 D4
Park Hotel Post	27 B3

EATING	
Alnatura	28 C5
Chang	29 D4
Englers Weinkrügle	30 D4
Greiffenegg-Schlössle	31 D4
Harem	32 C4
Hausbrauerei Feierling	33 D4
Más y Más	34 C4
Markthalle	35 C4
Martin's Bräu	(see 35)

Münsterplatz Food Market	36 D3
Reis Garten	37 D5
Rücker Käse und Wein	38 D4
Schwarzwald City	39 C3
Tacheles	40 C4
Zylinder Feinkost	41 D4

DRINKING	
Alte Wache	42 D4
Café Movie	43 D4
Café Ruef	44 D5
Gioia	45 C3
Schlappen	46 C4
White Rabbit Club	47 D3

ENTERTAINMENT	
BZ-Kartenservice	48 C4
Jazzhaus	49 A4
Konzerthaus	50 A3

TRANSPORT	
Bus Station	51 A3
Mobile	52 A3

COLD FEET OR WEDDED BLISS?

Freiburg is made for serendipitous strolls. Streets that will have you grappling for the digital camera include the wisteria-draped **Konviktstrasse**, punctuated by 15th-century town houses harbouring antique shops and wine bars. Nowhere is Freiburg's medieval past more tangible than in the canalside **Fischerau** and **Gerberau**, the former fishing and tanning quarters, where the cobbled lanes are lined with one-of-a-kind galleries, alfresco cafes and beer gardens. On balmy days, the banks of the **Dreisam River** attract inline skaters, cyclists and picnickers.

As you wander the mostly pedestrianised Altstadt, watch out for the gurgling **Bächle**, streamlets once used to water livestock and extinguish fires. Today they provide welcome relief for hot feet on sweltering summer days. Just be aware that you could get more than you bargained for: legend has it that if you accidentally step into the *Bächle*, you'll marry a Freiburger or a Freiburgerin. Keep an eye out, too, for the cheerful pavement **mosaics** in front of many shops – a cow is for a butcher, a pretzel for a baker, a diamond marks a jewellery shop, and so on.

The medieval **Martinskirche**, once part of a Franciscan monastery, demands attention on the northern side of Rathausplatz. Across the street on Franziskanergasse is its architectural antithesis, the extravagant **Haus zum Walfisch** (House of the Whale), whose late-Gothic oriel is garnished with two impish gargoyles.

In a sculpture-dotted park further west sits the neo-Gothic **Colombischlössle** villa, housing the **Archäologisches Museum** (Archaeology Museum; ☎ 201 2571; www.museen.freiburg.de, in German; Rotteckring 5; adult/concession €2/1; ☾ 10am-5pm Tue-Sun). A cast-iron staircase leads to a stash of archaeological finds from Celtic grave offerings to Roman artefacts.

Tours

Freiburg Kultour (☎ 290 7447; www.freiburg-kultour.com; Rathausplatz 2-4), based in the tourist office, where tours start, offers 1½- to two-hour **walking tours** (adult/12-18yr €7/6; ☾ 10.30am Mon-Fri & 10am Sat Apr-Oct, 10am Sat & 10.30am Sun Nov-Mar) of the Altstadt and the Münster in German and English.

Fahrradtaxi (☎ 0172-768 4370; ☾ mid-Apr–Oct) charges €6.50 for a 15-minute, two-person spin of the Altstadt in a pedicab. Call ahead or look for one on Rathausplatz or Münsterplatz.

Sleeping

Charismatic hotels abound in the Altstadt, but it's wise to book ahead in summer. The tourist office offers a booking service (€3) and has a list of good-value private guesthouses.

Hirzberg Camping (☎ 350 54; www.freiburg-camping.de; Kartäuserstrasse 99; per person/tent €7/5; ☾ year-round) Pitch a tent at this quiet meadow campsite, where facilities include bike rental, a cafe and a laundry. Take tram 1 to Stadthalle, walk north and cross the river.

ourpick Black Forest Hostel (☎ 881 7870; www.blackforest-hostel.de; Kartäuserstrasse 33; dm €13-22, s €29, d €48; ☐) Groove is in the heart of these cheerful backpacker digs, housed in a revamped factory five minutes' walk from the Altstadt. Reggae tunes, a well-equipped kitchen, and instruments for strumming add to the sociable vibe. The space-age showers are something else. Bike hire costs €5 per day.

Hotel Dionysos (☎ 293 53; www.hoteldionysos.de, in German; Hirschstrasse 2, Günterstal; d with shower €45, s/d with basin €28/40) For no-frills, spotless rooms, this hotel with a Greek restaurant is a good deal. It's an easy 3km ride south of the Altstadt to streamside Günterstal on tram line 4.

Hotel Goldene Krone (☎ 137 6083; www.hotelpension-goldene-krone.de, in German; Mattenstrasse 2a; s/d €49/71; ☐P) A friendly pick 10 minutes' walk from the centre, this hotel has comfortable if poky rooms with parquet floors.

Hotel Schwarzwälder Hof (☎ 380 30; www.schwarzwaelder-hof.eu; Herrenstrasse 43; s €45-70, d €75-105; ☐) Down the cobbled lane and up the wrought-iron staircase lie well-kept quarters. Choose between 'basic' (but rather nice) and 'modern' rooms with dark-wood floors, flat-screen TVs and Altstadt views. The rustic tavern (mains €8.80 to €16.50) serves regional fare and wines.

Hotel Barbara (☎ 296 250; www.hotel-barbara.de; Poststrasse 4; s €79-95, d €98-119; ☎) A grandfather clock, curvy staircases and high ceilings give this art-nouveau town house a nostalgic feel. It's a homely, family-run place with old-fashioned rooms and free wi-fi.

Hotel Minerva (☎ 386 490; www.minerva-freiburg.de, in German; Poststrasse 8; s €75-90, d €105-115) Up front the Minerva is all art-nouveau flair with arched windows and polished wood. Rooms are run-of-the-mill by comparison, though immaculate and comfy. There's a small sauna and free wi-fi.

Hotel Oberkirch (☎ 202 6868; www.hotel-oberkirch.de; Münsterplatz 22; s €95-118, d €139-161; P ☐) Our readers sing the praises of this green-shuttered, 250-year-old hotel, with the Münster views of a million postcards. The countrified rooms reveal a Laura Ashley love of florals and bathrooms positively sparkle.

Park Hotel Post (☎ 385 480; www.park-hotel-post.de; Am Colombipark 63; s €109-139, d €129-189; P ☐) Slip back to the more graceful age of art nouveau at this refined pile overlooking Colombipark, with summery rooms decorated in pastel blues and yellows. Attentive service and generous breakfasts sweeten the deal.

Hotel zum Roten Bären (☎ 387 870; www.roter -baeren.de; Oberlinden 12; s €110-125, d €152-172; P ☎) Billed as Germany's oldest guesthouse, this frescoed hotel near Schwabentor creaks under the weight of its 900-year history. The vaulted cellar is medieval, while the rooms are modern with sleek wood furnishings and wi-fi.

Eating

Freiburg is a festive town that enjoys eating out, preferably outdoors. The Altstadt is stacked with cafes, wine taverns, brewpubs and restaurants, many spilling out onto pavement terraces. The euro-conscious find cheap bites on Martinstor and Kartäuserstrasse.

Markthalle (Martinsgasse 235; ☒ 8am-8pm Mon-Thu, 8am-midnight Fri & Sat) A food court whose Mexican, Italian, Indian and French counters offer fast, tasty lunches.

Zylinder Feinkost (☎ 384 2624; Konviktstrasse 51; antipasti plate €8; ☒ 10am-noon & 2-6pm Tue-Thu, 10am-6pm Fri & Sat) Opera plays in this little Italian deli, where Matteo's passion for the minutiae of Chianti and antipasti is contagious. Pull up a stack of crates for a glass of *prosecco* and homemade focaccia with wafer-thin prosciutto.

Harem (☎ 225 33; Gerberau 7c; lunch €5.70, mains €6-9; ☒ 11.30am-midnight) No concubines here, just taste-bud-seducing Turkish specialities, like crispy *börek* (filled pastries) and baklava. Don't miss the original city walls out back.

Chang (☎ 137 9684; Grünwälderstrasse 21; mains €6-9.50; ☒ noon-11pm Mon-Sat, 1-10.30pm Sun) Same, same but different at this Thai restaurant, kissed with gold and scattered with tables inlaid with teak carvings. The curries, pad thai and smiles are as authentic as any you'll find in Bangkok's backstreets.

Reis Garten (☎ 208 8819; Kartäuserstrasse 3; mains €6.90-12.50; ☒ 11.30am-10.30pm Mon-Thu, 11.30am-11.30pm Fri & Sat, 2-10.30pm Sun) This Chinese haunt rolls out the usual suspects from chop suey to crispy duck. Lunch is a steal at €3.90. Sit in the courtyard when it's sunny.

Tacheles (☎ 319 6669; Grünwälderstrasse 17; schnitzel €7.50; ☒ 11.30am-2am Mon-Thu, 11.30am-5am Fri & Sat, 11.30am-1am Sun) Eat schnitzel and be merry is the motto at this laid-back courtyard-bar. On the menu: a mind-boggling 300 varieties of breaded veal. After 11pm, partygoers shuffle over to cave-like Club Daneben for grooving under the glitter balls.

Hausbrauerei Feierling (☎ 243 480; Gerberau 46; mains €7-13; ☒ 11am-midnight, to 1am Fri & Sat; V) Freiburg's best beer garden entices summertime crowds to this microbrewery, serving vegie options and monster-sized schnitzels. Take care not to fall in the stream after one too many or you may become dinner for the open-jawed crocodile.

Englers Weinkrügle (☎ 383 115; Konviktstrasse 12; mains €8-13.50; ☒ 11am-2pm & 5.30pm-midnight Tue-Sun) Wisteria drapes this woody Baden-style *Weinstube*, dishing up flavoursome regional fare like trout in various guises (for instance in riesling or almond-butter sauce).

Martin's Bräu (☎ 387 0018; Fressgässle 1; mains €7.50-16.50; ☒ 11am-midnight, to 2am Fri & Sat; ☎) Chefs whip up ox-tongue salad and half-metre-long bratwursts in the show kitchen of this bustling microbrewery. Such carnivorous fare goes well with home-brewed pilsners.

Más y Más (☎ 514 6022; Adelhauserstrasse 29; mains €10.90-29.90; ☒ noon-midnight) This slinky monochrome bistro is a grown-up choice for Med-inspired dishes, from plump scallops to creamy mozzarella risotto and rose-petal sorbet. The cobbled terrace facing a church is a pleasing spot to sip a glass of something.

Greiffenegg-Schlössle (☎ 327 28; Schlossbergring 3; mains €21-27) This perky hilltop villa tantalises with full-bodied wines and southern flavours like tender lamb with olive polenta. Sunset is primetime viewing on the terrace overlooking Freiburg's blushing red rooftops.

Self-caterers can grab picnic goodies at the following places:

Alnatura (Kaiser-Joseph-Strasse 26) Organic supermarket

Münsterplatz food market (☒ until 1pm Mon-Fri, to 1.30pm Sat) Farmers come to sell local produce. Stalls are particularly numerous and varied on Saturday. Various versions of wurst-in-a-bun (€2), topped with fried onions, are sold here.

Rücker Käse und Wein (Münzgasse 1; ☻ 9am-6.30pm
Mon-Fri, 9am-3pm Sat) For wine and cheese.

Schwarzwald City (Schiffstrasse 5; ☻ 10am-7pm
Mon-Fri, 10am-6pm Sat; ☝) Central shopping mall with
a supermarket, bakery, juice bar and free wi-fi.

Drinking

While folk in neighbouring Black Forest villages are already tucked up in bed, Freiburg's
restless student population keep steins a-
swinging in the beer gardens and bars and
clubs pumping until the wee hours.

Alte Wache (☎ 202 870; Münsterplatz 38; ☻ 10am-
7pm) Taste local Pinot noir wines and gaze
up to the Münster's gargoyles on the cobbled terrace of this 18th-century guardhouse
turned buzzy wine bar.

Café Movie (☎ 382 210; Oberlinden 22; ☻ 11am-
2am Mon-Thu & Sun, to 3am Fri & Sat) Bob Marley and
Che Guevara beam down from the walls at
this chilled-out dive, where the landlord's
love of reggae and big-screen sports shines.

Café Ruef (☎ 336 63; Kartäuserstrasse 2; ☻ 6am-1am
Mon-Sat, 6am-7pm Sun) Mellow and well-worn,
with armchairs for crashing and watching
Fussball, Ruef is a bakery with tasty pies
(around €2) by day and a pub with occasional live music by night.

Gioia (☎ 137 5588; Unterlinden 3; ☻ 9am-midnight
Mon-Fri, to 1am Sat & Sun) This slick Italian bar
has an attractive patio for lingering over a
caipirinha or gelato.

Schlappen (☎ 334 94; Löwenstrasse 2; ☻ 11am-1am
Mon-Thu, 11am-3am Fri & Sat, 3pm-1am Sun) Posters
cover every inch of this funky watering hole,
which attracts a mixed bunch. Some come
for the *Flammkuchen*, some to sample different types of absinthe, and some to check
out the wacky men's urinal – look in the
mirror and watch the water flow…

White Rabbit Club (☎ 590 0628; www.white-rabbit
club.de, in German; Leopoldring 1; ☻ 9pm-2am Tue & Thu,
5pm-2am Wed, 9pm-3am Fri & Sat, 8am-noon Sun) It's
never too late to disappear down this rabbit
hole, a student wonderland of cheap beers,
DJs and gigs. Things get even curiouser at
Wednesday night's open jam sessions.

Entertainment

Get the free listings monthly, *Freiburg Aktuell*,
at hotels and the tourist office.

BZ-Kartenservice (☎ 01805-55 66 56; www.freiburg
ticket.de, in German; Bertoldstrasse 7; ☻ 9am-6pm Mon-Fri,
9am-4pm Sat).

Jazzhaus (☎ 349 73; www.jazzhaus.de, in German;
Schnewlinstrasse 1) Under the brick arches of a
wine cellar, this venue stages first-rate jazz,
rock and hip-hop concerts at 8pm at least
three nights a week. It morphs into a club from
11pm to 3am on Friday and Saturday nights.

Konzerthaus (☎ 388 1552; www.konzerthaus
.freiburg.de; Konrad-Adenauer-Platz 1) A hulking modern concert hall that doubles as a cultural
events centre.

Waldsee (☎ 736 88; www.waldsee-freiburg.de, in
German; Waldseestrasse 84; ☻ 11am-2am Mon-Thu, 11am-
3am Fri & Sat, 10am-1am Sun) This lakeside haunt,
30 minutes' walk south of the Altstadt, hosts
events from jazz sessions to club nights.

Getting There & Around

AIR

Freiburg shares **EuroAirport** (www.euroairport
.com) with Basel (Switzerland) and Mulhouse
(France). Low-cost airlines easyJet and
Ryanair fly to destinations including London,
Berlin, Rome and Alicante from here.

BICYCLE

Bike paths run along the Dreisam River, leading
westward to Breisach and then into France.

Mobile (☎ 292 7996; www.mobile-freiburg.com, in
German; Wentzingerstrasse 15; 4hr/day €8/15; ☻ 9am-6.30pm
Mon-Fri, 10am-4pm Sat), in a glass-enclosed pavilion
across the bridge from the Hauptbahnhof,
rents bikes and sells cycling maps.

BUS

The **Airport Bus** (☎ 500 500; www.freiburger-reisedienst.de)
goes hourly from Freiburg's bus station to
EuroAirport (€20, 55 minutes).

SüdbadenBus (☎ 3680 388 www.suedbadenbus.de,
in German) and **RVF** (☎ 207 280; www.rvf.de, in German)
operate bus and rail links to towns and villages
throughout the southern Black Forest. Single
tickets for one/two/three zones cost €2/3.40/4.80
(half that for children aged six to 14); a 24-hour
Regio24 ticket costs €5/10/10 for one person
and €8.50/17/17 for two to five people.

From Freiburg, bus 1066 travels at 4pm on
weekdays to Haslach, Hausach and Schiltach
(2¼ hours) in the Kinzig Valley. See the town
listings in the Southern Black Forest for other
bus options to/from Freiburg.

Bus and tram travel within Freiburg (www
.vag-freiburg.de) is charged at the one-zone rate.
Buy tickets from the vending machines or
from the driver and validate upon boarding.

BADEN-WÜRTTEMBERG

CAR & MOTORCYCLE

The Frankfurt–Basel A5 passes just west of Freiburg. The scenic B31 leads east through the Höllental to Lake Constance. The B294 goes north into the Black Forest.

Car-hire agencies include **Europcar** (☎ 515 100; Löracherstrasse 10) and **Avis** (☎ 197 19; St-Georgener-Strasse 7).

About 1.5km south of Martinstor, there's unmetered parking on some side streets (eg Türkenlouisstrasse). To get there from the Altstadt drive south on Günterstalstrasse (the southern continuation of Kaiser-Joseph-Strasse).

TRAIN

Freiburg is on a major north–south rail corridor with frequent departures for destinations such as Basel (€14.10 to €21.80, 45 to 65 minutes) and Baden-Baden (€17.80 to €27, 45 minutes to 1½ hours). Freiburg is also the western terminus of the Höllentalbahn to Donaueschingen via Titisee-Neustadt (€4.80, 38 minutes, twice an hour). There's a local connection to Breisach (€4.80, 26 minutes, at least hourly).

AROUND FREIBURG
Schauinsland

Freiburg seems tiny as you drift up above the city and a tapestry of meadows and forest on the 3.6km **Schauinslandbahn** (cable car; adult/6-14yr/concession return €11.50/7/10.50, one-way €8/5/7.50; ☯ 9am-5pm, to 6pm Jul-Sep) to the 1284m **Schauinsland peak** (www.bergwelt-schauinsland.de, in German). The lift provides a speedy link between Freiburg and the Black Forest highlands.

Up top there's a lookout tower commanding astounding views to the Rhine Valley and Alps, plus walking, cross-country and cycling trails that allow you to capture the scenery from many angles. For downhill action, try the bone-shaking 8km off-road **scooter track** (2pm & 5pm Sun May-Jun, Sat & Sun Jul & Sep, Wed-Sun Aug), which costs €18 including equipment hire. To reach Schauinslandbahn from Freiburg, take tram 4 to Günterstal and then bus 21 to Talstation.

ourpick Halde (☎ 07602-944 70; www.halde.com, in German; Oberried-Hofsgrund; s €133-155, d €196-208; P 🖥 🕿) sits pretty above the rippling hills. This Black Forest farmhouse is a chic retreat, with an open fire crackling in the bar, calm rooms dressed in local wood and a glass-walled spa overlooking the valley. Martin Hegar cooks market-fresh dishes from trout to wild boar with panache in the wood-

---

MOVE YOUR ASS

There's nothing like a mule with impeccable eco-credentials to get kids to trade their iPods for the trail for the weekend. The solution? Renting a donkey for a day or two from **Eselwanderungen** (☎ 0761-7075 717; www.eselwanderungen.de, in German; per day €50), near Freiburg/Kirchzarten, to head off into the valleys and woodlands of the southern Black Forest. The donkeys lug the bags, leaving you free to stride and enjoy the glorious scenery – at donkey pace, of course. The friendly owners supply directions and maps, lend you pack saddles and can help organise mule-friendly lodgings. Call or email ahead for details on where and when to pick up your donkey.

---

panelled restaurant (mains €14.50 to €25.50). Great news for foodies: a four-course dinner is included in the room rate.

Steinwasen Park

You'll probably spy the eye-popping, 218m-long hanging bridge before you even reach this **family park** (☎ 07602-944 680; www.steinwasen-park.de; Steinwasen 1, Oberried; adult/4-11yr €18/15 ☯ 9am-6pm May–mid-Sep, 10am-5pm late Mar-Apr & mid-Sep–early Nov). Here woodland trails wriggle past roomy enclosures alive with Black Forest and Alpine animals, such as marmots and nimble-footed chamois. Bouncing on the bridge aside, there's fun to be had on whizzy rides like Gletscherblitz and River Splash.

Todtnauer Wasserfall

Illuminating the forest with its brilliance, and cascading over craggy rock faces, the 97m-tall **waterfall** in Todnau-Aftersteg is not quite as high as its rival in Triberg, but every bit as beautiful, considerably wilder and free. For the best views over the falls, hike the zigzagging 3.5km trail to **Aftersteg**. It sure gets slippery here when the paths freeze over, so take extra care in winter. The car park for the waterfall is on the L126, a 10km detour south of Steinwasen Park.

WEST OF FREIBURG
Breisach
☎ 07667 / pop 14,350

Rising above vineyards and the Rhine Breisach is where the Black Forest spills into Alsace. Given its geographical and cultural proximity to France, it's little surprise that the locals share their neighbours' passion for a good bottle of plonk.

In the cobbled streets lined with pastel-painted houses you'd never guess that 85% of the town was flattened in WWII, so successful has been the reconstruction. Vauban's star-shaped French fortress-town of Neuf-Brisach (New Breisach), which made the Unesco World Heritage list in 2008, sits 4km west of Breisach.

High above the centre, the Romanesque and Gothic **St Stephansmünster** shelters a faded fresco cycle, Martin Schongauer's *The Last Judgment* (1491), and a magnificent altar triptych (1526) carved from linden wood. From the tree-shaded square outside, the Schänzletreppe leads down to **Gutgesellentor**, the gate where Pope John XXIII was scandalously caught fleeing the Council of Constance in 1415.

Boat excursions along the Rhine are run by **BFS** (☎ 942 010; www.bfs-info.de, in German; Rheinuferstrasse; ☼ Apr-Sep); the dock is 500m southwest of the tourist office.

The **tourist office** (☎ 940 155; www.breisach.de; Marktplatz 16; ☼ 9am-12.30pm & 1.30-6pm Mon-Fri, 10am-1pm Sat Apr-Dec, 9am-12.30pm & 1.30-5pm Mon-Fri Jan-Mar) can advise on wine tasting in the area and arrange well-stuffed picnic hampers for €15.

SLEEPING & EATING

You'll find a handful of so-so dining options between Gutgesellentor and the tourist office, plus a supermarket on Bahnhofstrasse opposite the train station.

DJH hostel (☎ 7665; www.jugendherberge-breisach.de; Rheinuferstrasse 12; dm 1st/subsequent night €21.90/18.60) On the banks of the Rhine, this hostel has first-rate facilities, including a barbecue hut, volleyball court and access to the swimming pool next door.

Kapuzinergarten (☎ 9300; www.kapuzinergarten.de; Kapuzinergasse 26; s €61-79, d €77-110; P ☐) Even standard 'monk cell' rooms sport oak-parquet floors, natural lime walls and restored monastic furnishings at this hilltop hotel. An upgrade buys you luxuries like a four-poster bed and balcony. Chef Paul Demarche puts his own stamp on regional cuisine using organic, home-grown ingredients in the rustic restaurant (mains €19.50 to €28.50). The terrace is inviting in summer.

GETTING THERE & AROUND

Breisach's train station, 500m southeast of Marktplatz, serves Freiburg (€4.80, 25 minutes, at least hourly) and towns in the Kaiserstuhl. Buses go to Colmar, 22km west.

Breisach is a terrific base for free-wheeling over borders. Great rides include crossing the Rhine to the delightful French town of Colmar, or pedalling through terraced vineyards to Freiburg. Hire your own set of wheels from **Funbike** (☎ 7733; Metzgergasse 1; 1/3 days €10/25; ☼ 9am-noon or on request) opposite the tourist office.

Kaiserstuhl

Squeezed between the Black Forest and French Vosges, these low-lying **volcanic hills** in the Upper Rhine Valley yield some highly quaffable wines including fruity *Spätburgunder* (Pinot noir) and *Grauburgunder* (Pinot gris) varieties.

The grapes owe their quality to a unique microclimate, hailed as Germany's warmest and sunniest, and fertile loess (clay and silt) soil that retains heat during the night. Nature enthusiasts should keep their peepers open for rarities like sand lizards, praying mantis and European bee-eaters.

The Breisach tourist office can advise on cellar tours, wine tastings, bike paths like the 55km **Kaiserstuhltour** circuit, and trails such as the **Winzerweg** (Wine Growers' Trail), an intoxicating 15km hike from Achkarren to Riegel.

The **Kaiserstuhlbahn** does a loop around the Kaiserstuhl. Stops (where you may have to change trains) include Sasbach, Endingen, Riegel and Gottenheim.

Europa-Park

Germany's largest **theme park** (☎ 01805-776 688; www.europapark.de; adult/4-14yr €34/30; ☼ 9am-6pm early Apr-early Nov & early Dec-early Jan, later in peak season), 35km north of Freiburg near Rust, is Europe in miniature. Get soaked fjord-rafting in Scandinavia before nipping across to Atlantis in Greece. Thrill-seekers are hurtled from zero to 100km in 2.5 seconds on the new adrenalin-loaded Blue Fire roller-coaster in Iceland, while Welt der Kinder pleases tots with gentle rides. Europa-Park even has its own mousy mascot, Euromaus.

Shuttle buses (hourly in the morning) link Ringsheim train station, on the Freiburg-Offenburg line, with the park. By car, take the A5 to Herbolzheim (exit 58).

Vitra Design Museum

Sharp angles contrast with graceful swoops and swirls on Frank Gehry's strikingly postmodern **Vitra Design Museum** (☎ 07621-702 3200; www.design-museum.de; Charles-Eames-Strasse 1; adult/concession €8/6.50; ☒ 10am-6pm, to 8pm Wed). The blindingly white edifice hosts thought-provoking contemporary design exhibitions. Buildings on the nearby Vitra campus, designed by prominent architects like Nicholas Grimshaw, Zaha Hadid and Alvaro Siza, can be visited on a two-hour **architectural tour** (admission €9.50, incl the museum €13.50; ☒ 11am, 1pm & 3pm).

To get there by car, exit the A5 at Weil am Rhein. It's a 15-minute walk from the museum to Weil am Rhein train station, an easy trip from Freiburg (€10.30, 50 minutes, hourly).

NORTHEAST OF FREIBURG

St Peter

☎ 07660 / pop 2500

The folk of the bucolic village of St Peter, on the southern slopes of Mt Kandel (1243m), are deeply committed to time-honoured traditions. On religious holidays, villagers (from toddlers to pensioners) still proudly don colourful, handmade *Trachten* (folkloric costumes).

The most outstanding landmark is the **former Benedictine abbey**, a rococo jewel designed by Peter Thumb of Vorarlberg. Many of the period's top artists collaborated on the sumptuous interior of the twin-towered redsandstone **church** (☒ daily), including Joseph Anton Feuchtmayer, who carved the gilded Zähringer duke statues affixed to pillars. Guided tours (€6; in German) to the monastery complex include the rococo library.

The **tourist office** (☎ 910 224; www.st-peter -schwarzwald.de, in German; Klosterhof 11; ☒ 9am-noon & 3-5pm Mon-Fri Easter-Oct, 10am-noon Sat Jul & Aug, 9am-noon Mon-Fri, 3-5pm during school holidays Nov-Easter) is under the archway leading to the **Klosterhof** (the abbey courtyard). A nearby information panel shows room availability.

By public transport, the best way to get from Freiburg to St Peter is to take the train to Kirchzarten (13 minutes, two an hour) and then bus 7216 (24 minutes, two an hour).

St Peter is on the **Schwarzwald Panoramastrasse** (Black Forest Panorama Rd; www.schwarzwald-panoramastrasse .de), a 50km-long route from Waldkirch (26km northeast of Freiburg) to Hinterzarten (5km west of Titisee) with giddy mountain views.

Triberg

☎ 07722 / pop 5400

Home to Germany's highest waterfall, heir to the original Black Forest cake recipe and nesting ground of the world's biggest cuckoos – Triberg lays on the superlatives with a trowel. It was here that in bleak winters past folk huddled in snowbound farmhouses to carve the clocks that would drive the planet cuckoo; and here that in a flash of brilliance the waterfall was harnessed to power the country's first electric street lamps in 1884. Josef Keller's original recipe for the must-eat cake now takes pride of place in Café Schäfer.

ORIENTATION & INFORMATION

Triberg's main drag is the B500, which runs more-or-less parallel to the Gutach River. The town's focal point is the Marktplatz, a steep 1.2km uphill walk from the Bahnhof.

Triberg markets itself as **Ferienland** (Holidayland; www.dasferienland.de) to visitors.

Post office On Marktplatz next to the Rathaus.

Tourist office (☎ 866 490; www.triberg.de, in German; Wahlfahrtstrasse 4; ☒ 10am-5pm Nov-Apr, 10am-6pm May-Oct) Inside the Schwarzwald-Museum, 50m uphill from the river.

SIGHTS

Niagara they ain't, but Germany's highest **waterfalls** (☎ 2724; adult/8-16yr/family €3/1.50/7; ☒ Mar-early Nov, 25-30 Dec) do exude their own wild romanticism. The Gutach River feeds the seven-tiered falls, which drop a total of 163m. It's annoying to have to pay to experience nature but the fee is at least worth it. The trail up through the wooded gorge is guarded by tribes of red squirrels after the bags of nuts (€1) sold at the entrance.

Triberg is the world's undisputed cuckoo clock capital. Two timepieces claim the title of *weltgröste Kuckucksuhr* (world's largest cuckoo clock), giving rise to the battle of the birds. Triberg's underdog **World's Biggest Cuckoo Clock** (☎ 4689; Untertalstrasse 28; adult/6-10yr €1.20/0.60; ☒ 9am-noon & 1-6pm), complete with gear-driven innards, is 1km up the hill in Schonach, inside a snug chalet. Its commercially savvy **rival** (☎ 962 20; www.uhren-park.de; Schonachbach 27; admission €1.50; ☒ 9am-6pm Mon-Sat, 10am-6pm Sun Easter-Oct, 9am-5.30pm Mon-Sat, 11am-5pm Sun Nov-Easter), listed in the *Guinness World Records*, is at the other end of town on the B33 between Triberg and Hornberg.

THE CHERRY ON THE CAKE

Claus Schäfer, confectioner at Café Schäfer (below) and heir to Josef Keller's original 1905 recipe for *Schwarzwälder Kirschtorte,* reveals the secret to baking a tasty Black Forest cake.

What makes your Black Forest cake unique? The original recipe, which I follow religiously. I bake just a couple of Black Forest cakes fresh every morning, as they're best eaten the same day. I do everything myself, from making the short pastry and chocolate sponge to adding finishing touches like chocolate shavings. Black Forest cake is like a woman – when it looks good, it gives you an appetite!

Any top tips for recreating the cake at home? The bottom layer of sponge should be twice as thick as the other two, so it can support the compote [morello cherries, cherry juice and wheat powder] without collapsing. Buy top-quality *Kirschwasser* [cherry schnapps] with at least 45% alcohol, then add two shot glasses to the cream (not the sponge), so the alcohol isn't overpowering. Whip the cream lightly until smooth and silky. Finally, never freeze the cake or you'll lose the aroma.

Favourite places to work off the cake? Within minutes I can be up in hills, woods and beautiful untouched valleys around Triberg. The Kaiserstühl (p459) is glorious in spring when the cherry trees are in full bloom.

Which other Black Forest specialities are worth trying? The fresh trout, smoked ham and *Kirchwasser* sold by local farmers. Their quality is higher and prices lower than in the supermarkets.

A glockenspiel bashes out melodies and a cuckoo greets his fans with a hopelessly croaky squawk on the hour at the **House of 1000 Clocks** (☎ 963 00; Hauptstrasse 81; 🕑 10am-5pm). Inside, the clocks range from classic to funky; the latest quartz models feature a sensor that sends the cuckoo to sleep after dark. Ah…peace at last!

SLEEPING & EATING

DJH hostel (☎ 4110; www.jugendherberge-triberg.de; Rohrbacher Strasse 35; dm 1st/subsequent night €19.10/15.90) A great base for hikers, this neat-and-tidy hostel sits on a scenic ridge above Triberg, 1.2km uphill from Marktplatz.

Kuckucksnest (☎ 869 487; Wallfahrtstrasse 15; d €50-56) Escapists flock to this quiet 'cuckoo nest' built by master woodcarver Gerald Burger (his shop is downstairs). The snug, pale-wood rooms have flat-screen TVs. The *Wurzelsepp* fir-tree root sculptures by the entrance supposedly ward off evil spirits.

our pick **Parkhotel Wehrle** (☎ 860 20; www.parkhotel-wehrle.de; Gartenstrasse 24; d €129-149; P 💻 🏊) A drop of style in Triberg's ocean of kitsch, this 400-year-old pile won Hemingway's approval. Rooms fuse Biedermeier or country-cottage romance with contemporary flourishes like sexy transparent showers. The spa is quite something, with a starlit ice chamber, a kidney-shaped pool playing underwater music, and treatments from *rhassoul* clay wraps to oxygen therapy. Several fine restaurants include the hand-carved Ochsenstube (mains €19 to €22) serving imaginative local cuisine: think hay-stuffed trout on fennel-tomato vegetables.

Café Schäfer (☎ 4465; www.cafe-schaefer-triberg.de; Hauptstrasse 33; 🕑 9am-6pm Mon-Fri, 8am-6pm Sat, 11am-6pm Sun, closed Wed) Other Black Forest cakes pale in comparison to Claus Schäfer's masterpiece: layers of moist sponge, fresh cream and sour cherries, with the merest suggestion of *Kirsch* (cherry liqueur). So light you can eat another slice (well it would be rude not to), the *Kirschtorte* at this old-world cafe is baked according to the original recipe.

GETTING THERE & AWAY

The Schwarzwaldbahn railway line loops southeast to Konstanz (€21.50, 1½ hours, hourly), and northwest to Offenburg (€10.30, 40 minutes, hourly).

Bus 7150 travels north through the Gutach and Kinzig valleys to Offenburg; bus 7265 heads south to Villingen via St Georgen. Local buses operate between the Bahnhof and Marktplatz, and to the nearby town of Schonach (hourly).

Around Triberg

STÖCKLEWALDTURM

Triberg's waterfall is the trailhead for an attractive 6.5km walk to **Stöcklewaldturm** (1070m). A steady trudge through spruce forest and pastures brings you to this 19th-century lookout tower (admission €0.50), where the 360-degree views stretch from the Swabian Alps to the snowcapped Alps. Footpaths head off in all directions from the summit, where there's a cafe providing light refreshments. The car park on the K5727 is a 10-minute stroll from the tower.

MARTINSKAPELLE

A secret even to many locals, Martinskapelle is a hot spot for cross-country skiing in winter and hiking when the snow melts. It's named after the tiny chapel at the head of the Bregtal (Breg Valley). The steep road up to the 1100m peak negotiates some pretty hairy switchbacks, swinging past wood-shingle farmhouses that cling to forested slopes. A scenic year-round **walk** is the 4km woodland stroll to **Brendturm** (1149m) which, on cloud-free days affords views reaching from Feldberg to the Vosges and Alps. After a seasonal dump of snow, cross-country skiers glide along waymarked *Loipen*, including a 2km floodlit track.

our pick **Höhengasthaus Kolmenhof** (☎ 07723-931 00; An der Donauquelle; mains €9.50-14.90; closed Wed dinner & Thu) fills up with ruddy-cheeked skiers and walkers, who pile into this rustic bolt-hole for *Glühwein* (mulled wine) and soul food. Despite what critics (who have argued until blue in the face since 1544) say, the Danube's main source is right here. This accounts for the freshness of the trout, served smoked, roasted in almond butter, or poached in white wine.

Bus 7270 runs roughly hourly from the Marktplatz in Triberg to Escheck (€1.80, 23 minutes); from here it's a 4.5km walk to Martinskapelle. If you're driving, take the B500 from Triberg following signs to Schwarzenbach, Weissenbach and the K5730 to Martinskapelle.

Villingen-Schwenningen

☎ Villingen 07721, Schwenningen 07720 / pop 81,000

Encircled by impenetrable walls that look as though they were built by the mythical local giant, Romäus, Villingen's Altstadt is a medieval time capsule, laced with cobbled streets and handsome patrician houses. Though locals nickname it the *Städtle* (little town), the name seems inappropriate during February's mammoth, weeklong *Fasnet* celebrations (see boxed text, opposite).

Villingen and Schwenningen trip simultaneously off the tongue, yet each town has its own flavour and history. Villingen once belonged to the Grand Duchy of Baden and Schwenningen to the duchy of Württemberg; conflicting allegiances that apparently can't be reconciled. Villingen, it must be said, is the more attractive of the twin towns.

ORIENTATION & INFORMATION

Surrounded by a ring road, Villingen's Altstadt is criss-crossed by mostly pedestrianised streets: north–south Obere Strasse and Niedere Strasse, and east–west Bickenstrasse and Rietstrasse. The Bahnhof and bus station are east of the ring on Bahnhofstrasse Schwenningen's centre is 5km east.

Post office (Bahnhofstrasse 6, Villingen)
Villingen tourist office (☎ 822 340; www.tourismus -vs.de; Rietgasse 2; 9am-5pm Mon-Sat, 11am-5pm Sat) In the Franziskaner Museum.

SIGHTS

Walking Villingen's Altstadt, guarded by remarkably well-preserved ring walls and city gates, can feel like time travel. The main crowd-puller is the red-sandstone **Münster** (Münsterplatz) with disparate spires: one overlaid with coloured tiles, the other spiky and festooned with gargoyles. The Romanesque portals with haut-relief doors depict dramatic biblical scenes.

Right opposite is the step-gabled **Altes Rathaus** and Klaus Ringwald's **Münsterbrunnen**, a bronze fountain and a tongue-in-cheek portrayal of characters that have shaped Villingen's history. The square throngs with activity on Wednesday and Saturday mornings when market stalls are piled high with local goodies.

Next to the 13th-century **Riettor** and occupying a former Franciscan monastery, the **Franziskaner Museum** (☎ 822 351; Rietgasse 2, adult/concession €3/2; 1-5pm Tue-Sat, 11am-5pm Sun) skips merrily through Villingen's history and heritage. Standouts include Celtic artefacts unearthed at **Magdalenenberg**, 30 minutes' walk south of the centre. Dating to 616 BC, the enigmatic site is one of the largest Hallstatt burial chambers ever discovered in Central Europe and is shaded by a 1000-year-old oak tree.

Tucked behind the Franziskaner is the **Spitalgarten**, a park flanked by the original city walls. Here your gaze will be drawn to **Romäusturm**, a lofty 13th-century thieves' tower

---

CELEBRATE THE FIFTH SEASON

Boisterous and totally bonkers, the **Swabian-Alemannic Fasnacht** or *Fasnet* (not to be confused with Carnival) is a 500-year-old rite to banish winter and indulge in pre-Lenten feasting, parades, flirting and all-night drinkathons. Starting on Epiphany, festivities reach a crescendo the week before Ash Wednesday. Dress up to join the party and memorise a few sayings to dodge the witches and catch the flying sausages – anything's possible, we swear. For *Fasnacht* at its traditional best, try the following:

■ **Elzach** (www.schuttig.com, in German) *Trallaho*! Wearing a hand-carved mask and a tricorn hat adorned with snail shells, *Schuttige* dash through Elzach's streets cracking *Saublodere* (pig bladders) – dodge them unless you wish for many children! Sunday's torchlit parade and Shrove Tuesday's afternoon *Schuttigumzug* are the must-sees.

■ **Rottweil** (www.narrenzunft.rottweil.de, in German) At Monday's 8am *Narrensprung,* thousands of jester-like *Narros* in baroque masques ring through Baden-Württemberg's oldest town. Look out for the devil-like *Federhannes* and the *Guller* riding a cockerel.

■ **Schramberg** (www.narrenzunft-schramberg.de, in German) Protagonists include the *hoorige Katz* (hairy cat), the hopping *Hans.*

---

named after fabled local leviathan Remigius Mans (Romäus for short).

If the sun's out, take a 3km walk northwest of the Altstadt to the tree-fringed **Kneippbad** (Lido; ☎ 534 41; Am Kneippbad 1, adult/concession €3.70/2.50; ⏰ 6.30am-8pm Mon-Fri, 8am-8pm Sat & Sun May-Sep), a family magnet with its outdoor pools, slides and volleyball courts.

To extend your ramble, follow the **woodland trail** shadowing the copper-coloured Brigach River upstream from the Kneippbad, passing **Feldner Mühle** watermill with its playground and ponies. Continue northwest through the forest to reach **Salvest**, a beloved picnic spot with a deer enclosure and **Ackerloch Grillschopf** in Unterkirnach (p464).

Villingen-Schwenningen is the southern terminus of the **Neckartal-Radweg** (see p403), one of Baden-Württemberg's premier bike trails.

SLEEPING & EATING

The Altstadt is dotted with restaurants and cafes, but the best sleeping options are northwest of the centre around the Kurgarten. Villingen's bar mile, Färberstrasse, gets pretty lively at the weekend.

Haus Bächle (☎ 597 29; Am Kneippbad 5; s/d €15/30; Ⓟ) Set in a half-timbered house beside the flower-strewn Kurgarten, the lovingly kept rooms here are a steal. It's right next to the Kneippbad, so ideal for early-morning dips.

our pick **Rindenmühle** (☎ 886 80; www.rinden muehle.de; Am Kneippbad 9; s €72, d €89-104; Ⓟ 🖥 🛜) Next to the Brigach and the Kneippbad, this converted watermill houses one of Villingen's top hotels, with spacious, countrified rooms with wi-fi. Downstairs, award-winning chef Martin Weisser cooks with finesse, using home-grown produce such as herbs, free-range rabbits and geese plucked fresh from his garden.

Zampolli (☎ 328 65; Rietstrasse 33; ⏰ 9.30am-11pm Mon-Sat, 10.30am-11pm Sun Feb–mid-Nov) For an espresso or creamy gelati (wild berries is superb), make for this Italian-run cafe. By night, the pavement terrace facing Riettor is a laid-back spot for a drink.

Don Antonio (☎ 506 084; Färberstrasse 18; mains €10.50-14.50; ⏰ 6pm-midnight) Flamenco plays as a jovial crowd tucks into paella and tapas in cave-like, candlelit alcoves at this vibrant Spanish haunt.

GETTING THERE & AROUND

Villingen's Bahnhof is on the scenic Schwarzwaldbahn railway line from Konstanz (€16.70, 70 minutes) to Triberg (€7, 25 minutes) and Offenburg (€15.20, 70 minutes). Trains to Stuttgart (€23.60, two hours) involve a change in Rottweil, and to Freiburg (€16.70, 1¾ hours) a change in Donaueschingen.

From Villingen, buses 7265 and 7270 make regular trips north to Triberg. Frequent buses (for example line 1) link Villingen with Schwenningen.

Villingen-Schwenningen is just west of the A81 Stuttgart–Singen motorway and is also crossed by the B33 to Triberg and the B27 to Rottweil.

BADEN-WÜRTTEMBERG

Around Villingen-Schwenningen

ROTTWEIL
☎ 0741 / pop 25,500

Baden-Württemberg's oldest town is the strapline of Roman-rooted Rottweil, founded in AD 73. Yet a torrent of bad press about the woofer with a nasty nip means that most folk readily associate it with the Rottweiler, which was indeed bred here as a hardy butchers' dog until recently. Fear not, the Rottweiler locals are much tamer.

The sturdy 13th-century **Schwarzes Tor** is the gateway to Hauptstrasse and the well-preserved Altstadt, a cluster of red-roofed, pastel-painted houses. Nearby at No 6, the curvaceous **Hübschen Winkel** will make you look twice with its 45-degree kink. Just west on Münsterplatz, the late Romanesque **Münster-Heiliges-Kreuz** features some striking Gothic stonework and ribbed vaulting. Equally worth a peek about 1km south is the **Roman bath** (Hölderstrasse; admission free; ☉ daylight hours), a 45m-by-42m bathing complex unearthed in 1967.

The **tourist office** (☎ 494 280; www.rottweil.de; Hauptstrasse 21; ☉ 9.30am-5.30pm Mon-Fri, 9.30am-12.30pm Sat Apr-Sep, 9.30am-12.30pm & 2-5pm Mon-Fri Oct-Mar) can advise on accommodation, tours and biking the **Neckartal-Radweg** (p403).

Rottweil is just off the A81 Stuttgart–Singen motorway, Trains run roughly hourly to Villingen (€2.80, 25 minutes), situated 25km north.

UNTERKIRNACH
☎ 07721 / pop 2819

Nestled among velvety green hills, low-key Unterkirnach appeals to families and outdoorsy types. Kids can slide and climb to their heart's content at the all-weather **Spielscheune** (☎ 800 855; Schlossbergweg 4; admission €3; ☉ 1-7pm Mon-Fri, 11am-7pm Sat & Sun), or toddle uphill to the **farm** to meet inquisitive goats and Highland cattle (feeding time is 3pm). In summer, the village is a great starting point for forest walks, while in winter there are 50km of *Loipen* (cross-country trails) to ski and some terrific slopes to sledge.

Perched above Unterkirnach and a wide valley, **our pick Ackerloch Grillschopf** (☎ 544 21; Unteres Ackerloch; snacks €3-8; ☉ 11.30am-midnight Thu-Tue) is a rickety barn that doubles as a butchers selling home-smoked Black Forest ham. The smell of suckling pig roasting on a spit or sausages might lure you in for meaty snacks, which you can grill yourself on the barbecue.

Bus 16 runs roughly hourly between Unterkirnach and Villingen (€2.80, 10 minutes).

SOUTHEAST OF FREIBURG

Titisee-Neustadt
☎ 07651 / pop 12,000

Titisee is a cheerful summertime playground with a name that makes English-speaking travellers giggle and a shimmering blue-green glacial lake, ringed by forest, which has them diving for their cameras.

Sure, the village is touristy, but tiptoe south along the flowery **Seestrasse** promenade and you'll soon leave the crowds and made-in-China cuckoo clocks behind to find secluded bays ideal for swimming and picnicking. For giddy views, head up to 1192m **Hochfirst** tower, which overlooks Titisee from the east.

A laid-back way to appreciate the lake's soothing beauty is to hire a **rowing boat** or pedalo at one of the set-ups along the lakefront; expect to pay around €6 per hour.

The forest trails around Titisee are hugely popular for **Nordic walking** which, for the uninitiated, is walking briskly with poles to simultaneously exercise the upper body and legs.

Set to make a €30-million splash in autumn 2010 is the **Schwarzwald Badeparadies**, a 600-sq-metre leisure and wellness complex, comprising lagoons, slides, a wave pool and a sauna area, sheltered in a gigantic conservatory with a retractable roof.

Snow transforms Titisee into a winter wonderland and a **cross-country skiing** magnet, with *Loipen* (tracks) threading through the hills and woods, including a 3km floodlit track for a starlit skate. The tourist office map pinpoints cross-country and Nordic walking trails in the area.

The **tourist office** (☎ 980 40; www.titisee-neustadt.de; Strandbadstrasse 4; ☉ 9am-6pm Mon-Fri, 10am-1pm Sat & Sun May-Oct, 9am-noon & 1.30-5pm Mon-Fri Nov-Apr) in the Kurhaus, 500m southwest of the train station, stocks walking and cycling maps.

SLEEPING & EATING

Titisee's best sleeping deals are slightly away from the main drag.

Bergseeblick (☎ 8257; www.bergseeblick-titisee.de; Erlenweg 3; s €25-32, d 50-60; P) This welcoming, family-run cheapie near the church offers peaceful slumber in humble rooms decorated in pine and floral fabrics. Don't miss the fabulously kitsch Snow White–gnome collection next door.

ourpick **Alemannenhof** (☎ 07652-911 80; www
hotel-alemannenhof.de; Hinterzarten am Titisee; s €77-129,
€112-168; P 🖳 🖳) A pool, private beach
and plush rooms with country charm invite relaxation at this farmhouse-style hotel.
Plump for a room with a balcony facing
Titisee. Opening onto a lakefront terrace,
he all-pine restaurant (mains €13.50 to €32)
serves regional cuisine with a twist, such as
organic chicken breast in thyme sauce with
chive pasta.

Seebachstüble (☎ 8231; Seebachstrasse 43; mains €8-
5) Markus Ketterer cooks fresh and seasonal at
his rustic bolt-hole, with fusion dishes such as
tender milk-fed lamb on apricot-ginger sauce
and rump steak garnished with Thai prawns.
Kids love the ice cream from a local farm.

Gutscher (cnr Strandbadstrasse & Seestrasse; ☑ daily)
Picnickers should try Gutscher for local specialities including ham, cheese, schnapps and
wagon wheel–sized bread loaves.

GETTING THERE & AROUND
Rail routes include the twice hourly
Höllentalbahn to Freiburg (€4.80, 40 minutes)
and Donaueschingen (€8.40, 50 minutes) and
the hourly Dreiseenbahn to Feldberg (€2, 12
minutes) and Schluchsee (€2, 22 minutes).

From Titisee train station, there are frequent services on bus 7257 to Schluchsee
(€2, 40 minutes) and bus 7300 to Feldberg-
Bärental (€2, 10 minutes).

Ski-Hirt (☎ 922 80; Titiseestrasse 26, Neustadt) rents
reliable bikes and ski equipment, and can supply details on local cycling options.

Feldberg
☎ 07655 / pop 1800
At 1493m Feldberg is the Black Forest's highest mountain – no surprise, then, that it's
the region's premier downhill skiing area.
The actual mountaintop is treeless and not
particularly attractive, looking very much
like a monk's tonsured skull, but on clear
days the view southward towards the Alps
is mesmerising.

Feldberg is also the name given to a cluster of five villages, of which **Altglashütten** is
the hub. Its Rathaus houses the **tourist office**
(☎ 8019; www.feldberg-schwarzwald.de; Kirchgasse 1;
☑ 8.30am-5.30pm Mon-Fri), which has stacks of
information on activities and rents Nordic
walking poles for €3 per day.

About 2km north is the postcard-perfect
Bärental, where traditional Black Forest farm-

houses snuggle against the hillsides. East of
Bärental in the Haslach Valley is **Falkau**, a
family-friendly resort with a small waterfall.
Windfällweiher, an attractive lake for a swim or
picnic, is 1km southeast of Altglashütten.

Around 9km west of Altglashütten is
Feldberg-Ort, in the heart of the 42-sq-km **nature reserve** that covers much of the mountain.
Most of the ski lifts are here, including the scenic **Feldbergbahn chairlift** (one-way/return €7.20/8.60)
to the **Bismarckdenkmal** (Bismarck monument).
The **tourist office** (☎ 07676-933 630) is in the
environment-oriented **Haus der Natur**.

ACTIVITIES
The Feldberg area is great **hiking** territory,
criss-crossed with marked trails such as the
rewarding 12km **Feldberg-Steig** from Haus der
Natur to Feldberg summit, affording bewitching views from Zugspitze to Mont Blanc on
clear days. Feldberg is largely a nature reserve,
so keep an eye out for rare wildflowers, mountain hens, deer and chamois.

The **Feldberg ski area** (adult/under 15yr per day
€25/13, from 1pm €17.50/9.50) comprises 28 lifts, accessible with the same ticket. Four groomed
cross-country trails are also available. To hire
skis, look for signs reading 'Skiverleih'. A reliable outlet is **Skiverleih Schubnell** (☎ 560; www
.skiverleih-feldberg.de; Bärentalerstrasse 1, Altglashütten).

Come winter Feldberg's snowy heights are
ideal for a stomp through twinkling woods.
Strap on **snowshoes** to tackle the pretty 3km
Seebuck-Trail or the more challenging 9km
Gipfel-Trail. The Haus der Natur rents
lightweight snowshoes for €10/5 per day
for adults/children.

SLEEPING
Pick up the *Hüttenverzeichnis*, listing good-value
huts and guesthouses, at the tourist office.

DJH hostel (☎ 07676-221; www.jugendherberge
-feldberg.de; Passhöhe 14; dm 1st/subsequent night
€20.60/17.50) This rustic chalet near the slopes
in Feldberg-Ort offers spick-and-span dorms,
a ski room and volleyball court. It's served
by bus 7300 from Bärental train station to
Hebelhof (10 minutes, hourly).

Landhotel Sonneck (☎ 211; www.sonneck-feldberg.de,
in German; Schwarzenbachweg 5, Altglashütten; d €76-80;
P) Immaculate, light-filled rooms with pine
furnishings and balconies are the deal at this
hotel opposite the tourist office. The quaint
restaurant (mains €8 to €15) rolls out hearty
local fare.

BADEN-WÜRTTEMBERG

GETTING THERE & AWAY

Bärental and Altglashütten are stops on the Dreiseenbahn, linking Titisee with Seebrugg (Schluchsee). From the train station in Bärental, bus 7300 makes trips at least hourly to Feldberg-Ort (€2, 10 minutes).

From late December until the end of the season shuttle buses, run by Feldberg SBG, link Feldberg and Titisee with the ski lifts (free with a lift ticket or Gästekarte).

If you're driving, take the B31 (Freiburg–Donaueschingen) to Titisee, then the B317. To get to Altglashütten, head down the B500 from Bärental.

Schluchsee

☎ 07656 / pop 2600

Photogenically poised above its namesake petrol-blue lake (the Black Forest's largest) and rimmed by thick fir forest, Schluchsee tempts outdoorsy types with pursuits including swimming, windsurfing, hiking, cycling and, ahem, skinny-dipping from the western shore's secluded bays. The placid resort leaps to life with sun-seekers in summer and cross-country skiers in winter.

Popular with families, the lakefront lido, **Aqua Fun Strandbad** (Fischbacherstrasse 8; adult/6-16yr/concession €3.80/2.20/2.20; ☺ 9am-7pm late May-Sep) has a heated pool, a sandy beach, a volleyball court and waterslides.

T Toth (☎ 92 30; www.seerundfahrten.de, in German; ☺ hourly 10am-5pm May-Oct) runs boat tours around Schluchsee, with stops in Aha, Seebrugg and the Strandbad. An hour-long round trip costs €6 (less for single stops). You can hire rowing boats and pedalos for the same price.

ORIENTATION & INFORMATION

The railway tracks and the B500 shadow the lake's eastern shore between the lakefront and the Schluchsee's town centre. The lake's western shore is accessible only by bike or on foot.

Tourist office (☎ 7732; www.schluchsee.de; Haus des Gastes, Fischbacher Strasse 7; ☺ 8am-6pm Mon-Thu, 9am-6pm Fri, also 10am-noon Sat & Sun mid-Jul–late Sep) Situated 150m uphill from the church, with maps, info on activities and accommodation, and free wi-fi.

SLEEPING & EATING

Decent beds are alas pretty slim in Schluchsee, though there are a few good-value pensions – ask the tourist office for a list.

DJH hostel (☎ 329; www.jugendherberge-schluchse -wolfsgrund.de; Im Wolfsgrund 28; dm 1st/subsequent nigh €19.10/15.90) Right by the lake, this wood-tile hostel has well-kept dorms and a barbe cue area. It's a 10-minute walk west of th train station.

Hotel Schiff (☎ 975 70; www.hotel-schiff-schluchsee.d Kirchplatz 7; s €37-40, d €56-106; P) Some of th more dated rooms are begging for a make over, but for location and friendliness thi hotel next to the church knows no rival Guests can rent bikes, sledges and Nordi walking poles.

Pizzeria Seehof (☎ 1261; Kirchsteige 4; pizza €7 11) Chirpy Italian staff keep the good vibes crisp pizza and ice cream coming at thi unpretentious pizzeria, with a fine terrac overlooking the lake.

GETTING THERE & AROUND

The hourly Dreiseenbahn train goes t Feldberg (€2, 10 minutes) and Titisee (€2, 2 minutes). Bus 7257 links Schluchsee three o four times daily with the Neustadt and Titise train stations (€2, 37 minutes).

Bikes can be rented from Hotel Schif (above) for €5/9 per half-/full day.

Wutachschlucht

The swift, serpentine **Wutach** (literally 'angr river') has carved this wild gorge of jagged near-vertical rock faces. The river rises a most at the summit of the Feldberg and flow into the Rhine near Waldshut, on the Swis border. Wildlife spotters will want their bin oculars handy in this **nature reserve**, wher a microclimate supports orchids and ferns rare birds from treecreepers to kingfishers and countless species of butterflies, beetle and lizards.

To truly appreciate the Wutachschlucht hike the 13km from **Schattenmühle** t **Wutachmühle** (or vice versa). Energy permit ting, you can add the lush, 2.5km **Lotenbach Klamm** (Lotenbach Glen) to your tour. May t September is the best time to tackle the walk Be sure to carry supplies as there's very littl between the trailheads.

The **tourist office** (☎ 07703-7607; www.bonndorf.de in German; Martinstrasse 5; ☺ 9am-noon & 2-6pm Mon-Fri 10am-noon Sat May-Oct, 9am-noon & 2-5pm Mon-Fri excep Wed afternoon Nov-Apr) in Bonndorf, 15km east o Schluchsee, has hiking information, maps an a list of places to stay.

Bus 7258 runs between Bonndorf and Neustadt train station (€4, 40 minutes, hourly Monday to Saturday, every two hours Sunday). Bus 7344 links Bonndorf to Schattenmühle and Wutachmühle (€2.90, 27 minutes, every hour or two Monday to Friday).

LAKE CONSTANCE

Three is the magic number for Lake Constance, Central Europe's third-largest lake straddling three countries: Germany, Austria and Switzerland. Sculpted by the Rhine Glacier during the last ice age and fed and drained by that same sprightly river today, this whopper of a freshwater lake measures 63km long, 14km wide and up to 250m deep.

And if its statistics amaze, its landscapes move the soul like a greatest hits of European scenery. Where else can you wake up on a pebbly bay in Germany, lazily paddle over to Switzerland for *Birchermüesli* and make it to Austria in time for snapshots of the Alps and strudel elevenses? For yet more contrasts, climb into a bicycle saddle to roll through gold-tinged meadows and vineyards, apple orchards and wetlands. Culture you cry? It's all here: from baroque churches to Benedictine abbeys, Stone Age dwellings to Roman forts, medieval castles to zeppelins.

Whether cloaked in mist or bathed in the warm light of late summer, Lake Constance never looks less than astonishing. Come in spring for blossom and autumn for new wine, fewer crowds and top visibility when the warm föhn blows. Summers are humid and packed, but best for swimming and camping. Almost everything shuts from November to February when fog descends and the first snowflakes dust the Alps.

Activities

CYCLING

In the warm months, little beats free-wheeling around Lake Constance, pausing for invigorating dips in the lake, pretty villages in the hinterland and Alpine views without the uphill struggle. Well-signposted and largely flat, the 273km **Bodensee-Radweg** (Lake Constance Cycle Route; www.bodensee-radweg.com) circumnavigates the lake, zipping through Germany, Austria and Switzerland as it traces the shoreline between vineyards and orchards, woodlands and beaches. If you'd rather join a group than pedal alone, see the website for tour details.

The entire route takes roughly a week, but ferries and trains make it possible to cover shorter chunks, for instance Friedrichshafen–Konstanz–Meersburg, in a weekend. Maps and bike hire (€10 to €15 per day) are available locally. May to October is the best time to cycle, but trails get choked during the summer holidays when Lycra rage is rife.

Getting There & Around

Ryanair flies from London Stansted to **Friedrichshafen** (www.fly-away.de).

The most enjoyable way to cross the lake is by ferry. Konstanz is the main hub, but Meersburg and Friedrichshafen also have plentiful ferry options.

The public transport system is well-organised and preferable to driving. Although most towns have a train station (Meersburg is an exception), in some cases buses provide the only land connections. **Euregio Bodensee** (www.euregiokarte.com, in German), which groups all Lake Constance–area public transport, publishes a free *Fahrplan* with schedules for all train, bus and ferry services.

The **Euregio Bodensee Tageskarte** (1 zone €15, all 4 zones €28, 6-15yr half-price) gets you all-day access to land transport around Lake Constance, including areas in Austria and Switzerland. It's sold at tourist offices, train stations and ferry docks.

PASSENGER FERRIES

The **Weisse Flotte** (☎ 281 389), a grouping of German, Swiss and Austrian companies, runs passenger and car-ferry lines that hop between towns along the lake, and link towns on opposite shores. Holders of rail passes get a 50% discount on certain services.

The most useful lines, run by German **BSB** (☎ 07531-364 0389; www.bsb-online.com) and Austrian **OBB** (www.bodenseeschifffahrt.at, in German), link Konstanz with ports such as Meersburg (€4.80, 30 minutes), Friedrichshafen (€10.40, 1¾ hours), Lindau (€13.40, three hours) and Bregenz (€14.10, 3½ hours); children aged six to 15 years pay half-price. There are seven daily runs from early July to early September, five from late May to early July and early September to early October, and three from early April to late May, making it possible to visit several places in a single day.

Other ferry runs, mostly operated by BSB, link Konstanz with Reichenau Island, and both Konstanz and Meersburg with Mainau Island and Überlingen.

Der Katamaran (☎ 07541-971 0900; www.der -katamaran.de, in German; adult/6-14yr €9.50/4.80) is a sleek passenger service that takes 50 minutes to make the Konstanz–Friedrichshafen crossing (hourly from 6am or 8am to 7pm, plus twice hourly from 8pm to midnight from May to early October).

CAR FERRIES

The roll-on-roll-off **Konstanz–Meersburg car ferry** (☎ 07531-8030; www.sw.konstanz.de; car up to 4m incl driver/bicycle/pedestrian €8/2.20/2.50) runs 24 hours a day, except when high water levels mean it can't dock properly. The frequency is every 15 minutes from 5.30am to 9pm, every 30 minutes from 9pm to midnight and every hour from midnight to 5.30am. The **Mini-Maxi Ticket** (one-way/return €4/8) gets pedestrians a ferry ride plus bus transport on either end (to and from Meersburg and Konstanz). The crossing, affording superb views from the top deck, takes 15 minutes.

The dock in Konstanz, served by local bus 1, is 4km northeast of the centre along Mainaustrasse. In Meersburg, car ferries leave from a dock 400m northwest of the old town.

KONSTANZ
☎ 07531 / pop 81,000
Hugging the northwestern shore of Lake Constance and clinging to the Swiss border, scored by the Rhine and outlined by the Alps, Konstanz is a natural stunner. Roman emperors, medieval traders and the bishops of the 15th-century Council of Constance all left their mark on this red-roofed town, merci-fully spared from the WWII bombings that obliterated other German cities.

When the sun pops its head out, Konstanz is a feel-good university town with a lively buzz and upbeat bar scene, particularly in the cobbled Altstadt and the harbour where the voluptuous *Imperia* turns. In summer locals, nicknamed *Seehasen* (lake hares) head outdoors to inline skate along the leafy promenade and enjoy lazy days in lakefront lidos.

Orientation
Konstanz is split in two by the Rhine, with the Altstadt on its south bank. The imperial-style Deutscher Bahnhof (German train station and ramshackle Schweizer Bahnhof (Swiss train station) are adjacent to each other on Bahnhofplatz, at the Altstadt's eastern edge. Delineating the southern edge of the Altstadt is Bodanstrasse; a few blocks south is the Swiss frontier.

Information
English Bookshop (☎ 150 63; Münzgasse 10) Stocks a good selection.

ReiseBank (Hauptbahnhof; ⏲ 8am-12.30pm & 1.30-6pm Mon-Fri, 8am-3pm Sat) Currency exchange, including Swiss francs.

Schweizer Bahnhof (Swiss train station; ⏲ 6.50am-7pm Mon-Sat, 8.50am-12.10pm & 1.40-6pm Sun & holidays) The ticket counter changes currency at good rates.

Tel Center (per hr €4.20) Bahnhofplatz 6 (⏲ 9am-10pm), Marktstätte 30 (⏲ 9am-10pm Mon-Sat, noon-10pm Sun) Internet access.

Tourist office (☎ 133 030; www.konstanz.de/tourismus; Bahnhofplatz 13; ⏲ 9am-6.30pm Mon-Fri, 9am-4pm Sat, 10am-1pm Sun & holidays Apr-Oct, 9am-12.30pm & 2-6pm Mon-Fri Nov-Mar) Just north of the train stations. Inside you can pick up a walking-tour brochure (€1), outside there's a hotel reservation board and free hotel telephone.

Waschsalon und Mehr (Hofhalde 3; ⏲ 10am-7pm Mon-Fri, 10am-4pm Sat) A self- or full-service laundry.

HIT THE HAY

If you want to pedal around Lake Constance but don't fancy schlepping camping equipment, you can kip on clean, sweet hay at about a dozen **Heuhotels** (www.strohtour.de, in German) in summer. Bring your own sleeping bag. Surrounded by glorious countryside, these family-friendly barns offer an authentic down-on-the-farm experience, often with animals that kids can pet and home-grown goodies like fresh eggs and apple juice at breakfast. A great pick is organic farm **Unterbühlhof** (☎ 07735-1318; www.unterbuehlhof.de, in German; Öhningen; adult/child €14.50/9.50; ⏲ Jun–mid-Sep) in the bucolic Höri area. For options across the border in Switzerland, visit the website www.abenteuer-stroh.ch.

KONSTANZ

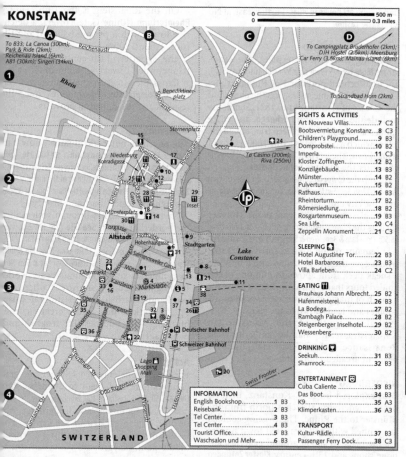

0   500 m
0   0.3 miles

SIGHTS & ACTIVITIES
Art Nouveau Villas	7	C2
Bootsvermietung Konstanz	8	C3
Children's Playground	9	C3
Domprobstei	10	B2
Imperia	11	C3
Kloster Zoffingen	12	B2
Konzilgebäude	13	B3
Münster	14	B2
Pulverturm	15	B2
Rathaus	16	B2
Rheintorturm	17	B2
Römersiedlung	18	B2
Rosgartenmuseum	19	B3
Sea Life	20	C4
Zeppelin Monument	21	C3

SLEEPING
Hotel Augustiner Tor	22	B3
Hotel Barbarossa	23	B3
Villa Barleben	24	C2

EATING
Brauhaus Johann Albrecht	25	B3
Hafenmeisterei	26	B2
La Bodega	27	B2
Rambagh Palace	28	B2
Steigenberger Inselhotel	29	B2
Wessenberg	30	B2

DRINKING
Seekuh	31	B3
Shamrock	32	B3

ENTERTAINMENT
Cuba Caliente	33	B3
Das Boot	34	B3
K9	35	A3
Klimperkasten	36	A3

TRANSPORT
Kultur-Rädle	37	B3
Passenger Ferry Dock	38	C3

INFORMATION
English Bookshop	1	B3
Reisebank	2	B3
Tel Center	3	B3
Tel Center	4	B3
Tourist Office	5	B3
Waschsalon und Mehr	6	B3

BADEN-WÜRTTEMBERG

Sights

WATERFRONT

At the merest hint of a sunray, the tree-ringed, sculpture-dotted **lakefront promenade** lures inline skaters, cyclists, walkers and ice cream–licking crowds.

At the eastern end of Marktstätte, a passageway links the lakefront to the Altstadt; just past it lies the white dormered **Konzilgebäude** (Council Building), built in 1388, which served as a granary and warehouse before Pope Martin V was elected here in 1417. Today it's a conference and concert hall.

At the end of the pier, giving ferry passengers a come-hither look from her rotating pedestal, stands **Imperia**. Peter Lenk's 9m-high sculpture of a buxom prostitute, said to have plied her trade in the days of the Council of Constance, is immortalised in a novel by Honoré de Balzac. In her clutches are hilarious sculptures of a naked (and sagging) Pope Martin V and Holy Roman Emperor Sigismund, symbolising religious and imperial power.

The nearby **Zeppelin Monument** shows the airship inventor Count Ferdinand von Zeppelin in an Icarus-like pose. He was born in 1838 on the **Insel**, an islet a short stroll north through the flowery **Stadtgarten** park, where there's a **children's playground**.

North of the Insel, the **Rheinbrücke** links the Altstadt with newer quarters across the Rhine. On the opposite bank, Seestrasse has a row of handsome **art nouveau villas**. Further east, at No 21, is the **casino**.

MÜNSTER & AROUND

Towering above Münsterplatz, the sandstone **Münster** (9am-6pm Mon-Sat, 10am-6pm Sun), an architectural potpourri of Romanesque, Gothic and baroque styles, was the church of the diocese of Konstanz until 1821. Standouts include the 15th-century **Schnegg**, an ornate spiral staircase in the northern transept, to the left of which a door leads to the 1000-year-old **crypt**. From the crypt's polychrome chapel, you enter the sublime **Gothic cloister**.

Climb the **tower** (adult/6-14yr €2/1; 10am-5.30pm Mon-Sat, 12.30-5pm Sun Mar-Oct) for far-reaching views over the city and lake.

The glass pyramid in front of the Münster shelters the **Römersiedlung** (133 026; tour in German €6.50; 11am & 3pm Wed & Sat), the 3rd-century-AD remains of the Roman fort Constantia, which gave the city its name. You'll only get a sneak peek from above, so join one of the guided tours that begin at the tourist office for a touch of magic as a staircase rises from the cobbles and leads down to the ruins.

Slightly south of the Münster on Kanzleistrasse, the flamboyantly frescoed Renaissance **Rathaus** (City Hall) hides a peaceful arcaded courtyard.

NIEDERBURG

Best explored on foot, Konstanz' historic heart, Niederburg, stretches north from the Münster to the Rhine. The twisting cobbled lanes lined with half-timbered town houses are the place to snoop around galleries, antique shops and 13th-century **Kloster Zoffingen** (Brückengasse 15), Konstanz' only remaining convent, still in the hands of Dominican nuns.

BODENSEE ERLEBNISKARTE

The three-day **Bodensee Erlebniskarte** (adult/6-15yr €69/37, not incl ferries €39/21), available at area tourist and ferry offices from early April to mid-October, allows free travel on almost all boats and mountain cableways on and around Lake Constance (including its Austrian and Swiss shores) and gets you free entry to around 180 tourist attractions and museums. There are also seven-day (adult/child €90/47) and 14-day (adult/child €123/61) versions.

On the Rheinsteig is the 15th-century **Rheintorturm** (Rhine Gate Tower), a defensive tower with a pyramid-shaped red-tile roof. About 200m west along the river is the squatter, 14th-century **Pulverturm** (Gunpowder Tower), with 2m-thick walls.

Cross the street to the orange-red, baroque **Dompropstei** (Rheingasse 20), once the residence of the cathedral provosts.

MUSEUMS

The one-time butchers' guildhall now harbours the **Rosgartenmuseum** (900 246; www.rosgartenmuseum-konstanz.de, in German; Rosgartenstrasse 3-5; adult/concession €3/1.50, 1st Sun of the month & after 2pm Wed free; 10am-6pm Tue-Fri, 10am-5pm Sat & Sun) spotlighting regional art and history.

Running a drag net through your wallet, the borderline kitsch **Sea Life** (128 270; www.sealifeeurope.com; Hafenstrasse 9; adult/3-14yr €13.95/9.95 10am-7pm Jul-mid-Sep, 10am-6pm May, Jun & mid Sep-Oct, 10am-5pm Mon-Fri, 10am-6pm Sat & Sun Nov-Apr) immerses you in an underwater world. Highlights include a shipwreck where you can handle starfish and get stingray close ups, a shark tunnel, and a creepy corner blubbing with oddities like frogfish and, ugh, giant isopods.

Activities

For some ozone-enriched summer fun, grab your bathers and head to **Strandbad Horn** (635 50; Eichhornstrasse 100; admission free; year round), near Campingplatz Bruderhofer (opposite), 4km northeast of the centre. The lakefront beach has sunbathing lawns, a kiddie pool, playground, volleyball courts and even a naturist area.

If you would prefer to trundle across the lake, hire a pedalo at **Bootsvermietung Konstanz** (218 81; per hr €8; 11am-sunset Easter–mid-Oct) in the Stadtgarten.

La Canoa (959 595; www.lacanoa.com, in German; Robert-Bosch-Strasse 4; canoe/kayak per hr €11/16, per day €28/39; 10am-6pm Mon-Fri, 10am-4pm Sat) rent high-quality canoes and kayaks in Konstanz and from various other Lake Constance locations, including Lindau and Friedrichshafen. Visit the website for canoe tour details.

Sleeping

Rock up between November and February and you may find some places closed. The tourist office has a free booking service.

Campingplatz Bruderhofer (☎ 313 88; www campingplatz-konstanz.de; Fohrenbühlweg 50; per person/ ent €4.50/6.80; ☻ Apr-Oct) Wake up to a pore-awakening splash in the lake at this leafy site n Staad, 4km northeast of the Altstadt.

DJH hostel (☎ 322 60; www.jugendherberge-konstanz de; Zur Allmannshöhe 18; dm 1st/subsequent night €21.90/18.60) Occupying a water tower, this hostel has neat dorms, a bistro and gardens. t's 4km northeast of the Altstadt, served by buses 1 and 4.

Hotel Barbarossa (☎ 128 990; www.barbarossa-hotel com, in German; Obermarkt 8-12; s €50-70, d €90-130; **P**) A makeover has brought the bright, parquet-floored rooms bang up to date at this central motel, though some kitsch remains and bathrooms can be a tight fit.

Hotel Augustiner Tor (☎ 282 450; www.hotel augustiner-tor.de; Bodanstrasse 18; s €80-100, d €110-140) This cleverly restored, turn-of-the-century hotel, offers unrivalled value for money. Streamlined rooms exude Scandinavian simplicity with clean lines, crisp white linens and wood floors.

Villa Barleben (☎ 942 330; www.hotel-barleben.de, in German; Seestrasse 15; s €95-215, d €165-265) Gregariously elegant, this 19th-century villa's sunny rooms and corridors are sprinkled with antiques and ethnic art. The rambling lakefront gardens are ideal for dozing in a *Strandkörb* (beach lounger), G&T in hand, or enjoying lunch on the terrace.

Riva (☎ 315 46; www.hotel-riva.de, in German; Seestrasse 25; s €130-150, d €200-260; **P ▯ ⟡ ▨**) This ultra-chic contender has crisp white spaces, glass walls and a snail-like stairwell. Zen-like rooms with hardwood floors feature perks including (like it!) free minibars and wi-fi. The rooftop pool and Mediterranean-style restaurant (four-course menu €49) overlook the lake.

Eating & Drinking

Münsterplatz and Markstätte are peppered with pizzerias, snack bars and gelatarias. Watch out for rip-offs around Stadtgarten.

La Bodega (☎ 277 88; Schreibergasse 40; tapas €2.50-6; ☻ 5pm-1am Tue-Sat) Squirreled away in Niederburg, this candy-bright bodega, with a pocket-sized terrace, whips up tapas from *papas canarias* (Canarian potatoes) to stuffed calamari.

Wessenberg (☎ 919 664; Wessenbergstrasse 41; mains €7-16.50; ☻ 9am-1am Mon-Thu, 9am-2am Fri, 9am-3am Sat, 10am-1am Sun) An art-slung interior, inner court-yard and clubby beats draw a lively crowd to Wessenburg. There are wines to match the global menu skipping from Thai curries to herby gnocchi.

Brauhaus Johann Albrecht (☎ 250 45; Konradigasse 2; mains €8-16) This step-gabled brewpub pairs light, hoppy beers with roll-me-out-the-door fare like fat pig trotters with sauerkraut. Sit on the terrace in summer.

Rambagh Palace (☎ 254 58; Brückengasse 1, 1st fl; mains €9.90-15.90; ☻ 6-11pm Tue-Sun; **V**) Bursts of hot pink and strings of beads add a bohemian touch to this Indian restaurant, occupying a former Gothic church. The Sri Lankan chef uses fresh, organic ingredients in his just-right curries and so-smooth lassis.

Hafenmeisterei (☎ 369 7212; Hafenstrasse 8; mains €10.90-22.50; ☻ 11am-1am, to 2am Fri & Sat) Hafenmeisterei blends beach-shack breezi-ness with a cool lounge vibe. Reggae grooves play as chefs sizzle up wok and fish dishes in the open kitchen. Chill with a glass of red on the lakefront terrace.

Steigenberger Inselhotel (☎ 1250; Auf der Insel 1; mains €23-31) Whether you have seasonal cuisine like halibut with asparagus or simply a coffee, you get the same unbeatable lake setting on the terrace of this former Dominican monas-tery. Don't miss the frescoed cloister.

Shamrock (☎ 246 22; Bahnhofstrasse 4; ☻ 5pm-1am Mon-Thu, 4pm-1am Fri & Sun, 2pm-3am Sat) Shamrock is the go-to pub for the *craic*, with Guinness, karaoke, live music, the works.

Seekuh (☎ 272 32; Konzilstrasse 1; ☻ 6pm-1am Sun-Thu, to 2am Fri, to 3am Sat) The rough and ready 'lake cow' is a Konstanz favourite for its beer garden, cheapest drinks and occasional gigs.

Entertainment

For the low-down on local nightlife see www .party-news.de (in German).

K9 (☎ 167 13; www.k9-kulturzentrum.de, in German; Obere Laube 71) A happening cultural-events venue with concerts from klezmer to tradi-tional Mongolian, as well as club nights and salsa parties.

Cuba Caliente (☎ 0151-5564 8937; www.cuba-caliente -konstanz.de, in German; Hussenstrasse 4; ☻ 9pm-late Wed-Sun) The gyrating hips don't lie at this sweaty *salsateca*, pumping out salsa and merengue (sometimes live) most nights, plus electro and hip hop on Thursday and Friday.

Klimperkasten (☎ 234 08; Bodanstrasse 40; ☻ 10am-1am, to 3am Sat) Indie kids, garage and old-school fans all hail this retro cafe, which gets clubbier after dark when DJs work the decks. Occasionally hosts gigs.

Das Boot (☎ 0172-724 2031; www.dasboot.de, in German; Am Hafen) A docked BSB ferry morphs into a disco on many Friday and Saturday nights from 11pm to 4am.

Getting There & Away
Konstanz is Lake Constance's main ferry hub; for ferry options see p467.

By car, Konstanz can be reached via the B33, which links up with the A81 to and from Stuttgart near Singen. Or you can take the B31 to Meersburg and then catch a car ferry.

Konstanz' Hauptbahnhof is the southern terminus of the scenic Schwarzwaldbahn, which trundles hourly through the Black Forest, linking Offenburg with towns such as Triberg and Villingen. To reach Lake Constance's northern shore, you usually have to change in Radolfzell. The Schweizer Bahnhof has connections to destinations throughout Switzerland.

Getting Around
The city centre is a traffic headache, especially at weekends. Your best bet is probably the free Park & Ride lot 3km northwest of the Altstadt, near the Flugplatz (airfield) on Max-Stromeyer-Strasse, where your only outlay will be for a bus ticket.

Local buses (www.sw.konstanz.de, in German) cost €2 for a single ticket (€3.50 at night); day passes are €3.90/6.60 for an individual/family. Bus 1 links the Meersburg car-ferry dock with the Altstadt. If you stay in Konstanz for at least two nights, your hotelier will give you a Gästekarte entitling you to free local bus travel.

For a taxi, ring ☎ 222 22.

Bicycles can be hired from **Kultur-Rädle** (☎ 273 10; Bahnhofplatz 29; per day €12; ☻ 9am-12.30pm & 2.30-6pm Mon-Fri, 10am-4pm Sat year-round, also 10am-12.30pm Sun & holidays Easter-Sep), 50m south of the tourist office.

AROUND KONSTANZ
Mainau Island
Jutting out over the lake and bursting with flowers, the lusciously green islet of **Mainau** (☎ 3030; www.mainau.de, in German; adult/under 12yr/concession/family €14.90/free/8/30; ☻ sunrise-sunset) is a 45-hectare Mediterranean garden dreamed up by the Bernadotte family, relatives of the royal house of Sweden.

Around two million visitors flock here every year to admire sparkly lake and mountain views from the **baroque castle**, wander sequoia-shaded avenues and hothouses bristling with palms and orchids. Crowd-pullers include the **Butterfly House**, where hundred of vivid butterflies flit amid the dewy foliage an **Italian Cascade** integrating patterned flowers with waterfalls, and a **petting zoo**. Tulips and rhododendrons are in bloom in spring hibiscus and roses in summer. Try to avoid weekends when the gardens get crowded.

You can drive, walk or cycle to Mainau 8km north of Konstanz. Take bus 4 from Konstanz' train station or hop aboard a passenger ferry.

Reichenau Island
☎ 07534 / pop 3200
In AD 724 a missionary named Pirmir founded a Benedictine monastery on **Reichenau** (www.reichenau.de), a 4.5km-by-1.5km island (Lake Constance's largest) about 11km west of Konstanz. During its heyday from 820 to 1050, the so-called Reichenaue School produced stunning illuminated manuscripts and vivid frescoes. Today, three surviving churches provide silent testimony to Reichenau's Golden Age. Thanks to them the island was declared a Unesco World Heritage Site in 2000.

Bring walking boots and binoculars, as this fertile isle of orchards and wineries is home to **Wollmatinger Ried**, a marshy nature reserve whose reed wetlands attract butterflies, migratory birds including kingfishers, grey herons and cuckoos, and even the odd beaver.

A 2km-long tree-lined causeway connects the mainland with the island, which is served by bus 7372 from Konstanz. The Konstanz–Schaffhausen and Konstanz–Radolfzell ferries stop off at Reichenau.

Marienschlucht
Well worth the 15km trek north of Konstanz, **Marienschlucht** (admission free; ☻ daylight hours) is a deep ravine wedged between the villages of Bodman and Wallhausen. A wooden staircase zigzags up through the chasm, past a babbling stream and 30m-high cliffs thick with lichen and ferns. The top rewards with snapshot views of Lake Constance through the beech trees. Bear left to follow the trail along the ridge and back

down to Wallhausen. There are picnic areas and a kiosk en route, as well as pebbly bays for refreshing dips in the lake.

Coming from Konstanz, Wallhausen is the best place to access the gorge, either by bicycle or bus 4 or 13 from the Hauptbahnhof (€2, 30 minutes). From Wallhausen it's a 3km walk to Marienschlucht.

MEERSBURG
☎ 07532 / pop 5500

Tumbling down vine-streaked slopes to Lake Constance and crowned by a perkily turreted medieval castle, Meersburg lives up to all those clichéd knights-in-armour, damsel-in-distress fantasies. And if its tangle of cobbled lanes and half-timbered houses filled with jovial banter don't sweep you off your feet, the local Pinot noir served in its cosy *Weinstuben* (wine taverns) will, we swear.

Orientation & Information
Walk downhill from the church opposite the tourist office to reach the Marktplatz, the heart of the Oberstadt (Upper Town). Go through the Rathaus arch and you're at the castles. Steigstrasse leads down to the Unterstadt (Lower Town) and the harbour.

Post office (Am Bleicheplatz) Across the intersection from the church.

Schickeria (☎ 6887; Stettener Strasse 3; per hr €4; ☼ noon-midnight) Internet access.

Tourist office (☎ 440 400; Kirchstrasse 4; www .meersburg.de; ☼ 9am-12.30pm & 2-6pm Mon-Fri, 10am-1pm Sat) Housed in a one-time Dominican monastery. Internet access costs €3 per hour.

Sights
ALTES SCHLOSS
Looking across the lake from its lofty perch, the **Altes Schloss** (☎ 800 00; adult/6-13yr/concession €8.50/4.50/6.50; ☼ 9am-6.30pm Mar-Oct, 10am-6pm Nov-Feb) is an archetypal medieval stronghold, complete with keep, drawbridge, knights' hall and dungeons. Founded by Merovingian king Dagobert I in the 7th century, the fortress is among Germany's oldest, which is no mean feat in a country with a *lot* of castles. The bishops of Konstanz used it as a summer residence between 1268 and 1803.

Other than contemplating the castle's fairy-tale qualities, rumoured to have inspired the Brothers Grimm, you can roam

the prim Biedermeier quarters of celebrated German poet Annette von Droste-Hülshoff (1797–1848), whose portrait once graced the DM20 note.

NEUES SCHLOSS
In 1710 Prince-Bishop Johann Franz Schenk von Stauffenberg, perhaps tired of the dinginess and rising damp, swapped the Altes Schloss for the dusky pink, lavishly baroque **Neues Schloss** (☎ 440 4900; www .schloesser-und-gaerten.de; adult/concession/family €4/1/8; ☼ 10am-1pm & 2-6pm Apr-Oct). A visit to the now state-owned palace takes in the extravagant bishops' apartments replete with stuccowork and frescoes, Bathasar Neumann's elegant staircase, and gardens with inspirational lake views.

On the 2nd floor, the **Städtische Galerie** presents the work of artists that were resident in Meersburg in the 1920s and 1930s.

LAKEFRONT
Stroll the **harbour** for classic snaps of Lake Constance or to hire a pedalo (€9 per hour). On the jetty, you can't miss – and the pious might prefer to – Peter Lenk's satirical **Magische Säule** (Magic Column). The sculpture is a comical, risqué depiction of characters who have shaped Meersburg's history, including buxom wine-wench Wendelgart and poet Annette von Droste-Hülshoff as a seagull.

It's a five-minute walk east along the Uferpromenade to **Meersburg Therme** (☎ 440 2850; www.meersburg-therme.de; Uferpromenade 12; thermal baths 3hr 4-15yr/concession €8/5.50/7, sauna 3hr €15.50; ☼ 10am-10pm Mon-Sat, 9am-10pm Sun), where the 34°C thermal waters, water jets and Swiss Alp views are soothing. Those who dare to bear all can skinny-dip in the lake and steam in saunas that are replicas of Unteruhldingen's Stone Age dwellings (p474).

Sleeping
Meersburg goes with the seasons, with some places closing from November to February.

Gasthaus zum Letzten Heller (☎ 6149; www .zum-letzten-heller.de, in German; Daisendorfer Strasse 41; s/d €36/56; ℗) This family-friendly guesthouse keeps it sweet 'n' simple in bright, cottage-like rooms with pine trappings. The restaurant serving home-grown fare (€8.20 to €12.50) has a tree-shaded patio. It's 1km north of the old town.

Aurichs (☎ 445 9855; www.aurichs.com, in German; Steigstrasse 28; s €43, d €67-73) Nice surprise: not only does Aurichs have a first-rate restaurant but also stylish rooms with flourishes like slanted beams and wool rugs. Choose from lake or castle views.

Haus Säntisblick (☎ 9277; www.tp-meersburg.de; Von Lassbergstrasse 1; s €48-60, d €64-95; ☯ closed Nov–mid-Feb; 🅿 🐾) Named after an Alpine peak across the lake, this chilled guesthouse has five bright rooms, an outdoor pool and a sauna. Situated 400m north of the old town, it also harbours Meersburg's scuba school (www.tauchschule-meersburg.de, in German).

Gasthof zum Bären (☎ 432 20; www.baeren -meersburg.de, in German; Marktplatz 11; s €48; d €89-108; ☯ closed Dec-Feb; 🅿) Straddling three 13th- to 17th-century buildings, this guesthouse near Obertor receives glowing reviews for its classic rooms, spruced up with stucco work, ornate wardrobes and lustrous wood; corner rooms, No 13 and 23, are most romantic.

Eating & Drinking

Inviting wine taverns cluster on Unterstadt-strasse. The lakefront Seepromenade has wall-to-wall pizzerias, gelatarias and restaurants with alfresco seating.

Winzerverein Meersburg (☎ 807 164; Unter-stadtstrasse 11; light bites €3-6; ☯ 10am-9pm Apr-Oct) Popping corks since 1884, the beamed tasting rooms and terrace of Meersburg's *Winzerverein* (wine cooperative) buzz with locals quaffing Pinot noirs and nibbling antipasti.

Weinhaus Hanser (☎ 7717; Unterstadtstrasse 28; Flammkuchen €7-8; ☯ closed Nov-Easter) Exposed red-brick and barrel tables create a cosy vibe at this 500-year-old *Torkel* (wine press), where you can taste five local wines for €5.80 or chomp pizza-like *Flammkuchen*.

Gasthof zum Bären (☎ 432 20; www.baeren-meersburg .de, in German; Marktplatz 11; mains €9-17.50 ☯ closed Feb & Mon) Antler lights, wood beams and a tiled oven set the scene in this rustic restaurant, popular for regional dishes like whitefish in grapefruit sauce.

Winzerstube zum Becher (☎ 9009; Höllgasse 4; mains €10.50-25.80; ☯ closed Mon) Vines drape the facade of this wood-panelled bolt-hole, run by the same family since 1884. Home-grown Pinot noirs accompany Lake Constance classics such as whitefish in

almond-butter sauce. The terrace affords Altes Schloss views.

our pick Aurichs (☎ 445 9855; Steigstrasse 28 mains €16.50-32; ☯ 5-11pm Tue-Sat, 11.30am-11pm Sun Christian Aurich has won foodies' heart at this contemporary, art-filled restaurant where he puts a Mediterranean spin on regional flavours. Starters such as sesame-crusted tuna carpaccio are followed by mains like beautifully tender Bodensee lamb with rosehip jus, and fruity desserts like black-berry *panna cotta*. The wine list and service are excellent, as are the lake views from the cliff-hanger of a terrace.

Getting There & Away

For details on the many ferry options from here, see p467.

Meersburg, which lacks a train station, is 18km west of Friedrichshafen.

From Monday to Friday, seven times a day express bus 7394 makes the trip to Konstanz (€3, 45 minutes) and Friedrichshafen (€2.95 26 minutes). Bus 7373 connects Meersburg with Ravensburg (€5, 40 minutes, four daily Monday to Friday, two Saturday). Meersburg's main bus stop is next to the church.

Getting Around

The best and only way to get around Meersburg is on foot. Even the large pay parking lot near the car-ferry port (€1.20 per hour) is often full in high season. You might find free parking north of the old town along Daisendorfer Strasse.

Hire bikes at **Hermann Dreher** (☎ 5176 Stadtgraben 5; per day €4.50; ☯ rental 9am-noon), down the alley next to the tourist office.

AROUND MEERSBURG
Pfahlbauten

Be catapulted back to the neolithic age and the Bronze Age at the **Pfahlbauten** (☎ 07556-8543; www.pfahlbauten.de; Strandpromenade 6 Unteruhldingen; adult/6-15yr/concession €7/4.50/5; ☯ 9am-7pm Apr-Sep, 9am-5pm Oct, 9am-5pm Sat & Sun Nov & 1-14 Mar, 9am-6pm 15-31 Mar, 11am & 2.30pm Mon-Fri Dec-Feb) carefully reconstructed pile dwellings based on the findings of local excavations. The 45-minute tours of the lakefront complex take in stilt dwellings that give an insight into the lives of farmers, fishermen and craftsmen Kids love the hands-on activities from axe making to starting fires using flints.

The Pfahlbauten are on the B31, which skirts the northern shore of the lake. The Bodensee–Gürtelbahn train serves Uhldingen-Mühlhofen, a 30-minute walk from the Pfahlbauten, hourly.

Birnau

Sitting on a bluff overlooking the lake and surrounded by vineyards, the exuberant, powder-pink **Birnau pilgrimage church** (admission free) is one of Lake Constance's architectural highlights. It was built by the rococo master Peter Thumb of Vorarlberg in 1746. When you walk in, the decor is so intricate and profuse you don't know where to look first. At some point your gaze will be drawn to the ceiling, where Gottfried Bernhard Göz worked his usual fresco magic.

Birnau is just off the B31, about 8km northwest of Meersburg and 7km southeast of **Überlingen**, which has an attractive lakefront promenade. Twice-hourly bus 7395 from Friedrichshafen (50 minutes) and Meersburg (20 minutes) stops near the church.

Affenberg Salem

No zoo-like cages, no circus antics, just happy Barbary macaques free to roam in a near-to-natural habitat is the concept behind the conservation-oriented **Affenberg Salem** (☎ 07553-381; www.affenberg-salem.de; Mendlishausen; adult/6-15yr/concession €7.50/4.50/6.50; ☼ 9am-6pm mid-Mar–Oct). Trails interweave the 20-hectare woodlands, where you can feed tail-less monkeys one piece of special popcorn at a time, observe their behaviour (you scratch my back, I'll scratch yours…) and get primate close-ups at hourly feedings. The park is also home to storks; listen for bill clattering and look out for their nests near the entrance.

Affenberg Salem is on the K776 in Mendlishausen, between Birnau and Salem. From May to early October, the ErlebnisBus runs hourly from Unteruhldingen and Salem to Mendlishausen (€2.10, 12 minutes).

Schloss Salem

Founded as a Cistercian monastery in 1134, the immense estate known as **Schloss Salem** (☎ 07553-814 37; www.salem.de; adult/6-16yr/student €7/3/4.50; ☼ 9.30am-6pm Mon-Sat, 10.30am-6pm Sun Apr-1 Nov) was once the largest and richest of its kind in southern Germany. The Grand Duchy of Baden sold out to the state recently,

but you can still picture the royals swanning around the hedge maze, gardens and extravagant rococo apartments dripping with stucco. The west wing shelters an elite boarding school, briefly attended by Prince Philip (Duke of Edinburgh and husband of Queen Elizabeth II).

Much of what you see in the convent buildings is baroque in excess, but the sublime **Münster** (Abbey Church) is Gothic except for the 26 neoclassical-style alabaster altars. The complex, which often hosts music festivals, also has a fire-fighting museum, old-time artisans' workshops and several restaurants.

The **Prälatenweg** (Prelates' Path) links Birnau to Schloss Salem, 9km northeast. From May to early October, the ErlebnisBus runs hourly between Schloss Salem and Salem (€1.80, five minutes) and Unteruhldingen (€2.10, 13 minutes). The Bodensee–Gürtelbahn train goes to Friedrichshafen (€3.65, 25 minutes, hourly).

FRIEDRICHSHAFEN

☎ 07541 / pop 58,000

Zeppelins, the cigar-shaped airships that first took flight in 1900 under the stewardship of high-flying Count Ferdinand von Zeppelin, will forever be associated with Friedrichshafen. An amble along the flowery lakefront promenade and a visit to the museum that celebrates the behemoth of the skies are the biggest draws of this industrial town, which was heavily bombed in WWII and rebuilt in the 1950s.

Orientation & Information

There are two train stations, the main-line Stadtbahnhof, 200m north of the lakefront, and, 800m southeast, the Hafenbahnhof, next to the Zeppelin Museum and the ferry port. The east–west lakefront promenade is called Seestrasse and then Uferstrasse. Friedrichstrasse runs between the train tracks and the lakefront.

ATMs Near the lakefront on Schanzstrasse.

Post office (Bahnhofplatz) To the right as you exit the Stadtbahnhof.

Tourist office (☎ 300 10; www.friedrichshafen.ws, in German; Bahnhofplatz 2; ☼ 9am-6pm Mon-Fri, 9am-1pm Sat May-Sep, 9am-noon & 2-5pm Mon-Thu, 9am-noon Fri Apr & Oct, 9am-noon & 2-4pm Mon-Thu, 9am-noon Fri Nov-Mar) On the square outside the Stadtbahnhof. Has a free internet terminal. Can book accommodation and zeppelin flights.

BADEN-WÜRTTEMBERG

Sights

Near the eastern end of Friedrichshafen's lakefront promenade, Seestrasse, is the **Zeppelin Museum** (☎ 380 10; www.zeppelin-museum.de; Seestrasse 22; adult/concession/family €7.50/3/17; ☺ 9am-5pm Tue-Sun May-Oct, 10am-5pm Tue-Sun Nov-Apr, also Mon Jul & Aug), housed in the Bauhaus-style former Hafenbahnhof, built in 1932.

The centrepiece is a full-scale mock-up of a 33m section of the *Hindenburg* (LZ 129), the largest airship ever built, measuring an incredible 245m long and outfitted as luxuriously as an ocean liner. The hydrogen-filled craft tragically burst into flames, killing 36, while landing in New Jersey in 1937.

Other exhibits provide technical and historical insights, including an original motor gondola from the famous *Graf Zeppelin*, which made 590 trips and travelled around the world in 21 days in 1929. An audioguide (€3) gives 1½ hours of English commentary (signage is in German). The top-floor art collection stars brutally realistic works by Otto Dix.

Kids can let off steam on the stainless-steel **Zeppelin sculpture** outside the museum. More sculptures are sprinkled around town, including in the lakefront **Stadtgarten** along Uferstrasse, a great spot for a picnic or stroll. Pedal and electric **boats** can be rented at the Gondelhafen (€8 to €30 per hour).

The western end of Friedrichshafen's promenade is anchored by the twin onion-towered, baroque **Schlosskirche**. It's the only accessible part of the Schloss, and is still inhabited by the ducal family of Württemberg.

Sleeping & Eating

The tourist office has a free booking terminal. For quick snacks, hit Seestrasse's beer gardens, pizzerias and ice-cream parlours.

Gasthof Rebstock (☎ 950 1640; www.gasthof-rebstock-fn.de, in German; Werastrasse 35; s/d €50/70; P) Geared up for cyclists, this family-run hotel has a beer garden and humble but tidy rooms with pine furnishings. It's situated 750m northwest of the Stadtbahnhof.

Buchhorner Hof (☎ 2050; www.buchhorn.de; Friedrichstrasse 33; s €82-210, d €100-260; P ▣) Many stifle a giggle (or a shriek) upon entering this hotel and coming face to face with an enormous moose head. The former owner, an avid hunter, lavishly decorated this traditional hotel with stuffed animals. Rooms are big if a tad bland. There's a sauna and a

COME FLY WITH ME

Real airship fans will justify the splurge on a trip in a high-tech, 12-passenger **Zeppelin NT** (☎ 590 00; www.zeppelinflug.de). Flights lasting 30/45/60/90/120 minutes cost €200/295/355/545/715. Shorter trips cover destinations on the lake such as Schloss Salem and Lindau, while longer ones drift across to Austria or Switzerland. Take-off and landing are in Friedrichshafen. The flights are not cheap, but nothing beats floating noiselessly over Lake Constance with the Alps on the horizon, so slowly that you can make the most of legendary photo ops.

restaurant (mains €18.50 to €26.50) serving regional fare.

Beach Club (Uferstrasse 1; snacks €6-8 ☺ 10am-midnight Apr-Oct) This lakefront shack is the place to unwind on the deck, mai tai in hand, and admire the *Klangschiff* sculpture and the not-so-distant Alps. Revive over tapas, salads and antipasti.

Getting There & Around

Ryanair flies from London Stansted to **Friedrichshafen's airport** (www.fly-away.de), frequently linked to the centre by buses 7586 and 7394. **InterSky** (www.intersky.biz) flies mainly to cities in Germany and Italy.

For details on ferry options, including the catamaran to Konstanz, see p467. Sailing times are posted on the waterfront just outside the Zeppelin Museum.

From Monday to Friday, seven times a day, express bus 7394 makes the trip to Konstanz (1¼ hours) via Meersburg (30 minutes). Birnau and Meersburg are also served almost hourly by bus 7395.

Friedrichshafen is on the Bodensee–Gürtelbahn rail line, which runs along the lake's northern shore from Radolfzell to Lindau. There are also regular services on the Bodensee–Oberschwaben–Bahn, which runs to Ravensburg (€3.65, 21 minutes) and Ulm (€17.80, 1¼ hours).

RAVENSBURG

☎ 0751 / pop 48,500

Ravensburg has puzzled the world for the past 125 years with its jigsaws and board games. The medieval Altstadt has toy-town appeal, studded with turrets, robber-knight towers and gabled patrician houses. For centuries dukes and wealthy merchants polished the cobbles of this Free Imperial City – now it's your turn.

Orientation & Information

The heart of Altstadt is the elongated, pedestrianised Marienplatz; almost all of Ravensburg's sights are nearby. The train station is six blocks to the west along Eisenbahnstrasse.

Tourist office (☎ 823 24; www.ravensburg.de; Kirchstrasse 16; ⏱ 9am-5.30pm Mon-Fri, 10am-1pm Sat) A block northeast of Marienplatz.

Sights & Activities

Slip back a few centuries taking in the sturdy towers and frescoed patrician houses framing **Marienplatz**. The 51m-high **Blaserturm** (adult/child €1/0.50; ⏱ 2-5pm Mon-Fri, 10am-3pm Sat Apr-Oct), part of the original fortifications, has superb views over the Altstadt from up top. Next door is the late-Gothic, step-gabled **Waaghaus**, while on the opposite side of Marienplatz sits the 15th-century **Lederhaus**, with its elaborate Renaissance facade, once the domain of tanners and shoemakers.

Ravensburg's newcomer is **Museum Humpis** (☎ 828 20; www.museum-humpis-quartier.de, in German; Marktstrasse 45; admission free; ⏱ 11am-6pm Tue-Sun, 8pm Thu), three blocks east of Marienplatz. Seven exceptional late-medieval houses set around a glass-covered courtyard shelter a permanent collection and rotating exhibitions focusing on Ravensburg's past as a trade centre.

At the northern end of Marienplatz is the round **Grüner Turm** (Green Tower), with its lustrous tiled roof, and the weighty, late-Gothic **Liebfrauenkirche**.

The all-white **Mehlsack** (Flour Sack) is a round tower marking the Altstadt's southern edge. From there a steep staircase leads up to the **Veitsburg**, a quaint baroque castle with outlooks over Ravensburg's mosaic of red-tiled roofs.

Sleeping & Eating

Marienplatz is lined with buzzy cafes, pizzerias and bars, many with pavement seating.

DJH hostel (☎ 253 63; www.jugendherberge-ravensburg.de; Veitsburgstrasse 1; dm 1st/subsequent night €19.10/15.90) Follow in dukes' footsteps to hillside Veitsburg castle, transformed into a hostel with creaky charm, well-kept dorms and gardens. It's a 25-minute uphill walk from the train station.

Gasthof Ochsen (☎ 254 80; www.ochsen-rv.de, in German; Eichelstrasse 17; s €52-62, d €82-92; 🛜) Just paces from Marienplatz, this 14th-century pile was once a butcher and baker. Today it's an inviting guesthouse with bright, parquet-floored rooms, free wi-fi and a wood-panelled *Stube* (lounge) serving hearty fare (mains €8 to €12).

Gasthof Obertor (☎ 366 70; www.hotelobertor.de; Marktstrasse 67; s €70-90, d €110-125) The affable Rimpps take pride in their lemon-fronted patrician house. Obertor is the pick of the Altstadt hotels, with spotless rooms, a sauna area, and generous breakfasts.

Sláinte (☎ 882 12 Eichelstrasse 4; snacks & mains €4.50-11; ⏱ 11am-1am Sun-Thu, 11am-2am Fri & Sat) Pop in for a pint, a bite to eat, or one of the regular concerts at this relaxed Irish watering hole.

Colours Café (☎ 352 6828; Bachstrasse 25; mains €7-15; ⏱ 9am-1am Mon-Sat, 10am-1am Sun; 🅥) The menu skips from drinks to tapas, pasta and blow-out brunches at this arty cafe with a covered patio.

Central (☎ 325 33; Marienplatz 48; mains €7.50-17; ⏱ 9am-1am Mon-Sat, 10am-1am Sun) Ravensburg hipsters head to this cafe-bistro for lounge grooves, cocktails and global cuisine from bouillabaisse to Thai curries.

Getting There & Away

Ravensburg is on the rail line linking Friedrichshafen (€3.65, 21 minutes, twice an hour) with Ulm (€15.20, 55 minutes, at least hourly) and Stuttgart (€30.70 to €40, 2¼ hours, at least hourly).

LINDAU

☎ 08382 / pop 24,300

Glossy brochures enthuse about Lindau being Germany's Garden of Eden and the Bavarian Riviera. Paradise and southern France it isn't, but you can believe at least some of the hype. Wedged into Lake Constance's northeastern corner, snuggling up to Austria and with an open attitude suggestive of warmer climes, the island's allure is undeniable. Never more so than when gazing across to the Alps at dusk from the lakefront promenade or meandering through the picture-book Altstadt.

Orientation

The *Insel* (island), home to the town centre and harbour, is connected to the mainland by the Seebrücke, a road bridge at its northeastern tip, and by the Eisenbahndamm, a

BADEN-WÜRTTEMBERG

rail bridge open to cyclists and pedestrians. The Hauptbahnhof lies to the east of the island, a block south of the pedestrianised, shop-lined Maximilianstrasse.

Information

ATMs There are several along Maximilianstrasse.

Lindauer Telecenter (Bahnhofplatz 8; per hr €2; ☑ 10am-7pm Mon-Fri, 11am-6pm Sat & Sun) Internet access; 100m to the left as you exit the Hauptbahnhof.

Post office (cnr Maximilianstrasse & Bahnhofplatz)

Tourist office (☎ 260 030; www.lindau.de; Alfred-Nobel-Platz 1; ☑ 9am-1pm & 2-6pm Mon-Fri, 2-6pm Sat early Apr–mid-Oct, plus 10am-2pm Sun late Jun–mid-Sep, 9am-noon & 2-5pm Mon-Fri mid-Oct–early Apr) Can make hotel bookings.

Sights

In summer the harbourside **Seepromenade** has Mediterranean flair, with its palms, bobbing boats and well-heeled tourists sunning themselves in pavement cafes.

Out at the harbour gates, looking across to the Alps, is Lindau's signature 33m-high **Neuer Leuchtturm** (New Lighthouse) and, just in case you forget which state you're in, a statue of the Bavarian lion. The square tile-roofed, 13th-century **Mangturm** (Old Lighthouse) guards the northern edge of the sheltered port.

Lions and voluptuous dames dance across the trompe l'oeil facade of the flamboyantly baroque **Haus zum Cavazzen**. Inside, the **Stadtmuseum** (☎ 944 073; Marktplatz 6; adult/concession €3/1.50; ☑ 11am-5pm Tue-Fri & Sun, 2-5pm Sat) showcases a fine collection of furniture, weapons and paintings.

Lindau's biggest stunner is the 15th-century, step-gabled **Altes Rathaus** (Bismarckplatz), a frescoed frenzy of cherubs, merry minstrels and galleons. Next door is the candy-pink, baroque **Neues Rathaus** where a glockenspiel plays at 11.45am daily.

Stepping north is **Peterskirche** (Schrannenplatz; ☑ daily), a millennium-old church that's now a war memorial, hiding exquisite time-faded frescoes of the Passion of Christ by Hans Holbein the Elder. The cool, dimly lit interior is a quiet spot for contemplation. Next door is the turreted, 14th-century **Diebsturm** (Brigand's Tower), once a tiny jail.

Sleeping

Lindau virtually goes into hibernation from November to February, when many hotels

close. Nip into the tourist office for a list of good-value holiday apartments.

DJH hostel (☎ 967 10; www.lindau.jugendherberge.de; Herbergsweg 11; dm €22.40, low season €18.90; ☑ closed Dec-early Feb; ☐) Housed partly in a 19th-century building and surrounded by gardens, this is an appealing hostel with a bistro and bike rental. It's served by bus line 1 or 2 from the Hauptbahnhof.

Hotel Anker (☎ 260 9844; www.anker-lindau.de; Bindergasse 10; s/d from €48/68) Shiny parquet floors, citrus colours and artwork have spruced up the bargain rooms at this peach-coloured guesthouse. Rates include a hearty breakfast.

Hotel Garni-Brugger (☎ 934 10; www.hotel-garni-brugger.de; Bei der Heidenmauer 11; s €49-62, d €85-98; ☑ closed Dec) Our readers rave about this 18th-century hotel, with bright rooms decked out in floral fabrics and pine. The family bends over backwards to please. Guests can unwind in the sauna (€10) in winter.

Hotel Medusa (☎ 932 20; www.medusa-hotel.com; Schafgasse 10; s €35-65, d €89-120) Not in the slightest bit scary, this Medusa pleases with lovingly renovated, high-ceilinged rooms with flat-screen TVs, and a downstairs Mexican restaurant.

Alte Post (☎ 934 60; www.alte-post-lindau.de; in German; Fischergasse 3; s €60-70, d €110-140; ☑ closed late Dec-late Mar) Sitting pretty on cobbled Fischergasse, this 300-year-old coaching inn was once a stop on the Frankfurt–Milan mail run. Well-kept, light and spacious, the rooms have chunky pine furnishings and perks like free tea. It's a short stroll from the harbour.

Eating & Drinking

For a drink with a cool view, head to Seepromenade. Maximilianstrasse's hordes can be avoided in quieter backstreets nearby where your euro will stretch further.

Alte Post (☎ 934 60; Fischergasse 3; mains €8.50-19.50) A dark-wood tavern with a cobbled terrace out front. Bring an appetite for soul food like Austrian *Tafelspitz* (boiled beef) and handmade *Maultaschen*, washed down with fruity local wines.

Valentin (☎ 504 3740; In der Grub 28; mains €13.50-26.90; ☑ closed Wed) Markus Allgaier uses the freshest local ingredients in Med-style dishes at this sleek vaulted restaurant. Signatures like monkfish medallions with pea-mint puree and lamb with wild-garlic risotto are uniformly delicious.

BADEN-WÜRTTEMBERG

Weinhaus Frey (☎ 947 9676; Maximilianstrasse 15; mains €15-32; ☽ closed Tue & Dec-Feb) This 500-year-old wine tavern oozes Bavarian charm in its wood-panelled tavern full of cosy nooks. Dirndl-clad waitresses serve up regional wines and fare such as Lake Constance trout. Sit on the terrace when the sun's out.

Marmor Saal (☎ 946 484; Maximilienstrasse 16; ☽ 9am-2am or 3am; ☞) The lakefront 'marble hall' once welcomed royalty and still has a feel of grandeur with its soaring columns, chandeliers and Biedermeier flourishes. Nowadays it's a relaxed cafe-bar with occasional live music and a chilled terrace.

Getting There & Away
For details on ferry services, see p467.

Lindau is on the B31 and is connected to Munich by the A96. The precipitous **Deutsche Alpenstrasse** (German Alpine Rd), which winds giddily eastward to Berchtesgaden, begins here.

Lindau is at the eastern terminus of the Bodensee–Gürtelbahn rail line, which goes along the lake's north shore via Friedrichshafen (€5.10, 25 minutes) westward to Radolfzell; and the southern terminus of the Südbahn to Ulm (€21.70, 1¾ hours) via Ravensburg (€8.40, 48 minutes).

Getting Around
The island is tiny and ideal for walking.

Buses 1 and 2 link the Hauptbahnhof to the main bus hub, known as ZUP. A single ticket costs €1.90, a 24-hour pass is €5.

To get to the island by car follow the signs to 'Lindau-Insel'. There's a large metered car park at the western end of the island, beyond the train tracks, but it may be easier to park on the mainland and either walk or catch a bus over.

Bikes and tandems can be rented at **Unger's Fahrradverleih** (☎ 943 688; Inselgraben 14; per day €6-15; ☽ 9am-1pm & 3-6pm Mon-Fri, 9am-1pm Sat & Sun).

Rhineland-Palatinate & Saarland

The state of Rhineland-Palatinate (Rheinland-Pfalz), patched together by the French aft WWII, united historically disparate bits of Bavaria, Hesse and Prussia that had only on thing in common – the Rhine (Rhein). The river meanders for 1390km from the Swiss Alp to Rotterdam, but nowhere else has it shaped the land and its people more profoundly tha along the 290km stretch traversing Rhineland-Palatinate.

Some of Europe's largest corporations dominate the banks of the Rhine south of Mainz, th state capital. But along here there's also a grand legacy of the Middle Ages: the magnifice Romanesque cathedrals of Mainz, Worms and Speyer. Northwest of Mainz is the river's mo picturesque stretch, the storied Romantic Rhine, whose vine-clad slopes, medieval hilltc castles and snug wine villages have drawn artists and tourists since the early 19th century

Most of Germany's wine is grown in Rhineland-Palatinate's six wine regions: the Ahr Valle Moselle-Saar-Ruwer, Middle Rhine, Nahe, Rheinhessen and, famed for its German Wine Roa the Rheinpfalz. The region's wines can all be sampled in a multitude of ambience-laden win taverns. The local people's *joie de vivre* finds expression in the many wine festivals.

Tiny Saarland, in the southwest, was once a centre for heavy industry but these days it better known for Saarbrücken's Frenchified urbane charms, and its verdant forests and fields ideal for hiking and cycling.

HIGHLIGHTS

- **Romantic Rhine** Cruise, cycle or ramble along the castle-studded Rhine (p499) between Koblenz and Bingen

- **Roman Relics** Explore the remarkable ruins of Roman Trier (p514)

- **Imperial Cathedrals** Marvel at the Romanesque cathedrals in Mainz (p484), Worms (p488) and Speyer (p490)

- **Five Rivers on Two Wheels** Cycle the Moselle, Saar, Kyll, Ruwer and Sauer Rivers from Trier (p517)

- **Floor It** Take a high-speed spin around the Nürburgring race track (p498)

- **Rusty, Not Rustic** Admire colourful art inside the Saarland's historic Völklinger Hütte ironworks (p525) in Völklingen

★ Nürburgring

Romantic Rhine ★

★ Mainz

★ Trier

Worms ★

★ Völklingen

Speyer ★

- RHINELAND-PALATINATE POPULATION: 4 MILLION
- RHINELAND-PALATINATE AREA: 19,853 SQ KM
- SAARLAND POPULATION: 1.04 Million
- SAARLAND AREA: 2569 SQ KM

RHINELAND-PALATINATE & SAARLAND

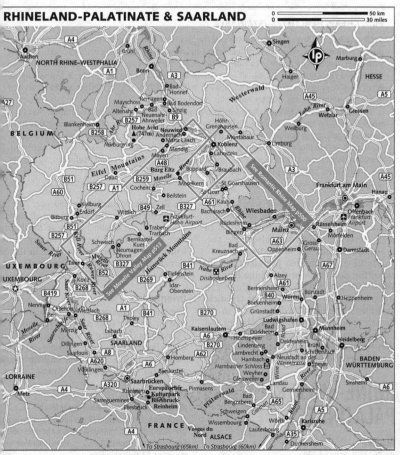

etting There & Away

eople complain that **Frankfurt-Hahn Airport** (irport code HHN; ☎ 06543-509 200; www.hahn-airport.de, ww.flyhahn.com), a Ryanair hub, is misleadingly amed because it's nowhere near Frankfurt, nd they have a point. But it *is* near many f the places covered in this chapter and linked by bus to destinations including ingen, Cochem, Idar-Oberstein, Koblenz us 610; €14, 65 minutes, six daily), Mainz €11, 70 minutes, 14 daily), Trier (stops at ells Park; see www.flibco.com for details; nline as cheap as €5, about one hour, 20 aily), Saarbrücken (see www.scherer-reisen le for details; €16, eight daily) and Worms. etails are available at www.hahn-airport.de – ick 'Getting There' and then 'By Bus'.

The *real* Frankfurt Airport (p542) is linked by easy public transport to places such as Mainz, Worms, Speyer, the German Wine Road (be prepared to transfer a few times) and some of the Romantic Rhine villages, especially right-bank ones served by direct trains from Wiesbaden.

Getting Around

With the **Rheinland-Pfalz-Ticket** (RP-Ticket; adult/ group of up to 5 €19/27), you can take any regional train (RE, IRE, RB and S-Bahn), tram, intercity bus or local bus anywhere within Rhineland-Palatinate and the Saarland for a full day – from 9am to 3am Monday to Friday and for the entire day on Saturdays, Sundays and holidays. On some rail routes it

---

FUN, CHEAP, HEALTHY, SUSTAINABLE

Cycling is *huge* in Rhineland-Palatinate and the Saarland, and for good reason. Delightful long-distance **bike trails** (www.radwanderland.de, in German) – many along decommissioned rail lines, with their mellow gradients – can be found along the Rhine (p500), the German Wine Road (p493) and the Ahr Valley (p496), all over Saarland (p521), and in the vicinity of towns such as Bernkastel-Kues (p518), Bingen (p510), Speyer (p492) and Trier (p517). Almost all the cities and towns mentioned in this chapter have bike rental shops.

You can bring your bicycle along for no charge on virtually all local trains, and for free (or a small charge) on boats sailing the Rhine, Moselle and Saar Rivers. Eight **RegioRadler bus lines** (www.regio-radler.de, in German; ☻ Apr-Oct) let you cycle one way and take the bus in the other. Mandatory reservations (€1.50 for up to five people) can be made via the website – tourist offices can help. Tourist offices can also supply you with cycling maps with useful details such as elevation charts and your public transport options.

---

costs less than the regular one-way fare, and for groups of up to five adults (or parents/grandparents with an unlimited number of their own children/grandchildren) the savings and flexibility are stupendous.

The RP-Ticket also lets you take the train along the right bank of the Rhine between Wiesbaden and St Goarshausen (this bit of track is officially in Hesse) and as far afield as Bonn, Mannheim, Karlsruhe and, in the French region of Alsace, Wissembourg and Lauterbourg. It is available from train station ticket machines, at local public transport offices and on buses.

RHINE-HESSE & PALATINATE

MAINZ

☎ 06131 / pop 198,000

The lively city of Mainz, capital of Rhineland-Palatinate, has a sizable university, fine pedestrian precincts and a certain *savoir vivre*, whose origins go back to Napoleon's occupation (1798–1814). Strolling along the Rhine and sampling local wines in a half-timbered Altstadt tavern are as much a part of any Mainz visit as viewing the fabulous Dom, Chagall's ethereal windows in St-Stephan-Kirche or the first printed Bible in the Gutenberg Museum, a bibliophile's paradise.

The Romans were the first to take advantage of Mainz' strategic location at the confluence of the Main and Rhine Rivers. In 12 BC, under Emperor Augustus, they founded a military camp called Moguntiacum as a base for the invasion of Germania. After the Romans, Mainz took a 250-year nap be fore being awoken by English missionary S Boniface, who established an archbishopri here in AD 746. In the 15th century, nativ son Johannes Gutenberg ushered in the in formation age by perfecting moveable typ (see the boxed text, p485).

Orientation

The mostly pedestrianised Altstadt is cen tred on the Dom (cathedral) and the adjacer Marktplatz (Domplatz), which are 1km ea of the Hauptbahnhof. Pedestrians-only thor oughfares include east–west Ludwigsstrass and north–south Augustinerstrasse.

Information

ATMs Several are situated along Grosse Bleiche.

ConAction (Grosse Bleiche 25; per hr €2; ☻ 9am-1am o later Mon-Sat, 10am-1am Sun & holidays) Internet cafe.

Eco-Express (Parcusstrasse 12; ☻ 6am-10pm Mon-Sat, closed Sun & holidays) Laundry.

Gutenberg Buchhandlung (☎ 270 330; Grosse Bleiche 27-31) Bookshop with English novels and Lonely Planet titles.

Internet Center (Bahnhofstrasse 11; per hr €1; ☻ 9am-11pm) One of several internet cafes near the Hauptbahnhof

Mainz Card (individual/group-of-5 €9.95/25) Available from the tourist office and valid for two days, it gets you admission to museums (some are free anyway), a walking tour, unlimited public transport plus various discounts.

Post office (Bahnhofstrasse 2; ☻ 8am-6pm Mon-Fri, 7.30am-noon & 12.30-3pm Sat) Has an ATM.

ReiseBank Currency exchange in the Hauptbahnhof.

Teleinternet Cafe (Kartäuserstrasse 13; per hr €2; ☻ 10am-11pm)

Tourist office (☎ 286 210; www.touristik-mainz.de, www.mainz.de; Brückenturm am Rathaus; ☻ 9am-6pm Mon-Fri, 10am-6pm Sat, 11am-3pm Sun) The Touristik

nelyplanet.com

MAINZ

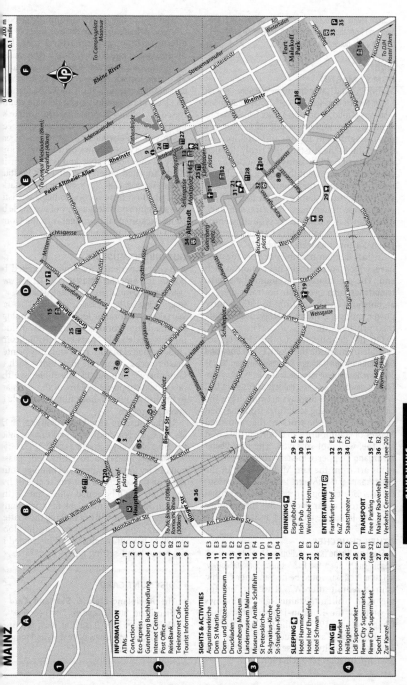

INFORMATION

ATMs	1 C2
ConAction	2 C2
Eco-Express	3 C2
Gutenberg Buchhandlung	4 C1
Internet Center	5 C2
Post Office	6 C2
ReiseBank	7 B2
Teleinternet Cafe	8 E3
Tourist Information	9 E2

SIGHTS & ACTIVITIES

Augustinerkirche	10 E3
Dom St Martin	11 E3
Dom- und Diözesanmuseum	12 E2
Druckladen	13 E2
Gutenberg Museum	14 E2
Landesmuseum Mainz	15 D1
Museum für Antike Schiffahrt	16 F4
St Peterskirche	17 D1
St-Ignatius-Kirche	18 F3
St-Stephan-Kirche	19 E2

SLEEPING

Hotel Hammer	20 B2
Hotel Hof Ehrenfels	21 E3
Hotel Schwan	22 E2

EATING

Food Market	23 E3
Heiliggeist	24 E2
Lidl Supermarket	25 D1
Rewe City Supermarket	26 B1
Rewe City Supermarket	(see 32)
Specht	27 E2
Zur Kanzel	28 E3

DRINKING

Eisgrubbräu	29 E4
Irish Pub	30 E4
Weinstube Hottum	31 E3

ENTERTAINMENT

Frankfurter Hof	32 E3
KuZ	33 F4
Staatstheater	34 D2

TRANSPORT

Free Parking	35 F4
Mainzer Radverleih	36 B2
Verkehrs Center Mainz	(see 20)

Centrale Mainz is across the pedestrian bridge (ie over the highway) from the Rathaus (town hall). English brochures include a self-guided tour map.

Sights

DOM ST MARTIN

Mainz' famed **cathedral** (Dom St Martin; ☺ 9am-6.30pm Mon-Fri, 9am-4pm Sat, 12.45-3pm & 4-6.30pm Sun & holidays Mar-Oct, to 5pm Sun-Fri Nov-Feb), entered from the Marktplatz, is one of Germany's most magnificent houses of worship. The focal point of the Altstadt, this richly detailed mountain of reddish sandstone, topped by an octagonal tower, went through a literal baptism by fire when the original burned down on the day of its consecration in 1009, an event whose millennium was marked in 2009. Much of what you see today is quintessential 12th-century Romanesque. Over the centuries seven coronations were held here.

Inside, a solemn ambience pervades the nave, which, surprisingly, has a choir at each end. The grandiose, wall-mounted **memorial tombstones** form a veritable portrait gallery of archbishops and other 13th- to 18th-century power mongers, many portrayed alongside their private putti.

Off the delicate, late-Gothic cloister, accessible from inside the Dom, is the **Dom- und Diözesanmuseum** (Cathedral & Diocesan Museum; ☎ 253 344; www.dommuseum-mainz.de, in German; ☺ 10am-5pm Tue-Sun, closed Mon & Catholic holidays; adult/student/family €3.50/3/7), which displays artwork from the cathedral, including sculptures from the rood screen (1239) – the work of the renowned Master of Naumburg – that portray the saved and the, well, not-so-saved. The new **Oberer Kreuzgang** (Upper Cloister) showcases religious art from the late Middle Ages. In the **Schatzkammer** (adult/student/family €3/2.50/6, combination ticket €5/4/10), you can see bejewelled ritual objects from as far back as the 10th century (English-language pamphlet available).

OTHER CHURCHES

St-Stephan-Kirche (Kleine Weissgasse 12; ☺ 10am-noon & 2-5pm Mon-Thu, 10am-5pm Fri & Sat, noon-5pm Sun Feb-Nov, to 4.30pm Dec & Jan) would be just another Gothic church rebuilt after WWII were it not for the nine brilliant, stained-glass windows created by the Russian-Jewish artist Marc Chagall (1887–1985) in the final years of his life. Bright blue and imbued with a mystical, meditative quality, they serve as a symbol of Jewish-Christian reconciliation.

Mainz also has a trio of stunning baroqu churches which illustrate the evolution of thi often over-the-top architectural style. Pa of the local Catholic seminary, the classi cally baroque **Augustinerkirche** (Augustinerstras 34; ☺ 8am-5pm Mon-Fri, may also open Sat & Sun whe the seminary is in session), built in 1768, feature an elaborate organ loft and a delicate ceilin fresco by Johann Baptist Enderle. Unlike s many churches in Germany, it has never bee destroyed. **St Peterskirche** (Petersstrasse 3; ☺ 9am 6pm, till 5pm in winter) shows off the sumptuou glory of the rococo style and is noted for it richly adorned pulpit and altars. **St-Ignatiu Kirche** (Kapuzinerstrasse 36; ☺ irregular hours) mark the transition from rococo to neoclassicism The sculpture outside is a copy of one made b Hans Backoffen (the original is in the Dom und Diözesanmuseum, see left).

GUTENBERG MUSEUM

A heady experience for anyone excited b books, the **Gutenberg Museum** (☎ 122 644; ww .gutenberg-museum.de; Liebfrauenplatz 5; adult/student senior/family €5/3/10; ☺ 9am-5pm Tue-Sat, 11am-3p Sun) takes a panoramic look at the technolog that made the world as we know it – includ ing this guidebook – possible. Highlights in clude medieval manuscripts and early printe masterpieces – kept safe in a vault – such a Gutenberg's original 42-line Bible (see th boxed text, opposite). Many of the signs ar in English; a quarter-hour film is available i seven languages.

In the museum's **Druckladen** (print shop; ☎ 12 686; www.gutenberg-druckladen.de; individual admissio free, group admission per person incl tour €5; ☺ 9am-5p Mon-Fri, 10am-3pm Sat), across tiny Seilergass you can try out Gutenberg's technology your self – on the condition that you're at least fiv years old. You'll be issued with a smock (th unique odour of printers' ink may, for many conjure up the nobility of making the writte word available to the masses, but the gloo is hell to get out of fabric) and instructed i the art of hand-setting type – backwards, ₑ

FORTY-TWO LINES THAT CHANGED THE WORLD

Johannes Gutenberg, the inventor of printing with moveable type, is one of those rare epochal figures whose achievements truly changed the course of human history.

Little is known about Gutenberg the man, who was born in Mainz in the very late 1300s, trained as a goldsmith and then, in the late 1420s, left for Strasbourg (now in France), where he first experimented with printing technology. By 1448 he was back in Mainz, still working on his top-secret project and in debt to some rather impatient 'venture capitalists'. But eventually his perseverance paid off and he perfected a number of interdependent technologies: metal type that could be arranged into pages; precision moulds to produce such type in large quantities; a metal alloy from which type could be cast; a type of oil-based ink suitable for printing with metal type; and press technology derived from existing wine, paper and bookbinding presses.

Despite several lawsuits, by 1455 Gutenberg had produced his masterpiece, the now-legendary Forty-Two-Line Bible, so-named because each page has 42 lines. Thus began a new era in human history, one in which the printed word – everything from Martin Luther's *Ninety-Five Theses* to pornography and the *Declaration of the Rights of Man and of Citizen* to Nazi propaganda – was to become almost universally accessible. In all of human history, arguably only two other inventions have come close to having the same impact on the availability of information: the alphabet and the internet.

ourse. Nearby, master craftsmen produce legant posters, certificates and cards using he labour-intensive technologies of another ge. Fascinating, especially in an era when rint' usually means 'Ctrl+P'.

ANDESMUSEUM MAINZ

he rich and far-reaching collection of the **andesmuseum Mainz** (State Museum; ☎ 285 70; ww.landesmuseum-mainz.de, in German; Grosse Bleiche 9-51; adult/student & senior/family €3/2/6, separate fee for ecial exhibitions, Sat free; ⏰ 10am-8pm Tue, 10am-5pm ed-Sun), housed in the former prince-elector's tables, traces the region's cultural history rom the Stone Age to the present. Treasures nclude the richly festooned facade of the **aufhaus am Brand**, a 14th-century trading ouse, and the famous **Jupitersäule** (on display gain in 2010), a Roman triumphal column rom the 1st century. Also of special interest re Dutch and Flemish paintings, faience and rt-nouveau glass.

USEUM FÜR ANTIKE SCHIFFAHRT

n 1981 excavations for a hotel unearthed he remains of five spectacular wooden ships f the Romans' Rhine flotilla, used around D 300 to thwart Germanic tribes trying to ntrude upon Roman settlements. They are ow on display, along with two full-size repcas, in the **Museum für Antike Schiffahrt** (Museum f Ancient Seafaring; ☎ 286 630; www.rgzm.de; Neutorstrasse b; admission free; ⏰ 10am-6pm Tue-Sun).

Tours

Walking tours of the city (€5) in German and English begin at the tourist office at 2pm on Saturday. From May to October, there are additional tours at 2pm on Monday, Wednesday, Friday and Sunday.

Sleeping

The tourist office has a **room reservations hotline** (☎ 286 2128; ⏰ 9am-1pm & 2-6pm Mon-Fri, 10am-4pm Sat, 11am-3pm Sun); bookings can be made in person, by phone or via www.touristik-mainz.de (under Accommodation).

Campingplatz Maaraue (☎ 06134-4383; www.krkg.de/camping.html; Auf der Maaraue 48, Mainz-Kostheim; adult/tent/car €4.50/3/3; ⏰ Apr-Oct) This grassy riverside camping ground is across the Rhine from the city centre. From the Hauptbahnhof take bus 54, 55, 56, 57, 68 or 91 to Brückenkopf; from there it's a 10-minute walk south.

DJH hostel (☎ 853 32; www.jugendherberge.de; Otto-Brunfels-Schneise 4; dm from €19.90; Ⓟ ☒) A modernised 166-bed hostel near a city park with two- and four-bed rooms, all with private bathroom. About 3.5km southeast of the Hauptbahnhof; take bus 62, 63 or 92.

Hotel Hammer (☎ 965 280; www.hotel-hammer.com; Bahnhofplatz 6; s/d from €99/119, weekends & low season from €79/89; Ⓟ ☒ ⌘ 💻) With an upbeat colour scheme, bright bathrooms and an urban skyline over each bed, the 37-room, business-oriented Hammer is convenient to the train station. The sauna is a welcome bonus.

Hotel Hof Ehrenfels (☎ 971 2340; www.hof-ehrenfels.de; Grebenstrasse 5-7; s/d/tr €80/100/120, €10 less Fri-Sun; ✗) Just steps from the cathedral, this 22-room place, housed in a 15th-century, one-time Carmelite nunnery, has Dom views that are hard to beat. A real treat if you love the tintinnabulation of the bells, bells, bells. Renovated in 2008.

our pick Hotel Schwan (☎ 144 920; www.mainz -hotel-schwan.de; Liebfrauenplatz 7; r €87-117) You can't get any more central than this family-run place, around since 1463. The 22 well-lit rooms have baroque-style furnishings.

Eating & Drinking
Cheap eateries can be found near the Hauptbahnhof and south of the Dom along Augustinerstrasse.

our pick Eisgrubbräu (☎ 221 104; www.eisgrub.de, in German; Weissliliengasse 1a; mains €5.80-17.90; ⌚ 9am-1am Sun-Thu, to 2am Fri & Sat) Grab a seat in this down-to-earth microbrewery's warren of vaulted chambers, order a mug of *Dunkel* (dark) or *Hell* (light) – or even a 3L/5L *Bierturm* (beer tower; €17.90/28.40) – and settle in for people watching. The Monday-to-Friday lunch (€5.90) – an all-you-can-eat buffet from October to March – and the daily breakfast buffet (€6.90; available 9am to noon) offer good value.

Heiliggeist (☎ 225 757; www.heiliggeist-mainz.de; Mailandsgasse 11; mains €6-20; ⌚ 4pm-1am Mon-Fri, 9am-1am or 2am Sat, Sun & holidays) Sit beneath the soaring Gothic vaults of a 15th-century hospital and enjoy a drink, snack or full meal from a menu filled with Italian-inspired creations.

Weinstube Hottum (☎ 223 370; Grebenstrasse 3; mains €7.50-13.50; ⌚ 4pm-midnight) One of the best of the Altstadt wine taverns, Hottum has a cosy, traditional atmosphere, delectable wines and a menu – half of which appears on a tiny slate tablet – with regional dishes such as *Saumagen* (pig's stomach stuffed with meat, potatoes and spices, then boiled, sliced and briefly fried) and *Winzersteak* (vintner-style pork steak).

Specht (☎ 231 770; Rotekopfgasse 2; mains €9.50-16; ⌚ 5pm-midnight Sun-Fri, 11.30am-midnight Sat) Thanks to its ancient wood beams, smoked walls and Fastnacht (carnival) medals, 'Woodpecker' has a 19th-century feel, though the building itself dates from 1557. It serves German and regional cuisine made with fresh products from the nearby market. If the ancient beam ceiling *doesn't* look uneven and wavy, you've had too much to drink.

our pick Zur Kanzel (☎ 237 137; Grebenstrasse mains €18.50-21.50; ⌚ 5pm-1am Mon-Fri, noon-1am Sa A classy place with a distinctly French fla and a nice courtyard, this *Weinstube* (win bar) serves upmarket French and region cuisine, including dishes made with *grün Sosse* (light sauce made with fresh herb sour cream and soft white cheese). All in gredients are fresh, so the menu evolves wit the seasons.

Irish Pub (☎ 231 430; Weissliliengasse 5; ⌚ 5pm-1a Sun-Thu, to 2am Fri & Sat) A candle-lit basemer watering hole – Irish owned and staffed with karaoke on Monday and Thursday, so musicians Tuesday and Wednesday, banc on Friday and Saturday and an open-mik night on Sunday (all from 9.30pm). Attrac a very international crowd, including US so diers from Wiesbaden.

Self-catering options:

Food market (Marktplatz & Liebfrauenplatz; ⌚ 7am-2pm Tue, Fri & Sat) Along the north and east sides of the Dom.

Lidl supermarket (Grosse Bleiche 41; ⌚ 8am-8pm Mon-Sat)

Rewe City supermarket (Augustinerstrasse 55; ⌚ 8am-10pm Mon-Sat)

Rewe City supermarket (Bonifatiusstrasse; ⌚ 8am-10pm Mon-Sat, bakery also open 8am-noon Sun) Near th train station.

Entertainment
Two free monthly mags with details o cultural events, *Fritz* and *Der Mainzer*, a available at the tourist office and in cafe and pubs. Tickets for most events are sol at the tourist office.

our pick KuZ (☎ 286 860; www.kuz.de, in Germa Dagobertstrasse 20b) Dance parties, live concert a summer beer garden with alfresco movi screenings, a world-music summer festiva kids' theatre…the happening *Kulturzentru* (cultural centre) has something for ever one. It's housed in a neat red-brick buil ing that began life in the 19th century as military laundry.

Frankfurter Hof (☎ 220 438; www.frankfurter-h -mainz.de, in German; Augustinerstrasse 55) This hug popular performance venue hosts everyon from up-and-coming artists to big-name ac such as Simply Red and Carlos Santana.

Staatstheater (☎ 285 1222; www.staatstheater-mai .com, in German; Gutenbergplatz 7) Mainz' city theatr stages plays, opera and ballet. Students ge significant discounts.

etting There & Away

rom the Hauptbahnhof, S-Bahn line 8 goes
Frankfurt Airport (€3.70, several times
ourly), 30km northeast of Mainz.

Details on public travel in the Mainz re-
ion are available at the **Verkehrs Center Mainz**
(☎ 127 777; www.mvg-mainz.de, in German; Bahnhofplatz
; ⊗ 7am-7pm Mon-Fri, 9am-2pm Sat).

A major IC rail hub, Mainz has at least
ourly regional services to Bingen (€5.70, 15
) 40 minutes) and other Romantic Rhine
wns, Koblenz (€16.70 by regional train, 50
) 90 minutes), Idar-Oberstein (€10.50, one
our), Saarbrücken (€27.40, 2½ hours) and
Vorms (€7.60, 26 to 43 minutes).

Mainz is encircled by a ring road with con-
ections to the A60, A63 and A66.

City-centre parking options are limited to
ricey underground garages and street spots
ith one- or two-hour limits. On the centre's
outheast edge, there's free parking on Am
Vinterhafen, just east of KuZ. You could also
esign your own Park & Ride by leaving your
ehicle outside the centre along a tram line.

For details on cruising the Rhine, see p500.

etting Around

1ainz operates a joint bus and tram system
ith Wiesbaden (www.mvg-mainz.de, in
erman). Single/five tickets cost €2.30/9.25;
ay passes are €5.60/8.40 for individuals/
roups of up to five.

Mainzer Radverleih (☎ 336 1225; Binger Strasse 19;
-/24-speed bicycle per day €7.50/8.50; ⊗ 8am-8pm Mon-Fri,
am-4pm Sat mid-Mar–early Oct), on the road bridge
vel of the round tower atop the CityPort
arkhaus (near the Hauptbahnhof), hires out
ikes and sells cycling maps.

VORMS

☎ 06241 / pop 82,300

Vorms (rhymes with 'forms'), one of
ermany's oldest cities, has played a pivotal
ole at various moments in European history.
n AD 413 it became capital of the legendary,
short-lived, Burgundian kingdom whose
ise and fall was creatively chronicled in
he 12th-century *Nibelungenlied*. Later hi-
cked by Wagner and the Nazis, the epic is
eatured in a local museum and the annual
ibelungen-Festspiele (www.nibelungenfestspiele.de, in
erman), a two-week festival held from late July
o mid-August.

After the Burgundians, just about every
ther tribe in the area had a go at ruling

Worms, including the Huns, the Alemans
and finally the Franks, and it was under the
Frankish leader, Charlemagne, that the city
flourished in the 9th century. The most impressive reminder of Worms' medieval heyday is its majestic, late-Romanesque Dom. A
Jewish community, renowned for the erudi-
tion of its rabbis, thrived here from the 10th
century until the 1930s, earning Worms the
moniker 'Little Jerusalem'.

In the Middle Ages, Worms – an important centre of commerce – hosted more
than 100 sessions of the imperial parliament (Diet), including one in 1521 at which
Luther famously refused to recant his views
and was declared an outlaw. An impressive
memorial (Lutherplatz) two blocks north of the
cathedral honours the Protestant reformer.

Orientation

Worms' basic layout dates from the Roman
period. Several streets are named for
Nibelungenlied characters, such as Kriemhild,
Siegfried and Hagen.

From the Hauptbahnhof and adjacent bus
station, pedestrianised Wilhelm-Leuschner-
Strasse leads 500m southeast to Lutherplatz,
on the northwest edge of the half-oval-
shaped Altstadt. From there, it's 150m
southeast to pedestrianised Kämmererstrasse,
the old city's main commercial thoroughfare,
and 300m south to the Dom. A plane-tree-
shaded promenade runs along the Rhine
about 800m east of the Dom.

Information

There are ATMs located inside the
Hauptbahnhof, along Wilhelm-Leuschner-
Strasse and at the Volksbank diagonally
across from the tourist office.

Internet Café (Neumarkt 5; per hr €1; ⊗ 10am-10pm
Mon-Sat, 11.30am-10pm Sun) Around the corner from
the Dom.

Internet und Telefonhaus (Hardtgasse 7; per hr €1;
⊗ 10am-11.30pm Mon-Sat, 11am-11.30pm Sun) Half a
block west of Kämmererstrasse, facing Woolworth.

Post office (Kaiserpassage, Am Römischen Kaiser) A
block east of Kämmererstrasse's Kaufhof department store.

TeleBistro (Kämmererstrasse 50; per hr €1; ⊗ 9.30am-
11pm) Internet access.

Tourist office (☎ 250 45; www.worms.de; Neumarkt
14; ⊗ 9am-6pm Mon-Fri, 10am-2pm Sat, Sun & holidays
Apr-Oct, 9am-5pm Mon-Fri Nov-Mar) Sells events tickets
and has a walking-tour brochure in English.

RHINELAND-PALATINATE & SAARLAND

Sights

KAISERDOM

Worms' skyline, such as it is, is dominated by the four towers and two domes of the magnificent **Dom St Peter und St Paul** (9am-5.45pm Apr-Oct, 10am-4.45pm Nov-Mar, closed during Sun morning Mass), built in the 11th and 12th centuries in the late-Romanesque style. Inside, the lofty dimensions impress as much as the lavish, canopied **high altar** (1742) in the east choir, designed by the baroque master Balthasar Neumann. In the south transept, a **scale model** shows the enormity of the original complex. Nearby stairs lead down to the stuffy **crypt**, which holds the stone sarcophagi of several members of the Salian dynasty of Holy Roman emperors.

In the *Nibelungenlied*, the **Kaiserportal** (open only during services) on the north side was the setting of a fierce quarrel between the Burgundian queens Kriemhild and Brünhild about who had the right to enter the Dom first. Trivial as it may seem, this little interchange ultimately led to their kingdom's downfall. Today, the main entrance is through the Gothic **Südportal** (south portal; 1300), richly decorated with biblical figures.

JEWISH SITES

Starting in the 900s, the Jewish community of Worms – known as Varmaiza in medieval Jewish texts – was centred on the northeast corner of the Altstadt (now a mostly Turkish quarter) along Judengasse and its side streets. Before 1933, 1100 Jews lived in the city; a Jewish community – now numbering 130 souls, almost all of them from the former USSR – was re-established in the late 1990s.

Worms' oldest synagogue, founded in 1034, was destroyed by the Nazis but in 1961 a new **Alte Synagoge** (Synagogenplatz; admission free; 10am-12.30pm & 1.30-5pm Apr-Oct, 10am-noon & 2-4pm Nov-Mar, closed to visitors every 2nd Sat morning) rose from its ashes. Men are asked to cover their heads. Around the side, stone steps lead down to a rare Romanesque **Mikwe** (ritual bath; admission free; same as Alte Synagoge) from the 1100s.

Behind the synagogue is the modern **Raschi-Haus**, built on the 14th-century foundations of a community wedding hall. It is named after Rashi (Rabbi Shlomo Yitzhaqi), a brilliant 11th-century Talmudic scholar who studied in Worms. Inside is the **Jüdisches Museum** (Jewish Museum; ☎ 853 4707; Hintere Judengasse 6;

adult/student €1.50/0.80; 10am-12.30pm & 1.30-5p Tue-Sun Apr-Oct, to 4.30pm Nov-Mar), which tell the history of the local Jewish community The singed Torah fragments were burnt i 1938 on Reichspogromnacht (Kristallnach see boxed text, p42). Signs are in Germa and English.

Just east of here is the arched **Raschito** (Rashi Gate; cnr Judengasse & Karolingerstrasse), a cit gate in the wall that still partially encircle the Altstadt.

Just outside the southwest corner of th Altstadt is the tranquil **Alter Jüdenfriedho** (Old Jewish Cemetery; Willy-Brandt-Ring 21; 9am-du Sep-Jun, to 8pm Jul & Aug, closed Jewish holidays), als known as the Heiliger Sand (meaning 'sa cred sand'), one of the oldest Jewish cem eteries in Europe (it was inaugurated i 1076). Men are asked to cover their head The most revered gravestone – it's one c two topped with large piles of pebbles, le by visitors as tokens of respect, and Wester Wall–style prayer notes – is that of Rabb Meir of Rothenburg (1215–93), who die in captivity after being imprisoned by Kin Rudolf of Habsburg for attempting to lead group of persecuted Jews to Palestine.

NIBELUNGEN MUSEUM

The *Nibelungenlied* is the ultimate ta of love and hate, treasure and treacher revenge and death, with a cast includ ing dwarves, dragons and bloodthirst *Überfrauen* (superwomen). Richard Wagne set it to music, Fritz Lang turned it into masterful silent movie (in 1924) and th Nazis abused its mythology, seeing i Siegfried the quintessential German hero.

The state-of-the-art **Nibelungen Museu** (☎ 202 120; www.nibelungen-museum.de; Fischerpförtche 10; adult/child/student €5.50/3.50/4.50; 10am-5pm Tu Fri, 10am-6pm Sat & Sun) seeks to rescue the epi from the Nazi's manipulations, bringing it t life in a surprisingly interesting multimed exhibit set up in two towers and along th ramparts of the medieval town wall. In th first tower you can listen to the anonymou poet tell his tale (in flawless English) whil watching excerpts from Lang's classic flic Signs are in German, English and French.

OTHER MUSEUMS

Two blocks south of the Dom (behind th youth hostel), the **Museum der Stadt Worms** (Cit Museum; ☎ 946 390; Weckerlingplatz 7; adult/studen

...mily €2/1/5, special exhibitions extra; ⊙ 10am-5pm Tue-...n), housed in the handsome Andreasstift ...irche (founded around AD 800), chroni-...es Worms' turbulent history from neolithi-...nd Roman times. Highlights include Bronze ...ge women's jewellery and delicate Roman ...ass excavated from local graves. Signs are ... German.

In the corner of a pretty park just north of ...e Dom, on the grounds of the former impe-...al and bishop's palace, is the **Museum Heylshof** ...⊙ 220 00; www.heylshof.de, in German; Stephansgasse 9; ...ult/student/family €3.50/1/5; ⊙ 11am-5pm Tue-Sun May-...p, 2-5pm Tue-Sat & 11am-5pm Sun mid-Feb–Apr & Oct-Dec). ...mong the paintings from the 15th to the 19th ...enturies are works by Tintoretto, Rubens ...nd Lenbach. The Venetian, Bohemian and ...erman glass, Frankenthal porcelain and ...eer steins (in the basement) are also worth ... look.

...eeping

...H hostel (☎ 257 80; www.jugendherberge.de; Dechanei-...sse 1; dm €18.90; ⊙ reception 7.30am-10pm Sun-Thu, ...l 11pm Fri & Sat; P ✕) A 140-bed hostel in an ...nbeatable location facing the south side of ...e Dom. The well-kept rooms have two to six ...eds and private bathrooms. Has free parking ...ut front.

Hotel Lortze-Eck (☎ 263 49; Schlossergasse 10-14; ...ww.lortzeeck.de, in German; s/d €46/65) This 14-...oom hotel is a practical choice, particu-...rly suitable if you like well-intentioned ...ke flowers. Situated half a block east of ...ämmererstrasse 22.

Hotel Kriemhilde (☎ 911 50; www.hotel-kriemhilde.de; ...ofgasse 2-4; s/d €52/74, s with hall toilet €39) Wake up to ...e peal of the Dom bells at this unassuming, ...mily-run inn. It faces the north side of the ...ighty cathedral, which is visible from some ...f the 19 rooms and audible everywhere.

Parkhotel Prinz Carl (☎ 3080; www.parkhotel ...rinzcarl.de; Prinz-Carl-Anlage 10-14; s/d from €85/125; ...P ✕) Housed in handsome barracks built – ...nd built to last – during the reign of the last ...aiser, this place has 90 pastel rooms that ...re spacious, comfortable and businesslike. ...n the northern edge of town, 500m north – ...hrough a chestnut-shaded park – from the ...auptbahnhof.

...ating & Drinking

...lthough the Diet of Worms was a sensa-...on in 1521, these days your culinary op-...ons are rather more varied. A cluster of

Italian restaurants can be found a block southeast of the Dom at the corner of Gerberstrasse and Wollstrasse. Cheap eats are available up towards the Hauptbahnhof along Wilhelm-Leuschner-Strasse.

Trattoria-Pizzeria Pepe e Sale (☎ 258 36; Wollstrasse 12; pizzas €3.10-6.20; ⊙ 11am-11.30pm) Serves 201 kinds of pizza, as well as pasta, including Spaghetti Robinson (tuna and garlic). Excellent value.

Café TE (☎ 597 633; Bahnhofstrasse 5; mains €4-13.30; ⊙ 8am-1am Mon-Thu, 8am-2am Fri & Sat, 9am-1am Sun) A trackside bar-cafe and beer garden half a block south of the Hauptbahnhof, this place – the name stands for 'Trans Europa' – is popular with students. Chic in an Italian sort of way, it features vegie dishes, 14 breakfast options and a different special each night. From October to May there's a Sunday breakfast buffet (€6.90).

our pick Hagenbräu (www.hagenbraeu.de, in German; Am Rhein 3; mains €5-10; ⊙ 9am-11pm Tue-Sun) This microbrewery, with hearty Rheinhessisch-style fare, is one of several hugely popular beer-garden-type eateries along the Rhine just north of the bridges. Nearby is a statue of Hagen tossing the Nibelung treasure into the Rhine.

For self-catering, try the **Kaufland supermarket** (Schönauerstrasse 8; ⊙ 7am-10pm Mon-Sat). To get to this big, new supermarket from the Dom, walk 400m south along Valckenbergstrasse and then 200m east.

Getting There & Around

Worms, about 50km south of Mainz, has frequent train connections with Mannheim (€4.70), a major rail hub, as well as Mainz (€7.60, 26 to 44 minutes, twice hourly), Bingen (€10.50, 70 minutes), Deidesheim (€7.10) and Neustadt an der Weinstrasse (€8.30). Going to Speyer (€8.30) requires a change in Ludwigshafen.

Seven **parking garages** (per 25min €0.50) are sprinkled around the city centre. There *may* be free parking at the Festplatz, just north of the twin Nibelungenbrücken (Rhine bridges).

Bicycles can be rented at **Radhaus-Mihm** (☎ 242 08; Von Steubenstrasse 8; 3-speed/all-terrain per day €5/12.50, per weekend €7.50/19, tandem per day €12.50; ⊙ 9.30am-12.30pm & 1.30-6pm Mon-Fri, 10am-1pm Sat), under the tracks from the Hauptbahnhof. The local **ADFC club** (www.adfc-worms.de, in German) organises group rides. The tourist office sells cycling maps.

SPEYER

☎ 06232 / pop 50,700

The dignified town of Speyer, about 50km south of Worms, has a walkable centre distinguished by a magnificent Romanesque cathedral, top-shelf historical museums and a medieval synagogue. Another highlight is the extraordinary Technik Museum, guaranteed to captivate kids and adults alike.

First a Celtic settlement, then a Roman market town, Speyer gained prominence in the Middle Ages under the Salian emperors, hosting 50 imperial parliament sessions (1294–1570).

In 1076 the king and later Holy Roman Emperor Heinrich IV – having been excommunicated by Pope Gregory VII – launched his penitence walk to Canossa in Italy from Speyer. He crossed the Alps in the middle of winter, an action that warmed even the heart of the pope, who revoked his excommunication. He lies buried in the Kaiserdom.

Orientation

Majestic Maximilianstrasse, the city centre's main commercial street, extends from the Altpörtel (a medieval city gate) 800m east to the Dom. The numbering of the buildings along Maximilianstrasse (from 1 to 100) begins at the Dom, runs sequentially along the south side to the Altpörtel, then it continues along the north side back to the Dom – be prepared for confusion! The Hauptbahnhof is about 1km north of the Altpörtel.

Information

For the price of a mobile phone call, you can get historical details on seven city sights by dialling ☎ 0911-810 940 043 and then the number marked on the attraction.

ATMs (Maximilianstrasse 47 & 49) Near the Altpörtel.

City-Call-Center (Bahnhofstrasse 3; per hr €1; ⏰ 10am-9pm Mon-Sat, noon-9pm Sun) Internet access, half a block north of the Altpörtel.

Post office (Wormser Strasse 4) Situated a block north of Maximilianstrasse 61.

Tourist office (☎ 142 392; www.speyer.de; Maximilianstrasse 13; ⏰ 9am-5pm Mon-Fri year-round, 10am-3pm Sat, 10am-2pm Sun & holidays Apr-Oct, 10am-noon Sat Nov-Mar) Next to the historic Rathaus, 200m west of the Dom.

Sights

KAISERDOM

In 1030 Emperor Konrad II of the Salian dynasty laid the cornerstone of the Romanesque

Kaiserdom (⏰ 9am-7pm Mon-Sat, 9am-5pm Sun Apr-Oc 9am or 10am-5pm daily Nov-Mar), whose square re towers and green copper dome float abov Speyer's rooftops. A Unesco World Heritag Site since 1981, its interior is startling for i awesome dimensions (it's an astonishin 134m long) and austere, dignified symmetr walk up the side aisles to the elevated alta area to get a true sense of its vastness.

Another set of steps, to the right of the alta leads down to the darkly festive **crypt** (adu under 17yr €2/free; ⏰ 9am-5pm, may open 10am or 11a in winter), whose candy-striped Romanesqu arches – like those on the west front – reca Moorish architecture (ask for an English language brochure). Stuffed into a side roon up some stairs, are the sandstone sarcopha of eight emperors and kings, along with som of their queens.

The most scenic way to approach the Dor is from Maximilianstrasse. Behind the Dor the large **Domgarten** (cathedral park) stretche towards the Rhine.

MAXIMILIANSTRASSE

Roman troops and medieval emperors onc paraded down 'Via Triumphalis'. Now know as Maximilianstrasse, Speyer's pedestrian only shopping precinct links the Dom wit the 55m-high, 13th-century **Altpörtel** (adu child €1/0.50; ⏰ 10am-noon & 2-4pm Mon-Fri, 10am-5p Sat & Sun Apr-Oct), the city's western gate an the only remaining part of the town wal The clock (1761) has separate dials fo minutes and hours. The views from up to are breathtaking.

A favourite with window-shoppers an strollers alike, Maximilianstrasse is lined wit baroque buildings, among which the **Rathau** (at No 13), with its red-orange facade an lavish rococo 1st floor (open for concerts an events), and the **Alte Münze** (Old Mint; at N 90) are worth a look.

A block south of the Rathaus is the **Judenh** (Jews' Courtyard; ☎ 291 971; Kleine Pfaffengasse 21; adu student/family €2/1/5; ⏰ 10am-5pm daily Apr-Oct, close Nov-Mar), where the excavated remains of Romanesque-style synagogue (consecrate in 1104 and used until 1450), its 13th-centur women's section and a **Mikwe** (ritual bath from the early 1100s – the oldest, largest an best preserved north of the Alps – hint at th glories of the city's storied medieval Jewis community. Signs are in German, English an French. A curious fact to note is that everyon

ith the surname of Shapira (or Shapiro) is
escended from Jews who lived in Speyer dur-
g the Middle Ages.

ISTORISCHES MUSEUM DER PFALZ
ne of the highlights of the superb **Historisches
useum der Pfalz** (Historical Museum of the Palatinate;
620 222; http://museum.speyer.de; Domplatz; adult/student
senior €4/3, incl special exhibitions €12/10; 10am-6pm
e-Sun), which prizes quality over quantity, is
e **Goldener Hut von Schifferstadt**, an ornate, per-
ctly preserved gilded hat, shaped like a giant
imble, that dates back to the Bronze Age (ie
e 14th century BC). The **Wine Museum** features
bottle containing an unappetising jellied sub-
ance from the 3rd century AD, purported
be the world's oldest wine. Two floors
elow is the **Domschatz** (cathedral treasury),
hose prized exhibit is Emperor Konrad II's
irprisingly simple bronze crown.

ECHNIK MUSEUM
t this amazing **museum** (670 80; www.technik
useum.de; Am Technik Museum 1; adult/under 6yr/6-14yr
3/free/11; 9am-6pm Mon-Fri, to 7pm Sat, Sun & holi-
ys), 1km south of the Dom (on the other side
f the A61 highway), you can climb aboard a
oeing 747-230 with navigational charts for
e British Crown Colony of Hong Kong in
e cockpit (how in the world did they get
e aircraft here and then mount it 28m off
e ground?); a 1960s U-boat that's claustro-
hobic even on dry land; and a mammoth
ntonov An-22 cargo plane with an all-
nalogue cockpit and a nose cone you can
eer out of. Other highlights include the
oviet space shuttle *Buran*, a superb collec-
on of vintage automobiles and fire engines,
nd military jets and helicopters from both
des of the Iron Curtain. A whole building is
lled with scale models, including ships, cars,
lanes and a destroyed German city c 1945.

The **Wilhelmsbau** showcases some truly ex-
aordinary automated musical instruments –
ll in working order – including a Hupfeld
honoliszt-Violina, a player-piano that also
ows and fingers two violins, and a Roland
rchestrion (1928), which simulates the sound
f a soprano accompanying an orchestra.

leeping
H hostel (615 97; www.jugendherberge.de; Geibstrasse
dm €19.90; reception 7.30am-8pm;) A
right, cheery hostel on the Rhine, a few hun-
red metres east of the Technik Museum and

next door to the new Bademaxx swimming
complex. Has 51 rooms, including 13 bunk
doubles, all with private bathroom. Linked
to the Hauptbahnhof and city centre by the
City-Shuttle bus.

Maximilian (100 2500; www.mein-maximilian.de,
in German; Korngasse 15; r €50-100) This cafe-bistro
rents out attractive rooms and two-person
apartments.

our pick **Hotel Zum Augarten** (754 58; www
.augarten.de, in German; Rheinhäuser Strasse 52; s €50-65,
d €68-85;) A cosy, family-run, family-
friendly hotel with 16 rooms, where you'll
enjoy German guest-house hospitality and observe suburban German life up close. Situated
1.7km south of the Dom – from the Technik
Museum take Industriestrasse and turn right
on Am Flugplatz.

Hotel Trutzpfaff (292 529; www.trutzpfaff-hotel
.de, in German; Webergasse 5; s/d €56/76; reception 8am-
8pm Mon-Fri, 8am-6pm Sat & Sun;) Centrally
situated just a block south of the tourist
office, this unassuming hostelry has eight
decent rooms. The Jewish tombstone given
pride of place at the entrance was brought to
this site, for use in reconstruction, after the
Napoleonic Wars.

Hotel am Technik Museum (671 00; www.hotel
-am-technik-museum.de; Am Technik Museum 1; s/d from
€62/78;) Part of the Technik Museum
complex, this place has 107 practical, worka-
day rooms. Got a campervan or tent? You can
stay at the adjacent *Stellplatz* (€20 per site),
open year-round. Linked to the Hauptbahnhof
and city centre by the City-Shuttle bus.

Hotel Domhof (132 90; www.domhof.de, in German;
Bauhof 3; s €95, d €116-125, cheaper Sun night;)
A hotel has stood on this spot next to the
Dom – an unbeatable location – since the
Middle Ages, once hosting emperors, kings
and councillors. The 49 comfortable rooms,
wrapped around an ivy-covered, cobbled
courtyard, have bright new bathrooms.

Eating & Drinking
A selection of dining options, including
outdoor cafes in the warm months, can be
found along Maximilianstrasse and nearby
streets, such as Kleine Pfaffengasse (near
the Judenhof).

Domhof-Hausbrauerei (674 40; Grosse Himmelsgasse
6; mains €4.90-14.50; 10am or 11am-midnight or 1am
Tue-Sat, to 11pm Sun & Mon) Speyer's loveliest beer
garden, shaded by chestnut trees, is just steps
west of the Dom and has a miniature children's

RHINELAND-PALATINATE & SAARLAND

playground. The menu features regional and German favourites, some prepared using the four beers brewed on the premises.

Hotel Trutzpfaff (☎ 292 529; Webergasse 5; mains €6.50-12.80; ⏰ lunch & dinner Mon-Fri, lunch Sun) The restaurant at Hotel Trutzpfaff (p491) serves up Palatine specialities such as *Saumagen*.

Maximilian (☎ 100 2500; Korngasse 15; mains €6.90-13.90; ⏰ 8am-midnight Sun-Wed, to 1am Thu-Sat) Just inside the Altpörtel (facing the Tengelmann supermarket), this convivial cafe-bistro serves up 10 different breakfasts, salads, grilled meats, Italian options and two reasonably priced dinner specials (€4.90 and €5.90).

our pick **Zweierlei** (☎ 611 10; www.das-zweierlei.de, in German; Johannesstrasse 1, cnr Salzgasse; mains €7.50-34; ⏰ noon-midnight daily Mar-Sep, closed Mon Oct-Apr) This innovative restaurant-cum-bistro, a block north of the tourist office, serves German nouvelle cuisine – made with the freshest ingredients – amid minimalist, ultramodern decor. If you go for the bistro's 'Tender' dinner offer, the chef will assign you an hors d'oeuvre, a main dish (you choose meat or fish) and a dessert (€7.50 each) built around what someone else is ordering in the pricier restaurant.

Backmulde (☎ 715 77; www.backmulde.de, in German; Karmeliterstrasse 11-13; mains €10-30; ⏰ 11.30am-2.30pm & 7-11.30pm Tue-Sun) Owner-chef Gunter Schmidt has a knack for spinning fresh, local products into gourmet dishes with a Mediterranean flavour – thus his motto, *cuisine sans frontières*. A block south of the western side of the Altpörtel.

For picnic supplies, check out **Tengelmann supermarket** (Maximilianstrasse 50; ⏰ 8am-9pm Mon-Sat), next to the Altpörtel.

Getting There & Around

An S-Bahn line links the Hauptbahnhof with Ludwigshafen (€4.70, 18 minutes) and Mannheim (€4.70, 25 minutes), both key rail hubs, and Heidelberg (50 minutes). Change trains in Schifferstadt to get to Neustadt an der Weinstrasse (€4.70, 25 minutes, twice hourly) and Deidesheim (€5.90).

Parking costs €1.50 per day at the Festplatz, 500m south of the Dom and across (under) the A61 from the Technik Museum.

The convenient City-Shuttle minibus (bus 565; day pass €1) links the Hauptbahnhof, Maximilianstrasse, the Dom, Festplatz, the Technik Museum and the youth hostel at 10- or 15-minute intervals from 6am (9am on Sunday) to 8pm.

Loaner cycling maps and information c pedal-driven touring options are enthusiast cally supplied at English-speaking **Radspo Stiller** (☎ 759 66; www.stiller-radsport.de, in Germa Gilgenstrasse 24; bike/tandem per day €10/20; ⏰ 9.30a 12.30pm & 2-6.30pm Mon-Fri, 9am-2pm Sat, also open demand to return bikes 2-6pm Sun), a bike rental sho a block southwest of the Altpörtel.

The circular **Kaiser-Konrad-Radweg** (Kais Konrad bicycle path) links Speyer's Dom wi Bad Dürkheim's Rathaus (about 30km eac way). **Veloroute Rhein** follows the Rhine nor to Worms. The excellent 1:150,000-scale cy cling map *Radtouren rund um Speyer* (Bicyc Touring around Speyer; €2) is sold at the tou ist office and bookshops.

GERMAN WINE ROAD

The **Deutsche Weinstrasse** (www.deutsche-weinstrasse.c in German) traverses the heart of the Palatina (Pfalz), a region of gentle forests, ruined castl and Germany's largest contiguous winegrow ing area. Starting in Bockenheim, about 15k west of Worms, it winds south for 85km Schweigen, on the French border, past welcon ing wine estates. Hiking and cycling optio are legion.

Blessed with a moderate climate that allov almonds, figs, kiwi fruit and even lemons thrive, the German Wine Road is especial pretty during the spring bloom (March mid-May). **Weinfeste** (wine festivals) ru from March to mid-November (especial on the weekends) – this is also a good tim to visit, especially around the grape harve (September and October).

In part because of its proximity to Franc the Palatinate is a renowned culinary destin tion, with restaurants serving everything fro gourmet German nouvelle cuisine to trad tional regional specialities, such as *Saumage* The **Pfälzerwald** (www.pfaelzerwald.de, in German), th hilly forest west of the Wine Road, was de clared (along with France's adjacent Vosg du Nord area) a Unesco Biosphere Reserv in 1993. Locals often plan a day outdoors i order to dine in a rustic **Waldhütte**, a trad tional rustic eatery found along forest trai such as the **Pfälzer Weinsteig**; tourist offices ca supply maps to find them.

GETTING THERE & AWAY

Neustadt an der Weinstrasse, a cen tral hub for exploring the German Win Road, is on the twice-an-hour railway lin

ROAD-TRIP RADIO IN ENGLISH

While tooling around Germany's southwest, you can crank up the car radio and tune in to a variety of often surprising programs in English.

When atmospheric conditions are right (as they almost always are at night), the **BBC World Service** can be picked up on 648kHz AM (medium wave) and, if you're lucky, **BBC Radio 4** can be heard on 198kHz long wave.

To feel like you're in Middle America (or to find out the weather in Baghdad or Kabul), just tune to a station run by the **AFN** (American Forces Network; www.afneurope.net), whose intended audience is US military personnel serving at places like Ramstein Air Base near Kaiserslautern and the Wiesbaden US Army Garrison. Programming you might come across includes NPR (National Public Radio) favourites such as *Car Talk*, pearls of populism from Rush Limbaugh, and news from AP Radio and the Pentagon Channel. One music show boasts that it plays 'music worth fighting for'. The public service advertisements, peppered with nanny-state announcements and unfathomable acronyms, give a taste of US military life in Germany. The most powerful relay frequencies to check are 873kHz AM (transmission from Frankfurt), 1107kHz (from Kaiserslautern) and 1143kHz (from Stuttgart). There are also a variety of local FM options.

Mannheim (€5.90, 30 minutes) and eidelberg (€8.30, 50 minutes) and also us train links to Saarbrücken (€17.60, 1½ ours via Kaiserslautern, hourly), Karlsruhe (10.30, 1¼ hours, twice hourly) and the rench town of Wissembourg (€8.30, one our, hourly). The trip from Speyer (€4.70, i minutes, twice hourly) requires a change Schifferstadt.

The **Rhein-Haardtbahn** (RHB; www.rhein-haardtbahn.de, German) light rail line links Bad Dürkheim with annheim (€4.70, 50 minutes, at least hourly); e **RNV-Express** (www.rnv-online.de) goes to all the ay to Heidelberg (80 minutes).

Ask at a train station about inexpensive gional train-tram-bus cards, good for 24 ours for up to five people.

ETTING AROUND

ne German Wine Road is most easily explored by car or, thanks to a multitude of *adwanderwege* (bike paths and cyclable back ads), bicycle. Area tourist offices carry the ee *Radkarte Pfalz* (Palatinate Cycling Map) d sell more detailed cycling maps.

Thanks to Germany's superb public transort system, however, it's possible to get almost everywhere – including *to* trail heads d *from* hike destinations – by public transort. Twice an hour, local trains that take cycles (free of charge) head from Neustadt orth to Deidesheim and Bad Dürkheim and uth to Landau.

A number of Pfälzerwald villages west of eustadt, including Lindenberg, are served bus 517.

Neustadt an der Weinstrasse
☎ 06321 / pop 53,700

The busy, modern town of Neustadt has a largely pedestrianised **Altstadt** teeming with half-timbered houses (eg along Mittelgasse, Hintergasse, Metzgergasse and Kunigundenstrasse). It is anchored by the **Marktplatz**, an attractive square flanked by the baroque **Rathaus** and the 14th- and 15th-century Gothic **Stiftskirche** (☺ sanctuary open during services, tower open with guide at noon Sat), a red-sandstone structure that's been shared by Protestant and Catholic congregations since 1708. The whimsical **Elwedritsche Brunnen** (fountain; Marstall) is two blocks northwest of the tourist office.

Just off the Marktplatz, **Haus des Weines** (☎ 355 871; www.haus-des-weines.com, in German; Rathausstrasse 6; ☺ 10am-6.30pm Tue-Fri, 10am-3pm Sat) is an excellent place to sample (€1 to €3 per glass) and buy regional wines and – believe it or not – drinkable vinegar, served in special tiny flutes.

From the Hauptbahnhof, cross Zwockelsbrücke (the road bridge a block west of the train station) to get to the **Eisenbahnmuseum** (Railway Museum; www.eisenbahnmuseum-neustadt.de, in German; ☺ 10am-1pm Tue-Fri, 10am-4pm Sat, Sun & holidays).

About 6km southwest of the centre, along the Deutsche Weinstrasse and then Eichstrasse, high atop a forested Pfälzerwald hill, stands the reconstructed **Hambacher Schloss** (Hambacher Castle; ☎ 926 290; www.hambacher-schloss.de; adult/student/family €4.50/1.50/9.50; ☺ 10am-6pm Apr-Oct, 11am-5pm Nov-Mar), known as the 'cradle of

German democracy'. It was here that idealistic students, local people, refugees from Poland and even some Frenchmen held massive protests for a free, democratic and united Germany on 27 May 1832, during which the German tricolour flag of black, red and gold was raised for the first time. Today an exhibition, opened in 2008, commemorates the event, known as the Hambacher Fest. Signs are in German, but audioguides (€3) are available in English, French and Polish. Bus 502 makes the trip here hourly from the train station.

INFORMATION

ATM Across the street from the tourist office in the Hetzelgalerie shopping mall.

Telecafe und Internetcafe (Friedrichstrasse 8; per hr €1; 🕙 11am-10pm) Around the corner from the tourist office.

Tourist office (☎ 926 892; www.neustadt.eu; Hetzelplatz 1; 🕙 9.30am-6pm Mon-Fri, 9.30am-noon Sat Apr-Oct, 9.30am-5pm Mon-Fri Nov-Mar) Diagonally across Bahnhofplatz from the Hauptbahnhof. Has ample information on town sights, hiking, cycling and wine festivals.

SLEEPING & EATING

Neustadt's nicest lodging options are in Haardt, a suburb northwest of the town centre. There are quite a few restaurants in Neustadt's Altstadt, especially along Mittelgasse and Hintergasse.

DJH hostel (☎ 2289; www.jugendherberge.de; Hans-Geiger-Strasse 27; dm €19.90; ✖ 🖳) A cheery, modern facility with 122 beds in rooms for one, two and four people, all with private bathroom. A 15-minute walk south of the Hauptbahnhof – cross the bridge over the tracks and head up Alter Viehberg.

Hotel Tenner (☎ 9660; www.hotel-tenner.de, in German; Mandelring 216, Haardt; d €79-92; P ✖) Surrounded by vineyards, this 32-room hotel, on a quiet suburban street, offers sweeping views of the Hambacher Schloss. In fine weather, breakfast is served on the pebbly panoramic patio. To get there from the town centre, take bus 512 (€1.80, twice hourly) or drive northeast on Maximilianstrasse and hang a left onto Haardter Strasse.

Liebstöckl (☎ 331 61; www.liebstoeckl.de, in German; Mittelgasse 22; mains €8.60-15.80; 🕙 lunch & dinner Wed-Mon, closed Tue) Has a beer garden and a hearty menu with Palatinate specialities and a few vegetarian choices (about €9).

For self-catering, there are food shops in Kellereistrasse and around Marktplatz, as well

as a **food market** (Marktplatz; 🕙 6am-1pm Tue & year-round, plus Thu May-Oct).

GETTING AROUND

The bus station (schedules posted) is in fro of the Hauptbahnhof.

Free parking is available along the stree northeast of the Hauptbahnhof (north Landauerstrasse).

Fahrrad Trimpe (🕙 487 070; Branchweilerhofstra∙ 11; per day €10; 🕙 9am-6.30pm Mon-Fri, 9am-4pm Sa∙ about 1.5km northeast of the Hauptbahnh∙ near Haltestelle Neustadt-Böbig (a stop on t∙ rail line to Ludwigshafen), rents bikes and c∙ deliver them to hotels.

Deidesheim
☎ 06326 / pop 3800

Awash in wisterias, diminutive Deideshei∙ one of the German Wine Road's most pi∙ turesque – and upscale – villages, is home 16 winemakers that welcome visitors; lo∙ for signs reading *Weingut* (winery), *Verka∙* (sale) and *Weinprobe* (wine tasting). The tov∙ is famed for its Christmas market.

The helpful **tourist office** (☎ 967 70; w∙ .deidesheim.de; Bahnhofstrasse 5; 🕙 9am-noon & 2-5∙ Mon-Fri Nov-Jul, 9am-12.30pm & 1.30-5pm Mon-Thu, to 6∙ Fri Aug-Oct, 9am-12.30pm Sat Apr-Oct), 150m across t∙ car park from the Bahnhof, has maps for ni∙ signposted **walking routes** through vineyar∙ and the Pfälzerwald. Down the block, t∙ **Sinneserlebnisgarten** (sense-experience garde∙ is set to open up in 2010.

Deidesheim is centred on the histor∙ Marktplatz, where you'll find a Gothic churc∙ **Pfarrkirche St Ulrich** (🕙 daily), and the 16th-centu∙ **Altes Rathaus**, noted for its canopied open-a∙ staircase. Inside the three-storey **Museum ∙ Weinkultur** (Museum of Wine Culture; ☎ 981 561; Marktpl∙ 8; admission free; 🕙 3-6pm Wed-Sun & holidays), featu∙ ing displays on winemakers' traditional lifest∙ and naive art portrayals of the German Wi∙ Road (English brochure available).

Down an alleyway across from the Ratha∙ the **Deutsches Film- und Fototechnik Museum** (F∙ & Photography Museum; ☎ 6568; www.dftm.de, in Germ∙ Weinstrasse 33; admission free; 🕙 2-6pm Wed-Sun & holid∙ Mar-Dec) has a truly impressive collection of hi∙ toric photographic and movie-making equi∙ ment. Veteran shutterbugs may be able to sp∙ every film camera they've ever used.

Galleries and artisans' studios (eg jewelle∙ makers) can be visited along the **Rundga∙ Kunst und Kultur** (Art and Culture Circuit); lo∙

r the black-on-yellow 'K' signs. A leaflet ailable at the tourist office has details and pening hours.

Near the tourist office, the whimsical eissbockbrunnen (Goat Fountain), erected 1985, celebrates a quirky local tradition. or seven centuries, the nearby town of ambrecht has had to pay an annual tribute f one goat for using pastureland belong- g to Deidesheim. The presentation of this at, which is auctioned off to raise funds r local cultural activities, culminates in the ucous **Geissbockfest** (Goat Festival), held on entecost Tuesday.

LEEPING & EATING

Gästehaus Ritter von Böhl (☎ 972 201; www.ritter-von oehl.de, in German; Weinstrasse 35; s €49, d €75-89; ☺ re- ption 8am-6pm; P ☒) Set around a delightful, isteria-wrapped courtyard, this guest house elongs to, and occupies part of the grounds , a charity hospital (now an old-age home), unded in 1494. Renovated in 2008, it has 2 rooms with pastel walls and parquet floors d a bright breakfast atrium.

our pick Deidesheimer Hof (☎ 968 70; www eidesheimerhof.de; Am Marktplatz; s/d from €120/165, low ason from €95/120; P ☒ ☒) This renowned ostelry has 28 elegant rooms, each unique, d two fine restaurants: St Urban (four- urse menu costs €41), whose regional offer- gs include *Saumagen*, made with chestnuts autumn; and the gourmet Schwarzer Hahn ve-/six-/seven-course menu costs €75/85/95; en for dinner Tuesday to Saturday), which ecialises in creative French- and Palatinate- yle dishes. Check out the photos of kings d presidents who have dined here.

our pick Turmstüb'l (☎ 981 081; Turmstrasse 3; mains .20-13.80; ☺ 6pm-midnight Tue-Sat, noon-11pm Sun & lidays) This contemporary, artsy wine cafe, own an alley opposite the church, serves sty hot dishes, including regional speciali- es such as *Saumagen*, and 22 wines by the ass (€3 to €4.50).

Gasthaus zur Kanne (☎ 966 00; www.gasthauszur nne.de, in German; Weinstrasse 31; mains €10-25; ☺ noon- m & 6-10pm Wed-Sun) Serves fresh, refined re- onal cuisine, with a menu that changes daily. ou can sit inside at hand-painted tables or the leafy courtyard.

ETTING AROUND

wned by Olympic cycling champion Stefan einweg, **Steinweg** (☎ 982 284; www.gepaeckservice

-pfalz.de, in German; Kirschgartenstrasse 49; ☺ Apr-Oct), 200m from the tourist office, rents bikes (€8 per day) and arranges cycling tours.

Bad Dürkheim
☎ 06322 / pop 18,900

Bad Dürkheim is a handsome, easily walk- able spa town, as famous for its salty ther- mal springs as for the annual **Dürkheimer Wurstmarkt** (sausage market; www.duerkheimer -wurstmarkt.de), held on the second and third weekends of September, which bills itself as the world's largest wine festival. Most of the action takes place around the **Dürkheimer Riesenfass**, a gargantuan wine cask that's had a restaurant inside since a master cooper built it in 1934 (its 75th anniversary was feted in 2009).

INFORMATION
Billard Café Valentino (Weinstrasse Sud 16; per hr €2; ☺ 3pm-1am or 2am Mon-Fri, 2pm-1am or 2am Sat & Sun) A pool hall and sports bar with internet access. One block up the hill (southeast) of the Obermarkt.

Tourist office (☎ 935 140; www.bad-duerkheim.com, in German; ☺ 9am-6pm Mon-Fri year-round, 11am-3pm Sat & Sun, 11am-1pm holidays May-Oct). In the Kurzentrum building. Has a worthwhile walking-tour map in English.

SIGHTS
Between the Hauptbahnhof and the tourist office lies the **Kurpark**, a grassy, azalea- and wisteria-filled park where you'll find a **chil- dren's playground** (in the corner nearest the Hauptbahnhof) and most of the town's spa and wellness facilities, including the **Kurzentrum** (spa centre; ☎ 9640; www.kurzentrum-bad -duerkheim.de, in German; Kurbrunnenstrasse 14).

The city-run **Salinarium** (☎ 935 865; www.salinarium .de, in German; pools adult/child over 6yr €5.50/3, saunas €11.50/9), a year-round complex of indoor and outdoor swimming pools (only one of which is saltwater) and seven saunas, is a few hundred metres northeast of the tourist office.

Walking options are legion and include **Weinwanderwege** (vineyard trails) from St Michaelskapelle, a chapel atop a little vine- clad hill just northeast of the tourist office, to Honigsäckel and Hochmess (two hours return); and **forest trails** to two historic ruins, **Limburg** (11km, three hours return) and **Hardenburg** (two hours one-way).

The **Kaiser-Konrad-Radweg** links Bad Dürkheim's Rathaus with Speyer's Dom (about 30km each way).

RHINELAND-PALATINATE & SAARLAND

SLEEPING & EATING

Bad Dürkheim has a good selection of reasonably priced hotels. Restaurants with warm-season terraces can be found on Römerplatz and along nearby Kurgartenstrasse.

Knaus Camping Park (☎ 613 56; www.knauscamp.de; In den Almen 3; site €7-12, person €6.40) A lakeside camping ground about 3.5km northeast of the centre.

ourpick Marktschänke (☎ 952 60; www.bd-markt schaenke.de, in German; s/d from €49/75; **P**) An especially friendly, family-run hotel with seven extra-large rooms and a playfully cluttered, rustic restaurant specialising in regional dishes (mains from €6.80). It's located about 250m southwest of the Hauptbahnhof, off the Obermarkt.

Hotel Weingarten (☎ 940 10; www.hotelwein garten.de; Triftweg 11a-13; d €88-105; **P** **X**) Situated 1km northeast of the Bahnhof along Manheimerstrasse, this aptly named, welcoming place has 18 lovingly cared-for rooms, most with balconies. Reception closes at 2pm on Sunday – call ahead if you'll be arriving after that. The same family runs a winery next door.

AHR VALLEY & THE EIFEL

The Eifel, a rural area of gentle hills, tranquil villages and volcanic lakes, makes for a great respite from the exuberant mass tourism of the Moselle and Rhine Valleys. Its subtle charms are best sampled on a bike ride or a hike, though it also has a few headline attractions, including a world-class car-racing track, a stunning Romanesque abbey and a lovely wine region, the Ahr Valley.

The Ahr River has carved a scenic 90km valley stretching from Blankenheim, in the High Eifel, to its confluence with the Rhine near Remagen. This is one of Germany's few red-wine regions – growing *Spätburgunder* (Pinot noir), in particular – with vineyards clinging to steeply terraced slopes along both banks. The quality is high but the yield small, so very few wine labels ever make it beyond the area – all the more reason to visit and try them for yourself.

For information on the region, see www.ahr-rhein-eifel.de (in German).

Getting Around

The best way to travel through the Ahr Valley is on the Ahrtalbahn, an hour. train serving most of the villages betwee Altenahr and Remagen (35 minutes), an Monday to Saturday, Bonn.

If you're driving, make your way to th B266/B267, which traverses the valley.

The scenic **Rotweinwanderweg** (Red Wi Hiking Trail; www.ahr-rotweinwanderweg.de, www.rotwe wanderweg.de, both in German), marked by sma signs with grape icons, takes hikers thoug luscious vineyard country on its 35km rou from Bad Bodendorf to Altenahr, via th hillsides above Bad Neuenahr and Ahrweil You can walk as far as you like and then r turn on the Ahrtalbahn. Tourist offices ha trail details and maps (€1).

Cycling options include the **Ahrtalradw** (Ahr-Radweg), which runs pretty mu along the Ahr, linking Sinzig (on the Rhin with Blankenheim, a distance of about 80k Bikes can be taken on the Ahrtalbahn fr of charge.

REMAGEN
☎ 02642 / pop 16,100

Remagen, 20km south of Bonn, was founde by the Romans in AD 16 as Rigomagus, b the town would hardly figure in the histor books were it not for one fateful day in ear March 1945. As the Allies raced across Fran and Belgium to rid Germany of Nazisr the Wehrmacht tried frantically to stave o defeat by destroying all bridges across th Rhine. But the **Brücke von Remagen** (the ste rail bridge at Remagen) lasted long enoug for Allied troops to cross the river, contri uting significantly to the collapse of Hitler western front. One of the bridge's survivi basalt towers now houses the **Friedensmuseu** (Peace Museum; ☎ 218 63 www.bruecke-remagen.de; adu student/family €3.50/1/7; 10am-5pm early Mar–mid-N to 6pm May-Oct), with a well-presented exhibit o Remagen's pivotal role in WWII.

BAD NEUENAHR & AHRWEILER
☎ 02641 / pop 27,600

Bad Neuenahr and Ahrweiler are a bit of a odd couple. Bad Neuenahr is a spa tow whose healing waters have been sought o by the moneyed and the famous (inclu ing Karl Marx and Johannes Brahms) for century and a half. Ahrweiler, by contras is an attractive medieval town encircled by

all and criss-crossed by pedestrianised lanes
ned with half-timbered houses. What the
vo do have in common, however, is wine,
hich can be enjoyed in both towns at taverns
nd restaurants.

rientation

rom Ahrweiler's Bahnhof (now just a train
op with a ticket machine), walk 600m west
ong Wilhelmstrasse to get to the old town;
ore convenient is the Ahrweiler Markt train
op, just north of the old town.

From the proper Bahnhof in Bad Neuenahr,
's a five-minute walk to the centre, which is
ound car-free Poststrasse.

nformation

t's Play (Ahrhutstrasse 23, Ahrweiler; per hr €2;
⌚ 9am-11pm) Internet access, across the square from the
urist office. This place doubles as a casino so you must be
er 18 to enter.
urist offices (☎ 917 10; www.ahrtaltourismus.de, in
rman; ⌚ 9am-5.30pm Mon-Fri, 10am-3pm Sat, Sun &
lidays) Ahrweiler (Blankartshof 1); Bad Neuenahr (Haupt-
asse 80) The Bad Neuenahr branch is a block to the right
hen exiting the Bahnhof. Both offices sell walking and
cling maps of the area.

ights & Activities

HRWEILER

hrweiler preserves a delightful, pedestrian-
ed **Altstadt**, almost entirely encircled by a
edieval **town wall** with four gates. The focal
oint is the **Marktplatz** and its yellow Gothic
hurch, **Pfarrkirche St Laurentius**, beautifully
ecorated with floral frescos from the 14th
ntury and luminous stained-glass win-
ows, some of which show farmers working
eir vineyards.

Ahrweiler's Roman roots spring to life at
e **Museum Roemervilla** (☎ 5311; Am Silberberg
adult/student/family €4/2/8; ⌚ 10am-5pm Tue-Sun
r–mid-Nov, closed mid-Nov-Mar) on the northwest
dge of town. Protected by a lofty glass and
ood structure are 1st- to 3rd-century ruins –
veritable Rhenish Pompeii – which reveal
e remarkable standard of living enjoyed by
ealthy Romans. A detailed English pamphlet
included in the price.

During the Cold War, there was no vast,
p-secret bunker complex bored into the
llside 500m up the slope from the Museum
oemervilla – at least not officially. Had you
sked a George Smiley type what was going on
p there, on a forested slope just 30km from

Bonn, you might have been told, 'I could tell
you but then I'd have to kill you'. Since 2008,
though, you can have a look for yourself – at a
200m section of the nuclear-proof 'Emergency
Seat of the Constitutional Organs of the Federal
Republic of Germany', rechristened (in inimitable bureaucratese) as the **Dokumentationsstätte
Regierungsbunker** (Government Bunker Documentation
Site; ☎ 917 10; www.ausweichstitz.de, www.bunker-doku.de,
in German; adult/under 13yr/13-16yr/student/senior/family €8/
free/3.50/5/7/20; ⌚ 10am-5pm Wed, Sat, Sun & holidays early
Mar–mid-Nov, closed mid-Nov–early Mar).

BAD NEUENAHR

The focal point of Bad Neuenahr, bisected by
the Ahr, is the stately **Kurhaus**, an art-nouveau
structure built in 1903; next door is the casino.
The nearby **river banks** are great for strolling.

Neuenahr owes its '*Bad* reputation' (ie its spa
status) to its mineral springs, whose soothing
qualities can be experienced in the **Ahr Resort**
(☎ 801 100; www.ahr-resort.de; Felix-Rütten-Strasse 3; week-
day/weekend day pass €15/17, sauna extra €5; ⌚ 9am-11pm or
midnight). Besides swimming pools, options include a surge channel, massage jets and all sorts
of saunas. Various discounts are available.

Sleeping & Eating

The town centres of Bad Neuenahr and
Ahrweiler (eg around Marktplatz) teem with
traditional German restaurants.

DJH hostel (☎ 349 24; www.jugendherberge.de; St-
Pius-Strasse 7; dm €19.90; ✗) This modern, 140-bed
hostel is on the south bank of the Ahr between
Ahrweiler and Bad Neuenahr (1.5km from
each). All rooms have a private bathroom.

Hotel Garni Schützenhof (☎ 90283; www.schuetzenhof
-ahrweiler.de, in German; Schützenstrasse 1, Ahrweiler; s/d
from €50/77; P ✗) Facing the Ahrtor, one of
Ahrweiler's landmark town gates, this unpretentious, welcoming family-run hotel has 14
spacious rooms. Excellent value.

our pick **Hotel & Restaurant Hohenzollern**
(☎ 9730; www.hotelhohenzollern.com, in German; Am
Silberberg 50, Ahrweiler; s €73-88, d €118-153; P ✗)
This elegant hillside hotel, right on the
Rotweinwanderweg, has unbeatable valley
views and a gourmet restaurant (four-/five-/
six-course menu €57/69/74) with local, French
and Italian dishes. From Ahrweiler's Museum
Roemervilla, head up the 1½-lane road 700m
through the forest.

Bell's WeinRestaurant (☎ 900 243; www.bells
-restaurant.de, in German; Niederhutstrasse 27a, Ahrweiler;
mains €9.50-17.90; ⌚ 11.30am-10pm Tue-Fri, to 10.30pm

Sat, to 9pm Sun, also open Mon in summer) The menu here includes soups, salads, potatoes, schnitzel, vegie plates and four options for kids. In fine weather, the chestnut-shaded beer garden has the nicest tables.

Eifelstube (☎ 348 50; www.eifelstube-ahrweiler.de, in German; Ahrhutstrasse 26, Ahrweiler; mains €13-23; ☽ Thu-Mon year-round, plus Wed Sep & Oct) Sample upmarket German and regional specialities in this cosy dining room, with its beam ceiling and tiled stove, run by the same family since 1905.

For self-catering, there's **Edeka Markt** (Ahrhutstrasse 8; ☽ 8.30am-6.30pm Mon-Fri, 8am-2pm Sat), a small supermarket just inside the Ahrtor.

Getting There & Away

Rail travel to Koblenz from the Ahrweiler Markt (€13), Ahrweiler (€13) and Bad Neuenahr (€11.50) train stations requires a change at Remagen (15 minutes). Direct trains from all three stations serve Bonn (€4.20, 35 minutes, hourly).

ALTENAHR

☎ 02643 / pop 1700

Surrounded on all sides by craggy peaks, steep vineyards and rolling hills, Altenahr may just be the most romantic spot in the Ahr Valley. The landscape is best appreciated by taking a 20-minute uphill walk from the Bahnhof to the 11th-century **Burgruine Are**, a ruined hilltop castle, whose weather-beaten stone tower stands guard over the valley.

Altenahr is the western terminus of the **Rotweinwanderweg** (p496). A dozen more **trails** can be picked up in the village centre (eg the 7km **Geologischer Wanderweg**) or at the top of the **Ditschardhöhe**, whose 'peak', at 354m, is most easily reached by the **Seilbahn** (chairlift; ☎ 8383; up only/return adult €3/5, 3-14yr €2/2.50; ☽ 10am-5pm or later Easter-Oct, closes earlier in stormy weather). In the town centre, parts of the Romanesque **Pfarrkirche Maria Verkündigung** (Church of the Annunciation) date from the late 1100s.

Altenahr's **tourist office** (Haus des Gastes; ☎ 8448; www.altenahr-ahr.de; ☽ 9am-4.30pm Mon-Fri, 10am-2pm Sat May & Aug-Oct, 10am-3pm Mon-Fri rest of year), inside the former Bahnhof building, sells hiking and cycling maps.

Sleeping & Eating

Campingplatz Altenahr (☎ 8503; www.camping-altenahr.de; Im Pappelauel; per tent & car/person €6/4.50; ☽ Apr-Oct). A grassy camping ground on the banks of the Ahr.

DJH hostel (☎ 1880; www.jugendherberge. Langfigtal 8; dm €19.90; ✗) Altenahr's 92-b hostel is beautifully located in the Langfig nature park, overlooking the Ahr.

Hotel-Restaurant Zum Schwarzen Kreuz (☎ 15 www.zumschwarzenkreuz.de, in German; Brückenstrasse 5- €35-95, d €58-95; **P** ✗) In the heart of town, th 30-room place offers retro flair, a quiet libra with overstuffed chairs (facing room 26) a rooms with balconies and groovy tapestri The restaurant does Eifel specialities (mai €8.50 to €18.50) and *Flammkuchen* (Alsatia pizza consisting of pastry topped with crea onion and bacon).

Getting There & Away

Trains go to Ahrweiler (€3.90, 19 minute and Bad Neuenahr (€4.85, 22 minutes).

NÜRBURGRING

This historic **Formula One race car track** (☎ 0269 302 630; www.nuerburgring.de), 60km west Koblenz, has hosted many spectacular rac with legendary drivers since its completio in 1927. The 20.8km, 73-curve **Nordschlei** (North Loop) was not only the longest circu ever built but also one of the most difficu earning the respectful moniker 'Green He from racing legend Jackie Stewart. After N Lauda's near-fatal crash in 1976, the Germa Grand Prix moved to the Hockenheimrin near Mannheim, but in 1995 Formula O returned (in odd-numbered years) to th 5148m **Grand-Prix-Strecke** (South Loop built in 1984. The complex hosts 100 rac a year.

You can get a glimpse behind the scen with a one-hour **Backstage Tour** (€6; ☽ 11am, 1p & 3pm daily), usually in German with printe material in English.

The new **Ring-Werk** (www.ring-werk.com; adult 11yr/family €19.50/11/49; ☽ 10am-6pm, till later wee ends & school holidays), opened in mid-2009, is motor-racing theme park featuring the late interactive, 3-D and tunnel-projection tec nologies and the **Ring-Racer**, which takes le than 2.5 seconds to accelerate from 0km/h an incredible 217km/h.

If you have your own car or motorcyc you can discover your inner Micha (Schumacher, that is) by taking a spin aroun the Nordschleife for €22 per circuit. Th Grand-Prix-Strecke costs €30 per 20 minut (motorcycles *verboten*). Check the website f **Open Nordschleife** times and dates.

Prefer to let someone else do the driving? ptions include the **BMW Ring-Taxi** (☎ 932 020, ffed 10am-noon Mon-Fri; http://bmw-motorsport.com/ ./ringtaxi.html; ☺ Mar-Nov, call for exact days). For 95, up to three people (children must be at ast 150cm tall) pile into a 507HP BMW M5, hich goes from 0km/h to 100km/h in under re seconds, and are 'chauffeured' around the ordschleife by a professional driver at speeds up to 320km/h. It's hugely popular so make servations early.

The Nürburgring is off the B258, reached a the B257 from Altenahr.

ARIA LAACH

bout 25km northwest of Koblenz, **Abteikirche aria Laach** (Maria Laach Abbey Church; ☎ 02652-590; ww.maria-laach.de, in German; admission free) is one of e finest examples of a Romanesque church Germany. Part of a nine-century-old enedictine abbey, it is next to a volcanic ke, the **Laacher See**, surrounded by a 21-sq-n nature reserve.

You enter the **church** (☺ 8.30-11.30am & 12.15-m Mon-Sat, 12.30-5pm Sun) via a large **Vorhalle** ortico; restored in 2009), a feature not usu-ly found north of the Alps. Note the quirky arvings on and above the capitals and the **wenbrunnen** (Lion Fountain), reminiscent Moorish architecture. The interior is sur-isingly modest, in part because the origi-al furnishings were lost during the 1800s. the west apse lies the late-13th-century, cumbent statue-adorned **tomb** of abbey under Heinrich II of Palatine (laminated formation sheets in six languages are avail-le nearby). The east apse shelters the high tar with its wooden canopy; overhead is an rly-20th-century Byzantine-style mosaic of hrist donated by Kaiser Wilhelm II. The trance to the 11th-century **crypt** (☺ 9-11am 2.30-5pm Mon-Sat, 12.30-2pm & 3.30-5pm Sun & holidays) to the left of the choir.

Across the path from the **Klostergaststätte** estaurant), a free 20-minute **film** (☺ begins -11.30am & 1.30-4.30pm Mon-Sat, 1.30-4.30pm Sun holiday) – available in German, English, rench and Dutch – looks at the life of the 5 monks, who take the motto *Ora et lab-ra* (pray and work) very seriously indeed. hey earn a living from economic activities ach as growing organic apples and raising ouse plants, available for purchase in the ostergärtnerei (nursery); and they pray five mes a day. Attending **Gottesdienst** (prayer services; hours posted at the church entrance) is worthwhile if only to listen to the ethereal chanting in Latin and German.

Various **trails** take walkers up the forested hill behind the abbey; options for circum-ambulating the Laacher See include the lakefront **Ufer-Rundweg** (8km) and two hillier trails (15km and 21km). You can swim near the camping ground.

Next to the car park, the **Bioladen** (organic grocery; ☺ 8.30am-6pm Mon-Sat, 10am-6pm Sun) sells fruits and vegies grown by the monks, as well as other organic edibles.

Maria Laach is served hourly by bus 312 from Mendig, the nearest town with a train station. By car, get off the A61 at the Mendig exit (No 34), 2km from Maria Laach. The car park (€1.50) is across the road from the church.

THE ROMANTIC RHINE

Between Koblenz and Bingen, the **Rhine** (www .romantischer-rhein.de) cuts deeply through the Rhenish slate mountains, meandering be-tween hillside castles and steep fields of wine to create a magical mixture of wonder and legend. This is Germany's landscape at its most dramatic – muscular forested hillsides alternate with craggy cliffs and nearly-vertical terraced vineyards. Idyllic villages appear around each bend, their neat half-timbered houses and proud church steeples seemingly plucked from the world of fairy tales.

High above the river, busy with barge traf-fic, and the rail lines that run along each bank are the famous medieval castles, some ruined, some restored, all mysterious and vestiges of a time that was anything but tranquil. Most were built by a mafia of local robber barons – knights, princes and even bishops – who extorted tolls from merchant ships by block-ing their passage with iron chains. Time and French troops under Louis XIV laid waste to many of the castles but several were restored in the 19th century, when Prussian kings, German poets and British painters discovered the gorge's timeless beauty. Today, some have been reincarnated as hotels and, in the case of Burg Stahleck, as a hostel (p508).

In 2002 Unesco designated these 65km of riverscape, more prosaically known as the **Oberes Mittelrheintal** (Upper Middle Rhine Valley; www.welterbe -mittelrheintal.de), as a World Heritage Site.

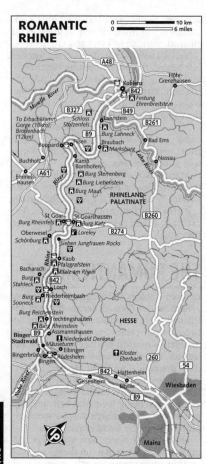

One of Germany's most popular tourist destinations, the area is often deluged with visitors, especially in summer and early autumn, but it all but shuts down in winter. Hotel prices are highest on weekends from September to mid-October.

Activities
CYCLING

The **Rhein-Radweg** (www.rheinradweg.eu) runs along the left (more-or-less west) bank of the Romantic Rhine and also along some sections of the right bank. It links up with two other long-distance bike paths, the **Nahe-Hunsrück-Mosel-Radweg** (www.naheland-radtouren.de, in German), which follows the Nahe River from Bingen southwest to Idar-Oberstein and beyond; and

the 311km **Mosel-Radweg** (www.mosel-radweg.c which runs along the banks of the Mose River from Koblenz to the French city Metz, passing through Bernkastel-Kues, Tri and Luxembourg.

Bicycles can be taken on regional trains, ferries and river ferries, making it possible ride one way (eg down the valley) and ta public transport the other way.

HIKING

The Rhine Valley is great hiking territor Each tourist office can supply suggestions a maps for superb local walks. A one-way hi can be turned into a circuit by mixing walki and public transport.

Four long-distance trails parallel the Rhi between Koblenz and Bingen, continui downriver to Bonn and upriver to Mainz a beyond. Each bank has a **Rheinhöhenweg** (Rh Heights Trail; www.rheinhoehenweg.de, in German), whi takes you from hill top to hill top – a bit aw from the river – and affords spectacular view Somewhat closer to the Rhine, along the ri erbank or on the hillsides just above it, r the **Rhein-Burgen-Wanderweg**, on the left ban and the **Rheinsteig** (www.rheinsteig.de), on the rig bank; the latter links Bonn with Wiesbaden distance of 320km.

Getting There & Away

Koblenz (for transport details, see p504) a Mainz (p487) are good starting points f touring the region.

Getting Around
BOAT

River travel is a relaxing and very roman way to see the castles, vineyards and villag of the Romantic Rhine.

Because of fast currents, shallows, narro channels and the many passing barges (t Rhine is still an important trade artery), m noeuvring a passenger ferry is a very tric business – and a fascinating one to see close. Vessels zipping downriver have prior over those steaming slowly upriver.

From about Easter to October (winter ser ices are very limited), 13 boats run by Kö **Düsseldorfer** (KD; ☎ 0221-2088 318; www.k-d.co link villages such as Bingen, St Goar a Boppard on a set timetable. You can trav to the next village or all the way from Mai to Koblenz (€46.50, downstream/upstrea 6/8½ hours). Within the segment you' aid for (for example, Boppard–Rüdesheim, hich costs €21.20 return), you can get on ad off as many times as you like, but make are to ask for a free stopover ticket each time ou disembark.

Many rail passes (such as Eurail) get you free ride on normal KD services. However, ou still need to obtain a ticket. Children up the age of four travel for free, while those up age 13 are charged a flat fee of €5. Students ader 27 get a 50% discount. From Monday Friday, seniors (over 60) also get a 50% dis-ount. Travel on your birthday is free. Return ckets usually cost only slightly more than 1e-way. To bring along a bicycle/dog, there's supplement of €2.50/3.50.

Several smaller companies, including ngen-Rüdesheimer (☎ 06721-14140; www.bingen edesheimer.com) and **Rössler Linie** (☎ 06722-2353; ww.roesslerlinie.de), also run passenger boats up ad down the river.

US & TRAIN

us and train travel, perhaps combined with inicruises by boat and car ferry, are a conven-nt way to go village hopping along the Rhine, get to a trail head, or to return to your lodg-gs at the end of a hike or bike ride.

Villages on the Rhine's left bank (eg ngen, Boppard and St Goar) are served ourly by local trains on the Koblenz–Mainz n, inaugurated in 1859. Right-bank villages ch as Rüdesheim, Assmannshausen and St oarshausen are linked every hour or two by oblenz–Wiesbaden services. It takes about ½ hours to travel by train from Koblenz to ther Mainz or Wiesbaden.

AR FERRY

nce there are no bridges over the Rhine be-veen Koblenz and Mainz (though there are ntroversial plans to build one near St Goar, ossibly endangering the area's Unesco World eritage status), the only way to cross the ver along this stretch is by *Autofähre* (car rry). The following services operate (from orth to south) every 15 or 20 minutes dur-g the day and every 30 minutes early in the orning and late at night:

ngen–Rüdesheim (www.bingen-ruedesheimer.com einfaehren; ☽ to 9.45pm Nov-Apr, to midnight or later y-Oct)

ppard–Filsen (www.faehre-boppard.de, in German; ☽ to n Oct-Mar, to 9pm Apr, May & Sep, to 10pm Jun-Aug)

ederheimbach–Lorch (☽ to 6.50pm Nov-Mar, to Opm Apr-Oct)

Oberwesel–Kaub (www.faehre-kaub.de, in German; ☽ to 6.50pm Oct-Mar, to 7.50pm Apr-Sep)

St Goar–St Goarshausen (www.faehre-loreley.de; ☽ to 9pm Oct-Apr, to 11pm May-Sep)

Prices vary slightly but you can figure on paying about €3.50 per car, including the driver; €1 per car passenger; €1.50 per pedes-trian (€0.70 for a child); and €2 for a bicycle, including the rider. This being well-organised Germany, the fare tables take into account the possibility, however remote, that you might want to bring along a horse or head of cattle (€3 or €4) or a horse-drawn cart (€4.50, including the driver).

KOBLENZ

☎ 0261 / pop 106,000

Koblenz is a modern town with roots that go all the way back to the Romans, who founded a military stronghold here around 10 BC. They called it, quite appropriately, Confluentes for its supremely strategic value – it lies at the confluence of the Moselle and the Rhine.

Today, Koblenz is the economic centre of the region. An eminently strollable town, it is the northern gateway to the Romantic Rhine and also affords access to the outdoor charms of three low mountain ranges – the Hunsrück, the Eifel and the Westerwald – which converge here.

In 2011, from mid-April to mid-October, Koblenz will host the prestigious **Bundes -gartenschau** (National Garden Show; www.buga2011. de), Germany's largest horticultural extrava-ganza, with focal points around the Deutsches Eck, the Kurfüstliches Schloss (on the Rhine 700m south of the Deutsches Eck) and Festung Ehrenbreitstein.

Orientation

Koblenz' core is shaped like the bow of a ship seen in profile, with the Rhine to the east, the Moselle to the north and the Deutsches Eck right where Leonardo DiCaprio would be kissing Kate Winslet if this were the *Titanic*. The area's southern border is Friedrich-Ebert-Ring; to the west it's de-lineated by Hohenfelderstrasse, which leads north to the Balduinbrücke, which spans the Moselle. The Altstadt is centred around the northern end of shop-lined, pedestrians-only Löhrstrasse, whose southern, cars-admitted section leads to the Hauptbahnhof, 600m south of Friedrich-Ebert-Ring.

Information

Eco-Express Waschsalon (Bahnhofstrasse 22; ⊙ 6am-10pm Mon-Sat, closed Sun & holidays) Self-service laundry, 400m north of the Hauptbahnhof.

JM Internet (Löhrstrasse 98; per hr €1.50; ⊙ 10am-midnight) One of several internet places on Löhrstrasse south of Friedrich-Ebert-Ring.

Post office (Bahnhofsplatz 16; ⊙ 8am-6.30pm Mon-Fri, 8.30am-1.30pm Sat)

Reuffel (Löhrstrasse 62; ⊙ 9.30am-7pm Mon-Sat) Carries English-language books.

Tourist office (www.touristik-koblenz.de) Hauptbahnhof (☎ 313 04; Bahnhofsplatz 17; ⊙ 9am-7pm daily May-Sep, 9am-6pm daily Apr & Oct, 9am-6pm Mon-Fri, 9am-2pm Sat Nov-Mar); Rathaus (☎ 130 920; Jesuitenplatz 2; ⊙ 9am or 10am-6pm daily May-Sep, 10am-6pm daily Apr & Oct, 9am-6pm Mon-Fri, 10am-4pm Sat Nov-Mar) The Hauptbahnhof branch is across the square and a bit to the right as you exit. Both have excellent maps in English and sell event tickets.

Sights

CITY CENTRE

The intersection of **Löhrstrasse**, Koblenz' main shopping drag, with Altengraben is known as **Vier Türme** (Four Towers) because each of the 17th-century corner buildings sports an ornately carved and painted oriel.

Turning east on Altengraben takes you to **Am Plan**, a broad square that has undergone various incarnations – as a butchers' market, a stage for religious plays, a place of execution and an arena for medieval tournaments. These days it's a fine place for sitting in cafes when the weather's warm.

The arched walkway at Am Plan's northeastern corner leads to the Catholic **Liebfrauenkirche** (www.liebfrauen-koblenz.de, in German; ⊙ 8am or 8.30am-6pm), built in a harmonious hotchpotch of styles: of Romanesque origin, it has a Gothic choir (check out the stained glass) and baroque onion-domed turrets. Note the fancy painted vaulting above the central nave.

A block to the north, **Florinsmarkt** is dominated by the Protestant **Florinskirche** (www.koblenz-mitte.de, in German; ⊙ 10.30am-5.30pm mid-May–Sep) and is home to the **Mittelrhein-Museum** (☎ 129 2520; www.mittelrhein-museum.de, in German; Florinsmarkt 15; adult/student & senior €2.50/1.50; ⊙ 10.30am-5pm Tue-Sat, 11am-6pm Sun & holidays), with eclectic displays reflecting the region's history. The collection of 19th-century landscape paintings of the Romantic Rhine by German and British artists is worth a look. For a bit of whimsy, check out the **Augenroller** (Eye Roller) figure beneath the

clock over the entrance to the museum, whic rolls its eyes and sticks out its tongue on th hour and half-hour. There are plans to mov the museum to the new **Kulturbau** (Zentralplatz), huge cultural complex, whose construction supposed to be completed in late 2012.

At Josef-Görres-Platz, six blocks southea of Florinsmarkt, the **Historiensäule** (Histo Column) portrays 2000 years of Kobler history in 10 scenes perched one atop th other – the WWII period, for instance, is rep resented by a flaming ruin. A nearby pan explains all (in English).

At the point of confluence of the Mosel and the Rhine is the **Deutsches Eck** (literall 'German corner'), dominated by a **statue Kaiser Wilhelm I** on horseback, in the bomba tic style of the late 19th century. After th original was destroyed in WWII, the ston pedestal remained empty – as a testament lost German unity – until, postreunificatio it was re-erected in 1993.

Further south, just in from the riverfro promenade, is the **Deutschherrenhaus**, once th property of the Deutscher Ritterorden (Ord of the Teutonic Knights). Today it's home to th **Ludwig Museum** (☎ 304 416; www.ludwigmuseum.o Danziger Freiheit 1; adult/student & senior €2.50/1.5 ⊙ 10.30am-5pm Tue-Sat, 11am-6pm Sun & holidays), whic showcases post-1945 and contemporary a from France and Germany. Just beyond ar the slender towers of 12th-century **Basilika Kastor** (⊙ 9am-6pm).

FESTUNG EHRENBREITSTEIN

On the right bank of the Rhine, looming 118 above the Deutsches Eck, the mighty **Festu Ehrenbreitstein** (Ehrenbreitstein Fortress; ☎ 6675 40 www.festungehrenbreitstein.de) proved indestructib to all but Napoleonic troops, who levelled it 1801. A few years later the Prussians, to prov a point, rebuilt it as one of Europe's might est fortifications. At the time of research, th complex was being renovated and some se tions were closed, in part to prepare for th 2011 National Garden Show (p501).

Behind the stone bulwarks, you'll find DJH hostel (closed until 2010), two resta rants and the **Landesmuseum** (☎ 667 50; ww .landesmuseumkoblenz.de, in German; adult/student & sen €4/3; ⊙ 9.30am-5pm late Mar-Oct), with exhibits the region's economic history, photograp and August Horch, founder of the Audi aut motive company. At the time of research, on the archaeology section was open.

Festung Ehrenbreitstein is accessible by car. ou can also take bus 9 or 10 to the Obertal bus op, where you can walk for 20 minutes or hop n the **Sesselbahn** (chairlift; adult/4-14yr & hostel guest e-way €5.30/3, return €7/4; 10am-5.50pm Jun-Sep, to 50pm Mar-May & Oct, closed Nov-Feb). A **Personenfähre** assenger ferry; adult/child €1.30/0.65; to 7pm May-t, to 6pm Apr, to 5pm Nov) links the right-bank hrenbreitstein quarter, below the fortress, ith the left-bank's Rheinpromenade.

There are plans to build a **Seilbahn** (aerial ble car) from near the Deutsches Eck up the Ehrenbreitstein plateau. Set to begin peration in 2011, the conveyance is supposed be dismantled in 2014 to avoid running oul of Unesco's World Heritage designation f this stretch of the Rhine.

CHLOSS STOLZENFELS

/ith its crenellated towers, ornate gables and edieval-style fortifications, **Schloss Stolzenfels** 516 56; www.burgen-rlp.de; interior closed until Apr 11), 5km south of the town centre above the hine's left bank, exudes the timeless, senti-ental beauty for which the Romantic Rhine famed. In 1823, the future Prussian king riedrich Wilhelm IV fell under its spell and ad the castle – ruined by the French – rebuilt his summer residence; during the Victorian a, guests included Queen Victoria. Today, e rooms remain largely as the king left them, ith paintings, weapons, armour and furnish-gs from the mid-19th century.

To get there, take bus 650 from the auptbahnhof to the castle car park, from here it's a 15-minute walk.

leeping

mpingplatz Rhein-Mosel (827 19; www.camping hein-mosel.de; Schartwiesenweg 6; per adult/tent/car .50/2.50/3; Apr–mid-Oct) On the north bank of e Moselle, facing the Deutsches Eck. Linked the city centre by a passenger ferry.

DJH hostel (972 870; www.jugendherberge.de;)) Situated inside historic Ehrenbreitstein ortress, this place is set to reopen in 2010 ter renovations. For transport details, see estung Ehrenbreitstein (opposite).

our pick **Hotel Jan van Werth** (365 00; www.hotel vanwerth.de, in German; Von-Werth-Strasse 9; s/d €43/64, thout bathroom €24/50;) This long-time udget favourite, with a lobby that feels ke someone's living room, offers excep-onal value – no surprise that the 16 rooms e often booked out, especially when the

weather's good. Situated four blocks north of the Hauptbahnhof and one block south of Friedrich-Ebert-Ring.

Hotel Hamm (303 210; www.hotel-hamm.de; St-Josef-Strasse 32-34; s €49-59, d €75-85, q €120;) Unpretentious and unsurprising, this 30-room hotel is popular with businesspeople and offers good value. It's located in a residential area three blocks south of the Hauptbahnhof and 1.5km from the Altstadt, to which it's linked by bus 1.

Diehl's Hotel (970 70; www.diehls-hotel.de; Rheinsteigufer 1; s €64-98, d €79-134, breakfast €13;) A family-run hotel on the Rhine's east bank, with a stylish 1980s vibe and 60 comfortable rooms offering watery views of Koblenz. The restaurant has a gorgeous terrace overlooking the Rhine – perfect for a romantic sunset dinner. Situated about 1km south of Festung Ehrenbreitstein.

Contel Koblenz (406 50; www.contel-koblenz.de; Pastor-Klein-Strasse 19; s/d from €75/79, buffet breakfast €11;) This 185-room hotel's exuberant bad taste begins with the electric-blue facade and gets wilder inside – some new outrage against bourgeois good taste awaits around every corner. Some rooms have kitchenettes and three rooms come with waterbeds. Situated 1km west along the Moselle from the Altstadt; served by bus 3, whose nearest stop is Ludwig-Erhard-Strasse.

Eating & Drinking

Many of Koblenz' restaurants and pubs are in the Altstadt, eg around Münzplatz and Burgstrasse, and along the Rhine. Diehl's Hotel has a romantic restaurant with lots of German dishes (mains €11.50 to €21.50).

Kaffeewirtschaft (914 4702; Münzplatz 14; mains €5.20-12.20, salads €4.40-8.70; 9am-midnight Mon-Thu, 9am-2am Fri & Sat, 10am-midnight Sun & holidays) An old-fashioned cafe with minimalist designer decor, old marble tables and weekly specials (including vegetarian options) that take advantage of whatever's in season.

our pick **Cafe Miljöö** (142 37; www.cafe-miljoeoe.de, in German; Gemüsegasse 12; mains €7.90-11.90; 8am-1am or later) 'Milieu' (pronounce it like the French) is a cosy, bistrolike cafe with fresh flowers, changing art exhibits, lots of vegie and vegan options, and a great selection of coffees, teas and homemade cakes. Breakfast is available until 5pm.

Irish Pub (973 7797; www.irishpubkoblenz.de; Burgstrasse 7; 4pm-1am or later Mon, Tue, Thu & Fri,

1pm–2am or later Wed, Sat & Sun) A Koblenz institution since 1985, this drinking establishment screens major sports events, hosts live music and has karaoke (Wednesday) and quiz nights (Tuesday in winter).

For self-catering, try **Aldi supermarket** (Bahnhofstrasse 50; 8am–8pm Mon–Sat), two blocks north of the Hauptbahnhof.

Getting There & Away

Koblenz' Hauptbahnhof is served by frequent regional/IC trains going north to destinations such as Bonn (€10.30/13.50) and Cologne (€16.70/20), south to Mainz (€16.70/20) and Frankfurt (€22.20/26), and southwest to Trier (€19.20/24). Regional trains serve villages on both banks of the Romantic Rhine, including Bingen (€11.30, 50 minutes). Some of the Rhine villages are also served by buses (www.rmv-bus.de, in German) that stop outside the Hauptbahnhof – bus 650 goes to Boppard via Schloss Stolzenfels, while bus 570 goes to Braubach/Marksburg.

Several boat companies have docks along Konrad-Adenauer-Ufer, along the Rhine south of the Deutsches Eck.

A number of highways converge in Koblenz, including the B9 from Cologne/Bonn. The nearest autobahns are the A61 (Koblenz-Nord exit) and the A48/A1 to Trier.

Getting Around

Bicycles can be rented from **Fahrrad Zangmeister** (323 63; Am Löhrrondell; 9am–6.30pm Mon–Fri, 10am–4pm Sat), half a block east of Löhnstrasse 89a.

Bus trips in the city centre cost €1.60; longer trips (eg to the hostel or Schloss Stolzenfels) are €2.40. Day passes cost €3.60/4.80 for one/two zones. Bus 1 links the Deutsches Eck with the Hauptbahnhof.

To avoid parking fees, you can leave your vehicle at a Park & Ride lot – options include Sporthalle-Stadion Oberwerth, 2.5km south of the Hauptbahnhof next to the stadium, from where bus 1 goes to the city centre.

BRAUBACH

02627 / pop 3200

Framed by forested hillsides, vineyards and Rhine-side rose gardens, the 1300-year-old town of Braubach, about 8km south of Koblenz on the right bank, is centred on the small, half-timbered **Marktplatz**. High above are the dramatic towers, turrets and crenellations of the 700-year-old **Marksburg** (206;

www.marksburg.de; adult/student/6–18yr €5/4.50/3.5 10am–5pm Easter–Oct, 11am–4pm Nov–Easter), one the area's most interesting castles becaus unique among the Rhine fastnesses, it wa never destroyed. The tour takes in the citade the Gothic hall and the large kitchen, plus grisly torture chamber, with its hair-raisin assortment of pain-inflicting nasties.

Bus 570 links Koblenz' Hauptbahnhof wit Braubach (€3.50, 35 minutes, half-hour Monday to Saturday, hourly Sunday and hol days), from where the castle is a 20-minut uphill walk (up the *Fussweg* from Hahnwe or a short drive.

BOPPARD

06742 / pop 16,000

Thanks to its historic sites and scenic locatio on a horseshoe bend in the river, Boppar about 20km south of Koblenz, makes a pa ticularly atmospheric stop. A gateway to lo of great hikes in the Hunsrück, it's also a re town complete with a small cinema and trav agencies – where locals can book flights where you're from. Be sure to sample the ex cellent riesling from grapes grown near he in some of the Rhine's steepest vineyards.

Information

ATMs On the parking-permitted part of the Marktplatz behind the tourist office.

Call-Shop (Oberstrasse 99; per hr €2; 11am–9pm Mon–Sat, 9am–5pm Sun) Has internet access.

Post office (Heerstrasse 177)

Tourist office (3888; www.boppard-tourismus.de; Marktplatz; 8am–6.30pm Mon–Fri, 10am–2pm Sat May–Sep, 9am–5pm Mon–Fri Oct–Apr) Inside the Altes Rathaus. Sells walking and cycling maps. Lists of hotels and cultural events and a map are posted outside.

Sights

Just off Boppard's main commerci street, the pedestrianised, east–west or ented **Oberstrasse**, is the ancient **Marktplat** whose modern fountain is a favourite loc hang-out. Still home to a weekly **food ma ket** (9am–1pm Fri), it's dominated by th pointy twin towers of the late Romanesqu **Severuskirche** (8am–6pm), an elegant 13th century church built on the site of Roma military baths. Inside are polychrome wa paintings, a hanging cross from 1225 an spiderweb-like vaulted ceilings.

Half a block east of the church, the cute of Boppard's half-timbered buildings, built i

CLASSIC, MODERN & TIMELESS

Faced with fickle fashion trends, few furniture styles retain their freshness and popularity for long. A rare exception is bentwood furniture, invented by a Boppard-born cabinetmaker named Michael Thonet (1796–1871).

Whether in modern-day Paris-style cafes or Toulouse-Lautrec paintings of real *fin de siècle* Paris cafes, we've all seen Thonet's minimalist Chair Number 14 looking curvaceous, elegant and sturdy. The secret of this model – of which tens of millions have been produced – and all other bentwood pieces, lies in a production process that involves stacking strips of veneer, soaking them in hot glue so they become pliable, and then drying them in the desired shape in metal moulds. Thonet began his experiments in his Boppard shop in about 1830, but it was the 1851 Great Exhibition in London's Crystal Palace that catapulted him and his Vienna-based firm, soon to be known as Gebrüder Thonet, into prominence.

Exquisite bentwood furniture produced by Thonet during the 19th century can be seen in the **Museum der Stadt Boppard** (below). **Gebrüder Thonet** (www.thonet.de) is now run by its founders' great-great-grandchildren.

19, now houses a tearoom called **Teehäusje** (5798; Untere Marktstrasse 10; 9.30am-6pm Mon-Fri, ᴀm-3pm Sat).

A couple of blocks east, in a 14th-century ᴘlace, the **Museum der Stadt Boppard** (103 69; ᴛgstrasse; admission free; 10am-12.30pm & 1.30-5pm ᴛ-Sun Apr-Oct) has displays on local history ᴅd an entire floor dedicated to bentwood ᴜrniture (see the boxed text, above).

Along the riverfront is the eminently ᴛollable **Rheinallee**, a promenade lined ᴛth ferry docks, neatly painted hotels and ᴛe taverns. There are grassy areas and a ᴀldren's playground a bit upriver from the ᴛ-ferry dock.

A block south of the Marktplatz, the ᴛmer-Kastell (Roman Fort; cnr Angertstrasse & ᴛhgasse; admission free; 24hr), also known as ᴛe Römerpark, has 55m of the original ᴛh-century Roman wall and graves from ᴛe Frankish era (7th century). A wall panel ᴏws what the Roman town of Bodobrica ᴏked like 1700 years ago.

ᴛivities

ᴜr a spectacular view that gives you the illu-ᴏn of looking at four lakes instead of a single ᴀer, take the 20-minute **Sesselbahn** (2510; ᴡw.sesselbahn-boppard.de; up only/return €4.20/6.50; 9.30am-6.30pm Jul & Aug, 10am-5pm or 6pm Apr-Jun, Sep ᴄt) from the upriver edge of town up to the ᴛrseenblick viewpoint. The nearby **Gedeonseck** ᴏords views of the Rhine's hairpin curve.

The **Klettersteig**, which begins near the ᴛsselbahn, is a 2½- to three-hour cliffside ᴛventure hike. Decent walking or climbing ᴏes are a must; optional climbing equip-

ment can be rented at the Aral petrol station for €3. If you chicken out at the critical vertical bits, some with ladders, less vertiginous alternatives are available – except at the *Kletterwand*, a hairy section with steel stakes underfoot. It's possible to walk back to town via the Vierseenblick.

The dramatically steep **Hunsrückbahn** train travels through five tunnels and across two viaducts on its 8km journey from Boppard's Bahnhof to Buchholz (adult/child up to 11 years one-way €2.25/1.30, 10 minutes, hourly). From there many people hike back via the **Mörderbachtal** to Boppard, but Buchholz is also the starting point of an excellent 17km hike via the romantic **Ehrbachklamm Gorge** to Brodenbach (on the Moselle), from where you can get back to Boppard by taking bus 301 to Koblenz and then the train or bus 650 (€4.85, half-hourly until 8pm Monday to Saturday, hourly Sunday and holidays) to Boppard.

The tourist office organises **wine tastings** (5 wines €6; 8pm Thu Apr-Oct), hosted each month by a different *Weingut* (winegrowing estate).

Bikes can be hired from **Fahrrad Studio** (4736; Oberstrasse 105; per day €7.50; 9am-6pm Mon-Fri, 9am-1pm Sat). The tourist office has lots of material on cycling options.

Sleeping & Eating

Hotels, cafes and restaurants line the Rheinallee, Boppard's riverfront promenade. To get there by car, follow the signs on the B9 to the *Autofähre* – that is, turn onto Mainzer Strasse at the upriver (eastern) edge of town.

Hotel Rebstock (4876; www.rheinhotel-rebstock.de, in German; Rheinallee 31; s €33-46, d €49-77, cheaper in winter;

reception 7am-10pm Wed-Sun, 7am-4pm Mon & Tue;) This family-run hotel, on the Rhine facing the car-ferry landing, has 10 bright, spacious rooms, many with river views and some with balconies. The restaurant (mains €10.50 to €17.90; open noon to 9pm Wednesday to Sunday) serves top-notch Rhenish and German dishes.

our pick **Hotel Günther** (☎ 890 90; www.hotel guenther.de; Rheinallee 40; s €49-89, d €64-112, cheaper in winter; closed most of Dec;) Watch boats and barges glide along the mighty Rhine from your balconied room at this bright, welcoming waterfront hotel. It's owned by an American fellow and his German wife, which makes communication a cinch – and explains why the breakfast buffet includes peanut butter.

Hotel Bellevue (☎ 1020; www.bellevue-boppard.de; Rheinallee 41; s/d from €80/112, cheaper in winter;) This classy, Best Western–affiliated hotel, built with grand art-nouveau flair in 1910, has 94 highly civilised rooms, half with views of the Rhine.

Weinhaus Heilig Grab (☎ 2371; www.heiliggrab.de; Zelkesgasse 12; snacks €3.50-7; 3-11pm or later Wed-Mon, closed Christmas–mid-Jan) Across the street from the Hauptbahnhof, Boppard's oldest wine tavern offers a cosy setting for sipping 'Holy Sepulchre' rieslings (from €2.30). When it's warm, you can sit outside under the leafy chestnut canopy. Also has snacks and five rooms for rent (doubles €66 to €76).

Weingut Felsenkeller (☎ 2154; www.felsenkeller -boppard.de, in German; Mühltal 21; 3-10pm or later Wed-Mon) Across the street from the chairlift station and next to a little stream, this place serves its own and other local growers' wines.

Severus Stube (☎ 3218; Untere Marktstrasse 7; mains €5.50-13.50; Fri-Wed) Serves up tasty, good-value German food in a cosy, rustic dining room.

For self-catering, try **Penny Markt supermarket** (Oberstrasse 171; 8am-8pm Mon-Sat), one of several food shops along Oberstrasse.

ST GOAR

☎ 06741 / pop 3000

St Goar, 10km upriver from Boppard and 28km downriver from Bingen, is lorded over by the sprawling ruins of **Burg Rheinfels** (☎ 383; Schlossberg; adult/6-14yr €4/2; 9am-6pm daily mid-Mar–early Nov, 11am-5pm Sat & Sun in good weather early Nov–mid-Mar), once the mightiest fortress on the Rhine. Built in 1245 by Count Dieter V of Katzenelnbogen as a base for his toll-collecti operations, its size and labyrinthine layout a truly astonishing. Not only kids will love e ploring the subterranean tunnels and galleri To get there, you can walk for 20 minutes the hill from the youth hostel or drive (parki fee required).

Another kid-pleasing stop is the **Deutsch Puppen- und Bärenmuseum** (German Doll & Tec Bear Museum; ☎ 7270; www.deutsches-puppen-u -baerenmuseum.de; Sonnengasse 8; adult/4-11yr/12-1 €3.50/1.50/2.50; 10am-5pm daily Apr-Dec, 2-5pm Sa Sun Jan-Mar).

The Protestant **Stiftskirche** (Am Marktpla across the street from the Bahnhof, is know for its late Gothic murals, neat vaulting a Romanesque crypt.

Walking options include the **Panoramaweg** to get there follow the signs from the Ratha or across the tracks from the Bahnhof.

The **tourist office** (☎ 383; www.st-goar.de; Heerstra 86; 9am-12.30pm & 1.30-6pm Mon-Fri May-Sep, to 5 Oct-Apr, closes 2pm Fri Nov-Mar, also open 10am-noon May-Sep), on the pedestrianised main street, c supply you with an English map-guide for t Via Sancti Goaris city-centre walking tour a offers internet access (€0.50 per 10 minute

Sleeping & Eating

Hotels line the waterfront; the three list below are all near the Stiftskirche.

DJH hostel (☎ 388; www.jugendherberge. Bismarckweg 17; dm €14.40; reception 7am-10p) This old-style, 126-bed hostel is at t northern end of town, on the hillside bel Burg Rheinfels.

Hotel Hauser (☎ 333; www.hotelhauser.de; Heerstra 77; s €26-30, d €52-66; reception closed Mon Nov-M hotel closed mid-Dec–mid-Feb) This slightly fad 13-room hotel feels like it's been lived-in wi humour and *joie de vivre*. The spacious roor come with compact plastic shower pods, an some have balconies. The restaurant serv regional specialities, including fish.

Hotel Zur Loreley (☎ 1614; www.hotel-zur-loreley Heerstrasse 87; s €47, d €60-70, apt per person €38-44, incl breakfast;) A central and welcomir place to hang your hat, this places has eig rooms with tasteful, modern decor and fi holiday apartments.

Hotel am Markt (☎ 1721; www.hotel-am-markt-sa -goar.de; Marktplatz 1; s/d/tr/q €50/65/90/99, s without ba room €38; closed Nov-Feb) Central and welcomir this family-owned hotel has 15 bright roor outfitted with simple wooden furniture

etting Around

icycles can be rented from **Goarbike** (☎ 1735; erstrasse 44; per half-/whole day €6/11.50; ◷ 9am-1pm 3-7pm Apr-Oct), near the Bahnhof.

T GOARSHAUSEN & LORELEY

☎ 06771 / pop 1600

: Goar's twin town on the right bank of the hine – the two are connected by car ferry – **St Goarshausen**, gateway to the most fabled ot along the Romantic Rhine, **Loreley**. his enormous slab of slate owes its fame a mythical maiden whose siren songs are id to have lured sailors to their death in the eacherous currents, as poetically portrayed y Heinrich Heine in 1823. At the very tip of narrow breakwater jutting into the Rhine, sculpture of the blonde buxom beauty erches lasciviously.

The Loreley outcrop can be reached by ir, by shuttle bus (one-way from St Goars-ausen's Marktplatz €2.40, hourly from Easter October) or via the **Treppenweg**, a steep,)0-step stairway that begins at the break-ater. At the **Loreley Besucherzentrum** (Visitor ntre; ☎ 599 093; www.loreley-besucherzentrum.de; ult/student €2.50/1.50; ◷ 10am-6pm Apr–mid-Nov, am-5pm Mar, 11am-4pm Sat & Sun Nov-Feb), which as a tourist office branch inside, exhibits ncluding an 18-minute 3-D film) examine e region's geology, flora and fauna, ship-ing, winemaking, the Loreley myth and rly Rhine tourism in an engaging, interac-ve fashion. To the left as you approach the ntre, a gravel path leads through the forest the **Loreleyspitze** (the tip of the Loreley utcrop), where you'll find spectacular pano-mic views and a **cafe** (◷ closed Nov-Mar). Far low, teeny-tiny trains slither along both nks of the Rhine, while miniature barges egotiate its waters.

Near St Goarshausen stand two rival astles. Burg Peterseck was built by the arch-ishop of Trier in an effort to counter the ll practices of the powerful Katzenelnbogen mily. In a show of medieval muscle flexing, e latter responded by building a much big-r castle high above St Goarshausen, Burg eukatzenelnbogen, which became known as **urg Katz** (Cat Castle; ◷ closed to the public) for short. nd so, to highlight the obvious imbalance of ower between the Katzenelnbogens and the rchbishop, Burg Peterseck soon came to be nown as **Burg Maus** (Mouse Castle).

These days, Burg Maus (interior closed) houses the **Adler- und Falkenhof** (Eagle & Falcon House; ☎ 7669; www.burg-maus.de, in German; adult/child over 6yr/family €8/6/22; ◷ falconry show 11am & 2.30pm Tue-Sun, also 4.30pm Sun & holidays mid-Mar–mid-Oct). It can be reached by a 20-minute walk from St Goarshausen-Wellmich.

St Goarshausen has its own **tourist office** (☎ 9100; www.loreley-touristik.de; Bahnhofstrasse 8; ◷ 9am-5pm Mon-Fri, 10am-noon Sat Apr-Oct, 9.30am-3pm Mon-Fri Nov-Mar) across the highway from the car-ferry landing. The hall is adorned with photos of recent Loreley beauty queens, all of them incredibly blonde.

About 8km upriver from Loreley stands fairly-tale **Pfalzgrafstein** (www.burgen-rlp.de; adult/under 18yr/family €2.10/0.70/4.80; ◷ 10am-6pm Tue-Sun Apr-Oct, to 5pm Mar, 10am-5pm Sat & Sun Nov, Jan & Feb, closed Dec), a boat-shaped toll castle perched on a island perfect for picnics in the middle of the Rhine. **Ferries** (☎ 0171 331 0375; adult/4-11yr/family €2.50/1/6) leave every half-hour from Kaub, next to the car ferry.

OBERWESEL

☎ 06744 / pop 3300

An impressive, 3km-long medieval **town wall**, sporting 16 guard towers, wraps around much of Oberwesel's Altstadt, which is sep-arated from the river by the rail line, laid in 1857. You can stroll on top of much of the wall.

Easily spotted on a hillside at the north-ern end of town is the 14th-century **St-Martins-Kirche**, known as the 'white church', which has painted ceilings, a richly sculpted main altar and a tower that once formed part of the town's defences. In the southern Altstadt, the **Liebfrauenkirche**, known as the 'red church' for the colour of its facade, is older by about 100 years and boasts an im-pressive carved gold altar.

Each April, Oberwesel crowns not a *Weinkönigin* (wine queen), as in most towns, but a *Weinhexe* (wine witch) – a good witch, of course – who is said to protect the vine-yards. Photos of all the *Weinhexen* crowned since the 1940s are on display in the modern **Oberwesel Kulturhaus** (☎ 714 726; www.kulturhaus -oberwesel.de; Rathausstrasse 23; adult/child/student €2.50/1/1.50; ◷ 10am-5pm Tue-Fri, 2-5pm Sat, Sun & holi-days Apr-Oct, closed Nov-Mar), whose well-presented local history museum features 19th-century engravings of the Romantic Rhine and models of Rhine riverboats. An excellent English visitors' guide is available at reception.

High above the town's upriver edge is the majestic **Schönburg** (www.hotel-schoenburg.com) castle, saved from total ruin when a New York real estate millionaire purchased it in 1885 (it's now a hotel). Legend has it that this was once the home of seven beautiful but haughty sisters who ridiculed and rejected all potential suitors until all seven of them were turned into stone and submerged in the Rhine. You may be able to spot them from the **Siebenjungfraublick** (Seven Virgins Viewpoint), reached via a lovely vineyard trail beginning at the town's downriver edge.

The **tourist office** (☎ 710 624; www.oberwesel.de; Rathausstrasse 3; ☉ 9am-5pm Mon-Fri Apr-Oct, to 2pm Fri Nov-Mar, plus 9am-1pm Sat Jul-Sep) is across the street from the Rathaus.

The 206-bed **DJH hostel** (☎ 933 30; www.jugendherberge.de; dm from €19.90) overlooks the town from near the Schönburg.

Half-timbered **Hotel Römerkrug** (☎ 7091; www.hotel-roemerkrug.rhinecastles.com; Marktplatz 1; s/d €50/80), run by three generations of a friendly local family, is in the most picturesque part of town, facing the Rathaus. The seven rooms have an antique feel and it has an excellent traditional **restaurant** (mains €12-25; ☉ daily May-Sep, Fri-Tue Oct-Dec, Mar & Apr, Sat & Sun Jan & Feb).

Picnic supplies are available a block from the Rathaus at the **Edeka Markt supermarket** (Koblenzstrasse 1; ☉ 8am-7pm Mon-Fri, 8am-4pm Sat).

Bicycles can be rented from **Höhn** (☎ 336; Liebfrauenstrasse 38).

BACHARACH
☎ 06743 / pop 2100

One of the prettiest of the Rhine villages, tiny Bacharach – 24km downriver from Bingen – conceals its considerable charms behind a time-worn, 14th-century wall. From the B9, go through one of the thick arched gateways under the train tracks and you'll find yourself in a medieval village graced with exquisite half-timbered mansions such as the **Altes Haus**, the **Posthof** and the off-kilter **Alte Münze** – all are along Oberstrasse, the main street, which runs parallel to the Rhine.

Also on Oberstrasse is the late-Romanesque **Peterskirche** (☉ 9am-6pm Easter-Oct), with some particularly suggestive capitals. Look for the naked woman with snakes sucking her breasts (a warning about the consequences of adultery) at the end of the left aisle. A path that begins in between the church and th• tourist office takes you uphill for 15 min• utes to the 12th-century **Burg Stahleck** (no• a hostel), and past the filigreed ruins of th• Gothic **Wernerkapelle**.

The best way to get a sense of the village an• its surrounds is to walk the new, signposte• **Stadtmauer Rundweg** (Town Wall Walkin• Circuit). The lookout tower on the upper se• tion of the wall affords panoramic views.

Bacharach's **tourist office** (☎ 919 303; www.rh• -nahe-touristik.de; Oberstrasse 45; ☉ 9am-5pm Mon-F• 10am-3pm Sat, Sun & holidays Apr-Oct, 9am-noon Mon-• Nov-Mar) has handy information about the e• tire area. There's an ATM across Oberstras• from the church.

Sleeping & Eating
There are places to eat along Oberstrasse.

Campingplatz Sonnenstrand (☎ 1752; www.campi• -sonnenstrand.de, in German; Strandbadweg 9; per perso• tent/car €5/3/3; ☉ Apr-Oct) On the Rhine abo• 500m south of (upriver from) town.

our pick DJH Burg Stahleck (☎ 1266; www.juge• herberge.de; Burg Stahleck; dm from €18.90; ☒) I• a dream setting inside the medieval Bur• Stahleck, this hostel has 168 beds in room• for one to six people, almost all with priva• bathrooms.

Rhein Hotel (☎ 1243; www.rhein-hotel-bacharach.c• Langstrasse 50; s €39-59, d €78-118; ☉ closed Jan & Fe• P ☒ ☒) Right on the town's mediev• ramparts, this homey, family-run hotel ha• 14 well-lit rooms with original artwor• and compact bathrooms. Those facing th• river, and thus the train tracks, have doub• double-glazing. The restaurant (mains €8.3• to €21; closed Tuesday) specialises in r• gional dishes such as *Rieslingbraten* (rieslin• marinated braised beef). Bikes are free f• guests to use.

Zum Grünen Baum (☎ 1208; Oberstrasse 63; snac• & light meals €2.40-7.50; ☉ closed Tue) An unpreter• tious wine tavern serving some of the be• whites in town. Try the *Weinkarussel*, a 1• wine sampler (€14).

For picnic supplies, **Nahkauf groce•** (Koblenzerstrasse 2; ☉ 8am-12.30pm & 2-6pm Mon-F• 8am-12.30pm Sat) is about 150m north alon• Oberstrasse from the church.

BACHARACH TO BINGEN
Along the southernmost stretch of the Rom• antic Rhine, three impressive castles affordin•

ectacular views grace the craggy left-bank
opes. First up (if you're coming from
e north) is the state-owned **Burg Sooneck**
(06743-6064; www.burgen-rlp.de; adult/concession guided
ur €2.60/1.30; 9am-6pm Apr-Sep, 9am-5pm Oct, Nov &
n-Mar, closed in Dec & 1st workday of each week, usually
on), carefully restored in the 19th century
id filled with neo-Gothic and Biedermeier
irniture and paintings.

Looming above the village of Trech-
ngshausen, the mighty **Burg Reichenstein**
(06721-6117; www.burg-reichenstein.de, in German;
ult/under 12yr €4/2.50; 10am-6pm Mar–mid-Nov,
osed Mon except perhaps Jul & Aug) now harbours
museum with a prized collection of fur-
ishings, armour, hunting trophies and even
ist-iron oven slabs. Also has a restaurant
id rooms for rent.

The most picturesque of the three is the
ivately owned **Burg Rheinstein** (06721-6348;
ww.burg-rheinstein.de; adult/child €4/2.80; 9.30am-
30pm mid-Mar–mid-Nov, 10am-4.30pm Sat & Sun mid-
ov–mid-Mar), which in the 1820s became
e first Rhine castle to be converted – by
russian royalty – into a romantic summer
esidence. The working drawbridge and a
ortcullis evoke medieval times but the in-
rior is mostly neo-Gothic.

INGEN
 06721 / pop 24,600
hanks to its strategic location at the conflu-
nce of the Nahe and Rhine Rivers, Bingen
as been coveted by warriors and mer-
hants since its founding by the Romans
1 11 BC. Repeatedly scarred by war,
ese days it's an attractive, flowery town
iat's rather less touristy than some of its
maller neighbours.

Bingen was the birthplace of the writer
tefan George (1868–1933) and, more no-
ibly, the adopted home of Hildegard von
ingen (see the boxed text, p510).

rientation & Information
ingen's centre is along the left (south) bank
f the Rhine, just east of its confluence with
ie Nahe River. The town has two train sta-
ons: the Hauptbahnhof, just west of the Nahe
1 Bingerbrück; and the more central Bahnhof
ingen Stadt, just east of the town centre.

ost office (Am Fruchtmarkt) Situated on the main street
ear the bridge. Has an ATM.

ourist office (184 205; www.bingen.de; Rheinkai
1; 9am-6pm Mon-Fri, 9am-5pm Sat Easter-Oct,

10am-1pm Sun May-Oct, 9am-12.30pm & 1.30-4pm Tue-
Thu, to 6pm Mon, to 1pm Fri Nov-Easter) Facing the Rhine
250m west of Bahnhof Bingen Stadt; it has brochures and
maps for hikers and cyclists.

Sights
Thanks to the 2008 State Garden Show, the
once-derelict bit of Bingen between the train
tracks and the Rhine has been turned into
a delightful **riverside promenade**, with lawns,
flower beds, a beer garden and a stylish
wine bar.

Bingen's commercial centre is centred
around pedestrians-only Basilikastrasse,
named after **Basilika St Martin**, a 15th-century,
Gothic-style church – built on the site of a
Roman temple – at its western end. Up a
staircase at the top of Rathausstrasse is the
town's most prominent landmark, **Burg Klopp**,
an imposing castle restored in the late 19th
century. The views are superb and the terrace is the perfect spot for a first kiss – or a
10,000th. To get a bit higher you can climb the
tower (admission free; 8am-6pm in the warm months),
which proudly flies the town's red-and-white
flag. The old Roman well seems bottomless
(it's actually 52m deep).

The **Historisches Museum am Strom** (991
531; Museumsstrasse 3; adult/concession/family €3/2/6;
 10am-5pm Tue-Sun), on the riverside promenade, has exhibits on Rhine romanticism,
both engraved and painted, and the life and
achievements of Hildegard von Bingen (see
the boxed text, p510). Another highlight is
a set of surgical instruments – from scalpels
and cupping glasses to saws – left behind by a
Roman doctor in the 2nd century AD.

High atop the **Rochusburg** (Rochus Hill),
2.5km southeast up Rochusallee from the
tourist office, is the neo-Gothic **Rochuskapelle**, a
pilgrimage church last rebuilt in the late 1800s.
It has a very sharp steeple and a splendid canopied altar showing scenes from the life of
Hildegard von Bingen. About 400m towards
Bingen is the **Hildegard Forum** (181 000; www
.hildegard-forum.de, in German; Rochusweg 1; admission free;
 11am-6pm Tue-Sun), run by Kreuzschwestern
nuns in black-and-white habits, which houses
Hildegard exhibits, a medieval herb garden
and a **restaurant** (buffet lunch €9.50; lunch 11.30am-
2pm, cafe 2-5pm Tue-Sun) serving wholesome foods
prepared just the way Hildegard liked them,
including dishes made with spelt, her favourite grain. The area is linked to Bahnhof
Bingen Stadt by bus 330 (once or twice hourly

HILDEGARD VON BINGEN

She's hip and holistic, a composer, a dramatist and a courageous campaigner for the rights of women. She heals with crystals and herbs, her music frequently hits the New Age charts...and she's been dead for more than 800 years.

Hildegard von Bingen (1098–1179) was born in Bermersheim (between Worms and Alzey), the 10th child of a well-off and influential family. At the age of three, she experienced the first of the visions that would occur over the course of her extraordinary – and extraordinarily long – life. As a young girl, she entered the convent at Disibodenberg on the Nahe River and eventually became an abbess, founding two abbeys of her own: Rupertsberg, above Bingen, in 1150; and Eibingen, across the Rhine near Rüdesheim, in 1165. During her preaching tours – an unprecedented activity for women in medieval times – she lectured both to the clergy and the common people, attacking social injustice and ungodliness.

Pope Eugene III publicly endorsed Hildegard, urging her to write down both her theology and her visionary experiences. This she did in a remarkable series of books that encompass ideas as diverse as cosmology, natural history and female orgasm. Her overarching philosophy was that humankind is a distillation of divinity and should comport itself accordingly. Her accomplishments are even more remarkable considering her lifelong struggle against feelings of worthlessness and the physical effects of her mysterious visions, which often left her near death.

Monday to Saturday, every two hours Sunday and holidays until 2pm).

On an island near the confluence of the Nahe and Rhine is the **Mäuseturm** (Mouse Tower; ☾ closed to the public), where, according to legend, Hatto II, the 10th-century archbishop of Mainz, was devoured alive by mice as punishment for his oppressive rule. In fact, the name is probably a mutation of *Mautturm* (toll tower), which was the building's medieval function.

The monumental statue on the wine slopes across the Rhine portrays a triumphant **Germania** (see opposite).

Activities

Eight **day-hike circuits**, 1.9km to 9.2km in length, including several through the vineyards, begin at the vineyard-adjacent car park at the corner of the Hildegard Forum complex (look for a map sign hidden by a row of bushes). You can also explore the **Binger Stadtwald**, a large forested area northwest of Bingerbrück.

Bingen is the meeting point of two major long-distance bike paths, the **Rhein-Radweg**, which hugs the Rhine's left bank, and the **Nahe-Hunsrück-Mosel-Radweg**, which follows the Nahe River to Idar-Oberstein.

Sleeping

Inexpensive places to sleep can be found on and around Basilikastrasse.

DJH hostel (☎ 321 63; www.jugendherberge.de; Herterstrasse 51, Bingerbrück; dm €19.90; ✗) Totally

renovated in 2006, this 121-bed hostel is 10-minute walk from the Hauptbahnho Rooms, all with bathrooms, are for one t four people.

Hotel-Café Köppel (☎ 147 70; www.hotel-koeppel.c Kapuzinerstrasse 12; s €45-55, d €65-78; ℗) In the hea of town across from the Kapuzinerkirch this place has a stylish *Konditorei* (cake cafe whose products will make your eyes go wid The rooms, renovated in 2009, are modest bu spotless and well kept.

Hotel Martinskeller (☎ 134 75; www.hotel-bing -rhein.com; Martinsstrasse 1-3; s €69-77, d €88-106; ℗ Creative use of some rather odd spaces give this family-run, 15-room hotel, two blocks u the hill from the tourist office, a quirky bu personal vibe. The comfortable rooms are bi and each is unique – one is African inspire another English.

Eating & Drinking

Vinotek (☎ 991 203; Hindenburganlage; light mains €4.8 7.50, wine per glass €3-6; ☾ 11am-11pm Tue-Sun Mai Oct, 5-11pm Wed-Sun Nov-Easter) A stylish riverfror wine bar – gorgeous on sunny evenings.

our pick **Gaggianer** (☎ 148 82; Badergasse 36; mair €6.50-12.90; ☾ 4pm-midnight or later, hot dishes to 10p Wed-Mon, closed Tue) A block inland from th Nahe, this informal restaurant serves win by the glass, salads and full meals in a lea beer garden and a rustic dining room, th latter with antique kitchen utensils, donate by friends and clients, dangling from the raf ers. Endemic specialities include *Zipfelche*

otato dough filled with fresh white cheese,
eam cheese and herbs) and *Viagra Naturell,*
hose ingredients include three eggs.

ÜDESHEIM

☎ 06722 / pop 10,000

üdesheim am Rhein, capital of the Rheingau
amous for its superior rieslings), is on the
hine's right bank across from Bingen, to
hich it's connected by passenger and car
rries. Administratively part of Hesse, it is
eluged by day-tripping coach tourists – three
illion a year – and for some its most famous
ature, **Drosselgasse**, brings to mind the words
ourist nightmare from hell'. If you're looking
r a souvenir thimble, this is definitely the
ace to come. That said, the exuberance can
e fun, at least for a while, and the town is also
good place to begin a variety of delightful
neyard walks.

The **tourist office** (☎ 906 150; www.ruedesheim.de;
isenheimer Strasse 22; ☼ 8.30am-6.30pm Mon-Fri & 10am-
m Sat, Sun & holidays Apr-Oct, 11am-3pm Mon-Fri Nov-Mar,
o 11am-3pm Sat & Sun late Nov-25 Dec) is 600m east
f Drosselgasse.

ights & Activities

rosselgasse, a tunnel-like alley so overloaded
ith signs that it looks like it might be in Hong
ong, is the Rhine at its most colourfully tour-
tic – bad German pop wafts out of the pubs,
hich are filled with rollicking crowds. The
oerstrasse, at the top of Drosselgasse, is simi-
rly overloaded with eateries and drinkeries,
ough to get away from the drunken mad-
ess all you have to do is wander a few blocks
any direction.

One island of relative calm, just 50m to the
ft from the top of Drosselgasse, is **Siegfried's**
echanisches Musikkabinett (☎ 492 17; www.siegfrieds
usikkabinett.de; Oberstrasse 29; tour adult/student €6/3;
☼ 10am-6pm Mar-Dec), a fun, working collec-
on of 18th- and 19th-century mechanical
usical instruments.

Near the Bingen car-ferry dock, in the
00-year-old Brömserburg castle, is the
einmuseum (Wine Museum; ☎ 2348; www.rheingauer
veinmuseum.de, in German; Rheinstrasse 2; adult/stu-
ent incl audioguide €5/3; ☼ 10am-6pm Apr-Oct),
lled with wine paraphernalia from Roman
mes onwards. The tower affords great
ver views.

For an even better panorama, head up to
he **Niederwald Denkmal** (inaugurated 1883),
bombastic monument on the wine slopes

west of town starring **Germania** and celebrating the creation of the German Reich in 1871.
You can walk up via the vineyards – trails,
including one that begins at the western
end of Oberstrasse, are signposted – but it's
faster to glide above the vineyards aboard the
Seilbahn (cable car; ☎ 2402; www.seilbahn-ruedesheim.de;
Oberstrasse; adult/5-13yr one-way €4.50/2, return €6.50/3;
☼ late Mar-early Nov & late Nov-23 Dec).

From the monument, a network of trails
leads to destinations such as the **Jagdschloss**
(hunting lodge; 2km) and, down the hill, the
romantic **Burg Ehrenfels** ruin.

From near the Jagdschloss you can catch
a trail down to **Assmannshausen**, a sedate burg
5km downriver from Rüdesheim that's known
for its *Spätburgunder* (Pinot noir) red wines.
Or you can head down the slope on the
Sesselbahn (chairlift; adult/child incl the Seilbahn €6.50/3)
and then head from Assmannshausen back
to Rüdesheim either by train or by passenger
ferry. A **Ring-Ticket** (adult/child €11/5.50) includes
the Seilbahn, the Sesselbahn and the ferry and
lets you stop in Bingen.

AROUND RÜDESHEIM
Eibingen

About 2km north of Rüdesheim, the wine
village of Eibingen is the burial place of medieval power woman **Hildegard von Bingen** (see
the boxed text, opposite). Her elaborate gold
reliquary shrine, containing her heart, hair,
tongue and skull, is prominently displayed inside the **parish church** (Marienthaler Strasse 3; ☼ daily),
attracting pilgrims from around the world,
especially on 17 September, the anniversary of
her death. Up the hill, the **St Hildegard Convent**
(www.abtei-st-hildegard.de, in German), with around 50
nuns, dates back to 1904.

Kloster Eberbach

If you saw the 1986 film *The Name of the
Rose*, starring Sean Connery, you've already
seen parts of this one-time Cistercian **monastery** (☎ 06723-917 80; www.kloster-eberbach.de;
adult/student incl English-language brochure €3.50/1.50,
1½hr audioguide for 1/2 people €3.50/5; ☼ 10am-6pm
Apr-Oct, 11am-5pm Nov-Mar), in which many of
the interior scenes were shot. Dating from
as far back as the 12th century and once
home to 150 or more monks and perhaps
400 lay brothers, this graceful complex –
in an idyllic little valley – went through
periods as a lunatic asylum, jail, sheep pen
and accommodation for WWII refugees.

Today visitors can explore the 13th- and 14th-century **Kreuzgang** (cloister), the monks' baroque **refectory** and their vaulted Gothic **Monchdormitorium** (dormitory), as well as the austere Romanesque **Klosterkirche** (basilica).

At the **Vinotek** (www.weingut-kloster-eberbach.de, in German), you can taste and buy the superb wines produced by the government-owned Hessische Staatsweingüter (Hessian State Winery).

Kloster Eberbach is about 20km northeast of (ie towards Wiesbaden from) Rüdesheim. From Rüdesheim or Wiesbaden, you can take bus 171 or the train either to Eltville, from where hourly bus 172 heads to the Kloster, or to Hattenheim, from which it's a 3km uphill walk.

THE MOSELLE VALLEY

While plenty of places in Germany demand that you hustle, the Moselle (in German, Mosel) gently suggests that you should, well…just mosey. The German section of the river, which rises in France and then traverses Luxembourg, runs 195km from Trier to Koblenz on a slow, serpentine course, revealing new scenery at every bend. Unlike the Romantic Rhine, it's spanned by plenty of bridges.

Exploring the vineyards and wineries of the Moselle Valley is an ideal way to get to know German culture, meet German people and, of course, acquire a taste for some wonderful wines. Slow down and experience sublime serial sipping – look for signs reading *Weingut, Weinprobe, Wein Probieren, Weinverkauf* and *Wein zu Verkaufen*. In spring luscious purple wisteria flowers, dangling from stone village houses, anticipate the bunches of grapes that will ripen in the fall.

Europe's steepest vineyard (the Bremmer Calmont near Bremm, with a 68% gradient) and Germany's most expensive one (the Bernkasteler Doctor in Bernkastel-Kues) are both located along the Moselle.

Activities
CYCLING
For details on some of the many superb cycling paths along and near the Moselle, see p500, p518 and the boxed text, p517.

HIKING
The Moselle Valley is especially scenic wall ing country. Expect some steep climbs if yc venture away from the river, but the view are worth a few sore muscles. A popul. long-distance hike is the **Moselhöhenweg**, ru ning on both sides of the Moselle for a tot of 390km. Good hiking maps are available most bookshops and tourist offices.

Getting There & Away
Frankfurt-Hahn Airport (p481) is only 20k from Traben-Trarbach and 30km fro Bernkastel-Kues.

Most people start their exploration the Moselle in either Trier or Koblenz. you have private transport and are con ing from the north, you might head u the Ahr Valley and cut through the Eif Mountains. If you're coming from th Saarland, your route will take you eith along the beautiful Saar River or throug the Hunsrück Mountains.

Getting Around
BUS & TRAIN
The rail line linking Koblenz with Tri (€19.20, 1½ to two hours, at least hourl follows the Moselle – and serves its vi lages – only as far upriver as Bullay (€10.3 45 to 65 minutes from Koblenz, 40 to 5 minutes from Trier). From there, hourl Moselwein-Strecke shuttle trains hea upriver to Traben-Trarbach (€3.10, 2 minutes, hourly).

The villages between Traben-Trarbac and Trier are served by bus 333 (at least si times daily Monday to Friday, twice dail Saturday and Sunday), run by **Moselbahn bus** (☎ 01805-131 619; www.moselbahn.de, in German).

CAR & MOTORCYCLE
Driving is the easiest way to see the Mosell From Trier, the B53 and then, from Bulla the B49 follow the river all the way t Koblenz, crossing it several times.

TRIER
☎ 0651 / pop 104,000
A Unesco World Heritage Site since 198 Trier is home to Germany's finest Roma monuments – including an extraordinar number of elaborate thermal baths – as we as architectural gems from later ages. Its prox imity to both Luxembourg and France ca

e tasted in the cuisine and felt in the local
sprit. About 21,000 students do their part to
ontribute to the lively atmosphere.

Founded by the Romans as Augusta
reverorum in 16 BC, Trier's rise was as me-
eoric as its citizens were well bathed. The
apital of the Belgian provinces of Roman
'iaul by the 2nd century, it served as the capi-
al of the Gallic Empire in the 3rd century and
s the residence of Constantine the Great in
he 4th century. A second heyday arrived in
he 13th century, when its archbishops ac-
uired the rank and power of prince-electors.
n the following centuries, the city see-sawed
etween periods of wealth and poverty. Karl
Marx (1818–83) lived here in bourgeois pros-
erity until age 17.

Orientation

The Hauptbahnhof, in a slightly seedy area
hat's being gentrified, is about 600m south-
ast of the landmark Porta Nigra and the
djacent tourist office. From there, the pe-
estrianised Simeonstrasse leads southwest
o the Hauptmarkt. The district of Olewig is
bout 2km southeast of the centre.

Information

fro Cosmetics Business (Karl-Marx-Strasse 32; per hr
1; ⏰ 11am-8pm Mon-Fri, noon-8pm Sat) Internet access.

TMs At the Kornmarkt; also in the Hauptbahnhof.

Combination Ticket – Roman Monuments (adult/
enior & student/family €6.20/3.10/14.80) Discounted
dmission to the Porta Nigra, Kaiserthermen, Amphi-
heater and Thermen am Viehmarkt. Sold at the tourist
ffice and each site.

S-Telecom (Bahnhofplatz 1; per hr €1; ⏰ 9am-11pm)
nternet access next to the Hauptbahnhof.

TS Internet Cafe (Porta-Nigra-Platz 4; per hr €1.50;
⏰ 9am-10pm Mon-Fri, 11am-9pm Sat, noon-10pm Sun)

Post office (Bahnhofplatz) Just north of the
Hauptbahnhof.

Tourist office (☎ 978 080; www.trier.de; An der Porta
.igra; ⏰ 9am-6pm Mon-Sat Mar-Dec, 10am-5pm Mon-Sat
an & Feb, 10am-5pm Sun & holidays May-Oct, 10am-3pm
un Mar, Apr & Nov-late Dec, 10am-1pm Sun late Dec-Feb)
Next to the Porta Nigra. Has a hotel-vacancies board outside
nd sells Moselle-area walking and cycling maps.

TrierCard (individual/family €9/19) For three consecutive
lays you get 25% off museum and monument admissions,
inlimited use of public transport and other discounts. Sold
only at the tourist office.

Waschsalon (Brückenstrasse 19-21; ⏰ 8am-10pm)
elf-service laundry.

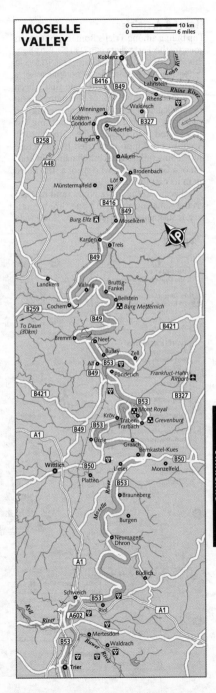

RHINELAND-PALATINATE & SAARLAND

Sights & Activities

Top billing among Trier's Roman monuments goes to the **Porta Nigra** (☎ 718 1459; Porta-Nigra-Platz; adult/7-18yr/senior & student/family €2.10/1/1.60/5.10; ☻ 9am-6pm Apr-Sep, to 5pm Mar & Oct, to 4pm Nov-Feb), a brooding 2nd-century city gate that's been blackened by time (hence the name, Latin for 'black gate'). A marvel of engineering and ingenuity, it's held together by nothing but gravity and iron rods. In the 11th century, Archbishop Poppo converted the structure into St Simeonkirche, a church named in honour of a Greek hermit who spent a stint holed up in its east tower.

Adjacent to the Porta Nigra (and reached via the same entrance), in a one-time monastery, is **Stadtmuseum Simeonstift** (☎ 718 1459; An der Porta Nigra; adult/under 10yr/student/family €5/free/3.60/4; ☻ 10am-6pm Tue-Sun). Completely renovated i 2007, it brings alive two millennia of loca history with carefully chosen objects, man of them exquisite. Highlights include the **Trie Kino** (Trier Cinema), where you can see 7 short films of Trier, some made as far back a 1904. Admission includes a free audioguid in German, English or French.

A block southwest is the 13th-centur **Dreikönigenhaus** (Simeonstrasse 19; ☻ interior closed public), a late Gothic residence with a geometri cally painted facade. Originally, the entranc was up on the 1st floor, reachable by stairs tha could be retracted in case of danger.

Two blocks further on is the **Hauptmarkt** where a food market is still held daily ex

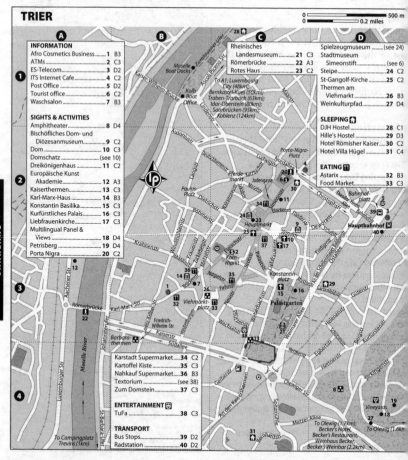

TRIER

0 ——— 500 m
0 ——— 0.2 miles

INFORMATION
Afro Cosmetics Business	**1** B3
ATMs	**2** C3
ES-Telecom	**3** D2
ITS Internet Cafe	**4** C2
Post Office	**5** D2
Tourist office	**6** C2
Waschsalon	**7** B3

SIGHTS & ACTIVITIES
Amphitheater	**8** D4
Bischöfliches Dom- und Diözesanmuseum	**9** C3
Dom	**10** C3
Domschatz	(see 10)
Dreikönigenhaus	**11** C2
Europäische Kunst Akademie	**12** A3
Kaiserthermen	**13** C3
Karl-Marx-Haus	**14** B3
Konstantin Basilika	**15** C3
Kurfürstliches Palais	**16** C3
Liebfrauenkirche	**17** C3
Multilingual Panel & Views	**18** D4
Petrisberg	**19** D4
Porta Nigra	**20** C2

Rheinisches Landesmuseum	**21** C3
Römerbrücke	**22** A3
Rotes Haus	**23** C2

SLEEPING
Spielzeugmuseum	(see 24)
Stadtmuseum Simeonstift	(see 6)
Steipe	**24** C2
St-Gangolf-Kirche	**25** C2
Thermen am Viehmarkt	**26** B3
Weinkulturpfad	**27** D4

SLEEPING
DJH Hostel	**28** C1
Hille's Hostel	**29** D3
Hotel Römisher Kaiser	**30** C2
Hotel Villa Hügel	**31** C4

EATING
Astarix	**32** B3
Food Market	**33** C3
Karstadt Supermarket	**34** C2
Kartoffel Kiste	**35** C3
Nahkauf Supermarket	**36** B3
Textorium	(see 38)
Zum Domstein	**37** C3

ENTERTAINMENT
TuFa	**38** C3

TRANSPORT
Bus Stops	**39** D2
Radstation	**40** D2

RHINELAND-PALATINATE & SAARLAND

ept Sunday. Anchored by a festive fountain
ledicated to St Peter and the Four Virtues,
t's surrounded by medieval and Renaissance
rchitectural treasures, such as the **Rotes
Haus** (Red House), home to an attractive
afe, and the **Steipe**, which now houses the
pielzeugmuseum (Toy Museum; ☎ 758 50; Dietrichstrasse
1, 2nd fl; adult/under 11yr/11-18yr €4/1.50/2; ☺ 11am-6pm
Je-Sun Apr-Oct, to 5pm Nov-Mar), chock full of minia-
ure trains, dolls and other childhood delights.
The Gothic **St-Gangolf-Kirche** (☺ daily) is reached
ia an angel-bedecked baroque portal.

A block east of the Hauptmarkt looms the
ortresslike **Dom** (www.dominformation.de; ☺ 6.30am-
pm Apr-Oct, 6.30am-5.30pm Nov-Mar), built above the
palace of Constantine the Great's mother,
Helena. The present structure is mostly
Romanesque with some soaring Gothic and
ye-popping baroque embellishments. To see
ome dazzling ecclesiastical equipment and
peer into early Christian history, head upstairs
o the **Domschatz** (cathedral treasury; adult/child €1.50/0.50;
☺ 10am-5pm Mon-Sat, 12.30-5pm Sun & religious holidays
pr-Oct, 1.30-4pm Mon, 11am-4pm Tue-Sat, 12.30-4pm Sun &
eligious holidays Nov-Mar) or go around the corner to
he **Bischöfliches Dom- und Diözesanmuseum** (☎ 710
255; www.bistum-trier.de/museum, in German; Windstrasse
-8; adult/student €3.50/2; ☺ 9am-5pm Tue-Sat, 1-5pm Sun
religious holidays, also open Mon Apr-Oct). The prized
exhibit here is a 4th-century Roman ceiling
rom Helena's palace, in vivid colours, that was
pieced together from countless fragments.

Just to the south is the **Liebfrauenkirche**
(☺ closed for repairs until mid-2010), one of Germany's
earliest Gothic churches. The cruciform struc-
ure is supported by a dozen pillars symbol-
sing the 12 Apostles and, despite its strict
ymmetry, has a light, mystical quality.

The brick **Konstantinbasilika** (Konstantinplatz;
☺ 10am-6pm Mon-Sat, noon-6pm Sun & holidays Apr-
Oct, 11am-noon & 3-4pm Tue-Sat, noon-1pm Sun & holidays Nov-Mar) was constructed in AD 310 as
Constantine's throne hall. Its dimensions
(67m long and 36m high) are truly mind-
blowing considering that it was built by the
Romans. Later part of the residence of Trier's
prince-electors, it is now a typically austere
Protestant church.

The adjacent **Kurfürstliches Palais** (Prince-Electors'
palace; interior €0.50; ☺ 9am-4pm Mon-Thu, 9am-1pm Fri),
a pink rococo confection entered from the
south (garden) side, looks out over the lawns,
pools and fountains of the formal **Palastgarten**
(palace garden), perfect for sunbathing on
warm summer days.

The adjacent **Rheinisches Landesmuseum**
(Roman Archaeological Museum; ☎ 977 40; www.landes
museum-trier.de, in German; Weimarer Allee 1; adult/student/
family incl audioguide €5/3/10; ☺ 9.30am-5.30pm Tue-Sun)
affords an extraordinary look at local Roman
life. Highlights include a scale model of 4th-
century Trier and rooms filled with tombstones, mosaics, rare gold coins and some
fantastic glass.

On the southern edge of the *Palastgarten*
stands the **Kaiserthermen** (☎ 436 2550; Weimarer Allee
2; adult/7-18yr/senior & student/family €2.10/1/1.60/5.10;
☺ 9am-6pm Apr-Sep, to 5pm Mar & Oct, to 4pm Nov-Feb),
a vast thermal bathing complex created by
Constantine. The striped brick-and-stone
arches, once part of the caldarium, make
you feel like you're at the Forum in Rome.
You can get a sense of the layout from the
lookout tower.

About 700m to the southeast is the Roman
Amphitheater (☎ 730 10; Olewiger Strasse; adult/7-18yr/
senior & student/family €2.10/1/1.60/5.10; ☺ 9am-6pm Apr-
Sep, to 5pm Mar & Oct, to 4pm Nov-Feb), once capable
of holding 20,000 spectators during gladiator
tournaments and animal fights – or when
Constantine the Great crowned his battlefield victories by feeding his enemies to
voracious animals.

Halfway up **Petrisberg**, the vine-covered hill
just east of the *Amphitheater*, you come to the
Weinkulturpfad (Wine Culture Path), which
leads through the grapes to Olewig (1.6km).
Further up, next to the stop for bus 14, a multilingual panel traces local history from the
first known human habitation (30,000 years
ago) through the last ice age to the Romans.
The panoramic views are tremendous.

Found by accident in the 1980s during the
construction of a parking garage, the **Thermen
am Viehmarkt** (☎ 994 1057; Viehmarktplatz; adult/7-
18yr/senior & student/family €2.10/1/1.60/5.10; ☺ 9am-5pm,
closed 1st workday of each week) are sheltered by a
dramatic glass cube.

The early-18th-century baroque town
house in which the author of *Das Kapital*
was born is now the **Karl-Marx-Haus** (☎ 970
680; www.fes.de/marx; Brückenstrasse 10; adult/student
€3/2; ☺ 10am-6pm Apr-Oct, 2-5pm Mon, 11am-5pm Tue-
Sun Nov-Mar), whose exhibits take a highbrow,
dialectical look at Marx, the meaning of his
intellectual and political legacy, and social
democracy. Admission includes a free audioguide that opens with the stirring cadences of
L'Internationale; it's available in six languages,
including that spoken by fully one third of

visitors, Chinese (not at all surprising if you think about it). Well worth a stop if you're trying to figure out whether Barack Obama really is bringing socialism to America – or if you're in the market for a bust of Marx, or a Marx coffee mug, or a Marx collector's plate… Gift shop profits (er, surplus value) go to a foundation affiliated with the SPD (Social Democratic Party), whose historical perspectives inform the exhibits.

The **Römerbrücke** still has five of the 2nd-century support columns (out of seven) that have been holding it up since legionnaires crossed on chariots. Parts of the arches date from the 1300s.

Courses

The **Europäische Kunst Akademie** (European Academy of Fine Arts; ☎ 998 460; www.en.eka-trier.de; Aachener Strasse 63) offers a wide variety of short courses (two days to nine weeks) in painting, sculpture, drawing, printmaking, photography and ceramics.

Tours

City Walking Tour (adult/6-14yr/student €7/3.50/6; ☉ 1.30pm Sat May-Oct) A two-hour city tour in English that begins at the tourist office.

Wine Tastings (4/6/8 wines €4.50/6.50/8.50; ☉ 10am-6pm) Each week four different vintners play host. Contact the tourist office for a schedule.

Sleeping

Campingplatz Treviris (☎ 820 0911; www.camping -treviris.de; Luxemburger Strasse 81; per adult/tent/car €6.25/4.30/2.25; ☉ year-round) On the Moselle's left bank 1.5km south of the Römerbrücke. To get there from the centre, walk or drive south along St-Barbara-Ufer and then turn right over the river at Konrad-Adenauer-Brücke.

Hille's Hostel (☎ 710 2785, 0171 329 1247; www .hilles-hostel-trier.de; Gartenfeldstrasse 7; dm from €14, d €28-50; ☉ reception 8am-noon & 4-6pm; ☒ ☐) An independent hostel with a 1970s vibe, this laid-back place has a piano in the kitchen and 10 brightly decorated rooms with private bathrooms. If arriving when reception is closed, call ahead and they'll leave a key.

DJH hostel (☎ 146 620; www.jugendherberge.de; An der Jugendherberge 4; dm €19.90; ℗ ☒) A spick-and-span, 228-bed hostel right on the Moselle, about 1km northeast of the tourist office. Rooms have bathrooms and up to six beds. Take bus 12 from the Hauptbahnhof or Porta Nigra.

Hotel Römischer Kaiser (☎ 977 0100; www.friedri -hotels.de, in German; Porta-Nigra-Platz; d €105-150; ☒ Right next to Porta Nigra, this 1894 build ing offers 43 bright, comfortable rooms wit solid wood furnishings, parquet floors an spacious bathrooms.

Becker's Hotel (☎ 938 080; www.beckers-trier.d Olewiger Strasse 206; d €110-170; ℗ ☒ ☐) Abou 2km east of the centre in the quiet wine distric of Olewig, across the creek from the old mon astery church, this Design Hotels–affiliate establishment pairs 32 supremely tastefu rooms – some ultramodern, others traditional with stellar dining. A swimming pool is bein added for 2010. Served by bus 6.

our pick **Hotel Villa Hügel** (☎ 937 100; www.hot -villa-huegel.de; Bernhardstrasse 14; d €128-185; ℗ ☒ ☒ A stylish, 30-room hillside villa, where yo can begin the day with a lavish Champagn breakfast buffet and end it luxuriating in th 12m indoor pool and Finnish sauna. Serve by buses 2 and 82.

Eating

In the warm months, cafes fill the old city' public squares, including the Kornmarkt.

Astarix (☎ 722 39; Karl-Marx-Strasse 11; pizza fror €4.10; ☉ noon-midnight or 1am Mon-Sat, from 1pm Sun) popular student cafe, in a funky part of town with good pizza and *Auflauf* (casserole; €4.8 plus €0.40 for each added ingredient). Ente through the arcade.

Textorium (☎ 474 82; Wechselstrasse 4-6; meal €6.20-16.90; ☉ noon-2.30pm & 6pm-1am or 2am) popular, industrial-chic eatery with outdoo seating and daily specials. Part of the TuF events venue.

Kartoffel Kiste (☎ 979 0066; www.kiste-trier.de, ir German; Fahrstrasse 13-14; mains €7.20-14.50; ☉ 11am midnight) A local favourite, this place special ises in baked, breaded, soupified and sauce engulfed potatoes, as well as steaks. Has ar extraordinary bronze fountain out front.

Zum Domstein (☎ 744 90; Am Hauptmarkt 5; main €8.80-16.90, Roman dinner €15-33; ☉ 8.30am-midnight A German-style bistro where you can ei ther dine like an ancient Roman or feast or more conventional German and interna tional fare. A cookbook of ancient Roman recipes, printed in Venice in 1498, is o display downstairs.

Becker's Hotel in Olewig affords thre excellent dining options: **Becker's Restauran** (5/8 courses €85/105; ☉ 7-9pm Tue-Sat) has two Michelin stars; **Weinhaus Becker** (1-/3-cours

CYCLE TOURING: FIVE RIVERS IN FIVE DAYS

Trier makes an ideal base for day trips by bike, with five different riverside bike paths to choose from. Trains and **RegioRadler buses** (www.regio-radler.de, in German; reservations required; ☯ Apr-Oct) make it possible to ride one way (eg downhill) and take public transport the other.

Kylltal-Radweg Heads 115km north along the Kyll River, paralleling the rail line to Cologne. Take the train between Erdorf and Kyllburg (five to seven minutes) to avoid a killer hill.

Mosel-Radweg (www.mosel-radweg.de) Heads down the Moselle River all the way to Koblenz or upriver along the Luxembourg border and into the French region of Lorraine. Served by RegioRadler bus 333.

Ruwer-Hochwald-Radweg (www.ruwer-hochwald-radweg.de) This recently completed, 50km bike path runs along a one-time rail line south along the Ruwer River and then west. Served by RegioRadler bus 200.

Saar-Radweg (VeloRoute SaarLorLux) Heads south along the gorgeous Saar River to Saarbrücken and, at Sarreguemines, into France.

Sauertal-Radweg This 53km path heads north, following a decommissioned rail line along the Sauer River into Luxembourg. Northern variants follow the Prüm and Nims Rivers. Served by RegioRadler bus 441.

---

nch €15/28; ☯ noon-2pm & 6-10pm) serves fresh, assy German cuisine; and ultramodern ecker's Weinbar (☯ 3pm-midnight, hot meals 6-pm) offers 60 wines by the glass and a more xperimental menu.

For picnic supplies:

od market (Viehmarktplatz; ☯ 7am-2pm Wed & Fri)

arstadt supermarket (Simeonstrasse 46; ☯ 9am-m Mon-Sat) In the basement.

ahkauf supermarket (Brückenstrasse 2; ☯ 8am-m Mon-Fri, 8am-7pm Sat)

ntertainment

op by the tourist office or go to www.trier oday.de for details on concerts and other ultural activities.

our pick **TuFa** (☎ 718 2412; www.tufa-trier.de, in rman; Wechselstrasse 4-6) This vibrant cultural 'ents venue, housed in a former *Tuchfabrik* owel factory) – thus the name – hosts abaret, live music of all sorts, theatre and ance performances.

etting There & Away

rier has several hourly train connections to aarbrücken (€15.20, one to 1½ hours), via ettlach, and to Koblenz (regional/IC trains 9.20/24, 1½ to two hours). There are also equent trains to Luxembourg (€10.40, 50 inutes, at least hourly), with onward con-ctions to Paris.

etting Around

rier has a comprehensive **bus system** (☎ 7172 ; www.swt.de, in German) but the city centre is eas-y explored on foot. Single tickets/day passes, old by drivers, cost €1.70/4.65. The Olewig ine district is served by buses 6 and 16.

Bikes in tip-top condition can be rented at the Hauptbahnhof's not-for-profit **Radstation** (☎ 148 856; per 24hr €9-12; ☯ 9am-7pm mid-Apr–Oct, 10am-6pm Mon-Fri Nov–mid-Apr), next to track 11. Staff are enthusiastic about cycling and can provide tips on routes.

BERNKASTEL-KUES
☎ 06531 / pop 6700

This charming twin town, some 50km down-river from Trier, is the hub of the middle Moselle region. Bernkastel, on the right bank, is a symphony in half-timber, stone and slate and teems with wine taverns. Kues, the birth-place of theologian Nicolaus Cusanus (1401–64), has little fairy-tale flair but is home to the town's most important historical sights.

The **tourist office** (☎ 500 190; www.bernkastel.de; Am Gestade 6, Bernkastel; ☯ 8.30am-12.30pm & 1-5pm Mon-Fri, 10am-5pm Sat, 10am-1pm Sun & holidays Easter-Oct, to 3pm Fri, closed weekends & holidays Nov-Easter), 100m downriver from the bridge, reserves hotel rooms, sells hiking and cycling maps, offers internet access and has a 24-hour ATM. A hotel reservation board with a free phone is just outside.

Sights & Activities

Bernkastel's pretty **Marktplatz**, a block inland from the bridge, is a romantic ensemble of half-timbered houses with beautifully deco-rated gables. Note the medieval iron rings, to which criminals were attached, on the facade of the old **Rathaus**.

On Karlstrasse, the alley to the right as you face the Rathaus, the tiny **Spitzhäuschen** re-sembles a giant bird's house, its narrow base topped by a much larger, precariously leaning, upper floor. More such crooked gems line

Römerstrasse and its side streets. Facing the bridge is the partly 14th-century **Pfarrkirche St Michael**, whose tower was originally part of the town's fortifications.

A rewarding way to get your heart pumping is by hoofing it from the Spitzhäuschen up to **Burg Landshut**, a ruined 13th-century castle – framed by vineyards and forests – on a bluff above town; allow 30 to 60 minutes. You'll be rewarded with glorious river valley views and a cold drink at the **beer garden** (✆ 10am-6pm mid-Feb–Nov).

In Kues, most sights are conveniently grouped next to the bridge in the late-Gothic **St-Nikolaus-Hospital** (☎ 2260; Cusanusstrasse 2; admission free; ✆ 9am-6pm Sun-Fri, 9am-3pm Sat), an old-age home founded by Cusanus in 1458 for 33 men (one for every year of Christ's life). You're free to explore the inner courtyard, Gothic *Kapelle* (chapel) and cloister at leisure, but the treasure-filled library can only be seen on a **guided tour** (€4; ✆ 10.30am Tue & 3pm Fri Apr-Oct), sometimes held in English.

The complex also houses the new, multimedia **Mosel-Weinmuseum** (Moselle Wine Museum; ☎ 4141; adult/under 12yr/13-18yr €5/free/3; ✆ 10am-6pm mid-Apr–Oct, 2-5pm Nov–mid-Apr), with interactive terminals (in German, English and Dutch) and attractions such as an Aromabar (you have to guess what you're smelling). In the cellar **Vinothek**, you can sample Moselle wines by the glass (about €2) or indulge in an 'all you can drink' wine tasting (€15).

Sleeping & Eating

In Bernkastel, places to eat can be found along the waterfront and on the Alstadt's squares and narrow, pedestrians-only streets. In Kues there are several restaurants near the bridge.

Campingplatz Kueser Werth (☎ 8200; www.camping-kueser-werth.de; Am Hafen 2, Kues; site/person/car €3/5/2.50; ✆ Apr-Oct) About 2km upriver from the bridge, next to the yacht harbour.

DJH hostel (☎ 2395; www.jugendherberge.de; Jugendherbergsstrasse 1, Bernkastel; dm €16.90; ✗) Fairly basic by today's standards. Scenically but inconveniently located above town next to Burg Landshut.

Hotel-Restaurant-Weinhaus St Maximilian (☎ 965 00; www.hotel-sankt-maximilian.de, in German; Saarallee 12, Kues; s €45, d €70-90; ✗) Run by a family of winemakers, this place has 17 quiet rooms, many with balconies, that look out on the courtyard of the restaurant, where you can dine on German, vegie and *moselländisch* dishes (mains €8 to €15.50).

our pick **Hotel Moselblümchen** (☎ 2335; www.ho -moselbluemchen.de; Schwanenstrasse 10, Bernkastel; s €3 65, d €66-110; ℗ ✗ 🖳) A traditional, family-ru hotel on a narrow old-town alley behind th tourist office. It has 20 tasteful rooms an a small sauna, and can arrange bike renta The restaurant's German and local specialiti include sauerkraut and homemade wurst.

Getting There & Around

The bus station is at Forumsplatz, on the Kue side 100m west of St-Nikolaus-Hospital.

From May to October, boats run b **Kolb** (☎ 4719; www.kolb-mosel.de, in German) lir Bernkastel with Traben-Trarbach (one-way return €11/17, two hours, five daily). You ca take along a bicycle for €2, making it easy ride the 24km back.

The **Mosel-Maare-Radweg** (www.maare-mos radweg.de, in German) links Bernkastel-Kues wi Daun (in the Eifel). From April to Octobe you can take the RegioRadler bus 300 up an ride the 55km back to Bernkastel-Kues.

Hire bikes at **Fun Bike Team** (☎ 940 24; www.f biketeam.de, in German; Schanzstrasse 22, Bernkastel; 7-spee tandem per day €11/20; ✆ 9am-6.30pm Mon-Wed & F to 7pm Thu, 9am-2pm & 6-6.30pm Sat), 500m upriv from the bridge.

TRABEN-TRARBACH

☎ 06541 / pop 6000

It's hard to imagine today that this peacef twin town, 24km downriver from Bernkaste Kues (but just 7km by foot over the hil was once in the crosshairs of warring fa tions during the late-17th-century War of th Palatine Succession (Nine Years War). Tw ruined fortresses are all that survive fro those tumultuous times, which were follow by a long period of prosperity as the tow became a centre of winemaking and trade

Traben lost its medieval look to thre major fires but was well compensated wi beautiful *Jugendstil* (art nouveau) villas and lots of wisteria. It united with Trarba in 1904.

Orientation & Information

Traben, on the Moselle's left bank, is whe you'll find the tourist office, the end-of-th line train shelter (linked to Bullay; see p51 the adjacent bus station and the commerc centre. Trarbach is across the bridge on th right bank.

The **tourist office** (☎ 839 80; www.traben-trarbach.de; ⁿ Bahnhof 5, Traben; ☒ 10am-5pm Mon-Fri May-Aug, to m Sep & Oct, to 4pm Nov-Apr, 11am-3pm Sat May-Oct), in ᵗᵉ Alter Bahnhof (old train station) 100m ᵉst (along Bahnhofstrasse) from the train ᵘᵉlter, sells walking and cycling maps, and ᵃs two internet terminals (€1 per hour). ᵖen daily until 10pm, the lobby offers ex-⁻llent English-language brochures (including ᵐap-guide) and an interactive informa-ᵒn screen. There are several ATMs in the ᵐmediate vicinity.

ᵍhts & Activities

ᵗhe ruined medieval **Grevenburg**, which, un-⁻ᵏe its Cochem cousin, survived the 19th ᵉntury without being 'restored', sits high ᵗ the craggy hills above Trarbach and is ᵃched from the Markt via a steep footpath. ᵉcause of its strategic importance, the castle ᵃanged hands 13 times, found itself under ᵉge six times and was destroyed seven ᵐes. No wonder two walls are all that are ᵗft! Across the river, the vast Vauban-style **ont Royal** fortress, built in the late 1600s ⁿder Louis XIV as a base from which to ᵣoject French power in the Rhineland, ᵣoved ruinously expensive and was soon ᵈsmantled by the French themselves.

Learn more about these castles at the **ittelmosel-Museum** (☎ 9480; Casinostrasse 2, ᵃrbach; adult/youth €2.50/1; ☒ 10am-5pm Tue-Sun ᵣ-early Nov, 10am-5pm Sat & Sun mid-Dec–mid-Jan), ᵒused in a furnished baroque villa proud ᵗ once having hosted Johann Wolfgang von ᵒethe for a few hours in 1792. Around the ᵒrner is the new **Fahrradmuseum** (☎ 819 9131; ᵃselstrasse 2, Trarbach; admission free; ☒ 2-6pm Tue-, 10am-3pm Sat, 10am-1pm Sun May-Oct), upstairs ᵗrough the Wein-Kontor wine shop.

Of Traben's sinuous **art-nouveau villas**, the ᵒst seductive – and the only one open to ᵉ public – is the **Hotel Bellevue** (Am Moselufer 11), ᵃsily recognised by its Champagne-bottle-ᵃaped slate turret. The oak-panelled lobby ᵃd stained-glass windows in the restaurant ᵗpify the style, brought to town by Berlin ᵃchitect Bruno Möhring. Historic flood crests ᵉ marked on the wall near the entrance.

Möhring also designed the medieval-style **ückentor** (1898) above the bridge on the ᵗrarbach side.

The tourist office organises daily **wine tast-ᵍs** (4/6/8 wines €6/8/10) and cellar tours with ᵃrious vintners.

Sleeping & Eating

Trarbach has quite a few restaurants in the area upriver from the bridge, eg along Moselstrasse and Weiherstrasse. In Traben, eateries can be found along Bahnhofstrasse and tiny parallel Neue Rathausstrasse.

DJH hostel (☎ 9278; www.jugendherberge.de; Hirtenpfad 6, Traben; dm €18.90; ☒ 🖳) All rooms at this modern, 172-bed hostel have private bathrooms. It's a 1.2km, signposted walk up from the train station, past the fire station.

Central Hotel (☎ 6238; www.central-hotel-traben.de, in German; Bahnstrasse 43, Traben; s €32-38, d €60-68; 🅟 ☒) In the same family for three genera-tions, this friendly hotel has 32 modest but spotless rooms. The owner, Iris, lived in Texas for eight years but somehow returned twang-less. Great budget value. Situated 200m south of the train shelter.

our pick Hotel Bellevue (☎ 7030; www.bellevue-hotel.de; Am Moselufer 11, Traben; d €135-190; ☒ 🖳 🖳) Classy, romantic and historic, this exquisite art-nouveau hotel, facing the river, offers perks that include bike and canoe hire, pool and sauna. The stained-glass-adorned gourmet restaurant (mains €11 to €27) serves regional and Mediterranean-inspired cuisine.

our pick Weingut Caspari (☎ 5778; www.weingut-caspari.de, in German; Weiherstrasse 18, Trarbach; mains €4.90-13.90; ☒ 5-10pm or later Mon-Fri, 11am-10pm or later Sat & holidays Easter-Oct) Six short blocks in-land from the bridge, this rustic, old-time *Strausswirtschaft* (winery-cum-eatery) serves hearty local specialities, such as *Feiner Grillschinken Moselart* (boiled ham with potato puree and sauerkraut).

Brücken-Schenke (☎ 818 435; Brückentor, Trarbach; mains €7.60-15.40; ☒ 11am-11pm Mon & Wed-Sat, 11am-10pm Sun) A range of solid, good-value German and regional favourites are served up inside the tower at the Trarbach end of the bridge. Great views.

For self-caterers, the **Edeka Neukauf super-market** (Am Bahnhof 44, Traben; ☒ 8am-9pm Mon-Sat, bakery also open 8-11am Sun) is diagonally across the tracks from the train shelter.

Getting There & Around

For details on boats to Bernkastel-Kues, see opposite.

You can hire bikes and buy or borrow cycling maps at **Zweirad Wagner** (☎ 1649; www.zweirad-wagner.de, in German; Brückenstrasse 42, Trarbach; city/mountain bike per day €8/12; ☒ 8am-12.30pm & 1.45-6pm Mon-Fri, 8.30am-1pm Sat year-round, also 10-11am Sun & holidays Easter-Oct), next to the bridge.

RHINELAND-PALATINATE & SAARLAND

COCHEM

☎ 02671 / pop 5100

Cochem, a picture-postcard village about 55km downriver from Traben-Trarbach, spends much of the year overrun with day trippers. If you're after narrow alleyways and half-timbered houses – well, there are less jaded locales to find them in.

Towering above steep vineyards, the city-owned **Reichsburg** (☎ 255; www.reichsburg-cochem.de; adult/6-17yr €4.50/2.50; ⏰ 9am-5pm mid-Mar–Oct, 10am or 11am-2pm or 3pm Nov-early Jan) – everyone's idealised version of a turreted medieval castle – is actually a neo-Gothic pastiche built in 1877, making it a full 78 years older than Disneyland (the 11th-century original fell victim to frenzied Frenchmen in 1689). It can be seen on a 40-minute guided tour (printed translation available in 12 languages). The walk up from town takes about 15 minutes.

AROUND COCHEM
Beilstein
pop 150

On the right bank of the Moselle about 12km upriver from Cochem, Beilstein (www.beilstein -mosel.de, in German) is a pint-sized village right out of the world of fairy tales. Little more than a cluster of houses surrounded by steep vineyards, its romantic, half-timbered townscape is enhanced by the ruined **Burg Metternich**, a hilltop castle reached via a staircase. During the Middle Ages, the **Zehnthauskeller** was used to store wine delivered as a tithe; it now houses a romantically dark, vaulted wine tavern. Also worth a look is the **Judenfriedhof** (Jewish cemetery).

Burg Eltz

Victor Hugo thought this fairy-tale castle, hidden away in the forest above the left bank of the Moselle, was 'tall, terrific, strange and dark'. Indeed, 850-year-old **Burg Eltz** (☎ 02672-950 500; www.burg-eltz.de; tour adult/student/family €8/5.50/24; ⏰ 9.30am-5.30pm Apr-Oct), owned by the same family for more than 30 generations, has a forbidding exterior, softened by turrets crowning it like candles on a birthday cake. The **treasury** features a rich collection of jewellery, porcelain and weapons.

By car, you can reach Burg Eltz – which has never been destroyed – via the village of Münstermaifeld; the castle is 800m from the car park (shuttle bus €1.50). Trains link Koblenz and Cochem with Moselkern (also

reachable by boat), where a 35-minute tra to the castle begins at the Ringelstein Mühle car park.

HUNSRÜCK MOUNTAIN:

IDAR-OBERSTEIN

☎ 06781 / pop 31,600

Agate mining in Idar-Oberstein goes ba to at least 1454, but the industry rea took off in the 1830s after local adventure left for South America (especially Brazil where they harvested raw precious ston (*Edelsteine*) and sent them back home – ships' ballast – to be processed. The loc mines have long since been exhausted, b Idar-Oberstein has remained a major gem cutting and jewellery-manufacturing centr If crystals really do have mysterious pov ers, though, you'd expect that a town wi so many – on display and for sale – wou look a lot better than this one does.

Orientation & Information

Idar-Oberstein is an unwieldy town, stretc ing for about 20km along the Idarbac creek and the Nahe River, which once po ered scores of stone-cutting mills. Linki Idar (in the northwest) with the Bahnh and, a few blocks northeast, the pedestr anised heart of old Oberstein (around th Marktplatz) is the 6km long Hauptstras (B422), numbered from 1 up to about 50 for a couple of kilometres it's paralleled the one-way Mainzerstrasse.

The **tourist office** (☎ 563 90; www.idar-oberstein. in German; Hauptstrasse 419, Oberstein; ⏰ 9am-6p Mon-Fri, 10am-3pm Sat, Sun & holidays mid-Mar–O 9am-5pm Mon-Fri Nov–mid-Mar) is near Oberstei Marktplatz.

Sights & Activities

A high point of any visit to Idar-Oberstein the **Deutsches Edelsteinmuseum** (☎ 900 980; ww .edelsteinmuseum.de; Hauptstrasse 118, Idar; adult/under 1 €4.20/1.60; ⏰ 9.30am-5.30pm May-Oct, 10am-5pm Nov-A closed Mon Nov-Jan), Europe's largest museum precious stones and gems. Among its ey popping, jaw-dropping examples of the sto carver's art: two incredibly lifelike stone toac some unbelievably fine agate cameos, natur and cut emeralds and rubies, a 12,555-car Brazilian topaz and some dazzling Australi opals. Take bus 301 or 302 to Börse.

The Jakob Bengel jewellery factory, built ɔore than a century ago, is now the charm-ɪgly decrepit **Industriedenkmal Bengel** (☎ 270); www.jakob-bengel.de; Wilhelmstrasse 42a, Oberstein; ıdult/child €4.50/3; 🕑 10am-noon & 2-4pm Tue-Fri), a ɛrry-built but engaging 'historic industrial lant' where you can imagine *fin de siècle* ɹorking-class life while watching ancient, lacking machines transform spools of wire ıto chains. To get there from the tour-ɪt office, cross the pedestrian bridge at lauptstrasse 466.

More minerals and crystals – including a ıodel of Manhattan made of rock crystal – ɾe on display at the **Museum Idar-Oberstein** ☎ 246 19; www.museum-idar-oberstein.de; Hauptstrasse 36, Oberstein; adult/6-14yr €3.90/2.40; 🕑 9am-5.30pm ɔr–mid-Jul, Sep & Oct, to 4.30pm Nov-Mar, to 7pm mid-l–Aug), 50m off the Marktplatz.

Tucked in a niche in the rock face is the 5th-century, Protestant **Felsenkirche** (Chapel the Rocks; ☎ 228 40; www.felsenkirche-oberstein.de, German; adult/6-16yr €2/0.50; 🕑 10am-6pm Apr-Oct, am-4pm 1st half Nov), said to have been built by local knight in atonement for the murder f his brother. It's a 216-step climb up from ıe Marktplatz.

Cutters lying belly down on tilting enches demonstrate how stones used to e cut at **Historische Weiherschleife** (☎ 901 8; www.edelsteinminen-idar-oberstein.de; Tiefensteiner ɾasse 87, Tiefenstein; 45min tour adult/student €3.50/2.50; 🕑 10am-6pm mid-Mar–mid-Nov, last tour 5pm), built ı the mid-1700s. There's also a mineral and emstone exhibit and a park that's perfect ɔr a picnic. Situated northwest of Idar in iefenstein and served by bus 301.

leeping & Eating

he local meat speciality, *Spiessbraten*, con-sts of a hunk of beef or pork marinated in ɪw onion, salt and pepper and then grilled ver a beech-wood fire, giving it a spicy, noky taste. It's available at restaurants ɾound Oberstein's Marktplatz.

DJH hostel (☎ 243 66; www.jugendherberge.de; Alte eibe 23, Oberstein; dm €18.90; 🅿 ☒) All the rooms ı this modern, 128-bed hostel have a private athroom. Situated on the hillside southeast f the Bahnhof, it's served by bus 301.

Edelstein-Hotel (☎ 502 50; www.edelstein-hotel.de; ıuptstrasse 302, Oberstein; d €65-80, q €110; 🅿 ☒) It's ɔt terribly stylish, but the owners of this 3-room place are enthusiastic and helpful, ıd the 26°C pool and sauna area offer a perfect retreat on a rainy day. Situated about 400m towards Idar from Oberstein's pedes-trian zone. Served by buses 301, 302, 303 and 304.

Gästehaus Amethyst (☎ 508 562; www.gaestehaus-amethyst.de, in German; Hauptstrasse 324, Oberstein; d €69-74; 🅿) This pocket-sized, bike-friendly *Pension*, 200m northwest of Oberstein's pedestrian zone, has welcoming owners, six nicely furnished rooms, a sauna and a free fitness room.

Getting There & Away

Idar-Oberstein, about 80km east of Trier and about 90km northeast of Saarbrücken, has rail links to Saarbrücken (€13.30, one hour) and Mainz (€10.50, one hour, hourly). The B41 and the B422 cross in Idar-Oberstein.

Along the **Nahe-Hunsrück-Mosel-Radweg**, it's a 75km bike ride to Bingen, on the Rhine.

SAARLAND

The tiny federal state of Saarland, long a land of coal and heavy industry, has in recent decades cleaned up its air and streams and reoriented its struggling economy towards high-tech industry and ecotourism. The capital, Saarbrücken, is a vibrant city with excellent museums and a fine, French-influenced culinary scene. Rolling hills and forest cover much of the countryside, which can be explored not only by car or public transport but also on foot or by bicycle; cycling paths include the 362km, circular **Saarland-Radweg** and the **Saar-Radweg** (VeloRoute SaarLorLux), along the mostly beautiful Saar River. The region's industrial heritage is celebrated in places such as the historic Völklinger Hütte ironworks (p525).

Over the centuries, France and Germany have played ping pong with the Saarland, coveting it for its valuable natural resources. In the 20th century, the region came under French control twice – after each of the world wars – but in both cases (in referendums held in 1935 and 1955) its people voted in favour of rejoining Germany.

Although now solidly within German boundaries, the influence of the land of the baguette is still felt in all sorts of subtle ways. Many locals are bilingual and the standard greeting is not *'hallo'* but *'salü'*, from the French *'salut'*. Their French heritage, although somewhat imposed, has softened the Saarlanders, who tend to be pretty relaxed folk with an appreciation of good food, wine and company – 'Saarvoir vivre', it's been called.

SAARBRÜCKEN
☎ 0681 / pop 179,000

The Saarland capital, though a thoroughly modern city, has considerable historical charm. Vestiges of its 18th-century heyday as a royal residence under Prince Wilhelm Heinrich (1718–68) survive in the baroque town houses and churches designed by his prolific court architect, Friedrich Joachim Stengel, and the historic centre around St Johanner Markt brims with excellent restaurants and cafes. All of the city's excellent museums have recently been comprehensively reinvigorated so, if you haven't seen them lately, you haven't really seen them.

Orientation

Central Saarbrücken is bisected by the Saar River and the A620, an ugly autobahn that disfigures the river's left bank. From the Hauptbahnhof, at the northwestern end of the commercial centre, pedestrians-only Reichsstrasse (in the process of desleazification) and Bahnhofstrasse (the main shopping street) lead 1km to St Johanner Markt, the city's street-life hub.

Information

ATMs are sprinkled along Kaiserstrasse.

Discount Waschsalon (Blumenstrasse 42; 🕑 7am-11pm) Self-service laundry.

Evangelisches Krankenhaus (EvK; ☎ 388 60; Grossherzog-Friedrich-Strasse 44) A hospital whose main entrance is on Neikestrasse.

Post office (Hauptbahnhof) Has an ATM.

ReiseBank (Hauptbahnhof; 🕑 7am-7.45pm Mon-Fri, 8.30am-4pm Sat) Exchanges currency.

Telecenter (Dudweilerstrasse 26; per hr €1; 🕑 9am-midnight) Internet access.

Telehouse (Obertorstrasse 1; per hr €1; 🕑 9.30am-midnight Mon-Sat, 10.30am-midnight Sun) Internet access.

Thalia Bücher (☎ 388 30; Bahnhofstrasse 54) Large bookshop with English titles, including Lonely Planet guides.

Tourist office (☎ 938 090; www.die-region-saarbruecken.de; Rathausplatz 1; 🕑 9am-6pm Mon-Fri, 10am-4pm Sat) Temporarily inside Rathaus St-Johann, but likely to move back to the rejuvenated Hauptbahnhof area. Sells tickets for cultural events.

Waschhaus (Nauwieserstrasse 22; 🕑 8am-10pm) Self-service laundry.

Sights

RIGHT BANK

The heart of Saarbrücken (and its nightlif hub) is the historic **St Johanner Markt**, a long narrow public square anchored by an ornat fountain designed by Stengel and flanked b some of the town's oldest buildings. Catholi **Basilika St Johann**, also by Stengel, is tw blocks northeast.

The city's main commercial street, pedes trianised Bahnhofstrasse, heads northwes from St Johanner Markt. From the corne with Betzenstrasse, you can see **Rathaus St Johann**, a red-brick neo-Gothic structure buil from 1897 to 1900.

The two museums on the right bank spe cialise in modern and contemporary art. A the southeastern end of St Johanner Markt i the **Stadtgalerie** (☎ 936 8327; www.stadtgalerie.de, German & French; St Johanner Markt 24, 2nd fl; admission fre 🕑 11am-7pm Tue & Thu-Sun, noon-8pm Wed), which pu on temporary exhibitions of contemporar photography, video and performance art.

One of Saarland's cultural highlights, th Saarland Museum's **Moderne Galerie** (☎ 99 40; www.saarlandmuseum.de; Bismarckstrasse 11-1 adult/student €1.50/1, Sat free, special exhibitions €5/3.5 🕑 10am-6pm Tue & Thu-Sun, 10am-10pm Wed) cov ers European art from the late 1800s to th present and is especially noteworthy for it German Impressionist (eg Slevogt, Corint and Liebermann), French Impressionist (e Monet, Sisley and Renoir) and expressioni works (eg by Kirchner, Marc and Jawlensky A new contemporary wing, Galerie de Gegenwart, is under construction.

The grandiose yellow **Staatstheater** (☎ 3 20; www.theater-saarbruecken.de, in German & Frenc Schillerplatz) was built on Hitler's orders to than the Saarlanders for their 1935 vote to rejoi Germany. It opened in 1938 with Richar Wagner's The Flying Dutchman and toda presents opera, ballet, musicals and drama

LEFT BANK

Crossing the Saar River via the pedestrians-on Alte Brücke takes you over the autobahn an up to the Stengel-designed baroque **Schlosspla** around which you'll find all the city's mus ums dealing with history and historic art. Th dominant building here is the **Saarbrücker Schloss** which mixes several architectural styles, fro

RHINELAND-PALATINATE & SAARLAND

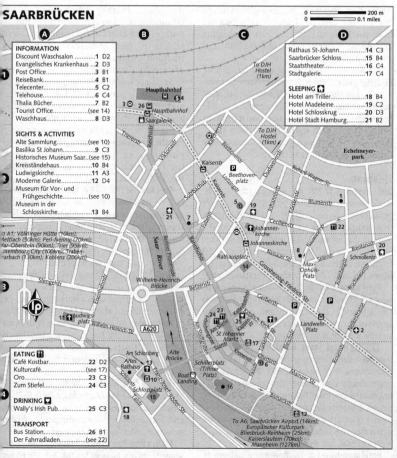

SAARBRÜCKEN

0 _____ 200 m
0 _____ 0.1 miles

INFORMATION
Discount Waschsalon	.........1 D2
Evangelisches Krankenhaus	...2 D3
Post Office	..........3 B1
ReiseBank	..........4 B1
Telecenter	..........5 C2
Telehouse	..........6 C4
Thalia Bücher	..........7 B2
Tourist Office	...........(see 14)
Waschhaus	..........8 D3

SIGHTS & ACTIVITIES
Alte Sammlung	.........(see 10)
Basilika St Johann	.........9 C3
Historisches Museum Saar	...(see 15)
Kreisständehaus	.........10 B4
Ludwigskirche	.........11 A3
Moderne Galerie	.........12 D4
Museum für Vor- und Frühgeschichte	.........(see 10)
Museum in der Schlosskirche	.........13 B4

Rathaus St-Johann	.........14 C3
Saarbrücker Schloss	.........15 B4
Staatstheater	.........16 C4
Stadtgalerie	.........17 C4

SLEEPING
Hotel am Triller	.........18 B4
Hotel Madeleine	.........19 C2
Hotel Schlosskrug	.........20 D3
Hotel Stadt Hamburg	.........21 B2

EATING
Café Kostbar	.........22 D2
Kulturcafé	.........(see 17)
Oro	.........23 C3
Zum Stiefel	.........24 C3

DRINKING
Wally's Irish Pub	.........25 C3

TRANSPORT
Bus Station	.........26 B1
Der Fahrradladen	.........(see 22)

To DJH Hostel (1km)

To DJH Hostel (1km)

Echelmeyerpark

Hauptbahnhof

Saargalerie

To AT; Völklinger Hütte (10km);
Mettlach (50km); Perl-Nennig (70km);
Idar-Oberstein (90km); Trier (95km);
Luxembourg City (100km); Traben-
Trarbach (130km); Koblenz (200km)

Saar River

Wilhelm-Heinrich-Brücke

Ludwigsplatz

Alte Brücke

Altes Rathaus

St Johanner Markt

Schillerplatz (Tiltiser Platz)

Boat Landing

Am Schlossberg

To A6; Saarbrücken Airport (14km);
Europäischer Kulturpark
Bliesbruck-Reinheim (25km);
Kaiserslautern (70km);
Mannheim (127km)

enaissance to baroque to neoclassical. The
orthern wing was once used by the Gestapo
s offices and detention cells.

The Schloss' basement and a modern annex
ouse the well-designed **Historisches Museum
aar** (☎ 506 4501; www.historisches-museum.org, in
rman; Schlossplatz 15; adult/student €5/3; ☼ 10am-6pm
e, Wed, Fri & Sun, 10am-8pm Thu, noon-6pm Sat). The
ction covering Saarland from 1870 to 1914
cludes a film of Saarbrücken street life – with
meo appearances by a surprising number
f dogs – made in 1904. From here you can
escend to the castle's massive bastions and
asematten (casemates; English brochure
vailable). Other exhibits look at Saarland
nder French rule (1920 to 1935) and the Nazi
a. Signs are in German and French.

The **Kreisständehaus** (Schlossplatz 16), completely
renovated in 2009, now houses two muse-
ums. The Saarland Museum's **Alte Sammlung**
(Old Collection) display's a millennium's
worth of paintings, porcelain, tapestries and
sculptures from southwest Germany and the
Alsace and Lorraine regions of France. Fans
of the Romans, the Celts and their predeces-
sors won't want to miss the **Museum für Vor-
und Frühgeschichte** (Museum of Early History & Prehistory;
☎ 954 050; www.vorgeschichte.de, in German & French).
The star exhibit here features resplendent
gold jewellery from around 400 BC, discovered in the tomb of a Celtic princess at
Bliesbruck-Reinheim (p526).

The **Museum in der Schlosskirche** (☎ 954 0518;
Am Schlossberg 6; admission free; ☼ 10am-6pm Tue &

Thu-Sun, 10am-10pm Wed), inside a desanctified late Gothic church, features religious art from the 13th to 19th centuries. Highlights include the elaborate tombs of three 17th- and 18th-century princes.

To the northwest is Stengel's handsome Ludwigsplatz, flanked by stately baroque town houses. **Ludwigskirche** (🕙 10am-5pm Tue-Sun, except during weddings), built in 1775, sports a facade festooned with biblical figures and a brilliant white interior with stylish stucco decoration. If the church is closed, you can sneak a peek through the windows of the vestibule.

Sleeping

DJH hostel (☎ 330 40; www.jugendherberge.de; Meerwiesertalweg 31; dm €20.40; ⊠) In Saarbrücken's green belt, this modern, 192-bed hostel is 100m from a supermarket, a 15-minute walk from the Hauptbahnhof and 1.5km northeast of Rathaus St-Johann. Served by buses 101, 102 and 150 from the Rathaus and, Monday to Friday, by buses 112 and 124 from the Hauptbahnhof.

Hotel Schlosskrug (☎ 367 35; www.hotel-schlosskrug.de, in German; Schmollerstrasse 14; s/d €36/59, s without bathroom €28) A friendly, if ordinary, midsize hotel with some of the cheapest rooms in town. Near a trendy student neighbourhood.

ourpick Hotel Stadt Hamburg (☎ 379 9890; www.hotel-stadt-hamburg-saarbruecken.de, in German; Bahnhofstrasse 71-73, 3rd fl; s/d €59/80; P ⊠) An unpromisingly small street door leads to a cheerful, well-kept establishment decorated with original watercolours, oils and collages (the owner is an artist). The 28 cheerful rooms are decorated in shades both pastel and saturated. Very central, but quiet.

Hotel Madeleine (☎ 322 28; www.hotel-madeleine.de, in German; Cecilienstrasse 5; d Mon-Thu €79-89, Fri-Sun €69-75; ⊠) Central and friendly, this family-run hotel has 28 well-kept rooms that are bright and comfortable but, shall we say, compact.

Hotel am Triller (☎ 580 000; Trillerweg 57; www.hotel-am-triller.de, in German; s/d Mon-Thu €118/146, Fri-Sun €90/110; P ⊠ 💻 🍸) This 110-room boutique hotel, on a quiet street uphill from Schlossplatz, has artsy public areas, creatively ultramodern rooms and an organic restaurant. The website offers discounts. To get there, take Eisenbahnstrasse to Vorstadtstrasse, then on to Trillerweg.

Eating & Drinking

Many local dishes revolve around the humble potato – look for *Hoorische* (potato dumplings, literally 'hairy ones'), *Gefill* (*Hoorische* filled with minced meat and liv sausage) and *Dibbelabbes* (a potato casserc with dried meat and leeks). In the Fren tradition, meals are often served with a bask of crunchy French bread.

Saarbrücken's lively restaurant, cafe ar bar scene centres on St Johanner Mar and nearby streets Saarstrasse, Am Stief and Kappenstrasse, with cheaper ea along Kaltenbachstrasse. Four long bloc northeast, Nauwieserstrasse is home to number of cutting-edge student cafes. C the Left Bank, cafes can be found arour the Schlossplatz.

Café Kostbar (☎ 374 360; Nauwieserstrasse 19; ma €5-8; 🕙 11am-1am, meals served noon-3pm & 6-11pm) a neighbourhood with a counter-cultural vib this courtyard establishment, popular wi impoverished students, serves a small sele tion of inexpensive but filling salads, mair vegie options and lunch specials.

Oro (🕙 938 8663; St Johanner Markt 7-9; daily specials mains €7.50-24.50; 🕙 10am-1am) A chic wine bar a upscale restaurant with a leafy courtyard, ge erous salads and about 30 wines by the glas

Kulturcafé (☎ 379 9200; St Johanner Markt 24; ma €6.90-12.90; 🕙 8.30am-1am) A cafe by day, this sty ish place attracts a youngish crowd after da with its black-and-red minimalism-mee gothic decor.

ourpick Zum Stiefel (☎ 936 450; www.stie gastronomie.de, in German; Am Stiefel 2; mains €8.50-21) T' *Gasthaus* features good-value classic Germ and *saarländische* dishes; adjacent Stiefel-Br is Saarbrücken's oldest brewery-pub.

Wally's Irish Pub (☎ 01577 195 4180; Katolisch-Kir Strasse 1; 🕙 2pm-midnight Sun-Thu, 2pm-2am Fri, noc 2am Sat) A welcoming pub, popular with loc Anglophones, that's owned by an Irish fellc whose name is *not* Wally.

Getting There & Away

Saarbrücken Airport (☎ 06893-832 72; www.flugha -saarbruecken.de, in German), about 14km east of tl city, offers mainly holiday charters and shc hops within Germany.

Saarbrücken's Hauptbahnhof has at lea hourly rail connections to Trier (€13.30, o' hour), Idar-Oberstein (€13.30, 50 minute and Mainz (€27.40, 1¾ hours). The city's ma bus station is outside the Hauptbahnhof.

Saarbrücken is on the A6 fro Kaiserslautern and Mannheim and the A from the Moselle Valley.

etting Around

he Saarland has an extensive integrated us and rail network (☎ 500 3377; www.saarbahn.de, ww.vgs-online.de, in German) that includes one am line, optimistically named S1. Tickets ithin the city (Zone 111) cost €2.10 (€1.90 r up to five stops); a day pass for one/five eople costs €4.80/8.20. Bus R10 goes from ie Hauptbahnhof out to the airport (€2.30, 5 minutes, hourly Monday to Friday, every vo or three hours Saturday and Sunday).

You can book a taxi on ☎ 330 33.

Bicycles can be hired from **Der Fahrradladen** ☎ 370 98; Nauwieserstrasse 19; per day/weekend/week 5/30/50; ☽ 2-7pm Mon, 10am-7pm Tue-Fri, 10am-2pm or m Sat), in the courtyard at Café Kostbar.

ÖLKLINGER HÜTTE

oth Dickensian and futuristic, dystopian id a symbol of renewal, the hulking former onworks of **Völklinger Hütte** (☎ 06898-910 0100; ww.voelklinger-huette.org; Völklingen; adult/7-16yr/stunt/family €12/3/10/25; ☽ 10am-7pm late Mar-Oct, 10amm Nov-late Mar), located in Völklingen, about)km northwest of Saarbrücken, are one of urope's great heavy-industrial relics. Opened 1873, 17,000 people worked here by 1965 – e height of Germany's post-WWII boom. he plant blasted its last pig iron in 1986 and as declared a World Heritage Site by Unesco 1994.

The plant's massive scale dwarfs mere huians, who nevertheless, though soft and tiny, anaged to master the forces of fire, wind and irth in order to smelt iron, without which vilisation as we know it could not exist. Fine ews of the whole rusty ensemble can be had om atop a 45m **blast furnace** (helmet required). arts of the vast complex are being reclaimed y trees, shrubs and mosses. Brochures and all gns are in German, English and French.

Colourful works of modern art make a par:ularly cheerful impression amid the ageing ncrete and rusted pipes, beams, conveyors id car-sized ladles. Check out the website for etails on exhibitions and events (eg summerie jazz concerts). At night the compound is ridly lit up like a vast science-fiction set.

Trains link the town of Völklingen with iarbrücken (€3, 10 minutes, twice an hour) id Trier (€13.30, one hour, at least hourly); ie ironworks are a three-minute walk from ie Bahnhof.

By car, take the A620 to Völklingen and illow the signs to the 'Weltkulturerbe'.

METTLACH

☎ 06864 / pop 12,600

Mettlach, on the Saar River about 50km northwest of Saarbrücken, is at the heart of the prettiest section of the Saarland. For the last two centuries, its history has been tied to the global ceramics firm **Villeroy & Boch** (www.villeroy -boch.com), whose headquarters has been in **Alte Abtei** (Saaruferstrasse), a former Benedictine abbey on the banks of the Saar River, since 1809.

Today, the abbey houses the **Erlebniscentrum** (Discovery Centre; ☎ 811 020; adult/family €3.50/6; ☽ 9am-6pm Mon-Fri, 9.30am-6pm Sat, Sun & holidays, parts closed until 2pm Sun Nov-Feb), which includes a multimedia exhibit called **Keravision**, introducing the company's history and products; the **Keramikmuseum** (www.keramikmuseum-mettlach. de, in German), with its collection of fine historical porcelain; the ornately tiled **Museumscafé**, a replica of a Dresden dairy shop decorated by Villeroy & Boch in 1892; and, out in the garden, a refreshingly quirky piece of walk-in art, **Living Planet Square**, whose giant bird topiary towers above six ceramictile walls representing the continents and their peopling in a rather, shall we say, graphic fashion.

The **tourist office** (Saarschleife Touristik; ☎ 8334; www.tourist-info.mettlach.de; Freiherr-vom-Stein-Strasse 64; ☽ 10am-noon & 2-5pm Mon-Fri, 10am-2pm Sat, Sun & holidays) is in Mettlach's pedestrian zone, which is also where you'll find a bunch of **factory outlet stores**.

Frequent regional trains link Mettlach with Saarbrücken (€7.40, 40 minutes) and Trier (€8.40, 45 minutes). By car from Saarbrücken, take the A8 to the Merzig-Schwemlingen exit and then follow the B51 north – look for signs to the 'Erlebniscentrum'. North of Mettlach, towards Trier, the B51 follows a drop-dead-gorgeous stretch of the Saar River.

AROUND METTLACH

The most scenic spot along the Saar River is the **Saarschleife**, where the river makes a spectacular, hairpin turn. It's in the community of **Orscholz**, in a large nature park about 5km northwest of Mettlach (towards Nennig). The best viewing point is **Cloef**, a short walk through the forest from the village.

PERL-NENNIG

☎ 06866 / pop 6600

Perl-Nennig, on the Luxembourg border about 20km west of Mettlach and 40km south of Trier, is the Saarland's only winegrowing community. The local specialities are made with grape varieties from Burgundy, introduced after the war when the region was under French control. On weekends between April and October, winegrowers open up their cellars for tastings on a rotating basis.

The best preserved and, perhaps, most lavish Roman mosaic north of the Alps can be seen in the reconstructed **Römische Villa** (Roman Villa; ☎ 1329; Römerstrasse 11; adult/child €1.50/0.75; ⊗ 8.30am-noon & 1-6pm Tue-Sun Apr-Sep, 9am-noon & 1-4.30pm Tue-Sun Oct, Nov & Mar). Comprising three million tiny stones, the stunning 160-sq-metre floor dates from the 3rd century AD.

The **tourist office** (☎ 1439; www.nennig.de, in German; Bübinger Strasse 5, Nennig; ⊗ 10am-noon & 2-5pm Mon-Fri Apr-Oct, 10am-noon Mon & Tue, 2-4pm Wed & Fri Nov–mid-Dec & mid-Jan–Mar), right by the Bahnhof in Nennig, can provide information on the villa, wine tastings and accommodation. It also hires out bicycles.

Perl-Nennig is linked by bus 210 with Merzig (€7.40 by rail from Saarbrücken). The train to/from Trier runs every hour or two

(€8.40, 40 minutes). By car take the A8 from Saarbrücken or the B419 from Trier.

EUROPÄISCHER KULTURPARK BLIESBRUCK-REINHEIM

Flanking the Franco-German border abou 25km southeast of Saarbrücken in the charm ing Blies Valley, the **Europäischer Kulturpar Bliesbruck-Reinheim** (European Archaeological Par ☎ 06843-900 221; www.kulturpark-online.de, in Germa www.archeo57.com, in French; Robert-Schuman-Strasse Gersheim-Reinheim; adult/student €5/3.50; ⊗ 10am-6p mid-Mar–Oct) showcases the ruins of a 1st- 4th-century Gallo-Roman crafts town. Mo of the artisans' houses, with their ovens, cella and heating systems, as well as thermal bath are on the French (Bliesbruck) side, but th area's most spectacular discovery, the tomb a Celtic princess from 400 BC, was unearthe on the German side. Her dazzling gold jewe lery can be seen at Saarbrücken's Museum f Vor- und Frühgeschichte (p523).

From Saarbrücken, take tram S1 Kleinblittersdorf, then bus 147 to Reinheir (total €6).

Hesse

About two-thirds of Hesse's population lives in the Rhine-Main region, a sprawling urban conglomeration, with excellent integrated public transport, that stretches from Frankfurt am Main in the north to Darmstadt in the south and Mainz (in Rhineland-Palatinate) and Wiesbaden in the west. The attractive spa-city of Wiesbaden is Hesse's political capital, but Frankfurt, home of the European Central Bank, wields the financial clout.

Contrary to Hesse's rather staid image, Wiesbaden's parliament was where Green Party former foreign minister Joschka Fischer raised eyebrows by taking his ministerial oath wearing tennis shoes; and, in the 1960s and '70s, Frankfurt was a hotbed of student politics.

International Frankfurt, although a banking powerhouse, is also known for its excellent quality of life, leafy parkland, lively nightlife and streets lined with laid-back cafes and beer gardens. Although perhaps Germany's most un-German city, it is ironically the first contact many will have with the country thanks to the presence of Europe's third-busiest airport.

The northern part of Hesse has some splendid green areas to explore on foot and by bicycle, including the picturesque Lahn River valley, the forested Nationalpark Kellerwald-Edersee and the gentle countryside around the baroque town of Fulda. Two university cities are of special interest: Marburg, famed for its hilltop old town; and Kassel, site of a baroque hillside park, innovative museums and the five-yearly documenta contemporary art exhibition.

HIGHLIGHTS

- **Urban Traditions** Check out Frankfurt am Main's trademarks: apple wine, smelly cheese, first-class museums and a big-city skyline (p528)

- **Architecture & Art** Explore Darmstadt's artists colony, surrounded by gardens and a gold-domed Russian chapel (p544)

- **Jugendstil Baths** Wander towel-clad between the saunas and pools of Wiesbaden's historic Kaiser-Friedrich-Therme (p547)

- **Cafe Culture** Wander from cafe to wine bar to beer garden in Frankfurt's Nordend and Bornheim neighbourhoods (p539)

- **Canoeing** Paddle along the Lahn River in Weilburg (p549)

- **Baroque Town** Take in the ornate baroque splendour of old Fulda (p553)

- **Water Show** Spend an hour chasing the water as it cascades down the slope from Kassel's towering Herkules statue (p556)

POPULATION: 6 MILLION	AREA: 21,115 SQ KM

HESSE

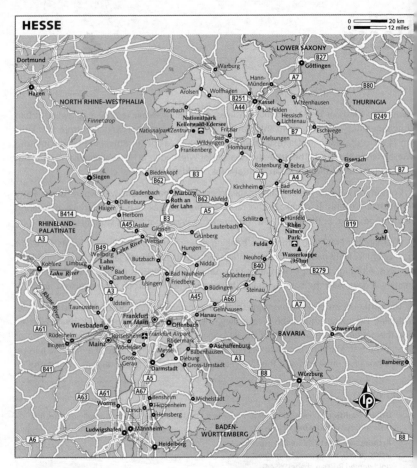

Getting Around

Deutsche Bahn's **Hessenticket** (€30) lets a group of up to five people take regional trains (ie any trains except D, IC, EC or ICE) anywhere within Hesse (plus Mainz and Worms) for a full day (except before 9am from Monday to Friday) – an incredible deal! The weekend version, known as a Schönes-Wochenende-Ticket, costs €37 and is valid on Saturday and Sunday. For one person the price is €13, making it a lot cheaper than many one-way train trips within Hesse (eg from Frankfurt north to Fulda, Kassel or Marburg).

Hesse bills itself as a 'Radwanderparadies' (cycling paradise). For help with planning an outing on two wheels, see www.radrouten planer.hessen.de (in German).

FRANKFURT AM MAIN

☎ 069 / pop 659,000

Unashamedly high-rise, Frankfurt-on-the-Main (pronounced 'mine') is unlike any other German city. Bristling with jagged skyscrapers, 'Mainhattan' – the focal point of an urban area with over 5 million inhabitants – is a true capital of finance and business, home base for one of the world's largest stock exchanges as well as the European Central Bank (www .ecb.int). It also hosts some of Europe's most important trade fairs, including the largest book and motorcar fairs anywhere.

Yet Frankfurt consistently ranks as one of the world's most liveable cities, with a rich collection of museums (second only to Berlin's), lots of parks and greenery, a lively student scene, ex-

ellent public transport, fine dining and plenty
o do in the evening. Nightspots range from cosy
neighbourhood apple-wine taverns to some of
Europe's most thumping techno-discos.

Frankfurt's airport, the region's biggest employer, is the third-largest in Europe, handling
some 53 million passengers per year.

Hotel prices rise precipitously during major
trade fairs (see p536), so plan ahead if you
don't want to spend €250 a night for a very
average double.

History

Around 2000 years ago Frankfurt was the site
of Celtic and Germanic settlement and then –
in the area known today as the Römerberg – a
Roman garrison town.

Mentioned in historical documents as far
back as 794, Frankfurt was an important centre of power in the Holy Roman Empire. With
the election of Frederick I (Barbarossa) in
1152, the city became the customary site of
the selection of German kings. International
trade fairs – attracting business from the
Mediterranean to the Baltic – were held here
beginning in the 12th century.

In 1372 Frankfurt became a 'free imperial
city', a status it enjoyed almost uninterruptedly
until the Prussian takeover of 1866. A stock exchange began operating in Frankfurt in 1585,
and it was here that the Rothschild banking
family began its ascent in the 1760s.

About 80% of the medieval city centre was
destroyed – and 1000 people were killed – by
Allied bombing raids in March 1944.

Orientation

The Main River flows from east to west, with
the Altstadt (old city) and the Innenstadt (city
centre) to the north and the Sachsenhausen
district, including the Museumsufer (Museum
Embankment), to the south. Frankfurt
Hauptbahnhof (the main train station), on the
eastern side of the partly sleazy Bahnhofsviertel
train station quarter), is about 1.3km west of
the Römerberg, a historic public square marking the centre of the Altstadt. About 500m to
the north of the Römerberg, the pedestrianised, east–west Zeil is the city's main shopping street and links two important U- and
S-Bahn stations with adjacent public squares,
Hauptwache and Konstablerwache.

Head northwest from the Innenstadt along
Bockenheimer Landstrasse and you get to the
well-off Westend neighbourhood and then,
2km northwest of Hauptwache, Bockenheim,
home to the university's new and old cam-

puses, respectively. North and northeast
of Konstablerwache are the Nordend and
Bornheim districts.

The airport is 12km southwest of the city
centre.

Information
BOOKSHOPS
British Bookshop (☎ 280 492; www.british-bookshop
.de; Börsenstrasse 17, Innenstadt; ◉ Hauptwache;
⏲ 9am-7pm Mon-Fri, 9.30am-6pm Sat) Largest selection
of English-language books in town.
Hugendubel (☎ 01801-484 484; Steinweg 12, Innenstadt; ◉ Hauptwache; ⏲ 9.30am-8pm Mon-Wed,
9.30am-9pm Thu-Sat) Multilevel, multilanguage bookstore.
Oscar Wilde Bookshop (☎ 281 260; www.oscar
-wilde.de; Alte Gasse 51, Innenstadt; ◉ Konstablerwache;
⏲ 11am-7pm Mon-Fri, 10am-4pm Sat) Gay and lesbian
books, plus local information.
Schmitt & Hahn Internationale Presse (☎ 2425
2345; ◉ Frankfurt Hauptbahnhof; ⏲ 4.30am-midnight)
Huge selection of newspapers and mags in many languages; it's inside the Hauptbahnhof, facing track 7.

DISCOUNT CARDS
FrankfurtCard (valid 1/2 days €8.70/12.50, for up to 5
people €15/24) Benefits include free public transport (including the airport – a big saving); 50% off at museums,
the Palmengarten and the zoo; and 15% off for the opera.
Available at the tourist office and the Verkehrsinsel (see
p530), the airport's Hotels & Tours desk and some hotels.

EMERGENCY
AIDS-Hilfe (☎ 295 959; www.frankfurt-aidshilfe.de, in
German; Alte Gasse 36, 1st fl, Innenstadt; ◉ Konstabler-
wache; ⏲ 11am-5pm Tue-Thu) Advice and AIDS help for
gay men.
Fire/ambulance (☎ 112)
Lesben Informations-und Beratungsstelle (LIBS;
☎ 282 883; www.libs.w4w.net, in German; Alte Gasse 38,
2nd fl, Innenstadt; ◉ Konstablerwache; ⏲ 5-7.30pm
Tue & Thu) Information and assistance for lesbians.
Police (☎ 110)
Women's hotline (☎ 709 494; www.frauennotrufe
-hessen.de, in German)

INTERNET ACCESS
In Bornheim, internet shops can be found
along Berger Strasse (eg at No 205).
CyberRyder (Töngesgasse 31, Innenstadt; ◉ Konstabler-
wache; per 15min €1-1.60; ⏲ 9.30am-10pm Mon-Fri,
10am-10pm Sat, noon-10pm Sun) Frankfurt's first internet
cafe, founded way back in 1995.
PTT Shop (Baseler Strasse 35-37, Bahnhofsviertel;
◉ Frankfurt Hauptbahnhof; per hr €2; ⏲ 8am-midnight)
Bright and pleasant. The entrance is on Mannheimerstrasse.

Telecafe Internet (Grosse Friedbergerstrasse 34, Innenstadt; ⊕ Konstablerwache; per hr €2; ⏲ 11am-11pm)

INTERNET RESOURCES
www.frankfurt.de Official Frankfurt website.
www.frankfurt-handicap.de Detailed information on
access for travellers with disabilities (in German).

LAUNDRY
SB Waschsalon Sachsenhausen (Wallstrasse 8; ⊕
Lokalbahnhof; ⏲ 6am-11pm except Sun & holidays);
Bornheim (Sandweg 41; ⊕ Merianplatz; ⏲ 6am-11pm
except Sun & holidays); Bockenheim (Grosse Seestrasse 46;
⊕ Bockenheimer Warte; ⏲ 6.30am-11pm except Sun
& holidays)

MEDICAL SERVICES
To find a duty pharmacy open after-hours,
check the window of any pharmacy, or consult the *Frankfurter Rundschau*.
Ärztlicher Bereitschaftsdienst (☎ 192 92;
www.bereitschaftsdienst-frankfurt.de, in German) A
24-hour doctor service.
Unfallklinik (Centre for Trauma Surgery; ☎ 4750;
www.bgu-frankfurt.de; Friedberger Landstrasse 430,
Seckbach) Accident treatment 4km northeast of the
centre. Served by bus 30.
Uni-Klinik (University Hospital; ☎ 630 11; www.kgu.de;
Theodor-Stern-Kai 7; ⊕ Stresemannallee; ⏲ 24hr) About
1.5km due south of the Hauptbahnhof, across the river. Take
tram 12 or 21.

MONEY
ReiseBank (⊕ Frankfurt Hauptbahnhof; ⏲ 7.30am-
9pm) Inside the Hauptbahnhof, behind track 1. Exchanges
cash and travellers cheques and makes credit-card cash
advances.

POST
Post office Hauptbahnhof (⊕ Frankfurt Hauptbahnhof;
⏲ 7am-7.30pm Mon-Fri, 8am-4pm Sat) Behind track 23;
Innenstadt (Goetheplatz 4; ⊕ Hauptwache; ⏲ 9.30am-
7pm Mon-Fri, 9am-2pm Sat)

TOURIST INFORMATION
Tourist office (☎ 2123 8800, for hotel reservations
2123 0808; www.frankfurt-tourismus.de) Hauptbahnhof
(⊕ Frankfurt Hauptbahnhof; ⏲ 8am-9pm Mon-Fri,
9am-6pm Sat & Sun) Behind track 13; Altstadt (Römerberg
27, inside Römer; ⊕ Dom/Römer; ⏲ 9.30am-5.30pm
Mon-Fri, 9.30am-4pm Sat & Sun)
Verkehrsinsel (☎ 01805-069 960; Zeil 129, Innenstadt;
⊕ Hauptwache; ⏲ 9am-8pm Mon-Fri, 9.30am-6pm
Sat) In a round, glass pavilion. Provides public transport
information and sells tickets. Staff are also happy to
provide tourist information.

TRAVEL AGENCIES
Hapag-Lloyd Reisebüro (☎ 216 216; Kaiserstrasse 22,
Innenstadt; ⊕ Willy-Brandt-Platz)
STA Travel (☎ 7430 3292; Berger Strasse 118, Nordend,
⊕ Höhenstrasse) Student travel agency.

Dangers & Annoyances
The area northeast of the Hauptbahnhof is
a base for Frankfurt's trade in sex and illegal drugs, and has *Druckräume*, special
rooms where needles are distributed and
the drug dependent can shoot up. Women
in particular might want to avoid Elbestrasse
and Taunusstrasse, the main red-light district. Frequent police and private security
patrols of the station and the surrounding
Bahnhofsviertel keep things under control
but it's always advisable to use big-city
common sense.

Sights & Activities
MAIN TOWER
A good place to start getting a feel for the city
is 200m above it, on the viewing platform
atop the **Main Tower** (☎ 3650 4777; www.maintower
-restaurant.de; Neue Mainzer Strasse 52-58; ⊕ Alte Oper;
elevator fee adult/student & senior €5/3.50; ⏲ 10am-9pm
Sun-Thu, 10am-11pm Fri & Sat late Mar-late Oct, 10am-7pm
Sun-Thu, 10am-9pm Fri & Sat late Oct-late Mar, weather permitting). The 53rd floor has a **cocktail bar** (⏲ 5.30pm-
1am, to 2am Fri & Sat, often closed for private events); you
have to reserve ahead for the restaurant.

From the platform, to the southeast you
can see the medieval-style Römberg, reconstructed after the war; beyond it, across the river
is Sachsenhausen. To the north and northeast is
the banking district, with its ever-changing vistas
of towers. The **Commerzbank Tower**, Europe's tallest office block at 258m high (298m including
the antenna), stands aloof at Kaiserplatz. Off
to the west is the 256m-high **Messeturm**, which
locals call the *Bleistift* (pencil).

ALTSTADT
The **Frankfurter Dom** (cathedral; www.dom-frankfurt.de,
in German; ⊕ Dom/Römer ⏲ officially 9am-noon & 2.30-
6pm, often opens earlier, closes later & stays open at noon)
one of the few structures to survive the 1944
bombing, is dominated by an elegant, Gothic-
style **tower** (95m), begun in the 1400s and
completed in the 1860s. Abutting the Dom's
west side is the **Historischer Garten** (Historical
Garden), where you can wander through excavated Roman and Carolingian foundations.

On the cathedral's southern side is the small
Wahlkapelle (Voting Chapel), where seven

lectors of the Holy Roman Empire chose he emperor from 1356 onwards. Adjoining it s a **choir** with beautiful wooden stalls.

The **Dommuseum** (cathedral museum; ☎ 1337 6816; ww.dommuseum-frankfurt.de, in German; adult/student 3/2; ◯ 10am-5pm Tue-Fri, 11am-5pm Sat, Sun & holidays) as a collection of precious liturgical objects nd sells tickets for Dom **tours** (in German; adult/ tudent €3/2; ◯ 3pm Tue-Sun).

The **Römerberg** (◉ Dom/Römer), a long block vest of the Dom, is Frankfurt's old central quare, where postwar-restored 14th- and 5th-century buildings, including the early Gothic, Protestant **Alte Nikolaikirche**, provide a limpse of how beautiful the city once was. In he centre is the **Gerechtigkeitsbrunnen** (Font of ustice); in 1612, at the coronation of Matthias, he fountain ran with wine! The Römerberg s especially lovely during December's Veihnachtsmarkt (Christmas market).

The old town hall, or **Römer**, in the northwest-rn corner of Römerberg, is made up of three ecreated step-gabled 15th-century houses. In he time of the Holy Roman Empire, it was he site of celebrations during the election and oronation of emperors; today it's the regis-ry office and houses the office of Frankfurt's nayor. Inside, the **Kaisersaal** (Imperial Hall; ☎ 2123 814; adult/student €2/1; ◯ 10am-1pm & 2-5pm, closed during vents) is adorned with portraits of 52 rulers.

The well-regarded **Museum für Moderne Kunst** Museum of Modern Art; ☎ 2123 0447; www.mmk-frankfurt de; Domstrasse 10; ◉ Dom/Römer; adult/student & senior 8/4; ◯ 10am-6pm Tue-Sun, to 8pm Wed), dubbed the slice of cake' because of its distinctive tri-ngular footprint, focuses on European and American art from the 1960s to the present, with frequent temporary exhibits. The per-nanent collection (not always on display) ncludes works by Roy Lichtenstein, Claes Oldenburg and Joseph Beuys.

In 2011 the **Historisches Museum** (☎ 2123 5599; www.historisches-museum.frankfurt.de, in German; Saalgasse 9; ◉ Dom/Römer; adult/concession €4/2; ◯ 10am-6pm ue-Sun, to 9pm Wed), established to showcase Frankfurt's long and fascinating history, will nove across the square to several old town ouses. The modern concrete monstrosity hat the museum's weak exhibits currently occupy – built, unsurprisingly, in 1972 – will hen be demolished and replaced.

NNENSTADT

The area delineated by the Alte Oper, Konstablerwache and Willy-Brandt-Platz

U-Bahn stations serves as the city's financial, business and commercial centre. The broad, pedestrians-only Zeil, Frankfurt's main shop-ping precinct, is great for strolling.

The famous old **Börse** (Stock Exchange; ☎ 2111 1515; visitors.centre@deutsche-boerse.com; Börsenplatz; ◉ Hauptwache; ◯ guided tour 10am, 11am & noon Mon-Fri, observation-platform visits 9.30am, 10.30am & 11.30am Mon-Fri) is an impressively colonnaded, neo-classical structure from 1843 whose porch is decorated with allegorical statues of the five continents. Frenzied buying and selling are a thing of the past but you can see the all-electronic trading floor on a free tour (in German and English). Book by telephone or email at least 24 hours ahead, and bring ID.

In the square out front, a sculpture entitled **Bulle und Bär** depicts a showdown between a bull and a bear in which the former clearly has the upper hoof.

Fans of the Enlightenment and German literature may want to drop by the **Goethe-Haus** (☎ 138 800; www.goethehaus-frankfurt.de; Grosser Hirschgraben 23-25; ◉ Willy-Brandt-Platz; adult/student €5/2.50; ◯ 10am-6pm Mon-Sat, 10am-5.30pm Sun), birthplace of Johann Wolfgang von Goethe (1749–1832). The furnishings are mainly reproductions but original pieces include Goethe's grandmother's writing desk and the great man's childhood puppet theatre. The **Gemäldegalerie** displays paintings from Goethe's time. PDA tours (€2) are available in German, English, Chinese, Japanese and Korean.

You can't go inside the 148m-high **Eurotower** (Kaiserstrasse 29; ◉ Willy-Brandt-Platz), home of the European Central Bank, but outside you can see the enormous blue-and-gold **euro symbol** beloved of TV talking heads reporting on EU financial news. At the ground-floor **Info Shop** (☎ 2440 4798) you can purchase euro coins from all over the eurozone.

Inaugurated in 1880, the Renaissance-style **Alte Oper** (Old Opera House; see p541) was burnt out in 1944, narrowly avoiding being razed and replaced with 1960s cubes, and was finally reconstructed (1976–81) to resemble the original, its facade graced with statues of Goethe and Mozart. The interior is modern.

In a square in the heart of the city's main gay and lesbian area is the **gay and lesbian memorial** (cnr Alte Gasse & Schäfergasse; ◉ Konstablerwache), in the form of an angel, which commemorates the many homosexuals persecuted and killed by the Nazis. It's deliberate that the statue's head is nearly severed from the body.

JEWISH SITES

Two notable museums take a look at nine centuries of Jewish life in Frankfurt. In 1933 the Jewish community here, numbering some 26,000, was Germany's second-largest.

The **Jüdisches Museum** (☎ 2123 5000; www.jewish museum.de; Untermainkai 14-15; ◉ Willy-Brandt-Platz; adult/student €4/2; ⊙ 10am-5pm Tue-Sun, to 8pm Wed),

on the north Main bank in the former residence of the Rothschild family, has exhibit on Jewish life in the city from the Middl Ages onward, with details on well-know Frankfurt Jews persecuted, exiled or mur dered by the Nazis.

At the **Museum Judengasse** (☎ 297 7419; Kur Schumacher-Strasse 10; ◉ Konstablerwache; adult/studer

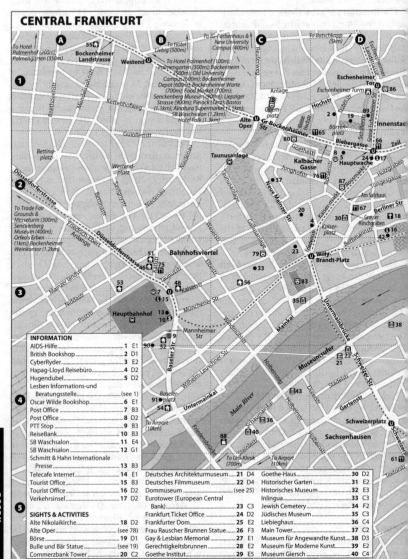

CENTRAL FRANKFURT

2/1, incl same-day entry to Jüdisches Museum €5/2.50; ☺ 10am-5pm Tue-Sun, to 8pm Wed), along the north-eastern boundaries of the old city fortifications, east of Altstadt, you can see the excavated remains of houses and ritual baths from the Jewish ghetto, most of which was destroyed by a French bombardment in 1796. Laws confining Jews to the ghetto were repealed in 1811.

Behind the Museum Judengasse, the western wall of the **Jewish Cemetery**, the **Wand der Namen** (Wall of Names) is studded with row upon row of metal cubes bearing the names of 11,000 Frankfurt Jews murdered during the Holocaust. Visitors often place pebbles atop the cubes to indicate, in accordance with Jewish tradition, that the deceased is still remembered.

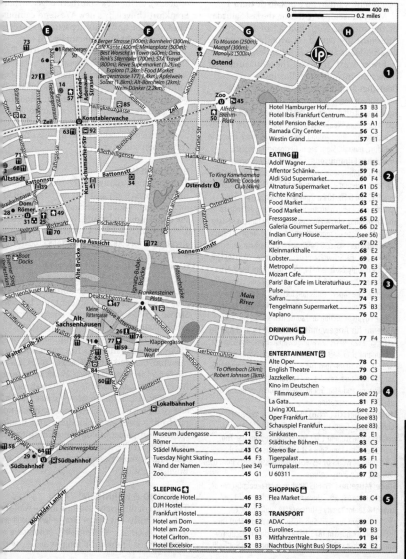

Hotel Hamburger Hof	**53**	B3
Hotel Ibis Frankfurt Centrum	**54**	B4
Hotel Pension Backer	**55**	A1
Ramada City Center	**56**	C3
Westin Grand	**57**	E1

EATING 🍴

Adolf Wagner	**58**	E5
Affentor Schänke	**59**	F4
Aldi Süd Supermarket	**60**	F4
Altnatura Supermarket	**61**	D5
Fichte Kränzi	**62**	E4
Food Market	**63**	E5
Food Market	**64**	E5
Fressgasse	**65**	D2
Galeria Gourmet Supermarket	**66**	D2
Indian Curry House	(see 56)	
Karin	**67**	D2
Kleinmarkthalle	**68**	E2
Lobster	**69**	E4
Metropol	**70**	E3
Mozart Cafe	**71**	E2
Paris' Bar Cafe im Literaturhaus	**72**	F3
Pulse	**73**	E1
Safran	**74**	F3
Tengelmann Supermarket	**75**	B3
Vapiano	**76**	D2

DRINKING 🍷

O'Dwyers Pub	**77**	F4

ENTERTAINMENT 🎭

Alte Oper	**78**	C1
English Theatre	**79**	C3
Jazzkeller	**80**	C2
Kino im Deutschen Filmmuseum	(see 22)	
La Gata	**81**	F3
Living XXL	(see 23)	
Oper Frankfurt	(see 83)	
Schauspiel Frankfurt	(see 83)	
Sinkkasten	**82**	E1
Städtische Bühnen	**83**	C3
Stereo Bar	**84**	E4
Tigerpalast	**85**	E1
Turmpalast	**86**	D1
U 60311	**87**	D2

SHOPPING 🛍

Flea Market	**88**	C4

TRANSPORT

ADAC	**89**	D1
Eurolines	**90**	B3
Mitfahrzentrale	**91**	B4
Nachtbus (Night Bus) Stops	**92**	E2

Museum Judengasse	**41**	E2
Römer	**42**	D2
Städel Museum	**43**	C4
Tuesday Night Skating	**44**	F3
Wand der Namen	(see 34)	
Zoo	**45**	G1

SLEEPING 🛏

Concorde Hotel	**46**	B3
DJH Hostel	**47**	F3
Frankfurt Hostel	**48**	B3
Hotel am Dom	**49**	E2
Hotel am Zoo	**50**	G1
Hotel Carlton	**51**	B3
Hotel Excelsior	**52**	B3

HESSE

Inside the cemetery, many of the remaining tombstones lean at crazy angles.

MUSEUMSUFER

In the northwest corner of Sachsenhausen, museums crowd the south bank of the Main along the Museumsufer (Museum Embankment). The nearest U-Bahn stations are 1km or so away, so from the Hauptbahnhof you might want to take bus 46 or tram 16.

Many museums are free on the last Saturday of the month. Note that all of Frankfurt's museums are closed on Monday *except* the Goethe-Haus and the Senckenberg Museum.

From west to east, the Museumsufer museums include the following:

Deutsches Architekturmuseum (☎ 2123 8844; www.dam-online.de; Schaumainkai 43; ◉ Schweizerplatz; adult/student €6/3; ♥ 11am-6pm Tue & Thu-Sun, 11am-8pm Wed) Puts on first-rate temporary exhibits on architecture from around the world. Not much relates to Frankfurt, though. Signs are in German and English.

Deutsches Filmmuseum (☎ 961 220 220; www .deutschesfilmmuseum.de, in German; Schaumainkai 41; ◉ Schweizerplatz; adult/student €2.50/1.30; ♥ 10am-5pm Tue, Thu & Fri, 10am-7pm Wed & Sun, 2-7pm Sat) A dynamic place with permanent and changing exhibitions on film-making, plus premieres and special film events (see p540). May close for renovations during the life of this guide.

Liebieghaus (☎ 650 0490; www.liebieghaus.de; Schaumainkai 71; ◉ Schweizerplatz; adult/under 12yr/student & senior/family €8/free/6/14; ♥ 10am-6pm Tue & Fri-Sun, 10am-9pm Wed & Thu) *The* place to come if you love sculpture. The superb collection includes Greek, Roman, medieval, Renaissance and baroque works, plus a recently redone Egyptian section and some items from East Asia.

Museum für Angewandte Kunst (Museum of Applied Arts; ☎ 2123 4037; www.angewandtekunst-frankfurt.de; Schaumainkai 17; ◉ Schweizerplatz; adult/concession €5/2.50; ♥ 10am-5pm Tue & Thu-Sun, 10am-9pm Wed) Displays furniture, textiles, metalwork, glass and ceramics from Europe and Asia. Set in lovely gardens, with a smart cafe and outdoor seating.

Museum Giersch (☎ 6330 4128; www.museum -giersch.de, in German; Schaumainkai 83; ◉ Schweizerplatz; adult/student €5/2.50; ♥ noon-7pm Tue-Thu, noon-5pm Fri, 11am-5pm Sat & Sun) Puts on special exhibitions of works by lesser-known Hesse artists from the 19th and early 20th centuries.

Städel Museum (☎ 605 0980; www.staedelmuseum.de; Schaumainkai 63; ◉ Schweizerplatz; adult/under 12yr/ student & senior/family €10/free/8/18, audioguide €4; ♥ 10am-6pm Tue & Fri-Sun, 10am-9pm Wed & Thu) This institution, founded in 1815, has a world-class collection of works by 14th- to 20th-century painters, including Botticelli, Dürer, Van Eyck, Rembrandt, Renoir, Rubens, Vermeer and Cézanne, plus Frankfurt natives such as Hans Holbein.

WESTEND

West of the Innenstadt, the well-heeled **Westend** (◉ Westend) – situated north and south of Bockenheimer Landstrasse – is known for its parks and tree-lined residential streets. The monumental **IG-Farbenhaus** (see the boxed text opposite), on the area's northern edge, anchors Frankfurt University's new Westend campus. The last of the university departments is set to move here from Bockenheim by 2014.

The 22-hectare botanical **Palmengarten** (Palm Garden; ☎ 2123 3939; www.palmengarten-frankfurt.de; Siesmayerstrasse 61 & Palmengartenstrasse; ◉ Bockenheimer Warte; adult/student/family €5/2/9.50; ♥ 9am-6pm Mon-Sa, Mar-Oct, 9am-4pm Nov-Feb), founded in 1868, has rose gardens, historic tropical hothouses, a playground for kids, a little pond with row boats and a mini-gauge train. It hosts open-air concerts in summer.

BOCKENHEIM

To see some strikingly ugly 1960s buildings that have aged badly and may not be around for long (and a few solid Wilhelmian ones), head to the old campus of Johann-Wolfgang-Goethe Universität (Frankfurt University), along the streets south of **Bockenheimer Warte** (◉ Bockenheimer Warte) – named after a medieval guard tower – between Gräfstrasse and Senckenberganlage. The university's departments are moving to the Westend, 1.5km to the northeast, but the area is still a centre of student life. **Leipziger Strasse** (◉ Bockenheimer Warte or Leipziger Strasse) is Bockenheim's lively main shopping street.

A solid neo-baroque building from the early 1900s houses Frankfurt's fine natural history museum, the **Senckenberg Museum** (☎ 754 20; www .senckenberg.de; Senckenberganlage 25; ◉ Bockenheimer Warte; adult/student/senior/family €6/3/5/15, audioguide €3; ♥ 9am-5pm Mon, Tue, Thu & Fri, to 8pm Wed, to 6pm Sat, Sun & holidays), which has full-sized dinosaur mock-ups out front – great for the kiddies – and, inside, exhibits on palaeontology (including fossils from the Grube Messel site, p546, outside Frankfurt), biology and geology. Most have English signs.

NORDEND & BORNHEIM

The heart of this lively, youthful area – well-off but not stuffy – is **Berger Strasse** (www.bornheim -mitte.de, in German; ◉ Merianplatz, Höhenstrasse or Bornheim Mitte), Frankfurt's longest street, with

IG-FARBENHAUS – KEEPING THE 'FINAL SOLUTION' RUNNING SMOOTHLY

Set in Frankfurt's leafy Westend, the monumental, Bauhaus-influenced **IG-Farbenhaus** (Furstenbergerstrasse 200; Holzhausenstrasse; 6am-8pm or later Mon-Sat), seven storeys tall and slightly curved, was erected in 1931 as the prestigious headquarters of IG-Farben, the mammoth German chemicals conglomerate whose constituents included Agfa, BASF, Bayer and Hoechst. White-collar staff based in this building carried out the banal work of coordinating the production of the company's most notorious product, Zyklon-B, the killing agent used in the gas chambers at Auschwitz.

After the war, IG-Farbenhaus served briefly as the headquarters of General Dwight D Eisenhower, Supreme Commander of Allied Forces in Europe, and later as the headquarters of US occupation forces and as a CIA bureau. Known as the 'Pentagon in Europe', the 'Casino' building was bombed by the Red Army Faction terrorist group (see p47) in the 1970s.

In 1995, with the Cold War over, US forces handed the building back to Germany's federal government. After refurbishment, it became the focal point of the new Westend campus of Johann-Wolfgang-Goethe-Universität (Frankfurt University) – and thus a bastion of the spirit of free inquiry and humanism that Nazism tried so hard to extinguish. Inside, you can check out the famed **paternoster lifts** and **exhibits** on the building's history.

Facing the southwest end of the building, the **Wollheim Memorial** (www.wollheim-memorial.de), in a little pavilion marked '107984', screens 24 interviews (also viewable on the excellent website) with former slave labourers who worked in IG-Farben factories such as IG Auschwitz, so big that it had its very own corporate concentration camp, Buna/Monowitz. Slave labourers who lived to write about their experiences with IG-Farben include Primo Levi and Elie Wiesel.

Photo panels installed in the IG-Farbenhaus gardens show German Jews enjoying life in the years before the Holocaust, unaware of what was to come.

the U4 line running underneath. Lined with eateries, cafes, wine bars, pubs and shops, it's ideal for a leisurely, well-irrigated stroll.

Explora (☎ 788 888; www.explora.info, in German; Glauburgplatz 1, Nordend; Glauburgstrasse; adult/concession €12/9; 11am-6pm Tue-Sun), 1.6km north of Konstablerwache, features mesmerising optical illusions and extraordinary images of all sorts. Highlights include stereoscopic slides of insects and mammals; holograms; 3-D X-ray photos of flowers; and feels-like-you're-there 3-D photos of turn-of-the-century Frankfurt, whose urban fabric was completely destroyed during WWII. The museum is housed in an above-ground WWII bomb shelter with reinforced concrete walls 2.15m thick.

ZOO

The **zoo** (Zoologisher Garten; ☎ 2123 3735; www.zoo frankfurt.de; Alfred-Brehm-Platz 16; Zoo; adult/student/family €8/4/20; 9am-7pm late Mar-late Oct, 9am-5pm late Oct-late Mar) isn't Germany's finest or prettiest but it does have kid-friendly houses for primates, nocturnal creatures, birds and amphibians.

EBBELWEI-EXPRESS

Run by Frankfurt's public transport company, the **Ebbelwei-Express** (Apple Wine Express; ☎ 2132 2425; www.ebbelwei-express.com; adult/child under 14yr €6/3;

 half-hourly 1.30-5.30pm Sat, Sun & holidays Apr-Oct & Sat Nov-Mar, approx hourly 1.30-5pm Sun & holidays Nov-Mar) is a historic tram whose 70-minute circuit takes in both banks of the Main between the Zoo and the Messe. Jump on at any stop – clockwise from the east, Zoo, Frankensteiner Platz, Lokalbahnhof, Südbahnhof, Hauptbahnhof and Börneplatz are convenient ones. As you'd expect, the price includes apple wine (*Ebbelwei*; or juice) and pretzels.

IN-LINE SKATING

No matter what the weather conditions, **Tuesday Night Skating** (www.tns-frankfurt.de, in German; Frankensteinerplatz, Sachsen-hausen; Lokalbahnhof; 8.30pm Tue late Mar-late Oct) brings out thousands of inline skaters for a sociable, 2½-hour (17km to 37km) circuit – with police escort – that begins at the southern end of Ignatz-Bubis-Brücke (served by tram 14).

Courses

The most respected place to study German is the **Goethe Institut** (☎ 961 2270; www.goethe.de; Diesterwegplatz 72, Sachsenhausen; Südbahnhof). German courses on offer at **Inlingua** (☎ 242 9200; www.inlingua-frankfurt.de, in German; Kaiserstrasse 37, Bahnhofsviertel; Willy-Brandt-Platz) include one that meets for four hours each morning from Monday to Friday (€440 for four weeks).

Festivals & Events

Some of Frankfurt's many festivals:

Christopher Street Day (www.csd-frankfurt.de, in German; ☽ mid-Jul) Colourful gay pride parade from the Römer to Konstablerwache, plus a street festival.

Frankfurt Book Fair (Frankfurter Buchmesse; www .frankfurt-book-fair.com; ☽ 5 days early or mid-October) World's largest book fair, with 7300 exhibitors from over 100 countries.

Weihnachtsmarkt (☽ late Nov–few days before Christmas) Christmas fair on the Römerberg, with mulled wine, choirs and traditional foods.

Sleeping

When it comes to accommodation prices, supply and demand reign supreme in Frankfurt. Hotels catering to business travellers tend to drop rates on weekends (Friday, Saturday and Sunday nights), on holidays and in August, but during major trade fairs prices can triple or even quadruple. To make sure your trip doesn't coincide with the book fair, when a modest double that usually costs €70 can set you back €280, go to www.frankfurt -tourismus.de, click 'Trade Shows & Events' and then 'Frankfurt Trade Shows'. Hotel websites give prices for specific dates.

The tourist office can help arrange hotel rooms (€3) but books private rooms only during trade fairs. At other times, you can find furnished rooms and apartments through a *Mitwohnzentrale* (accommodation finding service), such as www.city-mitwohnzentrale .de, www.mitwohnzentrale-mainhattan.de (in German) or www.allgemeine-mitwohnzentrale .de (in German).

Around the Hauptbahnhof, respectable hotels can be found along Poststrasse, Düsseldorferstrasse and Baseler Strasse.

BUDGET

Some of Frankfurt's low-end hotels are in the Bahnhofsviertel, the rather sleazy area northeast of the Hauptbahnhof.

DJH hostel (☎ 610 0150; www.jugendherberge-frankfurt .de; Deutschherrnufer 12, Sachsenhausen; ☒ Lokalbahnhof; dm €17-24.50, s/d €35.50/61, over 27yr €40/70; ☒ ☐) Advance bookings are advisable for the bustling, 434-room Jugendherberge Frankfurt, within easy walking distance of the city centre and nightspots. Has washing machines but doesn't allow cooking. From the Hauptbahnhof, take bus 46 to Frankensteiner Platz.

Frankfurt Hostel (☎ 247 5130; www.frankfurt-hostel .com; Kaiserstrasse 74, 3rd fl, Bahnhofsviertel; ◉ Frankfurt Hauptbahnhof; dm €17-25, s €30-55, d €45-75, s/d during fairs up to €100/140; ☒ ☐ ☞) Popular with young travellers, this lively, 230-bed establishment has bare-bones dorm rooms with metal bunks, wood-floored hallways that squeak, small shared kitchens and free, all you-can-eat spaghetti on Saturday.

Hotel Pension Backer (☎ 747 992; fax 747 900 Mendelssohnstrasse 92, Westend; ◉ Westend; s/d/tr with shared bathroom €25/40/45, breakfast per person €5) This no-frills, internet-challenged pension has 30 basic rooms that share five bathrooms, one on each floor. It's clean but don't expect an effusive welcome.

Hotel Carlton (☎ 241 8280; www.carlton-hotel -frankfurt.de; Karlstrasse 11, Bahnhofsviertel; ◉ Frankfurt Hauptbahnhof; s/d €50/70, weekends from €40/50, during fairs up to €190/250; ☒ ☐) In a century-old building the Carlton's 28 rooms are neat, practical and fairly large, but hardly romantic.

Hotel am Zoo (☎ 949 930; www.hotel-am-zoo.com Alfred-Brehm-Platz 6, Ostend; ◉ Zoo; s €50-70, d €70-90 s/d during fairs €168/198; ℗ ☒ ☒ ☐) Across the square from the zoo, this unpretentious hotel has 85 hypoallergenic rooms in white, yellow and blue. Near the eastern end of the Zeil.

our pick **Hotel Excelsior** (☎ 256 080; www.hotelexcelsior -frankfurt.de; Mannheimer Strasse 7-9, Bahnhofsviertel ◉ Frankfurt Hauptbahnhof; s/d €58/71, weekends €55/69 during fairs up to €220/259; ℗ ☒ ☐) Behind a brand-new, light-green facade, this 197-room place offers excellent value, with a free business centre, free coffee, tea, vegies and cakes in the lobby, and free landline phone calls throughout Germany.

Hotel Ibis Frankfurt Centrum (☎ 273 030; www.ibis hotel.de; Speicherstrasse 4, Bahnhofsviertel; ◉ Frankfurt Hauptbahnhof; s & d Mon-Fri €79, weekends & holidays €59, s/ during fairs up to €189/219, breakfast €10; ℗ ☒ ☐ ☒) You won't be swinging cats in the rooms of this 233-room chain hotel, but they are bright and some have nice views to the river or the quiet yard. An electronic scoreboard out front shows the day's prices.

MIDRANGE

Ramada City Center (☎ 310 810; www.ramada.com Weserstrasse 17, Bahnhofsviertel; ◉ Frankfurt Hauptbahnhof s/d from €65/112, weekends €65/85, during fairs from €199/299; ☒ ☐) Though unspectacular, this 108-room chain hotel offers all the fundamentals. Decent value for Frankfurt.

Hotel Hamburger Hof (☎ 2713 9690; www.hamburger hof.com; Poststrasse 10-12, Bahnhofsviertel; ◉ Frankfurt Hauptbahnhof; s/d €55/75, weekends, holidays & summer from €55/75, during fairs up to €240/250; ☐) A practical hotel with a spiffy new white-and-maroon lobby and 66 comfortable rooms.

Hotel am Dom (☎ 138 1030; www.hotelamdom.de; Kannengiessergasse 3, Altstadt; ⓜ Dom/Römer; s/d €90/120, apt €130) This unprepossessing, 30-room hotel has immaculate rooms, apartments with kitchenettes and four-person suites just a few paces from the cathedral.

Hotel Falk (☎ 7191 8870; www.hotel-falk.de; Falkstrasse 38a, Bockenheim; ⓜ Leipziger Strasse; s/d €100/130, weekends €65/85, during fairs up to €225/275; P ⊠ ⊠ ⊒) Near the Bockenheim shops and student eateries, this modern hotel has 29 rooms that are smallish but practical and comfy.

ourpick Hotel Liebig (☎ 2418 2990; www.hotel liebig.de; Liebigstrasse 45, Westend; ⓜ Westend; s €112-170, d €138-205, q €360, weekends s/d/q from €95/115/295, d during fairs up to €295; P ⊠) In the verdant Westend, this Italian-run family hotel has 19 bright rooms with wood floors and stylish bathrooms. Prices include breakfast only on the weekend.

TOP END

ourpick Villa Orange (☎ 405 840; www.villa-orange.de; Hebelstrasse 1, Nordend; ⓜ Musterschule; s/d from €128/158, weekends €90/99, during fairs up to €255/275; P ⊠ ⊠ ⊒) Offering tranquillity, modern German design and small-hotel comforts (eg a quiet corner library), this century-old villa has 38 spacious rooms. Breakfast is organic.

Concorde Hotel (☎ 242 4220; www.hotelconcorde.de; Karlstrasse 9, Bahnhofsviertel; ⓜ Frankfurt Hauptbahnhof; s/d from €110/160, weekends €65/100, during fairs up to €270/350; ⊠ ⊠ ⊒) Understated and friendly, this establishment in a restored century-old building has compact singles and spacious, sleek doubles with trendy washbasins and modern art photos on the walls.

Hotel Palmenhof (☎ 753 0060; www.palmenhof.com; Bockenheimer Landstrasse 89-91, Westend; ⓜ Westend or Bockenheimer Warte; s €119-149, d €159-175, weekends s €75-90, d €85-100, breakfast €16; P ⊠ ⊒) Built in 1890, this veteran establishment has 45 understated but tasteful rooms with classical furnishings. Also rents residential apartments (€33 to €50 plus taxes) for stays of at least two weeks.

Westin Grand (☎ 298 10; www.westin.com; Konrad-Adenauer-Strasse 5-7, Innenstadt; ⓜ Konstablerwache; d €179-600; P ⊠ ⊠ ⊒ ⊒) Convenient to the Zeil, this international standard business hotel has 371 large and very comfortable rooms with sparkling marble bathrooms. If your car is from the 1930s ask if you can park in the lobby. Breakfast is extra.

Eating & Drinking

During trade fairs restaurants fill up fast, so it's a good idea to call ahead.

BAHNHOFSVIERTEL

The train station area, some of it a bit insalubrious (at least at night), has quite a few cheap Mediterranean, Middle Eastern and Asian eateries. Part of Berlinerstrasse serves as a mini-Chinatown.

Indian Curry House (☎ 230 690; www.indiancurry house.de; Weserstrasse 17; ⓜ Frankfurt Hauptbahnhof; mains €7.10-13.50, weekday lunch special €6.90; ⊗ 11am-11pm Mon-Sat & during trade fairs Sun; Ⓥ) A popular sit-down-and-takeaway place with tasty meat and vegie dishes, both northern and southern.

For picnic supplies, try **Tengelmann supermarket** (Karlstrasse 4; ⓜ Frankfurt Hauptbahnhof; ⊗ 7am-9pm Mon-Fri, 8am-9pm Sat).

ALTSTADT

Mozart Café (☎ 291 954; Töngesgasse 23-25; ⓜ Hauptwache; cakes €2.90-3.80, light mains €6.90-16.50; ⊗ 8am-9pm Mon-Sat, 9am-8pm Sun) Join Frankfurt's 'granny scene' for coffee and cake or a light meal. Sit on red leather wing chairs inside or at Paris-cafe-style tables out front.

Metropol (☎ 288 287; Weckmarkt 13-15; ⓜ Dom/Römer; mains €9-15.50, 2-course lunch €8.50; ⊗ 9am-1am Tue-Thu, 9am-2am Fri & Sat, 9am-midnight Sun) Serves dishes from a changing menu that fluctuates between the inspired and bistro staples. Has a lovely courtyard out the back where children can chill out.

ourpick Paris' Bar Café im Literaturhaus (☎ 2108 5985; www.paris-literaturhaus.de, in German; Schöne Aussicht 2; ⓜ Dom/Römer; mains €15-23; ⊗ 11am-midnight Mon-Fri, 6pm-midnight Sat, 11am-6pm Sun) Inside an imposing, colonnaded venue for literary events, this semi-formal restaurant offers consistently excellent meat and fish, including superlative rump steak (€19). Served by tram 14.

ourpick Kleinmarkthalle (next to Hasengasse 9; ⓜ Dom/Römer; ⊗ 8am-6pm Mon-Fri, 8am-4pm Sat) This covered food market (the first in postwar Frankfurt) has fruit and vegie stands, ethnic specialities, wine and beer places (along the glass northern wall) and several *Wurst* (sausage) places, including the renowned *Gref Völsings Rindswurst* at the western end, not far from a large mural depicting impressions of Frankfurt. You can eat at narrow tables along the walls.

INNENSTADT

Known to locals as **Fressgasse** ('Munch Alley'; ⓜ Hauptwache), the wide, pedestrianised stretch of Kalbächer Gasse and its continuation, Grosse Bockenheimer Strasse, has lots of mid-priced and fast-food eateries with outdoor tables.

Vapiano (☎ 9288 7888; www.vapiano.com; Goetheplatz 1-3; ⊙ Hauptwache; pizza & pasta €5.75-8.75; ⊗ 10am-midnight, until 1am Fri & Sat) One of the best downtown deals, this stylish Italian chain has a unique system: at the door you get an electronic card used to calculate your food and wine tab when you leave. Keep it off your tray lest it gets whisked away.

Karin (☎ 295 217; Grosser Hirschgraben 28; ⊙ Willy-Brandt-Platz; mains €8-14; ⊗ 9am-midnight Mon-Sat, 10am-7pm Sun, 10am-midnight holidays) Across from the Goethe-Haus, this Frankfurt-style cafe serves German and international food and 18 different breakfasts (from €3). Payment is in cash only.

Pulse (☎ 1388 6802; www.pulse-frankfurt.de/page, in German; Bleichstrasse 38a; ⊙ Konstablerwache; mains €11.50-14.50; ⊗ 10am-1am Sun-Thu, 10am-4am Fri & Sat) A laid-back restaurant, bar and nightclub rolled into one. This place is officially gay but ends up very mixed, especially on weekends. The cuisine is seasonal and international. It has a wonderful warm-season patio out back.

For self-catering:

Food market (www.erzeugermarkt-konstablerwache.de, in German; Konstablerwache; ⊙ Konstablerwache; ⊗ 10am-8pm Thu, 8am-5pm Sat)

Galeria Gourmet supermarket (Zeil 116-126; ⊙ Hauptwache; ⊗ 9.30am-8pm Mon-Wed, 9.30am-9pm Thu-Sat) Under the Galeria Kaufhaus department store, two floors below street level.

SACHSENHAUSEN

Frankfurt's biggest food-and-drink district is **Alt-Sachsenhausen** (Old Sachsenhausen; ⊛ Lokalbahnhof), along pub- and eatery-packed side streets such as Grosse Rittergasse, Kleine Rittergasse, Klappergasse and Wallstrasse. People do imbibe to excess but the area is fairly safe and everyone-friendly (gays, lesbians, heteros, students, naked men with Walkmans, baked sun-studio worshippers).

The **Frau Rauscher Brunnen** (Klappergasse; ⊛ Lokalbahnhof) is a bulky, bitchy-looking Hausfrau who periodically spews a stream of water about 10m onto the footpath. When the street's busy – and the fountain, temporarily removed at press time, is back in place – you often see pedestrians get drenched. The idea is based on a popular Frankfurt song about apple wine (see the boxed text, opposite).

Safran (☎ 617 194; Klappergasse 8; ⊛ Lokalbahnhof; mains €8.90-13.90; ⊗ 6.30-11.30pm Mon-Sat, 12.30-10.30pm Sun; Ⓥ) A low-key Persian restaurant where the flavours are refined, the vegie options excellent, the service solicitous and the homemade green hot sauce positively lip-smacking.

our pick **Lobster** (☎ 612 920; Wallstrasse 21; ⊛ Lokal bahnhof; mains €15-20; ⊗ 6pm-1am Mon-Sat, hot dishes unt. 10.30pm) This cosy, friendly *Weinbistrot* serve up mouth-watering meat and fish dishes tha are 'a little bit French'. Offerings are listed on chalkboards.

O'Dwyers Pub (☎ 9623 3738; Klappergasse 19 ⊛ Lokalbahnhof; ⊗ 5pm-1am, until 3am Fri & Sat) Though not particularly Irish in ambience this Irish-owned place features on the drinking topography because it's loud and lively – even hellish sometimes. Monday is quiz nigh (at 9.30pm), and there's karaoke at 10.30pm (or when the footy's done) on Wednesday.

For self-catering:

Aldi Süd supermarket (Darmstadter Landstrasse 12; ⊛ Lokalbahnhof; ⊗ 8am-8pm Mon-Sat)

Alnatura supermarket (Schweizerstrasse 80; ⊙ Schweizerplatz; ⊗ 8am-8pm Mon-Sat) Sells upmarke organic and environmentally sustainable products.

Food market (Diesterwegplatz; ⊙ Südbahnhof; ⊗ 8am-6pm Tue & Fri) In front of the Südbahnhof.

BOCKENHEIM

Many university faculties have moved to the Westend but Bockenheim, especially **Leipziger Strasse** (⊙ Bockenheimer Warte or Leipziger Strasse) retains a string of inexpensive ethnic takeaways in what was, and to some extent still is Frankfurt's student stomping ground.

Bastos (☎ 7072 0004; www.bastos.de, in German Gräfstrasse 45; ⊙ Bockenheimer Warte; mains €6.90-9.50 ⊗ 9am-1am or later Sun-Thu, 9am-3am Fri & Sat) This contemporarily styled restaurant, cafe and night-owl drinking spot does good salads. pasta and mains, including vegie.

Pielok (☎ 776 468; www.restaurant-pielok.de, in German, Jordanstrasse 3; ⊙ Bockenheimer Warte; mains €8.20-15.30 ⊗ 11.30am-2.30pm & 5.30-10.30pm Mon-Fri & during trade fairs Sun, 5.30-10.30pm Sat; Ⓥ) Without claiming to be special, this place – run by the same family since 1945 – somehow is: loyal regulars, students and workers tread a path here for *bürgerlich* German fare at reasonable prices. Has a lovely grape-shaded back *Sommergarten*.

Orfeo's Erben (☎ 7076 9100; www.orfeos.de, in German; Hamburger Allee 45; ⊙ Westbahnhof; mains €11-19.50; ⊗ cafe noon-3pm & 6pm-midnight, closed Sun Jun-Aug) An arthouse cinema (p540), bar and restaurant with wood-slab tables and backlit beers. Dishes have an Italian inflection.

Bockenheimer Weinkontor (☎ 702 031; http:// bockenheimer-weinkontor.de, in German; Schlossstrasse 92; ⊙ Westbahnhof; ⊗ 7pm-1am, until 2am Fri & Sat) This mellow wine bar, in a 19th-century courtyard-cellar workshop, attracts a mixed crowd.

EBBELWEI & HANDKÄSE MIT MUSIK

Frankfurt delicacies are best experienced in the city's traditional taverns, which serve *Ebbelwei* (*Ebbelwoi;* Frankfurt dialect for *Apfelwein,* ie apple wine) along with local specialities like *Handkäse mit Musik* ('hand-cheese with music') and *Frankfurter Grüne Sosse* (Frankfurt green sauce).

   Handkäse mit Musik is the sort of name you could only find in Germany. It describes a round cheese marinated in oil and vinegar with onions, served with bread and butter and no fork. As you might imagine, this potent mixture tends to give one a healthy dose of wind – the release of which, ladies and gentlemen, is the music part.

   Frankfurter Grüne Sosse is made from parsley, sorrel, dill, burnet, borage, chervil and chives mixed with yoghurt, mayonnaise or sour cream; it's served with potatoes and ox meat or eggs, and was Goethe's favourite food.

   Atmospheric joints (most in Sachsenhausen) serving *Ebbelwei* and local dishes:

Adolf Wagner (☎ 612 565; www.apfelwein-wagner.com, in German; Schweizerstrasse 69, Sachsenhausen; Ⓖ Schweizerplatz) Warm and woody.

Affentor Schänke (☎ 627 575; www.affentor-schaenke.de; Neuer Wall 9, Sachsenhausen; Ⓡ Lokalbahnhof; mains €8.50-14; ☽ 5pm-midnight Mon-Sat, noon-11pm Sun & holidays) With a tree-shaded terrace.

Apfelwein Solzer (☎ 452 171; www.solzer-frankfurt.de; Berger Strasse 260, Bornheim; Ⓖ Bornheim Mitte; Handkäse €2.60; ☽ 6pm-midnight Mon-Sat, 1-10pm Sun May-Oct, winter from 5pm daily) With wood-panelled walls and a covered courtyard.

Fichte Känzi (☎ 612 778; www.fichtekraenzi.de; Wallstrasse 5, Sachsenhausen; Ⓡ Lokalbahnhof; ☽ 5pm-midnight) Has smoke-stained murals and great atmosphere.

There's a lovely vine-shaded summer courtyard, but the window ledge and the bar are the places to hang your buttocks and start gabbing. Serves light meals.

For self-catering:

Alnatura supermarket (Leipziger Strasse 19; Ⓖ Bockenheimer Warte; ☽ 8am-8pm Mon-Sat) A block northwest of Bockenheimer Warte.

Food market (Bockenheimer Warte; Ⓖ Bockenheimer Warte; ☽ 8am-6pm Thu)

NORDEND & BORNHEIM

Berger Strasse is lined with cafes and bars, especially northeast of **Merianplatz** (Ⓖ Merianplatz). The pub-lined stretch of Berger Strasse around No 237 (just past Rendeler Strasse) is known as **Alt-Bornheim** (Old Bornheim; Ⓖ Bornheim Mitte).

   Best Worscht in Town (☎ 1751 7318; www.best worschtintown.de; Berger Strasse 80; Ⓖ Merianplatz; Wurst €2.50-2.90; ☽ 11am-10pm Mon-Thu, 11am-11pm Fri & Sat) A worthy pun as this place does indeed serve some of Frankfurt's finest hot *Worscht* (known to non-Hessians as *Wurst*). The level of *Schärfehölle* (hellish hotness) goes up to FBI (Fucking Burning Injection).

   ourpick Café Kante (☎ 499 0083; Kantstrasse 13; Ⓖ Merianplatz; breakfast €2.80-6.50; ☽ 7am-8pm Mon-Fri, 7am-7pm Sat, 8.30am-7pm Sun) Walk into this classic neighbourhood cafe and you'll be overwhelmed by the delicious aroma of fantastic coffee, breads, cakes and croissants. Half a block east of Berger Strasse 48.

Eckhaus (☎ 491 197; Bornheimer Landstrasse 45; Ⓖ Merianplatz; mains €8-17.50; ☽ 5pm-midnight Mon-Thu, 5pm-1am Fri, 10am-1am Sat, 10am-midnight Sun) The smoke-stained walls and ancient floorboards suggest an inelegant, long-toothed past. We love this place, though others say the noise level saps their nerves. The hallmark *Kartoffelrösti* (shredded potato pancake; €9) has been served here for over 100 years.

   Manolya (☎ 494 0162; Habsburger Allee 6; Ⓖ Höhenstrasse; mains €9.50-18.50; ☽ 5pm-1am Mon-Thu, 11am-2am Fri & Sat, 11am-midnight Sun) This well-regarded Turkish restaurant, opened in 1992, has a convivial atmosphere and outdoor seating.

   Oma Rink's Sterntaler (☎ 4056 2290; www.oma rinks-sterntaler.de, in German; Musikantenweg 68; Ⓖ Merianplatz; mains from €9.80; ☽ 5pm-1am Mon-Fri, 5pm-2am Sat, 10am-midnight Sun) Outside there's a beer garden, inside a fireplace, brass candlesticks, big wooden tables and small crystal chandeliers. A good place for apple wine and local specialities such as *Rippchen mit Kraut* (grilled pork cutlet with sauerkraut and mashed potatoes). Sunday brunch (€12.90) is served until 4pm. Situated one-and-a-half short blocks southeast of Berger Strasse 84.

   Harvey's (☎ 4800 4878; www.harveys-ffm.de; Bornheimer Landstrasse 64; Ⓖ Merianplatz; mains €11.90-15.80; ☽ 10am-1am Mon-Thu, 10am-2am Fri & Sat, 10am-midnight Sun) Stylishly kitschy, with old-time chandeliers and bare-brick walls, this is a gay-friendly place that is modern but cosy, romantic but also

HESSE

great for dining on German favourites with old friends. Has warm-season outdoor seating.

our pick **Wein-Dünker** (☎ 451 993; Berger Strasse 265; ⊕ Bornheim Mitte; wine per glass from €2.10; ⊗ noon-2am or 3am Mon-Sat, 6pm-2am or 3am Sun) This musty little wine cellar, down to the right as you enter the courtyard, is not retro, it's real. Descend, rub your eyes and try some of Germany's finest. Food isn't served but you can bring your own and picnic atop an upturned barrel. A good place to meet real Frankfurters.

For self-catering:

Food market (Berger Strasse 177; ⊕ Bornheim Mitte; ⊗ 8am-6.30pm Wed, 8am-4pm Sat)

Food market (Friedbergerplatz; ⊕ Musterschule; ⊗ 10am-8pm Fri) Yuppies drop by in the late afternoon to chat each other up over a glass of wine.

Rewe supermarket (Berger Strasse 161; ⊕ Bornheim Mitte; ⊗ 8am-10pm Mon-Sat)

Entertainment

Frankfurt is a cultural magnet for the whole Rhine-Main region and this is reflected in the variety, verve and velocity of its concerts, clubs and cabarets. Oddly, Thursday is a big night out for workers who commute to Frankfurt for the week and go 'home' on Friday with drooping eyelids, scuffed dance shoes and wretched hangovers.

The best information source on what's on is the biweekly *Journal Frankfurt* (€1.80), available at newsstands and kiosks, with comprehensive listings, including a section for lesbians and gays, in German. *Prinz* (http://frankfurt. prinz.de), *Strandgut* (www.strandgut.de) and student-oriented *Frizz* (www.frizz-frankfurt .de) are German-language listings magazines available throughout the city.

Several dance clubs have summertime beach clubs along the Main River.

CABARET

Tigerpalast (☎ 920 0220; www.tigerpalast.com; Heiligkreuzgasse 16-20, Innenstadt; ⊕ Konstablerwache; adult Tue-Thu & Sun €53.25, Fri & Sat €58.75, child under 12yr half-price; ⊗ shows 7pm & 10pm Tue-Thu, 7.30pm & 10.30pm Fri & Sat, 5pm & 9pm Sun, closed late Jun-late Aug) One of Frankfurt's top venues for cabaret, music hall and *Varieté* theatre, with programs that often include acrobats and circus and magic performances.

Mouson (Künstlerhaus Mousonturm; ☎ 4058 9520; www.mousonturm.de, in German; Waldschmidtstrasse 4, Bornheim; ⊕ Merianplatz) This rambling former soap factory serves as a forum for younger artists and hosts contemporary dance, theatre

(sometimes in English) and cabaret, as well as concerts by up-and-coming bands.

CINEMAS

Films in the original language (ie non-dubbed) are denoted by 'OV' (original version) or 'OmU' (*Original mit Untertiteln*, ie subtitled). Look for posters in U-Bahn stations; if the description is in English, so is the movie. Listings can be found in the free weekly *Kino Journal Frankfurt* (www.kinojournal-frankfurt.de, in German), available at the tourist office (see p530), and at www .kinoservice.de (in German).

Turmpalast (☎ 01805-118 811; www.cinestar.de, in German; Bleichstrasse 57, Innenstadt; ⊕ Eschenheimer Tor) A seven-screen venue with first-run films in English, Turkish and Hindi.

Kino im Deutschen Filmmuseum (☎ 961 220 220; www.deutschesfilmmuseum.de, in German; Schaumainkai 41, Sachsenhausen; ⊕ Schweizerplatz) Art cinema attached to the Deutsches Filmmuseum.

Kino Mal Seh'n (☎ 597 0845; www.malsehnkino.de, in German; Adlerflychtstrasse 6, Nordend; ⊕ Musterschule; ⊗ 6pm, 8pm & 10pm) An 80-seat arthouse cinema with offbeat OV movies and an engaging wine bar.

Orfeo's Erben (☎ 7076 9100; www.orfeos.de, in German; Hamburger Allee 45, Bockenheim; ⊕ Westbahnhof; ⊗ 5pm, 7pm & 9pm) Screens arthouse films in OV. Has a restaurant (p538).

NIGHTCLUBS

King Kamehameha (☎ 4800 9610; www.king-kamehameha.de, in German; Hanauer Landstrasse 192; admission €8-10; ⊗ 9pm-4am Thu, 10pm-4am Fri & Sat) A strapping Leonardo DiCaprio–type guy might dash out and unexpectedly plough the length of the ornamental pool (clothed, take note) – it's been known to happen here. And much more too, for 'KingKa' is legendary, with its own live club band on Thursday and DJ dance beats on weekends. The door policy is pretty strict so the crowd, most in their 20s and early 30s, comes nicely turned-out. Situated about 2km southeast of the zoo; accessible by tram 11. Runs a summertime beach club in Offenbach.

U 60311 (☎ 297 060 311; www.u60311.net; cnr Rossmarkt & Am Salzhaus, Innenstadt; ⊕ Hauptwache; ⊗ from 10pm Wed-Sat) Deep underground in a decommissioned pedestrian passage (60311 is the postcode), this is one of the best (and most notorious) stops in town for hard-core techno.

Stereo Bar (☎ 617 116; www.stereobar.de, in German; Abtsgässchen 7, Sachsenhausen; ⊛ Lokalbahnhof; admission free; ☺ 10pm-4am Fri & Sat) This cellar bar has a 1970s vibe, a small dance floor, *nargileh* (water pipes) and music that's as eclectic as the decor. Dress is very informal.

Cocoon Club (☎ 900 200; www.cocoonclub.de; Carl-Benz-Strasse 21) This postmodern pulsating membrane-like miracle, about 5km east of the centre, is the home of techno legend Sven Väth. It throbs with music from the man himself or his guests Friday and Saturday, and other days in smaller format. To get there take tram 11 or 12 to Dieselstrasse.

Living XXL (☎ 242 9370; www.livingxxl.de; Kaiserstrasse 29, Innenstadt; ⊙ Willy-Brandt-Platz; ☺ 6pm-1am Wed, 6pm-3am Thu, 6pm-4am Fri, 6pm-5am Sat, dinner until 11pm) If the euro ever goes into freefall, it'll land here – this large, mainstream club, with a gallery restaurant and six bars, is in the basement of the Eurotower, home of the European Central Bank. Popular with bankers and wannabes. The no-techno disco hits its stride at around 1am. Has an after-work party (€6) with a buffet and happy hour on Wednesday.

Robert Johnson (☎ 821 123; www.robert-johnson.de, in German; Nordring 131, Offenbach; ⊙ Kaiserlai) On the south bank of the river, just over the line in Offenbach, this minimalist club attracts the best names in German electronic music and also has regular nights from the thriving Frankfurt-based Playhouse label.

GAY & LESBIAN VENUES

Frankfurt's gay life is concentrated north of the Zeil around **Schäfergasse** (⊙ Konstablerwache) and Alte Gasse, with a bevy of clubs and cafes. For details on the scene, see the free monthly magazine *Gab* (http://gab.publigayte.com, in German), www.frankfurt.gay-web.de or www.up-cityguide.de (in German).

Gay-oriented places include Harvey's (p539) and Pulse (p538).

La Gata (☎ 614 581; www.club-la-gata.de, in German; Seehofstrasse 3, Sachsenhausen; 🚋 Lokalbahnhof; ☺ 8pm-dawn Mon, Wed, Thu & Sun, 9pm-dawn Fri & Sat) Frankfurt's only women-only lesbian bar.

ROCK & JAZZ

Batschkapp (☎ 9521 8410; www.batschkapp.de; Maybachstrasse 24, Eschersheim; ⊙ Eschersheim) In its 30-plus years of staging live bands, the 'Batsch' has seen 'em come, go, burn out, gloriously self-destruct or simply rust to dust.

Jazzkeller (☎ 288 537; www.jazzkeller.com; Kleine Bockenheimer Strasse 18a, Innenstadt; ⊙ Hauptwache; admission €5-20; ☺ 9pm-2am Tue-Thu, 10pm-3am Fri & Sat,

8pm-2am Sun) Look hard to find this place – a great jazz venue with mood – hidden in a cellar under an alley that intersects Goethestrasse at an oblique angle. Concerts begin an hour after opening except on Friday, when there's dancing to Latin and funk. Founded in 1952.

Sinkkasten (☎ 0180-504 0300; www.sinkkasten -frankfurt.de, in German; Brönnerstrasse 5, Innenstadt; ⊙ Konstablerwache; disco admission €4.50) Has lots of live music as well as entertaining vinyl to dance to, especially if you love 1980s flavours. Since 1971.

Mampf (☎ 448 674; www.mampf-jazz.de, in German; Sandweg 64, Bornheim; ⊙ Merianplatz; ☺ 6pm-1am Sun-Thu, 6pm-2am Fri & Sat) You'll hear great jazz sounds in this tiny jazz club–cum–pub, running since 1972. Hosts live concerts two or three times a week, often from 8.30pm on Wednesday and Saturday.

THEATRE, CLASSICAL & DANCE

The Frankfurt theatre scene has all the hallmarks of high art – it bites back, it bitches, and occasionally an offended ego spontaneously and publicly explodes. There are over 30 different venues around town.

Tickets for operas, concerts, plays and sports events (except football) can be purchased from **Frankfurt Ticket** (☎ 134 0400; www .frankfurt-ticket.de, in German), which has a **ticket outlet** (⊙ Hauptwache; ☺ 9.30am-7pm Mon-Fri, 9.30am-4pm Sat, longer hr Dec, shorter hr Jul & Aug) underground on the B Level of the Hauptwache U-Bahn/S-Bahn station, facing KFC.

Last-minute tickets can generally be purchased an hour or so before performance time at each venue's *Abendkasse* (evening ticket window).

The city's major cultural institutions include the **Städtische Bühnen** (www.buehnen-frankfurt.de, in German; Untermainanlage 11; ⊙ Willy-Brandt-Platz), a huge cultural complex where you'll find the **Schauspiel Frankfurt** (www.schauspielfrankfurt.de, in German), a theatre company, and **Oper Frankfurt** (☎ 134 0400; www.oper-frankfurt.de), the city's main opera company. The **Alte Oper** (www.alteoper.de; Opernplatz 8; ⊙ Alte Oper) puts on performances of classical music.

The quality of the English-language plays and musicals at the **English Theatre** (☎ 2423 1620; www.english-theatre.de; Kaiserstrasse 34, entrance on Gallusanlage; ⊙ Willy-Brandt-Platz; tickets €21-44; ☺ season runs early Sep-early Jul, box office noon-6pm Mon, 11am-6.30pm Tue-Fri, 3-6.30pm Sat, 3-5pm Sun) is surprisingly high.

Bocken-heimer Depot (☎ 134 0400; www.bockenheimer -depot.de, in German; Carlo-Schmid-Platz 1, Bockenheim; 🚇 Bocken-heimer Warte), a century-old former tram depot, hosts innovative dance productions by the Forsythe Company (www.theforsythe company.com) as well as Städtische Bühnen theatre productions.

Shopping

When it comes to shopping, Frankfurt is not Berlin, Paris or Milan. The strollable **Zeil** (🚇 Hauptwache or Konstablerwache) is the main shopping precinct, but the really serious splurging takes place along **Goethestrasse** (🚇 Hauptwache) and other streets just west of Goetheplatz, which are lined with the city's priciest fashion boutiques and jewellery stores.

There's a weekly **flea market** (Schaumainkai; 🚇 Schweizerplatz; 🕙 8am-2pm Sat) located along the Museumsufer.

Getting There & Away

AIR

Frankfurt Airport (FRA; ☎ 01805-372 4636; www.frankfurt -airport.com; 🚇 Flughafen), 12km southwest of downtown, is Germany's busiest airport, with the highest cargo turnover and the third-highest passenger numbers in Europe (after London's Heathrow and Paris' Charles de Gaulle).

Gates beginning with A, B and C are in Terminal 1, which is dominated by Lufthansa, while gates beginning with D and E are in the newer Terminal 2. The terminals are linked by a poorly signposted, driverless elevated railway, the Sky Line, which runs every two minutes. Terminal 3 is being built on land that was part of the American Rhein-Main Air Base, which closed in 2005.

The airport has two train stations deep below Terminal 1, Hall B. The Regionalbahnhof handles regional-train and S-Bahn connections; services begin at about 4.30am and end at 12.30am. The Fernbahnhof is used by long-haul IC/EC and ICE trains.

Lufthansa buses (☎ 01803-803 803; www.lufthansa -airportbus.com) link the airport with Heidelberg, Mannheim and Strasbourg (France).

Services available at the airport:

Hotels & Tours (☎ 6907 0402; www.airport-travelnet .com; Terminal 1, Arrival Hall B; 🕙 7am-10.30pm) Helps with hotel bookings.

Post office (Terminal 1, Departure Hall B; 🕙 7am-10pm)

ReiseBank Terminal 1, Departure level (🕙 6am-10pm); Terminal 1, entrance to Regionalbahnhof (🕙 6am-9pm) Exchanges currency.

Showers (Duschen; Terminal 1, Departure Hall B; €6 or US$8)

Tegut supermarket (Terminal 1, btwn Halls B & C; 🕙 6am-10pm) Hidden away one floor below the Arrival level.

If your flight, eg on Ryanair, is to Frankfurt-Hahn Airport (airport code HHN; see p481), you'll land about 110km west of Frankfurt. Buses to/from Frankfurt's Hauptbahnhof (€12, 1¾ hours, hourly) stop on Mannheimer Strasse.

BUS

Long-distance buses leave from the south side of the Hauptbahnhof, where you'll find **Eurolines** (☎ 790 3253; www.eurolines.eu; Mannheimer Strasse 15; 🚇 Frankfurt Hauptbahnhof; 🕙 7.30am-7.30pm Mon-Fri, 7.30am-2pm Sat, 7.30am-1pm Sun), with services to most European destinations.

CAR & MOTORCYCLE

All major (and some minor) car-rental companies have offices in the Hauptbahnhof and at the airport.

ADAC (☎ 01805-101 112; www.adac.de, in German; Schillerstrasse 12; 🚇 Hauptwache; 🕙 9.30am-6.30pm Mon-Fri, 10am-1pm Sat), Germany's automobile association, provides free maps and route advice to members of partner automobile clubs, including the AAA in the US, the AA in the UK and eight state AAA groups in Australia.

The **Mitfahrzentrale** (☎ 194 40; Baselerplatz 🚇 Frankfurt Hauptbahnhof; 🕙 9.30am-6.30pm Mon-Fri 10am-2pm Sat) matches travellers with drivers going to the same destination. Typical all-up fares, including fees: Berlin (€30), Cologne (€17), London (€35), Munich (€15), Paris (€35) and Stuttgart (€10). It's best to make reservations (by phone or in person) two or three days ahead, but last-minute bookings are often possible. Drivers meet passengers at the office.

TRAIN

The Hauptbahnhof, west of the centre, handles more departures and arrivals than any other station in Germany, which means that there are convenient trains to pretty much anywhere, including Berlin (€111, four hours). The **Reisezentrum** (information office; 🕙 7am-10pm) faces platform 9. For train information call ☎ 01805-996 633.

HESSE

Long-haul services from Frankfurt Airport include ICE trains to Hamburg (€107, four hours), Hanover (€81, 2½ hours) and Stuttgart (€56, 1¼ hours) every two hours; to Cologne (€60, one hour) and Dortmund (€81, 2¼ hours) two or three times an hour; and south towards Basel (€70, three hours, hourly).

Getting Around

TO/FROM THE AIRPORT

S-Bahn lines S8 and S9 shuttle between the airport and the city centre (one-way €3.70, 15 minutes), stopping at Hauptbahnhof, Hauptwache and Konstablerwache, as well as Wiesbaden and Mainz. See right for details on other ticket types.

Bus 61 links the Südbahnhof in Sachsenhausen with Terminal 1 every half-hour.

For travel between the airport and the city centre, the taxi fare is €25 to €30 (a bit more from 10pm to 6am).

BICYCLE

Cycling is a great way to get around Frankfurt, which is well endowed with designated bike lanes.

With Deutsche Bahn's **Call-a-Bike** (☎ 07000-522 5522, without a German ID number 0345-2798 4907; www.callabike-interaktiv.de), you register by phone (€5, returned to you as a credit) and then, each time you want a bicycle, you go to a Call-a-Bike Station, which can be found all over the city centre, and phone to get the lock code. Costs are €0.08 a minute, €9 for 24 hours and €36 for four to seven days.

Next Bike (☎ 030-6920 5046; www.nextbike.de, in German; per 1hr/24hr €1/5) works in a similar manner. After you register using your credit card, you go to a pick-up point (eg next to the Römer tourist office or at Hauptwache) and phone to get the lock code; phone again when you return the bike.

In some parts of the Altstadt and Innenstadt, you can flag down (or reserve by phone) a pedal-powered, three-wheel **Velotaxi** (☎ 7158 8855; www.0700velotaxi.de, in German; per person 1st km €2.50, subsequent km €1.50, 30min €7.50; ☺ noon-8pm late Mar-Oct).

CAR & MOTORCYCLE

Traffic flows smoothly in central Frankfurt, but if you're behind the wheel the one-way system may drive you to distraction. To preserve your sanity, you may be better off parking your vehicle in a **Parkhaus** (parking garage; www.parkhaus-frankfurt.de, in German; per hr €2, overnight €3-5) and proceeding on foot. Throughout the centre you'll see signs with directions to the nearest garage and the number of places left.

City centre street parking costs €1 per 30 minutes and is generally limited to one hour.

To avoid hassles and/or parking fees, you may want to ditch your car out of the centre on a U-Bahn or S-Bahn line and use public transport.

PUBLIC TRANSPORT

Frankfurt's excellent transport network, run by **traffiQ** (☎ 01805-069 960; www.traffiq.de, in German), integrates all bus, tram, S-Bahn and U-Bahn lines (in general the U-Bahn is underground only in the city centre). The city centre's main transport hubs are Hauptwache, Konstablerwache and Frankfurt Hauptbahnhof. Each site mentioned in the Frankfurt am Main section has the nearest U-Bahn or S-Bahn station indicated right after the address, though in some cases (eg northern Sachsenhausen) a tram or bus will bring you closer.

Nachtbus (night bus; www.nachtbus-frankfurt.de, in German) lines leave from the east side of Konstablerwache (Konrad-Adenauer-Strasse) half-hourly (hourly for some suburban destinations) from 1.30am to 3.30am on Friday and Saturday nights and holiday eves.

Single or day tickets can be purchased from the machines at transit stops. Zone 50 encompasses most of Frankfurt, excluding the airport. An *Einzelfahrkarte* (single-ride ticket) costs €2.30 (€3.70 to the airport); a ticket for a *Kurzstrecke* (short trip; consult the list on machines) costs €1.50.

A *Tageskarte* (24-hour ticket) is €5.80 (€9.10 including the airport); a *Gruppentageskarte*, the version valid for up to five people, costs just €8.70 – a superb deal. A *Wochenkarte* (weekly pass, valid for any seven consecutive days) costs €21.10 (including the airport) and is also a great deal.

TAXI

Taxis are quite expensive. There's a €2.75 hire charge (€3.25 at night); travel costs €1.65 per kilometre (€1.75 at night), with a waiting charge of €0.35 per minute (€0.46 at night). There are taxi ranks throughout the city, or you can call ☎ 250 001, ☎ 203 04 or ☎ 7930 7999.

HESSE

DARMSTADT

☎ 06151 / pop 142,000

Jugendstil (art nouveau) architecture and a world-renowned technical university are hallmarks of this modest but interesting city about 35km south of Frankfurt. Despite some atrocious postwar architecture (the university has some real zingers), Darmstadt is a pretty city, and just the right size for strolling.

The super-heavy element Darmstadtium (Ds; atomic number: 110) was first created here in 1994. In its honour, the city's new conference centre was named the Darmstadtium.

Orientation

The Hauptbahnhof is connected to Luisenplatz, the focal point of the city centre, by a long walk (1.5km) or a short ride east along Rheinstrasse, which is 200m to the right as you exit the train station. Mathildenhöhe and its museums are 1.5km northeast of Luisenplatz, and about 500m north of the Grosser Woog (a lake).

Information

ATMs There are several around Luisenplatz.

Call Shop & Internet Cafe (Wilhelminenstrasse 8; internet access per hr €1; ☯ 10am-11pm Mon-Sat, 11am-11pm Sun) Facing the west side of the Luisencenter shopping mall, in the same passage as the cinema.

Post office (Luisenplatz) On the northwest corner.

Tourist office (☎ 4513; www.darmstadt-marketing.de; Luisenplatz 5; ☯ 10am-6pm Mon-Fri, 10am-4pm Sat, 10am-2pm Sun) In the north side of the Luisencenter shopping mall. Has tourist information and cultural events tickets.

Sights & Activities

Darmstadt's biggest attraction is the former *Künstlerkolonie* (artists colony) at **Mathildenhöhe** (www.mathildenhoehe.info), surrounded by a lovely hilltop park with fountains. Famous for its Darmstädter Jugendstil architecture and creations, it was established in 1899 at the behest of Grand Duke Ernst Ludwig. The area is linked to the centre by bus F.

The **Museum Künstlerkolonie** (☎ 133 385; Olbrichweg 13; adult/student €5/3; ☯ 10am-5pm Tue-Sun) displays stunningly elegant Jugendstil furniture, tableware, textiles, ceramics and jewellery. Nearby, the **Ausstellungsgebäude Mathildenhöhe** (☎ 132 778; adult €5-8, student €3-6; ☯ 10am-6pm Tue, Wed & Fri-Sun, to 9pm Thu) puts on temporary art exhibitions. The slope to the west is dominated by the three golden onion domes of the mosaic-adorned **Russian**

Orthodox chapel (☎ 424 235; Nikolaiweg 18; admission free; ☯ 10am-1pm & 2-4pm Tue-Sat, 2-4pm Sun), built from 1897–99 for the last Russian Tsar Nicholas II, who married a local gal, Princess Alix von Hessen (Grand Duke Ernst Ludwig's younger sister), in 1894.

Two blocks northeast of Luisenplatz, the **Hessisches Landesmuseum** (Hesse State Museum ☎ 165 703; www.hlmd.de, in German; Friedensplatz 1) has a wide-ranging collection that includes an exceptional display of works by Joseph Beuys (see p74). It is closed for renovations until 2011.

A long block east of Luisenplatz, the **Schlossmuseum** (☎ 240 35; www.schlossmuseum-darmstadt.de, in German; Marktplatz 15; adult/student €4/1.50), likely to be closed in 2010 and perhaps 2011, is packed with ornate furnishings, carriages and paintings. It occupies the southeast corner of the Schloss complex, rebuilt after WWII damage and now occupied by the **Technische Universität**, whose campus – some of it shiny-new, other sections postwar-ugly – is across the street to the east and northeast.

The historic **Jugendstilbad** (☎ 951 560; www.jugendstilbad.de, in German; Mercksplatz 1; swimming pools 2hr/4hr/all day €5/7/9, incl spa €7.50/10/12, incl spa & saunas €11/13.50/16, child under 1m tall free, child 1m-17yr 25% discount; ☯ 10am-10pm) is a swimming and spa complex that looks just as gorgeous as it did when it opened in 1909. It reopened in 2008 after meticulous restoration. It has a year-round outdoor pool, a superb Jugendstil indoor pool and 10 dry and wet saunas. Situated a long block east of the Schloss along Landgraf-Georg-Strasse.

Sleeping

DJH hostel (☎ 452 93; www.darmstadt.jugendherberge.de; Landgraf-Georg-Strasse 119; dm/s €24.40/36.40; ☒) This 130-bed hostel is 1km west of Luisenplatz on the shores of the Grosser Woog. Take bus L towards Ostbahnhof from the centre.

Hotel Prinz Heinrich (☎ 813 70; www.hotel-prinz-heinrich.de; Bleichstrasse 48; s/d/tr without breakfast €61/76/82; ☒) A traditional feel, modern furnishings and overall comfort make this 65-room hotel a solid choice. Midway between the Hauptbahnhof and Luisenplatz.

Best Western Hotel Darmstadt (☎ 281 00; www.hotel-darmstadt.bestwestern.de; Grafenstrasse 31, 4th fl, s/d from €105/130; ☒ ☒ ☒ ☒) The entrance, through a parking garage, is unpromising but inside the lobby is pristine and

LOCAL VOICE – BRIGITTE DURST

Germany didn't become a leader in environmental technologies – with wind farms dotting the landscape and solar panels on suburban rooftops – by accident. Consistent, long-term government strategies and subsidies have played a crucial role, but so has a broad-based environmental movement whose principles and vision have become part of everyday life.

Brigitte Durst, born in 1981 near Karlsruhe, grew up with green ideas. 'My father is very interested in environmental issues and I always was, too,' she explained. 'I remember that when I was maybe 11, I took the garbage from my grandmother to analyse it. I wanted to see what it consisted of – is it more organic, or more plastic? She was not really happy about that!'

Fast-forward to a decade later, when Brigitte had to make some career decisions. Pragmatically weighing her options, she decided to study for an environmental engineering degree, known in German as a 'Diplom-Ingenieur (FH) Umweltschutz', in the Rhine town of Bingen. Her favourite courses explored the economics of environmental protection, the life cycle of a consumer product, environmental law and exhaust-gas treatment.

During the fourth and final year of her program of study (2009), Brigitte did a company traineeship near Stuttgart. 'I worked on the digestion of organic waste by microbes in anaerobic conditions,' she said. 'The process I'm working on is called "wet digestion". Organic waste is brought to the plant. After recycled water is added, everything goes into the digester for 21 days and microbes try to degrade the mixture.' The resultant gases include not only methane, which can be fed into the natural gas grid, but also hydrogen sulphide (H_2S). 'My part is to eliminate the H_2S. It's a biological process using microbes that oxidise the H_2S so it becomes sulphur (S). It's an old technology but I'm trying to refine it.'

'There's lots of growth – and more and more jobs – in the renewable energy sector,' Brigitte observed. This is due to the urgent need to reduce greenhouse emissions and because Germany, like the rest of the EU, is seeking greater independence from potentially unreliable energy suppliers in Russia and the Middle East. 'In Germany, about 50% of organic waste is collected. To use it to produce energy – that's the way German government policy is going.'

the 77 rooms are spacious, modern and comfortable. Situated one block west of Luisenplatz – very central.

Eating & Drinking

In the warm season there are outdoor cafes two blocks southeast of Luisenplatz on the Marktplatz. Cheap eats can be found near the Technische Universität, eg east of the Schloss along Landgraf-Georg-Strasse.

City Braustübl (☎ 255 11; Wilhelminenstrasse 31; mains €7.90-15.50; ☽ 11am-midnight Mon-Fri, 11am-1am Sat & Sun) A classic brewery-affiliated restaurant, with wood-plank floors and hops hanging from the rafters. Strong on regional dishes that can be washed down with beers brewed over near the Hauptbahnhof. Situated three short blocks south of Luisenplatz.

An Sibin (☎ 204 52; www.ansibin.com; Landgraf-Georg-Strasse 25; ☽ 6pm-1am Sun-Wed, 6pm-3am Thu-Sat, may open earlier for sports events Sat & Sun) An Irish pub and live concert venue good for a few rounds and a yarn or four. Tuesday is quiz

night, on Thursday there's karaoke and on Sunday a traditional dinner is served.

For self-catering, try **Tegut supermarket** (cnr Marktplatz & Ludwigstrasse; ☽ 7am-9pm Mon-Sat).

Entertainment

Goldene Krone (☎ 213 52; www.goldene-krone.de; Schustergasse 18) An old favourite, with concerts, disco dance parties, a bar, billiards and lots more. The entrance is on Holzstrasse around the corner from the Schloss.

Centralstation (☎ 366 8899; www.centralstation-darmstadt.de, in German; Im Carree; ☽ cafe 10am-1am Mon-Thu, 10am-3am Fri & Sat) This cultural venue, housed in the city's first electric power plant (built 1888), has an excellent midday buffet restaurant (open noon to 2.30pm except Sunday), a cocktail lounge (open 8pm to 1am, until 3am on Friday and Saturday, closed Sunday except when there's a concert) and live music (especially jazz but also pop and classical). Situated in the courtyard across Luisenstrasse from the tourist office.

Getting There & Around

Frequent S-Bahn trains link Darmstadt with Frankfurt's Hauptbahnhof (€6.75, 30 minutes).

Trams 3 and 4 and bus H, among others, link the Hauptbahnhof with Luisenplatz.

There's free parking about 1km east of the centre around the Grosser Woog and the DJH hostel.

AROUND DARMSTADT

Kloster Lorsch

Founded in the 8th century, and Unesco-listed in 1991, **Kloster Lorsch** (Lorsch Abbey; ☎ 06251-103 820; www.kloster-lorsch.de; Nibelungenstrasse 35, Lorsch; adult/concession €4/3; ☒ 10am-5pm Tue-Sun) was an important religious site in its hey-day, especially for the Carolingian dynasty. A visit to the monastery makes a nice ex-cursion from Darmstadt, despite few of the original buildings having been preserved (the Königshalle and Altenmünster are the most accessible). The complex has three museum sections – one on the history of the abbey, the second on life in Hesse, and a third on tobacco, which was cultivated in Lorsch in the late 17th century. Lorsch is easily reached from Darmstadt along the A5 or the A67 south, or via the picturesque Bergstrasse (B3). The train from Darmstadt goes via Bensheim (25 minutes). The abbey is a 10-minute walk from the station.

Messel

Another Unesco monument, the Grube Messel (Messel Pit) fossil site contains a wealth of well-preserved animal and plant remains from the Eocene era, around 49 million years ago. It's best known for the specimens of early horses found here, which illustrate the evolutionary path towards the modern beast.

The most interesting fossils excavated are now held in the Hessisches Landesmuseum (see p533), in Darmstadt, the Senckenberg Museum (see p534) in Frankfurt, and Messel's own **museum** (☎ 06159-5119; www.messel museum.de; Langgasse 2; ☒ 2-6pm Tue-Sat & 10am-6pm Sun Apr-Oct, 2-4pm Sat, 10am-noon & 2-4pm Sun Nov-Mar) in a pretty half-timbered house. For tours of the site itself, contact the Messel museum.

Messel is about 10km northeast of Darmstadt and is served by city trams 4 and 5 from Hauptbahnhof to Siemenstrasse

(direction Kranichstein), where the bus U to Messel-Oberach departs.

WIESBADEN

☎ 0611 / pop 276,000

The spa-town capital of Hesse, 40km west of Frankfurt and across the Rhine from Mainz, has a handful of historic attractions, green parks to calm the weariest of urban eyes and a century-old thermal bath.

Dostoevsky messed himself up badly here in the 1860s (where didn't he, though?) when he amassed huge debts at the city's gambling tables, inspiring – so they say – his masterpiece, *The Gambler*.

For information on Rüdesheim, along the Romantic Rhine, and nearby Koster Eberbach, see p511 and p511.

Orientation

From the Hauptbahnhof, walk 1km north on Bahnhofstrasse to get to the city centre. The main shopping precinct is around Langgasse and its southern continuation, Kirchgasse. The Neroberg is 2km northwest of the centre.

Information

Laundrette (Dotzheimer Strasse 96) Situated 1.2km west of the centre.

Network Launch (Luisenstrasse 17; internet access per hr €2; ☒ 10am-4am Mon-Sat, noon-2am Sun)

Planet Callnet (Wellritzstrasse 22; per hr €1; ☒ 10am-10pm) In the heart of a lively Turkish neighbourhood.

Post office (Kaiser-Friedrich-Ring 98) Facing the Hauptbahnhof. Has an ATM.

ReiseBank (☎ 743 19; Hauptbahnhof; ☒ 9am-6.30pm Mon-Sat, 9am-12.30pm & 1.30-5.30pm Sun, closed 12.30-1.30pm Wed & Fri) Currency exchange.

Tourist office (☎ 172 9930; www.wiesbaden.de; Marktplatz 1; ☒ 10am-6pm Mon-Fri, 9.45am-3pm Sat, 11am-3pm Sun Apr-Sep)

Sights & Activities

CITY CENTRE

A nice place to start exploring is **Schlossplatz**, where you'll find the **Marktbrunnen** (Löwen-brunnen; Market Fountain; 1537), the **Altes Rathaus** (Old Town Hall; 1610) and the **Neues Rathaus** (New Town Hall; 1884–87). The Protestant neo-Gothic **Marktkirche** (1852–62) has a **Glockenspiel** (carillon; ☒ rings at 9am, noon & 5pm) and hosts **organ concerts** (☒ 11.30am Sat year-round). On the north side is the neoclassical **Stadtschloss** (1840), built for Duke Wilhelm

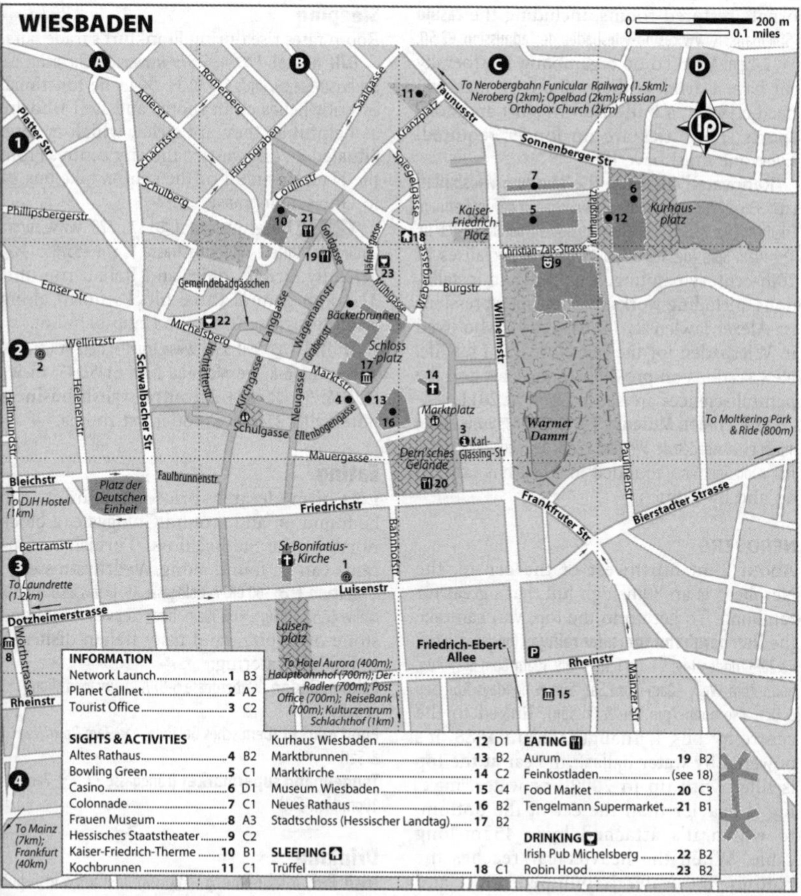
WIESBADEN
0 200 m
0 0.1 miles
A
B
C
D
1
2
3
4
To Nerobergbahn Funicular Railway (1.5km); Neroberg (2km); Opelbad (2km); Russian Orthodox Church (2km)
Platter Str
Adlerstr
Römerberg
Schachtstr
Hirschgraben
Saalgasse
Taunusstr
Kranzplatz
Sonnenberger Str
Schulberg
Coulinstr
Spiegelgasse
Phillipsbergerstr
Goldgasse
Häfnergasse
Kaiser-Friedrich-Platz
Kurhausplatz
Kurhaus-platz
Christian-Zais-Strasse
Gemeindebadgässchen
Emser Str
Mühlgasse
Webergasse
Burgstr
Bäckerbrunnen
Michelsberg
Langgasse
Wagemannstr
Grabenstr
Schloss-platz
Wilhelmstr
Wellritzstr
Schwalbacher Str
Hochstättenstr
Marktstr
Helenenstr
Hellmundstr
Kirchgasse
Neugasse
Ellenbogengasse
Marktplatz
Karl-Glässing-Str
Warmer Damm
To Moltkering Park & Ride (800m)
Schulgasse
Mauergasse
Dern'sches Gelände
Paulinenstr
Bleichstr
Faulbrunnenstr
Platz der Deutschen Einheit
Frankfruter Str
Bierstadter Strasse
To DJH Hostel (1km)
Friedrichstr
Bertramstr
St-Bonifatius-Kirche
Bahnhofstr
To Laundrette (1.2km)
Luisenstr
Dotzheimerstrasse
Luisen-platz
Wörthstrasse
Friedrich-Ebert-Allee
Rheinstr
Mainzer Str
To Hotel Aurora (400m); Hauptbahnhof (700m); Der Radler (700m); Post Office (700m); ReiseBank (700m); Kulturzentrum Schlachthof (1km)
To Mainz (7km); Frankfurt (40km)
INFORMATION
Network Launch 1 B3
Planet Callnet 2 A2
Tourist Office 3 C2
SIGHTS & ACTIVITIES
Altes Rathaus 4 B2
Bowling Green 5 C1
Casino 6 D1
Colonnade 7 C1
Frauen Museum 8 A3
Hessisches Staatstheater 9 C2
Kaiser-Friedrich-Therme 10 B1
Kochbrunnen 11 C1
Kurhaus Wiesbaden 12 D1
Marktbrunnen 13 B2
Marktkirche 14 C2
Museum Wiesbaden 15 C4
Neues Rathaus 16 B2
Stadtschloss (Hessischer Landtag) 17 B2
SLEEPING
Trüffel 18 C1
EATING
Aurum 19 B2
Feinkostladen (see 18)
Food Market 20 C3
Tengelmann Supermarket 21 B1
DRINKING
Irish Pub Michelsberg 22 B2
Robin Hood 23 B2

von Nassau and now the Hessischer Landtag (Hessian state parliament).

Built in 1913 as a municipal bathhouse on the site of a Roman steam bath, the gorgeous **Kaiser-Friedrich-Therme** (☎ 172 9660; Langgasse 38-40; 4hr €17.50; 🕑 10am-10pm Sat-Thu, 10am-midnight Fri) are fed by water naturally heated to 66.4°C. Ask for a sheet in English on 'bathing like the ancient Romans' by availing yourself of a succession of saunas and pools. Bathrobes and towels can be rented; swimsuits are unnecessary as, in keeping with *Saunakultur*, this place is 'textile-free'. Actually, bathing suits are completely forbidden only in the sauna (you just wear a towel); elsewhere, nudity is merely a recommendation. Tuesday is for women only. The minimum age is 16.

Want to actually taste the hot spa waters for which the city is known (indeed, named), said to have wonderful pharmacological powers? Head to the **Kochbrunnen** (Kranzplatz; 🕑 24hr) – inside the stone pavilion are four free-flowing spouts. A sign recommends drinking no more than 1L a day, though if you can down more than a mouthful you deserve a beer.

The neoclassical **Kurhaus Wiesbaden** (☎ 172 90; www.wiesbaden.de; Kurhausplatz 1; 🕑 24hr, closed during events), built in 1907, serves as the city's convention centre. On the plaza out front are the **Bowling Green** (a lawn for which locals have chosen a name that's as appropriate as it is English), a 129m-long **colonnade** and, opposite, the **Hessisches Staatstheater** (Hessian State Theatre). Pop inside to see some incredibly ornate restored rooms, including the **casino** (Spielbank; www.casino-wiesbaden.de; admission €2.50; ⊙ 2.45pm-4am). To do a gambling Dostoevsky (or have a drink at the casino bar), men will need a jacket, a button-down shirt and non-sports shoes; ties are no longer required. Everyone must have ID.

Renovated in 2006, the **Museum Wiesbaden** (☎ 335 2170; www.museum-wiesbaden.de, in German; Friedrich-Ebert-Allee 2; adult/child/student/family €5/2/3/10; ⊙ 10am-8pm Tue, 10am-5pm Wed-Sun) specialises in 20th-century painting, sculpture and installations, including works by Russian expressionist Alexei Jawlensky (1864–1941), who lived in Wiesbaden for the last 20 years of his life. New sections on pre-20th-century art and the natural sciences are set to open in 2011.

The **Frauen Museum** (☎ 308 1763; www.frauenmuseum-wiesbaden.de; Wörthstrasse 5; ⊙ noon-6pm Wed & Thu, noon-5pm Sun), founded in 1984, has exhibits on and by women.

NEROBERG

About 2km northwest of the centre, the Neroberg is an 80m-high hill that's great for rambling. To get up to the top, you can take the **Nerobergbahn funicular railway** (one-way/return €2.20/3, under 14yr €1.10/1.50; ⊙ 9.30am-8pm May-Aug, noon-7pm Wed, 10am-7pm Sat, Sun & holidays Apr, Sep & Oct, also noon-7pm Thu & Fri Sep), linked to the centre by bus 1. Inaugurated in 1888, it's powered by water ballast: the car at the top is filled with up to 7000L of water, making it heavier than the car at the bottom, to which it's attached by a 452m-long cable. When the heavier car reaches the bottom, the water is pumped out – and then pumped back up the hill. Elegant, ecological, ingenious!

Attractions up top include the **Opelbad** (adult/child 14-17yr €7/3; ⊙ 7am-8pm May-Sep), a Bauhaus-style outdoor swimming pool complex built in 1934, grassy expanses for sunbathing and one of the oldest vineyards in the area. The five-domed **Russian Orthodox Church** (Greek Chapel; adult/child €0.60/0.30; ⊙ 10am-5pm Apr-Oct, noon-4pm Sat, 10am-4pm Sun Nov-Mar) was built between 1847 and 1855.

Tours

The tourist office (p546) runs **walking tours** (adult/under 12yr €6.50/3.50; ⊙ 10am Sat). Free tours in German of the **Hessischer Landtag** (⊙ 3pm Sat) begin at the corner of the Stadtschloss facing the Marktbrunnen.

Sleeping

Room rates rise during Frankfurt's trade fairs.

DJH hostel (☎ 486 57; www.jugendherberge.de; Blücherstrasse 66; dm/s €19.50/33; ✗) The functional exterior belies clean rooms and staff who are as helpful as they are strict, which is very. Situated 1.2km west of the city centre. From the Hauptbahnhof or the centre, take bus 14 to Gneisenaustrasse.

ourpick Hotel Aurora (☎ 373 728; www.aurora-online.de; Untere Albrechtsstrasse 9; s/d €55/85; ✗) Friendly, bright, quiet and Italian-run, this 31-room gem is three blocks north along Bahnhofstrasse from the Hauptbahnhof.

Trüffel (☎ 990 550; www.trueffel.net, in German; Webergasse 6-8; s/d Mon-Thu from €115/145, Fri-Sun €90/115; ✗ 🖥 🖳) An ultra-stylish business hotel with 27 chic, modernist rooms.

Eating

Lots of moderately priced restaurants can be found on and around Goldgasse, a block north of the Stadtschloss. Turkish restaurants can be found along Wellritzstrasse.

Aurum (☎ 360 0877; Goldgasse 16; pizzas €5.50-10.50, mains €7.50-20.50; ⊙ 9.30am-1am) Serves very good stone-oven pizza and tasty Italian dishes.

For self-catering:

Feinkostladen (Webergasse 6-8) A luxury food shop and deli.

Food market (Dern'sches Gelände; ⊙ 7am-2pm Wed & Sat)

Tengelmann supermarket (Langgasse 32; ⊙ 7am-10pm Mon-Sat)

Drinking

Irish Pub Michelsberg (☎ 300 849; www.irish-pub-wiesbaden.de; Michelsberg 15; ⊙ 5pm-1am Sun-Thu, 5pm-2am Fri, 3pm-2am Sat) Verging on the grungy, this Irish-run establishment attracts an expat crowd. It has live music nightly from Wednesday to Saturday and karaoke at 9.30pm on Tuesday and Sunday.

Robin Hood (☎ 301 349; www.robin-wi.de, in German; Häfnergasse 3; ⊙ noon-1am Mon-Thu, noon-2am Fri & Sat, 3pm-1am Sun) It may not be stealing from the rich, but you'll certainly find a bunch of merry men in this hetero- and lesbian-friendly gay bar.

Kulturzentrum Schlachthof (☎ 974 450; www.schlachthof-wiesbaden.de, in German; Murnaustrasse 1) Live music, top-name DJs and a tumultuous program make this venue, one long block southeast of the train station, a draw for party animals.

Getting There & Around

S-Bahn trains link Wiesbaden with Frankfurt's Hauptbahnhof (€6.95, 50 minutes, every 15 minutes). S1 goes direct; S8 and S9 go via Frankfurt Airport; S8 also serves Mainz, a major rail hub. RE trains take just 34 minutes to Frankfurt.

Buses (www.eswe-verkehr.de, in German) linking the Hauptbahnhof with the city centre include 1, 4, 8, 14, 27 and 47. A single ticket costs €2.30 (€1.45 for up to three bus stops); a day pass for one/up to five people costs €5.60/8.40.

Bicycles can be rented from **Der Radler** (Hauptbahnhof; per hr/day €2/10, electric bikes €3/15; ☼ 7am-7pm Mon-Fri year-round, 8am-1pm Sat May-Sep), in an old blue rail car on what used to be track 11.

There's a Park & Ride on Moltkering, about 1.5km east of the Rathaus.

LAHN VALLEY

Hugely popular with cyclists, the majestic valley carved by the Lahn River (www.daslahntal.de, in German), which rises north of Marburg (right) and spills into the Rhine a bit south of Koblenz (p501), divides the Taunus hills (to the south) and the Westerwald hills (to the north). The 44km stretch between Weilburg and Limburg, known as the **Romantische Mittellahn** (Romantic Middle Lahn), is particularly alluring.

Virtually encircled by the river, the Altstadt section of **Weilburg** (www.weilburg.de, in German) – by car, follow the signs to 'Zentrum' – is dominated by the early-18th-century **Altes Rathaus** (Old City Hall; Marktplatz), painted burnt orange and cream, and the adjacent **Schloss** (☎ 06471-912 70; www.schloesser-hessen.de; adult/student/family €4/2.50/8; ☼ 10am-5pm Tue-Sun Mar-Oct, 10am-4pm Tue-Sun Nov-Feb), a sprawling rococo complex whose meticulously tended, 3.3-hectare **gardens** (☼ 8am-dusk) offer splendid and very romantic river views. Weilburg is home to Germany's only **ship tunnel**, a 195m-long structure built under the entrance to the Altstadt in 1847 as a short cut for river boats. This is a great place to embark on a trip downstream by canoe (☎ 06471-2277; www.dobi-trans.de, in German; Niedergasse 8, Weilburg; 1-/2-person kayak per day €18/23).

For details on the **Lahntal Radweg** (Lahn Valley Bike Path) and bike rental in the Marburg area, see p552. In Weilburg, bicycles can be rented at the **tourist office** (☎ 06471-314 67; Mauerstrasse; ☼ 9am-6pm Mon-Fr, 10am-noon Sat Apr-Oct, 10am-5pm Mon-Fri, 10am-noon Sat Nov-Mar).

A wing of Weilburg's Schloss has been turned into the **Schlosshotel Weilburg** (☎ 06471-509 00; www.schlosshotel-weilburg.de; Am Schloss, Langgasse 25; s/d from €63/94; (P) (X) (□) (☎)), with 50 comfortable rooms.

Weilburg is on a secondary rail line served by the Lahntalbahn, which links Koblenz with Limburg and Giessen (midway between Marburg and Frankfurt).

MARBURG

☎ 06421 / pop 79,000

Hilly, historic and humming at all hours, the university town of Marburg is some 90km north of Frankfurt. Narrow lanes wind through its vibrant Altstadt, which has a castle above it and a spectacular Gothic church below. Founded in 1527, Philipps-Universität – the world's oldest Protestant university – once counted the bookish Brothers Grimm among its students, of whom there are now 18,000. Thanks to them you'll find plenty of cafes and nightspots.

By an accident of history, this tranquil town has one of the world's grisliest haemorrhagic fevers named after it. In 1967 African green monkeys brought here from Uganda infected local lab workers with a close relative of the Ebola virus, and ever since the name 'Marburg virus' has been synonymous with 'bleeding from every orifice' and 'death'.

Orientation

The hilly Altstadt (Oberstadt, ie 'upper city'), situated west of Pilgrimstein and north of Universitätsstrasse, is centred on the Marktplatz. The area towers over the Unterstadt ('lower city'), whose centre is east of Pilgrimstein. The Hauptbahnhof is 1.5km northeast of the Altstadt. The Hauptbahnhof and Elisabethkirche are linked to the Altstadt by a cute, moderately sloping street known as Steinweg. The university is spread throughout the city.

Information

ATMs You'll find several around the Marburger Kunstverein.
Ch@rly's Internet TREFF (Pilgrimstein 29; per hr €3; ☼ 10am-1am Mon-Sat, noon-1am Sun)
Post office (Bahnhofstrasse 6)
Tourist information (☎ 991 20; www.marburg.de; Pilgrimstein 26; ☼ 9am-6pm Mon-Fri, 10am-2pm Sat) Has English brochures and sells events tickets.
Uni-Klinikum (☎ 283 697; Baldingerstrasse) The city's biggest hospital. Served by buses 7 and 16.

lonelyplanet.com

FAIRY-TALE ROAD

The 600km **Märchenstrasse** (www.deutsche-maerchenstrasse.de) is one of Germany's most popular tourist routes. It's made up of cities, towns and hamlets in four states (Hesse, Lower Saxony, North Rhine–Westphalia and Bremen), many of them associated with the works of Wilhelm and Jakob Grimm. Click on towns on the website's map for details. Public transport is designed for local commuting, so having a car is a big plus.

The Grimm brothers travelled extensively through central Germany in the early 19th century documenting folklore. Their collection of tales, *Kinder- und Hausmärchen*, was first published in 1812 and quickly gained international recognition. It includes such fairy-tale staples as *Hansel and Gretel*, *Cinderella*, *The Pied Piper*, *Rapunzel* and scores of others.

There are over 60 stops on the Fairy-Tale Road. Major ones include (from south to north): **Hanau**, about 15km east of Frankfurt, the birthplace of Jakob (1785–1863) and Wilhelm (1786–1859); **Steinau**, where the Grimm brothers spent their youth; **Marburg** (p549), in whose university the brothers studied for a short while; **Kassel** (p554), with a museum dedicated to the Grimms; **Göttingen** (p644), at whose university the brothers served as professors before being expelled in 1837 for their liberal views; **Bad Karlshafen** (p625), a meticulously planned white baroque village; **Bodenwerder**, whose rambling Münchhausen Museum is dedicated to the legendary Baron von Münchhausen, (in)famous for telling outrageous tales (see p625); **Hamelin** (Hameln; p623), forever associated with the legend of the Pied Piper; and **Bremen** (p663).

Universitätsbuchhandlung (☎ 170 90; Reitgasse 7-9) A bookshop with novels and Lonely Planet guides in English.

Sights

ELISABETHKIRCHE

Built between 1235 and 1283 (the twin spires were added later), the Protestant **Elisabethkirche** (www.elisabethkirche.de; adult/concession €2/1.50; ☉ 9am-6pm Apr-Sep, 10am-5pm Oct, 10am-6pm Dec, 10am-4pm Nov & Jan-Mar) is considered to be Germany's earliest pure-Gothic church. The highlight inside is the **Hohe Chor** (high choir), where you can see beautiful Gothic **stained glass** behind an astounding stone **Hochaltar** (high altar). The cathedral also houses the elegant **Elisabeth-Schrein** (Elisabeth Shrine), dedicated to St Elisabeth, whose burial here made the church a site of pilgrimage in the Middle Ages.

ALTSTADT

The focal point of the old city is the historic **Marktplatz**, elegantly adorned with a stone fountain; on the south side is the historic **Rathaus** (1512). From there it's a steep climb to the Lutheran **St-Marien-Kirche**, an imposing red-brick church with great views over the lower town. The terrace on the south side is the place to come at sunrise, particularly on weekends, when you'll often be joined by a motley crowd of students, late-night drinkers, early morning dog walkers and rough sleepers.

Perched at the highest point in town, a steep walk up from St-Marien-Kirche or the Marktplatz is the massive **Landgrafenschloss** (Landgraves' Castle; ☎ 282 5871; www.uni-marburg.de /uni-museum, in German; Schloss 1; adult/concession €4/2; ☉ 10am-6pm Tue-Sun Apr-Oct, until 4pm Nov-Mar), built between 1248 and 1300. It offers panoramic views of bucolic hills, jumbled Marburg rooftops and the **Schlosspark**, whose amphitheatre hosts concerts and open-air films. The **Universitätsmuseum für Kulturgeschichte** (University Cultural History Museum; incl in castle admission) inside the castle has exhibits on cultural history from prehistoric to modern times.

Eastward down the hill from the castle, in a half-hidden courtyard, you can see the excavated remains of a 13th- and 14th-century **synagogue** (Willy-Sage-Platz) under a giant glass cube.

UNTERSTADT

At the base of the Altstadt's Reitgasse are the **Universitätskirche** (early 1300s), a former Dominican monastery, and the neo-Gothic **Alte Universität** (1891), still a well-used and well-loved part of the university.

The **Universitätsmuseum für Bildende Kunst** (University Fine Arts Museum; ☎ 282 2355; www.uni-marburg .de/uni-museum; Biegenstrasse 11; adult/concession €4/2; ☉ 11am-1pm & 2-5pm Tue-Sun) focuses on artwork from the 20th century. The **Marburger Kunstverein** (☎ 258 82; www.marburger-kunstverein.de, in German; Biegenstrasse 1; ☉ 11am-5pm Tue, Thu-Sun, to 8pm Wed) puts on temporary exhibits of contemporary art.

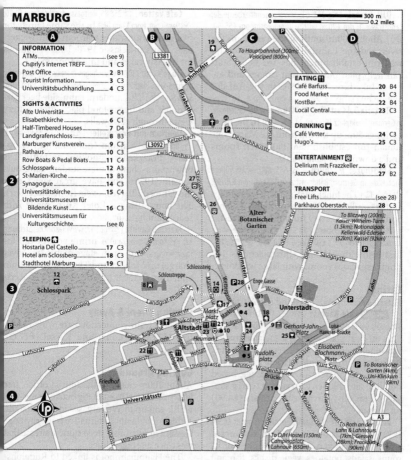

MARBURG

0 ——————— 300 m
0 ——————— 0.2 miles

INFORMATION
ATMs	(see 9)
Ch@rly's Internet TREFF	**1** C3
Post Office	**2** B1
Tourist Information	**3** C3
Universitätsbuchhandlung	**4** C3

SIGHTS & ACTIVITIES
Alte Universität	**5** C4
Elisabethkirche	**6** C1
Half-Timbered Houses	**7** D4
Landgrafenschloss	**8** B3
Marburger Kunstverein	**9** C3
Rathaus	**10** C3
Row Boats & Pedal Boats	**11** C4
Schlosspark	**12** A3
St-Marien-Kirche	**13** B3
Synagogue	**14** C3
Universitätskirche	**15** C4
Universitätsmuseum für Bildende Kunst	**16** C3
Universitätsmuseum für Kulturgeschichte	(see 8)

SLEEPING
Hostaria Del Castello	**17** C3
Hotel am Sclossberg	**18** C3
Stadthotel Marburg	**19** C1

EATING
Café Barfuss	**20** B4
Food Market	**21** C3
KostBar	**22** B4
Local Central	**23** C3

DRINKING
Café Vetter	**24** C3
Hugo's	**25** C3

ENTERTAINMENT
Delirium mit Frazzkeller	**26** C2
Jazzclub Cavete	**27** B2

TRANSPORT
Free Lifts	(see 28)
Parkhaus Oberstadt	**28** C3

Row boats and **pedal boats** (per hr €8) can be hired on the east bank of the Lahn, just south of Weidenhäuser Brücke. Nearby Weidenhäuser Strasse, in the heart of the oldest part of town (parts date from the 1400s), has some **half-timbered houses**.

The **Alter Botanischer Garten** (Old Botanical Garden), 300m north of the tourist office, is now a grassy public park. The university's new **Botanischer Garten** (☎ 282 1508; Karl-von-Frisch-Strasse; ◷ 9am-6.30pm Apr-Oct, 9am-3.30pm Nov-Mar), 4km from the centre near the Uni-Klinikum (university hospital), is served by buses 7 and 16.

East of the Lahn, you can walk up Blitzweg (served by bus 8) and a forest trail to the 36m sandstone **Kaiser-Wilhelm-Turm** (Spiegelslustturm; ◷ interior accessible 2-6pm except Tue Mar-Oct, 2-5pm except Tue Nov-Feb, weather permitting), an outlook tower erected on Marburg's highest point in 1890. Thanks to a 'Lichtkunstprojekt' (light-art-project) inaugurated in 2007, at night you can turn a romantic neon heart on the exterior, visible all over town, by phoning ☎ 09005-771 207 (costs per minute €0.49 from a landline, €0.79 to €2 from a mobile; proceeds go to charity). The phone number and the artwork's name, *Siebensiebenzwölfnullsieben*, refer to St Elisabeth's birthday on 7 July 1207.

Sleeping

The tourist office books **Privatzimmer** (private rooms; €20-40) for no charge.

HESSE

DJH hostel (☎ 234 61; www.jugendherberge.de; Jahnstrasse 1; dm €20, d with/without bathroom €55/50; ✗) About 500m south of the centre on the river and the Lahntal Radweg, this clean, well-run establishment has 163 beds. Staff can help plan outings, rent canoes and arrange bike hire. Take bus C to the Auf der Weide bus stop.

Hostaria Del Castello (☎ 243 02; www.del-castello.de, in German; Marktplatz 19; s €49-74, d €69-95) In the thick of things 50m up the hill from the Markt, this Italian-run establishment has seven rooms and a downstairs restaurant.

Stadthotel Marburg (☎ 685 880; www.village -hotels.de, in German; Bahnhofstrasse 14; s/d from €79/99; P ✗ 💻) The functional, modern furnishings at this family-run place are pleasant, if bland. Some rooms are away from the busy street.

Hotel am Schlossberg (☎ 9180; www.welcome-hotels .com; Pilgrimstein 29; s €90-110, d €110-130; P ✗ ✗) Just below the Altstadt, this place has 147 bright, spacious rooms with large windows.

Eating

Eateries are sprinkled around the Altstadt.

our pick **Café Barfuss** (☎ 253 49; Barfüsserstrasse 33; meals €4.90-6.20; 🕑 11am-1am, from 10am Sat; 🕸) This off-beat place attracts a sociable student crowd and serves up good vegetarian dishes, including *Kartoffelpuffer* (fried mashed potatoes) and *Spätzle* (a type of egg-based noodle), and a killer *Currywurst* (curry sausage). Has all-you-can-eat specials (€4.90) on Monday.

kostBar (☎ 161 170; Barfüsserstrasse 7; mains €6.90-15.90; 🕑 10am-1am) This modern restaurant and bar charges very reasonable prices for its soups, salads, potatoes, vegie dishes, fish and meat, all concocted from a creative blend of ingredients. Organic breakfasts are served until 3pm.

Local Central (☎ 253 90; Marktplatz 11; mains €6.90-16.90; 🕑 9.30am-midnight or later) The service here is young and friendly, the rump steak is especially delicious, and the room warbles with the sounds of lively conversation – a comfortable favourite for locals of all ages. Drinks include five beers on tap.

For self-catering, there's a **food market** (🕑 to 2pm Wed & Sat) on Marktplatz.

Drinking & Entertainment

For listings look no further than the free *Marburger Magazin Express* (www.marbuch -verlag.de, in German).

Café Vetter (☎ 258 88; Reitgasse 4; cakes from €1.70; 🕑 9am-6pm, from 11am Tue) In the same family for five generations, this tearoom with wicker-back chairs and classic 1970s lamps is famous for its tasty cakes and fine panoramas.

Hugo's (☎ 130 00; www.hugos-marburg.de, in German; Gerhard-Jahn-Platz 21a; 🕑 9am-midnight or 1am, from 10am Sat & Sun; 🕸) This modern, Lahn-side beer garden, bar and finger-food place offers watery views through glass walls.

Delirium mit Frazzkeller (☎ 649 19; Steinweg 3; 🕑 8pm-3am) Delirium (nonsmoking) is upstairs, Frazzkeller (smoking permitted) is downstairs – both of these student hang-outs scream '1970s' and have great views over the Unterstadt (yes, even from the cellar). The house drink is Roter Korn, made with redcurrant liqueur.

Jazzclub Cavete (☎ 661 57; www.jazzini.de; Steinweg 12; 🕑 8pm-1am or 2am) A prime port of call for jazz lovers, with open-stage nights (no cover charge) on Monday and Thursday from 9pm and, from October to June, frequent concerts (€10 to €20).

Getting There & Away

The best train connections are with Frankfurt (€21, one hour) and Kassel (€17.60, 1¼ hours).

Getting Around

About 100m north of the tourist office, **free lifts** (inside Parkhaus Oberstadt, Pilgrimstein; 🕑 6am-2am) whisk you up to Wettergasse in the Altstadt. A thigh-toughening alternative is nearby Enge Gasse, a monstrously steep stone staircase that was once a sewage sluice.

The Hauptbahnhof is linked to Rudolphsplatz (where Pilgrimstein meets Universitätsstrasse) by various bus lines, including 1, 2, 5, 6 and 7.

The 245km Lahntal Radweg runs along the Lahn all the way to the Rhine. Bicycles can be rented inside **Parkhaus Oberstadt** (☎ 205 155; Pilgrimstein & Wettergasse; per day Fri-Sun bicycle/tandem €7.50/16, Mon-Thu €6/13; 🕑 6am-2am) – go to the parking garage's glass-enclosed office on the 14th floor.

Velociped (☎ 245 11; www.velociped.de; Alte Kasseler Strasse 43), 400m north of the Hauptbahnhof, organises individual and guided cycling tours and hires out bicycles. About 7km south of Marburg, **Lahntours** (☎ 06426-928 00; www.lahntours .de, in German; Lahntalstrasse 45, Roth an der Lahn) arranges cycling and canoe trips.

NATIONALPARK KELLERWALD-EDERSEE

Hesse's first **national park** (www.nationalpark -kellerwald-edersee.de), established in 2004, encompasses one of the largest extant red beech forests in Central Europe, the **Kellerwald**, and the **Edersee**, a serpentine artificial reservoir 55km northeast of Marburg and about the same distance southwest of Kassel. Some 400 springs feed creeks that, as one brochure puts it, are 'a true paradise for the fire salamander'. Larger land animals include red deer; overhead you may see eagles and honey buzzards and, at night, various species of bat.

For information and insights into the area's ecosystems, head to the new **NationalparkZentrum** (☎ 05635-992 781; www.nationalparkzentrum-kellerwald .de, in German; B252, Vöhl-Herzhausen; ☻ 9am-6pm Apr-Oct, 10am-5pm Nov-Mar), a striking modern visitors centre at the western end of the Edersee, on the northern edge of Kirchlotheim.

A favourite family vacation spot, the national park's lush forests and flowery meadows offer excellent hiking. Hiking trails include the **Kellerwaldsteig** (marked 'K') and the **Urwaldsteig-Edersee** (marked 'UE'). Shorter hiking circuits are marked with animal or plant icons. The lake has swimming, canoeing and sailing.

The park is easiest to visit if you've got your own wheels but public transport (www .nvv.de, in German) is also an option. Buses lead into the park from the train stations in Bad Wildungen, Frankenberg and Korbach (linked to Kassel by the R4). Bus 555 (runs every hour or two Monday to Friday, six times on Saturday, two or three times on Sunday and holidays) links the NationalparkZentrum with both Frankenberg and Korbach. Bus 521 goes from Bad Wildungen to the Edersee.

FULDA

☎ 0661 / pop 64,000

Graced with elegant flower gardens and some transcendent baroque architecture, Fulda – founded as a Benedictine monastery in 744 – also has some good-value hotels, making it ideal for a romantic break that will leave you baroque but not broke.

During the Cold War, the famous 'Fulda Gap', the lowland area running northeast from Frankfurt via Fulda to the East German town of Eisenach, was seen by both sides as a potential Warsaw Pact invasion route. As a result, significant numbers of American troops were stationed in the area until the early 1990s.

Orientation & Information

The north–south Pauluspromenade separates the Stadtschloss and its gardens, to the east, from the Dom and Michaelskirche, to the west. The tourist office is at the southern end of Pauluspromenade; the attractive, pedestrianised Altstadt is a block further south. The Hauptbahnhof is about 600m east of the centre, at the northeastern end of Bahnhofstrasse.

ATMs There are several at the bottom of Bahnhofstrasse.

Tourist information (☎ 102 1813; www.tourismus -fulda.de; Bonifatiusplatz 1; ☻ 9.30am-6pm Mon-Fri, 9.30am-4pm Sat & Sun)

Sights

Across the street from the tourist office, the **Stadtschloss** (Town Castle; ☎ 102 1469) was built from 1706 to 1721 as the residence of Fulda's prince-abbots. It now houses the city administration and function rooms. Worth visiting are the ornate **Historische Räume** (historic rooms; adult/student €3/2; ☻ 10am-6pm, closed to 2pm Fri), which is a grandiose banquet hall. It's possible to climb the octagonal **Schlossturm** (tower; ☻ Apr-Oct) for great views of the town and the baroque and English-style **Schlossgarten** (palace gardens), where locals play *pétanque* (boules) and sunbathe in summer. On its northern edge are the baroque **Floravase** sculpture and the neoclassical **Orangerie** (now occupied by the Maritim Hotel).

Inside the baroque **Dom** (cathedral; ☻ 7am-6pm Mon-Sat, 7am-7.30pm Sun Apr-Oct, 7am-5pm Mon-Sat, 10.30am-7.30pm Sun Nov-Mar), built from 1704 to 1712, you'll find gilded furnishings, plenty of putti (figures of infant boys), some dramatic statues (eg to the left of the altar) and the tomb of St Boniface, who died a martyr in 754. There are **organ recitals** (www.orgelmusik.bistum-fulda.de, in German; adult/concession €3.50/2.50) here at noon every Saturday during May, June, September, October and December.

Treasures in the **Dommuseum** (Cathedral Museum; ☎ 872 07; adult/student €2.10/1.30; ☻ 10am-5.30pm Tue-Sat, 12.30-5.30pm Sun & holidays Apr-Oct, 10am-12.30pm & 1.30-4pm Tue-Sat, 12.30-4pm Sun Nov-Mar, closed mid-Jan–mid-Feb), reached through a delightful garden, include the spectacular Silver Altar and a spooky object reported to be part of the skull of St Boniface.

A short walk north is the chapel-sized **Michaelskirche** (☻ 10am-6pm Apr-Oct, 10am-noon & 2-5pm Nov-Mar), easy to spot thanks to its round witch's-hat tower. The rotunda and crypt are 9th-century Carolingian.

HESSE

Sleeping & Eating

Traditional eating options can be found in the Altstadt.

DJH hostel (☎ 733 89; www.jugendherberge.de; Schirrmannstrasse 31; dm from €21; ✗) Clean and friendly, this 45-room hostel is 3.5km southwest of the centre. Take bus 3 to the Stadion stop.

ourpick Wiesenmühle (☎ 928 680; www.wiesenmuehle .de, in German; Wiesenmühlenstrasse 13; s/d/tr €60/89/105; ✌ beer garden 10.30am-1am, restaurant 11am-2.30pm & 5.30-11pm) Four blocks down the hill (southwest) of the Stadtschloss on the banks of the Fulda, this one-time mill has a hugely popular beer garden, 26 hotel rooms, a working wooden waterwheel and two shiny copper vats for brewing Hell, Dunkel, Bock and Weizen beers.

Hotel Peterchens Mondfahrt (☎ 902 350; www.hotel-peterchens-mondfahrt.de; Rabanusstrasse 7, 4th fl; s/d/tr/q from €64/93/113/128, €10 less Sat & Sun; P ✗ 🖥 🖳) Facing the northeast corner of the Schloss and the new bus station, this bright, friendly hotel has 50 spacious rooms with big windows.

ourpick Hotel Goldener Karpfen (☎ 868 00; www .hotel-goldener-karpfen.com; Simpliziusbrunnen 1; s €95-155, d €130-230, ste €250-450; P ✗ 🖥 🖳) Great for a romantic getaway, the elegant, 60-room 'Golden Carp' playfully blends old and new, with creatively themed Designer rooms and more traditional Romantic rooms. The elegant restaurant (mains €10.50 to €28, open 11am to 10pm) is an excellent option for upmarket regional specialities.

For self-catering, try **Aldi Süd supermarket** (Bahnhofstrasse 17; ✌ 7.30am-8pm Mon-Sat), one block southwest of the train station.

Getting There & Around

Regular (but not all) ICEs plying the main north–south and Frankfurt–Erfurt lines link Fulda with Frankfurt (€29, one hour, hourly) and Kassel (€29, 30 minutes).

Bike path options are signposted down by the river. **Hahner Zweiradtechnik** (☎ 933 9944; www .hahner-zweirad.de, in German; Beethovenstrasse 3; ✌ 9am-6pm Mon-Fri, 9am-1pm Sat) rents out bicycles.

AROUND FULDA

The agricultural area northwest of Fulda, through which Soviet tanks rolled in serried ranks in countless NATO war-game scenarios, is quiet these days (as it was throughout the Cold War). The 245km **BahnRadweg Hessen**, a section of which is known as the **Vulkanradweg** (www.vulkanradweg.de), is a loopy bike path that follows old rail lines from Bad Hersfeld to Fulda and Schlitz and then southwest to Hanau.

The attractive village of **Schlitz**, 20km northwest of Fulda, has an **Altstadt** with just two gates, an 18th-century stone **Rathaus**, an austere Protestant **church** with colourful haut-relief panels behind the altar, and a 36m-high tower, the 14th-century **Hinterturm** (lift adult/child €1/0.50). The latter is turned into the 'world's largest candle' during the annual Christmas market. The **Marktplatz**, on the slope below the church, is surrounded by half-timbered houses. You can stay in the old town's cycle-friendly **Hotel Vorderburg** (☎ 06642-963 00; www.hotel -vorderburg.de, in German; s/d from €45/70).

Those who like hang-gliding, skiing or rock climbing will enjoy the beautiful **Rhön nature park** and its highest mountain, the **Wasserkuppe** (950m), east of Fulda.

KASSEL

☎ 0561 / pop 194,000

Postwar reconstruction left Kassel, on the Fulda River two hours north of Frankfurt, with lots of particularly unattractive 1950s buildings. Still, visitors will find a glorious baroque park and some surprisingly interesting museums, including one dedicated to death and another to the Brothers Grimm.

The Hessian mercenaries who fought for King George III in the American Revolution came from Kassel. Because of them, 'Hessian' became a household word, though not a title of honour, in the United States', as one 19th-century American historian put it.

Every five years Kassel hosts **documenta** (www.documenta.de), one of Europe's most important contemporary art exhibitions, which lasts 100 days. The next one will be held from 9 June to 16 September 2012.

Orientation

Kassel has two main train stations. Kassel Hauptbahnhof, on the northwest edge of the city centre, is served by regional (RE) trains, while the more important Kassel-Wilhelmshöhe (Fernbahnhof), 3km west of the centre, handles both regional and IC/ICE trains.

The focal point of the city centre's pedestrianised shopping precinct is fountain-adorned Königsplatz, from where Obere Königsstrasse runs southwest past Friedrichsplatz and the Rathaus (site of one of the tourist offices).

Wilhelmshöhe and its attractions are at the western end of 4.5km-long Wilhelmshöher Allee, which runs straight as an arrow from the centre westward to the Schloss.

Information

ATMs There are several at Königsplatz.

Call International (Untere Königsstrasse 72, 1st fl; per hr €1; 9am-midnight) Internet access just northwest of the city centre's pedestrian zone.

Kassel Card (1 or 2 people for 24hr/72hr €13/16, 4 people €18/24) Gets you discounts on attractions and free use of public transport. Sold only at the tourist office. An excellent deal.

Kassel Tourist Kassel-Wilhelmshöhe train station (340 54; www.kassel-tourist.de; 9am-6pm Mon-Fri, 9am-1pm Sat); Rathaus (707 707; Obere Königsstrasse 8; 9am-6pm Mon-Fri, 9am-2pm Sat) Tourist information office.

Post office (Untere Königsstrasse 95)

Wasch-Treff (Friedrich-Ebert-Strasse 81; 5am-midnight except Sun & holidays) Laundrette 1km west of the centre. Served by trams 4 and 8 (Querallee stop).

Sights

CITY-CENTRE MUSEUMS

Between the documenta exhibitions, **Museum Fridericianum** (707 2720; www.fridericianum-kassel.de; Friedrichsplatz 18) and, southeast across Friedrichsplatz, the striking **documenta Halle** (707 270; www.documentahalle.de, in German; Du-Ry-Strasse 1) host changing exhibitions of contemporary art.

Two long blocks southwest, the **Neue Galerie** (3168 0400; www.museum-kassel.de; Schöne Aussicht 1) showcases paintings and sculptures by German artists from 1750 to the present, as well as exhibits from past documenta exhibitions. Closed for repairs until late 2011.

Wilhelm and Jakob Grimm began compiling folk stories while living in Kassel. Their lives and stories, now available in almost 200 languages, are featured at the **Brüder Grimm-Museum** (Museum of the Brothers Grimm; 103 235; www.grimms.de; Schöne Aussicht 2; adult/student €1.50/1; 10am-5pm, to 8pm Wed), across the street from the Neue Galerie.

Billed as 'a meditative space for funerary art', the **Museum für Sepulkralkultur** (Museum of Sepulchral Culture; 918 930; www.sepulkralmuseum.de, in German; Weinbergstrasse 25-27; adult/child €5/3.50; 10am-5pm Tue & Thu-Sun, 10am-8pm Wed) is intended to bury the taboo on discussing death. The permanent collection includes headstones, hearses, dancing skeleton bookends and sculptures depicting death. Situated 300m west of the Neue Galerie, near trams 1 and 3 (Weigelstrasse stop).

WILHELMSHÖHE

Seven kilometres west of the centre, in the enchanting **Habichtswald** (Hawk Forest nature park), is the baroque, early-18th-century **Schlosspark Wilhelmshöhe** (316 800; www.museum-kassel.de, in German), a highlight of any visit to Kassel. You can spend an entire day here walking through the forest, enjoying a romantic picnic and exploring the castles, fountains, grottoes, a spectacular cascade and the city's symbol, a massive statue of Herkules atop a towering stone pyramid atop an octagonal amphitheatre atop an imposing hill. Until reunification, the hills here formed the border with the GDR.

Show a same-day entry ticket from one Wilhelmshöhe site at any other and you'll get a 25% discount.

Herkules

The 8.25m-high copper **Hercules statue** (312 456; adult/under 18yr/student €3/free/2; 10am-5pm Tue-Sun mid-Mar–mid-Nov), 600m above sea level, was erected between 1707 and 1717 as a symbol of regional power. From the top of the pyramid (which was set to reopen in late 2009), there's an unbelievable view in all directions, though fine views towards Kassel can also be had from the balconies on the west side of the statue's base. At the bottom you can see Schloss Wilhelmshöhe and, to its southwest, Löwenburg.

To get up here, take tram 3 to the Druseltal terminus and then bus 22 (runs once or twice an hour from 8am to 7pm or 8pm) to the Herkules stop.

Schloss Wilhelmshöhe

Home to Elector Wilhelm and later Kaiser Wilhelm II, this palace (1786–98) at the foot of the Wilhelmshöhe houses the **Gemäldegalerie Alte Meister** (Old Masters Gallery; 316 800; adult/under 18yr/student €6/free/2; 10am-5pm Tue-Sun). It has one of Germany's best collections (especially of Flemish and Dutch baroque painting), featuring works by Rembrandt, Rubens, Jordaens, Lucas Cranach the Elder, Dürer and many others. The **Antikensammlung** showcases Egyptian, Etruscan, Greek and Roman statuary and vases. In 1870, during the Franco-Prussian War, the French emperor Napoleon III was held here as a prisoner of war.

The 23 rooms of the **Weissensteinflügel** (316 800; adult/student €4/2; tours hourly 10am-4pm Tue-Sun, to 3pm Nov-Feb), which dates from 1790, are filled with original furnishings and paintings.

HESSE

To reach Schloss Wilhelmshöhe, you can either walk down from Herkules or, from the city, take tram 1 to the Wilhelmshöhe terminus. From there it's a short walk, or you can take bus 23 for one stop.

Schloss Löwenburg

Modelled on a medieval Scottish castle, tours of the **'Lions' Castle'** (☎ 316 800; adult/student €4/2; ⏱ tours hourly 10am-4pm Tue-Sun, to 3pm Nov-Feb) take in the Rüstkammer (Museum of Armaments) and Ritterzeitsmuseum (Museum of Chivalry). Situated less than 1km southwest (across the park) from Schloss Wilhelmshöhe, it is served by bus 23.

Fountains

Thanks to a 12km network of surface and subterranean channels, Wilhelmshöhe's gravity-powered, one-hour **Wasserspiele** (fountain show; admission free) takes place every Wednesday, Sunday and public holiday from May to 3 October. The water begins its tumble at 2.30pm from up top, near Herkules. From there you can walk down via the **Teufelsbrücke** (Devil's Bridge; 3.10pm) and the **Aquädukt** (3.20pm) to the **Grosse Fontäne** (Large Fountain; 3.30pm) to watch the water emerge in a 50m-high jet.

Sleeping

The tourist office books private rooms from around €25.

DJH hostel (☎ 776 455; www.jugendherberge.de; Schenkendorfstrasse 18; dm/s €21.20/31.20; P ☒ ☐) Has a leafy location, games in the basement and 209 beds, most with hall bathrooms. Situated about 1km west of Kassel Hauptbahnhof, or take tram 4 or 8 to Querallee.

Hotel Garni Kö 78 (☎ 716 14; www.koe78.de; Kölnische Strasse 78; s €34-48, d €69-78) Built in the 1890s, this clean, friendly place has a peaceful back garden and 24 rooms with practical furnishings. Situated about 500m west of Kassel Hauptbahnhof; from Kassel-Wilhelmshöhe take bus 52.

Hotel Domus (☎ 703 330; www.markhoteldomus.de; Erzbergerstrasse 1-5; s €49-99, d €59-109; P ☒) Beyond the Jugendstil foyer – with domed atrium, bar and billiard table – are 56 bright rooms with period-inspired furniture. Prices are without breakfast but do include an evening buffet dinner from Monday to Thursday. Situated one block northeast of Kassel Hauptbahnhof. There are two other hotels on the same block.

Arosa Hotel (☎ 7662 0590; www.arosa-hotel-kassel.de in German; Wilhelmshöher Allee 38; s/d €90/125) Opened in 2009, this place has a marble-floored lift and 27 rooms with large windows and curvaceous, wooden furniture. Situated 1.2km southwest of Kassel Hauptbahnhof; served by trams 1 and 3.

Eating & Drinking

The free monthly *Frizz* (www.frizz-kassel.de in German) has listings.

Lohmann (☎ 701 6875; www.lohmann-kassel.de, in German; Königstor 8; mains €5.50-15.70; ⏱ 11am-midnight or 1am Sun-Fri, from 4pm Sat) With roots that go back to 1888, this family-run *Kneipe* (pub) has an old-style birch- and maple-shaded beer garden with an outdoor grill. A great place for veal schnitzel and locally brewed Kasseler Premium Pils. Situated five blocks southwest of Kassel Hauptbahnhof.

Bolero (☎ 766 2242; www.bolerobar.de; Schöne Aussicht 1a; mains €7.90-22.90; ⏱ 10am-midnight Mon-Fri, 9am-1am Sat & Sun) A sleek, modern restaurant and bar serving tapas, meat and 'world food' – and lots of cocktails. Draws a trendy, upscale crowd. Situated behind the Neue Galerie.

Cafe-Bar Suspekt (☎ 104 522; Fünffensterstrasse 14; ⏱ 6pm-1am Tue-Thu, 1pm-2am Fri & Sat, 1pm-1am Sun) This hetero-friendly gay bar, painted in primary colours, has hip marble tables and mellow music. Situated five blocks south of Kassel Hauptbahnhof, at the southwestern edge of the pedestrian zone.

Getting There & Away

Rail destinations from Kassel Hauptbahnhof and/or Kassel-Wilhelmshöhe (Fernbahnhof) include Fulda (RE/ICE €19.20/29, 84/30 minutes), Marburg (€17.60, 1¼ hours) and Frankfurt am Main (RE/ICE €30.70/48, 125/80 minutes).

Getting Around

Tram 1 runs the length of Wilhelmshöher Allee, linking the city centre with Wilhelmshöhe. Trams 1, 3 and 4 go from Kassel-Wilhelmshöhe train station to the centre. Almost all the city's tram lines stop at Königsplatz.

You can rent city and trekking bikes and buy bike maps from **Fahrradhof** (☎ 313 083; www.fahrradhof.de, in German; per 24hr/week €10/40; ⏱ 9am-1pm & 2-6.30pm Mon-Fri year-round, 9am-3pm Sat Apr-Oct, 9am-1pm Sat Nov-Mar), on the east side of Kassel-Wilhelmshöhe train station just past track 11.

North Rhine–Westphalia

With a population greater than that of Austria and Switzerland combined, North Rhine–Westphalia feels almost like a country unto itself. Cobbled together in 1946 by the Allies from two Prussian provinces and a little fiefdom called Lippe-Detmold, it harbours within its boundaries flat, windswept expanses and forested hills high enough to hold onto snow during winter. Villages sweetly lost in time contrast with frenzied metropolises habitually on fast forward. There are places whose looks have remained largely unchanged since the Middle Ages and others fashioned completely from scratch in the wake of WWII. And through it all carves the muscular Rhine, fed by tributaries such as the Ruhr that gave an entire region its name.

The industrial age shaped North Rhine–Westphalia more than any other German region. For a hundred years, coal and steel fuelled the growth of Germany into one of Europe's most powerful nations. But starting in the mid-1960s, lower demand forced the region to focus its energies elsewhere. And so it did, banking instead on high-tech, media, retail and culture.

Must-sees include Cologne with its lofty Dom (cathedral), Bonn with its Beethoven legacy and fabulous museums, the Unesco-listed baroque palaces in Brühl, and Charlemagne's imperial capital of Aachen. The lively Ruhrgebiet and placid Lower Rhine are best for off-beat experiences. There are historical cities such as Münster, where the treaty that ended the Thirty Years' War was signed, and elegant ones such as Düsseldorf, the state capital. Paderborn and Soest are treasured for their churches and the Sauerland is the place to get your nature fix.

HIGHLIGHTS

- **Sucker for Soccer** Find out why football is a religion in the Ruhrgebiet when attending a Schalke 04 match in Gelsenkirchen (p599) or Borussia Dortmund game in Dortmund (p596)
- **Heavenly Heights** Feel your spirit soar when faced with the majestic loftiness of Cologne's Dom (cathedral; p569)
- **Regal Reception** Go behind the scenes of life at court on a tour of Schloss Augustus-burg (p579) in Brühl
- **Miraculous Metamorphosis** See urban planning in the making at Cologne's Rheinauhafen (p572)
- **Mine Madness** Experience a 21st-century spin on the industrial age at the Zeche Zollverein coal mine in Essen (p591)
- **Avant-Garde Art** Have your mind blown by cutting-edge exhibits in an old gas storage tower in Oberhausen (p597)

- POPULATION: 18 MILLION
- AREA: 34,080 SQ KM

NORTH RHINE–WESTPHALIA

NORTH RHINE–WESTPHALIA

Getting Around

There are several deals available for getting around North Rhine–Westphalia by public transport. The **SchönerTagTicket** buys one day of unlimited travel within the state from 9am to 3am the following day (midnight to 3am the next day on weekends). You can only use RE, RB and S-Bahn trains as well as buses, U-Bahn and trams. The ticket costs €25 for single travellers and €34 for groups of up to five people. There's also the **SchöneFahrtTicket** (€16), which gives you two hours to make a one-way trip to anywhere within North Rhine–Westphalia. Tickets are available at vending machines; if purchased from the ticket office, a €2 surcharge applies.

THE RHINELAND

DÜSSELDORF

☎ 0211 / pop 585,000

Düsseldorf, the state capital, dazzles with boundary-pushing architecture, zinging nightlife and an art scene to rival many large cities. It's a posh and modern city that seems all buttoned-up business at first glance: banking, advertising, fashion and telecommunications are among the fields that have made Düsseldorf one of Germany's wealthiest cities. Yet all it takes is a few hours of bar-hopping around the Altstadt (old town), the historical quarter along the Rhine, to realise that locals have no problem letting their hair down once they shed those Armani jackets.

The Altstadt may still be the 'longest bar in the world' but in recent times it's been getting competition from the Medienhafen, a redeveloped harbour area and a feast of international avant-garde architecture. Older neighbourhoods are changing too. Case in point: Flingern, which has gone from drab to fab in recent years and is developing a multifaceted arty boho scene. Highbrow types, meanwhile, can get more than their fill at the city's many world-class art museums and such venues as the renowned opera house, theatre and orchestra hall.

Orientation

The airport is about 7km north of the Altstadt; see p565 for details about getting into town. The Hauptbahnhof (main train station) is on the southeastern edge of the city centre. From here it's about a 20-minute walk along Bismarckstrasse and Blumenstrasse to the Königsallee, with the Altstadt just beyond. Alternatively, any U-Bahn from the Hauptbahnhof to Heinrich-Heine-Allee will put you right in the thick of things.

Information

BOOKSHOPS & INTERNET ACCESS
Buchhaus Stern-Verlag (☎ 388 10; Friedrichstrasse 24-26; per 15min €1; ⏰ 9.30am-8pm Mon-Sat) Awesome bookshop with huge international selection, a cafe and internet access.

DISCOUNT CARDS
Düsseldorf Welcome Card (per 24/48/72hr €9/14/19, group €18/28/38) Available at the tourist offices, hotels and public transport service points, this card buys unlimited public transport and free or discounted tickets for museums, tours and cultural events.

EMERGENCY
After-hours medical emergencies (☎ 192 92)
Dental emergencies (☎ 666 291)
Municipal Lost & Found (☎ 899 3285)

MONEY
ReiseBank (☎ 364 878; Hauptbahnhof; ⏰ 7am-10pm Mon-Sat, 8am-9pm Sun)

POST
Post office (Konrad-Adenauer-Platz 1; ⏰ 8am-8pm Mon-Fri, 8am-2pm Sat)

TOURIST INFORMATION
Staff stick around longer when big trade shows are in town. For pre-trip planning, go to www.duesseldorf-tourismus.de.
Tourist office Altstadt (☎ 1720 2840; cnr Marktstrasse & Rheinstrasse; ⏰ 10am-6pm)
Tourist office Hauptbahnhof (☎ 1720 2844; Immermannstrasse 65b; ⏰ 9.30am-6.30pm Mon-Sat)

Sights
ALTSTADT
Düsseldorf's Altstadt, a mostly pedestrianised web of lanes cuddling up to the Rhine, is rightly (in)famous for its raucous nightlife. Fortunately, it also brims with charming and quiet corners, a smattering of museums and historical sights, plus good shopping to boot.

At its centre is the historic Marktplatz, framed by the Renaissance **Rathaus** (town hall; 1573) and accented by an equestrian **statue of Jan Wellem**. The art-loving elector lies buried nearby in the late baroque **Andreaskirche** (Andreasstrasse 27; ⏰ 7.30am-6pm), which is drenched in fanciful white stucco. Six baroque saint-sculptures from the original altar were recently integrated into the sanctuary. More church art awaits in the new treasury in the upstairs gallery. A great time to visit is for the free organ concert at 4.30pm on Sundays.

A few steps west is the memorial **Mahn-und Gedenkstätte für die Opfer des Nationalsozialismus** (Memorial Exhibit to the Victims of the Nazi Regime; ☎ 899 6205; Mühlenstrasse 29; admission free; ⏰ 11am-5pm Tue-Fri & Sun, 1-5pm Sat), with an important but academic exhibit on local persecution and resistance during the Third Reich. Leaflets in English may be borrowed at no charge.

North of here looms the twisted tower of the 14th-century **St Lambertuskirche** (Church of St Lambert; Stiftsplatz) whose treasures span several centuries. Look for the Gothic tabernacle, the Renaissance marble tombs, baroque altars and modern windows.

Just beyond, on Burgplatz, the **Schlossturm** (Palace Tower) is all that's left of the electors' palace, which burned down in 1872. Now it makes an atmospheric backdrop for the **Schifffahrt Museum** (Navigation Museum; ☎ 899 4195; adult/child/concession €3/free/1.50; ⏰ 2-6pm Wed & Sat, 11am-6pm Sun) where nifty multimedia exhibits chronicle Rhine shipping from the Middle Ages until today. The 4th-floor cafe offers panoramic views.

DÜSSELDORF

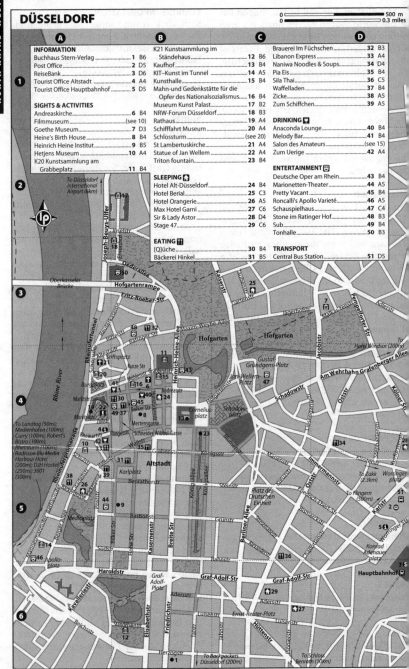

0 — 500 m
0 — 0.3 miles

INFORMATION
Buchhaus Stern-Verlag 1 B6
Post Office 2 D5
ReiseBank 3 D6
Tourist Office Altstadt 4 A4
Tourist Office Hauptbahnhof 5 D5

SIGHTS & ACTIVITIES
Andreaskirche 6 B4
Filmmuseum .... (see 10)
Goethe Museum 7 D3
Heine's Birth House 8 B4
Heinrich Heine Institut 9 B5
Hetjens Museum 10 A4
K20 Kunstsammlung am
    Grabbeplatz 11 B4

K21 Kunstsammlung im
    Ständehaus 12 B6
Kaufhof 13 B4
KIT–Kunst im Tunnel 14 A5
Kunsthalle 15 B4
Mahn-und Gedenkstätte für die
    Opfer des Nationalsozialismus... 16 B4
Museum Kunst Palast 17 B2
NRW-Forum Düsseldorf 18 B3
Rathaus 19 A4
Schifffahrt Museum 20 A4
Schlossturm .... (see 20)
St Lambertuskirche 21 A4
Statue of Jan Wellem 22 A4
Triton fountain 23 A4

SLEEPING
Hotel Alt-Düsseldorf 24 B4
Hotel Berial 25 C3
Hotel Orangerie 26 A5
Max Hotel Garni 27 C6
Sir & Lady Astor 28 D4
Stage 47 .... 29 C6

EATING
[Q]üche 30 B4
Bäckerei Hinkel 31 B5

Brauerei Im Füchschen 32 B3
Libanon Express 33 A4
Naniwa Noodles & Soups................ 34 D4
Pia Eis 35 B4
Sila Thai 36 C5
Waffelladen 37 B4
Zicke 38 A5
Zum Schiffchen 39 A5

DRINKING
Anaconda Lounge 40 B4
Melody Bar 41 B4
Salon des Amateurs .... (see 15)
Zum Uerige 42 A4

ENTERTAINMENT
Deutsche Oper am Rhein 43 B4
Marionetten-Theater 44 A5
Pretty Vacant 45 B4
Roncalli's Apollo Varieté................. 46 A5
Schauspielhaus 47 C4
Stone im Ratinger Hof 48 B3
Sub 49 B4
Tonhalle 50 B3

TRANSPORT
Central Bus Station 51 D5

Burgplatz marks the beginning of the **Rheinuferpromenade** (river walk), whose cafes and benches fill with people in fine weather, creating an almost Mediterranean flair. It follows the Rhine all the way to the Rheinpark and the 240m **Rheinturm** (Rhine Tower; Stromstrasse 20; lift adult/child €3.50/1.90) with a viewing platform and revolving restaurant at 172m. Just beyond are the **Landtag** (state parliament) and the sleek Medienhafen (Media Harbour; see right) with its dramatic blend of historic and postmodern architecture.

A short detour off the Rheinuferpromenade takes you to the **Hetjens Museum** (☎ 899 4210; Schulstrasse 4; adult/concession/family €3/1.50/6; 🕐 11am-5pm Tue & Thu-Sun, 11am-9pm Wed), known for its survey of 8000 years of ceramic art from around the world. An extension houses the **Filmmuseum** (☎ 899 2232; adult/concession €3/1.50; 🕐 11am-5pm Tue & Thu-Sun, 11am-9pm Wed), which trains the spotlight on the technology, history and mystery of movie-making. The integrated Black Box art-house cinema presents retrospectives, rare flicks and silent movies with live organ accompaniment (tickets €6.50/4.50).

For a literary kick, swing by the **Heinrich Heine Institut** (☎ 899 2902; Bilker Strasse 12-14; adult/concession €3/1.50; 🕐 11am-5pm Tue-Fri & Sun, 1-5pm Sat), where letters, portraits, first editions and manuscripts document this famed Düsseldorfer's career. **Heine's birth house** at Bolkerstrasse 53 now contains a literary bookshop and reading room.

ART MUSEUMS

Düsseldorf has long had a love affair with art and has several high-calibre museums to prove it.

A collection that spans the arc of 20th-century artistic vision gives the **K20 Kunstsammlung am Grabbeplatz** (☎ 838 1130; www.kunstsammlung.de; Grabbeplatz 5) an enviable edge in the art world. Paul Klee is well represented but walls are also graced by plenty of other western European and American big-shots, including Picasso, Matisse, Robert Rauschenberg, Jasper Johns and Düsseldorf's own Joseph Beuys. Displays should be even more impressive once the museum emerges from a major revamp, expected to be complete sometime in 2010.

Across the square, a hideous '60s cube houses the **Kunsthalle** (Art Hall; ☎ 899 6243; www.kunsthalle-duesseldorf.de; Grabbeplatz 4; admission prices vary; 🕐 noon-7pm Tue-Sat, 11am-6pm Sun), which hosts headline-grabbing contemporary art shows.

For the most Zeitgeist-capturing exhibits, though, swing by the **NRW-Forum Düsseldorf** (NRW Forum for Culture & Economics; ☎ 892 6690; www.nrw-forum.de; Ehrenhof 2; adult/concession €7.50/5; 🕐 11am-8pm Tue-Thu, Sat & Sun, 11am-midnight Fri). It targets the lifestyle-savvy crowd with changing exhibits on fashion, media, design and architecture.

Nearby, the once stuffy **museum kunst palast** (☎ 899 0200; www.museum-kunst-palast.de; Ehrenhof 5; adult/concession/family €8/6.50/18; 🕐 11am-6pm Tue-Sun) now takes an unconventional approach to presenting its well-respected collection. Old masters find themselves juxtaposed with contemporary young dogs and non-Western works to reveal unexpected connections between the ages and artistic trends. Temporary exhibitions further reinforce the theme.

Speaking of juxtaposition: a stately 19th-century parliament building forms the incongruous setting of the cutting-edge **K21 Kunstsammlung im Ständehaus** (☎ 838 1630; Ständehausstrasse 1; www.kunstsammlung.de; adult/concession/family €6.50/4.50/15; 🕐 10am-6pm Tue-Fri, 11am-6pm Sat & Sun), which brims with canvases, photographs, installations and video art created after 1980 by an international cast of artists. Look for works by Andreas Gursky, Candida Höfer, Bill Viola and the late Nam June Paik.

Young artists also get the nod in the city's newest space, the **KIT – Kunst im Tunnel** (☎ 892 0769; www.kunst-im-tunnel.de; Mannesmannufer 1b; adult/concession €4/3; 🕐 noon-7pm Tue-Sat, 11am-6pm Sun) in a spectacularly adapted tunnel below the river promenade. The entrance is via a glass pavilion that doubles as a restaurant.

MEDIENHAFEN

South of the Altstadt, the Medienhafen (Media Harbour) is an office quarter that's been wrought from the remains of the old city harbour. It's Düsseldorf's largest and most progressive urban construction project to get off the ground in the past 20 years. Despite a few trendy restaurants and design shops, there's little life in the streets as of yet, but if you're a fan of bold contemporary architecture, do swing by. The most eye-catching structure is clearly the warped **Neuer Zollhof**, a typically sculptural design by Frank Gehry. Moored nearby is Claude Vasconi's **Grand Bateau**, built to resemble an ocean liner. A new pedestrian bridge links to another quay dominated by William Alsop's **Colorium**, easily recognised by its kaleidoscopic glass facade. And

---

HAVE A FLING WITH FLINGERN

Altstadt too boisterous? Medienhafen too snooty? Head to Flingern, a charming neighbourhood near the Hauptbahnhof that's increasingly trading its working-class roughness for boho-chic hipness. The main strip is leafy Ackerstrasse, where retail therapy gets a unique twist in indie boutiques stocked with vintage frocks, edgy jewellery, whimsical tees, handmade accessories and gourmet foods. Stop off for coffee and a snack at retro-style **Beethoven** (☎ 2339 8687; Ackerstrasse 106; ☺ 10am-1am) or save your appetite for a plate of feistily flavoured *wot* (stew) at **Okra** (☎ 691 1856; Ackerstrasse 119; mains €10-12.50; ☺ dinner), an authentic Ethiopian restaurant. Getting there is easy: from the Hauptbahnhof it's either a 15-minute walk via Worringer Strasse or a short ride on tram 709 to Wetterstrasse (head north for a couple of minutes to get to Ackerstrasse).

---

the construction cranes are still pirouetting: in 2010 **Casa Stupenda** by Renzo Piano and **Sign** by Helmut Jahn are sure to make some headlines.

KÖNIGSALLEE & HOFGARTEN

Banks and boutiques are the ammo of the Königsallee (Kö for short), one of Germany's most expensive shopping strips. Otherwise there's little of actual merit here, although the art nouveau facade of the **Kaufhof** department store and the landmark **Triton fountain** deserve a glance.

The Kö spills out into the Hofgarten (palace garden), which is flanked by the opera house, the theatre and the eclectic **Goethe Museum** (☎ 899 6262; Jacobistrasse 2; adult/concession €3/1.50; ☺ 11am-5pm Tue-Fri & Sun, 1-5pm Sat) inside a piglet-pink yet dignified rococo palace. There's the usual assortment of letters, manuscripts, paintings and memorabilia that illustrate the spirit of this complex genius and his time. For more on the man, see the boxed text on p272.

SCHLOSS BENRATH

Elector Carl Theodor was a man of deep pockets and good taste, as reflected in his exquisite **pleasure palace and gardens** (☎ 899 3832; www.schloss-benrath.de; Benrather Schlossallee 104; ☺ 10am-6pm Tue-Sun mid-Apr–Oct, 11am-5pm Nov–mid-Apr), where he came to relax and frolic. Designed by Frenchman Nicolas de Pigage, the three-winged palace centres on the **Corps de Logis** (adult/concession €7/5), the former residential tract, where tours (in German) offer a glimpse of the elector's lifestyle. The other wings contain an old-school natural history museum (adult/concession €5/3) and a vaguely interesting museum of European garden history (adult/concession €5/3).

The complex is about 10km south of the city centre and reached by tram 701 from Jan-Wellem-Platz (near Altstadt and Kö) in about 30 minutes.

Tours

The tourist offices operate a variety of tours, many in English. The most popular is the 90-minute combined walking and boat tour of the Altstadt and the Medienhafen, offered daily at 2.30pm between April and mid-October (adult/child €10/5). Departure point is the Altstadt tourist office (see p559).

Sleeping

Düsseldorf's hotels cater primarily for the business brigade, which explains soaring prices during big trade shows held not only here but as far away as Cologne and Essen. On the bright side, bargains abound at weekends and in summer. Prices quoted here are applicable outside trade-show times. Rooms can be booked online at www.duesseldorf-tourismus.de or in person at the tourist offices (p559).

BUDGET

Backpackers Düsseldorf (☎ 302 0848; www.backpackers-duesseldorf.de; dm €22, incl linen, towel & breakfast; Ⓟ Ⓧ ▯ ☜) Düsseldorf's adorable indie hostel sleeps 45 in clean four to six-bed dorms outfitted with individual backpack-sized lockers. It's a low-key place with a homely kitchen and a relaxed lounge where cultural and language barriers melt quickly. The reception is generally staffed from 8am to 9pm.

DJH hostel (☎ 557 310; www.duesseldorf.jugendherberge.de; Düsseldorfer Strasse 1; dm/s/tw €25/42/62; Ⓟ Ⓧ ▯ ☜) Offering fine views of the Altstadt across the Rhine, this contender has emerged from a major revamp and scores igh for cleanliness, security, location and omforts. Each of the 96 rooms has its own hower and toilet, although party animals vill be better placed at Backpackers.

Hotel Berial (☎ 490 0490; www.hotel-berial.de; artenstrasse 30; s/d from €40/60; P ✕ 🖳 🛜) This vell-kept property is a fine choice for wallet-vatching nomads who have outgrown hostels. Room decor is nothing to write home about, ut all the expected comforts and amenities, ncluding free wi-fi, are here. The Hofgarten is couple of minutes away – perfect for jogging ff your jet lag.

Hotel Alt-Düsseldorf (☎ 133 604; www.alt-duesseldorf de; Hunsrückenstrasse 11; s €50-115, d €70-160; 🖳) If ou're happy to trade generic-ness for cen-rality, this family-run hotel should do in a nap. It's a small, good-value place where lays start with a big breakfast buffet served in un-yellow surroundings.

MIDRANGE & TOP END

Max Hotel Garni (☎ 386 800; www.max-hotelgarni.de; dersstrasse 65; s/d/tr €70/82/99; 🖳) Upbeat, con-emporary and run with personal flair, this harmer is one of our Düsseldorf favourites. The 11 rooms are good-sized and decked out n bright hues and warm woods. Rates in-lude coffee, tea, soft drinks and a regional ublic transport pass. The reception isn't lways staffed, so call ahead to arrange an rrival time.

ourpick Sir & Lady Astor (☎ 173 370; www.sir astor.de; Kurfürstenstrasse 18 & 23; s €83-170, d €95-40; P ✕ ✕ 🖳 🛜) Never mind the ho-um setting on a residential street near he Hauptbahnhof: this unique twin bou-ique hotel brims with class, originality and harm. Check-in is at Sir Astor, furnished n 'Scotland-meets-Africa' style, while Lady Astor across the street goes more for French loral sumptuousness. This place has a huge an base, so book early.

Hotel Windsor (☎ 914 680; www.sir-astor.de; rafenberger Allee 36; s €80-200, d €100-210; P ✕ 🖳 🛜) With the same owner as the Sir & Lady Astor, he Windsor commits itself to the British ountry tradition. Behind the sandstone fa-ade await 18 rooms where you can unwind eneath stucco-ornamented ceilings sur-ounded by antiques and plenty of plaid.

Radisson Blu Media Harbour Hotel (☎ 311 910; www.mediaharbour.duesseldorf.radissonsas.com; lammerstrasse 23; r weekday/weekend from €180/110; P ✕ ✕ 🖳 🛜) This hipster haven in the Medienhafen has 135 rooms flaunting the cut-ting-edge cool of Italian designer Matteo Thun. Even the 'standard' rooms are anything but, given the walk-in showers, full-length win-dows and other Zeitgeist-capturing features.

Hotel Orangerie (☎ 866 800; www.hotel-orangerie -mcs.de; Bäckergasse 1; s €110-165, d €130-210; ✕) Ensconced in a neoclassical mansion in a quiet corner of the Altstadt, this place puts you within staggering distance of pubs, the river and museums, yet offers a quiet and styl-ish refuge to retire to. Some of the 27 rooms skimp somewhat on size but all are as bright, modern and uncluttered as the lobby and breakfast room.

Stage 47 (☎ 388 030; www.stage47.de; Graf-Adolf-Strasse 47; s/d from €160/180; P ✕ 🖳 🛜) Behind the drab exterior, movie glamour meets design chic at this urban boutique hotel. Rooms are named for famous people, some of whom have actually stayed in environs dominated by black, white and grey tones. Nice touches: an iHome and a Nespresso coffeemaker.

Eating

Curry (☎ 303 2857; Hammer Strasse 2; meals under €6; 🕑 11.30am-11pm Sun-Thu, to midnight Fri & Sat) In this vibrant little kitchen, sausage is king. Get them big, spicy, hot and paired with your choice of gourmet sauce and possibly a mountain of fresh French fries. Avoid the lunchtime rush from the adjacent Media Harbour.

Zicke (☎ 324 056; Bäckerstrasse 5a; dishes €5-10; 🕑 9am-1am) Arty boho types jam this staple in a quiet corner tucked away from the Altstadt bustle. Linger over breakfast (served until 3pm, on weekends till 4pm) or come for salad, quiche and other light meals.

ourpick Brauerei im Füchschen (☎ 137 470; www .fuechschen.de; Ratinger Strasse 28; snacks €3, mains €5-14; 🕑 9am-1am) Boisterous, packed and drenched with local colour – the 'Little Fox' in the Altstadt is all you expect a Rhenish beer hall to be. The kitchen makes a mean *Schweinshaxe* (roast pork leg).

Zum Schiffchen (☎ 132 421; www.brauerei-zum -schiffchen.de; Hafenstrasse 5; mains €7-19; 🕑 11.30am-midnight) History pours from every nook and cranny in this almost ridiculously cosy Altstadt restaurant specialising in gut-busting German and Rhenish meals. Were portions as huge when Napoleon dropped by a couple of centuries ago? Reservations recommended.

Naniwa Noodles & Soups (☎ 161 799; www.naniwa.de; Oststrasse 55; mains €8-11; 🕑 noon-10.30pm Wed-Mon)

ALTSTADT SNACK FAVES

The Altstadt is chock-full of *Imbisse* (snack bars), mostly of the pizza-by-the-slice and doner-kebab variety, which are fine but nothing to rave about. We've ferreted out a few of the places where in-the-know locals feed their cravings. Those with a sweet tooth can't escape the magnetism of **Pia Eis** (Kasernenstrasse 1), the best ice-cream parlour around, bar none, with an incredible selection, quick service and modest prices. Another great sugar fix is the **Waffelladen** (Bolkerstrasse 8), an unimaginably tiny waffle kitchen in business for more than 40 years. Try one with a little powdered sugar or drenched in cherries or other toppings.

Bäckerei Hinkel (several branches, incl Hohe Strasse 31) is another institution that has people queuing patiently for its excellent breads and cakes. A great way to prepare the stomach for an extended pub crawl is by filling up on superb falafel sandwiches at **Libanon Express** (Berger Strasse 21). Trendy types, meanwhile, are drawn to **[Q]üche** (Kurze Strasse 3) for its fresh and healthful soups, salads and sandwiches.

The space is minimalist, the food is not. Soup's the thing and nearly every variety we tried – flavoured from mild to wild – had perfect pitch. Tables are usually packed with Japanese expats and plugged-in locals, but the wait's worth it. Or just make a reservation.

Robert's Bistro (☎ 304 821; Wupperstrasse 2; mains €10-22; 11.30am-midnight Tue-Fri, 10am-midnight Sat) Tables are squished together as tightly as lovers at this *très* French restaurant in the Media Harbour. Bring both an appetite for hearty Gallic fare (the fish soup is highly recommended) and some patience – it doesn't take reservations and a queue is guaranteed.

Sila Thai (☎ 860 4427; Bahnstrasse 76; mains €17.50-24; noon-3pm & 6pm-1am) Even simple curries become culinary poetry at this Thai gourmet temple with its fairy-tale setting of carved wood, rich fabrics and imported sculpture. Like a trip to Thailand without the passport. Reservations advised.

Drinking

At night, especially in good weather, the atmosphere in the Altstadt is electric and often raucous. The beverage of choice is *Altbier*, a dark and semi-sweet beer typical of Düsseldorf.

Zum Uerige (☎ 866 990; Berger Strasse 1; 10am-midnight) This cavernous beer hall is the best place to soak it all up. The suds flow so quickly from giant copper vats that the waiters – called *Köbes* – simply carry huge trays of brew and plonk down a glass whenever they spy an empty.

Anaconda Lounge (☎ 869 3939; Andreasstrasse 11; 8pm-2am Wed & Thu, to 5am Fri & Sat) The living room of hormone-happy hipsters, this designer cave is great for chilling or launching

a bar hop. Strong drinks, kick-ass music an complexion-friendly decor further loosen in hibitions. Insiders fuel up for the long nigh ahead with cheap pizza from Harlequino nex door (ok to bring inside bar).

Melody Bar (☎ 329 057; Kurze Strasse 12; Tue-Sun After 10pm you may have to shoehorn you way into this jewel of a cocktail bar that' an island of sophistication amid the boister ous Altstadt thirst parlours. The drinks ar excellent, the owner couple gracious and th crowd mixed.

Salon des Amateurs (☎ 899 6243; Grabbeplatz 4 noon-1am Tue-Sun) Tucked into the Kunsthalle this tunnel-shaped cafe-lounge pulls off a artsy vibe without a single canvas. Museum goers arrive in the afternoon for tea and cha while hipsters keep the bar and little danc floor hopping after dark.

Entertainment

Check the listings magazines *Prinz* an *Überblick* or the free *Coolibri* for curren goings-on in 'D-Town'. Gays and lesbi ans should look for *Rik Magazin*. All are i German only.

NIGHTCLUBS & LIVE MUSIC

our pick **Stone im Ratinger Hof** (☎ 210 7828; Ratinge Strasse 10; cover €5; Wed, Fri & Sat) After a stint a a techno temple in the '90s, the venerable Ratinger Hof has returned to its rock root and is now the 'it' place for lovers of indie an alt-sounds. Depending on the night, tousle hipsters, skinny-jean emos and sneaker-wear ing students thrash it out to everything from noise pop to neo-garage to indietronics.

Pretty Vacant (Mertensgasse 8; from 8pm) may be named for a Sex Pistols song, but thi

Altstadt haunt ain't no punk club. It's a shape-shifter really, whose cellar walls vibrate to different sounds nightly – glam rock to Britpop, electronica to R&B. Live bands, too.

Sub (☎ 865 890; Bolker Strasse 14; 🕒 from 8pm Wed, Fri & Sat) Getting past the door woman can be tough, but if you succeed you'll have a fine time inside this hip basement haunt designed to look like a subway station. Tip: dress nicely, smile and don't arrive drunk.

3001 (☎ 6882 4960; Franziusstrasse 7; 🕒 8pm-3am Thu, 11pm-5am Sat, also some Fri) A clubber's nirvana, this hot 'n' heavy club in Medienhafen has a giant dance floor where DJs whip shiny, happy and barely legal hotties into a frenzy with electro and sizzling light and video projections. The crowd's a bit older and admission is free during 'Milchbar' on Thursdays.

Zakk (☎ 973 0010; Fichtenstrasse 40; 🕒 Mon-Sat) Parties, concerts, readings, theatre, discussions – the menu sure varies at this well-established cultural centre in a former factory. The beer garden is a convivial place to spend a balmy summer night. It's a couple of kilometres east of the Hauptbahnhof; take tram 706 to Fichtenstrasse or the U-Bahn 75 to Kettwiger Strasse.

THEATRE

D:ticket (☎ 01805-644 332; www.dticket.de) is the central booking hotline.

Schauspielhaus (☎ 369 911; www.duesseldorfer-schauspielhaus.de; Gustaf-Gründgens-Platz 1; tickets €14-41) The main venue for drama and comedies, the Schauspielhaus enjoys a solid reputation nationwide.

Marionetten-Theater (☎ 328 432; www.marionetten-theater.duesseldorf.de; Bilker Strasse 7; tickets €13-20) Generations of kids and adults have been enthralled by the adorable marionettes that sing, dance and act their way through beautifully orchestrated operas and fairy tales at this venerable venue. Pure magic.

Roncalli's Apollo Varieté (☎ 828 9090; Apolloplatz 1; tickets €19-47) No German skills are needed to enjoy the line-up of acrobats, comedians, magicians, artistes and other variety acts performing under the starry-sky ceiling of a nostalgic theatre hall.

CLASSICAL MUSIC

Mozart to Monteverdi are the bread and butter of Düsseldorf's renowned opera house, the **Deutsche Oper am Rhein** (☎ 892 5211; www.rheinoper.de; Heinrich-Heine-Allee 16a; tickets €15-68),

while the imposing domed **Tonhalle** (☎ 899 6123; www.tonhalle-duesseldorf.de; Ehrenhof 1; tickets vary), in a converted 1920s planetarium, is the home base of the Düsseldorfer Symphoniker (Düsseldorf Symphony Orchestra).

Getting There & Away
AIR

Many domestic and international carriers serve **Düsseldorf International Airport** (☎ 4210; www.duesseldorf-international.de), which has all the expected infrastructure as well as wi-fi and even counselling for those suffering from fear of flying.

BUS

Düsseldorf's central bus station is on Worringer Strasse, about 250m north of the Hauptbahnhof main exit. From here, Eurolines services include daily buses to Paris (one-way/return from €41/74, 7½ hours), Warsaw (€63/95, 20 hours) and London (€63/114, 13½ hours).

CAR & MOTORCYCLE

Autobahns from all directions lead to Düsseldorf, including the A3 from Cologne and the A46 from Wuppertal and the eastern Ruhrgebiet.

TRAIN

Düsseldorf is part of a dense S-Bahn network in the Rhine–Ruhr region (see p590) and frequent services run to Cologne and Aachen as well. ICE train links include Berlin (€100, 4¼ hours), Munich (€127, 4¾ hours) and Frankfurt (€73, 1¾ hours).

Getting Around
TO/FROM THE AIRPORT

S-Bahns, regional RE and long-distance trains connect the airport with Düsseldorf Hauptbahnhof, and cities beyond, every few minutes. The free SkyTrain links the airport terminals with the station. A taxi into town costs about €16.

CAR & MOTORCYCLE

Central Düsseldorf is now a low-emission zone, meaning that your car needs to display an *Umweltplakette* (emission sticker). Rental cars automatically have one, but if you're driving your own vehicle, see p783 for details on how to obtain the sticker.

PUBLIC TRANSPORT

An extensive network of U-Bahn trains, trams and buses operates throughout Düsseldorf. Most trips within the city cost €2.30, longer trips to the suburbs are €4.50. Day passes are €5.30. Tickets are available from bus drivers and orange vending machines at U-Bahn and tram stops and must be validated upon boarding.

TAXI

For a taxi, call ☎ 333 33 or ☎ 212 121. Flag fall is €5.50, including the first 2km; additional kilometres are €1.70.

AROUND DÜSSELDORF

If you have a penchant for art in weird places, make the trip out to the **Langen Foundation** (☎ 02182-570 10; www.langenfoundation.de; Raketenstation Hombroich; adult/concession €7.50/5; ⏱ 10am-6pm). The location: a former NATO missile base where Pershing tanks armed with nuclear warheads held the line against the Soviet Union during the Cold War. The architecture: a minimalist glass, steel and concrete box by Japanese *Meister*-architect Tadao Ando. The art: a top collection of Japanese screens, scrolls and sculpture, plus works by 20th-century greats, such as Jawlensky, Klee and Ernst, presented in changing exhibits.

It's in the rural flatlands near the town of Neuss, about 20km west of Düsseldorf. Catch a train to Neuss Hauptbahnhof, then bus 860 or 877. By car, exit the A57 at Neuss-West and follow the signs to Raketenstation Hombroich.

LOWER RHINE

North of Düsseldorf, the Rhine widens and embarks on its final headlong rush towards the North Sea traversing the sparsely populated Lower Rhine (Niederrhein). It's a flat, windswept plain that feels like Holland without the windmills and yields a number of off-beat surprises.

The region has its own airport, the tiny **Niederrhein airport** (☎ 02837-666 000) in Weeze, which is used by RyanAir.

Xanten
☎ 02801 / pop 22,000

The hub of the Lower Rhine, Xanten was founded as a Roman military camp in 12 BC and within a century grew into a respectable settlement called Colonia Ulpia Traiana. At its peak, some 15,000 people milled about town, enjoying a surprisingly high standard of living. Xanten's medieval heyday is best symbolised by the majestic Dom that dominates the tangled old town with its stately gates, cheerful mills and historic fountains. The town is also the mythological birthplace of Siegfried, the dragon-slaying hero of the 12th-century Nibelungen epic, which became the subject of Richard Wagner's *Ring* opera cycle 700 years later. Starting in 2010, the new Museum Nibelungen(h)ort zeroes in on the saga and its impact through history.

ORIENTATION

Xanten is about 60km north of Düsseldorf. The compact Altstadt is about a 10-minute walk northeast of the Bahnhof (train station) via Hagenbuschstrasse or Bahnhofstrasse. The Archäologischer Park (Archaeological Park) is a further 15 minutes northwest of here.

INFORMATION

The **tourist office** (☎ 983 00; www.xanten.de; Kurfürstenstrasse 9; ⏱ 9am-1pm & 2-6pm Mon-Fri, 10am-4pm Sat noon-4pm Sun Apr-Oct, 10am-1pm & 2-5pm Mon-Fri, 10am-1pm Sat Nov-Mar) is right in the Altstadt, close to the Markt (market square) and Dom.

SIGHTS
Altstadt

The crown jewel of Xanten's Altstadt is the **Dom St Viktor** (☎ 713 10; Kapitel 8; ⏱ 10am-6pm Mon-Sat, 12.30-6pm Sun Apr-Oct, to 5pm Nov-Mar), which has Romanesque roots but is now largely Gothic. It is framed by a walled close, called an 'Immunity', which can only be entered from the Markt.

The soaring five-nave interior brims with treasures, reflecting the wealth Xanten enjoyed in the Middle Ages. Foremost among them is the **Marienaltar**, halfway down the right aisle, whose base features an intricately carved version of the *Tree of Jesse* by Heinrich Douvermann (1535). The candelabrum in the central nave, with its *Doppelmadonna* (Double Madonna, 1500), is another masterpiece. A stone sarcophagus in the crypt holds the remains of St Viktor, the Roman martyr who became Xanten's patron saint.

More treasures, including reliquaries, sculptures and graphics, will again be on view once the **Stiftsmuseum** (Monastic Museum) reopens in 2010.

Archäologischer Park

The old Roman colony has been reborn as the **Archäologischer Park** (Archaeological Park; ☎ 2999; Wardter Strasse 2; adult/child/family €9/4.50/18, incl RömerMuseum & Grosse Thermen; ☼ 9am-6pm Mar-Nov, 10am-4pm Dec-Feb), an open-air museum that features faithfully reconstructed structures to help amateurs visualise what the Roman town looked like. The originals were torn down and used in building the medieval town.

The self-guided tour takes you past such sites as the **Amphitheatre**, which seats 12,000 people during Xanten's summer music festival; the **Spielehaus**, where you can play early versions of backgammon and Nine Men's Morris; a Roman **hostel** complete with hot baths and restaurant; and the majestic **Hafentempel** (harbour temple). Kids will also enjoy the two imaginative playgrounds, one a Roman fort, the other a water-themed one (bring a towel). To get the most out of your visit, invest €2.50 in the audioguide, which uses narration and sound effects to recreate scenes from everyday life 2000 years ago.

RömerMuseum & Grosse Thermen

The extravagant building west of the park shelters the brand-new **RömerMuseum** (☎ 9881 7110; Siegfriedstrasse 39; see Archäologischer Park for hr & admission), which takes you on a journey through 400 years of Roman presence in the Lower Rhine region. Modern and interactive, the exhibit kicks off with the arrival of the Roman legions and ends with the colony's 4th-century demise at the hands of marauding Germanic tribes. Make your way along the floating ramps to learn how the Roman folk earned their money, how they worshipped, educated their kids, played and buried their dead. A highlight among the locally excavated treasures is the Roman ship.

The museum was built on the foundations of the **Grosse Thermen** thermal baths, which have been partly excavated and can be admired in an adjacent hall.

SLEEPING

DJH hostel (☎ 985 00; www.xanten.jugendherberge.de; Bankscher Weg 4; dm/s/d incl breakfast & linen €20.40/30.50/51; **P** 🗶) This hugely popular modern hostel has a pretty lakeside setting but is 3km from the Altstadt and often overrun with school kids. Rooms sleep two to five and come with their own bathrooms.

Klever Tor (☎ 983 00; Klever Strasse; apt €48, 2-night minimum; **P**) A romantic place to spend the night is inside the most striking of Xanten's surviving medieval town gates, now converted into holiday flats with small kitchens. Book through the tourist office.

Hotel van Bebber (☎ 6623; www.hotelvanbebber.de, in German; Klever Strasse 12; s €69-88, d €114-186; **P** 🗶) Queen Victoria and Churchill have slept in this old-school hotel where waiters wear tuxedos and the reception is past a gallery of mounted animal heads.

EATING

Cafe de Fries (☎ 2068; Kurfürstenstrasse 8; dishes €3.50-8; ☼ 8.30am-6.30pm Tue-Fri, 9am-6pm Sat & Sun) Newly updated, this cafe has a 180-year pedigree and is famous for its filled pancakes. Kids love the 'chocolate fountain' and the Easter-bunny centrifuge in the one-room museum (admission free; open 11am to 5pm).

Gotisches Haus (☎ 706 400; Markt 6; mains €9-20; ☼ 9am-1am) Xanten's top restaurant offers creative Austrian cuisine and artsy design flourishes within the wood-panelled walls of a centuries-old merchant house. The three-course lunch is a steal at €10 and tots love picking out their favourite dish from a menu designed just for them.

GETTING THERE & AROUND

Getting to Xanten from the Niederrhein airport (opposite) involves taking the bus to the Duisburg main train station (adult/child €12/7, hourly 9.30am to 12.30am), then catching the hourly train (€9.50, 45 minutes). Xanten is on route B57. If travelling on the A57, take the Alpen exit, then route B58 east to B57 north.

Zweirad Reineke (☎ 1474; Marsstrasse 19; ☼ 9am-1pm & 2.30-6.30pm Mon-Fri, 9am-2pm Sat) in the pedestrian zone near the Markt rents bikes for €7.50 per day.

Kalkar & Around
☎ 02824 / pop 11,500

About 15km north of Xanten, Kalkar boasts a pretty medieval core centred on a proud **Rathaus** and the **St Nikolaikirche** (Jan-Joest-Strasse 6; ☼ 10am-noon & 2-6pm Apr-Oct, 2-5pm Nov-Mar), famous for its nine masterful altars chiselled by members of the Kalkar woodcarving school. Top billing goes to the **High Altar**, which depicts the Passion of Christ in heart-wrenching detail. For a little comic relief, lift the first seat on the left in the back row of the choir chairs (with you facing the altar) to reveal a **monkey on a chamber pot**. Another eye-catcher is the **Seven Sorrows Altar** by Henrik Douvermann at the end of the right aisle. Note the oak-carved *Jesse's root*, which wraps around the entire altar.

Bus 44 makes regular trips from Xanten's Bahnhof to the Markt in Kalkar, but the service is infrequent at weekends.

SCHLOSS MOYLAND

With its Rapunzel towers, Romeo-and-Juliet balcony and creeping ivy, **Schloss Moyland** (☎ 02824-951 00; Am Schloss 4; www.moyland.de; adult/concession/family €7/3/15; ☟ 11am-6pm Tue-Fri, 10am-6pm Sat & Sun Apr-Sep, 11am-5pm Tue-Sun Oct-Mar) is a most unexpected sight amid the sweeping pastures and sleepy villages of the Lower Rhine flatlands. Medieval in origin, the palace got its fairy-tale looks in the 19th century and since 1997 has housed a private modern-art collection that includes the world's largest assortment of works by Joseph Beuys. 'Less is more' is definitely not a curatorial concept here, as every wall of the labyrinthine interior is smothered in drawings, paintings and etchings. If you need to clear your head, take a spin around the lovely park with its old trees and wacky sculptures.

The Schloss is about 4km northwest of Kalkar off the B57 and well signposted. Bus 44 heads out here from the Xanten Bahnhof or the Markt in Kalkar, but service is sketchy at weekends.

WUNDERLAND KALKAR

What do you do with a decommissioned nuclear power plant? Turn it into a convention hotel and amusement park, of course. So was the vision of a wily Dutchman who, in 1995, bought the so-called *Schneller Brüter* (Fast Breeder) reactor on a field in Kalkar. The behemoth never went live on account of opposition from environmentalists who convinced the authorities that it was unsafe. Reborn as **Wunderland Kalkar** (☎ 02824-9100; www.wunderland-kalkar.de), it offers utterly bizarre cruise-ship-meets-Vegas ambience where you can climb the cooling tower, ride a Ferris wheel and get wet on a log ride. A day pass, including unlimited rides, snacks and soft drinks, costs €22.50 for adults and €20.50 for kids (€2 more in July and August). Various hotel and dinner packages are also available.

The park is about 6km northeast of Kalkar and not served by public transport.

COLOGNE

☎ 0221 / pop 995,500

Cologne (Köln) is like a 3-D textbook on history and architecture. Drifting about town you'll stumble upon an ancient Roman wall, medieval churches galore, nondescript postwar buildings, avant-garde structures and now also a brand-new postmodern quarter right on the Rhine. Germany's fourth-largest city was founded by the Romans in 38 BC and given the lofty name Colonia Claudia Ara Aggripinensium. It grew into a major trading centre, a tradition it solidified in the Middle Ages and continues to uphold today. Cologne is also Germany's 'media capital', home to numerous TV and radio stations and over 600 production companies that collectively churn out over a third of all national programming.

For visitors, the city offers the mother lode of sightseeing attractions, led by its famous cathedral whose filigree twin spires dominate the Altstadt skyline. It's twice been voted the country's single most popular tourist attraction in polls conducted by the German Tourism Association. Cologne's museum landscape is especially strong when it comes to art but also has something in store for fans of chocolate, sports and history. Its people are well known for their liberalism and joie de vivre and it's easy to have a good time right along with them year-round in the beer halls of the Altstadt and especially in spring when everyone gets dressed up and drunk during one of Germany's most raucous Carnival celebrations.

Orientation

Köln Bonn Airport (Cologne Bonn Airport) is about 18km southeast of the city; see p579 for details on transport to/from the airport. Cologne's Hauptbahnhof sits just a Frisbee toss away from the landmark Dom. The pedestrianised Hohe Strasse – the main shopping strip – runs south of the Dom, as does the Altstadt, which hugs the river bank between the two bridges, Hohenzollernbrücke and Deutzer Brücke. Student-flavoured Zülpicher Viertel and the more grown-up Belgisches Viertel about 1.5km west of here are zinging bar and pub quarters.

nformation

BOOKSHOPS

Gleumes (Map p574; ☎ 211 550; Hohenstaufenring 17-51) Travel and map specialist.

Mayersche Buchhandlung (Map p570; ☎ 203 070; Neumarkt 2) There's another branch at Schildergasse 31-37.

DISCOUNT CARDS

Köln Welcome Card (per 24/48/72hr €9/14/19, group 18/28/38) Offers free public transport and discounted admission, tours, meals and entertainment. It's available at the tourist office and participating venues.

EMERGENCY

Dental emergencies (☎ 01805-986 700)
Gay Attack Hotline (☎ 192 28)
Medical emergencies (☎ 192 92)

INTERNET ACCESS

Giga-Center Köln (Map p574; ☎ 6502 6442; Hohenzollernring 7-11; per hr €0.50-1.50; ☼ 24hr) Huge entertainment centre with 130 high-speed computers.

LAUNDRY

Eleanicum (Map p574; Brüsseler Strasse 74-76; ☼ 8am-10pm Mon-Sat, noon-8pm Sun) Shares space with a streetwear store; has wi-fi.

Eco-Express Waschsalon (per load from €1.90, per 10min of dryer time €0.50; ☼ 6am-11pm Mon-Sat) Has branches at Friedrichstrasse 12 (Map p574), Richard-Wagner-Strasse 2 (Map p574) and Hansaring 68 (Map p570).

MEDICAL SERVICES

Uniklinik Köln (off Map p574; ☎ 4780; Kerpener Strasse 2; ☼ 24hr; ⊛ Lindenburg-Universitätskliniken) Major hospital located 1.6km southeast of Zülpicher Viertel.

MONEY

ReiseBank (Map p570; ☎ 134 403; Hauptbahnhof; ☼ 7am-10pm)

POST

Post office (Map p570; WDR Arkaden shopping mall, Breite Strasse 6-26; ☼ 9am-7pm Mon-Fri, 9am-2pm Sat)

TOURIST INFORMATION

Tourist office (Map p570; ☎ 2213 0400; www.koeln ourismus.de; Kardinal-Höffner-Platz 1; ☼ 9am-8pm Mon-Sat, 10am-5pm Sun)

Sights

KÖLNER DOM

Cologne's geographical and spiritual heart – and its single-biggest tourist draw – is the magnificent **Kölner Dom** (Cologne Cathedral; Map p570;

☎ 1794 0200; ☼ 6am-10pm May-Oct, 6am-7.30pm Nov-Apr). With its soaring twin spires, this is the Mt Everest of cathedrals, jam-packed with art and treasures. Its loftiness and dignified ambience leave only the most jaded of visitors untouched.

Construction began in 1248 in the French Gothic style but proceeded slowly and was eventually halted in 1560 when funds ran out. The half-built church lingered for nearly 300 years and even suffered a stint as a horse stable and prison when Napoleon occupied the town. A few decades later, a generous cash infusion from Prussian King Friedrich Wilhelm IV finally led to its completion in 1880. Luckily, it escaped WWII bombing raids with nary a shrapnel wound and has been a Unesco World Heritage Site since 1996.

The Dom is Germany's largest cathedral and must be circled to truly appreciate its dimensions. Note how its lacy spires and flying buttresses create a sensation of lightness and fragility despite its mass and height. This sensation continues inside, where a phalanx of pillars and arches supports the lofty nave. Soft light filters through the dazzling **stained-glass windows**, including the spectacular new one by Gerhard Richter in the transept – a kaleidoscope of 11,500 squares in 72 colours, Richter's abstract design has been called a 'symphony of light' and, in the afternoon especially, when the sun hits it just so, it's easy to understand why.

Among the cathedral's numerous treasures, the *pièce de résistance* is the **Shrine of the Three Kings** behind the main altar, a richly bejewelled and gilded sarcophagus said to hold the remains of the kings who followed the star to the stable in Bethlehem where Jesus was born. The bones were spirited out of Milan in 1164 as spoils of war by Emperor Barbarossa's chancellor and instantly turned Cologne into a major pilgrimage site.

Other highlights include the **Gero Crucifix** (970), notable for its monumental size and an emotional intensity rarely achieved in those early medieval days; the **choir stalls** from 1310, richly carved from oak; and the **altar painting** by local artist Stephan Lochner from around 1450.

To get more out of your visit, invest €1 in the information pamphlet or join a **guided tour**. Tours are offered in English (adult/concession €6/4) at 10.30am and 2.30pm (2.30pm only on Sunday) and more frequently in German.

For an exercise fix, climb the 509 steps up the Dom's **south tower** (adult/concession €2.50/1.50; ⏰ 9am-6pm May-Sep, 9am-5pm Mar-Apr & Oct, 9am-4pm Nov-Feb) to the base of the steeple that dwarfed all buildings in Europe until Gustave Eiffel built a certain tower in Paris. A good excuse to take a breather on your way up is the 24-tonne **Peter Bell** (1923), the largest

working bell in the world. Views from th 95m platform are so wonderful, you'll forge your vertigo.

Cologne is justifiably proud of its **Domschatz kammer** (Cathedral Treasury; ☎ 1794 0300; adult/conce sion/family €4/2/8; ⏰ 10am-6pm), whose reliquaries robes, sculptures and liturgical objects ar handsomely presented in medieval vaulte

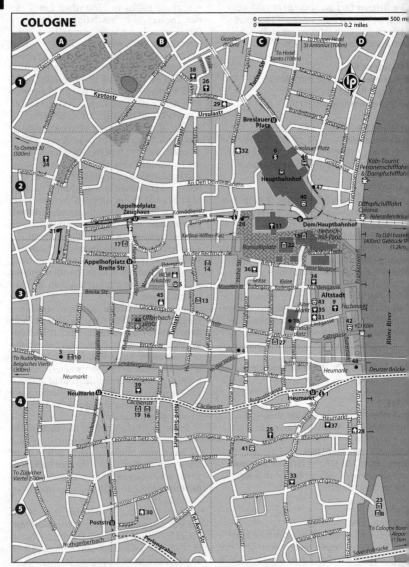

rooms. Standouts include a Gothic bishop's staff from 1322 and a 15th-century sword.

ROMANESQUE CHURCHES

Cologne's medieval heyday is reflected in its wealth of Romanesque churches, which were constructed between 1150 and 1250 and survived largely intact until WWII. About a dozen have been rebuilt since and offer many unique architectural and artistic features. Even if you're pushed for time, try seeing at least a couple of the ones mentioned here.

Winning top honours for most handsome exterior is **Gross St Martin** (Map p570; ☎ 1642 5650; An Gross-St-Martin 9; ⊗ 3-5pm Mon, 10am-noon & 3-5pm Tue-Fri, 10am-12.30pm & 1.30-5pm Sat, 2-4pm Sun), whose ensemble of four slender turrets grouped around a central spire towers above Fischmarkt in the Altstadt. Its striking clover-leaf choir is an architectural feature pioneered by **St Maria im Kapitol** (Map p570; ☎ 214 615; Marienplatz 19; ⊗ 9.30am-6pm), where major treasures include a carved door from the original 11th-century church and a spectacularly ornate Renaissance rood screen.

The most eccentric-looking church is **St Gereon** (Map p570; ☎ 134 922; Gereonskloster 2-4; ⊗ 10am-2pm & 3-5pm Mon-Fri, 10am-noon & 3-5pm Sat & Sun), which grew from a late-Roman chapel into a massive complex lidded by a decagonal dome decorated with delicate ribbed vaulting.

If you look at Cologne's coat of arms, you'll see what looks like 11 apostrophes

but in fact represents the Christian martyrs St Ursula and 10 virgins. The church of **St Ursula** (Map p570; ☎ 133 400; Ursulaplatz 24; ⊗ 10am-noon & 3-5pm Mon-Sat) stands atop the Roman graveyard where the virgins' remains were allegedly found. In the 17th century, the richly ornamented baroque **Goldene Kammer** (Golden Chamber; adult/child €1/0.50) was built to house their relics.

ROMAN COLOGNE

Anyone even remotely interested in Roman history should not skip the extraordinary **Römisch-Germanisches Museum** (Romano-Germanic Museum; Map p570; ☎ 2212 4438; Roncalliplatz 4; adult/concession €8/4; ⊗ 10am-5pm Tue-Sun), adjacent to the Dom. Sculptures and ruins displayed outside are merely the overture to a full symphony of Roman artefacts found along the Rhine. Highlights include the giant **Poblicius tomb** (AD 30–40), the magnificent 3rd-century **Dionysus mosaic** around which the museum was built, and astonishingly well-preserved glass items. Insight into daily Roman life is gained from such items as toys, tweezers, lamps and jewellery, the designs of which have changed surprisingly little since.

Plenty of remnants of the Roman city survive around the museum, including a street leading to the harbour and two wells. Other vestiges from the ancient settlement include a **Roman arch** (Map p570) from the former town wall outside the Dom and the

HARBOUR REDUX

London has its Docklands, Düsseldorf its Medienhafen, Hamburg is building HafenCity and now Cologne has jumped on the revitalised-harbour bandwagon with the Rheinauhafen. South of the Altstadt an entire new urban quarter has sprung up along a 2km stretch between the Severinsbrücke and Südbrücke bridges. Dozens of 19th-century brick buildings are taking on a second life as luxe office, living and entertainment spaces, juxtaposed with contemporary designs ranging from bland to avant-garde. The most dramatic change to Cologne's skyline comes courtesy of a trio of Kranhäuser (Crane Houses), huge inverted L-shaped structures that are an abstract interpretation of historic harbour cranes. There are a few shops, restaurants and cafes as well as a riverside promenade but, as with all projects of this type, it'll be a while before the quarter's true character and personality come into focus. Stay tuned.

Römerturm (Map p570), a tower standing among buildings at the corner of St-Apern-Strasse and Zeughausstrasse.

Finally, there's the **Praetorium** (Map p570; ☎ 2212 2394; Kleine Budengasse 2; adult/concession €2.50/1.50; ☉ 10am-5pm Tue-Sun), the relics of a Roman governor's palace below the Renaissance Rathaus (Map p570). The Praetorium will soon be part of a much larger subterranean archaeological museum that's taking shape beneath the Rathausplatz. Visitors will be able to get close-ups of remnants, ruins and foundations of both Roman Cologne and the Jewish quarter in their original locations. A 3-D model in the Praetorium illustrates the project that's expected to open in 2011.

KOLUMBA

Art, history, architecture and spirituality form a harmonious tapestry in spectacular new digs for the collection of religious treasures of the Archdiocese of Cologne. Called **Kolumba** (Map p570; ☎ 933 1930; Kolumbastrasse 4; adult/under 18yr/concession €5/free/3; ☉ noon-5pm Wed-Mon), the building encases the ruins of the late-Gothic church St Kolumba, layers of foundations going back to Roman times and the Madonna in the Ruins chapel, built on the site in 1950. It's yet another magnificent design by Swiss architect Peter Zumthor, 2009 winner of the Pritzker Prize, the 'architectural Oscar'. Exhibits span the arc of religious artistry from the early days of Christianity to the present. Coptic textiles, Gothic reliquary and medieval painting are juxtaposed with works by Bauhaus legend Andor Weiniger and edgy room installations. The overall effect is contemplative rather than instructive, inspirational rather than historical.

MUSEUM LUDWIG

The distinctive building facade and unorthodox roofline signal that the **Museum Ludwig** (Map p570; ☎ 2212 6165; Heinrich-Böll-Platz; adult/concession/family €9/6/18, audioguide €3; ☉ 10am-6pm Tue-Sun) is no ordinary museum. Considered a mecca of postmodern art, it actually presents a survey of all major 20th-century genres. There's plenty of American pop art, including Andy Warhol's *Brillo Boxes*, alongside a comprehensive Picasso collection and plenty of works by Sigmar Polke. Fans of German expressionism will get their fill here as much as those with a penchant for such Russian avant-gardists as Kasimir Malewitsch and Ljubow Popowa.

Admission is also good for the **Foto-Museum Agfa Foto-Historama**, an unusual collection of historic photographs and equipment, housed under the same roof.

WALLRAF-RICHARTZ-MUSEUM & FONDATION CORBOUD

A famous collection of paintings from the 13th to the 19th centuries, the **Wallraf-Richartz-Museum** (Map p570; ☎ 2212 1119; Obenmarspforten; admission varies, usually €6-9; ☉ 10am-6pm Tue, Wed & Fri, 10am-10pm Thu, 11am-6pm Sat & Sun) occupies a postmodern cube designed by the late OM Ungers. Works are presented chronologically, with the oldest on the 1st floor where standouts include brilliant examples from the Cologne School, known for its distinctive use of colour. Upstairs are Dutch and Flemish artists, including Rembrandt and Rubens, Italians such as Canaletto and Spaniards such as Murillo. The 3rd floor focuses on the 19th century, with evocative works by Caspar David Friedrich and Lovis Corinth. Thanks to a permanent loan from Swiss collector Gérard Corboud, there's also a respectable collection of impressionist paintings, including canvases by Monet and Cézanne.

KULTURQUARTIER AM NEUMARKT
East of the Neumarkt, the newly created Cultural Quarter encompasses an extension of the **Museum Schnütgen** (Map p570; ☎ 2212 3620; Cäcilienstrasse 29; adult/concession €3.20/1.90; ☉ 10am-5pm Tue-Fri, 11am-5pm Sat & Sun), a repository of medieval religious art and sculpture. Part of the exhibit will continue to be shown in the beautiful setting of the Romanesque Cäcilienkirche (Cecily Church). Also part of the complex is a new building that will house the non-European art and cultural collections of the **Rautenstrauch-Joest-Museum** (Map p570; ☎ 2213 1301; Cäcilienstrasse 29-33).

SCHOKOLADEN MUSEUM
You don't have to have a sweet tooth to enjoy the **Schokoladen Museum** (Chocolate Museum; Map p570; ☎ 931 8880; Am Schokoladenmuseum 1a; adult/concession/family €7.50/7/21; ☉ 10am-6pm Tue-Fri, 11am-7pm Sat & Sun), a high-tech temple to the art of chocolate-making. Exhibits on the origin of the 'elixir of the gods', as the Aztecs called it, and the cocoa-growing process are followed by a live-production factory tour and a stop at a chocolate fountain for a sample. Upstairs are departments on the cultural history of chocolate, advertising, and porcelain and other accessories. Stock up on your favourite flavours at the downstairs shop.

DEUTSCHES SPORT & OLYMPIA MUSEUM
In a 19th-century customs building near the Schokoladen Museum, the **Deutsches Sport & Olympia Museum** (German Sport & Olympic Games Museum; Map p570; ☎ 336 090; Im Zollhafen 1; adult/concession/family €5/2.50/12.50; ☉ 10am-6pm Tue-Fri, 11am-7pm Sat & Sun) is an imaginative, if Germany-focused, tribute to the sporting life from antiquity to today. There are exhibits on the 1936 Berlin and 1972 Munich Olympic Games and on such modern-day heroes as Steffi Graf and Michael Schumacher. Interactive displays allow you to experience a bobsled run or a bike race, and on the miniature football field on the rooftop you can kick with a view of the cathedral.

NS DOKUMENTATIONSZENTRUM
Cologne's Third Reich history is poignantly documented in the **Documentation Centre** (Map p570; ☎ 2212 6332; Appellhofplatz 23-25; adult/concession €3.60/1.50; ☉ 10am-4pm Tue, Wed & Fri, 10am-6pm Thu, 11am-4pm Sat & Sun). In the basement of the building was the local Gestapo prison where scores of people were interrogated, tortured and killed. Inscriptions on the basement cell walls offer a gut-wrenching record of the emotional and physical pain endured by inmates.

OTHER MUSEUMS
Inside a bank branch is the **Käthe-Kollwitz-Museum** (Map p570; ☎ 227 2899; Neumarkt 18-24; adult/concession €3/1.50; ☉ 10am-6pm Tue-Fri, 11am-6pm Sat & Sun), with graphics and sculptures by the acclaimed socialist artist. A highlight is the haunting cycle called *Ein Weberaufstand* (A Weavers' Revolt, 1897). Enter through the arcade, then take the glass-bubble lift to the 4th floor.

The **Kölnisches Stadtmuseum** (Cologne City Museum; Map p570; ☎ 2212 5789; Zeughausstrasse 1-3; adult/concession €4.20/2.60, incl audioguide; ☉ 10am-8pm Tue, 10am-5pm Wed-Sun), in the former medieval armoury, explores all facets of Cologne history. There are exhibits on Carnival, *Kölsch* (the local beer), eau de cologne and other things that make the city unique.

The **Museum für Angewandte Kunst** (Museum of Applied Arts; Map p570; ☎ 2212 6735; An der Rechtschule; adult/concession €4.20/2.60; ☉ 11am-5pm Tue-Sun) consists of a series of period rooms tracing European design from the Middle Ages to today. Keep an eye out for a 15th-century Venetian wedding goblet, a silver service by Henry van de Velde and life-sized animals made of Meissen porcelain.

Tours
From May to October, the tourist office runs 90-minute city walking tours in English every Saturday at 1pm (adult/concession €9/7). DIY types might prefer picking up an audiovisual iGuide, also available at the tourist office, for self-guided touring (per 4/8 hours €8/12).

Rent-A-Bike (Map p570; ☎ 0171-629 8796; Marksmanngasse) runs German/English three-hour bicycle tours (€15) daily at 1.30pm from April to October. Tours start in the Altstadt right below the Deutzer Brücke.

In the warmer months, several boat companies offer one-hour spins taking in the splendid Altstadt panorama (adult/child €7.80/3.90). Other options include sunset cruises and all-day trips to Königswinter. See the map for embarkation points.

NORTH RHINE–WESTPHALIA

ZÜLPICHER VIERTEL & BELGISCHES VIERTEL

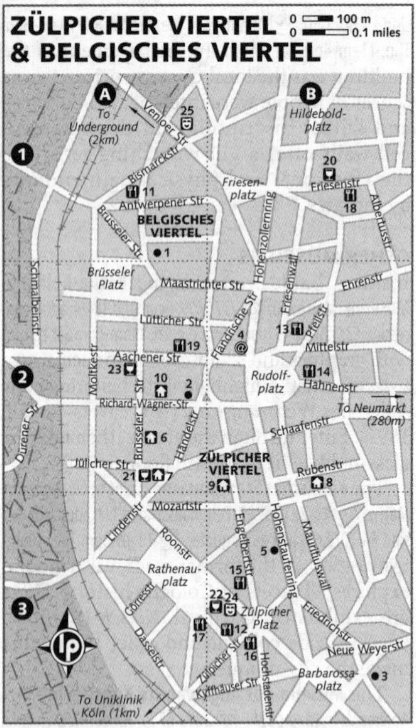

0 ———— 100 m
0 ———— 0.1 miles

Sleeping

Cologne is not a cheap city, especially during major trade shows (mostly in spring and autumn) when prices can be triple the standard rate.

BUDGET

Station – Hostel for Backpackers (Map p570; ☎ 912 5301; www.hostel-cologne.de; Marzellenstrasse 44-56; dm €17-20, s/d/tr €39/55/75; ✕ 🖳 ⃝) Near the Hauptbahnhof, this is a hostel as hostels should be: central, convivial and economical. A lounge gives way to clean, colourful rooms sleeping one to six people. The helpful staff speak fluent English, and there's lots of free stuff, including linen, internet access, lockers, city maps and guest kitchen.

Meininger City Hostel & Hotel (Map p574; ☎ 355 332 014; www.meininger-hostels.com; Engelbertstrasse 33-35; dm €17-24, s/d/tr from €43/68/84, breakfast €3.50; ✕ 🖳 ⃝) In a former hotel, this charming hostel in the cool Zülpicher Viertel is loaded with retro appeal coupled with modern rooms featuring lockers, reading lamps, a small TV and private bathrooms. Freebies include linen, towels and pasta that you can whip up in the small basement kitchen. The bar is a good spot for making friends.

Also recommended:

DJH hostel (off Map p570; ☎ 814 711; www.koeln -deutz.jugendherberge.de; Siegesstrasse 5; dm €25.30, s/d €43/63, incl linen & breakfast; ◉ Deutzer Freiheit; 🅿 ✕ 🖳 ⃝) Huge, state-of-the-art hostel.

Pension Jansen (Map p574; ☎ 251 875; www.pension jansen.de; Richard-Wagner-Strasse 18; s €31-45, d €62-65) Small B&B close to restaurants and nightlife; bathrooms are shared.

MIDRANGE

our pick Hotel Chelsea (Map p574; ☎ 207 150; www .hotel-chelsea.de; Jülicher Strasse 1; s €61-122, d €90-235; 🅿 ✕ 🖳 ⃝) Those fancying an artsy vibe will be well sheltered in this self-proclaimed 'hotel different'. Originals created by international artists in exchange for lodging grace the public areas and 38 rooms and suites. The eye-catching deconstructivist rooftop extension houses a spectacular penthouse.

Hotel Cristall (Map p570; ☎ 163 00; www.hotelcristall.de; Ursulaplatz 9-11; s €72-184, d €90-235; 🅿 ✕ 🅧 ⃝) This stylish boutique hotel makes excellent use of colour, customised furniture and light accents and manages to appeal both to the suit brigade and city-breakers. Alas, rooms won't it a tonne of luggage and light sleepers should get one facing away from the busy street.

Hotel Allegro (Map p570; ☎ 240 8260; www.hotel-allegro.com; Thurnmarkt 1-7; s €75-190, d €95-250; **P** ✕) Completely nonsmoking, this pleasant pit stop just south of the Altstadt has rooms that sport either a frilly Bavarian or sleek contemporary look. Some have river views, but those at the back are quieter.

Hotel Santo (off Map p570; ☎ 913 9770; www.hotelsanto.de; Dagobertstrasse 22-26; s €95-140, d €120-160; Ⓔ Ebertplatz; **P** ✕ ⌂) Despite the drab location near the Hauptbahnhof, this 69-room boutique hotel is an island of sassy sophistication. The design flaunts an edgy, urban feel tempered by playful light effects, soothing colours and natural materials. Bonus: the gourmet breakfast.

Hopper Hotel Et Cetera (Map p574; ☎ 924 400; www.hopper.de; Brüsseler Strasse 26; s €80-270, d €120-295; **P** ✕ ⌂) A waxen monk welcomes you to this former monastery whose 49 rooms sport eucalyptus floors, cherry furniture and marble baths along with lots of little pampering touches. The sauna and bar, both in the vaulted cellars, are great places for reliving the day's exploits.

Other recommendations:

Hotel Leonet (Map p574; ☎ 272 300; www.leonet-koeln.de; Rubensstrasse 33; s €65-160, d €85-225; **P** ✕ ⌂ ⌂) Modern hotel with good-sized rooms and extensive wellness area.

Lint Hotel (Map p570; ☎ 920 550; www.lint-hotel.de; Lintgasse 7; s/d €85/129; ✕) Cute, contemporary and eco-conscious (solar-panelled roof) hotel in the heart of the Altstadt.

TOP END

Hopper Hotel St Antonius (off Map p570; ☎ 166 00; www.hopper.de; Dagobertstrasse 32; s €105-290, d €175-315; Ⓔ Ebertplatz; **P** ✕ ⌂ ⌂) History and high-tech mix nicely at this posh retreat with plenty of eye candy for the style-conscious. The romantic courtyard garden and small wellness area in the brick-vaulted cellar are great blissout spots. Main drawback: the bland setting near the Hauptbahnhof.

Hotel Im Wasserturm (Map p570; ☎ 200 80; www.hotel-im-wasserturm.de; Kaygasse 2; r €236-385, breakfast €28; **P** ✕ ⌂ ⌂ ⌂) This is an extremely classy designer hotel cleverly converted from an old water tower, south of Neumarkt.

Eating

Cologne's multiculturalism lets you take a culinary journey around the world. Rhenish specialities and classic German food are best sampled in the beer halls (see p576).

La Bodega (Map p574; ☎ 257 3610; Friesenstrasse 51; tapas €2.20-5.70; ☒ 5pm-1am Sun-Thu, to 3am Fri & Sat) It's always fiesta time at this buzzy cantina with its cosy vaulted cellar and romantic courtyard. Gobble up the *jamón* (smoked ham), stuffed peppers, nut-encrusted goat cheese and other authentic tapas or go the whole nine yards and order a heaping paella. Locals invade for the Monday special: a pound of fat shrimp with four dipping sauces for €15.

Engelbät (Map p574; ☎ 246 914; Engelbertstrasse 7; crepes €2.50-7.50; ☒ 11am-1am) This cosy restaurant-pub is famous for its habit-forming crepes, which come in 30 varieties – sweet,

---

FOOLS, FLOATS & REVELRY

Carnival in Cologne is one of the best parties in Europe and a thumb in the eye of the German work ethic. Every year at the onset of Lent (late February/early March), a year of painstaking preparation culminates in the 'three crazy days' – actually more like six.

It all starts with *Weiberfastnacht*, the Thursday before Ash Wednesday, when women rule the day (and do things like chop off the ties of their male colleagues/bosses). The party continues through the weekend, with more than 50 parades of ingenious floats and wildly dressed lunatics dancing in the streets. By the time it all comes to a head with the big parade on *Rosenmontag* (Rose Monday), the entire city has come unglued. Those still capable of swaying and singing will live it up one last time on Shrove Tuesday before the curtain comes down on Ash Wednesday.

'If you were at the parade and saw the parade, you weren't at the parade', say the people of Cologne in their inimitable way. Translated, this means that you should be far too busy singing, drinking, roaring the Carnival greeting '*Alaaf!*' and planting a quick *Bützchen* (kiss) on the cheek of whoever strikes your fancy, to notice anything happening around you. Swaying and drinking while crammed like sardines in a pub, or following other costumed fools behind a huge bass drum leading to God-only-knows-where, you'll be swept up in one of the greatest parties the world knows.

meat or vegetarian. Also popular for breakfast (served until 3pm).

Metzgerei & Salon Schmitz (Map p574; ☎ 139 5577; dishes €4-10; Aachener Strasse 28; ☒ 10am-late) No matter whether you prefer sidling up to the long bar or grabbing an ultra-comfy sofa in the retro lounge, Schmitz is a perfect pit stop for relaxed chats over coffee or cocktails. If hunger strikes, pop next door to Metzgerei Schmitz, a deli in a former butcher's shop.

Alcazar (Map p574; ☎ 515 733; Bismarckstrasse 39; snacks €4-9, mains €7-17; ☒ noon-2am Mon-Fri, 6pm-3am Sat, 5pm-2am Sun) This is the kind of place that never goes out of fashion, thanks to its winning combination of freshly prepared international dishes, unpretentious ambience and chirpy service. No food service in the afternoon.

Feynsinn (Map p574; ☎ 240 9210; Rathenauplatz 7; lunch €7.50, dinner mains €10-17; ☒ 10am-1am) What used to be a small cafe famous for its eccentric glass-chard chandelier has morphed into a well-respected restaurant where organic ingredients are woven into sharp-flavoured dishes. Owners have even started to raise their own pigs and cattle!

Bagutta (Map p574; ☎ 212 694; Heinsbergstrasse 20a; mains around €20, 3-/4-/5-course menu €32/37/42; ☒ 6-11pm Wed-Mon) Leagues of local loyalists keep this knick-knack-filled charmer hopping. Do as they do: ignore the menu and just ask chef Stefan Bierl to put together a 'surprise menu'. With potential items including saffron risotto with scallops or guinea fowl with kohlrabi and chorizo stir-fry, you won't be disappointed.

Osman 30 (off Map p570; ☎ 5005 2080; Im Mediapark 8; 3-course menu €44; ☒ 6pm-1am Mon-Thu, 6pm-3am Fri & Sat, 11am-7pm Sun; ☺ Christoph-Strasse/Mediapark) The setting alone of this made-to-impress restaurant on the 30th floor of the KölnTurm is spectacular, but fortunately the Mediterranean food can hold its own with the views. Cap your meal with libations served in the wine salon with its stylish white leather armchairs. Reservations essential.

Other fine eating options:

Falafel Salam (Map p574; ☎ 240 2933; Zülpicher Platz 7; falafels €2.50-5; ☒ 11.30am-2am or later) The mother of all Cologne falafel snack bars.

Supa Salad (Map p570; ☎ 648 746; Gertrudenstrasse 33; mains €4-6.50; ☒ 10am-8pm Mon-Fri, noon-8pm Sat) Cheerful *Imbiss* (food stall) serving vitamin-packed salads and energy-restoring panini.

Drinking

Cologne's thirst parlours range from grungy to grand. Centres of action include the Altstadt, with its rollicking pubs and beer halls; the Friesenviertel along Friesenwall and Friesenstrasse; the 'Kwartier Lateng' (Cologne dialect for Latin Quarter, or student quarter), also known as Zülpicher Viertel, along Zülpicher Strasse, Roonstrasse and Kyffhäuser Strasse; and the Belgisches Viertel (Belgian Quarter) along Bismarckstrasse, Flandrische Strasse and Maastrichter Strasse.

BEER HALLS

Beer reigns supreme in Cologne, where over 20 breweries produce the local variety called *Kölsch*, which is served in skinny glasses called *Stangen*. Pick from a selection of stout Rhenish dishes to keep you grounded.

Brauhaus Peters (Map p570; ☎ 257 3950; Mühlengasse 1; dishes €4-13; ☒ 11am-12.30am) This relative youngster draws a somewhat less raucous crowd knocking back their *Kölsch* in a web of highly individualistic nooks, including a room lidded by a kaleidoscopic stained-glass ceiling. On Tuesday, insiders invade for the potato pancakes, freshly made and topped with anything from apple compote to smoked salmon.

Früh am Dom (Map p570; ☎ 261 30; Am Hof 12-14; breakfast €4-13, mains €4-20) This warren of a beer hall near the Dom epitomises Cologne earthiness. Sit inside amid loads of knick-knacks or on the terrace next to a fountain. It's also known for great breakfasts.

Päffgen (Map p574; ☎ 135 461; Friesenstrasse 64-66; mains €6.50-17; ☒ 10am-midnight) Busy, loud and boisterous, Päffgen has been pouring *Kölsch* since 1883 and hasn't lost a step since. In summer you can enjoy the refreshing brew and local specialities beneath starry skies in the beer garden.

Schreckenskammer (Map p570; ☎ 132 581; Ursulagartenstrasse 11; mains €8-15; ☒ 11am-1.45pm & 4.30-10.30pm Mon-Sat) Empty chairs are a rare sight at this locals' favourite that has better food than your average beer hall. New in 2009: the beer garden (enter from Ursulakloster 20).

Malzmühle (Map p570; ☎ 210 117; Heumarkt 6; mains €8-15; ☒ 10am-midnight) Expect plenty of local colour at this convivial beer hall off the beaten tourist track. It brews *Kölsch* with organic ingredients and is also known for its lighter *Malzbier* (malt beer, 2% alcohol).

PUBS & BARS

Scheinbar (Map p574; ☎ 923 9048; Brüsseler Strasse 10; ⓨ from 8pm) If you needed any proof that Cologne's nightlife is smoking hot, simply stop by this bar that's dressed in red satin, lava lamps and has sitting areas perfect for chilling.

Six Pack (Map p574; ☎ 254 587; Aachener Strasse 33; ⓨ 8pm-5am) This is a must-stop on any Belgian Quarter pub crawl. Belly up to the super-long bar and pick from several-dozen varieties of beer, all served by the bottle from a giant fridge. Things can get seriously jammed after midnight.

Sky Beach (Map p570; ☎ 1654 9904; above Aral petrol station, Cäcilienstrasse 32; ⓨ from noon, weather permitting, Apr-Sep) Check out the city skyline while wiggling your toes in Sahara sand on the upper deck of a parking garage at this quirky beach bar.

Shepheard (Map p574; ☎ 331 0994; Rathenauplatz 5; ⓨ 8pm-3am Tue-Sat) This glamorous cocktail bar lures chatty sophisticates huddled in intense conversation and grateful for the mellow lighting and jazz. Named for a colonial hotel in Cairo, it offers 190 different cocktails, including 40 original creations.

Flanagans (Map p570; ☎ 257 0674; Alter Markt 36; ⓨ 5pm-1am, to 3am Tue, Fri & Sat) Irish pub. Enough said.

Entertainment

For Cologne's main nightlife quarters, see Drinking (opposite). Major listings magazines are *Monatsvorschau* (bilingual, mainstream), *Kölner Illustrierte* (mainstream), *Prinz* (trendy) and *StadtRevue* (alternative), available at newsagents and bookshops.

NIGHTCLUBS & LIVE MUSIC

Gebäude 9 (off Map p570; ☎ 814 637; Deutz-Mülheimer Strasse 127; ⓞ Stegerwaldsiedlung) This ex-factory is an essential indie-rock concert venue in town. DJs take over at other times, and there's also an eclectic programme of nonmainstream plays and films. Take tram 3 or 4 to KölnMesse/Osthallen.

Stadtgarten (Map p574; ☎ 952 9940; Venloer Strasse 40) Surrounded by a small park, this Belgian Quarter favourite hosts vibrant dance parties and live jazz, soul and world music concerts in its cellar hall, but is also a great spot just for a drink (summer beer garden).

Underground (off Map p570; ☎ 542 326; Vogelsanger Strasse 200; ⓨ Mon & Wed-Sat; ⓞ Venloer Strasse/Gürtel) This complex combines a pub and two concert halls where indie and alternative rock bands hold forth several times a week. Otherwise it's party time with different music nightly (no cover). There's a beer garden in summer. To get here take U3 or U4 to Venloer Strasse/Gürtel.

GAY & LESBIAN COLOGNE

Next to Berlin, Cologne is Germany's gayest city, with the rainbow flag flying especially proudly in the so-called 'Bermuda Triangle' around Rudolfplatz, which explodes into a nonstop fun zone at weekends. Another major romping ground is the Heumarkt area (especially Pipinstrasse), which draws more sedate folks and leather and fetish lovers. The **Gay & Lesbian Street Festival** in June basically serves as a warm-up for the **Christopher Street Party & Parade** (usually in July), which brings more than a million people to Cologne.

A good place to start plugging into the scene is the information and health centre **Checkpoint** (Map p570; ☎ 9257 6868; www.checkpoint-cologne.de; Pipinstrasse 7; ⓨ 5-9pm Wed & Thu, 2-7pm Fri & Sat, 2-6pm Sun). The listings magazine **Rik** (www.rik-magazin.de) has good info and a database of hangouts, although unfortunately in German only.

Places worth checking out include: **Blue Lounge** (Map p570; ☎ 271 7117; Mathiasstrasse 4-6; ⓨ from 9pm Wed-Sun), a smooth dance and cocktail bar with a mixed crowd; **Barflo** (Map p574; ☎ 257 3239; Friesenwall 24d; ⓨ 10.30am-1am), a perennially popular all-day cafe with great breakfasts and cakes; **Brennerei Weiss** (Map p574; ☎ 257 4638; Hahnenstrasse 22; mains €5-14; ⓨ 3pm-1am Mon-Thu, 11am-open end Sat, 11am-1am Sun), a no-nonsense restaurant serving delicious German and regional cuisine; **Gezeiten** (off Map p570; ☎ 474 7703; Balthasarstrasse 1; mains €5-15; ⓨ from 7pm Tue-Sun; ⓞ Ebertplatz), which is favoured by lesbians and has a creative menu that changes weekly; and the men-only **Chains** (Map p570; ☎ 238 730; Stephanstrasse 4), the city's largest leather-and-fetish bar with house and techno on the turntable and an active darkroom.

Alter Wartesaal (Map p570; ☎ 912 8850; Johannisstrasse 11; ☼ Fri & Sat) In a former train station waiting hall, this is a stylish bar-disco-restaurant combo. Themed nights range from the erotic KitKatClub to Depeche Mode parties and '80s nights. The restaurant serves modern German with international touches (mains lunch €7.50 to €12, dinner €17 to €22; open noon to 1am).

Papa Joe's Klimperkasten (Map p570; ☎ 258 2132; Alter Markt 50) A piano player tickles the ivories nightly in this museum-like place where walls are strewn with yesteryear's photographs and there are lots of quirky things to discover (check out the wood-carved 'one-armed bandit' by the door).

Other recommendations:

Papa Joe's Em Streckstrump (Map p570; ☎ 257 7931; Buttermarkt 37; ☼ 8pm-3am Mon-Sat, from 3.30pm Sun) Free live jazz.

Roonburg (Map p574; ☎ 240 3719; Roonstrasse 33; ☼ Tue & Thu-Sat) High-octane party den with cheap beer and student crowd.

THEATRE & CLASSICAL MUSIC

Kölner Philharmonie (Map p570; ☎ 280 280; www .koelner-philharmonie.de; Bischofsgartenstrasse 1) The famous Kölner Philharmoniker is the 'house band' in this grand, modern concert hall below the Museum Ludwig. Buy tickets at www.koelnticket.de, by phone or at the box office.

Repertory theatre is based at the **Schauspielhaus** (Map p570; ☎ 2212 8400; www.buehnenkoeln.de; Offenbachplatz), in the same complex as the Opernhaus (opera). The box office for both is in the Opernhaus foyer.

Shopping

Cologne is a fantastic place to shop, with lots of eccentric boutiques, designer and vintage stores, plus the usual selection of chain and department stores. The last concentrate along Hohe Strasse, one of Germany's oldest pedestrianised shopping strips, and its side street, In der Höhle (Map p570). Schildergasse (Map p570) has smaller fashion and shoe shops and culminates in the Neumarkt (Map p570), where the Neumarkt-Galerie mall is easily recognised by the upturned ice-cream cone on the roof, designed by Claes Oldenburg and Coosje van Brugge. The best streets for maxing out your credit card are Mittelstrasse and Pfeilstrasse (Map p574), lined with exclusive fashion, jewellery and home-accessory shops. Ehrenstrasse (Map p574) is another interesting strip, even though it's increasingly taken over by international chains. Indie designer boutiques are scattered through the quiet streets of the Belgian Quarter around Brüsseler Platz (Map p574).

A classic gift for mum is a bottle of eau de cologne, the not terribly sophisticated but refreshing perfume created – and still being produced – in its namesake city. The most famous brand is called 4711, named after the number of the house where it was invented, which now houses a shop, **Haus 4711** (Map p570; ☎ 925 0450; Glockengasse 22-28). Outside, up on the facade, note the cutesy carillon with characters from Prussian lore parading hourly from 9am to 9pm.

The shops in the Hauptbahnhof stay open until 10pm.

Getting There & Away

AIR

About 18km southeast of the city centre, **Köln Bonn Airport** (Cologne Bonn Airport; off Map p570; ☎ 02203-404 001; www.airport-cgn.de) has direct flights to 130 cities and is served by 50 airlines, including budget carriers such as Germanwings, Air Berlin and easyJet.

BUS

Eurolines runs buses in all directions, including Paris (€43, 7½ hours) and Amsterdam (€23, 5¼ hours). The central bus station (Map p570) is on Breslauer Platz, behind the Hauptbahnhof.

CAR & MOTORCYCLE

Cologne is encircled by the heavily trafficked Kölner Ring, with exits to the A1, A3, A4, A57, A555 and A559 leading in all directions.

TRAIN

Cologne is linked to Bonn several times hourly by U-Bahn lines U16 and U18 and regional trains (€6.50, 30 minutes). There are also regional train services to Brühl (€3.30, 15 minutes), Düsseldorf (€9.60, 30 minutes) and Aachen (€14.40, 70 minutes). Cologne is also a major main-line hub with direct ICE service to Berlin (€106, 4¼ hours), Frankfurt (€63, 1¼ hours) and Munich (€127, 4½ hours).

Getting Around

TO/FROM THE AIRPORT

The S13 train connects the airport and the Hauptbahnhof every 20 minutes (€2.40, 15 minutes). Taxis charge about €25.

BICYCLE

Rent-A-Bike (Map p570; ☎ 0171-629 8796; Marksmanngasse; ☼ 10am-6pm Apr-Oct) hires out bikes for €2 per hour or €10 per day and also does tours (see p573).

Radstation (Map p570; ☎ 139 7190; Breslauer Platz; ☼ 5.30am-10.30pm Mon-Fri, 6.30am-8pm Sat, 8am-8pm Sun), at the Hauptbahnhof, has the same rates as Rent-A-Bike.

CAR & MOTORCYCLE

Central Cologne is now a low-emission zone, meaning that your car needs to display an *Umweltplakette* (emission sticker). Rental cars automatically have one, but if you're driving your own vehicle, see p783 for details on how to obtain the sticker.

Driving around Cologne can be an absolute nightmare. Unless you're careful, you could easily end up in a tunnel or on a bridge going across the Rhine. Most streets in the centre of the city are restricted to residents' parking only, so often your only option is an expensive public garage.

PUBLIC TRANSPORT

Cologne's mix of buses, trams, and U-Bahn and S-Bahn trains is operated by **VRS** (☎ 01803-504 030; www.vrsinfo.de) in cooperation with Bonn's system.

Short trips (up to four stops) cost €1.60, longer ones €2.40. Day passes are €6.90 for one person and €10.10 for up to five people travelling together. Buy your tickets from the orange ticket machines at stations and aboard trams; be sure to validate them.

TAXI

Taxis cost €2.50 at flag fall, plus €1.55 per kilometre (€1.65 between 10pm and 6am and all day Sunday). Call ☎ 2882 or ☎ 194 10.

BRÜHL

☎ 02232 / pop 44,600

Brühl, halfway between Cologne and Bonn, wraps an astonishing number of riches into a pint-size package. The town languished in relative obscurity until the 18th century, when archbishop-elector Clemens August

(1723–61) – friend of Casanova and himself a lover of women, parties and palaces – made it his residence. His two made-to-impress rococo palaces, at opposite ends of the elegant Schlosspark, landed on Unesco's list of World Heritage Sites in 1984.

The larger and flashier of the two, **Schloss Augustusburg** (☎ 440 00; Schlossstrasse 6; tours adult/student/family €5/4.50/12; ☼ 9am-1pm & 1.30-5pm Tue-Fri, 10am-6pm Sat & Sun, last admission 1hr before closing, closed Dec & Jan) is a little jewel box designed by François Cuvilliés. On guided tours you'll learn fascinating titbits about hygiene, dating and other aspects of daily life at court. The architectural highlight is a ceremonial staircase by Balthasar Neumann, a dizzying symphony in stucco, sculpture and faux marble.

Cuvilliés also dreamed up **Jagdschloss Falkenlust** (☎ 440 00; Schlossstrasse 6; adult/concession/family €3.50/3/8; ☼ 9am-1pm & 1.30-5pm Tue-Fri, 10am-6pm Sat & Sun, closed Dec & Jan), a hunting lodge where Clemens August liked to indulge his fancy for falconry. Though small, it's almost as opulent as the main palace. A particular gem is the adjacent chapel, which is awash in shells, minerals and crystals.

A short stroll from the palaces is the **Max Ernst Museum** (☎ 579 3110; www.maxernstmuseum.com; Comesstrasse 42; adult/concession/family €5/3/10; ☼ 11am-6pm Tue-Sun), where nine rooms trace all creative phases of the Brühl-born Dadaist and surrealist (1891–1976). We especially enjoyed examples of his artistic innovations such as frottage (floor-board rubbings) and the spooky collage novels, which are graphic works exploring the darkest crevices of the subconscious.

Brühl's other big drawcard is **Phantasialand** (☎ 362 00; www.phantasialand.de; Berggeiststrasse 31-41; adult/child €33.50/29.50; ☼ 9am-6pm Apr-Oct, last admission 4pm, extended hr possible in summer), one of Europe's earliest, most popular and best Disneyland-style amusement parks (since 1967). The park has six themed areas – Chinatown, Old Berlin, Mexico, Fantasy, Mystery and Deep in Africa – each with their own roller coasters, gondolas, flight simulators, water rides and other thrills, plus song and dance shows. To be admitted as a child you have to be shorter than 145cm; if you're younger than seven or it's your birthday, admission is free.

Brühl is regularly served by regional trains from Cologne (€3.30, 15 minutes) and Bonn (€4.20, 10 minutes). The Hauptbahnhof is opposite Schloss Augustusburg, with the compact town centre behind the palace. Shuttle buses to Phantasialand leave from outside the station. If you're driving, exit Brühl-Ost/Wesseling off the A553 or Godorf/Brühl off the A555, then follow the signs.

BONN
☎ 0228 / pop 311,000

When this friendly, relaxed city on the Rhine became West Germany's 'temporary' capital in 1949 it surprised many, including its own residents. When in 1991 a reunited German government decided to move to Berlin, it shocked many, *especially* its own residents. A generation later, no-one need feel sorry for Bonn. Change brings opportunity, and rather than plunge into the dark depths of provincialism, the ex-capital has reinvented itself with creativity and vigour. Its cosmopolitan openness has attracted an international cast of businesses, students, scientists and UN organisations. Bonn's progressive outlook is also reflected in its launch of a sustainability initiative, which ropes in hotels, caterers, venues and other businesses in an effort to create a 'conference location of sustainability'.

For visitors, the birthplace of Ludwig van Beethoven has plenty in store, not least the great composer's birth house, a string of top-rated museums, a lovely riverside setting and the nostalgic flair of the old government quarter. Bonn can be seen on an easy day trip from Cologne but also makes for an excellent jumping-off point to the Siebengebirge nature reserve and other area attractions.

Orientation
Cologne Bonn Airport is about 25km northeast of the city centre (see p585 for information on getting to/from the airport). The historic Altstadt extends north of the Hauptbahnhof with the Nordstadt just beyond, while the Museumsmeile (Museum Mile) and Bundesviertel (former government district) are south along the Rhine; Poppelsdorf is also south of the station but away from the Rhine.

Information
Bonn Regio WelcomeCard (per 24/48/72hr €9/14/19) Unlimited public transport, admission to over 20 museums, plus discounts on tours, thermal baths and more in Bonn and beyond. The group (three adults) or family (two adults, two kids) version is €18/28/38.
Bouvier (☎ 729 010; Am Hof 28) Bookshop.

Internet Several telephone-call shops near the Hauptbahnhof offer internet access.
Post office (Münsterplatz 17; ☉ 9am-8pm Mon-Fri, 9am-4pm Sat)
ReiseBank (☎ 632 958; Hauptbahnhof; ☉ 9am-7pm Mon-Fri, 9am-3pm Sat)
Tourist office (☎ 775 000; www.bonn.de; Windeckstrasse 1; ☉ 9am-6.30pm Mon-Fri, 9am-4pm Sat, 10am-2pm Sun) For pre-trip planning, go to www.bonn-region.de.
Uniklinikum Bonn (☎ 2870; Sigmund-Freud-Strasse 25; ☉ 24hr) Major hospital 4km south of the Hauptbahnhof.

Sights
ALTSTADT
A good place to start exploring Bonn's historic centre is on Münsterplatz, where the landmark **Münster Basilica** (☎ 985 880; www.bonner-muenster.de; admission free; ☉ 7am-7pm) was built on the graves of the two martyred Roman soldiers who later got promoted to be the city's patron saints. It got its Gothic look in the 13th century but the Romanesque origins survive beautifully in the ageing cloister (open till 5pm). On the square outside the church, a buttercup-yellow baroque Palais (palace; now the post office) forms a photogenic backdrop for the **Beethoven Monument** (1845).

The famous composer first saw the light of day in 1770 in the rather plain **Beethoven Haus** (Beethoven House; ☎ 981 7525; www.beethoven-haus-bonn.de; Bonngasse 20; adult/concession/family €4/3/10; ☉ 10am-6pm Mon-Sat, 11am-6pm Sun Apr-Oct, to 5pm Nov-Mar). It's now the repository of a pretty static array of letters, musical scores, instruments and paintings. The highlights – his last grand piano, the huge ear trumpets he used to combat his growing deafness and a famous portrait – are all on the 2nd floor. Tickets are also good for the **Digitales Beethoven-Haus** next door, where you can experience the composer's genius during a spacey, interactive 3-D multimedia show or deepen your knowledge in the digital archive.

In the Altstadt's other main square, the triangular Markt, the baroque **Altes Rathaus** (old town hall) stands pretty in pink with silver and gold trim. Politicians from Charles de Gaulle to John F Kennedy have waved to the crowds from its double-sided staircase.

To the south is the palatial 1705 **Kurfürstliche Residenz** (Electoral Residence; Regina-Pacis-Weg), once the immodest home of the archbishop-electors of Cologne and part of Bonn's university since 1818. Its south side opens up to

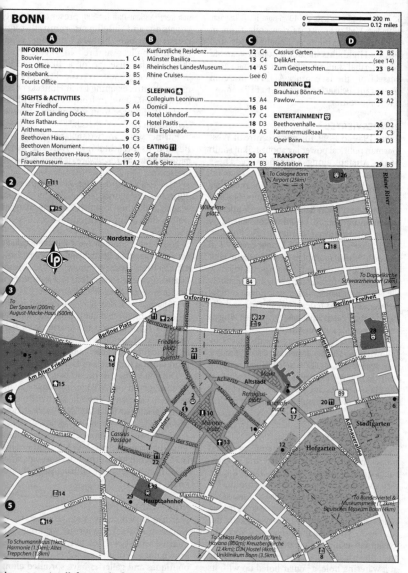

BONN

0 _____ 200 m
0 _____ 0.12 miles

INFORMATION		
Bouvier	**1**	C4
Post Office	**2**	B4
Reisebank	**3**	B5
Tourist Office	**4**	B4

SIGHTS & ACTIVITIES		
Alter Friedhof	**5**	A4
Alter Zoll Landing Docks	**6**	D4
Altes Rathaus	**7**	C4
Arithmeum	**8**	D5
Beethoven Haus	**9**	C3
Beethoven Monument	**10**	C4
Digitales Beethoven-Haus	(see 9)	
Frauenmuseum	**11**	A2

Kurfürstliche Residenz	**12**	C4
Münster Basilica	**13**	C4
Rheinisches LandesMuseum	**14**	A5
Rhine Cruises	(see 6)	

SLEEPING		
Collegium Leoninum	**15**	A4
Domicil	**16**	B4
Hotel Löhndorf	**17**	C4
Hotel Pastis	**18**	D3
Villa Esplanade	**19**	A5

EATING		
Cafe Blau	**20**	D4
Cafe Spitz	**21**	B3

Cassius Garten	**22**	B5
DelikArt	(see 14)	
Zum Gequetschten	**23**	B4

DRINKING		
Brauhaus Bönnsch	**24**	B3
Pawlow	**25**	A2

ENTERTAINMENT		
Beethovenhalle	**26**	D2
Kammermusiksaal	**27**	C3
Oper Bonn	**28**	D3

TRANSPORT		
Radstation	**29**	B5

the expansive **Hofgarten** (Palace Garden), a popular gathering place for students.

Off the far southwest corner, the **Arithmeum** (☎ 738 790; Lennéstrasse 2; adult/concession €3/2; ☺ 11am-5pm Tue-Sun) explores the symbiosis of science, technology and art. On view are hundreds of mechanical calculators and historic mathematics books but also an out-there exhibit

on the aesthetics of microchips. Design your own or study their beauty through a polarisation microscope. Work your way down from the top floor of this minimalist glass-and-steel cube.

South of the Hauptbahnhof, the **Rheinisches LandesMuseum** (Rhineland Regional Museum; ☎ 207 00; www.rlmb.lvr.de; Colmantstrasse 14-18; adult/under

18yr/student €5/free/3.50; ☼ 10am-6pm Tue & Thu-Sun, 10am-9pm Wed) presents its rich collections in such themed exhibits as Epochs, Gods, and Power. Highlights include a 40,000-year-old Neanderthal skull and a rare blue Roman glass vessel from the 1st century AD. The museum restaurant, **DelikArt** (mains €11 to €17), enjoys a fine reputation.

BUNDESVIERTEL

From 1949 to 1999, the nerve centre of West German political power lay about 1.5km south of the Altstadt along Adenauerallee. These days the former government quarter has reinvented itself as the home for UN and other international and federal institutions. The airy and modern **Plenary Hall**, where the Bundestag (German parliament) used to convene, now hosts international conferences. Nearby, the high-rise nicknamed **Langer Eugen** (Tall Eugen), where members of parliament kept their offices, is now a UN campus. Officially retaining their former purposes are the stately **Villa Hammerschmidt**, still a secondary official residence of the federal president, and the neoclassical **Palais Schaumburg**, now serving as the chancellor's Bonn office.

A handy way to explore the district is by following the **Weg der Demokratie** (Path of Democracy; www.wegderdemokratie.de), a self-guided walking tour taking in 18 key historic sites. It starts at the Haus der Geschichte der Bundesrepublik Deutschland. Explanatory panelling in English is provided.

MUSEUMSMEILE

Bonn's **Museum Mile**, one of the country's finest museum clusters, sits opposite the government quarter, on the western side of the B9. Across from the Villa Hammerschmidt, the **Museum Koenig** (☎ 912 20; www.zfmk.de; Adenauerallee 160; adult/concession €3/1.50; ☼ 10am-6pm Tue, Thu-Sun, 10am-9pm Wed) is a natural history museum but it's hardly your usual dead-animal zoo. The 'Savannah' exhibit re-creates an entire habitat with theatrical flourishes: elephants drinking at a watering hole, a jaguar holed up with its kill and vultures surveying the scene from above. Other highlights include a talking baobab tree in the 'Rainforest', a colossal sea elephant in the 'Arctic' and a condor with a 3m wingspan in the 'World of Birds'.

The **Haus der Geschichte der Bundesrepublik Deutschland** (Forum of Contemporary German History; ☎ 916 50; www.hdg.de; Willy-Brandt-Allee 14; admission free; ☼ 9am-7pm Tue-Sun) presents a highly engaging and intelligent romp through recent German history, starting when the final bullet was fired in WWII. Walk through the fuselage of a Berlin Airlift 'Rosinenbomber', watch classic clips in a 1950s movie theatre, examine Erich Honecker's arrest warrant, stand in front of a piece of the Berlin Wall or see John F Kennedy's famous 'Ich bin ein Berliner' speech.

Further south are two stellar art museums. Beyond its breathtaking foyer, the **Kunstmuseum Bonn** (☎ 776 260; www.kunstmuseum-bonn.de; Friedrich-Ebert-Allee 2; adult/concession/family €5/2.50/10; ☼ 11am-6pm Tue, Thu-Sun, 11am-9pm Wed) presents 20th-century works, especially by August Macke and other Rhenish expressionists, as well as such avant-gardists as Beuys, Baselitz and Kiefer.

Next door, the **Kunst-und Ausstellungshalle der Bundesrepublik Deutschland** (Art and Exhibition Hall of the Federal Republic of Germany; ☎ 917 1200; www.bundeskunsthalle.de; Friedrich-Ebert-Allee 4; adult/concession/family per exhibit €8/5/14, all exhibits €14/9/24.50; ☼ 10am-9pm Tue & Wed, 10am-7pm Thu-Sun) is another striking space that brings in blockbuster exhibits from around the world. It's easily recognised by the three sky-blue cones jutting from the rooftop garden and the 16 columns representing the states of Germany.

Did you know that the air bag, the computer tomograph and MP3 technology were invented in Germany? You will, after visiting the **Deutsches Museum Bonn** (☎ 302 255; www.deutsches-museum-bonn.de; Ahrstrasse 45; adult/child €4/2.50; ☼ 10am-6pm Tue-Sun), about 2km further south. This subsidiary of the Munich mother ship (p315) highlights German technology since WWII with plenty of buttons to push and knobs to pull.

NORDSTADT

Nordstadt, which is also referred to as Northern Altstadt, is a former working-class quarter whose web of narrow streets has grown pockets of hipness. Cafes, restaurants, boutiques and galleries have sprouted along Breite Strasse, Heerstrasse and the connecting side streets. The quarter is prettiest in spring when the cherry trees are in bloom.

The expressionist painter August Macke (1887–1914) lived in this neighbourhood in the three years before his untimely death on the battlefields in WWI. His neoclassical home is now the **August-Macke-Haus** (☎ 655 53;

www.august-macke-haus.de; Bornheimer Strasse 96; adult/concession/family €4/3/8; ☑ 2.30-6pm Tue-Fri, 11am-5pm Sat & Sun), where you can soak up the master's aura in his re-created studio and see some originals; the finest works, though, are at the Kunstmuseum Bonn (opposite).

Nordstadt is also home of the **Frauenmuseum** Women's Museum; ☎ 691 344; www.frauenmuseum.de; Im Krausfeld 10; adult/concession €4.50/3; ☑ 2-6pm Tue-Sat, 1am-6pm Sun), which supports and showcases the art of women through exhibits, lectures, readings and performances.

POPPELSDORF & AROUND

South of the Altstadt, elegant and leafy Poppelsdorf is anchored by **Schloss Poppelsdorf**, another electoral palace now used by the university. Students and neighbourhood folk populate the bars and restaurants along Clemens-August-Strasse, which runs south of the palace towards the hillside **Kreuzbergkirche** (Stationsweg 21; ☑ 9am-6pm Apr-Oct, to 5pm Nov-Mar). This rococo gem is lavishly decorated with gilded faux marble, frescoes and a Balthasar Neumann–designed version of the Holy Steps.

Fans of Robert Schumann (1810–56) might enjoy the small memorial exhibit in the **Schumannhaus** (☎ 773 656; Sebastianstrasse 182; admission free; ☑ 11am-1.30pm & 3-6pm Mon & Wed-Fri). It's in the former sanatorium he checked into following a suicide attempt in 1854. He and his wife Clara are buried in **Alter Friedhof** (Old Cemetery) on Bornheimer Strasse in the Nordstadt, as is Beethoven's mother Maria Magdalena.

DOPPELKIRCHE SCHWARZRHEINDORF

Across the river in the suburb of Schwarzrheindorf, the 12th-century **Doppelkirche Schwarzrheindorf** (☎ 461 609; Dixstrasse 41; ☑ 9am-4.30pm Tue-Sat, 11.30am-6.30pm Sun, upper church Sat & Sun only) is a magnificent 'double church' where the nobility sat on the upper level and the parishioners on the lower. The beautiful Romanesque architecture is impressive, as is the restored Old Testament fresco cycle in the lower church. Take bus 550 or 640 from the Hauptbahnhof to Schwarzrheindorf-Kirche.

Tours

The tourist office runs two English-language tours. The **Big City Tour** (adult/concession €15/7.50; ☑ 2pm daily Apr-Nov, less frequently Dec-Mar) is a com-

bined 2½-hour bus and walking tour. The **Altstadt Walking Tour** (adult/concession €7/4; ☑ 11am daily mid-Aug–Oct, 11am Sat & Sun May–mid-Aug, 3pm Sat Jun-Oct) takes 1½ hours.

Beethoven fans with a DIY streak can follow in their idol's footsteps, either via a free Beethoven Walk pamphlet or a one-hour MP3 audio tour (€5.90), both available at the tourist office (passport required).

Boats heading upriver to Königswinter and beyond leave from the Alter Zoll landing docks at the Brassertufer between April and October. **Bonner Personen Schiffahrt** (☎ 0228-636 363; www.b-p-s.de) and **KD** (☎ 0221-208 8318; www.k-d.com) are the main operators.

Sleeping

For phone bookings, call ☎ 0180-500 3365 or ☎ 910 4178; for online bookings go to www.bonn-region.de. Rates skyrocket during trade shows, while bargains are possible in summer and at weekends.

DJH hostel (☎ 289 970; www.bonn.jugendherberge.de; Haager Weg 42; dm €25.30, s €43-55, tw €63-70; P ☒ ☐) Bonn's modern hostel is about 4km south of the city centre next to a nature park. From the Hauptbahnhof, take bus 600 to Jugendherberge.

Hotel Pastis (☎ 969 4270; www.hotel-pastis.de, in German; Hatschiergasse 8; s/d €60/95) This little hotel-restaurant combo is so fantastically French, you'll feel like the Eiffel Tower is just around the corner. After dining on unfussy gourmet cuisine – paired with great wines, bien sûr – you'll sleep like a baby in snug, cosy rooms.

Hotel Löhndorf (☎ 634 726; www.hotel-loehndorf-bonn.de; Stockenstrasse 6; s/d from €65/95; ☒ ☐ ☎) This 13-room (all non-smoking) property is wonderfully quiet despite being close to the Hofgarten and the Rhine. The cheery breakfast room and the bamboo-lined patio are great for munching your morning croissants. Bonus: a handy honour bar in the lounge and free access to the adjacent gym and sauna.

Altes Treppchen (☎ 625 004; www.treppchen.de, in German; Endenicher Strasse 308; s/d €71/102; P) In the suburb of Endenich, this rustic inn is a true gem that's been in the same family for 500 years. The nine rooms are simple but squeaky clean and most of them are decent sized. The restaurant, all warm and snug with its wooden booths, is loaded with olde-worlde ambience and makes for a romantic dinner spot.

Villa Esplanade (☎ 983 800; www.hotel-villa-esplanade.de; Colmantstrasse 47; s/d/tr from €74/103/118; P ☒ ☎)

NORTH RHINE–WESTPHALIA

Inside a stately late-19th-century building, this charming hotel has 17 bright rooms with soft, feminine decor: think wicker chairs, pink bedspreads and lacy curtains. Days start with a heaping breakfast buffet served in a lovely room with ornate stucco ceilings.

Domicil (☎ 729 090; www.domicil-bonn.bestwestern.de; Thomas-Mann-Strasse 24/26; s/d from €85/120; P X ⊗) This classy hotel sprawls over several buildings grouped around a central courtyard. For something a little special, book the larger deluxe rooms, some of which have romantic stucco ceilings or a courtyard-facing terrace. The Jacuzzi and sauna are good unwinding options after a day of pavement-pounding.

Collegium Leoninum (☎ 629 80; www.leoninum -bonn.de, in German; Noeggerathstrasse 34; s €100-160, d €120-180; P X ⊗ ⊠) Until the late '90s, young men trained for the priesthood in this rambling neo-Gothic mansion near the Hauptbahnhof. Now parts of it have been converted into a comfortable, completely wheelchair-accessible hotel that cleverly mixes retro and modern touches.

Eating & Drinking

Bonn has several lively gastro zones. The largely pedestrianised historic Altstadt brims with mainstream options, but for less-touristed flair head to the Nordstadt (Breite Strasse, Heerstrasse), Poppelsdorf (Clemens-August-Strasse) or Endenich (Frongasse). The last is about 1.5km west of the Altstadt; take bus 634 from Hauptbahnhof to Frongasse.

Der Spanier (☎ 184 1542; Bornheimer Strasse 76; dishes €2-10; ⊙ dinner) It's a food store. It's a restaurant. It's both. Conversation flows as freely as the wine at this convivial eatery whose eclectic clientele shares a passion for chef Luis' grilled *gambas* (shrimp), crunchy fried calamari and other Iberian staples. If you help yourself to a bottle of wine from the shelf, the corkage fee is just €3.

Harmonie (☎ 614 042; Frongasse 28-30; mains €5-13; ⊙ 6pm-1am Mon-Sat, 5pm-1am Sun) The well-prepared comfort food – pizza, pasta, salads and meaty mains like schnitzel and pork chops – has vaulted this low-key pub to the top of many a local's fave list. In fine weather, the beer garden tables are the most coveted.

Cafe Spitz (☎ 697 430; Sterntorbrücke 10; mains €5-16; ⊙ 9am-1am Mon-Thu, to 2am Fri & Sat, 10am-midnight Sun) This place is often busy as a beehive, especially during the after-work cocktail happy hour. The menu revolves around salad, pizza and pasta supplemented by changing – and somewhat more inspired – blackboard specials.

Havana (☎ 721 8884; Clemens-August-Strasse 1; mains €6-12; ⊙ 10am-1am) This friendly contender in Poppelsdorf is a lively meet-and-greet zone that always hums with activity. Despite the name, the menu is more Italian than Cuban, but the cocktails are strong enough to give you the guts to chat up that cute guy or girl at the bar.

Brauhaus Bönnsch (☎ 650 610; Sterntorbrücke 4; mains €7-15; ⊙ 11am-1am) The unfiltered ale is a must at this congenial brew-pub adorned with photographs of famous politicians Willy Brandt to, yes, Arnold Schwarzenegger. Schnitzel, spare ribs and sausage dominate the menu, but the *Flammkuchen* (Alsatian pizza) is still a perennial bestseller.

Zum Gequetschten (☎ 638 104; Sternstrasse 78; mains €8-17; ⊙ noon-midnight) This traditional restaurant-pub is festooned with eye-catching blue tiles and is one of the most storied inns in town. The menu is back-to-basics German, all delicious and served in belt-loosening portions.

Pawlow (☎ 653 603; Heerstrasse 64; ⊙ 11am-1am Sun-Thu, 11am-open end Fri & Sat) Generations of *bon vivants* have followed the Pavlovian bell to this northern Altstadt institution. A cafe in the daytime, it morphs into a DJ bar at night with electro, punk and '60s sounds heating up a chatty, boozy crowd.

Other recommendations:

Cafe Blau (☎ 650 717; Franziskaner Strasse 9; dishes €4-8; ⊙ 9am-1am) Student bistro in the foyer of a public swimming pool.

Cassius Garten (☎ 652 429; Maximilianstrasse 28, Cassius-Passage; dishes per 100g €1.50; ⊙ 8am-8pm Mon-Sat; V) Self-service vegetarian buffet.

Entertainment

De Schnüss and *BonnJour* are the main listings magazines, available at newsagents and the tourist office. The central ticket hotline is ☎ 0180-500 1812.

Bonn's entertainment scene is especially strong in the field of classical music. A calendar highlight is the Beethovenfest in late September with several dozen concerts held in venues around town. These include the intimate **Kammermusiksaal** (☎ 981 7515; Bonngasse 24-26) next to the Beethoven Haus; the **Beethovenhalle** (☎ 722 20; Wachsbleiche 17), Bonn's premier concert hall; and the **Oper Bonn** (Bonn Opera; ☎ 778 000; Am Boeselagerhof 1), which also presents theatre, dance and opera.

Getting There & Away

Köln Bonn Airport (Cologne Bonn Airport; ☎ 02203-404 001; www.airport-cgn.de) has flights within Germany, Europe and beyond and is served by 50 airlines, including Germanwings, easyJet and Air Berlin.

Bonn is linked to Cologne several times hourly by U-Bahn lines U16 and U18 and regional trains (€6.50, 30 minutes). There are also frequent trains to the Ruhrgebiet cities and Koblenz (€10.30, 45 minutes).

Bonn is at the crossroads of the A59, A555 and A565. The B9 highway cuts north–south through the city.

Getting Around

Express bus SB60 makes the trip between the airport and Hauptbahnhof every 20 or 30 minutes between 4.45am and 12.30am (€6.50, 26 minutes). For a taxi to/from the airport budget between €35 and €40.

Buses, trams and the U-Bahn make up the public transport system, which is operated by the **VRS** (☎ 01803-504 030; www.vrsinfo.de). It extends as far as Cologne and is divided into zones. All you need to travel within Bonn is a City Ticket for €2.40 per trip or €6.90 for the 24-hour pass. All tickets must be validated when boarding.

For a taxi, ring ☎ 555 555. Bikes may be hired at **Radstation** (☎ 981 4636; Quantiusstrasse 26; per day €7; ☉ 6am-10.30pm Mon-Fri, 7am-10.30pm Sat, 8am-10.30pm Sun), on the south side of the Hauptbahnhof via the subterranean passageway.

AROUND BONN

Steeped in legend, the densely forested hills of the **Siebengebirge** (Seven Mountains) rise above the right bank of the Rhine, just a few kilometres south of Bonn. Closer inspection actually reveals about 40 peaks, but only the seven most prominent give the region its name.

At 461m, the Ölberg may be the highest, but the 321m **Drachenfels** is the most heavily visited of these 'mountains'. Since 1883, some 32 million peak-baggers have reached the top aboard the **Drachenfelsbahn** (☎ 02223-920 90; Drachenfelsstrasse 53; uphill/downhill/return €7.50/7.50/9; ☉ 9am-7pm May-Sep, shorter hr Oct-Apr), a nostalgic cogwheel train chugging along for 1.5km. Prices are a bit steep, but so is the paved path should you prefer to walk.

The walking route leads past restaurants and various attractions, including the 1913 **Nibelungenhalle** (☎ 02223-241 50; adult/child €5/3; ☉ 10am-6pm mid-Mar-Oct, 11am-4pm Sat & Sun Nov-

mid-Mar), a templelike shrine to the composer Richard Wagner decorated with scenes from his opera cycle *Ring of the Nibelungen*. Tickets include access to the **Drachenhöhle**, a cave inhabited by a 13m-long stone dragon, and a small **reptile zoo**.

Further uphill loom the fairy-tale turrets of the neo-Gothic **Schloss Drachenburg** (☎ 02223-901 970; adult/concession €3.50/2; ☉ 10am-6pm Tue-Sun Apr-Oct), which looks medieval but was actually built in the 1880s. It houses exhibits on the building's history, the ongoing restoration process and on the history of nature protection. Tours of the residential quarters cost an extra €3. Perhaps more interesting, though, are the lovely grounds with their terraces, fountains, and tower that can be climbed for expansive views.

Views are at least as nice (and free) from the medieval **Burg Drachenfels** at the top of the mountain, which has remained a ruin since the Thirty Years War (1618–48).

The Drachenfels rises above the town of Königswinter, which is served by the U66 from Bonn Hauptbahnhof. A more atmospheric approach is by one of the boats that leave from the Brassertufer in Bonn between April and October. **Bonner Personen Schiffahrt** (☎ 0228-636 363; one-way/return €7.50/10) and **KD** (☎ 0221-208 8318; www.k-d.com; one-way/return €7.60/9.70) are the main operators.

Right in Königswinter itself is **SeaLife** (☎ 02223-297 297, tickets 01805-6669 0101; Rheinallee 8; adult/child €14/9.50; ☉ 10am-6pm), a small and edutaining walk-through aquarium with a legend and fairy-tale theme. Kids love it.

AACHEN

☎ 0241 / pop 246,000

The Romans nursed their war wounds and stiff joints in the steaming waters of Aachen's mineral springs, but it was Charlemagne who put the city firmly on the European map. The emperor too enjoyed a dip now and then, but it was more for strategic reasons why, in 794, he made Aachen the geographical and political capital of his vast Frankish Empire – arguably the first empire with European dimensions. Today, Aachen is still a quintessentially international city, not in the least because of its location in the border triangle with the Netherlands and Belgium. Charlemagne's legacy lives on in the stunning Dom which, in 1978, became Germany's first Unesco World Heritage Site. Aachen is also the birthplace of the famous *Printen,* crunchy spiced cookies spiked with herbs or nuts and drenched in chocolate or frosting. Yum!

Orientation

Aachen's centre is contained within two concentric ring roads and is best explored on foot. The inner ring road encloses the Altstadt proper and is called Grabenring because it's composed of segments all ending in *'graben'* (meaning 'moat'). The outer ring is known as Alleenring, even though only some of its segments end in *'allee'* (meaning 'avenue'). The Hauptbahnhof is just south of this outer ring, on Römerstrasse. From here it's a 10- to 15-minute signed walk to the tourist office and the Altstadt.

Information

Mayersche Buchhandlung (☎ 477 00; Buchkremerstrasse 1-7) Books galore. Also at Pontstrasse 131.

Post office (☎ 01802-3333; Kapuzinerkarree, Kapuzinergraben 19) Inside a shopping mall.

ReiseBank (☎ 912 6872; Lagerhausstrasse 9; ⏲ 9.45am-2pm, 2.45-5.45pm Mon-Fri) Currency exchange.

Tourist office (☎ 180 2960/1; www.aachen-tourist.de; Elisenbrunnen, Friedrich-Wilhelm-Platz; ⏲ 9am-6pm Mon-Fri, 9am-2pm Sat, also 10am-2pm Sun Easter-Dec)

Universitätsklinikum Aachen (☎ 808 4444; Pauwelsstrasse 30) Major hospital, 2km northwest of the city centre.

Web (☎ 997 9210; Kleinmarschierstrasse 74-76; per 10min €0.50; ⏲ 10am-11pm Mon-Wed, to midnight Thu, to 3am Fri & Sat, 11am-10pm Sun) Internet access.

Sights

From April to October and in December, the tourist office runs 90-minute English-language walking tours for €6.

DOM

It's impossible to overestimate the significance of Aachen's magnificent **cathedral** (☎ 4770 9144; www.aachendom.de, in German; Münsterplatz; ⏲ 7am-6pm Nov-Mar, 7am-7pm Apr-Oct). The burial place of Charlemagne, it's where more than 30 German kings were crowned and where pilgrims have flocked since the 12th century.

The oldest and most impressive section is Charlemagne's palace chapel, the **Pfalzkapelle,** an outstanding example of Carolingian architecture. Completed in 800, the year of the emperor's coronation, it's an octagonal dome encircled by a 16-sided ambulatory supported by antique Italian pillars. The colossal brass **chandelier** was a gift from Emperor Friedrich Barbarossa during whose reign Charlemagne was canonised in 1165.

Pilgrims have poured into town ever since that time, drawn in as much by the cult surrounding Charlemagne as by the prized relics – said to include Christ's loincloth – that he had brought to Aachen. These are still displayed every seven years (next in 2014). To accommodate the flood of the faithful, a Gothic **choir** was docked to the chapel in 1414 and filled with such priceless treasures as the **pala d'oro,** a gold-plated altar-front depicting Christ's Passion, and the jewel-encrusted gilded copper **pulpit,** both fashioned in the 11th century. At the far end is the gilded **shrine of Charlemagne** that has held the emperor's remains since 1215. In front, the equally fanciful **shrine of St Mary** shelters the cathedral's four premium relics.

Unless you join a guided tour (adult/concession €3/2.50, 45 minutes), you'll only catch a glimpse of Charlemagne's white marble **imperial throne** in the upstairs gallery. Reached via six steps – just like King Solomon's throne – it served as the coronation throne of those 30 German kings between 936 and 1531. The 2pm tour is in English.

DOMSCHATZKAMMER

The **cathedral treasury** (☎ 4770 9127; Klostergasse; adult/concession €4/3; ⏲ 10am-1pm Mon, 10am-5pm Tue-Sun Jan-Mar, 10am-1pm Mon, 10am-6pm Tue, Wed, Fri-Sun, 10am-9pm Thu Apr-Dec) is a veritable mother lode of gold, silver and jewels. Focus your attention on the **Lotharkreuz,** a 10th-century processional cross, and the **marble sarcophagus** that held Charlemagne's bones until his canonisation; the relief shows the rape of Persephone.

RATHAUS

The Dom gazes serenely over Aachen's **Rathaus** (☎ 432 7310; Markt; adult/child/concession €2/free/1; ⏲ 10am-1pm & 2-5pm), a splendid Gothic pile festooned with 50 life-size statues of German rulers, including the 30 kings crowned in town. It was built in the 14th century atop the foundations of Charlemagne's palace of which only the eastern tower, the **Granusturm,** survives. Inside, the undisputed highlights are the **Kaisersaal** with its epic 19th-century **frescoes** by Alfred Rethel and the replicas of the **imperial insignia:** a crown, orb and sword (the originals are in Vienna).

AACHEN

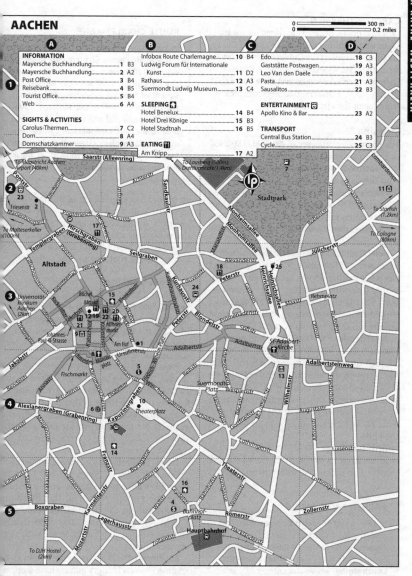

ART MUSEUMS

Of Aachen's two art museums, the **Suermondt Ludwig Museum** (☎ 479 800; www.suermondt-ludwig museum.de; Wilhelmstrasse 18; adult/concession €5/2.50; ☼ noon-6pm Tue, Thu & Fri, noon-8pm Wed, 10am-6pm Sat & Sun) is especially proud of its medieval sculpture but also has fine works by Cranach, Dürer, Macke, Dix and other masters.

In a former umbrella factory, the **Ludwig Forum für Internationale Kunst** (Ludwig Forum for International Art; ☎ 180 7104; www.ludwigforum.de; Jülicherstrasse 97-109; adult/concession €5/2.50; ☼ noon-6pm Tue, Wed & Fri, noon-8pm Thu, 11am-6pm Sat & Sun) trains the spotlight on contemporary art (Warhol, Immendorf, Holzer, Penck, Haring etc) and also stages progressive changing exhibits.

NORTH RHINE–WESTPHALIA

CAROLUS-THERMEN

Oriental pools, honey rubs, deep-tissue massages and soothing saunas are among the relaxation options at the **Carolus-Thermen** (Thermal Baths; ☎ 182 740; www.carolus-thermen.de; Passstrasse 79, Stadtgarten; admission with/without sauna from €22/11; ⏰ 9am-11pm), a snazzy bathing complex on the edge of the city park.

Sleeping

For room reservations call ☎ 0241-180 2950 or link to www.aachen-tourist.de.

DJH hostel (☎ 711 010; www.aachen.jugendherberge.de; Maria-Theresia-Allee 260; dm/s/tw €23/37/57; P ✕) Aachen's modernised hostel is nicely located in a park overlooking the city. About one third of the rooms have private bathrooms. Take bus 2 (direction Preuswald) to the Ronheide stop.

Hotel Stadtnah (☎ 474 580; http://hotelstadtnah.de; Leydelstrasse 2; s/d from €48/64; ✕ 🛜) The tab ain't steep but neither do you get the 'Ritz'. Still, if you're fine with basic decor and amenities, this 16-room cheapie near the Hauptbahnhof should do in a snap. Bonus: kids under eight stay free in their parents' room.

Hotel Benelux (☎ 400 030; www.hotel-benelux.de; Franzstrasse 21-23; s €94-109, d €120-154; P ✕ 🛜) Though on a busy street, this well-run place has 33 quiet, uncluttered rooms reached via art-filled floors. Fuel up with a generous breakfast served tableside and wrap things up with a sunset drink in the rooftop garden. There's even a small gym to work out the kinks.

Hotel Drei Könige (☎ 483 93; www.h3k-aachen.de, in German; Büchel 5; s €90-130, d €120-160, apt €130-240; ✕ 🛜) The radiant Mediterranean decor is

AACHEN FROM ABOVE

In fine weather, get off the asphalt and onto the trails of the densely forested spa garden north of the Altstadt. A brisk 20-minute walk takes you up the 264m-high **Lousberg** hill where the entire city panorama unfolds below you. For even more memorable 360-degree views, ride the lift up to the top of the old water tower, which is now the rotating **Drehturmcafe** (⏰ 10am-6pm). Get there by cutting north on Kupferstrasse from Ludwigsallee, then left on Belvedereallee.

ROUTE CHARLEMAGNE

In 2008 Aachen embarked on a multi-year project called Route Charlemagne to showcase its 1200-year tradition as a European city of culture and science. By 2012 a variety of themed exhibits will appear in such historic sites as the Rathaus (town hall), the cathedral and the Elisenbrunnen. Meanwhile, an information centre, the multimedia **Infobox** (Theaterplatz; admission free; ⏰ 11am-8pm Tue-Fri, 11am-6pm Sat, 1-6pm Sun), provides an overview.

an instant mood enhancer at this family-run favourite with its doesn't-get-more-central location. Some rooms are a tad twee but the two-room apartment sleeps up to four. Breakfast on the 4th floor comes with dreamy views over the rooftops and the cathedral.

Eating & Drinking

Sausalitos (☎ 160 5516; Markt 52-54; mains €5-15; ⏰ noon-1am) Park yourself on the patio of this perennially popular cantina overlooking Markt, sip a fruity cocktail and indulge in a dose of people-gawking. Pretty good Tex-Mex sustenance, too.

Pasta (☎ 288 91; Jakobstrasse 1; mains €6-12; ⏰ 10am-5pm Mon, 10am-9.30pm Tue-Sat) Fish-shaped ravioli paired with salmon creme is just one of the creative offerings at this popular pasta shop. All noodles are made fresh daily and available for take-away or for eating on the spot, preferably on the terrace. Avoid the lunch-hour rush.

Leo van den Daele (☎ 357 24; Büchel 18; dishes €7-11; ⏰ 9am-6.30pm Mon-Sat, 11am-6.30pm Sun) Leather covered walls, tiled stoves and antique forge the yesteryear flair of this rambling cafe institution. Come for all-day breakfast, a light lunch or divine cakes (the strudel and the Belgian Reisfladen, made with rice, are specialities).

Am Knipp (☎ 331 68; Bergdriesch 3; mains €8-17; ⏰ dinner Wed-Mon) Hungry grazers have stopped by this traditional inn since 1698 and you too will have a fine time spiking your cholesterol level with the hearty German cuisine served amid a flea market's worth of knick-knacks. Lovely beer garden as well.

Gaststätte Postwagen (☎ 350 01; Krämerstrasse 2; mains €10-20; ⏰ noon-midnight) This place, tacked onto the town hall, oozes olde-worlde flair rom every nook and cranny and is a good place for classic German meals. The downstairs is made to look like an 18th-century postal coach (hence the name).

Edo (☎ 478 70; Peterstrasse 71; mains €12.50-28, menu €36-77; ☻ lunch & dinner Mon-Sat) Aachen's Japanese food lovers have Edo, the city's first certified organic restaurant, on the speed dial. The sushi, the grilled duck and the tenderloin steak all get rave reviews. Or book a seat at the Teppan grill and go for the whole menu.

Entertainment

For listings pick up the free *Klenkes* in cafes, pubs and the tourist office. The main barhopping drag is student-flavoured Pontstrasse locals say 'Ponte').

Apollo Kino & Bar (☎ 900 8484; Pontstrasse 141-149; ☻ Mon-Sat) This cavernous basement joint does double duty as an art-house cinema and a sweaty dance club for the student brigade. Alt-sounds rule on Mondays, salsa on Tuesdays, but on other nights it could be anything from dancehall to disco, house to power pop.

Malteserkeller (☎ 257 74; Malteserstrasse 14; ☻ usually Tue-Sat) Elvin Jones and Bill Ramsey used to be regulars at what was once a venerable jazz venue. Changing tastes and financial realities have translated into an expanded musical menu that includes electro-funk, house, Nu skool and punk.

Starfish (☎ 938 900; Liebigstrasse 17-19; ☻ Fri & Sat) A cornerstone of Aachen's dance-club scene, Starfish keeps things interesting with four different dance floors playing house and charts, rock and soul. It's about 2.5km northeast of the city centre.

Getting There & Away

Tiny **Maastricht Aachen Airport** (MAA; ☎ 0031-3-358 9999 in Holland; www.maa.nl), about 35km northwest of the city, is served once daily by easyJet from Berlin. Flights are met by the Airport Shuttle (per trip €10) with service to the centre.

Regional trains to Cologne (€14.40, 70 minutes) run several times hourly, with some proceeding to Dortmund and other Ruhrgebiet cities. Trips to most cities south of Aachen require a change in Cologne.

For drivers, Aachen is easily reached via the A4 (east–west) from Cologne and the A44 (north–south) from Düsseldorf. The B57, B258 and B264 also meet here.

Getting Around

Bus tickets for travel within the area bounded by Alleenring cost a flat €1.55. All of Aachen and the adjoining Dutch communities of Vaals and Kelmis can be covered with a Zone 1 ticket for €2.30 (day pass €6.30). Drivers sell tickets. For bike hire, try **Cycle** (☎ 408 363; Heinrichsallee 66; per day €9.50).

For a taxi, call ☎ 344 41.

EIFEL NATIONAL PARK

Established in 2004, the **Eifel National Park** (☎ 02444-951 00; www.nationalpark-eifel.de) is North Rhine–Westphalia's only national park. It protects about 110 sq km of beech forest, rivers and lakes along with plenty of plant-and wildlife, including wild cats, beavers, kingfishers, bats and owls. In spring, a sea of wild narcissus floods the valleys. It's hard to imagine now that, until recently, Belgian troops used much of the area for military exercises.

A focal point of the park is **Vogelsang** (☎ 02444-915 790; www.vogelsang-ip.de; admission free, parking €3; ☻ 8am-8pm Apr-Oct, 10am-5.30pm Nov-Mar), a vast complex built by the Nazis as a party leadership training centre and later used as military barracks by the Belgians. It's being converted into Forum Vogelsang and will soon have exhibits on the national park and the Eifel region as well as a documentation centre about the indoctrination and educational system in the Nazi state. For now, German-speakers should join a **guided tour** (adult/child €4/free; ☻ 2pm, also 11am Sun) to learn more about the place, its history and architecture.

Vogelsang is also a good starting point for hikes in the national park. Staff at the **visitor centre** (☻ 10am-5pm) hand out suggestions and maps. Information is also available inside the Kall **train station** (☎ 02441-777 545; Bahnhofstrasse 13; ☻ 6am-6pm Mon-Fri, 8am-6pm Sat, 9am-5pm Sun).

The park is some 50km southeast of Aachen and 70km southwest of Cologne near the border with Belgium. From Cologne, regional trains make the trip to Kall several times daily (hourly on weekends), where you can switch to the Nationalparkshuttle bus SB82 to Vogelsang (€9.60, 90 minutes). From Aachen, bus SB63 also goes to Vogelsang, but only at weekends from Easter to October (€7.10, 90 minutes). The park website has full details and timetable information.

NORTH RHINE–WESTPHALIA

THE RUHRGEBIET

When the decision came down that the Ruhrgebiet – a metropolitan beehive of 53 cities and 5.3 million people – would be Cultural Capital of Europe in 2010, eyebrows were raised around the land. What kind of 'culture' could there possibly be in this region that, until not long ago, was primarily known for its belching steel works and dusty coal mines? Plenty.

Old Masters? World-class opera and drama? Great architecture from Gothic to Bauhaus to postmodern? Music festivals that draw visitors by the hundreds of thousands? Check, check, check and check again.

After the demise of the coal and steel industry in the 1960s, the Ruhrgebiet had to completely reinvent itself. These days, information technology, biomedicine, robotics and logistics are among the engines of the regional economy. Rather than eschew its heritage, though, the people have embraced it. Many of the dormant furnaces, steel works, coking plants and other vestiges of the industrial age have been rebooted in creative ways. You can see cutting-edge art in a huge converted gas tank or free-climb around a blast furnace. Or sip a martini in a former turbine house, go clubbing in a coal mine boiler room or listen to Mozart in a converted compressor machine hall.

For travellers with an open mind, a sense of adventure and a desire to get off the beaten track, the Ruhrgebiet delivers a treasure chest of surprises and unique sights, locations and experiences.

Information
DISCOUNT CARDS
The **RuhrTop-Card** (adult/child €44.90/29.90) gives free public transport and free one-time admission to 90 attractions, including theme parks, museums and tours during the course of a calendar year. It's available from local tourist offices and online at www.ruhrtopcard.de.

Getting Around
All cities covered in the Ruhrgebiet section have introduced low-emission zones in their city centres, meaning that your car needs to display an *Umweltplakette* (emission sticker). Rental cars have these, but if you're driving

your own, see p783 for details on how to obtain one.

Each Ruhrgebiet city has an efficient and comprehensive public transport system made up of U-Bahns, buses and trams. Cities are also connected to each other by S-Bahn and regional trains. The same tariffs apply within the entire region, which is divided into three zones. Study the displays on the orange ticket vending machines to determine which price applies for your trip. Single tickets are €2.30/4.50/9.20 for one/two/three zones. Single day passes are €5.30/10.50/21.40; group day passes for up to five people travelling together are €11.70/17.30/28.40.

ESSEN
☎ 0201 / pop 585,000
It's taken a few decades, but Germany's seventh-largest city has mastered the transition from industrial powerhouse to city of commerce and culture like few others. Van Gogh, anyone? Go to the Museum Folkwang. Fancy a look at Emperor Otto III's gem-studded childhood crown? Head for the cathedral treasury. A Unesco-listed Bauhaus-style coal mine? Look no further than the Zeche Zollverein.

According to no less an authority than *Men's Health* magazine, Essen is Germany's third-greenest city (after Hanover and Magdeburg), with 9.2% of its area claimed by nature. Make it out to the verdant green belt and the half-timbered suburbs and you too will believe it. Old images die hard, but even cynics would find lots to like about Essen. If only they'd come and see for themselves.

Orientation
The Hauptbahnhof's Nord (north) exit drops you right onto the centre's main drag, the pedestrianised Kettwiger Strasse. Essen's major sights are rather spread out, but all are accessible by U-Bahn, S-Bahn or trams. The handiest line is tram 107, which shuttles between the Zollverein coal mine, the Museum Folkwang and the Rüttenscheid restaurant and pub mile. The Baldeneysee and the suburb of Werden are further south and served by S-Bahn.

Information
Mayersche Buchhandlung (☎ 365 670; Markt 5-6) Bookshop.
Medical emergencies (☎ 192 92)

INDUSTRIAL HERITAGE TRAIL

Most of the smokestacks and mines are eerily silent today, but many of these 'cathedrals of industry' have taken on a new life as museums, concert halls, cinemas, restaurants, lookouts, playgrounds and other such venues. Dozens of them are linked along the 400km Industrial Heritage Trail that takes in such cities as Dortmund, Essen, Duisburg and Bochum. Most sites are also served by public transport.

Details are at www.route-industriekultur.de, or stop by the route's **central visitors' centre** (☎ 0180-400 0086; 🕐 10am-7pm Apr-Oct, 10am-5pm Nov-Mar) in the foyer of the Ruhr Museum at the Zollverein coal mine (below) in Essen. Information is also available at the **visitors centre** (☎ 429 1942; 🕐 10am-5pm Mon-Thu, 10am-9pm Fri-Sun Apr-Oct, reduced hr in winter) in the Landschaftspark Duisburg-Nord (p598).

Police headquarters (☎ 8290; Büscherstrasse 2-6)
Post office (Willy-Brandt-Platz 1; 🕐 8am-7pm Mon-Fri, 8.30am-3.30pm Sat) Near the Hauptbahnhof.
ReiseBank (☎ 202 671; Hauptbahnhof; 🕐 7.15am-7.45pm Mon-Fri, 8.15am-4pm Sat, 9.45am-1.15pm Sun)
Stadtbibliothek (☎ 884 2419; Hollestrasse 3; 🕐 10am-7pm Tue-Fri, 10am-2pm Sat) Internet access.
Tourist office (☎ 194 33, 887 2048; www.essen.de; Am Hauptbahnhof 2; 🕐 9am-5.30pm Mon-Fri, 10am-1pm Sat)

Sights

CITY CENTRE

Essen's medieval **Dom** (☎ 220 4206; Burgplatz 2; admission free; 🕐 6.30am-6.30pm Mon-Fri, 9am-7.30pm Sat, 9am-8pm Sun) is an island of quiet engulfed by the commercialism of pedestrianised Kettwiger Strasse, the main shopping strip. It has a priceless collection of Ottonian works, all about 1000 years old. Not to be missed is a hauntingly beautiful **Golden Madonna**, set in her own midnight-blue chapel matching the colour of her eyes. The revamped **treasury** (adult/concession/family €4/2/8; 🕐 10am-5pm Tue-Sat, 11.30am-5pm Sun) presents more fancy baubles, including a crown worn by Holy Roman Emperor Otto III, in a modern, intimate fashion.

East of the cathedral, the grand **Alte Synagoge** (☎ 884 5218; Steeler Strasse 29; admission free; 🕐 10am-6pm Tue-Sun) miraculously survived WWII largely intact. A memorial site since 1980, it was being revamped into a Jewish cultural centre and meeting place during our visit, but set to reopen in 2010.

MUSEUM FOLKWANG

A grand dame among Germany's art repositories, the **Museum Folkwang** (☎ 884 5314; www.museum-folkwang.de; Goethestrasse 41; adult/concession/family €5/3.50/10.50, under 14yr free; 🕐 10am-8pm Tue-Sun) is taking up residence in sparkling new digs designed by British star architect David Chipperfield in spring 2010. Galleries radiate out from inner courtyards and gardens of the glass-fronted building, providing a progressive setting for such 19th- and 20th-century masters as Gauguin, Caspar David Friedrich and Mark Rothko.

ZECHE ZOLLVEREIN

The former **Zollverein coal mine** (☎ 830 3636; www.zollverein.de; Gelsenkirchener Strasse 181; 🕐 visitors centre 10am-7pm Apr-Oct, 10am-5pm Nov-Mar) is a beautiful Bauhaus-style behemoth that was recognised as a Unesco World Heritage Site in 2001. In operation until 1986, it's since been rebooted as a cultural hub with museums, performance spaces, artist studios, a fine restaurant (see Casino Zollverein, p593) and some unusual playgrounds.

Start your visit at the former coal washing plant, which now provides an edgy setting for the **Ruhr Museum** (☎ 884 5200; www.ruhrmuseum.de, in German; adult/concession/family €5/3/10; 🕐 10am-6pm). Exhibits span the history of the Ruhr Region in an easily accessible and engaging fashion. Just as the coal was transported on conveyor belts, a long escalator whisks you up to the foyer from where you descend into the dark bowels of the building. With its raw stone walls, steep steel stairs, shiny aluminium ducts and industrial machinery, the space itself has all the drama and mystique of a movie set (*Blade Runner* comes to mind).

Another highlight is the **Red Dot Design Museum** (☎ 301 0425; adult/concession/family €5/3/15, under 12yr free; 🕐 11am-6pm Tue-Thu, 11am-8pm Fri-Sun) in the stoker's hall, creatively adapted by Lord Norman Foster. In a perfect marriage of space and function, this four-storey maze showcases the best in contemporary design right amidst the original fixtures: bathtubs balancing on grated walkways, bike helmets dangling from snakelike heating ducts, and beds perching atop a large oven. All objects are winners of the Red Dot award, the 'Oscar' of the design world.

One of the most unusual experiences you can have on the grounds is a ride aboard the Ferris-wheel-like **Sonnenrad** (Sun Wheel; adult/under 12yr €1/free; ☺ noon-8pm Sat & Sun May–mid-Oct) through the smelters of the coking plant. From mid-December to mid-January, there's an outdoor **ice skating rink** (€6.50), also at the coking plant.

Themed public tours (€4.50 to €15) zero in on the complex's industrial heritage, its architecture and its art, but for now they're in German only.

Tram 107 travels to Zollverein straight from the Hauptbahnhof.

BALDENEYSEE & VILLA HÜGEL

Essen's green belt follows the Ruhr River to the large **Baldeneysee**. OK, so it's not quite the Med, but on hot summer days there's an undeniable holiday feeling at the **Seaside Beach** (☎ 839 2836; Freiherr-vom-Stein-Strasse 384; adult/concession €3/2; ☺ from 10am), a 250m-long stretch of sand perfect for swimming, windsurfing, picnicking and playing beach volleyball. It's also a stop for the cruise boats plying the lake from April to September.

On the lake's north shore looms the imposing **Villa Hügel** (☎ 188 4823; www.villahuegel.de; Hügel 1; adult/under 14yr €3/free; ☺ 10am-6pm Tue-Sun), where the Krupp dynasty made its home from 1873 to 1945. You can wander around the partially furnished private quarters of the main building, which also hosts the occasional concert and internationally acclaimed art show (call or check the website for hours and admission). The former guesthouse presents an exhibit on the history of the family and the company. The lavish **park** (☺ 8am-8pm daily) is a pleasant place for a picnic or relaxing.

To get to the lake and the villa, take the S6 to Essen-Hügel from the Hauptbahnhof.

WERDEN

On the southern Ruhr bank, the half-timbered houses and cobbled lanes of the suburb of Werden intimate at what a pre-industrial Ruhrgebiet must have looked like. Students of the prestigious Folkwang School for Music, Dance and Drama fill the many pubs, cafes and restaurants, and the DJH hostel is here as well.

Werden's main sight is the 1175 **Abteikirche St Liudger** (☎ 491 801; Brückstrasse 54; ☺ 10am-noon & 3-5pm Tue-Sun), a beautiful late-Romanesque church named for the Frisian missionary buried here. It has an impressive exterior as well as a commendable **treasury** (adult/concession €2/1).

The S6 goes straight to Werden from the Hauptbahnhof.

Sleeping

Hotels in the centre cater for business visitors and are mostly nondescript and over-priced. The more charming places are in the suburbs.

DJH hostel (☎ 491 163; www.essen.jugendherberge.de; Pastoratsberg 2; dm/s/tw €23.70/37.50/58.40, incl linen & breakfast; P ⊠ ⌨) Essen's updated hostel is in the pretty but rather remote suburb of Werden. Many rooms have private bathrooms. Take the S6 to Essen-Werden, then bus 190 to Jugendherberge.

Welcome Hotel Essen (☎ 177 90; www.welcome-hotel-essen.de; Schützenbahn 58; s €83-123, d €113-153 P ⊠ ⌨ ⌨) Sure, this hulking property can't shake the business vibe, but its handsomely furnished rooms have plenty to offer those who've left their tie at home. Space cravers should opt for a 'superior room', which comes with such perks as a kettle, a fluffy robe and bottled water.

Hotel Margarethenhöhe (☎ 438 60; www.margarethenhoehe.com, in German; Steile Strasse 46; s €100-150, d €115-185; P ⊠ ⌨) A former Krupp guesthouse has been reborn as a cheerful hotel, filled with youthful flair, art and designer touches. It's about 5km south of the centre in the Margarethenhöhe, a gardenlike art nouveau workers' colony. Take the U17 to Laubenweg.

Hotel Résidence (☎ 02054-955 90; www.hotel-residence.de; Auf der Forst 1; s €110-190, d €157-210; P ⊠ ⌨) Posh and petite, this 18-room hotel in an art nouveau villa in the historic suburb of Kettwig appeals to refined tastes. Dinner in the restaurant, which boasts two Michelin stars, will likely cost more than your bed (five-course menu €110).

Eating

There's a dearth of interesting restaurants in the city centre, which is also pretty dead after dark. Head south to the Rüttenscheider Strasse (known as 'Rü' locally) where you have your pick from dozens of eateries. Take the U11 or tram 107 to Martinstrasse.

THE KRUPP DYNASTY – MEN OF STEEL

Steel and Krupp are virtual synonyms. So are Krupp and Essen. For it's this bustling Ruhrgebiet city that is the ancestral seat of the Krupp family and the headquarters of one of the most powerful corporations in Europe. (To avoid confusion, Krupp has nothing to do with the company that produces coffee-makers and other appliances – that's Krups.)

Through successive driven and obsessive generations, the Krupps amassed a huge private fortune, provided the German weaponry for four major wars and played a significant role in world economics and politics. At the same time, however, they established a relationship between workers and management that's still the basis for today's social contract in industrialised Germany.

It all began rather modestly in 1811 when Friedrich Krupp and two partners founded a company to process 'English cast steel' but, despite minor successes, he left a company mired in debt upon his death in 1826. Enter his son Alfred, then a tender 14, who would go on to become one of the seminal figures of the industrial age.

It was through the production of the world's finest steel that the 'Cannon King' galvanised a company that – by 1887 – employed more than 20,000 workers. In an unbroken pattern of dazzling innovation, coupled with ruthless business practices, Krupp produced the wheels and rails for America's railroads and the stainless steel plating on New York's Chrysler building. Krupp gave the world the first diesel engine and the first steam turbine locomotive. And – ultimately – it produced the fearsome weapons that allowed the Wehrmacht to launch the horror of the Blitzkrieg in WWII.

But in another pioneering move, Krupp also provided womb-to-tomb benefits to its workers at a time when the term 'social welfare' had not yet entered the world's vocabulary. Alfred realised that his company's progress and profit came at a price largely borne on the backs of his workers. He created a variety of measures, including company health insurance, a pension scheme, subsidised housing estates and company-owned retail shops.

Krupp will forever be associated, however, with the disastrous period in German history when a maniac from Austria nearly brought the world to its knees. Not only did the corporation supply the hardware for the German war machine, but it also provided much of the financial backing that Hitler needed to build up his political power base. Krupp plants were prime targets for Allied bombers. When the dust had settled, about two-thirds of its factories had either been destroyed or damaged. An American military court sentenced Alfried Krupp von Bohlen und Halbach (Alfred's great-grandson) to prison, releasing him in 1951. He resumed management of the firm in 1953.

An excellent source for an understanding of what the Krupp family has meant to Germany is William Manchester's brilliant chronicle *The Arms of Krupp* (1964).

Zodiac (☎ 771 212; Witteringstrasse 41; mains €8-16; ☯ dinner Fri-Wed; Ⓥ) People sharing laughs ver dinner are a common sight at this jungly anctuary where meat is a no-no and organic roduce standard. Dishes are inspired by the orld's cuisines and the pizzas are named for he signs of the zodiac. All can be calibrated o vegan needs.

Pfefferkorn (☎ 236 312; Rathenaustrasse 5; mains 1-19; ☯ 11am-10.30pm) If you find yourself n the city centre, this bustling place with ostalgic decor makes for a reliable pit stop. s speciality is steaks, but there are plenty f fish, salad and chicken dishes if you're ot a scorched-beast lover. Good for groups nd families.

raum.eins (☎ 455 3747; Rüttenscheider Strasse 154; tapas €2.30-6.20, mains €15-25; ☯ lunch Mon-Fri & dinner Mon-Sat) The chef puts substance over culinary pyrotechnics at this perennial favourite with an interesting tapas menu for grazers and meaty French-inflected mains for seriously growling tummies. There's a nice terrace, too.

our pick **Casino Zollverein** (☎ 830 240; www .casino-zollverein.de; Gelsenkirchener Strasse 181; mains €18-24; ☯ closed Mon) Cast iron, concrete and candlelight characterise this edgy restaurant inside the coal mine's former turbine house. The menu advertises 'new world cuisine', which translates mostly as inspired spins on German faves. If you want to keep it truly

NORTH RHINE–WESTPHALIA

local, order the dove-rabbit combo paired with sweet potato and turnip greens.

For the creamiest ice cream in town, stop by **Mörchens Eiscafe** (☎ 422 538; Rüttenscheider Strasse 202).

Drinking & Entertainment

our pick **Hotel Shanghai** (☎ 747 4756; Steeler Strasse 33; ☺ Wed, Fri & Sat) Electronic-music fans invade for ravetastic nights in this unpretentious joint where DJs spin in a lotus-shaped console, while you dance beneath Chinese lanterns. When your legs need a break, plonk down into a red leather booth and scan the crowd.

Zeche Carl (☎ 834 4410; Wilhelm-Nieswandt-Allee 100; ☺ nightly) The machine hall and washrooms of this former coal mine have been restyled as an alternative cultural centre with live concerts, parties, cabaret, theatre and art exhibits. Take U11 or U17 to Karlsplatz.

Ego Bar (☎ 770 708; Rüttenscheider Strasse 143; ☺ Wed, Fri & Sat) This modest-sized club on the 'Rü' has a high-octane dance floor where the DJs whip the crowd into a frenzy with house, R&B, dance and party hits.

For more fun, head here:

Aalto-Theater (☎ 812 2200; Operplatz 10) Opera and ballet in a famous building by Finnish architect Alvar Aalto.

Colosseum (☎ 887 2333; Altendorfer Strasse 1) Musical theatre in a late-19th-century factory.

GOP Varieté (☎ 247 9393; Rottstrasse 30) Jugglers, acrobats, ventriloquists and other artistes seize the stage.

Grillo-Theater (☎ 812 2200; Theaterplatz) Classic and contemporary drama and comedies.

Philharmonie Essen (☎ 812 2200; Huyssenallee 53) Classical, jazz and other concerts.

Getting There & Around

ICE trains leave in all directions hourly for such cities as Frankfurt (€81, two hours) and Berlin (€95, 3¾ hours). Essen is also efficiently linked to other Ruhrgebiet cities, as well as to Düsseldorf and Cologne.

The local autobahns A40, A42 and A52 are often clogged during rush hour. For rideshares, there's **Citynetz** (☎ 194 44; www.citynetz -mitfahrzentrale.de; Freiheit 5; ☺ 9am-7pm) outside the Hauptbahnhof's Süd (south) exit. Taxis are at ☎ 866 55.

DORTMUND

☎ 0231 / pop 580,500

Dortmund, the largest city in the Ruhrgebiet, once built its prosperity on coal, steel and beer. These days, the mines are closed,

the steel mills quiet and more Zeitgeist compatible high-tech industries have take their place. Only the breweries are going a strong as ever, churning out huge quanti ties of delicious beer and ale, much of i for export. Trading has always been big i Dortmund, which was a major stop on th Hellweg, a medieval trading route, and a bi player in the Hanseatic League. Even toda the city centre is tops for shopping. Footba (soccer) is another major passion. Borussi Dortmund, the city's *Bundesliga* (Germany first league) team, has been national cham pion six times, although not since th 2001–02 season. Its home base, the 67,00C seat Westfalenstadion (now Signal Idun Park), was one of a dozen FIFA World Cu venues in 2006.

Orientation

The airport is about 15km east of the cit centre (see p596 for transport to/from th airport). Most sights cluster within the cit centre bounded by a ring road consist ing of segments all ending in 'wall'. Th Hauptbahnhof, bus station and tourist of fice are on Königswall on the north sid of this ring. Just south of here, the pedes trianised Westenhellweg (which turns int Ostenhellweg further east) is the centre main thoroughfare and heart of a bustlin shopping district. The Kreuzviertel studen quarter, the trade fair grounds and the fa mous football stadium are all south of th centre and easily reached by public transpo (eg by U-Bahn 45).

Information

Dortmund hospital (Klinikum Dortmund; ☎ 9530; Beurhausstrasse 40) Centrally located hospital.

Internet Cafe (ICS; ☎ 141 069; Westenhellweg 121; per hr €1; ☺ 10am-8pm Mon-Sat, 2-8pm Sun)

Mayersche Buchhandlung (☎ 809 050; Westenhell weg 37-41) Bookshop.

Post office (Kurfürstenstrasse 2; ☺ 8am-7pm Mon-Fri 9am-2pm Sat) About 75m to the west of the Hauptbahn hof's north exit.

ReiseBank (☎ 138 8946; Königswall 18a; ☺ 10am-6pm Mon-Fri, 10am-3pm Sat) Next to the tourist office.

Stadtbücherei (public library; ☎ 502 3209; Königswa 18; per 30min €1, wi-fi per hr €3; ☺ 10am-7pm Tue-Fri 10am-3pm Sat) Internet terminals and wi-fi access.

Tourist office (☎ 189 990; www.dortmund-tourismus .de; Königswall 18a; ☺ 9am-6pm Mon-Fri, 9am-1pm Sa Opposite the Hauptbahnhof's south exit.

ights

DORTMUNDER U

You can see it from afar – the golden 'U' atop the tower of the defunct Union Brauerei. Once one of Dortmund's largest and most famous breweries, the protected landmark is being reinvented as a 'centre for art and creativity'. Three upper floors are the new home of the **Museum am Ostwall** (☎ 502 3247; www.museumam ostwall.dortmund.de; cnr Rheinische Strasse & Brinkhoffstrasse), an art-world star thanks to its far-reaching collection of all major 20th- and 21st-century genres – expressionism to art informel, luxus to op art to concrete art. For laypeople this translates into works by Macke, Nolde, Beuys and Paik, and living artists including Jochen Gerz and Anna and Bernhard Blume. It's expected to open in May 2010.

MEDIEVAL CHURCHES

Commerce coexists beautifully with religious treasures in Dortmund's city centre, just south of the Hauptbahnhof. The trio of churches described below conveniently line up along the pedestrianised Westenhellweg, a major trading route since the Middle Ages.

First up is the 14th-century **Petrikirche**, where the show-stopper is a massive Antwerp **altar** (1520) featuring 633 individually carved and gilded figurines in scenes depicting the Easter story. Note that the altar is closed in summer, exposing only the panels' painted outer side.

Following Westenhellweg east, past the **Krügerpassage**, a shopping arcade built in 1912 in exuberant neo-Renaissance style, leads to the **Reinoldikirche** (1280), named after the city's patron saint. As the story goes, after the man was martyred in Cologne, the carriage containing his coffin rolled all the way to Dortmund, stopping on the spot of the church. There's a statue of him, opposite Charlemagne, at the entrance to the choir. Of outstanding artistic merit is the late-Gothic **high altar** (ask nicely in the sacristy for a close-up look). The bell tower can be climbed.

Across the street, **Marienkirche** is the oldest of Dortmund's churches, and its Romanesque origins are still visible in the round-arched nave. The star exhibit here is the **Marienaltar** (1420), with a delicate triptych by local son Conrad von Soest. In the northern nave is the equally impressive **Berswordt Altar** (1385). Also note the rather frivolous wood reliefs on the choir stalls and the ethereal St Mary statue.

MUSEUM FÜR KUNST & KULTURGESCHICHTE

In a rambling art-deco bank building, the **Museum für Kunst & Kulturgeschichte** (Museum of Art & Cultural History; ☎ 502 6028; www.museendortmund.de; Hansastrasse 3; adult/concession €3/1.50, free Sat; ✆ 10am-5pm Tue, Wed, Fri & Sun, 10am-8pm Thu, noon-5pm Sat) is a repository of the kind of stuff that tracks the cultural history of a city. That might be boring were it not for such standout exhibits as sparkling Roman gold treasure, a Romanesque triumphal cross, period rooms and paintings by Caspar David Friedrich, Lovis Corinth and other outstanding artists.

MAHN-UND GEDENKSTÄTTE STEINWACHE

North of the Hauptbahnhof, just beyond the multiplex cinema, the **Mahn-und Gedenkstätte Steinwache** (☎ 502 5002; Steinstrasse 50; admission free; ✆ 10am-5pm Tue-Sun) uses the original rooms and cells of a Nazi prison as a backdrop for a bone-chilling memorial exhibit about Dortmund during the Third Reich. A free English-language pamphlet is available.

ZECHE ZOLLERN

The **Zollern II/IV Coal Mine** (☎ 696 1111; Grubenweg 5; adult/child/student €3.50/2/2.10; ✆ 10am-6pm Tue-Sun) was considered a 'model mine' when operation began in 1902. It boasted state-of-the-art technology and fantastic architecture, including an art nouveau machine hall and a castle-like administration building adorned with gables and onion-domed towers. An innovative exhibit documents the harsh realities of life as a miner, with plenty of interactive and child-oriented programs. To get here, take the U47 from Hauptbahnhof to Dortmund-Huckarde Bushof, then bus 462 direction Dortmund-Marten to Industriemuseum Zollern.

Sleeping

The tourist office makes free room reservations – call ☎ 1899 9111.

Ibis Dortmund City (☎ 185 770; www.ibishotel.com; Märkische Strasse 73; r from €59; ⓟ ⊠ ⊗ ⊚) This is one of the nicer contenders in this good-value chain. It's a 10-minute walk from the city centre and has a supermarket on the premises and a beer garden nearby.

Hotel Fürst Garden (☎ 477 3210; www.hotelfuerst garden.de; Beurhausstrasse 57; s/d €70/90; ⓟ ⊠) A bit outside the city centre, but not far from the stadium, this newly spiffed up 16-room place is cosy and mod in cheerful shades.

The bathrooms are tiny but rooms have all the expected amenities and the breakfast is a generous spread best enjoyed in the charming garden.

Cityhotel Dortmund (☎ 477 9660; www.cityhotel dortmund.de; Silberstrasse 37-43; s/d €83/103, breakfast €10; P ✕ ▯ ⏨) A mousy grey facade hides this jewel of a hotel where a palette evoking the ocean, sun and sand gives rooms and public areas a cheerful and fresh look. Non-smoking rooms facing the courtyard are quietest, but noise isn't really an issue here.

Eating & Drinking

Dortmund brims with pubs and restaurants, making it ideal for sampling the local brews and cuisine. Centres of action include the lively Brückstrassenviertel around the Konzerthaus, the area between Alter Markt and Kleppingstrasse and the alt-flavoured Kreuzviertel (U42 to Möllerbrücke).

BarRock (☎ 206 3221; Kreuzstrasse 87; dishes €5-13; ⏰ 5pm-1am Mon-Fri, 1pm-3am Sat, 10am-1am Sun) Painted cherubs frolicking on the ceiling survey the scene at this charismatic neighbourhood cafe in the Kreuzviertel. The food – baguettes to roast chicken – is a perfect counterbalance to the potent cocktails.

Stravinski (☎ 5844 9850; Brückstrasse 21; small plates €5-10, mains €14-25; ⏰ lunch & dinner) Right by the Konzerthaus, this stylish restaurant gets rushed for pre- and post-performance nosh frenzies. The menu is creative feel-good food, from small plates of antipasti to rump steak with herbed polenta.

Hövel's Hausbrauerei (☎ 914 5470; Hoher Wall 5-7; mains €8-15; ⏰ 11am-midnight Sun-Thu, 11am-1am Fri & Sat) This is a brew-pub for the 21st century – rustic yet infused with a touch of style. The menu is custom-made for hardcore meat lovers (try the suckling pig or the roast pork knuckle) washed down with the libation of choice, the tasty house-brewed *Bitterbier*.

Ristorante Bei Marija (☎ 751 9571; Am Beilstück 48; mains €10-22; ⏰ 6pm-midnight Tue-Sat) Like an embrace from an old friend, Marija is warm and welcoming. The place looks like an overstuffed living room, the owner is a character and the Italian country fare is mouth-watering. It's way off the tourist track; catch the U42 to An der Palmweide. Reservations advised.

Other chow spots:

Rigoletto (☎ 150 4431; Kleppingstrasse 9-11; mains €7-16; ⏰ 8.30am-1am Mon-Fri, 8.30am-3am Sat, 10am-

midnight Sun) High-energy bistro with Mediterranean classics, operatic decor and a see-and-be-seen crowd.

Zum Alten Markt (☎ 572 217; Markt 3; mains €8-14; ⏰ 11am-midnight Mon-Sat, 3pm-midnight Sun) Traditional Westphalian fare served in belt-loosening portions.

Entertainment

Domicil (☎ 862 9030; www.domicil-dortmund.de; Hansa strasse 7-11) The booking policy at this legendar music club in a former cinema is top-notch with quality jazz, world and avant-garde act featuring both promising newcomers an bona fide greats.

FZW (www.fzw.de, in German; Ritterstrasse 20 Generations of Dortmunders have partie at this legendary club that recently move to new digs near the Dortmunder U (p595) Catch tomorrow's headliners live in the big hall or get down to a 'Happy Feet' inducin dance mix in the club.

Konzerthaus Dortmund (☎ 2269 6200; www .konzerthaus-dortmund.de; Brückstrasse 21) This snazz steel-and-glass concert hall is home base o Dortmund's Philharmonic Orchestra and i also a stopover for top-flight internationa guest performers.

Borussia Dortmund (☎ 01805-309 000; www .bvb.de; Signal Iduna Park, Strobelallee 50; tickets €11 50) Dortmund's famous *Bundesliga* socce team plays its home games at the legendar Westfalenstadion, now renamed Signa Iduna Park. Guided tours (adult/child €6/3 take place at 4pm on Friday and at 2pm o Saturday and Sunday.

Getting There & Away

The only remaining budget carrier serv ing **Dortmund Airport** (☎ 921 301; www.dortmun -airport.de) is Air Berlin. The Airport Expres bus makes the trip to the Hauptbahnhof i about 20 minutes (adult/child €5.50/2, 5am to 10.30pm, mostly hourly).

There are frequent ICE and IC trains i all directions and RE and S-Bahn train to other Ruhrgebiet cities departing ever few minutes.

Dortmund is on the A1, A2 and A45. Th B1 runs right through the city and is the link between the A40 to Essen and the A4 to Kassel. It's very busy and often clogged.

Getting Around

For public transport, see p590. For a taxi ca ☎ 144 444 or ☎ 194 10. Bikes can be hire

From **Fahrradstation am Hauptbahnhof** (☎ 181
756; Königswall 15; per hr/day €4/12).

ELSEWHERE IN THE RUHRGEBIET
The Ruhrgebiet has plenty of other places
of interest, many of them on the Industrial
Heritage Trail (p591).

Bochum
☎ 0234 / pop 394,000
Industrial cities are not exactly the stuff
of heartfelt anthems, but that didn't stop
singer-songwriter Herbert Grönemeyer from
rhapsodising about his home town in the
1984 song 'Bochum'. The homage not only
boosted Grönemeyer's career but also the
image of this classic Ruhrgebiet city, halfway
between Essen and Dortmund.

Though indeed no beauty, as one of
the lyrics says, Bochum is worth a quick
stop if only to get 'down and dirty' in the
Deutsches Bergbau-Museum (German Mining Museum;
☎ 587 70; www.bergbaumuseum.de; Am Bergbaumuseum
8; adult/concession/family €6.50/3/14; ☺ 8.30am-5pm
Tue-Fri, 10am-5pm Sat & Sun), one of Germany's
most-visited museums. Besides learning
about all aspects of life *unter Tage* (below
ground), you can descend into the earth's
belly for a spin around a demonstration
pit followed by a ride up the landmark
winding tower for commanding views.
The U-Bahn 35 goes to the museum from
the Hauptbahnhof.

It's a bit away from the centre, but fans
of historic 'iron horses' have plenty to admire at the **Eisenbahnmuseum** (Train Museum;
☎ 492 516; Dr-C-Otto-Strasse 191; adult/child/family
€6/3/14; ☺ 10am-5pm Tue-Fri & Sun Mar–mid-Nov).
It displays around 180 steam and electric
locomotives, coaches and wagons dating
back as far as 1853. From the Hauptbahnhof
take tram 318 to Bochum-Dahlhausen, then
walk for 1200m or take the historic shuttle
Sundays only).

Bochum is also a Ruhrgebiet party hub,
with most of the action concentrated in the
so-called **Bermuda Dreieck** (Bermuda Triangle).
Formed by Kortumstrasse, Viktoriastrasse
and Brüderstrasse, it's just a five-minute
walk from the Hauptbahnhof. Nearby, the
Bochum Symphony is getting dramatic new
digs in the emerging **Viktoria Quartier** around
the Marienkirche, a church that's being converted into a cultural centre.

Oberhausen
☎ 0208 / pop 215,000
A barrel-shaped tower that once stored gas to
power blast furnaces, the **Gasometer Oberhausen**
(☎ 850 3730; www.gasometer.de; Arenastrasse 11; admission
varies; ☺ 10am-6pm Tue-Sun) has been reborn as one
of Germany's most exciting and popular art
and exhibit spaces. Since 1994, it has drawn
sizeable crowds with its site-specific installations by top artists, Bill Viola and Christo and
Jeanne-Claude included. Top off your visit –
literally – by riding a pair of elevators to a
117m-high platform for sweeping views over
the entire western Ruhrgebiet.

Down below, you'll see sprawling **CentrO**,
one of Europe's largest malls with more
than 200 shops, some 20 restaurants and
entertainment venues, including a multiplex cinema and the family-oriented **CentrO
Adventure Park** (☎ 456 780; Promenade 10; unlimited
rides under/over 1.2m tall €9.50/12.50; ☺ 10am-6pm or
7pm, days vary, call for details), a small amusement
park with rides, a Ferris wheel and a big
playground. Nearby, **SeaLife** (☎ 4448 8444; Zum
Aquarium 1; adult/child/concession €16/10/15; ☺ from
10am, closing time varies) is yet another instalment
in this chain of walk-through aquariums that
seems to be proliferating as inexorably as sea
slugs on Viagra.

Oberhausen is about 15km northwest of
Essen. From the Hauptbahnhof, take any bus
or tram going to Neue Mitte Oberhausen
from platform 1. By car, exit Oberhausen-
Zentrum off the A42 and follow the signs.

Duisburg
☎ 0203 / pop 496,000
Duisburg, about 25km west of Essen, is home
to Europe's largest inland port whose im-
mensity is best appreciated on a leisurely
boat tour (☎ 713 9667; adult/child €11/6; ☺ Apr-Nov).
Embarkation is at the Schwanentor, which
is also the gateway to the **Innenhafen Duisburg**
(inner harbour), now an increasingly dynamic
urban quarter with restaurants, bars, clubs
and museums set up in the old storage silos.

A highlight is the half-century of German art
on display at the **Museum Küppersmühle** (☎ 3019
4811; www.museum-kueppersmuehle.de; Philosophenweg 55; adult/concession €6/3, incl special exhibit €8/4;
☺ 2-6pm Wed, 11am-6pm Thu, Sat & Sun) in a mill
storage building converted by Swiss Pritzker
Prize–winning architects Herzog & de
Meuron. From Baselitz to Kiefer to Richter,
all the big names are showcased beneath the

lofty ceilings, as are up to six international art exhibits annually.

More great art awaits at the **Wilhelm-Lehmbruck-Museum** (☎ 283 3294; www.lehmbruck museum.de; Friedrich-Wilhelm-Strasse 40; adult/concession €6/3; ☻ 11am-5pm Tue-Sat, 10am-6pm Sun), which presents a survey of 20th-century international sculpture – think Giacometti, Calder, Ernst and Chillida. About 40 sculptures alone are planted throughout the lovely surrounding park. It's all a five-minute walk from the Hauptbahnhof.

Duisburg's other key sight is just a tram ride away: the **Landschaftspark Duisburg-Nord** (Landscape Park Duisburg-Nord; ☎ 429 1942; www.landschaftspark.de; Emscherstrasse 71; admission free, activities vary; ☻ 24hr). Molten iron used to flow 24/7 from the fiery furnaces of this decommissioned iron works that's now a unique performance space and an all-ages adventure playground. You can free-climb its ore bunkers, take a diving course in the former gas tank, climb to the top of the blast furnace, picnic in a flower garden and visit a petting zoo. On Friday, Saturday and Sunday a light installation by British artist Jonathan Park illuminates the complex after sundown.

There's also a **DJH hostel** (☎ 417 90; www.duisburg -meiderich.jugendherberge.de; Losörter Strasse 133; dm/s/tw €23.70/39.50/61.60, incl linen & breakfast; P X ⬛) on site, so you can stay the night if you want. To get to the park from Duisburg Hauptbahnhof, take tram 902 (direction Duisburg-Walsum) or 903 (direction Dinslaken) to Landschaftspark-Nord; from here it's a seven-minute walk via Emscherstrasse.

Bottrop
☎ 02041 / pop 118,000
About 13km north of Essen, Bottrop is the birthplace of Josef Albers (1888–1976), the Bauhaus artist famous for his explorations of colour and spatial relationships, squares in particular. With the **Josef Albers Museum** (☎ 297 16; Im Stadtgarten 20; admission free; ☻ 11am-5pm Tue-Sat, 10am-5pm Sun), the city honours its famous son, who fled the Nazis for the US in 1933 and later taught such notables as Robert Rauschenberg and John Cage. Presented in a starkly minimalist space are examples from Albers' key series 'Homage to the Square' as well as early lithographs from the Bottrop period. Get there from Bottrop Hauptbahnhof by taking bus SB16 to Im Stadtgarten.

It seems that Bottrop breeds an affinity for geometric shapes, for its other major attraction is the **Tetraeder** (Tetrahedron; admission free; ☻ 24hr), one of the more striking stops on the Industrial Heritage Trail. This 60m-high installation made from steel pipes and open space graces the top of a former slag heap turned landscape park, complete with trees, trails and benches. You can climb the Tetraeder via 'floating' staircases suspended from steel cables (yes, they swing when the wind's up), which lead to three viewing platforms. Not an experience recommended for vertigo sufferers! Views of the surprisingly green yet undeniably industrial surrounds are impressive rather than conventionally beautiful. At night, the Tetraeder becomes a light installation that you can see glowing from afar.

Right next to it, the **alpincenter Bottrop** (☎ 709 50; www.alpincenter.com, in German; Prosperstrasse 299; day pass weekday/weekend €30/40; ☻ 9.30am-midnight) is the world's longest indoor alpine ski run (630m); it's especially popular with teens and the Dutch (and Dutch teens, for that matter). Tickets include ski rental, unlimited food and drink, including beer and wine – is that really a good idea? Take bus 262 from Bottrop Hauptbahnhof to Brakerstrasse to get to both the centre and the Tetraeder.

More silly fun awaits at the **Movie Park Germany** (☎ 02045-8990; www.moviepark.de; Warner Allee 1; adult/senior & 4-11yr €31/27, parking €5; ☻ at least 10am-6pm, closed Nov-Mar), the Ruhrgebiet's version of Disneyland with thrill rides, live-action shows, restaurants and shops. There are direct RE train connections hourly from Essen; get off at Feldhausen. If you're driving, take the Kirchhellen-Nord exit off the A31, then follow the signs.

Gelsenkirchen
☎ 0209 / pop 262,000
We're not huge fans of zoos, but we make an exception for Gelsenkirchen's **Zoom Erlebniswelt** (☎ 954 50; www.zoom-erlebniswelt.de; Bleckstrasse 47; adult/child/concession €13/9/10, parking €3; ☻ 9am-6pm Mar & Oct, 9am-6.30pm Apr-Sep, 9am-5pm Nov-Feb). That's because the animals here don't roam in cages but in habitats that re-create their natural surroundings as closely as possible. 'Alaska' for instance, has rivers, a gushing waterfall, canyons and rock formations where grizzly bears lumber, timber wolves prowl, otters tumble and elks strut. Fencing is minimal and

unobtrusive – you can get surprisingly close to even the fiercer animals thanks to ditches and glass walls. Africa and Asia (set to open in 2010) are the other continents represented. From Gelsenkirchen Hauptbahnhof, tram 301 goes straight to the zoo.

To football (soccer) fans, Gelsenkirchen is of course synonymous with Schalke 04, the legendary club that's long been a mainstay in the *Bundesliga*. The team plays home games at the state-of-the-art **Veltins Arena** (☎ tickets 01805-150 810; www.schalke04.de; Ernst-Kuzorra-Weg 1; tickets €13-53). Tours run Tuesday to Sunday and cost €9 (under 21 €7), but you must call ☎ 389 2900 for specific times. Tour tickets include a visit to the newly revamped **club museum** (☎ 389 2900; adult/child €5/3; ☾ 10am-7pm Tue-Fri, 10am-5pm Sat & Sun). To get to the stadium, take tram 302 to Veltins Arena from Gelsenkirchen Hauptbahnhof.

WESTPHALIA

MÜNSTER
☎ 0251 / pop 281,000
When strolling around Münster's Altstadt, it's hard to imagine that nearly everything you see is only 60 years or so old. After near-total destruction in WWII, the cultural capital of Westphalia opted for creating a carbon copy of its medieval centre rather than embracing the ideas of modern town planning. Although the decision epitomises the rather conservative mindset of locals, Münster is not mired in nostalgia. Its 50,000 students definitely keep the cobwebs out and help make a success out of alternative projects such as the Hafenviertel (old harbour quarter) redevelopment. More than anything, though, it's the 500,000 bicycles – called *Leeze* in local dialect – that quite literally bring energy and movement to this pretty city.

Orientation
Münster's shared airport with Osnabrück is about 20km north of town in Greven (see p603 for travel between the airport and town). Many of the city's main sights are within the confines of the easy-to-walk Altstadt, a short walk northwest of the Hauptbahnhof via Windhorststrasse. The bus station is right outside the station's west exit. The Altstadt is encircled by the 4.8km Promenade, a car-free ring trail built on top

of the former city fortifications; it's hugely popular with cyclists.

Information
There are several banks in the centre, including a Sparkasse in the Münster Arkaden.
Poertgen Herder (☎ 490 140; Salzstrasse 56) Good selection of English books.
Post office (Domplatz; ☾ 9am-7pm Mon-Fri, 8.30am-2pm Sat) There's another branch at the Hauptbahnhof.
Raphaelsklinik (☎ 500 70; Loerstrasse 23) Medical services.
Stadtbücherei (☎ 492 4242; Alter Steinweg 11; per hr €0.50; ☾ 10am-7pm Mon-Fri, 10am-3pm Sat) Public library with internet access, international newspapers and magazines, and clean toilets.
Tourist office (☎ 492 2710; www.tourismus.muenster .de; Heinrich-Brüning-Strasse 9; ☾ 9.30am-6pm Mon-Fri, 9.30am-1pm Sat) Main office.
Tourist office Historisches Rathaus (☎ 492 2724; Prinzipalmarkt 10; ☾ 10am-5pm Tue-Fri, 10am-4pm Sat & Sun)

Sights
DOM ST PAUL
The two massive towers of Münster's cathedral, **Dom St Paul** (Domplatz; ☾ 6.30am-6pm Mon-Sat, 6.30am-7.30pm Sun), match the proportions of this 110m-long structure and the vast square it overlooks. It's a three-nave construction built at a time when Gothic architecture began overtaking the Romanesque style in popularity. Enter from Domplatz via the porch (called the 'Paradise'), richly festooned with sculptures of the apostles. Inside, pay your respects to the **statue of St Christopher**, the patron saint of travellers, then make your way to the southern ambulatory with its **astronomical clock**. This marvel of 16th-century ingenuity indicates the time, the position of the sun, the movement of the planets, and the calendar. Crowds gather daily at noon (12.30pm Sunday) when the carillon starts up.

The **Domkammer** (cathedral treasury; ☎ 495 333; admission €1; ☾ 11am-4pm Tue-Sun), which is reached via the cloisters, counts an 11th-century, gem-studded golden head reliquary of St Paul among its finest pieces.

AROUND DOMPLATZ
Northwest of the Dom, the **Überwasserkirche** (officially known as Liebfrauenkirche) is a 14th-century Gothic hall church with handsome stained-glass windows. The nickname

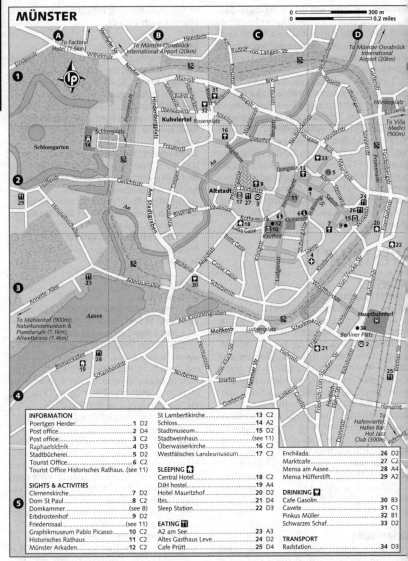

MÜNSTER

was inspired by its location right by the Aa, a tiny stream whose tree-lined promenade makes for relaxed strolling.

Many of the sculptures purged from the churches by the Anabaptists miraculously ended up at the **Westfälisches Landesmuseum** (Regional Museum; ☎ 590 701; Domplatz 10; admission varies; ☼ 10am-6pm Tue-Sun). The collection here spans

from the Middle Ages to the latest avant-garde creations and, not surprisingly, is especially strong when it comes to regional masters, most famously the painter Conrad von Soest. Fans of August Macke and other expressionists will get their fill on the 2nd floor.

One of the 20th century's most famous artists gets the spotlight at the **Graphikmuseum**

ablo Picasso (☎ 414 4710; www.graphikmuseum-picasso
muenster.de; Königsstrasse 5; adult/concession/family €8/6/12;
⏰ 10am-6pm Tue-Sun), the first German museum
ledicated to the Spanish artist. Changing ex-
ibits are drawn from the collection of some
*00 graphic works, including a near complete
eries of Picasso's lithographs.

RINZIPALMARKT

he most interesting street in Münster's
Altstadt is the Prinzipalmarkt, lined by re-
tored Patrician town houses with arcades
heltering elegant boutiques and cafes. The
ey building here is the Gothic **Historisches
athaus**, with its elegant filigree gable. In
648, an important subtreaty of the Peace of
Westphalia was signed here, marking the first
tep in ending the calamitous Thirty Years
Var. You can visit the splendidly wood-
arved hall where the historic moment took
lace; it's called the **Friedenssaal** (Hall of Peace;
☎ 492 2724; Prinzipalmarkt 8-9; adult/concession €1.50/1;
⏰ 10am-5pm Tue-Fri, 10am-4pm Sat & Sun). As you exit,
he beautifully porticoed Renaissance building
n your right is the **Stadtweinhaus** (City Wine
House). It was once used for wine storage and
s now a tourist-geared restaurant.

Continue north on from the Stadtweinhaus
o soon arrive at one of Münster's finest
hurches, the late-Gothic **St Lambertikirche**
☎ 448 93; ⏰ 8am-6.45pm Mon-Sat, 9.30am-7pm Sun),
uilt in 1450. See those three wrought-iron
ages dangling from the openwork spire? They
nce displayed the corpses of the Anabaptist
eader Jan van Leyden and his cohorts after
hey were defeated in 1535 by troops of the
rince-bishop. Before their execution, the trio
vas publicly tortured with red-hot tongs –
ow displayed 400m away at the **Stadtmuseum**
ity Museum; ☎ 492 4503; Salzstrasse 28; admission free;
⏰ 10am-6pm Tue-Fri, 11am-6pm Sat & Sun) – then stuck
n the cages and hoisted onto the church as a
eterrent to others.

Just south of Prinzipalmarkt is the **Münster
rkaden**, a small and elegant shopping mall
vith striking marble flooring and a central
lass dome.

AROQUE BUILDINGS

he architect who left his mark on Münster
nore than any other was Johann Conrad
chlaun (1695–1773). He was a master of
he Westphalian baroque, a more subdued,
ess exuberant expression of the style than
n southern Germany. A most exquisite

example of Schlaun's vision is the 1757
Erbdrostenhof (Salzstrasse 38), a lavish private
mansion. Nearby, the equally stunning 1753
Clemenskirche (Klemensstrasse) boasts a domed
ceiling-fresco supported by turquoise faux-
marble pillars. Less pristinely preserved is
the 1773 **Schloss** (Schlossplatz), the former residence of the prince-bishops and now the main
university building.

HAFENVIERTEL

A 10-minute walk southeast of the
Hauptbahnhof takes you to the **Hafenviertel**,
Münster's revitalised old harbour. What were
once derelict halls and brick warehouses have
been updated with avant-garde architectural
elements and now house a theatre, artist studios and offices alongside an eclectic mixture
of restaurants, bars and dance clubs. You can
promenade along the waterfront or watch
cargo barges cutting along the Dortmund-
Ems canal. In summer, there's even swimming
in the canal. To get to the Hafenviertel, exit
the Hauptbahnhof to the east via Bremer Platz,
follow Bremer Strasse south, cross Hansaring
and it will be on your left.

AASEE

Southwest of the Altstadt, the Aasee is another recreational getaway. Come for a picnic
by the lake, a stroll along its promenade or
to take your sweetie for a spin on the water
itself. Family-friendly attractions include the
Mühlenhof (☎ 981 200; Theo-Breider-Weg 1; adult/child/
student/family €4/2/2.50/10; ⏰ 10am-6pm Apr-Sep, 11am-
4pm Oct-Feb, closed Sat Nov-Feb), an open-air museum where you can stroll among historical
Westphalian buildings, including a mill and
bakery. Dinosaurs and the universe are the
stars at the **Naturkundemuseum & Planetarium**
(Natural History Museum; ☎ 591 05; Sentruper Strasse 285;
museum adult/concession €3.50/2, planetarium €4/2, both
€6.20/3.10; ⏰ 9am-6pm Tue-Sun), while highlights
of the **Allwetterzoo** (☎ 890 40; Sentruper Strasse 315;
adult/concession €12.50/6.30; ⏰ 9am-6pm Apr-Sep, 9am-
5pm Oct & Mar, 9am-4pm Nov-Feb) include the dolphin
tank and the horse museum with fun exhibits
on the region's equestrian heritage.

Sleeping

The tourist office operates a **reservation hotline**
(☎ 492 2726; ⏰ 8am-10pm).

Sleep Station (☎ 482 8155; www.sleep-station.de;
Wolbecker Strasse 1; dm €16-22, linen €3, s/d €40/52; ✉ ▣)
Münster's very own backpacker hostel is just

200m from the Hauptbahnhof above an erotic store (no worries, it's perfectly safe). Dorms are clean but basic and sleep three to eight; only a few singles and doubles have private bathrooms. Perks include free coffee and tea and kitchen use. Check-in is from 8am to 12.30pm and 5pm to 9pm.

Factory Hotel (☎ 418 80; www.factoryhotel.de; An der Germania Brauerei 5; r €80-150; P ⊠ ⊠ 🛜) This sleek new design hotel magically marries the historical with the contemporary in buildings of the defunct Germania Brewery. Gear up for the day in large and modern rooms that get texture from wood, leather and concrete and come with a balcony overlooking an artificial lake. Entertainment zones include three restaurants, a lounge and a club. It's about 2km north of the city centre.

Central Hotel (☎ 510 150; www.central-hotel-muenster .de, in German; Aegidiistrasse 1; s €90-140, d €110-190; P ⊠ 🛜) Small and personably run, this 20-room hotel offers soothing quarters at the end of the day. Alas, it has so many admirers that it's often fully booked. The owners are avid art supporters who don't mind sharing their collection with guests.

Hotel Mauritzhof (☎ 417 20; www.mauritzhof.de, in German; Eisenbahnstrasse 17; s €100-158, d €116-173, ste €188-203; ⊠ ⊠ 🛜) Bold hues, a harmonious interplay of glass and wood and extravagant designer furniture (Vitra, Driade, Kartell) give this 39-room property a mod edge. Rooms facing the promenade have a balcony, and XXL-sized beds are available upon request. Wind down the day in the reading room or over a drink in the lobby lounge.

Other places to unpack your bags:

DJH hostel (☎ 530 280; www.djh-wl.de/jh/muenster; Bismarckallee 31; dm/s/d €26/41/66; P ⊠ ▭) Modern hostel on the Aasee. Take bus 4 or 10 from the Hauptbahnhof to Jugendgästehaus Aasee.

Ibis (☎ 481 30; www.ibishotel.com; Engelstrasse 53; r €69; P ⊠ ⊠ ▭ 🛜) Attractive, good-value property near the Hauptbahnhof.

Eating

Cafe Prütt (☎ 665 588; Bremer Strasse 32; mains €4-9; ☽ noon-midnight Mon-Fri, 10am-midnight Sat & Sun) This alt-flavoured outpost feeds herbivores with wholewheat pizza, crunchy salads and globally inspired mains.

Marktcafe (☎ 575 85; Domplatz 6; mains €5-13; ☽ 9am-1am) In good weather, there's no better place to soak up the street action than the terrace of this been-here-forever cafe with free

views of the Dom. The food is fresh and tasty and Sunday's brunch buffet is an institution

Altes Gasthaus Leve (☎ 455 95; Alter Steinweg 3̄; mains €7-16; ☽ 11.30am-11pm) Münster's oldes inn (since 1607) is a trippy time-warp wher painted tiles, oil paintings and copper etching form a suitably rustic backdrop to the heart Westphalian fare. Dishes such as lima-bea stew and sweet-and-sour beef sound mor challenging than they are.

A2am See (☎ 284 6840; Annette-Allee 3; main €7.50-20; ☽ 11am-midnight Sun-Thu, open end Fri Sat) Location, location, location. A2, righ on the Aasee, certainly has got it. The glas walls and designer furniture scream trendy but this bar-bistro-restaurant actually ap peals as much to lifestyle-savvy types as t hip families and salt-and-pepper couples Stick to classics like steak or spaghetti o try something different, such as the yumm *fiocchi* (cheese-and-pear-stuffed pasta i gorgonzola sauce).

Enchilada (☎ 455 66; Arztkarrengasse 12; mains €8-1 ☽ dinner) The Tex-Mex fare is only so-so, bu the setting in a resurrected medieval bal room is truly stunning. Two happy hour (6pm to 8pm and after 11pm) ensure tha this place is never without a crowd. Nic terrace in summer.

Villa Medici (☎ 342 18; Ostmarkstrasse 15; main €25-40, five-course menu around €50; ☽ dinner Tue-Sat) I you're craving a first-class culinary journey report to this posh Italian *ristorante* whos reputation extends well beyond city border. Ambience-wise it's pretty old-school forma but even first-timers will relax after a warr welcome from the charming owners.

Not only students will enjoy a meal a one of Münster's superb *Mensen* (universit cafeterias) where you can fill up for €5 o less. Our favourites:

Mensa am Aasee (Bismarckallee 11; ☽ lunch & dinner Mon-Sat) Huge, modern with lake views, salad an vegetable bars and grill and wok stations.

Mensa Hüfferstift (Hüfferstrasse 27; ☽ 7.30am-2.30pm Mon-Fri) Paella, pasta, fish, schnitzel, salad and more with views over Münster's rooftops.

Drinking

Münster's party-happy students fuel an eclec tic pub and club scene.

Cafe Gasolin (☎ 510 5897; Aegidiistrasse 4 ☽ 11am-3am) This cleverly converted '5C gas station has yummy cakes and latte mac chiatos for a potent sugar fix and is also good place for that final drink when everything else is closed. Prices are low, quality is not.

Schwarzes Schaf (☎ 484 3577; Alter Fischmarkt 26; ☼ Mon-Sat) This is mostly a regular pub, but on Wednesday, Friday and Saturday the attached historic ballroom morphs into a full-on party den with several dance floors.

Hafen Bar (☎ 289 7810; Hafenweg 26a; ☼ from 10am Mon-Fri, from 8pm Sat) For a glamour vibe without the velvet rope, beat a trail to this stylish glass cube in the Hafenviertel. Soft lighting gives even pasty-faced hipsters a healthy glow.

Hot Jazz Club (☎ 6866 7909; Hafenweg 26b) Also in the trendy Hafenviertel, this subterranean bar keeps it real with live music of all stripes, not only jazz.

For a relaxed pint, steer to the Kuhviertel, the traditional student quarter north of the Dom. **Cavete** (☎ 457 00; Kreuzstrasse 38) and the brew-pub **Pinkus Müller** (☎ 451 51; Kreuzstrasse 4; ☼ closed Sun) with its wacky Westphalian decor have both been classics for generations.

Getting There & Away

The **Münster Osnabrück International Airport** (☎ 02571-943 360; www.fmo.de; Hüttruper Heide 71-81) has low-cost flights on Air Berlin to and from London, Rome, Barcelona and other destinations.

Münster is on an IC line with regular links to points north and south and frequent trains to the Ruhrgebiet cities. The city is on the A1 from Bremen to Cologne and is near the starting point of the A43, direction Wuppertal. It is also at the crossroads of the B51, B54 and B219.

Getting Around

Buses connect the airport and the Hauptbahnhof every half-hour (€5.60, 40 minutes). Drivers should take the Greven or Ladbergen exit off the A1 and follow the signs.

Bus drivers sell single tickets for €1.30 or €2.20, depending on the distance, as well as day passes for €3.60 (valid after 9am).

Hire bikes at **Radstation** (☎ 484 0170; Berliner Platz 27a; 1/3 days €7.50/17.50; ☼ 5.30am-11pm Mon-Fri, 7am-11pm Sat & Sun) at the Hauptbahnhof. The tourist office has cycling maps.

AROUND MÜNSTER

Münster is surrounded by the **Münsterland**, a flat and rural region that's home to about 100

castles and palaces, some of which are still owned and inhabited by blue bloods. Many are protected by water-filled moats, which was often the only way for local rulers to keep out the 'rabble' and rebels.

The region is a dream for cyclists, with over 4500km of well-signposted trails (called *Pättkes* in local dialect), including the scenic 100 Schlösser Route, which links, well, 100 palaces. Bicycles can be hired in Münster (left) and at practically all local train stations. Many castles are also served by public transport, though service can be sketchy or convoluted, especially at weekends.

For route planning, lodging and general information, call toll free ☎ 0800-939 2919, check www.100-schloesser-route.de or contact the Münster tourist office (p599). For public transport information, call ☎ 01803-504 030.

The following are snapshots of a quartet of castles that offer the greatest tourist appeal and, except for Schloss Nordkirchen, are relatively accessible from Münster.

Burg Hülshoff

In Havixbeck, about 10km west of Münster, **Burg Hülshoff** (☎ 02534-1052; Schonebeck 6; adult/concession/family €5/4.50/13; ☼ 11am-6.30pm Apr-Nov) is the birthplace of one of Germany's preeminent women of letters, Annette von Droste-Hülshoff (1797–1848). The red-brick Renaissance chateau is embedded in a lovely – partly groomed, partly romantic – park (admission free). The interior, which consists of period rooms furnished in the style of the poet's day, can be explored with an English-language audioguide. Alas, there's no public transport out here.

Haus Rüschhaus

Annette von Droste-Hülshoff did some of her finest writing at the smaller **Haus Rüschhaus** (☎ 02533-1317; Am Rüschhaus 81; adult/concession €5/2.50; ☼ tours hourly 10am-noon & 2-5pm Tue-Sun May-Oct, 11am, noon, 2pm, 3pm Tue-Sun Mar, Apr & Nov) where she lived for 20 years from 1826. The building was once the private home of star architect Johann Conrad Schlaun, who magically morphed a farmhouse into a baroque mini-mansion backed by a formal garden (always open). It's in the suburb of Nienberge, about 3km north of Burg Hülshoff, and served by bus 5 from Münster's Hauptbahnhof (€2.10, 20 minutes).

Burg Vischering

The quintessential medieval moated castle, **Burg Vischering** (☎ 02591-799 00; Berenbrok 1) is Westphalia's oldest (1271), and the kind that conjures romantic images of knights and damsels. Surrounded by a system of ramparts and ditches, the complex consists of an outer castle and the main castle, now a **museum** (adult/concession/family €2.50/2/6; ☺ 10am-12.30pm & 1-5.30pm Tue-Sun Apr-Oct, to 4.30pm Nov-Mar).

Burg Vischering is in Lüdinghausen, about 30km south of Münster. Catch bus S90/91 or S92 at the Hauptbahnhof to Lüdinghausen (€5.60, 45 minutes), then walk for about 10 minutes.

Schloss Nordkirchen

On an island surrounded by a sprawling, manicured park, **Schloss Nordkirchen** (☎ 02596-9330; tours €2; ☺ noon-5pm Sun May-Sep, 2-4pm Sun Oct-Apr & by prior arrangement) is an imposing baroque red-brick structure nicknamed the 'Westphalian Versailles'. On a nice day, the palace is well worth visiting for the gardens and the exterior alone. Since it's used as a state college for financial studies, the interior – with its stuccoed ceilings, festival hall and dining room – can only be seen on guided tours.

Schloss Nordkirchen is 8km southeast of Lüdinghausen in the hamlet of Nordkirchen, which is poorly served by public transport. Consult your bike map to find the route between Burg Vischering and Schloss Nordkirchen.

SOEST

☎ 02921 / pop 48,000

Soest is a tranquil town of half-timbered houses and a clutch of treasure-filled churches that reflect the wealth it enjoyed during its Hanseatic League days. Although heavily bombed in WWII, this maze of idyllic, crooked lanes has been beautifully rebuilt and preserves much of its medieval character. Soest is a 'green' town, not only because of its natural charms but also for the shimmering greenish shades of the local sandstone used in building its town wall, churches and other public structures. Its romantic looks have also charmed modern artists, including expressionists Emil Nolde, Karl Schmidt-Rottluff and native son Wilhelm Morgner. Only 45km east of Dortmund, Soest is compact enough to be explored on a day trip or as a side trip en route to somewhere else.

Orientation

The train and bus stations are on the north side of the ring road enclosing Soest's historic centre. Follow the pedestrianised Brüderstrasse south to the Markt, tourist office, Dom and the churches.

Information

There are several banks with ATMs around Markt.

Post office (Hospitalgasse 3)
Tourist office (☎ 6635 0050; www.soest.de; Teichsmühlengasse 3; ☺ 9.30am-4.30pm Mon-Fri, 10am-3pm Sat year-round, 11am-1pm Sun Apr-Oct)

Sights

Much of Soest's historic centre lies within a moated **defensive wall**, which today has a park-like appearance and is great for strolling and picnicking.

Soest is home to some of Westphalia's most important churches. Closest to the Hauptbahnhof is the exquisite late-Gothic hall church, **St Maria zur Wiese** (Wiesenstrasse; ☺ 11am-4pm Mon-Sat, noon-4pm Sun), also known as Wiesenkirche and easily recognised by its lacy neo-Gothic twin spires. These are undergoing restoration and will remain under wraps until at least 2023. The church restoration workshop also operates the **Grünsandstein-Museum** (Green Sandstone Museum; ☎ 150 11; Walburgerstrasse 56; admission free; ☺ 10am-5pm Mon-Sat, 2-5pm Sun), where you can learn about the origin of Soest's mysteriously green stone. Inside the church, its delicate proportions and vibrant stained-glass windows create an ethereal atmosphere. An endearing feature is the window above the north portal, which shows Jesus and his disciples enjoying a Westphalian Last Supper of ham, beer and rye bread.

On Hohe Gasse, **St Maria zur Höhe** (☺ 10am-5.30pm Mon-Fri, 10am-5pm Sat, noon-5pm Sun Apr-Sep, 10am-4pm Mon-Sat, noon-4pm Sun Oct-Mar), better known as Hohnekirche, is a squat, older and architecturally less refined 13th-century hall church. Its sombreness is brightened by beautiful ceiling frescoes, an altar ascribed to the Westphalian painter known as the Master of Liesborn, and the *Scheibenkreuz*, a huge wooden cross on a circular board more typically found in Scandinavian churches; in fact, it's the only such cross in Germany. Look for the light switch on your left as you enter to shed a little light on the matter.

Three more churches are near Markt, a short walk west via the **Grosser Teich**, a placid duck pond and park where the tourist office occupies an old water mill. The dignified tower of **St Patrokli** (Propst-Nübel-Strasse 2; 10am-6pm), a three-nave Romanesque structure partly adorned with delicate frescoes, looks down upon the **Rathaus**, a baroque confection with an arched portico on the western side.

Adjacent to this ensemble is the **Petrikirche** (Petrikirchhof 10; 9.30am-noon & 2-5.30pm Tue-Fri, to 4.30pm Sat, 2-5.30pm Sun), with Romanesque origins in the 8th century and a choir from Gothic times, all topped by a baroque onion dome. It's adorned with wall murals and features an unusual modern altar made from the local green sandstone, glass and brushed stainless steel.

The tiny **Nikolaikapelle** (Thomästrasse; 11am-noon Tue-Thu & Sun) is a few steps southeast of St Patrokli. It's a pity it's rarely open, for its almost mystical simplicity is enlivened by a masterful altar painting attributed to 15th-century master Conrad von Soest (who was born in Dortmund).

Sleeping

DJH hostel (162 83; www.djh-wl.de/jh/soest; Kaiser-Friedrich-Platz 2; dm under/over 26yr €19.10/21.80; P) Wallet watchers should check out this renovated yet still rather basic hostel.

Hotel im Wilden Mann (150 71; www.im-wilden-mann.de; Am Markt 11; s €49, d €78-85) This central landmark in a portly half-timbered town house offers the opportunity to connect to the magic of yesteryear in a dozen comfortable rooms furnished in rustic country style.

Pilgrim Haus (1828; www.pilgrimhaus.de, in German; Jakobistrasse 75; s/d/tr €79/105/128; P) This darling inn has been in the hospitality business since 1304 and hasn't lost its lustre. Pack your tummy with upscale German fare in the popular restaurant (mains €9 to €20), then report to hushed and elegant rooms decked out in soothing colours and attractive art.

Eating

Local specialities include the Soester pumpernickel, a rough-textured rye bread made entirely without salt, and the *Bullenauge* (bull's eye), a creamy mocha liqueur.

Der Kater (135 44; Nöttenstrasse 1; dishes €3-8; 10am-midnight Mon-Sat, 4pm-1am Sun) This kitty is cool and casual and feeds tasty pizza, sal-ads and other simple yet sustaining fare to its admirers.

Bontempi im Park (166 31; Im Theodor-Heuss-Park; pizza & pasta €7-9, mains €9-20; 10am-10pm) Let the good times roll in this modern bistro in an idyllic park next to a duck pond. The location may be the biggest selling point, but the Italian food convinces, too. Come for breakfast, snacks, ice cream, coffee or a full meal.

Brauerei Christ (155 15; Walburger Strasse 36; mains €10-20; noon-11pm) History oozes from every nook and cranny of this warren of living-room-style rooms stuffed with musical instruments, oil paintings and unique knick-knacks. Hunker down at polished tables for Westphalian specialities or any of its 15 schnitzel variations. Nice beer garden.

Getting There & Away

Soest is easily reached by train from Dortmund (€10.10, 45 minutes) and is also regularly connected to Paderborn (€10.10, 40 minutes) and Münster (€13.60, 50 minutes). If you're driving, take the Soest exit from the A44. Soest is also at the crossroads of the B1, B229 and B475.

PADERBORN

05251 / pop 144,000

About 50km east of Soest, Paderborn is the largest city in eastern Westphalia and offers an intriguing blend of medieval marvels and high-tech. It derives its name from the Pader which, at 4km, is Germany's shortest river. About 200 springs surfacing in the Paderquellgebiet, a landscaped park in the city centre, spurt out an average of 5000L per second.

Charlemagne used the royal seat and bishopric he had established here to control the Christianisation of the Saxon tribes. A visit by Pope Leo III in 799 led to the establishment of the Western Roman Empire, a precursor to the Holy Roman Empire, and Charlemagne's coronation as its emperor in Rome the following year. Paderborn remains a pious place to this day – churches abound, and religious sculpture and motifs adorn facades, fountains and parks. Many of the city's 14,000 students are involved in theological studies (economics and technology are other major fields).

Orientation

Paderborn/Lippstadt Airport is 18km southwest of town (see p607 for details on getting there and away). Most sights cluster in the largely pedestrianised Altstadt, which is small enough to explore on foot. To get to the Dom, the tourist office and other sights from the Hauptbahnhof, exit right onto Bahnhofstrasse and continue straight via busy Westernstrasse, the main shopping street. Alternatively, you can take bus 2, 4, 8 or 9 to Rathausplatz.

Information

Several banks with ATMs can be found along Westernstrasse and around the Dom and Rathaus.

Internet Bar (Kilianstrasse 5; per hr €2; ☼ 9.30am–1am)

Linnemann (☎ 285 50; Westernstrasse 31) Bookshop.

Post office (Liliengasse 2; ☼ 10am–6pm Mon–Fri, 10am–1pm Sat) Off Westernstrasse.

St-Vincenz Hospital (☎ 860; Am Busdorf 2)

Tourist office (☎ 882 980; www.paderborn.de; Marienplatz 2a; ☼ 10am–6pm Mon–Fri, 10am–2pm Sat Apr–Oct, 10am–5pm Mon–Fri, 10am–2pm Sat Nov–Mar)

Sights

CITY CENTRE

Paderborn's massive **Dom** (Markt 17; ☼ 10am–6.30pm), a three-nave Gothic hall church, is a good place to start your explorations. Enter through the southern portal (called 'Paradies'), adorned with delicate carved figures, then turn your attention to the **high altar** and the pompous **memorial tomb of Dietrich von Fürstenberg**, a 17th-century bishop. Signs point the way to the Dom's most endearing feature, the so-called **Dreihasenfenster**, a unique trompe l'oeil window in the cloister. Its tracery depicts three hares, ingeniously arranged so that each has two ears, even though there are only three ears in all.

The hall-like **crypt**, one of the largest in Germany, contains the grave and relics of St Liborius, the city's patron saint. To see the famous Liborius shrine, though, visit the **Erzbischöfliches Diözesanmuseum** (Museum of the Archdiocese; ☎ 125 1400; Markt 17; adult/concession/family €3/2.50/6; ☼ 10am–6pm Tue–Sun), housed in an incongruously modernist structure outside the Dom. Its surprisingly attractive interior brims with church treasures, the most precious of which are kept in the basement, including the gilded shrine and prized portable altars. Upstairs, the one piece not to be missed is the Imad Madonna, an exquisite 11th-century linden-wood statue.

Paderborn's proud **Rathaus** (1616) with ornate gables, oriels and other decorative touches is typical of the Weser Renaissance architectural style. South of the Rathaus is the **Marktkirche** (Market Church; Rathausplatz; ☼ 9am–6pm), aka Jesuitenkirche, a galleried basilica where pride of place goes to the dizzyingly detailed baroque high altar. A soaring symphony of wood and gold, it's an exact replica of the 17th-century original destroyed in WWII.

Rathausplatz blends into Marienplatz with its delicate **Mariensäule** (St Mary's Column) and **Heising'sche Haus**, an elaborate 17th-century patrician mansion that shares a wall with the tourist office. The **Abdinghofkirche** (Am Abdinghof; ☼ 11am–6pm) is easily recognised by its twin Romanesque towers. Once a Benedictine monastery, it's been a Protestant church since 1867 and is rather austere with its whitewashed and unadorned walls and a flat wooden ceiling.

At the foot of the Abdinghofkirche lies the **Paderquellgebiet**, a small park perfect for relaxing by the gurgling springs of the Pader and with nice views of the Dom. This is also the starting point of a lovely walk along the little river to **Schloss Neuhaus**, a moated palace about 5km northwest, which hosts frequent cultural events in summer.

East along Am Abdinghof to the north of the Dom are the remnants of the **Carolingian Kaiserpfalz**, Charlemagne's palace where that historic meeting with Pope Leo took place. It was destroyed by fire and replaced in the 11th century by the **Ottonian-Salian Kaiserpfalz**, which has been reconstructed as faithfully as possible atop the original foundations. Inside is the **Museum in der Kaiserpfalz** (☎ 105 110; Am Ikenberg 2; adult/concession €2.50/1.50; ☼ 10am–6pm Tue–Sun), which presents excavated items from the days of Charlemagne, including drinking vessels and fresco remnants. The only original palace building is the twee **Bartholomäuskapelle** (☼ 10am–6pm) next door. Consecrated in 1017, it's considered the oldest hall church north of the Alps and enjoys otherworldly acoustics.

HEINZ NIXDORF MUSEUMSFORUM

You don't have to be a techie to enjoy the engaging **Heinz Nixdorf Museumsforum** (HNF; ☎ 306 600; www.hnf.de; Fürstenallee 7; adult/concession/family €5/3/10; ☼ 9am–6pm Tue–Fri, 10am–6pm Sat & Sun), an amazing romp through 5000 years of information technology, from cuneiform to cyberspace. Established by the local founder of Nixdorf computers (since swallowed by bigger corporations), it displays calculating machines, typewriters, cash registers, punch-card systems, manual telephone exchanges, accounting machines and other time-tested gadgets, although the heart of the museum clearly belongs to the computer age. Most memorable is the full-scale replica of **Eniac**, a room-sized vacuum-tube computer developed for the US Army in the 1940s. These days, the data it held would fit onto a barely-there microchip.

There are plenty of machines to touch, push and prod as well as computer games and a virtual-reality theatre. English-language explanatory panels are only sporadic, but a comprehensive museum guide in English is available for €5. To get here, catch bus 11 from the Hauptbahnhof to Museumsforum.

Sleeping

DJH hostel (☎ 220 55; www.djh-wl.de/jh/paderborn; Meinwerkstrasse 16; dm under/over 26yr Mar-Oct €17.60/20.30, Nov-Feb €15.20/17.50; P ✗) Well-run and central hostel. Take bus 2 to Detmolder Tor.

Hotel Campus Lounge (☎ 892070; www.campuslounge.de, in German; Mersinweg 2; s/d from €80/90; P ✗ ☎) Great views and roomy digs with private balcony are among the assets of this warm and welcoming property near the university. Frolicking zones include a spa with sauna, steam room and ice grotto and a lounge-bar.

Galerie-Hotel Abdinghof (☎ 122 40; www.galerie-hotel.de, in German; Bachstrasse 1; s/d €80/100; P ✗) Hands-down our favourite in town, this charming hotel in a 1563 stone building overlooks the Paderquellgebiet. Famous artists – Michelangelo to Picasso – inspired the decor of the 11 rooms, furnished in styles ranging from country-rustic to elegant-feminine. Original art graces the downstairs cafe-restaurant.

Hotel Stadthaus (☎ 188 9910; www.hotel-stadthaus.de, in German; Hathumarstrasse 22; s/d €98/106; ✗ ☎) An air of quiet elegance pervades this 34-room hotel spread over two separate but equally delightful buildings. Free wine, bottled water and DSL are welcome perks, and so is the sauna for relaxing. The restaurant serves modern German cuisine.

Eating

Curry Company (☎ 387 7414; Kamp 10; dishes €2.50-9; ☺ 11am-midnight) 'Gourmet snack' is not an oxymoron at this artsy sausage parlour where you can pair your *Wurst* (sausage) with such freshly made gourmet sauces as

truffle mayonnaise, coriander-chilli sauce and roasted garlic honey sauce.

Deutsches Haus (☎ 221 36; Kisau 9; mains €7-19; ☺ 8.30am-1am) You won't leave hungry after a meal at this honest-to-goodness German inn souped up with rustic beams, wood booths and a mosaic inspired by Gustav Klimt. The hungry-man breakfasts (€6.50, including bottomless tea or coffee) could easily last you through to supper. Also come for lunch specials and meaty dinners.

Trattoria Il Postino (☎ 296 170; Rathauspassage; mains €10-22, 3-course lunch €12 or €14; ☺ lunch & dinner Mon-Sat) Locals intent on top-drawer Italian fare flock to this snazzy, glass-fronted restaurant anchored by a big central bar. Chef Domenico does creative things with pasta (made fresh daily), but his talent truly shines when it comes to meaty mains such as mustard-and-thyme-spiked roast pork. Enter from Jühenplatz.

Other recommended eateries:

Edoki Sushi Bar (☎ 873 073; An der Alten Synagoge 1; maki €4-7, nigiri €1.40-3.20, bento boxes €13-20; ☺ lunch & dinner Tue-Sun) The best place in town for sushi. Order à la carte or one of the bento boxes.

Kampus Cafe (☎ 892 9797; Kamp 12; ☺ 9am-1am) Friendly, all-purpose cafe no matter where the hands are on the clock.

Getting There & Away

Air Berlin offers direct flights between London-Stansted to **Paderborn/Lippstadt Airport** (Flughafen Paderborn/Lippstadt; ☎ 02955-770; www.airport-paderborn.com; Flughafenstrasse 33), which is connected to the Hauptbahnhof by bus 400 and 460.

Paderborn has direct IC every two hours to Kassel-Wilhelmshöhe (€24, 1¼ hours) and regional connections to Dortmund (€20.10, 1¼ hours) and other Ruhrgebiet cities. Trains to Soest (€10.10, 40 minutes) leave several times hourly.

Paderborn is on the A33, which connects with the A2 in the north and the A44 in the south. The B1, B64 and B68 also go through Paderborn.

Getting Around

Bus rides cost €1.25 for short trips, €2 for longer ones and €5.20 for a day pass. **Radstation** (☎ 870 740; Bahnhofstrasse 29; ☺ 5.30am-10.30pm) at the Hauptbahnhof rents bicycles for €9 per 24 hours.

NORTH RHINE–WESTPHALIA

SAUERLAND

Even if you've never heard of the Sauerland we bet you're familiar with its most famous product: beer. The best-known brew is Warsteiner Pils, made by Germany's largest brewery in the town of Warstein. Otherwise, this forested upland region southeast of Dortmund serves primarily as an easy getaway for nature-craving Ruhrgebiet residents and hill-craving Dutch tourists. There are a few museums and castles, but the Sauerland's primary appeal lies in the outdoors. Some 20,000km of marked hiking trails, mostly through beech and fir forest, spread across five nature parks. Cyclists and mountain bikers can pick their favourites from dozens of routes. Reservoirs and lakes are popular with swimmers, windsurfers and boaters, and in winter the higher elevations allow for decent downhill and Nordic skiing. The area is also rich in caves filled with ethereal formations.

The Sauerland is best explored under your own steam, although even the smallest towns are served by buses or trains. Almost every village has its own tourist office, but for pre-trip planning and room reservations go to www.sauerland.com or call the hotline at ☎ 01802-403 040.

ALTENA
☎ 02352 / pop 19,500

In a steep, narrow valley carved by the Lenne River, Altena has built its fortune on producing industrial wire since making mail-shirts for medieval knights. Still, despite its scenic setting, it would hardly be worth a stop were it not for the majestic **Burg Altena**. This fairy-tale medieval castle started out as the home of the local counts, then served military purposes under the Prussians before becoming, in 1912, the birthplace of the youth hostel movement. The world's first hostel, with dark dorms sporting wooden triple bunks, can be seen on a tour of the **castle museum** (☎ 966 7033; Fritz-Thomee-Strasse 80; adult/concession/family €5/2.50/10; 9.30am-5pm Tue-Fri, 11am-6pm Sat & Sun). There is a series of 31 themed rooms, each zeroing in on a different aspect of regional history, often in a visually pleasing and engaging fashion. You'll see some fancy historic weapons and armour, but also an exhibit on the Sauerland under the Nazis. Plan on spending at least 90 minutes to see it all.

Admission is also good at the **Deutsches Drahtmuseum**, about 300m downhill. It has hands-on displays on the many facets of wire, from its manufacture to its use in industry, communications and art.

Altena's **tourist office** (☎ 209 295; www.altena-tourismus.de; Lüdenscheider Strasse 22) keeps erratic hours, so call ahead if possible.

You won't have to sleep in triple bunks but staying at Altena's **DJH hostel** (☎ 235 22 www.djh-wl.de/jh/burg.altena, in German; Fritz-Thomee-Strasse 80; dm under/over 26yr €19.10/21.80;) which is inside the old castle, is still a nostalgic throw-back with two giant dorms sleeping 13 and 14, respectively.

The castle and hostel are about a 15-minute walk from the train station. Altena is served by regional trains from Hagen.

ATTENDORN
☎ 02722 / pop 24,800

The main attraction of Attendorn, a typical Sauerland town on the northern shore of the Biggesee, is the **Atta-Höhle** (☎ 937 50; www.atta-hoehle.de; Finnentroper Strasse 39; tours adult/child €7/4; 9.30am-4.30pm May-Aug, reduced hr Sep-Apr), one of Germany's largest and most impressive caves. The 40-minute tour takes you past a subterranean lake and stalagmites and stalactites shaped into curtains, domes, columns and shields.

The Biggesee is great for water sports as well as lake cruises, which are operated by **Personenschiffahrt Biggesee** (☎ 02761-965 90; www.personenschiffahrt-biggesee.de; cruises adult/child €9/4.50; Apr-Oct).

Attendorn's **tourist office** (☎ 4897; www.attendorn.net; Rathauspassage, Kölner Strasse 12a; 9am-5.30pm Mon-Fri year-round, 10am-noon Sat Jun-Sep) can help out with accommodation.

Fine options include **Landhotel Struck** (☎ 02721-139 40; www.landhotel-struck.de; Repetalstrasse 245; s €69-83, d €100-127;) in the suburb of Niederhelden. Everything speaks of sophistication at this family-owned hotel, from the grand wooden staircase to the fluffy duvets on your bed. Rooms in the annexe are cheaper but more basic (single/double €45/79).

A memorable place for a meal is the knight's hall in **Burg Schnellenberg** (☎ 6940; Schnellenberg 1; mains €17-28), a 13th-century castle perched high above town. It's quite formal, so bring your manners and evening finery. It also has rooms (from €125).

To get to Attendorn by regional train requires changing in Hagen and in Finnentrop.

WINTERBERG
☎ 02981 / pop 14,500

Winterberg, the main town in the Rothaargebirge nature park, is the Sauerland's winter sports centre. Its primary ski mountain is the 843m-high Kahler Asten. Besides skiing, attractions include a 1600m-long bobsled run that hosts international competitions and an indoor skating rink. In good winters, the season runs from December to March, helped along by snow-making machines if nature fails to perform. In summer, there's lots of good hiking, including a popular and moderately strenuous 5km trail to the top of the Kahler Asten.

For more ideas, stop by the **tourist office** (☎ 925 00; www.winterberg.de; Am Kurpark 6).

Winterberg is served directly by trains from Dortmund every two hours (€15.90, 1¾ hours).

SIEGERLAND

The hills and mountains of the Sauerland continue southward into the Siegerland region, with the city of Siegen as its focal point. Frankfurt, the Ruhrgebiet and Cologne are all about 100km away.

SIEGEN
☎ 0271 / pop 104,000

Wedged into a valley hemmed by dense forest, Siegen is the commercial hub of the Siegerland and birthplace of the painter Peter Paul Rubens (1577–1640). For centuries it was ruled by the Counts of Nassau-Oranien, the family that ascended to the Dutch throne in 1813. Two palaces from those glory days survived the bombing squadrons of WWII, but in every other respect Siegen is a thoroughly modern city. The hilly Altstadt has some appeal, but its streets are increasingly quiet as two giant shopping malls down by the Hauptbahnhof zap away the bulk of the business.

Orientation

Siegen's Altstadt slopes up from the Hauptbahnhof via pedestrianised Bahnhofstrasse and Kölner Strasse. For drivers, the main artery through town is Koblenzer Strasse (B54/62).

Information

Banks with ATMs are right outside the Hauptbahnhof along Bahnhofstrasse.

Post office (Hindenburgstrasse 9; ⏱ 9am-6.30pm Mon-Fri, 9am-1pm Sat)

Tourist office (☎ 404 1316; www.tourismus.gss-siegen.de, in German; Rathaus, Markt 2; ⏱ 9am-5pm Mon-Fri, 11am-3pm Sat & Sun)

Sights

A jailbird arriving in prison might well gripe: 'This sure ain't no palace'. Well, in Siegen, it is. The **Unteres Schloss**, a mustard-coloured baroque palace, now houses the local jail along with other city-government offices. The elegant three-wing structure originally served as the residence of the Protestant princes of Nassau-Oranien, who had split off from the family's Catholic branch in 1623.

Right next to the prison wing, the **Museum für Gegenwartskunst** (Museum of Contemporary Art; ☎ 405 770; www.kunstmuseum-siegen.de; Unteres Schloss 1; adult/concession/family €3.90/2.60/7.70; ⏱ 11am-6pm Tue, Wed & Fri-Sun, 11am-8pm Thu) mounts changing exhibits that zero in on the latest trends and players in the art world. Its permanent exhibition presents works by Francis Bacon, Lucian Freud and Cy Twombly, all of them recipients of the *Rubenspreis* (Rubens Prize) awarded by the city to an international artist every five years.

Halfway up the hill looms Siegen's signature landmark, the late Romanesque **Nikolaikirche** (Markt; ⏱ 10am-6pm Mon-Fri, 10am-noon Sat Apr-Oct). It's easily recognised by the golden crown atop the steeple, placed there by a local ruler in 1652 to commemorate his promotion from count to prince. The church itself has an unusual hexagonal floor plan but is otherwise rather plain on the inside.

From Markt, Burgstrasse slopes up to the **Oberes Schloss**, a classic medieval fortress and the ancestral home of the rulers of Nassau-Oranien. Its labyrinth of rooms now houses the **Siegerlandmuseum** (☎ 230 410; Burgstrasse; adult/concession/family €3/1.50/6; ⏱ 10am-5pm Tue-Sun), which would be a mediocre collection of old paintings were it not for its nine Rubens originals, including a self-portrait and a large-scale work viscerally depicting a lion hunt. Other rooms cover aspects of local history.

Sleeping & Eating

The local and the regional tourist offices can help with room reservations.

Berghotel Johanneshöhe (☎ 387 8790; www
.johanneshoehe.de; Wallhausenstrasse 1; s €50-95, d €86-120;
P ⊠ 🛜) Handy if you're motorised, this
hilltop hotel will treat you to sweeping views
(somewhat marred by the autobahn). Rooms
come in different sizes and comfort levels.
The nicest are large, stylish and have French
balconies overlooking the valley. Enjoy the
same views from the restaurant over creative
German fare (mains €10 to €20).

Park Hotel (☎ 338 10; www.parkhotel-siegen.best
western.de; Koblenzer Strasse 135; r €100-160; P ⊠ 🛜)
This modern 88-room property offers four-
star amenities at three-star prices. Although it
goes mostly after the business brigade, it offers
such welcome leisure facilities as a sauna and
steam room.

Laternchen (☎ 231 8000; Löhrstrasse 37; mains €10-20;
🕙 dinner Thu-Tue) This charismatic restaurant
is dressed in wood and candlelight and is
a romantic spot to enjoy delicious modern
German cuisine with the occasional French
touch. Its signature dish is a pungent garlic
soup. It's in one of Siegen's few historic buildings, with neat leaded-glass windows and a
slate-covered facade.

Piazza (☎ 303 0856; Unteres Schloss 1; lunch €6-12,
dinner €11-22; 🕙 11am-11pm) At the Museum für
Gegenwartskunst, Piazza brings a dash of
urban pizazz to sleepy Siegen. The chef uses
mostly regional ingredients to whip up an

inspired blend of German and Mediterranean
flavours. The late Josef Paul Kleihues designed
the sleek dining room.

Getting There & Away

Direct trains depart hourly for Cologne
(€18.70, 1½ hours), Frankfurt (€23.60,
1¾ hours) and Essen (€26.80, 2¼ hours).
Change in Hagen for Dortmund (€2.90, two
hours). Siegen is off the A45 connecting the
Ruhrgebiet with Frankfurt and is also easily
reached from Cologne via the A4.

AROUND SIEGEN
Freudenberg
☎ 02734 / pop 18,600

About 12km north of Siegen, Freudenberg
would be just another blip on the map were
it not for its gorgeous **Altstadt** (called *Alter
Flecken*, meaning 'old borough'), the 17th-
century equivalent of a planned community. Built in tidy rows, these half-timbered
houses all point in the same direction, are
approximately the same height and sport
the same white facades, the same pattern
of wooden beams and the same black-slate
roofs. Follow signs to *Historischer Stadtkern*
(historic town centre). For panoramic views
head to the Kurpark (spa garden), best accessed from the intersection of Am Kurpark
and Kölner Strasse.

Lower Saxony

The second largest state after Bavaria in terms of physical size, Lower Saxony (Niedersachsen) is characterised by broad, sweeping landscapes and its strong historical ties with Great Britain and Russia. Although it lacks spectacular 'must sees', this part of Germany offers the traveller a rich potpourri of experiences and, especially in the far north around the coast, an opportunity to slow down and engage with the landscape and people.

The capital, Hanover, hosts the enormous communications show, CeBit, and has a handful of museums and historic gardens that offer a window to the past and present. Wolfsburg, east of Hanover, is the home of one of the world's most successful automobile models (the Volkswagen Beetle), has an unusually relaxed character, and also has Phaeno, a cutting-edge science centre. A visit to the archaeological site of a Roman defeat at Osnabrück's Varusschlacht, graphically illustrating a spectacular collision of Roman and Germanic cultures during classical times, will appeal to young and old.

Lower Saxony also serves up some very unexpected cultural attractions, like Osnabrück's Felix-Nussbaum-Haus, an early example of the striking architecture of the American Daniel Libeskind, or historic towns like Celle or 'rat-ridden' Hamelin (of 'Pied Piper' fame). Meanwhile, its coast, river plains, moor and heath lend themselves perfectly to cycling, in a landscape that, like its inhabitants, tends towards understatement. In how many places, however, can you say that you've walked to an island? Head north to where Deutschland meets the North Sea, and Lower Saxony offers that opportunity, too.

HIGHLIGHTS

- **Open Stage** Carve your niche in Lower Saxony's entertainment scene at Göttingen's Nörgelbuff 'open stage' sessions (p647)
- **Quirky Old Town** Fall head over heels for the wobbly city of Lüneburg (p630)
- **Cycling Back in Time** Bicycle 15km from the Pied Piper's town of Hamelin to the Renaissance Schloss Hämelschenburg (p623)
- **Pilgrimage** Pay your respects to Anne Frank at the Bergen-Belsen concentration camp (p629)
- **Green Haven** Admire the Niki de Saint Phalle Grotto at Hanover's Herrenhäuser Gärten (p613)
- **Slow Travel** Grab a bicycle or kayak and ride or paddle through East Frisia (p653), or walk to the East Frisian Islands (p656)

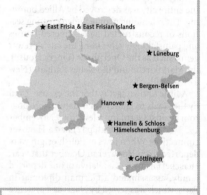

- ★ East Frisia & East Frisian Islands
- ★ Lüneburg
- ★ Bergen-Belsen
- Hanover ★
- ★ Hamelin & Schloss Hämelschenburg
- ★ Göttingen

■ POPULATION: 8 MILLION | ■ AREA: 47,613 SQ KM

HANOVER
☎ 0511 / pop 518,000

Fairly or not, Hanover tends to get a bad rap in Germany. Local comedians dismiss it as 'the Autobahn exit between Göttingen and Walsrode', it is reputed to have Germany's most boring parties, and when an Expo was held here about a decade back, even its spokesperson mused aloud about whether anyone would travel here if they had the choice.

To most of the world, Hanover is known for its huge CeBit information and communications technology fair, but the city also boasts acres of greenery and its spectacularly baroque Herrenhäuser Gärten (gardens) are a mini-Versailles, featuring a sparkly Niki de Saint Phalle Grotto. The compact centre, only partially reconstructed in a medieval style after WWII bombing, is adjoined to the east by the Eilenreide forest, and you can enjoy some good museums en route to the southern lake Maschsee.

History

Hanover was established around 1100 and became the residence of Heinrich der Löwe (p33) later that century. An early Hanseatic city, by the Reformation it had developed into a prosperous seat of royalty and a power unto itself.

Notably, it has links with Britain through a series of marriages. In 1714 the eldest son of Electress Sophie of Hanover, a granddaughter of James I of England (James VI of Scotland), ascended the British throne as George I while simultaneously ruling Hanover. This British-German union lasted until 1837.

In 1943, up to 80% of the centre and 50% of the entire city was destroyed by Allied bombing. The rebuilding plan included creating sections of reconstructed half-timbered houses and painstakingly rebuilding the city's prewar gems, such as the Opernhaus (Opera House), the Marktkirche and the Neues Rathaus (New Town Hall).

A little known fact is that the excuse given by the Nazis to launch their nationwide pogrom against Germany's Jews on 9 November 1938 (see the boxed text, p42) had a Hanover connection. When Jews of Polish origin were deported from Hanover in October that year, Herschel Grünspan, a relative of one deported family, assassinated a German diplomat in Paris, which was seized by Nazis as a pretence to begin a pogrom.

Orientation

The Hauptbahnhof (central train station) is located on the northeastern edge of the city centre. The centre contains one of the largest pedestrianised areas in Germany, focusing on Georgstrasse and Bahnhofstrasse. Bahnhofstrasse heads southwest from the Hauptbahnhof, and Georgstrasse runs west–east from Steintor via the Kröpcke square to Georgsplatz. There's a subterranean shopping strip running below Bahnhofstrasse, from the Hauptbahnhof to just south of Kröpcke, called the Niki de Saint Phalle Promenade.

The Herrenhäuser Gärten are situated about 4km northwest of the city centre. The Messegelände, the main trade fairgrounds, are in the city's southeast (see the boxed text, p618).

Information

DISCOUNT CARDS

HannoverCard (1/3 days €9.60/16) Available from the tourist office, this card offers unlimited public transport and discounted admission to museums etc. Group tickets for five are available, too.

EMERGENCY

Medical emergency service (☎ 314 044)

Police (☎ 110; Raschplatz) Beneath the overpass on the north side of the Hauptbahnhof.

INTERNET ACCESS

Teleklick Hannover (☎ 763 5201; Kurt-Schumacher-Strasse 11; per hr €1.80; ⏲ 9am-11pm) Comfortable place with Skype and telephones, plus muffins and coffee.

LAUNDRY

Wasch-Treff (cnr Friesenstrasse & Eichstrasse; per wash €3.50; ⏲ 6am-11pm) Conveniently opposite this laundry is an organic bakery-cafe.

MEDICAL SERVICES

Hospital (☎ 304 31; Marienstrasse 37)

MONEY

Reisebank (☎ 322 704; Hauptbahnhof; ⏲ 8am-10pm Mon-Sat, 9am-10pm Sun) ATMs plus currency exchange services, inside the station.

POST

Post office (Ernst-August-Platz 2; ⏲ 9am-7.30pm Mon-Fri, to 3pm Sat) Inside the Ernst-August-Galerie.

TOURIST INFORMATION

Tourist brochures are also available from the Neues Rathaus (below).

Hannover Tourismus (☎ information 1234 5111, room reservations 123 4555; www.hannover.de, www hannover-tourism.de; Ernst-August-Platz 8; ⊗ 9am-6pm Mon-Fri, 9am-2pm Sat, also 9am-2pm Sun Apr-Sep)

Dangers & Annoyances

The area behind the Hauptbahnhof and the red-light district near Steintor are well-policed but require care and common sense after dark.

Sights & Activities

ROTER FADEN

The city has painted a *Roter Faden* (red line) on pavements around the centre. Follow it with the help of the multilingual *Red Thread Guide* (€2.50), available from the tourist office, for a quick 4.2km, do-it-yourself tour of the city's main highlights.

NEUES RATHAUS

An excellent way to get your bearings in Hanover is to visit the Neues Rathaus (built in 1901–13) and travel 98m to the top in the **curved lift** (elevator; adult/concession €2.50/2; ⊗ 9.30am-5pm Mon-Fri, 10am-6pm Sat & Sun Apr-Nov) inside its green dome. There are several viewing platforms here, and while it's a novelty taking a lift that slants to stay within the dome, it's only on descent that you feel any gravitational swing. The cabin can take only five people at a time, so queues are inevitable.

In the downstairs lobby are four city models showing Hanover from the Middle Ages to today. Comparing the models from 1939 and 1945 drives home the dramatic extent of WWII devastation.

HERRENHÄUSER GÄRTEN

Largely modelled on the gardens at Versailles, the **Herrenhäuser Gärten** (☎ 1684 7576, 1234 5333; www.herrenhaeuser-gaerten.de; ⊗ 9am-sunset; ⓔ 4 or 5 to Herrenhäuser Gärten) truly rank among Hanover's most memorable attractions. You need a couple of hours to do them justice, but they combine a couple of treats.

On the one hand, the Grosser Garten (Large Garden), Berggarten (Mountain Garden) and Georgengarten (Georgian Garden) are prime examples of why Hanover calls itself a city 'in green'. On the other, the statues, fountains and coloured tile walls of the **Niki**

de Saint Phalle Grotto (opened after her death in 2002) provide a magical showcase of the artist's work that could one day outshine *Die Nanas* (see below).

With its fountains, neat flowerbeds, trimmed hedges and shaped lawns, the 300-year-old **Grosser Garten** (admission €3, incl entry to Berggarten €4, child free, Grosser Garten free mid-Oct–Mar) is the centrepiece of the experience. There's a maze near the northern entrance, while the **Grosse Fontäne** (Big Fountain; the tallest in Europe) at the southern end jets water up to 80m high. In summer, there are **Wasserspiele** (water games; ⊗ 11am-noon & 3-5pm Mon-Fri, 11am-noon & 2-5pm Sat & Sun Apr-late Oct) when all fountains are synchronised. During the **Illuminations** (adult/concession €4/3; ⊗ approximately 10pm Fri-Sun mid-May–Aug, also Tue Jul & Aug, call for exact times) the gardens and fountains are atmospherically lit at night. Meanwhile there are summer concerts, Shakespearean dramas and more. Call or check the Herrenhäuser website for details.

North of the Grosser Garten lies the **Berggarten** (admission €2, combined admission with Grosser Garten €4, child free), with its great assortment of flora from around the world. Amid the lake-dotted Georgengarten (admission free), you'll find the **Wilhelm-Busch-Museum** (☎ 1699 9916; www.wilhelm-busch-museum.de, in German; adult/ concession €4.50/2.50; ⊗ 11am-6pm Tue-Sun) containing a wealth of caricature, including works by Busch, Honoré Daumier and William Hogarth.

DIE NANAS

The city government was inundated with nearly 20,000 letters of complaint when these three earth-mama **sculptures** were first installed beside the Leine River in 1974. Now, the voluptuous and fluorescent-coloured 'Sophie', 'Charlotte' and 'Caroline', by French artist Niki de Saint Phalle, are among the city's most recognisable, and most loved, landmarks. Indeed, *Die Nanas* helped make de Saint Phalle famous, and devout fans of her work will find a direct trip to Leibnizufer (U-Bahn stop Markthalle Landtag) rewarding.

SPRENGEL MUSEUM

It's the building as much as the curatorial policy that puts the **Sprengel Museum** (☎ 1684 3875; www.sprengel-museum.de, in German; Kurt-Schwitters-Platz; adult/child under 12yr/concession €7/free/4; ⊗ 10am-6pm Wed-Sun, 10am-8pm Tue) in such high esteem.

LOWER SAXONY

Its huge interior spaces are brilliant for displaying its modern figurative, abstract and conceptual art, including a few works by Nolde, Chagall and Picasso. At the core of the collection are 300 works by Niki de Saint Phalle, a selection of which is usually on show. Take bus 100 from Kröpcke to the Sprengelmuseum/Maschsee stop.

MASCHSEE

This artificial lake, built by the unemployed in one of the earliest Nazi-led public works projects, is now a favourite spot for boating and swimming. It's certainly the most central at just 30 minutes' walk away; otherwise take bus 100 from Kröpcke to Sprengelmuseum/Maschsee.

Ferries (☎ 700 950; adult/child full tour €6/3, half-tour €3/1.50) – some solar-powered – ply the lake from Easter to October in good weather and there are sailing, pedal and rowing boats for hire. On the southeast bank there's a swimming beach, or **Strandbad** (adult/child €2.50/1.50; ☯ 9.30am-7.30pm May-Aug) while in-line skaters glide by under the neighbouring trees.

ALTSTADT

Despite WWII bombing, Hanover's restored Altstadt (old town) remains appealingly quaint. The red-brick, Gothic **Marktkirche** in the market square has original elements, as do both the **Altes Rathaus** (begun 1455) across the market, and the nearby **Ballhof** (1649-

www.kestner.org; Goseriede 11; adult/concession €5/2.50; 11am-6pm Tue, Wed & Fri-Sun, to 8pm Thu). Having exhibited works by Otto Dix, Georg Grosz, Wassily Kandinsky and Paul Klee before they became famous, the society is still originating shows that later tour Europe. Its wonderfully light, high-ceilinged premises were once a bathhouse.

Decorative arts through the ages are covered at the **Kestner Museum** (☎ 1684 2120; Trammplatz 3; adult/concession €5/3, Fri free; 11am-6pm Tue & Thu-Sun, to 8pm Wed), where you'll see everything from Bauhaus-style cutlery to a very impressive collection of Greek and Egyptian antiquities.

WAR MEMORIALS

In a city so devastated by war, it's not surprising to find a **peace bell**. Donated by sister city Hiroshima, it lies inside a steel-cross **Memorial to Our Dead** on Breite Strasse near the corner of Osterstrasse. Every 6 August at 8.15am, the date and time of the atomic detonation at Hiroshima, a delegation from both cities meets here to ring the bell. The neighbouring **Aegidienkirche Memorial** (1350) was bashed by artillery in 1943.

The winged angel **Waterloo Memorial** you see south of the Altstadt and west of the Neues Rathaus commemorates the German forces who fought at Waterloo.

Festivals & Events

The annual **Maschsee festival**, which includes drinking, performances and an enormous fireworks display, runs annually in early August.

Each year in summer pyrotechnic experts stage a handful of shows at the international **fireworks festival** and competition at Herrenhäuser Gärten.

People also come to Hanover from afar for the **Enercity Swinging Hannover** international jazz festival, held over two days around Ascension Day in May/June.

Sleeping

The tourist office books rooms for a €2.50 fee. Prices given here are those outside tradeshow periods. During shows, they can double, triple and even quadruple. Check on the city website (www.hannover.de) or better yet ask the tourist office directly to ensure you're not unintentionally arriving during a trade-fair period.

54), a hall originally built for 17th-century badminton-type games.

An entire row of **half-timbered houses** has been recreated along Kramerstrasse and Burgstrasse near the Marktkirche, and here you also find **Leibnizhaus**, once the home of mathematician and philosopher Gottfried Wilhelm Leibniz (1646–1716), with its reconstructed Renaissance facade.

In front of the Leibnizhaus is the **Oskar-Winter-Brunnen** (Oskar Winter Fountain). If you make a wish and turn the small brass ring embedded in the ironwork three times, local lore has it that the wish will come true.

OTHER MUSEUMS

It's always worth checking listings for the **Kestner Gesellschaft** (Kestner Society; ☎ 701 200;

LOWER SAXONY

BUDGET

Campingplatz Arnumer See (☎ 05101-3534; http://
camping-hannover.de; Osterbruchweg 5, Arnum-Hemmingen;
adult/car €6/4, tent €5; 🖵 🛜) In a pleasant leafy
lakeside location south of the city, this extremely well-equipped camping ground has
a playground and separate areas for tents and
caravans. Take bus 300 to Arnum Mitte, from
where it's a five-minute walk. By road, take
A7 south to Laatzen, or B3 from Arnum, and
follow the signs.

DJH hostel (☎ 131 7674; www.jugendherberge.de/jh
/hannover; Ferdinand-Wilhelm-Fricke-Weg 1; dm under/
over 27yr from €23.90/26.90; 🅿 ✕ 🖵 ; 🔴 3 or 7 to
Bahnhof Linden/Fischerhof) This huge, space-lab-
like structure houses a modern hostel with
breakfast room and terrace bar overlooking

the river. It's only a short walk from here to
the Maschsee.

GästeResidenz PelikanViertel (☎ 399 90; www
.gaesteresidenz-pelikanviertel.de; Pelikanstrasse 11; s €46-69
d €66-89, tr €92-109; 🅿 ✕ ; 🔴 3, 7 or 9 to Pelikanstrasse
Upmarket student residence meets budget
hotel, this well-managed complex alongside
the Arabella Sheraton has a wide range of
very pleasant Ikea-ish rooms, some split over
two levels. Long-term stays for seven days or
longer are excellent value.

our pick City Hotel am Thielenplatz (☎ 327 691
www.smartcityhotel.de, in German; Thielenplatz 2; s €58.50-
68.50, d €77-87; 🅿 ✕ 🛜) This very central
'budget boutique' beauty has a reception and
bar opulently re-styled with red leather seating, black-and-white leaf-patterned wallpaper

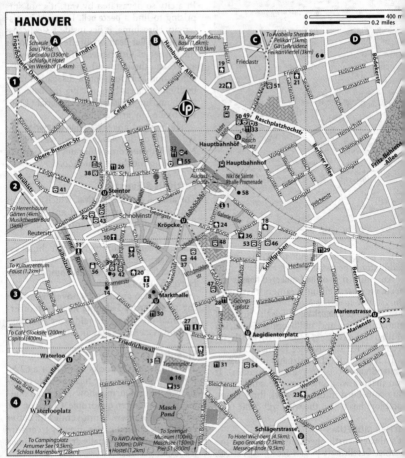

and lots of wood laminate. Most rooms have been renovated, all in a 1950s retro look, with a choice of wood laminate or carpet. There is wi-fi in the bar downstairs.

MIDRANGE

Hanns Lilje-Haus (☎ 124 1698; www.hanns-lilje-haus.de, in German; Knochenhauerstrasse 33; s/d from €66/82, breakfast per person €8; ✕ ☎) Though Church-owned, this hotel is fine about unmarried or gay couples staying; decorations are neutral, but rooms are large and make interesting use of space to create a bright and pleasant atmosphere.

Hotel Stella (☎ 811 2050; info@stella-hotel.de; Adelheidstrasse; s/d €64/84; P ✕ ☎ ; ☒ 1, 2 or 8 to Schlägerstrasse) Pleasant if unspectacular, the Stella is a small hotel with a big heart and decent-sized rooms in a quiet residential street. It's handily located on urban transport to the trade fairgrounds, but still close to the centre.

Hotel Königshof am Funkturm (☎ 339 80; www.koenigshof-hannover.de; Friesenstrasse 65; s €59-94, d €89-114; P ✕ ☒ ☎) Quirky religious statues and ethnic sculptures (plus an old Mercedes with Jesus in front of it) greet you in the foyer here. This rambling abode has 'economy', 'comfort', 'business' (with balcony) and 'deluxe' rooms (with sofa), decorated attractively with bright furnishings and subtle Toscana tones. The location is reasonably safe, but this is a red-light club district.

City Hotel Flamme (☎ 388 8004; www.city-hotel-flamme.de; Lammstrasse 3; s/d €69/99; P ✕ ☒ ☎) Most of the 24 rooms of this attractively mural-painted hotel-*Pension* open onto balconies facing a large atrium courtyard, which has a quirky eating area and glassed-in front wall. If you don't like the area around the train station, they will pick you up from there for free.

Hotel Wiehberg (☎ 879 990; www.hotel-wiehberg.de; Wiehbergstrasse 55a; s/d €72/87; P ✕ ☎ ; ☒ 1 or 2 to Dorfstrasse) Modernistic and evoking a 'Zen' feel, this hotel makes excellent use of natural lighting and shadow and even features low Japanese-style beds set on rails. These are designed for trade-fair guests who want to share rooms without getting too snug. If guests do get snug, though, they can push the beds together. The hotel's in a leafy residential neighbourhood.

Lühmanns Hotel am Rathaus (☎ 326 268; www.hotelamrathaus.de, in German; Friedrichswall 21; s €76.50-85, d €120, ste €150; ✕ ☒ ☎) Posters from the nearby Kestner Museum adorn the halls here, and the rooms themselves are tastefully decorated with liberal use of reds, blues and black, as well as the occasional bit of original art. Although the hotel's on a busy street, double-glazing keeps noise at bay.

Schlafgut Hotel im Werkhof (☎ 353 560; www.hotel-schlafgut.de; Kniesestrasse 33; s/d €82/118; P ✕ ☎ ; ☒ 6 or 11 to Kopernikusstrasse) Located in the Nordstadt

LOWER SAXONY

ALL THE FUN OF THE TRADE FAIR

Coming to Hanover for a trade fair (Messe)? You're part of a time-honoured tradition. The first export fair was held in August 1947 in the midst of all the rubble from WWII. As most hotels had been destroyed, the mayor made an appeal to citizens to provide beds for foreign guests. The people did, the money came and it's become a tradition; about a third more beds are available in private flats at fair time (the only time they're offered) than in hotels.

The pre-eminent fair today is CeBit, a telecommunications and office information gathering that organisers claim is 'the largest trade show of any kind, anywhere in the world'. It's held every March and during the dotcom boom of the late 1990s had as many as 800,000 attendees. (More recent shows have attracted smaller crowds of around half a million visitors.) Another biggie is Hannover Messe, an industrial show in late April.

The Messegelände, the main trade fairgrounds, are in the city's southeast, served by tram/U-Bahn 8 (and during fair times 18, both to Entrance Nord) as well as the S4 S-Bahn, and IC and ICE trains. Tram/U-Bahn 6 serves the eastern part of the fairgrounds near the former Expo site.

During major fairs there's a full-service tourist office at the airport and an information pavilion at the fairgrounds, in addition to the main tourist office (see p613).

Pressure on accommodation means you really need to book ahead – and be prepared for phenomenal price hikes too. Indeed, some visitors choose to stay instead in Hildesheim, Celle (both of which up their own prices during these times) or even in Hamburg, and commute.

As a first step, the website www.hannovermesse.de has full information in English. To organise a private room or hotel in Hanover, call ☎ 1234 5555.

in a former lift factory (remodelled along ecological principles), Schlafgut has a bright, open and colourful feel, along with a 1970s retro breakfast room. Rooms have conveniences like large writing surfaces and high-speed internet through the power socket – but bring your own cable or you'll need to buy one from reception for €5. There is wi-fi in the foyer.

our pick **Loccumer Hof** (☎ 126 40; www.loccumerhof.de, in German; Kurt-Schumacher-Strasse 14/16; s/d €99/129; P ☒ ⬜ ⬤) Some of the stylish and well-decorated rooms here are themed by nations ('Australia'), elements ('Air') and feng shui. Others are low-allergy, and the artwork (not for sale) is by the owner-manager, who has put together possibly Hanover's most interesting hotel. As well as these walk-in prices, rates are often one-third less for advanced booking.

Hotel Alpha (☎ 341 535; www.hotelalpha.de; Friesenstrasse 19; s/d/tr/apt €99/132/139/145; ☒) Situated at the end of the street away from the red-light clubs, this pleasant hotel has an assortment of sweet and quirky statues and marionettes. There's a trompe l'oeil of an Italian piazza in the breakfast room and the rooms are lovely and homey.

TOP END

Arabella Sheraton Pelikan (☎ 909 30; pelikanhotel@arabellasheraton.com; Podbielskistrasse 145; r €119-155; ☒ ☷ ⬜ ⬤ ; ⬤ 3, 7 or 9 to Pelikanstrasse) Fat beds

with thick mattresses and plump cushions dominate the rooms of this luxury hotel, although the high ceilings alleviate any feeling of being cramped. Set on a redeveloped factory site in the suburbs, it feels like a hideaway village, with the renowned restaurant 5th Ave and Harry's New York bar. There's a fitness centre (free use) next door, too.

Kastens Hotel Luisenhof (☎ 304 40; www.kastens-luisenhof.de; Luisenstrasse 1-3; s from €167, d from €187, junior ste from €290, ste from €390; P ☒ ☷ ⬜ ⬤) This grande dame looks pretty good in spite of being over 150 years old, possibly from the myriad of wellness offerings such as massages and its upper-level spa and fitness centre. Rooms reflect a timeless elegance, and prices vary according to demand, but are mostly below €200 for doubles in non-trade-fair periods.

Eating
RESTAURANTS

Sonderbar (☎ 3365 9700; Raschplatz 6; mains €3.50-15 ⬤ noon-11pm; ☒ ⬤ Ⓥ) This well-styled place has an assortment of Tex-Mex, Spanish and Italian snacks and mains, as well as oven potatoes in the upstairs, upmarket sports bar section (large screens). Downstairs is a lounge It's aimed at a business and pleasure crowd and close enough to the station to duck into between trains.

Georxx (☎ 306 147; Georgsplatz 3; dishes €5.50-15; ☻ from 9.30am; ✗) Popular with business-people, office workers, shoppers, tired travellers and even an arty crowd, Georxx has pleasant outdoor seating in summer, a menu offering a taste for everyone (a bit of Asia, a bit of Europe etc) and good lunch specials (€8.50 to €12). Breakfast is a staple, and served until 5pm.

our pick **Spandau** (☎ 1235 7095; Engelbosteler Damm 30; lunch special €6.50, mains €7.20-11.90; ☻ 10am-1am Sun-Wed, 10am-2am Thu-Sat; ✗ 🛜 Ⓥ) Retro-'70s Spandau in Hanover's Nordstadt is more like Berlin's Kreuzberg – a place where students from the nearby university and the local Turkish community rub shoulders. The menu is small-ish and features pasta, tofu curry and several more substantial meat dishes.

Mr Phung Kabuki (☎ 215 7609; Friedrichswall 10; sushi €2.50-6, mains €7.50-16; ☻ 11am-midnight Mon-Thu & Sun, 11am-2am Fri & Sat; ✗ Ⓥ) Boats bob by on the water-based sushi train, but you can order all manner of pan-Asian and wok dishes at this airy, trendy restaurant with an enormous range of spirits.

Besitos (☎ 169 8001; courtyard, Goseriede 4; tapas €2-5, mains €8-16; ☻ from 5pm; ✗ Ⓥ) Locals come to this warehouse-sized place to enjoy the city's best tapas under high ceilings and the watchful eye of gaucho and matador murals on the Mediterranean-coloured walls.

Basil (☎ 622 636; Dragonerstrasse 30; mains €12-25, menus from €25; ☻ dinner Mon-Sat; ✗) These former stables to the north of town now house a fabulous fusion restaurant, with a high arched ceiling and pressed tablecloths. Imaginative concoctions, such as coffee-marinated duck breast with chicory and pear ragout, are served to an in crowd. Take tram 1 or 2 to Dragonerstrasse.

Hiller (☎ 321 288; Blumenstrasse 3; mains €6.20-15, set menus €16-20; ☻ lunch & dinner Mon-Sat; ✗ Ⓥ) Germany's oldest vegetarian restaurant is such an institution it even has its logo – a carrot – carefully embroidered onto every linen napkin. Despite the modern interior, with swirly green painting and mustard-coloured walls, the atmosphere is quite hushed and the food a tad old-fashioned. That said, come with an appetite if ordering a set menu.

Pier 51 (☎ 807 1800; Rudolf von Bennigsen Ufer 51; starters €9-13, mains €21-23; ☻ noon-midnight; ✗) One of Hanover's loveliest restaurants, and very romantic at sundown, Pier 51 is walled with glass and juts out over the Maschsee. The menu is strong on fish, although you can also choose pasta or meat. In summer, there's an outside 'Piergarten', decked out with the old-fashioned *Strandkörbe* (straw basket seats) that you see on German beaches. Book at least a few days ahead if you want a window seat at dinner.

QUICK EATS & SELF-CATERING

our pick **Markthalle** (☎ 341 410; Kamarschstrasse 49; dishes €3.50-8; ☻ 7am-8pm Mon-Wed, to 10pm Thu & Fri, to 4pm Sat; ✗ Ⓥ) This huge covered market of food stalls and gourmet delicatessens is fantastic for a quick bite, both carnivorous and vegetarian.

Os Amigos (☎ 363 665; Ernst-August-Galerie; tapas €2.50-6.90, mains €6.90-12.50; ☻ 8am-8.45pm Mon-Sat; ✗ Ⓥ) This Spanish place is one of several inexpensive options alongside Hauptbahnhof inside the large shopping centre.

denn's Biomarkt (☎ 215 7866; Marktstrasse 45; ☻ 8.30am-8pm Mon-Fri, 8am-8pm Sat; Ⓥ) A large organic supermarket, denn's has everything from fruit and vegies to wines, aquaculture fish and meats – perfect for a wholesome picnic in Eilenriede forest or on the Maschsee.

Drinking
CAFES

Der Gartensaal (☎ 1684 8888; Neues Rathaus, Trammplatz 2; coffee with cake €5; ☻ 11am-10pm mid-May–mid-Sep, to 6pm mid-Sep–mid-May) A great place to sit and have a summer afternoon coffee overlooking the central *Stadtpark*.

Holländische Kakaostube (☎ 304 100; Ständehausstrasse 2-3; hot chocolate with cake €5; ☻ 9am-7.30pm Mon-Fri, 9am-6.30pm Sat) With the blue-and-white square-patterned floor matching the Delft pottery, and a curved ship's staircase and maritime paintings creating a subtle nautical feel, this historic Dutch coffee house has many fans, young and old.

BARS

Many of the cultural centres, clubs and rock and jazz venues listed under Entertainment (p620) are also good places to go just for a drink.

Brauhaus Ernst August (☎ 365 950; Schmiedestrasse 13; ☻ 8am-3am Sun-Thu, 8am-5am Fri & Sat; ✗) A Hanover institution, this sprawling brewpub makes a refreshing unfiltered Pilsner called Hannöversch. A party atmosphere reigns nightly, helped along by a varied roster of live bands and DJs.

Café Mezzo (☎ 314 966; Lister Meile 4; ⏰ 9am-2am Sun-Thu, 9am-3am Fri & Sat; ✕ 🛜) Inside the Pavillon (opposite), this classic bar and cafe used to be a student hang-out, but today Mezzo gets a balance of ages. It's popular any time of day (including for breakfast), but doubles well as a place to warm up in the evening before moving on to a club or performance.

HeimW (☎ 235 2301; Theaterstrasse 6; ⏰ 9am-1am Mon-Thu & Sun, 9am-2am Fri & Sat) This long, narrow bar has lights shaped like huge droplets of water about to land on your head, an atrium ceiling, potted palms beside cream leather banquettes, and intriguing artwork on the walls. Salads, breakfast and light meals are also served (€5 to €9.50).

Acanto (☎ 391 030; Dragonerstrasse 28; ⏰ from 8pm Thu-Sat) Next door to the restaurant Basil, you'll find one of Hanover's trendiest DJ bars, where fashionably dressed beautiful people sip caipirinhas under chandeliers and mirror balls. Take tram 1 or 2 to Dragonerstrasse.

Entertainment

For listings, check out the local edition of *Prinz*, in German.

NIGHTCLUBS

Hanover has two main clusters of clubs and bars. One place to head for is the red-light district of Steintor (cheekily nicknamed Stöhntor by locals, meaning 'Moaning Gate'), in a former strip- and sex-club stronghold. All these have free admission and are close together, so you can look in and take your pick.

Eve Klub (www.eve-klub.de, in German; Reuterstrasse 3-4; ⏰ from 9pm Thu, from 10pm Fri & Sat; ✕) is a former striptease bar that has kept the red lamps over the tables and red corduroy sofas; the **Kiez Klub** (☎ 353 5699; www.kiez-klub.de, in German; Scholvinstrasse 5; ⏰ from 10pm Wed, Fri & Sat) has minimal house, techno house and electro house, situated in a yard off the street; while **Sansibar** (www.sansibar-hannover.eu, in German; Scholvinstrasse 7; ⏰ from noon Mon-Sat) has soul and classics for 30-somethings. **Intensivstation** (☎ 301 59; Scholvinstrasse 9; ⏰ from 8pm Fri & Sat, plus some Wed & Thu; ✕) has staff dressed as nurses and medically themed surrounds – kinky.

Traditionally, the other main clubbing destination is in the revamped environs of Raschplatz (the so-called 'golden triangle') behind the train station. Here you find **Osho**

Diskothek (☎ 342 217; www.osho-disco.de, in German Raschplatz 7l; entry €2.50; ⏰ from 10pm; ✕), or 'Baggi as Hanoverians fondly call it, playing a mix of classic disco hits for the over-25s, as well as **Palo Palo** (☎ 331 073; www.palopalo.de, in German Raschplatz 8a; ⏰ from 10pm; ✕) for anyone wanting to see-and-be-seen.

3Raum (www.3raum-ballhof.de, in German; Ballhofstrasse 5; club nights €3; ⏰ 7pm-1am Tue-Thu, to 4am Fri & Sat) is a crossover place for the 25-to-40 age group, where early in the week you can enjoy drinks or theatre, and most get down in the club on Friday and Saturday.

CINEMAS

Anzeiger Hochhaus (☎ 144 54; Goseriede 9) This spacious, art-house cinema is on the top floor of a magnificent expressionist building designed by Fritz Höger, the architect of Hamburg's Chilehaus (p676). Check listing times, as the box office only opens just before screenings.

GAY & LESBIAN VENUES

More information can be found at http:// hannover.gay-web.de (in German) and, for lesbians, at www.hannoverfrauen.de (in German) or head to the lesbian and gay hang-outs **Café Konrad** (☎ 323 666; www.cafekonrad.de, in German Knochenhauerstrasse 34; weekly specials €6-10; ⏰ from 10am, breakfast till 4pm; ✕) or **Café Caldo** (☎ 151 73 Bergmanstrasse 7; ⏰ 6pm-2am Mon-Thu, 6pm-3am Fri, 8pm-3am Sat, 4pm-2am Sun; ✕) where the staff will be able to fill you in on the scene.

Schwule Sau (☎ 700 0525; Schaufelder Strasse 30a ✕) This alternative gay and lesbian centre regularly hosts concerts, theatre and club nights. The third Friday in the month is gay mixed, the third Saturday lesbian. Take the U6 or 11 to Kopernikusstrasse from Kröpcke.

Famous Club (☎ 1699 1888; Goseriede 4/Tiedthof; entry €3; ⏰ from 11pm Fri & Sat; ✕) This club catering for the gay and lesbian scenes offers up electro, house, R&B, '80s and other goodies with a top-class sound system and screens.

THEATRE & CLASSICAL MUSIC

Hanover's cultural firmament, **Staatsoper Hannover** (☎ tickets 9999 1111; www.staatsoperhannover .de, in German; Opernplatz 1; tickets €18-50), is housed in the 19th-century Opernhaus (Opera House) where classical music as well as ballet and opera are performed.

The Staatstheater Hannover performs or hosts international theatre in the **Schauspielhaus**

☎ tickets 9999 1111; www.schauspielhannover.de, in German; Prinzenstrasse 9; tickets €12-30), while the **Junges Schauspielhannover** (☎ tickets 9999 1111; www .schauspielhannover.de, in German; tickets €14.50-18) mainly uses two spaces on Ballhofplatz: **Ballhof eins** (Ballhofplatz 5), directly on the square, and **Ballhof zwei** (Knochenhauerstrasse 28), which adjoins it.

GOP Varieté (☎ 301 8670; www.variete.de/hannover, in German; Georgstrasse 36; tickets €15-35) is an old-school type of variety theatre with dancing, acrobatics, circus-style acts, magic, music and more, housed in the Georgspalast. It also boasts a much-lauded restaurant.

Those interested in seeing some cabaret should make tracks for **Marlene Bar & Bühne** (☎ 368 1687; www.marlene-hannover.de, in German; cnr Alexanderstrasse & Prinzenstrasse; free-€15), while German speakers into more serious drama should check out what's on at the **Neues Theater** (☎ 363 001; www.neuestheater-hannover.de, in German; Georgstrasse 54; tickets €10-30). Comedies and musical theatre are performed at **Theater am Aegi** (☎ 989 3333; www.theater-am-aegi.de, in German; Aegidientorplatz; tickets from €20).

LIVE MUSIC

Check the websites of the following venues (usually under 'Programm'), or listings, for dates and prices of events.

Café Glocksee (☎ 161 4712; www.cafe-glocksee.de, in German; Glockseestrasse 35; entry free-€20; ☒) Part live-music venue, part club, the Glocksee has everything from techno and trance DJs to grungy gigs. Friday nights go electronic.

Capitol (☎ 444 066; www.capitol-hannover.de, in German; Schwarzer Bär 2; entry with €3 purchase; ☒) This former movie theatre has rock, pop, house, soul and more on weekends and frequently during the week. Take tram 3, 7 or 9 to Schwarzer Bär.

Kulturzentrum Faust (☎ 455 001; www.faustev.de, in German; Zur Bettfedernfabrik 1-3, Linden; ☒) Ska from Uruguay, Chinese new year festivals, disco, reggae, heavy metal gigs, multimedia installations, quiz evenings, book readings – this all happens, and more, in this former factory complex. The 1960s concert hall is complemented by a pub-bar, Mephisto, beer garden and cafe. Take tram 10 to Leinaustrasse.

Musiktheater Bad (☎ 169 4138; www.musiktheater -bad.de, in German; Am Grossen Garten 60; ☒) In this large old building and its surrounding grounds, you'll find a mixed bag of live music, music theatre and dance offerings. It's great in summer when there's an outdoor stage.

Pavillon (☎ 344 558; Lister Meile 4; ☒) This huge circular venue has a cafe-bar (see opposite), theatre and various rooms used as venues where you can catch a wide program of jazz, off-beat rock, world music and whatever else anyone decides to put on there.

SPORT

AWD Arena (www.awdarena.de, in German) With a capacity of 44,000, this ground is one place where you can usually get last-minute seats (about €35) for matches between Hannover 96 and their opponents (not Bavaria Munich, rarely Schalke 04). Follow the stream of fans or take U-Bahn 3, 7 or 9 from Hauptbahnhof to Waterloo and follow the signs for about 500m.

Shopping

Hanover's compact city centre makes it ideal for shopping, although most of what you will find is modern, international fashion. A pedestrianised zone full of shops extends south from the Hauptbahnhof, along Bahnhofstrasse, Georgstrasse and Karmarschstrasse. The Niki de Sainte Phalle Promenade, a subterranean shopping strip running below Bahnhofstrasse, and **Ernst-August-Galerie** (Ernst-August-Platz 2) are also worth browsing.

There's a regular **flea market** (Hohen Ufer; ☼ 8am-4pm Sat) behind the Historisches Museum, along the Leine River Canal near Die Nanas.

Getting There & Away

AIR

Hanover Airport (HAJ; ☎ 977 1223; www.hannover -airport.de) has many connections, including **Lufthansa** (☎ 0180-380 3803), and the low-cost carriers **Air Berlin** (☎ 01805-737 800; www.airberlin.com) to/from London-Stansted and **TuiFly** (☎ 01805- 757 510; www.tuifly.com) to/from Newcastle in Great Britain.

The S-Bahn (S5) takes 18 minutes from the airport to the Hauptbahnhof (€2.80).

CAR & MOTORCYCLE

Nearby autobahns run to Hamburg, Munich, Frankfurt and Berlin, with good connections to Bremen, Cologne, Amsterdam and Brussels. Major car rental firms are in the Hauptbahnhof, including **Sixt** (☎ 01805-252 525; ☼ 7am-9pm Mon-Fri, 8am-6pm Sat, 9am-9.30pm Sun) and **Avis** (☎ 322 610; ☼ 7am-9.30pm Mon-Fri, 9am-4pm Sat, 4-9pm Sun).

TRAIN

Hanover is a major rail hub, with frequent ICE trains to/from Hamburg (€40, 1¼ hours), Munich (€116, 4¼ hours), Cologne (€64, 2¾ hours) and Berlin (€61, 1¾ hours), among others.

Getting Around

The transit system of buses and tram/U-Bahn lines is run by **Üstra** (☎ 166 80; www.uestra.de; ☺ 8am-9pm Mon-Fri, 8am-6pm Sat, 9am-5pm Sun). Most U-Bahn lines from the Hauptbahnhof are boarded in the station's north (follow signs towards Raschplatz), including U-Bahn 8 to the *Messe* (fairgrounds; €2.10, 19 minutes). Lines U10 and U17 are different. These are overground trams leaving south of the station near the tourist office.

Most visitors only travel in the central 'Hannover' zone, where single tickets are €2.10 and day passes €4.10. If you wish to travel in two/three zones, singles cost €2.80/3.50, while day passes cost €5.30/6.60.

For taxis call ☎ 8484, ☎ 2143 or ☎ 3811. From the centre to the fairgrounds a taxi costs about €35; to the airport it's about €20. **Fahrradstation am Bahnhof** (☎ 353 9640; Fernoroder Strasse 2; bicycle per day €7.50; ☺ 6am-11pm Mon-Fri, 8am-11pm Sat & Sun) has bicycle hire, alongside the Hauptbahnhof.

AROUND HANOVER

Nobles the world over will tell you that ancestral homes can be *such* a huge financial burden to maintain, especially when they're turreted castles. In late 2005, the family of Prince Ernst August of Hanover (Princess Caroline of Monaco's husband) auctioned off some 25,000 household objects to raise money for the upkeep of their 130-room neo-Gothic fancy. Now a small part of the palace, **Schloss Marienburg** (☎ 05069-407; www.schloss-marienburg.de; tour adult/under 16yr €6.50/5.50; ☺ 10.30am-5pm Apr-Oct), is open to members of the public interested in a behind-the-scenes glimpse of German aristocratic life. Admission is by a one-hour tour, either with a tour guide or using an audio guide (English, French, Polish and Russian available). Tours include the Knight's Hall, Queen's Library and more.

From Hanover, you can take the B3 28km south or alternatively the A7 south and exit 62 to Hildesheim. Take the B1 out of Hildesheim and continue 7km until you come to Mahlehrten. Turn right for

Nordstemmen and you should see the castle. By public transport, the best way out is by occasional direct bus 300 to the stop 'Marienburg Abzweig Nord'. A more frequent connection is to take bus 300 to the stop 'Pattensen', then change to bus 310 to stop 'Marienburg Abzweig Nord'. From there it's 1.5km to the castle (day card €6.60).

Dino Park Münchehagen (Dinosaur Open Air Museum; ☎ 05037-2073; www.dinopark.de; adult/under 12yr €9.50/8; ☺ 10am-6pm Mar-Oct, last entry 1hr before closing) has more than 200 life-size dinosaurs (*Brontosaurus, T rex*, raptors and so on) arranged around a walking trail where real dinosaurs once roamed.

By car, follow the A2 west of Hanover and take the No 40 exit to Wunstorf-Luthe. Continue along the 441 out of Wunstorf and you'll reach the park before Locum. By public transport, take S-Bahn 1 or 2 from Hanover to Wunstorf (€3.50, 19 minutes) then bus 716 to Saurier-Park (€2.10 one way, 30 minutes to one hour). Buses run more frequently at weekends; for timetable information check www.regiobus.de or call ☎ 0511-3688 8723.

FAIRY-TALE ROAD – SOUTH

This stretch of the **Märchenstrasse** (Fairy-Tale Road; www.deutsche-maerchenstrasse.de) is one of the prettiest. Connecting Hamelin, Bodenwerder and Bad Karlshafen, it hugs the Weser River for much of the way and is one of Germany's most popular cycling routes. South of Bodenwerder, the river is flanked by the east by the Solling-Vogler Naturpark, which is a great spot for hikers, too.

Hamelin is charming, if touristy, Bodenwerder is worth a quick stopover and Bad Karlshafen's a sleepy beauty.

See the boxed text, p550, for more information about this part of the Fairy-Tale Road.

Getting There & Away

What is a simple journey by car – take the B83 to/from Hamelin or Bad Karlshafen – requires a little planning with public transport. From Hamelin's Hauptbahnhof, bus 520 follows the Weser from Holzminden (€11.05, 1½ hours) via Bodenwerder (€5.15) hourly from 6.50am to 7.50pm during the week and every couple of hours on weekends. From Holzminden three to five trains leave daily for Bad Karlshafen (€7.05, 45 minutes), with a change at Ottbergen. Direct trains run every two hours from Bad Karlshafen to Göttingen (€9.05, one hour).

From April to October, boats operated by **Flotte Weser** (☎ 05151-939 999; www.flotte-weser.de, in German) also travel from Hamelin to Bodenwerder on Wednesday, Saturday and Sunday (€12.50, 3½ hours). Boats also do the run Fridays in the season in the downriver direction from Bad Karlshafen to Bodenwerder (€29.50, 6¼ hours).

Details of the much-loved **Weser Radweg** (Weser Cycle Path; http://weser-radweg.de, in German) can be found online. See p624 for details on bike hire.

HAMELIN & AROUND
☎ 05151 / pop 58,600

If you have a phobia about rats, you might give this picturesque town on the Weser River a wide berth. According to *The Pied Piper of Hamelin* fairy tale, in the 13th century the Pied Piper *(Der Rattenfänger)* was employed by Hamelin's townsfolk to lure its nibbling rodents into the river. When they refused to pay him, he picked up his flute again and led their kids away. In the meantime, the rats rule again here – rats that are stuffed, fluffy and cute rats, wooden rats, and even little rats that adorn the sights around town. In 2009 the town celebrated the 725th anniversary of the 'rat event', and work was beginning on revamping the centre. As well as having rats, Hamelin is a pleasant town with half-timbered houses and opportunities for cycling along the Weser River.

Orientation

On the eastern bank of the Weser River lies Hamelin's circular Altstadt. The main streets are Osterstrasse, which runs east–west, and Bäckerstrasse, the north–south axis.

The Hauptbahnhof is about 800m east of the centre. Turn right out of the station square (past the roundabout), follow Bahnhofstrasse to Diesterstrasse and turn left. Diesterstrasse becomes Diesterallee, where you'll find the tourist office, and then Osterstrasse. Buses 3, 4, 5 and 6 are just some of the lines that will take you into town.

Information

Hamelin Tourist Information (☎ 957 823, 0180-551 5150; www.hameln.de; Diesterallee 1; ☉ 9am-6.30pm Mon-Fri, 9.30am-4pm Sat, 9.30am-1pm Sun May-Sep, 9am-6pm Mon-Fri, 9.30am-1pm Sat & Sun Oct & Apr) On the eastern edge of the Altstadt (bus stop Bügergarten).

Sights & Activities
ALTSTADT

Look for the rat symbols cropping up throughout the streets along with information posts (currently only in German) offering a glimpse into the history of Hamelin and its restored 16th- to 18th-century architecture.

The ornamental Weser Renaissance style prevalent throughout the Altstadt has a strong Italian influence, and the finest example of this is the **Rattenfängerhaus** (Rat Catcher's House; Osterstrasse 28), from 1602, with its typically steep and richly decorated gable. Walking along Osterstrasse towards the Markt, you pass **Leisthaus** at No 9, built for a patrician grain trader in 1585–89 in the Weser Renaissance style and today housing the **Hamelin City Museum** (☎ 202 1215; Osterstrasse 8-9). This was being restored and upgraded at the time of publication, but in its new incarnation should be very worthwhile for more on the town's history. Next door is another Weser Renaissance beauty, the **Stiftsherrenhaus**, dating from 1558 and the only surviving building in Hamelin decorated with figures. It depicts two themes, one of planetary gods from classical times, and the other of biblical figures.

On the corner of Markt and Osterstrasse you find the **Hochzeitshaus** (1610–17), partly used today as city council offices and as a police station. The **Rattenfänger Glockenspiel** at the far end of the building chimes daily at 9.35am and 11.35am, while a **carousel of Pied Piper figures** twirls at 1.05pm, 3.35pm and 5.35pm.

The heart of Hamelin is the Markt (square) and its northern continuation, **Pferdemarkt** (Equestrian Square), where during the Middle Ages knights fought it out in tournaments. On the eastern side of Pferdemarkt is a sculpture by the eastern German artist Wolfgang Dreysse, *The Opening of the Iron Curtain,* dealing with the collapse of the East German border.

SCHLOSS HÄMELSCHENBURG

Some 15km southwest of Hamelin near a tributary of the Weser River is **Schloss**

LOWER SAXONY

Hämelschenburg (☎ 05155-951 690; www.schloss -haemelschenburg.de; Schlossstrasse 1, Emmerthal; tours adult/ concession €5.50/3.50; ⊙ tours 11am, noon, 2pm, 3pm & 4pm Tue-Sun Apr & Oct, also 10am & 5pm Tue-Sun May-Sep), a Renaissance residence dating from 1588–1613 set in pretty parkland. This is among the best of its ilk in Germany, and was built on a former pilgrimage road that eventually led to Santiago de Compostella in Spain. Tours, which are the only way to see the palace, take you through rooms decked out with original Renaissance furnishings and paintings, but getting there can be half the fun if you cycle along the Weser – follow the **Weser River bicycle path** (http://weser-radweg.de, in German) south, then the signs near Emmerthal – or take bus 40 (€2.60, 30 minutes) to the residence from the train station.

Sleeping & Eating

Ask the tourist office about camping, a 15-minute walk north of town.

DJH hostel (☎ 3425; www.jugendherberge.de /jh/hameln; Fischbeckerstrasse 33; dm under/over 27yr €19.10/22.10; ✗) Although there's not a lot of space in the dorms or bathrooms, this hostel enjoys excellent river views out the back. Take bus 2 from the Hauptbahnhof to Wehler Weg.

Hotel Garni Altstadtwiege (☎ 278 54; www.hotel -altstadtwiege.de; Neue Marktstrasse 10; s €36-47, d €60-90; P) This unprepossessing red-brick building contains charming, individually decorated rooms. The singles are narrow and get stuffy at night but the doubles are large and some have stained-glass windows – No 14 even has a four-poster bed.

Hotel-Garni Christinenhof (☎ 950 80; www.christinen hof-hameln.de, in German; Alte Marktstrasse 18; s/d €70/90; P ✗ 🖳 🖾) Historic on the outside, but to-tally modern in attitude, this hotel likes to pamper its guests, providing a small swimming pool in the vaulted cellar, a sauna, a generous buffet breakfast and compact but uncluttered rooms. High-speed internet is via the power sockets.

ourpick **Hotel La Principessa** (☎ 956 920; www .laprincipessa.de; Kupferschmiedestrasse 2; s €72, d €90-99; P ✗ 🛜) Cast-iron balustrades, tiled floors throughout and gentle Tuscan pastels and ochre shades make this Italian-themed hotel an unusual and distinguished option in Hamelin. A junior suite (€110) even has a whirlpool bath, and the buildings – with 30 rooms in all – have been completely restored and raised to modern environmental standards. Out the back are some giant rats for the kids to mess with.

Mexcal (☎ 428 06; Osterstrasse 15; mains €5.60-14.80; ⊙ noon-11pm Sun-Thu, to midnight Fri & Sat; ✗ V) Most dishes cost €8 to €12 in this cavernous restaurant where you are greeted with a com-plimentary bowl of tortilla chips and dip, and can fill up on generous portions of decent Tex-Mex. Lone diners will feel comfortable here.

Rattenfängerhaus (☎ 3888; Osterstrasse 28; mains €9-22; ⊙ lunch & dinner Mon-Thu, 10am-10pm Fri-Sun; ✗) Hamelin's traditional restaurants are unashamedly aimed at tourists, such as this cute half-timbered tavern with a speciality of 'rats' tails' flambéed at your table (fortunately, like most of the theme dishes here, it's based on pork). Schnitzels, herrings, vegie dishes and 'rat killer' herb liquor are also offered.

Getting There & Around

Frequent S-Bahn trains (S5) head to Hamelin from Hanover's Hauptbahnhof (€10.30, 45 minutes). Regular direct trains connect Hanover's airport with Hamelin (€13.30, one hour). By car, take the B217 to/from Hanover. See Getting There & Away on p622 earlier in this section for bus and boat lines.

Bikes can be hired from the **Jugendwerkstatt Hameln** (☎ 609 770; Ruthenstrasse 10; per day €4; ⊙ 7am-5pm Mon-Fri, 9am-1pm Sat May-Sep, 7.30am-4.30pm Mon-Fri, 7.30am-noon Sat Oct-Apr).

SOMETHING SPECIAL

ourpick **Schlosshotel Münchhausen** (☎ 05154-706 00; www.schlosshotel-muenchhausen.com; Schwöbber 9, Aerzen bei Hameln; s/d in Tithe barn from €105/135, in castle from €135/170, ste €345-445; P ✗ 🖾), 15km outside Hamelin, is worth staying at if you're driving through this region. As the name implies, it's set in a castle – the rooms are stylish and contemporary with historic touches, while the suites have tasteful period furnishings. Rooms in the adjacent Tithe barn are entirely modern. Two restaurants, one in the castle cellar with a traditional focus and the other Mediterranean, as well as spa facilities and two golf courses set in 8 hectares of parkland round off this luxurious option.

ODENWERDER

☎ 05533 / pop 5800

f Bodenwerder's most famous son were to ave described his small hometown, he'd robably have painted it as a huge, thriving metropolis on the Weser River. But then aron Hieronymous von Münchhausen 1720–97) was one of history's most shameess liars. He gave his name to a psychological condition – Münchhausen's syndrome, r compulsive exaggeration of physical illess – and inspired the cult film of British omedian Terry Gilliam, *The Adventures of aron Munchausen*.

Bodenwerder's principal attraction is the **Münchhausen Museum** (☎ 409 147; Münchhausenplatz ; adult/child €2/1.50; ☩ 10am-5pm Apr-Oct), which truggles a little with the difficult task of onveying the chaos and fun associated with he 'liar baron' – a man who liked to regale linner guests with his Crimean adventures, laiming he had, for example, tied his horse o a church steeple during a snow drift and idden around a dining table without breakng one teacup.

The museum houses a cannonball to illusrate the baron's most famous tale, in which e claimed to have hitched a lift on one imilar in an attempt to spy on a battlefield nemy. It also has paintings and displays of Münchhausen books in many languages. It's ll definitely more enjoyable if you first arm ourself with the English-language book, *Tall ales of Baron Münchhausen*, available at the nuseum shop.

In the garden by the museum, the simle **fountain** showing the baron riding half . horse relates to one such tale, where the aron noticed his horse seemed a bit thirsty, nd then realised the animal had been cut n two by a descending town gate, so the vater was pouring right through it. (In the tory the horse is sewn back together and ives happily ever after.)

The **Tourist Information Bodenwerder** (☎ 405 1; www.muenchhausenland.de; Münchhausenplatz 3; ☩ 9am-12.30pm & 2-5pm Mon-Fri, 10am-12.30pm Sat pr-Oct, 10am-12.30pm Mon-Fri Nov-Mar) has infornation on canoe and bicycle hire in town, rranges accommodation and can answer ther queries.

No trains travel to Bodenwerder; see >622 for transport information. The village s small and walkable.

BAD KARLSHAFEN

☎ 05672 / pop 4000

You'd be forgiven for thinking you'd stumbled into 18th-century France in this sleepy spa town. Little wonder, for Bad Karlshafen's orderly streets and whitewashed baroque buildings were built at that time for the local earl Karl by Huguenot refugees. The town was planned with an impressive harbour and a canal connecting the Weser with the Rhine to attract trade. But the earl died before his designs were completed and all that exists today is a tiny *Hafenbecken* (harbour basin) trafficked only by white swans. Add the town's *Gradierwerk*, a large pine-twig contraption poured with saltwater to create 'healthy' air, and this is the perfect place to escape the worries of the world for a few days.

Bad Karlshafen is strictly in Hesse, but it's at the end of the Fairy-Tale Road, just across the Lower Saxony border. For transport information, see p622.

The town is small and easily covered on foot. Most of it lies on the south bank of the Weser River, with the *Hafenbecken* and surrounding square, Hafenplatz, at its western end. To reach the **tourist office** (☎ 999 922; www .bad-karlshafen.de, in German; Hafenplatz 8; ☩ 9am-5.30pm Mon-Fri, 9.30am-noon Sat, 2.30-5pm Sun May–mid-Oct, 9am-noon & 2-4pm Mon-Fri mid-Oct–Apr) from the Hauptbahnhof, follow the road left for a few minutes after exiting the station and cross the bridge, right, over the river. Turn right again on the other side and continue straight ahead to Hafenplatz.

While here, take a stroll around the *Hafenbecken* and pop into the **Deutsches Huguenotten Museum** (German Huguenot Museum; ☎ 1410; www.hugenottenmuseum.de, in German; Hafenplatz 9a; adult/concession €3/2.50; ☩ 9am-5pm Tue-Sun mid-Mar–Oct, 2-5pm Sat & Sun Nov-Dec), which explains the history of the Huguenots in Germany.

The *Gradierwerk* lies to the left as you cross the bridge.

Sleeping

Am Rechten Weserufer (☎ 710; www.campingplatz -bad-karlshafen.de, in German; per adult/tent & car €4.50/5) This camping ground enjoys a prime position on the northern riverbank, extending south from the train station. It overlooks the town centre.

Helmarshausen DJH hostel (☎ 1027; helmarshausen@djh-hessen.de; Gottsbürener Strasse 15; dm under/over 27yr €18.50/21.50; ℗ ⌧ 🛜) Although

LOWER SAXONY

Bad Karlshafen doesn't have its own hostel, this one 3km from Hafenplatz (take bus 180 to Helmarshausen-Mitte) in the suburb of Helmarshausen is situated on the edge of the forest and the forest trails in a lovely half-timbered building.

Hotel-Pension Haus Fuhrhop (☎ 404; www.pension -fuhrhop.de, in German; Friedrichstrasse 15; s/d €37/74) This charming *Pension* has spacious and comfortable rooms with a modern, stylish character. Recent restorations mean that it is excellent value for money – especially considering its location. Go straight ahead after crossing the bridge – it's at the bend in the road.

Hotel zum Schwan (☎ 104 445; schwan1760@aol .com; Conradistrasse 3-4; s/d €48/86; P) Earl Karl's former hunting lodge, now one of the better hotels in towns, is a bit creaky around the staircase, but rooms have been given a make-over in recent years without losing a genuinely lived-in feel. It overlooks the *Hafenbecken* and has a lovely rococo dining room.

LÜNEBURGER HEIDE

North of Hanover along the sprawling Lüneburger Heide lies a land of attractive, historic villages and natural allure. Lower Saxony was ruled from here before the court moved to Hamburg, so royal treasures and exquisitely preserved buildings await you in Celle. In Lüneburg, you can observe the quirky side-effects of the salt-mining that made the town rich in the Middle Ages (the town visibly leans).

The area in between, along the Lüneburger Heide, can be covered on foot, by bike or in a boat.

CELLE
☎ 05141 / pop 70,850

With 400 half-timbered houses and its Ducal Palace dating back to the 13th century, Celle is graced with a picture-book town centre that is among the most attractive in the region. Many of the ornate houses were built in the 16th century by hard-working, pious folk who decorated them with stern mottos like 'Don't let widows and orphans suffer or you'll face the wrath of God', and 'This house was built from necessity not desire'. The white-and-pink Ducal Palace, Celle's centrepiece set in small gardens, contrasts with the ultra-modern Kunstmuseum op-

posite, which is illuminated at night into '24-hour' museum and successfully create an interesting contrast of old and new i this small but fascinating town.

Orientation
The mainly pedestrianised Altstadt is abou a 15-minute walk east of the Hauptbahnho reached by the rather unattractive Bahnhof strasse. Turning left at the street's end wi take you to the palace after 100m. Fron here, Stechbahn leads east to the nearb tourist office. The Aller River flows aroun the northern section of the Altstadt, with tributary encircling it to the south. Just sout of the Altstadt is the Französischen Garte (French Garden).

Information
Adunni Callshop & Internet (Bahnhofstrasse 38; inter net per hr €2; ☽ 10am-10pm Mon-Sat, noon-9pm Sun)

Main post office (Rundstrasse 7; ☽ 8.30am-6pm Mon Fri, to 1pm Sat) Diagonally opposite the Schloss.

Tourismus Region Celle (☎ 1212; www.region-celle .com; Markt 14-16; ☽ 9am-6pm Mon-Fri, 10am-4pm Sa 11am-2pm Sun May-Sep, 9am-5pm Mon-Fri, 10am-1pm Sat Oct-Apr) Runs guided tours (€5; in German) at 11am Saturday to Thursday, 4.30pm Friday May to October, 11am Saturday and Sunday November and April, and 11ar daily in December.

Sights
ALTSTADT
With row upon row of ornate half-timbere houses, all decorated with scrolls and alle gorical figures, Celle is a perfect place for stroll. Even the tourist office is located in striking building, the **Altes Rathaus** (1561–79) which boasts a wonderful Weser Renaissanc stepped gable, topped with the ducal coat o arms and a golden weather vane.

At the tourist office door, on the building' south side, there are two **whipping posts** wit shackles, used from 1786 to 1850 to punis minor offenders. Prisoners weren't in fac whipped but merely left here for 12 hours to allow their neighbours to spit at them o throw insults and eggs. Opposite, the statue o a man in shackles recreates the scene.

Jousting tournaments were held a little fur ther west on **Stechbahn**. The little horsesho alongside the iron horseshoe sculpture o the corner of the street's north side (outsid the *Apotheke*) marks the spot where a duke

vas slain during a tournament; step on it and
nake a wish, and local lore holds that the wish
vill come true.

One block south of the tourist office, on the
orner of Poststrasse and Runde Strasse, you'll
ind one of Celle's most magnificent build-
ngs, the ornate **Hoppener Haus** (1532). If you go
nother block southwards along Poststrasse
nd stop in the square in the corner, look
or the tiny alley between the two buildings:
ou'll see a little box with a window that was
baroque toilet.

Retrace your steps to the corner of
Poststrasse and Zöllnerstrasse, and turn right
nto Zöllnerstrasse. You'll pass **No 37** (built in
570, now the shop Reformhaus), with its
eart-warming inscription on the upper gable,
Work! No chatting, talking or gossiping!'.
'urn left into Rabengasse, and you'll come
o Neue Strasse. Highlights here include the
reen House (1478) with the crooked beam at
No 32 and the **Fairy-Tale House** at No 11. The fa-
ade of the latter is decorated with characters,
uch as a jackass crapping gold pieces.

If you'd like to continue walking, double
ack south, where Celle also has a lovely **French
arden** at the edge of the Altstadt.

Horse-drawn carriage rides (from €5
er person) depart between April and
October from the corner of Bergstrasse
nd Poststrasse.

CHLOSS

Celle's wedding-cake **Schloss** (Ducal Palace;
☎ 123 73; Schlossplatz; adult/concession €5/3, combined
esidenzmuseum, Bomann Museum & Kunstmuseum €8/5;
☑ 10am-5pm Tue-Sun) was built in 1292 by Otto
Der Strenge (Otto the Strict) as a town fortifi-
ation and in 1378 was expanded and turned
nto a residence. The last duke to live here
was Georg Wilhelm (1624–1705), and the
ast royal was Queen Caroline-Mathilde of
Denmark, who died here in 1775.

The Schloss is also used as government administrative offices, so the main part of the
palace you see is the **Residenzmuseum** (Palace
Museum). One-hour **guided tours** (adult/concession
6/4; ☑ 11am, 1pm & 3pm Tue-Fri, hourly 11am-3pm Sat
Apr-Oct, 11am & 3pm Tue-Fri, also 1pm Sat & Sun Nov-Mar)
take in about half of the museum, but also sections otherwise not accessible. One of these is
the **Renaissance Schlosskapelle** (Palace Chapel),
whose original Gothic form is evident in the
high windows and vaulted ceiling; the rest of
the intricate interior is pure Renaissance. The
duke's pew was above; the shutters were added
later so his highness could snooze during the
three-hour services. Tours also include the
19th-century **Schlossküche** (Palace Kitchen)
and – rehearsals permitting – the baroque
Schlosstheater (☎ tickets 127 14; www.schlosstheater
-celle.de, in German; Schlossplatz; ☑ closed Jul & Aug).

KUNSTMUSEUM & BOMANN MUSEUM

Celle's **Kunstmuseum** (Art Museum; ☎ 123 55; www
.kunst.celle.de; Schlossplatz 7; adult/concession incl Bomann
Museum €5/3; ☑ 10am-5pm Tue-Sun), situated across
the road from the Schloss, is dedicated to contemporary German artists. It has come up with
an interesting concept, calling itself a '24-hour
museum'. During the regular daytime opening
hours, you can stroll around and admire a collection of modern art that includes work from
the early 20th century to the present. A 'light
room' is the work of the artist Otto Piene, and
outside you find his tame *Firework for Celle*
sculptures, which are most effective at night.
As night does slowly descend, the 'nocturnal
museum' glows and oozes different colours,
morphing into its own quaint work of 'art'
with light and a few sounds.

In the older building adjacent, you'll find
the regional history **Bomann Museum** (☎ 125
44; www.bomann-museum.de, in German; Schlossplatz
7; adult/concession incl Kunstmuseum €3/2; ☑ 10am-
5pm Tue-Sun). Here, among other things, you
can wander through rooms furnished in
19th-century style.

STADTKIRCHE

Just west of the Rathaus is the 13th-century
Stadtkirche (☎ 7735; www.stadtkirche-celle.de, in German;
tower adult/concession €1/0.50; ☑ 10am-6pm Tue-Sat Apr-
Dec, to 5pm Jan-Mar, tower 10-11.45am & 2-4.45pm Tue-Sat
Apr-Oct). You can climb up the 235 steps to
the top of the church steeple for a view of
the city, or just watch as the city trumpeter
climbs the 220 steps to the white tower below
the steeple for a trumpet fanfare in all four
directions. The ascent takes place at 9.30am
and 5.30pm daily.

SYNAGOGUE

Dating back to 1740, Celle's **synagogue** (☎ 124
59; Im Kreise 24; admission free; ☑ noon-5pm Tue-Thu,
9am-2pm Fri, 11am-4pm Sun) is the oldest in northern Germany. Partially destroyed during
Kristallnacht (see the boxed text, p42), it looks
just like any other half-timbered house from
the outside, but a new Jewish congregation

LOWER SAXONY

formed in 1997 and services are held regularly. Changing exhibitions on Jewish history take place next door.

The synagogue is at the southeastern end of the Altstadt, in the town's former ghetto.

Sleeping

The tourist office can help with camping, 4km from the centre.

DJH hostel (☎ 532 08; www.jugendherberge.de/jh/celle; Weghausstrasse 2; dm under/over 27yr €17.80/20.80; ℗ ✗) In an ironic twist of fate, this rambling youth hostel inside a former school building gets mostly school groups in its six-bed dorms. Although the foyer and breakfast room are bright enough, corridors and rooms are a little bit gloomy. It's a 25-minute walk from the train station, or take bus 2 to Jugendherberge from the top of Bahnhofstrasse, opposite the station.

Hotel Neun ¾ (☎ 909 0731; www.hotel934.de, in German; Bahnhofstrasse 46; s/d/tr €42.50/75/92.50; ℗) The exterior of this budget abode near the main train station is unattractive and some of the window frames inside could do with work, but otherwise it is a very clean, well run and conveniently located place based on a Harry Potter theme – hence the name. Call ahead if arriving after 8pm.

Hotel Celler Hof (☎ 911 960; www.cellerhof.de, in German; Stechbahn 11; s €70-75, d €105, tr €125; ℗ ✗ 🖳 🛜) The friendly staff, Finnish sauna, tasteful furnishings and above all central location make this a good all-round option. All rooms have a writing desk, and there's a small lobby bar if you feel like letting your hair down in a public space without going anywhere. It's a good option for business travellers and tourists alike.

our pick **Hotel Utspann** (☎ 927 20; www.utspann.de; Im Kreise 13; s/d/ste €75/105/145; ℗ ✗) This remarkable half-timbered house evokes a staying-with-friends atmosphere. Individually sized rooms – named after towns – variously feature exposed wooden beams, antique desks and even a few alcove beds. The Gartenzimmer (Garden Room; €135) is little short of sensational – it backs onto the jungle-like growth, two walls are floor-to-ceiling glass, and you have your very own private sauna.

Hotel Fürstenhof (☎ 2010; www.fuerstenhof.de; Hannoversche Strasse 55/56; s from €160, d from €210, ste from €270; ℗ ✗ 🐾) A converted baroque palace, this renowned five-star hotel has floors featuring themes from 'Hunting' on the ground

floor to 'Golf' on the 6th. In the latter yo get a putter and carpet green for practicin your shots. 'Golf' rooms don't have bat tubs, though. The 'Heide' theme floor fea tures sheep on the carpet. That the place feel extremely elegant says something about th quality furnishings and the deft touch of th interior designer.

Eating

Explore the numerous eating and drinkin options along Schuhstrasse and Neue Strasse as well as those on Am Heiligen Kreuz.

Pasta (☎ 483 460; Neue Strasse 37; mains €4.50-6.5 🕑 9am-10pm Mon-Fri, to 4pm Sat May-Sep, 9am-5pr Mon-Fri, to 4pm Sat Oct-Apr; ✗ Ⓥ) Behind thi instant Celle hit lies one of those ideas tha is so simple it's genius. Mix your favourit pasta (tagliatelle, *penne rigate*, gnocchi, ra violi etc) with a sauce that takes your fanc (from *bolognese* or pesto to tuna and ca pers, or salmon cream). Crucially, it's al freshly homemade.

Cafe Central (☎ 22 320; Am Heiligen Kreuz 5; mair €9.60-21; 🕑 9am-1am Mon-Fri, to 2am Sat & Sun; ✗) Thi cafe-restaurant with a modern edge has a ver strong focus on meat dishes such as schnitze or medallions in a sauce, and most dishes ar well-priced at about €13. A lounge section i reserved for smokers.

India Haus (☎ 485 152; Neue Strasse 34; mains €8-1€ 🕑 lunch & dinner Mon-Fri, 11am-11pm Sat & Sun; ✗ Ⓥ) The combination of subcontinental interio decor and traditional, exposed medieval beam creates a surprisingly harmonious atmospher in this half-timber house. The dishes migh not be up to the exacting standards of nosher in London or New York, but it's excellent fo provincial Germany. Weekday lunch special cost €5.50.

Getting There & Away

Several trains each hour to Hanover take from 20 minutes (IC; €10.50) to 45 minutes (S Bahn; €8.40). There are also IC (€19, 40 min utes) and regional (€15.20, 1¼ hours) service to/from Lüneburg.

If you're driving, take the B3 straight int the centre.

Getting Around

City buses 2 and 4 run between the Haupt bahnhof and Schlossplatz, the two mai stations. Single tickets are €1.90 and day passes €4.75.

For a taxi call ☎ 444 44 or ☎ 280 01. Bicycle hire is available at **Fahrradhaus Jacaoby** (☎ 254 89; Bahnhofstrasse 27; bicycle per day €8.50; ⏱ 9am-1pm & 3-6pm Mon-Fri, 9am-1pm Sat).

BERGEN-BELSEN

Visiting a former concentration camp memorial in Germany is a moving but also challenging experience, and **Bergen-Belsen** (☎ 05051-6011; www.bergenbelsen.de; Lohheide; admission free; ⏱ 9am-5pm Apr-Sep, to 5pm Oct-Mar) is no exception – it provides a horrifying punch to the stomach through the sheer force of its atmosphere.

Unlike Auschwitz in Poland, none of the original buildings remain from the most infamous concentration camp on German soil. Yet the large, initially peaceful-looking lumps of grassy earth – covered in beautiful purple heather in summer – soon reveal their true identity as mass graves. Signs indicate approximately how many people lie in each – 1000, 2000, 5000, an unknown number…

In all, 70,000 Jews, Soviet soldiers, political hostages and other prisoners died here. Among them was Anne Frank, whose posthumously published diary became a modern classic.

Bergen-Belsen began its existence in 1940 as a POW camp, but was partly taken over by the SS from April 1943, to hold Jews as hostages in exchange for German POWs held abroad. Many Russian and Allied soldiers, then later Jews, Poles, homosexuals, Sinti and Roma all suffered here – beaten, tortured, starved and worked to death, or used as medical guinea pigs.

Tens of thousands of prisoners from other camps near the front line were brought to Belsen in the last months of WWII, causing overcrowding, an outbreak of disease and even more deaths. Despite the best attempts of the SS to hide evidence of their inhumane practices, by destroying documents and forcing prisoners to bury or incinerate their deceased fellow inmates, thousands of corpses still littered the compound when British troops liberated the camp on 15 April 1945.

After WWII, Allied forces used the troop barracks here as a displaced persons' (DP) camp, for those waiting to emigrate to a third country (including many Jews who went to Israel after its establishment in 1948). The DP camp was closed in September 1950.

The revamped **Documentation Centre** today is one of the best of its kind and deals sensitively but very poignantly with the lives of the people who were imprisoned here – before, during and after incarceration. The exhibition is designed to be viewed chronologically, and these days a better focus is placed on the role of Bergen-Belsen in the early years as a POW camp for mostly Soviet prisoners of war. About 40,000 POWs died here in 1939–42, largely due to atrocious conditions. As you move through the exhibition you listen to original-language descriptions through headphones (also subtitled on the screens), read documents and explanations, and watch a 25-minute documentary about the camp. This film includes a moving testimony from one of the British cameramen who filmed the liberation. Subtitled screenings rotate between different languages.

Also inside the centre, there's a book of names of those who were interned here, as well as guides and books for sale, including *The Diary of Anne Frank* (1947), plus the free *Guided Tour Memorial of Bergen-Belsen*.

In the several hectares of cemetery within the gates is a large stone **obelisk and memorial**, with inscriptions to all victims, a **cross** on the spot of a memorial initially raised by Polish prisoners and the **Haus der Stille**, where you can retreat for quiet contemplation.

A **gravestone for Anne Frank** and her sister, Margot, has also been erected (not too far from the cemetery gates, on the way to the obelisk). The entire family was initially sent to Auschwitz when their hiding place in Amsterdam was betrayed to police, but the sisters were later transferred to Belsen. Although no-one knows exactly where Anne lies, many pay tribute to their 15-year-old heroine at this gravestone.

Other monuments to various victim groups, including a **Soviet memorial**, are dotted across the complex.

Getting There & Away

Driving from Celle, take Hehlentorstrasse north over the Aller River and follow Harburger Strasse north out of the city. This is the B3; continue northwest to the town of Bergen and follow the signs to Belsen.

By public transport the journey is best done on a weekday, when you can take bus 1-15 at 10am weekdays from Schlossplatz in Celle direct to Bergen-Belsen Memorial (€5.60, 48 minutes). At 3.04pm, a direct bus returns to Celle. A few other buses run, requiring an easy change to a connecting bus in Bergen. Ask the driver when boarding. If you need to travel on a Saturday, ask the tourist office to help you with times. It is not usually possible on Sunday.

A **taxi** (☎ 05051-5555) to the camp from the village of Bergen will cost about €15.

For further details, ask at the Celle tourist office.

LÜNEBURG
☎ 04131 / pop 72,150

An off-kilter church steeple, buildings leaning on each other and houses with swollen 'beer-belly' facades: in parts it looks like the charming town of Lüneburg has drunk too much of the Pilsner lager it used to brew. Of course, the city's wobbly angles and uneven pavements have a more prosaic cause. For centuries until 1980, Lüneburg was a saltmining town, and as this 'white gold' was extracted from the earth, shifting ground and subsidence caused many buildings to tilt sideways.

Partly because of wobbly comic-book streets, Lüneburg is a lovely town with attractive stepped-gable facades and Hanseatic architecture. It has quite a lively student population, and doubles as a convenient gateway to the surrounding heath.

Orientation

The Ilmenau River sits between the Hauptbahnhof, which is on its eastern bank and the city centre to its west. To reach the Markt by foot from the train station, turn left when leaving the station, and take the first right into Altenbrückertorstrasse. This street leads across the river to Am Sande. From here, you'll find lots of billboard maps all over town.

Information

Lüneburg Tourist-Information Office (☎ 207 6620; www.lueneburg.de; Rathaus, Am Markt; ⏱ 9.30am-6pm Mon-Fri, 9am-2pm Sat Jan-Dec, 10am-4pm Sun May-Oct & Dec) Arranges city tours and trips to the surrounding Lüneburger Heide.

Main Post office (☎ 7270; Sülztorstrasse 21; ⏱ 8.30am-6pm Mon-Fri, 9am-1pm Sat) There's also a branch at the central bus station.

Stadt Krankenhaus (Hospital; ☎ 770; Bögelstrasse 1)

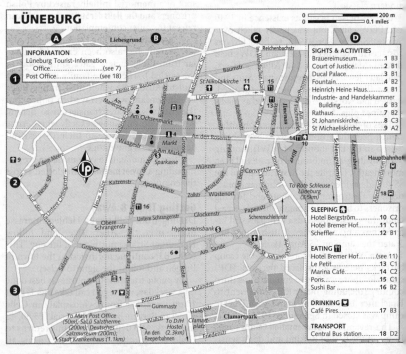

LÜNEBURG

0 ──── 200 m
0 ──── 0.1 miles

INFORMATION
Lüneburg Tourist-Information
Office.....................(see 7)
Post Office.................(see 18)

SIGHTS & ACTIVITIES
Brauereimuseum..............1 B3
Court of Justice.............2 B1
Ducal Palace................3 B1
Fountain....................4 B2
Heinrich Heine Haus.........5 B1
Industrie- and Handelskammer
Building...................6 B3
Rathaus.....................7 B2
St Johanniskirche...........8 C3
St Michaeliskirche..........9 A2

SLEEPING
Hotel Bergström.............10 C2
Hotel Bremer Hof............11 C1
Scheffler...................12 B1

EATING
Hotel Bremer Hof.........(see 11)
Le Petit....................13 C1
Marina Café.................14 C2
Pons........................15 C1
Sushi Bar...................16 B2

DRINKING
Café Pires..................17 B3

TRANSPORT
Central Bus station.........18 D2

Sights & Activities

ST JOHANNISKIRCHE

At the eastern edge of the square called Am Sande stands the clunky 14th-century **St Johanniskirche** (☎ 435 94; Am Sande; ☻ 10am-5pm Sun-Wed, to 6pm Thu-Sat Apr-Oct, 9am-6pm Thu-Sat, to 4pm Sun Nov-Mar), whose 108m-high spire leans 2.2m off centre. Local legend has it that the architect was so upset by this crooked steeple that he tried to do himself in by jumping off it. He fell into a hay cart and was saved, but, celebrating his escape later in the pub, drank himself into a stupor, fell over, hit his head and died after all.

The inside of the church is, well, a lot more believable than the legend; there's an impressive organ and stained-glass windows, both ancient and modern. Explanatory leaflets are provided in many languages.

AM SANDE

Moving westwards, the cobbled, slightly wobbly Am Sande is full of red-brick buildings with typically Hanseatic stepped gables. Even among these striking buildings, the black-and-white **Industrie- und Handelskammer** (Trade and Industry Chamber) at the far western end stands out; it's undoubtedly the most beautiful. Continue one block past the Handelskammer and turn right into restaurant-lined Schröderstrasse, which leads to the Markt.

RATHAUS & MARKT

The name Lüneburg hails from the Saxon word *hliuni* (refuge), which was granted at the Ducal Palace (right) to those fleeing other territories. However, many sources mistakenly assume the town's name has something to do with Luna, the Roman goddess of the moon. The city authorities at one time seem to have liked this idea, erecting a **fountain** with a statue of the Roman goddess in the town's Markt.

The statue sits in front of the medieval **Rathaus**, which has a spectacular baroque facade, added in 1720, decorated with coats of arms and three tiers of statues. The top row of statues on the facade represents (from left to right): Strength, Trade, Peace (the one with the staff), Justice and Moderation. The steeple, topped with 41 Meissen china bells, was installed on the city's 1000th birthday in 1956.

Rathaus tours (adult/concession/family €4.50/3.50/11.50) of the interior leave daily at 10am, 11.30am, 1.30pm and 3pm from the entrance on Am Ochsenmarkt.

Other buildings around the Markt include the **Court of Justice**, the little gated-in, grotto-like area with paintings depicting scenes of justice being carried out throughout the centuries; and the former **Ducal Palace**, now a courthouse. West of that, on the corner of Burmeisterstrasse and Am Ochsenmarkt, is the **Heinrich Heine Haus**, the home of the poet's parents. Heine, who hated Lüneburg, wrote the *Loreley* here (for more on the Loreley rock, see p507).

AUF DEM MEERE & ST MICHAELISKIRCHE

If you continue west along Waagestrasse from the Markt and veer left, you'll come to **Auf dem Meere**, a particularly striking Lüneburg street. Here the wavy pavements have pushed facades sideways or made buildings buckle in the middle. All the way to **St Michaeliskirche** (☎ 314 00; Johann-Sebastian-Bach-Platz; ☻ 10am-5pm Mon-Sat, 2-5pm Sun May-Sep, to 4pm Oct-Apr) the street feels wonky, like it's something from the 1919 German expressionist movie *The Cabinet of Dr Caligari*. Look at the steps leading to the church!

SPA BATHS

With Lüneburg having made its fortune from salt, where better to try the mineral's therapeutic properties than at the town's **SaLü Salztherme** (Spa Baths; ☎ 723 110; www.kurzentrum.de, in German; Uelzener Strasse 1-5; adult/child from €7.90/4.90; ☻ 10am-11pm Mon-Sat, 8am-9pm Sun). You can bathe in saltwater at 36°C, and try out the single-sex or mixed sauna area, water fountains and whirlpool.

CARRIAGE RIDES & CYCLING

Traditional **horse-drawn carriage rides** (☎ 04178-8542; adult/child €9/4.50; ☻ at 11.30am, 1pm & 2.30pm Tue, Thu & Fri) leave from the Markt. Call ahead or simply turn up.

Many tourists come to the Lüneburger Heide to go **cycling**; Lüneburg's tourist office has dozens of different pamphlets outlining routes.

MUSEUMS

The **Deutsches Salzmuseum** (☎ 450 65; www.salzmuseum.de; Sülfmeisterstrasse 1; adult/child/student €6/4/5; ☻ 9am-5pm Mon-Fri, 10am-5pm Sat & Sun May-Sep, 10am-5pm Oct-Apr) explains (in German only) how Lüneburg's precious food preservative made the town such an important player in the Hanseatic League.

There's also a **Brauereimuseum** (☎ 448 04; Heiligengeiststrasse 39; admission free; ☑ 1-4.30pm Tue-Sun) looking at the history of beer-making in this city, which once housed more than 80 breweries.

Sleeping

Rote Schleuse Lüneburg (☎ 791 500; www.camprote schleuse.de, in German; per adult/car & tent €5/6) This camping ground is about 3.5km south of the centre and offers a woodsy terrain scattered with fruit trees. Take bus 5600 to Rote Schleuse.

DJH hostel (☎ 418 64; www.jugendherberge.de/jh /lueneburg; Soltauer Strasse 133; dm under/over 27yr €23/26; P ☒ ☐ ☎) After sundown, the lights glow a warm welcome from the glass-walled stairwell of this spacious, modern and relatively luxurious hostel in the town's south, right near the university. Bus services – 5011 or 5012 from the train station to Scharnhorststrasse/DJH – don't run very late.

Scheffler (☎ 200 80; www.hotel-scheffler.de; Bardowicker Strasse 7; s €65, d €85-95; P ☒) The hotel most in keeping with Lüneburg's quirky character, this place just off the Markt greets you with brickwork, stained glass, carved wooden stair-rails, animal trophies and indoor plants. The rooms are low-ceilinged and cosy, and there's a restaurant on-site.

Hotel Bremer Hof (☎ 2240; www.bremer-hof.de; Lüner Strasse 12-13; s €50-106, d €93-135; P ☒ ☎) Easily the most versatile place in town, this hotel offers clean rooms for most budgets, from plain and inexpensive ones in an annex close-by to historic rooms in the main building. Staff are friendly and helpful, and it is popular among business and academic guests.

ourpick Hotel Bergström (☎ 3080; www.bergstroem .de, in German; Bei der Lüner Mühle; s €134-214, d €154-234; P ☒ ☐ ☎ ☒) Spread over a half-dozen warehouse buildings around the Ilmenau River, this four-star hotel offers good value for doubles, which cost only €20 more than single rooms. The pool is rather small (6m by 4m), but you also find wellness and sauna facilities.

Eating & Drinking

ourpick Sushi Bar (☎ 248 348; Schröderstrasse 8; sushi €1.60-15, large combinations €8.50-17, lunch wok dishes €6.70-7.50; ☑ noon-midnight Mon-Sat, 5pm-midnight Sun; ☒ ☑) All gleaming red-and-black lacquer, with blue up-lighting behind the bar, this chic restaurant is a long-time favourite locally,

both for its excellent sushi and for its elegant but comfortable atmosphere.

Le Petit (☎ 224 910; Am Stintmarkt 8; mains €8-17; ☑ 11am-11pm; ☒ ☎) While the cubicle for smokers is as diminutive as the name suggests, this relaxed place is reasonably roomy inside and positively sprawling outside, where tables spill across decking to the riverside. It even has its own pontoon. Expect a good range of German cuisine with differences: the rump steak is served with turnip and a port wine sauce. If you can't get a wi-fi signal, ask the owner to turn it on.

Hotel Bremer Hof (☎ 2240; Lüner Strasse 12-13; mains €8-20; ☑ lunch & dinner; ☒) Light and airy, with a lot of blue, the atmospheric restaurant here is strong on local specialities, including lamb which is from the heath (Heidschnucke), and comes in all shapes and sizes. Some meats are organic.

Marina Café (☎ 3080; Bei der Lüner Mühle; mains €17.50-24; ☒) The view over the Ilmenau would be reason enough for coming to the upmarket restaurant of the Hotel Bergström but the daily changing menu of international cuisine is also pretty good. For those who want to spend a little less but enjoy the views there's also a pleasant warehouse coffee shop attached to the hotel.

Pons (☎ 224 935; Salzstrasse am Wasser 1; ☑ from 5pm Mon-Fri, from 3pm Sat & Sun; ☒ ☑) If Pons looks this cracked, crooked and uneven when you walk in of an evening, just imagine how it will seem when you stagger out after a few drinks. This ex-1970s hippy joint has since cut its hair and mellowed into the upbeat student drinking strip known as the 'Stint' (Am Stintmarkt). It serves light dishes from 6pm (€3.90).

Also explore the numerous eating options on Schröderstrasse, or for something different in Lüneburg, drop into the Portuguese **Café Pires** (☎ 0173-606 8422; Rackerstrasse 7; mixed tapas €8.80; ☑ 9am-8pm Mon-Fri, 9am-midnight Sat).

Getting There & Away

There are frequent IC train services to Hamburg (€11.50, 30 minutes) and Hanover (€26, one hour) and a couple to Schwerin (€34, 1½ hours). There are also IC trains to/from Celle (€19, 40 minutes). Cheaper regional trains are also practical for all these routes.

If you're driving from Hamburg, take the A7 south to the B250. From Schwerin take the B6 south to the A24 west and then exit No 7 (Talkau). From there, turn south on the B209, and you'll eventually get to town. From Hanover, take the A7 north to the B209.

Getting Around

Buses leave from the ZOB central bus station at the Hauptbahnhof and from the busy bus stop on Am Sande. Most services stop running at around 7pm. Single tickets are €1.65; day tickets cost €3.80.

For a taxi, call ☎ 194 10. **Rad am Hauptbahnhof** (☎ 266 350; per day €10; ⏰ 6am-8pm Mon-Fri, 9am-6pm Sat & Sun) rents out bicycles.

NATURPARK ELBUFER-DRAWEHN

Bleckede and the Biosphärenreservat Niedersächsische Elbtalaue (Lower-Saxony Elbe Floodplain Biosphere) are located some 20km east of Lüneburg, in a wetland area of the Lüneburger Heide. The reserve is a haven for birdlife such as white storks, wild geese and cranes, and runs for 85km along the Elbe River. Cyclists and hikers will be well rewarded by this picturesque and interesting wetland, which is all part of the **Elberadweg** (www.elberadweg.de). See the boxed text, p228, for details on cycling in the area. If you intend to come out here, make sure you drop by the tourist office in Lüneburg first. You should find that it is well stocked with brochures on accommodation and activities that are available in the area.

For information by telephone or accommodation bookings, call the **tourist information office** (☎ 05852-958 458; www.elbtalaue-touristik.de, in German; ⏰ 8am-5pm) in Bleckede. The **Elbschloss Bleckede** (☎ 05852-951 40; www.elbschloss-bleckede.de, in German; Schlossstrasse 10; adult/child €5/2.50; ⏰ 10am-6pm Tue-Sun Apr-Oct, 10am-5pm Wed-Sun Nov-Mar) offers a telephone and walk-in information service on the biosphere.

Getting There & Around

No trains run to Bleckede, but the 5100 bus (€2.70, 30 minutes) leaves at least hourly from Lüneburg at Am Sande or the Hauptbahnhof.

If you're going by car, the B216 leads to the turn-off to Bleckede. A car ferry crosses the river at the turn-off and in Neu Darchau to the south.

SOUTH & EAST OF HANOVER

HILDESHEIM

☎ 05121 / pop 103,600

Though not an overly attractive or exciting city, Hildesheim has a couple of important sights that have visitors flocking to this former bishopric and market town: a pretty, post-WWII 'medieval' town centre, and genuinely ancient cathedral-door bas-reliefs, which were cleverly saved from the firebombing that razed Hildesheim to the ground on 22 March 1945. A legendary '1000-year-old' rosebush that re-emerged from the ashes of this attack also attracts pilgrims.

Orientation

The central Markt is 750m south of the Hauptbahnhof. To walk there from the station, take the pedestrianised Bernwardstrasse, which becomes Almsstrasse and Hoher Weg. Turning left, or east, from Hoher Weg into either Markstrasse or Rathausstrasse will lead you to Hildesheim's stunning centre, and the tourist office.

Continuing along Hoher Weg, instead of turning left for the tourist office, you hit Schuhstrasse, a central bus stop. To the right (west), the road heads to the cathedral and the Roemer- und Pelizaeus-Museum. Straight ahead across Schuhstrasse you'll find the drinking strip of Friesenstrasse and, 10 minutes further south, the old Jewish quarter.

Information

Main post office (Bahnhofsplatz 3-4; ⏰ 8.30am-6pm Mon-Fri, to 1pm Sat)

Netcafe (☎ 697 7044; Wollenweberstrasse 80; per hr €1.50; ⏰ 9am-10pm Mon-Fri, from 11am Sat & Sun) Internet access.

Tourist Office Hildesheim (☎ 179 80; www.hildesheim.de; Rathausstrasse 20; ⏰ 9am-6pm Mon-Fri, to 3pm Sat) Information and accommodation bookings.

Sights & Activities

For just €1, the tourist office sells the *Hildesheimer Rosenroute*, a very comprehensive guide to all of Hildesheim's sights. It's available in several languages, including English, and is particularly useful if you're staying a few days.

LOWER SAXONY

MARKT

One of the tragedies of Hitler's excursion into megalomania was the horrendous damage inflicted upon once-magnificent architectural gems such as Hildesheim. After WWII, key parts of the old town were lovingly reconstructed, and the result of this is especially visible on **Markt**. While you ooh and ah at the beauty of the historic houses, however, it is probably worth bearing in mind that much of it is, literally, younger than the original TV series of *Starsky & Hutch*. Clockwise (from north) you find the **Rokokohaus**, **Wollenweberhaus**, **Wedekindhaus**, **Knochenhauerhaus** (Butchers' Guild Hall) and **Bäckeramtshaus** (Bakers' Guild Hall). In many cases, you can see behind the facade, too: the Rokokohaus is now home to a hotel, and upstairs in the Knochenhauerhaus is the **Stadtmuseum** (☎ 301 163; Markt 7-8; adult/concession €2.50/1.50; ☺ 10am-6pm Tue-Sun).

One original feature is the **Marktbrunnen**, the fountain in front of the **Rathaus** on the east side of the square (bells play folk songs at noon, 1pm and 5pm daily).

DOM

There's a tiny entrance fee to see the **Tausend-jähriger Rosenstock** (1000-year-old rosebush; adult/concession €0.50/0.30) in the cloister of the **Hildesheimer Dom** (Hildesheim Cathedral; ☎ 179 1760; Domhof; ☺ 9.30am-5pm Mon-Sat, noon-5pm Sun May-Oct, 10am-4.30pm Mon-Sat, noon-5pm Sun Nov-Apr). However, the bas-reliefs on the cathedral's almost 5m-high **Bernwardstüren** (Bernward bronze doors) have much greater visual impact, and they aren't pay-per-view.

The allure of the rosebush lies in its supposed history as the very one on which Emperor Ludwig the Pious left his cloak and other effects in AD 815, where they miraculously stayed safe from theft. Its phoenix-like rise from the burnt-out cathedral remains after 1945 has only added to the bush's mystique.

Ultimately, though, it looks much like any other rose: something you wouldn't say about the bronze cathedral doors, which are Unesco-protected. Dating from 1015 and saved only because a concerned WWII prelate insisted they be stashed in a basement, they depict scenes from the Bible's Old and New Testaments in three-dimensional reliefs. A plaque to the left describes each scene in German, however, it's easy to identify each one yourself: from the creation of man, Adam and Eve's banishment from the Garden of Eden, and Cain and Abel, to the three wise men attending the birth of Christ, and Mary Magdalene attending his crucified body.

The church's **wheel-shaped chandelier** and the **Christussäule** (Column of Christ) are also original, and if you're really keen, there's an attached **Dom-Museum** (☎ 179 1640; www.dom-museum-hildesheim.de, in German; Domhof; adult/concession €4/2; ☺ 10am-1pm & 1.30-5pm Tue-Sat, noon-5pm Sun) with rotating exhibitions and the cathedral treasury.

OTHER CHURCHES

Like the cathedral doors, the Romanesque **St Michaeliskirche** (☎ 344 10; Michaelisplatz; admission free; ☺ 8am-6pm Mon-Sat, noon-6pm Sun Apr-Oct, 9am-4pm Mon-Sat, noon-4pm Sun Nov-Mar) is under Unesco protection. Built in 1022 and reconstructed after extensive war damage, it is undergoing another makeover and only partially open for viewing until at least 2010.

Off Hoher Weg is **St Andreaskirche** (☎ 124 34; Andreasplatz; adult/concession €1.50/1; ☺ tower 11am-4pm Mon-Sat, noon-4pm Sun Apr-Oct) whose lofty spire offers a sweeping view. There are 364 steps to the top.

LAPPENBERG

The former **Jewish Quarter** in and around Lappenberg Square is the oldest section of town. Most of it remains because, while local fire crews let the synagogue burn to the ground on Kristallnacht in November 1938, they rescued other houses around the square. These included the former **Jewish school**, now owned by St Godehard's Church, on the corner. In 1988, on the 50th anniversary, a memorial was installed on the site of the synagogue, following the outline of its foundations and topped by a model of Jerusalem.

While down this way, take time to check out the quaint **Wernesches Haus** on Hinterer Brühl, which is one of the oldest buildings in Hildesheim.

ROEMER- UND PELIZAEUS-MUSEUM

One of Europe's best collections of Egyptian art and artefacts is found in the **Roemer- und Pelizaeus-Museum** (☎ 936 90; www.rpmuseum.de, in German; Am Steine 1-2; adult/concession/family €8/6/16; ☺ 10am-6pm). There are dozens of mummies, scrolls, statues and wall hangings, but the life-size re-creation of an Egyptian tomb (of Sennefer) is a particular highlight.

Sleeping

Its proximity to Hanover means Hildesheim often takes overspill guests during trade fairs, when accommodation prices rise phenomenally.

DJH hostel (☎ 427 17; www.djh-niedersachsen.de /jh/hildesheim; Schirrmannweg 4; dm under/over 27yr €20.20/23.20, s €30.20, d €26.70; Ⓟ ✗ 및) In the morning, guests here often act as though they've just had an embarrassing one-night stand. It's a great hostel, really, with modern facilities and a good breakfast. But it's just so inconveniently located that many seem to be wondering what they're doing here and look in a hurry to leave. To get here catch bus 1 or 2 to Schuhstrasse and change to 4 in the direction of Im Koken-Hof. Get off at the Triftstrasse stop and walk the remaining 750m uphill.

Gästehaus Klocke (☎ 179 213; www.gaestehaus -klocke.de; Humboldtstrasse 11; s €48-55, d €75-80) This is a quirky gem, which feels a bit like a mini-castle upon entering, as its high-ceilinged stairwell has a landing with a stained-glass window, chess set and chairs. The rooms aren't quite as amazing but have character nevertheless. The hotel is just south over the canal from the Jewish quarter.

Gästehaus-Café Timphus (☎ 346 86; www.timphus -conditorei-hotel.de; Braunschweiger Strasse 90/91; s €52, d €74-84, tr €116; ✗ 🛜) This small *Pension* has walls bedecked with photos of artful chocolate displays, which might mean you keep going next door to the associated cafe for supplies. If you intend to arrive after 6pm, reserve ahead so you have a code for the key dispenser.

Novotel Hotel (☎ 171 70; www.accorhotels.com; Bahnhofsallee 38; s/d from €80/108; Ⓟ ✗ 🛜) Book early on the internet here and you can get even better prices than these in this spacious cloister building with exposed stone walls, gentle tones and cosy designer-chic style. It is set back from the street in quiet grounds and has excellent dining and bar facilities.

 ourpick **Van der Valk Hotel Hildesheim** (☎ 3000; www.vandervalk.de; Markt 4; s/d from €105/125; ✗ 및 🛜 🛋) Behind its historic frontage on the central market place, this luxury hotel reveals a surprisingly large interior. Its flagstone-floored atrium entrance (not all the stone on the walls is real, however) gives way to tasteful rooms in subtle shades of grey and turquoise. The pool and wellness areas (Finnish sauna) are a bonus.

Eating & Drinking

Café Desseo (☎ 399 27; Hindenburgplatz 3; tapas €3-9, other dishes €5.50-16; ✗ 🛜) Generally billed as a tapas bar, this excellent venue is actually more of an all-rounder. All-you-can-eat breakfasts (€6.80) and lunches (€7.70) are matched by sandwiches, delicious wraps, pasta, pizza and other dishes. In addition to all this there are smoking and nonsmoking areas and a good selection of cocktails.

 ourpick **Nil im Museum** (☎ 408 595; www.nil -restaurant.de, in German; Am Steine 1; mains €9.80-16.50; 🕙 10am-midnight; ✗) This relaxed restaurant in the Roemer- und Pelizaeus-Museum serves delicious antipasti, pasta and salads, along with poultry and red-meat main courses with a creative touch. It also has a regular program of jazz and blues.

Schlegels Weinstuben (☎ 331 33; Am Steine 4-6; mains €12.50-22.50; 🕙 dinner Mon-Sat; ✗) The lopsided walls of this rose-covered, 500-yearold house hunkering beside the Roemer- und Pelizaeus-Museum add to the sheer magic of the place. Inside are historic rooms and, in one corner, a round, glass-topped table fashioned from a well, where you can dine overlooking the water below. The ever-changing international cuisine is also exceptional, so book ahead.

Explore further options along the popular Friesenstrasse (just behind Schuhstrasse), where the pubs and bars usually sell cheap meals.

Getting There & Around

Frequent regional train services operate between Hildesheim and Hanover (€6.90, 30 minutes), while ICE trains head to Braunschweig (€13.50, 25 minutes) and Göttingen (€24.50, 30 minutes).

For those driving, the A7 runs right by town from Hanover, while the B1 goes to Hamelin.

Most sights in Hildesheim are within walking distance, but buses will take you to outlying restaurants and accommodation, as indicated. Single tickets cost €1.95, daily city tickets €4.20.

BRAUNSCHWEIG

☎ 0531 / pop 240,500

Still famous as the city of Heinrich der Löwe (Henry the Lion) nine centuries after this powerful medieval duke made it his capital, Braunschweig (Brunswick) reveals its past

LOWER SAXONY

as five separate settlements with a slightly meandering but pleasant historic old town.

Braunschweig has spent most of the post-WWII period nestled in the shadow of the Iron Curtain – in many an industrialist's eye, too close for comfort to be a candidate for locating an industry here. Today, despite its very provincial feel, it can be a pleasant place to while away a day or two, not least because of its handful of interesting museums and impressive buildings. These give a good insight into the history and lives of people in this part of Germany.

Orientation

Most sights are in the historic town centre, a distorted rectangle bounded by Konrad-Adenauer-Strasse to the south, Güldenstrasse to the west, Lange Strasse to the north and Bohlweg to the east. However, the arty quarter of the Magniviertel and the Herzog Anton Ulrich Museum lie just to the old town's east. A moat surrounds the centre, lending it the compact character of an island. One-way systems may cause problems if you're driving.

Information

Heimnet Internet Cafe (☎ 614 9739; Bohlweg 29; per hr €1.50; ◷ 9am-midnight Mon-Sat, from 10am Sun)
Main post office (Berliner Platz 12-16; ◷ 9am-7pm Mon-Fri, 10am-1pm Sat) Alongside the Hauptbahnhof.
Post office (Friedrich-Wilhelm-Strasse 3; ◷ 9am-7pm Mon-Fri, 9.30am-1pm Sat)
Tourist Service Braunschweig (☎ 470 2040; www.braunschweig.de; Vor der Burg 1; ◷ 10am-7pm Mon-Fri, to 4pm Sat)

Sights & Activities

Braunschweig's identity is intricately tied up with Heinrich der Löwe, a duke who was responsible for colonising the eastern regions of Germany beyond the Elbe and Saale as a secular ruler (that is, not strongly connected with the Church). The **Braunschweiger Löwe** (Brunswick lion) statue you see replicated around town, but most prominently on Burgplatz, is the city's symbol and based on the original lion Heinrich ordered to be built in 1166 as a symbol of his power and jurisdiction; you can see this original at Burg Dankwarderode (right).

DOM ST BLASII

Heinrich's tomb is in the crypt of **Dom St Blasii** (St Blasius Cathedral; ☎ 243 350; www.braunschweigerdom .de, in German; Domplatz 5; crypt admission €1; ◷ 10am-5pm), where he lies alongside his wife Mathilde. In a macabre postscript to the duke's life, the Nazis decided to co-opt his image and in 1935 exhumed his tomb to conduct an 'archaeological investigation'. Even Hitler paid a visit. However, the corpse found inside had one leg shorter than the other (it's known that Heinrich suffered a terrible horse-riding accident late in life) and dark hair, and the master-race propagandists went very quiet on the subject after that. There were also questions over the body's gender and some doubt as to whether it's really Heinrich in the sarcophagus.

On the cathedral's northern side is the largely Gothic building's only remaining Romanesque door, which sports so-called 'claw marks'. Legend has it these were left by the duke's pet lion, trying to get to its master when he lay in the cathedral after his death. A more realistic explanation is that soldiers sharpened their swords here.

BURG DANKWARDERODE

Heinrich's former **castle** (☎ 122 50; www.museum -braunschweig.de, in German; Burgplatz; adult/concession incl Herzog Anton Ulrich Museum €3/1.50; ◷ 10am-5pm Tue & Thu-Sun, 1-8pm Wed) is now a museum. It houses a glittering **medieval collection** (◷ 11am-5pm Tue & Thu-Sun, 1-2.30pm & 4-8pm Wed), including golden sculptures of arms, medieval capes and the original bronze lion statue cast in 1166.

Upstairs is a huge, spectacularly adorned **Knights' Hall** (◷ 10-11am Tue & Thu-Sun, 2.30-4pm Wed).

HERZOG ANTON ULRICH MUSEUM

Braunschweig is not only about Heinrich der Löwe. Another duke, Anton Ulrich (1633–1714) left Braunschweig with an impressive legacy too. Like Bruce Chatwin's compulsive collector Utz, Anton Ulrich had an eye for miniature porcelain figures – as well as for crockery, furniture and all types of painting, from Chinese to European. Now the thousands of pieces he assembled in his lifetime are found in the **Herzog Anton Ulrich Museum** (☎ 122 50; www.museum-braunschweig.de, in German; Museumstrasse 1; adult/concession incl Burg Dankwarderode €3/1.50; ◷ 10am-5pm Tue & Thu-Sun, 1-8pm Wed). Artefacts, including an ancient Roman onyx cup that survived some escapades through the years, and the most complete museum collection of Fürstenburg porcelain anywhere, are here. Unfortunately, lack of funding often means that opening times for different floors are staggered (as at Burg Dankwarderode), so ring ahead.

LANDESMUSEUM

The city's **Landesmuseum** (State Museum; ☎ 121 50; Burgplatz; adult/concession €2.50/1.30; ☉ 10am-5pm Tue, Wed & Fri-Sun, to 8pm Thu) covers German his-

tory from a regional perspective. Although the descriptions are only in German, the museum has lots of engaging exhibits that speak for themselves, starting with a large Foucault pendulum illustrating the principle of the Earth's rotation, and augmented by a myriad of artefacts assembled chronologically to tell the story of Germany's past. It is a fascinating

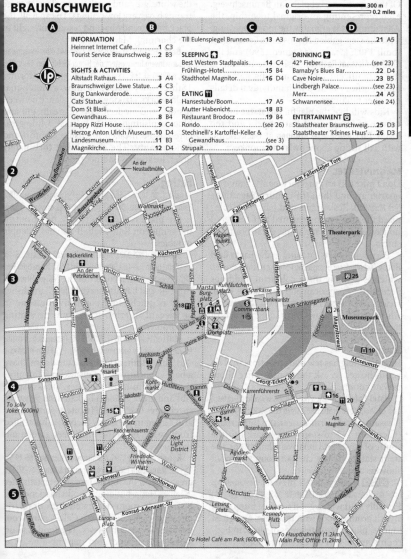

BRAUNSCHWEIG

0 — 300 m
0 — 0.2 miles

INFORMATION
Heimnet Internet Cafe..............1 C3
Tourist Service Braunschweig ...2 B3

SIGHTS & ACTIVITIES
Altstadt Rathaus.......................3 A4
Braunschweiger Löwe Statue....4 C3
Burg Dankwarderode................5 C3
Cats Statue..............................6 B4
Dom St Blasii...........................7 C3
Gewandhaus.............................8 B4
Happy Rizzi House 9 C4
Herzog Anton Ulrich Museum..10 D4
Landesmuseum.......................11 B3
Magnikirche...........................12 D4

Till Eulenspiegel Brunnen.....13 A3

SLEEPING
Best Western Stadtpalais........14 C4
Frühlings-Hotel......................15 B4
Stadthotel Magnitor..............16 D4

EATING
Hansestube/Boom...................17 A5
Mutter Habenicht...................18 B3
Restaurant Brodocz 19 B4
Rondo..............................(see 26)
Stechinelli's Kartoffel-Keller &
Gewandhaus...................(see 3)
Strupait.................................20 D4

Tandir....................................21 A5

DRINKING
42° Fieber.........................(see 23)
Barnaby's Blues Bar...............22 D4
Cave Noire............................23 B5
Lindbergh Palace................(see 23)
Merz.....................................24 A5
Schwannensee...................(see 24)

ENTERTAINMENT
Staatstheater Braunschweig.....25 D3
Staatstheater 'Kleines Haus'....26 D3

museum, not least because of eclectic objects like the strands of hair allegedly belonging to Heinrich der Löwe and Mathilde. They are in cases of silver, gold and marble, specially constructed in 1935 as part of Hitler's propaganda offensive to present Heinrich posthumously as one of his own.

OLD TOWN

Of the several market places in Braunschweig, each representing an original township, the Altstadtmarkt is arguably the most appealing, with the step-gabled Renaissance **Gewandhaus** (built 1303; facade redesigned 1590) and the Gothic **Altstadt Rathaus**. Inside the Rathaus is the magnificent Dronse meeting hall. The tourist office can help with individual details on other buildings.

Kids will like the playful **cats statue** on the corner of Damm and Kattreppeln and the lovely **Till Eulenspiegel Brunnen** at Bäckerklint, with Till sitting above owls and monkeys.

MAGNIVIERTEL

Don't miss this arty precinct–cum–traditional quarter around the 11th-century **Magnikirche** (Am Magnitor). Restaurants and bars have colonised the area's many restored half-timbered houses and there are some great boutique stores.

Particularly eye-catching is the **Happy Rizzi House** (Ackerhof, cnr Georg-Eckert-Strasse & Schlossstrasse), which is actually three colourful buildings decorated by American pop artist James Rizzi. Hearts are a recurring theme on the facade, while curved windows form integral parts of facial murals.

Sleeping

Braunschweig has few budget options and no youth hostel, so ask the tourist office about private rooms.

Hotel Café am Park (☎ 730 79; www.hotel-cafeampark.de; Wolfenbüttler Strasse 67; s/d/tr €60/80/91; P) This pleasant *Hotel Garni* is near the Bürgerpark (take tram M2 to stop 'Bürgerpark') to the south of town and relatively handy for the train station. It has cheaper rooms without showers and toilets.

ourpick Frühlings-Hotel (☎ 243 210; www.fruehlingshotel.de; Bankplatz 7; s €68-135, d €88-185; P X 💻 🛜) Friendly staff with a good sense of humour, a stylish ground floor with reception and guest lounge, plus three categories of pleasant bedrooms, make this an excellent choice. Some

of the cheaper accommodation on the top floor hasn't been refurbished but has good rooftop views.

Stadthotel Magnitor (☎ 471 30; www.stadthotel-magni.de; Am Magnitor 1; s €75-85, d €110-120; P X 🛜) Behind the historic black-and-white facade are carefully thought-out rooms with designer touches. The colours are low-key and furnishings keep things chic by rarely straying from the white, grey and black theme. Two or three rooms have very low ceilings. To cap it all, the place has a trendy bar and restaurant, right in the charming Magniviertel.

Best Western Stadtpalais (☎ 241 024; www.palais-braunschweig.bestwestern.de; Hinter Liebfrauen 1a; s €78-170, d €95-190, tr €135-220; P X 🛜) This former 18th-century palace is now a hotel that really works, striking a good balance between historic and modern. Lots of cream, gilt and blue furnishings create interest, while great care has been taken to ensure comfort and functionality. The central, but fortunately quiet, location is another plus.

Eating

Tandir (☎ 165 67; Südstrasse 24; 🕐 8am-2am Sun-Thu, 8am-5am Fri & Sat; X) This top takeaway Turk is the place to head to after a night out in the venues on Katenwall. It also has a couple of tables.

Strupait (☎ 2392 9494; Magnitorwall 8; soups €5-10; 🕐 9am-10pm Tue-Thu, 10am-10pm Fri & Sat, 10am-6pm Sun; X) Nestled on a corner in the Magniviertel, this cafe and bar also serves a few light dishes such as quiche to accompany the wine in an elegant interior. It has outside seating in summer.

Mutter Habenicht (☎ 459 56; Papenstieg 3; mains €5.75-18, weekday lunch menus €5.50; 🕐 11am-midnight; X) This 'Mother Hubbard' sure doesn't have a bare cupboard, as she dishes up filling portions of schnitzels, potatoes, steaks, spare ribs and the occasional Balkan dish. Seasonal specialities like *Spargel* (white asparagus) are also served in the dimly lit, bric-a-brac-filled front room, or in the small beer garden out the back.

Rondo (☎ 123 4595; Magnitorwall 18; mains €6-19.50; 🕐 11.30am-10pm Tue-Fri, from 6pm Sat & Sun; X V) A great find on the top floor of the Staatstheater 'Kleines Haus' building, Rondo has a modern bistro-style room decorated with dramatic photos of opera diva Maria Callas, plus a roof terrace offering city views. The food is plain and simple at lunch, but steps up a notch at dinner. Coffee and cake can be had when the kitchen closes from 3pm to 6pm.

Restaurant Brodocz (☎ 422 36; Stephanstrasse 1; soups €3.50-4.90, fish mains €9.30-23, vegetarian mains €5-14; ⏰ 11.30am-10pm Mon-Sat; ✗ Ⓥ) This Braunschweig institution specialises in salads and vegetarian soups and mains, augmented by piscine delights, with everything from English-style fish and chips to dorade, perch and salmon. The evening menu offers a smaller selection of dishes.

Stechinelli's Kartoffel-Keller & Gewandhaus (☎ 242 777; Altstadtmarkt 1-2; dishes €4-26; ⏰ 11.30am-10pm; ✗) In the basement of the Rathaus, these adjacent restaurants are touristy but ever-popular. You can indulge in potatoes over three courses in casual Stechinelli's, from potato soup to potato waffles for dessert. Gewandhaus has an identical menu but closes from 2pm to 6pm.

Hansestube/Boom (☎ 243 900; Güldenstrasse 7; mains €10.50-22.50; ⏰ 7am-11pm; ✗) Widely regarded as Braunschweig's leading restaurants, these sister establishments in a renovated half-timbered house serve a seasonally changing menu of modern international cuisine. Enjoy *Braunschweiger Mummebraten* (€13.50), a roast stuffed with mincemeat and served in a sauce based on Mumme, a local nonalcoholic malt extract. Rooms in the comfortable hotel cost €90 and €110 for singles and doubles, respectively.

Drinking

The Magniviertel is a good district to head to for drinks, with several traditional pubs. More listings can be found in *Cocktail*, *Da Capo* or *Subway*, the tourist office's *Braunschweig Bietet* or the quarterly *Hin & Weg*.

Barnaby's Blues Bar (☎ 356 9560; www.barnabys-bs.de, in German; Ölschlägern 20; entry free-€25; ⏰ from 6pm) A regular flow of artists take the stage each month in this poky, smoky blues bar that gets local unknowns to legends, like Mitch Ryder, on tour.

Merz (☎ 181 28; www.merz-bs.de, in German; Gieselerstrasse 3; entry €3; ⏰ 8pm-late Thu-Sat; ✗) Spacious and relaxed, Merz is a long-standing favourite especially among the student crowd, with table football, a beer garden, and a few snacks to nibble with inexpensive drinks. The lounge area opens at 10pm.

Schwannensee (☎ 458 33; entry €5; ⏰ 10pm-late Fri & Sat; ✗) In the same building as Merz, Schwannensee serves up hip-hop, house and rock.

Three venues stand cheek-by-jowl near Merz on Kalenwall and draw a mid-20s crowd. **Cave Noire** (Kalenwall 3; ⏰ 9pm-late Fri & Sat) is a champagne-style bar that also serves affordable beer and wine. Alongside it is **Lindbergh Palace** (entry free-€4; ⏰ 9pm-late Fri & Sat; ✗), where DJs turn soul and funk, and upstairs from here is **42° Fieber** (entry €4; ⏰ 11pm-very late Fri & Sat; ✗), with a round dance floor, red sofas and a demure mood where disco classics and house get a hearing.

Entertainment

Jolly Joker (☎ 281 4622; Broitzemerstrasse 220; entry for parties €6; ⏰ from 10pm Tue-Sat; ✗) This popular evergreen with a capacity of 4000 features four separate dance spaces, 10 bars including a huge cocktail bar, and several food outlets. Expect top-100 dance-chart hits. The same complex also houses a cinema.

Staatstheater Braunschweig (☎ ticket office 123 4567; www.staatstheater-braunschweig.de; Am Theater/Steinweg) is the historic venue for classical music, theatre, dance and opera. **Staatstheater 'Kleines Haus'** (Magnitorwall 18; ✗) is the second of its four performance spaces. Tickets range from €7 to €38 depending on venue, performance and seat. The tourist office also sells tickets, or turn up an hour before the event for rush tickets.

Getting There & Away

There are regular RE services to Hanover (€11.30, 45 minutes) and IC trains to Leipzig (€40, two hours). ICE trains go to Berlin (€53, one hour 20 minutes) and Frankfurt (€80, 2¾ hours).

The A2 runs east–west between Hanover and Magdeburg across the northern end of the city. This connects with the A39 about 25km east of the city, which heads north to Wolfsburg. The A39 also heads south from the city.

Getting Around

Braunschweig is at the heart of an integrated transport network that extends throughout the region and as far south as the Harz Mountains. Bus and tram ticket prices are determined by time, not distance: 90-minute tickets cost €2.10, 24-hour tickets €5.30.

Any bus or tram going to 'Rathaus' from the Hauptbahnhof will get you to the centre in 10 minutes; these leave from the same side as the public transport information booth just outside the train station. Trams 1 or 2 and bus 420 are among these. The M5 tram is useful, connecting the train station with Friedrich-Wilhelm-Platz via Am Magnitor and passing the Herzog Anton Ulrich Museum.

If driving, be aware that there are one-way systems all around the Altstadt. Alternatively, there's parking by the train station.

WOLFENBÜTTEL
☎ 05331 / pop 54,000

'Alles mit Bedacht' (everything with prudence) was the expression favoured by Duke August II (1579–1666), who founded Wolfenbüttel's famous library and turned the town into a cultural centre in the mid-17th century. This friendly, charming little city, about 10 minutes by train from Braunschweig, is worlds away in terms of its feel and architecture. First mentioned in 1118, Wolfenbüttel was virtually untouched by WWII, and it's almost a time capsule of half-timbered houses – there are over 600 of them, nearly all beautifully restored.

Orientation & Information
The Hauptbahnhof is a five-minute walk southwest of Stadtmarkt, the town centre. To get to **Tourist Information Wolfenbüttel** (☎ 862 80; www.wolfenbuettel.com; Stadtmarkt 7; ⏱ 9am-6pm Mon-Fri, 10am-4pm Sat), in Stadtmarkt, take Bahnhofstrasse north to Kommisstrasse. This joins Kornmarkt, the main bus transfer point. Stadtmarkt is just to the north. The Schloss and Herzog August Bibliothek are west of here.

Sights
The tourist office has German-language audioguides (€5.50 per day), or you can download an English, French or German MP3 guide from the website www.wolfenbuettel.tomis.mobi (click on the appropriate flag for your preferred language). The free tourist office brochure, *A walk through historic Wolfenbüttel*, is also an excellent guide. It starts at Wolfenbüttel's pretty **Schloss Museum** (☎ 924 60; Schlossplatz 13; adult/concession/family €3.50/1/7; ⏱ 10am-5pm Tue-Sun), where the living quarters of the Braunschweig-Lüneburg dukes have been preserved in all their glory of intricate inlaid wood, ivory walls, brocade curtains and chairs.

However, it's the **Herzog August Bibliothek** (☎ 808 214; www.hab.de; Lessingplatz 1; adult/concession €3/2; ⏱ 10am-5pm Tue-Sun), across the square, that will most interest bibliophiles. Not only is this hushed place one of the world's best reference libraries for 17th-century books (if you're a member that is), its collection of 800,000 volumes also includes what's billed as the 'world's most expensive book' (€17.50 million). This is the *Welfen Evangelial*, a gospel book once owned by Heinrich der Löwe. The original is only on show sporadically, as taking it out inevitably causes slight damage. However, an impressive facsimile is permanently displayed in the vault on the 1st floor.

From Schlossplatz, the walk suggested in the brochure continues east along Löwenstrasse to Krambuden and north up Kleiner Zimmerhof to **Klein Venedig** (Little Venice), one of the few tangible remnants of the extensive canal system built by Dutch workers in Wolfenbüttel in the late 16th century. From there the brochure continues to guide you past historic courtyards, buildings and squares. The entire walk takes around one hour (2km), excluding visits.

Getting There & Away
Trains connect Wolfenbüttel with Braunschweig's Hauptbahnhof (€3.20, 10 minutes) twice an hour.

WOLFSBURG
☎ 05361 / pop 120,000

Arriving in Wolfsburg by train, the first thing you see is an enormous, almost surreal, VW emblem on a building in a scene that could have come from Fritz Lang's classic film *Metropolis*. This is part of the Volkswagen company's nation-sized global headquarters. Wolfsburg is indeed a company town, and because of this it also has an earthy, working-class atmosphere that sets it apart from any other cities in the region.

Volkswagen is one of the world's most profitable and successful automotive manufacturers, and although it has been shedding employees locally over the past decade, about 40% of Wolfsburg still works for it. The company is even staking a claim to become the world's largest car manufacturer, currently producing 11% of the world's passenger vehicles. Wolfsburg is trying to diversify though, and tourism is seen as one way. As well as the hugely successful Autostadt theme park, the town boasts a Phaeno science centre, a sleek piece of futuristic architecture by celebrity architect Zaha Hadid.

Orientation

Wolfsburg's centre is just southeast of the Hauptbahnhof. Head diagonally left out of the train station to the partly pedestrianised main drag, Porschestrasse, and continue south. The Phaeno centre is impossible to miss, just to the left of the station. To get to Autostadt, walk under Phaeno and continue until you see the stairs across the railway tracks. These lead to the theme park.

Information

Babylon Tele- and Internet Shop (Porschestrasse 23; per hr €1.20; ☒ 9am-midnight Mon-Fri, from 10am Sat & Sun) Internet access.

Main post office (Porschestrasse 22-24; ☒ 8.30am-7pm Mon-Fri, 9am-1pm Sat)

Wolfsburg tourist office (☎ 899 930; www.wolfsburg .de; Willy Brandt-Platz 3; ☒ 9am-6pm Mon-Sat, 10am-3pm Sun) In the train station. Books hotels and has maps.

Sights & Activities

AUTOSTADT

Spread across 25 hectares, **Autostadt** (Car City; ☎ 0800-288678238; www.autostadt.de, in German; Stadtbrücke; adult/child/concession/family €15/6/12/38; ☒ 9am-6pm) is a celebration of all things VW. Conceived as a luxury centre for customers to collect new vehicles, it soon developed into a theme park with broad family appeal.

Things kick off with a broad view of automotive design and engineering in the Konzernforum, while the neighbouring Zeithaus looks back at the history of the Beetle (see the boxed text, p642) and other VW models. Then, in various outlying pavilions you can learn more about individual marques, including VW itself, Audi, Bentley, Lamborghini, Seat and Skoda. Many exhibits are interactive and most have signage in German and English.

Included in the entrance price is a 45-minute trip into the neighbouring Volkswagen factory, bigger than Monaco and the world's largest car plant. These leave at about 30-minute intervals from Monday to Friday only, and there's a daily tour in English (at 12.45pm, but call to confirm as this can change). The factory is so large that tours rotate through different workshop sections, so it's pot luck as to whether you'll see one of the 3000 cars produced each day roll off the assembly line or something less interesting, such as metal-pressing.

A **Turmfahrt** (Car Tower Discovery; adult/child/concession €8/4/6) involves sitting in a glass case and being freighted to the top of a 46m tower and down again – it's as if you're in one of the cars in this transparent tower, where vehicles are stored before being collected by eager new owners.

For a pure, competitive adrenaline rush, ring ahead to organise an English-speaking instructor for the park's **obstacle courses** and **safety training** (costing between €17 and €28 each). You'll need a valid licence, of course, and to be comfortable with a left-hand-drive car. The park even has a **mini-course**, with toy models that can be driven by kids.

AUTOMUSEUM

More low-key, the **AutoMuseum** (☎ 520 71; Dieselstrasse 35; adult/concession/family €6/3/15; ☒ 10am-6pm Fri-Sun, closed 24 Dec-1 Jan) has a collection that includes a vehicle used in the *Herbie, the Love Bug* movie, a Beetle built from wood, the original 1938 Cabriolet presented to Adolf Hitler on his 50th birthday, and the bizarre 'See-Golf', a Golf Cabriolet from 1983 with hydraulic pontoons that extend outwards to make it amphibious. Take bus 208 to Automuseum.

PHAENO

The glass-and-concrete building that houses the science centre **Phaeno** (☎ 0180-106 0600; www .phaeno.de; Willy Brandt-Platz 1; adult/child/concession/family €12/7.50/9/26.50; ☒ 9am-5pm Tue-Fri, 10am-6pm Sat & Sun, last entry 1hr before closing) is truly cutting edge. Sleek, curved and thin, it looks like a stretchy spaceship from Planet Minimalism.

Inside this building designed by British-based Iraqi architect Zaha Hadid are 300 hands-on physics exhibits and experiments (with instructions and explanations in both German and English) – and, frequently it seems, 10 times as many schoolchildren all pulling at them. You can wind up your own rocket, check your eyes by looking at bunnies, build an arched polystyrene bridge, watch thermal images of your body – and so on and so on. For the one really peaceful chance to savour the building's architecture, head to the canteen. Look for the window at the far end to see how it cleverly frames Porschestrasse.

BITTEN BY THE BUG

Cast-iron proof that Germans *do* have a sense of humour, the Volkswagen Beetle is truly greater than the sum of its parts. After all, the parts in question initially comprised little more than an air-cooled, 24-horsepower engine (maximum speed 100km/h) chucked in the back of a comically half-egg-shaped chassis. Yet somehow this rudimentary mechanical assembly added up to a global icon – a symbol of Germany's postwar *Wirtschaftswunder* (economic miracle) that owners the world over fondly thought of as one of the family.

Indeed, it's a testament to the vehicle's ability to run on the smell of an oily rag while rarely breaking down that few would even begrudge its Nazi provenance. Yes, in 1934 Adolf Hitler asked Ferdinand Porsche to design a 'Volkswagen' (people's car) affordable for every German household and, yes, the *Käfer* (bug) was the result. However, Beetle production only really began in the new Wolfsburg factory under British occupation in 1946.

Did the company realise then what a hit it had on its hands? By the early 1960s, the chugging, spluttering sound of VW engines could be heard across 145 nations.

Urged on by ads to 'Think Small', North Americans were particularly bitten by the bug, and this durable, cut-price vehicle became a permanent fixture on the hippie scene. Later in Europe, the Golf model cars that superseded the Beetle in the 1970s and '80s would prove a phenomenal success. (While Douglas Coupland talked about *Generation X*, the German equivalent, as identified by best-selling author Florian Illies in 2000, is *Generation Golf*). However the US never warmed to the usurper, pushing VW to introduce a sleek, trendy, state-of-the-art New Beetle in 1998.

Long after VW withdrew its bucket-of-bolts old Beetle (essentially the same beast despite improvements) from Western markets, the car remained a best seller in the developing world. Only on 31 July 2003 did the last one roll off the assembly line in Mexico, the 21,529,464th of its breed.

CITY CENTRE

As you walk south down Porschestrasse, you'll come to another great building, the **Kunstmuseum** (Art Museum; ☎ 266 90; www.kunstmuseum-wolfsburg.de; Porschestrasse 53; adult/concession €8/4; ⊗ 11am-8pm Tue, to 6pm Wed-Sun), which is home to temporary exhibitions of modern art. On the hill just southwest of the southern end of Porschestrasse is **Planetarium Wolfsburg** (☎ 219 39; www.planetarium-wolfsburg.de; Uhlandweg 2; adult/concession/family €5/3/10; ⊗ show times 3pm Wed, 4.30pm Sat & 3.30pm Sun), built in 1982 after VW bartered Golfs for Zeiss projectors with the GDR. It's got laser and rock shows, star shows and spoken-word performances set to the stars.

Next to it is the city's historic landmark, the **Esso Station**, built in 1951 and now restored to its original splendour.

SCHLOSS WOLFSBURG

In historic contrast to Autostadt's space-age sheen, Wolfsburg's castle dates from 1600 and today houses the **Stadtmuseum** (☎ 828 540; Schlossstrasse 8; admission free; ⊗ 10am-5pm Tue-Fri, 11am-6pm Sun). It has a rundown of the city's history from 1938, when the VW plant was founded, to the present day. There's also a small regional history museum and two **art**

galleries that host rotating exhibitions. The Schloss is five minutes northeast of Autostadt. Several buses, including 160, 201, 202, 208, 211 and 380, will get you here.

FALLERSLEBEN

Keen history students who speak German might want to visit this historic part of town to see **Fallersleben Schloss** and its **Hoffmann Museum** (☎ 05362-526 23; admission free; ⊗ 10am-5pm Tue-Fri, 1-5pm Sat, 11am-5pm Sun). In 1841, Fallersleben native August Heinrich Hoffman (1798–1874) wrote the lyrics to what would become the German national anthem (music courtesy of Joseph Hayden). Here you'll find discussion of how his words '*über alles*' ('above everything') were simply a call for an end to petty inter-German fiefdoms, and how they were expunged after the Third Reich's nationalistic excesses. Take bus 206 or 214 to Fallersleben.

Sleeping

Most tourists to Wolfsburg are day trippers, and the city's accommodation is geared towards business travellers.

DJH hostel (☎ 133 37; www.djh-niedersachsen.de/jh/wolfsburg; Lessingstrasse 60; dm under/over 27yr €22.20/24.20; P ☒ ▣) At its current location, this hostel has two- to four-bed dorms, but it expects to move into its new, refurbished premises around the corner at Kleiststrasse 18-20, some time after 2011, when you should find spanking new, upgraded facilities.

Global Inn (☎ 2700; www.globalinn.de; Kleiststrasse 46; s €62-67, d €93-114; **P** **✗**) While very much aimed at the corporate customer, the comfortable furnishings and facilities of this hotel, including a very decent Italian restaurant, Per Voi, make it suitable for leisure travellers, too. Book ahead.

Penthouse Hotel (☎ 2710; www.penthouse-hotel.de; Schachtweg 22; s €68, d €80-100, tr €120; **☜**) With basic kitchens, these central but quite plain-Jane apartments are popular among families or longer-stay international travellers in town on VW business. Discounts are given for extended stays.

ourpick **Hotel Goya** (☎ 266 00; www.goya-hotel.de; Poststrasse 34; s €77-91, d €94-106; **P** **✗** **☜**) Rooms in this very central and comfortable hotel are nicely furbished in subdued colours, using mirrors cleverly. Each room has a writing surface and if that's not sufficient, business guests can book a small office here. While facilities such as wi-fi cater for business guests, it actually does a very tasteful double-act as a quality tourist hotel.

Ritz-Carlton (☎ 607 000; www.ritzcarlton.com; Stadtbrücke; r from €205; **P** **✗** **✗** **☜** **☎**) This is a hard act to beat. Its swimming pool is integrated into the harbour basin of the canal, giving it a lakeside feel, the building forms a stunning arc on one side of Autostadt, and the decor is elegant, inspired and breathes natural tones. A bell hop will meet you and take your luggage as you approach, and once inside, full five-star facilities await, complemented by a Michelin-starred restaurant and numerous bars. Naturally, if you stay here admission to Autostadt is free. You can take high tea overlooking the harbour.

Eating & Drinking

Aalto Bistro (☎ 891 689; Porschestrasse 1; mains €6.50-9.50; **⏰** 11.30am-3pm & 6-11pm Mon-Sat; **✗**) Part of the Kulturhaus designed by star Finnish architect Alvar Aalto, this relaxing place serves pasta and seafood in a modern bistro environment.

ourpick **Vini D'Italia Marrone** (☎ 154 46; www.viniditalia-marrone.de, in German; Schillerstrasse 25; dishes €9.50-22; **⏰** 10am-10pm Mon-Wed, 10am-11pm Thu & Fri, 10am-4pm Sat; **✗**) This Italian *bottega* is a double

act, being a wine store but also a small eatery where antipasti and salads cost €5 to €8. You can choose from the main menu, do the daily lunch menu (€9.50), or simply treat yourself to whatever special is on offer that day.

Trattoria Incontri (☎ 437 254; Goethestrasse 53-55; most dishes €10-12; **⏰** 11.30am-midnight Mon-Sat, 4pm-midnight Sun; **✗**) While here, explore the handful of other culinary spots on Goethestrasse. Our tip in a town that does some of Germany's best Italian food is this hugely popular trattoria, but there's another Mediterranean-inspired one very close by (or grab your German dictionary and check out www.bistronando.de).

Altes Brauhaus (☎ 053362-3140; Schlossplatz, Fallersleben; mains €7.50-14; **⏰** from 11am; **✗**) If you're visiting the Hoffmann Museum in Fallersleben or simply dying for a German beer-hall atmosphere, come here. There's a good house brew and hearty fare including salads, sausages, potatoes and sauerkraut.

Most of the nine **Autostadt restaurants** (☎ 406 100; **✗**) stay open later than the park itself: within two hours of the park's closing time, you can buy an *Abendticket* (evening ticket, €7) and your admission fee is credited towards your restaurant meal. The restaurants are all operated by Mövenpick, use mostly organic ingredients, and serve a variety of cuisines. The **food hall** in the main forum building (right as you enter) does honest chow (steak and chips for €15; you don't need a ticket to eat here), while **Anan** in the 'Zeitreise' building (ticket required) does fantastic organic Japanese udon, soba and ramen noodle dishes (€8 to €13) in an intriguing 'plastic' environment.

Wolfsburgers do much of their drinking in Kaufhof – not the department store, but a small strip of bars, pubs and a few eateries west of Porschestrasse attracting a mostly young crowd. The best thing is to wander along and see what appeals.

Getting There & Away

Frequent ICE train services go to Berlin (€44, one hour). IC trains to Hanover (€17, 30 minutes) are cheaper and barely slower than the ICE. Frequent ICE trains, including some Berlin and Hanover ones, pass through Braunschweig (€11.50, 16 minutes). Regional trains are better value for Braunschweig (€4.60, 24 minutes).

From Braunschweig, take the A2 east to the A39 north, which brings you right into town. Alternatively, take the B248 north to the A39.

Getting Around

Single bus tickets, valid for 90 minutes, cost €2.10 and a day pass costs €5.30. The major bus transfer point (ZOB) is at the northern end of Porschestrasse. Buses 206 and 214 go regularly to Fallersleben from here.

Once you leave the pedestrianised centre, distances become difficult to cover easily by foot. In every sense, Wolfsburg was built for cars. The car park behind the Planetarium is free. Vehicles can be hired from **Europcar** (☎ 815 70; Dieselstrasse 19).

There are taxi ranks at the Hauptbahnhof and at the northern end of Porschestrasse. Alternatively, call **City Taxi** (☎ 230 223). **Zweirad Schael** (☎ 140 64; Kleiststrasse 5) hires out bicycles for €15 per day.

GÖTTINGEN

☎ 0551 / pop 121,500

Though short on sights, this historic town nestled in a corner of Lower Saxony near the Hesse border offers a good taste of university-town life in Germany's north. It was founded as a village in the mid-10th century, and since 1734, the year the Georg-August Universität was established here, Göttingen has sent more than 40 Nobel Prize winners into the world. As well as all those award-winning doctors and scientists, the fairy-tale-writing Brothers Grimm (as German linguistic teachers) and Prussian chancellor Otto von Bismarck (as a student) could quite rightly take their place at an alumni evening of all-time greats here.

Orientation

The circular city centre is surrounded by the ruins of an 18th-century wall and is divided by the Leinekanal (Leine Canal), an arm of the Leine River. The centre has a large pedestrianised mall, the hub of which is the Markt, a 10-minute walk east of the Hauptbahnhof.

Information

Gö-Card (1/3 days €5/12) Discount card offering free public transport and discounts on tours and museums.
Post office Groner Strasse (Groner Strasse 15-17; ⏰ 9am-6pm Mon-Fri, 10am-1pm Sat); main post office (Heinrich-von-Stephan-Strasse 1-5; ⏰ 8am-6pm Mon-Fri, 9am-1pm Sat) Near the Hauptbahnhof.
Tourist-Information Göttingen (☎ 499 800; www.goettingen-tourismus.de; Altes Rathaus, Markt 9;

⏰ 9am-6pm Mon-Fri, 10am-6pm Sat, 10am-4pm Sun Apr-Oct, 9.30am-6pm Mon-Fri, 10am-6pm Sat Nov-Mar) Has the bilingual English-German brochure Göttingen Komplett (€1) describing walks.
Universitätsklinikum (University hospital; ☎ 390; Robert-Koch-Strasse 40) Medical services.
Waschsalon (Ritterplan 3; per wash from €3.20; ⏰ 7am-10pm Mon-Sat) Laundry.

Sights & Activities

Rather than having any urgent must-sees, Göttingen is a mosaic of attractions that you'll most appreciate by walking around. Having existed since 953 at least, the town long had a protective network of walls and moats, and a walk around the 18th-century ramparts is recommended. These are earthy hummocks left from that time. It takes less than an hour to circumnavigate the city, the best starting point being the entrance near Cheltenham Park. This takes you past **Bismarckhäuschen** (Bismarck Cottages; ☎ 485 844; Im Hainberg; admission free; ⏰ 10am-1pm Tue, 3-5pm Thu & Sat), where the town fathers reputedly banished 18-year-old Otto for rowdy behaviour in 1833. This incident is probably apocryphal, but it's a matter of historical record that the future Iron Chancellor was later found guilty of witnessing an illegal duel. Nearby are two old **water mills**. The walk ends near the **Deutsches Theater** (☎ 496 90; Theaterplatz 11).

AROUND THE MARKT

The city's symbol, the **Gänseliesel** (the little goose girl) statue is hailed locally as the most kissed woman in the world – not a flattering moniker, some might think, but enough to make her iconic. After graduating, doctoral students climb up to peck her on the cheek – in icy conditions, some graduates go straight to the local clinic to repair a broken limb.

The nearby **Altes Rathaus** (⏰ 9.30am-6pm Mon-Fri, 10am-4pm Sat & Sun Apr-Oct, closed Sun Nov-Mar) was built in 1270 and once housed the merchants' guild; inside, later decorations added to its Great Hall include frescoes of the coats of arms of the Hanseatic cities and local bigwigs, grafted onto historic scenes.

BUILDINGS

Looking at some of Göttingen's half-timbered buildings is a pleasant way to while away some time. **Junkernschänke** (Barfüsserstrasse 5) is the prettiest, thanks to its colourful 16th-century Renaissance facade, behind

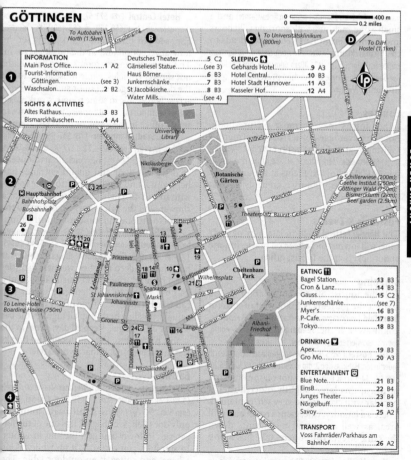

GÖTTINGEN

0 _____ 400 m
0 _____ 0.2 miles

INFORMATION
Main Post Office..................1 A2
Tourist-Information
Göttingen.....................(see 3)
Waschsalon.........................2 B2

SIGHTS & ACTIVITIES
Altes Rathaus.....................3 B3
Bismarckhäuschen.............4 A4

Deutsches Theater...............5 C2
Gänseliesel Statue.............(see 3)
Haus Börner........................6 B3
Junkernschänke..................7 B3
St Jacobikirche....................8 B3
Water Mills.......................(see 4)

SLEEPING
Gebhards Hotel...................9 A3
Hotel Central.....................10 B3
Hotel Stadt Hannover.......11 A3
Kasseler Hof......................12 A4

EATING
Bagel Station....................13 B3
Cron & Lanz......................14 B3
Gauss................................15 C2
Junkernschänke..............(see 7)
Myer's...............................16 B3
P-Cafe...............................17 B3
Tokyo................................18 B3

DRINKING
Apex.................................19 B3
Gro Mo.............................20 A3

ENTERTAINMENT
Blue Note.........................21 B3
EinsB................................22 B4
Junges Theater.................23 B4
Nörgelbuff........................24 B3
Savoy................................25 A2

TRANSPORT
Voss Fahrräder/Parkhaus am
Bahnhof...........................26 A2

LOWER SAXONY

---

which is an upmarket restaurant (see p647).
Haus Börner (Barfüsserstrasse 12) was built in 1536
and has the busy **Börnerviertel** alley behind it.
Kurze Strasse and Paulinerstrasse are also
worth exploring.

Among Göttingen's six Gothic churches,
the most interesting is the **St Jacobikirche**
(☎ 575 96; Jacobikirchhof; ☼ core hours 11am-3pm)
from 1361, off Weender Strasse. With eye-
catching red, white and grey angular striped
columns, it also features some contemporary
stained-glass windows.

PARKS & GARDENS
In the shadow of the old ramparts, the small
Botanische Gärten (Botanical Gardens; ☎ 395 755; www
.altgart.uni-goettingen.de, in German; Untere Karspüle 2; ad-

mission free; ☼ 8am-6.30pm) were Germany's first,
and there's a section devoted to mountain
plants, such as those from the Andes and
the Alps. The **tropical greenhouses** (admission free;
☼ 8am-3pm) are highly recommended in winter
for a shot of oxygen.

A 20-minute walk east of the Markt is the
Schillerwiese, a large park that backs onto forest. To reach it, follow Herzberger Landstrasse
east, then turn right into Merkelstrasse.

To enter **Göttinger Wald** (Göttingen Forest),
continue along Herzberger Landstrasse near
where it forms a hairpin bend, and turn into
Borheckstrasse. From there, a bitumen track
open to hikers and cyclists winds towards
Am Kehr, 45 minutes away, where there's
a small, Bavarian-style **beer garden** (☼ from

noon Mon-Fri, from 10am Sat & Sun, in fine weather) and a small game enclosure with snorting wild boars and Bambis. From Am Kehr a path leads to the **Bismarckturm** (www.bismarcktuerme.de, in German; adult/concession €2/1; 11.30am-6pm weekends & holidays Apr-Sep). This stone tower has pretty views over the Leine Valley.

Courses

Other towns may be more picture-book, but the advantages of learning German in Göttingen at its **Goethe Institut** (547 440; goettingen@goethe.de; Merkelstrasse 4) are that the town has 24,000 (fellow) students at the university and the university library is arguably the best in the country.

Festivals & Events

The **Händel Festival**, held in late May or early June, will interest those keen on music. Inquire about tickets at the tourist office.

Sleeping

Ask the tourist office about camping; the nearest site for tents is 15km west of town in **Dransfeld** (www.campingplatz-dransfeld.de). Another, 20km away at the **Seeburger See** (Lake Seeburg; www.seeburgersee.de, in German), is lakeside.

DJH hostel (576 22; www.djh-niedersachsen.de/jh /goettingen; Habichtsweg 2; dm under/over 27yr €23.20/26.20;) In a pleasant spot on the outskirts of town, this large, slightly older hostel is popular with cyclists and very self-contained. There's a laundry, cafe, games room and grill area, as well as several restaurants down the same street. To get here, take bus 6 or 9 to Jugendherberge.

Kasseler Hof (720 812; www.kasselerhof.de, in German; Rosdorfer Weg 26; s €55-59, d €79-89;) Most rooms in this once chintzy budget hotel have been refurbished and decorated to make it an appealing alternative to more expensive places in town. All rooms have bathrooms. Tucked away in a quiet corner not far from town, the hotel has its own restaurant.

Leine-Hotel Boarding House (505 10; www .leinehotel-goe.de; Groner Landstrasse 55; s €58-68, d €78-88, breakfast buffet €9.50;) A 10-minute walk from the centre on an insalubrious major street, this place is popular with visiting academics for longer stays (€540 per month), especially for the kitchenettes in every room and its business centre. It's large, with over 100 rooms, and generic looking, but a well-run operation.

Hotel Central (571 57; www.hotel-central.com; Jüdenstrasse 12; s €58-100, d €85-160;) Exposed red bricks and Miró prints set the tone at reception and in the breakfast room. The more expensive rooms here have baths not shower cubicles, while those at the top of the doubles range are junior suites. Free wi-fi access is available in some rooms, so ask ahead if this is important – otherwise you will have to set up office in the lobby or breakfast room.

Hotel Stadt Hannover (547 960; www.hotel stadthannover.de; Goetheallee 21; s €77-98, d €108-120, tr €145-165;) Beyond the art-nouveau etched glass door and quaint entrance hall here, you'll find modern, comfortable rooms with free wi-fi. There's a choice of bathtub or shower, and the prices vary according to the size of the room and standard of furnishing.

our pick Gebhards Hotel (496 80; www.romantik hotels.com/goettingen; Goetheallee 22-23; s €96-140, d €145-190;) This quaint, elegant four-star hotel has art-deco touches, wellness facilities like a large whirlpool and small sauna, and a 24-hour bar in its excellent restaurant. You can take breakfast any time of day here, so it's actually possible to stay up all night in the bar sipping champagne, sleep all day, sweat in the sauna, plunge into the whirlpool, and breakfast in the evening, if that's your style.

Eating

Bagel Station (489 4661; Weender Strasse 60; bagels €1.80-3.90; 8.30am-8pm Mon-Fri, 9am-7pm Sat, 11am-6pm Sun;) This small bagel joint not only does delicious bagels, it is one of the few eateries in town that gets the sun in winter. In summer, you can soak it up while taking a bagel and coffee at an outdoor table. The minimum order for delivery is between €8 and €15, depending on distance from the centre.

Cron & Lanz (560 22; Weender Strasse 25; cake €2.50 snacks €2-4, chocolate per 100g €5; 8am-7pm Mon-Fri 8.30am-6.30pm Sat, 1-7pm Sun;) This ornate Viennese-style cafe is Göttingen's dignified haunt for connoisseurs of chocolate and other calorie bombs, but it has a few snacks too.

P-Cafe (576 99; Nikolaikirchhof 11; cake €2.30, breakfast €3.50-16.50, light dishes €4-7.50; 9am-10pm Sun-Thu 9am-midnight Fri & Sat;) While the tables are cheek by jowl and it gets cramped in poor weather, this cafe-bar serving snacks is one of the nicest for outdoor seating in summer. If it gets cold, you can wrap up in one of the blankets provided. Its quiet location makes it especially good if you've got toddlers in tow.

Myer's (☎ 499 7888; Lange-Geismar-Strasse 47; dishes €4.40-11; ❂ 9am-midnight Mon-Sat, 10am-11pm Sun, closed Sun Jul-Aug; ✖ Ⓥ) This rambling cafe-bar and restaurant is great if you can handle the noise. Every now and again the very skilled chefs whip up a delicious surprise or two to complement pastas, salads, pancakes, pizzas and vegetarian or meat dishes on its large year-round or smaller seasonal menus. Smokers can sit upstairs.

Tokyo (☎ 999 5735; Gotmarstrasse 16; mains €8-14, sushi platters €16-21; ❂ lunch & dinner Tue-Sat, dinner Sun; ✖ Ⓥ) In the simple exposed-pine and bamboo interior here, the lone sushi chef works hard to turn out customers' orders, including the usual *maki* and *nigiri* sushi, tempura and *gyoza*. Tofu and vegetarian options are available, and there's even Korean beef and kimchi.

our pick **Junkernschänke** (☎ 384 8380; www.junkern schaenke.de, in German; Barfüsserstrasse 5; bistro mains €10-23, 3-7 course restaurant menus €45-79; ❂ 10am-midnight Mon-Thu, 10am-1am Fri & Sat, 10am-11pm Sun; ✖ Ⓥ) Behind the colourful timbers of one of the city's oldest buildings you find an Old World bistro and an upmarket restaurant, both sharpened up with a New World edge. Upstairs you can hang off the bar in fine style, sipping delicious wines and more, while a piano tinkles out a lounge feel. It also has classical and other music during its frequent events.

Gauss (☎ 566 16; www.restaurant-gauss.de; Obere Karspüle 22, enter on Theaterstrasse; 3-5 course menu €35-56; ❂ 6pm-midnight Tue-Sat; ✖ Ⓥ) Chef Jacqueline Amirfallah upholds this cellar restaurant's reputation as Göttingen's best gourmet experience with exquisite (and changing) haute cuisine, such as lamb in aubergine, mint yogurt, red lentils and couscous. There's a noticeable emphasis on seasonal ingredients.

Drinking

P-Cafe (opposite) and Myer's (left) are as much popular drinking holes as places to nibble and nosh, and Junkernschänke has a classy lounge bar. Explore eating and drinking options on the square in front of the Junges Theater or along Goetheallee.

Gro Mo (☎ 488 9232; Goetheallee 13a; ❂ 9.30am-midnight Mon-Thu, 9.30am-1am Fri, 9.30am-2am Sat, 10am-8pm Sun; ✖) Patrons nurse huge mugs of coffee or even bigger steins of beer at this funky Goetheallee hang-out. As they're strewn all over the place, it's a great spot to pick up flyers and local magazines. While on Goetheallee, also check out the other options near the small bridge.

Apex (☎ 447 71; Burgstrasse 46; ❂ from 5pm Mon-Sat, from 6pm Sun; ✖) An academic and generally older crowd (40s to 50s) comes to sup a range of wines in this dark-wood bistro, attached to a cabaret venue and art gallery. Mostly it's open till about midnight. The food can be hit and miss, but the chilli con carne is usually 'hit'.

LOWER SAXONY

KEEPING THE DAY JOB *Anthony Haywood*

Although quite a few pubs in Germany put on 'open stage' events, the ones in Göttingen at **Nörgelbuff** (☎ 384 8262; www.noergelbuff.de, in German; Groner Strasse 23; ❂ from 9pm or 9.30pm) can be a lot of fun.

Nörgelbuff mostly stages live music acts, especially local ones, but it's three of the regular spots that I enjoy the most. One of these is the Querbeat (Offbeat), held every second Monday of the month, which is a jam session for bands. Another, the Gong Show, is what it sounds like – open slather for young and old with the prospect of being 'gonged' humiliatingly off stage. Some weird and creative things happen during this round. The folks at Nörgelbuff were rethinking the show in 2009, so check the program or website to see if one's currently happening.

The Open Stage Unplugged events are my personal favourite. On a good night the cellar is packed with students, day-jobbers, hangers-out and discerning punters and drinkers. We've even seen the barman here get up to play guitar backing to Robbie Williams' 'Let Me Entertain You'. Some people arrive as audience and leave as 'artists'. If you want to run through a few covers or try out some of your own material, you'll find an acoustic guitar, usually a keyboard – sometimes even an old Fender Rhodes electric piano – and a mike at the ready. Sessions rarely end before 2am. Time your visit for the fourth or fifth (if there's one) Monday of the month.

Entertainment

German-language *Pony* is your best bet for information about individual gigs and club nights.

Savoy (☎ 789 6790; www.club-savoy.de; Berliner Strasse 5; entry €3-6; ⏰ 10pm-5am Wed, Sat & Sun; ✗) Dress up, for only sleek and trendy beings are waved through easily at Göttingen's leading and most glamorous club. Playing mainstream and house music, it's spread over a couple of levels, with a chilled-out lounge below the main floor (with bar and go-go podium).

EinsB (www.einsb.de; Nikolaistrasse 1b; ⏰ from 11pm Fri & Sat; ✗) Friday nights concentrate on new-wave guitar music, Britpop etc, while on Saturday things take a turn for the electronic in this laid-back, younger club above a pipe-smoking Turkish lounge.

Blue Note (☎ 469 07; www.club-bn.de; Wilhelmsplatz 3; entry €3.50-10; ⏰ from 9pm Wed-Sun; ✗) Right next to the university *Mensa* (canteen), the Blue Note has regular live bands and theme dance nights, including salsa, urban club, tropical and even Persian.

Junges Theater (☎ 495 015; www.junges-theater .de; Hospitalstrasse 6; entry €13) Göttingen's Junges Theater has been on the scene since the late 1950s and enjoys a high reputation throughout Germany; this was where Switzerland's most famous contemporary actor, Bruno Gans, began his career.

Getting There & Away

There are frequent direct ICE services north to Hanover (€32, 35 minutes) and Hamburg (€61, two hours) or south to Frankfurt (€58, 1¾ hours) and Munich (€100, 3¾ hours). ICE services also go to Berlin-Hauptbahnhof (€72, 2¼ hours). Direct regional services go to Kassel (€13.30, one hour) and Weimar (€26.10, two hours), but you'll have to change trains to get to Goslar (€15.20, 1¼ hours).

Göttingen is on the A7 running north–south. The closest entrance is 3km southwest along Kasseler Landstrasse, an extension of Groner Landstrasse. The Fairy-Tale Road (B27) runs southwest to the Weser River and northeast to the Harz Mountains.

Getting Around

Single bus tickets cost €1.90, while 24-hour tickets are €4.40.

There are taxi ranks at the Hauptbahnhof and behind the Altes Rathaus. To call one, ring ☎ 340 34.

Bikes can be hired from **Voss Fahrräder/ Parkhaus am Bahnhof** (☎ 59 994; Am Bahnhof; per day €11; ⏰ 9am-1pm & 2-7pm Mon-Fri, 10am-4pm Sat).

WEST OF HANOVER

OSNABRÜCK

☎ 0541 / pop 163,000

'Zum Glück komm' ich aus Osnabrück', locals boast of their good luck to come from this city; and that's something you most understand at night, wandering the winding lamp-lit streets of the old town, past ornate half-timbered houses.

But this historic heartland is now offset by a contemporary building that has overtaken interest in Osnabrück's native son Erich Maria Remarque, author of the WWI classic *All Quiet on the Western Front*, and truly eclipsed Osnabrück's claim to be where the Thirty Years' War ended in 1648. The construction in question is the Felix-Nussbaum-Haus, by leading world architect Daniel Libeskind.

Orientation

Osnabrück's egg-shaped city centre is divided into the northern Altstadt and the southern Neustadt, with the east–west Neumarkt drawing a line across the middle. The Hauptbahnhof is on the town's eastern edge. To reach the centre from the station takes about 15 minutes, going straight ahead along Möserstrasse, turning left at the Kaufhof building into Wittekindstrasse and then right into Grosser Strasse. When you come to the Domhof, continue left along Krahnstrasse to the tourist office. Pick up the free city map from the DB Service Point at the train station before setting out.

Information

There's an ATM in the Hauptbahnhof.
Main post office (Theodor-Heuss-Platz 6-9; ⏰ 8am-7pm Mon-Fri, to 2pm Sat)
Osnabrück Marketing & Tourismus (☎ 323 2202; www.osnabrueck.de, in German; Bierstrasse 22/23; ⏰ 9.30am-6pm Mon-Fri, 10am-4pm Sat)

Sights

FELIX-NUSSBAUM-HAUS

Shaped like an interconnected series of concrete shards, with slit windows and sloping floors, the **Felix-Nussbaum-Haus** (☎ 323 2207, 323

2237; Lotter Strasse 2; adult/concession €5/3; 🕙 11am-6pm Tue-Fri, 10am-6pm Sat & Sun) is an older, slightly more neglected sister of Libeskind's famous Jewish Museum Berlin. Inside is a collection of works by the Osnabrück-born Jewish painter Felix Nussbaum (1904–44). His works reveal shades of Van Gogh and Henri Rousseau, and Libeskind's 1988 building uses space magnificently to illustrate the absence of orientation in Nussbaum's eventful and tragic life. In 1944, after several years in exile, arrest in Belgium and successful escape in France, he was denounced and finally deported from Belgium to Auschwitz, where he died. Today the museum shares an entrance with the **Kulturgeschichtliches Museum** (entry included in price), which has graphics cabinets, also designed by Libeskind, holding works by Albrecht Dürer.

MARKT & AROUND

It was on the **Rathaus** (admission free; 🕙 8am-8pm Mon-Fri, 9am-4pm Sat, 10am-4pm Sun) steps that the Peace of Westphalia was proclaimed on 25 October 1648, ending the Thirty Years' War. The preceding peace negotiations were conducted partly in Münster, about 60km south, and partly in the Rathaus' **Friedenssaal** (Peace Hall). On the left as you enter the Rathaus are portraits of the negotiators. Also have a look around the **Schatzkammer** (Treasure Chamber) opposite, especially for the 13th-century *Kaiserpokal* (Kaiser goblet).

The four richly ornamented cross gables of the **Marienkirche** loom above the square, painstakingly rebuilt after burning down during WWII. Opposite, the small **Erich Maria Remarque Friedenszentrum** (Erich Maria Remarque Peace Centre; 🕾 323 2109; www.remarque.uos.de; Markt 6; admission free; 🕙 10am-1pm & 3-5pm Tue-Fri, 11am-5pm Sat & Sun) uses photos and documents to chronicle the writer's life (1898–1970) and work.

Various **half-timbered houses** survived WWII. At Bierstrasse 24 is the baroque Romantik Hotel Walhalla (p650), with a portal flanked by cheeky cherubs. At Krahnstrasse 4 you'll find a beautiful house (1533), with a cafe taking up the ground floor. The best of the bunch is the Renaissance **Haus Willmann** (1586) at No 7, with its carved circular motifs and small relief of Adam and Eve.

Just north of Heger Tor and Felix-Nussbaum-Haus you find the 28m-high **Bucksturm** (Bockturm; 🕾 323 2152; Bocksmauer; adult/concession €3/1; 🕙 11am-5pm Sun), built as a watch-tower inside the town wall in the 13th century and later used as a prison. Then, in the 16th and 17th centuries, those accused of being witches were tortured here. Today, it has an exhibition on the persecution of 'witches', explaining why and how it took place.

Sleeping

The free city map from the tourist office and DB Service Point has hotels marked and numbered. Ask the tourist office about camping, about 5km northeast of town.

Penthouse Backpackers (🕾 600 9606; www.penthouse bp.com; Möserstrasse 19; dm €14-16, s €28-32, d €36-40; 🖳) The furniture looks like it's been cobbled together from friends of the owner (because it has been!) and check-in is only from 8am to 11am and 5pm to 8pm (so call ahead), yet you can't beat the warmth of the welcome here. Handily located for the train station, this 4th-floor establishment has a kitchen, big guest lounge room, a sauna and a leafy terrace great for summer barbecues.

ourpick Intour Hotel (🕾 963 860; www.intour hotel.de; Maschstrasse 10; s €45-55, d €75-90; 🅿 ⊗ 🛜) Situated just outside the historic centre and handy to Felix-Nussbaum-Haus (see opposite), this hotel looks unprepossessing from the outside but is modern, cosy and immaculately clean inside. Above all, it is fantastic value and a 10-minute walk to the eating and drinking spots in the lively Heger-Tor-Viertel. Take buses 31, 32 or 33 to Weissenburgstrasse from the train station or Neuer Markt.

Dom Hotel (🕾 358 350; www.dom-hotel-osnabrueck.de; Kleine Domsfreiheit 5; s €57-75, d €87-97, tr €111; 🅿 ⊗ 🛜) Rooms here are comfortable and cheery in Mediterranean yellowy-orange, but they don't exude bags of atmosphere. That's left to the friendly owner, who always seems ready to help and chat, even when busy.

Advena Hotel Hohenzollern (🕾 331 70; www .advenahotels.com; Theodor-Heuss-Platz 5; s €76-90, d €116-155; 🅿 ⊗ 🛜 🍴) You won't have to stray far from the trains for one of the 113 rooms in this hotel – it is opposite the train station and therefore especially convenient for business and conference guests. But it also has a few surprises (which you wouldn't guess from the outside): functional but nevertheless pleasant rooms, an even more pleasant 8m-or-so pool and a sauna area (free), and an (unaffiliated) fitness space allowing guests use of workout facilities for €6 per day.

Romantik Hotel Walhalla (☎ 349 10; www.hotel
-walhalla.de; Bierstrasse 24; s €89-100, d €110-125, ste €295-
350; P ✗ ☎) If you're looking for historic
atmosphere, this hotel has it aplenty. The half
that's housed in a traditional half-timbered
building has higgledy-piggledy rooms with
low-beamed ceilings and rustic features. Even
rooms in the more modern half continue the
theme. Wi-fi is expensive but you can plug
your laptop into the high-speed internet connection in the foyer.

Steigenberger Hotel Remarque (☎ 609 60; www
.osnabrueck.steigenberger.de, in German; Natruper-Tor-Wall
1; s €82-219, d €99-335; P ✗ 🖳 ☎) Overlooking
the old town from a small hill, this modern
four-star hotel offers the unusual combination of quiet and convenience. A glass lift
takes you up to tasteful rooms decorated in
Mediterranean-style sienna and blues, with
portraits and mementos of Erich Maria
Remarque dotted around. Prices are subject
mainly to current demand, so check the web
or call.

Eating & Drinking

Ichiban Sushi Chami (☎ 259 9504; Kamp 80; sushi
€0.50-2.50, sushi combinations €6.80-17.50; ⓦ 11am-8pm
Mon-Fri, to 6pm Sat; ✗ V) It took some time for
sushi to make a landing in Osnabrück, and
this excellent eat-in and takeaway place was
the first to touch ground. It is popular with
workers and students alike, and with those
taking a break from reading in the nearby
university library.

Tristan (☎ 350 2401; Heger Strasse 12; pizza €5.50-
10.50, mains €16.50-22; ⓦ lunch & dinner Tue-Sun; ✗ V)
This homely, family-friendly Italian *osteria*
(inn) has chunky dark-wood tables and a tiled
floor that combine well with white walls hung
with art. It's so large that toddlers will find
enough room to explore. If dining alone, you'll
find *Der Spiegel* and other magazines here for
browsing. Beyond the pizza and pasta, the
menu is small, changing and meat-focused;
the house red wine, very decent.

Hausbrauerei Rampendahl (☎ 245 35; Hasestrasse
35; light meals €6.40-21; ⓦ 11am-11pm Mon-Sat, to 9.30pm
Sun; ✗) This restaurant and boutique brewery is about as hearty as they come, serving
full meals or substantial 'light' dishes to accompany the own-brew beers. It has various
cheaper and ever-changing lunch or dinner
deals like a *Stammessen* (staple; €5.95) –
typically a beer goulash with cabbage and
dumplings.

Arabesque (☎ 260 363; Osterberger Reihe 12; mains
€7-14.50; ⓦ 4.30pm-midnight Mon-Thu, 4.30pm-1am Fri,
11am-1am Sat, 3.30-11pm Sun; ✗ V) The friendly
couple who own this Middle Eastern restaurant and hookah place (you retreat to the
cushions in the special smoking room) once
lived in Sydney's Bondi Beach. It's a superb
haunt with good food and outdoor seating in
the self-styled 'Hanse Kogge' square. The latter takes its name from the boat that stands in
the children's playground out front – another
good reason to visit. While here, also check
out other places nearby.

ourpick **Restaurant La Vie** (☎ 331 150; www
.restaurant-lavie.de; Krahnstrasse 1/2; menu €114-158; ⓦ dinner Tue-Sat; ✗) La Vie, which has established itself
recently as one of Germany's top restaurants
(with two Michelin stars in 2009), is where
head chef Thomas Bühner and his Sri Lankan
partner Thayarni Kanagaratnam highlight
the aromas and harmony of European cuisine
with hints of the east. One of the specialities
is reindeer filet gently flavoured with garlic,
coriander, apple puree and Sichuan pepper oil.
Reserve at least one or two weeks ahead, and
for Friday and Saturday, at least three. You can
occasionally fill a cancellation at short notice
by calling on the day.

Osnabrück has a wonderful range of
pubs (most open in the evening only) that
also serve simple, inexpensive food. These
include the traditional **Grüne Gans** (☎ 239 14
Grosse Gildewart 15; mains €3.50-7.50; ⓦ from 6pm Mon-Sat
from 5pm Sun; ✗).

If you follow Grosse Gildewart south,
it becomes Rolandsmauer, where you find
Lagerhalle (☎ 338 740; www.lagerhalle-osnabrueck.de;
Rolandsmauer 26; ⓦ 8pm-1am Mon, 6pm-1am Tue-Thu
6pm-2am Fri & Sat, 9.30am-11pm Sun; ✗), a culture
venue, cinema and bar with everything
from readings through film to live jazz or
rock. *Cultcha* seekers of all ages simply
drink, snack or play pool here, too. Outside
is a board listing other places to go to in
Heger-Tor-Viertel, inviting exploration of
the quarter.

Getting There & Away

The low-cost carrier **Air Berlin** (www.airberlin
.com) is among those with services to **Münster-
Osnabrück airport** (FMO; www.flughafen.fmo.de). The
airport is 30km southwest of the centre
and reached by Schnellbus X150 (€9, 40
minutes), which leaves the airport almost
hourly between 3.30am and 11pm Monday

to Friday, from 8.10am Saturday and from 10am Sunday.

RE (€23, 1½ hours) and IC (€27, 1¼ hours) trains to Hanover leave twice an hour. Various services go to Hamburg (€46, one hour 50 minutes), Cologne (€40, two hours 10 minutes) and Dortmund (€23, 55 minutes). For Hamelin (€17.60, 1½ hours) you change at Bünde.

Osnabrück is well connected by road via the A1 (Bremen to Dortmund) and the B51, B65 and B68.

Getting Around

Single bus tickets cost €1.90 and day tickets €4 (so buy a day ticket).

Call a taxi on ☎ 277 81 or ☎ 320 11.

VARUSSCHLACHT MUSEUM & PARK KALKRIESE

You needn't be a history buff to come to the Varusschlacht Museum & Park Kalkriese (☎ 05468-920 4200; www.kalkriese-varusschlacht.de; Bramsche-Kalkriese; adult/concession/family €7/4/16; ⌚ 10am-6pm Apr-Oct, 10am-5pm Nov-Mar), although by the time you leave you'll have probably acquired an interest. It was long known that rebellious Germanic tribes had won a major victory over their Roman masters somewhere in the Osnabrück region in AD 9 – defeating three of military commander Publius Quinctilius Varus' legions.

However, only in 1987 was this likely candidate for the site of the so-called 'Battle of Teutoberg Forest' uncovered near Kalkriese. In 2000, the battlefield was opened as an archaeological park to display the Germans' dirt ramparts and explain how they did it. Two years later, a funky steel-clad museum was built by famous Swiss architectural duo Annette Gigon and Mike Guyer. In 2009 a new Visitor Center by the same architects was unveiled, and part of this building is used for changing exhibitions. Also in 2009, two millennia after the Battle of Teutoberg, an inaugural exhibition was held on the theme 'Conflict', which focused on why the Germanic tribes were so successful in battle against the Romans. Meanwhile, a permanent exhibition in a 40m rectangular tower from 2002 has also been revamped, and here you can find so-called Schlachtschrott (battle debris) such as battle masks, bells, spearheads and other finds.

The surrounding park and battlefield features three quirky pavilions, called 'seeing', 'hearing' and 'questioning'. Using a camera obscura, huge ear trumpet and video technology respectively, they give you a quirky perspective on the battlefield.

Unless you have your own car, you must plan your visit to Kalkriese carefully, as bus services are sparse. Take bus X275 from Osnabrück's main train station (€3.20, 50 minutes). Sometimes you will need to change at Herringhausen Leckermühle, but the bus driver will make an announcement. Check return bus times when you arrive. If you come in summer, there's a restaurant and beer garden where you can while away any waiting time.

OLDENBURG

☎ 0441 / pop 159,500

Being shuffled between Danish and German rule has left the relaxed capital of the Weser-Ems region with a somewhat difficult-to-pin-down identity. Most of its medieval buildings were destroyed in a huge fire in 1676, while others were later refashioned at various stages according to the prevailing architectural style of the time. Count Peter Friedrich Ludwig began redecorating the town in a neoclassical style in 1785, evidence of which still survives in the Schlosspark, its promenade and other nearby buildings.

Today it's principally a business destination, but you might make a day-trip from Bremen if you're a mummy fan, or stop over on the way to the East Frisian Islands.

Orientation

Oldenburg's pedestrianised core is bounded by Heiligengeistwall to the north, Theaterwall to the west and Schlosswall to the south. Turn right after you exit from the 'Stadtmitte' side of the Hauptbahnhof (Bahnhof Süd), which takes you along Moslestrasse. Turn left into Osterstrasse, which takes you to Achternstrasse in the city centre. Turn left and continue until you come to the Markt. The tourist office is in a street one block northwest of this; look for the signs.

Information

Main post office (Bahnhofsplatz 10; ⌚ 8am-6pm Mon-Fri, 9am-1pm Sat)

Oldenburg Tourismus (☎ 3616 1366; www.oldenburg-tourist.de; Kleine Kirchenstrasse 14; ⌚ 10am-6pm Mon-Fri, to 2pm Sat) Has maps and accommodation guides that are also available from the DB Service Point inside the train station.

Sights

The pale-yellow Renaissance-baroque **Schloss** (1607) at the southern end of the Altstadt shopping district (on Schlossplatz, just south of the Markt) was once home to the counts and dukes of Oldenburg. Part of the same family governed Denmark briefly in the 15th century.

Inside is the **Landesmuseum für Kunst und Kulturgeschichte** (Museum of Art & Cultural History; ☎ 220 7300; www.landesmuseum-oldenburg.niedersachsen.de, in German; adult/concession incl Augusteum & Prinzenpalais €3/1.50; ✆ 9am-5pm Tue, Wed & Fri, to 8pm Thu, 10am-5pm Sat & Sun), which chronicles the area's history from the Middle Ages. On the 1st floor, you'll find the Idyllenzimmer with 44 paintings by court artist Heinrich Wilhelm Tischbein, a friend of Goethe, which explains why he was often known by his double-banger moniker 'Goethe-Tischbein'. Take bus 315 from the train station (platform B) to Festungsgraben.

Behind the Schloss is the sprawling English-style **Schlosspark**. The neoclassical building you see across the square from the Schloss is **Die Neue Wache** (1839), once a city guardhouse but now part of a bank.

Just across the bridge, the revivalist **Augusteum** (☎ 220 7300; Elisabethstrasse 1; included in Landesmuseum ticket; ✆ same hours) was built in 1857 in the style of the Italian Renaissance expressly as Oldenburg's first art gallery. Today it showcases European paintings – with a strong focus on Italian and Dutch masters – from the 16th to the 18th century. The gallery also features changing exhibitions. The third in the Landesmuseum triumvirate is the **Prinzenpalais** (☎ 220 7300; Damm 1; included in Landesmuseum ticket; ✆ same hours), which focuses on German artists, beginning with Romanticism and neoclassicism of the mid-19th century and culminating in post-1945 artists such as Ernst Wilhelm Nay (1902–68) and Willy Baumeister (1889–1955), and GDR artists popular in the 1980s, like Bernhard Heisig (b 1935). Damm runs southeast from Schlossplatz. Both of these are near the corner of Elisabethstrasse (take bus 315 to Staatsarchiv stop).

Another highlight of Oldenburg is the **Landesmuseum Natur und Mensch** (Natural History Museum; ☎ 924 4300; www.naturundmensch.de, in German; Damm 38-44; adult/concession €5/2.50; ✆ 9am-5pm Tue-Fri, 10am-5pm Sat & Sun). Covering the ecology of Lower Saxony's various landscapes, its most famous exhibit is a huge chunk (or wall) of peat bog, with three niches containing bod-

ies from the Roman period originally found preserved in surrounding moors in the 1930s and '40s.

Sleeping & Eating

DJH hostel (☎ 871 35; http://oldenburg.jugendherberge-nordwesten.de; Alexanderstrasse 65; dm under/over 27yr €18.90/21.90; P ✗) It is highly advisable to book ahead for this large and rambling hostel. Drawbacks are that it closes at midnight and is also closed for check-in between noon and 5pm. Staff, though, is helpful and it is about 20 minutes by foot north of the Hauptbahnhof, or take bus 302 or 303 to Von-Finckh-Strasse.

Hotel Tafelfreuden (☎ 832 27; www.tafelfreuden-hotel.de; Alexanderstrasse 23; s €63-75, d €90-100, apt €129; P ✗ ✆ V) This interesting hotel changes concepts every couple of years. One time its rooms were styled on the theme of countries, more recently it takes the theme of colour (and mostly food), with things like 'vanilla', 'chilli' and 'lavender' providing the inspiration for tones. Rooms are mostly a good size, and the atmosphere is chirpy, enhanced by a large glass-enclosed seating area and an outdoor terrace. The menu of the restaurant downstairs also changes considerably, but always offers two meat and two fish mains, plus a vegetarian dish and pastas (mains €12 to €25). Take bus 315 to Humboldtstrasse stop.

For eating options simply cruise along pedestrianised **Wallstrasse**, north of the Markt.

Getting There & Around

There are trains at least once an hour to Bremen (€7.10, 30 minutes) and Osnabrück (€19.40, 1¼ hours). From Oldenburg, there are trains north to Emden (€15.20, 70 minutes) and beyond.

Oldenburg is at the crossroads of the A29 to/from Wilhelmshaven and the A28 (Bremen–Dutch border).

Single bus tickets (valid for one hour) for the entire city cost €2; short trips are only €1.50, and day passes €5.60. Buy your tickets from the driver. **Fahrrad Station Oldenburg** (☎ 218 8250; Hauptbahnhof; ✆ 6.30am-8pm Mon-Sat) rents out bicycles for €7 per day.

EMDEN & AROUND

☎ 04921 / pop 51,700

You're almost in Holland here, and it shows from the flat landscape, dikes and windmills outside Emden to the lackadaisical manner in

SLOW TRAVEL IN EAST FRISIA

Train connections are pretty good in parts of the East Frisian region, but to really get out and explore it, you're better off walking, riding a bicycle, paddling or, if the legs are too tired from walking the Wadden Sea (see the boxed text, p656), taking a bus. During the season from mid-March to October, the *Urlauberbus* service allows you to travel on any bus, no matter how far it's going, for €1. Each time you change buses, you pay again, but if you're in no rush, you can go, say, from Oldenburg to Emden (€3) and via the 'dike country' along the coast down to Jever (from Emden, €4) on a slow jaunt over a few days. Pick up a free copy of the *Urlauberbus für'n euro* map from Jever, Emden or another of the local tourist offices, or check out the website www.urlauberbus. info (in German). This is one region where you might have a good time getting stranded.

If you want to combine kayaking or Canadian canoe paddling with cycling in East Frisia, the easiest way to do it is by using some of the 21 **'Paddel und Pedal' stations** (www.paddel-und-pedal .de, in German). You can paddle to one, hire another kayak there, or switch to bicycle, and choose your next destination/station, making for a varied and environmentally friendly way of getting around. To give just one of many options, from **Emden** (Paddel- und Pedalstation Emden; ☎ 0160-369 2739, 04921-890 7219; Marienwehrster Zwinger 13) you can hire a single kayak (€17), paddle about 11km (three hours) to the quarry lake **Grosses Meer** (Paddel- und Pedalstation Grosses Meer; ☎ 04942-576 838; Langer Weg 25, in Südbrookmerland), which is in parts a nature reserve, then change to a bicycle (€6.50 per day) and ride back, or further into East Frisia. Local tourist offices can help if you need planning or language help.

which locals pedal their bikes across the town's canal bridges. The Dutch as well as Germans have shaped Emden, and the local Plattdütsch dialect sounds like a combination of English, German and – guess what? – Dutch. While in most senses Emden stoically defies the adjective 'spectacular', two museums (both closed on Mondays, so avoid coming on that day) here and the pretty coastal landscape of its environs do make it fascinating.

Orientation

Emden's train and bus stations are about a 10-minute walk west of the city centre. As you exit, take the road heading right, which will lead to Grosse Strasse and the small medieval harbour and centre called Ratsdelft.

Information

Tourist-Information Emden im Pavillon am Stadtgarten (10am-6pm Mon-Fri, 10am-2pm Sat) Just north of the central Ratsdelft harbour, near the car park and taxi stand.

Tourist-Information im Bahnhof (☎ 974 00; www.emden-touristik.de; Bahnhofsplatz 11; 8am-6pm Mon-Fri, 10am-4pm Sat, also 11am-3pm Sun Apr-Oct) Main tourist office, with an efficient hotel and private-room booking service.

Sights & Activities

Most people visit Emden for two reasons: either business with its mainstay, the local Volkswagen factory, or en route to the East Frisian Islands. Emden, though, has an unusually good **Kunsthalle** (☎ 975 050; www .kunsthalle-emden.de, in German; Hinter dem Rahmen 13; adult/concession €8/6; 10am-5pm Tue-Fri, 11am-5pm Sat & Sun), thanks to local boy Henri Nannen. The founder of the magazine *Stern* (a glossy news weekly à la *Time* or *Newsweek*), he made his private collection available to the town when he retired. Focusing on 20th-century art, its white-and-exposed-timber, light-flooded rooms show off a range of big, bold canvases. There are some works by Max Beckmann, Erich Heckel, Alex Jawlensky, Oskar Kokoschka, Franz Marc, Emil Nolde and Max Pechstein, although most of the artists are more obscure. Several times a year, the museum closes its doors for a week while exhibitions are changed. Follow the signs from the tourist office.

The award-winning **Ostfriesisches Landesmuseum** (Regional History Museum; ☎ 872 058; www .landesmuseum-emden.de, in German; Rathaus, Brückstrasse 1; adult/child under 12yr €6/free; 10am-6pm Tue-Sun) is another highlight. This has an interesting and varied collection illustrating themes of local history and life in the region. Not surprisingly, its picture gallery has a strong focus on Dutch artists. In the late 16th century a large number of Protestant Dutch fled to Emden to escape religious persecution in the Spanish-ruled low countries, and ships even set out from Emden,

LOWER SAXONY

the so-called 'Sea Beggars', to prey on Spanish and Dutch trading vessels. Glass painting established itself here during that time, and later the Emden-born painter Ludolf Backhuysen returned to work here. Today his work forms the backbone of the picture gallery. Other sections of the museum cover the Frisian coast and cartography, prehistory and 20th-century landscape painting; a highlight is a stunning collection of armour.

The labyrinth of WWII civilian air-raid shelters at the **Bunkermuseum** (☎ 322 25; www .bunkermuseum.de, in German; Holzsägerstrasse; adult/child €2/1; ⏱ 10am-1pm & 3-5pm Tue-Fri, 10am-1pm Sat & Sun May-Oct) includes testimonies from those who sheltered here, offering a moving insight into part of recent history.

Harbour cruises run by **EMS** (☎ 890 70; www .ag-ems.de, in German) leave several times daily between early April and late October from the Delfttreppe steps in the harbour (adult/child €6.90/3). The company also runs services to the East Frisian Island of Borkum (p659) and North Frisian Island of Helgoland (p724).

The tourist offices have information on canal tours and canoe hire, and can give tips on a favoured East Frisian past-time – cycling (see the boxed text, p653).

Sleeping & Eating

The tourist office at the train station is a well-run outfit with a walk-in and advance room-booking service. Options are not abundant, so it pays to use it.

DJH hostel (☎ 237 97; www.jugendherberge.de/jh /emden; An der Kesselschleuse 5, off Thorner Strasse; dm under/ over 27yr €18.10/21.10; ⏱ closed Nov-Feb; P ✗ ☐) With some dorms in stand-alone bungalows, this place feels more like a holiday camp than a hostel. Popular with schools and other groups, its canal-side location offers plenty of swimming, canoeing and cycling opportunities. Take bus 3003 to Realschule/Am Herrentor.

Heerens Hotel (☎ 237 40; www.heerenshotel.de, in German; Friedrich-Ebert-Strasse 67; s €55-79, d €69-103, ste €128; P ✗ ☎) The generously sized rooms here are comfortable, better value and as good as – if not better than – those of other hotels in its vicinity. Next door is an inexpensive Serbian restaurant. Wi-fi, though, is with a credit card and expensive.

Goldener Adler (☎ 927 30; Neutorstrasse 5; s/d from €73/88) Rooms here are comfortable but tending to small; it is right in the centre of town and on the water.

Hotel am Boltentor (☎ 972 70; fax 972 733; Hinter dem Rahmen 10; s/d €76/98; P ✗) Hidden by trees from the main road nearby and just a minute from the Kunsthalle, this homey red-brick hotel has possibly the best location in town plus comfy and well-equipped rooms.

Carlino Osteria Enoteca (☎ 923 080; Alter Markt 9; pizza & pasta €5-9, meat & fish mains €16.50-22; ⏱ lunch & dinner Tue-Sun; ✗ V) This Italian restaurant near the tourist office pavilion offers more than the run-of-the-mill traditional fish and meat dishes you find around the centre.

Emden is not really the place for outrageous nights, but if you came here under the delusion it was, then explore Neuer Markt, where you can unearth a place to hip-hop and a couple of cafes and bars.

Getting There & Around

Emden is connected by rail to Oldenburg (€15.20, 70 minutes) and Bremen (€23, 1¾ hours). Despite its relative remoteness, the town is easily and quickly reached via the A31, which connects with the A28 from Oldenburg and Bremen. The B70/B210 runs north from Emden to other towns in Friesland and to the coast.

Emden is small enough to be explored on foot but also has a bus system (€1.10 per trip). The best transport method is the bicycle (see the boxed text, p653).

JEVER

☎ 04461 / pop 13,900

Famous for its pilsner beer, the capital of the Friesland region also has a secondary motif. The face of 'Fräulein Maria' peers out from attractions and shop windows alike. She was the last of the so-called *Häuptlinge* (chieftains) to rule the town in the Middle Ages, and although Russia's Catherine the Great got her hands on Jever for a time in the 18th century, locals always preferred their home-grown queen. Having died unmarried and a virgin, Maria is the German equivalent of England's (in truth more worldly) Elizabeth I.

With its Russian-looking castle, Jever is worth a brief visit, probably en route to the East Frisian Islands.

Orientation

Most of Jever's attractions are within a few hundred metres of each other in the eastern section of the Altstadt around the Schloss. There are map boards at the small train sta tion. Follow the signs to the centre along Schlosserstrasse to the beginning of the pedestrianised streets. Continue along the cobbled streets until you come across yet more signposts, or ask for Alter Markt.

Information

Tourist Information Jever (☎ 710 10; www.stadt-jever.de; Alter Markt 18; ☺ 9am-6pm Mon-Fri, 9am-1pm Sat Apr-Oct, 9am-5pm Mon-Fri Nov-Mar)

Sights

SCHLOSS

Looking like a prop from the film *Doctor Zhivago*, the onion-shaped dome is literally the crowning feature of Jever's 14th-century **Schloss** (☎ 969 350; www.schlossmuseum.de; adult/concession €3.50/1.80; ☺ 10am-6pm Tue-Sun year-round, 10am-6pm Mon Jul & Aug). The town's 18th-century Russian rulers added it to a building built by Fräulein Maria's grandfather, chieftain Edo Wiemken the Elder. Today the palace houses the **Kulturhistorische Museum des Jeverlandes**, a mildly diverting cultural-history museum with objects chronicling the daily life and craft of the Frieslanders, including a vast porcelain collection.

The *pièce de résistance* is the magnificent **audience hall**, with a carved, coffered, oak ceiling of great intricacy. Fräulein Maria retained the Antwerp sculptor Cornelis Floris to create this 80-sq-metre Renaissance masterpiece.

FRIESISCHES BRAUHAUS ZU JEVER

A brewery that has been producing dry pilsner since 1848 is worth a visit, and the **Friesisches Brauhaus** (☎ 137 11; www.jever.de, in German; Elisabethufer 18; tours adult/child €7/2.50; ☺ frequent tours 9am-6pm Mon-Fri, 9am-2pm Sat) allows visitors a peek behind the scenes. Two-hour weekday tours travel through the production and bottling facilities, as well as a small museum, whereas 1½-hour Saturday tours only include the museum. Reservations are essential.

OTHER ATTRACTIONS

Many of Jever's sights are in some way connected to Fräulein Maria. The most spectacular is in the **Stadtkirche** (☎ 933 80; Am Kirchplatz 3; ☺ 8am-6pm), where you'll find the lavish memorial tomb of her father, Edo Wiemken (1468–1511). The tomb is another opus by Cornelis Floris and miraculously survived eight fires. The church itself succumbed to the flames and was rebuilt in a rather modern way; the main nave is opposite the tomb, which is now behind glass.

Near the tourist office, you'll see a **statue of Fräulein Maria**. Her image also joins that of her father and other historic figures in the town's **Glockenspiel** (☺ carillon 11am, noon, 3pm, 4pm, 5pm & 6pm), opposite the tourist office on the facade of the Hof von Oldenburg.

An interesting Frisian craft is on show at the **Blaudruckerei shop** (☎ 713 88; www.blaudruckerei.de, in German; Kattrepel 3; ☺ 10am-1pm & 2-6pm Mon-Fri, 10am-2pm Sat). This is owned by former teacher Georg Stark, who 20 years ago revived the long-lost art and tradition of Blaudruckerei, a printing and dying process whose results vaguely resemble batik.

Sleeping & Eating

DJH hostel (☎ 909 202; www.jugendherberge.de/jh/jever; Dr-Fritz-Blume-Weg 4; dm under/over 27yr €22/25; ☺ closed Dec-Feb; P ☒ ☐) Jever's cute *Jugendherberge* is like a little village, with a series of green and red-brick bungalows grouped around the reception. Dorms are as clean, modern and comfortable in buildings dating from 2006.

Hotel Pension Stöber (☎ 5580; www.hotel-stoeber.de, in German; Hohnholzstrasse 10; s €40-45, d €68-74; P ☒) In a leafy neighbourhood a 10-minute walk south of the centre, this whitewashed building has traditionally German rustic rooms.

Am Elisabethufer (☎ 949640; www.jever-hotel-pension .de; Elisabethufer 9a; s €42-48, d €72-78; P ☒ ☏) Frilly lampshades, floral duvet covers and an assortment of knick-knacks are par for the course in Jever's *Pensionen*, and exactly what you'll find in this attractive and comfortable place with free internet (using an adapter in the power socket) and wi-fi. From the tourist office, it's a short walk north along Von-Thünen-Ufer.

Im Schützenhof (☎ 9370; www.schuetzenhof-jever.de, in German; Schützenhofstrasse 47; s €44-55, d €74-90; P ☒) For something a little more upmarket, this hotel, a 10-minute walk south (away from the centre) of the train station, has comfortable modern rooms. It's favoured for local celebrations because of its excellent restaurant, Zitronengras.

Balu (☎ 700 709; Kattrepel 1a; mains €10-19; ☺ 5.30pm-midnight) Whitewashed walls and tasteful decoration give this African restaurant understated style. Tex-Mex and Italian fare are also on the menu, and once the kitchen settles down, Moses, who comes from Nigeria and runs Balu with his German wife, strolls around for a chat with

LOWER SAXONY

WALKING TO THE ISLANDS

When the tide recedes on Germany's North Sea coast, it exposes the mudflats connecting the mainland to the East Frisian Islands, and that's when hikers and nature lovers make their way barefoot to Baltrum and its sister 'isles'. This involves wallowing in mud or wading knee-deep in seawater, but it's one of the most popular outdoor activities in this flat, mountainless region. The Wadden Sea in the Netherlands and Germany became a World Heritage Site in 2009.

Wattwandern, as such trekking through the Wadden Sea National Park is called, can be dangerous as the tide follows channels that will cut you off from the mainland unless you have a guide who knows the tide times and routes. Tourist offices in Jever and Emden can provide details of state-approved ones, including **Martin Rieken** (☎ 04941-8260; www.wattfuehrer-rieken.de, in German) and **Johann Behrends** (☎ 04944-913 875; www.wattwandern-johann.de, in German). Or call **Strandkasse Schillig** (☎ 04426-987 174), a central office in Schillig for organising hikes on the Wadden Sea, and they can help you find a guide.

Coastal tours cost from €7 to €10, but if a ferry is needed for one leg of the trip, count on paying about €25. Necessary gear includes shorts or short trousers and possibly socks or trainers (although many guides recommend going barefoot). In winter, gumboots are necessary.

---

his guests – even about Wole Soyinka and Chinua Achebe, if Nigerian writers happen to be one of your interests.

Haus der Getreuen (☎ 3010; Schlachtstrasse 1; mains €13.50-22.50; ✗) With a historic dining room and outside seating, Haus der Getreuen is well known for its good regional dishes, especially fish.

For a drink, the area around Markt offers a few options.

Getting There & Around

The train trip to Jever from Bremen (€15.70, two hours) involves at least one change, in Sande, and sometimes one in Oldenburg, too. Ask the tourist office for the free *Urlauberbus* map (see the boxed text, p653). By road, take the exit to the B210 from the A29 (direction: Wilhelmshaven).

Jever is small enough to explore on foot.

EAST FRISIAN ISLANDS

Trying to remember the sequence of the seven East Frisian Islands, Germans – with a wink of the eye – recite the following mnemonic device: '*Welcher Seemann liegt bei Nanni im Bett?*' (which translates rather saucily as 'Which seaman is lying in bed with Nanni?').

Lined up in an archipelago off the coast of Lower Saxony like diamonds in a tiara, the islands are (east to west): Wangerooge, Spiekeroog, Langeoog, Baltrum, Norderney, Juist and Borkum. Their long sandy beaches, open spaces and sea air make them both a nature lovers' paradise and a perfect retreat for those escaping the stresses of the world. Like their North Frisian cousins Sylt (p724), Amrum (p724) and Föhr (p723), the islands are part of the Wadden Sea (Wattenmeer) National Park. Along with coastal areas of the Netherlands, Germany's Wadden Sea is a Unesco World Heritage Site.

The main season runs from mid-May to September. Beware, however, that the opening hours of tourist offices in coastal towns change frequently and without notice. Call ahead if possible.

Getting There & Away

Most ferries sail according to tide times rather than on a regular schedule, so it's best to call the local ferry operator or **Deutsche Bahn** (DB; www.bahn.de/nordseeinseln, in German) for information on departure times on a certain day. Tickets are generally offered either as returns for those staying on the island (sometimes valid for up to two months) or cheaper same-day returns.

In most cases (apart from Borkum, Norderney and Juist) you will need to change from the train to a bus at some point to reach the harbour from where the ferry leaves. Sometimes those are shuttle buses operated by the ferry company, or scheduled services from **Weser-Ems Bus** (☎ 04921-974 00; www.weser-ems-bus.de, in German). For more details see Getting There & Away for each island. For planning bus connections from Norden and Esens to ferry harbours, the tourist office in Emden runs a useful transport information service (p653).

Light aircraft also fly to every island except Spiekeroog. Contact **Luftverkehr Friesland Harle** (☎ 04464-948 10; www.inselflieger.de, in German).

RESORT TAX

Each of the East Frisian Islands charges a *Kurtaxe* (resort tax), entitling you to entry onto the beach and offering small discounts for museums etc. It's a small amount, typically €3 a day, and if you're staying overnight it's simply added to your hotel bill. Remind your hotel to give you your pass should they forget.

Getting Around

Only Borkum and Norderney allow cars, so heading elsewhere means you'll need to leave your vehicle in a car park near the ferry pier (about €3.50 per 12 hours).

WANGEROOGE

The second-smallest of the East Frisian Islands – after Baltrum – is inhabited by just under 1000 people and is the easternmost of the group, lying about 7km off the coast in the region north of Jever. While crunching sand between your toes and watching huge tanker ships lumber past on their way to and from the ports at Bremerhaven, Hamburg and Wilhelmshaven, it's easy to feel like a willing castaway here.

Two good sources of information are the **Kurverwaltung** (spa administration; ☎ 04469-990; www .wangerooge.de, in German; Strandpromenade 3; ⊙ 9am-5pm Mon-Fri, to noon Sat & Sun Apr-Oct, 9am-noon & 3-4.30pm Mon-Fri Nov-Mar) and the **Verkehrsverein** (☎ 04469-948 80; info@westturm.de; Hauptbahnhof; ⊙ 9am-5pm Mon-Fri, also 9am-noon Sat & Sun Apr-Oct), which handles room reservations as well.

If you're feeling active you can climb the 161 steps of Wangerooge's 39m-tall **lighthouse** (☎ 04469-8324; www.leuchtturm-wangerooge.de; adult/child €2/1; ⊙ 10am-noon & 2-5pm Mon-Fri, Apr-Oct, 10am-noon Nov-Mar) from 1855, take to the seawater adventure pool or indulge in a long list of sports activities. For more of a learning experience, head to the **Nationalparkhaus** (☎ 04469-8397; www.nationalparkhaus-wangarooge .de, in German; Friedrich-August-Strasse 18; admission free; ⊙ 9am-1pm & 2-6pm Tue-Fri, 10am-noon & 2-5pm Sat & Sun Mar-Oct, 10am-1pm Mon-Fri, 2-5pm Sat & Sun Nov-Feb).

Getting There & Away

The ferry to Wangerooge leaves from Harlesiel two to five times daily (1½ hours), depending on the tides. An open return ticket costs €28.80 (two-month time limit), and a same-day return ticket is €18.80. This includes the tram shuttle to the village on the island (4km). Large pieces of luggage are an extra €2.80 each, and a bike €10.50 each way. The ferry is operated by **DB** (☎ in Harlesiel 04464-949 411, on Wangerooge 04469-947 411).

To reach Harlesiel, take bus 211 from Jever train/bus station (€3.10, 30 minutes).

SPIEKEROOG

Rolling dunes dominate the landscape of minuscule Spiekeroog; about two-thirds of its 17.4 sq km is taken up by these sandy hills. It's the tranquillity of this rustic island that draws people, although you can distract yourself with the **Pferdebahn** (adult/child return €3/2; ⊙ departs 10am, 10.45am, 3pm & 3.45pm Tue-Sun Apr-Sep), a horse-drawn train that runs on rails and dates back to 1885. There are also plenty of baths for swimming.

The **tourist office** (☎ 04976-919 3101; www .spiekeroog.de, in German; Noorderpad 25; ⊙ 9am-12.30pm & 2-5pm Mon-Fri, 9am-noon Sat & Sun Apr-Oct, 10am-noon Mon-Fri, 11am-1pm Sat & Sun Nov-Mar) is in the 'Haus Kogge', where there's also a **Mussel Museum** (☎ 04976-919 3225; admission €1; ⊙ 9am-12.30pm & 2-5pm Mon-Fri) with more than 3000 shells of all varieties.

Spiekeroog is not only car-free but discourages bicycles, too.

Getting There & Away

From the ferry departure point in Neuharlingersiel it takes 40 to 55 minutes to reach Spiekeroog. Ferry times depend on the tides, so same-day returns aren't always possible. Prices are €12 each way or €20 for same-day return tickets. Each piece of luggage over the two-bag limit costs an extra €2 return. Call ☎ 04974-214 or ☎ 04976-919 3133, or email reederei@spiekeroog.de for details and tickets.

To get to the ferry, catch a train to Esens (from Jever €5.10, 22 minutes) or Norden (from Emden €5.10, 15 minutes), and change there for a bus (from Esens €3.70, 30 minutes; from Norden €6.40, one hour). Buses outside summer months are infrequent, so check before setting out (see opposite).

LOWER SAXONY

LANGEOOG

Floods and pirates make up the story of Langeoog, whose population was reduced to a grand total of two following a horrendous storm in 1721. By 1830 it had recovered sufficiently to become a resort town.

The island boasts the highest elevation in East Frisia – the 20m-high **Melkhörndüne** – and the **grave** of Lale Anderson, famous for being the first singer to record the WWII song 'Lili Marleen'. Nautical tradition is showcased in the **Schiffahrtsmuseum** (☎ 04972-693 211; adult/concession €2.50/1.50; ⊙ 10am-noon & 3-5pm Mon-Thu, 10am-noon Fri & Sat mid-Mar–Oct), and you can also view a **sea rescue ship** (☎ 04972-330; admission free; ⊙ 10.30am-12.30pm Tue, Thu & Sun). In sunshine, the 14km-long **beach** is clearly the biggest attraction.

Langeoog's **tourist office** (☎ 04972-6930; kurverwaltung@langeoog.de; Hauptstrasse 28; ⊙ 8am-noon & 2-4.30pm Mon-Thu, 8am-noon Fri) is in the Rathaus, while **room reservations** (☎ 04972-693 201; zimmernachweis@langeoog.de; ⊙ 9am-6.30pm Mon-Fri, 10am-3pm Sat & Sun) can be dealt with on the 1st floor of the island's 'train station'.

Getting There & Away

The ferry shuttles between Bensersiel and Langeoog at least four times daily. The trip takes about one hour and costs €23 return, or €19.50 for a same-day return. Luggage is €2.50 per piece, bikes €15 return. For details, call ☎ 04971-928 90 or see www.schiffahrt-langeoog.de.

To get to Bensersiel, take the train to Esens or Norden, and change to a shuttle bus (from Esens €3.10, 15 minutes; from Norden €5, 50 minutes).

BALTRUM

The smallest inhabited East Frisian Island, Baltrum is just 1km wide and 5km long and peppered with dunes and salty marshland. It's so tiny that villagers don't bother with street names but make do with house numbers instead. Numbers have been allocated on a chronological basis; houses No 1 to 4 no longer exist so the oldest is now No 5.

There's little to do except go on walks or to the beach, or visit the exhibition on the national-park environment in **house No 177** (☎ 04939-469; admission free; ⊙ 10am-noon & 3-7pm Tue-Thu, 3-7pm Sat & Sun). As the island closest to the mainland, Baltrum is the most popular destination for *Wattwanderungen* guided tours (see the boxed text, p656).

The **Kurverwaltung** (☎ 04939-800; www.baltrum.de in German; house No 130; ⊙ 8.30am-noon & 2-4pm Mon-Thu, 8.30am-noon Fri) can provide information. For room reservations, call ☎ 04931-938 3400 (in Norden) or see www.zimmervermittlung-baltrum.de.

Getting There & Away

Ferries (and *Wattwanderungen*) leave from Nessmersiel. Ferries take 30 minutes. Departures depend on the tides, which mean day trips aren't always possible. Tickets are €13 one way or €16.50/25 for a same-day/open return. Bikes cost €5 each way and luggage is usually free. More details are available from **Reederei Baltrum** (☎ Baltrum 04939-9130, Nessmersiel 04931-938 3400; www.baltrum-linie.de, in German).

To get to Nessmersiel change from the train in Norden to a bus (€3.60, 20 minutes).

NORDERNEY

'Queen of the East Frisian Islands', Norderney was Germany's first North Sea resort. Founded in 1797 by Friedrich Wilhelm II of Prussia, it became one of the most famous bathing destinations in Europe, after Crown Prince Georg V of Hanover made it his summer residence and personalities such as Chancellor Otto von Bismarck and composer Robert Schumann visited in the 19th century.

Now 'Lüttje Welt' – 'Little World', as the 6200 islanders call Norderney for the way fog makes it seem like it's the only place on earth – is complementing its image of tradition and history with some decidedly modern touches. Its wonderful art-deco **Kurtheater** was built as a private theatre in 1893 but with the advent of film it morphed gradually from 1923 into a cinema, which is what it is mainly used for today. Another gem is the neoclassical **Conversationshaus** (1840), which today houses the tourist office.

The jewel in the crown is indisputably the **Bade:haus** (☎ 04932-891 162, 891 141; Am Kurplatz 3; pool/sauna per 4hr €13/19; ⊙ 9.30am-9.30pm, women only from 2pm Wed), in the former art-nouveau sea-water baths. This sleek stone-and-glass complex is now an enormous thalassotherapy centre, with warm and cold swimming pools, a rooftop sauna with views over the island, relaxation areas where you can lie back on lounges and drink Frisian tea, and much more – all split between the 'Wasserebene' (Water Level), where you can bathe in the pools or bob around in the wave pool, and the 'Feuerebene' (Fire Level) zone for saunas.

Norderney's **tourist office** (☎ 04932-891 131, 891
32, room reservations 04932-891 300; Conversationshaus;
✆ core hours 9am-5pm Mon-Fri, 10am-1pm Sat, 11am-1pm
un, closed Sun Nov-mid-Mar) can provide more de-
ails or book rooms. A **harbour service centre**
☎ 04932-927 237; ✆ 9am-6pm) has information
ut no room-booking service.

The **Nationalpark-Haus** (☎ 04932-2001; www
nationalparkhaus-norderney.de, in German; Am Hafen 1;
dmission free; ✆ 9am-6pm Tue-Sun), directly on
he harbour, has a small exhibition and
egularly offers walks into the Wadden Sea
check ahead, as visitor hours are shorter in
ome months).

Getting There & Away

To get to Norderney you have to catch the
erry in Norddeich. **Reederei Frisia** (☎ 04931-
870; www.reederei-frisia.de, in German; adult/child return
17/8.50, bikes €7.50) leaves Norddeich every one
o two hours roughly from 6am to 6pm daily
later some days in summer). The journey
akes 50 minutes and any DB office can
rovide details.

There are trains (€7.60 to €9.70, 40 min-
tes) from Emden to Norddeich Mole, the
erry landing stage.

UIST

uist, shaped like a snake, is 17km long and
nly 500m wide. The only ways to travel are
y bike, horse-drawn carriage or on your own
wo feet. Here, you're often alone with the
creeching seagulls, the wild sea and the howl-
ng winds. Forest, brambles and elderberry
ushes blanket large sections of the island.

One peculiarity of Juist is the idyllic
ammersee – a bird sanctuary and the only
reshwater lake on all the islands (no swim-
ning). In 1651 Juist was torn in two by a
torm tide, but in the early 20th century it was
ecided to close off the channel with dunes,
ventually creating a freshwater lake. There's
lso the **Juister Küstenmuseum** (Coastal Museum;
☎ 04935-1488; www.kuestenmuseum-juist.de, in German;
oogster Pad 29; adult/concession €2.50/1.50; ✆ 9.30am-1pm
2.30-5pm Tue-Fri, 9.30am-2pm Sat, 2.30-5pm Sun Apr-Oct,
.30-5pm Tue-Sat Nov-Mar).

Juist's main **tourist office** (☎ 04935-809 107;
www.juist.de, in German; Strandstrasse 5; ✆ 9am-12.30pm
1on-Fri year-round, plus 10am-12.30pm Sat mid-May–Sep
. 10am-12.30pm Sun Jul & Aug) is in the Rathaus.

It also has a room-reservation service
(☎ 04935-809 222).

Getting There & Away

Reederei Frisia (☎ 04931-9870; www.reederei-frisia.de,
in German) operates the ferries from Norddeich
to Juist (adult day/normal return €18/29.50,
1½ hours); children are half-price and bikes
cost €11 return. You can also ask any DB
office for details.

Trains from Emden (€7.60 to €9.70, 40
minutes) travel straight to the landing dock
in Norddeich Mole.

BORKUM

The largest of the East Frisian Islands – once
even larger before it was ripped apart by a
flood in the 12th century – has a tough seafaring and whaling history. Reminders of those
frontier times are the whalebones that you'll
occasionally see, stacked up side by side, or
as unusual garden fences. In 1830, however,
locals realised that reinventing itself as a 'seaside' resort was a safer way to earn a living,
and today many of the island's 5500 inhabitants are involved in the tourism industry in
one way or another.

To learn about the whaling era and
other stages in the life of Borkum, visit the
Heimatmuseum (Local History Museum; ☎ 04922-4860;
adult/concession €3/1.50; ✆ 10am-5pm Tue-Sun Apr-Oct,
3-5pm Tue & Sat Nov-Mar) at the foot of the old lighthouse (€1.50). Also of interest is the museum
fire ship **Borkumriff** (☎ 04922-2030; www.feuerschiff
-borkumriff.de, in German; Am Nordufer; adult/child €3/2;
✆ 9.45am-5.45pm Tue-Sun Apr-Oct), with its exhibition
on the Wadden Sea National Park.

The **tourist office** (☎ 04922-9330; www.borkum.de,
in German; Am Georg-Schütte-Platz 5; ✆ 9am-6pm Mon-
Fri, 10am-noon & 3-5pm Sat, 10am-noon Sun Mar-Oct, 9am-
5pm Mon-Fri, 10am-noon Sat Nov-Feb) also handles
room reservations.

Getting There & Away

All-year boats depart twice daily to/from
Emden for Borkum. **AG-Ems** (☎ 01805-180 182;
www.ag-ems.de, in German) has both car ferries (adult
same-day/open return €17.60/33.60, two
hours) and faster catamarans (€27.80/55.60,
one hour). Transporting a car costs from €61
to €180 return (depending on size), while a
bike costs €11.50.

LOWER SAXONY

Bremen

Bremen is the smallest of Germany's three city-states and convincing proof that good thing come in small packages. Like Hamburg, it evolved into a separate state after being a move and shaker in the powerful Hanseatic League, and to this day it retains the character of free spirit. Unlike Hamburg, however, Bremen is less a compact whole than a pair of distinc flecks dotted on the Lower Saxony landscape: industrial Bremerhaven at the Weser River' mouth, and riverside Bremen, 65km south. They've been linked politically since 1827, whe Bremen's mayor cleverly bought the river delta from Hanover. Since that time, these two cities have complemented each other, with Bremen playing the lead role as the commercia cultural and political centre of the state, and Bremerhaven providing a sea gateway to the world beyond.

In Bremen, the compact and picturesque red-brick capital, you can explore an unusual ex pressionist street, move on to a quaint district of winding medieval lanes and continue to a alternative student quarter via a small but interesting 'museum mile', all within minutes.

To the north, Bremerhaven has an impressive Emigration Centre that's a perfect compan ion piece to the one on New York's Ellis Island. Economically, this city's lifeline is the long container quay, one of the world's largest, while its historic Alter Hafen and Neuer Hafe (Old Harbour and New Harbour), off the mainstream of the Weser River, now accommodate museums, and invite the visitor to stroll and explore.

HIGHLIGHTS

- **Grand Designs** Marvel at the golden archangel and red-brick angles of Böttcherstrasse (p663)

- **Coffee with a Murky Splash** Catch a ferry to Café Sand (p667) for a coffee on the golden sands of the Weser River 'beach'

- **Alternative Chic** Nosh or sip a drink at a restaurant (p666) or bar (p667) in Das Viertel, Bremen's fashionable alternative quarter

- **Off-Beat Experience** Peek in at the black-ened mummies in the Dom St Petri's Bleikeller (p663)

- **Roots Attack** Follow an ancestor across the ocean at the German Emigration Centre (p670) in Bremerhaven

★ German Emigration Centre

★ Dom St Petri
Böttcherstrasse ★ ★ Café Sand
★ Das Viertel

| POPULATION: 663,082 | AREA: 404 SQ KM |

BREMEN CITY

☎ 0421 / pop 550,000

Bremen has a highly justified reputation for being one of Germany's most outward-looking and hospitable places, and the people of Bremen seem to strike a very good balance between style, earthiness and good living.

Nature is never far away here, but Bremen is better known for its fairy-tale character, a unique expressionist quarter and (it must be said, because the Bremen folk are avid football fans) one of Germany's most exciting football teams. That nature would get its chance to win back a few urban patches did seem likely from the late 1960s, when the population, having peaked at over 600,000, began to decline. Something else happened, however, to clinch it: in 1979 Bremen – the city-state – was the first to elect Green Party candidates to its state parliament, unwittingly becoming the cradle of a worldwide movement to put 'Greens' in parliaments.

Today, Bremen is growing again – the city just scrapes in among Germany's largest 10 – and offers an unhurried and relaxed lifestyle, some very lively areas where you can enjoy good food, culture and a drink, a lovely old town with one section where the streets are way too narrow to risk swinging cats, and some tall tales to complement its history – likely proof that the people of Bremen are also among Germany's most gregarious.

HISTORY

Bremen's origins go back to a string of settlements that developed near today's centre from about 100 AD, and one settlement in particular that in 787 was given its own bishop's seat by Charlemagne. In its earliest days, it was known as the 'Rome of the North' and developed as a base for Christianising Scandinavia. Despite this, it gradually shed its religious character, enjoying the greater freedom of being an imperial city from 1186, joining the Hanseatic League in 1260, and in 1646 coming directly under the wing of the Kaiser as a free imperial city; today it is a 'Free Hanseatic City'.

ORIENTATION

Bremen is compact and can be walked or crossed by tram. The Altstadt (old town) lies south of the Hauptbahnhof (central train station), on the

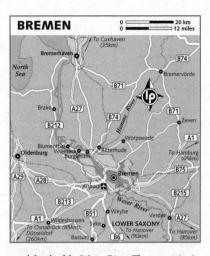

north bank of the Weser River. The expressionist Böttcherstrasse lies directly south of Altstadt's central Markt and the popular Schlachte promenade southwest of this. Domsheide, just southeast of Markt, and the tram and bus stops in front of Hauptbahnhof are the two main interchanges for urban public transport.

The Schnoor maritime quarter is to the southeast, and the art galleries and student nightlife district of Das Viertel lie to the east along Ostertorsteinweg (also known, for obvious reasons, as O-Weg).

INFORMATION

ErlebnisCARD (adult incl up to 2 children for 1/2 days €8.90/10.90, group €17.50/22) Free public transport and discounts on sights; available from tourist offices.

Moneymaker (Bahnhof; per hr €3; ☒ 24hr) Internet access in the northern end of the main train station.

Police (☎ 3621; Am Wall 201)

Post office (Domsheide 15; ☒ 8am-7pm Mon-Fri, 9am-1pm Sat)

Post office (Bahnhofplatz 21; ☒ 9am-7pm Mon-Fri, 9am-1pm Sat)

Schnell & Sauber (Vor dem Steintor 105; per wash €4.30; ☒ 6am-11pm) Laundry, just east of centre.

Tourist-Info Bremen (☎ 01805-101 030; www .bremen-tourism.de) City (Obernstrasse/Liebfrauenkirchhof; ☒ 10am-6.30pm Mon-Fri, 10am-4pm Sat & Sun) Hauptbahnhof (Hauptbahnhof; ☒ 9am-7pm Mon-Fri, 9.30am-6pm Sat & Sun)

DANGERS & ANNOYANCES

Bremen is a safe town to walk around day or night, but the teenage club mile of Rembertiring,

BREMEN CITY

0 ————————— 400 m
0 ————————— 0.2 miles

INFORMATION
Moneymaker **1** C3
Post Office **2** C5
Post Office **3** C4
Tourist-Info Bremen **4** C3
Tourist-Info Bremen **5** B5

SIGHTS & ACTIVITIES
Bleikeller **6** C5
Dom St Petri **7** C5
Gerhard Marcks Haus **8** C6
Glockenspiel .... (see 16)
Hal Över Schreiber Reederei **9** B5
Haus Atlantis **10** B5
Haus der Bürgerschaft **11** B5
Kirche Unser Lieben Frauen **12** B5
Knight Roland Statue **13** B5
Kunsthalle **14** C6
Lichtbringer **15** B5
Paula Modersohn-Becker Haus ... **16** B5
Rathaus **17** B5
Roselius Haus .... (see 16)
Schnoor **18** C6
Town Musicians of Bremen
    Statue **19** B5
Übersee Museum **20** C4
Weserburg Museum für Moderne
    Kunst **21** A5

Wilhelm Wagenfeld
    Haus **22** C6
Windmill **23** B4

SLEEPING 🏠
Bremer Backpacker
    Hostel **24** C4
Hotel Bölts am Park **25** D3
Hotel Bremer Haus **26** D4
Hotel Lichtsinn **27** D5
Hotel Residence **28** D4
Hotel Überfluss **29** A5
Jugendherberge
    Bremen **30** A4

EATING 🍴
Cafe Engel **31** D6
Casablanca **32** D6
Delano **33** D6
Energie Cafe **34** C5
Freudenhaus .... (see 29)
Gallo Nero **35** A5
Katzen Cafe **36** C6
Luv **37** B5
Osteria **38** B5
Schröter's **39** C6
Ständige Vertretung **40** B5

DRINKING 📷 📺
2raumlounge **41** D5
Bodega Del Puerto **42** A5
Cafe Kweer **43** B5
Cafe Tölke **44** C6
Feldmann's **45** B5
Lagerhaus **46** D6
Wohnzimmer **47** D6

ENTERTAINMENT 🎭
Brauhaskeller **48** D6
Die Glocke **49** C5
Lila Eule **50** D6
Neues Schauspielhaus **51** D6
NFF Cream Club **52** C6
Theater am Goetheplatz **53** C6

SHOPPING 🛍️
Hachez **54** B5

TRANSPORT
Agentur Grajan **55** C4
Avis **56** C3
Central Bus Station **57** C4
Domsheide **58** C5
Hal Över Schreiber Reederei .. (see 9)
Radstation **59** C3

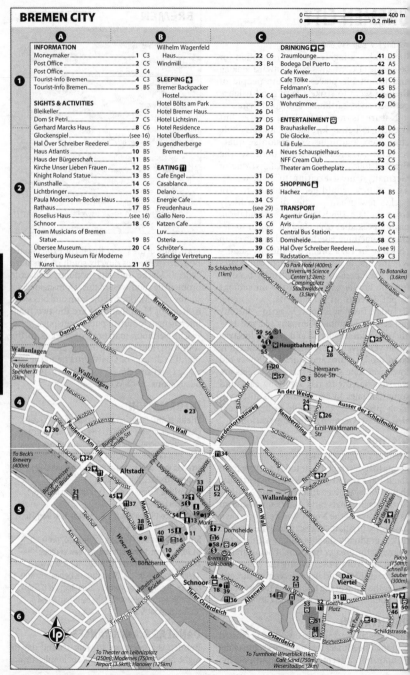

BREMEN

near the main train station, has been a problem zone in recent years. Video cameras, a strong police presence and a ban on carrying 'dangerous objects' in this vicinity – meaning knives, baseball bats, handguns and the like, as yellow signs make graphically clear – point to its potential for sudden violence. Use big-city sense here.

SIGHTS & ACTIVITIES
Markt
With high, historic buildings looming over a relatively small space, Bremen's Markt is one of the most remarkable in northern Germany. The two towers of the 1200-year-old **Dom St Petri** (St Petri Cathedral; ☾ 10am-5pm Mon-Fri, 10am-2pm Sat, 2-5pm Sun), see also right, dominate the northeastern edge, beside the ornate and imposing **Rathaus** (town hall). Although the Rathaus was first erected in 1410, the Weser Renaissance balcony in the middle, crowned by three gables, was added between 1595 and 1618.

Bremers boast that the 13m-high **Knight Roland statue** (1404) in front of the Rathaus is Germany's tallest representation of this just, freedom-loving knight, and his belt buckle is certainly in an interesting position. However, it's the statue tucked away on the Rathaus' western side, in front of the **Kirche Unser Lieben Frauen** (Church of our Beloved Lady) that people more readily identify with this city. Sculptor Gerhard Marcks has cast the **Town Musicians of Bremen** (1951) in their famous pose – one on top of the other, on the shoulders of the donkey (see the boxed text below). The donkey's nose and front legs are incredibly shiny after being touched by visitors for good luck.

The one obviously modern building on the Markt is the **Haus der Bürgerschaft** (State Assembly; 1966), whose geometrical steel-and-concrete structure features artfully moulded pieces of metal attached to its facade, suggesting a Gothic style that blends in with the other architecture of the historic square.

CATHEDRAL CELLAR
What's most unusual about Dom St Petri is what lies beneath. In the incredibly dry air of its **Bleikeller** (Lead Cellar; ☎ 365 0441; adult/concession €1.40/1; ☾ 10am-5pm Mon-Fri, 10am-2pm Sat, noon-5pm Sun Easter-Oct) corpses mummify, and you can still spy eight preserved bodies in open coffins here. The figures include a Swedish countess, a soldier with his mouth opened in a silent scream, and a student who died in a duel in 1705. The Bleikeller has its own entrance, to the south of the main door. The 265 steps to the top of the cathedral's **tower** (adult/child €1/0.70; ☾ 10am-5pm Mon-Fri, 10am-2pm Sat, 2-5pm Sun Easter-Oct) can also be climbed.

Böttcherstrasse
If Bremen's Markt is striking, the nearby Böttcherstrasse (1931) is unique. A charming lane with a golden entrance and staggered red-brick walls as you approach from Markt, it's a superb example of expressionism.

This 110m-long street was commissioned in 1931 by Ludwig Roselius, a merchant who made his fortune by inventing decaffeinated coffee and founding the company Hag in the early 20th century. Most of the street's design was by Bernhard Hoetger (1874–1959), including the **Lichtbringer** (Bringer of Light), the golden relief at the

BREMEN

THE FANTASTIC FOUR

In the Brothers Grimm fairy tale, the *Bremer Stadtmusikanten* (Town Musicians of Bremen) never actually make it to Bremen, but when you arrive in the city you might enjoy a quick reminder of what the fuss is about. Starting with a donkey, four overworked and ageing animals, fearing the knacker's yard or the Sunday roasting pan, run away from their owners. They head for Bremen intending, like many young dreamers, to make their fortune as musicians.

On their first night on the road, they decide to shelter in a house. It turns out to be occupied by robbers, as our heroes discover when they climb on the donkey to peer through the window. The sight of a rooster atop a cat, perched on a dog, which is sitting on a donkey – and the 'musical' accompaniment of braying, barking, meowing and crowing – startles the robbers so much, they flee. The animals remain and make their home 'where you'll probably still find them today'.

On Sunday from May to early October, this story is charmingly re-enacted (at noon and 1.30pm) in Bremen's Markt.

northern entrance, showing a scene from the Apocalypse with the Archangel Michael fighting a dragon.

Hoetger's **Haus Atlantis** (now the Bremen Hilton) features a show-stopping, multi-coloured, glass-walled **spiral staircase** (tours 10am-noon & 2-4pm Mon).

Hoetger worked around the existing, 16th-century **Roselius Haus**, and the **Paula Modersohn-Becker Haus**, with its rounded edges and wall reliefs, is his design too. Today these two houses are adjoining **museums** (336 5077; combined ticket adult/concession €5/3; 11am-6pm Tue-Sun). The first contains Roselius' private collection of medieval art. The second showcases the art of the eponymous painter, Paula Modersohn-Becker (1876–1907), an early expressionist and member of the Worpswede colony (p672).

Outside, the **Glockenspiel** (carillon; hourly noon-6pm May-Dec, noon, 3pm & 6pm Jan-Apr) chimes while a panel honouring great sea explorers, such as Leif Eriksson and Christopher Columbus, rotates.

Böttcherstrasse is all the more enjoyable for having survived a Nazi destruction order. Roselius convinced the authorities to save the 'degenerate' street as a future warning of the depravity of 'cultural Bolshevism'.

Schnoor

Over the years, Bremen's former maritime and then red-light district transmogrified into a quaint maze of restaurants, cafes and boutique shops. It's a honey-pot for tourists, but its restaurants are also popular with locals in the evenings.

The name 'Schnoor' is north German for 'string', and refers to the way the 15th- and 16th-century cottages – once inhabited by fisherfolk, traders and craftspeople – are 'strung' along the alleyways.

Beck's Brewery

Germany has well over 1200 breweries, and about half of these are found in Bavaria, not the north. The beer of one brewery in particular, though, has long washed beyond the shores of Germany to establish itself as an international brand. You can see where the wares come from during a two-hour tour of the **Beck's brewery** (5094 5555; Am Deich; tours €9; 2pm & 3.30pm Thu & Fri, 12.30pm, 2pm, 3.30pm & 5pm Sat Jan-Apr, additionally 11am & 12.30pm Thu & Fri, 9.30am & 11am Sat May-Dec). Take tram 1 or 8 to Am Brill. *Prost!*

Museums

Bremen has a strong aerospace industry and space buffs will enjoy the eye-catching oyster-shaped **Universum Science Center** (334 60; www.universum-bremen.de; Wiener Strasse 1a; adult/child €18.50/12.50; 9am-6pm Mon-Fri, 10am-7pm Sat & Sun), where you can make virtual trips to the stars, as well as to the ocean floor or the centre of the earth. Take tram 6 from the main train station to Universität/NW1 stop.

The **Übersee Museum** (Overseas Museum; 1603 8101; www.uebersee-museum.de, in German; Bahnhofplatz 13; adult/child/concession €6.50/2.50/4.50; 9am-6pm Tue-Fri from 10am Sat & Sun) takes you to all continents of the world and offers an insight into natural evolution with its dazzling collection of exotic artefacts, brought together in the tradition of a Hanseatic city. It can call on about 1.1 million objects, including African art, tropical plants and gold from South America.

Meanwhile, the **Hafenmuseum Speicher XI** (Harbour Museum Warehouse 11; 303 8279; www.speicherelf.de, in German; Am Speicher XI; adult/concession €4.50/3.50; 11am-6pm Tue-Sun) expounds on Bremen's waterside history. Take bus 26 to Speicher XI.

For art lovers, Bremen's *Kulturmeile* (Cultural Mile) boasts the **Kunsthalle** (329 080; www.kunsthalle-bremen.de; Am Wall 207; closed to late 2010/early 2011), which at the time of publication was being given two new wings and a revamped cafe. When it reopens, you can expect to find a large permanent collection of paintings, sculpture and copperplate engraving from the Middle Ages into the modern as well as changing exhibitions. The nearby **Gerhard Marcks Haus** (327 200; Am Wall 208; adult/concession €3.50/2.50; 10am-6pm Tue-Sun) showcases sculpture, while **Wilhelm Wagenfeld Haus** (338 8116; Am Wall 209; adult/concession €3.50/1.50; 3-9pm Tue, 10am-6pm Wed-Sun) features household objects from this Bauhaus luminary.

On an island in the Weser River, across from the Schlachte promenade, you'll find the **Weserburg Museum für Moderne Kunst** (Weserburg Museum of Modern Art; 598 390; www.weserburg.de, Teerhof 20; adult/concession €7/5; 10am-6pm Tue, Wed & Fri, 10am-9pm Thu, 11am-6pm Sat & Sun) with changing exhibitions of hot-off-the-press art.

Other Attractions

The city's typical **Dutch Windmill** (Am Wall) today houses a restaurant and adds a pleasant rural flavour to the parkland. Plant-lovers shouldn't miss a trip to **botanika** (4270 6610; www.botanika.net, in German; in Rhododendron-Park, Deliusweg adult/child €8/5; 9am-6pm Wed-Fri, 10am-6pm Sat & Sun Mar-Oct, 9am-4pm Wed-Fri, 10am-4pm Sat & Sun Nov-Feb) and its replicated Asian landscapes from the Himalayas to New Guinea. Admission to the rhododendron park itself, where you find 2000 rhododendron and azaleas, is free. To get here, take tram 4 to Horner Kirche.

TOURS

Leaving from the Hauptbahnhof, a **city bus tour** (adult/child under 12yr/family €17.20/11.50/44; 10.30am Tue-Sun) run by the tourist office has English and German commentary. Otherwise, ask the office about its many German-language tours.

Hal Över Schreiber Reederei (☎ 338 989; www.hal-oever.de; Martinianleger, Schlachte 2; 9am-5pm Mon-Fri) operates a 75-minute **Weser and harbour tour** (adult/child €9.80/7.50) up to five times daily between April and October. It also runs the ferry across the river to Café Sand (p667). The tourist office has a full schedule of candlelight cruises and boat trips to the islands of Helgoland and Sylt. Hal Över Schreiber Reederei also runs scheduled services along the river in summer (see Getting There & Away, p669).

SLEEPING

Budget

Camping Stadtwaldsee (☎ 841 0748; www.camping-stadtwaldsee.de; Hochschulring 1; per adult/tent/car €9/4/3) This rebuilt camping ground features modern amenities, a supermarket, and a cafe with a lakeside terrace. By car, take the A27 to the university exit in Bremen Nord. Tram 6 to Universität/NW1 is close, or change here to bus 28 to reach the doorstep.

Bremer Backpacker Hostel (☎ 223 8057; www.bremer-backpacker-hostel.de; Emil-Waldmann-Strasse 5-6; dm/s/d €17/28/46; P X L) This private hostel is simply furnished but spotless, with a kitchen, communal room and a small courtyard out front for soaking up the sun.

Jugendherberge Bremen (☎ 163 820; www.jugendherberge.de/jh/bremen; Kalkstrasse 6; dm under/over 27yr €23.50/26.50, s/d €36.50/63; X L) Looking like a work of art from the exterior, with a yellow and orange Plexiglas facade and slit windows, this hostel has comfortable rooms, a rooftop terrace and a bar–breakfast room with huge glass windows overlooking the Weser River.

Midrange

our pick Hotel Bölts am Park (☎ 346 110; www.hotel-boelts.de, in German; Slevogtstrasse 23; s/d €70/90;

P X) This cosy family-run hotel in a leafy neighbourhood has real character, from the wonderfully old-fashioned breakfast hall to its well-proportioned doubles. A few singles with hall showers and toilets start from €50.

Turmhotel Weserblick (☎ 790 300; www.turmhotel-weserblick-bremen.de; Osterdeich 53; s €70-80, d €85-95; P X) This tower-topped hotel right on the Weser River foreshore has heaps of atmosphere, with bare floorboards and Persian carpets in renovated and extremely spacious rooms. The tower rooms overlook the river and have a kitchen. Take tram 2, 3 or 10 to Sielwall.

Hotel Residence (☎ 348 710; www.hotelresidence.de; Hohenlohestrasse 42; s €75-98, d €95-145; P X L) Many celebrities have stayed in this century-old terrace converted to a charming hotel, including Destiny's Child and writer Harry Rowohlt – check out the photos near reception. The main building has rooms to the street, while the newer extension backs onto the railway line but is still reasonably quiet. A sauna, solarium, bar and dining room complete the package.

Hotel Lichtsinn (☎ 368 070; www.hotel-lichtsinn.com; Rembertistrasse 11; s/d €85/110; P X L) Wooden floorboards, Persian carpets and vaguely Biedermeier-style furniture characterise most of this hotel's rooms, a favourite with the theatre world. To use the wi-fi, you'll need a PCMCIA (PC Card) slot.

Hotel Bremer Haus (☎ 329 40; www.hotel-bremer-haus.de; Löningstrasse 16/20; s €85-126, d €110-150; P X L) The yellow exterior of this place is somewhat unappealing, but it gives way to modern, clean and comfortable rooms inside that are especially favoured by business travellers. It has a small foyer lounge for mulling over the newspapers and a 24-hour reception; some doubles are more like junior suites.

Top End

our pick Hotel Überfluss (☎ 322 860; www.hotel-ueberfluss.com; Langenstrasse 72/Schlachte 36; s €139-154, d €184-199, ste €359; X L) Quite literally 7m above river level, this designer hotel has black bathrooms (some with transparent shower areas) and stunning views from its more expensive rooms. For splashy fun, the magnificently designed suite has its own sauna and whirlpool. This one is perfect for a honeymoon.

Park Hotel (☎ 340 80; www.park-hotel-bremen.de; Im Bürgerpark; s €145-290, d €195-340, ste from €585;

BREMEN

P X ▯ 🛜 🏋) This domed lakeside mansion, surrounded by parkland, impresses through its sheer extravagance. It offers access to excellent spa, fitness and beauty facilities, a heated outdoor pool and views over the lake in a traditional 'spa resort' ambience.

EATING
Town Centre
Energie Cafe (☎ 277 2510; www.energiecafe.de, in German; Sögestrasse 59-61; mains €6-15.50; ⏰ 9am-10pm Mon-Fri, 10am-10pm Sat; X 🛜 V) A delightfully upbeat cafe run by a local power company, this place serves delicious pizza, pasta, lunch specials (€6 to €8) and meat mains (from €10.50). It has regular jazz sessions and a whiz interior.

Delano (☎ 338 7400; Queerenstrasse 1; mains €6-22; ⏰ noon-midnight; X V) The black wood furniture, fat columns and ringed black-and-white lampshades lend this Italian brasserie sophistication. Each menacingly large pizza (€8 to €13) comes in an elongated oval shape and is *meant* to be eaten between two.

Ständige Vertretung (☎ 320 995; Böttcherstrasse 3-5; mains €8-16; ⏰ 11.30am-11pm; X) An offshoot of Berlin's best-known restaurant for homesick Rhineland public servants, this large, bustling place thrives on its political theme and solid cuisine washed down with Rhineland wines and beer – the photos of movers and shakers on the walls will keep you guessing.

Schlachte & Around
ourpick Freudenhaus (☎ 322 860; Langenstrasse 72/ Schlachte 36; mains €11-28; ⏰ 7am-midnight; X) This upmarket restaurant inside Hotel Überfluss (p665) is a very classy act and serves gourmet dishes, such as *coq au vin* of Bresse poulard with chick-pea mousse, white cabbage in cider and champignons prepared with rosé wine (€17). This is complemented by a seafood menu and lighter dishes.

Gallo Nero (☎ 957 9958; Heimlichenstrasse 1; pasta €7.50-13, mains €16-22; ⏰ lunch & dinner; X) A delicious haricot-bean cream soup with a peppery bite and reasonably priced *saltimbocca alla Romana* are for the asking in this friendly Italian restaurant. If you're eating alone, retreat into the niche on the left as you enter, away from the main dining area.

Luv (☎ 165 5599; Schlachte 15-18; lighter mains under €10, mains €15-24; ⏰ from 11am Mon-Fri, from 10am Sat & Sun; X) A friendly atmosphere reigns in this large, upbeat bistro with a menu strong on salads and pasta, which is complemented by

more-substantial fare with a Central European focus. A Texas burger can be found alongside the *Wiener Schnitzel* and *nouveau hearty* dishes, some with good old *Bratkartoffeln* (pan-fried potatoes).

Osteria (☎ 339 8207; Schlachte 1; veg menu €28, 5-course menu €38; ⏰ from noon; X V) Crisp tablecloths and good service are hallmarks of this more formal, upmarket Italian restaurant that has won acclaim beyond the region, especially for its grilled seafood. For vegetarians it has a good selection of pasta dishes without meat as mains for €7 to €10. The open kitchen and tiled floor lend a pleasant, relaxed feel; most people dress up for this one.

Schnoor
Schröter's (☎ 326 677; Schnoor 13; mains €11.50-23.50; ⏰ lunch & dinner; X) A modern bistro with artful decoration, Schröter's is known for its antipasti and abundant Mediterranean mains, from risotto to fish. It is a veritable warren of rooms, including a Toulouse-Lautrec room upstairs, decorated with plenty of copies of the painter's pictures.

Katzen Cafe (☎ 326 621; Schnoor 38; mains €13.50-24.50, 3-course lunch menu €15; ⏰ noon-11pm; X) This popular Moulin Rouge–style restaurant opens out into a rear sunken terrace bedecked with flowers. The menu runs the gamut from Alsatian to Norwegian, with seafood a strong theme.

Das Viertel
This arty, student neighbourhood is where to head for cheaper meals or simply a glass of wine or beer over something light.

Casablanca (☎ 326 429; Ostertorsteinweg 59; mains €4-17; ⏰ 9am-midnight Mon-Sat, 10am-midnight Sun X V) The emphasis is on the 'Casa' in this homey Bremen institution, where goths, grannies and particularly students while away the hours within scuffed walls painted to look like marble, and under a ceiling that's a trompe l'oeil jungle canopy. Upstairs is a glass booth for smokers that begs for a 'Do Not Feed!' sign. It's usually open later weekends and on theatre nights.

ourpick Piano (☎ 785 46; Fehrfeld 64; mains €5.50-9.50; ⏰ from 9am; X V) Another enduringly popular cafe, this bustling place serves pizza, pasta, steaks and vegie casseroles to a broad neighbourhood mix, from media types checking proofs to young mums. Breakfast can also be ordered until 4pm Saturday and 5pm Sunday.

Cafe Engel (☎ 766 15; Ostertorsteinweg 31; mains €6-15; ⏰ from 10am; ✗ 🛜 Ⓥ) Housed in a former pharmacy, this is a popular hang-out that co-ordinates tasteful black-and-white tiled floors with dark wood furniture. In summer, tables spill onto the pavement.

DRINKING

The waterfront Schlachte promenade has a respectably long line of bars catering to all tastes. For either a slightly older, alternative feel or for a student vibe, head to Das Viertel and just walk along O-Weg. Auf den Höfen, north of O-Weg and also part of Das Viertel, has a good selection of bars. Check listings mags, such as *Prinz*, *Bremen4U* or *PortO*, for more details.

our pick **Wohnzimmer** (☎ 163 2064; Ostertorsteinweg 99; ⏰ from 2pm) This bar and lounge mostly gets a relaxed 20s and 30s crowd, who hang out on the sofas – which explains the name 'Living Room' – or lounge around on the mezzanine levels in non-smoker and smoker areas.

2raumlounge (☎ 745 77; Auf den Höfen; ⏰ from 7pm; ✗ 🛜) This is the jiving lynchpin of the Auf den Höfen scene. Sitting in the space-age orange chairs, you can gaze at the regularly changing art on the walls and even buy a piece if you feel inclined to do so. Though the crowd is largely mid-20s, a few older regulars dig in here, especially when football team Werder Bremen is playing – Werder matches are always screened here. Thursday is student night.

Lagerhaus (☎ 702 168; www.kulturzentrum-lagerhaus .de, in German; Schildstrasse 12/19; ⏰ from 6pm Mon-Sat, from 4pm Sun; ✗) This once-dilapidated warehouse off Ostertorsteinweg was squatted by young revolutionaries in the 1970s and later became a cultural centre. Although the young revolutionaries grew long in the tooth, the building actually got younger – or rather, was reprieved from the developer's demolition ball and given a face lift, thanks to their efforts. Today it houses a pub with an alternative flavour downstairs and upstairs has regular parties (about €3, from 11pm or midnight) for a 20s to 30-something crowd. Concerts are held here, too.

Bodega Del Puerto (☎ 178 3797; Schlachte 31a; ⏰ from 5pm Mon-Sat, from 10am Sun; ✗) Essentially, the point of the Schlachte is exploration – to walk along it and see which bar you most like the look of. However, this one is the prime choice for a Spanish-style place with good tapas.

Feldmann's (☎ 168 9192; Schlachte 19-20; dishes €4.60-14; ⏰ 10.30am-midnight Sun-Thu, 10.30am-1am Fri, 10.30am-2am Sat; ✗) A slightly older crowd can be found chatting and lingering over the wide range of Haake-Beck beers in this modern *Bierhaus*, which also sells food.

our pick **Café Sand** (☎ 556 011; Strandweg 106; Pommes & Becks €4.40; ⏰ from 10am May-Sep, noon-6pm Fri & Sat, 10am-6pm Sun Jan-Apr, Oct & Nov; ✗) Situated on an island in the Weser River, this cafe makes you feel light years away from the city. In fact, it serves the local swimming holes – the 'golden sands' of the Weser beach in summer, as well as the lake (which you can also swim in), a 10-minute walk inland on the island. Families come here for cake and coffee, but it also kicks on some evenings. If that's the case, keep an ear open for the announcement of the last ferry back or you'll have to walk west and cross at Wilhelm-Kaisen-Brücke.

Cafe Tölke (☎ 324 330; Schnoor 23a; ⏰ 10am-7.30pm; ✗) This taste of a Viennese coffee house in Bremen will please even the most discerning tipplers of the regally roasted bean. Furnishings are original sofas, mirrors and chairs from the Austrian capital, but offering a less stuffy, more Hanseatic interpretation. It's a long-time favourite in the Schnoor and lends itself to unwinding between sights.

BREMEN

GAY & LESBIAN BREMEN

Bremen's gay scene is, like the city itself, relatively small but friendly. A handful of bars and clubs in the streets An der Weide and its extension Ausser der Schleifmühle make up the main quarter for guys. The lesbian scene is very small and centres on **Cafe Kweer** (Rat & Tat Zentrum; ☎ 700 008; www.ratundtat-bremen.de/events.php, in German; Theodor-Körner-Strasse 1; ⏰ 8pm-midnight Tue & Wed, 8pm-1am Fri), part of the information centre for gays and lesbians. It becomes a lesbian cafe from 9pm every third Saturday of the month, and from 3pm to 6pm each Sunday (with football screenings if Werder Bremen happens to be playing). Other events are also held here for gays and lesbians, so it's worthwhile checking out the website.

ENTERTAINMENT
Nightclubs

Clubbing in Bremen is relatively cheap; expect to pay €4 to €8 at the door for regular nights, although special events may cost more. Rembertiring, near the main train station, has a string of clubs for a very young crowd. See Dangers & Annoyances (p661).

ourpick **Lila Eule** (☎ 794 0664; www.lilaeule.de, in German; Bernhardstrasse 10; admission free, parties €3-6, bands €8-10; ☽ from 8pm, plus special events) A decade or more is a long time to be a hot tip, but this gem off Sielwall has pulled it off. A student crowd gathers here for parties and events, but it's also a very alternative place to watch the Werder Bremen football team; most Werder matches are shown here. Thursday night is the legendary student bash.

Modernes (☎ 505 553; www.modernes.de, in German; Neustadtwall 28; ☽ from 11pm Fri & Sat, plus special events) South of the river in Neustadt, this converted old movie theatre also hosts live music, and remains Bremen's best club, bar none. The centrepiece is the domed roof that can be opened to let in some much-needed air towards the end of the evening.

NFF Cream Club (☎ 345 199; Katherinenstrasse 12-14; ☽ Fri & Sat, plus special events) With a futuristic-looking bar, a chic dance floor and lots of cocktails, Nur Für Freunde (Just for Friends) is the place for house, dance and electro. It's also where famous German and international DJs come to spin tunes.

Theatre & Music

Bremen's main theatre company is **Theater Bremen** (☎ tickets 365 3333; www.bremertheater.com, in German; Goetheplatz 1-3; ☽ 11am-6pm Mon-Fri, 11am-2pm Sat), which performs across three venues. The main theatre, which stages opera, operettas and musicals, is Theater am Goetheplatz, where the famous 1970s film director, Rainer Werner Fassbinder honed his craft with the company. In the attached Neues Schauspielhaus you'll find new interpretations of classics and avant-garde drama, while the Brauhauskeller, the smallest venue, is used for anything from Elvis musicals to Edward Albee.

Die Glocke (☎ 336 699; www.glocke.de, in German; Domsheide) Bremen's concert hall stages classical concerts, opera and a large variety of special events, many by visiting performers, in a venue whose acoustics are considered to be among Europe's very best.

Schlachthof (☎ 377 750; www.schlachthof-bremen.de Findorffstrasse 51) Ethnic and world-music concerts, theatre, cabaret and variety are all complemented here by parties, art exhibitions and a cafe. Take bus 25 to Theodor-Heus-Allee.

Theater am Leibnizplatz (☎ 500 333; www .shakespeare-company.com; Am Leibnizplatz) Here the highly acclaimed Bremer Shakespeare Company mixes the Bard (in German) with fairy tales and contemporary works. Take tram 4, 5 or 6 to Leibnizplatz.

Sport

The local *Bundesliga* team **Werder Bremen** (☎ 01805-937 337; www.werder.de) is less a football team than a sporting religion. Worship takes place at the **Weserstadion** (www.weserstadion .de; Franz-Böhmert-Strasse 1a), where a seat costs about €40; these are almost impossible to come by, so your best bet is to beg outside the stadium. Take tram 3 to Weserstadion, or tram 2 or 10 to St Jürgen-Strasse.

SHOPPING

Reacquaint yourself with the Brothers Grimm fairy tale of *The Town Musicians of Bremen* (see the boxed text on p663) via one of the many English-language editions. Otherwise, the most obvious buy in Bremen is sweets. **Hachez** (☎ 339 8898; Am Markt 1) is a good port of call, as the local purveyor of chocolate and specialities such as *Kluten* (peppermint sticks covered in dark chocolate).

Both Böttcherstrasse and the Schnoor Viertel are full of interesting jewellery, from antique silver and oodles of amber to modern designer pieces. Ostertorsteinweg, in Das Viertel, is the place to look for funky streetwear.

There's also a renowned flea market on the Bürgerweide, north of the Hauptbahnhof (7am to 2pm most Sundays; check exact dates at the tourist office).

GETTING THERE & AWAY
Air

Bremen's **airport** (☎ 559 50; www.airport-bremen .de) is about 3.5km south of the centre and has flights to destinations in Germany and Europe. Airline offices here include **Air Berlin** (☎ 0421-552 035) and **Lufthansa Airlines** (☎ 01803-803 803). Low-cost carrier **RyanAir** (www .ryanair.com) flies to Edinburgh and London Stansted.

Boat

Hal Över Schreiber Reederei (☎ 338 989; www
.hal-oever.de, Martinianleger, Schlachte 2) operates
scheduled services along the Weser between
April and September. Boats from Bremen to
Bremerhaven (one-way/return €14.80/23.80,
3½ hours), with numerous stops en route,
depart at 8.30am every Wednesday, Thursday
and Saturday, and 9.30am on Sunday. Shorter
trips ending at Brake (€10.50/16.50, 2½ hours)
depart on Tuesday at 12.30pm. Students and
children pay half-price.

Bus

Agentur Grajan (☎ 157 00; Bahnhofsplatz 15) inside
the main train station sells **Eurolines** (☎ 069-790
3501; www.eurolines.com) tickets. Services run from
Bremen to Amsterdam (one way €38, five
hours), and other European destinations, departing and arriving from Breitenweg in front
of the Hauptbahnhof. Check prices online as
they are extremely variable.

Car & Motorcycle

The A1 (from Hamburg to Osnabrück) and
the A27/A7 (Bremerhaven to Hanover) intersect in Bremen. The city is also on the B6
and B75. All major car-rental agencies have
branches at the airport, including **Avis** (☎ 558
055), **Budget** (☎ 597 0016), **Europcar** (☎ 557 440),
Hertz (☎ 555 350) and **Sixt** (☎ 01805-252 525). **Avis**
(☎ 163 3699; Hauptbahnhof; ☼ 7am-8pm) also has an
office inside the main train station.

Train

Frequent trains go to Hamburg (€20.80 to €28,
one hour to 1¼ hours), Hanover (€21 to €30,
one hour to 80 minutes) and Cologne (€60,
three hours).

GETTING AROUND

Tram 6 travels between the Hauptbahnhof and
the airport (€2.20, 15 minutes). A **taxi** (☎ 140
14, 144 33) from the airport costs about €15.

Buses and trams are operated by **Verkehrs-
verbund Bremen/Niedersachsen** (☎ 01805-826 826;
www.bsag.de). Main hubs are in front of the
Hauptbahnhof and at Domsheide near the
Rathaus. A €2.20 single covers most of the
Bremen city area, while a day pass (Tageskarte)
costs €5.90.

For bike rental, contact the **Radstation** (☎ 169
0100; www.1-2-3rad.de; per day from €9.50; ☼ 8am-
10pm Mon-Fri, 9am-8pm Sat & Sun) just outside the
Hauptbahnhof (bring your passport).

AROUND BREMEN

BREMERHAVEN
☎ 0471 / pop 115,000

Anyone who has dreamt of running away to
sea will love Bremerhaven's waterfront – part
machinery of the trade, part glistening glass
buildings pointing to a more recent understanding of its harbour as a recreation spot.
Although it is best seen on a day trip, the city
has an unusual zoo and many boats you can
clamber over, so it's a hit with kids.

Most of all, Bremerhaven's German
Emigration Centre and the new Klimahaus
Bremerhaven 8° Ost (Climate House) are
worth coming to see. Bremerhaven has long
been a conduit that gathered the 'huddled
masses' from the verdant but poor countryside and poured them into the world outside. Of the millions who landed at New
York's Ellis Island, a large proportion sailed
from here, and an enticing exhibition at the
Emigration Centre allows you to share their
history. The new Climate House (looking in
plan a bit like the bubbly Kunsthaus in Graz,
Austria) and the new Atlantic Hotel SAIL
City (like a mini-version of Dubai's Burj Al-
Arab) have added a new dimension to the
interesting waterfront.

Orientation

The **bus ticket office** (☎ 300 3513; Friedrich-Ebert-Strasse
73 D-F; ☼ 7am-6pm Mon-Fri, 8am-1pm Sat), outside
Bremerhaven's train station, has free maps. The
city runs north–south along the eastern bank of
the Weser River. For the museums and zoo, get
on any bus leaving from in front of the Sparkasse
building outside the train station and disembark at the 'Havenwelten' stop, about 1.7km
northwest of the train station. Havenwelten
comprises the main harbours (Alter Hafen and
Neuer Hafen). The Schaufenster Fischereihafen
(fishing harbour) is 2km southwest of the station. See p672 for more details.

Information

Bremerhaven Touristik (☎ 414 141; www.bremer
haven-tourism.de; H-H-Meier-Strasse 6; ☼ 9.30am-6pm
mid-Mar–Oct, 9am-5pm Mon-Fri, 10am-4pm Sat & Sun
Nov–mid-Mar) When you cross from the bridge behind
the Auswandererhaus, this is in the building ahead, but is
unhelpfully hidden on the far side.
Tourist-Info Havenplaza (Am Längengrad;
☼ 9.30am-6pm Mon-Fri, to 4pm Sat mid-Feb–Mar,
9.30am-6pm Apr-Nov; hr might be extended to whole year)

BREMEN

GETTING BACK TO THE ROOTS

About 42 million US citizens are descendents of German emigrants, according to the US census of 2000. Each year, says Dr Simone Eick, who heads the German Emigration Centre in Bremerhaven, over 700,000 of these come to Germany. Many will find their way to the Centre, which opened its doors to visitors in 2005.

'We kept in mind two things when we started working on the concept of the Center', Simone Eick explains. 'The theme of migration can be frightening, so we wanted the visitor to get in touch. It's why the visitor can personally accompany an individual emigrant on the journey to the New World. You feel what it was like and become sensitive to the theme.'

Over 7 million emigrants left from Bremerhaven between 1830 and 1974, but who were they exactly? They were a wide group, Dr Eick says. In the mid-19th century many emigrants were looking for land and work. Later emigrants were Jews who came from Eastern Europe, especially Russian Jews escaping pogroms from 1871 until the 1930s. During the Nazi period many were Jewish refugees, who up until 1939 left from Bremerhaven for the USA, Great Britain or other countries.

Until 1900, entering the USA was relatively straightforward for any European, Dr Eick says. 'But after 1900 you had to have money and you couldn't be in ill health. On Ellis Island, if the immigration inspector saw you were disabled, for example, a C for *Crippled* was marked on your jacket – after that, you had to return to Europe. The steamship company was forced to pay the passage, so the companies began having their own doctors at the harbours.' Later, in 1921, a quota act was introduced in the USA. Under a system aimed at regulating the inflow of nationalities, only 3% of the total number of any ethnic group already in America could enter each year. Based on the census of 1910 – about 8 million Americans born in Germany or of German descent lived in the United States at that time.

BREMEN

Tourist-Info Schaufenster Fischereihafen

(☉ 9am-6pm mid-Mar–Oct, 10am-5pm Nov–mid-Mar) Located at the Fischkai, near the FMS 'Gera' ship. Also rents bicycles: to 6pm on day of rental €6.50.

Sights & Activities
GERMAN EMIGRATION CENTRE

'Give me your tired, your poor, your huddled masses,' invites the Statue of Liberty in New York harbour. Well, Bremerhaven is one place that most certainly did. Millions of those landing at Ellis Island departed from here, and the **Deutsches Auswandererhaus** (German Emigration Centre; ☎ 902 200; www.dah-bremerhaven .de; Columbusstrasse 65; adult/child/concession/family €10.50/6/8.50/26; ☉ 10am-6pm Mar-Oct, to 5pm Nov-Feb) now chronicles and commemorates some of their stories.

This is Europe's largest exhibition on emigration, and it does a superb job of conjuring up the experience. For added piquancy, it's located on the very spot where more than 7 million people set sail, for the USA and other parts of the world, between 1830 and 1974.

The exhibition recreates their travelling conditions, as you move from a 3rd-class passengers' waiting room, to dockside, to the gangway, into the bowels of a ship. You also stop in the huge 'Gallery of the 7 Million', which contains emigrants' personal details (a few thousand of them) in pull-out drawers and tries to explain why people left home. Your electronic entry card contains the biographical details of one particular traveller, whom you can follow throughout the exhibition. Everything is available in both German and English.

The early sections are especially interesting, so take your time to read and listen to the descriptions. A later section lands you in the reception centre at Ellis Island, with a moderately interesting film. If your forebears moved from Germany to the States, you can start doing research here; although some trips must be investigated at the **Historisches Museum Bremerhaven/Morgenstern Museum** (Bremerhaven Museum of History; ☎ 308 160; www.historisches-museum-bremerhaven.de; An der Geeste 1; adult/child/concession/family €4/2.50/3/10; ☉ 10am-6pm Tue-Sun).

Unfortunately, information about emigrants to countries other than the States is sketchier.

Getting *out* of Germany was not always easy either, she says. Until 1871 you were not a citizen, you belonged to the German ruler and needed a special release form before you could leave. In the days of sailing ships, the boats could be delayed and passengers had to wait in Bremerhaven – there were no exact departure dates. 'There was a lot of waiting. This was a danger for people. A lot left Bremerhaven without any money at all, having spent it on food and on a hotel. It was tragic.' This situation improved, however, with the introduction of steam shipping and good timetables, she says.

So what about conditions on the boats? 'At the beginning of the 19th century, few German boats left for the US. Most emigrants left on British, French or Belgian ships. These were overcrowded and had no cook on board. Each family cooked for itself, but no one knew how much food they'd need for the journey. Most didn't have enough with them and had no choice but to buy overpriced food from the captain. This was big business for the companies. It's another reason why many emigrants arrived in the USA with nothing.'

'In the 1830s some companies began employing a cook, and in Bremerhaven a law stated that only ships with a cook could depart. Another reason Bremerhaven was very popular among migrants was that in the 1840s a special hotel was built – it was cheap and very good.' Also from the 1840s, she says, the ships got better, because the owners realised they could earn more money from treating migrants well.

As well as offering an experience of what it was like to emigrate from Germany, the Centre has databases to help visitors look up their ancestors. Equipped with a surname and year of departure, visitors can find the ship their ancestors took and begin delving deeper into their German ancestry.

Finally, we asked the head of the German Emigration Centre where in Bremerhaven she likes to go to relax? 'To the wall on the foreshore', she says without hesitating a second. 'It's nice, because we're just two minutes from the river and close to the sea.'

OTHER SIGHTS

Behind the Emigration Centre, the **Zoo am Meer** (☎ 308 410; www.zoo-am-meer-bremerhaven.de; H-H-Meier-Strasse 6; adult/child €6.50/3.50; ⏱ 9am-7pm Apr-Sep, 9am-6pm Mar & Oct, 9am-4.30pm Nov-Feb, last entry 30min before closing) isn't spectacular on the face of things, but all the kids we saw there during shockingly inclement weather were enthralled, partly because the enclosures are cleverly built into one big artificial 'rock' formation. They'll see a polar bear (or if he's sleeping, a fluffy pile of fur on a rock), polar foxes, seals, penguins, pumas and chimpanzees. Check the website or ask the tourist office for feeding times.

The space-age and slug-like **Klimahaus Bremerhaven 8° Ost** (Climate House; ☎ 902 0300; www .klimahaus-bremerhaven.de; Am Längengrad 8; adult/concession/family €12.50/8.50/36; ⏱ 9am-7pm Mon-Fri, 10am-7pm Sat & Sun Apr-Oct, 10am-6pm daily Nov-Mar) is a fascinating new arrival in Bremerhaven. It opened in mid-2009 and offers a journey around the world along the 8° east longitude through climate zones in Switzerland (rather than on-the-nose due to cow pats), Italy, Niger, Cameroon, Antarctica, Samoa, Alaska and Germany. The displays have an educational aspect and are very much aimed at kids but are enjoyable

for adults, too. The temperatures do soar and plummet considerably (Cameroon gets pretty sweaty), so along with sensible shoes to scale Swiss mountains, and cross stepping stones and rope bridges in Africa, wear two layers of clothing. In fact, any wardrobe choice will be the wrong one at some point of the journey! Other sections focus on climate change and the elements. Late afternoon is the best time to visit because the queues are shorter, and plan about three hours here to get the most out of the experience.

For a spectacular view over Bremerhaven, go up the new **Aussichtslattform SAIL City** (Viewing Platform SAIL City; ☎ 309 900; Am Strom 1; adult/child €3/2; ⏱ 10am-8pm Apr-Sep, 11am-5pm Nov-Mar). This is part of the Atlantic Hotel SAIL City (p672).

A highlight of the **Deutsches Schiffahrtsmuseum** (German Maritime Museum; ☎ 482 070; www.dsm.museum; Hans-Scharoun-Platz 1; adult/concession €6/4; ⏱ 10am-6pm daily Apr-Oct, closed Mon Nov-Mar, last entry 30min before closing) is the reconstructed *Bremer Hansekogge*, a merchant boat from 1380, reassembled (in part) from pieces rescued from the deep. The collection of 500 boats inside is complemented by a harbour bobbing with museum ships and a submarine. Some have additional entrance fees.

BREMEN

Sleeping & Eating

If you do decide to stay in town, you might like to treat yourself to the **Atlantic Hotel SAIL City** (☎ 309 900; www.atlantic-hotels.de; Am Strom 1; s €160-300, d €220-400; ⊠ ⎙). Beige is the dominant tone here in rooms with vast panorama windows. The interiors are tasteful without being ostentatious, and there's a sauna and wellness area with quite good views, too.

Succulently fresh fish is served at the many restaurants of the remodelled Schaufenster Fischereihafen (Fishing Harbour) complex. (There's also an aquarium and puppet theatre; the on-site tourist office can help with details.) Between Fischereihafen I and Fischereihafen II of the Fishing Harbour, near the Comfort Hotel, is one of Bremerhaven's better fish restaurants, **Natusch** (☎ 710 21; www.natusch.de, in German; Am Fischbahnhof 1; mains €16.50-25.50; ⌚ closed Monday). Take bus 504 south to Fischbahnhof or 505 or 506 to Schaufenster Fischereihafen. Connoisseurs of delicious smoked fish can head for the family-run **Räucherei Herbert Franke** (☎ 742 06; Am Pumpwerk 2; small/large baskets €5/15; ⌚ 7am-4.30pm Mon-Fri, 7am-1pm Sat), where a long tradition of hand-smoking makes this another culinary highlight. Cats will be following you around for days afterwards.

Getting There & Around

Frequent trains connect Bremen and Bremerhaven (€10.60, 52 minutes), but consider buying a €20 return Niedersachsen Single ticket.

Travelling by car, Bremerhaven is quickly reached via the A27 from Bremen; get off at the Bremerhaven-Mitte exit. An alternative is a leisurely boat ride from Bremen (see Getting There & Away, p669).

Within Bremerhaven, single tickets/day passes cost €2.10/5.60. From the train station, buses 502, 505, 506 and 508 stop at Havenwelten, near the Alter Hafen and Neuer Hafen. Buses 504, 505 and 506 also go to Schaufenster Fischereihafen, in the other direction.

WORPSWEDE

☎ 04792 / pop 9450

Worpswede was originally a settlement of turf diggers, but from 1894 an artists colony was established here by the architects and painters who became associated with Bremen's Böttcherstrasse. Today it is a cute artisans town that lends to mooching around in sunny weather. Outside Germany, the community's most famous member was the poet Rainer Maria Rilke, who dedicated several books to this pretty Niedersachsen village. Other major names involved include Paula Modersohn-Becker (p664) and her husband Otto Modersohn, plus the future designer of Böttcherstrasse, Bernhard Hoetger, architect and painter Heinrich Vogeler, and the first to move here, painter Fritz Mackensen.

Today, not only can you visit their buildings and view their art in some seven museums, but you can also shop for porcelain, jewellery, posters, soap made from moor products and other trinkets. Throw in plenty of opportunities to stop for coffee and cakes, enjoy a spa, or go hiking, cycling or canoeing, and Worpswede makes a pleasant outing for anyone.

The **tourist office** (☎ 935 820; www.worpswede .de; Bergstrasse 13; ⌚ 10am-5pm May-Oct, 10am-5pm Mon-Fri, 10am-2pm Sat & Sun Nov-Mar) can provide more details, but one highlight is the stroll to the 55m-tall **Weyerberg dune**, less than a kilometre from the centre, where Hoetger's **Niedersachsenstein** sculpture looms like a giant eagle. A memorial to the fallen of WWI, it's a controversial beast for both the way it 'spoils' the natural landscape and for its original purpose as a victory column.

Even easier to reach is the revamped **Grosse Kunstschau** (☎ 1302; www.grosse-kunstschau .de; adult/concession €4/3; ⌚ 10am-6pm mid-Mar-Oct, 10am-5pm Tue-Sun Nov-mid-Mar), designed by Bernhard Hoetger in 1927. It is part art deco and part tepee, has a round skylight that complements wooden floors and, like most things in Worpswede, has attractively curved forms. Its permanent exhibition is a who's who of the artists' colony, but there is also a regularly changing exhibition, included in the admission. Part of the complex is a cafe known locally as Cafe Verrückt (Cafe Crazy).

The creative heart of the colony was the **Barkenhoff** (☎ 3968; Ostendorfer Strasse 10; adult/concession €4/2; ⌚ 10am-6pm), a half-timbered structure remodelled in the art-nouveau style by its owner Heinrich Vogeler. Today, it's a museum. Meanwhile, Vogeler's beautiful **art nouveau train station** (www.worpsweder-bahnhof.de) has been transformed into a restaurant. The Moor Express (see opposite) stops here.

Sleeping & Eating

Worpswede has several charming hotels, many of them integrated with art galleries.

DJH (☎ 1360; http://worpswede.jugendherbergen
-nordwesten.de; Hammeweg 2; dm under/over 27 €17.70/20.80, s/d €30.80/51.60; P ✕ 🖳) This hostel is located in a brick farm-style building where the bus from Bremen terminates (800m from the town centre).

Village Hotel am Weyerberg (☎ 935 00; www
.village-worpswede.de; Bergstrasse 22; s/d/tr €76/125/145; P ✕ Ⓥ) Rooms here are divided into split-level living and mezzanine sleeping areas, above a restaurant and basement art gallery. Its modern restaurant-cum-bar (open from 8am to 10pm, kitchen closed from 2.30pm to 5.30pm) has a drifty lounge feel and serves pasta, baked potatoes, salads and other light dishes (€5.50 to €9.50).

Getting There & Around

From Bremen's central bus station, bus 670 (€3.70 one-way) makes the 50-minute trip 23 times a day during the week and every two hours on weekends. From Bremen, the first direct bus is just before 6am and the last at 10.50pm weekdays. First and last buses are 8.50am and 9.50pm Saturday, 9.50am and 10.50pm Sunday. From Worpswede, weekday services run from 4.41am to 11.25pm, Saturdays from 7.53am to 11.31pm and Sundays from 10.53am to 9.53pm. Ask the driver to drop you near the tourist office ('Insel'). The vintage train, **Moor Express** (☎ 04761-993 116; www
.moorexpress.net; one-way adult/child/family €5.50/2.80/12) runs between Worpswede and Bremen (and on to Stade) four times each way every Saturday and Sunday from May to October. First and last services from Worpswede to Bremen are 8.07am and 6.07pm. First and last services to Worpswede from Bremen are 9.05am and 7.05pm. The train station is about 1km north of the tourist office on Bahnhofstrasse (follow Strassentor or Bauernreihe north).

Fahrradladen Eckhard Eyl (☎ 2323; Finddorfstrasse 28) hires out bikes from €6 a day. From the tourist office, you can walk there in less than 10 minutes by taking the path between the bank and the Village Hotel am Weyerberg to Finddorfstrasse and going right.

BREMEN

Hamburg

'The gateway to the world' might be a bold claim, but Germany's second-largest city and biggest port has never been shy. Hamburg has engaged in business with the world ever since it joined the Hanseatic League trading bloc back in the Middle Ages, and this 'harbourpolis' is now the nation's premier media hub and its wealthiest city, with its container ports growing rapidly thanks to burgeoning Eastern European business.

Hamburg's maritime spirit infuses the entire city – from its architecture (especially the redbrick, copper-roofed neo-Gothic warehouses rising above the canal-woven Speicherstadt, and buildings shaped like cruise liners and stacked shipping crates) to its rowdy fish market, along with the billowing spinnakers of sailboats gracing the Alster Lakes, and ships the size of city blocks sounding their horns as they navigate the mighty Elbe River. It's also given rise to vibrant immigrant neighbourhoods awash with multicultural eateries, as well as the gloriously seedy Reeperbahn red-light district. Hamburg nurtured the early promise of the Beatles, and today its distinctive live and electronic music scene thrives in unique harbourside venues.

That maritime spirit also continues to shape the city's evolution, including the all-new HafenCity waterside precinct, hip industrial-style restaurants strung along the Elbmeile docks, and mould-breaking design hotels and hostels that are seeing Hamburg steal the international limelight from Munich and Berlin. Visitor numbers (particularly city breakers) are booming, as the construction of new hotels races to keep up with demand.

The world, it seems, is finally returning some of its gateway's attentions.

HIGHLIGHTS

- **Go Up...** Ride up the spire of St Nikolai (p676) to its panoramic viewing platform

- **...And Up** Take to the skies above the Speicherstadt aboard Hamburg's moored High Flyer Balloon (p677)

- **Float your Boat** Rent a row boat (p684) to explore the Alster Lakes

- **Get Back** Time travel through the Beatles' career at the Beatlemania Museum (p682) near the venues where they once performed

- **Fast Forward** Peer into Hamburg's future through architectural plans and scale models at HafenCity (p681)

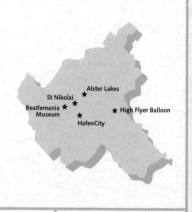

| ■ TELEPHONE CODE: 040 | ■ POPULATION: 1.77 MILLION | ■ AREA: 755 SQ KM |

HISTORY

Dubbed the world's 'most mercantile city', Hamburg's commercial character was forged in 1189, when local noble Count Adolf III persuaded Emperor Friedrich I (Barbarossa) to grant the city free trading rights and an exemption from customs duties. This transformed the former missionary settlement and 9th-century moated fortress of Hammaburg into an important port and member of the Hanseatic League.

The city prospered until 1842, when the Great Fire destroyed a third of its buildings. While it managed to recover in time to join the German Reich in 1871, this then saw it involved in two devastating world wars. After WWI, most of Hamburg's merchant fleet (almost 1500 ships) was forfeited to the Allies. WWII saw more than half of Hamburg's housing, 80% of its port and 40% of its industry reduced to rubble, and tens of thousands of civilians killed.

In the postwar years, Hamburg harnessed its resilience to participate in Germany's economic miracle *(Wirtschaftswunder)*. Its harbour and media industries are now the backbone of its wealth. The print media are especially prolific: the majority of Germany's largest publications are produced here, including news magazines *Stern* and *Der Spiegel* and the newspaper *Die Zeit*. The city is also a major Airbus base.

About 15% to 20% of the population are immigrants, giving the city a vibrant international flavour.

ORIENTATION

Hamburg is as watery as Venice and Amsterdam. Set around two lakes, the Binnenalster and Aussenalster (Inner and Outer Alster Lakes) in the city centre, it's also traversed by three rivers – the Elbe, the Alster and the Bille – and a grid of narrow canals called *Fleete*.

The half-moon-shaped city centre arches north of the Elbe and is bisected diagonally by the Alsterfleet, the canal that once separated the now almost seamless Altstadt (old town) and Neustadt (new town).

The Hauptbahnhof (central train station) is on Glockengiesserwall on the centre's northeastern edge; the ZOB (central bus station) is behind it to the southeast. Three other mainline stations lie west (Altona), south (Harburg) and north (Dammtor) of the centre. A network of S-Bahn (suburban trains), U-Bahn (urban rail) and buses criss-cross the city.

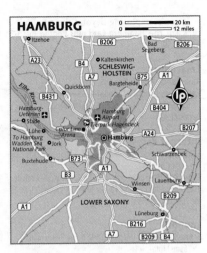

Within the sprawling city are distinct neighbourhoods. East of the Hauptbahnhof is St Georg, a gradually gentrifying red-light district and hub of the city's gay scene. The immense HafenCity development is evolving south of the Hauptbahnhof. West of the centre, St Pauli is home to the Reeperbahn, as well as clubs and bars. Further west St Pauli merges with the lively Altona district, which stretches south to the Elbmeile waterfront. To the north of St Pauli are its trendy and creative neighbours, the Schanzenviertel and Karolinenviertel.

Select neighbourhoods hug the 160-hectare Aussenalster north of the city centre, with Winterhude and Uhlenhorst on the eastern shores and Harvestehude and Rotherbaum on the western shores. The Universitätsviertel (University Quarter) takes up the western section of Rotherbaum.

INFORMATION

Bookshops

Dr Götze Land & Karte (Map pp678-9; ☎ 357 4630; www.mapshop-hamburg.de; Alstertor 14-18) Enormous range of guidebooks and maps.

Thalia Bücher (Map pp678-9; ☎ 3020 7160; Grosse Bleichen 19) Stocks English books.

Discount Cards

Tourist offices and some hostels and hotels sell the **Hamburg Card** (per 1/3/5 days €8.50/18.90/33.90). In addition to free public transport in the greater city area, it provides discounts on museums, tours and more.

If you're exploring beyond the city limits, pick up the **Hamburg Card plus Region** (per 1/3 days €18.50/51).

Emergency
Ambulance/Fire/Police (☎ 110)
Police Hauptbahnhof (Map pp678-9; Kirchenallee exit); St Pauli (Davidwache; Map pp678-9; Spielbudenplatz 31, cnr Davidstrasse)

Internet Access
Hamburg teems with call shops offering internet access.
Cyber Zob (Map p686; ☎ 2442 3768; www.cyber-zob.de, in German; Adenauerallee 78; per hr €2; ☒ 10am-10pm) In the ZOB (central bus station).

Laundry
Schnell & Sauber (Map pp678-9; Neuer Pferdemarkt 27; ☒ 6am-11pm)
St Pauli Waschsalon (Map pp678-9; Hein-Hoyer-Strasse 12; ☒ 6am-10pm)

Medical Services
Ärztlicher Notfalldienst (Emergency Doctor Service Hamburg; ☎ 228 022) Provides 24-hour medical advice.
Internationale Apotheke (Map pp678-9; ☎ 309 6060; Ballindamm 39; ☒ 8am-8pm Mon-Fri, 8am-9pm Sat, noon-6pm Sun) Pharmacy.

Money
There are ATMs at the Hauptbahnhof, the airport and all over town.

Post
Main Post Office (Map pp678-9; ☎ 01802-3333; Dammtorstrasse 14; ☒ 8.30am-6pm Mon-Fri, 9am-noon Sat)
Post Office (Map pp678-9; ☎ 01802-3333; Mönckebergstrasse 7; ☒ 9am-7pm Mon-Fri, 9am-3pm Sat)

Tourist Information
Hamburg Tourismus (☎ 3005 1300; www.hamburg-tourismus.de) airport (arrivals hall; ☒ 6am-11pm); Hauptbahnhof (Map p686; Kirchenallee exit; ☒ 8am-9pm Mon-Sat, 10am-6pm Sun); Landungsbrücken (Map pp678-9; btwn Brücke 4 & Brücke 5; ☒ 8am-6pm Apr-Oct, 10am-6pm Nov-Mar)
Information booth (Map pp678-9; Dammtor train station, Dag-Hammarskjöld-Platz; ☒ 8am-7.45pm Mon-Fri, 10am-4pm Sat) No hotel bookings.

DANGERS & ANNOYANCES
Although safe and wealthy, Hamburg is also undeniably sleazy in parts, with red-light districts around the Hauptbahnhof and Reeperbahn. The Kirchenallee exit of the Hauptbahnhof and Hansaplatz in St Georg are also dicey, both day and night. Fortunately, there's a strong police presence in these areas, too.

As in any big city, pickpockets prey on people in busy places, so stay alert.

SIGHTS
Altstadt, Merchant's District & Around
Hamburg's baroque **Rathaus** (Town Hall; Map pp678-9; ☎ 428 312 010; Rathausmarkt; tour adult/child €3/0.50; ☒ English-language tours hourly 10.15am-3.15pm Mon-Thu, to 1.15pm Fri, to 5.15pm Sat, to 4.15pm Sun) is one of Europe's most opulent, renowned for the Emperor's Hall and the Great Hall, with its spectacular coffered ceiling. There are no fewer than 647 rooms here, but the guided 40-minute tours only take in a small number.

To the northwest, the elegant Renaissance-style arcades of the **Alsterarkaden** shelter shops and cafes alongside a canal.

One of the city's most remarkable buildings lies to the south in the Merchant's District. The brown-brick **Chilehaus** (Map pp678-9; www.chilehaus-hamburg.de, in German; Burchardstrasse) is shaped like an ocean liner, with remarkable curved walls meeting in the shape of a ship's bow and staggered balconies that look like decks. Designed by architect Fritz Höger for a merchant who derived his wealth from trading with Chile, the 1924 building is a leading example of German expressionist architecture. It's situated alongside other so-called 'Backsteingotik' buildings (*Backstein* refers to a specially glazed brick; *gotik* means 'Gothic').

Keep an eye out for special exhibitions in the museums along Hamburg's **Kunstmeile** (Art Mile), extending from Glockengiesserwall to Deichtorstrasse between the Alster Lakes and the Elbe, such as contemporary art and photography in the converted market halls of the **Deichtorhallen** (Map pp678-9; ☎ 321 030; Deichtorstrasse 1-2; adult/under 18yr €7/free; ☒ 11am-6pm Tue-Sun).

Hamburg's Great Fire of 1842 broke out further west in **Deichstrasse**, which features a few restored 18th-century homes, most now housing restaurants.

Nearby **St Nikolai** (Map pp678-9; ☎ 371 125; Ost-West-Strasse; adult/child €3.70/2; ☒ 10am-8pm May-Sep, 10am-6pm Oct-Apr), not to be confused with the new Hauptkirche St Nikolai in Harvestehude, was the world's tallest building from 1874 to 1876, and remains Hamburg's second-tallest structure (after the TV tower). Badly damaged in WWII, it now houses a war memorial. A glass lift zips you up to its 75.3m-high viewing platform inside the surviving spire.

At the eastern edge of the Altstadt, near the Hauptbahnhof and St Georg neighbourhood, are some of the city's best museums. A treasure trove of art from the Renaissance to the present day, Hamburg's **Kunsthalle** (Map p686; ☎ 428 131 200; www.hamburger-kunsthalle.de; Glockengiesserwall; adult/concession/under 18yr €8.50/5/free; ☥ 10am-6pm Tue, Wed & Fri-Sun, to 9pm Thu) spans two buildings – one old, one new – linked by an underground passage. The main building houses works ranging from medieval portraiture to 20th-century classics, such as Klee and Kokoschka. There's also a memorable room of 19th-century landscapes by Caspar David Friedrich. Its stark white new building, the **Galerie der Gegenwart**, showcases contemporary German artists, including Rebecca Horn, Georg Baselitz and Gerhard Richter, alongside international stars, including David Hockney, Jeff Koons and Barbara Kruger. The view out of the gallery's huge picture windows is also worthy of framing. Special exhibitions incur an extra charge.

The **Museum für Kunst und Gewerbe** (Museum of Arts & Crafts; Map p686; ☎ 428 542 732; www.mkg -hamburg.de; Steintorplatz 1, St Georg; adult/student/under 18yr €8/5/free, adult from 5pm Wed & Thu €5; ☥ 11am-5pm Tue & Fri-Sun, to 9pm Wed & Thu) isn't quite so exalted, but is still lots of fun. Its vast collection of sculpture, furniture, fashion, jewellery, posters, porcelain, musical instruments and household objects runs the gamut from Italian to Islamic, Japanese to Viennese and medieval to pop art, and includes an art-nouveau salon from the 1900 Paris World Fair. The museum cafe is integrated into the exhibition space.

North of the Altstadt, the newly refurbished, **Museum für Völkerkunde** (Museum of Ethnology; ☎ 01805-308 888; www.voelkerkundemuseum.com; Rothenbaumchaussee 64; adult/concession/under 17yr €7/3/free; ☥ 10am-6pm Tue, Wed & Fri-Sun, to 9pm Thu; ⊕ Hallerstrasse) demonstrates seafaring Hamburg's acute awareness of the outside world. Modern artefacts from Africa, Asia and the South Pacific are displayed alongside traditional masks, jewellery, costumes and musical instruments, including carved wooden canoes and giant sculptures from Papua New Guinea, and a complete, intricately carved Maori meeting hall. The approach is refreshingly respectful of the cultures it presents.

Speicherstadt

The seven-storey redbrick warehouses lining the Speicherstadt archipelago are a well-recognised Hamburg symbol, stretching to Baumwall in the world's largest continuous warehouse complex. Their neo-Gothic gables and (mostly) green copper roofs are reflected in the narrow canals of this free-port zone.

A separate free port became necessary when Hamburg joined the German Customs Federation on signing up to the German Reich in 1871. An older neighbourhood was demolished – and 24,000 people displaced – to make room for the construction of the Speicherstadt from 1885 to 1927.

You can simply wander through its intriguing streets, look down on it from the **High Flyer Balloon** (Map pp678-9; ☎ 3008 6968; www .highflyer-hamburg.de; Deichtorstrasse 1-2; adult/student/child per 15min €15/10/8; ☥ 10am-10pm, weather permitting), which lifts you 150m into the air while remaining tethered to the ground, or take a *Barkassen* (small barge) trip up its canals.

Kapitän Prüsse (Map pp678-9; ☎ 313130; www.kapitaen -pruesse.de, in German; Landungsbrücken 3; tours from €12.50) offers regular Speicherstadt tours, leaving from the port. Other *Barkassen* operators drum up business opposite the archipelago, near Hohe Brücke. The area is beautifully lit at night.

In the post-industrial age, many of the warehouses have been put to new use as museums. The centrepiece is the new **International Maritime Museum** (Map pp678-9; ☎ 3009 2300; www.internationales -maritimes-museum.de; Koreastrasse 1; adult/child €10/7; ☥ 10am-6pm Tue-Wed & Fri-Sun, 10am-9pm Thu) It takes 10 floors to house this, the world's largest private collection of maritime treasures. Professor Peter Tamm Sr has amassed an astonishing 26,000 model ships, 50,000 construction plans, 5000 illustrations, 2000 films, 1.5 million photographs and much more, including innumerable nautical devices, uniforms, military and other objects documenting 3000 years of maritime history.

Other Speicherstadt museums include the following:

Dialog im Dunkeln (Dialogue in Darkness; Map pp678-9; ☎ 0700-443 3200, 309 6340; www.dialog-im-dunkeln.de; Alter Wandrahm; adult/student/child €15/9/6; ☥ 9am-5pm Tue-Fri, 10am-8pm Sat, 11am-7pm Sun, phone reservation required) Hour-long, pitch-black journey with a blind guide through recreated natural and urban landscapes, giving you a memorable impression of what it's like not to see.

HAMBURG

HAMBURG CITY

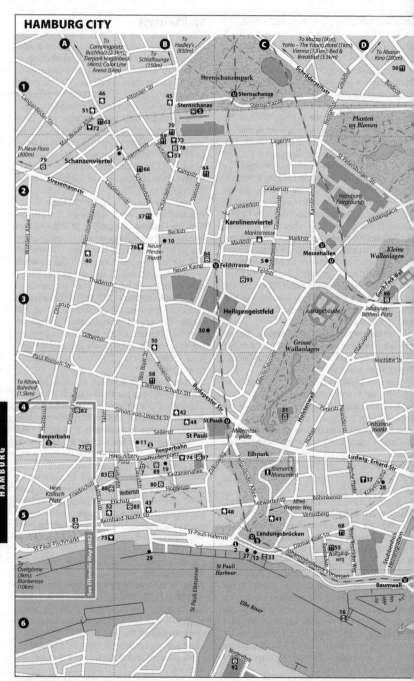

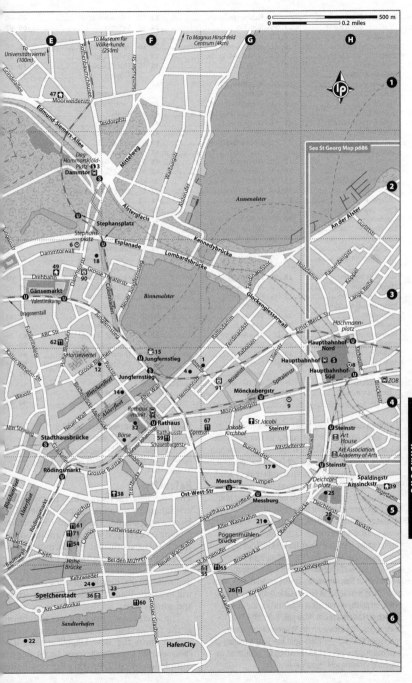

HAMBURG

Hamburg Dungeon (Map pp678-9; ☎ information 3600 5500, tickets 3005 1512; www.thedungeons.com; Kehrwieder 2; adult/concession/child €18.95/17.95/13.95; ⏱ 10am-6pm Jul & Aug, 10am-5pm Mar-Jun & Sep-Dec, 11am-5pm Jan & Feb) Camped-up chamber of horrors brought to life by actors, incorporating various rides. Tours depart every seven minutes and last around one hour. Older kids will get a kick out of it, but it's not recommended for those under 10.

Miniatur-Wunderland (Map pp678-9; ☎ 300 6800; www.miniatur-wunderland.de; Kehrwieder 2; adult/concession/under 16yr/child under 1m tall €10/7/5/free; ⏱ 9.30am-6pm Mon & Wed-Fri, 9.30am-9pm Tue, 8am-9pm Sat, 8.30am-8pm Sun) Kids and trainspotters will delight at this, the world's largest model railway, with astonishing recreations of recognisable landmarks. In busy times, prepurchase your ticket online to skip the queues.

Speicherstadtmuseum (Map pp678-9; ☎ 321 191; www.speicherstadtmuseum.de; St Annenufer 2; adult/concession €3/1.90; ⏱ 10am-5pm Tue-Sun) A century-old warehouse is the atmospheric backdrop for exhibitions on Hamburg's trading role (mostly in German).

Spicy's Gewürzmuseum (Map pp678-9; ☎ 367 989; www.spicys.de; Am Sandtorkai 32; adult/child €3/1; ⏱ 10am-5pm Tue-Sun) This spice and herb museum invites you to exercise your olfaction to the fullest.

HafenCity

The Speicherstadt merges into Europe's biggest inner-city urban development, **HafenCity**. Here, a long-abandoned area of 155 hectares is being redeveloped with restaurants, shops, apartments and offices in an enormous regeneration project encompassing 12 distinctive quarters. In the next 20 years, it's anticipated that some 40,000 people will work and 12,000 will live here. Plans include a primary school and a university.

The squat brown-brick former warehouse at the far west of the zone is being transformed into the new **Elbphilharmonie** (Elbe Philharmonic Hall; http://elbphilharmonie-bau.de), due for completion by 2012. Pritzker Prize–winning

Swiss architects Herzog & de Meuron are responsible for the design, which, like their Tate Modern building in London, boasts a glass top. This time, however, they're being far more ambitious, as the glass facade should be taller than its brick base and the roof line will rise in wavelike peaks to reflect the waterfront location.

HafenCity will be connected to the Hauptbahnhof and several other central transport hubs when the new U-Bahn line (U4) opens in late 2011.

You can pick up brochures (in German and English) and check out detailed architectural models and installations at the **HafenCity InfoCenter** (☎ 3690 1799; www.hafencity.com; Am Sandtorkai 30; admission free; ♡ 10am-6pm Tue, Wed & Fri-Sun, to 8pm Thu May-Sep), which also has a cafe. The centre offers a program of free guided tours through the evolving district.

Port of Hamburg

Sprawling over 75 sq km (12% of Hamburg's entire surface area), each year some 12,000 ships deliver and take on some 70 million tonnes of goods at Hamburg's huge port.

Climbing the steps above the Landungsbrücken U-/S-Bahn station to the Stintfang stone balcony offers an interesting snapshot, while dozens of **port and Elbe River cruises**, starting at the St Pauli Harbour Landungsbrücken, put you right in the middle of the action.

Operators at the Landungsbrücken include the following:

Abicht (☎ 317 8220; www.abicht.de; Brücke 1; 1hr tour adult/child €12/6; ♡ English-language tours noon Apr-Oct) Also offers Saturday evening tours taking you past the illuminated warehouses (departure times vary according to tides).

Hadag (☎ 311 7070; www.hadag.de; Brücke 2; adult/under 16yr 1hr tour incl audioguide €11/5; ♡ up to 4 times daily year-round) Has a Lower Elbe service (see p683), too.

Maritime Circle Line (☎ 2849 3963; www.maritime-circle-line.de; Brücke 10 adult/under 15yr €8/5; ♡ 3-5 times daily) Harbour shuttle service connecting Hamburg's maritime cultural attractions. The entire loop takes around 95 minutes; you can hop on or off at any of its stops.

At the piers, you'll also find the 1886 three-masted steel windjammer **Rickmer Rickmers** (☎ 319 5959; www.rickmer-rickmers.de; Brücke 1; adult/child €3/2; ♡ 10am-6pm), now a museum ship and restaurant. The nearby 10,000-tonne **Cap San Diego** (☎ 364 209; adult/child €6/2.50) hosts some

interesting temporary exhibitions on immigration and shipping.

Near the landing piers, the grey structure topped by a copper cupola is the entrance to the **St Pauli Elbtunnel** (1911), a twinset of 426m-long passageways with original tiling beneath the Elbe River. It's still used by vehicles (from 5.30am to 8pm Monday to Friday) and pedestrians and bicycles (24 hours), although most cars take the New Elbe Tunnel further west.

Northeast of the landing piers, the **St Michaeliskirche** (Map pp678-9; ☎ 3767 8100; www.st-michaelis.de, in German; Englische Planke 1a; adult/under 16yr tower €3/2, tower & crypt €5/3; ♡ 9am-7.30pm May-Oct, 10am-5.30pm Nov-Apr), or 'Der Michel' as it's commonly called, is one of Hamburg's most recognisable landmarks and northern Germany's largest Protestant baroque church. Ascending the tower's steps (or catching the lift) rewards with great panoramas across the canals.

Below St Michaeliskirche, in an alley off Krayenkamp 10, are the **Krameramtswohnungen** (Map pp678-9), a row of tiny half-timbered houses from the 17th century that, for nearly 200 years, were almshouses for the widows of members of the Guild of Small Shopkeepers. Today they house shops and restaurants, plus a little summer-only museum.

Reeperbahn

Even those not interested in strip shows usually pay a quick trip to the red-light **Reeperbahn** to see what the fuss is all about. Sure, it's tamer than the Amsterdam scene (which is itself becoming tamer), but it's still Europe's biggest. Long established as a party place for incoming sailors, crowds of thousands start to stream in from around 4pm, cruising the rip-roaring collection of bars, sex clubs, variety acts, pubs and cafes collectively known as the 'Kiez'.

Just north of the S-Bahn station is the **Grosse Freiheit** (literally 'great freedom') street, with its bright lights, dark doorways and live sex shows. Doormen try to lure the passing crowd into strip clubs; if you're interested, check the conditions of entry. Admission tends to be fairly low (around €5), but it's the mandatory drink minimum (usually at least €25) that drives up the cost. Ask at the bar how much drinks cost; we've heard reports of people being charged around €100 for a couple of watery cocktails.

South of the Reeperbahn stands the star of many a German crime film and TV show,

HAMBURG

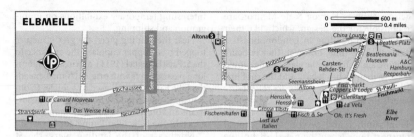

the **Davidwache** (Map pp678-9; Spielbudenplatz 31, cnr Davidstrasse). This brick police station, festooned with ornate ceramic tiles, is the base for 150 officers.

One of the most frequented shops in the area is the **Condomerie** (Map pp678-9; Spielbudenplatz 18), with its mind-boggling collection of sex toys and flavoured condoms.

Along Davidstrasse, a painted tin wall bars views into **Herbertstrasse**, a block-long bordello that's off-limits to men under 18 and to women of all ages (this is no joke: women have been met not only with verbal abuse but buckets of urine).

While the sex industry is still in full swing, some of the harsher edges (loitering pimps, for example) are gone. Mainstream musicals now play to sold-out houses on the eastern edge, and stylish nightclubs and bars entertain a hip, moneyed clientele until dawn. For comprehensive coverage of the area, pick up the free brochure *Hamburg St Pauli – The Reeperbahn Experience* from tourist offices, which even has a perforated 'adults only' sealed section (advising the going rates for sex, where to catch live sex shows and so on).

In the swinging '60s, the Beatles cut their musical teeth at the area's now-defunct Star-Club (see the boxed text, p684). At the intersection of the Reeperbahn and Grosse Freiheit, the new **Beatles-Platz** (Map p682) is designed like a vinyl record. Standing on this circular, 29m-diameter black-paved plaza are abstract steel sculptures resembling cookie cutters of the fab four (including a hybrid of Ringo Starr and Pete Best) plus Stuart Sutcliffe.

You can take a slightly surreal journey through the Beatles' career at the **Beatlemania Museum** (Map p682; ☎ 8538 8888; www.beatlemania -hamburg.de, in German; Nobistor 10; adult/child €10/6; ☽ 10am-10pm). In addition to entertaining interactive exhibits (including recreated Abbey Road Studios), and rare memorabilia (such as the Beatles' first record contract, which was

signed in Hamburg), it stages concerts and fashion shows. Look for the giant yellow submarine bulging from the building's facade.

East of the Reeperbahn, the kid-friendly (and kid-at-heart-friendly) **Museum für Hamburgische Geschichte** (Museum of Hamburg History; Map pp678-9; ☎ 428 412 380; www.hamburg museum.de; Holstenwall 24; adult/concession/under 18y €7.50/4/free, adult Fri €4; ☽ 10am-5pm Tue-Sat, to 6pm Sun) is chock-full of intricate ship models, has a large model train set (only open at certain times; check ahead), and even the actual bridge of the steamship *Werner*, which you can clamber over. As it chronicles the city's evolution, it reveals titbits such as the fact that the Reeperbahn was once the home of rope makers (*Reep* means 'rope'). There's a reduced admission price of €6.50 for ticket-holders to Miniatur-Wunderland (p680).

Schanzenviertel & Karolinenviertel
North of St Pauli lie the lively **Schanzenviertel** and **Karolinenviertel** districts, bordered by the U-Bahn Feldstrasse, S-/U-Bahn Sternschanze, and Stresemannstrasse, which retain a strong sense of Hamburg's countercultural scene. Creative media types mix with students amid a landscape of multicultural cafes and restaurants, as well as funky retro and vintage clothing and music shops, particularly along **Marktstrasse**, where you'll find everything from '70s sportswear to Bollywood fashions.

One of the most outstanding remnants of the area's rougher days, the graffiti- covered **Rote Flora** (Map pp678-9; ☎ 439 5413; www.rote-flora.de in German; Schulterblatt 71) looks one step away from demolition. Once the famous Flora Theatre, it's now an alternative cultural centre.

Altona
To the west of the Schanzenviertel, **Altona** is more gentrified but also has its share of off-beat shops (especially along the western

stretch of Ottenser Hauptstrasse) and buzzing restaurants, as well as a unique cultural centre, **abrik** (Map p683; ☎ 391 070; www.fabrik.de; Barnerstrasse 6), in a former foundry. Altona stretches from he villagelike centre around its S-Bahn and rain stations to the waterfront, where a string of industrial-style restaurants stretch along he Elbmeile.

Blankenese

Once a former fishing village and haven for ut-throat pirates, **Blankenese**, west of Altona, now boasts some of the finest and most expensive houses in Germany. For visitors, the area's attractiveness lies in its hillside labyrinth of narrow, cobbled streets, with a network of 58 stairways (4864 steps in total) connecting them. The best views of the Elbe (nearly 3km wide here) and its container ships are from the 75m-high **Süllberg** hill. To get to Süllberg, ake the S-Bahn to Blankenese, then bus 48 to Waseberg – having passed the clutch of beachfront restaurants and cafes – where you'll see a sign pointing to the nearby Süllberg. If you alight at the Krögers Treppe (Fischerhaus) bus stop, head up the Bornholldt Treppe and Süllbergweg. Or you can get off once the road starts winding and just explore.

Alternatively, **Hadag** (p681; adult one-way/return €5.30/10.60, under 16yr €2.65/5.30; ☼ 10.30am & 2.30pm Sat, Sun & public holidays Apr-Sep) runs Lower Elbe boat trips from the port stop at Blankenese.

ACTIVITIES

The 7.6km paved path around the Aussenalster is a popular jogging, in-line skating and cycling route.

Dr Götze Land & Karte (p675) stocks a wide range of local cycling maps and itineraries. For bike hire, see p698.

Hamburgers prefer not to call **Tierpark Hagenbeck** (Map p675; ☎ 530 0330; www.hagenbeck tierpark.de; Lokstedter Grenzstrasse 2, Hamburg-Stellingen; adult/under 16yr €16/11; ☼ 9am-7pm Jul & Aug, 9am-6pm Sep-Oct & Mar-Jun, 9am-4.30pm Nov-Feb; ☻ Hagenbecks Tierpark) a zoo. That's because its 2500 animals live in very open enclosures over 27 hectares. In addition to elephants, tigers, orang-utans, toucans and other creatures, you'll find a replica Nepalese temple, Japanese garden, art-deco gate and other similar attractions. A petting zoo, pony rides, a miniature railway and playground mean you'll have to drag the kids away at the end of the day.

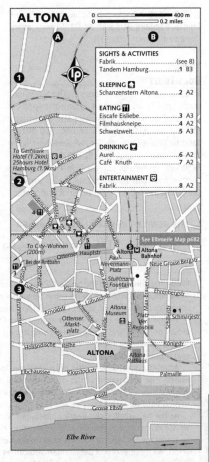

Hamburg's huge **Color Line Arena** (Map p675; www.colorline-arena.com, in German; Sylvesterallee 7, Bahrenfeld) was extensively refurbished for the 2006 football World Cup, and is home to Bundesliga club Hamburger SV. The stadium lies in the city's northwest, just off the E45/7/27 by car. Alternatively, take S-Bahn 21 or 3 to 'Stellingen', which is linked by free shuttle buses with the stadium.

Favourite local team **FC St Pauli** (www.fcstpauli .com) plays at home in the **Millerntor-Stadion** (Map pp678-9; ☎ tickets 3178 7451; Heiligengeistfeld).

COURSES

Hamburg has several German-language schools offering short and long courses for all levels, including **Colón Language Center** (Map

HAMBURG

pp678-9; ☎ 345 850; www.colon.de; Colonnaden 96), and **Tandem Hamburg** (Map p683; ☎ 381 959; www.tandem -hamburg.de; Schmarjestrasse 33).

TOURS
Boat Tours
In addition to the boat tours in the Speicher- stadt (p677) and Port of Hamburg (p681), you can also float past elegant buildings aboard an Alster Lakes cruise. **ATG Alster- Touristik** (Map pp678-9; ☎ 3574 2419; www.alstertouristik .de; adult/under 16yr single stage €1.50/0.75, 2hr round trip €9.50/4.25; ☯ Apr-Sep) runs a hop-on, hop-off service between nine landing stages around the lakes, as well as various canal and water-

way tours. Free English-language pamphlets and taped commentaries are available.

If you're the DIY kind, hire your own boat some travellers tell us it's the most fun they've had in Hamburg. **Segelschule Pieper** (Map p686 ☎ 247 578; www.segelschule-pieper.de, in German; An de Alster; per hr from €15) rents row boats and sail- boats, though you'll need a sailing certificate for the latter. The tourist office maintains a list of other rental outlets, including canoe and kayak rental.

Bus Tours
A bus tour is a stress-free way to piece to- gether this sprawling jigsaw of a city. As with boats, there are numerous tours; the best for

---

THE BEATLES IN HAMBURG – FOREVER

I was born in Liverpool, but I grew up in Hamburg.

John Lennon

It was the summer of 1960 and a fledgling band from Liverpool had been assured a paying gig in Hamburg, if only they could come up with a drummer. After a frantic search, Pete Best joined John, Paul, George and Stuart (Sutcliffe) in August that year.

Within days, the band opened at the Indra Club on the notorious Grosse Freiheit to a seedy crowd of drunks and whores. After being egged on by the club's burly owner to 'put on a show', John went wild, screaming, leaping and shouting, and performing in his underwear with a toilet seat around his neck.

After 48 consecutive nights of six-hour sessions, the Beatles' innate musical genius had been honed. The magnetism of the group that would rock the world began drawing huge crowds. When police shut down the Indra, they moved a block south to the Kaiserkeller – and the crowds moved with them.

At the Kaiserkeller, the Beatles alternated with a band called Rory Storm and the Hurricanes, whose drummer was one Ringo Starr. But they hardly had time to get to know each other before an underage George was deported in November, and Paul and Pete were arrested for attempted arson. All three escaped the German authorities and returned to England. There, as 'The Beatles: Direct from Hamburg', they had their Merseyside breakthrough.

In 1961 the Beatles returned to Hamburg, this time to the Top Ten Club on the Reeperbahn. During their 92-night stint, they made their first professional recording. Around this time, man- ager extraordinaire Brian Epstein and the recording genius (now Sir) George Martin arrived on the scene. The Beatles' recording contract with German producer Bert Kaempfert was bought out and they began their career with EMI, with one proviso: exit Pete Best, enter Ringo, a more professional drummer. Stuart Sutcliffe had also quit the band, and not long afterwards died of a brain haemorrhage.

In the spring of 1962, the final constellation of the Beatles logged 172 hours of performance over 48 nights at Hamburg's Star-Club (once at Grosse Freiheit 39, but now long gone). But with their increasing fame in England, they began to shuttle off more regularly for home and foreign shores. To usher in the new year of 1963, the Beatles gave their final concert at the Star-Club, immortalised in what would become known as the 'Star-Club tapes'.

The Beatles returned occasionally to Hamburg in later years. But it was the 800 hours of live performance on grimy red-light district stages that burned away their rough edges to reveal their enduring brilliance.

Beatlemaniacs can relive the Beatles' career at the **Beatlemania Museum** (p682).

on–German speakers, with reliable recorded commentary in several languages, is **Hamburg City Tour** (☎ 3231 8590; www.hamburg-city-tour.de; adult/under 12yr €15/free; ⊙ half-hourly 9.30am-5pm). ts open-topped double-decker buses pass all he leading sights over 1½ hours; tickets (sold on the bus) allow you to jump on and jump off all day. You can board at stops including the Hauptbahnhof (Kirchenallee exit), Landungsbrücken and the Rathaus.

Walking Tours

Dozens of walking tours operate throughout he city, many with specific themes, such as ed-light tours, 'historic hooker' tours, Beatles tours, culinary tours and more. Tourist offices maintain a list of seasonal departures. The Hauptbahnhof tourist office also rents DIY **GPS walking tours** (€8 per 4hr).

FESTIVALS & EVENTS

The city's biggest annual event is the three-day **Hafengeburtstag** (Harbour Birthday; www.hafengeburtstag de) in early May. It commemorates Emperor Barbarossa granting Hamburg customs exemption and is energetically celebrated with harbourside concerts, funfairs and gallons of beer.

Established in 1329, the **Hamburger Dom** www.hamburger-dom.de), held in late March, ate July and late November, is one of Europe's largest and oldest funfairs. It's held on Heiligengeistfeld, between St Pauli and Schanzenviertel.

SLEEPING

Booking ahead is a good idea any time of year, and is essential on weekends, during festivals and throughout summer.

If you'll be in Hamburg for a while, try **Bed & Breakfast** (☎ 491 5666; www.bed-and-breakfast de; Müggenkampstrasse 35) for rentals of up to one month, and **HomeCompany** (Map pp678-9; ☎ 194 45; hamburg@homecompany.de; Schulterblatt 112) or **City-Wohnen** (☎ 194 30; www.city-wohnen.de; Fischersallee 70) for stays over one month.

Budget

CITY CENTRE

A&O Hamburg Hauptbahnhof (Map pp678-9; ☎ 030-809 475 110; www.aohostel.com; Amsinckstrasse 10; dm from €12, linen €3, s/d incl linen from €26/32, breakfast €6; P ⊠ ▢ ⊙) A 300m suitcase drag from the Hauptbahnhof, this central branch of the institutional-style A&O chain has some

---

> ### SIGHTSEEING ON THE CHEAP
>
> This maritime city offers a bewildering array of boat trips, but locals will tell you that you don't have to book a cruise to see the port – the city's harbour ferries will take you up the river on a cheap and ordinary public transport ticket.
>
> One oft-recommended route is to catch ferry 62 from Landungsbrücken to Finkenwerder, then change for the 64 to Teufelsbrücke. From Teufelsbrücke you can wander along the Elbe eastwards to Neumühlen, from where you can catch bus 112 back to the Altona S-Bahn station or ferry 62 back to Landungsbrücken.
>
> On land, the U3 U-Bahn line is particularly scenic, especially the elevated track between the St Pauli and Rathaus U-Bahn stations.

---

900 beds in rooms with private bathrooms. Those deep inside the labyrinthine building can feel claustrophobic; try for one overlooking the street. Prices can skyrocket depending on demand. Two other Hamburg branches, A&O Hamburg Reeperbahn (Map p682; Reeperbahn 154), and A&O Hamburg Hammer Kirche (Hammer Landstrasse 170) 2.8km east of St Georg, are contactable through the same central reservation number and website.

ST GEORG

our pick Superbude (☎ 380 8780; www.superbude.de; dm €16-22, d €59-89, breakfast €7; P ⊠ ▢ ⊙ ; ⊙ ⊛ Berliner Tor) A games room (with Wii, table football and punching bags), large-screen cinema (and seat covers stitched from old jeans) and an open-plan kitchen and dining area (with bar stools made from recycled beer crates) are among the innovations at Hamburg's hippest hostel–budget hotel. Rooms, all with private bathrooms, are painted in candy-coloured shades like pink, orange or red, and all have flat-screen TVs. Laundry facilities are free; bike rental costs €4 per day.

Hotel Pension Annenhof (Map p686; ☎ 243 426; www.hotelannenhof.de; Lange Reihe 23; s €40-50, d €70-80) Behind this place's peeling facade lie 13 simple but attractive rooms, with polished floorboards and brightly painted walls. None have private toilets, though a few have shower cabins in the room. Breakfast isn't served, but free coffee and tea is available, and there are

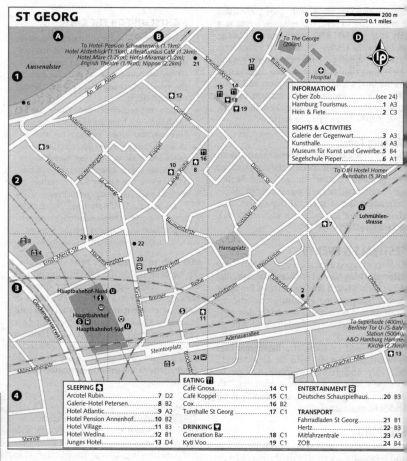

ST GEORG

Aussenalster

To Hotel-Pension Schwanenwik (1.1km);
Hotel Alsterblick (1.1km); Literaturhaus Café (1.2km);
Hotel Mare (1.2km); Hotel-Miramar (1.2m);
English Theatre (1.9km); Nippon (2.2km)

To The George
(200m)

Hospital

INFORMATION
Cyber Zob.....................................(see 24)
Hamburg Tourismus.............................1 A3
Hein & Fiete...2 C3

SIGHTS & ACTIVITIES
Galerie der Gegenwart........................3 A3
Kunsthalle...4 A3
Museum für Kunst und Gewerbe.5 B4
Segelschule Pieper..............................6 A1

To DJH Hostel Horner
Rennbahn (5.3km)

Lohmühlen-strasse

Hansaplatz

Hauptbahnhof-Nord

Hauptbahnhof

Hauptbahnhof-Süd

To Superbude (400m),
Berliner Tor U-/S-Bahn
Station (500m);
A&O Hamburg Hammer
Kirche (2.7km)

Steintorplatz

Mönckebergstr

Steinstr

SLEEPING		**EATING**		**ENTERTAINMENT**	
Arcotel Rubin.........................7 D2		Café Gnosa..........................14 C1		Deutsches Schauspielhaus.........20 B3	
Galerie-Hotel Petersen........8 B2		Café Koppel 15 C1			
Hotel Atlantic.......................9 A2		Cox.......................................16 B2		**TRANSPORT**	
Hotel Pension Annenhof...10 B2		Turnhalle St Georg 17 C1		Fahrradladen St Georg.............21 B1	
Hotel Village.......................11 B3				Hertz....................................22 B3	
Hotel Wedina......................12 B1		**DRINKING**		Mitfahrzentrale 23 A3	
Junges Hotel.......................13 D4		Generation Bar...................18 C1		ZOB.......................................24 B4	
		Kyti Voo..............................19 C1			

dozens of cafes in this increasingly gentrified part of St Georg.

SCHANZENVIERTEL & ST PAULI
Instant Sleep Backpacker Hostel (Map pp678-9; ☎ 4318 2310; www.instantsleep.de; Max-Brauer-Allee 277; dm/s/d €16.50/37/52; 🖳 🛜) Artistic murals – from green stripes to golden Buddhas – adorn this chilled-out pad in the happening Schanzenviertel. Airy dorms and private rooms house 53 proper beds (no bunks), though all share bathrooms.

Schanzenstern (Map pp678-9; ☎ 439 8441; www.schanzenstern.de; Bartelsstrasse 12; dm/s/d/tr €19/38/54/64, breakfast €4.50-6.50, mains €7-17; 🗡 🖳 🛜) Unlike its Altona counterpart (opposite), accommodation here is worn, but it rates a mention for

its handy location and on-site *bio* (organic) restaurant.

Backpackers St Pauli (Map pp678-9; ☎ 2351 7043; www.backpackers-stpauli.de; Bernstorffstrasse 98; dm €19.50-24, d tr from €60/75, linen €2, breakfast & snacks €2-4.30; 🗡 🖳) Entered via a bright cafe, this is a great new addition to Hamburg's hostel scene, which has a cool, subterranean maritime-themed lounge containing a small kitchenette, a sunny outdoor terrace, table football, and light-filled rooms (some with private bathrooms) with good-sized lockers.

DJH hostel (Auf dem Stintfang; Map pp678-9; ☎ 313 488; www.jugendherberge.de; Alfred-Wegener-Weg 5; dm without/with bathroom from €19.90/22.70, d with bathroom €59; 🗡 🖳) When you're not gazing out over the Elbe and harbour in the lounge of

HAMBURG

his squeaky-clean 357-bed hostel, you can shoot pool or play a life-size game of chess using knee-high pieces. It attracts lots of rambunctious school groups, but access is 24 hours. To get here, it's a 100-stair climb from Landungsbrücken U-/S-Bahn station. There's another DJH hostel in town (Horner Rennbahn; Rennbahnstrasse 100) but it's nowhere near as convenient.

Kogge (Map pp678-9; ☎ 312872; www.kogge-hamburg .de; Bernhard-Nocht-Strasse 59; s €29.50-33, d €48.40-55; ☎) At this rock-and-roll pub deep in noisy, grungy Reeperbahn territory, sleepyhead young party-goers can check out as late as 2pm from 'Bollywood', 'Punk Royal', 'Disco Dream' or other artist-designed rooms. None of the 12 rooms have bathrooms, but all have sinks. The bar is the hang-out of Hamburg's movers and shakers in the music industry.

Etap Hotel (Map pp678-9; ☎ 3176 5620; www.etaphotel .com; Simon-von-Utrecht-Strasse 64; s €49-59, d €59-69, breakfast €6; P ▣ ☎) Two minutes' walk from the Reeperbahn, this six-storey hotel, accessed by a glass lift is unusually central for the budget Etap chain. Industrially carpeted rooms have the typical single-bunk over a double bed set-up and ship-cabin-like bathrooms, but they're bright and clean, and wi-fi's free.

UNIVERSITÄTSVIERTEL
Hadley's (☎ 417 871; www.hadleys.de; Beim Schlump 85; s/d without bathroom from €65/75, breakfast €5; P ☎; ⊙ Schlump) With mattresses set on tall mezzanine platforms (accessed by ladders), there's enough space for you to have your own living room in this simple but stylish B&B. One of its four rooms has a private bathroom (yet surprisingly costs the same); shared bathrooms are lined with grey slate. While you can have breakfast in your room, Hadley's fantastic cafe (p692) is on your doorstep.

ALTONA
Schanzenstern Altona (Map p683; ☎ 3991 9191; www .schanzenstern.de; Kleine Rainstrasse 24-26; dm/s/tw/d/tr €19/44/59/69/74, apt €79-95, breakfast €6.50; ☒ ▣ ☎) A mix of families and slightly more grown-up backpackers inhabit these sparkling rooms with private bathrooms, and self-catering apartments. *National Geographic* prints decorate the common room's yellow walls, while wooden chairs are also painted in parrot colours. Staff are wired into what's happening around Hamburg. Two small ca-

veats: there are no lockers, and wi-fi doesn't extend to the rooms.

Seemannsheim Altona (Seaman's Home Altona; Map p682; ☎ 306 220; altona@seemannsmission.de; Grosse Elbstrasse 132; s/d without bathroom €30/55, s/d with bathroom €45/70; ☒) Christian sailors lodge between trips at this friendly, freshly refurbished seamen's home overlooking the river, and you can, too. Visitors (especially women) shouldn't confuse this with the Seemannsheim near St Michaeliskirche, which can feel intimidating.

OUT OF TOWN
Campingplatz Buchholz (☎ 540 4532; www.camping -buchholz.de; Kieler Strasse 374, Stellingen; per person/car €6.50/5, tent €11-15, s/d €62.50/77.50; ⊙ Hagenbecks Tierpark) This small, family-run camping ground has decent washing facilities, lots of shade and some cosy rooms in the reception building. It's well connected to the city by public transport. If driving, take the A45/E45 then exit 26 to Hamburg-Stellingen.

Midrange
ST GEORG
ourpick Galerie-Hotel Petersen (Map p686; ☎ 249 826, 0173 200 0746; www.ghsp.de; Lange Reihe 50; s/d without bathroom €49/69, s with bathroom €88-155, d with bathroom €98-165, breakfast €9.50; ☒ ▣ ☎) This delightful *Pension* inside a historic 1790 town house is an extension of its welcoming artist-owner's personality, whose paintings decorate the walls of his 'gallery of dreams'. Furnishings include a mix of contemporary, antique and art-deco styles. Our pick of its five rooms is the top-floor terrace studio, with a romantic rooftop terrace, kitchenette and separate living area.

Hotel Village (Map p686; ☎ 480 6490; www.hotel-village .de; Steindamm 4; s without/with bathroom incl breakfast from €52/72, d without/with bathroom incl breakfast from €68/95; ☎) You can tell this edgy gem was once a bordello: boudoirs feature various kitsch mixes of red velvet, gold flock wallpaper and leopard prints, and several have huge mirrors above the bed. It attracts a mix of gay and straight guests. For night owls, free, freshly brewed coffee is available around the clock.

Hotel Wedina (Map p686; ☎ 280 8900; www.wedina .de; Gurlittstrasse 23; s/d main Bldg incl breakfast from €98/118, other Bldg incl breakfast from €108/138; P ☎) You might find a novel instead of a chocolate on your pillow at this literary hotel. Margaret Atwood, Jonathan Safran Foer, Jonathan

Franzen, Michel Houellebecq, Vladimir Nabokov and JK Rowling are just some of the authors who've stayed and left behind signed books. The hotel's 59 rooms are spread over four buildings, offering a choice of traditional decor in the main red building, which opens to a leafy garden, or modern, urban living in its green, blue and yellow houses.

Junges Hotel (Map p686; ☎ 419 230; www.junges -hotel.de; Kurt-Schumacher-Allee 14; s/d incl breakfast €105/118; Ⓟ ▣ 🖳 ⌨) Yellow, pale-pink and orange window panels complement lots of blond wood in this airy, modern hotel less than five minutes' walk from the Berliner Tor U-Bahn/S-Bahn station. It's most memorable for the way extra guests can be accommodated in some double rooms, where beds drop down from the wall as in a train sleeper compartment. For adults, these beds costs €28 per person; kids under 12 stay free.

ALSTER LAKES

Hotel-Pension Schwanenwik (☎ 220 0918; www.hotel -schwanenwik.de; Schwanenwik 29; s/d without bathroom €50/75, s/d with bathroom €85/108; ⌨) Enjoy a luxury location and views for less at this humble but spotless *Pension*, whose breakfast room overlooks the Aussenalster. Framed pictures, especially by Miró, brighten the historic building. Rooms 19 and 20 also have lake views. Rates include breakfast. Take bus 6 to Mundsburger Brücke.

Hotel Mare (☎ 5190 0940; www.hotel-mare.de; Armgartstrasse 14; s/d €80/100; Ⓟ ⌨) A few doors from the long-established Hotel Miramar (below), the same mother-and-daughter team recently opened Hotel Mare, with fresh, contemporary styling in its large rooms. Take bus 6 to Mundsburger Brücke.

Hotel Miramar (☎ 5190 0940; www.hotelmiramar.de; Armgartstrasse 20; s/d incl breakfast €85/110; Ⓟ ⌨) On the same leafy street as Hotel Mare (above), the 'little taste of England' promised here means a choice of quintessential English rose or colonial decor (lots of ruffles and cut crystal).

Hotel Alsterblick (☎ 2294 8989; www.hotel-alster blick.de; Schwanenwik 30; s €85, d €100-160 incl break-fast; ⌨) Through an elegant stained-glass lobby with a caged wrought-iron lift, accommodation at this historic lakeside hotel blends original herringbone floors with contemporary furnishings and mod cons. Two rooms have balconies – one, amusingly, is off the bathroom. Catch bus 6 to Mundsburger Brücke.

Nippon (☎ 227 1140; www.nippon-hotel-hh.de; Hofwe 75; s €104-127, d €122-158, breakfast €15; Ⓟ ⌨) White walls, low futon beds, rice-paper screens tatami flooring and occasional splashes o cherry red create a Zen recipe here, as does its well-regarded Japanese restaurant, Wa-Yo. In addition to dinner (mains €16.50 to €23.30; Tuesday to Sunday), guests have the option of a traditional Japanese breakfast from Wednesday to Monday, and its che runs regular five-hour cooking classes (€89) Take bus 6 to Zimmerstrasse.

SCHANZENVIERTEL & ST PAULI

Fritz Hotel (Map pp678-9; ☎ 8222 2830; www.fritzhote .com; Schanzenstrasse 101-103; s/d €80/90) Run by fun friendly staff, this stylish town-house hote is as cool as a cucumber in shades of white and grey, and splashes of red. It's great fo 'urbanistas' who'll be happy finding their own breakfast at neighbourhood cafes (fresh frui and cappuccinos are laid on for free), and who aren't perturbed by a bit of street noise (some rooms have balconies overlooking the action; ask for one of the quieter rooms ou the back).

Hotel St Annen (Map pp678-9; ☎ 3177130; www.stanner .de; Annenstrasse 5; s €78-98, d €88-139; Ⓟ ☒ ▣) Tucked away in one of the few quiet streets between the Reeperbahn and Schanzenviertel this 36-room hotel is a favourite with business people and middle-class travellers fo its whitewashed, glossy-timber-furnished modern rooms and oasislike shaded back garden and terrace. Good-value family rates can be arranged.

Hotel Hafen (Map pp678-9; ☎ 311 1370; www.hotel -hafen-hamburg.de; Seewartenstrasse 9; r from €120, breakfas €16; Ⓟ ☒ ⌨) Location, location, location This privately owned behemoth of a hotel (353 rooms) looms over the heart of Hamburg's harbour from a small hill. If you're lucky enough to score a harbour-facing room (no guarantees, but it's worth asking) the views are extraordinary. In addition to the refurbished, historic main building, a former seamen's home, there are newer modern wings.

UNIVERSITÄTSVIERTEL

YoHo – The Young Hotel (☎ 284 1910; www.yoho-hamburg .de; Moorkamp 5; s/d €85/99, breakfast €12; Ⓟ ☒ ; 🚇 Schlump) Tasteful splashes of orange – the winged retro chairs and walls in reception and the burnt-sienna blankets draped across the beds – don't detract from he minimalist feel at this urban pad, where ersonal touches include miniature bags of elly beans on the pillows. The only outra- geous eye candy is found in its 'Occidental' breakfast room.

Schlaflounge (☎ 3868 5387; www.schlaflounge.de, in German; Vereinstrasse 54b; s/d €65/89, breakfast €10; ✕ ; ⊕ Christuskirche) Live like a local in this stylish, streamlined B&B in an appealing residential quarter with relaxed neighbourhood bars and excellent restaurants nearby. Attractive rooms incorporate blond wood and either brown and ochre or dark red and aqua colour schemes. Breakfast includes organic fruit and homemade jam.

Hotel Fresena (Map pp678-9; ☎ 410 4892; www.hotel-fresena.de; 3rd fl, Dammtorpalais, Moorweidenstrasse 34; s €75-99, d €88-139, breakfast €9; ✕) African sculptures and interesting photos greet you at this otherwise old-fashioned hotel, one of five hotels occupying the same historic former apartment building.

Hotel Bellmoor (☎ 413 3110; www.hotel-bellmoor.de; 4th fl, Dammtorpalais, Moorweidenstrasse 34; s/d/tr incl breakfast from €82/100/140; ☎) White embossed wallpaper and vintage advertising posters line the halls of this traditional hotel in the same converted apartment building as Hotel Fresena (above). Rooms 14 (single) and 34 (twin) feature art-nouveau bathrooms with stained-glass windows and tiled tubs. Views over Hamburg's rooftops unfurl from the sunlit breakfast room.

ALTONA

25hours Hotel Hamburg (☎ 855 870; www.25hours-hotel.de; Paul-Dessau-Strasse 2; r €105-135, breakfast €14; P ✕ ☎ ; ⊞ Bahrenfeld) Funky decor and an upbeat atmosphere attract models and fashion types to this design hotel. The reception features bright pink chairs and a desk that looks like it's wearing a studded belt, but the rooms are a little less Barbie meets Barbarella, with white, blues and exposed concrete. The biggest drawback is the location, in a suburban business park, but you can rent bikes for €7 per day. Room rates drop by around 15% if you're under 26.

Clipper Elb Lodge (Map p682; ☎ 809 010; www.clipper-boardinghouse.de; Carsten-Rehder-Strasse 71; apt €126-225; ✕ reception 7am-10pm Mon-Fri, 9am-5pm Sat, Sun & public holidays; P ✕ ☎) Designed for extended stays (when rates drop accordingly), these spacious turn-of-the-millennium apartments are kitted out with cream stone bathrooms, black kitchen cupboards and dishwashers, and TVs that swivel in the wall between the sleeping and living areas. Some have fabulous river views through floor-to-ceiling windows. You can unwind in the free sauna, steam room and solarium; laundry facilities are also free.

Top End
CITY CENTRE
Hotel SIDE (Map pp678-9; ☎ 309 990; www.side-hamburg.de; Drehbahn 49; r incl breakfast €170-300; P ✕ ☎ ⊟ ☎ ☎) A stylish alternative to the city centre's chain hotels, this Matteo Thun–designed stunner is built around a soaring prism-shaped central atrium. Suites feature vividly coloured free-standing bath-tubs. The 8th-floor chill-out lounge, strewn with 1950s-style saucers-from-outer-space sofas, opens to a panoramic sun deck. On weekends you can enjoy a decadent breakfast until 2pm, and check out as late as 8pm on Sunday evening for no extra cost. Its Fusion restaurant (mains €16 to €38; lunch Monday to Friday, dinner nightly) serves Asian-inspired cuisine.

ST GEORG
Arcotel Rubin (Map p686; ☎ 241 9290; www.arcotel.at; Steindamm 63; r €125-270; P ✕ ☎ ⊟ ☎) Privately owned Austrian chain Arcotel has arrived in Hamburg in style at this snazzy hotel. Done out in gleaming Middle Eastern marble, cherry-coloured carpets are woven with the names of Hamburg landmarks, while the smallish rooms are dominated by giant, circular red-leather 'sunset' bedheads. You can work off the exquisite home-baked pastries at its authentic Viennese coffee house (7am to midnight) in the high-tech gym.

The George (☎ 280 0300; www.thegeorge-hotel.de; Barcastrasse 3; s incl breakfast €139-209, d incl breakfast €146-216, lunch menus €14.50, dinner mains €17-38; P ✕ ☎ ⊟ ☎ ; ⊕ Lohmühlenstrasse, Uhlandstrasse) The concave caffe-latte-coloured facade of this design hotel, built in 2008, might be austere, but, inside, every one of its 125 rooms has individual wallpaper, and all come with free DVD rental and iPod docking stations. You can recharge yourself at the on-site spa, the classical Italian restaurant, DaCaio, the stately book-shelf-lined British-themed bar, or rooftop terrace with stunning lake views.

Hotel Atlantic (Map p686; ☎ 288 80; www.kempinski.atlantic.de; An der Alster 72-79; s €270-370, d €300-500, ste from €500, breakfast €33; P ✕ ☎ ☎ ☎) Imagine yourself aboard a luxury ocean liner in this

HAMBURG

grand 252-room hotel, which opens onto Holzdamm. Built for cruise passengers, it has ornate stairwells, wide hallways and subtle maritime touches. Suites – including BMW and James Bond suites – are a big leap up from the standard accommodation. Significantly cheaper rates are often available online.

SCHANZENVIERTEL & ST PAULI

East (Map pp678-9; ☎ 309 930; www.east-hamburg.de; Simon-von-Utrecht-Strasse 31; r €155-420, breakfast €17; P ✗) Even those who've seen a few design hotels in their time will be impressed by East. The walls, lamps and huge pillars of this hotel's public areas emulate organic forms – droplets, flowers, trees – giving it a warm, rich and enveloping feel. Floors are themed by plants and spices, and rooms have open bathroom areas, divided by flowing curtains. Its wellness centre, Japanese garden, and sunken restaurant (p692) are equally stunning.

Empire Riverside (Map pp678-9; ☎ 311 190; www .empire-riverside.de; Bernhard-Nocht-Strasse 97; r from €159, breakfast €18; P ✗ 🛜) This glittering glass edifice rose from an old brewery site in the rejuvenated Hafenkrone (harbour crown) precinct in 2008. Sparing splashes of colour brighten its restaurant, bars, and streamlined rooms (many of which take in the twinkling harbour lights).

ALTONA

Gastwerk Hotel (☎ 890 620; www.gastwerk.com; Beim Alten Gaswerk 3, Daimlerstrasse, Altona; r €136-181, ste €192-370, breakfast €18; P ✗ 🛜 🖥 🛜 🍽) Fashioned from a former gasworks, warmly coloured furnishings and quirky touches like the huge milling chute above the bar offset the exposed steel, concrete and brick at Hamburg's original design hotel. Located in a suburban business park, the place feels a little stranded, but it's fine if you have your own car or just want to cocoon. Catch bus 2 from Altona to Stresemannstrasse.

EATING

Unsurprisingly, seafood is this port city's strong suit, with everything from traditional regional specialties to sushi.

The city centre is (with a few exceptions) a culinary desert, but Schanzenviertel, the Port and Speicherstadt, and the Elbmeile teem with local and international eateries.

City Centre

Café Paris (Map pp678-9; ☎ 3252 7777; Rathausstrasse 4 mains €5.50-26; ✆ from 9am Mon-Fri, from 10am Sat, clos ing times vary) Within a spectacularly tiled 188 butchers' hall and adjoining art-deco salon this elegant yet relaxed brasserie serves clas sical French fare like *croque-monsieur* (toasted ham-and-cheese sandwich), *croque-madam* (the same, but with a fried egg), and *steak tar tare* (minced meat, but pan-fried, not raw). It breakfast for two (€23.90) is a veritable feast.

Mr Cherng (Map pp678-9; ☎ 3987 0366; Speersort 1 lunch/dinner menu €8.90/14.90; ✆ lunch & dinner Mon-Fr noon-11pm Sat, 4-11pm Sun; V) A favourite with city office workers, high-quality Chinese Thai and Japanese cuisine is served at impres sively low prices, especially its all-you-can-ea sushi buffet.

Die Bank (Map pp678-9; ☎ 238 0030; Hohe Bleichen 17 mains €22-27.50; ✆ 11.30am-late Mon-Sat) The banking industry no longer has the cachet it once did but don't let that dissuade you from dining in this 1st-floor former bank. Flanked by mag nificent marble columns and gleaming timber and opening onto a large terrace, the financ theme continues in the outsize sepia-tone photos of piles of coins, and 'banker's platters (prawns, crabs, more prawns and lobster), a well as rich dishes like truffle-infused vea which you can check out on the computerise menu at street level.

St Georg

Café Koppel (Map p686; ☎ 249 235; Lange Reihe 66; dishe €3.30-13.60; ✆ 10am-11pm; V) Set back from bus Lange Reihe, with a garden in summer, thi largely vegie cafe is a refined oasis, where yo can hear the tinkling of spoons in coffee cup midmorning on the mezzanine floor. The menu includes great breakfasts, lots of salads stews, jacket potatoes, curries and pasta.

Turnhalle St Georg (Map p686; ☎ 2800 8480; Lange Reihe 107; mains €9.50-25.50, brunch Sat/Sun €11.90/17.90 ✆ 9.30am-midnight Mon-Sat, 11am-midnight Sun Intimate is not a word you could use for this converted gymnasium, inside an elegant 1882 redbrick building, serving modern interna tional cuisine – but you still sometimes have trouble getting a seat. Exercise rings and rope remain hanging from one of the thick white beams under the vaulted A-line roof, but de signer lampshades and huge, potted trees have been added to the mix. Great cocktails, too.

Cox (Map p686; ☎ 249 422; Lange Reihe 68; mains lunch €9.50-18.50, dinner €16.50-23; ✆ lunch Mon-Fri, dinner daily

HISTORY OF THE HAMBURGER

A classic *Calvin and Hobbes* comic strip once asked if hamburgers were made out of people from Hamburg. And while Hamburg's citizens are, of course, known as Hamburgers, it was the city's role as an international port that gave rise to its most famous namesake.

The origins of the ubiquitous fast food date back to the 12th century. The Tartars (Mongolian and Turkish warriors) wedged pieces of beef between their saddles and the horses' backs, softening the meat as they rode until it was tender enough to be eaten raw. When they later invaded Moscow in 1238, the Russians incorporated the tenderised meat into their cuisine. By the 17th century, Hamburg ships called into the Russian port, bringing 'steak tartare' (named after the Tartars) back to Germany, which visiting seafarers then referred to as 'steak in the Hamburg style'. These patties of salted minced beef – usually slightly smoked and mixed with breadcrumbs and onions – were highly durable, making them ideal for long sea voyages.

Emigrants to America on the Hamburg shipping lines continued making the patties, which they served in bread. (As for who in the America officially launched the burger and whether the first burgers were served between bread slices or in a bun is unclear: various claims rest largely on anecdotal stories.)

Today, the hamburger has come full circle. American chains have propagated in Hamburg, as they have throughout the rest of the world. Although known here, too, as hamburgers or burgers, the original style of patty is rarely called Hamburg steak in Germany, but *Frikadelle*, *Frikandelle* or *Bulette*.

The hamburger's history explains the anomaly over the name of its key ingredient (namely, that it doesn't contain ham), compared to descriptive spin-offs like cheeseburgers, chicken burgers, vegie burgers and so on. But it doesn't answer the question of what you would call a burger that actually did contain ham – a ham hamburger?

behind its opaque glass doors, this upmarket bistro was part of the original vanguard of St Georg's gentrification. Its frequently changing menu of dishes, like swordfish with passionfruit and chilli vinaigrette, and semolina almond strudel with rhubarb, continue to lure discerning clientele.

Alster Lakes

Literaturhaus Café (☎ 220 1300; Schwanenwik 38; dishes €5.50-18.50, menus €24.50-38.70; ☻ 9am-midnight Mon-Fri, 10am-midnight Sat & Sun) If you're strolling around the Outer Alster, be sure to stroll in here, where creaky parquet floors lead you to a beautiful baroque cafe, with marble columns, high moulded ceilings, huge chandeliers and leafy garden views. Bistro fare ranges from antipasto and risotto to tarts and salads.

Port & Speicherstadt

Ti Breizh (Map pp678-9; ☎ 3751 7815; Deichstrasse 39; galettes €4.50-8.90, crêpes €3.10-7.20; ☻ noon-10pm; **V**) Once you get past the souvenir shop selling striped Breton sailors' tops, there's some cool, contemporary Breton artwork on the walls of this canalside restaurant. You can wash down galettes (savoury crêpes, made from buckwheat), such as a *Brocéliande* (Roquefort

cheese and walnuts), and sweet crêpes, like *Morgane* (caramelised apples and chestnut cream), with Dan Armor Breton cider. *Yec'hed mat* (cheers)!

Fleetschlösschen (Map pp678-9; ☎ 3039 3210; Brooktorkai 17; snacks €3.80-7.50; ☻ 10am-8pm) One of the cutest cafes you ever saw, this former customs post overlooks a Speicherstadt canal and has a narrow, steel spiral staircase to the toilets. There's barely room for 20 inside, but its outdoor seating areas are brilliant in sunny weather. The owner's collection of *Kleinods* (small treasures) includes centuries-old Dutch pottery unearthed during the construction of HafenCity.

Chilli Club (Map pp678-9; ☎ 3570 3580; Am Sandtorkai 54; dishes €6.50-23.50; ☻ food served noon-11pm; **V**) This trendy noodle bar is tucked away in the industrial-looking HafenCity. Asian tapas, dim sum and sushi are served within the restaurant's red-and-black interior and sailcloth-shaded waterside terrace.

Deichgraf (Map pp678-9; ☎ 364 208; Deichstrasse 23; lunch mains €7-14.50, dinner mains €14.50-24.50; ☻ lunch & dinner Mon-Fri, noon-10pm Sat) In a prime setting, with the water on one side and long street-side tables on the other, Deichgraf excels in Hamburg specialities cooked to a high standard.

HAMBURG

Aquario (Map pp678-9; ☎ 3600 6500; Rambachstrasse 4; mains €9.90-19.90; noon-11pm Tue-Sun) Looking like a retro underwater world with its exposed bricks and giant shells on the ceiling, Aquario is a family-friendly favourite for its heaping portions of fresh seafood. Enter via Wolfgangsweg.

Panthera Rodizio (Map pp678-9; ☎ 378 6370; Ditmar-Koel-Strasse 3; mains €10-23, buffet €23.50; noon-1am; V) At the eastern end of one of Hamburg's liveliest and most multicultural eat streets, the best way to experience a feast at this high-tempo Brazilian restaurant is to order the *Spezialität Rodizio* buffet, whereby huge skewers of meat are brought around to your table and carved onto your plate. Vegetarian dishes are available too, but that would be missing the point.

Alt Hamburger Aalspeicher (Map pp678-9; ☎ 362 990; Deichstrasse 43; mains €12-26.50, set menus €29.50-47.50; lunch & dinner) Despite its tourist-friendly canalside location, the knick-knack-filled dining room and warm service at this avocado-coloured restaurant make you feel like you're dining in your *Oma's* (grandma's) house. *Aalsuppe* (see p81) is among its local specialties.

Schanzenviertel & St Pauli

Café Mimosa (Map pp678-9; Clemens-Schultz-Strasse 87; dishes €2.20-8.50; 11am-7pm Tue-Sun; V) A welcome change from the greasy fast-food joints on the nearby Reeperbahn, this gem of a neighbourhood cafe serves delicious pastas, healthy salads, proper coffee and homemade cakes in a theatrical space of stripped floors, bare wooden tables with brass candlesticks and red-and-cream-painted walls. There's a clutch of pavement tables.

Die Herren Simpel (Map pp678-9; ☎ 3868 4600; Schulterblatt 75; dishes €3.60-7.90; 9am-late Mon-Fri, 10am-late Sat & Sun; V) The sky-blue mural with huge white flowers behind the bar has become this cafe's signature. Its tiny entrance opens to an unexpectedly spacious series of retro rooms, plus a winter garden niche and al fresco tables out back. There's a fantastic range of breakfasts, from the fishy *Sylter* (from Sylt) to the healthy *Frucht* (fruit), along with light meals.

Erikas Eck (Map pp678-9; ☎ 433 545; Sternstrasse 98; mains €5.90-17.90; 5pm-2am) Wood-lined Erikas has been serving up traditional home cooking since the golden oldies on its radio were first-time hits. Most of its filling fare, including schnitzels, herrings and *Schweinebraten* (roas pork), costs under €10.

East (Map pp678-9; ☎ 309 930; Simon-von-Utrech Strasse 31; lunch mains €9.50-18.50, dinner mains €20.50-2 noon-11pm Sun-Wed, 2pm-midnight Thu-Sat) House in a converted 19th-century iron factory the Euro-Asian restaurant at this desig hotel (p690) is bathed in ethereal light from cathedral-style pink, purple, orange and yel low stained-glass windows, while wavy treelik striated columns stretch from the basemen floor to the ceiling above the mezzanin Yakshi's bar. Private lounges are hidden i the white honeycomb wall. Book ahead.

La Sepia (Map pp678-9; ☎ 432 2066; Schulterblatt 3 mains €12-20; noon-3am) The aroma of fresh fis wafting from this neighbourhood restauran stops you in your tracks. Its enormous dinin space is adorned with a hotchpotch of mari time relics, like old wooden boats suspende from the ceiling, while dishes incorporat Portuguese and Spanish influences.

Also recommended:

Bok (Map pp678-9; ☎ 4318 3597; Schulterblatt 3; lunch mains €5.70-9.20, dinner mains €9.30-14.70; V) A popu lar Hamburg minichain. Duck makes a frequent appearanc on its pan-Asian menu.

Shikara Quick (Map pp678-9; ☎ 430 2353; Susannenstrasse 20; mains €5.90-8.50; noon-midnight; V) Another excellent Hamburg minichain, cooking tasty Indian curries.

Thai Cowboy's (Map pp678-9; ☎ 430 8025; Susannenstrasse 18; mains €6.20-8.50; 11.30am-10pm; V) Fragrant stand-up Thai fare.

Universitätsviertel

Hadley's (☎ 450 5075; Beim Schlump 84a; dishes €2.90-8.50, brunch Sun €16.80; 10am-late Mon-Sat, 11am-lat Sun; Schlump; V) This stylish yet relaxed cafe bar was once the emergency room of a histori Wilhelminian-style former hospital, now hotel (see p687). Through the door curtains the enveloping dining room and mezzanin open onto a terrace and leafy garden. Home baked treats features on the simple but stel lar menu. Regular events include live jazz o Monday nights from 8pm.

Balutschi (Map pp678-9; ☎ 452 479; Grindelallee 3 mains €5.50-14.50; lunch & dinner; V) Out the bacl of this Pakistani restaurant, there's an over the-top *Arabian Nights*–style grotto, where you remove your shoes and sit on carpets and low benches. The multicourse banquet menu are particularly good value if there are two o more of you.

HAMBURG

HAMBURG'S UNIQUE FISH MARKET

Every Sunday morning, in the wee hours, an unusual ritual unfolds along the banks of the Elbe. A fleet of small trucks rumbles onto the cobbled pavement. Hardy types emerge from the drivers' cabins and set out to turn their vehicles into stores on wheels. They artfully arrange their bananas, apples, cauliflower and whatever else they've harvested that week. Others pile up slippery eels, smoked fish fillets and fresh shrimp in tasteful displays. In another corner, cacti, flowers and leafy plants wait for customers. It's not yet 5am as the first customers begin to trundle in, hyper from a night of partying in adjacent St Pauli. Let the trading begin!

The **Fischmarkt** (Map p682; ⏰ 5am-9.30am Sun Apr-Sep, 7am-9.30am Sun Oct-Mar) in St Pauli has been a Hamburg institution since 1703 and still defines the city's life and spirit. Locals of every age and walk of life join curious tourists, and you can buy everything from cheap sweatshirts to tulips.

The undisputed stars of the event – and great, free entertainment – are the boisterous *Marktschreier* (market criers) who hawk their wares at the top of their lungs. 'Don't be shy, little girl,' they might say with a lascivious wink to a rotund 60-year-old, waggling a piece of eel in front of her face. Almost always, the 'girl' blushes before taking a hearty bite as the crowd cheers her on. It's all just part of the show.

More entertainment takes place in the adjoining Fischauktionshalle (Fish Auction Hall), where a live band cranks out ancient German pop songs. Down in the pit, sausage fumes waft and beer flows as if it were evening and not just past dawn. For those who actually know what time it is, breakfast is served on the gallery.

Vienna (☎ 439 9182; Fettstrasse 2; mains €10-20; ⏰ dinner Tue-Sun; Ⓜ Christuskirche) Hidden in a quiet residential street, with an overgrown garden screening its outdoor terrace, this German-Austrian restaurant is renowned Hamburg-wide for its authentic schnitzels, venison and fish. It doesn't take reservations; your best bet for getting a table is to turn up early, at 6.45pm, or late, at 9pm.

Mazza (☎ 2841 9191; Moorkamp 5; lunch/dinner menu €11.50/28; ⏰ lunch & dinner; Ⓥ; Ⓜ Schlump) In the same swish building as YoHo – The Young Hotel (p688) but separately owned, this Syrian restaurant sticks to a simple formula when it comes to food, offering a choice of three-course lunch menus and five-course dinner menus made up of dishes like potatoes in lemon, olive oil and thyme, carrot in rose water, and lamb with mint yoghurt. The extensive wine list spans Lebanon to South Africa.

Altona

In the villagelike area around Altona's S-Bahn and train stations, you'll find dozens of international eateries. For restaurants along Altona's waterfront, see the Elbmeile section (right).

our pick **Eiscafe Eisliebe** (Map p683; ☎ 3980 8482; Bei der Reitbahn 2; ice cream from €1.30; ⏰ noon-9pm) Some of the yummiest ice cream you'll ever taste is scooped from this little hole in the wall (look for the queues). On any given day, you'll find around a dozen of its handmade, all-natural flavours like cherry-rippled poppy-seed or sticky crème brûlée.

Filmhauskneipe (Map p683; ☎ 3990 8025; Friedensallee 7; mains €5-9.20; ⏰ noon-1am, kitchen closes 11pm) Within Altona's Zeisehallen (cultural centre), wrapped around an old ship-propeller factory, this chilled cafe-bar is a favourite hang-out of students from the centre's film school for its simple but wholesome food. In summer it spills onto a 100-seater terrace.

Schweizwelt (Map p683; ☎ 3990 7000; Grosse Rainstrasse 2; mains €5.50-17.90; ⏰ 10am-midnight Tue-Sat, 10am-6pm Sun) Noodle, meat and especially cheese dishes, along with homemade chocolate mousse, are the mainstays of this cute basement Swiss restaurant.

Elbmeile

Hamburg's western riverfront, from Altona to Övelgönne, known as the Elbmeile (Elbe Mile), has a dense concentration of mostly fish-oriented restaurants in a stark, industrial-style setting.

our pick **Fisch & So** (Map p682; ☎ 389 3109; Grosse Elbstrasse 117; dishes €2.90-11.50; ⏰ 9am-5pm Mon-Fri, 11am-6pm Sat) For fresh fish at fantastically low prices, head to this little cafe's clutch of blue-clothed tables to savour simple but delicious fish sandwiches, or perhaps *Tintenfisch* (calamari) with *Bratkartoffeln* (sautéed potatoes).

It's tucked away on the river side of the redbrick Fischmarkt Hamburg-Altona market hall.

Oh, It's Fresh (Map p682; ☎ 3803 7861; Carsten-Rehder-Strasse 71; dishes €3.95-14.50; ⓨ 6.30am-6.30pm Mon-Fri, 8am-6pm Sat & Sun; Ⓥ) Part of a rapidly growing, health-food-oriented Hamburg minichain, red floral wallpaper and a series of world clocks decorate this light-filled, airy space. In addition to international breakfasts, it serves salads, bagels and baked treats, such as melt-in-your-mouth brownies, to eat in or take away.

Das Weisse Haus (Map p682; ☎ 390 9016; Neumühlen 50; lunch mains €6.90-10, dinner menus €28-42; ⓨ lunch & dinner Mon-Sat) A converted fisherman's cottage, the 'White House' is (unlike its US namesake) surprisingly cramped, given its status as a major culinary player. Diners book a month ahead to submit themselves to 'surprise' dinners (vegetarian and other dietary requirements can be accommodated to a limited degree). Lunch is a simpler, à la carte affair, but reservations are still advised. The best seats among the artfully low-key rooms are in the front winter garden.

Lust auf Italien (Map p682; ☎ 382 811; Grosse Elbstrasse 133; mains €7-17; ⓨ noon-midnight; Ⓥ) Plonk yourself down at one of the communal wooden benches at this unpretentious, family-friendly restaurant. The pasta and fish dishes are homey rather than gourmet, but the seafood tastes like it's just leapt from the sea.

La Vela (Map p682; ☎ 3869 9393; Grosse Elbstrasse 27; mains €8.50-23.50; ⓨ noon-11pm; Ⓥ) Cruise and container ships glide by just outside the window of this buzzing, semiformal Italian restaurant. With such unusually close-up views, it keeps most other things simple: the redbrick interior is uncluttered and the menu is sparse, with about a dozen choices for mains. The only complicated thing is the enormous wine list.

Fischereihafen (Map p682; ☎ 381 816; Grosse Elbstrasse 143; lunch mains €8.50-14.50, dinner mains €18.50-28.50; ⓨ lunch & dinner) Traditional and incredibly elegant, Fischereihafen serves some of Hamburg's finest fish, including regional specialities, to a mature, well-heeled clientele. Its 1st-floor, subtly maritime-themed dining room overlooks the Elbe.

Henssler & Henssler (Map p682; ☎ 3869 9000; Grosse Elbstrasse 160; mains €12.50-26; ⓨ lunch & dinner Mon-Sat) This smart-casual spot doesn't really 'do' views: it's across the road from the water and has an opaque frontage. But couples, business people and young families all pack its minimalist concrete-floored milieu for its delectable sushi.

Le Canard Nouveau (Map p682; ☎ 8812 9531; Elbchaussee 139; mains €32-36, menus €48-99; ⓨ lunch & dinner Tue-Fri, dinner Sat) Turkish-born chef Ali Güngörmüs has deservedly claimed a Michelin star for his intricate dishes, such as turbot with polenta soufflé, duck with apple-ginger purée, and chocolate cake with rhubarb jelly, marinated strawberries and honey-and-sour-cream ice cream. Definitely book ahead. Güngörmüs also runs regular cooking classes, which cost €200 for five hours, including meal and wines.

DRINKING

Listings in *Prinz* (http://hamburg.prinz.de), *Oxmox* (www.oxmoxhh.de) and *Szene* (www.szene-hamburg.de), and their websites, are in German, but non-German speakers will also find them helpful for navigating the enormous bar scene.

Nachtasyl (Map pp678-9; ☎ 814 444; Alstertor 1; ⓨ from 7pm) Hamburg's city centre is usually like the *Mary Celeste* of an evening, but it does boast this unusual beauty, with its high-arched ceiling and embossed wallpaper.

Dual (Map pp678-9; ☎ 4320 8829; Schanzenstrasse 53; ⓨ from 11.30am Mon-Fri, from 10am Sat, from 4pm Sun) Within its chic orange, 1970s retro interior, the loungey vibe at this elongated space is perfect for an espresso or cocktails.

Nouar (Map pp678-9; ☎ 430 8949; Max-Brauer-Allee 275; ⓨ from 7pm) A popular late-night bar with students and other denizens of the nearby Schanzenviertel, this place has that relaxed secondhand look going on and a fondness for football during the week.

Zoë 2/Summun Bonum (Map pp678-9; Neuer Pferdemarkt 17; ⓨ from noon) The share-house decor here is such a home from home for students that you'll often see them snoozing in its battered secondhand sofas.

Meanie Bar (Map pp678-9; ☎ 310845; www.molotowclub.com, in German; Spielbudenplatz 5; ⓨ from 6pm) One of the few venues along the Reeperbahn with local cred, the retro Meanie Bar is a hang-out for musos and artists.

Tower Bar (Map pp678-9; www.hotel-hafen-hamburg.de; Seewartenstrasse 9; ⓨ 6pm-1am Mon-Thu, 6pm-2.30am Fri-Sun) For a more elegant, mature evening, repair to this 14th-floor eyrie at

HAMBURG'S UNLIKELY BEACH BARS

When it comes to city beaches, you have to hand it to Hamburgers for their can-do spirit. Undeterred by the cranes, shipbuilding docks and steel containers decorating their city's workaholic port, and renowned *Schmuddelwetter* (drizzly weather), they've begun shipping in tonnes of sand to the industrial waterfront.

The city beach season kicks off in spring and lasts until at least September, as hipsters come to drink, listen to music, dance and simply lounge on these artificial beaches. Ibiza it ain't, but it does have its own special buzz.

Leading venues, open daily (weather permitting), include the following:

Central Park (Map pp678–9; www.centralpark-hamburg.de, in German; Max-Brauer-Allee 277) A beach bar without water? 'No problem', said its enterprising owners, who built this summer garden smack bang in the grungy Schanzenviertel. Music, snacks, massages and a kid's playground are often joined by sculpture exhibitions.

StrandPauli (Map pp678–9; www.strandpauli.de, in German; St-Pauli-Hafenstrasse 84) Tuesday is tango night at this *Gilligan's Island* stretch of sand overlooking the heart of the busy docks. The reed-thatched shack looks a bit out of place, but the beer, cocktails and sausages hit the spot.

Strandperle (Map p682; www.strandperle-hamburg.de, in German; Schulberg 2) The mother of Hamburg's beach bars is little more than a kiosk, but the people watching is tops, as patrons linger over the *MOPO* (*Hamburger Morgenpost* newspaper) with a snack, coffee, beer or local fritz-kola.

the Hotel Hafen (p688) for unbeatable harbour views.

Café Knuth (Map p683; ☎ 4600 8708; Grosse Rainstrasse 21; ☼ from 10am) Altona stakes its own claim on the olive-green retro style seen across the city. Students, creative types and work colleagues come to chat in its split-level lounge areas.

Aurel (Map p683; ☎ 390 2727; Bahrenfelder Strasse 15; ☼ from 11am) This cosy red-tinged bar is a long-standing Altona favourite for its cheap cocktails and crowd-pleasing music.

ENTERTAINMENT
Nightclubs & Live Music

Opening hours and admission prices for Hamburg's clubs vary depending on what's on. Check program details on the online gig guide www.clubkombinat.de (in German).

Astra Stube (Map pp678–9; www.astra-stube.de; Max-Brauer-Allee 200; ☼ from 9.30pm Mon-Sat) This graffiti-covered red building underneath the railway tracks looks totally unpromising, but it's actually a pioneer of Hamburg's underground scene, with DJs playing experimental electro, techno and drum and bass.

Beat Club (Map pp678–9; ☎ 3339 6959; www.myspace.com/beati; Hopfenstrasse 32; ☼ from 10pm) Identified by its London Underground–style logo, this little cellar bar is a bastion of rock 'n' roll in Hamburg.

China Lounge (Map p682; ☎ 3197 6622; www.china-lounge.de, in German; Nobistor 14; ☼ from 11pm Thu-Sat) Stylish without being snootily exclusive, this

leading mainstream venue boasts four areas playing electro, house, hip hop and R&B. A huge laughing Buddha looks down on the main floor.

Golden Pudel Club (Map pp678–9; ☎ 3197 9930; www.pudel.com, in German; St-Pauli-Fischmarkt 27; ☼ from 10pm) In a ramshackle wooden fisherman's hut, this bar-club was established by members of legendary Hamburg band Die Goldenen Zitronen and gets packed to the rafters for its quality electro, hip-hop, R&B and reggae gigs.

Hafenklang (Map p682; www.hafenklang.de, in German with English sections; Grosse Elbstrasse 84) A collective of Hamburg industry insiders, including Jan Drews (see p696), present established and emerging DJs and bands, as well as clubbing events and parties. Look for the spray-painted name on the dark-brick harbour store above a blank metal door.

Knust im Schlachthof (Map pp678–9; ☎ 8797 6230; www.knusthamburg.de, in German; Neuer Kamp 30) In addition to excellent live music gigs and experimental DJ sets, this former slaughterhouse hosts anything from football fan parties to spoken word.

Komet Musik Bar (Map pp678–9; ☎ 2786 8686; www.komet-st-pauli.de, in German; Erichstrasse 11; ☼ from 9pm) Vinyl and only vinyl spins at this treasure of a music bar. Nightly themes range from ska and rocksteady to '60s garage punk and hip hop.

Molotow Club (Map pp678–9; ☎ 310845; www.molotowclub.com, in German; Spielbudenplatz 5) An alternative,

HARBOUR SOUND

The Beatles may have anchored Hamburg's musical reputation (see the boxed text, p684), but the distinctive electro-punk sound for which the harbour city is known today kicked off some two decades after the Liverpool lads left town. Born and bred Hamburger Jan Drews DJ'd his first gig back when it began in the early '80s, and today books acts at harbourside club Hafenklang (p695), in addition to hitting the decks around town himself. Hamburg's music scene still revolves around the same central quarters where the Beatles performed, although it now faces a daunting battle, according to Drews.

The authorities want to turn inner-city quarters like St Pauli into 'family quarters'. Rents for venues are going up – sometimes a 100% increase from year to year – and leases are getting shorter. There's no money from the government; venues have to pay performers, staff wages, royalties; they survive only from drinks. Young audiences often buy drinks nearby at petrol stations or drink before going into the venues, so there's no money in the club. I get requests from bands and DJs from all over the world to play at Hafenklang, but we're very lucky; we make enough money from big parties that we don't have to make a profit from concerts. The income from putting on parties means I can book quality acts attracting only a small crowd to keep the diversity of the scene in Hamburg. The Molotow Club (p695) is one of Hamburg's most important music venues; it's been breaking in new bands and DJs for decades, but recently it had big financial problems and nearly closed down. Other venues helped save it with donations and cross-promotions. Now it works, but it's an ongoing challenge for all venues.

Despite the challenges, Drews believes that 'Hamburg's bands and DJs are strong enough to survive – even if it means moving to the other side of the Elbe.'

Aside from the Molotow Club, and, of course, Hafenklang, Drews' favourite venues include Knust im Schlachthof (p695; 'it hosts really well-known bands, but in an interactive atmosphere'), Komet Musik Bar (p695; 'the best range of drinks and the best DJs, who are real collectors') and the Golden Pudel Club (p695; 'it has cult status').

independent music scene thrives at this much-loved basement venue at Meanie Bar (p694).

Also recommended:

Grosse Freiheit 36/Kaiserkeller (Map pp678–9; ☎ 3177 7811; www.grossefreiheit36.de, in German; Grosse Freiheit 36; ⊙ from 10pm Tue–Sat) The Beatles once played in the basement Kaiserkeller at this now-mainstream venue mounting pop and rock concerts.

King Calavera (Map pp678–9; www.kingcalavera.de, in German; Hans-Albers-Platz 1) Rockabilly, trash, outlaw country and much, much more.

Mobile Blues Club (www.mobile-blues-club.de, in German) An old shipping container is this blues club's roving home.

Queen Calavera (Map pp678–9; www.queen-calavera.de; Gerhardstrasse 7; ⊙ from 9pm Thu–Sat) Tasteful burlesque.

Uebel & Gefährlich (Map pp678–9; www.uebelund gefaehrlich.com, in German; Feldstrasse 66) DJ sets, live music and parties rock this soundproof WWII bunker.

Cinema

Several cinemas screen movies in the original language with subtitles. Look for the acronym 'OmU' (*Original mit Untertiteln*). Venues include **Abaton Kino** (☎ 4132 0320; www.abaton.de, in German; cnr Grindelhof & Allende Platz, Universitätsviertel) and **3001** (Map pp678–9; ☎ 437 679; www.3001-kino.de, in German; Schanzenstrasse 75).

Theatre

Deutsches Schauspielhaus (Map p686; ☎ 248 710; www.schauspielhaus.de, in German; Kirchenallee 39) Germany's largest and most important theatre presents imaginative interpretations of the classics (Shakespeare, Goethe, Chekhov et al) alongside new works.

Thalia Theater (Map pp678–9; ☎ 3281 4444; www.thalia-theater.de, in German; Alstertor 1) This intimate, galleried venue with a central stage is fond of cutting-edge adaptations of classics and cinema (for example, from Krzysztof Kieślowski and Lars von Trier).

English Theatre (☎ 227 7089; www.englishtheatre.de; Lerchenfeld 14; ⊙ Mundsburg) Predominantly British actors perform mysteries, comedies and the occasional classic, such as Tennessee Williams' *The Glass Menagerie*, at this venue in Winterhude.

Schmidt Theater (Map pp678-9; ☎ 3177 8899; www tivoli.de, in German; Spielbudenplatz 24) This plush former ballroom now stages a cornucopia of saucy musical reviews, comedies, soap operas and variety shows. Midnight shows follow the main performance, and there's a smaller cabaret-comic venue, Schmidt's Tivoli, attached.

MUSICALS

Big, glossy Broadway and West End productions (generally performed in German) are immensely popular in Hamburg, the nation's musical capital'.

Venues include:

Theater im Hafen Hamburg (Map pp678-9; ☎ 0180-544 44; www.loewenkoenig.de, in German; Norderelbstrasse 6) Across the harbour, the yellow tent resembling a giant bee hosts *Der König der Löwen* (*The ion King*). A ferry shuttles here from Landungsbrücke 1.

Neue Flora (☎ 0180-544 44; www.stage-entertainment de, in German; Stresemannstrasse 159a) One of Europe's largest theatres.

Operettenhaus (Map pp678-9; ☎ 01805-114 113; www stage-entertainment.de, in German; Spielbudenplatz 1)

Opera & Classical Music

Staatsoper (Map pp678-9; ☎ 356 868; www.hamburgische staatsoper.de; Grosse Theaterstrasse 25) Among the world's most respected opera houses, the Staatsoper has been directed by the likes of Gustav Mahler and Karl Böhm during its 325-year-plus history.

Musikhalle (Map pp678-9; ☎ 346 920; www.laeiszhalle .de, in German; Johannes-Brahms-Platz) The premier address for classical concerts is this splendid neobaroque edifice, home to the State Philharmonic Orchestra, among others. Along with the opera house, it's now artistically directed by the world's leading female conductor, Australian Simone Young.

SHOPPING

Central Hamburg has two main shopping districts. West of the Hauptbahnhof, along Spitalerstrasse and Mönckebergstrasse (known as the 'Mö'), you'll find the large department stores and mainstream boutiques. Further west again, more upmarket shops are located within the triangle created by Jungfernstieg, Fuhlentwiete and Neuer Wall. Most of them are in a network of elegant shopping arcades.

For secondhand, retro and up-and-coming fashion and music, see p682.

GETTING THERE & AWAY

Air

Hamburg Airport (HAM; ☎ 507 50; www.flughafen -hamburg.de) has frequent flights to domestic and European cities, including on Lufthansa, British Airways and Air France, and low-cost carriers Air Berlin and Germanwings (see p774 for airline details).

The small Hamburg-Uetersen airfield has flights to/from Helgoland (p724).

For flights to and from Lübeck airport (sometimes called 'Hamburg-Lübeck'), see p706.

HAMBURG

GAY & LESBIAN HAMBURG

Hamburg has a thriving gay and lesbian scene; look out at venues for the free listings magazine *hinnerk* (www.hinnerk.de, in German).

Men can find out more at the gay centre **Hein & Fiete** (Map p686; ☎ 240 333; www.heinfiete.de, in German; Pulverteich 21; ⊙ 4-9pm Mon-Fri, to 7pm Sat), while women can contact the lesbian centre **Intervention** (Map pp678-9; ☎ 245 002; www.intervention-hamburg.de, in German; Glashüttenstrasse; ⊙ hours vary). Both men and women can pick up information from the social cafe at the **Magnus Hirschfeld Centrum** (MHC; ☎ 2787 7800; http://mhc-hamburg.de, in German; Borgweg 8; dishes €2.90-4.20; ⊙ 5.30-11pm Mon-Thu, 5pm-late Fri, 3-8pm Sun).

With its abstract art and in-house bakery, **Café Gnosa** (Map p686; ☎ 243 034; Lange Reihe 93; dishes €6.20-13; ⊙ 10am-1am) is a good starting point for gay and lesbian visitors to Hamburg.

Also recommended:

136 Degrees (Map pp678-9; Reeperbahn 136; ⊙ Fri & Sat from midnight) Party-hard disco.

Generation Bar (Map p686; ☎ 2880 4690; Lange Reihe 81; ⊙ from 6pm) Popular gay bar.

Kyti Voo (Map p686; ☎ 2805 5565; Lange Reihe 8; ⊙ from 10am) This bar attracts a mixed crowd.

Bus

The **ZOB** (Busbahnhof; Central Bus Station; Map p686; ☎ 247 576; www.zob-hamburg.de, in German; Adenauerallee 78; ⓨ ticket counters 5am-10pm Mon-Tue, Thu, Sat & Sun, to midnight Wed & Fri) is southeast of the Hauptbahnhof. Domestic and international buses arrive and depart around the clock. **Eurolines** (☎ 4024 7106; www.eurolines.com) has buses to Prague (one-way/return €59/108; 8½ hours) and Warsaw (€50/82; 13 hours), for example; web specials can bring the price down dramatically. Other destinations include Amsterdam, Copenhagen and Paris.

Polen Reisen (☎ 241 427; www.polenreisen-hamburg.de, in German; ⓨ 9am-8pm Mon-Fri, 9.30am-8pm Sat, 4-8pm Sun) is one of several Eastern European specialists in the building.

Autokraft (☎ 208 8660; www.autokraft.de, in German) operates numerous services within Germany.

Car & Motorcycle

The major A1 and A7 autobahns cross south of the Elbe River. Three concentric ring roads manage traffic flow.

For ride-shares, try the **Mitfahrzentrale** (Map p686; ☎ 194 40; www.citynetz-mitfahrzentrale.de; Ernst-Merck-Strasse 12; ⓨ 9am-8pm Mon-Fri, 10am-8pm Sat, 11am-6pm Sun). Destinations include Berlin (€18.50), Frankfurt (€27.50), Cologne (€28) and Munich (€42).

Train

Hamburg has four mainline train stations: the Hauptbahnhof, Dammtor, Altona and Harburg. Remember this as you read the timetables or you may end up at the wrong station.

Frequent trains serve Lübeck (€18.50, 40 minutes), Kiel (€27, 1¼ hours), Hanover (€40, 1¼ hours) and Bremen (€20.80 to €28, 55 minutes). A direct service to Westerland on Sylt Island leaves every two hours (€44, 3¼ hours).

The Hamburg, Schleswig-Holstein-Ticket (p701) and Mecklenburg-Vorpommern-Ticket (p726), and Bremen, Niedersachsen-Ticket (used in Bremen and Lower Saxony) day passes are valid in Hamburg state, including public transport in Hamburg's city centre.

There are direct ICE services to Berlin-Hauptbahnhof (€68, 2¼ hours), Cologne (€79, four hours), Munich (€127, six hours) and Frankfurt (€106, three hours). A direct service to Copenhagen runs several times a day (€78.80, five hours). The fastest rail con nection to Paris (€182, 8½ hours) requires change in Frankfurt.

GETTING AROUND
To/From the Airport

The S1 S-Bahn connects the airport di rectly with the city centre, including th Hauptbahnhof. The journey takes 24 min utes and costs €2.70; see below for ticke information.

Bicycle

Many hostels and some hotels arrange bik rental for guests, or try **Fahrradladen St Geor** (Map p686; ☎ 243 908; Schmilinskystrasse 6; per 24hr €10 12, refundable €50 cash deposit; ⓨ 10am-7pm Mon-Fr 10am-1pm Sat).

StadtRAD Hamburg (www.stadtradhamburg.de), ru by Deutsche Bahn (called Call in Bike at othe major German cities) operates from U-Bah and S-Bahn stations and other key point across the city. Rental of its bright-red, seven gear bikes will be free for the first 30 minutes €0.04 per minute for the next 30 minutes, an €0.08 per minute each hour thereafter.

Car & Motorcycle

Driving around town is easy: thoroughfare are well signposted, and parking station plentiful.

All the major car-hire agencies hav branches in Hamburg. **Europcar** (☎ 01805-500C is at the Hauptbahnhof and airport. The cit office of **Hertz** (Map p686; ☎ 01805-333 535; Kirchenalle 34-36) is just opposite the Hauptbahnhof.

Public Transport

The **HVV** (☎ 194 49; www.hvv.de) operates buses ferries, U-Bahn and S-Bahn (plus A-Bah commuter services), and has several offices including at the Jungfernstieg S-/U-Bahn sta tion, and the Hauptbahnhof.

The city is divided into 'rings' (zones) Ring A covers the city centre and inner sub urbs, while ring B covers the Grossbereich (Greater Hamburg area), encompassing th city centre plus outlying communities like Blankenese. The Gesamtbereich (rings C, I and E) covers the entire Hamburg state. Kid under six travel free. Day Passes (Tageskarten both after 9am and all day) cover travel fo: one adult and up to three children aged si› to 14.

S-/U-Bahn tickets must be purchased from machines at station entrances; bus tickets are available from the driver. Ticket types include the following:

Ticket	Gross-bereich	Gesamt-bereich
Short Journey (no transfers)	€1.30	–
Single	€2.70	€7.20
Day Pass (after 9am)	€5.30	€13.80
Day Pass (all day)	€6.30	€16
3-Day Pass	€15.60	–
Group Day Pass (after 9am, up to 5 people of any age)	€8.95	€22.50

If you catch an express bus (Schnellbus), it costs an extra €1.40.

Services run around the clock on weekends and the night before a public holiday, but between approximately 12.30am and 4am Sunday to Thursday the night bus network takes over, converging on Rathausmarkt.

Bikes are allowed free of charge aboard S-/U-Bahn trains and buses outside peak hours (6am to 9am and 4pm to 6pm) and on ferries any time.

Taxi

Taxis can be found at the Hauptbahnhof, Dammtor and Altona train stations, and many larger S-Bahn and U-Bahn stations. You can book one through **Taxiruf** (☎ 441 011; www.autoruf.de, in German), or **Taxi Hamburg** (☎ 666 666; www.taxihamburg.de, in German).

AROUND HAMBURG

Although dominated by its namesake city, Hamburg State does encompass part of the **Altes Land**, a fertile area reclaimed from marshy ground by Dutch experts in the Middle Ages.

And, at the mouth of the Elbe, you can hunt for amber at the **Hamburg Wadden Sea National Park**, the smallest of Germany's three mud-flat national parks. In the same vein as the Schleswig-Holstein Wadden Sea National Park (p719) and the Lower Saxony Wadden Sea National Park (p656), you can also climb dunes, hike along dykes, seal spot, take a horse-and-carriage ride across the seabed or, at low tide, *Wattwandern* (see p656).

Ask the Hamburg tourist office for more information if you're interested in either of these options (Altes Land and Hamburg Wadden Sea National Park).

With Germany's excellent train system and great-value day passes (see opposite), destinations in surrounding states make easy day trips, such as Lüneburg (p630), Bremen (p660) and Lübeck (p701).

Among Germans, one very popular day trip from Hamburg is by boat to **Helgoland** (p724), operated by **FRS Helgoline** (☎ 0462-864 602; www.helgoline.de, in German). From April to October, you can catch the fast 'Halunder Jet' (return €74.80) from Landungsbrücken 3 or 4.

HAMBURG

Schleswig-Holstein

Sandy beaches, jaunty red-and-white striped lighthouses, deep fjords carved by glaciers, sandpipers and seals have made this sweeping peninsula between the North and Baltic Seas Germany's most elite summer retreat.

Much of the peninsula's interior is comprised of seemingly never-ending expanses of flat, green farmland interrupted only by wind farms and grazing black-and-white-splotched cows. But its coastline – and especially the North Frisian Islands off Schleswig-Holstein's western coast – remain the country's answer to the Côte d'Azur.

Of course, the fickle northern European climate makes for a funny sort of answer, as cold winds and dark clouds periodically drive the hardiest holidaymakers from their *Strandkörbe* (sheltered straw 'beach basket' seats). Yet there's something unusually hypnotic about the state's wide horizons, grass-covered dunes, meandering canals and glistening lakes. Over 200 lakes are scattered throughout the protected Naturpark Holsteinische Schweiz, which sprawls south of the busy port city and state capital, Kiel.

Schleswig-Holstein belonged to neighbouring Denmark until 1864 and you'll find Scandinavian overtones throughout the region, particularly in Flensburg and Schleswig, home to a superbly recreated Viking settlement, as well as the state's finest art museum.

Local artists have embraced the moodier side of Schleswig-Holstein's beauty for centuries. At home in Seebüll, Emil Nolde swirled his brushes into stormy oil-paint waves; author Theodor Storm captured the weather-beaten Husum coast in his poetry and prose; and contemporary literary giant Günter Grass has long been based in Thomas Mann's birthplace, Lübeck, the magnificently preserved medieval headquarters of the Hanseatic League.

HIGHLIGHTS

- **Wave Riding** Windsurf (p720) off Sylt's North Sea coast

- **Planet Watching** See the 17th-century night sky spin at Schleswig's Schloss Gottorf (p712)

- **Puppet Watching** Catch a show at Lübeck's endearing puppet theatre (p706), and visit its puppet museum (p704)

- **Border Crossing** Hike across the Schusterkate (p715) bridge connecting Germany and Denmark just north of Flensburg

- **Halligen Hopping** Sail to Schleswig-Holstein's tiny Halligen (islets) from Nordstrand, near historic Husum (p718)

- POPULATION: 2.37 MILLION
- AREA: 15,729 SQ KM

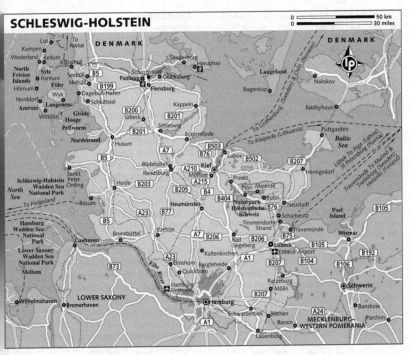

Getting There & Around

Lübeck has an airport serving low-cost airlines, as well as international ferries – see p706. Nearby Travemünde also has international ferry services (p707), as does Kiel (p711). Rail links with Denmark include a direct Lübeck–Copenhagen service.

Within northern Germany, up to five people travelling together can make enormous savings with a **Hamburg, Schleswig-Holstein-Ticket** (€30), which is good for rail journeys from 9am until 3am the following day (from midnight on weekends) anywhere in the states of Hamburg, Schleswig-Holstein and Mecklenburg–Western Pomerania on all regional trains. There are no single rates, but it still often works out cheaper than a regular ticket, even for solo travellers.

LÜBECK
☎ 0451 / pop 212,207

A 12th-century gem boasting more than 1000 historical buildings, Lübeck's picture-book appearance is an enduring reminder of its role as one of the founding cities of the mighty Hanseatic League (see boxed text, p36) and its

moniker of the 'Queen of the Hanse'. Behind its landmark Holstentor (gate), you'll find streets lined with medieval merchants' homes and spired churches forming Lübeck's 'crown'.

Recognised by Unesco as a World Heritage Site in 1987, today this thriving provincial city retains many enchanting corners to explore.

Orientation

Lübeck's Altstadt (old town) is on an island encircled by the canalised Trave River. The Holstentor forms the western gateway to the Altstadt; the Hauptbahnhof (central train station) and central bus station are several hundred metres west.

Information

Ärztlicher Bereitschaftsdienst (☎ 710 81; An der Untertrave 98) Medical services.
Buchhaus Weiland (☎ 160 060; Königstrasse 67a) Good selection of foreign-language books.
Lübeck & Travemünde tourist office (☎ 01805-882 233; www.luebeck-tourism.de; Holstentorplatz 1; ☼ 9.30am-7pm Mon-Fri, 10am-3pm Sat, 10am-2pm Sun Jun-Sep, 9.30am-6pm Mon-Fri, 10am-3pm Sat Oct-May) Sells the Happy Day Card (per 1/3 days €7/14) offering

free public transport and museum discounts. Also has a cafe and internet terminals.

Netzwerk (☎ 409 5552; Wahmstrasse 58; per hr €2; 🕑 10am-10pm Mon-Sat) Internet access.

Post office (Königstrasse 46)

Sights & Activities

HOLSTENTOR & AROUND

Built in 1464 and looking so settled-in that it appears to sag, Lübeck's charming redbrick **Holstentor** city gate is a national icon. Its twin pointed cylindrical towers, leaning together across the stepped gable that joins them, captivated Andy Warhol (his print is in the St Annen Museum; see p704), and have graced postcards, paintings, posters, marzipan souvenirs and even the old DM50 note, as you'll discover inside its **Museum Holstentor** (☎ 122 4129; adult/concession/child under 18yr €5/2.50/2; 🕑 10am-6pm Apr-Dec, 11am-5pm Tue-Sun Jan-Mar).

Just behind the Holstentor (to the east) stand the **Salzspeicher**: six gabled brick buildings once used to store salt transported from Lüneburg. It was then bartered for furs from Scandinavia and used to preserve the herrings that formed a substantial chunk of Lübeck's Hanseatic trade.

MARKT & AROUND

Sometimes described as a 'fairy tale in stone', Lübeck's 13th- to 15th-century **Rathaus** (town hall; ☎ 122 1005; Breite Strasse; guided tours in German adult/concession €3/1.50; 🕑 tours 11am, noon & 3pm Mon-Fri) is widely regarded as one of the most beautiful in Germany. Unfortunately, the impact of its facade is diminished by new buildings around the marketplace, which block previously open views. Inside, a highlight is the Audienzsaal (audience hall), a light-flooded hall decked out in festive rococo.

Across the street from the Markt, **Café Niederegger** (☎ 530 1126; www.niederegger.de; Breite Strasse 89; 🕑 9am-7pm Mon-Fri, 9am-6pm Sat, 10am-6pm Sun) is Lübeck's mecca for marzipan lovers, the almond confectionery from Arabia, which has been made in Lübeck for centuries. Even if you're not buying, the shop's elaborate foil-wrapped displays (many of them maritime-themed) are a feast for the eyes. In its **Marzipan-Salon** (admission free) you'll learn that in medieval Europe marzipan was considered medicine, not a treat. At the back of the shop there's an elegant cafe (p705).

CHURCHES

Near the Markt rise the 125m twin spires of Germany's third-largest church, the **Marienkirche** (Schüsselbuden 13; admission €1; 🕑 10am-6pm Apr-Sep, to 5pm Oct, 10am-4pm Tue-Sun Nov-Mar). It's most famous for its shattered bells, which have been left where they fell after a WWII bombing raid, as a peace memorial. Turn left upon entering the church and go to the end of the aisle. Outside there's a little devil sculpture with an amusing folk tale (in German and English).

Panoramic views over the city unfold from the **Petrikirche** (Schmiedstrasse; lift adult/concession €2.50/1.50; 🕑 9am-9pm Apr-Sep, 10am-7pm Oct-Mar), which has a tower lift to the 7th floor.

The **Dom** (cathedral; 🕑 10am-6pm Apr-Oct, 10am-4pm Nov-Mar) was founded in 1173 by Heinrich der Löwe (see p33) when he took over Lübeck. Locals like to joke that if you approach the Dom from the northeast, you have to go through *Hölle* (hell) and *Fegefeuer* (purgatory) – the actual names of streets – to see **Paradies**, the lavish vestibule to the Dom. Otherwise, the building is quite spartan.

Art lovers will enjoy the towerless **Katharinenkirche** (cnr Glockengiesserstrasse & Königstrasse; admission free; 🕑 10am-5pm Tue-Sun) for its sculptures by Ernst Barlach and Gerhard Marcks, plus *The Resurrection of Lazarus* by Tintoretto.

COURTYARDS & MEWS

In the Middle Ages, Lübeck was home to numerous craftspeople and artisans. Their presence caused demand for housing to outgrow the available space, so tiny single-storey homes were built in courtyards behind existing rows of houses. These were then made accessible via little walkways from the street.

Almost 90 such *Gänge* (walkways) and *Höfe* (courtyards) still exist, among them charitable housing estates built for the poor, the *Stiftsgänge* and *Stiftshöfe*. The most famous of the latter are the beautiful **Füchtingshof** (Glockengiesserstrasse 25; 🕑 9am-noon & 3-6pm) and the **Glandorps Gang** (Glockengiesserstrasse 41-51), which you can peer into.

If you head south along An der Obertrave southwest of the Altstadt, you'll pass one of Lübeck's loveliest corners, the **Malerwinkel** (Painters' Quarter), where you can take a break on garden benches among blooming flowers, gazing out at the houses and white picket fences across the water.

LITERARY MUSEUMS

There must be something in the water in Lübeck, or maybe it's all that marzipan. The city has connections to two Nobel Prize–winning authors (as well as Nobel Peace Prize–winning former chancellor Willy Brandt).

The winner of the 1929 Nobel Prize for Literature, Thomas Mann, was born in Lü-

beck in 1875 and his family's former home is now the **Buddenbrookhaus** (☎ 122 4190; www.buddenbrookhaus.de; Mengstrasse 4; adult/concession/child under 18yr €5/2.50/2; ⏰ 11am-6pm Apr-Dec, 11am-5pm Jan-Mar). Named after Mann's novel of a wealthy Lübeck family in decline, *The Buddenbrooks* (1901), this award-winning museum is a monument not only to the

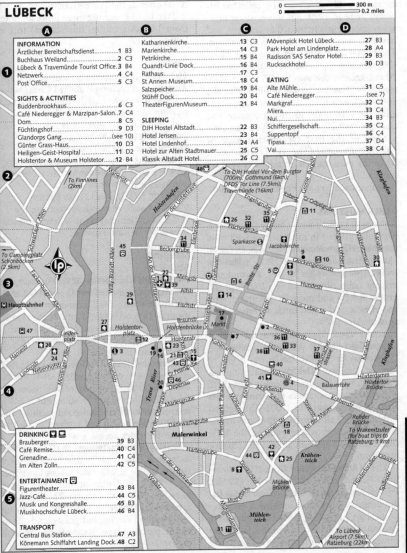

LÜBECK

0 _____ 300 m
0 _____ 0.2 miles

author of such classics as *Der Tod in Venedig* (Death in Venice) and *Der Zauberberg* (The Magic Mountain), but also to his brother Heinrich, who wrote the story that became the Marlene Dietrich film *Der Blaue Engel* (The Blue Angel). There's a rundown of the rather tragic family history, too.

Born in Danzig (now Gdansk), Poland, Günter Grass had been living just outside Lübeck for 13 years when he collected his Nobel Prize in 1999. But this postwar literary colossus initially trained as an artist, and has always continued to draw and sculpt. The **Günter Grass-Haus** (Günter Grass House; ☎ 122 4192; www.guenter-grass-haus.de; Glockengiesserstrasse 21; adult/concession/child under 18yr €5/2.50/2; 🕐 10am-5pm Apr-Dec, 11am-5pm Jan-Mar) is filled with the author's leitmotifs – flounders, rats, snails and eels – brought to life in bronze and charcoal, as well as in prose. You can view a copy of the first typewritten page of *Die Blechtrommel* (The Tin Drum; 1959), while the man himself occasionally appears for readings.

Both museums have English annotations.

OTHER MUSEUMS

If you're travelling with children, or have a particular interest in marionettes, don't miss the **TheaterFigurenMuseum** (☎ 786 26; Am Kolk 14; adult/concession/child under 18yr €5/2.50/2; 🕐 10am-6pm Apr-Dec, 11am-5pm Tue-Sun Nov-Mar), a wondrous private collection of some 1200 puppets, props, posters and more from Europe, Asia and Africa; and try to catch a performance at its theatre (p706).

You're most likely to enter the former **Heiligen-Geist-Hospital** (Königstrasse; admission free; 🕐 10am-5pm Tue-Sun, 10am-4pm Dec-Feb) if you're here for December's **Christmas market**. Although the building is largely an elegant shell these days, there are resonances of Germany's first hospital (dating back to 1227). Through an early-Gothic hall church, you come to the hospital hallway, where you see the little chambers that were built around 1820 to give the infirm privacy.

The **St Annen Museum** (☎ 122 4137; St-Annen-Strasse 15; adult/concession/child under 18yr €5/2.50/2; 🕐 10am-5pm Tue-Sun Apr-Dec, 11am-5pm Tue-Sun Jan-Mar) houses a browsable mishmash of ecclesiastical art (including Hans Memling's 1491 Passion Altar), historical knick-knacks and contemporary art in its modern Kunsthalle wing. The latter houses the Andy Warhol print of Lübeck's Holstentor.

GOTHMUND

Lined with fishermen's cottages, this little village on Lübeck's outskirts is impossibly quaint. After strolling along Fischerweg, a path running in front of the cottages, take the same path west, which leads through a nature reserve beside the Trave River.

Take bus 12 (leaving three times an hour from Lübeck's central bus station) to the last stop.

Tours

The Trave River forms a moat around the Altstadt, and cruising it aboard a boat is the best way to get a feel for the city. You start off viewing an industrial harbour, but soon float past beautiful leafy surrounds.

Quandt-Linie (☎ 777 99; www.quandt-linie.de; adult/child under 15yr €10/6) Leaves from just south of the Holstenbrücke bridge. One-hour city tours leave every half-hour between 10am and 6pm from May to October (plus limited services November to April).

Stühff (☎ 707 8222; www.luebecker-barkassenfahrt.de, in German; adult/concession/child under 12yr €7.50/6.50/3.50) Runs boat tours up to six times daily (call ahead outside the summer months).

Sleeping

BUDGET

Campingplatz Schönböcken (☎ 893 090; campingplatz.luebeck@gmx.de; Steinrader Damm 12; per tent €4-5, adult/child €5/2, electricity €2.50) This modern camping ground is a good bet for its grassy sites, kiosk, restaurant, entertainment room and children's playground. It's a 10-minute bus ride west of the city centre (take bus 7).

Rucksackhotel (☎ 706 892; www.rucksackhotel-luebeck.de; Kanalstrasse 70; dm €13-15, s €28, d €34-40, linen €3, breakfast €3-5, 💻 📶) None of the rooms at this 30-bed hostel are en suite, but it has a relaxed atmosphere and good facilities including a well-equipped kitchen, as well as round-the-clock access.

Hotel zur Alten Stadtmauer (☎ 737 02; www.hotelstadtmauer.de, in German; An der Mauer 57; s/d with shared bathroom from €37/55, with private bathroom from €55/65; P ⊠ 💻 📶) With pine furniture and splashes of red or yellow, this simple 22-room hotel is bright and cheerful. The wooden flooring means sound carries, but guests tend not to be the partying type. Back rooms overlook the river.

Lübeck has two DJH hostels:

DJH hostel Vor dem Burgtor (☎ 334 33; www
.jugendherberge.de/jh/luebeck-jh; Am Gertrudenkirch-
hof 4; dm under/over 26yr incl breakfast €18.40/21.40;
🏠 early-Jan–mid-Dec; P 🖳) Huge, modern hostel
popular with school groups, just outside the Altstadt.

DJH hostel Altstadt (☎ 702 0399; www.jugend
herberge.de/jh/luebeck-jgh; Mengstrasse 33; dm under/
over 26yr incl breakfast €19.70/22.70) Central hostel in the
Altstadt. Not particularly new, but cosy and comfortable.

MIDRANGE

A unique way to absorb Lübeck's history is
stay in one of the restored *Gänghäuser* (mews
houses) in the Stiftsgänge courtyards (see
p702). These self-contained properties cost
€50 to €95 per night for two people. The tourist office can help with bookings, but there
aren't many so reserve ahead (see p701).

Park Hotel am Lindenplatz (☎ 871 970; www
.parkhotel-luebeck.de; Lindenplatz 2; s €59-99, d €79-130 incl
breakfast; P ✖ 🖳 📶) Inside a well-preserved
art nouveau building, this small, intimate
hotel has 24 low-lit, neutral-toned rooms
that – like Lübeck itself – are ideal for a
romantic interlude.

Hotel Lindenhof (☎ 872 100; www.lindenhof-luebeck
.de; Lindenstrasse 1a; s €65-95, d €85-135 incl breakfast; P ✖ 🖳) Rooms at this family-run
hotel in a quiet side street are small, but
a healthy breakfast buffet, friendly service
and little extras (such as free biscuits and
newspapers) propel the Lindenhof into a
superior league.

Hotel Jensen (☎ 702 490; www.hotel-jensen.de; An
der Obertrave 4-5; s €75-85, d €93-115 incl breakfast) This
old *Patrizierhaus* (mansion house) dating
from the early 14th century overlooks the
Salzspeicher across the Trave River. Alas,
rooms aren't as characterful as the gabled
exterior suggests, with modern and comfortable if somewhat pedestrian furnishings.
Beautiful stained glass and tiling, however,
adorn its excellent regional restaurant,
Yachtzimmer (mains €9.75 to €24.50). Ask
about nearby private parking.

Klassik Altstadt Hotel (☎ 702 980; www.klassik-altsta
dt-hotel.de; Fischergrube 52; s/d €76/138, ste from €135;
P ✖ 🖳 📶) Each room at this elegantly
furnished boutique hotel is dedicated to a
different, mostly German writer or artist,
such as Thomas Mann and Johann Sebastian
Bach, as well as international luminaries
like Denmark's Hans Christian Andersen.
It's close to many of the city's best din-

ing options, but it also has a solid in-house
restaurant (mains €11.50 to €14.50).

TOP END

Mövenpick Hotel Lübeck (☎ 150 40; www.moevenpick
-luebeck.com; Willy-Brandt-Allee 1-5; s €112-237, d €154-274,
ste from €240; P ✖ 🖳 🐕 📶) Sure, it's a chain
with a concrete exterior so ugly it's almost
(almost) beautiful. But this hotel's superior
rooms are startlingly stylish and designer-
looking in slate grey and burnt sienna tones
with abstract works from local artists, while
suites in plum and chocolate are stunning.
Ordinary rooms are, well, fairly ordinary
(if comfortable), but the location near the
Holstentor couldn't be more convenient.

Radisson SAS Senator Hotel (☎ 1420; www.senator
hotel.de; Willy-Brandt-Allee 6; s €131-179, d €142-198;
P ✖ 🐕 🖳 📶 🖳) The Lübeck option that
really wows, the Senator resembles something
from *War of the Worlds* with its three parallel
rectangular wings cantilevered out into the
Trave River. Plate-glass windows in the riverfront restaurant and the lofty atrium ensure
front-row views of the old town (beautiful at
night or in winter), while rooms are done out
in Southeast Asian colonial style.

Eating

Café Niederegger (dishes €2.40-11.60) Milky marzipan coffee, marzipan ice cream and a host
of other sweet and savoury snacks and light
meals are served at the cafe inside Lübeck's
marzipan centre (see p702).

Suppentopf (☎ 400 8136; Fleischhauerstrasse 36;
soups €3.60-4.10; 🏠 11am-4pm Mon-Fri Sep-Jun;
Ⓥ) Join Lübeck's office workers for delicious, often spicy soup, in this terrific
little hole-in-the-wall.

Alte Mühle (☎ 707 2592; Mühlendamm 24; mains
€4.80-13.50; 🏠 from 3pm Mon-Sat, from 12.30pm Sun;
Ⓥ) In a historic old mill on the banks of the
Trave River, this rustic bistro serves fabulous *Flammkuchen* (Alsatian pizzas) along
with steaks and seasonal specialities. There's
a clutch of garden-set tables in summer.
Definitely worth the detour.

Tipasa (☎ 706 0451; Schlumacherstrasse 12-14; lunch
mains €7.50-8.50, dinner mains €8.50-17.50; 🏠 from
noon; Ⓥ) International dishes like pizzas
and curries are served below the Australian
Aboriginal dot paintings and faux cave-
man frescoes of animals. The eclectic decor
comes together surprisingly well to create a
relaxed ambience.

SCHLESWIG-HOLSTEIN

ourpick Schiffergesellschaft (☎ 767 76; Breite Strasse 2; mains €11.50-24.50; ☯ 10am-11pm) Opened in 1535 as the dining room for the Blue Water Captains' Guild, Lübeck's best restaurant is a veritable museum. Ships' lanterns, original model ships dating from 1607 and orange Chinese-style lamps with revolving maritime silhouettes adorn the wood-lined rooms, which include an elevated banquet room up the back. As you sit on long benches resembling church pews, staff in long white aprons bring you Frisian specialities. On balmy nights, head up a flight of steps to the hidden garden out back.

Nui (☎ 203 7333; Beckergrube 72; sushi €1.80-15.50, mains €11.90-14.50; ☯ lunch & dinner Mon-Fri, 3-10pm Sat, closed Sun; V) Tempting aromas waft from artfully arranged plates in this trendy but relaxed Thai/Japanese restaurant.

Miera (☎ 772 12; Hüxstrasse 57; mains €14.50-23.50, 3-/4-/5-course menu €33/38/45; ☯ 9am-10pm; V) You can sit down for a platter of antipasti or pick up gourmet picnic goodies at this sophisticated delicatessen-bistro. Reserve ahead to dine in the formal restaurant on elegant Italian fare.

Markgraf (☎ 706 0343; Fischergrube 18; mains €14.50-23.50, 3-/4-/5-course menu €33/41/48; ☯ dinner Tue-Sun) White tablecloths and silverware are laid out under the chandeliers and black ceiling beams of this historic, ochre-coloured 14th-century house. Exquisitely presented dishes include the likes of grain-fed chicken with sherry tomato fondue, and lemon ricotta mousse for dessert.

Vai (☎ 400 8083; Hüxstrasse 42; lunch mains €8-16.50, dinner mains €16-26, 3-/4-course menu €35/42; ☯ noon-11pm) Glossy, richly grained timber lines the walls, tables and even the alfresco courtyard of this sleek restaurant. Veal braised in red wine with puréed potatoes is a highlight of its contemporary menu.

Drinking

Grenadine (☎ 307 2950; Wahmstrasse 40; ☯ 9am-midnight Mon-Thu, 9am-1am Fri & Sat, 9am-3pm Sun) This narrow, elongated bar leads through to a garden out back. A recent transformation has seen its decor pared down in chic, retro-minimalist style, such as carpet panels cladding the walls. Similarly simple German/Italian dishes are served at lunch (€6 to €12.90).

Café Remise (☎ 777 73; Wahmstrasse 43-45; ☯ 9am-late Mon-Fri, 10am-late Sat & Sun) An arty crowd sips wine in the vine-draped courtyard of this

split-level cafe, but it also serves decent bistro fare (dishes €3.30 to €10.70).

Im Alten Zolln (☎ 723 95; Mühlenstrasse 93-95; ☯ 11am-late; ⊜) There's a slightly alternative vibe at this classic pub, where patrons people-watch from the terrace in summer and watch bands inside in winter.

Brauberger (☎ 702 0606; Alfstrasse 36; ☯ 5pm-midnight Mon-Thu, 5pm-late Fri & Sat) This traditional German brewer has been serving its own golden amber since 1225.

Entertainment

Local listings magazines include *Piste* (www .piste.de) and *Ultimo* (www.ultimo-luebeck .de), both in German.

MUSIC

Ask the tourist office about church organ concert dates.

Musikhochschule Lübeck (☎ 150 50; www.mh -luebeck.de; Grosse Petersgrube 17-29) High-calibre concerts (mostly free) take place throughout the summer and winter semesters at this music academy.

Musik und Kongresshalle (☎ 790 40; www.muk .de; Willy-Brandt-Allee 10) Notable for the colourful statues on its roof, this concrete monolith is where big international names perform when in town.

Jazz-Café (☎ 707 3734; Mühlenstrasse 62; ☯ 4pm-late Sun-Fri, noon-late Sat) Live jazz plays at least once a month at this chilled spot.

THEATRE

Figurentheater (☎ 700 60; www.figurentheater-luebeck .de, in German; Am Kolk 20-22; tickets €5-7; ☯ Tue-Sun) This adorable puppet theatre puts on a children's show at 3pm, and another for adults on some evenings at 7.30pm, as well as occasional performances in English.

Getting There & Away

AIR

Low-cost carriers **Ryanair** (www.ryanair.com) and **Wizzair** (www.wizzair.com) serve **Lübeck airport** (www .luebeckairport.com), which they euphemistically call Hamburg-Lübeck. Destinations include London, Dublin, Frankfurt-Hahn Airport, and many other European cities.

Synchronised shuttle buses take passengers straight to Hamburg (one-way €9, 55 minutes), while scheduled bus 6 (€2.50) serves Lübeck's Hauptbahnhof and central bus station. Frequent trains run from the airport train station (300m from the terminal) north to Lübeck's Hauptbahnhof, and south as far as Büchen, from where there are connections to Hamburg.

BOAT

Ferries sail from Lübeck to Riga and St Petersburg – see p778 for details.

Könemann Schiffahrt (☎ 280 1635; www.koenemann schiffahrt.de; Teerhofinsel 14a) has three ferries to, and two ferries from, Travemünde (one-way/return €10/15) daily from April to mid-October. Tickets are sold on-board.

BUS

Regional buses stop opposite the local buses on Hansestrasse, around the corner from the Hauptbahnhof. Kraftomnibusse services to/from Wismar terminate here, as do the Autokraft buses to/from Hamburg, Schwerin, Kiel, Rostock and Berlin.

CAR & MOTORCYCLE

Lübeck is reached via the A1 from Hamburg. The town also lies at the crossroads of the B75, the B104 to Schwerin, the B206 to Bad Segeberg and the B207 to Ratzeburg.

TRAIN

Lübeck has connections every hour to Hamburg (€18.50, 40 minutes), Kiel (€15.20, 1¼ hours) and Rostock (€22.90, two hours 20 minutes) with a change in Bad Kleinen.

Getting Around

Lübeck's centre is easily walkable, and since many streets are pedestrianised and off limits to all but hotel guests' vehicles, many people just park their cars and go on foot.

Bus tickets cost €1.50 to €2.50, depending on the distance you travel, and day cards cost €4.50 to €8.20. Higher-priced tickets are valid for Travemünde.

AROUND LÜBECK

Travemünde

☎ 04502

Writer Thomas Mann declared that he spent his happiest days in Travemünde, just outside Lübeck (which bought it in 1329 to control the shipping coming into its harbour), and its 4.5km of sandy beaches at the point where the Trave River flows into the Baltic Sea make it easy to see why. Water sports are the main draw, along with a colourful **sailing regatta** (www.travemuenderwoche.de) in the last week of July.

The town takes great pride in its historic four-masted sailing ship-turned-museum, **Passat** (☎ 122 5202; www.passat.luebeck.de; 🕑 10am-5pm mid-May–mid-Sep, 11am-4.30pm Sat & Sun Easter–mid-May & mid-Sep–Oct), which used to do the run around South America's Cape Horn in the early to mid-20th century. The **Passat Choir** (www.passatchor.de, in German) performs concerts of sea shanties aboard the ship or on land.

The **Lübeck & Travemünde tourist office** (☎ 01805-882 233; www.travemuende-tourismus.de; Strandbahnhof; 🕑 9.30am-7pm Mon-Fri, 10am-3pm Sat, 10am-2pm Sun Jun-Sep, 9.30am-6pm Mon-Fri, 10am-3pm Sat Oct-May) can advise on choir practice times and locations, and also help with accommodation.

Camping at beachfront sites is particularly fun; try **Strand Priwall** (☎ 717 92; www.strand camping-priwall.de, in German; adult/tent/car €5.50/8/3.50; 🕑 May-Sep). The town's most famous hotel is the luxurious **Columbia Hotel Casino Travemünde** (☎ 3080; www.columbia-hotels.de; Kaiserallee 2; s €135-275, d €210-320; P ⊠ ✱ 💻 📶 🏊) in a historic, 19th-century building with three restaurants, including the Michelin-starred La Belle Epoque (dinner Wednesday to Sunday by reservation).

GETTING THERE & AWAY

Könemann Schiffahrt (☎ 0451-280 1635; www .koenemannschiffahrt.de; Teerhofinsel 14a, Lübeck) has two ferries going to, and three from, Lübeck (one-way/return €10/15) daily from April to mid-October.

Regular trains connect Lübeck to Travemünde, which has several train stations, including Skandinavienkai (for ferries) and Strandbahnhof (for the beach and tourist office); the latter is sometimes covered by bus. Buses 30 and 31 provide direct services from Lübeck's central bus station. The B75 leads northeast from Lübeck to Travemünde.

Travemünde is a gateway to Scandinavia, with major ferry lines sailing from its Skandinavienkai – see p778.

Ratzeburg

☎ 04541 / pop 13,700

Scenically located on an island and connected to the surrounding land by three narrow causeways, Ratzeburg makes a relaxing day trip from Lübeck. Highlights of this historic town include the Dom built by

Heinrich der Löwe and a former residence of the Dukes of Mecklenburg.

Boat tours (☎ 0451-793 885; www.wakenitz-schiffahrt -quandt.de, in German; Wakenitzufer 1c) sail from Lübeck up the 14.5km Wakenitz River to the Ratze-burger Lake (adult/child €10/6, four departures daily each way between approximately mid-April to mid-October).

If you'd like to stay, **Ratzeburg Information** (☎ 800 0886; www.ratzeburg.de, in German; Rathaus, Unter den Linden 1; ☺ 9am-5pm Mon-Fri Oct-Apr, 9am-5pm Mon-Fri, 11am-4pm Sat & Sun May-Sep) can help with accommodation.

NATURPARK HOLSTEINISCHE SCHWEIZ

Sprawling over 75,328 hectares between Lübeck to the south and Kiel to the north, the **Naturpark Holsteinische Schweiz** (www.naturpark -holsteinische-schweiz.de, in German) is the state's largest outdoor playground. Germany's propensity to label its most scenic areas 'Swiss' (the name translates as 'Holstein Switzerland') reflects the park's undulating green hills, golden fields and wildflower-strewn meadows, and hedge walls dating from 18th-century farming laws. This chocolate-box-pretty landscape is interspersed with a string of some 200 lakes, of which 70 are over one hectare in size. Visitors heading off the beaten track will also find caves, red beech forests, and (if you're lucky) rare white-tailed eagles and shy bitterns, as well as small green tree frogs.

The park's three main towns, each in idyllic lakeside settings, are **Eutin** (www .eutin.de), famed for its baroque castle amid English-style gardens; the spa resort of **Malente** (www.bad-malente.de, in German); and **Plön**, on the shores of the park's largest lake, the Grosser Plöner See.

Plön's comprehensive **Tourist Info Grosser Plöner See** (☎ 04522-509 50; www.touristinfo-ploen.de; Bahnhofstrasse 5, Plön; ☺ 8am-6pm Mon-Fri, 10am-2pm Sat & Sun May-Sep, 9am-6pm Mon-Fri Oct-Apr) can help with accommodation (including camping grounds) and a wealth of water-based activities from boat trips to fishing, swimming, windsurfing, kayaking and scuba diving. The website www.holsteinischeschweiz.de is a good source of information.

Hiking and cycling trails criss-cross the park, as does a well-signed road network. Lübeck–Kiel trains stop in Eutin, Malente (Bad Malente-Gremsmühlen) and Plön.

KIEL

☎ 0431 / pop 233,800

Rapidly rebuilt after its U-Boot (submarine) base meant that it was shattered during WWII, some locals admit the Schleswig-Holstein capital's city centre is *grottenhässlich* (ugly as sin). There *are* actually some pretty quarters inland (if you look hard enough), but 'Kiel Sailing City's' most romantic aspect is the water. Huge ferries transport millions of passengers to and from Scandinavia, while summer sees locals strolling the waterfront Kiellinie promenade. And, thanks to some 23,000 university students, you'll find a lively pub scene year-round.

Orientation

Kiel's main thoroughfare is the pedestrianised Holstenstrasse, about 100m inland from the firth. It runs between the Sophienhof, a vast, glass-roofed shopping mall opposite the Hauptbahnhof on Sophienblatt, to Kieler Schloss (Kieler Castle) about 1.5km north. The central bus station is just to the north of the Hauptbahnhof, through the 'City/Fernbus' exit leading to Auguste-Viktoria-Strasse.

Information

Callshop & Internet Café (☎ 248 5099; Sophienblatt 42a; per hr €1.60; ☺ 9am-11pm Mon-Fri, 10am-11pm Sat & Sun) Cheap internet access just across from the Hauptbahnhof.

Kiel tourist office (☎ 679 100; www.kiel-tourist.de; main office Neues Rathaus Andreas-Gayk-Strasse 31; ☺ 9am-6pm Mon-Fri, 10am-2pm Sat; Hauptbahnhof ☺ 8am-8pm) Both branches have free city maps and sell the FördeCard (bus/bike and ferry €9.40/12), including free public transport and museum discounts.

Post office (Stresemannplatz 5; ☺ 9am-7pm Mon-Fri, 9am-2pm Sat)

University Medical Clinic (Universitäts-Klinikum; ☎ 5970; Brunswiker Strasse 10)

Wasch-Treff (cnr Exerzierplatz & Kronshagener Weg; per load €3.50; ☺ 6am-10pm) Laundry.

Sights & Activities

DIE KIELLINIE & FERRY RIDES

The waterfront promenade known as the Kiellinie begins north of the pedestrian zone, past the Schloss (castle) and through the Schlossgarten (behind the overpass crossing Düsternbrooker Weg).

Sailing clubs and restaurants line the way, but the only real attraction is the **aquarium** (☎ 600 1637; Düsternbrooker Weg 20; admission free).

It has seals in an outside tank, where public feedings take place at 10am and 2.30pm Saturday to Thursday.

From the Revenloubrücke, ferries will take you back into town or on to Laboe (p711). If you continue along the Kiellinie past Blücherbrücke, you'll come to the sailing harbour used during the 1936 Olympics, now full of yachts.

PARKS

Peaceful expanses of greenery include the **Schrevenpark** and **Old Botanical Gardens**. One of the few postcard views of Kiel city (as opposed to Kiel firth) can be enjoyed from the intersection of Lorenzdamm and Legienstrasse, situated between the two **Kleiner Kiel** lakes. Children will love the playful **Jeppe Hein Fountain** in the **Hiroshimapark** next to the westerly lake and behind the Opera House.

CITY CENTRE

The pedestrian zone is unattractive but usually unavoidable (you have to traverse it to get to the much more appealing waterfront Kiellinie). As you wander from the Sophienhof, through Holstenplatz and along Holstenstrasse, you'll pass the **Altes Rathaus** (Old Town Hall) to your left down Fleethörn, with its 106m tower.

Outside the **Nikolaikirche** (Church of St Nicholas) on the Alter Markt (Old Square) stands a striking Ernst Barlach statue. **Der Geistkämpfer** (Ghost Fighter) was removed during the Third Reich as 'degenerate art', but was later found buried in the Lüneburg Heath.

Dänische Strasse, at the far left corner of the Alter Markt, is one of the more successfully restored sections of old Kiel. The **Schloss** (closed to the public) isn't so exciting: the west wing is the only original section still surviving.

GALLERIES & MUSEUMS

Next to the main tourist office, Kiel's **Stadtgalerie** (☎ 901 3400; Andreas-Gayk-Strasse 31; adult/concession €3/1.50; ✆ 10am-5pm Tue-Wed & Fri, 7pm Thu, 11am-5pm Sat & Sun) features attention-grabbing displays of contemporary art.

The **Kunsthalle** (☎ 880 5756; www.kunsthalle-kiel.de; Düsternbrooker Weg; adult/concession €6/3; ✆ 10am-6pm Tue & Thu-Sun, 10am-8pm Wed), near the start of the Kiellinie, is also impressive. Individual sections are dedicated to Emil Nolde, Antony Gormley and Bridget Riley, and it hosts

frequently changing temporary exhibitions (charging extra admission).

The **Schiffahrtsmuseum** (Maritime Museum; ☎ 901 3425; Am Wall 65; adult/concession €3/1.50; ✆ 10am-6pm Apr-Oct, 10am-5pm Nov-Mar), atmospherically located in a former fish market, has its own pier, where three historic ships are moored from April to October.

NORD-OSTSEE-KANAL

Kiel lies at the point at which the 99km-long Nord-Ostsee-Kanal enters the Baltic Sea from the North Sea. Inaugurated in 1895, the canal is now the third-most trafficked in the world, after the Suez and Panama Canals, with some 60,000 ships passing through every year.

The best way to appreciate this marvel of engineering is on an eight-hour journey with the **Raddampfer Freya** (☎ 04651-987 00; www.raddampfer-freya.de; adult/child €32.90/16.45; ✆ 3-4 times weekly Jun-Sep). This historic steamship sails along the canal to Rendsburg and back from Bahnhofsbrücke in Kiel (some services are aboard regular boats).

If you're on a tight schedule but would like a closer look at the canal, you can see the *Schleusen* (locks) at Holtenau, north of Kiel. The **viewing platform** (adult/child €1/0.50) here is open from sunrise to sunset. There's a **museum** (Nord-Ostsee-Kanal Ausstellung Schleusenmuseum; ☎ 360 30; adult/concession €2.30/1.50) on the southern side of the canal. German-speakers may be interested in **tours of the locks** (☎ 360 30; adult/concession €2.30/1.50). These depart at 9am, 11am, 1pm and 3pm daily from March to October from the northern side. To get to the locks, take bus 11 to Wik, Kanal. A free ferry shuttles back and forth between the southern and northern banks.

Festivals & Events

Kiel's biggest annual event is the giant **Kieler Woche** (Kiel Week; ☎ 679 100; www.kieler-woche.de) held during the last full week of June. Revolving around a series of yachting regattas, it's attended by more than 4000 of the world's sailing elite and half a million spectators. Even if you're not into boats, it's one nonstop party. Some concerts are free; book ahead for other events.

Sleeping

The tourist office has a list of private rooms starting from around €25 per night. Kiel has a **DJH hostel** (☎ 731 488; www.jugendherberge.de/jh/kiel;

Johannesstrasse 1; 😊 closed mid-Dec–early Jan). Take bus 11 from the Hauptbahnhof to the Karlstal stop, or walk 900m along Hörnbrücke.

Campingplatz Falckenstein (☎ 392 078; www .campingkiel.de, in German; Palisadenweg 171; adult €4.50, tent €4.90-7.50; 😊 Apr-Oct; 🛜) Situated on the western bank of Kiel firth, 17km north of the city centre, facilities at this waterside camping ground include a solarium and sauna.

Peanuts Hostel (☎ 364 2208; www.peanuts-hostel.de; Harriesstrasse 2; dm €18, s/d €28/48; 🍴) With just eight beds and a snug lounge room, this little locally run hostel inside an 1895 town house gives you the feeling you're staying with friends. It's an easy walk from the ferries and Hauptbahnhof, as well as cosy neighbourhood pubs and restaurants. Call ahead to confirm your arrival time.

Bekpek Kiel (☎ 888 8009; www.bekpek-kiel.de; Kronshagener Weg 130a; dm €21-27, s €30, d €52-65, linen €3.50; 😊 reception 8am-noon & 4-8pm or by arrangement; 🅿 🍴 💻) To get to this independent hostel, you have to take a bus from the centre (bus 34, 100 or 101 to Dehnckestrasse). But it's worth it for the sociable atmosphere, sunshine-coloured modern rooms and little extras like fresh peppermint tea.

Basic Hotel City (☎ 986 800; www.nordic-hotels.com, in German; Muhliusstrasse 95; s €45-135, d €65-180 incl breakfast; 🅿 🍴 💻) Despite its prosaic name, rooms here are modern and spacious, and nothing is too much for the friendly staff, whether organising a courier or feeding a hungry guest after hours.

Hotel Berliner Hof (☎ 663 40; www.berlinerhof -kiel.de; Ringstrasse 6; s €65-100, d €95-125 incl breakfast; 🅿 🍴 🛜) Although completely modern, this epicentral hotel has been in the same family since it opened in 1902. Above the faux-marble reception area with red leather lounges, there are two main room types: newer, lighter rooms with funky abstract quilts and splashes of bright colours, and a cheaper, more mainstream variety. Three of the 103 rooms are equipped for wheelchairs.

Hotel Am Schwedenkai (☎ 986 4220; www.hotel -am-schwedenkai.de; Holstenbrücke 28; s €67-118, d €88-190 incl breakfast; 🅿 🍴 🛜) Kiel's portside atmosphere is evoked at this central hotel, 100m from the Sophienhof shopping centre, which has fabulous views of the waterfront from the front rooms, and direct access to the ferry docks. Rooms are simple but appealing, with Nordic blue, white and pale timber colour schemes.

A MOVEABLE MUSICAL FEAST

During the statewide **Schleswig-Holstein Music Festival** (www.shmf.de) you might find yourself down on a farm listening to a chamber orchestra instead of lowing cattle. Over seven weeks each summer, leading international musicians and promising young artists perform in venues ranging from the castle in Kiel and music academy in Lübeck to churches, warehouses and animal stalls, and sometimes even ferries to the North Frisian Islands.

Each year, the festival takes a different country as a theme. Performances are largely classical, but you'll also find pop, rock and jazz on the program.

---

ourpick Romantik Hotel Kieler Kaufmann (☎ 88 10; www.kieler-kaufmann.de, in German; Niemannsweg 102 s €119-200, d €159-310; 🅿 🍴 🛜 🍽) Kiel's mos romantic place to stay is indeed this vine-covered 1911-built gem. Warm, rich, striped and printed fabrics adorn the individually decorated guest rooms, plus there's a decaden wellness centre and an excellent restauran (mains €17.50 to €29, open lunch and dinner serving local produce with a Mediterranean twist. It's set in a leafy park adjoining the firth 5km north of the Hauptbahnhof.

Eating

Louf (☎ 551 178; Reventloualle 2, cnr Kiellinie; main €8.10-16.30; 😊 10am-late, reduced hours winter; Ⓥ) Ir summer, Kiel's hipsters lounge around on th deckchairs on the lawn, while behind them everyone from skiving businessmen to young mothers (there's a good kids' menu) tucks into waffles, Thai curries, meat dishes and more Outdoor heaters and blankets keep thing going in cooler seasons.

Club 68 (☎ 617 39; Ringstrasse 68; mains €8.40-11.80 😊 from 6pm; Ⓥ) This little *urige Kneipe* (down to-earth, authentic pub) is decked out like th local hang-out in popular cartoon *Werner* Even those unfamiliar with the strip will ge a kick out of the unusual decor, including ol Mercedes car seats with wooden armrests and copper light fittings. The menu spans pastas and salads to *Schnitzels*.

Fuego del Sur (☎ 364 6036; An der Halle 400, Willy Brand-Ufer; mains €11-19.80, Sunday brunch €11.40; 😊 din ner nightly, brunch from 11am Sun; Ⓥ) Its open gril means this Argentine *parilla* (grill) establishment is as steaming as the pampas it evokes. So in summer the huge noisy crowd decamps from the indoor dining area and low gaucho-style seating to the terrace. Big, bloody steaks are accompanied on the menu by polenta, and crème caramel made from *dulce de leche* (a thickened condensed-milk confection).

Ratskeller (☎ 971 0005; Rathaus; mains €11.90-22.90; ☙ from 11am) Local specialities like sour duck with cranberries, cabbage and potatoes, or salmon and shrimp ragout in herb-infused garlic sauce, and an atmospheric backdrop of rough-hewn walls and dark-beamed ceilings, make Kiel's *Ratskeller* (town hall restaurant) better than most.

Lüneburg-Haus (☎ 982 600; Dänische Strasse 22; mains 12.80-30.50; ☙ lunch & dinner Mon-Sat) Despite the designer touches, there are still historic hints in this lovely century-old restaurant. Locally sourced sweet-and-sour regional cuisine is accompanied by creative international dishes and delicious desserts like poached vanilla pudding with warm chocolate sauce, and double-chocolate mousse.

Drinking

Prinz Willy (Lutherstrasse 9; ☙ from 5.30pm Tue-Sun) A cool little cafe-bar patronised by book-reading arty types and students. Prinz Willy is in one of Kiel's tucked-away historic quarters, and puts on regular live music.

Two Irish pubs, **O'Dwyer's Irish Pub** (☎ 556 227; Bergstrasse 15; ☙ 6pm-1am Mon, Wed & Thu, 6pm-2am Tue, 6pm-3am Fri, 1pm-3am Sat, 1pm-1am Sun) and **McLang's Irish Pub** (☎ 828 456; Lange Reihe 17; ☙ 5pm-midnight Mon-Thu, 1pm-2am Fri-Sun), are local stalwarts. The latter has regular whisky-tasting evenings.

Also recommended:

Forstbaumschule (☎ 333 496; Dvelsbeker Weg 46; ☙ from 10am) Huge beer garden in a rambling park 3.5km north of the city centre (take bus 32, 33, 41, 42, 61 or 62).

Kieler Brauerei (☎ 906 290; Alter Markt 9; ☙ 10am-midnight Mon-Fri, 10am-1am Fri & Sat, noon-8pm Sun) Historic premises brewing its own flavoursome beer.

Oblomov (☎ 801 467; Hansastrasse 82; ☙ 11.30am-1am Mon-Fri, 6pm-1am Sat, 10am-1am Sun) Legendary student pub.

Getting There & Away

AIR

The bus service **Kielius** (☎ 666 2222; www.kielius.de) shuttles 18 times in each direction between Hamburg airport and Kiel's central bus station (one-way/return €17.50/30). Lübeck airport (see p706) is also convenient.

BOAT

See p778 for details of ferry services between Kiel and Gothenburg, Oslo, and Klaipeda in Lithuania.

BUS

Interglobus Reisen (☎ 661 1576; Auguste-Viktoria-Strasse) operates buses to Poland. Many other services head from the central bus station to towns in Schleswig-Holstein, although the train is generally more convenient.

CAR & MOTORCYCLE

Kiel is connected with the rest of Germany via the A210 and A215, which merge with the A7 to Hamburg and beyond.

TRAIN

Numerous trains shuttle between Kiel and Hamburg (€27, 1¼ hours). Trains to Lübeck leave hourly (€15.20, 1¼ hours). There are regular local connections to Schleswig, Husum, Schwerin and Flensburg.

Getting Around

Local bus trips cost from €1.50 one-way or €4.30 for a day card. To hire a taxi, call ☎ 680 101.

A ferry service along the firth runs daily until around 6pm (to 5pm on weekends) from the Bahnhofsbrücke pier behind the Hauptbahnhof. The trip to Laboe is €3.70.

Bikes can be rented from the Hauptbahnhof.

AROUND KIEL

Laboe

☎ 04343 / pop 5300

At the mouth of the Kiel firth, on its eastern bank, the village of Laboe is home to a WWII-serving **U-Boot** (☎ 427 00; adult/child €2.50/1.80; ☙ 9.30am-6pm Apr-Oct, 9.30am-4pm Nov-Mar) and associated **Marine Ehrenmal** (adult/child €4/2.50, combined admission with U-Boot adult/child €5/3.50). The sub is the kind featured in Wolfgang Petersen's seminal film *Das Boot* (1981). It's now a museum where you can climb through its claustrophobic interior. From Kiel, take the ferry (see p701) or bus 100 or 101.

Schleswig-Holsteinisches Freilichtmuseum

South of Kiel, in Molfsee, is the excellent **Schleswig-Holsteinisches Freilichtmuseum** (Schleswig-Holstein Open-Air Museum; ☎ 0431-659 660; Alte Hamburger

Landstrasse 97; adult/child/family €6/2/13 Apr-Oct, adult/child €3/1.50 Nov-Mar; 🕑 9am-6pm Apr-Oct, 11am-4pm Sun & holidays Nov-Mar), featuring some 70 traditional houses typical of the region, relocated from around the state, and providing a thorough introduction to the northern lifestyle. Take bus 501/502 from Kiel's central bus station.

SCHLESWIG
☎ 04621 / pop 24,036

Neat redbrick houses and manicured lawns give this 'Viking town' on the Baltic Sea's longest fjord a Nordic look, while the tall cathedral spire rising proudly above the water hints that little Schleswig wasn't always this sleepy.

This is certainly true. Founded in 804, after a major Viking community put down roots across the Schlei fjord, it was the continent's economic hub for some 200 years.

The Dukes of Gottorf, who made Schleswig their power base from the 16th to 18th centuries, have also come and gone, as have generations of fishermen and their families. All have left distinctive reminders of their time here that add to the town's charm.

Information

There are late-opening internet cafes at the Bahnhof and bus station.

Post office (Poststrasse 1a)

Tourist office (☎ 850 056; www.schleswig.de; in German; Plessenstrasse 7; 🕑 10am-6pm Mon-Fri, 10am-2pm Sat May-Sep, 10am-4pm Mon-Fri Oct-Apr) In the town centre. City maps and hotel brochures are available outside after hours.

Sights & Activities
SCHLOSS GOTTORF

Wartime destruction of Kiel meant that the treasures from the **Schleswig-Holstein Landesmuseum** (☎ 8130; www.schloss-gottorf.de; adult/concession/family €8/5/17, audioguide €2; 🕑 10am-6pm Apr-Oct, 10am-4pm Tue-Fri, 10am-5pm Sat & Sun Nov-Mar) were moved to the Dukes of Gottorf's 12th-century castle in Schleswig. The collection fitted perfectly and the museum has been based here ever since.

A roomful of paintings by Lucas Cranach the Elder and a wood-panelled 17th-century wine tavern from Lübeck create a memorable first impression. There's also the rococo **Plöner Saal**, with faïence from the Baltic region; the stunning **Schlosskapelle** (room 26); and the elegant **Hirschsaal**, the former banquet hall named for the bas-reliefs of deer on the walls.

The more contemporary collection is equally noteworthy, including an entire **Jugendstil Abteilung** (Art Nouveau Department) and 20th-century paintings, sketches, lithographs and woodcuts from German artists such as Emil Nolde and Ernst Barlach.

And we haven't even reached the museum's two main highlights: the first is the **Nydam-Boot**, a reconstructed and preserved 28-oar rowing boat from 350 BC, which is housed in its own hall (and sometimes goes on loan to other museums); while the second is a reconstruction of the famous **Gottorfer Globus** (Gottorf Globe; adult/child Sat & Sun €14/11, Tue-Thu €11/8.50, Mon & Fri €10/7.50; 🕑 10am-6pm Apr-Oct), which has been placed in its own house a five-minute walk behind the castle grounds. The original 17th-century globe was lauded as one of the wonders of the world – its first planetarium – but through war ended up being taken from Schleswig to St Petersburg. It's still there (albeit fire-damaged) in the Lomonosov Museum. The exterior of the 3m-diameter reconstruction shows how the continents and seas were thought to look in the 17th century. The real magic is inside, however. Several people can fit on a bench inside the globe and watch the Renaissance night sky change as the globe spins around them; it takes eight minutes to simulate a day.

You'll need at least half-a-day to do Schloss Gottorf justice. Kids can rent a special audioguide that weaves together fairy-tale-like stories as it interprets the collections. There's a cafe and restaurant on-site.

The Schloss is 2km south of the centre (1km north of the Bahnhof).

WIKINGER MUSEUM

It would have been rather dangerous venturing into this area some 1000 to 1200 years ago, when Vikings ruled the roost from their base here at Haithabu, across the Schlei from Schleswig. Fortunately, these days the local warriors are a lot less fearsome, being merely actors and exhibits at the **Wikinger Museum** (Viking Museum; ☎ 813 222; www.haithabu.de; adult/concession/family €6/3.50/13; 🕑 9am-5pm Apr-Oct, 10am-4pm Tue-Sun Nov-Mar).

Located just outside the historic settlement (now an archaeological site), this kid-friendly museum features replica huts showing how the Viking families lived their daily lives. There are also seven exhibition halls (designed to resemble Viking boat sheds) with multilingual multimedia displays and artefacts discovered nearby. One of these includes a 30m longboat, since reconstructed.

Seasonal events include an autumn *Messe* (fair) of Viking crafts, Midsummer's Day eve and New Year's Eve, and celebrations during Schleswig's 'Viking Days' festival in August of even-numbered years.

The museum lies east of the B76 that runs between Schleswig and Kiel, about 3km from Schleswig's Hauptbahnhof. Between May and September, the easiest way to arrive is by ferry (see p714). Otherwise, bus 4810 to Kiel runs all year. Alight at Haddeby.

STADTMUSEUM SCHLESWIG

Another favourite with littlies, **Schleswig's City Museum** (☎ 936 820; www.stadtmuseum-schleswig.de, in German; Friedrichstrasse 9-11; adult/concession/family €4/2/8.50) incorporates an adorable 'Teddy Bear Haus' in a half-timbered building off the courtyard. In addition to historic, well-loved bears (some a little worse for wear), there's a 'zoo' of dozens of other stuffed, furry creatures. The museum's main building charts the history of northern Europe's oldest city through multimedia exhibits, audiovisual presentations (also in English) and artefacts. It's signposted a five-minute walk north of the Bahnhof.

HOLM

This quaint-as-can-be traditional fishing village southeast of the Altstadt sits on a peninsula that until 1935 was an island. Its centrepiece is an almost toy-sized **chapel** in the middle of a small cemetery, which is ringed by a cobbled road and tiny fishermen's houses.

A handful of locals still fish here, and their colourful nets hanging out to dry are a memorable sight. Continue further east, and you'll come to the **Johanniskloster** (convent; ☎ 242 36; Süderholmstrasse; admission by donation; ☼ by appointment) and its beautiful 'bible garden'.

DOM ST PETRI & AROUND

With its steeple towering above the town, the **Dom St Petri** (☎ 989 585; Süderholmstrasse 2; ☼ 9am-5pm Mon-Sat, 1.30-5pm Sun May-Sep, 10am-4pm Mon-Sat, 1.30-4pm Sun Oct-Apr) provides an excellent point of orientation. It's also home to the intricate **Bordesholmer Altar** (1521), a carving by Hans Brüggemann. The 12.6m by 7.14m altar, on the wall furthest from the entrance, shows more than 400 figures in 24 scenes relating the

story of the Passion of Christ – the result of extraordinary craftsmanship and patience.

While here, don't forget to explore the cobbled cluster of streets behind the cathedral, especially **Rathhausmarkt**.

Tours

Several companies offer a vast array of boat trips up the 40km Schlei between April and October from varying landing docks (onboard commentary is in German).

Operators are:

Schlei-Ausflugsfahrten (☎ 6184; www.schlei-ausflugsfahrten.de, in German)

Schleischiffahrt A Bischoff (☎ 233 19; www.schleischifffahrt.de, in German)

Schleswiger Hafenrundfahrten (☎ 275 30; www.schleifahrten.de, in German)

Sleeping

Many hotels in Schleswig close their reception at 10pm (some as early as 6pm). You can still phone them after closing time, but it's always better to call at least half a day ahead.

Campingplatz Haithabu (☎ 324 50; www.campingplatz-haithabu.de, in German; per adult/tent/car €3.50/6/2; ☼ Mar-Oct; **P**) This well-equipped camping ground is right on the southern shore of the Schlei in Haddeby, with a great view of the Schleswig skyline. Take bus 4810 or catch a ferry (see p714) in summer.

DJH hostel (☎ 238 93; www.jugendherberge.de/jh/schleswig; Spielkoppel 1; under/over 26yr €17.20/21.20 incl breakfast; ☼ closed Dec-Jan; ✗) Noise is an afternoon phenomenon at this renovated hostel that's popular with families and school groups. The nearest bus stop is Stadttheater, from where it's a 10- to 15-minute walk.

Hotel Alter Kreisbahnhof (☎ 302 00; www.hotel-alter-kreisbhahnhof.de, in German; Königstrasse 9; s/d incl breakfast €54/93; **P** ✗ ☎) Some of the spacious rooms at this new boutique hotel-restaurant, based in a turreted former railway station, have water views. Splashes of vivid colours like fuchsia brighten the restaurant (mains €8.40 to €14.90), which serves creative regional cuisine.

Bed & Breakfast am Dom (☎ 485 992; www.bb-schleswig.de; Töpferstrasse 9; s/d incl breakfast €60/85; **P** 💻) You'd scarcely guess there's a building behind all the ivy, let alone one this spacious. From the long, narrow dining room, the six bedrooms and guest sitting room stretch back to the private garden, with a pretty summerhouse pavilion. Decor in the 200-year-old town house combines historic, romantic and designer touches.

Zollhaus (☎ 239 47; www.zollhaus-schleswig.de, in German; Lollfuss 110; s €79-95, d €95-109 incl breakfast; P ✗ ☎ �🛜) Culture vultures coming to neighbouring Schloss Gottorf will enjoy the refined (but totally unstuffy) atmosphere and comfortable rooms at this 200-year-old customs house. Its highly regarded restaurant (mains €16.50 to €28.50) specialises in seafood.

Waldschlösschen (☎ 3830; www.hotel-waldschloesschen.de; Kolonnenweg 152; s €80-90, d €95-149; P ✗ ☎ 🛜 🍽) At the western edge of Schleswig, 2km from the town centre, you can set about the serious business of relaxing at this elegant, family-run hotel on the Schlei. The most appealing of its rooms are themed (such as maritime or Africa), you can steam or soak in its wellness centre, sip cocktails in the bar and dine on gourmet cuisine (mains €14 to €21.50).

Eating & Drinking

Several of Schleswig's hotels (p713) have excellent restaurants. You'll also find appealing restaurants around the main 'square' of pint-sized Holm (p713).

Panorama (☎ 245 80; Plessenstrasse 15; mains €7.90-13.50; 🕑 lunch & dinner Mon-Fri, 11.30am-11pm Sat & Sun; V) Panorama's crispy wood-fired pizzas provide an antidote for anyone tired of seafood. Weekday lunch specials cost just €4.50 to €5.50.

ourpick Senator-Kroog (☎ 222 90; Rathausmarkt 9-10; mains €7.90-18.50; 🕑 10am-midnight Mar-Dec, 5-10pm Mon-Fri, 10am-midnight Sat & Sun Jan & Feb) Angus beef and rump steak are among the hearty meat dishes at this local favourite, but there's also a melange of regional specialities, such as its signature *Labskaus* (a minced dish of salt herring, corned beef, pig lard, potato and beetroot, topped with gherkins and a fried egg). Fronted by alfresco tables overlooking Schleswig's market square, the 1884 property – one half painted white, the other red, both with duck-egg-blue window trim – is a picture.

Speicher (☎ 305 184; Am Hafen 5; mains €8.90-15.20; 🕑 11.30am-10pm; 🛜 V) A converted grain silo now houses Schleswig's newest restaurant. The sound of clinking masts from the boats bobbing out the front on the harbour provides a fitting backdrop for its extensive range of fish specialities.

Asgaard (☎ 292 06; Königstrasse 27; mains €8.90-16.90; 🕑 from 5pm Tue-Fri, from 11am Sat, 1-10pm Sun; V)

Tables in the split-level dining room overlook this contemporary brewery's copper boilers. It's inside an atmospheric 1880-built brick former freight-train station. In addition to its full-flavoured lager, Das Göttliche ('the Divine'), and smooth Pils, try the fruity Kleiner Wikinger ('Little Viking') blending Das Göttliche and mead. Soak them up with its house speciality pork *Schnitzel*, or lighter meals such as salads or vegie gratin.

La Dom (☎ 276 09; Rathausmarkt 17; mains €9-15.50, tapas €1.90-7.50; 🕑 11am-10pm; V) Stretching from the Rathausmarkt to just behind the Dom St Petri, you'll find a series of airy rooms (including a canopied winter garden) at this stylish yet relaxed cafe/restaurant, along with succulent steaks, lobster and a vast array of tapas dishes.

Café im Wikingturm (☎ 330 40; 26th fl, Wikingturm, Wikingeck 5; menus from €11; 🕑 lunch & dinner, seasonal hours vary) Across the Schlei, Schleswig's octagonal tower with garish bright-blue panels is an eyesore, but absolves its architectural sins with superb-value three-course menus and awesome views from the top-floor restaurant.

Getting There & Away

Schleswig's Bahnhof is 3km south of the centre and connected to it by buses and a long, well-signed footpath. In town, the central bus station is on the corner of Königstrasse and Plessenstrasse, just northeast of the Altstadt, although regional bus services are infrequent.

Direct trains to Hamburg (€21.20, 1½ hours) run every two hours, while trains to Flensburg (€6.80, 30 minutes), Kiel (€9.70, 40 minutes) and Husum (€6.80, 45 minutes) leave every 30 minutes.

If you're driving, take the A7 (Hamburg–Flensburg) to the Schuby exit, then continue east on the B201.

Getting Around

Tickets for Schleswig's bus system cost €1.40 per trip, or €7.20 for a six-ticket strip. You'll find taxis at the Bahnhof and the central bus station. A taxi from the Bahnhof to the town centre costs around €8.

Between May and September, ferries cross the Schlei from Schleswig Hafen (just south of the Dom) between 10.30am to 5pm daily (adult one-way/return €2.50/4).

Bike rental outlets include **Fahrradverleih Röhling** (☎ 993 030; www.fahrradverleih-schleswig.de, in

German; Knud-Laward-Strasse 30; per day €7.50; 🕑 9am-6pm Mon-Fri, 9am-12.30pm Sat).

FLENSBURG

☎ 0461 / pop 87,065

Flensburg might not be as stereotypically pretty as Schleswig, but this port city is certainly livelier. Situated on a busy industrial firth just a handful of kilometres south of the Danish border, it's sometimes still dubbed 'Rumstadt' for its prosperous 18th-century trade in liquor with the Caribbean. The city was the Third Reich's last seat of power, when shortly before VE Day in 1945 a cornered Hitler handed power to Flensburg-based Admiral Karl Dönitz. Little is made of this dark snippet, but reminders of its sea-faring, rum-trading days can be found across town.

Orientation

Most attractions run north–south parallel to the western bank of the firth. The central bus station is across from the firth, which extends along Norderhofenden (becoming Schiffbrücke). The pedestrian zone is just inland; following Rathausstrasse (adjacent to the tourist office) for one block west (uphill) brings you to the main drag, whose name changes from Holm at the southern end to Grosse Strasse in the centre and Norderstrasse to the north.

Information

Flensburg tourist office (☎ 909 0920; www.flensburg-tourismus.de; Europa-Haus, Rathausstrasse 1; 🕑 9am-6pm Mon-Fri year-round, 10am-4pm Sat Jun-Aug, 10am-2pm Sat May & Sep) Across from the northwestern corner of the central bus station.

Post office (Schiffbrückstrasse 2)

Zuckerspeicher (☎ 840 1188; Grosse Strasse 69; per hr €3; 🕑 10am-8pm Mon-Sat, noon-7pm Sun) Internet access.

Sights

A Flensburg highlight, literally as well as figuratively, is the hilltop **Museumsberg Flensburg** (Municipal Museum; ☎ 852 956; www.museumsberg-flensburg.de, in German; Museumsberg 1; adult/child/family €4/1.50/8, extra for special exhibitions; 🕑 10am-5pm Tue-Sun Apr-Oct, 10am-4pm Tue-Sun Nov-Mar). The museum is divided into the Heinrich-Sauermann-Haus and the Hans-Christiansen-Haus. The first building contains a collection of rooms and furniture from Schleswig-Holstein history, including a remarkably painted cembalo

(early piano covered in murals; room 25). In the second building, you'll find excellent art nouveau works by Flensburg-born painter Hans Christiansen, as well as an Emil Nolde room.

Combination tickets (adult/child/family €5/2.50/10) are good for both Museumsberg Flensburg and the **Schiffahrtsmuseum** (Maritime Museum; ☎ 852 970; www.schiffahrtsmuseum.flensburg.de; Schiffbrücke 39; adult/child/family €4/1.50/8, extra for special exhibitions; 🕑 10am-5pm Tue-Sun Apr-Oct, 10am-4pm Tue-Sun Nov-Mar), which has a small **rum museum** (included in admission) in the basement.

Flensburg's other main highlight is checking out the town's charming **Kaufmannshöfe** (Merchants' Courtyards). These date from the 18th century, when Danish-ruled Flensburg provided supplies to the Danish West Indies (St Thomas, St Jan and St Croix) in exchange for sugar and rum. Designed to make it easier to load goods into ships, they typically consisted of a tall warehouse on the harbourside, behind which was a series of low workshops, wrapped around a central courtyard and leading to the merchant's living quarters.

Free town maps from the tourist office mark nearly every *Hof* (courtyard), or ask for its *Käpitans Weg* brochure (also free), which follows a captain's route around town as he was preparing for a trip.

Just off Grosse Strasse 24 is a courtyard that houses the attractive **Westindien-speicher** (West Indian Warehouse). If you continue south along Grosse Strasse it becomes Holm, where at No 17 you'll also find the **Borgerforeningen Hof.**

The prettiest courtyards can be found off picturesque **Rote Strasse** (continue south along Holm through Südermarkt). While here, you have a chance to buy rum at **Weinhaus Braasch** (☎ 141 600; www.braasch-rum.de, in German; Rote Strasse 26-28; 🕑 10am-7pm Mon-Fri, 10am-4pm Sat).

Activities

Today, when most of us fly across borders, or whiz across by road, rail or sea, it's fun to have the opportunity to cross one on foot. Just 6.5km north of Flensburg's city centre you can hike (or cycle) across the **Schusterkate**. Northern Europe's smallest border post sits on the only bridge connecting Germany and Denmark. It's unmanned following the open-border Schengen Agreement, but as with all cross-border travel, you're still required to carry your passport.

The Schusterkate is part of the 74km-long **Gendarmenpfad** trail, which starts west of Flensburg in the otherwise uninspiring Danish truck-stop town of Padborg. From Padborg, it heads east to the Schusterkate and then follows the coastline to Høruphav, Denmark. Ask the tourist office for information, including its free *Gendarmenpfad* booklet. It's in German and Danish only, but the maps are easily navigable.

Tours

The **MS Viking** (☎ 167 2674; www.viking-schifffahrt.de, in German; adult/child return €7/4) operates scenic cruises to Glücksburg (one hour each way), departing from where Norderhofenden meets Schiffbrücke. Boats leave at least four times daily from March to December (none in January or February).

Slightly closer to the bus station, the **MS Möwe** (☎ 629 45; www.ms-moewe.net, in German; adult/child €7/4) offers hour-long cruises around the firth five times daily from June to August, and three times daily in April, May, September and October.

Sleeping

DJH hostel (☎ 377 42; www.djh-nordmark.de/jh/flensburg; Fichtestrasse 16; under/over 26yr €18/21 incl breakfast; ❍ closed mid-Dec–mid-Feb; **P** ✗ ☎) Hidden down a leafy lane near the local football stadium, this is very popular with school sporting teams, so brace yourself for lots of noise and restless activity. Facilities are tip-top, though, and the ride from town (on bus 3, 5 or 7 to the Stadion bus stop) only takes about five minutes.

Hotel Handwerkerhaus (☎ 144 800; www.hotel-handwerkerhaus.de, in German; Augustastrasse 2; s €47.50-55, d €67.50-75; ✗) Although this small, redbrick hotel is more characterful on the outside than it is inside, its old-fashioned, built-in timber-furnished rooms are spotlessly clean and it's in a quiet side street just one block east of the bus station.

Hotel Xenia (☎ 160 620; www.hotelxenia.de, in German; Süderhofenden 38; s/d incl breakfast €55/82; **P** ✗ 🖳) At the eastern edge of the Altstadt, just south of the historic Johanniskirche (built from fieldstones in the 12th century), this whitewashed hotel has just nine charming rooms under its sloping roof, and opens to a private, flower-filled garden.

Hotel Dittmer's Gasthof (☎ 240 52; www.dittmers gasthof.de; Neumarkt 2-3; s/d €60/95; **P**) This flower-festooned historic inn at the southern edge of

the city centre has been run by the same family for more than 100 years. Rooms are cosy and the welcome particularly warm.

For all-out luxury, head to the Strandhotel Glücksburg (opposite) in nearby Glücksburg.

Eating & Drinking

Marien-Café (☎ 500 9711; Norderstrasse 11-13; dishes €2.90-13.90; ❍ 8am-6pm; **V**) Splurge on a sumptuous slice of homemade cake or linger over a long breakfast beneath the china teapots hanging from the ceiling of this quaint tearoom.

Hansens Brauerei (☎ 222 10; Schiffbrücke 16; meals €7.80-15.80; ❍ 11.30am-midnight) Simple but hearty German fare – homemade meatballs, roast pork, herrings – is served at this brewery opposite the waterfront, although most people order food to accompany the wide range of beers (including some great seasonal beers) amid the copper boilers.

Porterhouse im Gnomenkeller (☎ 221 16; Holm 3; mains €11.90-32.50; ❍ 11.30am-11pm) Heading through the metal gates inconspicuously set in the blank facade of a row of shops and descending the short flight of stairs brings you to this cross-vaulted cellar with tables in low-lit corners. Even the heartiest of appetites will be challenged by the XXL-sized steaks.

Piet Henningsen (☎ 245 76; Schiffbrücke 20; mains €14.50-29.50; ❍ 11.30am-11.30pm) Locals say tha *Wer dat Piet nicht kennt, hat de Tied verpennt* (He who doesn't know Piet's has missed the tide). Heed their advice: this atmospheric spot is crammed with exotic souvenirs brought home by sailors: African statues and ceramics Indonesian wall hangings, ship models, empty rum bottles, a leopard skin and a stuffed croc odile. Argentine steaks aside, the menu is a smorgasbord of seafood.

On the eastern bank of the firth are two excellent restaurants in neighbouring waterfront locations:

Mäder's (☎ 150 7900; Ballastkai 9; mains €13.90-24.50 ❍ 10am-11.30pm; **V**) One of northern Germany's very few all-organic restaurants, serving Mediterranean-inspired dishes.

Jessen's Fischperle (☎ 182 8230; Ballastkai 4-6; main €16.70-19.50; ❍ 11.30am-9.30pm) Outstanding seafood

Getting There & Away

Flensburg has rail connections with Kie (€15.20, 1½ hours), and with Schleswig (€6.80 30 minutes), from where trains continue to Hamburg. Trips to Husum (€13.20, 1½ hours require a change at Jübek.

COASTAL COFFEE

If the cold wind's biting, warm up with one of the region's specialities, rum-laced coffee topped with cream, known as a *Pharisäer*. So the stories go, chilly locals in the region infused their strong, sweetened coffee with a shot of rum. But, to hide the presence of alcohol from their priest, they smothered the top with cream. The priest, however, quickly caught on, decrying them as Pharisees (his point being that they were following the letter, not the spirit, of the law). The name stuck, as did the surreptitious drinking technique – don't stir it; instead, slurp the hot coffee through the cream.

Autokraft (☎ 690 69; www.autokraft.de, in German) has regular buses to Husum (€6.10, one hour), Niebüll (€6.10, one hour) and Kiel (€8.70, two hours) from the central bus station.

Flensburg is at the beginning of the A7, which leads south to Hamburg, Hanover and beyond. The town can also be reached via the B76, B199 and B200.

Getting Around

Buses cost €1.70/4.90 for a single/day pass, but you can easily cover Flensburg on foot. To walk from the Bahnhof, which takes around 15 minutes, follow the small blue signs reading 'Altstadt/Zentrum'.

GLÜCKSBURG
☎ 04631 / pop 5985

Overlooking the water 10km northeast of Flensburg, this small spa town is renowned for its horseshoe-shaped Renaissance **Wasserschloss** (Moated Palace; ☎ 442 330; adult/concession €5/3.50; � 10am-6pm May-Sep), which appears to float in the middle of a large lake. The rest of the town is equally charming, and it's a pleasant stroll around the lake up to the beach.

ourpick **Strandhotel Glücksburg** (☎ 614 10; www.strandhotel-gluecksburg.de; Kirstenstrasse 6; s/d from €130/180; P X 🖴 🛜), the fabled 'white castle by the sea', counts Thomas Mann among its former guests. Rooms at this resplendent beachfront villa are now decked out in cool, minimalist Scandinavian style. Decadences include a spa and gastronomic restaurant serving a daily changing menu utilising fresh produce. Foodies should ask about special

bon vivant packages incorporating gourmet evening meals.

Buses run hourly between Glücksburg and Flensburg's central bus station (€2.40). For boat services to Glücksburg, see opposite.

HUSUM & THE HALLIGEN
☎ 04841 / pop 21,000

The 19th-century German novelist and poet Theodor Storm (1817–88) called his hometown 'the grey town by the sea'. But although its *Aussenhafen* (outer harbour) has some hulking industrial monoliths, warmly toned buildings huddle around its delightful *Binnenhafen* (inner harbour), colourful gabled houses line its narrow, cobbled lanes, and in late March and early April millions of purple crocuses bloom in Husum's Schlosspark.

After retracing Storm's footsteps through Husum and seeing where his seminal North Frisian novella *Der Schimmelreiter* (The Rider on the White Horse) was written, it's easy to head offshore from nearby Nordstrand to the tiny islets known as Halligen.

Orientation

Husum is compact and extremely well signposted. The Bahnhof lies 700m south of the city centre. Head north along Herzog-Adolf-Strasse (passing the library and the central bus station) and turn left at Ludwig-Nissen-Strasse, following the sign reading Zentrum, to the *Binnenhafen*; the *Aussenhafen* is just west of here. Alternatively, continue north along Herzog-Adolf-Strasse and turn left into Nordstrasse for the Markt, Gross Strasse and tourist office.

Information

Husum tourist office (☎ 898 70; www.tourismus -husum.de; Historisches Rathaus, Gross Strasse 27; � 9am-6pm Mon-Fri, 10am-4pm Sat Apr-Oct, 9am-5pm Mon-Fri, 10am-4pm Sat Nov-Mar)

Sights
HUSUM

Even if you're not too familiar with the author, the **Theodor-Storm-Haus** (Theodor Storm House; ☎ 803 8630; www.storm-gesellschaft.de; Wasserreihe 31-35; adult/concession €3/2; � 10am-5pm Tue-Fri, 11am-5pm Sat, 2-5pm Sun & Mon Apr-Oct, 2-5pm Tue, Thu & Sat Nov-Mar) will whet your appetite. Well-placed literary snippets and biographical titbits fill in the life of this novelist, poet and proud Schleswig-Holstein citizen in the small, intimate rooms where he lived and wrote.

Ask at the tourist office for a map highlighting other stops along the town's 'cultural trail'. Many also focus on Theodor Storm, right down to the **fountain** in the Markt, which shows Tine, a young Frisian woman who figures in a Storm novella. Even the **Marienkirche** (1829) featured in a couple of his novellas. The church tower is supposed to symbolise a lighthouse.

Kids – and kids at heart – will be enchanted by the puppets on display at the **Poppenspäler Museum** (☎ 632 42; www.pole-poppenspaeler.de, in German; Erichsenweg 23; adult/child/family €2/1/5; ⌚ 2-5pm Sun-Fri Apr-Dec, 2-5pm Mon, Wed & Fri Jan-Mar). In summer, it presents a series of outdoor shows from its century-old 'puppet wagon' – check with the museum for annual schedules.

THE HALLIGEN

Is it an island? Is it a sandbank? No, it's a *Hallig*, one of about 10 tiny wafer-flat 'islets' scattered across the Schleswig-Holstein Wadden Sea National Park (Nationalpark Schleswig-Holsteinisches Wattenmeer) and home to seal colonies. In the Middle Ages some 50 Halligen existed, but the sea has swallowed up most of them. Up to 60 times a year, floods drown the beaches and meadows, leaving the few reed-thatched farms stranded on the artificial knolls, or 'wharves', that they're built on. An aerial shot of such stranded farms is a favourite postcard image.

Most people visit the islets on day excursions. The prettiest destination is **Hallig Hooge**, which once sheltered a Danish king from a storm in the handsome **Königshaus**, with its blue and white tiles and baroque ceiling fresco. Other popular Halligen include Langeness and Gröde.

Between April and October, boat trips run by **Adler Schiffe** (☎ 04842-900 00; www.adler-schiffe.de, in German) sail from Nordstrand to Hallig Hooge (€19.50 return). See opposite for bus connections from Husum to Nordstrand, as well as boat trips from Nordstrand to the North Frisian Islands.

Some Halligen can also be reached directly from the North Frisian Islands (see p721).

Sleeping & Eating

The tourist office can help book private rooms and holiday apartments.

DJH hostel (☎ 2714; www.jugendherberge.de/jh/husum; Schobüller Strasse 34; dm under/over 26yr €18.20/21.20 incl linen & breakfast; ⌚ closed late Dec-early Jan; P ⊠) Husum's hostel is set in a typical and very atmospheric Frisian building with wood-beamed ceilings. It's a 35-minute walk northwest of the city centre, or take the Schobüll bus from the central bus station to the Westerkamp stop.

Hotel Hinrichsen (☎ 890 70; www.hotel-hinrichsen.de, in German; Süderstrasse 35; s €49.50-52, d €68-98 incl breakfast; P ⊠ wi-fi) A hop, skip and a jump from the Bahnhof (less than five minutes' walk), this flower-bedecked, white-painted hotel has clean, modern rooms. Bathrooms are largely moulded-plastic constructions, but the friendly welcome makes up for it.

Hotel am Schlosspark (☎ 2022; www.hotel-am-schlosspark-husum.de; Hinter der Neustadt 76-86; s €59-65, d €89-99 incl breakfast; P ⊠ wi-fi) Laid out like a sprawling motel, this smart hotel one block from the Schlosspark has stylish, contemporary decor in pistachio and chocolate tones, and offers pampering beauty and fitness treatments.

Hotel Altes Gymnasium (☎ 8330; www.altes-gymnasium.de; Süderstrasse 6; s €105-145, d €160-235; P ⊠ wi-fi) This five-star hotel is a splendidly historic former high school, with Persian carpets, flagstones, tapestries and chandeliers in the entrance hall, an exalted gourmet restaurant (five-course menu €77, dinner Wednesday to Sunday), cheaper winter-garden restaurant and a cocktail bar. Rooms are as luxurious as you'd expect, but definitely request one in the atmospheric older building rather than the new wing.

Brauhaus Husum (☎ 896 60; Neustadt 60-68; mains €6.50-19.50; ⌚ 3pm-late summer, 5pm-late winter) Frothy beers including a thirst-quenching *Husumer Weizen* (wheat beer) are made on-site at this brilliant local brewery. Specialities include pizzas made from brewers yeast, and spare ribs with honey and mandarin sauce. Serious beer lovers should ask about regular brewery tours (€5).

Cafes and restaurants ring the St Marienkirche and the Markt; you'll find more around the *Binnenhafen*. Pick up fresh food at Husum's **market** (⌚ Thu year-round plus Sat Mar-Dec), which has been held on the Markt since 1465.

AT HOME WITH EMIL NOLDE

Bright flowers, stormy seas, red-lipped women with jaunty hats and impressionistic seaside watercolours: these are some of the recurring themes of great Schleswig-Holstein painter Emil Nolde. Born in 1867 in Nolde village near the Danish border (from whence he took his name), he first gained fame for producing postcards in which he gave mountains human features. In 1906, after spending much of his early life in Berlin, Munich and Karlsruhe, Nolde joined the expressionist group Die Brücke.

In 1927 Nolde and his wife Ada built their own home and studio in Seebüll. Here, banned from working by the Nazis, he proceeded to produce 1300 'unpainted pictures' in secret. He died in 1956.

Nowadays Nolde is considered one of the great 20th-century watercolourists, and his work is found across Schleswig-Holstein (and far beyond), including in Kiel's Kunsthalle (p709), the Schleswig-Holstein Landesmuseum in Schleswig (p712) and the Museumsberg Flensburg (p715).

By far the biggest and most impressive collection is in Nolde's former atelier at Seebüll, now the **Emil Nolde Stiftung** (☎ 04664-983 930; www.nolde-stiftung.de; Neukirchen bei Seebüll; adult/child €8/3; ⏰ 10am-6pm Apr-Nov, to 8pm Thu Jun-Sep). The exhibition is worth a half to whole day's excursion, which is lucky because that's what it will take you, depending on where you're coming from. The closest train stations are Niebüll (15km from Seebüll) or Klanxbüll (8km from Seebüll), from where you can catch a taxi to Seebüll. Some buses (included in the admission price) run by **Niebüller Verkehrsbetriebe** (☎ 04661-980 8890; www.nvb-niebuell.de, in German) come from Niebüll via Klanxbüll, and from Westerland via Klanxbüll to the museum, but must be confirmed directly with the bus company at least one day ahead. By road, follow the B199 and then the B5 from Niebüll.

Getting There & Around

There are regular direct rail connections to Kiel (€15.20, 1½ hours), Hamburg (€31, two hours) and Schleswig (€6.80, 30 minutes), plus several links daily to Westerland on Sylt (€13.20, one hour).

From Nordstrand, **Adler Schiffe** (☎ 04842-900 00; www.adler-schiffe.de, in German) has boat trips to Amrum (€22.50 return) and Hörnum, Sylt (€26.50 return). Up to seven buses daily connect Husum with Nordstrand (€4.30, 43 minutes).

Husum has many bus connections with other towns in North Friesland, but service is sporadic to say the least. For timetables, contact **Autokraft** (☎ 0431-666 222; www.autokraft.de, in German).

Husum is at the crossroads of the B5, the B200 and the B201.

Bikes can be rented at the Bahnhof from **Rad Station** (☎ 805 550; per day from €4.50; ⏰ 6.15am-6pm Mon-Fri & by appointment).

NORTH FRISIAN ISLANDS

With their grass-covered dunes, shifting sands, birds, seal colonies, lighthouses and rugged cliffs, you'd imagine Germany's North Frisian Islands to be the domain of intrepid nature lovers. Instead, these North Sea islands are a favourite of the German jet set. On glamorous Sylt in particular, you'll find designer boutiques housed in quintessential reed-thatched cottages, gleaming Porches and Mercedes jamming the car parks, luxurious accommodation and some of the country's most extravagant restaurants.

Those with less cash to splash can still enjoy the pure sea air, especially in Sylt's remoter corners. The islands of Amrum and Föhr are more peaceful still.

SYLT

☎ 04651 / pop 21,000

The anchor-shaped island of Sylt is attached to the mainland by a narrow causeway. On its west coast, the North Sea's fierce surf and strong winds gnaw mercilessly at the shoreline. By contrast, Sylt's eastern Wadden Sea shore is tranquil and serene. At low tide, the retreating shallows expose vast mudflats.

Sylt's candy-striped lighthouses rise above wide expanses of shifting dunes, fields of gleaming yellow-gold rape flower and expanses of heath. Dotted along its beaches, the island also has several saunas, where the idea is to heat up and then run naked into the chilly North Sea!

Despite its glut of upmarket restaurants and designer boutiques, it's easy enough to lose the glamour and crowds on the beaches, in the dunes or on a hiking or bike trail.

Orientation

Sylt is 38.5km long and measures only 700m at its narrowest point. The largest town, commercial hub and train terminus is Westerland on the island's central west coast. Keitum is on the central east coast. North of Westerland is Wenningstedt, while Kampen is north again, and List still further north. Rantum is south of Westerland; Hörnum is at the narrow southern tip.

Information

All communities on Sylt charge visitors a *Kurtaxe* (resort tax) of €3.50 per day. In return you receive a *Kurkarte* (resort card), which you need to get onto the beach; it also entitles you to small discounts at museums. If you're staying overnight, your hotel will automatically obtain a pass for you, adding the *Kurtaxe* to the room rate. Day-trippers will need to buy a *Tageskarte* (day pass) from tourist offices or the kiosks at entrances to the beach.

The **Kampen tourist office** (☎ 469 80; www.kampen .de, in German; Hauptstrasse 12; ☉ 10am-5pm Mon-Fri, 10am-1pm Sat & Sun, reduced hours in winter) produces a quirky illustrated map of the 'in' restaurants, bars and clubs. Information is also available from the **Keitum tourist office** (☎ 337 74; www.sylt -ost.de; Am Tipkenhoog 5; ☉ 9am-4.30pm Mon-Fri, 10am-1pm Sat), the **Wenningstedt tourist office** (☎ 4470; www .wenningstedt.de, in German; Strandstrasse 25; ☉ 8.30am-4pm Mon-Fri, 9am-4pm Sat) and Westerland's three **tourist offices** (☎ 9980; www.westerland.de):

Main tourist office (Strandstrasse 35; ☉ 9am-6pm Mon-Fri May-Oct, 9am-5pm Mon-Fri Nov-Apr) Has internet terminals.

Tourist information booth (Friedrichstrasse 44; ☉ 9am-5pm Mon-Thu, to 2pm Fri) On Westerland's main pedestrianised shopping and restaurant strip. Hours can fluctuate.

Tourist information desk (Bahnhof; ☉ 9am-1pm & 2-6pm daily year-round) Inside the train station's *Reisezentrum* (travel centre).

Sights & Activities

WESTERLAND

People have been complaining about the overdevelopment of Westerland ever since it became Sylt's first resort in the mid-19th century. Their protestations seem to have gone unheeded: the island's largest town (with 8927 permanent residents) is now a forest of concrete towers, often blocking sea views. It has a laidback holiday atmosphere, though, and makes a convenient base. The pedestrianised Friedrichstrasse is awash with shops and restaurants; and if you want to go anywhere else on the island, this is the easiest place to start from.

Windsurfing off Sylt is known as the most radical on the World Cup tour, when the final tour takes place here each September, with wild winds and waves. Yet even beginners shouldn't be deterred. The island has numerous water-sports schools, including Westerland's **Surf Schule Westerland Sunset Beach** (☎ 271 72; www.sunsetbeach.de; Brandenburger Strasse 15), which offer lessons and also rent out equipment for windsurfing as well as kitesurfing, regular surfing and catamaran sailing.

Indoors, get wet on water slides or in the swimming pools – or steamy in the saunas – at the **Sylter Welle** (☎ 0180-500 9980; Strandstrasse 32; admission with/without sauna €16.50/9.50; ☉ 10am-9pm Mon, 10am-10pm Tue-Sun).

KEITUM

Historic reed-thatched houses strangled with ivy, lush gardens of colourful blooms, stone walls and the occasional garden gate made from two curving whalebones combine to create the island's prettiest village.

Keitum was once Sylt's most important harbour, which is recalled in its late-Romanesque sailors' church **St Severin**, with its Gothic altar and chancel, and heritage-listed gravestones in its cemetery; and in the historic **Altfriesisches Haus** (Old Frisian House; ☎ 328 05; Am Kliff 13; adult/concession/child €3.50/3/1.75; ☉ 10am-5pm Mon-Fri, 11am-5pm Sat & Sun Easter-Oct, noon-5pm Wed-Sun Nov-Easter).

WENNINGSTEDT

The best of Sylt's Stone Age graves are in the family-oriented resort town of Wenningstedt. You can enter its 4000-year-old **Denghoog** (Am Denghoog; ☉ 10am-5pm May-Sep), next to the town church, which measures 3m by 5m and is nearly 2m tall in parts. The outer walls consist of 12 40-tonne stones. How Stone Age builders moved these is a Stonehenge kind of mystery.

KAMPEN

Hermès, Cartier and Louis Vuitton boutiques ensconced in traditional reed-thatched houses mmediately signal that this little village is the sland's ritziest. Each summer, aristocrats and German celebrities come to see and be seen long the main promenade, Stroenwai, aka Whiskey Alley.

People-watching aside, the principle reason o visit is the stunning **Uwe Dune**, at 52.5m sylt's highest natural elevation. You can climb he wooden steps to the top for a 360-degree iew over Sylt and, on a good day, to neighouring Amrum and Föhr islands.

Kampen's **Strandsauna** (Beachside Sauna; ☎ 4787; a Grande Plage; admission €14; ☼ 10am-6pm) is, unusually, open year-round.

.IST

Everything in List is dubbed 'Germany's northernmost' – harbour, beach, restaurant tc... It's a windswept, tranquil land's end, but hings usually liven up in the harbour when he ferry from Rømø (Denmark) deposits lay-tripping Danes.

Nordic walking, using poles to propel your ıpper body forward as if you were skiing, s hugely popular all over Sylt, but espeially along the grass-covered dunes of the **Vanderdünengebiet**. The **List tourist office** (☎ 952 0; www.list.de, in German; Am Brünk 1; ☼ 9am-noon & 2-pm Mon-Fri year-round, 9am-noon Sat Apr-Sep) has maps ınd details of rental outlets.

List's newest attraction is the whiz-bang **rlebniszentrum Naturgewalten** (☎ 836 190; www naturgewalten-sylt.de, in German; Hafenstrasse 37; adult/child ınder 15yr €11/6.50; ☼ 10am-10pm Jul & Aug, 10am-6pm ʲep-Jun), a state-of-the-art ecological museum ɟedicated to the North Sea with multimedia ʲxhibits that keep both kids and adults enterⱦained (especially on rainy days). It's housed n a vivid-blue 'wave'-like building powered ıy renewable energy including solar.

The privately owned Ellenbogen ('elbow') ⱦeninsula is Sylt's far northern tip (there's ı €5 toll if you enter by car). The beaches here ıre off limits for swimming because of danⱬerous currents, but are dramatically backed ıy 35m-high shifting dunes. En route you'll ⱦass List's **Strandsauna** (☎ 877 174; admission €16; ☼ 11am-5pm Easter-Oct) – take the road branch-ng off the main route about 4km southwest ɟf List.

ⱦours

Tickets are available from the **Info-Pavillon** ☎ 846 1029; ☼ 9am-4pm Jun-Aug, reduced hours winter) ɟn the Westerland Bahnhof forecourt.

BOAT

There's a head-spinning array of boat cruises, mostly operated by **Adler-Schiffe** (☎ 987 00; www .adler-schiffe.de; Boysenstrasse 13, Westerland). Highlights include the following:

Amrun & Föhr (adult/child under 14yr from €24/free; ☼ daily Easter–mid-Oct from Hörnum) Choose one or both islands.

Hallig Hooge (adult/family from €23.50/62.50; ☼ daily Apr-Oct from Hörnum) Other Halligen can be combined with Amrun/Föhr tours.

Seal Colonies (adult/child under 14yr from €14.50/11.50; ☼ daily Apr-Oct from Hörnum) See seals bask in the sun on their regular sandbank on this 1½-hour tour.

Wattwandern tours (adult/child under 14yr/family €28.50/18/75; ☼ allocated days only mid-May–mid-Oct) At low tide wander across the seabed between Amrun and Föhr.

BUS

Grosse Inselrundfahrt (Big Island Tour; adult/child €15/10; ☼ 2pm Feb-Nov, 1pm Dec-Jan) Comprehensive 3¼-hour tour.

Kleine Inselrundfahrt (Small Island Tour; adult/child €13/10; ☼ 11am Apr-Oct) Two-hour tour.

SVG (☎ 836 100; www.svg-sylt.de, in German) Runs two bus tours.

Sleeping

Tourist offices have details of the island's plethora of accommodation options including holiday apartments and private rooms.

DJH hostel (☎ 835 7825; www.jugendherberge.de/jh/ westerland; Fischerweg 36-40, Westerland; dm under/over 26yr incl breakfast €20.10/23.10; ☼ closed mid-late Dec; **P** **X**) Set amid the dunes is Westerland's brand-new hostel, a 45-minute walk from the Bahnhof. Alternatively, take bus 2 in the direction of Rantum/Hörnum to the Dikjen Deel stop. If you're after something even further away from it all, there are also DJH hostels at List-Mövenberg (www.jugend herberge/jh/list) and Hörnum (www.jugend herberge/jh/hoernum).

Single Pension (☎ 920 70; www.singlepension.de, in German; Trift 26, Westerland; s €46-70, d €63-79 incl breakfast; **P**) Not only for singles, but certainly a social spot for solo travellers young and old, who can strike up a rapport over tea or lounging in the garden. The rooms are humble, but the location central and breakfast is served to 1pm. Some cheaper single rooms sharing bathrooms are available from as little as €27.

Hotel Gutenberg (☎ 988 80; www.hotel-gutenberg.de, in German; Friedrichstrasse 22, Westerland; s €55-95, d €120-155 incl breakfast; P X) This gabled hotel with sea-green stained timber furniture has an epicentral location on Westerland's main pedestrian drag. Doubles with shared (albeit spotless) bathrooms cost €72 to €105 – be sure to specify your requirements when booking.

Raffelhüschen Hotel (☎ 836 210; www.sylthotel -raffelhueschen.de, in German; Boysenstrasse 8, Westerland; s €72-102, d €98-169 incl breakfast; P X) Ground-floor rooms at this stylish, breezy hotel have wooden floors and garden terraces with *Strandkörbe* 'beach basket' seats. Upstairs, there are carpets and balconies. Guests can use the three saunas and solarium, and enjoy free afternoon coffee and cake.

Landhaus Sylter Hahn (☎ 928 20; www.sylter-hahn.de, in German; Robbenweg 3, Westerland; s €75-95, d €115-170 incl breakfast; P X 🛜 🐾) The exterior doesn't give much away, but inside, the Landhaus Sylter Hahn is done out in ultrachic country house style, with contemporary artworks, designer wallpaper, friezes and tiling. In a peaceful location 250m from the beach, facilities including a wellness centre and hammocks in the garden make it a fantastic deal.

Long Island House Sylt (☎ 995 9550; www.sylthotel.de, in German; Eidumweg 13, Westerland; s €88-116, d €126-196 incl breakfast; P X) A perfect blend of pure contemporary design and subtle nautical touches. Porthole-shaped mirrors, unpolished wood hinting at ship's timbers and a carved Moby Dick are complemented by quilted or faux-fur throws, painted wicker chairs, orchids and green apples. Most of the individually decorated rooms are small but you can unwind in the garden or by the Scandinavian fireplace on chilly nights.

ourpick **Romantik Hotel Jörg Müller** (☎ 277 88; www.hotel-joerg-mueller.de, in German; Südermarkt Strasse 8, Westerland; r incl breakfast €160-260; P X) Gourmands are in for a treat at this boutique establishment run by one of Germany's best-known foodie families. Its pastel-hued rooms are romantic hideaways, but the real lure is the gourmet breakfast and three restaurants, including Jörg Müller's signature gastronomic restaurant (menus from €32 up to €118 for a six-course blow-out). If you're inspired, Müller also offers cooking classes (six-hour class €240 including five-course meal and paired wines).

Of Sylt's numerous camping grounds, those in idyllic beachside locations include:

Campingplatz Rantum (☎ 807 55; www.camping -rantum.de, in German; Hörnumer Strasse 3, Rantum; per person €3.50-4.60, tent €4.70-6.10, car €2.20-2.60; 🌤 Apr-Oct; P) Great facilities including a bakery, restaurant and sauna.

Campingplatz Kampen (☎ 420 86; www.campen-in -kampen.de, in German; Möwenweg 4, Kampen; per person €3.05, tent €8.70-16, car €3; 🌤 Easter-Oct; P) Among the dunes at the southern end of Kampen.

Eating

Sylt has some sterling restaurants, such as Jörg Müller's Michelin-starred digs (left). But the island's most quintessential dish is a simple and delicious fish sandwich from home-grown chain, Gosch (see the boxed text, opposite). Look out too for local oysters from Germany's only oyster farm, in List.

Kupferkanne (☎ 410 10; Stapelhooger Wai, Kampen; snacks & dishes €4-13; 🌤 from 10am summer, from noon winter) Giant mugs of coffee and huge slices of cake (including scrumptious plum cake) are served in the magical gardens of this *Alice in Wonderland*-style cafe where wooden tables surrounded by a maze of low bramble hedges overlook the Wadden Sea and the Braderup Heide (heath). Meals are also served in the attached Frisian house.

Sansibar (☎ 964 646; Hörnumer Strasse 80, Rantum; mains €11-42; 🌤 from noon) Dining among the dunes in this large grass-roof pavilion on the beach, on the likes of whole North Sea sole or salmon and wild prawns in white crustacean sauce is an unforgettable experience (book well ahead). Alternatively, stop by for a drink on its terrace at sunset, with a view of the crashing waves.

Alte Friesenstube (☎ 1228; Gaadt 4, Westerland; mains €19-25; 🌤 from 6pm Tue-Sun) You won't find sojourning celebs at this charmingly old fashioned, family-run restaurant. Set inside Sylt's oldest reed-thatched cottage (1648) lined with decorative wall tiles and tile ovens, what you will find are homely regional specials listed on a largely incomprehensible handwritten menu in *Plattdütsch* dialect (helpfully translated by staff).

Gogärtchen (☎ 412 42; Stroenwai, Kampen; mains €29-38, 8-/10-course tasting menu €108/124; 🌤 from 1pm) The thatch-roofed Gogärtchen is renowned as a favourite haunt of the nation's holidaying glitterati, not least for its exquisitely presented contemporary dishes like foie gras with marinated grapes and brioche, followed by monkfish with macadamia nuts, wasabi potato foam and coconut milk.

GOSCH: A SYLT SUCCESS STORY

Coming to Sylt without visiting **Gosch** (www.gosch-sylt.de, in German) would be like coming to Germany without ordering a beer. Established by eel seller Jürgen Gosch some three decades ago, this nation-wide chain of 'fast-fish' outlets is a Sylt institution, and its seafood tastes exceptionally fresh here.

The site of Gosch's original kiosk in List harbour is now its maritime-themed flagship, **Alte Bootshalle** (☎ 870383; Hafenstrasse 16, List; dishes €2.50-14.50; ☺ from 11am). But across the island you'll find branches offering its range of delicious fish sandwiches, seafood pasta, smoked salmon and *Rösti* (potato cakes), lobster and caviar.

Also recommended:

Badezeit (☎ 834 020; Strandpromenade, Westerland; mains €8.90-19.50; ☺ from 11am Mon-Fri, from 10am Sat & Sun; Ⓥ) Bang on the beach in Westerland, serving tapas, pastas and, yes, fish.

Jungo Willms (☎ 995 282; Elisabethstrasse 4, Westerland; mains €14.50-28, menus from €29.50; ☺ lunch & dinner Mon-Sat) Sophisticated Westerland restaurant creating inventive, modern German cuisine.

Getting There & Away

Sylt/Westerland airport (www.flughafen-sylt.de, in German) is served by **Air Berlin** (www.airberlin.com) from Berlin and Düsseldorf; **TUIfly** (www.tuifly.com) flies from Hannover, Cologne-Bonn and Stuttgart; and **Lufthansa** (www.lufthansa.com) from Frankfurt, Hamburg and Munich, among others. Flights are more frequent in summer.

Otherwise, Sylt is connected to the mainland by a causeway catering exclusively for trains. IC trains serve Hamburg Hauptbahnhof (€44, 3¼ hours), while regional trains have regular direct services to Hamburg Altona (€30, 3¼ hours). Alternatively, change at Elmshorn for Hamburg Dammtor and the Hauptbahnhof (€30, 3½ hours). *Important:* make sure you're sitting in the correct part of the train, as they sometimes split en route, and you may find yourself making an unexpected stopover (trust us…).

If you're driving, you must load your vehicle onto a **car train** (☎ 995 0565; www.syltshuttle.de) in Niebüll (one-way/return €45/83 Friday to Monday, return €70 Tuesday to

Thursday). There are constant crossings (usually at least once an hour) in both directions; it doesn't take reservations.

Alternatively, catch the **car ferry** (☎ 0180-310 3030; www.sylt-faehre.de) from Rømø in Denmark to List (one-way per foot passenger/car and passengers €7/43.50).

For ships to/from Amrun and Föhr, see p721.

Getting Around

Sylt is well covered by **buses** (☎ 836 100; www.svg-sylt.de). The two main north–south connections run at 20-minute intervals during the day: Line 1 (Westerland-Wenningstedt-Kampen-List) and Line 2 (Westerland-Rantum-Hörnum). There are four other lines; prices are calculated by zone, ranging from €1.60 to €6.40. Tell the driver your destination. Some buses have bicycle hangers.

Cycling is extremely popular and *Fahrradverleih* (bike-hire) outlets abound. Westerland alone has more than half-a-dozen places, such as **Veloquick** (☎ 215 06; Kirchenweg 13, Westerland; per day from €7).

Trains to/from Westerland stop in Keitum.

FÖHR

☎ 04681 / pop 8700

Closer to the mainland, cloud-shaped Föhr is known as the green isle, although there's also a good sandy beach in the south. Its main village, Wyk, has plenty of windmills. In the north you'll find 16 tiny Frisian hamlets tucked behind dikes up to 7m tall. In the old days, Föhr's men went out to sea to hunt whales, an epoch you can learn more about at the **Friesenmuseum** (☎ 2571; www.friesen-museum.de, in German; Rebbelstieg 34, Wyk; adult/concession €3.50/2; ☺ 10am-5pm daily Jul & Aug, 10am-5pm Tue-Sun mid-Mar–Oct, 2-5pm Tue-Sun Nov–mid-Mar).

The church of **St Johannis** in Nieblum dates from the 12th century and is sometimes called the 'Frisian Cathedral' because it seats up to 1000 people.

Föhr's main **tourist office** (☎ 300 3040; www.foehr.de; Wyk harbour; ☺ 10am-1pm & 2-5.45pm) is open daily year-round and can help with accommodation. Föhr does not have a camping ground.

Getting There & Around

To get to Föhr, you catch a ferry operated by **WDR** (☎ 01805-080 140; www.faehre.de) from Dagebüll Hafen (reached via Niebüll; one-way

€6.25). Up to 13 boats make the trip daily in the high season, taking 45 minutes to Wyk. Bikes are an extra €4.50 return (no single rates available), while cars (prior reservation necessary) start from €57.15 return.

There are also regular ferries between Föhr and Amrum (one-way/return €6.40/8); cars start from €50.65 return (prior reservation also necessary).

For information on getting to Föhr from Sylt, see p721.

There's an hourly bus service to all villages on Föhr (less frequent in winter). You'll find bike-rental outlets in every village.

AMRUM
☎ 04682 / pop 2300
Amrum is the smallest North Frisian Island; you can walk around it in a day. It's also the prettiest, with reed-thatched Frisian houses, a patchwork of dunes, woods, heath and marsh, and glorious Kniepsand – 12km of fine, white sand, sometimes up to 1km wide – that takes up half the island.

Crowning the central village of Wittdün is northern Germany's tallest lighthouse, which stands 63m tall. The island's largest village is Nebel.

Much of Amrum is under protection, so you must stick to the marked paths. There are some fine walks, including the 10km walk from the lighthouse to the village of Norddorf through the pine forest, or the 8km return hike from Norddorf along the safe swimming beach to the tranquil **Ood Nature Reserve**, an ideal place to observe bird life.

The **tourist office** (☎ 940 30; www.amrum.de; ferry landing, Wittdün; ✆ hours vary) can help with accommodation on the island. Options include two camping grounds (one for nudists) amid the dunes, a **DJH hostel** (☎ 2010; www.jugendherberge.de/jh/wittduen; Mittelstrasse 1, Wittdün; under/over 26yr incl breakfast €19.20/22.20; ✆ mid-Feb–mid-Nov; ✗) and several hotels.

Getting There & Around
To reach Amrum from the mainland, take the ferry operated by **WDR** (☎ 01805-080 140; www.faehre.de) from Dagebüll Hafen (change in Niebüll; one-way €8.85). The trip to Wittdün usually goes via Wyk on Föhr and takes 1½ hours.

For information on getting to Amrum from Sylt, see p721.

Buses take you around the island; there are bike-rental places in every village.

HELGOLAND
☎ 04725 / pop 1333
Helgoland's former rulers, the British, re ally got the better deal in 1891 when the swapped it for then German-ruled Zanziba But Germans today are very fond of this lone some North Sea outcrop of red sandstone roc and its fresh air and warm weather, courtes of the Gulf Stream.

The 80m-tall Lange Anna (Long Anna rock on the island's southwest edge is a com pelling sight, standing alone in the ocean There are also WWII bunkers and tunnels t explore, and resurging numbers of Atlanti grey seals. Cycling is not permitted on th tiny 4.2-sq-km island.

As Helgoland is still covered by an agree ment made in 1840 and economically isn part of the EU, most visitors indulge in som **duty-free shopping** in the outlets lining the mai drag, Lung Wai ('long way'). To swim, man head to neighbouring **Düne**, a blip in the ocea that is popular with nudists. Little boats (one way €4) make regular trips between May an mid-October from Helgoland's northeaster landing stage.

Helgoland makes an easy and enjoyable da trip, but if you want to stay, the **Kurverwaltun** (☎ 01805-643 737; www.helgoland.de; Lung Wai 28 ✆ 9am-noon Mon-Fri & by appointment) can help fin a room or tent pitch.

Getting There & Away
For high-speed ferries from Hamburg, se p699. **Reederei Rahder** (☎ 04834-3612; www.rahder.de in German) and **Helgoland Reisen** (☎ 04834-938 220 www.helgolandreisen.de, in German) have ferries from Büsum (return from €34 and €36 respectively) The latter also has ferries from Cuxhaven ir Lower Saxony (return from €38). Other ferr services include **Helgoline** (☎ 0180-522 1445; www .helgoline.de, in German) from Cuxhaven (return from €36.50) and **Helgoland Linie** (☎ 01805-228 661; www .helgolandlinie.de, in German) from Wilhelmshaven ir Lower Saxony (return from €36.50).

Adler Schiffe (☎ 987 00; www.adler-schiffe.de, in German puts together full-day trips departing from the Westerland Bahnhof, Sylt (€45.50), which include around four hours on Helgoland.

Alternatively, you can fly from Büsum (one-way/return/day trip €80.50/159/149) and from Bremerhaven in Bremen (€86/170/155) with **OLT** (☎ 0471-771 88; www.olt.de), or from the small Hamburg-Uetersen airfield with **Air Hamburg** (☎ 04070-708 890; www.air-hamburg.de, ir German; from €79 one-way).

Mecklenburg–
Western Pomerania

ll clichés aside, this spectacular stretch of the Baltic coast is certainly one of Germany's bet-
er-kept secrets. Domestic tourists make up a whopping 97% of all visitors to Mecklenburg–
Western Pomerania (Mecklenburg-Vorpommern), who flock in summer to its dazzling clean,
white sand and glittering seas.

Hotspots during the all-too-brief beach-going season include the magnificent strand ad-
oining the quaint fishing village-turned-Rostock seaside suburb of Warnemünde, as well
s three leafy resort islands: romantic, villa-lined Rügen; car-free Hiddensee; and Usedom
(which Germany shares with Poland). The charming gateway town to the first two islands,
tralsund, is effectively an island itself, encircled by water.

While you can simply take in the brisk air, sunshine and bracing seas (or take to an
door *Bad* – spa and swimming pool complex – for a longer and infinitely warmer soak),
he region has much more to offer. The state capital, Schwerin, has an incredible castle at
s heart and is among the most striking little cities anywhere in the country. The gracious
niversity town of Greifswald retains some exquisite medieval architecture, as do Wismar
nd Stralsund, whose medieval cores are both Unesco-listed. And Rostock, once a gritty
hipbuilding town, is building a reputation as a party city, thanks to an exuberant student
opulation. Nature lovers can head into Mecklenburg–Western Pomerania's delightfully wild
ational parks, or encounter its marine life on boating and diving trips.

Trust the locals' judgment and discover a corner of the country that is only going to
ecome more popular once the rest of the world catches on.

HIGHLIGHTS

- **Bay Watching** Scale the spiralling staircase of Warnemünde's 19th-century lighthouse (p736)
- **Time Keeping** Watch Rostock's extraordinary 1472-built astrological clock (p735) in action as it strikes noon
- **Picnicking** Pick up fresh fish (p743) from the boats bobbing in Wismar's harbour
- **Paddling** Dip your oars in the peaceful waterways of Müritz National Park (p733) on a paddle-and-camp trip
- **Night Swimming** Stay in a 'swimming holi-day home' (p752) in Lauterbach on Rügen Island

- POPULATION: 1.68 MILLION
- AREA: 23,170 SQ KM

Getting There & Around

Mecklenburg–Western Pomerania's largest city, Rostock, has an airport, as well as an international ferry port – see p739. International ferries also sail from Sassnitz on Rügen Island (p748). Direct trains from Stralsund serving the German side of Usedom Island terminate in Świnoujście (Swinemünde in German) just over the Polish border, which is home to Poland's largest international ferry terminal.

Within northern Germany, if you're travelling by train you can make huge savings with a **Mecklenburg-Vorpommern-Ticket** (single/group up to 5 people €18/26), which is good for travel from 9am until 3am the following day (from midnight on weekends) on all regional trains throughout the state, as well as in neighbouring Hamburg state.

MECKLENBURGER SEENPLATTE

At the doorstep of the state capital, Schwerin, the wilderness area of the Mecklenburg Lake Plains spreads across the centre of the state, and shelters the pristine Müritz National Park. Meandering through charming little villages and hamlets, many roads in the area are canopied by trees that were planted by medieval fish merchants to shield wagons from the heat of the summer sun.

SCHWERIN

☎ 0385 / pop 95,855

Picturesquely sited around seven lakes (or possibly more depending on how you tally them), the centrepiece of this engaging city is its Schloss (castle), built in the 14th century during the city's time as the former seat of the Grand Duchy of Mecklenburg.

Schwerin has shrugged off the 45 years of communist rule that followed WWII. Today there's an upbeat, vibrant energy on its streets that befits its role as the reinstated capital of Mecklenburg–Western Pomerania (beating Rostock for the mantle), and creative new shops and restaurants occupy its preserved 16th- to 19th-century buildings.

Orientation

The partly pedestrianised Altstadt (old town) sits south of the rectangular Pfaffen-

teich (a pretty, artificial lake) and nort west of Burg Island. Burg Island connected to two gardens further south the Schlossgarten and the lesser-know Grüngarten.

Information

Helios Kliniken Schwerin (☎ 5200; Wismarsche Strasse 397) Medical services.
Main post office (Mecklenburgstrasse 4-6)
Netz-Games (☎ 593 6960; Ritterstrasse 1; per hr €2; ☯ 3pm-midnight) Internet access.
Tourist-Information Schwerin (☎ 592 5212; www.schwerin.com; Rathaus, Am Markt 14; ☯ 9am-7p Mon-Fri, 10am-6pm Sat & Sun Apr-Oct, 9am-6pm Mon-I 10am-4pm Sat & Sun Nov-Mar)

Sights

SCHLOSS & GARDENS

Gothic and Renaissance turrets, Slavic onio domes, Ottoman features and terracot Hanseatic step gables are among the mis mash of architectural styles that make u Schwerin's inimitable **Schloss** (☎ 525 292 www.schloss-schwerin.de; adult/concession €4/2.50, au oguide €2; ☯ 10am-6pm mid-Apr–mid-Oct, 10am-5p Tue-Sun mid-Oct–mid-Apr), which is crowned b a main golden dome. Nowadays the Schlo earns its keep as the state's parliamei building.

Schwerin derives its name from a Slav castle known as Zuarin (Animal Pastur that was formerly on the site, and which wε first mentioned in 973 AD. In a niche ove the main gate, the **statue of Niklot** depicts Slavic prince, who was defeated by Heinric der Löwe in 1160.

Inside the castle's opulently furnishe rooms, highlights include a huge collectio of Meissen porcelain.

The park immediately surrounding th palace is known as the Burggarten an most notably features a wonderful **orangeri** overlooking the water, with a conservator restaurant and terrace cafe (open May t October). A handful of statues, a grotto an lookout points are also here.

Crossing the causeway south from th Burggarten brings you to the baroqu **Schlossgarten** (Palace Garden), intersected b several canals.

Continuing southeast you'll come to th **Schleifmühle** (☎ 562 751; adult/concession €2.50/1.5 ☯ 10am-5pm Apr-Oct), a small local histor

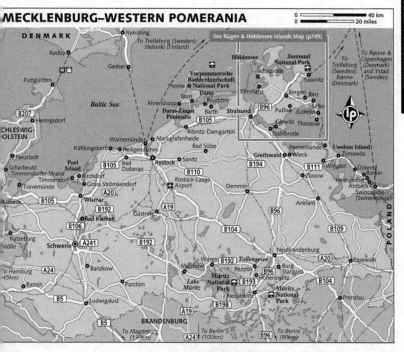

museum located in a carefully restored 9th-century mill.

TAATLICHES MUSEUM

the Alter Garten, opposite the Schloss, the **taatliches Museum** (State Museum Schwerin; ☎ 595 80; www.museum-schwerin.de; Alter Garten 3; adult/concession 5/4; ☉ 10am-6pm Tue-Sun Apr-Oct, 10am-5pm Tue-Sun ov-Mar) has a substantial collection spaning the ages. The 15 statues in the Ernst arlach room (see the boxed text, p731) rovide a small taste of the sculptor's work. here's also a typically amusing and irrevernt Marcel Duchamp collection. Those with nore traditional tastes will prefer the oils by ucas Cranach the Elder, as well as works by embrandt and Rubens.

DOM

bove the Markt, the tall 14th-century iothic **Dom** (cathedral; Am Dom 4; ☉ 11am-2pm Monri, 11am-4pm Sat, noon-3pm Sun) is a superb example of north German redbrick architecture. ou can climb up to the viewing platform €1.50) of its 19th-century cathedral tower 118m), which is a mere 50cm taller than

Rostock's Petrikirche. Check with the tourist office, as hours can vary.

ALTSTADT

The bustling Markt is home to the **Rathaus** (town hall) and the colonnaded neoclassical **Neues Gebäude** (1780–83), which houses a classy cafe. The latter is fronted by a lion monument honouring the town's founder, Heinrich der Löwe. A walk southwest of the Rathaus to the appropriately named **Engestrasse** (Narrow Street) brings you past a lovely example of the city's earliest half-timbered houses at Buschstrasse 15.

SCHELFSTADT

North of the Markt along Puschkinstrasse is Schelfstadt, a planned baroque village that was autonomous until Schwerin's mid-19th-century expansion. The restored 1737 **Schleswig-Holstein-Haus** (☎ 555 527; Puschkinstrasse 12; admission varies; ☉ 10am-6pm) contains a gallery that features changing contemporary art exhibitions. Just north of here is the baroque **Schelfkirche** (Nikolaikirche; 1708–13) and **Schelfmarkt**, the former town market.

MECKLENBURG–
WESTERN POMERANIA

SCHWERIN

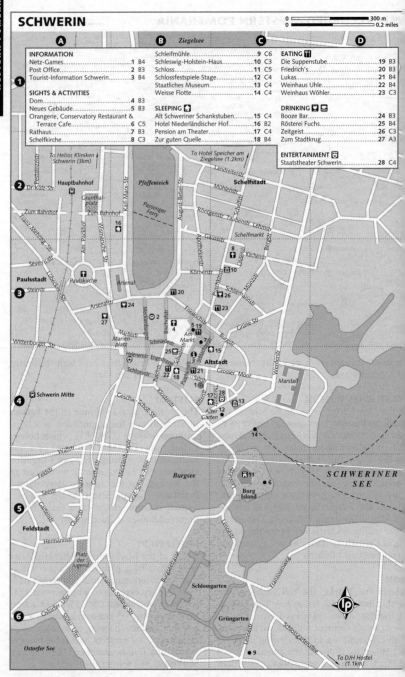

INFORMATION	
Netz-Games	1 B4
Post Office	2 B3
Tourist-Information Schwerin	3 B4

SIGHTS & ACTIVITIES	
Dom	4 B3
Neues Gebäude	5 B3
Orangerie, Conservatory Restaurant & Terrace Cafe	6 C5
Rathaus	7 B3
Schelfkirche	8 C3
Schleifmühle	9 C6
Schleswig-Holstein-Haus	10 C3
Schloss	11 C5
Schlossfestspiele Stage	12 C4
Staatliches Museum	13 C4
Weisse Flotte	14 C4

SLEEPING	
Alt Schweriner Schankstuben	15 C4
Hotel Niederländischer Hof	16 B2
Pension am Theater	17 C4
Zur guten Quelle	18 B4

EATING	
Die Suppenstube	19 B3
Friedrich's	20 B3
Lukas	21 B4
Weinhaus Uhle	22 B4
Weinhaus Wöhler	23 C3

DRINKING	
Booze Bar	24 B3
Rösterei Fuchs	25 B4
Zeitgeist	26 C3
Zum Stadtkrug	27 A3

ENTERTAINMENT	
Staatstheater Schwerin	28 C4

ours

From May to September, **Weisse Flotte** (☎ 557 0; www.weisseflotteschwerin.de; late Apr-Oct) opates a regular hour-long **Inseltour** (island tour; ult/child under 14yr €9.50/4) on the Schweriner See. from Tuesday to Sunday between May and eptember, there are a handful of additional ½-hour tours (€14/4).

The tourist office organises several guided alking tours in German, including 90-minute **ty tours** (per person €4.50; 11am) and **evening alks** (per person €6; 8.30pm Thu Apr-Oct, 6.30pm Thu v-Mar) from Weinhaus Wöhler (right).

estivals & Events

he highlight of Schwerin's cultural calenar is the **Schlossfestspiele** (www.theater-schwerin.de): pen-air opera concerts performed on a stage ected in front of the theatre and state muum in June and July. Punters gather across e water in the Burggarten to listen in.

From June to December, concerts and vents are held across the state as part of the **stspiele Mecklenburg-Vorpommern** (☎ 591 8585; ww.festspiele-mv.de).

leeping

H hostel (☎ 326 0006; www.jh-schwerin.de; Waldschulweg dm under/over 26yr incl breakfast €17.50/20.50; P) hough popular with school groups, this 90-d hostel is in a peaceful, leafy location south f the city centre. Take bus 14.

Pension am Theater (☎ 593 680; www.pension ntheater.m-vp.de, in German; Theaterstrasse 1-2; s €52-68, €69-90 incl breakfast; P) In the shadow of the uge theatre building and (just) within sight f the castle, this privately run establishment oasts cheerful, stylish and spacious rooms, lthough you may miss little things like soap a the bathrooms.

Zur guten Quelle (☎ 565 985; www.zur-guten-quelle n-vp.de, in German; Schusterstrasse 12; s €51-55, d €74-82, €95-107; P) One of Schwerin's prettiest half-mbered houses, bang in the heart of the ltstadt. Zur guten Quelle is best known for s cosy traditional restaurant, but it also has alf a dozen simple but comfortable rooms. If ou're staying here, a two-course evening meal s a bargain at €10 per person, per night.

Alt Schweriner Schankstuben (☎ 592 5313; www chankstuben.de, in German; Am Schlachtermarkt 9-13; €55-65, d €78-94, f €132-140 incl breakfast; P) nother historic half-timbered house in the ltstadt. Sixteen charming rooms are tucked bove Schankstuben's restaurant, which opens

to a flower-filled terrace. It's renowned for its regional specialities; romantics can go all-out with a candlelight dinner (€28 per person) and/or champagne breakfast (€8.50 per person).

Hotel Speicher am Ziegelsee (☎ 500 30; www.speicher -hotel.de, in German; Speicherstrasse 11; s €77-100, d €97-130 incl breakfast; P) This tall heritage-listed former warehouse on the waterfront with its own pier has been fitted out with streamlined rooms in Mediterranean hues. You can unwind in its sauna, solarium, gym, English bar and fine-dining restaurant, whose cuisine is also inspired by the Med.

Hotel Niederländischer Hof (☎ 591 100; www.nieder laendischer-hof.de; Karl-Marx-Strasse 12-13; s €87-124, d €125-170 incl breakfast; P) Overlooking the Pfaffenteich, this regal 1901-established hotel has 32 elegant rooms with marble bathrooms, a library warmed by an open fire, and a lauded restaurant.

Eating

our pick **Die Suppenstube** (☎ 0172-382 5038; Puschkinstrasse 55; mains €3.20-4; 11am-5pm Mon-Fri; V) Funky stainless-steel light fittings made from cutlery, stripped floorboards and bare tables provide a minimalist contrast with the historic half-timbered walls of this house on the edge of the Markt. The menu is equally sparing but stylish – eight steaming kettles of homemade soups (with optional sliced sausage), and three desserts (including a deliciously rich chocolate pudding).

Friedrich's (☎ 555 473; Friedrichstrasse 2; mains €7.50-15.50; 11am-midnight; V) Spilling onto an alfresco terrace with water views of the Pfaffenteich, this Parisian-style cafe has art-deco trimmings, a casual atmosphere and an uncomplicated selection of brasserie fare including salads, fish and grills.

Weinhaus Wöhler (☎ 555 830; Puschkinstrasse 26; mains €8.50-19.90; 11am-1pm;) In addition to wood-lined dining rooms, a large covered courtyard and a tapas/cocktail bar, this historic, half-timbered inn also shelters six luxury double rooms (€80 to €130) and an apartment (€150). Poached salmon in Riesling, and shredded pork with bacon, potato and cucumber are among the standouts of its regional menu.

Weinhaus Uhle (☎ 562 956; www.weinhaus-uhle.de; Schusterstrasse 13-15; mains €9-18; from 10am) Step back in time at this traditional family wine merchant, where the pianist plays beneath stained-glass windows and barrel-vaulted ceilings in the formal restaurant (with tables divided by olive-coloured velvet curtains) and the occasional customer still wears an opera cloak in the wood-lined *Weinstube* (traditional wine bar). Specialities include chateaubriand, carved at the table, as well as venison and fish.

Lukas (☎ 565 935; Grosser Moor 5; mains €9.80-15.40; ☉ from 11am) Framed by giant glass windows, this conservatory restaurant feels a bit like dining inside a fishbowl. Future meals similarly swim in a large aquarium – before appearing on laden seafood platters.

Drinking

Schwerin's watering holes are concentrated along Arsenalstrasse, Mecklenburgstrasse and Puschkinstrasse.

Zum Stadtkrug (☎ 593 6693; Wismarsche Strasse 126; ☉ from 11am) The homebrew at this 1936-established microbrewery/pub consistently rates among the best in Germany. It's full of antique brewing equipment, and opens to a convivial beer garden.

Booze Bar (☎ 562 576; Arsenalstrasse 16; ☉ from 5pm) Connected to the somewhat cheesy Madison Club, this central cocktail bar has an eye-catching Marc Chagall-style mural behind the bar and an extensive – and inventive – drinks list.

Zeitgeist (Puschkinstrasse 22; ☉ from 6pm Tue-Thu, from 7pm Fri & Sat) Young and contemporary – this hip bar has an alternative, creative bent.

Rösterei Fuchs (☎ 593 8444; Am Markt 4; ☉ 10am-7pm Mon-Fri, 10am-5pm Sat) The aroma of freshly roasted coffee fills this small, chic place, which roasts its own coffee in-house, and also sells beans (ground or unground) as well as gourmet chocolates. At the very least, drop by for an espresso, which comes with an individually wrapped chocolate-covered coffee bean.

Entertainment

Staatstheater Schwerin (☎ 530 00; www.theater-schwerin.de; Alter Garten) The state theatre offers a varied range of concerts and theatrical performances.

Getting There & Around

Schwerin has two train stations in the city centre: Schwerin Mitte, southwest of the Altstadt, and the Schwerin Hauptbahnhof (central train station), northwest of the Altstadt. Bear this in mind when you check timetables.

Trains arrive regularly from Hambu (from €21.50, one hour), Rostock (fro €15.20, one hour), Stralsund (from €26.3 two hours) and Wismar (€6.90, 30 minutes with less frequent direct connections to/fro Berlin (€32.30, 2¾ hours).

Schwerin is signposted off the A241.

City buses and trams cost €1.50/4.60 for single/day pass. A ferry crosses the Pfaffenteic (€1) from late April to mid-October.

LUDWIGSLUST

☎ 03874 / pop 12,500

Such was the allure of Ludwigslust's sturd **ducal residence** (☎ 571 90; www.schloss-ludwigslust.c adult/child €5/3; ☉ 10am-6pm daily mid-Apr–mid-O 10am-5pm Tue-Sun mid-Oct–mid-Apr) that when th ducal seat moved 36km north to Schwer in 1837, some family members continued live here until 1945. Now part of the Schwer State Museum, its high point is the statel gilt-columned, high-ceilinged **Golden Hall**.

A planned baroque town, Ludwigslust neat, orderly layout is an attraction in itsel

Trains run from Schwerin every tw hours (€6.90, 30 minutes). To get to the ca tle from Ludwigslust station, walk south o Bahnhofstrasse to Platz des Friedens, cros the canal to Kanalstrasse and turn righ on Schlossstrasse.

GÜSTROW

☎ 03843 / pop 31,083

Best known for its small but statel Renaissance Schloss, this charming 775-plus year-old town is also the place where sculpte Ernst Barlach (see the boxed text, opposite spent most of his working life, and invites yo to view dozens of his works, including in h former atelier.

Güstrow Information (☎ 681 023; www.guestro -tourismus.de, in German; Franz-Parr-Platz 10; ☉ 9am-7p Mon-Fri, 10am-5pm Sat, 11am-5pm Sun May-Sep, 9am-6p Mon-Fri, 10am-4pm Sat, 11am-4pm Sun Oct-Apr) can hel with accommodation.

Sights & Activities

Güstrow's 16th-century **Schloss** (☎ 7520; ww .schloss-guestrow.de; adult/concession €3/2; ☉ 10am-6p daily mid-Apr–mid-Oct, 10am-5pm Tue-Sun mid-Oct–mi Apr) is home to an historical museum a well as a cultural centre, art exhibitions an occasional concerts.

Built between 1226 and 1335, the Gothi **Dom** (☎ 682 433; www.dom-guestrow.de, in Germa

ERNST BARLACH

One of the most important German expressionists, Ernst Barlach's sculptures and drawings are found across Germany, but it's especially hard not to notice him in Güstrow, where he spent the last 28 years of his life.

Born in 1870 outside Hamburg, Barlach visited Russia in 1906, soon after finishing his art studies, and this trip was to forever influence his work. Based on sketches he made there, his squarish sculptures began bearing the same expressive gestures and hunched-over, wind-blown postures of the impoverished people he encountered.

Although Barlach greeted WWI with enthusiasm, he soon came to realise the horrors of war, which also became a recurring theme in his work. He gained widespread fame for the WWI memorial in Magdeburg's cathedral (p219). His profoundly humanist approach did not sit well with Nazi aesthetics, however. He was declared a degenerate artist in the 1930s and banned from working, while 381 of his works were destroyed.

Barlach died in 1938 in Rostock at the peak of the ideological frenzy, without ever seeing his work resurrected, as it was after WWII. He is buried in Ratzeburg (p707).

hilipp-Brandin-Strasse 5; ⊗ 10am-5pm Mon-Sat, 2-4pm un mid-May–mid-Oct, reduced hours rest of year) contains a copy of Ernst Barlach's *Hovering Angel*, a memorial for the fallen soldiers of WWI; this copy was made secretly from the original mould after the Nazis destroyed the original sculpture.

The Barlach memorial in the **Gertrudenkapelle** (☎ 844 000; Gertrudenplatz 1; adult/concession/family 4/2.50/6.50; ⊗ 10am-5pm Tue-Sun Apr-Oct, 11am-4pm ue-Sun Nov-Mar) displays many of his original works. More of his bronze and wood carvings re housed along with a biographical exhibion at his former studio, the **Atelierhaus** (☎ 822 9; www.ernst-barlach-stiftung.de, in German; Heidberg 15; dult/concession/family €5/3.50/8.50; ⊗ 10am-5pm Tue-Sun pr-Oct, 11am-4pm Tue-Sun Nov-Mar), 4km south of the ity at Inselsee; take bus 204 or 205.

etting There & Around

Trains leave for Güstrow once or twice an our from Rostock's Hauptbahnhof (€6.90, 25 ninutes). Hourly services to/from Schwerin €13.30, one hour) require a change in Bad Kleinen.

NEUBRANDENBURG

☎ 0395 / pop 67,517

Neubrandenburg has few pretensions. It bills itself as 'the city of four gates on the Tollensesee Lake', and that's pretty well what t is. A largely intact medieval wall, with four gates, encircles the 13th-century Altstadt although you have to peer hard through some harsh GDR architecture to see it), and he lake is great for boating or swimming. Although there's little else to detain you,

the town also makes a handy staging post for forays into the Müritz National Park to the south.

Orientation

Consider the circular city wall as the rim of a clock face. The train station is at 12 o'clock; to get to the tourist office and the middle of the Altstadt, you simply have to walk straight down Stargarder Strasse to the middle of the face. The four gates are located as follows: Friedländer Tor at 2 o'clock, Neues Tor at 3 o'clock, Stargarder Tor at 6 o'clock and Treptower Tor at 9 o'clock. Inside the walls is a grid of north–south and east–west streets with the Marktplatz in the centre.

Information

Main post office (Marktplatz 2)
Stadt Info (☎ 194 33; www.neubrandenburg.de; Stargarder Strasse 17; ⊗ 10am-7pm Mon-Fri, 10am-6pm Sat, 10am-2pm Sun) Tourist information.

Sights & Activities

CITY WALL

Neubrandenburg was founded in 1248 by Herbord von Raven, a Mecklenburg knight granted the land by Brandenburg Margrave Johann I, and building progressed in the usual order: defence system, church, town hall, pub. The security system was the 2.3km-long, 7.5m-high stone wall that survives today, with four city gates and 56 sentry posts built into it.

The **Friedländer Tor**, begun in 1300 and completed in 1450, was the first gate. **Treptower Tor** is the largest and contains the **Regionalmuseum**

(☎ 555 1271; adult/concession €3/1.50; ⊙ 10am-5pm Tue-Sun), which is essentially an archaeological collection.

At the southern end of the city is the gaudy **Stargarder Tor**. The simple brick **Neues Tor** fronts the east side of the Altstadt and houses a small **Fritz Reuter exhibition** (admission free; ⊙ 9am-5.30pm Mon-Fri) on the writer and satirist (1810–74). There's a 2m-high bronze **statue** of 'uns Fritzing' ('our mate Fritz') near the train station.

Southwest of the train station (at about 11 o'clock) is the city's former dungeon, the **Fangelturm**. You'll recognise it by its pointy tower.

Wedged into the stone circumference are the 27 sweet **half-timbered houses** that remain of the original sentry posts. When firearms rendered such defences obsolete in the 16th century, the guardhouses were converted into *Wiekhäuser*, homes for the poor, disadvantaged and elderly. Most of the surviving homes are now craft shops, galleries and cafes.

TOLLENSESEE

In the summer months, locals decamp to this large lake southwest of the centre.

The best **swimming** places are both fun and free: Strandbad Broda at the northwest tip of the lake and Augustabad on the northeastern side.

Ferries (☎ 350 0524; www.neu-sw.de, in German; oneway €4.50) travel around the lake three times daily: click on 'Linienschiff', or ask the tourist office for the latest timetable, which also lists lakeside attractions. **Cruise boats** (☎ 584 1218; www.fahrgastschiff-mudderschulten.de, in German; 1½hr tours from €10; ⊙ Tue-Sun May-Sep) also circumnavigate the lake.

DIY types can hire all kinds of boats, including canoes. Operators include **Freizeittreff am Kulturpark** (☎ 566 5352; www.freizeittreff-behn.de, in German; Parkstrasse 15; ⊙ 10am-7pm May-Oct), which also rents bikes.

Sleeping

Camping Gatsch-Eck (☎ 566 5152; www.camping-gatsch -eck.de, in German; per adult/car €4.80/2.30, tents €3.80-4.80) Down the western side of the lake, this leafy site has new bathroom facilities, and a laundry hut with washing machines and dryers. There's a ferry landing nearby and lots of sports facilities.

Wiekhaus 28 (☎ 566 6571; www.wiekhaus.ws; 3rd Ringstrasse; s/d €43/55, breakfast from €4) Another of the city wall's former sentry posts, this

homely little apartment also has a min mum two-night stay and full self-caterin facilities.

Wiekhaus 49 (☎ 581 230; www.hotel-weinert.d in German; 4th Ringstrasse; d €65; **P**) This histori half-timbered former sentry post near th Neues Tor has a cosy upstairs bedroom mid-level lounge (with extra beds) and lowe level kitchen, plus good bathroom facilitie There's a minimum two-night stay (phon bookings required), but kids under 12 sta free, while it's just €5 per night for thos under 18.

Parkhotel Neubrandenburg (☎ 559 00; ww .parkhotel-nb.de; Windbergsweg 4; s/d €65/90; **P** 🗶 🖳 One of the few larger hotels in town tha doesn't betray its GDR roots (at least o the inside). This place has stylish an well-planned modern rooms, with double boasting two bathrooms to save domestic a guments. It's in the Kulturpark between th old town and the Tollensesee, and rooms a the front have the best views.

Eating & Drinking

Café im Reuterhaus (☎ 582 3245; Stargarder Strasse 3 mains €7.20-10.50; ⊙ 7am-6pm Mon-Sat, 11am-6pm Sun This old-fashioned cafe, ensconced in th one-time home of Fritz Reuter, has a tanta lising array of cakes to enjoy over coffee.

Wiekhaus 45 (☎ 566 7762; 4th Ringstrasse; main €8.95-17.80; ⊙ from 11am) Easily the best place t eat in Neubrandenburg is this lovely reno vated guardhouse. Waiters zip up and dow the narrow stairwell carrying huge portion of delicious Mecklenburg specialities (star with the tasty onion soup served with fres bread). There are delightful garden-set table in summer.

Entertainment

Within the war-damaged shell of the 13th century Marienkirche, Neubrandenburg' stunning new **Konzertkirche** (concert church ☎ tickets 559 5127; www.konzertkirche-nb.de; cn Stargarder Strasse & Grosse Wollweberstrasse) has goose bump-raising acoustics. The ticket service in the tourist office handles bookings.

Getting There & Away

Trains leave every two hours for Berlin (€25.50, two hours). There are also service every two hours to/from Rostock (€20.90 two hours), via Güstrow, and Stralsund (€15.20, 1¼ hours).

By road from Berlin take the A20 north-
est then take the B96 north (follow the
igns for Stralsund). From Stralsund or
ireifswald, head south on the B96. From
ostock, take the A19 south to Güstrow
hen follow the B104 southeast.

1ÜRITZ NATIONAL PARK

⅃üritz is commonly known as the land –
r paradise – of a thousand lakes. While
hat's an exaggeration, there are well over
00 lakes here, as well as countless ponds,
treams and rivers.

Declared a protected area in 1990, this
erene **national park** (☎ 039824-2520; www.national
ark-mueritz.de) consists of bog and wetlands,
nd is home to a wide range of waterfowl,
ncluding ospreys, white-tailed eagles and
ranes. Its two main sections sprawl over
00 sq km to the east and (mainly) west of
⅃eustrelitz, where the park's waterway be-
ins on the Zierker See.

Tourist offices throughout the region have
rail and park maps and offer recommen-
lations for the main activity: self-guided
addle-and-camp trips. Paddlers should pick up
he brochure *Paddeln im Land der Tausend
een* (Paddling in the Land of 1000 Lakes).
his includes tips for 13 tours and places to
tay along the way; although it's in German,
ssential information such as maps, dis-
ances, camp site icons and telephone
umbers are easy to read. Rental places are
verywhere; prices start from €6 per day. If
ou'd rather have company, tourist offices
nd national park offices also have lists of
uides who lead various trips.

When camping, you must use designated
sites. Many are operated by **Haveltourist**
(☎ 03981-247 90; www.haveltourist.de; adult/tent only/tent
& car from €4.10/3.40/6.10), which also rents canoes
and bikes and runs organised trips.

Timetables for park-wide **Müritz Linie**
(☎ 03991-6450; www.mueritz.de, in German) bus and
ferry services are available from tourist offices. Day passes cost €8 for buses only, or
€16 for buses and ferries.

Neustrelitz
☎ 03981 / pop 22,275
Situated on the Zierker See within the national park, the pretty, planned baroque
town of Neustrelitz centres on its circular
Markt, from which streets radiate like the
spokes of a wheel.

The town's Schloss fell victim to WWII,
but its beautiful Schlossgarten retains its 18th-
century orangerie (with a restaurant open
Tuesday to Sunday May to September), and
hosts the **Schlossgartenfestspiele** (☎ 2393; www
.schlossgartenfestspiele.de, in German), a series of classical and various other concerts (such as Beatles
tunes) from mid-June to mid-August.

The **tourist office** (☎ 253 119; www.neustrelitz.de;
Strelitzer Strasse 1; ☉ 9am-6pm Mon-Fri, 9.30am-1pm Sat
& Sun May-Sep, 9am-noon & 1-4pm Mon-Thu, 9am-noon Fri
Oct-Apr) shares space with a branch of the **na-
tional park office** (☎ 253 106; ☉ 9.30am-6pm Mon-Sat
May-Sep, 9.30am-4pm Mon-Fri early–mid-Apr & Oct), and
can help with accommodation in town and
throughout the park.

Fish plucked fresh from the lake is the
highlight of two wonderfully rustic water-
side eateries: **Zum Fischerhof** (☎ 200 842; Seestrasse
15a; mains €6-10; ☉ 11am-8pm) and **Bootshaus
Neustrelitz** (☎ 239 860; Useriner Strasse 1; mains €9-10;
☉ from 11am; ☎). The latter also has breezy,
pine-furnished guest rooms (doubles €70).

Trains to/from Neubrandenburg (€6.90,
30 minutes) continue to Stralsund (€21,
two hours).

COASTAL MECKLENBURG

ROSTOCK
☎ 0381 / pop 200,413
Rostock, the largest city in northeastern
Germany, *does* have a small but very attractive historic core – redbrick and pastel-
coloured buildings harking back to the
14th- and 15th-century Hanseatic era – but
you generally have to wade past a landscape
of concrete and industrial eyesores to reach
it. As a major port and shipbuilding centre,
the city was devastated in WWII and later
pummelled by socialist architectural 'ideals'.
It's extremely clean and safe, though, and has
several other winning cards up its sleeve.

Its trump card is the former fishing village
of Warnemünde, with its vibrant harbour
and one of Germany's most stunning and
accessible beaches, which is now proudly
claimed by Rostock as its own seaside suburb. And the city's venerable university,
which helps biotech replace its shipyards,
ensures some of the best nightlife for miles
around. Rostock is also a good base for day
trips further afield, such as Güstrow, and
Bad Doberan and nearby coastal resorts.

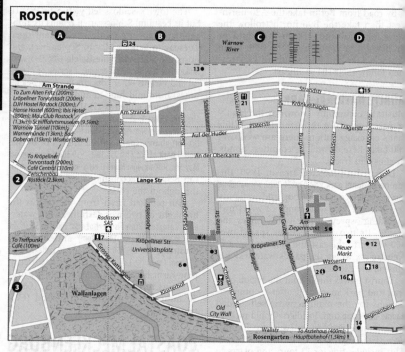

ROSTOCK

Orientation

Rostock is on the last stretch of the Warnow River before it flows into the Baltic Sea. The egg-shaped Altstadt sits below an east–west bend in the river. West of the Altstadt lies the student and nightlife district Kröpeliner Torvorstadt, commonly known as KTV. The city's harbour is north along the top of the Altstadt and KTV. From this point, both the river and the city head north to seaside Warnemünde, around 13km northwest, on Mecklenburger Bucht (Mecklenburg Bay). Most of Rostock is on the western riverbank, including Warnemünde, although the ferry port is on the east side of the Warnow, and some of Warnemünde's accommodation lies across the river mouth at Hohe Düne.

The Hauptbahnhof is about 1.5km south of the Altstadt. Rosa-Luxemburg-Strasse runs north from the station to Steintor, in the old town's southeast corner. The airport is some 30km south of town.

Information

Tourist offices sell the Rostock Card (€10), which is good for 48 hours of pub-lic transport and offers discounts to some attractions.

Ärztehaus (☎ 456 1622; Paulstrasse 48) Medical services.

Main post office (Neuer Markt 3-8)

Tourist-Information Rostock (☎ 381 2222; www.rostock.de; Neuer Markt 3; ⏰ 10am-7pm Mon-Fri, 10am-4pm Sat & Sun Jun-Aug, 10am-6pm Mon-Fri, 10am-4pm Sat & Sun May & Sep, 10am-6pm Mon-Fri, 10am-3pm Sat Oct-Apr)

Tourist office Warnemünde (☎ 548 000; www.warnemuende.de; Am Strom 59, cnr Kirchstrasse; ⏰ 9am-6pm Mon-Fri, 10am-4pm Sat & Sun Mar-Oct, 10am-5pm Mon-Fri, 10am-3pm Sat Nov-Feb)

Treffpunkt Café (☎ 643 8066; Am Vögenteich 23; ⏰ 9am-7pm Mon-Fri, 10am-1pm Sat) Twenty minutes' free internet access with any order.

Sights

It takes just a couple of hours or so to see the city sights, after which it's worth making a beeline for Warnemünde. The way to the sea is lined with *Plattenbauten*, stunningly ugly concrete apartment blocks that were built to house GDR workers, but the beach and harbour are, fortunately, very different.

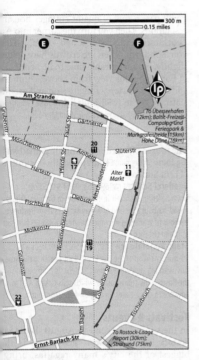

MARIENKIRCHE

Central Rostock's pride and joy is the 13th-century **Marienkirche** (☎ 453 325; Am Ziegenmarkt; admission by donation; ☺ 10am-6pm Mon-Sat, 11.15am-5pm Sun May-Sep, 10am-noon & 2-4pm Mon-Sat, 11.15am-noon Sun Oct-Apr), the only main Rostock church to survive WWII unscathed. Behind the main altar, the church's 12m-high **astrological clock**, built in 1472 by Hans Düringer, is the only working clock of its kind in the world still with its original mechanisms. At the very top of the clock is a series of doors. At noon and midnight the innermost right door opens and six of the 12 apostles march out to parade around Jesus (Judas is locked out). Zodiac symbols and moon phases feature in the centre, while the lower section has a disc that tells the exact day on which Easter falls in any given year. The replaceable discs are accurate for 130 years – the current one expires in 2017, and the University of Rostock already has a new one ready. Look out too for the unusually tall, organically shaped **baroque organ** (1770).

NEUER MARKT

Rostock's large, open central square is dominated by the splendid 13th-century **Rathaus**. The building's Baroque facade was added in 1727 after the original brick Gothic structure collapsed.

Opposite the Rathaus is a series of restored **gabled houses** and a stylised, sea-themed fountain, the **Möwenbrunnen** (2001), by artist Waldemar Otto. The explanatory plaque says the four figures are Neptune and his sons, although many believe they represent the four elements.

KRÖPELINER STRASSE & UNIVERSITÄTSPLATZ

Kröpeliner Strasse, a broad, lively, cobblestone pedestrian mall lined with 15th- and 16th-century burghers' houses, runs from Neuer Markt west to Kröpeliner Tor.

At the centre of the mall is **Universitätsplatz**, and its centrepiece, the crazy rococo **Brunnen der Lebensfreude** (Fountain of Happiness). True to its name, the square is lined with university buildings, including the handsome terracotta **Hauptgebäude** (1866–70), which replaced the famous 'White College'. The university itself is the oldest on the Baltic (founded in 1419), and currently has about 11,000 students.

At the northern side of Universitätsplatz are the **Five-Gables Houses**, modern interpretations of the residences that lined the square before WWII.

At the southwestern end is the Kloster Zum Heiligen Kreuz, a convent established in 1270 by Queen Margrethe of Denmark. Today it houses the city's cultural history museum, the **Kulturhistorische Museum Rostock** (☎ 203 590; www .kulturhistorisches-museum-rostock.de, in German; Klosterhof 18; admission free; ☯ 10am-6pm Tue-Sun), with an interesting collection including Victorian furniture and a few sculptures by Ernst Barlach.

CITY WALLS & GATES

Today only two of 32 gates, plus a small brick section, remain of the old city wall. The 55m-high **Kröpeliner Tor** stands at the western end of Kröpeliner Strasse. From here, you can follow the *Wallanlagen* (city walls) through the pleasant park to Wallstrasse and the other surviving gate, the **Steintor**.

PETRIKIRCHE

The Gothic **Petrikirche** (☎ 211 01; Alter Markt; tower admission €2; ☯ 9am-noon & 2-5pm Mon-Fri, 11am-5pm Sat & Sun) has a 117m-high steeple – a mariner's landmark for centuries – that was restored in 1994, having been missing since WWII. You can climb the steps or take the lift up to the viewing platform.

SCHIFFFAHRTSMUSEUM

Rostock's excellent **Schifffahrtsmuseum** (Ship Museum; ☎ 1283 1364; www.schifffahrtsmuseum-rostock.de, in German; MS Dresden, IGA Park, Liegeplatz Schmarl; admission €4, park only €1; ☯ 10am-6pm Tue-Sun) is moored on the shores of the flower-filled **IGA Park** on the northwest riverbank. Aboard the ship, there's a rundown on shipping from the Hanseatic period to today, plus the chance to play captain and other hands-on activities.

Take the S-Bahn to Lütten Klein and then bus 31 or 35.

WARNEMÜNDE

Warnemünde is all about promenading, eating fish, sipping cocktails, and lazing in a *Strandkörbe* (sheltered straw 'beach basket' seat) on its long, wide and startlingly white beach.

Walking from Warnemünde's train station along **Alter Strom**, the boat-lined main canal,

you'll pass a row of quaint cottages housin restaurants. Then you turn the corner into A Leuchtturm and Seestrasse and – bam! – it hi you. Sundown, when the crowds have abate slightly, is a memorable time to be here.

For a fabulous view from above, climb th spiralling 135-step wrought-iron and granit staircase of the 1898-built **lighthouse** (adult/cor cession/family €2/1/4; ☯ 10am-6.30pm May-Sep).

Tours

The tourist office runs 90-minute guided **walk ing tours** (in German; €4) at 2pm daily in summe (11am Sunday).

Reederei Schütt (☎ 690 953, 0173-917 9178; www.hafenrundfahrten-in-rostock.de, in German) Offers round-harbour trips and one-way services from Rostock's harbour to Warnemünde (one-way/return €8/12) between May and October.

Stadt-Rundfahrten (☎ 312 6507; €10) Does a 50-minute circuit of the city in an 18-seater 'panorama bus' with big viewing windows. It departs from outside the Rostock city tourist office, which sells tickets. Call in advance to check times for English-language tours.

Festivals & Events

In the second weekend in August, **Hanse Sa Rostock** (☎ 208 5233; www.hanse-sail.com) is the biggest of the city's many regattas, bring ing countless sailing ships to the city an Warnemünde harbours.

Rostock is also a venue for the state's clas sical music **Festspiele Mecklenburg-Vorpommer** (☎ 0385-591 8585; www.festspiele-mv.de) each June to September.

Sleeping

Rostock city and Warnemünde have scads o accommodation, including many chains (e Ibis, Radisson SAS). Tourist offices can help with bookings, including private rooms.

CITY

Hanse Hostel (☎ 128 6006; www.hanse-hostel.de Doberaner Strasse 136; dm €14-18, s/d with shared bathroom €24/44, breakfast €4, linen €2; ☒ ▣ ☯) On the edge of Rostock's trendy bar district, the KTV, is this clean, family-run operation, with great facilities and lots of board games. Its popularity has seen it recently expand into a second, bigger building up the road. From the Hauptbahnhof, take tram 4 or 5 to the Volkstheater stop.

DJH hostel Rostock (Jugendgästeschiff Georg Buchner; ☎ 670 0320; www.jugendgaesteschiff-rostock.jugendherberge

e; Am Stadthafen 72-3; dm under/over 26yr incl breakfast
9/22; ☼ closed mid-late Dec; ✗) The dorms aboard
ais unique 1950s cargo ship-turned-hostel are
▸mewhat claustrophobic, but keen sailors
▸ight want to give it a whirl. Take tram 4 or 5
▸ Kabutzenhof.

Hotel Kleine Sonne (☎ 497 3153; www.die-kleine
▸onne.de; Steinstrasse 7; s €52-82, d €104-164, breakfast
▸1; P ✗ 🖳 ⬱) This lovely place lives up
▸ its name with sunny yellow and red detail-
▸g, and semaphore prints by Berlin artist
Jils Ausländer. If you're cycling, you can get
▸vo nights' accommodation, a packed lunch,
▸ree-course dinner, cycling itineraries and
ike storage for €159/238 per single/double.
▸ll guests have free use of the wellness centre
▸ the Steigenberger Hotel Sonne (below).

Hotel Verdi (☎ 252 240; www.hotel-verdi.de;
Jollenweberstrasse 28; s/d/studio/apt incl breakfast
▸om €59/79/84/119; P ✗ ⬱) Opening to an
▸mbrella-shaded, timber-decked terrace is this
▸parkling little hotel just near the Petrikirche
▸nd Alter Markt, with a handful of attrac-
▸ively decorated rooms, larger studios with
▸itchenettes, and a ground-floor holiday
▸partment sleeping up to four people. All are
▸reat value.

Altes Hafenhaus (☎ 493 0110; www.altes-hafenhaus
▸e, in German; Strandstrasse 93; s €64-100, d €79-130 incl
▸reakfast; ✗) Stained-glass windows, polished
▸vooden floors and embroidered towels give
▸he 10 rooms in this butter-coloured baroque
▸illa considerable charm, as do the beamed
▸eilings in some rooms, while bathrooms are
▸right and contemporary. Some rooms at this
▸Old Port House' overlook the water, although
▸'s not the most scenic stretch of river.

Steigenberger Hotel Sonne (☎ 497 30; www.hotel
▸onne-rostock.de; Neuer Markt 2; s/d from €79/158, breakfast
▸17; P ✗ 🖳 ⬱) It's hard for the interior to
▸ompete with the ornate facade at this hotel
- a confection of stepped gables and iron lace-
▸work topped with a golden 'sun', which rises
▸above Rostock's main square. However, the
▸rooms do their best, in tones of brown, red
and yellow, and there's a clutch of classy res-
▸taurants and bars as well as a wellness centre
▸with a sauna and steam room.

WARNEMÜNDE

Baltic-Freizeit Camping und Ferienpark (☎ 04544-800
313; www.baltic-freizeit.de; Dünenweg 27, Markgrafenheide;
sites incl person & car from €11, cottages per person from €55;
P) On the eastern bank of the Warnow River,
across from Warnemünde, this enormous

city-run affair has over 1200 pitches, plus 80
cottages sleeping up to six people, as well as
minigolf, tennis courts, a sauna, and several
restaurants and bars.

DJH hostel Warnemünde (☎ 548 170; www.warne
muende.jugendherberge.de; Parkstrasse 47; dm under/over 26yr
€25.20/30.80; P ✗ 🖳) This decade-old, family-
friendly hostel is in a converted weather station near the western end of the Warnemünde
beach. Take the S-Bahn to Warnemünde S-
Bahn to the Lichtenhagen stop, then change
to bus 36 to Warnemünde beach.

Hotel-Pension Zum Kater (☎ 548 210; www.pension
-zum-kater.de, in German; Alexandrinenstrasse 115; s €50-72,
d €72-129, breakfast €8; P) Less than 10 minutes'
stroll from the beach, and even closer to the
harbour, this guesthouse manages to be sweet
and cosy without straying into Laura Ashley
territory. It's possible to stay less than three
nights over weekends in the high season, but
there's a supplement of €21/16 per person
for the first/second nights. Look for the cute
black cat logo.

Residenz Strandhotel (☎ 548 060; www.residenz
-strandhotel.de, in German; Seestrasse 6; s €69-85, d without
sea view €70-110, d with sea view €78-155, ste €165-229;
P ✗ 🗮 🖳 ⬱) The balcony-clad exterior of
this new hotel reflects and updates the fishermen's cottages along Alter Strom. Inside,
you'll find stylish, sound-insulated rooms
with flat-screen TVs, plus a library. Spa treatments and physiotherapy are available, as is
free 'energised' water.

Hotel am Leuchtturm (☎ 543 70; www.hotel-am
-leuchtturm.de; Am Leuchtturm 16; s €95-125, d €110-215;
P ✗) There are sea or harbour views from
every room, but the corner ones are especially panoramic at this place by the lighthouse. The oft-used colours of yellow and
blue are given a designer twist in the spacious,
light-filled accommodation.

Hotel Neptun (☎ 7770; www.hotel-neptun.de;
Seestrasse 19; s/d from €115/174; P ✗ 🖳 ⬱ 🐾) As
hideous as this enormous concrete boxlike
building is, its balconies are cleverly angled
so that each room has a beach view. Inside,
it's a haven of luxuriously renovated rooms,
numerous bars and restaurants (including
a panoramic 64m-high cafe), and a spa and
supervised gym. Past guests have included
Fidel Castro and Franz Beckenbauer.

Strand-Hotel Hübner (☎ 543 40; www.hotel-huebner.de;
Seestrasse 12; s €135-175, d €175-220; P ✗ ⬱ 🐾)
Fabulous views unfold from the balconies of
this cruise-liner-like beachside hotel. Highlights

include a glassed-in wellness centre and guest lounge overlooking the Baltic Sea, where in winter you can enjoy coffee, cakes, fondue, baked apples or *Feuerzangenbowle* punch (see boxed text, p87).

Eating

CITY

Zum Alten Fritz (☎ 208 780; Warnowufer 65; mains €7.60-18.90; ⏰ from 11am) With a good range of standards, plus organic meats and specials like turkey in beer, this big pub-restaurant down on the docks is part of an expanding local brewery chain.

Ratskeller (☎ 510 8460; Rathaus, Neuer Markt 1; mains €8.50-14.50; ⏰ from 11am) Descending the steps to Rostock's circa-eight-century-old *Ratskeller* (town hall restaurant) brings you into a vast, low-lit series of cross-vaulted rooms that provide an atmospheric backdrop for dining on its hearty German fare (lots of pork, *lots* of sauerkraut).

Zur Kogge (☎ 493 4493; Wokrenterstrasse 27; mains €8.60-14.80; ⏰ 11.30am-midnight; Ⓥ) At this Rostock institution, cosy wooden booths are lined with stained-glass Hanseatic coats of armour and monster fish threatening sailing ships, while life preservers hang from the walls, and ships lanterns are suspended from the ceiling. Local fish dishes (rollmops and so on) dominate the menu, or you can stop by for coffee and cake between meal times. There's an above-average kids' menu, too.

Albert & Emile (☎ 493 4373; Altschmiedestrasse 28; mains €10.90-16.90; ⏰ from 6.30pm Tue-Sat) Rostock's most romantic place to dine is this French jewel. Behind the ivy-covered facade it's a haven of black-and-white marble tiles and dark timber, *chansonniers* crooning from the speakers and accomplished haute cuisine on the handwritten menu.

Amberg 13 (☎ 490 6262; Amberg 13; mains €14.30-15.90; ⏰ 5-11pm Tue-Sun plus brunch from 11am 2nd & 4th Sun of month) This relaxed, unassuming restaurant is locally renowned for its ambitious and creative cuisine, with dishes such as *Kalbshaxe* (knuckle of veal) accompanied by polenta and capsicum, onion, rosemary and sherry ragout, or rabbit with chanterelle mushrooms, garlic gnocchi and green beans. It's accessed via an archway and courtyard.

WARNEMÜNDE

Fish – fresh, fried, baked, smoked, you name it – is the order of the day here. Both banks of

the harbour are lined with kiosks and caravan selling inexpensive fish sandwiches – perfect you're heading to the beach or a nearby bencl along the harbourfront, though not so good i you're dining in one of the restaurants behind as they often block the views.

Fischerhaus (☎ 778 8474; Am Bahnhof 1d; main €6.95-14.50; ⏰ 11am-10pm) In one of the newe developments along the eastern bank of Alte Strom (where the food is at least as good a the traditional western bank), this relaxe canteen-style place serves simple but deliciou dishes: salmon in beer batter, fried Baltic eel and – for a change from fish – fried liver with apples, onions and mash.

Fischerklause (☎ 525 16; Am Strom 123; main €8.80-14.95; ⏰ from 11.30am) Fischerklause is one of the atmospheric old fishermen's cottage lining the western bank of Alter Strom, an attracts plenty of tourists (but then so does a of Warnemünde). Still, its ship's cabin decor and its succulent seafood make it worth seek ing out. Afterwards pop in for a drink at the adjoining bar fronted by thatched umbrellas

La Villa (☎ 510 9944; Am Bahnhof 1b; tapas €2.50-9.6(mains €14.90-26; ⏰ from 11.30am) Fish dishes have a modern Mediterranean accent at this designer cafe/restaurant, where meals are served in a stripped interior of bare boards, banquettes and high-backed wicker chairs. Its extensive tapas menu is best sampled over a glass of freshly made strawberry punch.

Drinking

CITY

Krahnstöver Likörfabrik (☎ 4377 7654; Grubenstrasse 1; 🕸) Rostock's oldest family-run wine merchant owns this multifaceted bistro-bar-cafe, next to an artificial stream near the city wall. It also has a brasserie in the Steigenberger Hotel Sonne (p737).

Studentenkeller (☎ 455 928; www.studentenkeller.de, in German; Universitätsplatz 5; ⏰ Tue-Sat) This cellar and garden joint has been rocking Rostock's learned youth for years. Check the website for parties, DJ sets and other events.

Café Central (☎ 490 4648; Leonhardstrasse 20; ⏰ from 9.30am Mon-Sat, from 10am Sun) In the heart of the scene, Café Central has cult status among Rostock locals. Students, artists, hipsters and suited-up professionals all loll around sipping long drinks on the banquettes below black-and-white photos or enjoy a tall beer over a game of backgammon at the tables in the centre.

WARNEMÜNDE

chuster's (☎ 700 7835; Im Teepott; ⏲ from 11am) Head
here for sunset cocktails. It has a hip summer
pavilion on the beach a few metres from its
main location in the quirky, mollusc-shaped
Teepott building.

Sky-Bar (19th fl, Hotel Neptun; ⏲ hours vary) Live
music plays at this ritzier venue, where the
roof opens up to reveal the star-filled sky).

Entertainment
Live gigs, DJs, concerts and a host of other
events are listed in *Szene* (www.szenerostock
.de) and *Piste* (www.piste.de/rostock), both
in German.

MS Stubnitz (☎ 490 7475; www.stubnitz.com;
Stadthafen, Liegeplatz 82; ⏲ hours vary) A former fishing trawler has been converted into Rostock's
most unusual and most alternative, grunge-
style venue, with bands, DJs and performances
over three decks. Beware that the boat sometimes sails off to entertain other cities, too.

Mau Club Rostock (☎ 202 3576; www.mauclub.de,
in German; Warnowufer 56; ⏲ Fri, Sat & special events)
Everything from indie to punk to disco attracts a wide-ranging crowd to this former
storage hall. It's well known for its support
of up-and-coming acts and hosts many free
local band evenings.

Zwischenbau Rostock (☎ 377 8737; www.zwischen
bau.com, in German; Erich-Schlesinger-Strasse 19a, Südstadt;
⏲ Fri, Sat & special events) A temple for serious
dance music of various shades and flavours.

In Warnemünde, Hotel Neptun (p737) has
a classy disco, **Da Capo** (⏲ Tue, Fri & Sat).

Getting There & Away
AIR
Rostock's airport, **Rostock-Laage** (RLG; ☎ 01805-
007 737; www.rostock-airport.de), has scheduled services to Cologne-Bonn, Munich, Stuttgart and
Zürich, plus seasonal charter flights to holiday
resorts in Bulgaria, Greece, Spain, Tunisia and
Turkey, among others.

BOAT
Ferries sail to/from Denmark, Sweden, Latvia
and Finland – see p778.

Boats depart from the **Überseehafen** (overseas
seaport; www.rostock-port.de), which is on the east
side of the Warnow. Take tram 1, 2, 3 or 4
to Dierkower Kreuz (tram 3 or 4 from the
Hauptbahnhof), then change for bus 49 to
Seehafen. There is an S-Bahn to Seehafen, but
it's a 20-minute walk from the station to the
piers (not fun if you're dragging heavy bags).

CAR & MOTORCYCLE
The A19 runs south from Rostock to connect
with the A24 to Berlin. For a lift, get in touch
with the ride-sharing agency **Mitfahrzentrale**
(☎ 194 40; www.mitfahrgelegenheit.de, in German).

TRAIN
There are frequent direct trains to Rostock
from Berlin (from €35.10, 2½ hours) and
Hamburg (from €30.90, 2½ hours), and hourly
services to Stralsund (€13.30, one hour),
Wismar (€10.30, 1¼ hours) and Schwerin
(€15.20, one hour).

Private company **InterConnex** (www.interconnex
.com, in German) has one train a day between
Berlin and Rostock's Hauptbahnhof as well
as Warnemünde's Bahnhof, costing an
astonishingly cheap €12.

Getting Around
TO/FROM THE AIRPORT
Bus 127 connects Rostock's Hauptbahnhof
and central bus station with the airport (one-
way €9.10). A taxi costs around €50.

BICYCLE
Cycling can be hair-raising in the centre
because of heavy traffic, but things quickly
improve outside the city. Rental stations include outlets at Rostock's Hauptbahnhof and
Warnemünde's Bahnhof.

CAR & MOTORCYCLE
With complicated one-way systems, confusing street layouts and dedicated parking-
ticket police, Rostock is not a driver-friendly
city. There are several convenient parking
lots off Lange Strasse. The **Warnow Tunnel**
(www.warnowtunnel.de, in German; toll €2.90) crosses
beneath the river in the north of the city and
links to the A19.

PUBLIC TRANSPORT
Journeys within Rostock, including Warnemünde, cost €1.70/4.50 for a single/day pass,
valid on the Warnow ferries as well as land
transport, including frequent double-decker S-
Bahn services to Warnemünde (22 minutes).

Trams 5 and 6 travel from the Hauptbahnhof
up Steinstrasse, around Marienkirche and down
Lange Strasse to the university. Lines 4 and 5 go
from the train station to the KTV district.

TAXI
For a taxi, ring **Hanse-Taxi** (☎ 685 858).

BAD DOBERAN & COASTAL RESORTS

☎ 038203 / pop 11,600

The former summer ducal residence of Bad Doberan, about 15km west of Rostock, was once the site of a powerful Cistercian monastery. Today, it's a tourist town with a mighty *Münster* (large church) and horse races in July and August.

Bad Doberan is also the starting point for the Molli Schmalspurbahn, a popular narrow-gauge steam train that travels to the coastal resorts of Heiligendamm and Kühlungsborn. Catching the train and walking along the coast between some stops makes for a pleasant and undemanding day trip from Rostock.

The Bad Doberan **tourist office** (☎ 621 54; www .bad-doberan-heiligendamm.de, in German; Severinstrasse 6; ◷ 9am-6pm Mon-Fri, 10am-3pm Sat mid-May–mid-Sep, 9am-4pm Mon-Fri mid-Sep–mid-May) is a five-minute walk from the train station.

Sights & Activities

MÜNSTER

Construction of Bad Doberan's magnificent Gothic church hall, the **Münster** (☎ 627 16; www .doberanermuenster.de; Klosterstrasse 2; adult/concession/child under 18yr €2/1.50/0.50; ◷ 9am-6pm Mon-Sat, 11am-6pm Sun May-Sep, 10am-5pm Mon-Sat, 11am-5pm Sun Mar-Apr & Oct, 10am-4pm Mon-Sat, 11am-4pm Sun Nov-Feb), started in 1280 but the scale of the building (incorporating some 1.2 million bricks) meant it wasn't consecrated until 1368. Its treasures include a lovely high altar and an ornate pulpit. There's at least one hour-long guided tour in German per day (€3/2.50/1); call ahead to enquire about English-language tours.

Organ recitals, choirs and bands perform from May to September, usually on Friday evenings – contact the Bad Doberan tourist office for tickets.

ZAPPA MEMORIAL

Since 1989, Bad Doberan's racecourse has been the unlikely venue each July for the **Zappanale** (www.arf-society.de), Germany's only Frank Zappa festival. A **Zappa memorial** was erected in the town centre in 2002 amid much psychedelic rejoicing.

MOLLI SCHMALSPURBAHN

In 1886, the steam train 'Molli', as she's affectionately known, began huffing and puffing her way to Heiligendamm, carrying Germany's elite. Then in 1910, the line was extended west along the coast to Kühlungsborn. Today the train goes by the full name of **Mecklenburge Bäderbahn Molli** (☎ 4150; www.molli-bahn.de), witl services departing Bad Doberan's train statio on average 11 times a day year-round.

With a maximum speed of 45km/h, th journey takes 15 minutes to reach the coast a Heiligendamm (one-way/return €4/7) and 4 minutes in total to Kühlungsborn/West (€6/11` with interim stops in Steilküste, Kühlungsborn East and Kühlungsborn/Mitte. Concessions an family fares are also available. Children love th dinky engine and carriages. There's a salon ca on many journeys and the scenery is lovely.

To help plan your day, pick up a pocket sized timetable when you buy your ticket a Bad Doberan's train station.

For a particularly easy and enjoyable walk you can get off at Heiligendamm and walk tc the Steilküste station before picking up th train again.

HEILIGENDAMM

The 'white town on the sea' is Germany's oldest seaside resort, founded in 1793 by Mecklenburg duke Friedrich Franz I anc fashionable throughout the 19th century as a playground of the nobility.

In the 21st century, it has been reborn with the opening of the exclusive **Grand Hotel Heiligendamm** (☎ 7400; www.grandhotel-heiligendamm .de; s/d from €225/260; P ✕ ♨ ☐ ☎ ☒). With cool, contemporary rooms housed in five gleaming white, heritage-listed buildings, the palatial hotel is continuing the resort's tradition and hosted a G8 summit in 2007. Even for those not staying here, the hotel is an attraction, with some seven restaurants and bars, its own pier, pristine beach and surrounding parkland.

KÜHLUNGSBORN

Kühlungsborn, the biggest Baltic Sea resort, with some 7453 inhabitants, is also home to some lovely art-deco buildings and adjoins a dense 130-hectare forest. The east and west parts of town are linked by the Ostseeallee promenade, lined with hotels and restaurants. In the eastern part of town you'll find a pier running 240m out to sea and a newly built yacht harbour.

All sorts of water sports, including diving, are on offer. For more information, contact the **Kurverwaltung** (spa resort administration; ☎ 8490; www.kuehlungsborn.de; Ostseeallee 19; ◷ 9am-6pm Mon-Fri, 10am-4pm Sat & Sun May-Sep, 9am-4pm Mon-Fri, 10am-1pm Sat & Sun Oct-Apr).

Getting There & Around

Trains connect Bad Doberan with Rostock Hauptbahnhof (€6.90, 25 minutes) and Wismar (€6.90, 45 minutes) roughly hourly. By car, take the B105 towards Wismar.

See opposite for details of the Molli Schmalspurbahn steam train linking Bad Doberan with the coastal resorts.

WISMAR

☎ 03841 / pop 45,182

With its gabled facades and cobbled streets, this small, photogenic city looks essentially Hanseatic. But although it joined the Hanseatic trading league in the 13th century, it spent most of the 16th and 17th centuries as part of Sweden. There are numerous reminders of this era all over town, including some striking buildings, a clock and a tomb. The entire Altstadt was Unesco-listed in 2002.

Wismar has been long popular with filmmakers and its picturesque *Alter Hafen* (old harbour) starred in the 1922 Dracula movie *Nosferatu*; and today it's not unusual to stumble across movie crews around town.

Orientation

Wismar's Altstadt centres on the Markt, said to be the largest medieval town square in northern Germany. The Bahnhof is at the northeastern corner of the Altstadt and the *Alter Hafen* port is at the northwestern corner; a canal runs from *Alter Hafen* almost due east across the Altstadt's northern half. The streets around the Markt are pedestrianised; the main dining and entertainment area is around *Alter Hafen*.

Information

Main post office (Mecklenburger Strasse 18-20)
Tourist-Information (☎ 251 3025; www.wismar.de, with English sections; Am Markt 11; ⏰ 9am-6pm Mar-Dec, 9am-6pm Mon-Sat, 10am-4pm Sun Jan & Feb)

Sights

MARKT

Dominating the middle of the Markt is the 1602-built **Wasserkunst** (waterworks), an ornate, 12-sided well that supplied Wismar's drinking water until 1897. Today it remains the town's landmark.

Behind it stands the redbrick **Alter Schwede**, which dates from 1380 and features a striking step buttress gable facade. Today it houses a restaurant and guesthouse (p743), as well as

a copy of one of the so-called 'Swedish Heads' (see the boxed text, p742).

Other gabled houses around the Markt have also been lovingly restored. The large **Rathaus** at the square's northern end was built between 1817 and 1819 and today houses the excellent **Rathaus Historical Exhibition** (adult/concession €1/0.50; ⏰ 10am-6pm) in its basement. Displays include an original 15th-century *Wandmalerei* (mural) uncovered by archaeologists in 1985, a glass-covered medieval well, and the Wrangel tomb – the coffin of influential Swedish General Helmut V Wrangel and his wife, with outsized wooden figures carved on top.

CHURCHES

Of the three great redbrick churches that once rose above the rooftops before WWII, only the enormous redbrick **St-Nikolai-Kirche** (admission by donation; ⏰ 8am-8pm May-Sep, 10am-6pm Apr & Oct, 11am-4pm Nov-Mar), the largest of its kind in Europe, was left intact. Today it contains a font from its older sister church, the St-Marien-Kirche.

All that remains of the 13th-century **St-Marien-Kirche** (admission by donation; ⏰ 10am-8pm Jul & Aug, 10am-6pm Mar-Jun & Sep-Dec, 10am-6pm Mon-Sat, 10am-4pm Sun Jan & Feb) is its great brick steeple (1339), which rises above the city. A multimedia exhibit on medieval church-building techniques is housed in the tower's base.

The massive red shell of the **St-Georgen-Kirche** (admission by donation; ⏰ 10am-8pm Jul & Aug, 10am-6pm Mar-Jun & Sep-Dec, 10am-6pm Mon-Sat, 10am-4pm Sun Jan & Feb) has been extensively renovated for combined use as a church, concert hall and exhibition space and is set to reopen in May 2010. In 1945 a freezing populace was driven to burn what was left of the church's beautiful wooden statue of St George and the dragon.

FÜRSTENHOF

Between the St-Marien and St-Georgen churches lies the restored Italian Renaissance **Fürstenhof** (1512–13), now the city courthouse. The facades are slathered in terracotta reliefs depicting episodes from folklore and the town's history.

HISTORICAL MUSEUM

The town's historical museum is in the Renaissance **Schabbellhaus** (☎ 282 350; www.schabbellhaus.de; Schweinsbrücke 8; adult/concession/child under 18yr €2/1/free; ⏰ 10am-8pm Tue-Sun May-Oct, to 5pm Nov-Apr) in a former brewery (1571), just south

---

A SWEDISH HEADS-UP

A 'Swedish head' isn't (in this case, at least) something you need to successfully assemble a flat-pack IKEA bookcase. In Wismar, Swedish Heads refers to two baroque busts of Hercules, which once stood on mooring posts at the harbour entrance.

Semi-comical, with great curling moustaches and wearing lions as hats, and painted in bright colours (one red-and-white, the other yellow-and-blue), the statues are believed to have marked either the beginning of the harbour or the navigable channels within it. It's thought that before this they were ships' figureheads.

The original heads were damaged when a Finnish barge rammed them in 1902, at which time replicas were made. One original is now in the **Schabbellhaus** (Historical Museum; p741), while two replicas guard the Baumhaus in Wismar's *Alter Hafen*. They're also a boon for Wismar's souvenir manufacturers, adorning all manner of gifts.

---

of St-Nikolai-Kirche across the canal. Pride of place goes to one of the original Swedish Heads (see the boxed text, above).

Regional artist Christian Wetzel's four charming metal **pig statuettes** grace the **Schweinsbrücke** between the church and the museum.

Activities

Fritz Reuter (☎ 05254-808 500; www.ms-fritz-reuter.de, in German) organises wreck dives along the Baltic coast.

The huge water park, **Wonnemar** (☎ 327 623; www.wonnemar.de, in German; Bürgermeister-Haupt-Strasse 38; day ticket adult/child/concession/family €10.50/9.50/8.50/31; ☒ 10am-9pm May-Sep, 10am-8pm Oct-Apr), has lots of fun water slides as well as pools, tennis, bowling, badminton, a wellness centre and four restaurants.

Tours

BOAT TOURS

Clermont Reederei (☎ 224646; www.reederei-clermont.de, in German) operates hour-long harbour cruises five times daily from May to September, leaving from the *Alter Hafen* (adult/child €8/4). It also runs boats to **Poel Island** up to four times daily (adult one-way/return €8/14, bicycle €2/3), which despite its close proximity to Wismar has the atmosphere of a remote fishing community.

Various other companies run tours on historic ships during summer; contact the **harbour** (☎ 389 082; www.alterhafenwismar.de, in German) for details.

MINIBUS TOURS

High-roofed **minibuses** (adult/child under 12yr €8.50/4.30; ☒ 10am-4.30pm) with panoramic glass windows circumnavigate the city's sights over

40 minutes. The vans depart half-hourly from outside the tourist office, which sells ticket Commentary is in German, but the tou ist office can provide an English-languag audioguide and leaflet (see p741).

WALKING TOURS

From Easter to October there are two-hou walking tours of the city (in German) lea ing the tourist office at 10.30am (adult/con cession €4/3) plus 2pm Saturday, Sunda and holidays.

Festivals & Events

Annual events include Wismar's **Hafenfe** (Harbour Festival) in mid-June, featuring o and new sailing ships and steamers, music an food, and a free **street theatre** festival in Jul August. Wismar also holds a **Schwedenfest** o the third weekend of August, commemoratir the end of Swedish rule in 1903.

Sleeping

Private rooms starting from €20 are bookab through the tourist office.

DJH hostel (☎ 326 80; www.wismar.jugendherberge.c Juri-Gagarin-Ring 30a; dm incl breakfast & linen under/ov 26yr €20.50/25.10; ℗ ☒ ▣) Wismar's hostel is i a pretty, old brick building 15 minutes' wa west of town, not far from the Wonnema The Schwedenstein (Swedish Stone) next do is another reminder of Swedish hegemony.

Pension Chez Fasan (☎ 213 425; www.pensi -chez-fasan.de, in German; Bademutterstrasse 20a; s wi out bathroom €21, s/d with bathroom €24/45, breakfast € ℗) The 25 simple but perfectly comfortab rooms in these three linked houses, just on block north of the Markt, are fantastic valu Call ahead to make sure someone's arour to let you in.

Hotel Reuterhaus (☎ 222 30; www.hotel-reuterhaus.de, German; Am Markt 19; s €50-70, d €80-110 incl breakst) Right on the Markt overlooking the Vasserkunst, this historic family-run establishnent has modernised (if fairly prosaic) rooms nd a good restaurant (mains €8 to €20).

ourpick Bio Hotel Reingard (☎ 284 972; www eingard.de, in German; Weberstrasse 18; s €58-62, d €86-88 cl breakfast; P X) Wismar's most charming lace to stay is this boutique hotel with its andful of artistic rooms, leafy little garden nd gourmet *bio* (organic) restaurant (menus om €30 for two people; by arrangement). here's even a small adjoining museum conaining the owner's 300,000-strong collection f buttons and vintage belt buckles.

Steigenberger Hotel Stadt Hamburg (☎ 2390; ww.wismar.steigenberger.de; Am Markt 24; s €83-88, d €97-3; P X X 🛜) Abstract sculptures decoate the lobby, restaurant and wellness centre f Wismar's swishest hotel. Rooms are fresh, reamlined and contemporary, and some njoy great views over the Markt.

ating & Drinking

you're feeling adventurous, try *Wismarer oickaal* (young eel smoked in a way that's nique to the region). And if you're in celebratory mood, look out for locally roduced Hanse-Sektkellerei champagne from dry (Hanse Tradition) to extra dry lanse Selection).

Along the *Alter Hafen,* seafood (includg delicious fish sandwiches from as little €2) is sold directly from a handful of bobing boats. Most are open 9am to 6pm daily, nd from 6am on Saturday during Wismar's eekly fish market.

You'll also find a concentration of resurants along the nearby pedestrianised m Lohberg.

Avocados (☎ 303 333; Hinter dem Chor 1; mains .90-12; 🕒 8am-3.30pm Mon-Fri, 10am-4pm Sat; V) iagonally opposite the Schabbellhaus muum, this little corner cafe is a treat for vegerians for its organic fare, including warming ups, and vitamin-packed salads.

Zum Weinberg (☎ 283 550; Hinter dem Rathaus mains €8.20-14.90; 🕒 noon-10pm) This lovely enaissance house, with painted ceiling, ained-glass windows, and uneven walls and one floors, serves huge portions of fruity ecklenburg specialities such as *Rippenbraten* olled roast pork stuffed with lemon, apple d plums).

To'n Zägenkrog (☎ 282 716; Ziegenmarkt 10; mains €9.10-13.50; 🕒 dinner) Excellent fish dishes are the mainstay of this cosy 1897-established pub. It's crammed with maritime mementoes and has some of Wismar's best harbour views.

Brauhaus am Lohberg (☎ 250 238; Kleine Hohe Strasse 15; mains €9.20-12.80; 🕒 11am-late) This building was once home to the town's first brewery, which opened in 1452. It's now brewing again, with enormous copper vats and trailing vines occupying its central room, where you can soak it up with local seafood dishes. Live music regularly cranks up throughout summer.

Alter Schwede (☎ 283 552; Am Markt 19; mains €10.80-20.50; 🕒 11.30am-late; V) Baltic eel with herbed potatoes, catfish with mustard and a 'captain's bowl' of pork, beef and turkey medallions served on beans with bacon and potatoes are among the specialities of this landmark spot, but there are also a few decent vegetarian choices. Upstairs is a clutch of appealing en suite rooms (singles/doubles €30/45) and a self-contained apartment (€60).

Getting There & Around

Trains travel every hour to/from Rostock (€10.30, 70 minutes) and Schwerin (€6.90, 40 minutes). The fastest connection to Hamburg (€26.30, 1¾ hours) requires a change in Bad Kleinen.

Bikes can be rented from the Bahnhof.

DARSS-ZINGST PENINSULA

Nature lovers and artists will be captivated by the **Darss-Zingst Peninsula** (Fischland-Darss-Zingst; www.fischland-darss-zingst.de). This far-flung splinter of land is part of the 805-sq-km Vorpommersche Boddenlandschaft (Western Pomeranian Boddenlandschaft) National Park, which also encompasses the island of Hiddensee (see p753) and the west coast of Rügen Island (see p753).

The 'Bodden' are lagoons that were once part of the sea here, but have been cut off by shifting landmasses and are now rich with fish life. The seawards peninsula is raw and bracing, with trees growing sideways away from the constant winds. Further inland you'll find charming 'captains' houses' – reed-thatched houses with colourfully painted doors depicting sunflowers, fish and other regional motifs. Also common are *Zeesenboote* (drag-net fishing boats) with striking brown sails.

The area looks a picture, so not surprisingly it's home to an artists' colony in **Ahrenshoop** (www.ostseebad-ahrenshoop.de), whose century-old **Kunstkaten** (www.kunstkaten.de, in German; Strandweg 1; 🕙 10am-1pm & 2-5pm) gallery is in one of the region's most strikingly painted reed-thatched houses.

Baltic coastlines are the source of almost all the world's amber. As well as the jewellery on sale throughout Mecklenburg–Western Pomerania, you'll find the **Deutsches Bernsteinmuseum** (German Amber Museum; www.deutsches-bernsteinmuseum.de, in German; Im Kloster 1-2; adult/concession/child under 16yr €6/3.50/2.50; 🕙 9.30am-6pm Mar-Oct, 9.30am-5pm Tue-Sun Nov-Feb) in the 'amber town' of **Ribnitz-Damgarten** (www.ribnitz-damgarten.de).

The delightful town of **Prerow** (www.ostsee bad-prerow.de, in German) is renowned for its seamen's church and lighthouse.

Some 60,000 migratory cranes stop over in the park every spring and autumn, their biggest resting ground in Central Europe. For more information, contact the park authority, **Nationalparkamt Vorpommersche Boddenlandschaft** (☎ 038234-5020; www.nationalpark-vorpommersche-boddenlandschaft.de, in German), which has nine information offices spread across the park.

WESTERN POMERANIA

STRALSUND
☎ 03831 / pop 57,613

Stralsund was once the second-most important member of the Hanseatic League, after Lübeck, and its square gables interspersed with Gothic turrets, ornate portals and vaulted arches make it one of the leading examples of *Backsteingotik* (classic redbrick Gothic gabled architecture) in northern Germany. It has been classified as a Unesco World Heritage Site since 2002.

As the main gateway to Rügen and Hiddensee islands, the added sight of holidaymakers in shorts and flip-flops wandering along its historic cobbled streets offers a rare, but thoroughly enjoyable, combination indeed.

Orientation
The Altstadt is effectively on its own island, surrounded by lakes and the sea. Its main hubs are Alter Markt in the north and Neuer Markt in the south; a few blocks south of the latter is the central bus station. The Hauptbahnhof is across the Tribseer Damm causeway, west of Neuer Markt. The harbour is on the Altstadt eastern side.

Information
Main post office (Neuer Markt 4)
Toffi's Web Café (☎ 309 385; Am Lobshagen 8a; per €3; 🕙 noon-10pm)
Tourismuszentrale (☎ 246 90; www.stralsund.de; Alter Markt 9; 🕙 10am-6pm Mon-Fri, 10am-4pm Sat & Sun May-Oct, 10am-5pm Mon-Fri, 10am-4pm Sat Nov-Ap) Tourist information and room bookings.
Waschcafé (☎ 309 159; Wasserstrasse 18; 🕙 10am-8pm Mon-Fri, 10am-6pm Sun) Serviced laundry with internet terminals.

Sights
ALTER MARKT
Seven copper turrets and six triangular gable grace the redbrick Gothic facade of Stralsund splendid **Rathaus** (1370). The upper portion the northern facade, or *Schauwand* (show wall), has openings to prevent strong wind from knocking it over. Inside, the sky-lit co onnade boasts shiny black pillars on carve and painted bases; on the western side of th building is an ornate portal.

Through the Rathaus' eastern walkwa you'll come to the main portal of the 127 **Nikolaikirche** (☎ 297 199; 🕙 10am-5pm Mon-Sat, 11ar noon & 2-4pm Sun Apr-Sep, 10am-noon & 2-4pm Mon-S. 11am-noon & 2-4pm Sun Oct-Mar), which was modelle on Lübeck's Marienkirche and is filled with a treasures. The **main altar** (1708), designed t the baroque master Andreas Schlüter, show the eye of God flanked by cherubs and cappe by a depiction of the Last Supper. Also worth closer look are the **high altar** (1470), 6.7m wie and 4.2m tall, showing Jesus' entire life, an behind the altar, a 1394-built (but no long operational) **astronomical clock**.

Opposite the Rathaus you'll find th **Wulflamhaus** (Alter Markt 5), a beautiful 15th century town house named after an o mayor. Its turreted step gable imitates th Rathaus facade.

OTHER CHURCHES & CLOISTERS
The Neuer Markt is dominated by the ma sive 14th-century **Marienkirche** (☎ 293 52 Neuer Markt; 🕙 10am-5pm Mon-Sat, 11.30am-5pm Su another superb example of north Germa redbrick construction. You can climb th steep wooden steps up the tower (adult/ch €4/2) for a sweeping view of the town, wi its lovely red-tiled roofs, and Rügen Islan

On Schillstrasse, reached via Külpstrasse, the **Johanniskloster** (☎ 294 265; Schillstrasse 27; adu

STRALSUND

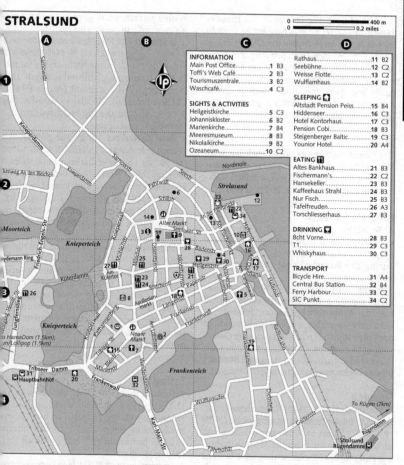

INFORMATION	
Main Post Office	1 B3
Toffi's Web Café	2 B3
Tourismuszentrale	3 B2
Waschcafé	4 C3

SIGHTS & ACTIVITIES	
Heilgeistkirche	5 C3
Johanniskloster	6 B2
Marienkirche	7 B4
Meeresmuseum	8 B3
Nikolaikirche	9 B2
Ozeaneum	10 C2

Rathaus	11 B2
Seebühne	12 C2
Weisse Flotte	13 C2
Wulflamhaus	14 B2

SLEEPING	
Altstadt Pension Peiss	15 B4
Hiddensee	16 C3
Hotel Kontorhaus	17 C3
Pension Cobi	18 B3
Steigenberger Baltic	19 C3
Younior Hotel	20 A4

EATING	
Altes Bankhaus	21 B3
Fischermann's	22 C2
Hansekeller	23 B3
Kaffeehaus Strahl	24 B3
Nur Fisch	25 B3
Tafelfreuden	26 A3
Torschliesserhaus	27 B3

DRINKING	
8cht Vorne	28 B3
T1	29 C3
Whiskyhaus	30 C3

TRANSPORT	
Bicycle Hire	31 A4
Central Bus Station	32 B4
Ferry Harbour	33 C2
SIC Punkt	34 C2

ncession €2.10/0.50; 🕙 10am-6pm Wed-Sun May-Oct), a ⸱rmer Franciscan monastery that's now a ⸱ncert venue. It's famous for its 'smoking ⸱tic' (there was no chimney), chapter hall ⸱d cloister.

Be sure to peek at the lovely ivy-covered ⸱ce of the **Heilgeistkirche** (Wasserstrasse).

⸱QUARIUMS

⸱ralsund is home to two of the country's ⸱p aquariums. Combination tickets per ⸱ult/child cost €18/11.

In a stylised arctic-white wavelike building ⸱at leaps out from the surrounding redbrick ⸱arehouses, the state-of-the-art **Ozeaneum** 🔊 2650 610; www.ozeaneum.com; Hafenstrasse 11; adult/ ⸱ld €14/8; 🕙 9.30am-9pm Jun-Sep, 9.30am-7pm Oct-May)

takes you into an underwater world of creatures from the Baltic and North Seas and the Atlantic Ocean up to the polar latitudes.

By contrast, the **Meeresmuseum** (Oceanographic Museum; ☎ 265 0210; www.meeresmuseum.de; Katharinenberg 14-20; adult/child €7.50/5; 🕙 10am-6pm Jun-Sep, 10am-5pm Oct-May) aquarium is in the basement of a 13th-century convent building, and is filled with colourful tropical fish.

Activities

Weisse Flotte (☎ 268 10; www.weisse-flotte.com, in German; Fährstrasse 16; adult/child €7/4) offers four one-hour harbour cruises a day from May to October, circling the island of Dänholm, between Stralsund and Rügen.

West of Tribseer Damm is the massive **HanseDom** (☎ 373 30; www.hansedom.de; Grünhufer Bogen 18-20; adult/concession/child under 15yr per 2hr from €10.50/9.50/8; ☻ 9.30am-11pm), boasting numerous pools including a wave pool, water slides, an array of Oriental-style saunas, massage treatments and sports facilities, as well as several restaurants and bars and a four-star hotel (singles/doubles from €78/118).

Tours

The tourist office rents out English-language MP3 audioguide tours (€7; leave your passport as a deposit). It also offers guided walking tours in German (€4) at 11am daily.

Festivals & Events

A *Seebühne* (floating stage) is erected in the harbour each June to August for opera, operetta and classical music performances during the **Ostseefestspiele** (☎ 264 6150; www .ostseefestspiele.de).

In the third week of July, Stralsund celebrates repelling an enemy invasion in 1628 with the **Wallensteintage** historic festival.

In early September, some 50 public buildings open their doors all night and welcome visitors with light displays, concerts, performing art, dance and cabaret during the **Lange Nacht des Offenen Denkmals** (Long Night of the Open Monuments).

Sleeping

Younior Hotel (☎ 0800-233 388 234; www.younior-hotel.de, in German; Tribseer Damm 78; dm incl breakfast €20-25; Ⓟ ⓧ 🖵) In an expanse of parkland just around the corner from the Hauptbahnhof, a grand old 1897 building that once housed Stralsund's railway offices now has a much more active life as a 300-bed hostel. Dorms have comfy, capsule-like triple-decker bunks, and fun facilities include a guest-only bar, table tennis, pool tables, a barbecue area and a sandy beach volleyball court.

Pension Cobi (☎ 278 288; www.pension-cobi.de, in German; Jakobiturmstrasse 15; s €35-45, d €50-70 incl breakfast; Ⓟ 🛜) In the shadow of the Jakobikirche, this is a great location for exploring the Altstadt. Rooms are smart and clean, and some have balconies.

Altstadt Pension Peiss (☎ 303 580; www.altstadt -pension-peiss.de, in German; Tribseer Strasse 15; s €50-70, d €65-95; Ⓟ ⓧ) Spacious rooms with terracotta-coloured linen, Paul Gauguin prints and sparkling bathrooms combine with friendly, familiar service at this appealing guesthouse.

With a terrace, small garden and bike rack it's especially popular with cyclists.

Hiddenseer (☎ 289 2390; www.hotel-hiddenseer.d◾ in German; Hafenstrasse 12; s €55-90, d €80-120 incl break fast; Ⓟ ⓧ 🛜) A prime harbourside locatio by the Ozeaneum, comfortable rooms and highly regarded restaurant (mains €9.80 t €22.80, open 11am Monday to Saturday, fro 5pm Sunday) make the Hiddenseer one c Stralsund's best options.

Hotel Kontorhaus (☎ 289 800; www.kontorha -stralsund.de; Am Queerkanal 1; s/d €80/118, ste €120 incl brea fast; ⓧ 🛜) This sleek harbour hotel states i nautical intent from the outset, with brow Hamburg-style brick and lots of window some shaped like portholes. Developed by cruise-liner interior designer, the rooms fe◾ like upmarket cabins, especially those ove looking Rügen Island.

Steigenberger Baltic (☎ 2040; www.stralsur .steigenberger.de; Frankendamm 22; s/d incl breakfast fro €89/119; Ⓟ ⓧ 🛜) Try for a north-facin room at central Stralsund's most upmark◾ hotel for breathtaking views (especially ◾ twilight) over the Altstadt's rooftops an across the harbour to Rügen. Contemporar rooms are spacious and well equipped, wit huge desks and minibars, and service impressively personalised.

Eating

Kaffeehaus Strahl (☎ 278 566; Mönchstrasse 46; cak €1.60-3.20; ☻ 10am-8pm early Jul–mid-Sep, 10am-6p mid-Sep–early Jul; 🛜) Displays of huge hom◾ made cakes tempt you into this charm◾ ing, old-fashioned cafe and on down to i medieval cellar.

Fischermann's (☎ 292 322; An der Fährbrücke 3; mai €9-16.50; ☻ from 10am; 🛜) Don't be dissuade by Fischermann's touristy location in a ta redbrick warehouse on the waterfront. Mar of the diners packing its terrace like sardine on sunny days are locals, who head here for ◾ small but stellar selection of fish dishes – th views across to Rügen are just the bonus.

Hansekeller (☎ 703 840; Mönchstrasse 48; mai €9.80-13.90; ☻ 11am-midnight; Ⓥ) Entering an i◾ conspicuous archway and descending a flig◾ of steps brings you to this 16th-century cros vaulted brick cellar illuminated by glowi◾ lamps and flickering candles. Taking a se near the open kitchen lets you watch its che prepare regional specialities.

Altes Bankhaus (☎ 303 388; Heilgeiststrasse 4 mains €11.90-18.90; ☻ lunch & dinner; Ⓥ) This sle◾

1odern bistro housed in a 1913-built bank
1rns out creative dishes such as goat's cheese
1d smoked salmon gnocchi with whisky-
1ustard sauce, and Baileys ice cream with
1int leaves for dessert.

ourpick Tafelfreuden (☎ 299 260; Jungfernstieg 5a;
nch menu €15, dinner menus €37-46.50; ⊙ lunch & dinner Tue-
n) This sunflower-yellow, poppy-red-trimmed
'ooden villa was built in 1870 as a summer
ouse and is now home to a wonderfully con-
vial restaurant where set menus utilise fresh
roduce and are accompanied by an inspired
ine list. If you can't drag yourself away, it also
as three charming guest rooms (singles €45
» €60, doubles €60 to €75) with beach themes:
ghthouse', 'shell' and 'Strandkörbe', for the
·gion's iconic sheltered 'beach basket' seats.

Also recommended:

ur Fisch (☎ 306 609; Heilgeiststrasse 92; dishes €2.50-
.90; ⊙ 10am-6pm Mon-Fri, 11am-2pm Sat) Simple
nteen-style bistro dedicated to marine delights – from
h sandwiches to sumptuous platters of seafood.

orschliesserhaus (☎ 293 032; Am Kütertor 1; mains
.90-11.30; ⊙ lunch & dinner; ☎) Photogenic 1281
lf-timbered gatehouse in the city wall, dishing up solid
ples such as steaks.

·inking & Entertainment

hiskyhaus (☎ 289 280; Wasserstrasse 25; ⊙ 10am-6pm
n-Fri, 10am-4pm Sat, 2-5pm Sun) Deliberate over more
an 500 different whiskies at this specialist
/hisky house', which has a small bar for tast-
gs and organises regular talks and events.

8cht Vorne (☎ 281 888; www.carpediem-hst.de, in German;
denstrasse 45; ⊙ from 8pm) A scene stalwart that
rnishes Stralsund's student population with
Js, dancing and plenty of drinks specials.

T1 (☎ 282 8111; www.t1-stralsund.de, in German;
ilgeiststrasse 64; ⊙ from 8pm) A (somewhat) older
owd heads to this hip bar inside a central,
ep-gabled town house.

Fun/Lollipop (☎ 399 039; Grünhufer Bogen 11-14;
· from 9pm Wed-Sun) Stralsund's only large-
ale club is inside a shopping complex out
/ the HanseDom.

·tting There & Away

OAT
·e p748 for details of services to Rügen Island,
id p753 for boat services to Hiddensee
land.

AR & MOTORCYCLE
coming from the west – Lübeck, Wismar or
ostock – take the A20, then the B96.

TRAIN
Regional trains travel to/from Rostock
(€13.30, 1¼ hours), Berlin Hauptbahnhof
(from €36.50, 3½ hours) and Hamburg (from
€39.10, 3½ hours) at least every two hours.
There are frequent trains to Sassnitz (from
€8.40, 50 minutes) and Binz (from €10.30, 50
minutes), on Rügen Island.

Getting Around
Your feet will do just fine in the Altstadt.
Bicycle rental outlets include the **train station**
(☎ 625 81) and **SIC Punkt** (☎ 280 155; Harbour).

RÜGEN ISLAND
With its white-sand beaches, canopies of
chestnut, oak, elm and poplar trees, charming architecture and even its own national
park, Rügen is a microcosm of Mecklenburg–
Western Pomerania.

Frequented in the late 19th and early 20th
centuries by luminaries including Bismarck,
Thomas Mann and Albert Einstein, its chalk
coastline was also immortalised by Romantic
artist Caspar David Friedrich in 1818.
Unfortunately, Hitler was also beguiled by
Germany's largest island, choosing one of its
most beautiful beaches to build a monstrous
holiday resort for his troops. Later, GDR governments made Rügen their holiday choice.

Although summer draws thousands to its
shores, Rügen's lush 1000-sq-km surface area
fringed by 574km of coastline means there are
plenty of quiet corners to escape the crowds.

Orientation
Rügen's main and most accessible resort,
Binz, is in the centre of the island's east coast.
Southeast of Binz is the Mönchgut Peninsula,
where you'll find most of the other resorts,
such as Sellin and Göhren. North of Binz is the
Stubbenkammer area of white chalk cliffs in
the Jasmund National Park. In the west is the
more remote area of Wittow, with Germany's
most northeasterly point, Kap Arkona (Cape
Arkona). Altefähr lies just across the water
from Stralsund on the southwestern coast.

The island's official capital is Bergen (often
written Bergen auf Rügen), in the centre, but
it's of little interest to visitors other than as a
transport hub.

Information
Every town has at least one tourist office dis-
pensing local information. **Tourismuszentrale**

**MECKLENBURG–
WESTERN POMERANIA**

Rügen (☎ 03838-807 780; www.ruegen.de) can provide island-wide information.

Rügen's communities levy a tax on overnight guests of around €2.60 per person per night from May to September (dropping to around €1.50 from October to April; the tax varies slightly between resorts). Book accommodation *well* ahead in the busy summer months. Alternatively, good transport links make it possible to base yourself in Stralsund and take day trips from there.

Getting There & Away
BOAT

Weisse Flotte (☎ 268 10; www.weisse-flotte.com, in German) operates passenger and car ferries to Rügen. Passenger ferries leave Stralsund harbour for the village of Altefähr on Rügen's southwestern shore (one-way/return €2.50/3.80, bicycle €1.50/2.50, hourly 8.45am to 7pm mid-May to October). Car ferries leave from Stahlbrode, 15km southeast of Stralsund, for Glewitz (car/passenger/bicycle €4.50/1.20/1.20, approximately every 20 minutes between 6am and 8pm early April to late October).

Adler Schiffe (☎ 038378-477 90; www.adler-schiffe.de, in German) connects Peenemünde on Usedom Island with Göhren, Sellin and Binz (one-way €11.50) once daily from Easter to October.

For ferries from Rügen to Hiddensee, see p753.

Ferries to Trelleborg, Sweden, and Rønne, Denmark, sail from Sassnitz Mukran, about 7km south of Sassnitz' Bahnhof (linked by buses 18 and 20) – see p778.

CAR & MOTORCYCLE

The Rügenbrücke (2007) and neighbouring Rügendamm (1936) bridges cross the Strelasund channel from Stralsund onto the island. Both are toll-free. From Stralsund, take Karl-Marx-Strasse.

TRAIN

Direct IC trains connect Binz with Hamburg (€55, 3¾ hours), stopping in Stralsund. Local trains run hourly from Stralsund to Binz (€10.30, one hour) and also to Sassnitz (€10.30, one hour). To get to Putbus, change RE trains in Bergen.

On the island, a number of destinations are served by the Rasender Roland steam train (see right).

Getting Around
BICYCLE

Sharing roads with cars cannot always b avoided. Ask at tourist offices for the *Fahrra & Nahverkehrskarte* map, which include route recommendations and a list of hire ar repair shops.

BOAT

Reederei Ostsee-Tour (☎ 038392-3150; www.reede -ostsee-tour.de, in German) will carry you around th coast from Göhren to Sassnitz, via Sellin an Binz between April and October. Sample far include Göhren–Binz (€7), Göhren–Sassni (€8) and Sassnitz–Binz (€6).

BUS

RPNV Buses (☎ 03838-822 90; www.rpnv.de, in Germa link practically all communities, though ser ice can be sporadic.

Fares are according to distance: Binz Göhren, for example, costs €4.30. A day ca for the whole network is often a good de at €11. Local tourist offices have timetabl and maps (€1).

CAR & MOTORCYCLE

If you don't have much time, a car is the mo convenient (if not the most environmenta friendly) mode of transport on Rügen Islan The main artery is the B96.

TRAIN

More than just a tourist attraction, the **Rasend Roland** (☎ 038301-801 12; www.ruegensche-baederba .de, in German) steam train serves as a handy mo of transport as it chuffs between Putbus an Göhren (check online or with tourist offic for seasonal schedules). En route, it stops Binz, Jagdschloss Granitz, Sellin and Baab several services a day also go beyond Putb to Lauterbach Mole. Much of the narrow tra passes through sun-dappled forest.

The route is divided into five zones, ea costing €1.60. Bikes cost €2.10. There are d counts for families.

Binz
☎ 038393 / pop 5600

Rügen's largest and most celebrated seasi resort, 'Ostseebad' (Baltic Sea spa) Binz is romantic confection of ornate, white 19t century villas, white sand and blue water. roads are signed in Gothic script and lin with coastal pines and chestnut trees. Even

RÜGEN & HIDDENSEE ISLANDS

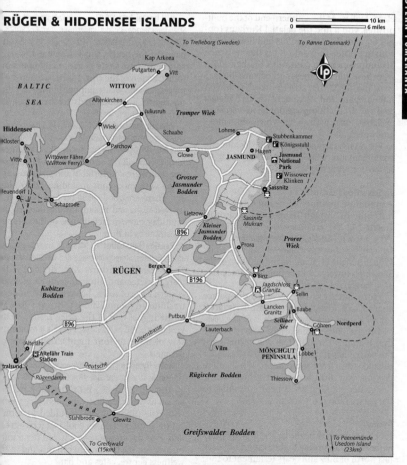

the signs of 21st-century capitalism abound, pecially along jam-packed Hauptstrasse, you n still feel the pull of history.

The town's spruced-up *Bäderarchitektur* pa architecture) – as the villas with their rought-iron latticework or carved wooden lconies are collectively called – is sepa-ted from the beach by the long tree-lined randpromenade. Once you step onto the nd, you have glorious views of Prorer Wiek y and its white chalk cliffs.

INFORMATION

urist information (www.ostseebad-binz.de; ☾ 9am-m Mon-Fri, 10am-6pm Sat & Sun Apr-Oct, 9am-4pm Mon-, 11am-4pm Sat & Sun Nov-Apr) is available from e following:

Fremdenverkehrsein (☎ 665 740; Paulstrasse 2) Room bookings.

Kurverwaltung (☎ 148 148; Heinrich-Heine-Strasse 7) General information. Has internet access.

Rügener Reiselotse (☎ 337 89; Proraer Chaussee 3f) Room bookings and holiday apartment rental.

Note that Binz has two train stations, the main Ostseebad Binz Bahnhof, serving RE and IC trains, and the Kleinbahnhof, 2km southeast, serving the Rasender Roland steam train (see opposite). Both are well signposted.

SIGHTS & ACTIVITIES
Strandpromenade

A highlight of Binz is simply strolling its 4km-long north–south beach promenade lined with elegant villas. At the southern end of the built-up area, you'll find the palatial Kurhaus (opposite), a lovely-looking 1908 building housing a luxury hotel. In front of it is the long pier. Strandpromenade continues further south from here, but becomes markedly less busy.

At the northern end of the beach is the IFA holiday park and its state-of-the-art **Vitamar pool** (☎ 911 02; Strandpromenade 74; adult per hr €3; ☯ 7.30am-10pm), with slides, whirlpool, saunas and waterfalls.

For catamaran and windsurfing lessons and equipment hire, contact **Sail & Surf Rügen** (☎ 411 30; www.segelschule-ruegen.de, in German).

Jagdschloss Granitz

A grandiose hunting palace built in 1723 on top of the 107m-high Tempelberg, **Jagdschloss Granitz** (☎ 2263; adult/concession/child €3/2.50/1.50; ☯ 9am-6pm Tue-Sat May-Sep, 10am-4pm Tue-Sun Oct-Apr) was significantly enlarged and altered by Wilhelm Malte I (including the addition of the 38m-high tower). Malte's flights of fancy also gave Rügen the grandiose Putbus.

From Binz, you can travel to the palace aboard the forest-green **Jagdschlossexpress** (☎ 338 80; www.jagdschlossexpress.de, in German; adult/child return €7.50/4), a motorised tourist 'train' that trundles through town. Alternatively, the palace has its own stop on the Rasender Roland steam train route (see p748). If you're driving, you must leave your vehicle in the designated parking areas before heading to the palace (about a 10-minute walk).

Prora

Prora was going to be the largest holiday camp in the world, according to the Nazis. The beach just north of Binz still bears testament to this: running parallel to the beautiful coast is a wall of six hideous six-storey buildings, each 500m long. Begun in 1936, this was intended as a *Kraft-durch-Freude* (strength through joy) resort for 20,000 people. The outbreak of WWII stopped its completion; after the war, Soviet troops tried to blow it up but failed.

What to do with the buildings is an ongoing debate. The Museumsmeile (Museum Row) occupies a portion of the buildings, but at the time of writing various development proposals were under consideration. Check the latest with Rügen's tourist offices.

SLEEPING

Binz' abundant accommodation includes private rooms (many in beautiful historic properties) starting from €15 per person.

DJH hostel (☎ 325 97; www.binz.jugendherberge.d Strandpromenade 35; dm under/over 26yr €22.90/28, €53.80/64.60 incl breakfast; ℗ ☒ ☐ ☜) As it bang on the beach, this hostel has the sam stunning views as its elegant neighbours b for a fraction of the cost. It's been extensivel revamped with well-equipped lounge and din ing rooms, and bunk beds creatively painte with a sea-green wash.

Villa Schwanebeck (☎ 2013; www.villa-schwanebeck.c in German; Margaretenstrasse 18; s €39-60, d €50-98 ir breakfast; ℗ ☒ ☜) The decor at this centra family-run villa is somewhat old-fashione but rooms are comfortable and spacious, an come with mod cons including DVD play ers. There are good deals on half-pension a its well-respected restaurant, particularly f multiday stays; in fact, it's one of the cheape guesthouses in Binz.

Pension Haus Colmsee (☎ 325 56; www.hauscolms .de, in German; Strandpromenade 8; d incl breakfast €6 95; ℗ ☒) This historic villa, situated at th leafy, quieter and altogether most pleasar eastern edge of town, has relatively moder uncluttered rooms. Those with a sea view a at the higher end of the price scale, but a well worth the extra cost. There's a minimu stay of three or four nights, depending o demand.

Hotel Nymphe (☎ 122 0000; www.hotel-nymphe.c in German; Strandpromenade 48; s €69-94, d €90-122 ir breakfast; ℗ ☒ ☐ ☜) Binz' newest hotel is vision of white, with streamlined, airy room with pale timber floors, moulded furnitur subtle colours such as cool pistachio-gree and iPod docking stations. If you're taking break from the beach, you can unwind in th wellness centre, cafes and bar.

Strandhotel (☎ 3810; www.strandhotelbinz.de, German; Strandpromenade 33; d €82-159; ℗ ☒ ☜) Son of the guest rooms at this boutique beac front gem have period detailing, while othe are ultra-contemporary. Its excellent bas ment restaurant, Fischmarkt (mains €11.9 to €17.90, open from noon), is reached via short flight of steps below its sun-drenche front terrace.

Hotel am Meer & Spa (☎ 440; www.hotel-a -meer.de; Strandpromenade 34; s €110-200, d €140-26 ℗ ☒ ☜ ☒) Light-filled rooms at this swis spa hotel – some over two floors – are decke out with porthole windows, striking shades red, yellow, green and blue, and Bose soun systems. Prebooking online entitles you to free beer, wine or coffee and cake.

Kurhaus Binz (☎ 6650; www.travelcharme.de; trandpromenade 27; s/d/ste from €102/164/226; P ⊠ 🖳 🛜 🕿) For the ultimate in traditional style and luxury, this lemon-yellow ındmark is it. Many of its sand-and-sky-ɔned rooms have balconies or terraces. And 'ith indoor and outdoor pools, a library with n open fireplace, and no fewer than six res-aurants, you might find it hard to step any ırther away than the beach out front.

ATING

'he beachfront Strandpromenade is lined 'ith restaurants serving everything from izzas and ice creams to gastronomic xtravaganzas.

Fischräucherei Kuse (☎ 322 49; Strandpromenade dishes from €1.30; ⏱ 9am-8pm) For some of the ıost delicious and certainly the cheapest fish ı Rügen, follow your nose – literally – to the ır southern end of the Strandpromenade, 'here fish has been freshly smoked in its utdoor smokehouse since 1900. Choose ·om simple fish sandwiches and meals to ine at its indoor tables, on the terrace, or ıke to the beach.

Münsterteicher (☎ 143 80; Strandpromenade 17-18; ains €9.90-19.80; ⏱ from noon) The Strandhalle's ister restaurant, fronted by a terrace strewn 'ith green-and-white-canopied *Strandkörbe* ɔeach chairs), serves Argentine steaks, pasta, sh and sushi.

Poseidon (☎ 337 10; Lottumstrasse 1; mains €11.50-".50; ⏱ from noon) One of the most respected ɛstaurants in Binz, this lovely historic villa ne block west of the Strandpromenade serves ımously fresh catches of the day and even as a menu section that takes you 'round the ɛrring'. For those who don't eat fish, venison another speciality.

ourpick Strandhalle (☎ 315 64; Strandpromenade mains €11.90-18.40; ⏱ noon-11pm) Toni Münster-ɛicher's Strandhalle is a local legend that romises – and delivers – fine cooking t everyday prices. At the quiet southern nd of Strandpromenade, the atmospheric all's vaulted-ceiling and wood-lined inte-or is eclectically decked out with church tatues, chandeliers, curtains of fairy lights nd shelves of antiquarian books. Don't pass p Münsterteicher's signature pear-and-ɛlery soup with red peppercorns followed by altic cod cooked in a potato crust and the *cheiterhaufen* ('pyre') dessert of baked and ıaramelised apple.

South Rügen

SELLIN
☎ 038303 / pop 18,586

The symbol of 'Ostseebad' Sellin is its *Seebrüucke* (pier), an ornate, turreted pavilion sitting out over the water at the end of a long wooden causeway. The original pier was built in 1906, following a boating accident while bringing visitors to shore (the only access to Sellin at the time). Twice destroyed by storms, what you see today is a 1998 reproduction based on a model from 1927, which now houses cafes and bars.

To reach the pier from Sellin's southern shores (and the Sellin Ost steam train station), follow the long Seepark Promenade through grassy parkland until you reach the covered archway of the Seepark Passage, flanked by ice cream shops. Continuing straight ahead takes you uphill along the main street, Wilhelmstrasse, lined with elegant villas. The pier is at the far northern end of Wilhelmstrasse, as is Sellin's loveliest white-sand beach.

Sellin's **Kurverwaltung** (☎ 160; www.ostseebad -sellin.de; Warmbadstrasse 4; ⏱ 8.30am-8pm Mon-Fri, 1-5pm Sat & Sun Jun-Sep, 8.30am-4pm Mon-Fri, 1-5pm Sat Oct-May) has tourist information and can help you find a room.

Plentiful accommodation includes a **DJH hostel** (☎ 950 99; www.sellin.jugendherberge.de; Kiefernweg 4; dm under/over 26yr incl breakfast €25.20/30.80; ⊠) 400m from the sea. Rising above the pier is the town's most famous hotel, the **Kurhaus Sellin** (☎ 951 00; www.travelcharme.com; Wilhelmstrasse 27; s €69-149, d €98-238, ste from €138 incl breakfast; ⏱ Mar-Nov; P ⊠ 🖳 🛜), sister property of Binz' iconic Kurhaus (left), with nostalgic wicker-furnished rooms, spa treatments, and romantic suites tucked inside its tower.

The Rasender Roland steam train (see p748) stops in Sellin West and Ostseebad Sellin (also known as Sellin Ost), four minutes apart. Disembark at the latter for the town centre.

GÖHREN
☎ 038308 / pop 1278

On the Nordperd spit, Göhren's stunning 7km-long stretch of sand – divided into the sleepier Südstrand and the more developed Nordstrand – lives up to its hype as Rügen's best resort beach.

Apart from its beach, Göhren has a collection of four sites: the historical Heimats-museum and the Museumshof farm (open year-round), and the unusual chimney-less Rookhus and the museum ship *Luise* (open mid-April to mid-October), which together make up the **Monchgüter Museen** (☎ 2175; www .moenchguter-museen-ruegen.de, in German; single museum adult/concession €3/2.50, combined ticket €8/6). Check individual opening hours for each at the **Kurverwaltung** (☎ 667 90; www.ostseebad-goehren.de, in German; Poststrasse 9; ☙ 9am-6pm Mon-Fri, 9am-noon Sat May-Sep, 9am-noon & 1-4.30pm Mon, Wed & Thu, 9am-noon & 1-6pm Tue, 9am-3pm Fri Oct-Apr), which can also help with hotel and private room bookings.

The **Regenbogen Resort** (☎ 901 20; www.regen bogen-camps.de, in German; Nordstrand; adult €4.50-8.45, tent €3-12.60, car €2.10-4.30) is the island's largest camping ground, idyllically situated in the woods behind the dunes. You'll find cafes and restaurants by the beach and up in the town.

Göhren is the eastern terminus of the steam train route Rasender Roland (see p748).

PUTBUS
☎ 038301 / pop 2700

Putbus appears like a sci-fi mirage from the middle of modest farming villages. At its heart lies a gigantic circular plaza, known as the **Circus**, resembling a roulette wheel, with its alternating wedges of green and paving, and 16 large white neoclassical buildings dotted around it. Nearby, the town's 75-hectare **English park** is filled with ginkgos, cypresses, Japanese spruces and other exotic botanical species. This civic oddity was conceived and realised in the 19th century by ambitious local prince, Wilhelm Malte I of Putbus (1783–1854), and stands today as the last European town to be purpose-built as a royal seat. Priding itself on being Rügen's cultural centre, it has the island's only **theatre** (☎ 8080; www.theater-putbus.de, in German; Markt 13), built in 1819.

Although hotels are limited and hence the town is best seen on a day trip, you can make accommodation enquiries at **Putbus Info** (☎ 431; www.putbus.de, in German; Orangerie, Alleestrasse 35; ☙ 9am-5pm Mon-Fri, 11am-5pm Sat & Sun May-Oct, 9am-4pm Mon-Fri, 11am-4pm Sat & Sun Nov-Apr). It's inside the **Orangerie** (☎ 745; adult/concession/child €2.50/2/1; ☙ hours same as Putbus Info) gallery, a town highlight.

The Rasender Roland steam train (see p748) and RE trains to/from Bergen (€2.10, nine minutes) use the same train station.

LAUTERBACH
☎ 038301

The standout feature of the yacht harbou southeast of Putbus is its **Schwimmende Ferienhäuser** (Swimming Holiday Homes; ☎ 809 www.im-jaich.de; Am Yachthafen; apt 2-4 people €6 115, 6 people €80-140 plus final cleaning fee €35): ne Scandinavian-style bungalows and two-store huts that float in the harbour on individu pontoons. The same company also runs sailing school and organises boat hire, an has land-based accommodation.

Lauterbach Mole is the westerly terminus the Rasender Roland steam train (see p748

North Rügen
JASMUND NATIONAL PARK & AROUND

The rugged beauty of Jasmund Nationa Park first came to national attention than to the romanticised paintings of Casp David Friedrich in the early 19th centur His favourite spot was the **Stubbenkammer**, a area at the northern edge of the park, whe jagged white-chalk cliffs plunge into th jade-coloured sea.

By far the most famous of the Stubbe kammer cliffs is the **Königsstuhl** (King's Chair; adm sion €1) – at 117m, it's Rügen's highest poin although the scenery is often marred b everyone else trying to see it too. Fewer peop make the trek a few hundred metres east to th **Victoria-Sicht** (Victoria View), which provide the best view of the Königsstuhl itself.

The **Nationalpark-Zentrum Königsstu** (☎ 38392-661 70; www.koenigsstuhl.com; adult/child und 14yr €6/3; ☙ 9am-7pm Easter-Oct, 10am-5pm Nov-Easte has multimedia displays on environment themes, a 'climbing forest' and a restaurant

Buses 20 (from Göhren, Sellin and Bin Prora and Sassnitz) and 23 (from Bergen, Bin Prora and Sassnitz) go to the Königsstuh and offer a Königsstuhl Ticket (adult/fami €15/30) that includes bus travel and entry the Nationalpark-Zentrum Königsstuhl.

From April to October, **Reederei Ostsee-To** (☎ 038392-3150; www.reederei-ostsee-tour.de, in Germa operates several daily trips from Göhren (€17 Sellin (€16.50), Binz (€15.50) and Sassni (€11.50) around the chalk cliffs.

If you're feeling energetic, a spectacular wa to approach the area is by making the 10km tre from Sassnitz along the coast through the ar cient forest of Stubnitz. The trail also takes yo past the gorgeous **Wissower Klinken** chalk clif another vista famously painted by Friedrich.

Drivers must leave vehicles in the (paid) arking lot in Hagen, then either catch the nuttle bus or walk 2.5km past the Herthasee ke through the forest.

Panorama-Hotel Lohme (☎ 038302-9221; www hme.com; Dorfstrasse 35, Lohme; s €52-62, d €68-136; P)), west of the national park in Lohme, is ptly named. The hotel has stunning views om rooms at the higher end of the price cale, and from what may be the island's lost romantic restaurant (mains €9.40 to 20.60, open 7.30am to 9.30pm), particu- rly when the sun sets over Kap Arkona on mmer nights.

While most people only pass through ssnitz (population 10,747), at the south- rn end of the national park, the town has een redeveloping its Altstadt and its har- our is home to a British submarine-turned- useum, the **HMS Otus** (☎ 038392-315 16; www.hms tus.com; Hafenstrasse 12; admission €5.50; 10am-7pm or-Oct, 10am-4pm Nov-Mar). Find out more from e **tourist office** (www.insassnitz.de) Bahnhofstrasse a (☎ 038392-6490; 9am-6pm Mon-Fri, 10am-6pm t, 2-6pm Sun); Strandpromenade 12 (☎ 038392-669 45; 10am-5pm), which can also help with room ookings. See p748 for transport details, icluding international ferries.

AP ARKONA

ügen ends at the rugged cliffs of **Kap Arkona**, ith its famous pair of lighthouses: the square, quat **Schinkel-Leuchtturm**, completed in 1827, nd the cylindrical **Neuer Leuchtturm**, in busi- ess since 1902.

A few metres east of the lighthouses is e **Burgwall**, a complex that harbours the emains of the Tempelburg, a Slavic temple nd fortress. The castle was taken over by e Danes in 1168, paving the way for the hristianisation of Rügen.

Most people sail around the cape (with- ut landing) on boat tours. **Reederei Ostsee- our** (☎ 038392-3150; www.reederei-ostsee-tour.de, in erman; tour €21; Tue-Fri May-Sep) operates four- our tours from Binz at 1.15pm and Sassnitz t 2pm.

Driving all the way to the cape is not al- wed for environmental reasons. You must ave your vehicle in the gateway village of utgarten, then take the gas-powered **Arkona ahn** (☎ 038391-132 13; www.arkonabahn.de, in German; ult/child €2/0.50) or make the 1.5km journey by ot or bicycle. Putgarten is served by bus 11 om Altenkirchen in central Wittow. (To get

to Altenkirchen, you will need to travel from Sassnitz or Bergen.)

Unusual adventure tours run by **Rügen Safari** (☎ 038309-708 62; www.ruegen-safari.de, in German) in- clude jeep safaris, mountain biking or Indian canoe tours with real tepees!

HIDDENSEE ISLAND
☎ 038300 / pop 1076

'Dat söte Länneken' (the sweet little land) is much mythologised in the German national imagination. This tiny patch off Rügen's west- ern coast measures 18km long and just 1.8km at its widest point. What makes it so sweet is its breathtaking, remote landscape. The heath and meadows of the 'Dornbush' area, with the island's landmark lighthouse and wind- buckled trees, extend north of the village of Kloster, while dunes wend their way south from the main village of Vitte to Neuendorf. In the 19th and early 20th centuries, Hiddensee bewitched artists and writers including Thomas Mann and Bertolt Brecht, as well as Gerhart Hauptmann, who is buried here.

Cars are banned on Hiddensee but bike hire places are everywhere. Alternatively, you can see the island at a gentle pace aboard the island's clip-clopping horse-drawn carriages; you'll find them around the harbours and in Kloster.

The **tourist office** (☎ 642 26; www.seebad-hiddensee .de; Norderende 162, Vitte; 9am-5pm Mon-Fri, 10am-noon Sat May-Sep, 9am-4pm Mon-Fri Apr & Oct, 9am-3pm Nov-Mar) has a seasonal **branch** (10am-12.30pm & 1.30-5pm Mon-Fri, 10am-12.30pm Sat & Sun May-Sep, 10am-noon & 1-4pm Mon-Fri, 10am-12.30pm Sat Easter-end Apr, 10am- noon & 1-5pm Fri Oct) at Kloster harbour. A spa tax of €1.50 from April to October (€1 from November to March) is levied by hotels for overnight guests, and by ferry companies for day-trippers.

There are no camp sites on Hiddensee, but inexpensive private rooms are available in the villages, or you can rock to sleep in dorm-style cabins aboard the **Hotelschiff Caprivi 93** (☎ 501 62; www.hotelschiff-hiddensee.de, in German; Springe 39, Vitte; dm incl breakfast from €20). In a charming timbered building, the **Hotel Hitthim** (☎ 6660; www.hitthim.de; Hafenweg, Kloster; s €52.50-72.50, d €90-155 incl half- pension, breakfast €12) is one of Hiddensee's best accommodation options, with floral wall- papered rooms, and home-cooked meals in its lamp-lit restaurant.

Ferries run by **Reederei Hiddensee** (☎ 0180- 321 2150; www.reederei-hiddensee.de, in German) leave

Schaprode, on Rügen's western shore, up to 12 times daily year-round. Return fares to Neuendorf are €14.30, to Kloster and Vitte €16.60. The same company offers services from Stralsund up to three times daily between April and October. Return tickets to Neuendorf cost €17.90; to Vitte and Kloster €18.70. Check the website for other services.

GREIFSWALD
☎ 03834 / pop 54,200

The old university town of Greifswald, south of Stralsund, was largely unscathed by WWII thanks to a courageous German colonel who surrendered to Soviet troops (a move usually punishable by execution).

The skyline of this former Hanseatic city – as once perfectly captured by native son Caspar David Friedrich – is defined by three churches: the 'Langer Nikolas' ('Long Nicholas'), 'Dicke Marie' ('Fat Mary') and the 'Kleine Jakob' ('Small Jacob').

Greifswald also has a pretty harbour in the charming district of Wieck, reached by a Dutch-style wooden drawbridge, and its medieval city walls have been turned into a wide, tree-shaded promenade. The town is a convenient gateway for the island of Usedom.

Orientation & Information

Greifswald's Altstadt is northeast of the train station, on the bank of the Ryck River. The mostly pedestrianised Lange Strasse bisects the Altstadt from east to west. Around 4km east is the gull- and mast-filled harbour neighbourhood of Wieck. The ruins of the 1225 Eldena cloister famously portrayed by Caspar David Friedrich are a few minutes' walk south of Wieck.

Helpful **Greifswald Information** (☎ 521 380; www .greifswald.de; Markt; ⏰ 9am-6pm Mon-Fri, 10am-2pm Sat May-Sep plus 10am-2pm Sun Jul & Aug, 9am-5pm Mon-Fri Oct-Apr) is in the Rathaus.

Sights
DOM ST NIKOLAI

The 100m onion-domed tower of the **Dom St Nikolai** (☎ 2627; Domstrasse; ⏰ 10am-6pm Mon-Sat, 10am-12.30pm & 3-6pm Sun) rises above a row of historic facades, giving the cathedral the nickname 'Long Nicholas'. It has an austere, whitewashed interior with a large and solitary golden cross. You can climb the tower (adult/concession €2/1.50) and, yes, there's a great view from the top.

MARKT & AROUND

The historic buildings ringing the Markt hi• at Greifswald's stature in the Middle Age The **Rathaus**, at the western end, started li• as a 14th-century department store wit characteristic arcaded walkways. Among th redbrick **gabled houses** on the eastern side, th **Coffee House** (No 11) is gorgeous and a goo example of a combined living and storag house owned by Hanseatic merchants.

Greifswald's outstanding **Pommersch• Landesmuseum** (Pomeranian State Museum; ☎ 831 2 www.pommersches-landesmuseum.de, in German; Rakow Strasse 9; adult/concession €6/4; ⏰ 10am-6pm Tue-Su links three Franciscan monastery building via a 73m-long, glassed-in hall. There's major gallery of paintings, including half dozen by Caspar David Friedrich, as well a history and natural history exhibits.

Northeast of the Markt is the 12th-centu• redbrick **Marienkirche** (☎ 2263; Brüggstrass ⏰ 10am-4pm Mon-Fri, 11am-3pm Sat, 10.15am-1pm Sur a square three-nave tower trimmed with tu rets. It's easy to see why it's teasingly calle 'Fat Mary'.

UNIVERSITY AREA

Close to the train station is the university di trict, with Rubenowplatz at its heart. There a fanciful neo-Gothic **monument** to Heinric Rubenow, the university's founder, in th middle of the little park. The university's mai building flanks the square's south side. Th resplendently restored baroque **Aula** (assemb hall) is the highlight of a 45-minute **guided to•** (☎ 861 123; €2.50; ⏰ phones staffed 9am-1pm Mon-Fr English-language tours can be arranged if yo call in advance.

East of Rubenowplatz is the 'Kleine Jakob• the modest **Jakobikirche** (☎ 502 209; Karl-Marx-Pla 4; ⏰ 10am-4pm Mon & Thu, 10am-2pm Tue, 10am-3pm F 10am-noon Sat, 10.30am-noon Sun, closed Wed).

Sleeping & Eating

Greifswald has some lovely hotels (many i beautiful historic buildings), with more i the pretty harbourside precinct of Wieck; th tourist office can make bookings.

Hotel Alter Speicher (☎ 777 00; www.alter-speich .de, in German; Rossmühlenstrasse 25; s €69-74, d €84-8 🅿 🗶 🛜) In a renovated warehouse ove looking the river just outside the centre, sim ple but appealing timber-furnished roon and a good regional restaurant make the Alt• Speicher great value for money.

Hotel Galerie (☎ 773 7830; www.hotelgalerie.de, in
rman; Mühlenstrasse 10; s/d €78/98; P ✗) Rooms
this sparkling modern property across from
ie state museum are filled with a changing
illection of works by contemporary artists.

Zum Alten Fritz (☎ 578 30; Am Markt 13; mains
.90-15.90; ⏰ from 11am) Greifswald's branch of
is wonderful local brewery chain occupies
ie of the most striking step-gabled redbrick
iildings on the Markt. Many of its dishes are
ioked in its own beer.

Fischer-Hütte (☎ 839 654; An der Mühle 8; mains
.90-23.40; ⏰ from 11.30am) An exquisitely pre-
nted meal at the 'fisherman's house' in
'ieck might start with potato soup with a
ied scallop and black caviar and move onto
ie house speciality – smoked herring with
iango in creamy curry sauce, topped off by
iarzipan parfait with sesame seed brittle on
ied apricot salsa.

etting There & Away
here are regular train services to Stralsund
:9, 25 minutes), Rostock (from €17.80,
½ hours) and Berlin Hauptbahnhof (from
i2.90, 2½ to three hours).

The A20 connects Greifswald with Lübeck
id Rostock, and links with the A11 to
erlin.

etting Around
's easy to get around Greifswald's centre on
ot, but to reach outlying areas you may want
► make use of the bus system. Single/day
ckets cost €1.70/3.50. You can reach Wieck
.a a 4km foot/bike path, or by bus 6 or 7. If
iu're driving, head east towards Wolgast; the
irn-off is on your left.

SEDOM ISLAND

sedom (Uznam in Polish) lies in the delta of
e Oder River about 30km east of Greifswald,
id is separated from the German main-
nd by the wide Peene River. The island's
istern tip lies across the border in Poland.
lthough the German side accounts for 373
₁ km of the island's total 445-sq-km sur-
ce area, the population of the Polish side is
rger (45,000 compared with 31,500 on the
erman side).

Nicknamed *Badewanne Berlins* (Berlin's
athtub) in the prewar period, the island

was a sought-after holiday spot in GDR days
for its 42km stretch of beautiful beach and
average 1906 annual hours of sunshine that
make it the sunniest place in Germany. As
sprucing up continues it's coming into its
own. Elegant 1920s villas with wrought-
iron balconies grace many traditional resorts along its northern spine, including
Zinnowitz, Ückeritz, Bansin, Heringsdorf
and Ahlbeck. All have tourist offices. **Usedom
Tourismus** (☎ 038378-477 10; www.usedom.de) can
book accommodation island-wide.

It was at Peenemünde, on the island's western tip, that Wernher von Braun developed
the V2 rocket, first launched in October 1942.
It flew 90km high and a distance of 200km
before plunging into the Baltic – the first
time in history that a flying object exited the
earth's atmosphere. The research and testing complex was destroyed by the Allies in
July 1944, but the Nazis continued their research in Nordhausen in the southern Harz
(see Mittelbau Dora, p253). At the **Historisch-
Technisches Informationszentrum** (Historical &
Technological Information Centre; ☎ 038371-5050; www
.peenemuende.de; adult/concession €6/4; ⏰ 10am-6pm
Apr-Sep, 10am-4pm Oct, 10am-4pm Tue-Sun Nov-Mar)
Peenemünde is immodestly billed as 'the
birthplace of space travel'. The Peenemünde
harbour is another popular spot, with plenty
of boats and the battered Russian **U461 submarine** (☎ 285 66; www.u-461.de; adult/family €6/11;
⏰ 10am-6pm Apr-Jun & mid-Sep–Oct, 9am-9pm Jul–mid-
Sep, 10am-4pm Nov-Mar).

Getting There & Away
Direct **UBB** (Usedomer Bäderbahn; www.ubb-online.com, in
German) trains from Stralsund (and Greifswald)
traverse the German side of Usedom, stopping at coastal resorts before terminating
in Świnoujście (Swinemünde in German)
just over the Polish border. Peenemünde is
on a branch line; change in Züssow. You'll
also need to change in Züssow for Usedom
if you're arriving from points south or west.
UBB's Usedom day card costs €12.

See p748 for ferries between Peenemünde
and Rügen Island.

Polferries (☎ in Poland +48-94-3552119; www.pol
ferries.com) connect Świnoujście with Rønne
and Copenhagen in Denmark, and Ystad
in Sweden.

Directory

CONTENTS

ACCOMMODATION

Germany has all types of places to unpack your suitcase, from hostels, camping grounds and family hotels to chains, business hotels and luxury resorts. Reservations are a good idea between June and September, around major holidays (p766), festivals and cultural events (mentioned throughout this book and also on p24) and trade shows.

This book lists accommodation as budget, midrange and top end. Listings are in ascending order of price. Unless noted, rates include VAT and breakfast, which is usually a generous all-you-can-eat buffet. Places we consider extra special have been identified as **our pick**.

Some regional variation notwithstanding, budget stays will have you checking in at hostels, country inns, *Pensionen* (B&Bs or small hotels) or simple family hotels charging €80 or less (per double, less in rural areas).

Midrange properties generally offer the best value for money. Expect to pay between €80 and €150 for a clean, comfortable, decent-sized double with at least a modicum of style, a private bathroom, cable TV and direct-dial telephone. Communal saunas and basic fitness facilities are quite common as well.

Top-end places start at €150 and offer luxurious amenities, perhaps a scenic location, special decor or historical ambience. Many also have pools, saunas, business centres or other upmarket facilities.

To help you determine whether a property listed in this book is right for you, we've devised a handful of icons. Hotels with on-site parking, for instance, sport the parking icon **P**. Properties with designated nonsmoking rooms or floors are identified with ☒. These are very common now and the number of properties that are completely nonsmoking is on the rise. By contrast, rooms with air-con are exceedingly rare, except in upmarket chain hotels; properties that do have at least some rooms with air-con are denoted with ☒. Hostels and hotels offering guest PCs with internet access are identified with an internet icon ☐, while ☎ indicates the availability of wi-fi. Places with their own swimming pool are denoted by ☒.

Prices listed in this book do not take into account promotional discounts. City hotels geared to the suit brigade often try to lure leisure travellers with lower weekend rates. Also check hotel websites (listed throughout this book) for discount rates or packages.

Reservations

Many tourist office and hotel websites let you check for room availability and make advance reservations. Quite a few of those reviewed in this book can also be booked via Lonely Planet's own website (see the boxed text, p759). Other online booking services include www.venere.com and www.hotel.de. Last-minute bargains can often be found at www.hrs.de (in German). For independent hostels, try www.hostelworld.com, www.gomio.com and www.hostels.com.

PRACTICALITIES

- Electrical supply is 220V AC, 50 Hz.

- Widely read daily newspapers include the *Süddeutsche Zeitung*, *Die Welt* and *Der Tagesspiegel* (all quite centrist), as well as the more conservative *Frankfurter Allgemeine Zeitung*. *Die Zeit* is a high-brow weekly with in-depth reporting.

- *Der Spiegel* and *Focus* magazines are popular German news weeklies, and *The Economist*, *Time* and *Newsweek* are sold in train stations and major news-stands.

- Radio stations are regional with most featuring a mixed format of news, talk and music.

- Germany uses the metric system (see conversion chart on inside front cover).

- GSM 900/1800 is used for mobile (cell) phones.

- For women's clothing sizes, a German size 36 equals size 6 in the US and size 10 in the UK, then increases in increments of two, making size 38 a US 8 and UK 12.

If you're already in town, swing by the tourist office, where staff can assist you in finding last-minute lodging. After hours, vacancies may be posted in the window or in a display case.

When making a room reservation directly with a property, tell your host what time they can expect you and stick to your plan or ring again. Many well-meaning visitors have lost rooms by showing up late.

Camping

Camping grounds are generally well maintained but may get jammed in summer. The core season runs from May to September, although quite a few remain open year-round. Book early or show up before noon to snap up any spots that may have been vacated that morning. Having your own wheels is definitely an asset, as many sites are in remote locales that are not, or only poorly, served by public transport.

There are usually separate charges per person (between €3 and €6), tent (€2.50 to €8, depending on size) and car (€2 to €4) and additional fees for hot showers, resort tax, electricity and sewage disposal. A Camping Card International (see p765) may yield some savings.

The *ADAC Camping & Caravaning Führer,* available in bookshops, is a comprehensive German-language guide. Other handy sources include www.eurocampings.de and www.alanrogers.com.

Camping on public land is not permitted. Pitching a tent on private property requires the consent of the landowner.

Farm Stays

A holiday on a working farm (*Urlaub auf dem Bauernhof*) is inexpensive and a great opportunity to get close to nature in relative comfort. This type of vacation is especially popular with families. Kids get to interact with their favourite barnyard animals and maybe help with everyday chores. Accommodation ranges from bare-bones rooms with shared facilities to fully-furnished holiday flats. Minimum stays are common. A variety of farm types are on offer, including organic, dairy and equestrian farms as well as wine estates. Places advertising *Landurlaub* (country holiday) no longer actively work their farms. The best establishments are quality controlled by the Deutsche Landwirtschafts-Gesellschaft (DLG; German Agricultural Association). To learn more about farm holidays, check www.landtourismus.de, www.bauernhofurlaub-deutschland.de or www.bauernhofurlaub.com (in German).

Holiday Flats & Homes

If you want to get to know a place better, renting for a week or two can be ideal, especially for budget-minded travellers, self-caterers,

THE 'CURSE' OF THE KUR

Most German resort and spa towns charge their overnight guests a so-called *Kurtaxe* (resort tax). Fees range from €1 to €4 per person per night and are added to your hotel bill. The money subsidises visitor-oriented events and services, such as concerts, lectures and walking tours, and sometimes free public transportation.

SMOKE & MIRRORS

Germany was one of the last countries in Europe to legislate smoking, which it did in 2007–08, and, by all accounts, it hasn't done a very effective job. Each of the 16 states was allowed to introduce its own antismoking laws, creating a rather confusing patchwork. In most states, smoking is a no-no in schools, hospitals, airports, train stations and other public facilities. But when it comes to bars, pubs, cafes and restaurants, every state does it just a little differently. Bavaria has the toughest laws, which ban smoking practically everywhere, although an exception was made for Oktoberfest tents; so-called 'smoking clubs' are also permitted. In most states, lighting up is allowed in designated smoking rooms. However, in July 2008 Germany's highest court ruled this scheme unconstitutional because it discriminates against one-room establishments. These may now allow smoking provided they serve no food and only admit patrons over 18. So far only Berlin has introduced this compromise, but other states are likely to follow suit. In any case, enforcement has been sporadic, to say the least, despite the threat of fines. The situation is fluid.

---

families and small groups. Tourist offices have lists of holiday flats *(Ferienwohnungen* or *Ferien-Appartements)*. Some *Pensionen*, inns, hotels and even farmhouses also rent out apartments. Stays under a week usually incur a surcharge, and there's almost always a 'cleaning fee' payable at the end. A central online booking service is www.atraveo.de.

Hostels
DJH HOSTELS

Germany's 600 Hostelling International–affiliated hostels are run by the **Deutsches Jugendherbergswerk** (DJH; www.jugendherberge.de) and are open to people of all ages, although they're especially popular with school and youth groups, families and sports clubs. Most have recently been modernised but often can't quite shake that institutional feel. Still, smaller dorms and private rooms for families and couples, often with private bathroom, are increasingly common. Almost all hostels can accommodate mobility-impaired travellers.

Rates in gender-segregated dorms or in family rooms range from €13 to €29 per person, including linen and breakfast; optional lunch and dinner cost around €5 extra each. People over 27 are charged an extra €3 or €4. If space is tight, hostels may give priority to people under 27, except for those travelling as a family.

Unless you're a member of your home country's HI association, you need to buy either a Hostelling International Card for €15.50 (valid for one year) or six individual stamps costing €3.10 per night. Both are available at any DJH hostel. Around half of German DJH hostels can now be booked online at www.jugendherberge.de and about 60 can also be booked on the HI website (www.hihostels.com). Alternatively, just contact the hostel directly by phone, fax or email.

INDEPENDENT HOSTELS

Germany was slow to embrace the backpacker hostel concept, but in recent years indies have been popping up all over the country. Although they sometimes accept school groups, they generally cater for individual travellers, welcome people of all ages and attract a more convivial, international crowd than DJH hostels. Most now offer private quarters with bathrooms, and even apartments with kitchens, alongside multi-bed dorms, making them an excellent budget choice even if you've traded your backpack for a rolling suitcase.

No two hostels are alike, but typical facilities include communal kitchens, bars, cafes, TV lounges, lockers, internet terminals and laundry facilities. There are no curfews, and staff tend to be savvy, energetic, eager to help and multilingual. Dorms are mixed, although women-only dorms can usually be set up on request. Most hostels charge an extra fee (around €3) for linen; some also serve optional breakfast but no other meals.

Several dozen indies have joined together in an alliance known as the **Backpacker Network** (www.backpackernetwork.de, partly in English). Some hostels can also be booked via this site. Other recommended online booking systems are www.gomio.com, www.hostelworld.com, www.hostels.com and www.hostels.net.

Hotels

Hotels range from small family-run properties to cookie-cutter international chains to luxurious designer abodes. Those serving only breakfast are called *Hotel garni*. An official classification system exists, based on a scale of one to five stars, but it's voluntary and few hotels participate. Even so, this being Germany, you can generally expect even budget abodes to be spotlessly clean, comfortable and well run.

In older, family-run hotels, individual rooms often vary dramatically in terms of size, decor and amenities. The cheapest may have shared facilities, while others come with a shower cubicle installed but no private toilet; only the pricier ones have their own bathrooms. If possible, ask to see several rooms before committing.

If you're the romantic type, consider staying in a *Schlosshotel,* a modernised castle, palace or country manor that drips with character and history. Some belong to an association called Romantik Hotels (www.romantikhotels com). Also try www.castles.de.

Long-Term Rentals

If you're going to stay in any particular German city for a month or longer, consider renting a room or a flat through a *Mitwohnzentrale* (flat-sharing agency). These agencies match up visitors with fully furnished vacant flats, houses or rooms in shared houses. Rates vary by agency, city and type of accommodation, but the final tally is likely to be less than what you'd pay for a similar standard in a hotel. Many *Mitwohnzentralen* now also arrange short-term stays, although prices are higher.

Home Company (www.home-company.de, in German and English) is a nationwide network of agencies; its website has all the details. **Apartments Apart** (www apartmentsapart.com) arranges Europe-wide holiday rentals. Do-it-yourself types with some German skills could also try www.zwischenmiete.de.

Pensionen, Inns & Private Rooms

Pensionen and *Gasthöfe/Gasthäuser* (inns) are smaller and less formal, and are an excellent low-cost alternative to hotels; the latter usually have restaurants serving regional and German food to a local clientele. Expect clean rooms but minimal amenities – maybe a radio, sometimes a small TV, almost never a phone. Facilities may be shared. What rooms lack in amenities, though, they often make up for in charm and authenticity, often augmented by friendly hosts who take a personal interest in ensuring that you enjoy your stay. Rates always include breakfast.

Privatzimmer – essentially guest rooms in private homes – are ubiquitous and great for catching a glimpse into how locals live, although privacy seekers may find these places a bit too intimate. Tourist offices keep lists of available rooms; you can also look around for 'Zimmer Frei' (rooms available) signs in house or shop windows. They're usually quite cheap, with per-person rates starting at €13 and usu-

BOOK YOUR STAY ONLINE

For more accommodation reviews and recommendations by Lonely Planet authors, check out the booking service at www.lonely planet.com/hotels. You'll find the true, insider low-down on the best places to stay. Reviews are thorough and independent. Best of all, you can book online.

ally topping out at €25, including breakfast. If a landlord is reluctant to rent for a single night, offer to pay a little extra. For advance reservations, try www.bed-and-breakfast.de or www.bedandbreakfast.de.

ACTIVITIES

No matter what kind of activity gets you off that couch, you'll be able to pursue it in this land of lakes, rivers, mountains and forests. There's plenty to do year-round, with each season offering its own special delights, be it hiking among spring wildflowers, swimming in a lake warmed by the summer sun, biking among a kaleidoscope of autumn foliage or celebrating winter by schussing through deep powder. Wherever you go, you'll find outfitters and local operators eager to gear you up.

Cycling

Strap on your helmet! Germany is superb cycling territory, no matter whether you're off on a leisurely spin along the beach, an adrenaline-fuelled mountain exploration or a multiday bike-touring adventure. Practically every town and region has a network of signposted bike routes. For day tours, staff at local tourist offices can supply you with ideas, maps and advice. Most towns have at least one bike-hire station (often at or near the train station); many are listed throughout this book. The folks at bike shops are also great for getting the inside scoop on the local scene.

Germany is also criss-crossed by more than 200 long-distance trails covering 70,000km, making it ideal for *Radwandern* (bike touring). Routes are well signposted and are typically a combination of lightly travelled back roads, forestry tracks and paved highways with dedicated bike lanes. Many traverse nature reserves, meander along rivers or venture into steep mountain terrain.

For inspiration and route planning, check out www.germany-tourism.de/cycling, which

---

TOP FIVE LONG-DISTANCE CYCLING ROUTES

Altmühltal Radweg (190km) This easy to moderate route goes from Rothenburg ob der Tauber to Beilngries, following the Altmühl River through the Altmühltal Nature Park.

Bodensee–Königssee Radweg (414km) Lindau to Berchtesgaden; a moderate route running along the foot of the Alps with magnificent views of the mountains, lakes and forests.

Elberadweg (860km) Follows the Elbe River from Saxon Switzerland to Hamburg through wine country, heath and marshland and past such cities as Dresden, Dessau and Wittenberg. Also see the boxed text, p228.

Donauradweg (434km) Travelling from Neu-Ulm to Passau, this is a delightful, easy to moderate riverside trip along one of Europe's great streams.

Romantische Strasse (359km) Würzburg to Füssen; this easy to moderate route is one of the nicest ways to explore Germany's most famous holiday route, though it can get busy during the summer peak season.

---

provides, in English, an overview of routes, helpful planning tips, a route finder and free downloads of route maps and descriptions.

For on-the-road navigating, the best maps are those published by the national cycling organization **Allgemeiner Deutscher Fahrrad Club** (ADFC; www.adfc.de, in German). Their regional maps for day and weekend tours and cycle tour maps for longer excursions are available in book stores, at tourist offices and online. They indicate inclines, the condition of the track, how busy it is and the location of repair shops. GPS users should find the UTM grid coordinates useful.

ADFC also publishes a useful online directory called **Bett & Bike** (www.bettundbike.de, in German) that lists thousands of bicycle-friendly hotels, inns and hostels. Bookstores carry the printed version.

For an overview of transporting your bike within Germany, see p780.

Hiking & Nordic Walking

Got wanderlust? With lovely scenery throughout, Germany is perfect for exploring on foot. Ramble through romantic river valleys, hike among fragrant pines, bag Alpine peaks or simply go for a walk by the lake or through the dunes. Many of the nicest trails traverse national and nature parks or biosphere reserves. Nordic walking, where you strut with poles just like a cross-country skier, has taken Germany by storm in recent years.

Trails are usually well signposted, sometimes with symbols quaintly painted on tree trunks. To find a route matching your fitness level and time frame, pick the brains of local tourist office staff, who can also supply you with maps and tips. Many also offer multiday 'hiking without luggage' packages that include accommodation and luggage transfer between hotels.

The German National Tourist Office website (www.deutschland-tourismus.de) should

be your first port of call, with inspirational information in English on walking throughout Germany. Other excellent hiking websites include www.wanderbares-deutschland.de which features comprehensive information on dozens of walking trails throughout Germany. It's mostly in German, but some routes are also detailed in English. Also have a look at www.tourentipp.de (in German) with mountain weather forecasts, mapping information and walks searchable by region.

Mountaineering

'Climb every mountain...' the Mother Superior belts out in the *Sound of Music*, and the Bavarian Alps – the centre of mountaineering in Germany – will give you plenty of opportunity to do just that. You can venture out on day treks or plan multiday clambers from hut to hut as long as you keep in mind that hiking in the Alps is no walk in the park. You need to be in reasonable condition and come equipped with the right shoes, gear, and topographic maps or GPS. Trails can be narrow, steep and have icy patches, even in summer.

Before heading out, seek local advice on trails, equipment and weather and take all precautions concerning clothing and provisions. Always let someone know where you're going. If you're inexperienced, ask at the tourist offices about local outfitters offering instruction, equipment rental and guided tours. These are usually run by energetic, English-speaking folks with an infectious love for, and deep knowledge of, the mountains. For potential problems and how to deal with hypothermia, see p790.

The **Deutscher Alpenverein** (DAV; German Alpine Club; ☎ 089-140 030; www.alpenverein.de, in German) is a goldmine of information on hiking and mountaineering and has local chapters in practically every German town. It also maintains hundreds of Alpine mountain huts, many of them open to the public, where you can spend the night and get a meal. Local DAV chapters also organise various courses (climbing, mountaineering etc), as well as guided treks, with which you can link up. Staff at local tourist offices should be able to hook you up with local DAV branches. If you're planning multiday treks, becoming a member of the organisation can yield a 30% to 50% discount on Alpine huts and other benefits, including insurance.

Rock Climbing

Clambering around steep rock faces chiselled and carved by time and the elements is a popular pursuit in various parts of the country. Rock hounds, from beginner to expert, test their mettle on the Jurassic limestone cliffs in the Naturpark Altmühltal (p383) and in Saxon Switzerland (Sächsische Schweiz; p190) in Saxony. Wherever you go, there are local outfitters that can set you up with equipment and advice.

Snow Sports

Modern lifts, primed ski slopes from 'Sesame Street' to 'Death Wish', solitary cross-country trails through untouched nature, cosy mountain huts, steaming mulled wine, hearty dinners by a crackling fire – all these are the hallmarks of a German skiing holiday.

The Bavarian Alps, only an hour's drive south of Munich, offer the best downhill slopes and most reliable snow conditions. The most famous resort town here is, of course, Garmisch-Partenkirchen (p356), which hosted the 1936 Olympic Games and is popular with the international set. Other major resorts are Oberstdorf (p360) in the Allgäu Alps and Berchtesgaden (p362).

There's also plenty of skiing, snowboarding and cross-country skiing to be done elsewhere in the country, where the mountains may not soar as high as in the Alps, but assets include cheaper prices, smaller crowds and a less frenetic atmosphere. Among Germany's lower mountain ranges, the Bavarian Forest (p400) has the most reliable snow levels, with plenty of good downhill action on the Grosser Arber mountain. Cross-country skiing is especially wonderful in the Bavarian Forest National Park. In snowy winters, the Black Forest (p443), the Harz (p242), the Thuringian Forest (p280) and the Sauerland (p608) also attract scores of snow fans.

At higher elevations, the season generally runs from late November/early December to March, but, thanks to global warming, snow levels are becoming less reliable, especially in the lower-lying resorts. Most try to trick Mother Nature by installing snowmaking

---

RESPONSIBLE HIKING *Kerry Christiani*

Follow these tips to tread lightly and minimise your impact in the Alps and other fragile natural environments.

Rubbish

■ Carry out all rubbish (including cigarette butts, tin foil, plastic wrappers and sanitary pads).

■ Burying rubbish disturbs soil and ground cover and encourages erosion. It may be dug up by animals (potentially harming them).

■ Take reusable containers or stuff sacks. Avoid plastic bags and bottles.

Human Waste Disposal

■ Make an effort to use toilets in huts and refuges where provided.

■ Where there is none, bury your waste. Dig a small hole 15cm deep and at least 100m from any watercourse. Cover the waste with soil and a rock. Use toilet paper sparingly and bury that, too. In snow, dig down beneath the soil.

Erosion

■ Stick to existing tracks and avoid short cuts that bypass a switchback. If you blaze a new trail straight down a slope, it will turn into a watercourse with the next heavy rainfall.

■ Avoid removing the plant life that keeps topsoil in place.

SOAKIN' & SWEATIN'

If the road has left you frazzled and achy, a trip to a day spa may just be what the doctor ordered. Every place has its own treatment menu of massages (shiatsu, deep tissue, Swedish, hot stone, etc) and beauty treatments (facials, wraps, botanical baths, mud baths, etc). Many hotels, especially in the countryside, have so-called 'wellness areas', with a sauna, perhaps a whirlpool, a steam room or even a swimming pool. Massage services are often available on request. Note that not a stitch of clothing is worn in German saunas, so leave your modesty in the locker. And always bring or hire a towel.

'Taking a cure', ie booking a multi-week regimen of sauna, bath, massage and exercise in a spa resort *(Kurort)*, has been a German tradition for more than 100 years. Visitors can pick and choose from treatments offered through the local spa centres *(Kurzentrum)* or spa administrations *(Kurverwaltung)*. Bookings can usually be made at short notice.

Water parks, which seem to be proliferating faster than rabbits on Viagra, are also good for getting pummelled into a state of bliss. Most have several indoor and outdoor pools (often filled with thermal water from local mineral springs), hot tubs, surge channels, massage jets, waterfalls and multiple saunas, plus a big menu of pampering options. A few hours in such a wellness oasis can do wonders to brighten your mood on a rainy afternoon.

---

equipment, which works up to a point but gobbles up tons of water and energy. All resorts have equipment-hire facilities. Rates for downhill gear start at about €10 per day, with discounts for longer rental periods. Cross-country equipment costs slightly less. Daily ski-lift passes start at around €20.

Water Sports

Germany's coasts, lakes, rivers and canals are all popular playgrounds for water-based pursuits, even if the swimming season is relatively short (June to September) since water temperatures rarely climb above 21°C.

Canoeing and kayaking are popular in such places as the Spreewald (p166) in Brandenburg, the Naturpark Altmühltal (p382) in Bavaria and the Müritz National Park (p733) in Mecklenburg–Western Pomerania.

Sailors and windsurfers should steer towards the North Sea or, if you prefer calmer waters, the Baltic Sea and such lakes as the Chiemsee (p334), Lake Constance (p467) and Starnberger See (p332).

BUSINESS HOURS

Most shops open between 9am and 10am, except for bakeries and kiosks that may open as early as 6am and some supermarkets which open at 7am or 8am. Closing times vary from 6pm or 6.30pm (1pm or 2pm on Saturday) for shops in rural areas and suburbs to 8pm or 9pm for malls, department stores and stores in the bigger city centres. There is no Sunday shopping except in December and a

few times throughout the year. After hours and on Sundays you can get basic (and overpriced) supplies at petrol stations and larger train stations. Bakeries open for a few hours on Sunday mornings.

Banks do business from 8.30am to 4pm Monday to Friday (sometimes 6pm on Thursday), while core hours at post offices are 9am to 6pm Monday to Friday and to noon or 1pm on Saturday (also see p769).

Travel agencies and other service-oriented businesses unlock doors from 9am to 6pm weekdays and till 1pm or 2pm on Saturday. Public servants, on the other hand, often shut down their PCs as early as 1pm on Friday. Museums usually take Monday off but stay open late one evening a week.

In villages and suburbs, shops and businesses often observe a two- to three-hour lunch break. And speaking of lunch, it's generally served between 11.30am and 2pm, while dinner feedings are from 5.30pm to 9.30pm, although many restaurants continue to dish up throughout the afternoon. Some also observe a *Ruhetag* (day of rest), usually Monday or Tuesday.

Pubs and bars pour libations from around 6pm, unless they serve food, in which case they're also open during the day. In cities without closing hours, such as Hamburg and Berlin, bars stay open until the last tippler leaves; otherwise, 1am or 2am are typical closing times. Big-city clubs open around 11pm but don't kick into high gear until 1am or 2am and keep buzzing until sunrise or later. Cities like Berlin have a growing number of daytime clubs, so it's quite possible not to go home at all at weekends!

Variations on the above are noted in individual reviews.

CHILDREN

(Tiny) hands down, travelling to Germany with tots can be child's play, especially if you keep a light schedule and involve the little ones in the day-to-day trip planning. Plus they're a great excuse if you secretly yearn to ride roller coasters or go ape in a zoo. Lonely Planet's *Travel with Children* offers a wealth of tips and tricks on the subject. The websites www .travelwithyourkids.com and www.flyingwith kids.com are also good general resources.

Practicalities

Germany is a very family-friendly destination and most places are happy to cater for kids, whether with smaller dinner portions, a high chair, special attention on a tour, making up a special bed or giving them a little extra attention. That said, amenities and services specifically geared to children are rare.

Overall, children enjoy lots of discounts for everything from museum admissions to bus fares and tour tickets, although the cut-off age can be anything from six to 18. Many hotels have family rooms with three or four beds or large doubles with a sofa bed. Practically everyone can provide cots, though sometimes for a small charge. Some properties, especially those in the countryside, don't charge extra for small children staying in their parents' room without requiring extra bedding. In vehicles, children's safety seats are compulsory and available through the car-hire companies, but book them in advance.

Baby food, infant formulas, soy and cow's milk, disposable nappies (diapers) and the like are widely available in supermarkets and chemists (drugstores). Breastfeeding in public is practised, especially in the cities, although most women are discreet about it. Most tourist offices can lead you to local resources for children's programs, child-care facilities and English-speaking paediatricians. If you need a babysitter, ask staff at your hotel for a referral.

Also see Eating with Kids on p89.

Sights & Activities

It's easy to keep the kids entertained no matter where you travel in Germany. The great outdoors, of course, yield endless possibilities. A day spent swimming, cycling, windsurfing, walking or otherwise engaging in physical activity is sure to send the little ones quickly off to dreamland. Farm holidays (p757) are an excellent way for city kids to get fully immersed in nature. Germany's legend-shrouded castles, including the medieval fortresses along the Romantic Rhine (p499), the stately Wartburg (p281) in Thuringia or dreamy Schloss Neuschwanstein (p352) in Bavaria, are sure to fuel the imagination of many a Harry Potter fan.

Theme parks are also perennially popular playgrounds. Phantasialand (p579) in Brühl and Europa-Park (p459) in the Black Forest are among the best ones. Older kids might get a kick out of Hollywood magic at Filmpark Babelsberg (p161) in Potsdam near Berlin and Movie Park Germany (p598) in the Ruhrgebiet.

Even in the cities, possibilities for keeping kids entertained abound. Take them to parks, playgrounds, swimming pools, zoos or such kid-friendly museums as the Schokoladen Museum (Chocolate Museum; p573) in Cologne, the Spielzeugmuseum (Toy Museum; p367) in Nuremberg or the technology museums in Munich (Deutsches Museum; p315), Speyer (Technik Museum; p491) and Berlin (Deutsches Technikmuseum; p125).

Berlin (p128), Münster (p601), Leipzig (p198) and Gelsenkirchen (p598) are among those cities with wonderful zoos.

CLIMATE CHARTS

The German weather is highly capricious: on any given day it can be cold or warm, sunny or rainy, windy or calm – or any combination thereof. Meteorologists blame this lack of stability on colliding maritime and continental air masses, but for you this simply means packing a wardrobe that's as flexible as possible.

The weather tends to be most pleasant in summer, which is rarely suffocatingly hot (usually around 28°C/82°F), the occasional heat wave notwithstanding. Humidity levels tend to be quite high, making afternoon thunderstorms fairly common. Spring is beautiful but it can be slow to arrive, even if jackets are sometimes stripped off as early as April. Autumn arrives in September and brings the added bonus of bright foliage.

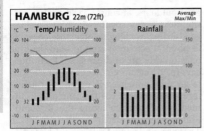

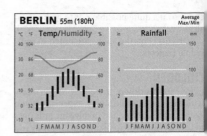

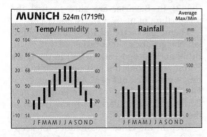

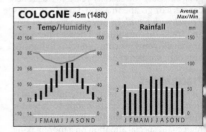

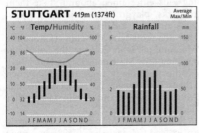

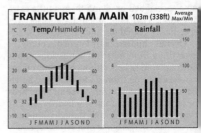

Temperatures can still be quite pleasant, which may keep beer gardens and outdoor cafes open until October. Predictably, December to February is the coldest period, when the mercury can plunge well below 0°C/32°F. At the higher elevations, snowfall is possible from November.

For general advice on the best times to travel around the country, see p20. The climate charts p764 provide a snapshot of local weather patterns.

COURSES

Plenty of courses are offered throughout Germany, including hands-on sessions that don't require fluency in German. Options are literally endless. How about learning rock climbing in Saxon Switzerland, taking a workshop in porcelain painting in Meissen, joining a wine seminar in a Mosel village, getting a tutorial in woodcarving in the Black Forest or taking cooking lessons in Berlin? Tourist offices are usually the best sources for what's on offer locally, although the classifieds in listings magazines and local newspapers may also yield some leads.

If learning German is your aim, you could hire a private tutor or join a language school. Among the most respected are those run by the **Goethe Institut** (www.goethe.de), a government-subsidised nonprofit organisation promoting German language and culture abroad. Programs cater for all levels of proficiency, usually last a few weeks and are offered in 12 German cities, including Berlin, Dresden and Munich.

Many universities offer summer courses, which are sometimes held in English. The website of the **Deutscher Akademischer Austauschdienst** (DAAD; German Academic Exchange Service; www.daad.de) has a searchable database of available programs.

CUSTOMS & REGULATIONS

Most articles that you take to Germany for your personal use may be imported free of duty and tax. Duty-free allowances for goods purchased in a non–European Union country were recently changed. Anyone over 17 may now bring in 1L of strong liquor *or* 2L of less than 22% alcohol by volume *plus* 4L of wine *plus* 16L of beer. Duty-free tobacco imports are capped at 200 cigarettes *or* 100 cigarillos *or* 50 cigars *or* 250g of loose tobacco. If you're over 15, you may also bring in other products up to the value of €300 if arriving by land or €430 if arriving by sea or air. The limit for those under 15 is €175.

DANGERS & ANNOYANCES

Germany is a very safe country in which to live and travel, with crime rates that are quite low by international standards. Theft and other crimes against travellers occur rarely. Of course, you should still take all the usual sensible precautions, such as locking hotel rooms and cars, not leaving valuables unattended, keeping an eye out for pickpockets in crowded places and not taking midnight strolls in city parks. Many hostels provide lockers, but you need your own padlock. Train stations tend to be magnets for the destitute and drug dependent who might harass you or make you feel otherwise uncomfortable, especially if you are in the area at night.

In big cities, especially Berlin, large-scale political protests and demonstrations are quite common. Despite a high police presence, these can turn rowdy or violent on rare occasions, so it's best to stay away from them altogether. Police are also very visible on game days of soccer matches to prevent clashes between fans of rival teams. Always avoid groups of intoxicated hooligans, as many belong to neo-Nazi and skinhead organisations and are erratic, unpredictable and often violent. Although they do not target tourists, innocent bystanders they perceive as 'foreign looking' or as members of rivalling left-wing groups could potentially be harassed. If you do find yourself in a threatening situation, try not to provoke these aggressors, get away from the scene as fast as possible and notify the police.

DISCOUNT CARDS

If you're a full-time student, the **International Student Identity Card** (ISIC; www.isic.org) is your ticket to savings on airfares, travel insurance and many local attractions. The **International Youth Travel Card** (IYTC; www.istc.org) grants similar savings and benefits for non-students under 26, while the **Euro<26 Youth Card** (www.euro26.org) is available to anyone under 30, despite the name. All cards are issued online, by student unions, hostelling organisations and youth-oriented travel agencies such as STA Travel.

Discounts are also available for seniors, children, families and the disabled. Although no special cards are needed, you may be asked to show ID to prove your age.

In cities, many tourist offices sell **Welcome Cards** entitling visitors to discounts on museums, sights and tours, plus unlimited trips on local public transportation. They can be good value if you plan on taking advantage of most of the benefits and don't qualify for any of the standard discounts.

Frequent campers can save up to 25% in camping fees with the **Camping Card International** (www.campingcardinternational.com). It's available from your local camping or motoring association and includes third-party liability insurance while in camping grounds.

EMBASSIES & CONSULATES

All foreign embassies are in Berlin, but many countries have consular offices in such cities as Frankfurt, Munich, Hamburg and Düsseldorf. Call the embassy number listed here to find out which consulate is closest to your location. For German missions around the world, as well as foreign missions in Germany not listed here, go to www.auswaertiges-amt.de (click on 'English', then 'Addresses').

Australia (Map p108; ☎ 030-880 0880; www.germany .embassy.gov.au; Wallstrasse 76-79)

Canada (Map pp110-11; ☎ 030-203 120; www.kanada -info.de; Leipziger Platz 17)

Czech Republic (Map p108; ☎ 030-226 380; www .mzv.cz/berlin; Wilhelmstrasse 44)

France (Map p108; ☎ 030-590 039 000; www.botschaft -frankreich.de; Pariser Platz 5)

Ireland (Map p108; ☎ 030-220 720; www.embassy ofireland.de; Friedrichstrasse 200)

Italy (Map p108; ☎ 030-254 400; www.ambberlino .esteri.it; Hiroshimastrasse 1)

Japan (Map p108; ☎ 030-210 940; www.botschaft -japan.de; Hiroshimastrasse 6)

Netherlands (Map p108; ☎ 030-209 560; www .niederlandeweb.de; Klosterstrasse 50)

New Zealand (Map p108; ☎ 030-206 210; www .nzembassy.com/germany; Friedrichstrasse 60)

Poland (☎ 030-223 130; www.botschaft-polen.de; Lassenstrasse 19-21)

Russia (Map p108; ☎ 030-229 111 029; www.russische -botschaft.de; Unter den Linden 63-65)

South Africa (Map p108; ☎ 030-220 730; www .suedafrika.org; Tiergartenstrasse 18)

Spain (Map pp106-7; ☎ 030-254 0070; www.spanische botschaft.de; Lichtensteinallee 1)

Switzerland (Map p108; ☎ 030-390 4000; www.eda .admin.ch; Otto-von-Bismarck-Allee 4a)

UK (Map p108; ☎ 030-204 570; www.britischebotschaft .de; Wilhelmstrasse 70)

USA (Map p108; ☎ 030-830 50; www.usembassy.de; Pariser Platz 2)

FOOD

Eating recommendations in this guide match all tastes and travel budgets. Budget eateries include takeaways, delis, cafes, *Imbisse* (snack bars), markets and basic restaurants where you can get a meal (defined as a main course and one drink) for less than €10. At midrange establishments expect tablecloths, full menus, beer and wine lists and a bill that shouldn't exceed €20 per person. Top-end places tend to be full gourmet affairs with expert service, creative and freshly prepared food and matching wine lists. Main courses alone here will cost €20 or more; set three- or four-course menus are usually a better deal. Places with a good selection for vegetarians are denoted with Ⓥ.

If our reviews do not mention opening hours, standard hours (11am to 11pm) apply. Note that food service may stop earlier, depending on how busy the place is that night.

For more on cuisine and eating customs, see p79.

GAY & LESBIAN TRAVELLERS

Germany is a magnet for gay travellers with the rainbow flag flying especially proudly in Berlin, which is helmed by Germany's first openly gay mayor, Klaus Wowereit. For an overview of the Berlin scene, see the boxed text on p150; for Cologne, flick to p577; for Hamburg, p697. All of these hubs have humming nightlife scenes, magazines, associations and support groups, and major Gay Pride celebrations. Frankfurt, Munich (p328) and Bremen (p667) have smaller but still vibrant scenes.

Overall, Germans are tolerant of gays (*Schwule*) and lesbians (*Lesben*) although, as elsewhere in the world, cities are more liberal than rural areas, and younger people tend to be more open-minded than older generations.

Homophobic hostility is more likely in eastern Germany and in the conservative south where gays and lesbians tend to keep a lower profile.

Local gay and lesbian magazines and centres are listed throughout this book. For online info, listings and contacts, see www .gayscape.com, a search tool with hundreds of links, www.gay-web.de or www.blu.fm, the online version of the magazine. Lesbians should check out www.lesarion.de and the online version of *L-Mag* (www.l-mag.de), a bimonthly magazine. An LGBT travel specialist is www.damronvacations.com. Another good general source is www.outtraveler.com.

HOLIDAYS
Public Holidays

Germany observes eight religious and three secular holidays nationwide. Shops, banks, government offices and post offices are closed on these days. States with predominantly Catholic populations, such as Bavaria and Baden-Württemberg, also celebrate Epiphany (6 January), Corpus Christi (10 days after Pentecost), Assumption Day (15 August) and All Saints' Day (1 November). Reformation Day (31 October) is only observed in eastern Germany (but not in Berlin).

The following are *gesetzliche Feiertage* (public holidays):

Neujahrstag (New Year's Day) 1 January

Ostern (Easter) March/April; Good Friday, Easter Sunday and Easter Monday

Christi Himmelfahrt (Ascension Day) 40 days after Easter

Maifeiertag/Tag der Arbeit (Labour Day) 1 May

Pfingsten (Whit/Pentecost Sunday & Monday) 50 days after Easter

Tag der Deutschen Einheit (Day of German Unity) 3 October

Weihnachtstag (Christmas Day) 25 December

Zweiter Weihnachtstag (Boxing Day) 26 December

School Holidays

Each state sets its own school holidays but, in general, kids get six weeks off in summer and two weeks each around Christmas, Easter and October. In some states, schools are also closed for a few days in February and around Whitsun/Pentecost.

Traffic is worst at the beginning of school holidays in population-rich states like North Rhine–Westphalia and can become a nightmare if several states let out their schools at the same time.

Germans are big fans of mini-holidays built around public holidays, when you can expect heavy crowds on the roads, in the towns, on boats, in beer gardens and everywhere else. Lodging is at a premium at these times as well.

INSURANCE

No matter how long or short your trip, make sure you have adequate travel insurance. EU citizens should obtain the European Health Insurance Card (EHIC), which entitles you to reduced-cost or free medical treatment due to illness or accident, although not for emergency repatriation home. See p789 for details. Non-EU citizens should check if a similar reciprocal agreement exists between their country and Germany, or if their policy at home provides worldwide health-care coverage.

If you do need to buy travel health insurance, be sure to get a policy that also covers emergency flights back home. While some plans pay doctors or hospitals directly, some health-care providers may still require immediate payment from non-locals. Most do not accept credit cards. Except in emergencies, call around for a doctor willing to accept your insurance. Check your policy for what supporting documentation you need to file a claim and be sure to keep all receipts.

Also consider coverage for luggage theft or loss. If you already have a homeowners or renters policy, check what it will cover and only get supplemental insurance to protect against the rest. If you have prepaid a large portion of your vacation, trip cancellation insurance is a worthwhile expense.

Worldwide travel insurance is available at www.lonelyplanet.com/travel_services. You can buy, extend and claim online anytime – even if you're already on the road.

For information about what kind of insurance coverage you need while driving in Germany, see p784.

INTERNET ACCESS

Internet cafes are listed throughout the destination chapters, but most have about the lifespan of a fruit fly, so please forgive us if our listings are outdated and ask staff at your hotel for a recommendation. Public libraries offer free terminals and sometimes wi-fi access, but downsides may include time limits, reservation requirements and queues. Internet access is also available at slightly seedy 'telephone call shops', which cluster near train stations.

In hotels and hostels, broadband and wi-fi (*W-LAN* in German) have become quite commonplace. Some hotels, especially in eastern Germany, have ISDN data service which was state-of-the-art in the '90s but has since been supplanted by DSL. Unless you have an ISDN-compatible modem, access may be difficult, if not impossible. Laptop users may also need adapters for German electrical outlets and telephone sockets, which are widely available in such electronics stores as Saturn and Media Markt.

Wi-fi is available on select ICE train routes, including Frankfurt to Hamburg and Frankfurt to Munich. More than 20 stations, including those in Berlin, Munich, Hamburg and Frankfurt, also offer wi-fi in their DB Lounges.

Throughout this book, we use 🖳 to indicate that a place has PCs with internet access for public use and 🛜 for places with wi-fi. Access fees range from free to exorbitant, with some top-end business chain hotels charging as much as €25 per day.

To locate wi-fi hot spots, check the directories at www.jiwire.com or www.hotspot-locations.com. For a full rundown on connectivity issues, see www.kropla.com or www.teleadapt.com. Useful trip-planning websites are listed on p23.

LEGAL MATTERS

By law you must carry some form of photographic identification, such as your passport, national identity card or driving licence. Reporting theft to the police is usually a simple, if occasionally time-consuming, matter. Remember that the first thing to do is show some form of identification.

If driving in Germany, you should carry your driving licence and obey road rules carefully (see p784). The permissible blood-alcohol

---

THE LEGAL AGE FOR...

- Drinking beer or wine: 14
- Being served beer or wine in a pub: 16
- Buying cigarettes: 18
- Driving a car: 18
- Military service: 17
- Sexual consent: 14 (with restrictions)
- Voting in an election: 18

limit is 0.05%; drivers caught exceeding this amount are subject to stiff fines, a confiscated licence and even jail time. Drinking in public is not illegal, but please be discreet about it.

Illegal drugs are widely available, especially in clubs. Cannabis possession is a criminal offence and punishment may range from a warning to a court appearance. Dealers face far stiffer penalties, as do people caught with any other 'recreational' drugs.

If you are arrested, you have the right to make a phone call and are presumed innocent until proven guilty. If you don't know a lawyer, contact your embassy (p765).

MAPS

Most tourist offices distribute free (but often very basic) maps. For driving around Germany, however, you'll need a detailed road map or atlas such as those published by Falk, RV Verlag or ADAC. Look for them at bookshops, tourist offices, newsagents and petrol stations. Find downloadable maps and driving directions at www.maps.google.de, www.stadtplandienst.de or www.viamichelin.de.

MONEY

Euros come in seven notes (€5, €10, €20, €50, €100, €200 and €500) and eight coins (€0.01, €0.02, €0.05, €0.10, €0.20, €0.50, €1 and €2). At press time, the euro was a strong and stable currency, although some minor fluctuations are common. A guide to exchange rates is given on the inside front cover of this book; for pointers on costs, see p20.

Cash is still king in Germany, so you can't really avoid having at least some notes and coins, say €100 or so, on you at all times. Plan to pay in cash almost everywhere.

You can exchange money at airports, some banks and currency exchange offices, such as ReiseBank. In rural areas, such facilities are rare, so make sure you have plenty of cash.

For an overview of the costs you can expect in Germany, see p20.

ATMs

The easiest and quickest way to obtain cash is by using your debit (bank) card at an ATM (Geldautomat) linked to international networks such as Cirrus, Plus, Star and Maestro. ATMs are ubiquitous and accessible 24/7.

Make sure you know your PIN and check with your bank for fees, daily withdrawal limits and contact information for reporting lost or stolen cards. Some shops, hotels, restaurants and other businesses also accept payment by debit card. Since 2006 nearly all cards use the 'chip and pin' system: instead of signing, you enter your PIN. If you're from overseas and your card isn't chip-and-pin enabled, you may be able to sign it in the usual way, although not all places will accept your card, so enquire first.

Credit Cards

Credit cards are becoming more widely accepted, but it's best not to assume that you'll be able to use one – enquire first. Even so, a piece of plastic is vital in emergencies and also useful for phone or internet bookings. Visa and MasterCard are more commonly accepted than American Express. Avoid getting cash advances on your credit card via ATMs since fees are steep and you'll be charged interest immediately (in other words, there's no grace period as with purchases). Report lost or stolen cards to the following:
American Express (☎ 01805-840 840)
MasterCard (☎ 0800-819 1040)
Visa (☎ 0800-811 8440)

Tipping

Restaurant bills always include a Bedienung (service charge) but most people add 5% or 10% unless the service was truly abhorrent. At hotels, bellboys get about €1 per bag and it's also nice to leave some cash for the room cleaners. Tip bartenders about 5% and taxi drivers around 10%.

Travellers Cheques

Travellers cheques are becoming increasingly obsolete in the age of network-linked ATMs. It doesn't help that German businesses generally don't accept them, even if denominated in euros, and banks charge exorbitant fees for cashing them (currency exchange offices are usually better). American Express offices cash Amex cheques free of charge.

PHOTOGRAPHY

Germany is a photographer's dream, with its gorgeous countryside, fabulous architecture, quaint villages, exciting cities, lordly cathedrals, lively cafes and picture-perfect castles, palaces and old towns. A good general reference guide is Lonely Planet's *Travel Photography* by Richard I'Anson.

Germans tend to be deferential around photographers and will make a point of not walking in front of your camera, even if you want them to. No one seems to mind being photographed in the context of an overall scene, but if you want a close-up shot, you should ask first.

POST

Main post offices, which are often near train stations, are usually open from 9am to 6pm Monday to Friday and till noon or 1pm on Saturday. Suburban and rural branches often close at lunchtime and at 5pm or 5.30pm weekdays and noon on Saturday. Our destination chapters list only opening hours deviating from this standard.

Mailing standard-sized postcards to destinations within Europe costs €0.65, a 20g letter costs €0.70 and a 50g letter costs €1.25. Mail sent outside Europe costs €1 for postcards, €1.70 for a 20g airmail letter and €2.20 for a 50g airmail letter. A surcharge applies to oversized envelopes. Parcels up to 2kg are charged at €8.60 to destinations within Europe and €13.90 to destinations beyond. For full details, see www.deutsche-post.de.

Letters sent within Germany take one to two days for delivery; those addressed to destinations within Europe or to North America take three to five days and those to Australasia five to seven days.

SHOPPING

Germany is a fun place to shop, with a big selection of everyday and unique items. Much of the shopping is done in pedestrianised shopping areas in the city centres rather than in big shopping malls, which are often relegated to the suburbs. Famous shopping strips include the Kurfürstendamm in Berlin, the Königsallee in Düsseldorf, the Hohe Strasse in Cologne; Kaufingerstrasse, Neuhauser Strasse and Maximilianstrasse in Munich and the Zeil in Frankfurt.

There's really nothing you can't buy in Germany, but even in the age of globalisation, there are still some treasures you'll unearth here better than anywhere else.

Regional products include traditional Bavarian outfits, including dirndl dresses, lederhosen and loden jackets. Beer mugs are the classic souvenir, no matter whether made

TAXES & REFUNDS

Prices for goods and services include a value-added tax (VAT), called *Mehrwertsteuer*, which is 19% for regular goods and 7% for food and books. If your permanent residence is outside the European Union, you can have a large portion of the VAT refunded, provided you shop at a store displaying the 'Tax-Free for Tourists' sign and obtain a tax-free form for your purchase from the sales clerk. At the airport, show this form, your unused goods and your receipt to a custom official before checking your luggage. The customs official will stamp the form, which you can then take straight to the cash refund office at the airport.

of glass or stoneware, plain or decorated, with or without pewter lids – the choice is endless. Famous food products include marzipan from Lübeck, *Lebkuchen* (gingerbread) from Nuremberg and Printen (spicy cookies) from Aachen.

The Black Forest is the birthplace of German clockmaking, and not only of the cuckoo variety. Precision instruments, such as microscopes and binoculars, are also a speciality. Cutlery is first-rate, with Wüsthof and JA Henckels being leading brands.

Good-quality woodcarvings are widely available in the Alpine regions (Oberammergau's are especially famous, p358). Fans of the fragile can pick up exquisite china made by Meissen, Villeroy & Boch, Rosenthal, KPM or Porzellanmanufaktur Nymphenburg. The glass artisans in the Bavarian Forest make beautiful vases, bowls and ornaments.

Famous toy brands include stuffed animals by Steiff (the inventor of the teddy bear) and collectible Käthe Kruse dolls. At Christmas markets you'll discover wonderful ornaments, classic nutcrackers and other decorations.

German wine is another excellent purchase, especially since some of the best bottles are not available outside the country. If you're into street fashion, head to Berlin, which makes the most Zeitgeist-capturing outfits.

Bargaining almost never occurs, except at flea markets.

SOLO TRAVELLERS

There are no particular problems or difficulties associated with travelling alone in

DIRECTORY

Germany. Germans are generally friendly but rather reserved and not likely to initiate a conversation with strangers. This shouldn't stop you from approaching them, though, since most will quite happily respond and even be extra helpful once they find out you're a traveller. And don't let your lack of German deter you. Young people especially speak at least some English and many are keen to practise it. For more on the subject, check out the website of the nonprofit **Connecting: Solo Travel Network** (www.cstn.org).

TELEPHONE & FAX
Fax
Faxes can be sent from and received at most hotels, photocopy shops, internet cafes and telephone call shops.

Mobile Phones
Mobile (cell) phones are called 'Handys' and work on GSM 900/1800. If your home country uses a different standard, you'll need a multi-band GSM phone in Germany. If you're staying for a while and have an unlocked multi-band phone, buying a prepaid, rechargeable SIM card with a local number might work out cheaper than using your own network. Cards are available at any telecommunications store (eg T-Online, Vodafone, E-Plus or O_2). These places also sell prepaid GSM900/1800 phones, including some credit, starting at €30. Recharge credit by buying scratch-off cards sold at newsagents, supermarkets, petrol stations and general stores.

Calls made to a mobile phone are more expensive than those to a landline, but incoming calls are free.

Phone Codes
German phone numbers consist of an area code, which starts with ☎ 0, and the local number. Area codes can be up to six digits long; local numbers, up to nine digits. If dialling from a landline within the same city, you don't need to dial the area code. If using a mobile, you must dial it.

If calling Germany from abroad, first dial your country's international access code, then ☎ 49 (Germany's country code), then the area code (dropping the initial ☎ 0) and the local number. Germany's international access code is ☎ 00.

Deutsche Telekom directory assistance charges a ridiculous €1.39 per minute for numbers within Germany (☎ 118 37 for an English-speaking operator; ☎ 118 33 for German-speaking) and €1.99 for numbers outside Germany (☎ 118 34). Get the same information for free at www.telefonbuch.de. A much cheaper provider is the fully automated Telix (☎ 118 10), which charges €0.39 per minute.

Numbers starting with ☎ 0800 are toll free, ☎ 01801 numbers are charged at €0.046 per minute, ☎ 01803 at €0.09 and ☎ 01805 at €0.14. Calls to numbers starting with ☎ 01802 cost a flat €0.06, while those to ☎ 01804 numbers cost a flat €0.20. Avoid numbers starting with ☎ 0190 or ☎ 900, which are charged at exorbitant rates. Direct-dialled calls made from hotel rooms are also usually charged at a premium.

If you have access to a private phone, you can benefit from cheaper rates by using a 'Call-by-Call' access code (eg ☎ 01016 or ☎ 010090). Rates change daily and are published in the newspapers or online at www .billigertelefonieren.de (in German).

Telephone call shops, which tend to cluster around train stations, may also offer competitive calling rates but often charge steep connection fees. Always make sure you understand the charges involved.

With a high-speed internet connection, you can talk for free via **Skype** (www.skype.com), or use their SkypeOut service, which allows you to call landlines from your computer.

Phonecards
Most public pay phones only work with Deutsche Telekom (DT) phonecards, available in denominations of €5, €10 and €20 from DT stores, as well as post offices, newsagents and tourist offices. Occasionally you'll see non-DT pay phones, but these may not necessarily offer better rates.

For long-distance or international calls, prepaid calling cards issued by other companies tend to offer better rates than DT's phonecards. Look for them at newsagents and telephone call shops. Most of these cards also work with payphones but usually at a surcharge – read the fine print on the card itself. Those sold at ReiseBank outlets have some of the most competitive rates.

TIME
Clocks in Germany are set to central European time (GMT/UTC plus one hour).

Daylight-saving time kicks in at 2am on the last Sunday in March and ends on the last Sunday in October. Without taking daylight-saving times into account, when it's noon in Berlin, it's 11am in London, 6am in New York, 3am in San Francisco, 8pm in Tokyo, 9pm in Sydney and 11pm in Auckland. The use of the 24-hour clock (eg 6.30pm is 18.30) is the norm.

TOURIST INFORMATION

The best pre-trip planning source is the **German National Tourist Office** (GNTO; www.deutschland -tourismus.de), whose comprehensive website is available in almost 30 languages and has links to sub-sites catering specifically for visitors from various countries. Regional websites and tourist organisations are listed at the start of each destination chapter throughout this book.

Local Tourist Offices

Just about every community in Germany has a walk-in tourist office where you can get advice and pick up maps and pamphlets, sometimes in English. Many also offer a room and ticket reservation service, usually free but sometime for a small fee. With few exceptions, there's at least one staff member more or less fluent in English and willing to make the effort to help you. Contact details are listed throughout this book in the Information section of each town.

TRAVELLERS WITH DISABILITIES

If you happen to be in a wheelchair, use crutches or can't see or hear so well, Germany is a mixed bag. The mobility impaired will find access ramps and/or lifts in many public buildings, including train stations, museums, theatres and cinemas, especially in the cities. In historic towns, though, cobblestone streets make getting around quite cumbersome.

Newer hotels have lifts and rooms with extra-wide doors and spacious bathrooms. Trains, trams, underground trains and buses are becoming increasingly accessible. Some stations also have grooved platform borders to assist blind passengers. Seeing-eye dogs are allowed on all forms of public transport. For the hearing impaired, upcoming station names are often displayed electronically on all forms of public transport.

Some car-rental agencies offer hand-controlled vehicles and vans with wheelchair lifts at no charge, but you must reserve them well in advance. In parking lots and garages, look for designated disabled spots marked with a wheelchair symbol.

Many local and regional tourist offices have special brochures for people with disabilities, although usually in German. Good general resources include:

Deutsche Bahn Mobility Service Centre (☎ 01805-512 512, 01805-996 633, ext 9 for English operator; www.bahn.de; ☺ 8am-8pm Mon-Fri, 8am-4pm Sat) Train access information and help with route planning. The website has useful information in English.

German National Tourism Office (www.deutschland -tourismus.de) Has an entire section (under Travel Tips) about barrier-free travel in Germany.

Natko (☎ 0211-336 8001; www.natko.de, in German) Central clearing house for inquiries about 'tourism without barriers' in Germany.

VISAS

Most EU nationals only need their national identity card or passport to enter, stay and work in Germany. Citizens of Australia, Canada, Israel, Japan, New Zealand, Poland, Switzerland and the US are among those countries that need only a valid passport but no visa if entering Germany as tourists for up to three months within a six-month period. Passports should be valid for at least another four months from the planned date of departure from Germany.

Nationals from most other countries need a so-called Schengen Visa, named for the 1995 Schengen Agreement that abolished passport controls between Austria, Belgium, Denmark, Finland, France, Germany, Iceland, Italy, Greece, Luxembourg, Netherlands, Norway, Portugal, Spain and Sweden. In late 2007, the following nine countries joined the agreement: Czech Republic, Estonia, Hungary, Latvia, Lithuania, Malta, Poland, Slovakia and Slovenia. Switzerland joined in 2008.

Applications for a Schengen Visa must be filed with the embassy or consulate of the country that is your primary destination. It is valid for stays up to 90 days. Legal residency in any Schengen country makes a visa unnecessary, regardless of your nationality.

Visa applications are usually processed within two to 10 days, but it's always best to start the process as early as possible. For details, see www.auswaertiges-amt.de and check with a German consulate in your country.

DIRECTORY

WOMEN TRAVELLERS

Germany is a safe place for women to explore, even solo. Of course, this doesn't mean you can let your guard down and trust your life to every stranger. Simply use the same common sense you would at home. Getting hassled in the streets happens infrequently and is usually limited to wolf whistles and unwanted stares. In crowded situations, like public transport and events, groping is possible but rare.

German women are quite outspoken and emancipated. There's no need to be afraid of initiating a conversation, not even with men. Unless you're overtly coquettish, this most likely won't be interpreted as a sexual advance. It's quite normal to split dinner bills, even on dates, or for a woman to start talking to a man. Going alone to cafes and restaurants is perfectly acceptable, even at night, although how comfortable you feel doing so depends entirely on you. In bars and nightclubs, solo women are likely to attract some attention, but if you don't want company, most men will respect a firm 'no, thank you'. If you feel threatened, protesting loudly will often make the offender slink away with embarrassment – or at least spur other people to come to your defence. Unfortunately, drinks spiked with so-called 'date-rape drugs' can be a problem in some bars and clubs, so don't leave your drink unattended.

If assaulted, call the police (☎ 110) or contact a women's crisis hotline (selected numbers follow). They can help you deal with the emotional trauma and make referrals to medical, legal and social-service providers. For a complete list, see www.frauennotrufe.de (click to 'Hilfsangebote') or call ☎ 030-3229 9500. They're not staffed around the clock, but don't get discouraged – try again later or leave a message and someone will call you back.

Berlin (☎ 030-216 8888)
Cologne (☎ 0221-562 035)
Frankfurt am Main (☎ 069-709 494)
Hamburg (☎ 040-255 566)
Hanover (☎ 0511-332 112)
Leipzig (☎ 0341-391 1199)
Mainz (☎ 06131-221 213)
Munich (☎ 089-763 737)
Nuremberg (☎ 0911-284 400)
Stuttgart (☎ 0711-285 9002)

WORK

Non-EU citizens cannot work legally in Germany without a residence permit (Aufenthaltserlaubnis) and a work permit (Arbeitserlaubnis). EU citizens don't need a work permit but they must have a residence permit, although obtaining one is a mere formality. Since regulations change from time to time, it's best to contact the German embassy in your country for the latest information.

Because of fairly high unemployment, finding skilled work in Germany can be a full-time job in itself. A good place to start is at the local employment office (Arbeitsamt), which maintain job banks of vacancies. The classified sections of the daily papers are another source, as are private placement and temp agencies such as **Randstad** (www.randstad .de), **Adecco** (www.adecco.de) and **Persona** (www .persona.de). All have comprehensive websites (in German) that allow you to search for job openings. Computer specialists might want to visit www.computerjobs24.de, a data bank that allows you to search for jobs or list your services at no cost. Obviously, the better your German, the greater your chances.

If you're not in the market for a full-time job but simply need some cash to replenish your travel budget, consider babysitting, house cleaning, English tutoring, operating tours, bartending, yoga teaching, donating sperm or perhaps nude modelling for art classes. You won't get rich, but neither will you need a high skill level, much training, or fluent German. Start by placing a classified ad in a local newspaper or listings guide. Other places to advertise include noticeboards at universities, photocopy shops and supermarkets.

Au pair work is relatively easy to find and can be done legally even by non-EU citizens. Fluent German is not expected, although you should have some basic language skills. For the full story, get Lonely Planet's *The Big Trip,* or the latest edition of *The Au Pair and Nanny's Guide to Working Abroad* by Susan Griffith and Sharon Legg. The website www .au-pair-agenturen.de (in German) has links to numerous agencies in Germany.

Citizens of Australia, New Zealand, Japan, South Korea and Hong Kong between the ages of 18 and 30 may apply for a Working Holiday Visa, which entitles them to work in Germany for up to 90 days in a 12-month period. A similar scheme is available for Canadians up to age 35. Contact the German embassy in your country for details.

Also check out the 'Living & Working Abroad' thread on the Thorn Tree forum at www.lonelyplanet.com.

Transport

CONTENTS

GETTING THERE & AWAY

ENTERING THE COUNTRY

Entering Germany is usually a very straightforward procedure. If you're arriving in Germany from any of the 25 Schengen countries, such as the Netherlands or Austria, you no longer have to show your passport or go through customs in Germany, no matter which nationality you are. For a list of Schengen countries, as well as an overview of visa requirements, see p771.

Passport

Passports must be valid for at least six months after the end of your trip. Citizens of most Western countries can enter Germany without a visa; other nationals may need a Schengen Visa; see p771 for details.

AIR
Airports

Frankfurt International Airport (FRA; ☎ 01805-372 4636; www.frankfurt-airport.de) is the main gateway for transcontinental flights, although **Düsseldorf** (DUS; ☎ 0211-4210; www.duesseldorf-international.de) and **Munich** (MUC; ☎ 089-975 00; www.munich-airport.de) also receive their share of overseas air traffic. Berlin has two international airports, **Tegel** (TXL; ☎ 0180-500 0186; www.berlin-airport.de) and **Schönefeld** (SXF; ☎ 0180-500 0186; www.berlin-airport.de). There are also sizeable airports in **Hamburg** (HAM; ☎ 040-

507 50; www.flughafen-hamburg.de), **Cologne/Bonn** (CGN; ☎ 02203-404 001; www.airport-cgn.de) and **Stuttgart** (STR; ☎ 01805-948 444; www.stuttgart-airport.com), and smaller ones in such cities as Bremen, Dresden, Erfurt, Hanover, Leipzig, Münster-Osnabrück and Nuremberg.

Some of the budget airlines – Ryanair in particular – keep their fares low by flying to remote airports, which are often recycled military airstrips. The biggest of these is **Frankfurt-Hahn** (HHN; ☎ 06543-509 200; www.hahn-airport.de), which is actually near the Moselle River, about 110km northwest of Frankfurt proper.

For details about individual German airports, including information about getting to and from them, see the destination chapters.

Airlines

The main airline serving Germany is the national flagship carrier and Star Alliance member **Lufthansa** (LH; ☎ 01805-838 426; www.lufthansa.de), which operates a vast network of domestic and international flights and has one of the world's best safety records. Of the many other national and discount carriers also serving Germany, the main ones are listed here along with their telephone numbers in Germany for reservations, flight changes and information. For contact information in your home country, see the airlines' websites.

NATIONAL CARRIERS

Aeroflot (SU; ☎ 0180-375 5555; www.aeroflot.com)
Air Canada (AC; ☎ 069-2711 5111; www.aircanada.ca)
Air France (AF; ☎ 01805-830 830; www.airfrance.com)

Air India (AI; ☎ in the UK 0208-560 9996; www
.airindia.com)

Air Lingus (EI; ☎ 01805-133 209; www.airlingus.com)

Air New Zealand (NZ; ☎ 0800-181 7778; www.airnz
.co.nz)

Alitalia (AZ; ☎ 01805-074 747; www.alitalia.com)

American Airlines (AA; ☎ 069-5098 5070; www
.aa.com)

British Airways (BA; ☎ 01805-266 522; www
.britishairways.com)

Cathay Pacific (CX; ☎ 01805-288 285; www.cathay
pacific.com)

Continental Airlines (CO; ☎ 0180-321 2610; www
.continental.com)

Delta (DL; ☎ 01803-337 880; www.delta.com)

Iberia (IB; ☎ 01805-442 900; www.iberia.com)

KLM (KL; ☎ 01805-254 750; www.klm.com)

LOT (LO; ☎ 01803-000 346; www.lot.com)

Malev Hungarian Airlines (MA; ☎ 01805-363 586;
www.malev.hu)

Olympic Airlines (OA; ☎ 069-970 670; www.olympic
airlines.com)

Qantas (QF; ☎ 01805-250 620; www.qantas.com.au)

Scandinavian Airlines/SAS (SK; ☎ 01805-117 002;
www.scandinavian.net)

Singapore Airlines (SQ; ☎ 069-719 5200; www
.singaporeair.com)

South African Airways (SA; ☎ 069-2998 0320; www
.flysaa.com)

Swiss (LX; ☎ 01803-000 337; www.swiss.com)

Turkish Airlines (TK; ☎ 01805-849 266; www
.turkishairlines.com)

United Airlines (UA; ☎ 069-5007 0387; www.united.com)

US Airways (US; ☎ 01803-000 609; www.usairways.com)

DISCOUNT CARRIERS

Air Berlin (AB; ☎ 01805-737 800; www.air-berlin.com)

Cirrus (C9; ☎ 0180-444 4888; www.cirrusairlines.de)

Condor (DE; ☎ 01805-767 757; www.condor.com)

easyJet (EZY; ☎ 0900-1100 161; www.easyjet.com)

Flybe (BE; ☎ in the UK 004413-9226 8513; www.flybe.com)

Germanwings (4U; ☎ 0900-19 19 100; www.german
wings.com) Calls cost €0.99 per minute.

Norwegian Air Shuttle (DY; ☎ in Norway 0047-2149
0015; www.norwegian.no)

Ryanair (FR; ☎ 0900-116 0500; www.ryanair.com) Calls
cost €0.62 per minute.

TUIfly (X3; ☎ 01805-787 510; www.tuifly.com)

Wizz Air (W6; ☎ 0900-120 4021; www.wizzair.com)
Calls cost €1.03 per minute.

Tickets

Everybody loves a bargain and timing is key
when it comes to snapping up cheap airfares.
You can generally save a bundle by booking early, travelling midweek (Tuesday to
Thursday) or in low season (October to
March/April in the case of Germany), or flying in the late evening or early morning.

Your best friend in ferreting out deals is
the internet. Start by checking fares at www
.expedia.com, www.travelocity.com, www
.orbitz.com or www.zuji.com, then run the
same flight request through meta-search engines such as www.sidestep.com, www.kayak
.com or www.openjet.com. If you're not tied
to particular travel dates, use the flexible-date
search tool to find the lowest fares or consult
www.itasoftware.com.

Many airlines now guarantee the lowest
fares on their own websites, so check these
out as well. A good way to learn about late-
breaking bargain fares is by signing up to airlines' free weekly email newsletters. To get the
skinny on which low-cost airlines fly where,
go to www.whichbudget.com and then book
tickets on the airline website.

If you're based in North America and flexible with regard to the airline and departure
times or dates, you might be able to save a
bundle through www.priceline.com and its
'Name Your Own Price' scheme. Enter the
fare you're willing to pay, then wait and see
if any airline bites.

And don't forget about travel agents, who
can be especially helpful when planning complex itineraries since they know the system,
the options, the special deals and so on.

INTERCONTINENTAL (RTW) TICKETS

Coming from Australia or New Zealand,
round-the-world (RTW) tickets may work out
cheaper than regular return fares, especially
if you're planning on visiting other countries
besides Germany. They're of most value for
trips that combine Germany with Asia or
North America.

Official airline RTW tickets are usually
put together by a combination of airlines or
an entire alliance and permit you to fly to
a specified number of stops and/or a maximum mileage, so long as you don't backtrack.
Tickets are usually valid for one year. Some
airlines 'black out' a few heavily travelled
routes. Online agencies to consult include
www.airbrokers.com, www.airtreks.com and
www.circletheplanet.com.

Australia & New Zealand

The dominant carriers to central Europe
are Qantas, British Airways and Singapore
Airlines. Flights go either via Asia or the

CLIMATE CHANGE & TRAVEL

Climate change is a serious threat to the ecosystems that humans rely upon, and air travel is the fastest-growing contributor to the problem. Lonely Planet regards travel, overall, as a global benefit, but believes we all have a responsibility to limit our personal impact on global warming.

Flying & Climate Change

Pretty much every form of motor travel generates CO_2 (the main cause of human-induced climate change) but planes are far and away the worst offenders, not just because of the sheer distances they allow us to travel, but because they release greenhouse gases high into the atmosphere. The statistics are frightening: two people taking a return flight between Europe and the US will contribute as much to climate change as an average household's gas and electricity consumption over a whole year.

Carbon Offset Schemes

Climatecare.org and other websites use 'carbon calculators' that allow jetsetters to offset the greenhouse gases they are responsible for with contributions to energy-saving projects and other climate-friendly initiatives in the developing world – including projects in India, Honduras, Kazakhstan and Uganda.

Lonely Planet, together with Rough Guides and other concerned partners in the travel industry, supports the carbon offset scheme run by climatecare.org. Lonely Planet offsets all of its staff and author travel.

For more information check out our website: lonelyplanet.com.

Middle East (with possible stopovers in such cities as Singapore or Dubai), or across Canada or the US (with possible stopovers in Honolulu, Los Angeles or San Francisco). Fares in high/low season hover around AUD$2100/1300. RTW tickets may work out cheaper than straightforward return fares.

Canada

Lufthansa and Air Canada fly to Frankfurt and Munich from all major Canadian airports. Cheaper flights with other airlines usually involve a stopover or change of plane in a US, Canadian or European airport.

Continental Europe

Lufthansa and other national carriers connect all major European cities with destinations in Germany. The dominant discount carriers – Air Berlin, easyJet, Germanwings and Ryanair – have flights to all major and minor German airports from throughout Europe. Smaller airlines servicing less busy routes include Norwegian Air Shuttle from Scandinavia and Wizz Air from Eastern Europe.

UK & Ireland

Numerous airlines fly to destinations throughout Germany from practically every airport in the UK and Ireland. Lufthansa and British Airways are the main national carriers, but prices are usually lower on Ryanair, easyJet, TUIfly, Air Berlin and Germanwings. Their extensive route networks have made travelling even to smaller, regional destinations, such as Dortmund, Nuremberg and Münster, very inexpensive. Rock-bottom fares start as low as £20 one way, including airport taxes.

USA

Lufthansa and all major US carriers operate flights from nearly every big US city to Germany. In addition, German carriers Air Berlin and Condor operate seasonal (ie summer) services from selected US cities. (Condor flies from Anchorage and Fairbanks, for instance.) Good fares are often available from Asia-based airlines, such as Air India and Singapore Airlines, which stop in the US en route to their final destination.

Most flights land in Frankfurt, but Düsseldorf and Munich are also seeing more incoming traffic. But even if you land in Frankfurt – and it's not your final destination – it's a snap to catch a connecting domestic flight or continue your travels on Germany's ever-efficient train system.

Airfares rise and fall in a cyclical pattern. The lowest fares are available from early

---

SMART TRAVELS

Flying has become second nature in this era of low-cost airlines and few of us stop to consider using alternative travel methods and doing our bit for the environment. Yet, depending on where you're based, getting to Germany without an aeroplane is easier and more comfortable than you might think and leaves a much smaller carbon footprint.

Take the trip from London to Frankfurt, for instance. If you're flying, you're generating 0.349 tons of emissions. If you're driving, it's still 0.223 tons. But by travelling by rail or bus, you can cut that number down dramatically to just 0.092 tons. Just catch the Eurostar (opposite) in the afternoon, then switch to a night train in Paris and be in Germany for breakfast. There are also direct overnight trains from Warsaw, Vienna, Munich, Paris and Brussels, as well as frequent daytime connections from many other cities.

Buses are slower and less comfortable, but they're another option, especially if you're travelling at short notice or live in an area poorly served by air or train. The main operator within Europe is Eurolines (below).

November to mid-December and then again from mid-January to Easter, gradually rising in the following months. Peak months are July and August, after which prices start to drop again. Fares to Frankfurt start at around US$600/450 return in high/low season from New York, US$850/550 from Chicago and US$1000/650 from Los Angeles.

STA Travel (☎ 800-781-4040; www.statravel.com) and **Flight Centre** (☎ 877-233-9999; www.flightcentre .us) are both reliable budget travel agencies offering online bookings and brick-and-mortar branches throughout the country.

LAND
Border Crossings
Germany is bordered anticlockwise by Denmark, the Netherlands, Belgium, Luxembourg, France, Switzerland, Austria, the Czech Republic and Poland. The Schengen Agreement (p771) abolished passport and customs formalities between Germany and all bordering countries.

Bus
Eurolines (www.eurolines.com) is the umbrella organisation of 32 European coach operators connecting 500 destinations across Europe. Its website has links to each national company's site with detailed fare and route information, promotional offers, contact numbers and, in most cases, an online booking system. Children between the ages of four and 12 pay half price, while teens, students and seniors get 10% off regular fares. In Germany, Eurolines is represented by **Deutsche Touring** (☎ 069-790 3501; www.touring.de).

Sample Eurolines fares:

Route	Price	Duration (hr)
Budapest-Frankfurt	€98	13-18
Florence-Munich	€76	9
London-Cologne	£60	13
Paris-Munich	€61	13
Warsaw-Berlin	€58	11

If Germany is part of your Europe-wide itinerary, a **Eurolines Pass** (www.eurolines-pass.com) may be a ticket to savings. It offers unlimited travel between 41 cities within a 15- or 30-day period. From late June to early September, the cost is €310/410 (15/30 days) for those over 26 years and €260/340 for travellers under 26 years. Lower prices apply during the rest of the year; the website has full details. The pass is available online and from travel agents.

Berlin-based **Berlin Linien Bus** (☎ 030-861 9331; www.berlinlinienbus.de) is a similar organisation with some 55 national and Europe-wide companies serving 350 destinations all over the continent. There is some overlap between services provided by Berlin Linien Bus and Eurolines.

Backpacker-geared **Busabout** (☎ in the UK 08450 267 514; www.busabout.com) is a hop-on, hop-off service that runs coaches along three interlocking European loops between May and October. Germany is part of the northern loop, which includes stops in Berlin, Dresden, Munich and Stuttgart. Loops can be combined. In Munich, for instance, the northern loop intersects with the southern loop to Italy. Trips on one loop cost €419, on two loops €719 and on three €879.

If you don't like travelling along predetermined routes, you can buy the Flexitrip

Pass, which allows you to travel between cities across different loops. It costs €369 for six stops. Check the website for the full low-down or to buy a pass. Passes are also available from travel agencies, such as STA Travel and Flight Centre.

In many cities, buses drop off and pick up at centrally located hostels.

Car & Motorcycle

When bringing your own vehicle to Germany, you need a valid driving licence, your car registration certificate and proof of insurance. Foreign cars must display a nationality sticker unless they have official European plates. You also need to carry a warning (hazard) triangle and a first-aid kit. For road rules and other driving-related information, see p781.

Coming from the UK, the fastest way to the continent is via the **Eurotunnel** (☎ in the UK 08705-353 535, in Germany 01805-000 248; www.eurotunnel .com). These shuttle trains whisk cars, motorbikes, bicycles and coaches from Folkestone in England through the Channel Tunnel to Coquelles (near Calais, in France) in about 35 minutes. From there, you can be in Germany in about three hours. Loading and unloading takes about one hour.

Shuttles run daily around the clock, with several departures hourly during peak periods. Fares are calculated per vehicle, including passengers, and depend on such factors as time of day, season and length of stay. Expect to pay between £90 and £155 for a standard one-way ticket. Promotional fares often bring the cost down to around £50. The website and travel agents have full details.

For details about bringing your car across the Channel by ferry, see p779.

Hitching

Lonely Planet does not recommend hitching. Travellers intending to hitch shouldn't, however, have too many problems getting to and from Germany via the main autobahns and highways. See p784 for a discussion of potential risks and for information on ridesharing, which is an economical and much safer alternative to hitchhiking.

Train

Long-distance trains connecting major German cities with those in other countries are called EuroCity (EC) trains. Seat reservations are highly recommended, especially during the peak summer season and around major holidays (p766).

There are direct overnight trains (City Night Line, CNL) to Germany from such cities as Amsterdam, Copenhagen, Belgrade, Budapest, Bucharest, Florence, Milan, Prague, Rome, Venice and Vienna. You can choose between *Schlafwagen* (sleepers; €40 to €100 supplement), which are comfortable compartments for up to three people; *Liegewagen* (couchettes; €20 to €30 supplement), which sleep four to six people; and *Sitzwagen* (seat carriage; €4 to €10 supplement), which have roomy reclining seats. If you have a rail pass, you only pay the supplement. Women can ask for a berth in a single-sex couchette when booking, but book early. For full details, contact Deutsche Bahn's **night train specialists** (☎ in Germany 01805-141 514; www.nachtzugreise.de, in German).

EURAIL PASS

If you want to cover lots of territory in and around Germany within a specific time, **Eurail Passes** (www.eurail.com) are a convenient and good-value option. They're valid for travel on national railways, and some private lines, ferries and river boat services. Available only to non-residents of Europe, they should be bought before leaving your home country, although a limited number of outlets, listed on their website, also sell them in Europe.

A bewildering variety of Eurail Passes is now available. The Eurail Global Pass, for instance, provides unlimited 1st-class travel in 21 countries and is available for 15 or 21 consecutive days or one, two or three months. There are also Flexi Passes, giving you 10 days of travel within a one-month period or 15 days within two months. Eurail Select Passes limit travel to within three, four or five bordering countries. Regional passes, meanwhile, get you around two neighbouring countries, eg Germany and France or Germany and the Czech Republic. Groups of two to five travelling together save 15% off the regular adult fares. If you're under 26, prices drop 35%, but you must travel in 2nd class. Children aged between four and 11 years get a 50% discount on the adult fare. Children under four years travel for free.

The website has all the details, as well as a ticket purchasing function allowing you to pay in US or Australian dollars, as well as euros.

EUROSTAR

The Channel Tunnel makes train travel between the UK and Germany a fast and enjoyable option. High-speed **Eurostar** (☎ in the UK 08705-186 186; www.eurostar.com) passenger trains hurtle at least 10 times daily between London and Paris (the journey takes 2½ hours) or Brussels (two hours). At either city you can change to regular or other high-speed trains to destinations in Germany.

Eurostar fares depend on such factors as class, time of day, season and destination. Children, rail-pass holders and those aged between 12 and 25 and over 60 qualify for discounts. For the latest fare information, including promotions and special packages, check the website.

INTERRAIL PASS

InterRail Passes (www.interrailnet.com) may be purchased by anyone who's been a permanent resident of a European country (including Russia, Estonia, Turkey and several others; see the website for details). As with the Eurail Pass, you can pick from several schemes. The InterRail Global Pass entitles you to unlimited travel in 30 countries and is available either for 22 days (€469) or one month (€599) of continuous travel, for five travel days within a 10-day period (€249) or for 10 travel days within a 22-day period (€359).

The other option is the One Country Pass, eg the InterRail Germany pass, which buys three, four, six or eight days of travel within a one-month period. The cost is €189/209/269/299 respectively. This pass is not available if you are a resident of Germany.

Prices quoted are for one adult travelling in 2nd class. Different prices apply to 1st class tickets and for travellers under 26. Children aged between four and 11 years get a 50% discount on the adult fare. Children under four years travel for free.

LAKE

The Romanshorn–Friedrichshafen car ferry provides the quickest way across Lake Constance between Switzerland and Germany. It's operated year-round by **Schweizerische Bodensee Schifffahrt** (☎ in Switzerland 071-466 7888; www.boden seeschiffe.ch), takes 40 minutes and costs €7.50 per person (children €3.50). Bicycles are €5, cars start at €28.50.

SEA

Germany's main ferry ports are Kiel and Travemünde (near Lübeck) in Schleswig-Holstein, and Rostock and Sassnitz (on Rügen Island) in Mecklenburg–Western Pomerania. All have services to Scandinavia and the Baltic states. Return tickets are often cheaper than

two one-way tickets. Prices fluctuate dramatically according to the season, the day and time of departure and, for overnight ferries, cabin size, location and amenities. All prices quoted are for one-way fares. Car prices are for a standard passenger vehicle up to 6m in length and include all passengers. Also see the individual port towns' Getting There & Away sections in the destination chapters.

Denmark
GEDSER–ROSTOCK
Scandlines (☎ 01805-116 688; www.scandlines.de) runs year-round ferries every two hours to/from Gedser, about 100km south of Copenhagen. The 1¾-hour trip costs €87 per car in high season. Walk-on passengers pay €7/5 per adult/child. It's €16 for a bike and you.

RØDBY–PUTTGARDEN
Scandlines (☎ 01805-116 688; www.scandlines.de) operates a 45-minute ferry every half-hour for €64 for a regular car. Foot passengers pay €6/4 per adult/child in peak season one-way or same-day return. It's €13 if you bring a bicycle.

RØNNE–SASSNITZ
From March to October, **Scandlines** (☎ 01805-116 688; www.scandlines.de) operates three daily ferries to/from Rønne on Bornholm Island. The trip takes 3¾ hours and costs from €134 per car, €26 per person (kids €13) and €33 with a bike, all in peak season.

Finland
HELSINKI–TRAVEMÜNDE
Finnlines (☎ 04502-805 43; www.finnlines.de) goes to Travemünde (near Lübeck) daily, year-round in 27 to 36 hours. Berths start at €196; food is another €60. Bikes are €20, cars start at €100.

Latvia
RIGA–TRAVEMÜNDE
DFDS Lisco (☎ 0431-2097 6420; www.dfdslisco.com) operates this epic 35-hour journey twice weekly, with berths starting at €75, sleeper seats at €45 and cars at €126.

VENTSPILS–ROSTOCK
Scandlines (☎ 01805-116 688; www.scandlines.de) also runs this route, which costs from €105 per car, €40 for a Pullman seat and €140 per cabin berth in peak season. Bikes are €10. Kids pay half price. Ferries run four times weekly and make the journey in 27 hours.

Lithuania
KLAIPĖDA–KIEL
DFDS Lisco (☎ 0431-2097 6420; www.dfdslisco.com) makes 22-hour runs on this route six times weekly. Passengers pay from €70 per berth or €35 for sleeper seat. Cars start at €73.

KLAIPĖDA–SASSNITZ
DFDS Lisco (☎ 0431-2097 6420; www.dfdslisco.com) also operates this 19-hour ferry ride once a week in either direction. Costs start at €70 per berth in peak season, €35 for a sleeper seat and €62 for a regular car.

Norway
OSLO–KIEL
Color Line (☎ 0431-730 0300; www.colorline.de) makes this 20-hour journey almost daily. The fare, including a berth in the most basic two-bed cabin, is around €225. Children, seniors and students pay half-price on selected departures. Cars start at €84.

Sweden
GOTHENBURG–KIEL
The daily overnight ferry run by **Stena Line** (☎ 0431-9099, 01895-916 666; www.stenaline.de) takes 14 hours and costs €71 for foot passengers (€46 for children, students and seniors). Taking your car will cost €171 in peak season, including all passengers. Berths are compulsory and start at €78.

MALMÖ–TRAVEMÜNDE
Finnlines (☎ 04502-805 43; www.finnlines.de) makes the trip in nine hours. It's primarily geared to passengers travelling with their own car. Tickets start at €60 for daytime sailings and €120 for overnight departures, including car and one person.

TRELLEBORG–ROSTOCK
This **Scandlines** (☎ 01805-116 688; www.scandlines.de) service runs up to three times daily, takes between six and 7½ hours and in peak season costs €144 per car and all passengers. Foot passengers pay €25 (kids €13) or €26 if you bring a bike.

TT-Line (☎ 04502-801 81; www.ttline.de) makes the same crossing in 5½ hours and charges €95 per car with passengers. Adult walk-ons pay €30; children, seniors and students pay €15. Bikes are €5.

TRELLEBORG–SASSNITZ
Scandlines (☎ 01805-116 688; www.scandlines.de) operates a quick ferry to Sweden, popular with day trippers. There are five departures daily and the trip takes 3¾ to 4½ hours. Peak season fares are €114 for regular cars and all passengers, €16/8 for adult/child foot passengers and €23 for you and a bike.

TRELLEBORG–TRAVEMÜNDE
TT-Line (☎ 04502-801 81; www.ttline.de) operates up to five ferries daily on this route, which takes 7½ hours and costs €30 for adult foot passengers and €15 for students, seniors and children. Cars, including all passengers, start at €135. Bicycles are €5.

UK
There are no longer any direct ferry services between Germany and the UK, but you can just as easily go via the Netherlands, Belgium or France and drive or train it from there. Competition from Eurotunnel and budget airlines has forced ferry operators to significantly lower their fares, meaning great bargains may be available at quiet times of the day or year. Check the ferries' websites for fare details or check www.ferrybooker.com, a single site covering all sea-ferry routes and operators, plus Eurotunnel.

TO FRANCE
P&O Ferries (☎ in the UK 08716-645 645, in Germany 01805-500 9437; www.poferries.com) Dover–Calais; 75 minutes.
SeaFrance (☎ 0871-423 7119; www.seafrance.com) Dover–Calais; 75 minutes.
Norfolkline (☎ in the UK 0844-499 007, in Germany 01801-600 31; www.norfolkline.com) Dover–Dunkirk; two hours.

TO BELGIUM
P&O Ferries (☎ in the UK 08716-645 645, in Germany 01805-500 9437; www.poferries.com) Hull–Zeebrugge; 13½ hours.

TO THE NETHERLANDS
P&O Ferries (☎ in the UK 08716-645 645, in Germany 01805-500 9437; www.poferries.com) Hull–Rotterdam; 14 hours.
Stena Line (☎ 0431-9099, 01895-916 666; www.stenaline.co.uk) Harwich–Hoek van Holland; 3¾ hours.
DFDS Seaways (☎ 0871-522 9955; www.dfds.co.uk) Newcastle–Amsterdam; 15 hours.

TRANSPORT

TRANSPORT

GETTING AROUND

Germans are whizzes at moving people around, and the public transport network is among the best in Europe. The two best ways of getting around the country are by car and by train. Regional bus services fill the gaps in areas not well served by the rail network.

AIR

Most large and many smaller German cities have their own airports (see also p773) and numerous carriers operate domestic flights within Germany. Lufthansa, of course, has the most dense route network. Other airlines offering domestic flights include Air Berlin, Cirrus Air and Germanwings.

Unless you're flying from one end of the country to the other, say Berlin to Munich or Hamburg to Munich, planes are only marginally quicker than trains if you factor in the time it takes to get to and from the airports.

BICYCLE

Cycling is allowed on all roads and highways but not on the autobahns (motorways). Cyclists must follow the same rules of the road as cars and motorcycles. Helmets are not compulsory, not even for children, but wearing one is simply common sense.

Hire & Purchase

Most towns and cities have some sort of bicycle-hire station, which is often at or near the train station. Hire costs range from €9 to €25 per day and €35 to €85 per week, depending on the model of bicycle you hire. A minimum deposit of €30 (more for fancier bikes) and/or ID are required. Many agencies are listed in the Getting Around sections of the destination chapters in this book. Some outfits also offer repair service or bicycle storage facilities.

Hotels, especially in resort areas, sometimes keep a stable of bicycles for their guests, often at no charge.

If you plan to spend several weeks or longer in the saddle, buying a second-hand bike may work out cheaper than renting one and be easier than bringing your own. You can get a cheap, basic two-wheeler for around €60, although for good reconditioned models you'll probably have to shell out at least €200. The hire stations sometimes sell used bicycles

or may be able to steer you to a good place locally. Flea markets are another source, as are the classified sections of daily newspapers and listings magazines. Notice boards at universities, hostels or supermarkets may also yield some leads. A useful website for secondhand purchases is www.zweitehand. de, although it's in German only.

Transport

Bicycles may be taken on most trains but require purchasing a separate ticket (Fahrradkarte). These cost €9 per trip on long-distance trains (IC and EC; reservations required) and €4.50 per day on local and regional trains (IRE, RB, RE and S-Bahn; see the boxed text, p788, for train types). Bicycles are not allowed on high-speed ICE trains. There is no charge at all on some trains. For full details, enquire at a local station or call ☎ 01805-151 415. Free lines are also listed in DB's complimentary Bahn & Bike brochure (in German), as are the almost 250 stations where you can rent bikes. Both are available for downloading from www.bahn.de/bahnundbike.

Many regional companies use buses with special bike racks. Bicycles are also allowed on practically all boat and ferry services on Germany's lakes and rivers.

For additional information on cycling in Germany, see p759.

BOAT

With two seas and a lake- and river-filled interior, don't be surprised to find yourself in a boat at some point. For basic transport, boats are primarily used when travelling to or between the East Frisian Islands in Lower Saxony; the North Frisian Islands in Schleswig-Holstein; Helgoland, which also belongs to Schleswig-Holstein; and the islands of Poel, Rügen and Hiddensee in Mecklenburg–Western Pomerania. Scheduled boat services operate along sections of the Rhine, the Elbe and the Danube. There are also ferry services in areas with no or only a few bridges as well as on major lakes such as the Chiemsee and Lake Starnberg in Bavaria and Lake Constance in Baden-Württemberg.

From around April to October, local operators run scenic river or lake cruises lasting from one hour to a full day. For details, see the individual entries in the destination chapters.

BUS

Local & Regional

Basically, wherever there is a train, take it. Buses are generally slower, less dependable and more polluting than trains, but in some rural areas they may be your only option for getting around without your own vehicle. This is especially true of the Harz Mountains, sections of the Bavarian Forest and the Alpine foothills. Separate bus companies, each with its own tariffs and schedules, operate in the different regions.

The frequency of services varies from 'rarely' to 'constantly'. Commuter-geared routes offer limited or no service in the evenings and at weekends, so keep this in mind or risk finding yourself stuck in a remote place on a Saturday night. Make it a habit to ask about special fare deals, such as daily or weekly passes or tourist tickets.

In cities, buses generally converge at the *Busbahnhof* or *Zentraler Omnibus Bahnhof* (ZOB; central bus station), which is often near the Hauptbahnhof (central train station).

Long Distance

Deutsche Touring (☎ 069-790 3501; www.touring .de) runs daily overnight services between Hamburg and Mannheim via Hannover, Frankfurt, Göttingen, Kassel and Heidelberg. If you book early, trips between any two cities cost just €9. Fares top out at €49 for the full Hannover–Mannheim route for tickets bought on the bus. Children under 12 pay half-price.

Berlin Linien Bus (☎ 030-861 9331; www.berlinlinien us.de) connects major cities (primarily Berlin, but also Munich, Düsseldorf and Frankfurt) with each other as well as holiday regions such as the Harz, the islands of Rügen and Usedom and the Bavarian Alps. One of the most popular routes is the express bus to Hamburg, which makes the journey from Berlin in 3¼ hours 12 times daily with one-way fares ranging from €9 to €21.50.

Tickets are available online and from travel agencies. Children under four years travel for free and discounts are available for older children, students, those over 60 and groups of six or more.

For details on the Europabus service along the Romantic Road, see p337.

CAR & MOTORCYCLE

German roads are excellent and motoring around the country can be a lot of fun. The country's pride and joy is its 11,000km network of autobahns (motorways, freeways). Every 40km to 60km, you'll find elaborate service areas with petrol stations, toilet facilities and restaurants; many are open 24 hours. In between are rest stops *(Rastplatz)*, which usually have picnic tables and toilet facilities. Orange emergency call boxes are spaced about 2km apart. Simply lift the metal flap and follow the (pictorial) instructions.

Autobahns are supplemented by an extensive network of *Bundesstrassen* (secondary 'B' roads, highways) and smaller *Landstrassen* (country roads). These are generally more scenic and fun as you wind through the countryside from village to village – ideal for car or motorcycle touring. You can't travel fast, but you won't care. No tolls are charged on any public roads.

If your car is not equipped with a navigational system, having a good map or road atlas is essential, especially when negotiating the tangle of country roads. Navigating in Germany is not done by the points of the compass. That is to say that you'll find no signs saying 'north' or 'west'. Rather, you'll see signs pointing you in the direction of a city, so you'd best have that map right in your lap to stay oriented. Maps cost a few euros and are sold at bookstores, train stations, airports and petrol stations. The best are published by Freytag & Berndt, ADAC, Falk and Euromap. Free maps available from tourist offices or rental agencies are generally inadequate.

Seat belts are mandatory for all passengers and there's a €30 fine if you get caught not wearing one. If you're in an accident, not wearing a seatbelt may invalidate your insurance. Children need a child seat if under four years and a seat cushion if under 12; they may not ride in the front until age 13. Motorcyclists must wear a helmet. The use of hand-held mobile phones while driving is very much *verboten* (forbidden).

Driving in the cities is not nearly as much fun as in the countryside thanks to congestion and the expense and overall scarcity of parking. In the city centre, parking is usually limited to parking lots and garages charging

TRANSPORT

GERMAN AUTOBAHNS

between €0.50 and €2 per hour. Note that some garages and parking lots close at night and charge an overnight fee.

Many cities have electronic parking guidance systems directing you to the nearest garage and indicating the number of available spaces. Street parking usually works on the pay-and-display system and tends to be

short-term (one or two hours) only. For long-term and overnight parking, consider leaving your car outside the centre in a Park & Ride (P+R) lot, which are free or low cost.

Automobile Associations

Germany's main motoring organisation, the **Allgemeiner Deutscher Automobil-Club** (ADAC; ☎ for

GREENING CITY CENTRES

To decrease air pollution caused by fine particles, 32 cities throughout Germany have introduced so-called Green Zones, which are low emission zones that may only be entered by cars displaying an *Umweltplakette* (emissions sticker; sometimes also called *Feinstaubplakette*). And yes, this includes foreign vehicles.

The easiest way to obtain the sticker is by ordering it online from the TÜV (Technical Inspection Authority) at www.tuev-sued.de or www.tuev-nord.de, both of which provide easy instructions in English. The cost is €14.99 per car. In Germany, stickers are also available from designated repair centres, car dealers and vehicle licensing offices. Drivers caught without one will be fined €40.

Cities currently participating include: Augsburg, Berlin, Bochum, Bottrop, Bremen, Cologne, Dortmund, Duisburg, Düsseldorf, Essen, Frankfurt am Main, Freiburg, Gelsenkirchen, Hanover, Heidelberg, Heilbronn, Karlsruhe, Mannheim, Munich, Oberhausen, Pforzheim, Regensburg, Reutlingen, Schwäbisch Gmünd, Stuttgart, Tübingen and Ulm. Dozens more are expected to create their own zones in the coming years. See www.umweltbundesamt.de and www.bmu.de for the latest information.

oadside assistance 0180-222 2222, from a mobile phone 222 22; www.adac.de) has offices in all major cities and many smaller ones. Its roadside assistance program is also available to members of its affiliates, including the British (AA), American (AAA) and Canadian (CAA) ones.

Driving Licence

Drivers need a valid driving licence. International Driving Permits (IDP) are not compulsory, but having one may help Germans make sense of your home licence (always carry that one, too) and may simplify the car or motorcycle hire process. IDPs are inexpensive, valid for one year and issued by your local automobile association – bring a passport photo and your home licence.

Fuel & Spare Parts

Petrol stations, nearly all of which are self-service, are generally ubiquitous except in sparsely populated rural areas. Petrol is sold in litres.

Finding spare parts should not be a problem, especially in the cities, although availability, of course, depends on the age and model of your car. Be sure to have some sort of roadside emergency assistance plan (opposite) in case your car breaks down.

Hire

As anywhere, rates for car hire vary quite considerably by model, pick-up date and location, but you should be able to get an economy-size vehicle from about €35 per day, plus insurance and taxes. Expect surcharges for hire cars originating at airports and train stations, additional drivers and one-way hire. Child or infant safety seats may be hired for about €5 per day and should be reserved at the time of booking.

In order to hire your own wheels, you'll need to be at least 25 years old, and possess a valid driving licence and a major credit card. Some companies hire out to drivers between the ages of 21 and 24 for an additional charge (about €12 to €20 per day). Younger people or those without a credit card are often out of luck, although some local car-rental outfits may accept cash or travellers-cheque deposits. Taking your rental car into an Eastern European country, such as the Czech Republic or Poland, is often a no-no, so check in advance if that's where you're planning to head.

All the main international companies, including **Avis** (☎ 01805-217 702; www.avis.com), **Europcar** (☎ 01805-8000; www.europcar.com), **Hertz** (☎ 01805-333 535; www.hertz.com) and **Budget** (☎ 01805-244 388; www.budget.com), maintain branches at airports, major train stations and towns.

You could make a booking when calling the reservation agent, although it may be worth checking directly with a local branch for special promotions the agent may not know about. Smaller local agencies sometimes offer better prices, so it's worth checking into that as well.

Pre-booked and prepaid packages arranged in your home country usually work out much cheaper than on-the-spot rentals. The same is true of fly/drive packages. Check for deals with the online travel agencies, travel agents or car-rental brokers, such as the US-based company **Auto Europe** (☎ in the US 888-223-5555; www.autoeurope.com) or the UK-based **Holiday Autos** (☎ in the UK 0871-472 5229; www.holidayautos.co.uk).

Insurance

German law requires that all registered vehicles carry third-party liability insurance. You could get seriously screwed by driving uninsured or underinsured. Germans are very fussy about their cars, and even nudging someone's bumper when jostling out of a tight parking space may well result in you having to pay for an entirely new one.

When hiring a vehicle, make sure your contract includes adequate liability insurance at the very minimum. Rental agencies almost never include insurance that covers damage to the vehicle itself, called Collision Damage Waiver (CDW) or Loss Damage Waiver (LDW). It's optional but driving without it is not recommended. Some credit-card companies cover CDW/LDW for a certain period if you charge the entire rental to your card. Always confirm with your card issuer what coverage it provides in Germany.

Road Rules

Driving is on the right-hand side of the road and standard international signs are in use. If you're unfamiliar with these, pick up a pamphlet at your local motoring organisation. Obey the road rules and speed limits carefully. Speed and red-light cameras are common and notices are sent to the car's registration address wherever that may be. If you're renting a car, the police will obtain your home address from the rental agency. There's a long list of finable actions, including using abusive language or gestures and running out of petrol on the autobahn.

The usual speed limits are 50km/h on city streets and 100km/h on highways, unless they are otherwise marked. And yes, it's true, there really are no speed limits on autobahns. However, there are many stretches where slower speeds must be observed (eg near towns, road construction), so be sure to keep an eye out for those signs or risk getting ticketed. And remember, the higher the speed, the higher the fuel consumption and emissions.

Drivers unaccustomed to the high speeds on autobahns should be extra careful when passing another vehicle. It takes only seconds for a car in the rear-view mirror to close in at 200km/h. Pass as quickly as possible, then quickly return to the right lane. Try to ignore those annoying drivers who will flash their headlights or tailgate you to make you drive faster and get out of the way. It's an illegal practice anyway, as is passing on the right.

The highest permissible blood-alcohol level for drivers is 0.05%, which for most people equates to one glass of wine or two small beers.

Pedestrians at crossings have absolute right of way over all motor vehicles. Always watch out for bicyclists when turning right; they have the right of way. Right turns at a red light are only legal if there's a green arrow pointing to the right.

HITCHING & RIDE-SHARE

Hitching *(trampen)* is never entirely safe in any country and we don't recommend it. That said, in some rural areas in Germany poorly served by public transport – such as sections of the Alpine foothills and the Bavarian Forest – it is not uncommon to see people thumbing for a ride. If you do decide to hitch, understand that you are taking a small but potentially serious risk. Remember that it's safer to travel in pairs and be sure to let someone know where you are planning to go. It's illegal to hitchhike on autobahns and their entry/exit ramps.

A safer, inexpensive and eco-conscious form of travelling is ride-shares, where you travel as a passenger in a private car in exchange for some petrol money. Most arrangements are now set up via free online ride boards, such as www.mitfahrzentrale. de, www.mitfahrgelegenheit.de (in German) and www.drive2day.de. You can advertise a ride yourself or link up with a driver going to your destination. **Citynetz** (☎ 01805-194 444; www. citynetz-mitfahrzentrale.de, in German) still maintains a few staffed offies in major cities, but they do charge a small commission for linking you up with a driver.

LOCAL TRANSPORT

Most towns have efficient public transport systems. Bigger cities, such as Berlin and Munich, integrate buses, trams, U-Bahn (underground, subway) trains and S-Bahn (suburban) trains into a single network.

Fares are either determined by zones or time travelled, or sometimes by both. A

ROAD DISTANCES (KM)

	Bamberg	Berlin	Bonn	Bremen	Cologne	Dresden	Erfurt	Essen	Frankfurt am Main	Freiburg	Hamburg	Hanover	Koblenz	Leipzig	Mainz	Munich	Nuremberg	Rostock	Saarbrücken	Stuttgart
Berlin	395																			
Bonn	353	596																		
Bremen	471	376	335																	
Cologne	377	558	28	307																
Dresden	275	187	549	460	565															
Erfurt	147	277	335	332	351	216														
Essen	416	514	105	246	69	547	336													
Frankfurt am Main	196	507	177	407	347	451	238	396												
Freiburg	388	778	393	673	419	662	509	488	269											
Hamburg	502	282	476	115	413	453	354	356	482	750										
Hanover	354	273	314	115	288	357	213	243	327	593	150									
Koblenz	300	564	61	392	88	508	295	153	106	332	492	344								
Leipzig	240	160	591	354	472	109	123	438	359	627	354	250	415							
Mainz	226	542	142	437	166	487	273	228	39	261	512	357	80	394						
Munich	225	576	561	696	569	457	371	646	392	332	777	629	473	422	394					
Nuremberg	60	425	412	531	397	304	206	446	216	355	561	417	320	270	246	157				
Rostock	580	226	614	290	587	408	430	532	613	882	175	300	641	357	645	762	609			
Saarbrücken	359	688	215	552	243	633	419	312	182	267	657	503	165	540	146	423	349	792		
Stuttgart	222	613	318	591	345	492	350	410	183	167	650	495	258	457	180	228	182	780	212	
Würzburg	82	475	271	463	294	358	208	339	114	305	504	350	217	320	143	257	102	656	276	141

TRANSPORT

multi-ticket strip (*Streifenkarte*) or a day pass (*Tageskarte*) generally offers better value than a single-ride ticket. Normally, tickets must be stamped upon boarding in order to be valid. Fines are levied if you're caught without a valid ticket. For details, see the Getting Around sections in the destination chapters.

Bicycle

From nuns to Lance Armstrong wannabes, Germans love to cycle, be it for errands, commuting, fitness or pleasure. Many cities have dedicated bicycle lanes, which must be used unless obstructed. There's no helmet law, not even for children, although using one is recommended, for obvious reasons. Bicycles must be equipped with a white light in the front, a red one in the back and yellow reflectors on the wheels and pedals. See p780 and p759 for additional cycling information.

Bus & Tram

Buses are the most ubiquitous form of public transport and practically all towns have their own comprehensive network. Buses run at regular intervals, with restricted services in the evenings and at weekends. Some cities operate night buses along the most popular routes to get night owls safely back home.

Occasionally, buses are supplemented by trams, which are usually faster because they travel on their own tracks, largely independent of other traffic. In city centres, they sometimes go underground. Bus and tram drivers normally sell single tickets and day passes only.

S-Bahn

Metropolitan areas, such as Berlin and Munich, have a system of suburban trains called the S-Bahn. They are faster and cover a wider area than buses or trams but tend to be less frequent. S-Bahn lines are often linked to the national rail network and sometimes connect urban centres. Rail passes are generally valid on these services. Specific S-Bahn lines are abbreviated with 'S' followed by the number (eg S1, S7) in the destination chapters.

Taxi

Taxis are expensive and, given the excellent public transport systems, not recommended unless you're in a real hurry. (They can actually be slower than trains or trams if you're stuck in rush-hour traffic.) Cabs are metered and charged at a base rate (flag fall) plus a per-kilometre fee. These charges are fixed but vary from city to city. Some cabbies charge extra for bulky luggage or night-time rides. It's rarely possible to flag down a taxi. Rather, order one by phone (look up *Taxiruf* in the phone book) or board at a taxi rank. The phone numbers of local taxi companies are often listed in the Getting Around sections of the destination chapters.

U-Bahn

Underground (subway) trains are known as U-Bahn in Germany and are generally the fastest form of travel in big cities. Route maps are posted in all stations and at many you'll be able to pick up a printed copy from the stationmaster or ticket office. The frequency of trains usually fluctuates with demand, meaning there are more trains during commuter rush hours than, say, in the middle of the day. Buy tickets from vending machines and validate them before the start of your journey. Specific U-Bahn lines are abbreviated with 'U' followed by the number (eg U1, U7) in the destination chapters.

TRAIN
Deutsche Bahn

Germany's rail system is operated almost entirely by **Deutsche Bahn** (DB; ☎ 01805-996 633, free automated timetable information 0800-150 7090; www.bahn.de), with a variety of train types serving just about every corner in the country (see the boxed text, p788). The DB website has detailed information (in English and other languages), as well as a ticket purchasing function with detailed instructions. Tickets may be bought using a credit card up to 10 minutes before departure at no surcharge. You will need to present a printout of your ticket, as well as the credit card you used to buy it, to the conductor.

Otherwise, tickets are available from vending machines and agents at the *Reisezentrum* (travel centre) in train stations. The latter charge a service fee but are useful if you need assistance with planning your itinerary (ask for an English-speaking clerk). Smaller stations may only have a few ticket windows and the smallest ones may have only vending machines. English instructions are normally provided. Tickets sold on board incur

a surcharge and are not available on regional trains (RE, RB, IRE) and the S-Bahn. Agents, conductors and machines usually accept major credit cards.

Most train stations have coin-operated lockers ranging in cost from €1 to €4 per 24-hour period. Larger stations have staffed left-luggage offices *(Gepäckaufbewahrung)*, but these are more expensive than lockers. If you leave your suitcase overnight, you're charged for two full days.

See p780 for details on taking your bicycle on the train.

Classes

German trains have 1st and 2nd class cars, both of them modern and comfortable. Paying extra for 1st class is usually not worth it, except perhaps on busy travel days (eg Friday, Sunday afternoon and holidays) when 2nd-class cars can get very crowded. Seating is either in compartments of up to six people or in open-plan carriages with panoramic windows. On ICE trains you'll enjoy such extras as reclining seats, tables, free newspapers and audio systems in your armrest. Newer generation ICE trains also have individual laptop outlets, unimpeded cell phone reception in 1st class and, on some routes, wi-fi access.

Trains and stations are completely non-smoking. ICE, IC and EC trains are fully air-conditioned and have a restaurant or self-service bistro.

For details about sleeper cars, see p777.

Costs

Standard, non-discounted train tickets tend to be quite expensive, but promotions, discounted tickets and special offers become available all the time. Always check www.bahn.de for the latest rail promotions. Permanent rail deals include the Schönes-Wochenende-Ticket and Ländertickets.

SCHÖNES-WOCHENENDE-TICKET

The 'Nice-Weekend-Ticket' is Europe's finest rail deal. It allows you and up to four accompanying passengers (or one or both parents or grandparents plus all their children or grandchildren up to 14 years) to travel anywhere in Germany on *one day* from midnight Saturday or Sunday until 3am the next day for just €37. The catch is that you can only use IRE, RE, RB and S-Bahn trains in 2nd class, plus local buses and other forms of public transport.

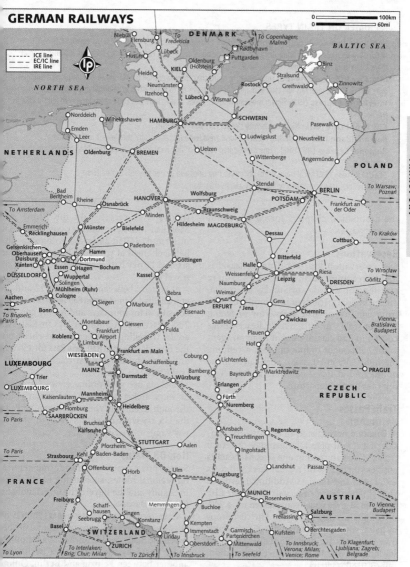

GERMAN RAILWAYS

---- ICE line
- - - EC/IC line
—— IRE line

NORTH SEA

NETHERLANDS

To Amsterdam

LUXEMBOURG

FRANCE

To Paris

To Paris

To Lyon

DENMARK

BALTIC SEA

To Copenhagen;
Malmö

POLAND

To Warsaw;
Poznań

To Kraków

To Wrocław

CZECH
REPUBLIC

Vienna;
Bratislava;
Budapest

PRAGUE

AUSTRIA

To Vienna;
Budapest

SWITZERLAND

TRANSPORT

ÄNDERTICKETS

These are essentially a variation of the Schönes-Wochenende-Ticket, except that they are valid any day of the week and are limited to travel within one of the German states (or, in some cases, also in bordering states). Prices vary slightly from state to state but are in the €26 to €34 range.

Some states also offer cheaper tickets for solo travellers costing between €18 and €25. Night passes, valid from 6pm until 6am the following day, are available in Berlin-Brandenburg and Bavaria. Travel is always in 2nd class, except in Berlin-Brandenburg and Mecklenburg–Western Pomerania where 1st class versions are available. See

TRANSPORT

A PRIMER ON TRAIN TYPES

Here's the low-down on the alphabet soup of trains operated by Deutsche Bahn (DB):

InterCity Express (ICE) Long-distance, space-age bullet trains that can reach a top speed of 300km/h, stop at major cities only and run at one- or two-hour intervals.

InterCity (IC), EuroCity (EC) Long-distance trains that are slower than the ICE (up to 200km/h); also run at one- and two-hour intervals and stop in major cities. EC trains go to major cities in neighbouring countries.

InterRegio-Express (IRE) Slower medium-distance trains connecting cities and linking local with long-distance trains.

City Night Line (CNL) Night trains with sleeper cars and couchettes.

RegionalBahn (RB) Local trains, mostly in rural areas, with frequent stops; the slowest in the system.

Regional Express (RE) Local trains with limited stops that link rural areas with metropolitan centres and the S-Bahn.

StadtExpress (SE) Local trains primarily connecting cities and geared towards commuters.

S-Bahn Local trains operating within a city and its suburban area.

---

the destination chapters for details about specific passes.

Reservations

Seat reservation for long-distance travel is highly recommended, especially if you're travelling on a Friday or Sunday afternoon, during holiday periods or in summer. Choose from window or aisle seats, row or facing seats, or seats with a fixed table. Reservations cost €4 in 2nd class if bought from an agent and €2 if bought online or from a vending machine (€5/3 in 1st class). They can be made online and at ticket counters as late as 10 minutes before departure.

Train Passes

BAHNCARD

A **Bahncard** (www.bahn.de) may be worth considering if you plan a longer stay or return trips to Germany within one year. **BahnCard 25** entitles you to 25% off regular fares and costs €57/114 in 2nd/1st class. Additional cards for your children between ages six and 18 are €10. **BahnCard 50** gives you – you guessed it – a 50% discount and costs €225/450. The cost drops by half if you're a student under 27 or a senior over 60. Cards are available at all major train stations and online. For further information, call ☎ 01805-340 035.

GERMAN RAIL PASSES

If your permanent residence is outside Europe, you qualify for the **German Rail Pass**. It entitles you to unlimited 1st- or 2nd-class travel for four to 10 days within a one-month period. The pass is valid on all trains within Germany and some Köln-Düsseldorfer

(p500) river services on the Rhine and Moselle Rivers. The four-day pass costs €236 in 1st and €180 in 2nd class, with extra days being charged at €32/22. Children between six and 11 pay half-fare. Children under six travel free.

If you are between the ages of 12 and 25, you qualify for the **German Rail Youth Pass**, which costs €150 for four days and is only good for 2nd-class travel. Additional days are €10. Two adults travelling together should check out the four-day **German Rail Twin Pass** for €270 in 2nd class and €370 in 1st class. More days cost €30/42.

Tickets are sold online (www.bahn.de), at some ticket counters in Germany and through agents in your home country. In the US, try www.raileurope.com; in the UK www.raileurope.co.uk.

Non-DB Trains

Several private operators provide train services on regional routes, such as the LausitzBahn in Saxony and the Bayerische Oberlandbahn (p334) in Bavaria.

In eastern Germany, **Interconnex** (☎ 01805-10 616; www.interconnex.com) runs one train daily between the Baltic seaside town of Warnemünde (near Rostock) and Leipzig via Berlin and another between Leipzig and Berlin. Online tickets cost just €12 for either the Berlin–Warnemünde route or the Berlin–Leipzig route and €21 for trips from Warnemünde to Leipzig. Fares are a bit higher (€17/17/29.50) if purchased through the hot line or at agents (see website for addresses), and are higher again on the train itself (€20/20/35). Seat reservations are €2.50.

Health

CONTENTS

BEFORE YOU GO

While Germany has excellent health care, prevention is the key to staying healthy while abroad. A little planning before departure, particularly for pre-existing illnesses, will save trouble later. Bring medications in their original, clearly labelled containers. A signed and dated letter from your physician describing your medical conditions and medications, including generic names, is also a good idea. If carrying syringes or needles, be sure to have a physician's letter documenting their medical necessity. Carry a spare pair of contact lenses and glasses, and take your optical prescription with you.

INSURANCE

If you're an EU citizen, an E111 form, available from health centres or, in the UK, post offices, covers you for most medical care. E111 will not cover you for non-emergencies, or emergency repatriation home. Citizens from other countries should find out if there is a reciprocal arrangement for free medical care between their country and Germany. If you do need health insurance, make sure you get a policy that covers you for the worst possible case, such as an accident requiring an emergency flight home. Find out in advance if your insurance plan will make payments directly to providers or reimburse you later for overseas health expenditures.

RECOMMENDED VACCINATIONS

No jabs are required to travel to Germany. The World Health Organization (WHO), however, recommends that all travellers should be covered for diphtheria, tetanus, measles, mumps, rubella and polio, regardless of their destination.

IN TRANSIT

DEEP VEIN THROMBOSIS (DVT)

Blood clots may form in the legs during plane flights, chiefly because of prolonged immobility. The longer the flight, the greater the risk. The chief symptom of DVT is swelling or pain of the foot, ankle or calf, usually but not always on just one side. When a blood clot travels to the lungs, it may cause chest pain and difficulty breathing. Travellers with any of these symptoms should immediately seek medical attention.

To prevent the development of DVT on long flights you should walk about the cabin, contract the leg muscles while sitting, drink plenty of fluids and avoid alcohol and tobacco.

JET LAG & MOTION SICKNESS

To avoid jet lag (common when crossing more than five time zones) try drinking plenty of non-alcoholic fluids and eating light meals. Upon arrival, get exposure to natural sunlight and readjust your schedule (for meals, sleep etc) as soon as possible.

Antihistamines such as dimenhydrinate (Dramamine) and meclizine (Antivert, Bonine) are usually the first choice for treating motion sickness. A herbal alternative is ginger.

IN GERMANY

AVAILABILITY & COST OF HEALTH CARE

Excellent health care is readily available but rather expensive. For minor illnesses, pharmacists are able to dispense valuable advice

HEALTH

MEDICAL CHECKLIST

All of the following are readily available in Germany. If you are hiking out of town, these items may come in handy.

- antibiotics
- antidiarrhoeal drugs (eg loperamide)
- acetaminophen (Tylenol) or aspirin
- anti-inflammatory drugs (eg ibuprofen)
- antihistamines (for hay fever and allergic reactions)
- antibacterial ointment (eg Bactroban; for cuts and abrasions)
- steroid cream or cortisone (for poison ivy and other allergic rashes)
- bandages, gauze, gauze rolls

- adhesive or paper tape
- scissors, safety pins, tweezers
- thermometer
- pocket knife
- DEET-containing insect repellent for the skin
- pyrethrin-containing insect spray for clothing, tents and bed nets
- sun block
- oral rehydration salts
- acetazolamide (Diamox; for altitude sickness)

---

and over-the-counter medication. They can also advise when more specialised help is required and point you in the right direction.

TRAVELLERS' DIARRHOEA

If you develop diarrhoea, drink plenty of fluids, preferably in the form of an oral rehydration solution such as Dioralyte. If diarrhoea is bloody, persists for more than 72 hours or is accompanied by fever, shaking, chills or severe abdominal pain, seek medical attention.

ENVIRONMENTAL HAZARDS
Heat Illness

Heat exhaustion occurs following excessive fluid loss with inadequate replacement of fluids and salt. Symptoms include headache, dizziness and tiredness. Dehydration is already happening by the time you feel thirsty – aim to drink sufficient water to produce pale, diluted urine. To treat heat exhaustion drink water and/or fruit juice, and cool the body with cold water and fans.

Cold Illness

Hypothermia occurs when the body loses heat faster than it can produce it. As ever, proper preparation will reduce the risks of getting it. Even on a hot day in the mountains, the weather can change rapidly, so always carry waterproof garments, warm layers and a hat and inform others of your route.

Hypothermia starts with shivering, loss of judgment and clumsiness. Unless rewarming occurs, the sufferer deteriorates into apathy,

confusion and coma. Prevent further heat loss by seeking shelter, warm dry clothing, ho sweet drinks and shared bodily warmth.

SEXUAL HEALTH

Emergency contraception is available with doctor's prescription in Germany. It is mos effective if taken within 24 hours after un protected sex. Condoms are readily availabl throughout the country.

TRAVELLING WITH CHILDREN

Make sure the children are up to date wit routine vaccinations, and discuss possibl travel vaccines well before departure as som vaccines are not suitable for children age under one year.

If your child has vomiting or diarrhoe lost fluid and salts must be replaced. It ma be helpful to take rehydration powders wit boiled water.

WOMEN'S HEALTH

Emotional stress, exhaustion and travellin through different time zones can all contribut to an upset in a woman's menstrual pattern

If using oral contraceptives, remembe some antibiotics, diarrhoea and vomitin can stop the pill from working. Time zones gastrointestinal upsets and antibiotics do no affect injectable contraception.

Travelling during pregnancy is usually pos sible but always consult your doctor befor planning your trip. The most risky times fo travel are during the first 12 weeks of preg nancy and after 30 weeks.

Language

German belongs to the Germanic branch of the Indo-European language family and is spoken by over 100 million people worldwide, mainly in Germany, Austria and Switzerland. There are also ethnic-German communities in neighbouring Eastern European countries, such as Poland and the Czech Republic, although expulsions after 1945 reduced their numbers dramatically.

Today's standard German (High German) comes from a regional Saxon dialect. It developed into an official bureaucratic language and was used by Luther in his translation of the Bible, gradually spreading throughout Germany. The impetus Luther gave to the written language through his translations was followed by the establishment of language societies in the 17th century, and later by the 19th-century work of Jacob Grimm, the founder of modern German philology. With his brother, Wilhelm Grimm, he also began work on the first German dictionary.

Regional dialects still thrive throughout Germany, especially in Cologne, rural Bavaria, Swabia and parts of Saxony. The Sorb minority in eastern Germany has its own language. In northern Germany it is common to hear Plattdeutsch (Low German) and Frisian spoken.

German and its dialects are distant relatives of English, and the fact that many Germanic words survive in the English vocabulary today makes things a lot easier for native English speakers.

That's the good news; the bad news is that, unlike English, German has retained clear distinctions in gender and case for nouns. Though not as difficult as Russian, for instance, which has more cases, German does have its tricky moments. Germans are used to hearing foreigners – and a few notable indigenous sports personalities – make a hash of their grammar, however, and any attempt to speak the language is always well received.

All German school children learn a second language – usually English – which means most can speak it to a certain degree; some, very well. You might have problems finding English speakers in eastern Germany, however, where Russian was the main foreign language taught in schools before the *Wende* (change).

The words and phrases included in this language guide should help you through the most common travel situations (see also p90 for food vocabulary). Those with the desire to delve further into the language should get a copy of Lonely Planet's *German Phrasebook*.

GRAMMAR

German grammar can be a nightmare for speakers of other languages. Nouns come in three genders: masculine, feminine and neutral. The corresponding forms of the definite article ('the' in English) are *der*, *die* and *das*, with the universal plural form, *die*. Nouns and articles will alter according to complex grammatical rules relating to the noun's function within a phrase – known as 'case'. In German there are four cases: nominative, accusative, dative and genitive. We haven't allowed for all possible permutations of case in this language guide – it really is language-course material and simply too complex to cover here. However, bad German is a whole lot better than no German at all, so even if you muddle your cases, you'll find that you'll still be understood – and your efforts will be warmly appreciated.

If you've noticed that written German seems to be full of capital letters, the reason is that all German nouns begin with a capital letter (not just proper nouns, as in English).

PRONUNCIATION

It's not difficult to pronounce German because almost all sounds can be found in English. Follow the pronunciation guide and you should have no trouble getting your message across.

Vowels

German Example	Pronunciation Guide
hat	**a** (eg the 'u' in 'run')
habe	**aa** (eg 'father')
mein	**ai** (eg 'aisle')
Bär	**air** (eg 'hair', with no 'r' sound)
Boot	**aw** (eg 'saw')
leben	**ay** (eg 'say')
Bett/Männer/kaufen	**e** (eg 'bed')
fliegen	**ee** (eg 'thief')
schön	**eu** (eg 'her', with no 'r' sound)
zurück	**ew** ('ee' said with rounded lips)
mit	**i** (eg 'bit')
Koffer	**o** (eg 'pot')
Leute/Häuser	**oy** (eg 'toy')
Schuhe	**oo** (eg 'moon')
Haus	**ow** (eg 'how')
unter	**u** (eg 'put')

Consonants

The only two tricky consonant sounds in German are **ch** and **r**. All other consonants are pronounced much the same as their English counterparts (except **sch**, which is always as the 'sh' in 'shoe').

The **ch** sound is generally like the 'ch' in *Bach* or Scottish *loch* – like a hiss from the back of the throat. When **ch** occurs after the vowels **e** and **i** it's more like a 'sh' sound, produced with the tongue more forward in the mouth. In this book we've simplified things by using the one symbol **kh** for both sounds.

The **r** sound is different from English, and it isn't rolled like in Italian or Spanish. It's pronounced at the back of the throat, almost like saying a 'g' sound, but with some friction – it's a bit like gargling.

Word Stress

As a general rule, word stress in German mostly falls on the first syllable. To remove any doubt, the stressed syllable is shown in italics in the pronunciation guides for th following words and phrases.

ACCOMMODATION

Where's a ...?	Wo ist ...?	vaw ist ...
bed and breakfast	eine Pension	ai·ne paang·zyaw
camping ground	ein Campingplatz	ain kem·ping·pla
guest house	eine Pension	ai·ne paang·zyaw
hotel	ein Hotel	ain ho·tel
inn	ein Gasthof	ain gast·hawf
room in a private home	ein Privatzimmer	ain pri·vaat·tsi·me
youth hostel	eine Jugendherberge	ai·ne yoo·gent·her·ber·g

What's the address?
Wie ist die Adresse?   vee ist dee a·dre·se
I'd like to book a room, please.
Ich möchte bitte ein   ikh meukh·te bi·te ain
Zimmer reservieren.   tsi·mer re·zer·vee·ren
For (three) nights/weeks.
Für (drei) Nächte/   fewr (drai) nekh·te/
Wochen.   vo·khen

Do you have a ... room?	Haben Sie ein ...?	haa·ben zee ain ...
single	Einzelzimmer	ain·tsel·tsi·mer
double	Doppelzimmer mit einem	do·pel·tsi·mer mit ai·nem
	Doppelbett	do·pel·bet
twin	Doppelzimmer mit zwei	do·pel·tsi·mer mit tsvai
	Einzelbetten	ain·tsel·be·ten

How much is it per ...?	Wie viel kostet es pro ...?	vee feel kos·tet es praw ...
night	Nacht	nakht
person	Person	per·zawn

May I see it?
Kann ich es sehen?   kan ikh es zay·en
Can I get another room?
Kann ich ein anderes   kan ikh ain an·de·res
Zimmer bekommen?   tsi·mer be·ko·men
It's fine. I'll take it.
Es ist gut. Ich nehme es.   es ist goot ikh nay·me es
I'm leaving now.
Ich reise jetzt ab.   ikh rai·ze yetst ap

CONVERSATION & ESSENTIALS

You should be aware that German uses polite and informal forms for 'you' (*Sie* and *du* respectively). When addressing people you don't know well you should always use the polite form (though younger people will be less inclined to expect it). In this language guide we use the polite form unless indicated by 'inf' (for 'informal') in brackets.

If you need to ask for assistance from a stranger, always remember to introduce your request with a simple *Entschuldigung* (Excuse me).

Hello.	*Guten Tag./*	goo-ten taak/
	Grüss Gott.	grews got
	(in the south)	
Hi.	*Hallo.*	ha-lo
Goodbye.	*Auf Wiedersehen.*	owf vee-der-zay-en
See you later.	*Bis später.*	bis shpay-ter
Bye.	*Tschüss./Tschau.*	chews/chow

Good ...	*Guten ...*	goo-ten ...
day	*Tag*	taak
morning	*Morgen*	mor-gen
afternoon	*Tag*	taak
evening	*Abend*	aa-bent

How are you?
Wie geht es Ihnen?/ vee gayt es ee-nen/
Wie geht es dir? (inf) vee gayt es deer
Fine, thank you.
Danke, gut. dang-ke goot
And you?
Und Ihnen?/ unt ee-nen/
Und dir? (inf) unt deer
What's your name?
Wie ist Ihr Name?/ vee ist eer naa-me/
Wie heisst du? (inf) vee haist doo
My name is ...
Mein Name ist .../ main naa-me ist .../
Ich heisse ... ikh hai-se ...

Yes.	*Ja.*	yaa
No.	*Nein.*	nain
Please.	*Bitte.*	bi-te
Thank you.	*Danke.*	dang-ke
You're welcome.	*Bitte.*	bi-te
Excuse me.	*Entschuldigung.*	ent-shul-di-gung
Sorry.	*Entschuldigung.*	ent-shul-di-gung

DIRECTIONS
Could you help me, please?
Können Sie mir bitte keu-nen zee meer bi-te
helfen? hel-fen
Where's (a bank)?
Wo ist (eine Bank)? vaw ist (ai-ne bangk)
I'm looking for (the cathedral).
Ich suche (den Dom). ikh zoo-khe (dayn dawm)

Which way's (a public toilet)?
In welcher Richtung ist in vel-kher rikh-tung ist
(eine öffentliche toilette)? (ai-ne eu-fent-li-khe to-a-le-te)
How can I get there?
Wie kann ich dahin vee kan ikh daa-hin
kommen? ko-men
How far is it?
Wie weit ist es? vee vait ist es
Can you show me (on the map)?
Können Sie es mir keu-nen zee es meer
(auf der Karte) zeigen? (owf dair kar-te) tsai-gen

left	*links*	lingks
right	*rechts*	rekhts
near	*nahe*	naa-e
far away	*weit weg*	vait vek
here	*hier*	heer
there	*dort*	dort
on the corner	*an der Ecke*	an dair e-ke
straight ahead	*geradeaus*	ge-raa-de-ows
opposite ...	*gegenüber ...*	gay-gen-ew-ber ...
next to ...	*neben ...*	nay-ben ...
behind ...	*hinter ...*	hin-ter ...
in front of ...	*vor ...*	fawr ...
north	*nord*	nort
south	*süd*	zewt
east	*ost*	ost
west	*west*	vest

Turn ...	*Biegen Sie ... ab.*	bee-gen zee ... ap
left/right	*links/rechts*	lingks/rekhts
at the next	*an der nächsten*	an dair naykhs-ten
corner	*Ecke*	e-ke
at the traffic	*bei der Ampel*	bai dair am-pel
lights		

SIGNS

Ausgang	Exit
Eingang	Entrance
Geschlossen	Closed
Kein Zutritt	No Entry
Offen	Open
Polizei	Police
Polizeiwache	Police Station
Rauchen Verboten	No Smoking
Toiletten (WC)	Toilets
Damen	Women
Herren	Men
Verboten	Prohibited

EATING OUT

Can you recommend...?	*Können Sie ... empfehlen?*	keu·nen zee ... emp·fay·len
a restaurant	*ein Restaurant*	ain res·to·rang
a bar/pub	*eine Kneipe*	ai·ne knai·pe
Where would you go for ...?	*Wo kann man hingehen, um ...?*	vaw kan man hin·gay·en um ...
local specialities	*örtliche Spezialitäten zu essen*	eut·li·khe shpe·tsya·li·tay·ten tsoo e·sen
a cheap meal	*günstig zu essen*	gewn·stikh tsoo e·sen
a celebration	*etwas zu feiern*	et·vas tsoo fai·ern
I'd like to reserve a table for ...	*Ich möchte einen Tisch für ... reservieren.*	ikh meukh·te ai·nen tish fewr ... re·zer·vee·ren
(two) people	*(zwei) Personen*	(tsvai) per·zaw·nen
(eight) o'clock	*(acht) Uhr*	(akt) oor
Do you have ...?	*Haben Sie ...?*	ha·ben zee ...
a menu in English	*eine englische Speisekarte*	ai·ne eng·li·she shpai·ze·kar·te
kosher food	*koscheres Essen*	kaw·she·res e·sen
vegetarian food	*vegetarisches Essen*	ve·ge·ta·ri·shes e·sen

I'm starving!
Ich bin am Verhungern!   ikh bin am fer·hung·ern

Are you still serving food?
Gibt es noch etwas zu essen?   gipt es nokh et·vas tsoo e·sen?

What would you recommend?
Was empfehlen Sie?   vas emp·fay·len zee

What's in that dish?
Was ist in diesem Gericht?   vas ist in dee·zem ge·rikht

Is it cooked in meat stock?
Ist es in Fleischbrühe?   ist es in flaish·brew·e

Does it take long to prepare?
Dauert das lange?   dow·ert das lang·e

I'd like a local speciality.
Ich möchte etwas typisches aus der Region.   ikh meukh·te et·vas tew·pi·shes ows dair re·gyawn

That was delicious!
Das hat hervorragend geschmeckt!   das hat her·fawr·raa·gent ge·shmekt/
Das war sehr lecker!   das var zair le·ker

My compliments to the chef!
Mein Kompliment an den Koch!   main kom·pli·ment an dayn kokh

The bill, please.
Die Rechnung, bitte.   dee rekh·nung bi·te

I'd like ..., please.	*Ich möchte ..., bitte.*	ikh meukh·te ... bi·te
a cup of tea/coffee	*eine Tasse Tee/Kaffee*	ai·ne ta·se tay/ka·fay
with (milk)	*mit (Milch)*	mit (milkh)

HEALTH

Where's the nearest ...?	*Wo ist der/die/das nächste ...? (m/f/n)*	vaw ist dair/die/das naykhs·te ...
chemist	*Apotheke (f)*	a·po·tay·ke
dentist	*Zahnarzt (m)*	tsaan·artst
doctor	*Arzt (m)*	artst
hospital	*Krankenhaus (n)*	krang·ken·hows

I need a doctor (who speaks English).
Ich brauche einen Arzt (der Englisch spricht).   ikh brow·khe ai·nen artst (dair eng·lish shprikht)

Is there a (night) chemist nearby?
Gibt es in der Nähe eine (Nacht)Apotheke?   gipt es in dair nay·e ai·ne (nakht·)a·po·tay·ke

I'm allergic to ...	*Ich bin allergisch gegen ...*	ikh bin a·lair·gish gay·gen ...
antibiotics	*Antibiotika*	an·ti·bi·aw·ti·ka
aspirin	*Aspirin*	as·pi·reen
penicillin	*Penizillin*	pe·ni·tsi·leen

I'm sick.
Ich bin krank.   ikh bin krangk

It hurts here.
Es tut hier weh.   es toot heer vay

I have diarrhoea/a fever/a headache.
Ich habe Durchfall/Fieber/Kopfschmerzen.   ikh haa·be durkh·fal/fee·ber/kopf·shmer·tsen

(I think) I'm pregnant.
(Ich glaube) ich bin schwanger.   (ikh glow·be) ikh bin shvang·er

LANGUAGE DIFFICULTIES

Do you speak English?
Sprechen Sie Englisch?   shpre·khen zee eng·lish

Does anyone here speak English?
| Spricht hier jemand | shprikht heer *yay*·mant |
| Englisch? | eng·lish |

Do you understand (me)?
| Verstehen Sie (mich)? | fer·*shtay*·en zee (mikh) |

I (don't) understand.
| Ich verstehe (nicht). | ikh fer·*shtay*·e (nikht) |

How do you say ... in German?
| Wie sagt man ... auf | vee zagt man ... owf |
| Deutsch? | doytsh |

Could you	Könnten Sie ...?	keun·ten zee ...
please ...?		
speak more	bitte langsamer	bi·te *lang*·za·mer
slowly	sprechen	shpre·khen
repeat that	das bitte	das bi·te
	wiederholen	vee·der·*haw*·len
write it down	das bitte	das bi·te
	aufschreiben	owf·shrai·ben

NUMBERS

1	eins	aints
2	zwei	tsvai
3	drei	drai
4	vier	feer
5	fünf	fewnf
6	sechs	zeks
7	sieben	zee·ben
8	acht	akht
9	neun	noyn
10	zehn	tsayn
11	elf	elf
12	zwölf	zveulf
13	dreizehn	drai·tsayn
14	vierzehn	feer·tsayn
15	fünfzehn	fewnf·tsayn
16	sechzehn	zeks·tsayn
17	siebzehn	zeep·tsayn
18	achtzehn	akh·tsayn
19	neunzehn	noyn·tsayn
20	zwanzig	tsvan·tsikh
21	einundzwanzig	ain·unt·tsvan·tsikh
22	zweiundzwanzig	tsvai·unt·tsvan·tsikh
30	dreizig	drai·tsikh
31	einunddreizig	ain·und·drai·tsikh
40	vierzig	feer·tsikh
50	fünfzig	fewnf·tsikh
60	sechzig	zekh·tsikh
70	siebzig	zeep·tsikh
80	achtzig	akh·tsikh
90	neunzig	noyn·tsikh
100	hundert	hun·dert
1000	tausend	tow·zent
2000	zwei tausend	tsvai tow·zent

EMERGENCIES

Help!
| Hilfe! | hil·fe |

It's an emergency!
| Es ist ein Notfall! | es ist ain *nawt*·fal |

Call the police!
| Rufen Sie die Polizei! | roo·fen zee dee po·li·*tsai* |

Call a doctor!
| Rufen Sie einen Arzt! | roo·fen zee *ai*·nen artst |

Call an ambulance!
| Rufen Sie einen | roo·fen zee *ai*·nen |
| Krankenwagen! | krang·ken·vaa·gen |

Leave me alone!
| Lassen Sie mich in Ruhe! | la·sen zee mikh in roo·e |

Go away!
| Gehen Sie weg! | gay·en zee vek |

I'm lost.
| Ich habe mich verirrt. | ikh haa·be mikh fer·*irt* |

Where are the toilets?
| Wo ist die Toilette? | vaw ist dee to·a·*le*·te |

PAPERWORK

name	Name	naa·me
nationality	Staats-	shtaats·
	angehörigkeit	an·ge·heu·rikh·kait
date of birth	Geburtsdatum	ge·burts·daa·tum
place of birth	Geburtsort	ge·burts·ort
sex/gender	Sex	seks
passport	(Reise)Pass	(rai·ze·)paas
visa	Visum	vee·zum

QUESTION WORDS

Who?	Wer?	vair
What?	Was?	vas
Where?	Wo?	vo
When?	Wann?	van
How?	Wie?	vee
Why?	Warum?	va·*rum*
Which?	Welcher?	vel·kher
How much?	Wie viel?	vee feel
How many?	Wie viele?	vee *fee*·le

SHOPPING & SERVICES

I'm looking for ...
| Ich suche ... | ikh *zoo*·khe ... |

Where's the (nearest) ...?
| Wo ist der/die/das | vaw ist dair/dee/das |
| (nächste) ...? (m/f/n) | (*naykhs*·te) ... |

Where can I buy ...?
| Wo kann ich ... kaufen? | vaw kan ikh ... *kow*·fen |

I'd like to buy ...
| Ich möchte ... kaufen. | ikh *meukh*·te ... *kow*·fen |

LANGUAGE

How much (is this)?

Wie viel (kostet das)?   vee feel (kos·tet das)

That's too much/expensive.

Das ist zu viel/teuer.   das ist tsoo feel/toy·er

Can you lower the price?

Können Sie mit dem   keu·nen zee mit dem
Preis heruntergehen?   prais he·run·ter·gay·en

Do you have something cheaper?

Haben Sie etwas   haa·ben zee et·vas
Billigeres?   bi·li·ge·res

I'm just looking.

Ich schaue mich nur um.   ikh show·e mikh noor um

Can you write down the price?

Können Sie den Preis   keu·nen zee dayn prais
aufschreiben?   owf·shrai·ben

Do you have any others?

Haben Sie noch andere?   haa·ben zee nokh an·de·re

Can I look at it?

Können Sie es   keu·nen zee es
mir zeigen? (n)   meer tsai·gen

more	*mehr*	mair
less	*weniger*	vay·ni·ger
smaller	*kleiner*	klai·ner
bigger	*grosser*	gro·ser

Do you accept ...? *Nehmen Sie ...?*   nay·men zee ...
   credit cards *Kreditkarten*   kre·deet·kar·ten
   travellers *Reiseschecks*   rai·ze·sheks
   cheques

I'd like to ... *Ich möchte ...*   ikh meukh·te ...
   change money *Geld umtauschen*   gelt um·tow·shen
   cash a cheque *einen Scheck*   ai·nen shek
     einlösen   ain·leu·zen
   change some *Reiseschecks*   rai·ze·sheks
     travellers *einlösen*   ain·leu·zen
     cheques

an ATM	*ein Geldautomat*	ain gelt·ow·to·maat
a bank	*eine Bank*	ai·ne bangk
the ... embassy	*die ... Botschaft*	dee ... bot·shaft
an exchange	*eine Geldwechsel-*	ai·ne gelt·vek·sel·
office	*stube*	shtoo·be
the market	*der Markt*	dair markt
the police	*die Polizei*	dee po·li·tsai
the post office	*das Postamt*	das post·amt
a public phone	*ein öffentliches*	ain eu·fent·li·khes
	Telefon	te·le·fawn
a public toilet	*eine öffentliche*	ain eu·fent·li·khe
	Toilette	to·a·le·te

Where's the local internet cafe?

Wo ist hier ein   vaw ist heer ain
Internet-Café?   in·ter·net·ka·fay

What time does it open/close?

Wann macht es   van makht es
auf/zu? (n)   owf/tsoo

I want to buy a phonecard.

Ich möchte eine   ikh meukh·te ai·ne
Telefonkarte kaufen.   te·le·fawn·kar·te kow·fen

I'd like to ... *Ich möchte ...*   ikh meukh·te ...
   get internet *Internetzugang*   in·ter·net·tsoo·gang
     access *haben*   haa·ben
   check my email *meine E-Mails*   mai·ne ee·mayls
     checken   che·ken

TIME & DATES

What time is it?

Wie spät ist es?   vee shpayt ist es

It's (one) o'clock.

Es ist (ein) Uhr.   es ist (ain) oor

Twenty past one.

Zwanzig nach eins.   tsvan·tsikh naakh ains

Half past one.

Halb zwei. ('half two')   halp tsvai

Quarter to one.

Viertel vor eins.   fir·tel fawr ains

am

morgens/vormittags   mor·gens/fawr·mi·taaks

pm

abends/nachmittags   aa·bents/naakh·mi·taaks

now	*jetzt*	yetst
today	*heute*	hoy·te
tonight	*heute Abend*	hoy·te aa·bent
tomorrow	*morgen*	mor·gen
morning	*Morgen*	mor·gen
afternoon	*Nachmittag*	naakh·mi·taak
evening	*Abend*	aa·bent

Monday	*Montag*	mawn·taak
Tuesday	*Dienstag*	deens·taak
Wednesday	*Mittwoch*	mit·vokh
Thursday	*Donnerstag*	do·ners·taak
Friday	*Freitag*	frai·taak
Saturday	*Samstag*	zams·taak
Sunday	*Sonntag*	zon·taak

January	*Januar*	yan·u·aar
February	*Februar*	fay·bru·aar
March	*März*	merts
April	*April*	a·pril
May	*Mai*	mai
June	*Juni*	yoo·ni
July	*Juli*	yoo·li
August	*August*	ow·gust
September	*September*	zep·tem·ber
October	*Oktober*	ok·taw·ber
November	*November*	no·vem·ber
December	*Dezember*	de·tsem·ber

TRANSPORT
Public Transport

metro	*U-Bahn*	oo·baan
(metro) station	*(U-)Bahnhof*	(oo-)baan·hawf
suburban railway	*S-Bahn*	es·baan
tram	*Strassenbahn*	shtraa·sen·baan
tram stop	*Strassenbahn-*	shtraa·sen·baan·
	haltestelle	hal·te·shte·le

What time does	*Wann fährt ...*	van fairt ...
the ... leave?	*ab?*	ap
boat	*das Boot*	das bawt
bus	*der Bus*	dair bus
train	*der Zug*	dair tsook

What time's	*Wann fährt*	van fairt
the ... bus?	*der ... Bus?*	dair ... bus
first	*erste*	ers·te
last	*letzte*	lets·te
next	*nächste*	naykhs·te

Where's the nearest metro station?

Wo ist der nächste   vaw ist dair naykhs·te
U-Bahnhof?   oo·baan·hawf

Which (bus) goes to ...?

Welcher (Bus) fährt   vel·kher (bus) fairt
nach ...?   nakh ...

A ... ticket to	*Eine ... nach*	ai·ne ... naakh
(Berlin).	*(Berlin).*	(ber·leen)
one-way	*einfache*	ain·fa·khe
	Fahrkarte	faar·kar·te
return	*Rückfahrkarte*	rewk·faar·kar·te
1st-class	*Fahrkarte erster*	faar·kar·te ers·ter
	Klasse	kla·se
2nd-class	*Fahrkarte zweiter*	faar·kar·te tsvai·ter
	Klasse	kla·se

The ... is cancelled.

... ist gestrichen.   ... ist ge·shtri·khen

The ... is delayed.

... hat Verspätung.   ... hat fer·shpay·tung

Is this seat free?

Ist dieser Platz frei?   ist dee·zer plats frai

Do I need to change trains?

Muss ich umsteigen?   mus ikh um·shtai·gen

Are you free? (to taxi)

Sind Sie frei?   zint zee frai

How much is it to ...?

Was kostet es bis ...?   vas kos·tet es bis ...

Please take me to (this address).

Bitte bringen Sie mich   bi·te bring·en zee mikh
zu (dieser Adresse).   tsoo (dee·zer a·dre·se)

Private Transport

Where can I hire	*Wo kann ich ...*	vaw kan ikh ...
a/an ...?	*mieten?*	mee·ten
I'd like to hire	*Ich möchte ...*	ikh meukh·te ...
a/an ...	*mieten.*	mee·ten
automatic	*ein Fahrzeug mit*	ain faar·tsoyk mit
	Automatik	ow·to·maa·tik
bicycle	*ein Fahrrad*	ain faar·raat
car	*ein Auto*	ain ow·to
4WD	*ein*	ain
	Allradfahrzeug	al·raat·faar·tsoyk
manual	*ein Fahrzeug mit*	ain faar·tsoyk mit
	Schaltung	shal·tung
motorbike	*ein Motorrad*	ain maw·tor·raat

How much is it	*Wie viel kostet es*	vee feel kos·tet es
per ...?	*pro ...?*	praw ...
day	*Tag*	taak
week	*Woche*	vo·khe

diesel	*Diesel*	dee·zel
LPG	*Autogas*	ow·to·gaas
petrol (gas)	*Benzin*	ben·tseen

Where's a petrol station?

Wo ist eine Tankstelle?   vaw ist ai·ne tangk·shte·le

Does this road go to ...?

Führt diese Strasse   fewrt dee·ze shtraa·se
nach ...?   naakh ...

(How long) can I park here?

(Wie lange) kann ich   (vee lang·e) kan ikh
hier parken?   heer par·ken

Where do I pay?

Wo muss ich bezahlen?   vaw mus ikh be·tsaa·len

I need a mechanic.

Ich brauche einen   ikh brow·khe ai·nen
Mechaniker.   me·khaa·ni·ker

I had an accident.

Ich hatte einen Unfall.   ikh ha·te ai·nen un·fal

LANGUAGE

The car has broken down (at ...).

Ich habe (in ...) eine Panne mit meinem Auto.	ikh *haa*·be (in ...) *ai*·ne *pa*·ne mit *mai*·nem *ow*·to

The car/motorbike won't start.

Das Auto/Motorrad springt nicht an.	das *ow*·to/*maw*·tor·raat shpringkt nikht an

I have a flat tyre.

Ich habe eine Reifenpanne.	ikh *haa*·be *ai*·ne *rai*·fen·pa·ne

I've run out of petrol.

Ich habe kein Benzin mehr.	ikh *haa*·be kain ben·*tseen* mair

TRAVEL WITH CHILDREN

I need ...	*Ich brauche ...*	ikh *brow*·khe ...
Is there ...?	*Gibt es ...?*	gipt es ...
a baby change room	*einen Wickelraum*	*ai*·nen *vi*·kel·rowm
a baby seat	*einen Babysitz*	*ai*·nen *bay*·bi·zits
a booster seat	*einen Kindersitz*	*ai*·nen *kin*·der·zits
a child-minding service	*einen Babysitter-Service*	*ai*·nen *bay*·bi·si·ter-ser·vis
a children's menu	*eine Kinderkarte*	*ai*·ne *kin*·der·kar·te
an (English-speaking) babysitter	*einen (englisch-sprachigen) Babysitter*	*ai*·nen (*eng*·lish-shpra·khi·gen) *bay*·bi·si·ter
a highchair	*einen Kinderstuhl*	*ai*·nen *kin*·der·shtool
infant formula (milk)	*Trockenmilch für Säuglinge*	*tro*·ken·milkh fewr *soyg*·ling·e
a potty	*ein Kindertöpfchen*	ain *kin*·der·teupf·khen

Do you mind if I breastfeed here?

Kann ich meinem Kind hier die Brust geben?	kan ikh *mai*·nem kint heer dee brust *gay*·ben

Are children allowed?

Sind Kinder erlaubt?	zint *kin*·der er·*lowpt*

Glossary

(pl) indicates plural

Abtei – abbey
ADAC – Allgemeiner Deutscher Automobil Club; German Automobile Association
Allee – avenue
Altstadt – old town
Apotheke – pharmacy
Arbeitsamt – employment office
Arbeitserlaubnis – work permit
Ärztehaus – medical clinic
Ärztlicher Notfalldienst – emergency medical service
Aufenthaltserlaubnis – residency permit
Ausgang, Ausfahrt – exit
Autobahn – motorway, freeway
Autofähre – car ferry

Bad – spa, bath
Bahnhof – train station
Barkassen – small barge
Bau – building
Bedienung – service; service charge
Berg – mountain
Besenwirtschaft – seasonal wine restaurant indicated by a broom above the doorway
Bezirk – district
Bibliothek – library
Bierkeller – cellar pub
Bierstube – traditional beer pub
bio – organic
BRD – Bundesrepublik Deutschland or, in English, FRG (Federal Republic of Germany); the name for Germany today; before reunification it applied to West Germany
Brücke – bridge
Brunnen – fountain, well
Bundesliga – Germany's premier football (soccer) league
Bundesrat – upper house of the German parliament
Bundestag – lower house of the German parliament
Bundeswehr – German National Army
Burg – castle
Busbahnhof – bus station

CDU – Christlich Demokratische Union Deutschlands; Christian Democratic Union
Christkindlmarkt – Christmas market; also called *Weihnachtsmarkt*
City Night Line (CNL) night trains with sleeper cars and couchettes
CSU – Christlich-Soziale Union; Christian Social Union; Bavarian offshoot of CDU

DB – Deutsche Bahn; German national railway
DDR – Deutsche Demokratische Republik or, in English, GDR (German Democratic Republic); the name for former East Germany
Denkmal – memorial
Dirndl – traditional women's dress (Bavaria only)
DJH – Deutsches Jugendherbergswerk; German youth hostels association
Dom – cathedral
Dorf – village

Eiscafé – ice-cream parlour

Fahrplan – timetable
Fahrrad – bicycle
FDP – Freie Demokratische Partei; Free Democratic Party
Ferienwohnung, Ferienwohnungen (pl) – holiday flat or apartment
Fest – festival
FKK – Freikörperkultur; nude bathing area
Fleete – canals in Hamburg
Flohmarkt – flea market
Flughafen – airport
Forstweg – forestry track
FRG – see *BRD*
Fussball – football, soccer
Fussweg – footpath

Garten – garden
Gasse – lane, alley
Gästehaus – guesthouse
Gaststätte, Gasthaus – informal restaurant, inn
GDR – see *DDR*
Gedenkstätte – memorial site
Gepäckaufbewahrung – left-luggage office

Hafen – harbour, port
Hauptbahnhof – central train station
Heide – heath
Hof, Höfe (pl) – courtyard
Höhle – cave
Hotel Garni – hotel without a restaurant where you are only served breakfast

Imbiss – stand-up food stall; also called *Schnellimbiss*
Insel – island
InterCity (IC), EuroCity (EC) long-distance trains that are slower than the ICE and stop in major cities; EC trains go to major cities in neighbouring countries

InterCity Express (ICE) long-distance, space-age bullet trains that stop at major cities only
InterRegio-Express (IRE) slower medium-distance trains connecting cities and linking local with long-distance trains

Jugendgästehaus – youth guesthouse of a higher standard than a youth hostel
Jugendherberge – youth hostel

Kanal – canal
Kapelle – chapel
Karte – ticket
Kartenvorverkauf – ticket booking office
Kino – cinema
Kirche – church
Kletterwand – climbing wall
Kloster – monastery, convent
Kneipe – pub
Konditorei – cake shop
Konzentrationslager (KZ) – concentration camp
KPD – Kommunistische Partei Deutschlands; German Communist Party
Krankenhaus – hospital
Kreuzgang – cloister
Kunst – art
Kurhaus – literally 'cure house', usually a spa town's central building, used for social gatherings and events and often housing the town's casino
Kurort – spa resort
Kurtaxe – resort tax
Kurverwaltung – spa resort administration
Kurzentrum – spa centre

Land, Länder (pl) – state
Landtag – state parliament
Lederhosen – traditional leather trousers with attached braces (Bavaria only)
Lesbe, Lesben (pl) – lesbian (n)
lesbisch – lesbian (adj)

Markt – market; often used instead of *Marktplatz*
Marktplatz – marketplace or square; often abbreviated to *Markt*
Mass – 1L tankard or stein of beer
Meer – sea
Mehrwertsteuer (MwST) – value-added tax
Mensa – university cafeteria
Mitfahrzentrale – ride-sharing agency
Mitwohnzentrale – accommodation-finding service that is usually for long-term stays
multi-kulti – multicultural
Münster – minster, large church, cathedral

Neustadt – new town
Nord – north

NSDAP – Nationalsozialistische Deutsche Arbeiterpartei; National Socialist German Workers' Party

Ossi – nickname for an East German
Ost – east

Palais, Palast – palace, residential quarters of a castle
Paradies – literally 'paradise'; architectural term for a church vestibule or anteroom
Parkhaus – car park
Passage – shopping arcade
Pension, Pensionen (pl) – relatively cheap boarding house
Pfand – deposit for bottles and sometimes glasses (in beer gardens)
Pfarrkirche – parish church
Platz – square
Putsch – revolt

Radwandern – bicycle touring
Radweg – bicycle path
Rathaus – town hall
Ratskeller – town hall restaurant
Regional Express (RE) local trains with limited stops that link rural areas with metropolitan centres and the S-Bahn
RegionalBahn (RB) local trains, mostly in rural areas, with frequent stops
Reich – empire
Reisezentrum – travel centre in train or bus stations
Ruhetag – literally 'rest day'; closing day at a shop or restaurant
Rundgang – tour, route

Saal, Säle (pl) – hall, room
Sammlung – collection
Säule – column, pillar
S-Bahn – suburban-metropolitan trains; short for 'Schnellbahn'
Schatzkammer – treasury room
Schiff – ship
Schiffahrt – shipping, navigation
Schloss – palace, castle
Schnellimbiss – stand-up food stall; also called *Imbiss*
schwul – gay (adj)
Schwuler, Schwule (pl) – gay (n)
SED – Sozialistische Einheitspartei Deutschlands; Socialist Unity Party
See – lake
Sesselbahn – chairlift
SPD – Sozialdemokratische Partei Deutschlands; Social Democratic Party
Speisekarte – menu
Stadt – city, town
Stadtbad, Stadtbäder (pl) – public pool
StadtExpress (SE) local trains primarily connecting cities and geared towards commuters

Stadtwald – city or town forest
Stehcafé – stand-up cafe
Strand – beach
Strasse – street; often abbreviated to Str
Strausswirtschaft – seasonal wine pub indicated by wreath above the doorway
Süd – south

Tageskarte – daily menu; day ticket on public transport
Tal – valley
Teich – pond
Tor – gate
trampen – hitchhike
Turm – tower

U-Bahn – underground train system
Ufer – bank (of river etc)

verboten – forbidden
Verkehr – traffic
Verkehrsamt/Verkehrsverein – tourist office
Viertel – quarter, district

Wald – forest
Wäscherei – laundry
Wattenmeer – tidal flats on the North Sea coast
Weg – way, path
Weihnachtsmarkt – Christmas market; also called *Christkindlmarkt*
Weingut – wine-growing estate
Weinkeller – wine cellar
Weinprobe – wine tasting
Weinstube – traditional wine bar or tavern
Wende – 'change' of 1989, ie the fall of communism that led to the collapse of the GDR and German reunification
Wessi – nickname for a West German
West – west
Wiese – meadow

Zahnradbahn – cogwheel railway
Zimmer frei – rooms available
Zimmervermittlung – a room-finding service, primarily for short-term stays
ZOB – Zentraler Omnibusbahnhof; central bus station

AUTHORS

The Authors

ANDREA SCHULTE-PEEVERS
Coordinating Author, Berlin, Brandenburg, Saxony-Anhalt, Thuringia, North Rhine–Westphalia

Andrea has logged countless miles travelling in nearly 60 countries on five continents and carries her dog-eared passport like a badge of honour. Born and raised in Germany and educated in London and at UCLA, she's built a career on writing about her native country for almost two decades. She's authored or contributed to more than 40 Lonely Planet titles, including all six editions of this book as well as the *Berlin* city guide, the *Berlin Encounter* guide and the *Munich, Bavaria & the Black Forest* guide. For this trip she again traded her house in Los Angeles for a teensy rooftop apartment in Berlin – and didn't regret a day of it.

KERRY CHRISTIANI
Baden-Württemberg

Big wilderness, the promise of snow in winter and a husband born in Villingen lured Kerry from London to the Black Forest four years ago. When not on the road, Kerry can be found hiking, cycling or cross-country skiing in the woods and hills close to her home. For this edition, she was delighted to rediscover Baden-Württemberg, from canoeing on Lake Constance to testing – well it would be rude not to! – Black Forest cake in Triberg. Kerry's incurably itchy feet have taken her to some 40 countries, inspiring numerous travel articles, online features and around 15 guidebooks, including Lonely Planet's *Austria, Switzerland, Munich, Bavaria & the Black Forest* and *Portugal*.

MARC DI DUCA
Saxony, Bavaria

From a library job in the Ruhrgebiet during the summer of '89 to scrambling up the Alps for this guide, Germany and German have been with Marc throughout his adult life. Marc has explored many corners of Germany over the last 20 years, but it's to the variety and friendliness of Bavaria that he returns most willingly. During research, Marc also enjoyed the opportunity to explore Saxony where he became smitten with the Trabant. When not Trabi hugging in Zwickau or leaving beer rings in Munich, Marc can usually be found in Sandwich, Kent, where he lives with his Kievite wife, Tanya, and son Taras. This is Marc's fourth Lonely Planet title after *Russia, Trans-Siberian Railway* and *Cycling Britain*.

ANTHONY HAYWOOD
History, The Culture, Harz Mountains, Lower Saxony, Bremen

Anthony was born in the port city of Fremantle, Western Australia, and pulled anchor early on to hitchhike through Europe and the USA. Aberystwyth in Wales and Ealing in London were his wintering grounds at the time. He later studied comparative literature in Perth and Russian language in Melbourne. In the 1990s, fresh from a spell in post-Soviet, pre-anything Moscow, he moved to Germany. Today he works as a German-based freelance writer and journalist and divides his time between Göttingen (Lower Saxony) and Berlin. Anthony worked on the first and most subsequent editions of *Germany*.

CATHERINE LE NEVEZ
Hamburg, Schleswig-Holstein, Mecklenburg–Western Pomerania

Catherine road-tripped across Europe aged four and has been hitting the road at every opportunity since, completing her Doctorate of Creative Arts in Writing, Masters in Professional Writing, and postgrad qualifications in editing and publishing along the way. Catherine has authored or co-authored over a dozen Lonely Planet guidebooks, including two editions of *Munich, Bavaria & the Black Forest*. For this book, she jumped at the chance to celebrate Hamburg's Hafengeburtstag, head into northern Germany's national parks, and soak up the sea air and scenery on the spectacular Baltic and North Sea coastline and islands.

DANIEL ROBINSON
Hesse, Rhineland-Palatinate & Saarland

Brought up in Northern California, Illinois and Israel, Daniel holds degrees from Princeton and Tel Aviv University and now lives with his wife Rachel in Los Angeles and Tel Aviv. In his two decades with Lonely Planet, he has covered both sides of the Franco–German border and has had his work translated into 10 languages. The Moselle's medieval wine villages and the area's many *Radwege* (cycling paths) keep bringing Daniel back to Rhineland-Palatinate, but he's equally enchanted by the trains that slither along both banks of the Romantic Rhine, past cargo barges and car ferries. In the Saarland he's as captivated by the hulking Völklinger Hütte ironworks as he is at peace on the leafy Saar River.

CAROLINE SIEG
Food & Drink, Environment, Welcome to Germany

Half-American and half-Swiss, Caroline has spent most of her life moving back and forth across the Atlantic Ocean, with lengthy stops in Zürich, Miami and New York City. When not cycling around Berlin's Tiergarten or Hamburg's waterways in an effort to work off a daily dose of *Kaffee und Kuchen*, Caroline spends her days writing and editing, with a focus on anything involving travel and food.

LONELY PLANET AUTHORS

Why is our travel information the best in the world? It's simple: our authors are passionate, dedicated travellers. They don't take freebies in exchange for positive coverage so you can be sure the advice you're given is impartial. They travel widely to all the popular spots, and off the beaten track. They don't research using just the internet or phone. They discover new places not included in any other guidebook. They personally visit thousands of hotels, restaurants, palaces, trails, galleries, temples and more. They speak with dozens of locals every day to make sure you get the kind of insider knowledge only a local could tell you. They take pride in getting all the details right, and in telling it how it is. Think you can do it? Find out how at **lonelyplanet.com**.

Behind the Scenes

THIS BOOK

The 1st edition of *Germany* was written by Steve Fallon, Anthony Haywood, Andrea Schulte-Peevers and Nick Selby. This 6th edition was written by Andrea Schulte-Peevers, Kerry Christiani, Marc Di Duca, Anthony Haywood, Catherine Le Nevez and Daniel Robinson. The 5th edition was written by Jeremy Gray, Anthony Haywood, Sarah Johnstone and Daniel Robinson, also under the expert co-ordination of Andrea Schulte-Peevers. This guidebook was commissioned in Lonely Planet's London office, and produced by the following:

Commissioning Editors Joanna Potts, Caroline Sieg, Clifton Wilkinson

Coordinating Editor Robyn Loughnane

Coordinating Cartographer Marc Milinkovic

Coordinating Layout Designer Gary Newman

Managing Editor Annelies Mertens

Managing Cartographer Adrian Persoglia

Managing Layout Designer Indra Kilfoyle

Assisting Editors Judith Bamber, Carolyn Boicos, Victoria Harrison, Helen Koehne, Anne Mulvaney, Alan Murphy

Assisting Cartographers Alissa Baker, Enes Basic, Marion Byass, Diana Duggan, Karen Grant

Assisting Layout Designer Carol Jackson

Cover Research Naomi Parker, lonelyplanetimages.com

Internal Image Research Jane Hart, lonelyplanet images.com

Project Managers Craig Kilburn, Anna Metcalfe

Thanks to Lucy Birchley, Melanie Dankel, Wayne Murphy, Amanda Rogerson, Herman So, Lyahna Spencer

THANKS
ANDREA SCHULTE-PEEVERS

Big thanks to friends, family, tourist office staff and complete strangers who've shared their expertise, favourite spots and insights with me while researching this book. David, you've once again been my rock and I will never be able to thank you enough for your endless love, support and encouragement. Finally, a big hug and thanks to Christina Rasch and Holm Friedrich for letting us camp out in their Berlin flat.

KERRY CHRISTIANI

A heartfelt *Dankeschön* to my friends and family in the Black Forest for their valuable insight, especially Imke and Sebastian for showing me another side to Heidelberg. In Triberg, special thanks to Claus Schäfer for the interview and delicious cake. Thank you to all of the tourist professionals who helped in one way or another, particularly the tourist boards in Konstanz, Baden-Baden, Freiburg and Karlsruhe, as well as Caroline Sieg at Lonely Planet for entrusting me with the gig. Finally, a great big thank you to Andy, my terrific husband and travel companion, for all of his tips, driving and tireless support.

THE LONELY PLANET STORY

Fresh from an epic journey across Europe, Asia and Australia in 1972, Tony and Maureen Wheeler sat at their kitchen table stapling together notes. The first Lonely Planet guidebook, *Across Asia on the Cheap*, was born.

Travellers snapped up the guides. Inspired by their success, the Wheelers began publishing books to Southeast Asia, India and beyond. Demand was prodigious, and the Wheelers expanded the business rapidly to keep up. Over the years, Lonely Planet extended its coverage to every country and into the virtual world via lonelyplanet.com and the Thorn Tree message board.

As Lonely Planet became a globally loved brand, Tony and Maureen received several offers for the company. But it wasn't until 2007 that they found a partner whom they trusted to remain true to the company's principles of travelling widely, treading lightly and giving sustainably. In October of that year, BBC Worldwide acquired a 75% share in the company, pledging to uphold Lonely Planet's commitment to independent travel, trustworthy advice and editorial independence.

Today, Lonely Planet has offices in Melbourne, London and Oakland, with over 500 staff members and 300 authors. Tony and Maureen are still actively involved with Lonely Planet. They're travelling more often than ever, and they're devoting their spare time to charitable projects. And the company is still driven by the philosophy of *Across Asia on the Cheap*: 'All you've got to do is decide to go and the hardest part is over. So go!'

MARC DI DUCA

Big thanks to Caroline Sieg for entrusting me with such a hefty chunk of the guide, and to Andrea Schulte-Peevers for her support throughout; huge thanks to Oleksandr Kalinin for use of his apartment in Erding, for the trips into the wilds of Eastern Bavaria and for the hours of 'research' over pints of Erding's finest. A huge thank you also goes to Liane Mautner in Dresden, Dirk Marky in Franconia, Andy Mayston in Munich and Rüdi Poschlod for his insights into life in Germany and the trip to Saxon Switzerland. I'd also like to express my gratitude to all the dedicated staff at tourist offices around Bavaria and Saxony, including Günther Schulz in Würzburg, Anne Riedler in Oberstdorf, Michael Henger in Bamberg, Kreszentia Struber in Berchtesgaden, Christina Sprenger in Garmisch-Partenkirchen, Theresa Appoltshauser in Regensburg, Sabine Garau in Munich, Hedda Manhard in Munich and Barbara Geier of the German National Tourist Office in London. Last but certainly not least, heartfelt thanks must go to my wife Tanya and son Taras for all the days we spend apart.

ANTHONY HAYWOOD

In large and small ways, many different people were very helpful in researching my chapters of this new edition of Germany. First and foremost, thanks go to the folks at the tourist offices who were a useful source of orientation in my regions, but especially to Timo Soik in Wolfsburg, Diana Lichtner in Wernigerode, Kathrin Friedling in Thale, Astrid Müller in Gernrode, Anna Mrozek in Braunschweig, and Frau Kerstin Makrosch in Worpswede. Special thanks to Dr Simone Eick of the German Emigration Center for agreeing to be interviewed for Lonely Planet. As well as these, I'd like to thank my co-authors, in particular Andrea Schulte-Peevers, and commissioning editor Caroline Sieg, Herman So in mapping, Eoin Dunlevy and managing editor Bruce Evans. Finally, special thanks to Sylvia Möhle for ongoing support on the project and valuable insights.

CATHERINE LE NEVEZ

Vielen Dank to all the locals, tourism professionals and fellow travellers in Hamburg, Schleswig-Holstein and Mecklenburg–Western Pomerania who offered insights, assistance and inspiration along the way. *Danke* in particular to Jan Drews and Thorsten in Hamburg and André in Stralsund, as well as Claudia for the Hamburg meet-up, and the Bavarian (Franconian!) crew – (Saint) Dirk, Harry, Holger, and Daniel – for the northern tips. Major thanks to Caroline Sieg for giving me the gig, as well as Cliff Wilkinson, Craig Kilburn, Herman So, Andrea and the *Germany* team, and everyone at LP. As ever, *merci surtout* to my family.

DANIEL ROBINSON

Special thanks to Agnetha Weidler (Schlitz, Hesse), Brigitte Durst (Stuttgart), Cheri Mersey (Frankfurt), Claudia Kuhnen (Trier), Esther Riepert (Kassel), Eugen Hahn (Jazzkeller, Frankfurt), Dr Katerina Wolf (Saarlandmuseum, Saarbrücken), Hubert and Karin Braun (Lauterbach, Hesse), Jim Sunthimer (Boppard), Leonard Hill (Darmstadt), M Brensing (Alte Synagoge, Worms), Michael Congdon (Wiesbaden), Stephan Olk (Radstation, Trier) and Ute Goerg (Deutsches Edelsteinmuseum, Idar-Oberstein) for their enthusiasm and generosity with their time. Michael Benz and Kirstin Göring (Frankfurt) were the most generous of hosts.

As usual, it was a pleasure working with my consummately professional LP colleagues Caroline Sieg, this volume's commissioning editor, and Andrea Schulte-Peevers, its coordinating author.

What can I say about my wife's support and forbearance, both while I was nine time zones away and during the long write-up nights, except *'elef todot, Chell!'*

OUR READERS

Many thanks to the travellers who used the last edition and wrote to us with helpful hints, useful advice and interesting anecdotes:

A Carolyn Agocs, Lesley Ashley, Jodean Ator **B** Fiammetta Battaglia, André Bauer, Manuel Biewald, Ellen Birger, Anthony Bradbury, Angela Broeders, John Bulcock, Jonathan Butlin **C** Lilo Ccoyllor, Frauke Certa, Ann Clark, Alessandro Coggi, Guilherme Cohn **D** Claire Davies, Mrs M J A De Koster, Catherine Dignam, Nadine Dwyer **E** Albrecht Eisen, Horst Eisfelder, Dylan Esson **F** Fanli Fanli, Malcolm Faul, Kay Fuchs **G** Surabhi Ganguly, Mario Garcia Ramirez, Jay Geller, Rick Green **H** Gareth Hamilton, Will Harwood, Clemens Hellenschmidt, Willemyn Hoebert, Felix Hoffmann, Lucia Hoymann **J** Sam James **K** Katharine Kirkland, Jessica Kirsch **L** Sw Lam, Joel Lopez-Ferreiro, Andrew Lucas **M** Tony Mason, Trevor Mazzucchelli, David Mccormick, Gary Mcdade, Christopher Mcdonald, Ann and James Mchenry, Cynthia Meketa, Adele Melander-Dayton, Kerstin Meyer, Sarah Mitchell, Heather Monell, Lucia Mussi **N** Lisa Nolan **P** Gavin Parnaby, Veronica Pellacini **R** Jørgen Rantorp, Janice Rossen, Gary Russ **S** Bekir Salgin, Robert Sanderson, Claudia Scano, Christiane Scheuer, Steffi Schmidt, Adrian Schmohl, M Schweuzer, John Slevin, Adam Smith, Helen Smithson, B M Sorgo, Miss Deborah Spooner, Pamela Stokes, Darius Sunawala, Egor Sviridenko **T** Stephan Tautz, Daniel Theus, James Thomson **V** Jan Van Wandelen, Guy Voets **W** Leticia Weizenegger, Ruben Wickenhäuser, Sophie Wilson, Franka Winter, Jeff Wolf **X** Zigor Xabier **Y** Nadia Yoshioka, Margaret Young

ACKNOWLEDGMENTS

Many thanks to the following for the use of their content:

Globe on title page ©Mountain High Maps 1993 Digital Wisdom, Inc.

Berlin S+U-Bahn Map © 2009 Berliner Verkehrsbetriebe (BVG)

Internal photographs p429 Sigrid Dauth/Alamy; p431 (#2) Imagebroker/Alamy; p431 (#3) StockFood/Picture Media; p433 (#3) Imagebroker/Alamy; p434 (#1) INSADCO Photography/Alamy; p436 (#2) Caro/Alamy. All other photographs by Lonely Planet Images, and by John Borthwick p430; Alfredo Maiquez p432 (#1); Izzet Keribar p432 (#2); Feargus Cooney p434 (#2); Martin Moos p435 (#3); Bruce Esbin p435 (#5).

All images are the copyright of the photographers unless otherwise indicated. Many of the images in this guide are available for licensing from Lonely Planet Images: www.lonelyplanetimages.com.

Index

INDEX

000 Map pages
000 Photograph pages

INDEX

GreenDex

The following sights, attractions, lodging, eating places and transport options have been selected by Lonely Planet authors because they demonstrate a commitment to sustainability. Restaurants and cafes get the nod because of their use of seasonal, organic and locally sourced produce on their menus. We've also highlighted farmers markets and the local producers themselves. In addition, we've covered accommodation that we deem to be environmentally friendly, for example for their commitment to recycling or energy conservation. Attractions are listed because they're involved in conservation or environmental education or have been given an ecological award. For more tips about travelling sustainably in Germany, turn to the Getting Started chapter (p21). For national parks and nature reserves, see p95 and the Index. For information on Green Zones in Germany's cities, see p783. We are committed to further developing our sustainable-travel content. If you would like to comment on our selection or think we've omitted someone who should be listed here, email us at http://www.lonelyplanet.com/contact. For more information about sustainable tourism and Lonely Planet, see www.lonelyplanet.com/responsibletravel.

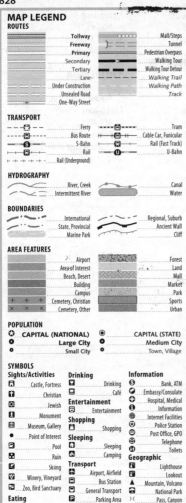

MAP LEGEND

ROUTES

Tollway	Mall/Steps
Freeway	Tunnel
Primary	Pedestrian Overpass
Secondary	Walking Tour
Tertiary	Walking Tour Detour
Lane	Walking Trail
Under Construction	Walking Path
Unsealed Road	Track
One-Way Street	

TRANSPORT

Ferry	Tram
Bus Route	Cable Car, Funicular
S-Bahn	Rail (Fast Track)
Rail	U-Bahn
Rail (Underground)	

HYDROGRAPHY

River, Creek	Canal
Intermittent River	Water

BOUNDARIES

International	Regional, Suburb
State, Provincial	Ancient Wall
Marine Park	Cliff

AREA FEATURES

Airport	Forest
Area of Interest	Land
Beach, Desert	Mall
Building	Market
Campus	Park
Cemetery, Christian	Sports
Cemetery, Other	Urban

POPULATION

◎ **CAPITAL (NATIONAL)**	◉ CAPITAL (STATE)
● **Large City**	◉ Medium City
○ Small City	○ Town, Village

SYMBOLS

Sights/Activities	Drinking	Information
🔲 Castle, Fortress	🔲 Drinking	🄑 Bank, ATM
🔲 Christian	🔲 Café	🄐 Embassy/Consulate
🔲 Jewish	**Entertainment**	🄗 Hospital, Medical
🔲 Monument	🔲 Entertainment	🄘 Information
🔲 Museum, Gallery	**Shopping**	🄒 Internet Facilities
● Point of Interest	🔲 Shopping	🄟 Police Station
🔲 Pool	**Sleeping**	🄟 Post Office, GPO
🔲 Ruin	🔲 Sleeping	🄣 Telephone
🔲 Skiing	🔲 Camping	🄣 Toilets
🔲 Winery, Vineyard	**Transport**	**Geographic**
🔲 Zoo, Bird Sanctuary	🔲 Airport, Airfield	🄛 Lighthouse
Eating	🔲 Bus Station	🄛 Lookout
🔲 Eating	🔲 General Transport	▲ Mountain, Volcano
	🄟 Parking Area	National Park
	🔲 Taxi Rank	)(Pass, Canyon
		→ River Flow

LONELY PLANET OFFICES

Australia (Head Office)
Locked Bag 1, Footscray, Victoria 3011
☎ 03 8379 8000, fax 03 8379 8111
talk2us@lonelyplanet.com.au

USA
150 Linden St, Oakland, CA 94607
☎ 510 250 6400, toll free 800 275 8555
fax 510 893 8572
info@lonelyplanet.com

UK
2nd fl, 186 City Rd,
London EC1V 2NT
☎ 020 7106 2100, fax 020 7106 2101
go@lonelyplanet.co.uk

Published by Lonely Planet
ABN 36 005 607 983

© Lonely Planet 2010

© photographers as indicated 2010

Cover photograph: Burg Hohenzollern perched high on a hill near Stuttgart, Greg Gawlowski/Lonely Planet Images. Many of the images in this guide are available for licensing from Lonely Planet Images: lonelyplanetimages.com.